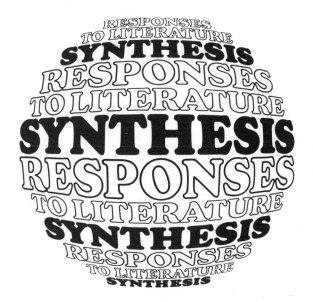

Edited with introductions by

Charles Sanders, Robin R. Rice, and Watt J. Cantillon

The University of Illinois at Urbana

Alfred A. Knopf  New York

RESPONSES
TO LITERATURE
SYNTHESIS
RESPONSES
TO LITERATURE
SYNTHESIS
RESPONSES
TO LITERATURE
SYNTHESIS
RESPONSES
TO LITERATURE
SYNTHESIS

This is a Borzoi Book  Published by Alfred A. Knopf, Inc.

ISBN: 0–394–31044–6

Library of Congress Catalog Card Number: 75–144003

Manufactured in the United States

First Edition

987654321

Acknowledgments

FICTION

"The Dream of a Ridiculous Man," by Fyodor Dostoevsky, from *The Best Short Stories of Fyodor Dostoevsky*. Translation copyright © by David Magarshack. All rights reserved. Reprinted by permission of the translator and Random House, Inc.

"The Legend of St. Julian the Hospitaler," by Gustave Flaubert, from *French Stories*, edited and translated by Wallace Fowlie. Copyright © 1960 by Bantam Books, Inc. All rights reserved. Reprinted by permission of Bantam Books, Inc.

"The Altar of the Dead," by Henry James, from *The Novels and Tales of Henry James*, Vol. XVII. Copyright 1909 by Charles Scribner's Sons; renewal copyright 1937 Henry James. Reprinted by permission of Charles Scribner's Sons.

"The Secret Sharer," by Joseph Conrad, from *'Twixt Land and Sea*. Reprinted by permission of J. M. Dent & Sons Ltd., and the Trustees of the Joseph Conrad Estate.

"The Darling," by Anton Chekhov, from *The Darling and Other Stories*, translated by Constance Garnett. Copyright 1916 by The Macmillan Company. Renewed in 1944 by Constance Garnett. Reprinted by permission of The Macmillan Company, Mr. David Garnett, and Chatto and Windus Ltd.

" 'They,' " by Rudyard Kipling, from *Traffics and Discoveries*. Reprinted by permission of Doubleday & Company, Mrs. George Bambridge, and the Macmillan Company of Canada.

"Loneliness," by Sherwood Anderson, from *Winesburg, Ohio*. Copyright 1919 by B. W. Huebsch, Inc., renewed 1947 by Eleanor Copenhaver Anderson. Reprinted by permission of The Viking Press, Inc.

"Two Gallants," by James Joyce, from *Dubliners*. Originally published by B. W. Huebsch, Inc., in 1916. Copyright © 1967 by The Estate of James Joyce. All rights reserved. Reprinted by permission of The Viking Press, Inc.

"The Judgment," by Franz Kafka, from *The Penal Colony*, translated by Willa and Edwin Muir. Copyright © 1948 by Schocken Books Inc. Reprinted by permission of Schocken Books Inc., and Martin Secker & Warburg Ltd.

"Second Best," by D. H. Lawrence, from *The Complete Short Stories of D. H. Lawrence*, Vol. I. All rights reserved. Reprinted by permission of Laurence Pollinger Ltd., The Viking Press, Inc., and the Estate of the Late Frieda Lawrence.

"Theft," by Katherine Anne Porter, from *Flowering Judas and Other Stories*. Copyright 1935; renewed 1963 by Katherine Anne Porter. Reprinted by permission of Harcourt Brace Jovanovich, Inc.

"In a Grove," by Ryūnosuke Akutagawa, from *Rashomon and Other Stories*, translated by Takashi Kojima. Copyright 1952 by the Liveright Publishing Corp. Reprinted by permission of the Liveright Publishing Corp.

"Di Grasso," by Isaac Babel, from *The Collected Stories of Isaac Babel*, translated by Walter Morison. Copyright 1955 by S. G. Phillips, Inc. Reprinted by permission of S. G. Phillips, Inc.

"Theater," by Jean Toomer, from *Cane*. Copyright ® 1951 by Jean Toomer. Reprinted by permission of the Liveright Publishing Corp.

"Wash," by William Faulkner, from *Collected Stories of William Faulkner*. Copyright 1934 and renewed 1962 by William Faulkner. Reprinted by permission of Random House, Inc.

"The Lottery in Babylon," by Jorge Luis Borges, from *The Labyrinths: Selected Stories and Other Writings*, translated by John M. Fein, edited by Donald A. Yates and James E. Irby; originally published by Penguin Books Ltd. Copyright © 1962 by New Directions Publishing Corporation. Reprinted by permission of New Directions Publishing Corporation and Laurence Pollinger Ltd.

"Mysterious Kôr," by Elizabeth Bowen, from *Ivy Gripped the Steps*. Copyright 1941, 1946 by Elizabeth Bowen. Reprinted by permission of Alfred A. Knopf, Inc., and Jonathan Cape Ltd. "A Natural History of the Dead," by Ernest Hemingway, from *Winner Takes Nothing*. Copyright 1932, 1933 Charles Scribner's Sons; renewal copyright © 1960 Ernest Hemingway, © 1961 Mary Hemingway. Reprinted by permission of Charles Scribner's Sons.

"Stones," by Samuel Beckett, from *Three Novels by Samuel Beckett: Molloy, Malone Dies, The Unnamable*, translated from the French by Patrick Bowles in collaboration with the author. Copyright © 1955, 1956, 1958 by Grove Press, Inc. Reprinted by permission of Grove Press, Inc.

"Big Boy Leaves Home," by Richard Wright, from *Uncle Tom's Children*. Copyright 1936, by Richard Wright. Reprinted by permission of Harper & Row, Inc.

"The Guest," by Albert Camus, from *Exile and the Kingdom*, translated by Justin O'Brian. Copyright © 1957, 1958 by Alfred A. Knopf, Inc. Reprinted by permission of Alfred A. Knopf, Inc.

"The Renegade," by Shirley Jackson, from *The Lottery, or The Adventures of James Harris*. Copyright 1949 by Shirley Jackson. Reprinted by permission of Farrar, Straus & Giroux, Inc.

"My Side of the Matter," by Truman Capote, from *A Tree of Night and Other Stories*. Copyright 1945 by Truman Capote. Reprinted by permission of Random House, Inc.

"Novotny's Pain," by Philip Roth. Copyright © 1962 by Philip Roth. Reprinted by permission of Robert Lantz-Candida Donadio Literary Agency, Inc., and the author.

DRAMA

The Bacchae, by Euripedes, from *The Bacchae and Other Plays*, translated by Philip Vellacott. Copyright © 1954 by Philip Vellacott. Reprinted by permission of Penguin Books Ltd.

Tartuffe, by Molière, from *Tartuffe*, translated by Renee Waldinger. Copyright © 1959 by Barron's Educational Series, Inc. Reprinted by permission of Barron's Educational Series, Inc.

The Master Builder, by Henrik Ibsen, from *The Oxford Ibsen*, Vol. VII, translated by James Walter McFarlane. Copyright © 1966 Oxford University Press. Reprinted by permission of Oxford University Press, Inc.

Three Sisters, by Anton Chekhov, translated by Elisaveta Fen, from *Plays.* Reprinted by permission of Penguin Books Ltd.

Henry IV, by Luigi Pirandello, translated by Edward Storer, from *Naked Masks: Five Plays,* edited by Eric Bentley. Copyright 1922, 1952 by E. P. Dutton & Co., Inc. Renewal 1950, in the names of Stefano, Fausto, and Lietta Pirandello. Dutton Paperback Edition. Reprinted by permission of E. P. Dutton & Co., Inc.

America Hurrah, by Jean-Claude van Itallie. Copyright © 1966, 1967 by Jean-Claude van Itallie. *America Hurrah* is the sole property of the author and is fully protected by copyright. It may not be acted either by professionals or amateurs without written consent. Public readings, radio and television broadcasts likewise are forbidden. All inquiries should be addressed to International Famous Agency, 1301 Avenue of the Americas, New York, New York. Reprinted by permission of Coward-McCann, Inc.

POETRY

"The Gentian Weaves Her Fringes," "I Never Lost As Much But Twice," "I Taste a Liquor Never Brewed," "I Reason, Earth Is Short," "I Heard a Fly Buzz—When I Died," "I Like to See It Lap the Miles," "Because I Could Not Stop for Death," and "A Narrow Fellow in the Grass," by Emily Dickinson, from *Complete Poems of Emily Dickinson,* edited by Thomas H. Johnson. "After Great Pain a Formal Feeling Comes," by Emily Dickinson, from *Complete Poems of Emily Dickinson.* Copyright 1929, © 1957 by Mary L. Hampton. Reprinted by permission of Little, Brown and Company.

"The Subalterns," "The Ruined Maid," "By Her Aunt's Grave," and "The Oxen," by Thomas Hardy, from *Collected Poems.* Copyright 1925 by The Macmillan Company. Reprinted by permission of the Macmillan Company, Macmillan & Co. Ltd., London, The Macmillan Company of Canada Ltd., and Trustees of the Estate of Thomas Hardy.

"The Cap and Bells," copyright 1906 by The Macmillan Company, renewed 1934 by William Butler Yeats. "Adam's Curse," copyright 1903 by The Macmillan Company, renewed 1931 by William Butler Yeats. "The Second Coming," copyright 1924 by The Macmillan Company, renewed 1952 by Bertha Georgie Yeats. "Among School Children," copyright 1928 by The Macmillan Company, renewed 1956 by Georgie Yeats. "Crazy Jane Talks with the Bishop," copyright 1933 by The Macmillan Company, renewed 1961 by Bertha Georgie Yeats. "Lapis Lazuli," and "A Bronze Head," copyright 1940 by Georgie Yeats, renewed 1968 by Bertha Georgie Yeats, Michael Butler Yeats, and Anne Yeats. The above poems by William Butler Yeats, from *Collected Poems,* are reprinted by permission of The Macmillan Company, The Macmillan Company of Canada Ltd., Mr. Michael Yeats, and A. P. Watt & Son.

"The Man Against the Sky," copyright 1916 by Edwin Arlington Robinson, renewed 1944 by Ruth Nivison. "The Sheaves," copyright 1925 by Edwin Arlington Robinson, renewed 1952 by Ruth Nivison and Barbara R. Holt. The above poems by Edwin Arlington Robinson, from *Collected Poems,* are reprinted by permission of The Macmillan Company. "The Clerks," by Edwin Arlington Robinson, from *The Children of the Night,* is reprinted by permission of Charles Scribner's Sons.

" 'Out, Out—,' " "To Earthward," and "Acquainted with the Night," by Robert Frost, from *Complete Poems of Robert Frost.* Copyright 1916, 1923, 1928 by Holt, Rinehart and Winston, Inc. Copyright 1944, 1951, © 1956 by

Archibald MacLeish. Reprinted by permission of the Houghton Mifflin Company.

"Chanson Innocente" and "Portrait," by E. E. Cummings, from *Poems 1923–1954*, copyright 1923, 1951 by E. E. Cummings. "anyone lived in a pretty how town" and "what freedom's not," by E. E. Cummings. Copyright 1940 by E. E. Cummings; renewed 1968 by Marion Morehouse Cummings. "i sing of Olaf glad and big," by E. E. Cummings, from *Poems 1923–1954*, copyright 1931, 1959 by E. E. Cummings. "no time ago," by E. E. Cummings, from *Poems 1923–1954*. Copyright 1950 by E. E. Cummings. Reprinted by permission of Harcourt Brace Jovanovich, Inc.

"Ulysses," "Leda," and "To Juan at the Winter Solstice," by Robert Graves. Copyright © 1955 by Robert Graves. Reprinted by permission of Collins-Knowlton, Wing, Inc.

"VI" ("Where icy and bright dungeons lift") from *Voyages*, "For the Marriage of Faustus and Helen," and "National Winter Garden," from *The Bridge*, by Hart Crane from the *Complete Poems of Hart Crane*. Copyright 1933, 1958, 1966 by Liveright Publishing Corporation. Reprinted by permission of Liveright Publishing Corporation.

"Strange Hurt" and "Trumpet Player," by Langston Hughes, from *Selected Poems*. Copyright 1947 by Langston Hughes. "Daybreak in Alabama," by Langston Hughes, from *Selected Poems*. Copyright 1948 by Alfred A. Knopf, Inc. Reprinted by permission of Alfred A. Knopf, Inc.

"Pursuit" and "Original Sin: A Short Story," by Robert Penn Warren, from *Selected Poems: New and Old, 1923–1966*. Copyright 1942 by Robert Penn Warren. Reprinted by permission of Random House, Inc.

"Musée des Beaux Arts" and "In Memory of W. B. Yeats," by W. H. Auden, from *Collected Shorter Poems, 1927–1957*. Copyright 1940 and renewed 1968 by W. H. Auden. "Pur," by W. H. Auden, from *Collected Shorter Poems, 1927–1957*. Copyright 1934 and renewed 1962 by W. H. Auden. Reprinted by permission of Random House, Inc., and Faber Faber Ltd.

"I Knew a Woman," copyright 1954 by Theodore Roethke. "In a Dark Time," copyright © 1960 by Beatrice Roethke as Executrix of the Estate of Theodore Roethke. "The Waking," copyright 1948 by Theodore Roethke. The above poems by Theodore Roethke, from *The Collected Poems of Theodore Roethke*, are reprinted by permission of Doubleday & Company, Inc.

"An Elementary School Classroom in a Slum" and "Thoughts During an Air Raid," copyright 1942 by Stephen Spender. "Seascape," copyright 1946 by Stephen Spender. The above poems by Stephen Spender, from *Collected Poems 1928–1953*, are reprinted by permission of Random House, Inc., and Faber Faber Ltd.

"A Miracle for Breakfast" and "Roosters," by Elizabeth Bishop, from *Complete Poems*. Copyright 1937, 1941, by Elizabeth Bishop, copyright renewed 1968 by Elizabeth Bishop. Reprinted by permission of Farrar, Straus & Giroux, Inc.

"The Stranger," by William Everson (Brother Antoninus), from *The Residual Years*. Copyright 1948 by New Directions Publishing Corporation. Reprinted by permission of New Directions Publishing Corporation. "I Am Long Weaned," by William Everson (Brother Antoninus), from *The Hazards of Holiness*. Copyright © 1962 by The Poetry Seminar, Inc. Reprinted by permission of Doubleday & Company, Inc.

"Effort At Speech Between Two People," by Muriel Rukeyser, from *Theory of Flight*. Copyright © 1935 by Yale University Press,

Preface

First shot: a panoramic view of a large, land-grant university, 12:45 P.M., any Monday, Wednesday, or Friday. We zoom in and focus on individual students. One group is sitting in the middle of the quad, listening to a radio and playing with the stray dogs. Over them, three or four boys are throwing a football; there's a good deal of laughter. In the Union, a boy is standing in line at the snack bar, having spent forty-five minutes planning what to do with the next fifteen: "If I can find a place to sit down, I can read that short story and get a letter off to Joyce. He'll just ask the names, anyway." Another student is gathering up his books in a local bar, having lost seventeen consecutive pinball games to his fraternity brothers. A girl discusses the strategy of getting a date for Saturday night with a guy in her next class. Some students are protesting job policy in front of a dean's office, others protesting student representation in front of a chancellor's office, others protesting their arrest in front of the president's office. Waking up, dozing off. Flying kites, snake-dancing, strumming guitars, cleaning up the litter from a creek that trickles through the campus, performing impromptu dances, mimes, and sketches outdoors on the steps of the center for the performing arts, speaking of women's rights, civil rights, emancipation, repression, war, trips, love, pollution, sensitivity training. Writing papers, building collages. Worrying. Reading—something else. Writing an exposé for an underground newspaper. Shooting a film of the quad at 12:45 P.M.

The ten-minute bell paralyzes, then scatters them all off with a purpose —getting across campus before roll is taken.

Camera rolls down a hall, peering into classrooms. Literature sections, talking, rustling of paper.

"Now I'm sure you all read 'The Judgment' as the simple story of a man with an Oedipus complex. But, viewing the work as a whole, and taking into account the abnormal circumstances of Kafka's life, I'm sure we can arrive at the truer, hidden meaning. Let's consider the river at the end of the story. It obviously symbolizes a return to the womb, a desperate attempt at rebirth. (Since Freud, an author knows not to use a body of water unless he's got that meaning in mind.) All such scenes are returns to the womb. The author-surrogate, George, makes a leap into the eternal feminine because of his father's rejection of him for his alter ego, his daimon, almost his Doppelgänger . . ."

". . . Flaubert's 'St. Julian' seems to me to exemplify the lesson we have learned from our great authors Hawthorne and Dostoevsky, that you must love your neighbor as yourself. Through the trial and deprivation of a true commitment and vocation Julian emerges almost as a Christ figure, a truly great saint . . ."

". . . Today we'll ignore the elementary problems of plot and theme, having spent a class on them already. Rather we will talk about the conceptual basis for the comedy in Molière. Traditional comedy is based upon the stability and uniformity of human nature. It has a historically-funded knowledge of human potentiality which it articulates in terms of ethical–sociological categories and terms. Therefore our primary interests are epistemological . . ."

". . . Forget what the syllabus says. Study guides just keep garbagemen working. What I want to know is did you like it, did you *feel* it . . ."

"O. K. Now you read Yeats' 'The Second Coming.' And you think like he's weird, it's out of sight—falcons, gyres, *Spiritus Mundi*, out there in the stratosphere, right? But he's *where it's at* . . . he's rapping with us. I mean . . . this beast across the desert. It's like . . . the people's time has come! . . ."

". . . Let's all draw our desks up into a circle, make a closer-knit group, be a real democracy. Jim, you take *Bacchae* for Monday, Sally, *The Master Builder* for Wednesday, Betsy, *Henry IV* for Friday . . . but . . ."

"In conclusion, we should never forget that Swift says: 'Satire is a sort of glass, wherein beholders do generally discover everybody's face but their own.' "

There is no transition.

This book and its accompanying manual have been composed in the belief that if we want our students to appreciate literature and to respond perceptively and enjoyably to it, then we must transfer to the classroom some part of that vitality, excitement, and creativity that students all too often leave behind them in the quad or, as in some stimulus-response experiment, unconsciously submerge when the class bell rings. Thus our manual, while providing sequenced questions that probe the structures of literature, suggestions for class discussion, and theme assignments, also proposes that students may respond in some forms other than writing—in dance, film, games, musical settings, painting, to name but a few—and demonstrate their "literacy." Thus in our introductions to the stories, plays, and poems anthologized here we have tried to draw the student *into* his reading, to lead him to look at literature from several vantage points, to allow him a participation on his terms rather than on his teachers' definitions. The fiction section views short stories through the authors' principles of construction, their manipulation of point of view, plot, symbol, and theme. We try to alert the students to the writers' building processes.

The drama and poetry sections, on the other hand, are concerned with a writer's relation to his audience. What, we ask, are the elements of a play besides a good script? And how does one cope with a work which, like an iceberg, is over half invisible? As the play script engages the reader in creation when he must invent and envision a production of costumes, lights, props, movement, and motivation, so a poem becomes a joint enterprise between the reader and writer in still another way. The poet insists on the reader's intuition, his outside impressions: he maneuvers the reader, we try to show, into a partnership of invention, allows him a poem composed partially of his own experiences.

In this book, then, we are attempting to show that a work of art is not an artifact complete in itself. Its completion is dependent upon its audience. The author may have created it for himself as reader. But another reader brings to it another shape, a new essence, a different finish. This integrity of work and reader is what we mean by *synthesis:* the necessary re-creation of art.

Urbana, Illinois 1970

CHARLES SANDERS
ROBIN R. RICE
WATT J. CANTILLON

Contents

DRAMA 253

POETRY 501

xvii   Contents

xix Contents

Witnesses give evidence about a rape and murder.

A schoolteacher refuses to turn over a political prisoner to the authorities.

A retired civil servant dies in a church.

An old man kills the father of his granddaughter's illegitimate child.

All the events reported in the four sentences above could be items in today's newspapers, selections from the letters to an advice column, neighborhood gossip, or an afternoon's episodes on *Search for Life*. They are in fact summaries of the action in four of the short stories anthologized here: respectively, Akutagawa's "In a Grove," Camus' "The Guest," James' "The Altar of the Dead," and Faulkner's "Wash." Presented without ramifications, these events are stereotypes, daily, routine occurrences to us. But pressed into the form of a story, a plot arranged from just such passing incidents, these stereotypes take on a particular significance, dictated and illuminated by the author's perception.

In Sherwood Anderson's story "Loneliness," Enoch Robinson lives in a room with his own creations, first with his paintings and then with his imaginary friends. They are conjured up "out of real people he had seen and who had for some obscure reason made an appeal to him. There was a woman with a sword in her hand, an old man with a long white beard who went about followed by a dog, a young girl whose stockings were always coming down and hanging over her shoe tops." Enoch's creations are like the stories in this volume. His "child-mind" creates from reality as the artist's does, forming reality to his own needs and his own expression.

The short-story writer is attempting to influence his reader, to move him to reach a similar vision of reality. His approach to the reader is therefore more structured than a poet's, since he is leading the reader in a specific direction rather than simply pointing out the way. As Edgar Allan Poe noted in a review of Nathaniel Hawthorne's work, the short story is concentrated around a specific effect; the story is perfectly suited to this end because it can be read in one sitting and so envelops the reader, while a novel, or a long poem, takes longer to read and cannot sustain its hold on the imagination.

Such a necessary concentration obviously requires discipline of the writer. How, he may ask himself, can he manage to direct his reader so firmly that every word tells? Isaac Babel ponders the problem of artistic effect in "Di Grasso." He tells the story of a boy working for a theatrical promoter, Nick Schwarz, who has to book a last-minute substitute company. But the company, playing an old-fashioned melodrama on a Sicilian shepherd, his love, and her seducer, creates a sensation. Nick views the show primarily as a source of income; his wife views it as a romantic, fairy-tale world she can never reach with her mercenary husband. But her dreaming prompts her to action—she forces Nick to return the boy's watch, which he had offered to Nick as loan security; even after repaying the money, he had not been allowed to reclaim the watch. The wife's action instantaneously evokes a response from the boy: "I saw the columns of the Municipal Building soaring up into the heights, the gas-lit foliage of the boulevard, Pushkin's bronze head touched by the dim gleam of the moon; saw for the first time the things surrounding me as they really were: frozen in silence and ineffably beautiful." In such a pose, the boy may almost be an author's perfect reader: he sees as the author wants him to see, sees things revealed "as they really are," not as they seem to others. The reader is here intended to share the writer's insight: a poet may prompt toward a more general perception, but Babel insists on a specific reaction, on the author's terms.

In "Di Grasso" there is only one sympathetic view. The boy who has the experience is also the storyteller, and his final vision of a higher reality does not coincide with any other character's. Certainly not with Mrs. Schwarz's, for she sees beauty and reality in the Sicilian folk drama and nothing but "beastliness today and beastliness tomorrow" in her actual life. We are sorry for her, but she is present only as a catalyst. The slant, the point of view of the story, is exclusively the boy's; all information filters through him, and we learn nothing he does not.

By using a first-person narrator, Babel throws attention on the "I," makes his problems and observations the center of the universe presented to the reader. Point of view is the basic tool of the fiction writer, for the reader gains access to the writer's world only through an acceptance of the latter's place of observation. The slant may come from a first-person narrator (as in Kipling's " 'They' " or Beckett's "Stones"), or from a third-person storyteller who never enters the tale (as in Flaubert's "The Legend of St. Julian" or Chekhov's "The Darling"), but there is, inevitably, some principle of focus.

A conventional distinction divides authors into those who show and those who tell—those who simply show the reader the situation, and those who tell him what to think about it. But how one tells the difference between the two may initially appear difficult. An intrusive author is fairly easy to categorize. His comments come directly from the eighteenth-century tradition of the familiar essay. Essentially, he makes explicit the implicit relation of the reader to his story by addressing the reader openly. He describes the setting and characters, notes information that none of the characters reveals, and, above all, comments. He has opinions, and he states them repeatedly, just as the persona (assumed character of the author) argues his case in a familiar essay, or explores his ideas in a poem.

In "Wakefield," for example, Hawthorne deliberately presents himself as the intrusive author. He has come across a "true story" and has formed his own impressions about it, which he wishes to present to the reader. His most effective method is through use of an omniscient point of view, for then his reader gets both the facts and a specific interpretation. Since Hawthorne wants the reader to see Wakefield's story only one way, he chooses the highly subjective "intrusive" method which, as the term implies, constitutes an imposition on the reader.

Hawthorne is not actually specifying what the reader will think. He is, nevertheless, limiting his reader's speculations far more greatly than a poet would, by limiting the ideas he himself is willing to entertain. In Hawthorne's own words: "If the reader choose, let him do his own meditation; or if he prefer to ramble with me through the twenty years of Wakefield's vagary, I bid him welcome." It becomes immediately apparent, however, that this will not be just a leisurely stroll; Hawthorne has both a path and a destination in mind: "What sort of a man was Wakefield? We are free to shape out our own idea, and call it by his name. He was now in the meridian of life; his matrimonial affections, never violent, were sobered into a calm, habitual sentiment . . . his mind occupied itself in long and lazy musings, that ended to no purpose, or had not vigor to attain it . . . Had his acquaintances been asked, who was the man in London the surest to perform nothing to-day which should be remembered on the morrow, they would have thought of Wakefield." In less than a paragraph, Hawthorne has announced his intention of creating a fictional character, and sketched him in; no matter that the real Wakefield might have had a dozen urgent reasons for leaving home, from the melodramatic to the simply maudlin. Hawthorne's Wakefield must be consciously motiveless, and so successful is the artist in his drawing that the creation of imaginary friends to vouch for Hawthorne's description of an equally imaginary Wakefield seems logical. We have been drawn into the author's world.

But an author may not want to insert himself so obviously into his story. In that case, he can choose another first-person narrator: either a participant in the action, like the boy in "Di Grasso" or Dostoevsky's Ridiculous Man; or perhaps a first-person narrator who is an observer of the action rather than a participant, like the narrator of Borges' "The Lottery in Babylon," who lived there, but who has only a very superficial connection with the events. A narrator may be either reliable or unreliable: the reader may be intended to believe him, to see more than he does, or to see through him to the real situation. For instance, the narrators of "The Lottery in Babylon" and "Stones" are reliable. We are meant to accept their stories and accounts of themselves as real, incredible as the situation in Babylon and the personality of the narrator of "Stones" may seem. But the narrator of Capote's "My Side of the Matter" is no more right than the other characters, perhaps just because he protests his superiority to the grotesques around him so much.

Similarly, third-person narrators may be limited or omniscient; they may know only the outside of events as they know only the outside of the characters; or they may read the inside of a mind as easily as they recognize a character's face. Most authors alternate, using the omniscient and limited points of view as a movie director uses a camera: close-ups, panoramic vistas, even subtitles and superimpositions are useful to the writer. In "Two Gallants" James Joyce moves in and out of Lenehan's mind during the last part of the story, focusing first on the early evening, then on the appearance of the two men, next on their conversation, and finally on Lenehan's thoughts. Thus Joyce's point of view is third-person omniscient: he surveys Dublin, sees Lenehan and Corley, and can penetrate their consciousness. But his point of view is also highly selective, since he chooses to note only Lenehan's thoughts. "Two Gallants" records the changes in Lenehan, places the emphasis on him rather than on Corley's successful attempt to get money from a serving girl.

Though Lenehan's part in that attempt is secondary or peripheral, Joyce must make it obvious that most of our attention should be given to him rather than Corley, so he chooses to reveal Lenehan's dreams. His hopes to get out of the present, to find a "simple-minded girl with a little of the ready," show more sides of him, while Corley, in contrast, is viewed only from the outside as a rude, single-minded man who sometimes crowds Lenehan off the sidewalk. "He always stared straight before him as if he were on parade and, when he wished to gaze after someone in the street, it was necessary for him to move his body from the hips."

A character like Lenehan, described from several sides and in several situations, is usually termed "round." We know enough about him to guess at what he will do in a given situation, though he is as unpredictable as any real person. Corley is less fully pictured, less often seen. We know his opinions of women and his reaction to Lenehan, but we know nothing of how he works. And about the serving girl we know nothing but the essentials—only her clothes and her money. Both Corley and the girl are "flatter" characters, less fully explored than Lenehan. Only one side is presented; we are left free to conjecture about the other facets of their personalities, while not allowed enough data to make an inquiry complete.

One of the most common "flat" characters is the first-person narrator. He gives little information about himself, so the only thing the reader knows is his bias on the situation described. Sometimes, if the character is active in the plot, other characters will comment on him, although the narrator has the privilege of editing their remarks. If the narrator has no part in his story, he fades. The speaker in "The Lottery in Babylon" is almost a disembodied voice, while all we know about Hemingway's persona in "A Natural History of the Dead" is his loathing of war and its accompanying stupidity.

Such manipulation of viewpoints is one of the author's tools in shaping his theme (underlying statement) as well as in guiding his reader. The essential conflict (the protagonist's attempt to reach his goals—for further discussion, see the introduction to drama) of any story is developed and elaborated according to the larger necessities of the theme. As the author moves away from telling the reader his intentions and progresses further toward demonstrating, or showing, his conclusions, he relies more heavily on other devices, especially the imagery patterns we call symbolism. We can never remove the concept of an author from fiction: even if he is writing an "antinovel," viewing his work as mere reporting, he has still chosen what to report on.

His choice of plot, action, setting, determines his symbols; sometimes, however, the author chooses a symbol first, then builds a setting around it. A symbol is an extended simile or metaphor. The simile points out an explicit likeness, such as the one Eliot uses in the first lines of his poem "The Love Song of J. Alfred Prufrock": "Let us go then, you and I, / When the evening is spread out against the sky / *Like a patient etherised upon a table*" [editors' italics]. A metaphor goes a step further, for it asserts that something is *in fact* something else. It sets up an impossible equation, operating on analogy. For instance, in "The Dry Salvages" Eliot equates the future with several objects: ". . . *the future is a faded song, a Royal Rose or a lavender spray / Of wistful regret for those who are not yet here to regret*" [editor's italics]. Finally, a symbol is an extension of such an analogy; we start with a concrete object that can be equated with another simple object or idea. Reading the story, poem, or play, we find that the concrete object has one or more definite, related equals. Such a prescribed symbol is usually termed "nondiscursive." But in another story another author may refuse any definite equation for the object; instead he lays out boundaries, so that it cannot be greater than one thing or less than another. Such an expanding, complex symbol is "discursive": its associations/definitions are much greater than the nondiscursive sort of analogy.

In light of these remarks, let us consider one of the simplest stories in this book, Katherine Anne Porter's "Theft." On reading the title, we are immediately on the alert for some valuable object that may have been lost, and the opening sentence of the story ("She had the purse in her hand when she came in") confirms our first impression. References to money, and specifically to the purse, pile up throughout the story: Camilo has no more money than the nameless heroine does, Roger compliments her on the purse, she argues with Bill about money he owes her, it was in the purse that she kept a letter from a man who once loved her, and the purse was itself a present, perhaps from him. By the time she realizes the purse is missing and goes into the basement to ask the janitoress to return it, the purse has collected a number of meanings for the reader. It has intruded on every moment of the woman's life shown us by the author. It is connected not only with money, but with love, and finally it is designated as her life, equated with all the other things, material and spiritual, she has "lost." The woman even tells us, "I was right not to be afraid of any thief but myself, who will end by leaving me nothing."

The purse in "Theft" is a nondiscursive symbol; that is, it stands for something reasonably specific, easily labeled or paraphrased. But in another story, "Two Gallants," the symbolism is much more complex. At the end, Corley has acquired both a gold piece and a disciple. How are the two linked? By the symbolism of the coin. "Disciple" calls up the whole question of Judas, Christ, and the thirty pieces of silver. But who is Judas? And is there a savior? The coin is evidence of the woman's relation to Corley, as it is the reason for Lenehan's following him. It also confirms the attitude of both men toward the character of women in general, and proves Corley's superiority. Its roundness and golden glow are an obvious contrast to the silver moon, at which Lenehan was gazing earlier in the evening. These limitations of the situation will have to take the place of a definition of the symbol; it is too complex to be translated as anything more specific than "a price." But whose?

A discursive symbol can function even more intricately than the coin in "Two Gallants." In "The Altar of the Dead," Henry James focuses on the unique relation between George Stransom, who has assembled votary candles at an altar to commemorate his dead friends, and a mysterious lady who prays in the same place for his one dead enemy. The major symbol in the story is obviously the blazing altar, with its multitude of candles. Probably as soon as James settled on the idea of candles, he began arranging their implications. A flame as a representation of the soul is a commonplace. But Stransom wants bodies. He wants to tie down his dead friends, to remember them, to have conversations with them, to assure them life on his terms. And on his terms, such a memorial requires a large amount of money. So his candles also illuminate his materialism, his refusal to view anything except in his own way, those character traits that will be so important in the story. The symbols here are flagrantly discursive. They widen, affect, and reflect each other to the fullest extent, showing a mastery of the indefinable.

And the indefinable, wrapped around with plot, point of view, character, and symbol, is really the theme of the artist. Perhaps the story that supports this generalization best in the present book is Ryūnosuke Akutagawa's "In a Grove." In his story Akutagawa recounts differing versions of a rape and murder and the evidence given about them. These versions range from an interview with the woodcutter who found the body to a seance with the murdered man. All three principals—the man, his wife, and the robber who attacked them—express varying points of view about who did what to whom and why. The robber says that he attacked the two to rape the wife, not to kill the husband, having only tied him up. But, he continues, she begged them to fight for her, so that only one man would know her dishonor, and she would be the wife of the winner. The husband was killed, but she ran away from the thief.

The wife says she killed the husband. She was planning to kill herself in any case, but she realized that she could not let him live when she saw loathing in his eyes. So she stabbed him and afterwards did not have the courage to kill herself.

Finally, the murdered man complains that no one has the story right. He explains that his wife wanted to go with the thief after her rape, but she tried to persuade him to kill her husband. When both men were amazed at this lack of honor, she ran off into the woods, the robber following to kill her. But he released the husband's bonds and the husband, honorably, killed himself.

As in any popular murder case, so in "In a Grove" there are varying stories, each witness seeing what he wishes or what he most fears. There is no Truth in this story. Every viewpoint is true for the character who holds it, just as there is no one reality but a continually reshaped past. Flannery O'Connor once commented that a writer must have a certain essential "stupidity," a slowness of perception: he stares at things, takes longer to realize and see their basic form. Akutagawa is showing us the process, forcing us through that long stare—at a wall? at Truth? at a mirror?—to apprehend his perception. He sees pieces, the indefinables of life that we all collect for our own mosaics, our separate realities, our "fictions."

NATHANIEL HAWTHORNE

Wakefield

In some old magazine or newspaper I recollect a story, told as truth, of a man—let us call him Wakefield—who absented himself for a long time from his wife. The fact, thus abstractedly stated, is not very uncommon, nor—without a proper distinction of circumstances—to be condemned either as naughty or nonsensical. Howbeit, this, though far from the most aggravated, is perhaps the strangest, instance on record, of marital delinquency; and, moreover, as remarkable a freak as may be found in the whole list of human oddities. The wedded couple lived in London. The man, under pretence of going on a journey, took lodgings in the next street to his own house, and there, unheard of by his wife or friends, and without the shadow of a reason for such self-banishment, dwelt upwards of twenty years. During that period, he beheld his home every day, and frequently the forlorn Mrs. Wakefield. And after so great a gap in his matrimonial felicity—when his death was reckoned certain, his estate settled, his name dismissed from memory, and his wife, long, long ago, resigned to her autumnal widowhood—he entered the door one evening, quietly, as from a day's absence, and became a loving spouse till death.

This outline is all that I remember. But the incident, though of the purest originality, unexampled, and probably never to be repeated, is one, I think, which appeals to the generous sympathies of mankind. We know, each for himself, that none of us would perpetrate such a folly, yet feel as if some other might. To my own contemplations, at least, it has often recurred, always exciting wonder, but with a sense that the story must be true, and a conception of its hero's character. Whenever any subject so forcibly affects the mind, time is well spent in thinking of it. If the reader choose, let him do his own meditation; or if he prefer to ramble with me through the twenty years of Wakefield's vagary, I bid him welcome; trusting that there will be a pervading spirit and a moral, even should we fail to find them, done up neatly, and condensed into the final sentence. Thought has always its efficacy, and every striking incident its moral.

What sort of a man was Wakefield? We are free to shape out our own idea, and call it by his name. He was now in the meridian of life; his matrimonial affections, never violent, were sobered into a calm, habitual sentiment; of all husbands, he was likely to be the most constant, because a certain sluggishness would keep his heart at rest, wherever it might be placed. He was intellectual, but not actively so; his mind occupied itself in long and lazy musings, that ended to no purpose, or had not vigor to attain it; his thoughts were seldom so energetic as to seize hold of words. Imagination, in the proper meaning of the term, made no part of Wakefield's gifts. With a cold but not depraved nor wandering heart, and a mind never feverish with riotous thoughts, nor perplexed with originality, who could have anticipated that our friend would entitle himself to a foremost place among the doers of eccentric deeds? Had his acquaintances been asked, who was the man in London the surest to perform nothing to-day which should be remembered on the morrow, they would have thought of Wakefield. Only the wife of his bosom might have hesitated. She, without having analyzed his character, was partly aware of a quiet selfishness, that had rusted into his inactive mind; of a peculiar sort of vanity, the most uneasy attribute about him; of a disposition to craft, which had seldom produced more positive effects than the keeping of petty secrets, hardly worth revealing; and, lastly, of what she called a little strangeness, sometimes, in the good man. This latter quality is indefinable, and perhaps nonexistent.

Let us now imagine Wakefield bidding adieu to his wife. It is the dusk of an October evening. His equipment is a drab greatcoat, a hat covered with an oilcloth, top-boots, an umbrella in one hand and a small portmanteau in the other. He has informed Mrs. Wakefield that he is to take the night coach into the country. She would fain inquire the length of his journey, its object, and the probable time of his return; but, indulgent to his harmless love of mystery, interrogates him only by a look. He tells her not to expect him positively by the return coach, nor to be alarmed should he tarry three or four days; but, at all events, to look for him at supper on Friday evening. Wakefield himself, be it considered, has no suspicion of what is before him. He holds out his hand, she gives her own, and meets his parting kiss in the matter-of-course way of a ten years' matrimony; and forth goes the middle-aged Mr. Wakefield, almost resolved to perplex his good lady by a whole week's absence. After the door has closed behind him, she perceives it thrust partly open, and a vision of her husband's face through the aperture, smiling on her, and gone in a moment. For the time, this little incident is dismissed without a thought. But, long afterwards, when she has been more years a widow than a wife, that smile recurs, and flickers across all her reminiscences of Wakefield's visage. In her many musings, she surrounds the original smile with a multitude of fantasies, which make it strange and awful: as, for instance, if she imagines him in a coffin, that parting look is frozen on his pale features; or, if she dreams of him in heaven, still his blessed spirit wears a quiet and crafty smile. Yet, for its sake, when all others have given him up for dead, she somehow doubts whether she is a widow.

But our business is with the husband. We must hurry after him along the street, ere he lose his individuality, and melt into the great mass of London life. It would be vain searching for him there. Let us follow close at his heels, therefore, until, after several superfluous turns and doublings, we find him comfortably established by the fireside of a small apartment, previously bespoken. He is in the next street to his own, and at his journey's end. He can scarcely trust his good fortune, in having got thither unperceived—recollecting that, at one time, he was delayed by the throng, in the very focus of a lighted lantern; and, again, there were footsteps that seemed to tread behind his own, distinct from the multitudinous tramp around him; and, anon, he heard a voice shouting afar, and fancied that it called his name. Doubtless, a dozen busybodies had been watching him, and told his wife the whole affair. Poor Wakefield! Little knowest thou thine own insignificance in this great world! No mortal eye but mine has traced thee. Go quietly to thy bed, foolish man; and, on the morrow, if thou wilt be wise, get thee home to good Mrs. Wakefield, and tell her the truth. Remove not thyself, even for a little week, from thy place in her chaste bosom. Were she, for a single moment, to deem thee dead, or lost, or lastingly divided from her, thou wouldst be wofully conscious of a change in thy true wife forever after. It is perilous to make a chasm in human affections; not that they gape so long and wide—but so quickly close again!

Almost repenting of his frolic, or whatever it may be termed, Wakefield lies down betimes, and starting from his first nap, spreads forth his arms into the wide and solitary waste of the unaccustomed bed. "No,"—thinks he, gathering the bedclothes about him,—"I will not sleep alone another night."

In the morning he rises earlier than usual, and sets himself to consider what he really means to do. Such are his loose and rambling modes of thought that he has taken this very singular step with the consciousness of a purpose, indeed, but without being able to define it sufficiently for his own contemplation. The vagueness of the project, and the convulsive effort with which he plunges into the execution of it, are equally characteristic of a feeble-minded man. Wakefield sifts his ideas, however, as minutely as he may, and finds himself curious to know the progress of matters at home—how his exemplary wife will endure her widowhood of a week; and, briefly, how the little sphere of creatures and circumstances, in which he was a central object, will be affected by his removal. A morbid vanity, therefore, lies nearest the bottom of the affair. But, how is he to attain his ends? Not, certainly, by keeping close in this comfortable lodging, where, though he slept and awoke in the next street to his home, he is as effectually abroad as if the stage-coach had been whirling him away all night. Yet, should he reappear, the whole project is knocked in the head. His poor brains being hopelessly puzzled with this dilemma, he at length ventures out, partly resolving to cross the head of the street, and send one hasty glance towards his forsaken domicile. Habit —for he is a man of habits—takes him by the hand, and guides him, wholly unaware, to his own door, where, just at the critical moment, he is aroused by the scraping of his foot upon the step. Wakefield! whither are you going?

At that instant his fate was turning on the pivot. Little dreaming of the doom to which his first backward step devotes him, he hurries away, breathless with agitation hitherto unfelt, and hardly dares turn his head at the distant corner. Can it be that nobody caught sight of him? Will not the whole household —the decent Mrs. Wakefield, the smart maid servant, and the dirty little footboy—raise a hue and cry, through London streets, in pursuit of their fugitive lord and master? Wonderful escape! He gathers courage to pause and look homeward, but is perplexed with a sense of change about the familiar edifice, such as affects us all, when, after a separation of months or years, we again see some hill or lake, or work of art, with which we were friends of old. In ordinary cases, this indescribable impression is caused by the comparison and contrast between our imperfect reminiscences and the reality. In Wakefield, the magic of a single night has wrought a similar transformation, because, in that brief period, a great moral change has been effected. But this a secret from himself. Before leaving the spot, he catches a far and momentary glimpse of his wife, passing athwart the front window, with her face turned towards the head of the street. The crafty nincompoop takes to his heels, scared with the idea that, among a thousand such atoms of mortality, her eye must have detected him. Right glad is his heart, though his brain be somewhat dizzy, when he finds himself by the coal fire of his lodgings.

So much for the commencement of this long whim-wham. After the initial conception, and the stirring up of the man's sluggish temperament to put it in practice, the whole matter evolves itself in a natural train. We may suppose him, as the result of deep deliberation, buying a new wig, of reddish hair, and selecting sundry garments, in a fashion unlike his customary suit of brown, from a Jew's old-clothes bag. It is accomplished. Wakefield is another man. The new system being now established, a retrograde movement to the old would be almost as difficult as the step that placed him in his unparalleled position. Furthermore, he is rendered obstinate by a sulkiness occasionally incident to his temper, and brought on at present by the inadequate sensation which he conceives to have been produced in the bosom of Mrs. Wakefield. He will not go back until she be frightened half to death. Well; twice or thrice has she passed before his sight, each time with a heavier step, a paler cheek, and more anxious brow; and in the third week of his non-appearance he detects a portent of evil entering the house, in the guise of an apothecary. Next day the knocker is muffled. Towards nightfall comes the chariot of a physician, and deposits its bigwigged and solemn burden at Wakefield's door, whence, after a quarter of an hour's visit, he emerges, perchance the herald of a funeral. Dear woman! Will she die? By this time, Wakefield is excited to something like energy of feeling, but still lingers away from his wife's bedside, pleading with his conscience that she must not be disturbed at such a juncture. If aught else restrains him, he does not know it. In the course of a few weeks she gradually recovers; the crisis is over; her heart is sad, perhaps, but quiet; and, let him return soon or late, it will never be feverish for him again. Such ideas glimmer through the mist of Wakefield's mind, and render him indistinctly conscious that an almost impassable gulf divides his hired apartment from his former home. "It is but in the next street!" he sometimes says. Fool! it is in another world. Hitherto, he has put off his return from one particular day to another; henceforward, he leaves the precise time undetermined. Not to-morrow—probably next week—pretty soon. Poor man! The dead have nearly as much chance of revisiting their earthly homes as the self-banished Wakefield.

Would that I had a folio to write, instead of an article of a dozen pages! Then might I exemplify how an influence beyond our control lays its strong hand on every deed which we do, and weaves its consequences into an iron tissue of necessity. Wakefield is spellbound. We must leave him, for ten years or so, to haunt around his house, without once crossing the threshold, and to be faithful to his wife, with all the affection of which his heart is capable, while he is slowly fading out of hers. Long since, it must be remarked, he had lost the perception of singularity in his conduct.

Now for a scene! Amid the throng of a London street we distinguish a man, now waxing elderly, with few characteristics to attract careless observers, yet bearing, in his whole aspect, the handwriting of no common fate, for such as have the skill to read it. He is meagre; his low and narrow forehead is deeply wrinkled; his eyes, small and lustreless, sometimes wander apprehensively about him, but oftener seem to look inward. He bends his head, and moves with an indescribable obliquity of gait, as if unwilling to display his full front to the world. Watch him long enough to see what we have described, and you will allow that circumstances—which often produce remarkable men from nature's ordinary handiwork—have produced one such here. Next, leaving him to sidle along the footwalk, cast your eyes in the opposite direction, where a portly female, considerably in the wane of life, with a prayer-book in her hand, is proceeding to yonder church. She has the placid mien of settled widowhood. Her regrets have either died away, or have become so essential to her heart, that they would be poorly exchanged for joy. Just as the lean man and well-conditioned woman are passing, a slight obstruction occurs, and brings these two figures directly in contact. Their hands touch; the pressure of the crowd forces her bosom against his shoulder; they stand, face to face, staring into each other's eyes. After a ten years' separation, thus Wakefield meets his wife!

The throng eddies away, and carries them asunder. The sober widow, resuming her former pace, proceeds to church, but pauses in the portal, and throws a perplexed glance along the street. She passes in, however, opening her prayer-book as she goes. And the man! with so wild a face that busy and selfish London stands to gaze after him, he hurries to his lodgings, bolts the door, and throws himself upon the bed. The latent feelings of years break out; his feeble mind acquires a brief energy from their strength; all the miserable strangeness of his life is revealed to him at a glance: and he cries out, passionately, "Wakefield! Wakefield! You are mad!"

Perhaps he was so. The singularity of his situation must have so moulded him to himself, that, considered in regard to his fellow-creatures and the business of life, he could not be said to possess his right mind. He had contrived, or rather he had happened, to dissever himself from the world—to vanish—to give up his place and privileges with living men, without being admitted among the dead. The life of a hermit is nowise parallel to his own. He was in the bustle of the city, as of old; but the crowd swept by and saw him not; he was, we may figuratively say, always beside his wife and at his hearth, yet must never feel the warmth of the one nor the affection of the other. It was Wakefield's unprecedented fate to retain his original share of human sympathies, and to be still involved in human interests, while he had lost his reciprocal influence on them. It would be a most curious speculation to trace out the effect of such circumstances on his heart and intellect, separately, and in unison. Yet, changed as he was, he would seldom be conscious of it, but deem himself the same man as ever; glimpses of the truth, indeed, would come, but only for the moment; and still he would keep saying, "I shall soon go back!"—nor reflect that he had been saying so for twenty years.

I conceive, also, that these twenty years would appear, in the retrospect, scarcely longer than the week to which Wakefield had at first limited his absence. He would look on the affair as no more than an interlude in the main business of his life. When, after a little while more, he should deem it time to reenter his parlor, his wife would clap her hands for joy, on beholding the middle-aged Mr. Wakefield. Alas, what a mistake! Would Time but await the close of our favorite follies, we should be young men, all of us, and till Doomsday.

One evening, in the twentieth year since he vanished, Wakefield is taking his customary walk towards the dwelling which he still calls his own. It is a gusty night of autumn, with frequent showers that patter down upon the pavement, and are gone before a man can put up his umbrella. Pausing near the house, Wakefield discerns, through the parlor windows of the second floor, the red glow and the glimmer and fitful flash of a comfortable fire. On the ceiling appears a grotesque shadow of good Mrs. Wakefield. The cap, the nose and chin, and the broad waist, form an admirable caricature, which dances, moreover, with the up-flickering and down-sinking blaze, almost too merrily for the shade of an elderly widow. At this instant a shower chances to fall, and is driven, by the unmannerly gust, full into Wakefield's face and bosom. He is quite penetrated with its autumnal chill. Shall he stand, wet and shivering here, when his own hearth has a good fire to warm him, and his own wife will run to fetch the gray coat and small-clothes, which, doubtless, she has kept carefully in the closet of their bed chamber? No! Wakefield is no such fool. He ascends the steps—heavily!—for twenty years have stiffened his legs since he came down—but he knows it not. Stay, Wakefield! Would you go to the sole home that is left you? Then step into your grave! The door opens. As he passes in, we have a parting glimpse of his visage, and recognize the crafty smile, which was the precursor of the little joke that he has ever since been playing off at his wife's expense. How unmercifully has he quizzed the poor woman! Well, a good night's rest to Wakefield!

This happy event—supposing it to be such —could only have occurred at an unpremeditated moment. We will not follow our friend across the threshold. He has left us much food for thought, a portion of which shall lend its wisdom to a moral, and be shaped into a figure. Amid the seeming confusion of our mysterious world, individuals are so nicely adjusted to a system, and systems to one another and to a whole, that, by stepping aside for a moment, a man exposes himself to a fearful risk of losing his place forever. Like Wakefield, he may become, as it were, the Outcast of the Universe.

FEODOR DOSTOEVSKY

The Dream of a Ridiculous Man

A Fantastic Story

Translated by David Magarshack

I

I am a ridiculous man. They call me a mad-man now. That would be a distinct rise in my social position were it not that they still regard me as being as ridiculous as ever. But that does not make me angry any more. They are all dear to me now even while they laugh at me—yes, even then they are for some reason particularly dear to me. I shouldn't have minded laughing with them—not at myself, of course, but because I love them—had I not felt so sad as I looked at them. I feel sad because they do not know the truth, whereas I know it. Oh, how hard it is to be the only man to know the truth! But they won't understand that. No, they will not understand.

And yet in the past I used to be terribly distressed at appearing to be ridiculous. No, not appearing to be, but being. I've always cut a ridiculous figure. I suppose I must have known it from the day I was born. At any rate, I've known for certain that I was ridiculous ever since I was seven years old. Afterwards I went to school, then to the university, and—well—the more I learned, the more conscious did I become of the fact that I was ridiculous. So that for me my years of hard work at the university seem in the end to have existed for the sole purpose of demonstrating and proving to me, the more

deeply engrossed I became in my studies, that I was an utterly absurd person. And as during my studies, so all my life. Every year the same consciousness that I was ridiculous in every way strengthened and intensified in my mind. They always laughed at me. But not one of them knew or suspected that if there were one man on earth who knew better than anyone else that he was ridiculous, that man was I. And this—I mean, the fact that they did not know it—was the bitterest pill for me to swallow. But there I was myself at fault. I was always so proud that I never wanted to confess it to anyone. No, I wouldn't do that for anything in the world. As the years passed, this pride increased in me so that I do believe that if ever I had by chance confessed it to any one I should have blown my brains out the same evening. Oh, how I suffered in the days of my youth from the thought that I might not myself resist the impulse to confess it to my schoolfellows. But ever since I became a man I grew for some unknown reason a little more composed in my mind, though I was more and more conscious of that awful characteristic of mine. Yes, most decidedly for some unknown reason, for to this day I have not been able to find out why that was so. Perhaps it was because I was becoming terribly disheartened owing to one circumstance which was beyond my power to control, namely, the conviction which was gaining upon me that nothing in the whole world *made any difference.* I had long felt it dawning upon me, but I was fully convinced of it only last year, and that, too, all of a sudden, as it were. I suddenly felt that it made *no* difference to me whether the world existed or whether nothing existed anywhere at all. I began to be acutely conscious that *nothing existed in my own lifetime.* At first I couldn't help feeling that at any rate in the past many things had existed; but later on I came to the conclusion that there had not been anything even in the past, but that for some reason it had merely seemed to have been. Little by little I became convinced that there would be nothing in the future, either. It was then that I suddenly ceased to be angry with people and almost stopped noticing them. This indeed disclosed itself in the smallest trifles. For instance, I would knock against people while walking in the street. And not because I was lost in thought—I had nothing to think about—I had stopped thinking about anything at that time: it made no difference to me. Not that I had found an answer to all the questions. Oh, I had not settled a single question, and there were thousands of them! But *it made no difference to me,* and all the questions disappeared.

And, well, it was only after that that I learnt the truth. I learnt the truth last November, on the third of November to be precise, and every moment since then has been imprinted indelibly on my mind. It happened on a dismal evening, as dismal an evening as could be imagined. I was returning home at about eleven o'clock and I remember thinking all the time that there could not be a more dismal evening. Even the weather was foul. It had been pouring all day, and the rain too was the coldest and most dismal rain that ever was, a sort of menacing rain—I remember that—a rain with a distinct animosity towards people. But about eleven o'clock it had stopped suddenly, and a horrible dampness descended upon everything, and it became much damper and colder than when it had been raining. And a sort of steam was rising from everything, from every cobble in the street, and from every side-street if you peered closely into it from the street as far as the eye could reach. I could not help feeling that if the gaslight had been extinguished everywhere, everything would have seemed much more cheerful, and that the gaslight oppressed the heart so much just because it shed a light upon it all. I had had scarcely any dinner that day. I had been spending the whole evening with an engineer who had two more friends visiting him. I never opened my mouth, and I expect I must have got on their nerves. They were discussing some highly controversial subject, and suddenly got very excited over it. But it really did not make any difference to them. I could see that. I knew that their excitement was not genuine. So I suddenly blurted it out. "My dear fellows," I said, "you don't really care a damn about it, do you?" They were not in the least offended, but they all burst out laughing at me. That was because I had said it without meaning to rebuke them, but simply because it made no difference to me. Well, they realized that it made no difference to me, and they felt happy.

When I was thinking about the gaslight in the streets, I looked up at the sky. The sky was awfully dark, but I could clearly distinguish the torn wisps of cloud and between them fathomless dark patches. All of a sudden I became aware of a little star in one of those patches and I began looking at it intently. That was because the little star gave me an idea: I made up my mind to kill myself that night. I had made up my mind to kill myself already two months before and, poor as I am, I bought myself an excellent revolver and loaded it the same day. But two months had elapsed and it was still lying in the drawer. I was so utterly indifferent to everything that I was anxious to wait for the moment when I would not be so indifferent and then kill myself. Why—I don't know. And so every night during these two months I thought of shooting myself as I was going home. I was only waiting for the right moment. And now the little star gave me an idea, and I made up my mind then and there that it should *most certainly* be that night. But why the little star gave me the idea—I don't know.

And just as I was looking at the sky, this little girl suddenly grasped me by the elbow. The street was already deserted and there was scarcely a soul to be seen. In the distance a cabman was fast asleep on his box. The girl was about eight years old. She had a kerchief on her head, and she wore only an old, shabby little dress. She was soaked to the skin, but what stuck in my memory was her little torn wet boots. I still remember them. They caught my eye especially. She suddenly began tugging at my elbow and calling me. She was not crying, but saying something in a loud, jerky sort of voice, something that did not make sense, for she was trembling all over and her teeth were chattering from cold. She seemed to be terrified of something and she was crying desperately, "Mummy! Mummy!" I turned round to look at her, but did not utter a word and went on walking. But she ran after me and kept tugging at my clothes, and there was a sound in her voice which in very frightened children signifies despair. I know that sound. Though her words sounded as if they were choking her, I realized that her mother must be dying somewhere very near, or that something similar was happening to her, and that she had run out to call someone, to find someone who would help her mother. But I did not go with her; on the contrary, something made me drive her away. At first I told her to go and find a policeman. But she suddenly clasped her hands and, whimpering and gasping for breath, kept running at my side and would not leave me. It was then that I stamped my foot and shouted at her. She

just cried, "Sir! Sir! . . ." and then she left me suddenly and rushed headlong across the road: another man appeared there and she evidently rushed from me to him.

I climbed to the fifth floor. I live apart from my landlord. We all have separate rooms as in an hotel. My room is very small and poor. My window is a semicircular skylight. I have a sofa covered with American cloth, a table with books on it, two chairs and a comfortable armchair, a very old armchair indeed, but low-seated and with a high back serving as a headrest. I sat down in the armchair, lighted the candle, and began thinking. Next door in the other room behind the partition, the usual bedlam was going on. It had been going on since the day before yesterday. A retired army captain lived there, and he had visitors—six merry gentlemen who drank vodka and played faro with an old pack of cards. Last night they had a fight and I know that two of them were for a long time pulling each other about by the hair. The landlady wanted to complain, but she is dreadfully afraid of the captain. We had only one more lodger in our rooms, a thin little lady, the wife of an army officer, on a visit to Petersburg with her three little children who had all been taken ill since their arrival at our house. She and her children were simply terrified of the captain and they lay shivering and crossing themselves all night long, and the youngest child had a sort of nervous attack from fright. This captain (I know that for a fact) sometimes stops people on Nevski Avenue and asks them for a few coppers, telling them he is very poor. He can't get a job in the Civil Service, but the strange thing is (and that's why I am telling you this) that the captain had never once during the month he had been living with us made me feel in the least irritated. From the very first, of course, I would not have anything to do with him, and he himself was bored with me the very first time we met. But however big a noise they raised behind their partition and however many of them there were in the captain's room, it makes no difference to me. I sit up all night and, I assure you, I don't hear them at all—so completely do I forget about them. You see, I stay awake all night till daybreak, and that has been going on for a whole year now. I sit up all night in the armchair at the table—doing nothing. I read books only in the daytime. At night I sit like that without even thinking about anything in particular: some thoughts wander in and out of my mind, and I let them come and go as they please. In the night the candle burns out completely.

I sat down at the table, took the gun out of the drawer, and put it down in front of me. I remember asking myself as I put it down, "Is it to be then?" and I replied with complete certainty, "It is!" That is to say, I was going to shoot myself. I knew I should shoot myself that night for certain. What I did not know was how much longer I should go on sitting at the table till I shot myself. And I should of course have shot myself, had it not been for the little girl.

II

You see, though nothing made any difference to me, I could feel pain, for instance, couldn't I? If anyone had struck me, I should have felt pain. The same was true so far as my moral perceptions were concerned. If anything happened to arouse my pity, I should have felt pity, just as I used to do at the time when things did make a difference to me. So I had felt pity that night: I should most decidedly have helped a child. Why then did I not help the little girl? Because of a thought that had occurred to me at the time: when she was pulling at me and calling me, a question suddenly arose in my mind and I could not settle it. It was an idle question, but it made me angry. What made me angry was the conclusion I drew from the reflection that if I had really decided to do away with myself that night, everything in the world should have been more indifferent to me than ever. Why

then should I have suddenly felt that I was not indifferent and be sorry for the little girl? I remember that I was very sorry for her, so much so that I felt a strange pang which was quite incomprehensible in my position. I'm afraid I am unable better to convey that fleeting sensation of mine, but it persisted with me at home when I was sitting at the table, and I was very much irritated. I had not been so irritated for a long time past. One train of thought followed another. It was clear to me that so long as I was still a human being and not a meaningless cipher, and till I became a cipher, I was alive, and consequently able to suffer, be angry, and feel shame at my actions. Very well. But if, on the other hand, I were going to kill myself in, say, two hours, what did that little girl matter to me and what did I care for shame or anything else in the world? I was going to turn into a cipher, into an absolute cipher. And surely the realisation that I should soon cease to exist *altogether*, and hence everything would cease to exist, ought to have had some slight effect on my feeling of pity for the little girl or on my feeling of shame after so mean an action. Why after all did I stamp and shout so fiercely at the little girl? I did it because I thought that not only did I feel no pity, but that it wouldn't matter now if I were guilty of the most inhuman baseness, since in another two hours everything would become extinct. Do you believe me when I tell you that that was the only reason why I shouted like that? I am almost convinced of it now. It seemed clear to me that life and the world in some way or other depended on me now. It might almost be said that the world seemed to be created for me alone. If I were to shoot myself, the world would cease to exist—for me at any rate. To say nothing of the possibility that nothing would in fact exist for anyone after me and the whole world would dissolve as soon as my consciousness became extinct, would disappear in a twinkling like a phantom, like some integral part of my consciousness, and vanish without leaving a trace behind, for all this world and all these people exist perhaps only in my consciousness.

I remember that as I sat and meditated, I began to examine all these questions which thronged in my mind one after another from quite a different angle, and thought of something quite new. For instance, the strange notion occurred to me that if I had lived before on the moon or on Mars and had committed there the most shameful and dishonorable action that can be imagined, and had been so disgraced and dishonored there as can be imagined and experienced only occasionally in a dream, a nightmare, and if, finding myself afterwards on earth, I had retained the memory of what I had done on the other planet, and moreover knew that I should never in any circumstances go back there—if that were to have happened, should I or should I not have felt, as I looked from the earth upon the moon, that *it made no difference* to me? Should I or should I not have felt ashamed of that action? The questions were idle and useless, for the gun was already lying before me and there was not a shadow of doubt in my mind that *it* was going to take place for certain, but they excited and maddened me. It seemed to me that I could not die now without having settled something first. The little girl, in fact, had saved me, for by these questions I put off my own execution.

Meanwhile things had grown more quiet in the captain's room: they had finished their card game and were getting ready to turn in for the night, and now were only grumbling and swearing at each other in a half-hearted sort of way. It was at that moment that I suddenly fell asleep in my armchair at the table, a thing that had never happened to me before.

I fell asleep without being aware of it at all. Dreams, as we all know, are very curious things: certain incidents in them are presented with quite uncanny vividness, each detail executed with the finishing touch of a jeweller, while others you leap across as though entirely unaware of, for instance, space and time. Dreams seem to be induced not by reason but by desire, not by the head but by the heart, and yet what clever tricks my reason has sometimes played on me in dreams! And furthermore what incomprehensible things happen to it in a dream. My brother, for instance, died five years ago. I sometimes dream about him: he takes a keen interest in my affairs, we are both very interested, and yet I know very well all through my dream that my brother is dead and buried. How is it that I am not surprised that, though dead, he is here beside me, doing his best to help me? Why does my reason accept all this without the slightest hesitation? But enough. Let me tell you about my dream. Yes, I dreamed that dream that night. My dream of the third of November. They are making fun of me now by saying that it was only a dream. But what does it matter whether it was a dream or not, so long as that dream revealed the Truth to me? For once you have recognized the truth and seen it, you know it is the one and only truth and that there can be no other, whether you are asleep or awake. But never mind. Let it be a dream, but remember that I had intended to cut short by suicide the life that means so much to us, and that my dream—my dream —oh, it revealed to me a new, grand, regenerated, strong life!

Listen.

III

I have said that I fell asleep imperceptibly and even while I seemed to be revolving the same thoughts again in my mind. Suddenly I dreamed that I picked up the gun and, sitting in my armchair, pointed it straight at my heart—at my heart, and not at my head. For I had firmly resolved to shoot myself through the head, through the right temple, to be precise. Having aimed the gun at my breast, I paused for a second or two, and suddenly my candle, the table and the wall began moving and swaying before me. I fired quickly.

In a dream you sometimes fall from a great height, or you are being murdered or beaten, but you never feel any pain unless you really manage somehow or other to hurt yourself in bed, when you feel pain and almost always wake up from it. So it was in my dream: I did not feel any pain, but it seemed as though with my shot everything within me was shaken and everything was suddenly extinguished, and a terrible darkness descended all around me. I seemed to have become blind and dumb. I was lying on something hard, stretched out full length on my back. I saw nothing and could not make the slightest movement. All round me people were walking and shouting. The captain was yelling in his deep bass voice, the landlady was screaming and—suddenly another hiatus, and I was being carried in a closed coffin. I could feel the coffin swaying and I was thinking about it, and for the first time the idea flashed through my mind that I was dead, dead as a doornail, that I knew it, that there was not the least doubt about it, that I could neither see nor move, and yet I could feel and reason. But I was soon reconciled to that and, as usually happens in dreams, I accepted the facts without questioning them.

And now I was buried in the earth. They all went away, and I was left alone, entirely alone. I did not move. Whenever before I imagined how I should be buried in a grave, there was only one sensation I actually associated with the grave, namely, that of damp and cold. And so it was now. I felt that I was very cold, especially in the tips of my toes, but I felt nothing else.

I lay in my grave and, strange to say, I did not expect anything, accepting the idea that a dead man had nothing to expect as an incontestable fact. But it was damp. I don't know how long a time passed, whether an hour, or several days, or many days. But suddenly a drop of water, which had seeped through the lid of the coffin, fell on my closed left eye. It was followed by another drop a minute later, then after another minute by another drop, and so on. One drop every minute. All at once deep indignation blazed up in my heart, and I suddenly felt a twinge of physical pain in it. "That's my wound," I thought. "It's the shot I fired. There's a bullet there. . . ." And drop after drop still kept falling every minute on my closed eyelid. And suddenly I called (not with my voice, for I was motionless, but with the whole of my being) upon Him who was responsible for all that was happening to me:

"Whoever Thou art, and if anything more rational exists than what is happening here, let it, I pray Thee, come to pass here too. But if Thou are revenging Thyself for my senseless act of self-destruction by the infamy and absurdity of life after death, then know that no torture that may be inflicted upon me can ever equal the contempt which I shall go on feeling in silence, though my martyrdom last for aeons upon aeons!"

I made this appeal and was silent. The dead silence went on for almost a minute, and one more drop fell on my closed eyelid, but I knew, I knew and believed infinitely and unshakably that everything would without a doubt change immediately. And then my grave was opened. I don't know, that is, whether it was opened or dug open, but I was seized by some dark and unknown being and we found ourselves in space. I suddenly regained my sight. It was a pitch-black night. Never, never had there been such darkness! We were flying through space at a terrific speed and we had already left the earth behind us. I did not question the being who was carrying me. I was proud and waited. I was telling myself that I was not afraid, and I was filled with admiration at the thought that I was not afraid. I cannot remember how long we were flying, nor can I give you an idea of the time; it all happened as it always does happen in dreams when you leap over space and time and the laws of nature and reason, and only pause at the points which are especially dear to your heart. All I remember is that I suddenly beheld a little star in the darkness.

"Is that Sirius?" I asked, feeling suddenly unable to restrain myself, for I had made up my mind not to ask any questions.

"No," answered the being who was carrying me, "that is the same star you saw between the clouds when you were coming home."

I knew that its face bore some resemblance to a human face. It is a strange fact but I did not like that being, and I even felt an intense aversion for it. I had expected complete nonexistence and that was why I had shot myself through the heart. And yet there I was in the hands of a being, not human of course, but which *was*, which existed. "So there is life beyond the grave!" I thought with the curious irrelevance of a dream, but at heart I remained essentially unchanged. "If I must *be* again," I thought, "and live again at someone's unalterable behest, I won't be defeated and humiliated!"

"You know I'm afraid of you and that's why you despise me," I said suddenly to my companion, unable to refrain from the humiliating remark with its implied admission, and feeling my own humiliation in my heart like the sharp prick of a needle.

He did not answer me, but I suddenly felt that I was not despised, that no one was laughing at me, that no one was even pitying me, and that our journey had a purpose, an unknown and mysterious purpose that concerned only me. Fear was steadily growing in my heart. Something was communicated to me from my silent companion—mutely but agonizingly—and it seemed to permeate my whole being. We were speeding through dark and unknown regions of space. I had long since lost sight of the constellations familiar to me. I knew that there were stars in the heavenly spaces whose light took thousands and millions of years to reach the earth. Possibly we were already flying through those

spaces. I expected something in the terrible anguish that wrung my heart. And suddenly a strangely familiar and incredibly nostalgic feeling shook me to the very core: I suddenly caught sight of our sun! I knew that it could not possibly be *our* sun that gave birth to our earth, and that we were millions of miles away from our sun, but for some unknown reason I recognized with every fibre of my being that it was precisely the same sun as ours, its exact copy and twin. A sweet, nostalgic feeling filled my heart with rapture: the old familiar power of the same light which had given me life stirred an echo in my heart and revived it, and I felt the same life stirring within me for the first time since I had been in the grave.

"But if it is the sun, if it's exactly the same sun as ours," I cried, "then where is the earth?"

And my companion pointed to a little star twinkling in the darkness with an emerald light. We were making straight for it.

"But are such repetitions possible in the universe? Can that be nature's law? And if that is an earth there, is it the same earth as ours? Just the same poor, unhappy, but dear, dear earth, and beloved for ever and ever? Arousing like our earth the same poignant love for herself even in the most ungrateful of her children?" I kept crying, deeply moved by an uncontrollable, rapturous love for the dear old earth I had left behind.

The face of the poor little girl I had treated so badly flashed through my mind.

"You shall see it all," answered my companion, and a strange sadness sounded in his voice.

But we were rapidly approaching the planet. It was growing before my eyes. I could already distinguish the ocean, the outlines of Europe, and suddenly a strange feeling of some great and sacred jealousy blazed up in my heart.

"How is such a repetition possible and why? I love, I can only love the earth I've left behind, stained with my blood when, ungrateful wretch that I am, I extinguished my life by shooting myself through the heart. But never, never have I ceased to love that earth, and even on the night I parted from it I loved it perhaps more poignantly than ever. Is there suffering on this new earth? On our earth we can truly love only with suffering and through suffering! We know not how to love otherwise. We know no other love. I want suffering in order to love. I want and thirst this very minute to kiss, with tears streaming down my cheeks, the one and only earth I have left behind. I don't want, I won't accept life on any other! . . ."

But my companion had already left me. Suddenly, and without as it were being aware of it myself, I stood on this other earth in the bright light of a sunny day, fair and beautiful as paradise. I believe I was standing on one of the islands which on our earth form the Greek archipelago, or somewhere on the coast of the mainland close to this archipelago. Oh, everything was just as it is with us, except that everything seemed to be bathed in the radiance of some public festival and of some great and holy triumph attained at last. The gentle emerald sea softly lapped the shore and kissed it with manifest, visible, almost conscious love. Tall, beautiful trees stood in all the glory of their green luxuriant foliage, and their innumerable leaves (I am sure of that) welcomed me with their soft, tender rustle, and seemed to utter sweet words of love. The lush grass blazed with bright and fragrant flowers. Birds were flying in flocks through the air and, without being afraid of me, alighted on my shoulders and hands and joyfully beat against me with their sweet fluttering wings. And at last I saw and came to know the people of this blessed earth. They came to me themselves. They surrounded me. They kissed me. Children of the sun, children of their sun—oh, how beautiful they were! Never on our earth had I beheld such beauty in man. Only perhaps in our children during the very first years of their life could one have found a remote,

though faint, reflection of this beauty. The eyes of these happy people shone with a bright lustre. Their faces were radiant with understanding and a serenity of mind that had reached its greatest fulfillment. Those faces were joyous; in the words and voices of these people there was a childlike gladness. Oh, at the first glance at their faces I at once understood all, all! It was an earth unstained by the Fall, inhabited by people who had not sinned and who lived in the same paradise as that in which, according to the legends of mankind, our first parents lived before they sinned, with the only difference that all the earth here was everywhere the same paradise. These people, laughing happily, thronged round me and overwhelmed me with their caresses; they took me home with them, and each of them was anxious to set my mind at peace. Oh, they asked me no questions, but seemed to know everything already (that was the impression I got), and they longed to remove every trace of suffering from my face as soon as possible.

IV

Well, you see, again let me repeat: All right, let us assume it was only a dream! But the sensation of the love of those innocent and beautiful people has remained with me for ever, and I can feel that their love is even now flowing out to me from over there. I have seen them myself. I have known them thoroughly and been convinced. I loved them and I suffered for them afterwards. Oh, I knew at once even all the time that there were many things about them I should never be able to understand. To me, a modern Russian progressive and a despicable citizen of Petersburg, it seemed inexplicable that, knowing so much, they knew nothing of our science, for instance. But I soon realized that their knowledge was derived from, and fostered by, emotions other than those to which we were accustomed on earth, and that their aspirations, too, were quite different. They desired nothing. They were at peace with themselves. They did not strive to gain knowledge of life as we strive to understand it because their lives were full. But their knowledge was higher and deeper than the knowledge we derive from our science; for our science seeks to explain what life is and strives to understand it in order to teach others how to live, while they knew how to live without science. I understood that, but I couldn't understand their knowledge. They pointed out their trees to me, and I could not understand the intense love with which they looked on them; it was as though they were talking with beings like themselves. And, you know, I don't think I am exaggerating in saying that they talked with them! Yes, they had discovered their language, and I am sure the trees understood them. They looked upon all nature like that—the animals which lived peaceably with them and did not attack them, but loved them, conquered by their love for them. They pointed out the stars to me and talked to me about them in a way that I could not understand, but I am certain that in some curious way they communed with the stars in the heavens, not only in thought, but in some actual, living way. Oh, these people were not concerned whether I understood them or not; they loved me without it. But I too knew that they would never be able to understand me, and for that reason I hardly ever spoke to them about our earth. I merely kissed the earth on which they lived in their presence, and worshipped them without any words. And they saw that and let me worship them without being ashamed that I was worshipping them, for they themselves loved much. They did not suffer for me when, weeping, I sometimes kissed their feet, for in their hearts they were joyfully aware of the strong affection with which they would return my love. At times I asked myself in amazement how they had managed never to offend a person like me and not once arouse in a person like me a feeling of jealousy and envy.

Many times I asked myself how I—a braggart and a liar—could refrain from telling them all I knew of science and philosophy, of which of course they had no idea? How it had never occurred to me to impress them with my store of learning, or impart my learning to them out of the love I bore them?

They were playful and high-spirited like children. They wandered about their beautiful woods and groves, they sang their beautiful songs, they lived on simple food—the fruits of their trees, the honey from their woods, and the milk of the animals that loved them. To obtain their food and clothes, they did not work very hard or long. They knew love and they begot children, but I never noticed in them those outbursts of *cruel* sensuality which overtake almost everybody on our earth, whether man or woman, and are the only source of almost every sin of our human race. They rejoiced in their newborn children as new sharers in their bliss. There were no quarrels or jealousy among them, and they did not even know what the words meant. Their children were the children of them all, for they were all one family. There was scarcely any illness among them, though there was death; but their old people died peacefully, as though falling asleep, surrounded by the people who took leave of them, blessing them and smiling at them, and themselves receiving with bright smiles the farewell wishes of their friends. I never saw grief or tears on those occasions. What I did see was love that seemed to reach the point of rapture, but it was a gentle, self-sufficient, and contemplative rapture. There was reason to believe that they communicated with the departed after death, and that their earthly union was not cut short by death. They found it almost impossible to understand me when I questioned them about life eternal, but apparently they were so convinced of it in their minds that for them it was no question at all. They had no places of worship, but they had a certain awareness of a constant, uninterrupted, and living union with the

Universe at large. They had no specific religions, but instead they had a certain knowledge that when their earthly joy had reached the limits imposed upon it by nature, they—both the living and the dead—would reach a state of still closer communion with the Universe at large. They looked forward to that moment with joy, but without haste and without pining for it, as though already possessing it in the vague stirrings of their hearts, which they communicated to each other.

In the evening, before going to sleep, they were fond of gathering together and singing in melodious and harmonious choirs. In their songs they expressed all the sensations the parting day had given them. They praised it and bade it farewell. They praised nature, the earth, the sea, and the woods. They were also fond of composing songs about one another, and they praised each other like children. Their songs were very simple, but they sprang straight from the heart and they touched the heart. And not only in their songs alone, but they seemed to spend all their lives in perpetual praise of one another. It seemed to be a universal and all-embracing love for each other. Some of their songs were solemn and ecstatic, and I was scarcely able to understand them at all. While understanding the words, I could never entirely fathom their meaning. It remained somehow beyond the grasp of my reason, and yet it sank unconsciously deeper and deeper into my heart. I often told them that I had had a presentiment of it years ago and that all that joy and glory had been perceived by me while I was still on our earth as a nostalgic yearning, bordering at times on unendurably poignant sorrow; that I had had a presentiment of them all and of their glory in the dreams of my heart and in the reveries of my soul; that often on our earth I could not look at the setting sun without tears. . . . That there always was a sharp pang of anguish in my hatred of the men of our earth; why could I not hate them without loving them too? why

could I not forgive them? And in my love for them, too, there was a sharp pang of anguish: why could I not love them without hating them? They listened to me, and I could tell that they did not know what I was talking about. But I was not sorry to have spoken to them of it, for I knew that they appreciated how much and how anxiously I yearned for those I had forsaken. Oh yes, when they looked at me with their dear eyes full of love, when I realized that in their presence my heart, too, became as innocent and truthful as theirs, I did not regret my inability to understand them, either. The sensation of the fullness of life left me breathless, and I worshipped them in silence.

Oh, everyone laughs in my face now and everyone assures me that I could not possibly have seen and felt anything so definite, but was merely conscious of a sensation that arose in my own feverish heart, and that I invented all those details myself when I woke up. And when I told them that they were probably right, good Lord, what mirth that admission of mine caused and how they laughed at me! Why, of course, I was overpowered by the mere sensation of that dream and it alone survived in my sorely wounded heart. But none the less the real shapes and forms of my dream, that is, those I actually saw at the very time of my dream, were filled with such harmony and were so enchanting and beautiful, and so intensely true, that on awakening I was indeed unable to clothe them in our feeble words so that they were bound as it were to become blurred in my mind; so is it any wonder that perhaps unconsciously I was myself afterwards driven to make up the details which I could not help distorting, particularly in view of my passionate desire to convey some of them at least as quickly as I could. But that does not mean that I have no right to believe that it all did happen. As a matter of fact, it was quite possibly a thousand times better, brighter, and more joyful than I describe it. What if it was only a dream? All that couldn't possibly not have been. And do you know, I think I'll tell you a secret: perhaps it was no dream at all! For what happened afterwards was so awful, so horribly true, that it couldn't possibly have been a mere coinage of my brain seen in a dream. Granted that my heart was responsible for my dream, but could my heart alone have been responsible for the awful truth of what happened to me afterwards? Surely my paltry heart and my vacillating and trivial mind could not have risen to such a revelation of truth! Oh, judge for yourselves: I have been concealing it all the time, but now I will tell you the whole truth. The fact is, I—corrupted them all!

V

Yes, yes, it ended in my corrupting them all! How it could have happened I do not know, but I remember it clearly. The dream encompassed thousands of years and left in me only a vague sensation of the whole. I only know that the cause of the Fall was I. Like a horrible trichina, like the germ of the plague infecting whole kingdoms, so did I infect with myself all that happy earth that knew no sin before me. They learnt to lie, and they grew to appreciate the beauty of a lie. Oh, perhaps, it all began *innocently*, with a jest, with a desire to show off, with amorous play, and perhaps indeed only with a germ, but this germ made its way into their hearts and they liked it. The voluptuousness was soon born, voluptuousness begot jealousy, and jealousy—cruelty. . . . Oh, I don't know, I can't remember, but soon, very soon the first blood was shed: they were shocked and horrified, and they began to separate and to shun one another. Recriminations began, reproaches. They came to know shame, and they made shame into a virtue. The conception of honor was born, and every alliance raised its own standard. They began torturing animals, and the animals ran away from them into the forests and became their enemies. A struggle began for separation, for isolation, for personality, for mine and thine. They began talking in different languages. They came to know sorrow, and they loved sorrow. They thirsted for suffering, and they said that Truth could only be attained through suffering. It was then that science made its appearance among them. When they became wicked, they began talking of brotherhood and humanity and understood the meaning of those ideas. When they became guilty of crimes, they invented justice, and drew up whole codes of law, and to ensure the carrying out of their laws they erected a guillotine. They only vaguely remembered what they had lost, and they would not believe that they ever were happy and innocent. They even laughed at the possibility of their former happiness and called it a dream. They could not even imagine it in any definite shape or form, but the strange and wonderful thing was that though they had lost faith in their former state of happiness and called it a fairy tale, they longed so much to be happy and innocent once more that, like children, they succumbed to the desire of their hearts, glorified this desire, built temples, and began offering up prayers to their own idea, their own "desire," and at the same time firmly believed that it could not be realized and brought about, though they still worshipped it and adored it with tears. And yet if they could have in one way or another returned to the state of happy innocence they had lost, and if someone had shown it to them again and had asked them whether they desired to go back to it, they would certainly have refused. The answer they gave me was, "What if we are dishonest, cruel, and unjust? We *know* it and we are sorry for it, and we torment ourselves for it, and inflict pain upon ourselves, and punish ourselves more perhaps than the merciful Judge who will judge us and whose name we do not know. But we have science and with its aid we shall again discover truth, though we shall accept it only when we perceive it with our reason. Knowledge is higher than feeling, and the consciousness of life is higher than life. Science will give us wisdom. Wisdom will reveal to us the laws. And the knowledge of the laws of happiness is higher than happiness." That is what they said to me, and having uttered those words, each of them began to love himself better than anyone else, and indeed they could not do otherwise. Every one of them became so jealous of his own personality that he strove with might and main to belittle and humble it in others; and therein he saw the whole purpose of his life. Slavery made its appearance, even voluntary slavery: the weak eagerly submitted themselves to the will of the strong on condition that the strong helped them to oppress those who were weaker than themselves. Saints made their appearance, saints who came to these people with tears and told them of their pride, of their loss of proportion and harmony, of their loss of shame. They were laughed to scorn and stoned to death. Their sacred blood was spilt on the threshold of the temples. But then men arose who began to wonder how they could all be united again, so that everybody should, without ceasing to love himself best of all, not interfere with everybody else and so that all of them should live together in a society which would at least seem to be founded on mutual understanding. Whole wars were fought over this idea. All the combatants at one and the same time firmly believed that science, wisdom, and the instinct of self-preservation would in the end force mankind to unite into a harmonious and intelligent society, and therefore, to hasten matters, the "very wise" did their best to exterminate as rapidly as possible the "not so wise" who did not understand their idea, so as to prevent them from interfering with its triumph. But the instinct of self-preservation began to weaken rapidly. Proud and voluptuous men appeared who frankly demanded all or nothing. In order to obtain everything they did not hesitate to resort to violence, and if it failed—to suicide. Religions were founded to propagate the cult of nonexistence and self-destruction for the sake of the everlasting peace in nothingness. At last these people grew weary of their senseless labors and suffering appeared on their faces, and these people proclaimed that suffering was beauty, for in suffering alone was there thought. They glorified suffering in their songs. I walked among them, wringing my hands and weeping over them, but I loved them perhaps more than before when there was no sign of suffering in their faces and when they were innocent and—oh, so beautiful! I loved the earth they had polluted even more than when it had been a paradise, and only because sorrow had made its appearance on it. Alas, I always loved sorrow and affliction, but only for myself, only for myself; for them I wept now, for I pitied them. I stretched out my hands to them, accusing, cursing, and despising myself. I told them that I alone was responsible for it all—I alone; that it was I who had brought them corruption, contamination, and lies! I implored them to crucify me, and I taught them how to make the cross. I could not kill myself; I had not the courage to do it; but I longed to receive martyrdom at their hands. I thirsted for martyrdom, I yearned for my blood to be shed to the last drop in torment and suffering. But they only laughed at me, and in the end they began looking upon me as a madman. They justified me. They said that they had got what they themselves wanted and that what was now could not have been otherwise. At last they told me that I was becoming dangerous to them and that they would lock me up in a lunatic asylum if I did not hold my peace. Then sorrow entered my soul with such force that my heart was wrung and I felt as though I were dying, and then— well, then I awoke.

It was morning, that is, the sun had not risen yet, but it was about six o'clock. When I came to, I found myself in the same armchair, my candle had burnt out, in the captain's room they were asleep, and silence, so rare in our house, reigned around. The first thing I did was to jump up in great amazement. Nothing like this had ever happened to me before, not even so far as the most trivial details were concerned. Never, for instance, had I fallen asleep like this in my armchair. Then, suddenly, as I was standing and coming to myself, I caught sight of my gun lying there ready and loaded. But I pushed it away from me at once! Oh, how I longed for life, life! I lifted up my hands and called upon eternal Truth—no, not called upon it, but wept. Rapture, infinite and boundless rapture intoxicated me. Yes, life and—preaching! I made up my mind to preach from that very moment and, of course, to go on preaching all my life. I am going to preach, I want to preach. What? Why, truth. For I have beheld truth. I have beheld it with mine own eyes, I have beheld it in all its glory!

And since then I have been preaching. Moreover, I love all who laugh at me more than all the rest. Why that is so, I don't know and I cannot explain, but let it be so. They say that even now I often get muddled and confused and that if I am getting muddled and confused now, what will be later on? It is perfectly true. I do get muddled and confused and it is quite possible that I shall be getting worse later. And, of course, I shall get muddled several times before I find out how to preach, that is, what words to use and what deeds to perform, for that is all very difficult! All this is even now as clear to me as daylight, but, pray, tell me who does not get muddled and confused? And yet all follow the same path, at least all strive to achieve the same thing, from the philosopher to the lowest criminal, only by different roads. It is an old truth, but this is what is new: I cannot even get very much muddled and confused. For I have beheld the Truth. I have beheld it and I know that people can be happy and beautiful without losing their ability to live on earth. I will not and I cannot believe that evil is the normal condition among men. And yet they all laugh at this faith of mine. But how can I help believing it? I have beheld it—the Truth—it is not as though I had invented it with my mind: I have beheld it, I have beheld it, and the *living image* of it has filled my soul for ever. I have beheld it in all its glory and I cannot believe that it cannot exist among men. So how can I grow muddled and confused? I shall of course lose my way and I'm afraid that now and again I may speak with words that are not my own, but not for long: the living image of what I beheld will always be with me and it will always correct me and lead me back on to the right path. Oh, I'm in fine fettle, and I am of good cheer. I will go on and on for a thousand years, if need be. Do you know, at first I did not mean to tell you that I corrupted them, but that was a mistake—there you have my first mistake! But Truth whispered to me that I was *lying*, and so preserved me and set me on the right path. But I'm afraid I do not know how to establish a heaven on earth, for I do not know how to put it into words. After my dream I lost the knack of putting things into words. At least, into the most necessary and most important words. But never mind, I shall go on and I shall keep on talking, for I have indeed beheld it with my own eyes, though I cannot describe what I saw. It is this the scoffers do not understand. "He had a dream," they say, "a vision, a hallucination!" Oh dear, is this all they have to say? Do they really think that is very clever? And how proud they are! A dream! What is a dream? And what about our life? Is that not a dream too? I will say more: even—yes, even if this never comes to pass, even if there never is a heaven on earth (that, at any rate, I can see very well!), even then I shall go on preaching. And really how simple it all is: in one day, *in one hour*, everything could be arranged at once! The main thing is to love your neighbor as yourself—that is the main thing, and that is everything, for nothing else matters. Once you do that, you will discover at once how everything can be arranged. And yet it is an old truth, a truth that has been told over and over again, but in spite of that it finds no place among men! "The consciousness of life is higher than life, the knowledge of happiness is higher than happiness" —that is what we have to fight against! And I shall, I shall fight against it! If only we all wanted it, everything could be arranged immediately.

And—I did find that little girl.... And I shall go on! I shall go on!

GUSTAVE FLAUBERT

The Legend of St. Julian the Hospitaler

Translated by Wallace Fowlie

I

Julian's father and mother lived in a castle, in the middle of a forest, on the slope of a hill.

The four towers at the corners had pointed roofs covered with scales of lead, and the base of the walls rested on shafts of rock which fell steeply to the bottom of the moat.

The pavement of the courtyard was as clean as the flagstones of a church. Long gutter-spouts, representing dragons, with their mouths hanging down, spat rainwater into the cistern; and on the window ledges, at every floor, in a pot of painted earthenware, a basil or heliotrope blossomed.

A second enclosure, made with stakes, contained first an orchard of fruit trees, then a flower-bed where flowers were patterned into the form of figures, and then a trellis with arbors where you could take a walk, and a mall where the pages could play. On the other side were the kennels, the stables, the bakery, the wine-presses and the barns. A pasture of green grass spread round about, itself enclosed by a stout thorn-hedge.

They had lived at peace for so long that the portcullis was never lowered. The moats were full of water, birds made their nests in the cracks of the battlements, and when the blaze of the sun was too strong, the archer, who all day long walked back and forth on the curtain wall, went into the watch-tower and slept like a monk.

Inside, the ironwork glistened everywhere. Tapestries in the bedrooms were protection against the cold. Cupboards overflowed with linen, casks of wine were piled up in the cellars, and oak coffers creaked with the weight of bags of money.

In the armory, between standards and heads of wild beasts, you could see weapons of every age and nation, from the slings of the Amalekites and the javelins of the Garamantes, to the short swords of the Saracens and the Norman coats-of-mail.

The large spit in the kitchen could roast an ox. The chapel was as sumptuous as the oratory of a king. There was even, in a remote corner, a Roman steam-bath; but the good lord did not use it, considering it a pagan practice.

Always wrapped in a coat lined with fox fur, he walked about his house, meting out justice to his vassals and settling the quarrels of his neighbors. During the winter, he would watch the snowflakes fall or have stories read to him. With the first fine days he went off on his mule along the small lanes, beside the wheat turning green, and chatted with the peasants, to whom he gave advice. After many adventures, he had taken as his wife a young lady of high lineage.

Her skin was very white, and she was a bit proud and serious. The horns of her coif grazed the lintel of the doors, and the train of her dress trailed three paces behind her. Her household was run like the inside of a monastery. Each morning she distributed the work to her servants, supervised the preserves and unguents, span at her distaff or embroidered altar-cloths. After much praying to God, a son was born to her.

There was great rejoicing then, and a banquet which lasted three days and four nights, on leaves strewn about, under the illumination from torches and the playing of harps. They ate the rarest spices, with chickens as fat as sheep. For amusement, a dwarf came out of a pastry-pie, and as the bowls gave out because the crowd was constantly increasing, they were obliged to drink from horns and helmets.

The new mother was not present at this festivity. She quietly stayed in her bed. One evening she awoke and saw, under a moonbeam which came through the window, something like a moving shadow. It was an old man in a frieze robe, with a rosary at his side, a wallet on his shoulder, and resembling a hermit. He came near to her bedside and said to her, without opening his lips:

"Rejoice, O mother, your son will be a saint!"

She was going to cry out, but, gliding along the moonbeam, he gently rose up into the air and disappeared. The banquet songs broke out louder. She heard the voices of angels and her head fell back on her pillow over which hung a martyr's bone in a frame of carbuncles.

The next day all the servants were questioned and declared they had seen no hermit. Dream or reality, it must have been a message from heaven, but she was careful to say nothing about it, for fear she would be accused of pride.

The guests departed at day-break. Julian's father was outside of the postern gate where he had just accompanied the last one to go, when suddenly a beggar rose up before him in the mist. He was a Gypsy with plaited beard and silver rings on his two arms, and flaming eyes. Like one inspired, he stammered these disconnected words:

"Ah, ah! your son! . . . much blood! . . . much glory! . . . always happy! an emperor's family."

And bending down to pick up his alms, he was lost in the grass and disappeared.

The good castellan looked right and left, and called as loud as he could. No one! The wind whistled and the morning mist flew away.

He attributed this vision to the weariness of his head for having slept too little. "If I speak of this, they will make fun of me," he said to himself. Yet the glory destined to his son dazzled him, although the promise was not clear and he even doubted he had heard it.

The husband and wife kept their secret. But both cherished the child with an equal love, and respecting him as one marked by God, they had infinite care for his person. His crib was padded with the finest down, a lamp in the form of a dove burned over it, three nurses rocked him, and, tightly wrapped in his swaddling-clothes, with rosy face and blue eyes, dressed in a brocade mantle and a bonnet set with pearls, he looked like a little Lord Jesus. He teethed without crying once.

When he was seven, his mother taught him to sing. To make him brave, his father lifted him up on to a large horse. The child smiled with pleasure and was not long in knowing everything about chargers.

A very learned old monk taught him Holy Scripture, Arabic numerals, Latin letters, and how to make charming pictures on vellum. They worked together, high up in a turret, away from noise.

When the lesson was over, they went down into the garden where they studied flowers as they walked slowly about.

Sometimes they saw, passing below in the valley, a file of beasts of burden, led by a man walking, dressed in an Oriental fashion. The castellan, recognizing him for a merchant, would send a page to him. The stranger, when he felt confidence, turned off from his road. When led into the parlor, he would take out of his coffers strips of velvet and silk, jewelry, spices and strange things of unknown use. After this, the fellow, having suffered no violence, would go off, with a large profit. At other times, a group of pilgrims would knock at the door. Their wet clothes steamed before the hearth. When they had eaten heartily, they told the story of their travels: the courses of the ships on the foamy sea, the journeyings on foot in the burning sand, the cruelty of the pagans, the caves of Syria, the Manger and the Sepulcher. Then they would give the young lord shells from their cloaks.

Often the castellan would give a feast for his old companions-at-arms. As they drank, they recalled their wars, the storming of fortresses with the crash of war machines and huge wounds. As he listened to them, Julian uttered cries; his father then did not doubt that one day he would be a conqueror. But at evening, coming from the Angelus, when he passed among the poor, with their heads bowed, he took money from his purse with such modesty and so noble an air, that his mother was sure she would see him one day an archbishop.

His place in chapel was beside his parents, and no matter how long the services, he remained kneeling on his prayer-stool, his cap on the floor and his hands clasped.

One day, during mass, he saw, on raising his head, a small white mouse coming out of a hole in the wall. It trotted over the first step of the altar and after two or three turns to right and left, scampered back from where it had come. The next Sunday, he was disturbed by the thought that he might see it again. It came back, and each Sunday, he waited for it, was upset by it, grew to hate it and made up his mind to get rid of it.

So, having shut the door and spread on the steps some cake-crumbs, he took his place in front of the hole, with a stick in his hand.

After a long time, a pink nose appeared, and then the entire mouse. He struck a light blow, and stood lost in stupefaction before the small body that did not move again. A drop of blood spotted the pavement. He quickly wiped it with his sleeve, threw the mouse outdoors, and did not mention the matter to anyone.

All kinds of small birds were pecking at the seeds in the garden. He had the idea of putting peas in a hollow reed. When he heard the birds chirping in a tree, he came up to it quietly, then raised his pipe and blew out his cheeks. The little creatures rained down on his shoulders in such numbers that he could not keep from laughing with delight over his malice.

One morning, as he was coming back along the curtain wall, he saw on the top of the rampart a fat pigeon strutting in the sun. Julian stopped to look at it. The wall at that spot had a breach and a fragment of stone lay close to his fingers. He swung his arm and the stone struck down the bird which fell like a lump into the moat.

He rushed down after it, tearing himself on the undergrowth, ferreting about everywhere, more nimble than a young dog.

The pigeon, its wings broken, hung quivering in the branches of a privet.

Its persistence to live irritated the boy. He began to strangle it. The bird's convulsions made his heart beat and filled him with a wild tumultuous pleasure. When it stiffened for the last time, he felt himself fainting.

During the evening meal, his father declared it was time for him to learn venery, and went to look for an old copybook containing, in the form of questions and answers, the entire pastime of hunting. In it a teacher demonstrated to his pupil the art of training dogs and taming falcons, of setting traps, of how to recognize the stag by his droppings, the fox by its track, the wolf by its scratchings; the right way to make out their tracks, the way in which to start them, where their lairs are usually found, which winds are the most favorable, with a list of the calls and the rules for the quarry.

When Julian could recite all these things by heart, his father made up a pack of hounds for him.

First you could see twenty-four greyhounds from Barbary, swifter than gazelles, but subject to over-excitement; then seventeen pairs of Breton hounds, with red coats and white spots, unshakably dependable, broad-chested and great howlers. For an attack on the wild boar and for dangerous redoublings, there were forty griffons, as shaggy as bears. Mastiffs from Tartary, almost as tall as asses, flame-colored, with broad backs and straight legs, were intended to hunt aurochs. The black coats of the spaniels shone like satin. The yapping of the talbots was equal to the chanting of the beagles. In a yard by themselves, as they shook their chains and rolled their eyes, growled eight Alain bulldogs, formidable beasts which fly at the belly of a horseman and have no fear of lions.

All ate wheat bread, drank from stone troughs, and bore sonorous names.

The falconry, possibly, was better chosen than the pack. The good lord, thanks to money, had secured tercelets from the Caucasus, sakers from Babylonia, gerfalcons from Germany, and peregrines, caught on the cliffs, at the edge of cold seas, in distant countries. They were housed in a shed with a thatched roof, and attached according to size on the perching-bar. Before them was a strip of grass where from time to time they were placed to unstiffen their legs.

Rabbit-nets, hooks, wolf-traps and all kinds of snares were constructed.

They often took into the country setters which quickly came to a point. Then grooms, advancing step by step, cautiously spread over their motionless bodies an immense net. A word of command made them bark; the quail took wing; and ladies from nearby, invited with their husbands, children, handmaids,—the entire group fell on the birds and easily caught them.

On other occasions, to start the hares, they would beat drums. Foxes fell into pits, or a trap would spring and catch a wolf by its paw.

But Julian scorned these easy devices. He preferred to hunt far from the others, with his horse and falcon. It was almost always a large Scythian tartaret, white as snow. Its leather hood was topped with a plume, gold bells shook on its blue feet. It stood firm on its master's arm while the horse galloped and the plains unrolled. Julian, untying the jesses, would suddenly release it. The bold bird rose straight as an arrow into the air, and you saw two uneven specks turn, meet and disappear in the high blue of the sky. The falcon was not long in coming down, tearing apart some bird, and returned to perch on the gauntlet, its two wings quivering.

In this way, Julian flew his falcon at the heron, the kite, the crow and the vulture.

As he blew his horn, he loved to follow his dogs when they ran over the side of the hills, jumped the streams, and climbed back to the woods. When the stag began to groan under the bites of the dogs, he killed it quickly and then revelled in the fury of the mastiffs as they devoured it, cut into pieces on its steaming skin.

On foggy days he would go down into a marsh to ambush geese and otters and wildduck.

At dawn three squires were waiting for him at the foot of the steps, and the old monk, leaning out of his dormer-window, vainly made signs to call him back. Julian would not turn. He went out in the heat of the sun, in the rain, in storms, drank the water of the springs out of his hand, ate crab-apples as he trotted, rested under an oak if he were tired; and came back in the middle of the night, covered with blood and mire, with thorns in his hair and the smell of wild beasts on him. He became one of them. When his mother kissed him, he accepted her embrace coldly and seemed to be dreaming of deep things.

He killed bears with blows of his knife, bulls with the axe, wild boars with the boar-spear, and once, even, with only a stick he defended himself against wolves which were gnawing corpses at the foot of a gibbet.

One winter morning, he left before daybreak, well equipped, with a crossbow on his shoulder and a bunch of arrows at his saddle-bow.

His Danish jennet, followed by two bassets, made the earth resound under its even tread. Drops of ice stuck to his cloak. A strong wind was blowing. One side of the horizon lighted up, and in the whiteness of the early light, he saw rabbits hopping at the edge of their burrows. Immediately the two bassets rushed on them, and quickly throwing them back and forth broke their backs.

Soon he went into a forest. At the end of a branch, a wood grouse, numbed by the cold, slept with its head under its wing. With a back-stroke of his sword, Julian cut off its two feet, and without picking it up, went on his way.

Three hours later, he was on the top of a mountain, so high that the sky seemed almost black. In front of him, a rock like a long wall sloped down, hanging over a precipice. At its farther end, two wild rams were looking into the chasm. Since he did not have his arrows (his horse had stayed behind), he decided to go down to them. Barefoot and half bent-over, he finally reached the first of the rams, and plunged a dagger under its ribs. The second, terrified, jumped into the chasm. Julian jumped in order to strike it, and slipping on his right foot, fell over the body of the other one, his face over the abyss and his two arms spread out.

Coming down again onto the plain, he followed a line of willows which bordered a river. Cranes, flying very low, passed overhead from time to time. Julian killed them with his whip and did not miss one.

In the meantime the warmer air had melted the hoarfrost, broad streaks of mist floated in the air and the sun came out. At a distance he saw a still lake glistening as if it were of lead. In the middle of the lake there was an animal which Julian did not know, a beaver with a black snout. In spite of the distance, an arrow killed it, and he was disconsolate at not being able to carry off the skin.

Then he advanced along an avenue of tall trees, forming with their tops a kind of triumphal arch, at the entrance of a forest. A roebuck bounded out of a thick wood, a deer appeared at a crossing, a badger came out of a hole, a peacock spread its tail on the grass; and when he had slain them all, more roebucks appeared, more deer, more badgers, more peacocks, and blackbirds, jays, polecats, foxes, hedgehogs, lynxes, an endless number of animals, more numerous at every step. They circled around him, trembling and looking at him gently and entreatingly. But Julian did not tire of killing, by turns bending his crossbow, unsheathing his sword, thrusting with his cutlass, and having no thought, no memory of anything at all. He had been hunting in some vague country, for an indefinite time, by the sole fact of his own existence, and everything had been accomplished with the ease you experience in dreams. An extraordinary spectacle brought him to a halt. A valley in the form of an amphitheater was filled with stags crowded close together and warming one another with their breath which could be seen steaming in the fog.

The perspective of such a slaughter choked him with pleasure for a few minutes. Then he dismounted, rolled up his sleeves and began to shoot.

At the whistle of the first arrow, all the stags turned their heads at once. Some openings were made in their mass. Plaintive cries rose up and a great stir shook the herd.

The brim of the valley was too high to climb. They leapt about in the enclosure, trying to escape. Julian kept aiming and shooting, and his arrows fell like shafts of rain in a storm. The maddened stags fought, reared, and climbed over each other. Their bodies with their entangled antlers made a broad hillock which collapsed as it moved about.

At last they died, stretched out on the sand, frothing at the nostrils, their entrails coming out, and the heaving of their bellies slowly diminishing. Then all was motionless.

Night was approaching. Behind the woods, in the interspaces of the branches, the sky was red like a cloth of blood.

Julian leaned against a tree. With staring eyes he looked at the vastness of the massacre, and did not understand how he could have done it.

On the other side of the valley, on the edge of the forest, he saw a stag, a hind and its fawn.

The stag, which was black and huge in size, carried antlers of sixteen tines and a white beard. The hind, of a dull yellow like dead leaves, was grazing, and the spotted fawn, without hindering her walk, was suckling her udder.

Once more the crossbow hummed. The fawn was killed at once. Then its mother, raising her head toward the sky, belled with a deep, heart-rending, human cry. Exasperated, Julian, with one shot full in the breast, stretched her out on the ground.

The large stag had seen this and made one bound. Julian shot his last arrow at him. It pierced him in the forehead and stuck fast there.

The large stag did not seem to feel it. Stepping over the dead bodies, it kept coming, and was going to charge and disembowel him. Julian drew back in unspeakable fear. The monstrous animal stopped. With his eyes flaming, as solemn as a patriarch and a judge, he repeated three times, while a bell tolled far off:

"A curse on you! A curse on you! A curse on you! One day, ferocious heart, you will murder your father and your mother!"

His knees bent, he gently closed his eyes, and died.

Julian was stupefied and then crushed by a sudden fatigue. Disgust and an immense sadness overcame him. His head in his two hands, he wept for a long time.

His horse was lost, his dogs had abandoned him, and the solitude which surrounded him seemed to threaten him with vague perils. Impelled by fright, he made his way across the countryside, chose a path at random, and found himself almost immediately at the gate of the castle.

That night he did not sleep. In the flickering of the hanging lamp he kept seeing the large black stag. Its prophecy obsessed him. He fought against it. "No, no, no, it is impossible for me to kill them!" Then he thought, "And yet, what if I wished to . . . ?" And he feared that the devil might inspire him with this desire.

For three months his anguished mother prayed by his bedside, and his father with groans walked back and forth in the corridors. He sent for the most famous master physicians who prescribed quantities of drugs. They said that the malady of Julian had been caused by some deadly wind or by a love-desire. But the young man, at every question, shook his head.

His strength came back, and he was taken for walks in the courtyard, the old monk and the good lord supporting him on either side.

When he had completely recovered, he stubbornly refused to hunt.

His father, wanting to cheer him, made him a present of a large Saracen sword.

It was at the top of a pillar, in a trophy-stand. To reach it, a ladder was necessary. Julian climbed up. The sword was so heavy that it slipped from his fingers as it fell, it grazed the good lord so close that it cut his greatcoat. Julian thought he had killed his father and fainted.

From then on, he dreaded weapons. The sight of a bare blade made him turn pale. This weakness was a sorrow for his family.

Finally the old monk, in the name of God, of his honor and his ancestors, ordered him to resume his exercises of a noble.

Every day the squires amused themselves by practising with the javelin. Very soon Julian excelled in this. He could hurl his into the neck of bottles, or break off the teeth of weather-vanes, or hit the nails on doors at a hundred paces.

One summer evening, at the hour when the fog makes things indistinct, he was under the vine-arbor of the garden and saw at the end of it two white wings fluttering at the same height as the espalier. He thought beyond doubt it was a stork, and threw his javelin.

A piercing cry rang out.

It was his mother whose bonnet with long flaps was nailed to the wall.

Julian fled from the castle and was not seen there again.

II

He joined up with a troop of adventurers who happened to pass by. He knew hunger, thirst, fever and vermin. He grew accustomed to the din of fights, and to the sight of dying men.

The wind tanned his skin. His limbs hardened through contact with armor; and as he was very strong, courageous, temperate and prudent, he received without difficulty the command of a company.

At the beginning of the battles, he would urge on his soldiers with a flourish of his sword. With a knotted rope he scaled the walls of citadels, at night, swinging with the wind, while sparks of Greek fire stuck to his cuirass, and boiling resin and molten lead poured from the battlements. Often a stone would strike and shatter his shield. Bridges overladen with men collapsed under him. By swinging his mace, he got rid of fourteen horsemen. In the lists, he overcame all his challengers. More than twenty times he was believed dead.

Thanks to divine favor, he always recovered, because he protected churchmen, orphans, widows, and most of all, old men. When he saw one walking in front of him, he called out to see his face, as if he were afraid of killing him by mistake.

Runaway slaves, peasants in revolt, bastards without fortune, all kinds of daring men crowded under this banner, and he formed an army of his own.

It grew large. He became famous. He was sought after.

In turn, he helped the French Dauphin and the King of England, the Templars of Jerusalem, the Surena of the Parthians, the Negus of Abyssinia, and the Emperor of Calicut. He fought Scandinavians covered with fish-scales, Negroes equipped with round shields of hippopotamus hide and mounted on red asses, gold-colored Indians brandishing over their diadems broadswords brighter than mirrors. He conquered the Troglodytes and the Anthropophagi. He crossed lands so torrid that under the burning sun the hair on the head caught fire of itself, like a torch. And other regions were so glacial that the arms snapped from the body and fell to the ground. And still other countries where there was so much fog that you walked surrounded by ghosts.

Republics in distress consulted him. When he interviewed ambassadors, he obtained unhoped-for terms. If a monarch behaved too badly, Julian appeared suddenly and admonished him. He liberated peoples. He freed queens locked in towers. It was he, and no other, who slew the viper of Milan and the dragon of Oberbirbach.

Now, the Emperor of Occitania, having triumphed over the Spanish Moslems, had taken as concubine the sister of the Caliph of Cordova. By her he had a daughter whom he had brought up as a Christian. But the Caliph, pretending he wanted to be converted, came to visit him, accompanied by a numerous escort, and massacred his entire garrison. He threw the Emperor into a dungeon underground where he treated him harshly in order to extort treasures from him.

Julian hastened to his aid, destroyed the army of the Infidels, besieged the city, killed the Caliph, cut off his head, and threw it like a ball over the ramparts. Then he released the Emperor from prison and set him back on his throne, in the presence of his entire court.

For such a service, the Emperor presented him with a great deal of money in baskets. Julian wanted none of it. Believing that he desired more, he offered him three quarters of his wealth. He was refused again. Then he offered to share his kingdom and Julian declined. The Emperor wept through vexation, not knowing how to express his gratitude, when suddenly he tapped his forehead, and said some words in a courtier's ear. The curtains of a tapestry lifted and a young girl appeared.

Her large black eyes shone like two very gentle lamps. Her lips parted in a charming smile. The ringlets of her hair caught in the jewels of her half-opened dress, and under the transparency of her tunic the youthfulness of her body could be guessed. She had a slim figure and was entrancing and soft.

Julian was dazzled with love, all the more so because he had lived until then very chastely.

So, he took the Emperor's daughter in marriage, and a castle which she received from her mother. When the wedding was over, the two families separated after endless courtesies on both sides.

It was a palace of white marble, built in the Moorish style, on a promontory, in a grove of orange trees. Terraces of flowers sloped down to the edge of a bay, where pink shells crunched underfoot. Behind the castle, a forest spread in the shape of a fan. The sky was continually blue, and the trees bent by turns under the sea breeze and the wind from the mountains which enclosed the horizon far off.

The bedrooms, full of twilight, were lighted from inlays in the walls. High columns, as slender as reeds, supported the vault of the cupolas, decorated with bas-reliefs imitating stalactites in caves.

There were fountains in the large rooms, mosaics in the courtyards, festooned partitions, numberless delicacies of architecture, and everywhere such silence that you heard the rustle of a scarf or the echo of a sigh.

Julian no longer waged war. He rested, in the midst of a quiet people. Each day a crowd passed in front of him with genuflections and hand-kissing in the Oriental style.

Dressed in purple, he remained leaning on his elbows in the embrasure of a window, recalling the hunts he used to go on. He would have liked to race over the desert after gazelles and ostriches, hide in the bamboo to wait for leopards, go through forests full of rhinoceroses, climb to the summit of the most inaccessible mountains in order to take better aim at eagles, and fight white bears on ice floes.

Sometimes, in a dream, he saw himself as

our father Adam in the middle of Paradise, among all the animals. By stretching out his arm, he had them die. Or they would file by, two by two, according to size, from elephants and lions to ermines and ducks, as on the day when they entered Noah's Ark. In the dark of a cavern, he hurled on them infallible javelins. Others appeared, and there was no end to them. He woke up rolling his wild eyes.

Some princes among his friends invited him to hunt. He always refused, believing that by this kind of penance, he would turn aside his misfortune, for it seemed to him that the fate of his parents depended upon the slaughter of animals. But he was grieved at not seeing them, and his other desire became unbearable.

His wife had jugglers and dancing-girls come to amuse him.

She traveled with him, in an open litter, throughout the countryside. On other occasions, lying over the edge of a shallop they would watch fish swimming aimlessly in water as clear as the sky. Often she threw flowers in his face, or crouching at his feet she drew melodies from a three-stringed mandolin. Then, placing her two clasped hands on his shoulders, said timidly:

"What troubles you, dear lord?"

He did not answer, or burst into sobs. At last, one day he confessed his horrible thought.

She fought it with good arguments. His father and mother were probably dead. If ever he did see them again, by what chance or for what reason, would he perform that abomination? So, his fears had no cause and he should take up hunting again.

Julian smiled as he listened to her, but did not decide to fulfil his desire.

One evening in the month of August when they were in their room, she had just gone to bed and he was kneeling for his prayers when he heard the yapping of a fox and then light steps under the window. In the shadows he caught a glimpse of something like the forms of animals. The temptation was too strong. He took down his quiver.

She showed surprise.

"It is to obey you!" he said. "I shall be back at sunrise."

Yet she feared a fatal adventure.

He reassured her and then left, surprised at the inconsistency of her mood.

Shortly afterwards, a page came to announce that two strangers were insisting upon seeing the wife of the lord immediately, since the lord was absent.

Soon there came into the room an old man and an old woman, bent over, covered with dust, dressed in rough cloth and each leaning on a staff.

They took courage and declared they were bringing Julian news of his parents.

She leaned over in order to hear them.

But first, exchanging glances of agreement, they asked her if he still loved them and if he ever spoke of them.

"Oh, yes!" she said.

Then they cried:

"We are his parents!"

And they sat down, being very weary and exhausted with fatigue.

There was nothing to assure the young wife that her husband was their son.

They gave proof of this by describing some particular marks he had on his body.

She leapt from her bed, called her page and had food served to them.

Although they were very hungry, they could hardly eat; and, off to one side, she watched the trembling of their bony hands as they took the goblets.

They asked countless questions about Julian. She answered each one, but was careful to conceal the deadly idea in which they were concerned.

When he did not return home, they had left their castle and had been walking for several years, on vague clues, without losing hope. So much money had been needed for river-tolls and for hostelries, for the taxes of princes and the demands of thieves, that the bottom of their purse was empty and now they begged. But this was of no consequence, since they would soon embrace their son. They extolled his happiness at having such a pretty wife, and did not grow weary of looking at her and kissing her.

The richness of the apartment astonished them, and the old man, examining the walls, asked why the coat-of-arms of the Emperor of Occitania was on them.

She replied:

"He is my father!"

At that he trembled, remembering the prophecy of the Gypsy, and the old woman thought of the hermit's words. Her son's glory doubtless was only the dawn of eternal splendor. Both of them sat open-mouthed, under the light of the candelabrum on the table.

They must have been very handsome in their youth. The mother still had all her hair and its fine plaits, like drifts of snow, hung to the bottom of her cheeks. The father, with his tall figure and long beard, resembled a church statue.

Julian's wife urged them not to wait for him. She herself put them into her own bed, and then closed the casement window. They fell asleep. The day was about to dawn and on the other side of the stained-glass window, small birds were beginning to sing.

Julian had crossed the park and he walked with a nervous stride in the forest enjoying the softness of the grass and the mildness of the air.

Shadows from the trees spread over the moss. At times the moon made white spots in the glades, and he hesitated to continue, thinking he saw a pool of water, or the surface of the still ponds merged with the color of the grass. A deep silence was everywhere. He found not one of the beasts which a few minutes earlier were wandering around his castle.

The wood thickened and the darkness grew more dark. Puffs of warm wind passed by, full of enervating smells. He sank into piles of dead leaves, and he leaned against an oak in order to catch his breath.

Suddenly, behind his back, a blacker mass leapt out. It was a wild boar. Julian had only time enough to seize his bow, and he was grieved at this as if by a misfortune.

Then, after leaving the woods, he saw a wolf trotting along a hedge.

Julian shot an arrow at it. The wolf stopped, turned its head to look at him, and went on again. As it trotted on, it always kept the same distance, stopped from time to time, and as soon as it was aimed at, began again to run.

In this manner, Julian covered an endless plain, then some small sand-hills, and finally came out on a plateau which looked over a large expanse of country. Flat stones were scattered about between ruined burial vaults. You stumbled over bones of dead men. In some places worm-eaten crosses leaned over in a mournful way. But forms stirred in the indistinct shadows of the tombs. Hyenas, terrified and panting, rose out of them. With their nails clattering on the paving-stones, they came up to him and sniffed at him, showing their gums as they yawned. He unsheathed his sword. They went off at once in every direction, and continuing their limping precipitous gallop, they disappeared in a distant cloud of dust.

One hour later, in a ravine he came upon a mad bull, its horns lowered and pawing the sand with its foot. Julian thrust his lance under its dew-lap. The weapon was shattered as if the animal had been of bronze. He closed his eyes, expecting his death. When he opened them again, the bull had disappeared.

Then his soul sank with shame. A superior power was destroying his strength. In order to return home, he went back into the forest.

It was tangled with creepers. He was cutting them with his sword when a marten slipped abruptly between his legs. A panther made a bound over his shoulder and a serpent coiled its way up an ash tree.

A monstrous jackdaw in the foliage was looking at Julian. Here and there, between the branches appeared quantities of large sparks, as if the firmament had showered all of its stars into the forest. They were eyes of animals, wildcats, squirrels, owls, parrots and monkeys.

Julian shot his arrows at them, and the arrows with their feathers alighted on the leaves like white butterflies. He threw stones at them, and the stones, without touching anything, fell to the ground. He cursed himself, wanted to fight, shouted imprecations, and choked with rage.

And all the animals he had hunted appeared again forming around him a narrow circle. Some sat on their haunches and others were fully erect. He stayed in the middle, frozen with horror, incapable of the slightest movement. Through a supreme effort of his will, he took one step. The ones perched on trees opened their wings, those treading the ground stretched their limbs, and all went with him.

The hyenas walked in front of him, the wolf and the boar behind. The bull, on his right, swayed its head, and on his left, the serpent wound through the grass, while the panther, arching its back, advanced with long velvet-footed strides. He went as slowly as possible in order not to irritate them. He saw coming out from the dark of the bushes porcupines, foxes, vipers, jackals and bears.

Julian began to run, and they ran. The serpent hissed, the stinking beasts slavered. The boar rubbed Julian's heels with his tusks, the wolf the inside of his hands with the hairs of its snout. The monkeys pinched him and made faces. The marten rolled over his feet. A bear, with a backhanded swipe of its paw, knocked off his hat, and the panther scornfully dropped an arrow which it had been holding in its mouth.

An irony was apparent in their sly movements. While watching him from the corner of their eyes, they seemed to be meditating a plan of revenge. Deafened by the buzzing of insects, lashed by the tails of birds, suffocated by all the breathing around him, he walked with his arms stretched out and his eyes closed like a blind man, without even having the strength to cry for mercy.

The crow of a cock rang through the air. Others answered it. It was day and he recognized, beyond the orange trees, the ridge of his palace roof.

Then, at the edge of a field he saw, three paces off, some red-legged partridge fluttering in the stubble. He unfastened his cloak and cast it over them like a net. When he uncovered them, he found only one, dead for a long time and rotten.

This disappointment exasperated him more than all the others. His thirst for slaughter seized him again. Since there were no animals, he would willingly massacre humans.

He climbed the three terraces, broke open the door with a blow of his fist, but at the bottom of the staircase, the thought of his dear wife softened his heart. She was doubtless sleeping and he would surprise her.

Taking off his sandals, he gently turned the lock and went in.

The pallor of the dawn was darkened as it came through the leaded stained-glass windows. Julian's feet caught in some clothes on the floor, and a bit farther on, he knocked against a buffet still laden with dishes. "She must have been eating," he said to himself, and he moved toward the bed which was lost in the darkness at the end of the room. When he reached the edge of the bed, in order to kiss his wife, he leaned over the pillow where the two heads were lying one close to the other. Then against his mouth he felt the touch of a beard.

He drew back, believing that he was losing his mind. But he came back close to the bed, and as his fingers felt about, they touched very long hair. To convince himself of his error, he again slowly passed his hand over the pillow. It was really a beard this time and a man! A man in bed with his wife!

Overcome with unbounded rage, he leaped on them and struck with his dagger. He stamped and foamed, with roars of a wild beast. Then he stopped. The dead, pierced to the heart, had not even moved. He listened closely to their death-rattles which were almost the same, and as they grew feebler, another groan from far off took them up. At first indistinct, this plaintive long-drawn voice came closer, swelled and became cruel. Terrified, he recognized the belling of the large black stag.

As he turned around, he thought he saw, in the frame of the door, his wife's ghost, with a light in her hand.

She had been drawn there by the din of the murder. In one wide glance she understood everything, and fleeing in horror, dropped her torch.

He picked it up.

Before him his mother and father were lying on their backs, with a hole in their breasts. Their faces, of a majestic gentleness, seemed to be keeping an eternal secret. Splashes and pools of blood spread over their white skin, over the sheets of the bed, on the floor, and over an ivory crucifix hanging in the alcove. The scarlet reflection from the stained-glass window, which the sun was striking, lit up the red patches and cast many others throughout the apartment. Julian walked toward the two dead figures, saying to himself, and wanting to believe, that this was not possible, that he was mistaken, that at times there are inexplicable resemblances. Finally he bent down slightly to look at the old man close to, and he saw, between the partly closed eyelids, a glazed eyeball which burned him like fire. Then he went to the other side of the bed, where the other body lay, whose white hair covered a part of her face. Julian passed his fingers

under the plaits and raised the head. He looked at it as he held it at arm's length in one hand, while in his other hand he held up a torch for light. Drops, oozing from the mattress, fell one by one on the floor.

At the end of the day, he presented himself before his wife. In a voice not his own, he first ordered her not to answer him, not to approach him, not even to look at him, and to follow, under pain of damnation, all his instructions, which were irrevocable.

The funeral was carried out according to the directions he had left in writing, on a prie-Dieu, in the chamber of the dead. He left to her his palace, his vassals, all his possessions, without even retaining the clothes of his body and his sandals which would be found at the head of the stairs.

She had obeyed the will of God in causing his crime, and she was to pray for his soul because henceforth he did not exist.

The dead were buried with great pomp, in the church of a monastery three days' journey from the castle. A monk, with his hood pulled down, followed the procession, far from all the others, and no one dared to speak to him.

During the mass, he remained flat on his stomach, in the middle of the portal, his arms like a cross and his forehead in the dust.

After the burial, they saw him take the road which led to the mountains. He turned to look back several times, and finally disappeared.

III

He went off, begging his way through the world.

He held out his hand to horsemen on the roads, and approached harvesters with genuflections, or remained motionless before the gate of courtyards. His face was so sad that he was never refused alms.

In a spirit of humility, he would tell his story. Then all would flee from him, as they made the sign of the cross. In villages which he had already passed through, as soon as he was recognized, people would shut their doors, threaten him with words, and throw stones at him. The most charitable placed a bowl on their window-sill, then closed the shutters so as not to see him.

Being repulsed everywhere, he avoided men. He lived on roots, plants, spoiled fruit and shellfish which he found along the beaches.

Sometimes, at the turn of a hillside, he saw down below a jumble of crowded roofs, with stone spires, bridges, towers, dark streets criss-crossing, from which a continuous hum rose up to him.

The need to mingle with other beings made him go down into the town. But the brutish expressions on the faces, the uproar of the crafts, the emptiness of the words froze his heart. On feast days, when the ringing of the cathedral bells made everyone joyful from daybreak, he watched the inhabitants leave their houses, and the dancing on the squares, the barley-beer jugs at the crossroads, the damask hangings in front of the houses of princes; and when evening came, he watched through the windows of the ground floor the long family tables where grandparents held small children on their knees. Sobs would choke him and he would go back toward the country.

With feelings of love he watched the colts in the pasture, birds in their nests, insects on the flowers. But all, as he drew near, would run off, or hide in terror or quickly fly away.

He sought solitary places. But the wind brought to his ears sounds like the death-rattle. The drops of dew falling to the ground reminded him of other drops of heavier weight. Every evening the sun spread blood over the clouds, and every night, in his dreams, his parricide began over again.

He made himself a hair shirt with iron spikes. On his knees he climbed every hill which had a chapel at the top. But his pitiless thought darkened the splendor of the tabernacles, and tortured him throughout the maceration of his penance.

He did not revolt against God who had inflicted this action on him, and yet he was in despair through having been able to commit it.

His own person filled him with such horror that, hoping for release from it, he risked his life in dangers. He saved paralytics from fires and children from the bottom of chasms. The abyss threw him back and the flames spared him.

Time did not relieve his suffering. It grew intolerable. He resolved to die.

One day when he was on the brink of a fountain and leaning over in order to judge the depths of the water, he saw appear opposite him an emaciated old man, with a white beard and so sorrowful a look that he could not hold back his weeping. The other also was weeping. Without recognizing his image, Julian vaguely remembered a face which resembled that one. He uttered a cry. It was his father. He thought no more of killing himself.

Thus, bearing the weight of his memory, he traveled through many countries. He came to a river which was dangerous to cross because of its violence and because there was on its banks a large stretch of mud. For a long time no one had dared cross it.

An old boat, whose stern was embedded, raised its prow among the reeds. On examining it, Julian discovered a pair of oars, and the thought came to him to spend his life in the service of others.

He began by constructing on the banks a kind of roadway which would permit people to reach the channel. He broke his nails in moving gigantic stones, and pressed them against his stomach in order to carry them, slipped in the mud, sank into it, and almost perished several times.

Then he repaired the boat with pieces of ship wreckage and made a hut for himself with clay and tree-trunks.

43 Gustave Flaubert

Since the crossing was known, travelers appeared. They called to him from the other bank, by waving flags. Quickly Julian jumped into his barge. It was very heavy, and they would overweigh it with all kinds of baggage and bundles, not to mention the beasts of burden which increased the crowding as they kicked in fear. He asked nothing for his work. Some would give him the remains of food which they pulled out of their wallets or worn-out clothes they no longer wanted. The roughest of them shouted blasphemies. Julian reproved them gently and they answered with words of abuse. He was content to bless them.

His only furniture was a small table, a stool, a bed of dry leaves and three clay cups. Two holes in the wall served as windows. On one side barren plains stretched out as far as the eye could see, dotted here and there with pale ponds. In front of him, the great river rolled forth its greenish waves. In the spring, the damp earth had a smell of decay. Then, a riotous wind raised up the dust in whirling clouds. It came in everywhere, muddied the water, and made a crunching sound under the gums. A little later, there were swarms of mosquitoes, which did not stop buzzing and stinging day or night. Then, terrible frosts would come which gave to everything the rigidity of stone, and aroused a mad need to eat meat.

Months passed when Julian saw no one. He often closed his eyes and tried in his memory to return to his youth. The courtyard of the castle would appear with greyhounds on the steps, page boys in the armory, and, under a vine arbor, a blond-haired adolescent between an old man dressed in furs and a lady wearing a large coif. Suddenly, the two corpses were there. He threw himself flat on his stomach, on his bed, and repeated through his tears:

"Ah! poor father! poor mother! poor mother!"

And fell into a drowsiness where funereal visions continued.

One night when he was sleeping, he thought he heard someone calling him. He listened and could only make out the roar of the waves.

But the same voice called out again:

"Julian!"

It came from the other bank, which seemed extraordinary to him, considering the breadth of the river.

A third time someone called:

"Julian!"

And that loud voice had the resonance of a church bell.

He lit his lantern and went out of the hut. A furious hurricane filled the night. There was total darkness, pierced here and there by the whiteness of the leaping waves.

After a moment's hesitation, Julian untied the painter. Instantly the water became calm. The barge glided over it and reached the other bank where a man was waiting.

He was wrapped in a tattered cloth. His face was like a plaster mask and his two eyes were redder than coals. As he brought the lantern close to him, Julian saw that he was covered with a hideous leprosy; yet his bearing had the majesty of a king.

As soon as he entered the barge, it sank prodigiously, overwhelmed by his weight. It rose again with a shake, and Julian began to row.

At each stroke of the oar, the backwash of the waves raised its bow. Blacker than ink, the water raced furiously on both sides of the planking. It hollowed out chasms and made mountains. The shallop leaped over them, then went down again into the depths where it whirled, tossed about by the wind.

Julian bent his body, stretched out his arms, and propping himself with his feet, swung back with a twist of his waist, in order to get more power. The hail lashed his hands, the rain rolled down his back, the fierceness of the wind stifled him and he stopped. Then the boat was set adrift. But, feeling that something momentous was at stake, an order which he should not disobey, he took up his oars again. The banging of the tholes cut through the uproar of the storm.

The small lantern burned in front of him. Birds as they fluttered about hid it from time to time. But he could always see the eyeballs of the Leper who stood at the stern, motionless as a pillar.

That lasted a long time, a very long time.

When they came to the hut, Julian shut the door. He saw the Leper sitting on the stool. The kind of shroud which covered him had fallen to his hips. His shoulders, his chest and his thin arms were hidden under a coating of scaly pustules. Immense wrinkles furrowed his brow. Like a skeleton, he had a hole in place of a nose, and his bluish lips exhaled a breath as thick as fog and nauseous.

"I am hungry!" he said.

Julian gave him what he had, an old gammon of bacon and the crusts of a loaf of black bread.

When he had devoured them, the table, the bowl and knife handle bore the same spots that were seen on his body.

Next, he said:

"I am thirsty."

Julian went to get his pitcher, and as he took it, it gave forth an aroma which dilated heart and nostrils! It was wine—what luck! But the Leper put out his arm and emptied the whole pitcher at one draught.

Then he said:

"I am cold!"

With his candle Julian lighted a pile of fern in the middle of the hut.

The Leper drew near to warm himself. Crouching on his heels, he trembled in every limb and grew weaker. His eyes no longer shone, his ulcers ran, and in an almost lifeless voice, he murmured:

"Your bed!"

Julian helped him gently to drag himself to it and even spread over him, to cover him, the sail from his boat.

The Leper groaned. His teeth showed at the corners of his mouth, a faster rattle shook his chest, and his stomach at each breath was hollowed to his backbone.

Then he closed his eyelids.

"It is like ice in my bones! Come close to me!"

And Julian, lifting the sail, lay down on the dry leaves, near him, side by side.

The Leper turned his head.

"Undress, so that I can have the warmth of your body!"

Julian took off his clothes; then, naked as on the day of his birth, got back into the bed. And he felt against his thigh the Leper's skin, colder than a serpent and rough as a file.

He tried to give him courage, and the other answered panting:

"Ah! I am dying! . . . Come closer, warm me! Not with your hands! no! with your whole body."

Julian stretched out completely over him, mouth to mouth, chest to chest.

Then the Leper clasped him and his eyes suddenly took on the light on the stars. His hair became as long as the rays of the sun. The breath of his nostrils was as sweet as roses. A cloud of incense rose up from the hearth and the waves sang. Meanwhile an abundance of happiness, a superhuman joy came down like a flood into Julian's soul as it swooned. The one whose arms still clasped him grew and grew until he touched with his head and his feet the two walls of the hut. The roof flew off, the firmament unrolled, and Julian ascended toward the blue spaces, face to face with Our Lord Jesus, who carried him to heaven.

And that is the story of St. Julian the Hospitaler, more or less as you find it, on a stained-glass window of a church in my town.

HENRY JAMES

The Altar of the Dead

I

He had a mortal dislike, poor Stransom, to lean anniversaries, and loved them still less when they made a pretence of a figure. Celebrations and suppressions were equally painful to him, and but one of the former found a place in his life. He had kept each year in his own fashion the date of Mary Antrim's death. It would be more to the point perhaps to say that this occasion kept *him:* it kept him at least effectually from doing anything else. It took hold of him again and again with a hand of which time had softened but never loosened the touch. He waked to his feast of memory as consciously as he would have waked to his marriage-morn. Marriage had had of old but too little to say to the matter: for the girl who was to have been his bride there had been no bridal embrace. She had died of a malignant fever after the wedding-day had been fixed, and he had lost before fairly tasting it an affection that promised to fill his life to the brim.

Of that benediction, however, it would have been false to say this life could really be emptied: it was still ruled by a pale ghost, still ordered by a sovereign presence. He had not been a man of numerous passions, and even in all these years no sense had grown stronger with him than the sense of being bereft. He had needed no priest and no altar to make him for ever widowed. He had done many things in the world—he had done almost all but one: he had never, never forgotten. He had tried to put into his existence whatever else might take up room in it, but had failed to make it more than a house of which the mistress was eternally absent. She was most absent of all on the recurrent December day that his tenacity set apart. He had no arranged observance of it, but his nerves made it all their own. They drove him forth without mercy, and the goal of his pilgrimage was far. She had been buried in a London suburb, a part then of Nature's breast, but which he had seen lose one after another every feature of freshness. It was in truth during the moments he stood there that his eyes beheld the place least. They looked at another image, they opened to another light. Was it a credible future? Was it an incredible past? Whatever the answer it was an immense escape from the actual.

It 's true that if there were n't other dates than this there were other memories; and by the time George Stransom was fifty-five such memories had greatly multiplied. There were other ghosts in his life than the ghost of Mary Antrim. He had perhaps not had more losses than most men, but he had counted his losses more; he had n't seen death more closely, but had in a manner felt it more deeply. He had formed little by little the habit of numbering his Dead: it had come to him early in life that there was something one had to do for them. They were there in their simplified intensified essence, their conscious absence and expressive patience, as personally there as if they had only been stricken dumb. When all sense of them failed, all sound of them ceased, it was as if their purgatory were really still on earth: they asked so little that they got, poor things, even less, and died again, died every day, of the hard usage of life. They had no organised service, no reserved place, no honour, no shelter, no safety. Even ungenerous people provided for the living, but even those who were called most generous did nothing for the others. So on George Stransom's part had grown up with the years a resolve that he at least would do something, do it, that is, for his own—would perform the great charity without reproach. Every man *had* his own, and every man had, to meet this charity, the ample resources of the soul.

It was doubtless the voice of Mary Antrim that spoke for them best; as the years at any rate went by he found himself in regular communion with these postponed pensioners, those whom indeed he always called in his thoughts the Others. He spared them the moments, he organised the charity. Quite how it had risen he probably never could have told you, but what came to pass was that an altar, such as was after all within everybody's compass, lighted with perpetual candles and dedicated to these secret rites, reared itself in his spiritual spaces. He had wondered of old, in some embarrassment, whether he had a religion; being very sure, and not a little content, that he had n't at all events the religion some of the people he had known wanted him to have. Gradually this question was straightened out for him: it became clear to him that the religion instilled by his earliest consciousness had been simply the religion of the Dead. It suited his inclination, it satisfied his spirit, it gave employment to his piety. It answered his love of great offices, of a solemn and splendid ritual; for no shrine could be more bedecked and no ceremonial more stately than those to which his worship was attached. He had no imagination about these things but that they were accessible to any one who should feel the need of them. The poorest could build such temples of the spirit—could make them blaze with candles and smoke with incense, make them flush with pictures and flowers. The cost, in the common phrase, of keeping them up fell wholly on the generous heart.

II

He had this year, on the eve of his anniversary, as happened, an emotion not unconnected with that range of feeling. Walking home at the close of a busy day he was arrested in the London street by the particular effect of a shop-front that lighted the dull brown air with its mercenary grin and before which several persons were gathered. It was the window of a jeweller whose diamonds and sapphires seemed to laugh, in flashes like high notes of sound, with the mere joy of knowing how much more they were "worth" than most of the dingy pedestrians staring at them from the other side of the pane. Stransom lingered long enough to suspend, in a vision, a string of pearls about the white neck of Mary Antrim, and then was kept an instant longer by the sound of a voice he knew. Next him was a mumbling old woman, and beyond the old woman a gentleman with a lady on his arm. It was from him, from Paul Creston, the voice had proceeded: he was talking with the lady of some precious object in the window. Stransom had no sooner recognised him than the old woman turned away; but just with this growth of opportunity came a felt strangeness that stayed him in the very act of laying his hand on his friend's arm. It lasted but the instant, only that space sufficed for the flash of a wild question. Was *not* Mrs. Creston dead?—the ambiguity met him there in the short drop of her husband's voice, the drop conjugal, if it ever was, and in the way the two figures leaned to each other. Creston, making a step to look at something else, came nearer, glanced at him, started and exclaimed—behaviour the effect of which was at first only to leave Stransom staring, staring back across the months at the different face, the wholly other face, the poor man had shown him last, the blurred ravaged mask bent over the open grave by which they had stood together. That son of affliction was n't in mourning now; he detached his arm from his companion's to grasp the hand of the older friend. He coloured as well as smiled in the strong light of the shop when Stransom raised a tentative hat to the lady. Stransom had just time to see she was pretty before he found himself gaping at a fact more portentous. "My dear fellow, let me make you acquainted with my wife."

Creston had blushed and stammered over it, but in half a minute, at the rate we live in polite society, it had practically become, for our friend, the mere memory of a shock. They stood there and laughed and talked; Stransom had instantly whisked the shock out of the way, to keep it for private consumption. He felt himself grimace, he heard himself exaggerate the proper, but was conscious of turning not a little faint. That new woman, that hired performer, Mrs. Creston? Mrs. Creston had been more living for him than any woman but one. This lady had a face that shone as publicly as the jeweller's window, and in the happy candour with which she wore her monstrous character was an effect of gross immodesty. The character of Paul Creston's wife thus attributed to her was monstrous for reasons Stransom could judge his friend to know perfectly that he knew. The happy pair had just arrived from America, and Stransom had n't needed to be told this to guess the nationality of the lady. Somehow it deepened the foolish air that her husband's confused cordiality was unable to conceal. Stransom recalled that he had heard of poor Creston's having, while his bereavement was still fresh, crossed the sea for what people in such predicaments call a little change. He had found the little change indeed, he had brought the little change back; it was the little change that stood there and that, do what he would, he could n't, while he showed those high front teeth of his, look other than a conscious ass about. They were going into the shop, Mrs. Creston said, and she begged Mr. Stransom to come with them and help to decide. He thanked her, opening his watch and pleading an engagement for which he was already late, and they parted while she shrieked into the fog "Mind now you come to see me right away!" Creston had had the delicacy not to suggest that, and Stransom hoped it hurt him somewhere to hear her scream it to all the echoes.

He felt quite determined, as he walked away, never in his life to go near her. She was perhaps a human being, but Creston ought n't to have shown her without precautions, ought n't indeed to have shown her at all. His precautions should have been those of a forger or a murderer, and the people at home would never have mentioned extradition. This was a wife for foreign service or purely external use; a decent consideration would have spared her the injury of comparisons. Such was the first flush of George Stransom's reaction; but as he sat alone that night—there were particular hours he always passed alone—the harshness dropped from it and left only the pity. *He* could spend an evening with Kate Creston, if the man to whom she had given everything could n't. He had known her twenty years, and she was the only woman for whom he might perhaps have been unfaithful. She was all cleverness and sympathy and charm; her house had been the very easiest in all the world and her friendship the very firmest. Without accidents he had loved her: without accidents every one had loved her: she had made the passions about her as regular as the moon makes the tides. She had been also of course far too good for her husband, but he never suspected it, and in nothing had she been more admirable than in the exquisite art with which she tried to keep every one else (keeping Creston was no trouble) from finding it out. Here was a man to whom she had devoted her life and for whom she had given it up—dying to bring into the world a child of his bed; and she had had only to submit to her fate to have, ere the grass was green on her grave, no more existence for him than a domestic servant he had replaced. The frivolity, the indecency of it made Stransom's eyes fill; and he had that evening a sturdy sense that he alone, in a world without delicacy, had a right to hold up his head. While he smoked, after dinner, he had a book in his lap, but he had no eyes for his page: his eyes, in the swarming void of things, seemed to have caught Kate Creston's, and it was into their sad silences he looked. It was to him her sentient spirit had turned, knowing it to be of her he would think. He thought for a long time of how the closed eyes of dead women could still live— how they could open again, in a quiet lamplit room, long after they had looked their last. They had looks that survived—had them as great poets had quoted lines.

The newspaper lay by his chair—the thing that came in the afternoon and the servants thought one wanted; without sense for what was in it he had mechanically unfolded and then dropped it. Before he went to bed he took it up, and this time, at the top of a paragraph, he was caught by five words that made him start. He stood staring, before the fire, at the "Death of Sir Acton Hague, K.C.B.," the man who ten years earlier had been the nearest of his friends and whose deposition from this eminence had practically left it without an occupant. He had seen him after their rupture, but had n't now seen him for years. Standing there before the fire he turned cold as he read what had befallen him. Promoted a short time previous to the governorship of the Westward Islands, Acton Hague had died, in the bleak honour of this exile, of an illness consequent on the bite of a poisonous snake. His career was compressed by the newspaper into a dozen lines, the perusal of which excited on George Stransom's part no warmer feeling than one of relief at the absence of any mention of their quarrel, an incident accidentally tainted at the time, thanks to their joint immersion in large affairs, with a horrible publicity. Public

indeed was the wrong Stransom had, to his own sense, suffered, the insult he had blankly taken from the only man with whom he had ever been intimate; the friend, almost adored, of his University years, the subject, later, of his passionate loyalty: so public that he had never spoken of it to a human creature, so public that he had completely overlooked it. It had made the difference for him that friendship too was all over, but it had only made just that one. The shock of interests had been private, intensely so; but the action taken by Hague had been in the face of men. To-day it all seemed to have occurred merely to the end that George Stransom should think of him as "Hague" and measure exactly how much he himself could resemble a stone. He went cold, suddenly and horribly cold, to bed.

III

The next day, in the afternoon, in the great grey suburb, he knew his long walk had tired him. In the dreadful cemetery alone he had been on his feet an hour. Instinctively, coming back, they had taken him a devious course, and it was a desert in which no circling cabman hovered over possible prey. He paused on a corner and measured the dreariness; then he made out through the gathered dusk that he was in one of those tracts of London which are less gloomy by night than by day, because, in the former case, of the civil gift of light. By day there was nothing, but by night there were lamps, and George Stransom was in a mood that made lamps good in themselves. It was n't that they could show him anything, it was only that they could burn clear. To his surprise, however, after a while, they did show him something: the arch of a high doorway approached by a low terrace of steps, in the depth of which —it formed a dim vestibule—the raising of a curtain at the moment he passed gave him a glimpse of an avenue of gloom with a glow of tapers at the end. He stopped and looked up, recognising the place as a church. The thought quickly came to him that since he was tired he might rest there; so that after a moment he had in turn pushed up the leathern curtain and gone in. It was a temple of the old persuasion, and there had evidently been a function—perhaps a service for the dead; the high altar was still a blaze of candles. This was an exhibition he always liked, and he dropped into a seat with relief. More than it had ever yet come home to him it struck him as good there should be churches.

This one was almost empty and the other altars were dim; a verger shuffled about, an old woman coughed, but it seemed to Stransom there was hospitality in the thick sweet air. Was it only the savour of the incense or was it something of larger intention? He had at any rate quitted the great grey suburb and come nearer to the warm centre. He presently ceased to feel intrusive, gaining at last even a sense of community with the only worshipper in his neighbourhood, the sombre presence of a woman, in mourning unrelieved, whose back was all he could see of her and who had sunk deep into prayer at no great distance from him. He wished he could sink, like her, to the very bottom, be as motionless, as rapt in prostration. After a few moments he shifted his seat; it was almost indelicate to be so aware of her. But Stransom subsequently quite lost himself, floating away on the sea of light. If occasions like this had been more frequent in his life he would have had more present the great original type, set up in a myriad temples, of the unapproachable shrine he had erected in his mind. That shrine had begun in vague likeness to church pomps, but the echo had ended by growing more distinct than the sound. The sound now rang out, the type blazed at him with all its fires and with a mystery of radiance in which endless meanings could glow. The thing became as he sat there his appropriate altar and each starry candle an appropriate vow. He numbered them, named them, grouped them—it was the silent roll-call of his Dead. They made together a brightness vast and intense, a brightness in which the mere chapel of his thoughts grew so dim that as it faded away he asked himself if he should n't find his real comfort in some material act, some outward worship.

This idea took possession of him while, at a distance, the black-robed lady continued prostrate; he was quietly thrilled with his conception, which at last brought him to his feet in the sudden excitement of a plan. He wandered softly through the aisles, pausing in the different chapels, all save one applied to a special devotion. It was in this clear recess, lampless and unapplied, that he stood longest—the length of time it took him fully to grasp the conception of gilding it with his bounty. He should snatch it from no other rites and associate it with nothing profane; he would simply take it as it should be given up to him and make it a masterpiece of splendour and a mountain of fire. Tended sacredly all the year, with the sanctifying church round it, it would always be ready for his offices. There would be difficulties, but from the first they presented themselves only as difficulties surmounted. Even for a person so little affiliated the thing would be a matter of arrangement. He saw it all in advance, and how bright in especial the place would become to him in the intermissions of toil and the dusk of afternoons; how rich in assurance at all times, but especially in the indifferent world. Before withdrawing he drew nearer again to the spot where he had first sat down, and in the movement he met the lady whom he had seen praying and who was now on her way to the door. She passed him quickly, and he had only a glimpse of her pale face and her unconscious, almost sightless eyes. For that instant she looked faded and handsome.

This was the origin of the rites more public, yet certainly esoteric, that he at last found himself able to establish. It took a long time, it took a year, and both the process and the result would have been—for any who knew—a vivid picture of his good faith. No one did know, in fact—no one but the bland ecclesiastics whose acquaintance he had promptly sought, whose objections he had softly overridden, whose curiosity and sympathy he had artfully charmed, whose assent to his eccentric munificence he had eventually won, and who had asked for concessions in exchange for indulgences. Stransom had of course at an early stage of his enquiry been referred to the Bishop, and the Bishop had been delightfully human, the Bishop had been almost amused. Success was within sight, at any rate from the moment the attitude of those whom it concerned became liberal in response to liberality. The altar and the sacred shell that half encircled it, consecrated to an ostensible and customary worship, were to be splendidly maintained; all that Stransom reserved to himself was the number of his lights and the free enjoyment of his intention. When the intention had taken complete effect the enjoyment became even greater than he had ventured to hope. He liked to think of this effect when far from it, liked to convince himself of it yet again when near. He was not often indeed so near as that a visit to it had n't perforce something of the patience of a pilgrimage; but the time he gave to his devotion came to seem to him more a contribution to his other interests than a betrayal of them. Even a loaded life might be easier when one had added a new necessity to it.

How much easier was probably never guessed by those who simply knew there were hours when he disappeared and for many of whom there was a vulgar reading of what they used to call his plunges. These plunges were into depths quieter than the deep sea-caves, and the habit had at the end of a year or two become the one it would have cost him most to relinquish. Now they had really, his Dead, something that was indefeasibly theirs; and he liked to think that they might in cases be the Dead of others, as well as that the Dead of others might be invoked

there under the protection of what he had done. Whoever bent a knee on the carpet he had laid down appeared to him to act in the spirit of his intention. Each of his lights had a name for him, and from time to time a new light was kindled. This was what he had fundamentally agreed for, that there should always be room for them all. What those who passed or lingered saw was simply the most resplendent of the altars called suddenly into vivid usefulness, with a quiet elderly man, for whom it evidently had a fascination, often seated there in a maze or a doze; but half the satisfaction of the spot for this mysterious and fitful worshipper was that he found the years of his life there, and the ties, the affections, the struggles, the submissions, the conquests, if there had been such, a record of that adventurous journey in which the beginnings and the endings of human relations are the lettered mile-stones. He had in general little taste for the past as a part of his own history; at other times and in other places it mostly seemed to him pitiful to consider and impossible to repair; but on these occasions he accepted it with something of that positive gladness with which one adjusts one's self to an ache that begins to succumb to treatment. To the treatment of time the malady of life begins at a given moment to succumb; and these were doubtless the hours at which that truth most came home to him. The day was written for him there on which he had first become acquainted with death, and the successive phases of the acquaintance were marked each with a flame.

The flames were gathering thick at present, for Stransom had entered that dark defile of our earthly descent in which some one dies every day. It was only yesterday that Kate Creston had flashed out her white fire; yet already there were younger stars ablaze on the tips of the tapers. Various persons in whom his interest had not been intense drew closer to him by entering this company. He went over it, head by head, till he felt like the shepherd of a huddled flock, with all a shepherd's vision of differences imperceptible. He knew his candles apart, up to the colour of the flame, and would still have known them had their positions all been changed. To other imaginations they might stand for other things—that they should stand for something to be hushed before was all he desired; but he was intensely conscious of the personal note of each and of the distinguishable way it contributed to the concert. There were hours at which he almost caught himself wishing that certain of his friends would now die, that he might establish with them in this manner a connexion more charming than, as it happened, it was possible to enjoy with them in life. In regard to those from whom one was separated by the long curves of the globe such a connexion could only be an improvement: it brought them instantly within reach. Of course there were gaps in the constellation, for Stransom knew he could only pretend to act for his own, and it wasn't every figure passing before his eyes into the great obscure that was entitled to a memorial. There was a strange sanctification in death, but some characters were more sanctified by being forgotten than by being remembered. The greatest blank in the shining page was the memory of Acton Hague, of which he inveterately tried to rid himself For Acton Hague no flame could ever rise on any altar of his.

IV

Every year, the day he walked back from the great graveyard, he went to church as he had done the day his idea was born. It was on this occasion, as it happened, after a year had passed, that he began to observe his altar to be haunted by a worshipper at least as frequent as himself. Others of the faithful, and in the rest of the church, came and went, appealing sometimes, when they disappeared, to a vague or to a particular recognition; but this unfailing presence was always to be observed when he arrived and still in possession when he departed. He was surprised, the first time, at the promptitude with which it assumed an identity for him— the identity of the lady whom two years before, on his anniversary, he had seen so intensely bowed, and of whose tragic face he had had so flitting a vision. Given the time that had passed, his recollection of her was fresh enough to make him wonder. Of himself she had of course no impression, or rather had had none at first: the time came when her manner of transacting her business suggested her having gradually guessed his call to be of the same order. She used his altar for her own purpose—he could only hope that, sad and solitary as she always struck him, she used it for her own Dead. There were interruptions, infidelities, all on his part, calls to other associations and duties; but as the months went on he found her whenever he returned, and he ended by taking pleasure in the thought that he had given her almost the contentment he had given himself. They worshipped side by side so often that there were moments when he wished he might be sure, so straight did their prospect stretch away of growing old together in their rites. She was younger than he, but she looked as if her Dead were at least as numerous as his candles. She had no colour, no sound, no fault, and another of the things about which he had made up his mind was that she had no fortune. Always black-robed, she must have had a succession of sorrows. People weren't poor, after all, whom so many losses could overtake; they were positively rich when they had had so much to give up. But the air of this devoted and indifferent woman, who always made in any attitude, a beautiful accidental line, conveyed somehow to Stransom that she had known more kinds of trouble than one.

He had a great love of music and little time for the joy of it; but occasionally, when workaday noises were muffled by Saturday afternoons, it used to come back to him that there were glories. There were moreover friends who reminded him of this and side by side with whom he found himself sitting out concerts. On one of these winter afternoons, in St. James's Hall, he became aware after he had seated himself that the lady he had so often seen at church was in the place next him and was evidently alone, as he also this time happened to be. She was at first too absorbed in the consideration of the programme to heed him, but when she at last glanced at him he took advantage of the movement to speak to her, greeting her with the remark that he felt as if he already knew her. She smiled as she said "Oh yes, I recognise you"; yet in spite of this admission of long acquaintance it was the first he had seen of her smile. The effect of it was suddenly to contribute more to that acquaintance than all the previous meetings had done. He had n't "taken in," he said to himself, that she was so pretty. Later, that evening—it was while he rolled along in a hansom on his way to dine out—he added that he had n't taken in that she was so interesting. The next morning in the midst of his work he quite suddenly and irrelevantly reflected that his impression of her, beginning so far back, was like a winding river that had at last reached the sea.

His work in fact was blurred a little all that day by the sense of what had now passed between them. It was n't much, but it had just made the difference. They had listened together to Beethoven and Schumann; they had talked in the pauses, and at the end, when at the door, to which they moved together, he had asked her if he could help her in the matter of getting away. She had thanked him and put up her umbrella, slipping into the crowd without an allusion to their meeting yet again and leaving him to remember at leisure that not a word had been exchanged about the usual scene of that coincidence. This omission struck him now as natural and then again as perverse. She might n't in the least have allowed his warrant for speaking to her, and if she had n't he would have judged her an underbred woman. It was odd that when nothing had really ever brought them together he should have been able successfully to assume they were in a manner old friends—that this negative quantity was somehow more than they could express. His success, it was true, had been qualified by her quick escape, so that there grew up in him an absurd desire to put it to some better test. Save in so far as some other poor chance might help him, such a test could be only to meet her afresh at church. Left to himself he would have gone to church the very next afternoon, just for the curiosity of seeing if he should find her there. But he was n't left to himself, a fact he discovered quite at the last, after he had virtually made up his mind to go. The influence that kept him away really revealed to him how little to himself his Dead *ever* left him. He went only for *them*—for nothing else in the world.

The force of this revulsion kept him away ten days: he hated to connect the place with anything but his offices or to give a glimpse of the curiosity that had been on the point of moving him. It was absurd to weave a tangle about a matter so simple as a custom of devotion that might with ease have been daily or hourly; yet the tangle got itself woven. He was sorry, he was disappointed: it was as if a long happy spell had been broken and he had lost a familiar security. At the last, however, he asked himself if he was to stay away for ever from the fear of this muddle about motives. After an interval neither longer nor shorter than usual he re-entered the church with a clear conviction that he should scarcely heed the presence or the absence of the lady of the concert. This indifference did n't prevent his at once noting that for the only time since he had first seen her she was n't on the spot. He had now no scruple about giving her time to arrive, but she did n't arrive, and when he went away still missing her he was profanely and consentingly sorry. If her absence made the tangle more intricate, that was all her own doing. By the end of another year it was very intricate indeed; but by that time he did n't in the least care, and it was only his cultivated consciousness that had given him scruples. Three times in three months he had gone to church without finding her, and he felt he had n't needed these occasions to show him his suspense had dropped. Yet it was, incongruously, not indifference, but a refinement of delicacy that had kept him from asking the sacristan, who would of course immediately have recognised his description of her, whether she had been seen at other hours. His delicacy had kept him from asking any question about her at any time, and it was exactly the same virtue that had left him so free to be decently civil to her at the concert.

This happy advantage now served him anew, enabling him when she finally met his eyes—it was after a fourth trial—to predetermine quite fixedly his awaiting her retreat. He joined her in the street as soon as she had moved, asking her if he might accompany her a certain distance. With her placid permission he went as far as a house in the neighbourhood at which she had business: she let him know it was not where she lived. She lived, as she said, in a mere slum, with an old aunt, a person in connexion with whom she spoke of the engrossment of humdrum duties and regular occupations. She was n't, the mourning niece, in her first youth, and her vanished freshness had left something behind that, for Stransom, represented the proof it had been tragically sacrificed. Whatever she gave him the assurance of she gave without references. She might have been a divorced duchess—she might have been an old maid who taught the harp.

V

They fell at last into the way of walking together almost every time they met, though for a long time still they never met but at church. He could n't ask her to come and see him, and as if she had n't a proper place to receive him she never invited her friend. As much as himself she knew the world of London, but from an undiscussed instinct of privacy they haunted the region not mapped on the social chart. On the return she always made him leave her at the same corner. She looked with him, as a pretext for a pause, at the depressed things in suburban shop-fronts; and there was never a word he had said to her that she had n't beautifully understood. For long ages he never knew her name, any more than she had ever pronounced his own; but it was not their names that mattered, it was only their perfect practice and their common need.

These things made their whole relation so impersonal that they had n't the rules or reasons people found in ordinary friendships. They did n't care for the things it was supposed necessary to care for in the intercourse of the world. They ended one day—they never knew which of them expressed it first—by throwing out the idea that they did n't care for each other. Over this idea they grew quite intimate; they rallied to it in a way that marked a fresh start in their confidence. If to feel deeply together about certain things wholly distinct from themselves did n't constitute a safety, where was safety to be looked for? Not lightly nor often, not without occasion nor without emotion, any more than in any other reference by serious people to a mystery of their faith; but when something had happened to warm, as it were, the air for it, they came as near as they could come to calling their Dead by name. They felt it was coming very near to utter their thought at all. The word "they" expressed enough; it limited the mention, it had a dignity of its own, and if, in their talk, you had heard our friends use it, you might have taken them for a pair of pagans of old alluding decently to the domesticated gods. They never knew—at least Stransom never knew—

how they had learned to be sure of each other. If it had been with each a question of what the other was there for, the certitude had come in some fine way of its own. Any faith, after all, has the instinct of propagation, and it was as natural as it was beautiful that they should have taken pleasure on the spot in the imagination of a following. If the following was for each but a following of one it had proved in the event sufficient. Her debt, however, of course was much greater than his, because while she had only given him a worshipper he had given her a splendid temple. Once she said she pitied him for the length of his list—she had counted his candles almost as often as himself—and this made him wonder what could have been the length of hers. He had wondered before at the coincidence of their losses, especially as from time to time a new candle was set up. On some occasion some accident led him to express this curiosity, and she answered as if in surprise that he had n't already understood. "Oh for me, you know, the more there are the better—there could never be too many. I should like hundreds and hundreds —I should like thousands; I should like a great mountain of light."

Then of course in a flash he understood. "Your Dead are only One?"

She hung back at this as never yet. "Only One," she answered, colouring as if now he knew her guarded secret. It really made him feel he knew less than before, so difficult was it for him to reconstitute a life in which a single experience had so belittled all others. His own life, round its central hollow, had been packed close enough. After this she appeared to have regretted her confession, though at the moment she spoke there had been pride in her very embarrassment. She declared to him that his own was the larger, the dearer possession—the portion one would have chosen if one had been able to choose; she assured him she could perfectly imagine some of the echoes with which his silences were peopled. He knew she could n't; one's

relation to what one had loved and hated had been a relation too distinct from the relations of others. But this did n't affect the fact that they were growing old together in their piety. She was a feature of that piety, but even at the ripe stage of acquaintance in which they occasionally arranged to meet at a concert or to go together to an exhibition she was not a feature of anything else. The most that happened was that his worship became paramount. Friend by friend dropped away till at last there were more emblems on his altar than houses left him to enter. She was more than any other the friend who remained, but she was unknown to all the rest. Once when she had discovered, as they called it, a new star, she used the expression that the chapel at last was full.

"Oh no," Stransom replied, "there's a great thing wanting for that! The chapel will never be full till a candle is set up before which all the others will pale. It will be the tallest candle of all."

Her mild wonder rested on him. "What candle do you mean?"

"I mean, dear lady, my own."

He had learned after a long time that she earned money by her pen, writing under a pseudonym she never disclosed in magazines he never saw. She knew too well what he could n't read and what she could n't write, and she taught him to cultivate indifference with a success that did much for their good relations. Her invisible industry was a convenience to him; it helped his contented thought of her, the thought that rested in the dignity of her proud obscure life, her little remunerated art and her little impenetrable home. Lost, with her decayed relative, in her dim suburban world, she came to the surface in distant places. She was really the priestess of his altar, and whenever he quitted England he committed it to her keeping. She proved to him afresh that women have more of the spirit of religion than men; he felt his fidelity pale and faint in comparison with hers. He often said to her that since he had so little time to live he rejoiced in her having so much; so glad was he to think she would guard the temple when he should have been called. He had a great plan for that, which of course he told her too, a bequest of money to keep it up in undiminished state. Of the administration of this fund he would appoint her superintendent, and if the spirit should move her she might kindle a taper even for him.

"And who will kindle one even for me?" she then seriously asked.

VI

She was always in mourning, yet the day he came back from the longest absence he had yet made her appearance immediately told him she had lately had a bereavement. They met on this occasion as she was leaving the church, so that postponing his own entrance he instantly offered to turn round and walk away with her. She considered, then she said: "Go in now, but come and see me in an hour." He knew the small vista of her street, closed at the end and as dreary as an empty pocket, where the pairs of shabby little houses, semi-detached but indissolubly united, were like married couples on bad terms. Often, however, as he had gone to the beginning he had never gone beyond. Her aunt was dead—that he immediately guessed, as well as that it made a difference; but when she had for the first time mentioned her number he found himself, on her leaving him, not a little agitated by this sudden liberality. She was n't a person with whom, after all, one got on so very fast: it had taken him months and months to learn her name, years and years to learn her address. If she had looked, on this reunion, so much older to him, how in the world did he look to her? She had reached the period of life he had long since reached, when, after separations, the marked clock-face of the friend we meet announces the hour we have tried to forget. He could n't have said what he expected as,

at the end of his waiting, he turned the corner where for years he had always paused; simply not to pause was a sufficient cause for emotion. It was an event, somehow; and in all their long acquaintance there had never been an event. This one grew larger when, five minutes later, in the faint elegance of her little drawing-room, she quavered out a greeting that showed the measure she took of it. He had a strange sense of having come for something in particular; strange because literally there was nothing particular between them, nothing save that they were at one on their great point, which had long ago become a magnificent matter of course. It was true that after she had said "You can always come now, you know," the thing he was there for seemed already to have happened. He asked her if it was the death of her aunt that made the difference; to which she replied: "She never knew I knew you. I wished her not to." The beautiful clearness of her candour—her faded beauty was like a summer twilight—disconnected the words from any image of deceit. They might have struck him as the record of a deep dissimulation; but she had always given him a sense of noble reasons. The vanished aunt was present, as he looked about him, in the small complacencies of the room, the beaded velvet and the fluted moreen; and though, as we know, he had the worship of the Dead, he found himself not definitely regretting this lady. If she was n't in his long list, however, she was in her niece's short one, and Stransom presently observed to the latter that now at least, in the place they haunted together, she would have another object of devotion.

"Yes, I shall have another. She was very kind to me. It's that that's the difference."

He judged, wondering a good deal before he made any motion to leave her, that the difference would somehow be very great and would consist of still other things than her having let him come in. It rather chilled him, for they had been happy together as they were. He extracted from her at any rate an intimation that she should now have means less limited, that her aunt's tiny fortune had come to her, so that there was henceforth only one to consume what had formerly been made to suffice for two. This was a joy to Stransom, because it had hitherto been equally impossible for him either to offer her presents or contentedly to stay his hand. It was too ugly to be at her side that way, abounding himself and yet not able to overflow—a demonstration that would have been signally a false note. Even her better situation too seemed only to draw out in a sense the loneliness of her future. It would merely help her to live more and more for their small ceremonial, and this at a time when he himself had begun wearily to feel that, having set it in motion, he might depart. When they had sat a while in the pale parlour she got up— "This is n't *my* room: let us go into mine." They had only to cross the narrow hall, as he found, to pass quite into another air. When she had closed the door of the second room, as she called it, he felt at last in real possession of her. The place had the flush of life—it was expressive; its dark red walls were articulate with memories and relics. These were simple things—photographs and water-colours, scraps of writing framed and ghosts of flowers embalmed; but a moment sufficed to show him they had a common meaning. It was here she had lived and worked, and she had already told him she would make no change of scene. He read the reference in the objects about her—the general one to places and times; but after a minute he distinguished among them a small portrait of a gentleman. At a distance and without their glasses his eyes were only so caught by it as to feel a vague curiosity. Presently this impulse carried him nearer, and in another moment he was staring at the picture in stupefaction and with the sense that some sound had broken from him. He was further conscious that he showed his companion a white face when he turned round on her gasping: "Acton Hague!"

She matched his great wonder. "Did you know him?"

"He was the friend of all my youth—of my early manhood. And *you* knew him?"

She coloured at this and for a moment her answer failed; her eyes embraced everything in the place, and a strange irony reached her lips as she echoed: "Knew him?"

Then Stransom understood, while the room heaved like the cabin of a ship, that its whole contents cried out with him, that it was a museum in his honour, that all her later years had been addressed to him and that the shrine he himself had reared had been passionately converted to his use. It was all for Acton Hague that she had kneeled every day at his altar. What need had there been for a consecrated candle when he was present in the whole array? The revelation so smote our friend in the face that he dropped into a seat and sat silent. He had quickly felt her shaken by the force of his shock, but as she sank on the sofa beside him and laid her hand on his arm he knew almost as soon that she might n't resent it as much as she 'd have liked.

VII

He learned in that instant two things: one being that even in so long a time she had gathered no knowledge of his great intimacy and his great quarrel; the other that in spite of this ignorance, strangely enough, she supplied on the spot a reason for his stupor. "How extraordinary," he presently exclaimed, "that we should never have known!"

She gave him a wan smile which seemed to Stransom stranger even than the fact itself. "I never, never spoke of him."

He looked again about the room. "Why then, if your life had been so full of him?"

"May n't I put you that question as well? Had n't your life also been full of him?"

"Any one's, every one's life who had the wonderful experience of knowing him. *I* never spoke of him," Stransom added in a moment, "because he did me—years ago—an unforgettable wrong." She was silent, and with the full effect of his presence all about them it almost startled her guest to hear no protest escape her. She accepted his words; he turned his eyes to her again to see in what manner she accepted them. It was with rising tears and a rare sweetness in the movement of putting out her hand to take his own. Nothing more wonderful had ever appeared to him than, in that little chamber of remembrance and homage, to see her convey with such exquisite mildness that as from Acton Hague any injury was credible. The clock ticked in the stillness—Hague had probably given it to her—and while he let her hold his hand with a tenderness that was almost an assumption of responsibility for his old pain as well as his new, Stransom after a minute broke out: "Good God, how he must have used *you!*"

She dropped his hand at this, got up and, moving across the room, made straight a small picture to which, on examining it, he had given a slight push. Then turning round on him with with her pale gaiety recovered, "I 've forgiven him!" she declared.

"I know what you 've done," said Stransom; "I know what you 've done for years." For a moment they looked at each other through it all with their long community of service in their eyes. This short passage made, to his sense, for the woman before him, an immense, an absolutely naked confession; which was presently, suddenly blushing red and changing her place again, what she appeared to learn he perceived in it. He got up and "How you must have loved him!" he cried.

"Women are n't like men. They can love even where they 've suffered."

"Women are wonderful," said Stransom. "But I assure you I 've forgiven him too."

"If I had known of anything so strange I would n't have brought you here."

"So that we might have gone on in our ignorance to the last?"

"What do you call the last?" she asked, smiling still.

At this he could smile back at her. "You 'll see—when it comes."

She thought of that. "This is better perhaps; but as we were—it was good."

He put her the question. "Did it never happen that he spoke of me?"

Considering more intently she made no answer, and he knew then he should have been adequately answered by her asking how often he himself had spoken of their terrible friend. Suddenly a brighter light broke in her face and an excited idea sprang to her lips in the appeal: "You *have* forgiven him?"

"How, if I had n't, could I linger here?"

She visibly winced at the deep but unintended irony of this; but even while she did so she panted quickly: "Then in the lights on your altar——?"

"There 's never a light for Acton Hague!"

She stared with a dreadful fall, "But if he 's one of your Dead?"

"He 's one of the world's, if you like—he 's one of yours. But he 's not one of mine. Mine are only the Dead who died possessed of me. They 're mine in death because they were mine in life."

"*He* was yours in life then, even if for a while he ceased to be. If you forgave him you went back to him. Those whom we 've once loved——"

"Are those who can hurt us most," Stransom broke in.

"Ah, it 's not true—you 've *not* forgiven him!" she wailed with a passion that startled him.

He looked at her as never yet. "What was it he did to you?"

"Everything!" Then abruptly she put out her hand in farewell. "Good-bye."

He turned as cold as he had turned that night he read the man's death. "You mean that we meet no more?"

"Not as we 've met—not *there!*"

He stood aghast at this snap of their great bond, at the renouncement that rang out in the word she so expressively sounded. "But what 's changed—for you?"

She waited in all the sharpness of a trouble that for the first time since he had known her made her splendidly stern. "How can you understand now when you did n't understand before?"

"I did n't understand before only because I did n't know. Now that I know, I see what I 've been living with for years," Stransom went on very gently.

She looked at him with a larger allowance, doing this gentleness justice. "How can I then, on this new knowledge of my own, ask you to continue to live with it?"

"I set up my altar, with its multiplied meanings," Stransom began; but she quickly interrupted him.

"You set up your altar, and when I wanted one most I found it magnificently ready. I used with the gratitude I 've always shown you, for I knew it from of old to be dedicated to Death. I told you long ago that my Dead were n't many. Yours were, but all you had done for them was none too much for *my* worship! You had placed a great light for Each—I gathered them together for One!"

"We had simply different intentions," he returned. "That, as you say, I perfectly knew, and I don't see why your intention should n't still sustain you."

"That 's because you 're generous—you can imagine and think. But the spell 's broken."

It seemed to poor Stransom, in spite of his resistance, that it really was, and the prospect stretched grey and void before him. All he could say, however, was: " I hope you 'll try before you give up."

"If I had known you had ever known him I should have taken for granted he had his candle," she presently answered. "What 's changed, as you say, is that on making the discovery I find he never has had it. That makes *my* attitude"—she paused as thinking how to express it, then said simply—"all wrong."

"Come once again," he pleaded.

"Will you give him his candle?" she asked.

He waited, but only because it would sound ungracious; not because of a doubt of his feeling. "I can't do that!" he declared at last.

"Then good-bye." And she gave him her hand again.

He had got his dismissal; besides which, in the agitation of everything that had opened out to him, he felt the need to recover himself as he could only do in solitude. Yet he lingered—lingered to see if she had no compromise to express, no attenuation to propose. But he only met her great lamenting eyes, in which indeed he read that she was as sorry for him as for any one else. This made him say: "At least, in any case, I may see you here."

"Oh yes, come if you like. But I don't think it will do."

He looked round the room once more, knowing how little he was sure it would do. He felt also stricken and more and more cold, and his chill was like an ague in which he had to make an effort not to shake. Then he made doleful reply: "I must try on my side— if you can't try on yours." She came out with him to the hall and into the doorway, and here he put her the question he held he could least answer from his own wit. "Why have you never let me come before?"

"Because my aunt would have seen you, and I should have had to tell her how I came to know you."

"And what would have been the objection to that?"

"It would have entailed other explanations; there would at any rate have been that danger."

"Surely she knew you went every day to church," Stransom objected.

"She did n't know what I went for."

"Of me then she never even heard?"

"You 'll think I was deceitful. But I did n't need to be!"

He was now on the lower door-step, and his hostess held the door half-closed behind him. Through what remained of the opening he saw her framed face. He made a supreme appeal. "What *did* he do to you?"

"It would have come out— *she* would have told you. That fear at my heart—that was my reason!" And she closed the door, shutting him out.

VIII

He had ruthlessly abandoned her—that of course was what he had done. Stransom made it all out in solitude, at leisure, fitting the unmatched pieces gradually together and dealing one by one with a hundred obscure points. She had known Hague only after her present friend's relations with him had wholly terminated; obviously indeed a good while after; and it was natural enough that of his previous life she should have ascertained only what he had judged good to communicate. There were passages it was quite conceivable that even in moments of the tenderest expansion he should have withheld. Of many facts in the career of a man so in the eye of the world there was of course a common knowledge; but this lady lived apart from public affairs, and the only time perfectly clear to her would have been the time following the dawn of her own drama. A man in her place would have "looked up" the past —would even have consulted old newspapers. It remained remarkable indeed that in her long contact with the partner of her retrospect no accident had lighted a train; but there was no arguing about that; the accident had in fact come: it had simply been that security had prevailed. She had taken what Hague had given her, and her blankness in respect of his other connexions was only a touch in the picture of that plasticity Stransom had supreme reason to know so great a master could have been trusted to produce.

This picture was for a while all our friend saw: he caught his breath again and again as it came over him that the woman with whom he had had for years so fine a point of con-tact was a woman whom Acton Hague, of all men in the world, had more or less fashioned. Such as she sat there to-day she was ineffaceably stamped with him. Beneficent, blameless as Stransom held her, he could n't rid himself of the sense that he had been, as who should say, swindled. She had imposed upon him hugely, though she had known it as little as he. All this later past came back to him as a time grotesquely misspent. Such at least were his first reflexions; after a while he found himself more divided and only, as the end of it, more troubled. He imagined, recalled, reconstituted, figured out for himself the truth she had refused to give him; the effect of which was to make her seem to him only more saturated with her fate. He felt her spirit, through the whole strangeness, finer than his own to the very degree in which he might have been, in which she certainly had been, more wronged. A woman, when wronged, was always more wronged than a man, and there were conditions when the least she could have got off with was more than the most he could have to bear. He was sure this rare creature would n't have got off with the least. He was awestruck at the thought of such a surrender—such a prostration. Moulded indeed she had been by powerful hands, to have converted her injury into an exaltation so sublime. The fellow had only to die for everything that was ugly in him to be washed out in a torrent. It was vain to try to guess what had taken place, but nothing could be clearer than that she had ended by accusing herself. She absolved him at every point, she adored her very wounds. The passion by which he had profited had rushed back after its ebb, and now the tide of tenderness, arrested for ever at flood, was too deep even to fathom. Stransom sincerely considered that he had forgiven him; but how little he had achieved the miracle that she had achieved! His forgiveness was silence, but hers was mere unuttered sound. The light she had demanded for his altar would have broken his silence with a blare; whereas all the lights in the church were for her too great a hush.

She had been right about the difference—she had spoken the truth about the change: Stransom was soon to know himself as perversely but sharply jealous. *His* tide had ebbed, not flowed; if he had "forgiven" Acton Hague, that forgiveness was a motive with a broken spring. The very fact of her appeal for a material sign, a sign that should make her dead lover equal there with the others, presented the concession to her friend as too handsome for the case. He had never thought of himself as hard, but an exorbitant article might easily have rendered him so. He moved round and round this one, but only in widening circles—the more he looked at it the less acceptable it seemed. At the same time he had no illusion about the effect of his refusal; he perfectly saw how it would make for a rupture. He left her alone a week, but when at last he again called this conviction was cruelly confirmed. In the interval he had kept away from the church, and he needed no fresh assurance from her to know she had n't entered it. The change was complete enough: it had broken up her life. Indeed it had broken up his, for all the fires of his shrine seemed to him suddenly to have been quenched. A great indifference fell upon him, the weight of which was in itself a pain; and he never knew what his devotion had been for him till in that shock it ceased like a dropped watch. Neither did he know with how large a confidence he had counted on the final service that had now failed: the mortal deception was that in this abandonment the whole future gave way.

These days of her absence proved to him of what she was capable; all the more that he never dreamed she was vindictive or even resentful. It was not in anger she had forsaken him; it was in simple submission to hard reality, to the stern logic of life. This came home to him when he sat with her again in the room in which her late aunt's conversation lingered like the tone of a cracked piano. She tried to make him forget how much they were estranged, but in the very presence of what they had given up it was impossible not to be sorry for her. He had taken from her so much more than she had taken from him. He argued with her again, told her she could now have the altar to herself; but she only shook her head with pleading sadness, begging him not to waste his breath on the impossible, the extinct. Could n't he see that in relation to her private need the rites he had established were practically an elaborate exclusion? She regretted nothing that had happened; it had all been right so long as she did n't know, and it was only that now she knew too much and that from the moment their eyes were open they would simply have to conform. It had doubtless been happiness enough for them to go on together so long. She was gentle, grateful, resigned; but this was only the form of a deep immoveability. He saw he should never more cross the threshold of the second room, and he felt how much this alone would make a stranger of him and give a conscious stiffness to his visits. He would have hated to plunge again into that well of reminders, but he enjoyed quite as little the vacant alternative.

After he had been with her three or four times it struck him that to have come at last into her house had had the horrid effect of diminishing their intimacy. He had known her better, had liked her in greater freedom, when they merely walked together or kneeled together. Now they only pretended; before they had been nobly sincere. They began to try their walks again, but it proved a lame imitation, for these things, from the first, beginning or ending, had been connected with their visits to the church. They had either strolled away as they came out or gone in to rest on the return. Stransom, besides, now faltered; he could n't walk as of old. The omission made everything false; it was a dire mutilation of their lives. Our friend was frank and monotonous, making no mystery of his remonstrance and no secret of his predicament. Her response, whatever it was, always came to the same thing —an implied invitation to him to judge, if he spoke of predicaments, of how much comfort she had in hers. For him indeed was no comfort even in complaint, since every allusion to what had befallen them but made the author of their trouble more present. Acton Hague was between them—that was the essence of the matter, and never so much between them as when they were face to face. Then Stransom, while still wanting to banish him, had the strangest sense of striving for an ease that would involve having accepted him. Deeply disconcerted by what he knew, he was still worse tormented by really not knowing. Perfectly aware that it would have been horribly vulgar to abuse his old friend or to tell his companion the story of their quarrel, it yet vexed him that her depth of reserve should give him no opening and should have the effect of a magnanimity greater even than his own.

He challenged himself, denounced himself, asked himself if he were in love with her that he should care so much what adventures she had had. He had never for a moment allowed he was in love with her; therefore nothing could have surprised him more than to discover he was jealous. What but jealousy could give a man that sore contentious wish for the detail of what would make him suffer? Well enough he knew indeed that he should never have it from the only person who to-day could give it to him. She let him press her with his sombre eyes, only smiling at him with an exquisite mercy and breathing equally little the word that would expose her secret and the word that would appear to deny his literal right to bitterness. She told nothing, she judged nothing; she accepted everything but the possibility of her return to the old symbols. Stransom divined that for her too they had been vividly individual, had stood for particular hours or particular attributes—particular links in her chain. He made

it clear to himself, as he believed, that his difficulty lay in the fact that the very nature of the plea for his faithless friend constituted a prohibition; that it happened to have come from *her* was precisely the vice that attached to it. To the voice of impersonal generosity he felt sure he would have listened; he would have deferred to an advocate who, speaking from abstract justice, knowing of his denial without having known Hague, should have had the imagination to say: "Ah, remember only the best of him; pity him; provide for him." To provide for him on the very ground of having discovered another of his turpitudes was not to pity but to glorify him. The more Stransom thought the more he made out that whatever this relation of Hague's it could only have been a deception more or less finely practised. Where had it come into the life that all men saw? Why had one never heard of it if it had had the frankness of honourable things? Stransom knew enough of his other ties, of his obligations and appearances, not to say enough of his general character, to be sure there had been some infamy. In one way or another this creature had been coldly sacrificed. That was why at the last as well as the first he must still leave him out and out.

IX

And yet this was no solution, especially after he had talked again to his friend of all it had been his plan she should finally do for him. He had talked in the other days, and she had responded with a frankness qualified only by a courteous reluctance, a reluctance that touched him, to linger on the question of his death. She had then practically accepted the charge, suffered him to feel he could depend upon her to be the eventual guardian of his shrine; and it was in the name of what had so passed between them that he appealed to her not to forsake him in his age. She listened at present with shining coldness and all her habitual forbearance to insist on her terms; her deprecation was even still tenderer, for it expressed the compassion of her own sense that he was abandoned. Her terms, however, remained the same, and scarcely the less audible for not being uttered; though he was sure that secretly even more than he she felt bereft of the satisfaction his solemn trust was to have provided her. They both missed the rich future, but she missed it most, because after all it was to have been entirely hers; and it was her acceptance of the loss that gave him the full measure of her preference for the thought of Acton Hague over any other thought whatever. He had humour enough to laugh rather grimly when he said to himself: "Why the deuce does she like him so much more than she likes me?"—the reasons being really so conceivable. But even his faculty of analysis left the irritation standing, and this irritation proved perhaps the greatest misfortune that had ever overtaken him. There had been nothing yet that made him so much want to give up. He had of course by this time well reached the age of renouncement; but it had not hitherto been vivid to him that it was time to give up everything.

Practically, at the end of six months, he had renounced the friendship once so charming and comforting. His privation had two faces, and the face it had turned to him on the occasion of his last attempt to cultivate that friendship was the one he could look at least. This was the privation he inflicted; the other was the privation he bore. The conditions she never phrased he used to murmur to himself in solitude: "One more, one more —only just one." Certainly he was going down; he often felt it when he caught himself, over his work, staring at vacancy and giving voice to that inanity. There was proof enough besides in his being so weak and so ill. His irritation took the form of melancholy, and his melancholy that of the conviction that his health had quite failed. His altar moreover had ceased to exist; his chapel, in his dreams, was a great dark cavern. All the lights had gone out—all his Dead had died again. He could n't exactly see at first how it had been in the power of his late companion to extinguish them, since it was neither for her nor by her that they had been called into being. Then he understood that it was essentially in his own soul the revival had taken place, and that in the air of this soul they were now unable to breathe. The candles might mechanically burn, but each of them had lost its lustre. The church had become a void; it was his presence, her presence, their common presence, that had made the indispensable medium. If anything was wrong everything was—her silence spoiled the tune.

Then when three months were gone he felt so lonely that he went back; reflecting that as they had been his best society for years his Dead perhaps would n't let him forsake them without doing something more for him. They stood there, as he had left them, in their tall radiance, the bright cluster that had already made him, on occasions when he was willing to compare small things with great, liken them to a group of sea-lights on the edge of the ocean of life. It was a relief to him, after a while, as he sat there, to feel they had still a virtue. He was more and more easily tired, and he always drove now; the action of his heart was weak and gave him none of the reassurance conferred by the action of his fancy. None the less he returned yet again, returned several times, and finally, during six months, haunted the place with a renewal of frequency and a strain of impatience. In winter the church was unwarmed and exposure to cold forbidden him, but the glow of his shrine was an influence in which he could almost bask. He sat and wondered to what he had reduced his absent associate and what she now did with the hours of her absence. There were other churches, there were other altars, there were other candles; in one way or another her piety would still operate; he could n't absolutely have deprived her of her rites. So he argued, but without contentment; for he well enough knew there was no other such rare semblance of the mountain of light she had once mentioned to him as the satisfaction of her need. As this semblance again gradually grew great to him and his pious practice more regular, he found a sharper and sharper pang in the imagination of her darkness; for never so much as in these weeks had his rites been real, never had his gathered company seemed so to respond and even to invite. He lost himself in the large lustre, which was more and more what he had from the first wished it to be—as dazzling as the vision of heaven in the mind of a child. He wandered in the fields of light; he passed, among the tall tapers, from tier to tier, from fire to fire, from name to name, from the white intensity of one clear emblem, of one saved soul, to another. It was in the quiet sense of having saved his souls that his deep strange instinct rejoiced. This was no dim theological rescue, no boon of a contingent world; they were saved better than faith or works could save them, saved for the warm world they had shrunk from dying to, for actuality, for continuity, for the certainty of human remembrance.

By this time he had survived all his friends; the last straight flame was three years old, there was no one to add to the list. Over and over he called his roll, and it appeared to him compact and complete. Where should he put in another, where, if there were no other objection, would it stand in its place in the rank? He reflected, with a want of sincerity of which he was quite conscious, that it would be difficult to determine that place. More and more, besides, face to face with his little legion, reading over endless histories, handling the empty shells and playing with the silence—more and more he could see that he had never introduced an alien. He had had his great compassions, his indulgences—there were cases in which they had been immense; but what had his devotion after all been if it had n't been at bottom a respect? He was, however, himself surprised at his stiffness; by the end of the winter the responsibility of it was what was uppermost in his thoughts. The refrain had grown old to them, that plea for just one more. There came a day when, for simple exhaustion, if symmetry should demand just one he was ready so far to meet symmetry. Symmetry was harmony, and the idea of harmony began to haunt him; he said to himself that harmony was of course everything. He took, in fancy, his composition to pieces, redistributing it into other lines, making other juxtapositions and contrasts. He shifted this and that candle, he made the spaces different, he effaced the disfigurement of a possible gap. There were subtle and complex relations, a scheme of cross-reference, and moments in which he seemed to catch a glimpse of the void so sensible to the woman who wandered in exile or sat where he had seen her with the portrait of Acton Hague. Finally, in this way, he arrived at a conception of the total, the ideal, which left a clear opportunity for just another figure. "Just one more—to round it off; just one more, just one," continued to hum in his head. There was a strange confusion in the thought, for he felt the day to be near when he too should be one of the Others. What in this event would the Others matter to him, since they only mattered to the living? Even as one of the Dead what would his altar matter to him, since his particular dream of keeping it up had melted away? What had harmony to do with the case if his lights were all to be quenched? What he had hoped for was an instituted thing. He might perpetuate it on some other pretext, but his special meaning would have dropped. This meaning was to have lasted with the life of the one other person who understood it.

In March he had an illness during which he spent a fortnight in bed, and when he revived a little he was told of two things that had happened. One was that a lady whose name was not known to the servants (she left none) had been three times to ask about him; the other was that in his sleep and on an occasion when his mind evidently wandered he was heard to murmur again and again: "Just one more—just one." As soon as he found himself able to go out, and before the doctor in attendance had pronounced him so, he drove to see the lady who had come to ask about him. She was not at home; but this gave him the opportunity, before his strength should fail again, to take his way to the church. He entered it alone; he had declined, in a happy manner he possessed of being able to decline effectively, the company of his servant or of a nurse. He knew now perfectly what these good people thought; they had discovered his clandestine connexion, the magnet that had drawn him for so many years, and doubtless attached a significance of their own to the odd words they had repeated to him. The nameless lady was the clandestine connexion—a fact nothing could have made clearer than his indecent haste to rejoin her. He sank on his knees before his altar while his head fell over on his hands. His weakness, his life's weariness overtook him. It seemed to him he had come for the great surrender. At first he asked himself how he should get away; then, with the failing belief in the power, the very desire to move gradually left him. He had come, as he always came, to lose himself; the fields of light were still there to stray in; only this time, in straying, he would never come back. He had given himself to his Dead, and it was good: this time his Dead would keep him. He could n't rise from his knees; he believed he should never rise again; all he could do was to lift his face and fix his eyes on his lights. They looked unusually, strangely splendid, but the one that always drew him most had an unprecedented lustre. It was the central voice of the choir, the glowing heart of the brightness, and on this occasion it seemed to expand, to spread great wings of flame. The whole altar flared—dazzling and blinding; but the source of the vast radiance burned clearer than the rest, gathering itself into

form, and the form was human beauty and human charity, was the far-off face of Mary Antrim. She smiled at him from the glory of heaven—she brought the glory down with her to take him. He bowed his head in submission and at the same moment another wave rolled over him. Was it the quickening of joy to pain? In the midst of his joy at any rate he felt his buried face grow hot as with some communicated knowledge that had the force of a reproach. It suddenly made him contrast that very rapture with the bliss he had refused to another. This breath of the passion immortal was all that other had asked; the descent of Mary Antrim opened his spirit with a great compunctious throb for the descent of Acton Hague. It was as if Stransom had read what her eyes said to him.

After a moment he looked round in a despair that made him feel as if the source of life were ebbing. The church had been empty —he was alone; but he wanted to have something done, to make a last appeal. This idea gave him strength for an effort; he rose to his feet with a movement that made him turn, supporting himself by the back of a bench. Behind him was a prostrate figure, a figure he had seen before; a woman in deep mourning, bowed in grief or in prayer. He had seen her in other days—the first time of his entrance there, and he now slightly wavered, looking at her again till she seemed aware he had noticed her. She raised her head and met his eyes: the partner of his long worship had come back. She looked across at him an instant with a face wondering and scared; he saw he had made her afraid. Then quickly rising she came straight to him with both hands out.

"Then you *could* come? God sent you!" he murmured with a happy smile.

"You 're very ill—you should n't be here," she urged in anxious reply.

"God sent me too, I think. I was ill when I came, but the sight of you does wonders."

He held her hands, which steadied and quickened him. "I 've something to tell you."

"Don't tell me!" she tenderly pleaded; "let me tell you. This afternoon, by a miracle, the sweetest of miracles, the sense of our difference left me. I was out—I was near, thinking, wandering alone, when, on the spot, something changed in my heart. It 's my confession—there it is. To come back, to come back on the instant—the idea gave me wings. It was as if I suddenly saw something—as if it all became possible. I could come for what you yourself came for: that was enough. So here I am. It 's not for my own—that 's over. But I 'm here for *them*." And breathless, infinitely relieved by her low precipitate explanation, she looked with eyes that reflected all its splendour at the magnificence of their altar.

"They're here for you," Stransom said, "they're present to-night as they 've never been. They speak for you—don't you see?—in a passion of light; they sing out like a choir of angels. Don't you hear what they say?— they offer the very thing you asked of me."

"Don't talk of it—don't think of it; forget it!" She spoke in hushed supplication, and while the alarm deepened in her eyes she disengaged one of her hands and passed an arm round him to support him better, to help him to sink into a seat.

He let himself go, resting on her; he dropped upon the bench and she fell on her knees beside him, his own arm round her shoulder. So he remained an instant, staring up at his shrine. "They say there 's a gap in the array—they say it 's not full, complete. Just one more," he went on, softly—"is n't that what you wanted? Yes, one more, one more."

"Ah no more—no more!" she wailed, as with a quick new horror of it, under her breath.

"Yes, one more," he repeated, simply; "just one!" And with this his head dropped on her shoulder; she felt that in his weakness he had fainted. But alone with him in the dusky church a great dread was on her of what might still happen, for his face had the whiteness of death.

JOSEPH CONRAD

The Secret Sharer

I

On my right hand there were lines of fishing stakes resembling a mysterious system of half-submerged bamboo fences, incomprehensible in its division of the domain of tropical fishes, and crazy of aspect as if abandoned forever by some nomad tribe of fishermen now gone to the other end of the ocean; for there was no sign of human habitation as far as the eye could reach. To the left a group of barren islets, suggesting ruins of stone walls, towers, and blockhouses, had its foundations set in a blue sea that itself looked solid, so still and stable did it lie below my feet; even the track of light from the westering sun shone smoothly, without that animated glitter which tells of an imperceptible ripple. And when I turned my head to take a parting glance at the tug which had just left us anchored outside the bar, I saw the straight line of the flat shore joined to the stable sea, edge to edge, with a perfect and unmarked closeness, in one leveled floor half brown, half blue under the enormous dome of the sky. Corresponding in their insignificance to the islets of the sea, two small clumps of trees, one on each side of the only fault in the impeccable joint, marked the mouth of the river Meinam we had just left on the first preparatory stage of our homeward journey; and, far back on the inland level, a larger and loftier mass, the grove surrounding the great Paknam pagoda, was the only thing on which the eye could rest from the vain task of exploring the monotonous sweep of the horizon. Here and there gleams as of a few scattered pieces of silver marked the windings of the great river; and on the nearest of them, just within the bar, the tug steaming right into the land became lost to my sight, hull and funnel and masts, as though the impassive earth had swallowed her up without an effort, without a tremor. My eye followed the light cloud of her smoke, now here, now there, above the plain, according to the devious curves of the stream, but always fainter and farther away, till I lost it at last behind the miter-shaped hill of the great pagoda. And then I was left alone with my ship, anchored at the head of the Gulf of Siam.

She floated at the starting point of a long journey, very still in an immense stillness, the shadows of her spars flung far to the eastward by the setting sun. At that moment I was alone on her decks. There was not a sound in her—and around us nothing moved, nothing lived, not a canoe on the water, not a bird in the air, not a cloud in the sky. In this breathless pause at the threshold of a long passage we seemed to be measuring our fitness for a long and arduous enterprise, the appointed task of both our existences to be carried out, far from all human eyes, with only sky and sea for spectators and for judges.

There must have been some glare in the air to interfere with one's sight, because it was only just before the sun left us that my roaming eyes made out beyond the highest ridges of the principal islet of the group something which did away with the solemnity of perfect solitude. The tide of darkness flowed on swiftly; and with tropical suddenness a swarm of stars came out above the shadowy earth, while I lingered yet, my hand resting lightly on my ship's rail as if on the shoulder of a trusted friend. But, with all that multitude of celestial bodies staring down at one, the comfort of quiet communion with her was gone for good. And there were also disturbing sounds by this time— voices, footsteps forward; the steward flitted along the main-deck, a busily ministering spirit; a hand bell tinkled urgently under the poop deck. . . .

I found my two officers waiting for me near the supper table, in the lighted cuddy. We sat down at once, and as I helped the chief mate, I said:

"Are you aware that there is a ship anchored inside the islands? I saw her mastheads above the ridge as the sun went down."

He raised sharply his simple face, overcharged by a terrible growth of whisker, and emitted his usual ejaculations: "Bless my soul, sir! You don't say so!"

My second mate was a round-cheeked, silent young man, grave beyond his years, I thought; but as our eyes happened to meet I detected a slight quiver on his lips. I looked down at once. It was not my part to encourage sneering on board my ship. It must be said, too, that I knew very little of my officers. In consequence of certain events of no particular significance, except to myself, I had been appointed to the command only a fortnight before. Neither did I know much of the hands forward. All these people had been together for eighteen months or so, and my position was that of the only stranger on board. I mention this because it has some bearing on what is to follow. But what I felt most was my being a stranger to the ship; and if all the truth must be told, I was somewhat of a stranger to myself. The youngest man on board (barring the second mate), and untried as yet by a position of the fullest responsibility, I was willing to take the adequacy of the others for granted. They had simply to be equal to their tasks; but I wondered how far I should turn out faithful to that ideal conception of one's own personality every man sets up for himself secretly.

Meantime the chief mate, with an almost visible effect of collaboration on the part of his round eyes and frightful whiskers, was trying to evolve a theory of the anchored ship. His dominant trait was to take all things into earnest consideration. He was of a painstaking turn of mind. As he used to say, he "liked to account to himself" for practically everything that came in his way, down to a miserable scorpion he had found in his cabin a week before. The why and the wherefore of that scorpion—how it got on board and came to select his room rather than the pantry (which was a dark place and more what a scorpion would be partial to), and how on earth it managed to drown itself in the inkwell of his writing desk—had exercised him infinitely. The ship within the islands was much more easily accounted for; and just as we were about to rise from table he made his pronouncement. She was, he doubted not, a ship from home lately arrived. Probably she drew too much water to cross the bar except at the top of spring tides. Therefore she went into that natural harbor to wait for a few days in preference to remaining in an open roadstead.

"That's so," confirmed the second mate, suddenly, in his slightly hoarse voice. "She draws over twenty feet. She's the Liverpool ship *Sephora* with a cargo of coal. Hundred and twenty-three days from Cardiff."

We looked at him in surprise.

"The tugboat skipper told me when he came on board for your letters, sir," explained the young man. "He expects to take her up the river the day after tomorrow."

After thus overwhelming us with the extent of his information he slipped out of the cabin. The mate observed regretfully that he "could not account for that young fellow's whims." What prevented him telling us all about it at once, he wanted to know.

I detained him as he was making a move.

For the last two days the crew had had plenty of hard work, and the night before they had very little sleep. I felt painfully that I—a stranger—was doing something unusual when I directed him to let all hands turn in without setting an anchor watch. I proposed to keep on deck myself till one o'clock or thereabouts. I would get the second mate to relieve me at that hour.

"He will turn out the cook and the steward at four," I concluded, "and then give you a call. Of course at the slightest sign of any sort of wind we'll have the hands up and make a start at once."

He concealed his astonishment. "Very well, sir." Outside the cuddy he put his head in the second mate's door to inform him of my unheard-of caprice to take a five hours' anchor watch on myself. I heard the other raise his voice incredulously—"What? The Captain himself?" Then a few more murmurs, a door closed, then another. A few moments later I went on deck.

My strangeness, which had made me sleepless, had prompted that unconventional arrangement, as if I had expected in those solitary hours of the night to get on terms with the ship of which I knew nothing, manned by men of whom I knew very little more. Fast alongside a wharf, littered like any ship in port with a tangle of unrelated things, invaded by unrelated shore people, I had hardly seen her yet properly. Now, as she lay cleared for sea, the stretch of her maindeck seemed to me very fine under the stars. Very fine, very roomy for her size, and very inviting. I descended the poop and paced the waist, my mind picturing to myself the coming passage through the Malay Archipelago, down the Indian Ocean, and up the Atlantic. All its phases were familiar enough to me, every characteristic, all the alternatives which were likely to face me on the high seas—everything! . . . except the novel responsibility of command. But I took heart from the reasonable thought that the ship was like other ships, the men like other men, and that the sea was not likely to keep any special surprises expressly for my discomfiture.

Arrived at that comforting conclusion, I bethought myself of a cigar and went below to get it. All was still down there. Everybody at the after end of the ship was sleeping profoundly. I came out again on the quarterdeck, agreeably at ease in my sleeping suit on that warm breathless night, barefooted, a glowing cigar in my teeth, and, going forward, I was met by the profound silence of the fore end of the ship. Only as I passed the door of the forecastle I heard a deep, quiet, trustful sigh of some sleeper inside. And suddenly I rejoiced in the great security of the sea as compared with the unrest of the land, in my choice of that untempted life presenting no disquieting problems, invested with an elementary moral beauty by the absolute straightforwardness of its appeal and by the singleness of its purpose.

The riding light in the forerigging burned with a clear, untroubled, as if symbolic, flame, confident and bright in the mysterious shades of the night. Passing on my way aft along the other side of the ship, I observed that the rope side ladder, put over, no doubt, for the master of the tug when he came to fetch away our letters, had not been hauled in as it should have been. I became annoyed at this, for exactitude in some small matters is the very soul of discipline. Then I reflected that I had myself peremptorily dismissed my officers from duty, and by my own act had prevented the anchor watch being formally set and things properly attended to. I asked myself whether it was wise to interfere with the established routine of duties even from the kindest of motives. My action might have made me appear eccentric. Goodness only knew how that absurdly whiskered mate would "account" for my conduct, and what the whole ship thought of that informality of their new captain. I was vexed with myself.

Not from compunction certainly, but, as it were mechanically, I proceeded to get the ladder in myself. Now a side ladder of that sort is a light affair and comes in easily, yet my vigorous tug, which should have brought it flying on board, merely recoiled upon my body in a totally unexpected jerk. What the devil! . . . I was so astounded by the immovableness of that ladder that I remained stock-still, trying to account for it to myself like that imbecile mate of mine. In the end, of course, I put my head over the rail.

The side of the ship made an opaque belt of shadow on the darkling glassy shimmer of the sea. But I saw at once something elongated and pale floating very close to the ladder. Before I could form a guess a faint flash of a phosphorescent light, which seemed to issue suddenly from the naked body of a man, flickered in the sleeping water with the elusive, silent play of summer lightning in a night sky. With a gasp I saw revealed to my stare a pair of feet, the long legs, a broad back immersed right up to the neck in a greenish cadaverous glow. One hand, awash, clutched the bottom rung of the ladder. He was complete but for the head. A headless corpse! The cigar dropped out of my gaping mouth with a tiny plop and a short hiss quite audible in the absolute stillness of all things under heaven. At that I suppose he raised up his face, a dimly pale oval in the shadow of the ship's side. But even then I could only barely make out down there the shape of his black-haired head. However, it was enough for the horrid, frost-bound sensation which had gripped me about the chest to pass off. The moment of vain exclamations was past, too. I only climbed on the spare spar and leaned over the rail as far as I could, to bring my eyes nearer to that mystery floating alongside.

As he hung by the ladder, like a resting swimmer, the sea lightning played about his limbs at every stir; and he appeared in it ghastly, silvery, fishlike. He remained as mute as a fish, too. He made no motion to get out of the water, either. It was inconceivable that he should not attempt to come on board, and strangely troubling to suspect that perhaps he did not want to. And my first words were prompted by just that troubled incertitude.

"What's the matter?" I asked in my ordinary tone, speaking down to the face upturned exactly under mine.

"Cramp," it answered, no louder. Then slightly anxious, "I say, no need to call anyone."

"I was not going to," I said.

"Are you alone on deck?"

"Yes."

I had somehow the impression that he was on the point of letting go the ladder to swim away beyond my ken—mysterious as he came. But, for the moment, this being appearing as if he had risen from the bottom of the sea (it was certainly the nearest land to the ship) wanted only to know the time. I told him. And he, down there, tentatively:

"I suppose your captain's turned in?"

"I am sure he isn't," I said.

He seemed to struggle with himself, for I heard something like the low, bitter murmur of doubt. "What's the good?" His next words came out a hesitating effort.

"Look here, my man. Could you call him out quietly?"

I thought the time had come to declare myself.

"*I* am the captain."

I heard a "By Jove!" whispered at the level of the water. The phosphorescence flashed in the swirl of the water all about his limbs, his other hand seized the ladder.

"My name's Leggatt."

The voice was calm and resolute. A good voice. The self-possession of that man had somehow induced a corresponding state in myself. It was very quietly that I remarked:

"You must be a good swimmer."

"Yes. I've been in the water practically since nine o'clock. The question for me now is whether I am to let go this ladder and go on swimming till I sink from exhaustion, or —to come on board here."

I felt this was no mere formula of desperate speech, but a real alternative in the view of a strong soul. I should have gathered from this that he was young; indeed, it is only the young who are ever confronted by such clear issues. But at the time it was pure intuition on my part. A mysterious communication was established already between us two —in the face of that silent darkened tropical sea. I was young, too; young enough to make no comment. The man in the water began suddenly to climb the ladder, and I hastened away from the rail to fetch some clothes.

Before entering the cabin I stood still, listening in the lobby at the foot of the stairs. A faint snore came through the closed door of the chief mate's room. The second mate's door was on the hook, but the darkness in there was absolutely soundless. He, too, was young and could sleep like a stone. Remained the steward, but he was not likely to wake up before he was called. I got a sleeping suit out of my room and, coming back on deck, saw the naked man from the sea sitting on the main hatch, glimmering white in the darkness, his elbows on his knees and his head in his hands. In a moment he had concealed his damp body in a sleeping suit of the same gray-stripe pattern as the one I was wearing and followed me like my double on the poop. Together we moved right aft, barefooted, silent.

"What is it?" I asked in a deadened voice, taking the lighted lamp out of the binnacle, and raising it to his face.

"An ugly business."

He had rather regular features; a good mouth; light eyes under somewhat heavy, dark eyebrows; a smooth square forehead; no growth on his cheeks; a small, brown mustache, and a well-shaped, round chin. His expression was concentrated, meditative, under the inspecting light of the lamp I held up to his face; such as a man thinking hard in solitude might wear. My sleeping suit was just right for his size. A well-knit young fellow of twenty-five at most. He caught his lower lip with the edge of white, even teeth.

"Yes," I said, replacing the lamp in the binnacle. The warm, heavy tropical night closed upon his head again.

"There's a ship over there," he murmured.

"Yes, I know. The *Sephora*. Did you know of us?"

"Hadn't the slightest idea. I am the mate of her——" He paused and corrected himself. "I should say I *was*."

"Aha! Something wrong?"

"Yes. Very wrong indeed. I've killed a man."

"What do you mean? Just now?"

"No, on the passage. Weeks ago. Thirty-nine south. When I say a man——"

"Fit of temper," I suggested, confidently.

The shadowy, dark head, like mine, seemed to nod imperceptibly above the ghostly gray of my sleeping suit. It was, in the night, as though I had been faced by my own reflection in the depths of a somber and immense mirror.

"A pretty thing to have to own up to for a Conway boy," murmured my double, distinctly.

"You're a Conway boy?"[1]

"I am," he said, as if startled. Then, slowly . . . "Perhaps you too——"

It was so; but being a couple of years older I had left before he joined. After a quick interchange of dates a silence fell; and I thought suddenly of my absurd mate with his terrific whiskers and the "Bless my soul —you don't say so" type of intellect. My double gave me an inkling of his thoughts by saying: "My father's a parson in Norfolk. Do you see me before a judge and jury on that charge? For myself I can't see the necessity. There are fellows that an angel from heaven—— And I am not that. He was one of those creatures that are just simmering all the time with a silly sort of wickedness. Miserable devils that have no business to live at

---

[1] *Conway boy:* a graduate of a training ship. [All notes, unless otherwise identified, are editors'.]

all. He wouldn't do his duty and wouldn't let anybody else do theirs. But what's the good of talking! You know well enough the sort of ill-conditioned snarling cur——"

He appealed to me as if our experiences had been as identical as our clothes. And I knew well enough the pestiferous danger of such a character where there are no means of legal repression. And I knew well enough also that my double there was no homicidal ruffian. I did not think of asking him for details, and he told me the story roughly in brusque, disconnected sentences. I needed no more. I saw it all going on as though I were myself inside that other sleeping suit.

"It happened while we were setting a reefed foresail, at dusk. Reefed foresail! You understand the sort of weather. The only sail we had left to keep the ship running; so you may guess what it had been like for days. Anxious sort of job, that. He gave me some of his cursed insolence at the sheet. I tell you I was overdone with this terrific weather that seemed to have no end to it. Terrific, I tell you—and a deep ship. I believe the fellow himself was half crazed with funk. It was no time for gentlemanly reproof, so I turned round and felled him like an ox. He up and at me. We closed just as an awful sea made for the ship. All hands saw it coming and took to the rigging, but I had him by the throat, and went on shaking him like a rat, the men above us yelling, 'Look out! look out!' Then a crash as if the sky had fallen on my head. They say that for over ten minutes hardly anything was to be seen of the ship— just the three masts and a bit of the forecastle head and of the poop all awash driving along in a smother of foam. It was a miracle that they found us, jammed together behind the forebitts. It's clear that I meant business, because I was holding him by the throat still when they picked us up. He was black in the face. It was too much for them. It seems they rushed us aft together, gripped as we were, screaming 'Murder!' like a lot of lunatics, and broke into the cuddy. And the ship run-

ning for her life, touch and go all the time, any minute her last in a sea fit to turn your hair gray only a-looking at it. I understand that the skipper, too, started raving like the rest of them. The man had been deprived of sleep for more than a week, and to have this sprung on him at the height of a furious gale nearly drove him out of his mind. I wonder they didn't fling me overboard after getting the carcass of their precious shipmate out of my fingers. They had rather a job to separate us, I've been told. A sufficiently fierce story to make an old judge and a respectable jury sit up a bit. The first thing I heard when I came to myself was the maddening howling of that endless gale, and on that the voice of the old man. He was hanging on to my bunk, staring into my face out of his sou'wester.

"'Mr. Leggatt, you have killed a man. You can act no longer as chief mate of this ship.'"

His care to subdue his voice made it sound monotonous. He rested a hand on the end of the skylight to steady himself with, and all that time did not stir a limb, so far as I could see. "Nice little tale for a quiet tea party," he concluded in the same tone.

One of my hands, too, rested on the end of the skylight; neither did I stir a limb, so far as I knew. We stood less than a foot from each other. It occurred to me that if old "Bless my soul—you don't say so" were to put his head up the companion and catch sight of us, he would think he was seeing double, or imagine himself come upon a scene of weird witchcraft; the strange captain having a quiet confabulation by the wheel with his own gray ghost. I became very much concerned to prevent anything of the sort. I heard the other's soothing undertone.

"My father's a parson in Norfolk," it said. Evidently he had forgotten he had told me this important fact before. Truly a nice little tale.

"You had better slip down into my stateroom now," I said, moving off stealthily. My double followed my movements; our bare feet made no sound; I let him in, closed the door with care, and, after giving a call to the second mate, returned on deck for my relief.

"Not much sign of any wind yet," I remarked when he approached.

"No, sir. Not much," he assented, sleepily, in his hoarse voice, with just enough deference, no more, and barely suppressing a yawn.

"Well, that's all you have to look out for. You have your orders."

"Yes, sir."

I paced a turn or two on the poop and saw him take up his position face forward with his elbow in the ratlines of the mizzen rigging before I went below. The mate's faint snoring was still going on peacefully. The cuddy lamp was burning over the table on which stood a vase with flowers, a polite attention from the ship's provision merchant—the last flowers we should see for the next three months at the very least. Two bunches of bananas hung from the beam symmetrically, one on each side of the rudder casing. Everything was as before in the ship—except that two of her captain's sleeping suits were simultaneously in use, one motionless in the cuddy, the other keeping very still in the captain's stateroom.

It must be explained here that my cabin had the form of the capital letter L, the door being within the angle and opening into the short part of the letter. A couch was to the left, the bed place to the right; my writing desk and the chronometers' table faced the door. But anyone opening it, unless he stepped right inside, had no view of what I call the long (or vertical) part of the letter. It contained some lockers surmounted by a bookcase; and a few clothes, a thick jacket or two, caps, oilskin coat, and such like, hung on hooks. There was at the bottom of that part a door opening into my bathroom, which could be entered also directly from the saloon. But that way was never used.

The mysterious arrival had discovered the advantage of this particular shape. Entering my room, lighted strongly by a big bulkhead lamp swung on gimbals above my writing desk, I did not see him anywhere till he stepped out quietly from behind the coats hung in the recessed part.

"I heard somebody moving about, and went in there at once," he whispered.

I, too, spoke under my breath.

"Nobody is likely to come in here without knocking and getting permission."

He nodded. His face was thin and the sunburn faded, as though he had been ill. And no wonder. He had been, I heard presently, kept under arrest in his cabin for nearly seven weeks. But there was nothing sickly in his eyes or in his expression. He was not a bit like me, really; yet, as we stood leaning over my bed place, whispering side by side, with our dark heads together and our backs to the door, anybody bold enough to open it stealthily would have been treated to the uncanny sight of a double captain busy talking in whispers with his other self.

"But all this doesn't tell me how you came to hang on to our side ladder," I inquired, in the hardly audible murmurs we used, after he had told me something more of the proceedings on board the *Sephora* once the bad weather was over.

"When we sighted Java Head I had had time to think all those matters out several times over. I had six weeks of doing nothing else, and with only an hour or so every evening for a tramp on the quarter-deck."

He whispered, his arms folded on the side of my bed place, staring through the open port. And I could imagine perfectly the manner of this thinking out—a stubborn if not a steadfast operation; something of which I should have been perfectly incapable.

"I reckoned it would be dark before we closed with the land," he continued, so low that I had to strain my hearing near as we were to each other, shoulder touching shoulder almost. "So I asked to speak to the old man. He always seemed very sick when he came to see me—as if he could not look me in the face. You know, that foresail saved the ship. She was too deep to have run under bare poles. And it was I that managed to set it for him. Anyway, he came. When I had him in my cabin—he stood by the door looking at me as if I had the halter round my neck already—I asked him right away to leave my cabin door unlocked at night while the ship was going through Sunda Straits. There would be the Java coast within two or three miles, off Angier Point. I wanted nothing more. I've had a prize for swimming my second year in the Conway."

"I can believe it," I breathed out.

"God only knows why they locked me in every night. To see some of their faces you'd have thought they were afraid I'd go about at night strangling people. Am I a murdering brute? Do I look it? By Jove! If I had been he wouldn't have trusted himself like that into my room. You'll say I might have chucked him aside and bolted out, there and then—it was dark already. Well, no. And for the same reason I wouldn't think of trying to smash the door. There would have been a rush to stop me at the noise, and I did not mean to get into a confounded scrimmage. Somebody else might have got killed—for I would not have broken out only to get chucked back, and I did not want any more of that work. He refused, looking more sick than ever. He was afraid of the men, and also of that old second mate of his who had been sailing with him for years—a gray-headed old humbug; and his steward, too, had been with him devil knows how long—seventeen years or more—a dogmatic sort of loafer who hated me like poison, just because I was the chief mate. No chief mate ever made more than one voyage in the *Sephora*, you know. Those two old chaps ran the ship. Devil only knows what the skipper wasn't afraid of (all his nerve went to pieces altogether in that hellish spell of bad weather we had)—of what the law would do to him —of his wife, perhaps. Oh, yes! she's on board. Though I don't think she would have meddled. She would have been only too glad to have me out of the ship in any way. The 'brand of Cain' business, don't you see. That's all right. I was ready enough to go off wandering on the face of the earth—and that was price enough to pay for an Abel of that sort. Anyhow, he wouldn't listen to me. 'This thing must take its course. I represent the law here.' He was shaking like a leaf. 'So you won't?' 'No!' 'Then I hope you will be able to sleep on that,' I said, and turned my back on him. 'I wonder that *you* can,' cries he, and locks the door.

"Well after that, I couldn't. Not very well. That was three weeks ago. We have had a slow passage through the Java Sea; drifted about Carimata for ten days. When we anchored here they thought, I suppose, it was all right. The nearest land (and that's five miles) is the ship's destination; the consul would soon set about catching me; and there would have been no object in bolting to these islets there. I don't suppose there's a drop of water on them. I don't know how it was, but tonight that steward, after bringing me my supper, went out to let me eat it, and left the door unlocked. And I ate it—all there was, too. After I had finished I strolled out on the quarter-deck. I don't know that I meant to do anything. A breath of fresh air was all I wanted, I believe. Then a sudden temptation came over me. I kicked off my slippers and was in the water before I had made up my mind fairly. Somebody heard the splash and they raised an awful hullabaloo. 'He's gone! Lower the boats! He's committed suicide! No, he's swimming!' Certainly I was swimming. It's not so easy for a swimmer like me to commit suicide by drowning. I landed on the nearest islet before the boat left the ship's side. I heard them pulling about in the dark, hailing, and so on, but after a bit they gave up. Everything quieted down and the anchorage became as still as death. I sat down on a stone and began to think. I felt certain they would start searching for me at daylight. There was no place to hide on those stony things—and if there had been, what would have been the good? But now I was clear of that ship, I was not going back. So after a while I took off all my clothes, tied them up in a bundle with a stone inside, and dropped them in the deep water on the outer side of that islet. That was suicide enough for me. Let them think what they liked, but I didn't mean to drown myself. I meant to swim till I sank—but that's not the same thing. I struck out for another of these little islands, and it was from that one that I first saw your riding light. Something to swim for. I went on easily, and on the way I came upon a flat rock a foot or two above water. In the daytime, I dare say, you might make it out with a glass from your poop. I scrambled up on it and rested myself for a bit. Then I made another start. That last spell must have been over a mile."

His whisper was getting fainter and fainter, and all the time he stared straight out through the porthole, in which there was not even a star to be seen. I had not interrupted him. There was something that made comment impossible in his narrative, or perhaps in himself; a sort of feeling, a quality, which I can't find a name for. And when he ceased, all I found was a futile whisper: "So you swam for our light?"

"Yes—straight for it. It was something to swim for. I couldn't see any stars low down because the coast was in the way, and I couldn't see the land, either. The water was like glass. One might have been swimming in a confounded thousand-feet deep cistern with no place for scrambling out anywhere; but what I didn't like was the notion of swimming round and round like a crazed bullock before I gave out; and as I didn't mean to go back . . . No. Do you see me being hauled back, stark naked, off one of these little islands by the scruff of the neck and fighting like a wild beast? Somebody would have got killed for certain, and I did not want any of that. So I went on. Then your ladder——"

"Why didn't you hail the ship?" I asked, a little louder.

He touched my shoulder lightly. Lazy footsteps came right over our heads and stopped. The second mate had crossed from the other side of the poop and might have been hanging over the rail for all we knew.

"He couldn't hear us talking—could he?" My double breathed into my very ear, anxiously.

His anxiety was in answer, a sufficient answer, to the question I had put to him. An answer containing all the difficulty of that situation. I closed the porthole quietly, to make sure. A louder word might have been overheard.

"Who's that?" he whispered then.

"My second mate. But I don't know much more of the fellow than you do."

And I told him a little about myself. I had been appointed to take charge while I least expected anything of the sort, not quite a fortnight ago. I didn't know either the ship or the people. Hadn't had the time in port to look about me or size anybody up. And as to the crew, all they knew was that I was appointed to take the ship home. For the rest, I was almost as much of a stranger on board as himself, I said. And at the moment I felt it most acutely. I felt that it would take very little to make me a suspect person in the eyes of the ship's company.

He had turned about meantime; and we, the two strangers in the ship, faced each other in identical attitudes.

"Your ladder——" he murmured, after a silence. "Who'd have thought of finding a ladder hanging over at night in a ship anchored out here! I felt just then a very unpleasant faintness. After the life I've been leading for nine weeks, anybody would have got out of condition. I wasn't capable of swimming round as far as your rudder chains. And, lo and behold! there was a ladder to get hold of. After I gripped it I said to myself, 'What's the good?' When I saw a man's head looking over I thought I would swim away presently and leave him shouting —in whatever language it was. I didn't mind being looked at. I—I liked it. And then you speaking to me so quietly—as if you had expected me—made me hold on a little longer. It had been a confounded lonely time —I don't mean while swimming. I was glad to talk a little to somebody that didn't belong to the *Sephora*. As to asking for the captain, that was a mere impulse. It could have been no use, with all the ship knowing about me and the other people pretty certain to be round here in the morning. I don't know—I wanted to be seen, to talk with somebody, before I went on. I don't know what I would have said. . . . 'Fine night, isn't it?' or something of the sort."

"Do you think they will be round here presently?" I asked with some incredulity.

"Quite likely," he said, faintly.

He looked extremely haggard all of a sudden. His head rolled on his shoulders.

"H'm. We shall see then. Meantime get into that bed," I whispered. "Want help? There."

It was a rather high bed place with a set of drawers underneath. This amazing swimmer really needed the lift I gave him by seizing his leg. He tumbled in, rolled over on his back, and flung one arm across his eyes. And then, with his face nearly hidden, he must have looked exactly as I used to look in that bed. I gazed upon my other self for a while before drawing across carefully the two green serge curtains which ran on a brass rod. I thought for a moment of pinning them together for greater safety, but I sat down on the couch, and once there I felt unwilling to rise and hunt for a pin. I would do it in a moment. I was extremely tired, in a peculiarly intimate way, by the strain of stealthiness, by the effort of whispering and the general secrecy of this excitement. It was three o'clock by now and I had been on my feet since nine, but I was not sleepy; I could not have gone to sleep. I sat there, fagged out, looking at the curtains, trying to clear my mind of the confused sensation of being in two places at once, and greatly bothered by an exasperating knocking in my head. It

was a relief to discover suddenly that it was not in my head at all, but on the outside of the door. Before I could collect myself the words "Come in" were out of my mouth, and the steward entered with a tray, bringing in my morning coffee. I had slept, after all, and I was so frightened that I shouted, "This way! I am here, steward," as though he had been miles away. He put down the tray on the table next the couch and only then said, very quietly, "I can see you are here, sir." I felt him give me a keen look, but I dared not meet his eyes just then. He must have wondered why I had drawn the curtains of my bed before going to sleep on the couch. He went out, hooking the door open as usual.

I heard the crew washing decks above me. I knew I would have been told at once if there had been any wind. Calm, I thought, and I was doubly vexed. Indeed, I felt dual more than ever. The steward reappeared suddenly in the doorway. I jumped up from the couch so quickly that he gave a start.

"What do you want here?"

"Close your port, sir—they are washing decks."

"It is closed," I said, reddening.

"Very well, sir." But he did not move from the doorway and returned my stare in an extraordinary, equivocal manner for a time. Then his eyes wavered, all his expression changed, and in a voice unusually gentle, almost coaxingly:

"May I come in to take the empty cup away, sir?"

"Of course!" I turned my back on him while he popped in and out. Then I unhooked and closed the door and even pushed the bolt. This sort of thing could not go on very long. The cabin was as hot as an oven, too. I took a peep at my double, and discovered that he had not moved, his arm was still over his eyes; but his chest heaved; his hair was wet; his chin glistened with perspiration. I reached over him and opened the port.

"I must show myself on deck," I reflected.

Of course, theoretically, I could do what I liked, with no one to say nay to me within the whole circle of the horizon; but to lock my cabin door and take the key away I did not dare. Directly I put my head out of the companion I saw the group of my two officers, the second mate barefooted, the chief mate in long India-rubber boots, near the break of the poop, and the steward halfway down the poop ladder talking to them eagerly. He happened to catch sight of me and dived, the second ran down on the main-deck shouting some order or other, and the chief mate came to meet me, touching his cap.

There was a sort of curiosity in his eye that I did not like. I don't know whether the steward had told them that I was "queer" only, or downright drunk, but I know the man meant to have a good look at me. I watched him coming with a smile which, as he got into point-blank range, took effect and froze his very whiskers. I did not give him time to open his lips.

"Square the yards by lifts and braces before the hands go to breakfast."

It was the first particular order I had given on board that ship; and I stayed on deck to see it executed, too. I had felt the need of asserting myself without loss of time. That sneering young cub got taken down a peg or two on that occasion, and I also seized the opportunity of having a good look at the face of every foremast man as they filed past me to go to the after braces. At breakfast time, eating nothing myself, I presided with such frigid dignity that the two mates were only too glad to escape from the cabin as soon as decency permitted; and all the time the dual working of my mind distracted me almost to the point of insanity. I was constantly watching myself, my secret self, as dependent on my actions as my own personality, sleeping in that bed, behind that door which faced me as I sat at the head of the table. It was very much like being mad, only it was worse because one was aware of it.

I had to shake him for a solid minute, but when at last he opened his eyes it was in the full possession of his senses, with an inquiring look.

"All's well so far," I whispered. "Now you must vanish into the bathroom."

He did so, as noiseless as a ghost, and then I rang for the steward, and facing him boldly, directed him to tidy up my stateroom while I was having my bath—"and be quick about it." As my tone admitted of no excuses, he said, "Yes, sir," and ran off to fetch his dustpan and brushes. I took a bath and did most of my dressing, splashing, and whistling softly for the steward's edification, while the secret sharer of my life stood drawn up bolt upright in that little space, his face looking very sunken in daylight, his eyelids lowered under the stern, dark line of his eyebrows drawn together by a slight frown.

When I left him there to go back to my room the steward was finishing dusting. I sent for the mate and engaged him in some insignificant conversation. It was, as it were, trifling with the terrific character of his whiskers; but my object was to give him an opportunity for a good look at my cabin. And then I could at last shut, with a clear conscience, the door of my stateroom and get my double back into the recessed part. There was nothing else for it. He had to sit still on a small folding stool, half smothered by the heavy coats hanging there. We listened to the steward going into the bathroom out of the saloon, filling the water bottles there, scrubbing the bath, setting things to rights, whisk, bang, clatter—out again into the saloon—turn the key—click. Such was my scheme for keeping my second self invisible. Nothing better could be contrived under the circumstances. And there we sat; I at my writing desk ready to appear busy with some papers, he behind me out of sight of the door. It would not have been prudent to talk in daytime; and I could not have stood the excitement of that queer sense of whispering to myself. Now and then, glancing over my shoulder, I saw him far back there, sitting rigidly on the low stool, his bare feet close together, his arms folded, his head hanging on his breast—and perfectly still. Anybody would have taken him for me.

I was fascinated by it myself. Every moment I had to glance over my shoulder. I was looking at him when a voice outside the door said:

"Beg pardon, sir."

"Well!" . . . I kept my eyes on him, and so when the voice outside the door announced, "There's a ship's boat coming our way, sir," I saw him give a start—the first movement he had made for hours. But he did not raise his bowed head.

"All right. Get the ladder over."

I hesitated. Should I whisper something to him? But what? His immobility seemed to have been never disturbed. What could I tell him he did not know already? . . . Finally I went on deck.

II

The skipper of the *Sephora* had a thin red whisker all round his face, and the sort of complexion that goes with hair of that color; also the particular, rather smeary shade of blue in the eyes. He was not exactly a showy figure; his shoulders were high, his stature but middling—one leg slightly more bandy than the other. He shook hands, looking vaguely around. A spiritless tenacity was his main characteristic, I judged. I behaved with a politeness which seemed to disconcert him. Perhaps he was shy. He mumbled to me as if he were ashamed of what he was saying; gave his name (it was something like Archbold—but at this distance of years I hardly am sure), his ship's name, and a few other particulars of that sort, in the manner of a criminal making a reluctant and doleful confession. He had had terrible weather on the passage out—terrible—terrible—wife aboard, too.

By this time we were seated in the cabin and the steward brought in a tray with a bottle and glasses. "Thanks! No." Never took liquor. Would have some water, though. He drank two tumblerfuls. Terrible thirsty work. Ever since daylight had been exploring the islands round his ship.

"What was that for—fun?" I asked, with an appearance of polite interest.

"No!" He sighed. "Painful duty."

As he persisted in his mumbling and I wanted my double to hear every word, I hit upon the notion of informing him that I regretted to say I was hard of hearing.

"Such a young man, too!" he nodded, keeping his smeary blue, unintelligent eyes fastened upon me. "What was the cause of it—some disease?" he inquired, without the least sympathy and as if he thought that, if so, I'd got no more than I deserved.

"Yes; disease," I admitted in a cheerful tone which seemed to shock him. But my point was gained, because he had to raise his voice to give me his tale. It is not worth while to record that version. It was just over two months since all this had happened, and he had thought so much about it that he seemed completely muddled as to its bearings, but still immensely impressed.

"What would you think of such a thing happening on board your own ship? I've had the *Sephora* for these fifteen years. I am a well-known shipmaster."

He was densely distressed—and perhaps I should have sympathized with him if I had been able to detach my mental vision from the unsuspected sharer of my cabin as though he were my second self. There he was on the other side of the bulkhead, four or five feet from us, no more, as we sat in the saloon. I looked politely at Captain Archbold (if that was his name), but it was the other I saw, in a gray sleeping suit, seated on a low stool, his bare feet close together, his arms folded, and every word said between us falling into the ears of his dark head bowed on his chest.

"I have been at sea now, man and boy, for seven-and-thirty years, and I've never heard of such a thing happening in an English ship. And that it should be my ship. Wife on board, too."

I was hardly listening to him.

"Don't you think," I said, "that the heavy sea which, you told me, came aboard just then might have killed the man? I have seen the sheer weight of the sea kill a man very neatly, by simply breaking his neck."

"Good God!" he uttered, impressively, fixing his smeary blue eyes on me. "The sea! No man killed by the sea ever looked like that." He seemed positively scandalized at my suggestion. And as I gazed at him certainly not prepared for anything original on his part, he advanced his head close to mine and thrust his tongue out at me so suddenly that I couldn't help starting back.

After scoring over my calmness in this graphic way he nodded wisely. If I had seen the sight, he assured me, I would never forget it as long as I lived. The weather was too bad to give the corpse a proper sea burial. So next day at dawn they took it up on the poop, covering its face with a bit of bunting; he read a short prayer, and then, just as it was, in its oilskins and long boots, they launched it amongst those mountainous seas that seemed ready every moment to swallow up the ship herself and the terrified lives on board of her.

"That reefed foresail saved you," I threw in.

"Under God—it did," he exclaimed fervently. "It was by a special mercy, I firmly believe, that it stood some of those hurricane squalls."

"It was the setting of that sail which——" I began.

"God's own hand in it," he interrupted me. "Nothing less could have done it. I don't mind telling you that I hardly dared give the order. It seemed impossible that we could touch anything without losing it, and then our last hope would have been gone."

The terror of that gale was on him yet. I let him go on for a bit, then said, casually— as if returning to a minor subject:

"You were very anxious to give up your mate to the shore people, I believe?"

He was. To the law. His obscure tenacity on that point had in it something incomprehensible and a little awful; something, as it were, mystical, quite apart from his anxiety that he should not be suspected of "countenancing any doings of that sort." Seven-and-thirty virtuous years at sea, of which over twenty of immaculate command, and the last fifteen in the *Sephora*, seemed to have laid him under some pitiless obligation.

"And you know," he went on, groping shame-facedly amongst his feelings, "I did not engage that young fellow. His people had some interest with my owners. I was in a way forced to take him on. He looked very smart, very gentlemanly, and all that. But do you know—I never liked him, somehow. I am a plain man. You see, he wasn't exactly the sort for the chief mate of a ship like the *Sephora*."

I had become so connected in thoughts and impressions with the secret sharer of my cabin that I felt as if I, personally, were being given to understand that I, too, was not the sort that would have done for the chief mate of a ship like the *Sephora*. I had no doubt of it in my mind.

"Not at all the style of man. You understand," he insisted, superfluously, looking hard at me.

I smiled urbanely. He seemed at a loss for a while.

"I suppose I must report a suicide."

"Beg pardon?"

"Sui-cide! That's what I'll have to write to my owners directly I get in."

"Unless you manage to recover him before tomorrow," I assented, dispassionately. . . . "I mean, alive."

He mumbled something which I really did not catch, and I turned my ear to him in a puzzled manner. He fairly bawled:

"The land—I say, the mainland is at least seven miles off my anchorage."

"About that."

My lack of excitement, of curiosity, of surprise, of any sort of pronounced interest, began to arouse his distrust. But except for the felicitous pretense of deafness I had not tried to pretend anything. I had felt utterly incapable of playing the part of ignorance properly, and therefore was afraid to try. It is also certain that he had brought some ready-made suspicions with him, and that he viewed my politeness as a strange and unnatural phenomenon. And yet how else could I have received him? Not heartily! That was impossible for psychological reasons, which I need not state here. My only object was to keep off his inquiries. Surlily? Yes, but surliness might have provoked a point-blank question. From its novelty to him and from its nature, punctilious courtesy was the manner best calculated to restrain the man. But there was the danger of his breaking through my defense bluntly. I could not, I think, have met him by a direct lie, also for psychological (not moral) reasons. If he had only known how afraid I was of his putting my feeling of identity with the other to the test! But, strangely enough—(I thought of it only afterwards)—I believe that he was not a little disconcerted by the reverse side of that weird situation, by something in me that reminded him of the man he was seeking—suggested a mysterious similitude to the young fellow he had distrusted and disliked from the first.

However that might have been, the silence was not very prolonged. He took another oblique step.

"I reckon I had no more than a two-mile pull to your ship. Not a bit more."

"And quite enough, too, in this awful heat," I said.

Another pause full of mistrust followed. Necessity, they say, is mother of invention, but fear, too, is not barren of ingenious suggestions. And I was afraid he would ask me point-blank for news of my other self.

"Nice little saloon, isn't it?" I remarked, as if noticing for the first time the way his eyes roamed from one closed door to the other.

"And very well fitted out, too. Here, for instance," I continued, reaching over the back of my seat negligently and flinging the door open, "is my bathroom."

He made an eager movement, but hardly gave it a glance. I got up, shut the door of the bathroom, and invited him to have a look round, as if I were very proud of my accommodation. He had to rise and be shown round, but he went through the business without any raptures whatever.

"And now we'll have a look at my stateroom," I declared, in a voice as loud as I dared to make it, crossing the cabin to the starboard side with purposely heavy steps.

He followed me in and gazed around. My intelligent double had vanished. I played my part.

"Very convenient—isn't it?"

"Very nice. Very comf . . ." He didn't finish and went out brusquely as if to escape from some unrighteous wiles of mine. But it was not to be. I had been too frightened not to feel vengeful; I felt I had him on the run, and I meant to keep him on the run. My polite insistence must have had something menacing in it, because he gave in suddenly. And I did not let him off a single item; mate's room, pantry, storerooms, the very sail locker which was also under the poop—he had to look into them all. When at last I showed him out on the quarter-deck he drew a long, spiritless sigh, and mumbled dismally that he must really be going back to his ship now. I desired my mate, who had joined us, to see to the captain's boat.

The man of whiskers gave a blast on the whistle which he used to wear hanging round his neck, and yelled, "*Sephora's* away!" My double down there in my cabin must have heard, and certainly could not feel more relieved than I. Four fellows came running out from somewhere forward and went over the side, while my own men, appearing on deck too, lined the rail. I escorted my visitor to the gangway ceremoniously, and nearly overdid it. He was a tenacious beast. On the very ladder he lingered, and in the unique, guiltily conscientious manner of sticking to the point:

"I say . . . you . . . you don't think that——"

I covered his voice loudly:

"Certainly not. . . . I am delighted. Good-by."

I had an idea of what he meant to say, and just saved myself by the privilege of defective hearing. He was too shaken generally to insist, but my mate, close witness of that parting, looked mystified and his face took on a thoughtful cast. As I did not want to appear as if I wished to avoid all communication with my officers, he had the opportunity to address me.

"Seems a very nice man. His boat's crew told our chaps a very extraordinary story, if what I am told by the steward is true. I suppose you had it from the captain, sir?"

"Yes. I had a story from the captain."

"A very horrible affair—isn't it, sir?"

"It is."

"Beats all these tales we hear about murders in Yankee ships."

"I don't think it beats them. I don't think it resembles them in the least."

"Bless my soul—you don't say so! But of course I've no acquaintance whatever with American ships, not I, so I couldn't go against your knowledge. It's horrible enough for me. . . . But the queerest part is that those fellows seemed to have some idea the man was hidden aboard here. They had really. Did you ever hear of such a thing?"

"Preposterous—isn't it?"

We were walking to and fro athwart the quarter-deck. No one of the crew forward could be seen (the day was Sunday), and the mate pursued:

"There was some little dispute about it. Our chaps took offense. 'As if we would harbor a thing like that,' they said. 'Wouldn't you like to look for him in our coal-hole?' Quite a tiff. But they made it up in the end. I suppose he did drown himself. Don't you, sir?"

"I don't suppose anything."

"You have no doubt in the matter, sir?"

"None whatever."

I left him suddenly. I felt I was producing a bad impression, but with my double down there it was most trying to be on deck. And it was almost as trying to be below. Altogether a nerve-trying situation. But on the whole I felt less torn in two when I was with him. There was no one in the whole ship whom I dared take into my confidence. Since the hands had got to know his story, it would have been impossible to pass him off for anyone else, and an accidental discovery was to be dreaded now more than ever. . . .

The steward being engaged in laying the table for dinner, we could talk only with our eyes when I first went down. Later in the afternoon we had a cautious try at whispering. The Sunday quietness of the ship was against us; the stillness of air and water around her was against us; the elements, the men were against us—everything was against us in our secret partnership; time itself—for this could not go on forever. The very trust in Providence was, I suppose, denied to his guilt. Shall I confess that this thought cast me down very much? And as to the chapter of accidents which counts for so much in the book of success, I could only hope that it was closed. For what favorable accident could be expected?

"Did you hear everything?" were my first words as soon as we took up our position side by side, leaning over my bed place.

He had. And the proof of it was his earnest whisper, "The man told you he hardly dared to give the order."

I understood the reference to be to that saving foresail.

"Yes. He was afraid of it being lost in the setting."

"I assure you he never gave the order. He may think he did, but he never gave it. He stood there with me on the break of the poop after the main topsail blew away, and whimpered about our last hope—positively whimpered about it and nothing else—and the night coming on! To hear one's skipper go on like that in such weather was enough to drive any fellow out of his mind. It worked me up into a sort of desperation. I just took it into my own hands and went away from him, boiling, and—— But what's the use telling you? *You* know! . . . Do you think that if I had not been pretty fierce with them I should have got the men to do anything? Not it! The bo's'n perhaps? Perhaps! It wasn't a heavy sea—it was a sea gone mad! I suppose the end of the world will be something like that; and a man may have the heart to see it coming once and be done with it—but to have to face it day after day—— I don't blame anybody. I was precious little better than the rest. Only—I was an officer of that old coal wagon, anyhow——"

"I quite understand," I conveyed that sincere assurance into his ear. He was out of breath with whispering; I could hear him pant slightly. It was all very simple. The same strung-up force which had given twenty-four men a chance, at least, for their lives, had, in a sort of recoil, crushed an unworthy mutinous existence.

But I had no leisure to weigh the merits of the matter—footsteps in the saloon, a heavy knock. "There's enough wind to get under way with, sir." Here was the call of a new claim upon my thoughts and even upon my feelings.

"Turn the hands up," I cried through the door. "I'll be on deck directly."

I was going out to make the acquaintance of my ship. Before I left the cabin our eyes met—the eyes of the only two strangers on board. I pointed to the recessed part where the little campstool awaited him and laid my finger on my lips. He made a gesture—somewhat vague—a little mysterious, accompanied by a faint smile, as if of regret.

This is not the place to enlarge upon the sensations of a man who feels for the first time a ship move under his feet to his own independent word. In my case they were not unalloyed. I was not wholly alone with my command; for there was that stranger in my cabin. Or rather, I was not completely and wholly with her. Part of me was absent. That mental feeling of being in two places at once affected me physically as if the mood of secrecy had penetrated my very soul. Before an hour had elapsed since the ship had begun to move, having occasion to ask the mate (he stood by my side) to take a compass bearing of the pagoda, I caught myself reaching up to his ear in whispers. I say I caught myself, but enough had escaped to startle the man. I can't describe it otherwise than by saying that he shied. A grave, preoccupied manner, as though he were in possession of some perplexing intelligence, did not leave him henceforth. A little later I moved away from the rail to look at the compass with such a stealthy gait that the helmsman noticed it—and I could not help noticing the unusual roundness of his eyes. These are trifling instances, though it's to no commander's advantage to be suspected of ludicrous eccentricities. But I was also more seriously affected. There are to a seaman certain words, gestures, that should in given conditions come as naturally, as instinctively as the ,winking of a menaced eye. A certain order should spring on to his lips without thinking; a certain sign should get itself made, so to speak, without reflection. But all unconscious alertness had abandoned me. I had to make an effort of will to recall myself back (from the cabin) to the conditions of the moment. I felt that I was appearing an irresolute commander to those people who were watching me more or less critically.

And, besides, there were the scares. On the second day out, for instance, coming off the deck in the afternoon (I had straw slippers on my bare feet) I stopped at the open pantry door and spoke to the steward. He was doing something there with his back to me. At the sound of my voice he nearly jumped out of his skin, as the saying is, and incidentally broke a cup.

"What on earth's the matter with you?" I asked, astonished.

He was extremely confused. "Beg your pardon, sir. I made sure you were in your cabin."

"You see I wasn't."

"No, sir. I could have sworn I had heard you moving in there not a moment ago. It's most extraordinary . . . very sorry, sir."

I passed on with an inward shudder. I was so identified with my secret double that I did not even mention the fact in those scanty, fearful whispers we exchanged. I suppose he had made some slight noise of some kind or other. It would have been miraculous if he hadn't at one time or another. And yet, haggard as he appeared, he looked always perfectly self-controlled, more than calm—almost invulnerable. On my suggestion he remained almost entirely in the bathroom, which, upon the whole, was the safest place. There could be really no shadow of an excuse for anyone ever wanting to go in there, once the steward had done with it. It was a very tiny place. Sometimes he reclined on the floor, his legs bent, his head sustained on one elbow. At others I would find him on the campstool, sitting in his gray sleeping suit and with his cropped dark hair like a patient, unmoved convict. At night I would smuggle him into my bed place, and we would whisper together, with the regular footfalls of the officer of the watch passing and repassing over our heads. It was an infinitely miserable time. It was lucky that some tins of fine preserves were stowed in a locker in my stateroom; hard bread I could always get hold of; and so he lived on stewed chicken, *pâté de foie gras*, asparagus, cooked oysters, sardines—on all sorts of abominable sham delicacies out of tins. My early-morning coffee he always drank; and it was all I dared do for him in that respect.

Every day there was the horrible maneuvering to go through so that my room and then the bathroom should be done in the usual way. I came to hate the sight of the steward, to abhor the voice of that harmless man. I felt that it was he who would bring on the disaster of discovery. It hung like a sword over our heads.

The fourth day out, I think (we were then working down the east side of the Gulf of Siam, tack for tack, in light winds and smooth water)—the fourth day, I say, of this miserable juggling with the unavoidable, as we sat at our evening meal, that man, whose slightest movement I dreaded, after putting down the dishes ran up on deck busily. This could not be dangerous. Presently he came down again; and then it appeared that he had remembered a coat of mine which I had thrown over a rail to dry after having been wetted in a shower which had passed over the ship in the afternoon. Sitting stolidly at at the head of the table I became terrified at the sight of the garment on his arm. Of course he made for my door. There was no time to lose.

"Steward," I thundered. My nerves were so shaken that I could not govern my voice and conceal my agitation. This was the sort of thing that made my terrifically whiskered mate tap his forehead with his forefinger. I had detected him using that gesture while talking on deck with a confidential air to the carpenter. It was too far to hear a word, but I had no doubt that this pantomime could only refer to the strange new captain.

"Yes, sir," the pale-faced steward turned resignedly to me. It was this maddening course of being shouted at, checked without rhyme or reason, arbitrarily chased out of my cabin, suddenly called into it, sent flying out of his pantry on incomprehensible errands, that accounted for the growing wretchedness of his expression.

"Where are you going with that coat?"

"To your room, sir."

"Is there another shower coming?"

"I'm sure I don't know, sir. Shall I go up again and see, sir?"

"No! never mind."

My object was attained, as of course my other self in there would have heard everything that passed. During this interlude my two officers never raised their eyes off their respective plates; but the lip of that confounded cub, the second mate, quivered visibly.

I expected the steward to hook my coat on and come out at once. He was very slow about it; but I dominated my nervousness sufficiently not to shout after him. Suddenly I became aware (it could be heard plainly enough) that the fellow for some reason or other was opening the door of my bathroom. It was the end. The place was literally not big enough to swing a cat in. My voice died in my throat and I went stony all over. I expected to hear a yell of surprise and terror, and made a movement, but had not the strength to get on my legs. Everything remained still. Had my second self taken the poor wretch by the throat? I don't know what I could have done next moment if I had not seen the steward come out of my room, close the door, and then stand quietly by the sideboard.

"Saved," I thought. "But, no! Lost! Gone! He was gone!"

I laid my knife and fork down and leaned back in my chair. My head swam. After a while, when sufficiently recovered to speak in a steady voice, I instructed my mate to put the ship round at eight o'clock himself.

"I won't come on deck," I went on. "I think I'll turn in, and unless the wind shifts I don't want to be disturbed before midnight. I feel a bit seedy."

"You did look middling bad a little while ago," the chief mate remarked without showing any great concern.

They both went out, and I stared at the steward clearing the table. There was nothing to be read on that wretched man's face. But why did he avoid my eyes, I asked myself. Then I thought I should like to hear the sound of his voice.

"Steward!"

"Sir!" Startled as usual.

"Where did you hang up that coat?"

"In the bathroom, sir." The usual anxious tone. "It's not quite dry yet, sir."

For some time longer I sat in the cuddy. Had my double vanished as he had come? But of his coming there was an explanation, whereas his disappearance would be inexplicable. . . . I went slowly into my dark room, shut the door, lighted the lamp, and for a time dared not turn round. When at last I did I saw him standing bolt-upright in the narrow recessed part. It would not be true to say I had a shock, but an irresistible doubt of his bodily existence flitted through my mind. Can it be, I asked myself, that he is not visible to other eyes than mine? It was like being haunted. Motionless, with a grave face, he raised his hands slightly at me in a gesture which meant clearly, "Heavens! what a narrow escape!" Narrow indeed. I think I had come creeping quietly as near insanity as any man who has not actually gone over the border. That gesture restrained me, so to speak.

The mate with the terrific whiskers was now putting the ship on the other tack. In the moment of profound silence which follows upon the hands going to their stations I heard on the poop his raised voice: "Hard alee!" and the distant shout of the order repeated on the main-deck. The sails, in that light breeze, made but a faint fluttering noise. It ceased. The ship was coming round slowly: I held my breath in the renewed stillness of expectation; one wouldn't have thought that there was a single living soul on her decks. A sudden brisk shout, "Mainsail haul!" broke the spell, and in the noisy cries and rush overhead of the men running away with the main brace we two, down in my cabin, came together in our usual position by the bed place.

He did not wait for my question. "I heard him fumbling here and just managed to squat myself down in the bath," he whispered to me. "The fellow only opened the door and put his arm in to hang the coat up. All the same——"

"I never thought of that," I whispered back, even more appalled than before at the closeness of the shave, and marveling at that something unyielding in his character which was carrying him through so finely. There was no agitation in his whisper. Whoever was being driven distracted, it was not he. He was sane. And the proof of his sanity was continued when he took up the whispering again.

"It would never do for me to come to life again."

It was somthing that a ghost might have said. But what he was alluding to was his old captain's reluctant admission of the theory of suicide. It would obviously serve his turn —if I had understood at all the view which seemed to govern the unalterable purpose of his action.

"You must maroon me as soon as ever you can get amongst these islands off the Cambodge shore," he went on.

"Maroon you! We are not living in a boy's adventure tale," I protested. His scornful whispering took me up.

"We aren't indeed! There's nothing of a boy's tale in this. But there's nothing else for it. I want no more. You don't suppose I am afraid of what can be done to me? Prison or gallows or whatever they may please. But you don't see me coming back to explain such things to an old fellow in a wig and twelve respectable tradesmen, do you? What can they know whether I am guilty or not—or of *what* I am guilty, either? That's my affair. What does the Bible say? 'Driven off the face of the earth.' Very well, I am off the face of the earth now. As I came at night so I shall go."

"Impossible!" I murmured. "You can't."

"Can't? . . . Not naked like a soul on the Day of Judgment. I shall freeze on to this sleeping suit. The Last Day is not yet—and . . . you have understood thoroughly. Didn't you?"

I felt suddenly ashamed of myself. I may say truly that I understood—and my hesitation in letting that man swim away from my ship's side had been a mere sham sentiment, a sort of cowardice.

"It can't be done now till next night," I breathed out. "The ship is on the off-shore tack and the wind may fail us."

"As long as I know that you understand," he whispered. "But of course you do. It's a great satisfaction to have got somebody to understand. You seem to have been there on purpose." And in the same whisper, as if we two whenever we talked had to say things to each other which were not fit for the world to hear, he added, "It's very wonderful."

We remained side by side talking in our secret way—but sometimes silent or just exchanging a whispered word or two at long intervals. And as usual he stared through the port. A breath of wind came now and again into our faces. The ship might have been moored in dock, so gently and on an even keel she slipped through the water, that did not murmur even at our passage, shadowy and silent like a phantom sea.

At midnight I went on deck, and to my mate's great surprise put the ship round on the other tack. His terrible whiskers flitted round me in silent criticism. I certainly should not have done it if it had been only a question of getting out of that sleepy gulf as quickly as possible. I believe he told the second mate, who relieved him, that it was a great want of judgment. The other only yawned. That intolerable cub shuffled about so sleepily and lolled against the rails in such a slack, improper fashion that I came down on him sharply.

"Aren't you properly awake yet?"

"Yes, sir! I am awake."

"Well, then, be good enough to hold yourself as if you were. And keep a lookout. If there's any current we'll be closing with some islands before daylight."

The east side of the gulf is fringed with islands, some solitary, others in groups. On the blue background of the high coast they seem to float on silvery patches of calm water, arid and gray, or dark green and rounded like clumps of evergreen bushes, with the larger ones, a mile or two long, showing the outlines of ridges, ribs of gray rock under the dank mantle of matted leafage. Unknown to trade, to travel, almost to geography, the manner of life they harbor is an unsolved secret. There must be villages— settlements of fishermen at least—on the largest of them, and some communication with the world is probably kept up by native craft. But all that forenoon, as we headed for them, fanned along by the faintest of breezes, I saw no sign of man or canoe in the field of the telescope I kept on pointing at the scattered group.

At noon I gave no orders for a change of course, and the mate's whiskers became much concerned and seemed to be offering themselves unduly to my notice. At last I said:

"I am going to stand right in. Quite in—as far as I can take her."

The stare of extreme surprise imparted an air of ferocity also to his eyes, and he looked truly terrific for a moment.

"We're not doing well in the middle of the gulf," I continued, casually. "I am going to look for land breezes tonight."

"Bless my soul! Do you mean, sir, in the dark amongst the lot of all them islands and reefs and shoals?"

"Well—if there are any regular land breezes at all on this coast one must get close inshore to find them, mustn't one?"

"Bless my soul!" he exclaimed again under his breath. All that afternoon he wore a dreamy, contemplative appearance which in him was a mark of perplexity. After dinner I went into my stateroom as if I meant to take some rest. There we two bent our dark heads over a half-unrolled chart lying on my bed.

"There," I said. "It's got to be Koh-ring. I've been looking at it ever since sunrise. It has got two hills and a low point. It must be inhabited. And on the coast opposite there is what looks like the mouth of a biggish river

—with some towns, no doubt, not far up. It's the best chance for you that I can see."

"Anything. Koh-ring let it be."

He looked thoughtfully at the chart as if surveying chances and distances from a lofty height—and following with his eyes his own figure wandering on the blank land of Cochin-China, and then passing off that piece of paper clean out of sight into uncharted regions. And it was as if the ship had two captains to plan her course for her. I had been so worried and restless running up and down that I had not had the patience to dress that day. I had remained in my sleeping suit, with straw slippers and a soft floppy hat. The closeness of the heat in the gulf had been most oppressive, and the crew were used to seeing me wandering in that airy attire.

"She will clear the south point as she heads now," I whispered into his ear. "Goodness only knows when, though, but certainly after dark. I'll edge her in to half a mile, as far as I may be able to judge in the dark——"

"Be careful," he murmured, warningly— and I realized suddenly that all my future, the only future for which I was fit, would perhaps go irretrievably to pieces in any mishap to my first command.

I could not stop a moment longer in the room. I motioned for him to get out of sight and made my way on the poop. That unplayful cub had the watch. I walked up and down for a while thinking things out, then beckoned him over.

"Send a couple of hands to open the two quarter-deck ports," I said, mildly.

He actually had the impudence, or else so forgot himself in his wonder at such an incomprehensible order, as to repeat:

"Open the quarter-deck ports! What for, sir?"

"The only reason you need concern yourself about is because I tell you to do so. Have them open wide and fastened properly."

He reddened and went off, but I believe made some jeering remark to the carpenter as to the sensible practice of ventilating a ship's quarter-deck. I know he popped into the mate's cabin to impart the fact to him because the whiskers came on deck, as it were by chance, and stole glances at me from below—for signs of lunacy or drunkenness, I suppose.

A little before supper, feeling more restless than ever, I rejoined, for a moment, my second self. And to find him sitting so quietly was surprising, like something against nature, inhuman.

I developed my plan in a hurried whisper.

"I shall stand in as close as I dare and then put her round. I will presently find means to smuggle you out of here into the sail locker, which communicates with the lobby. But there is an opening, a sort of square for hauling the sails out, which gives straight on the quarter-deck and which is never closed in fine weather, so as to give air to the sails. When the ship's way is deadened in stays and all the hands are aft at the main braces you will have a clear road to slip out and get overboard through the open quarter-deck port. I've had them both fastened up. Use a rope's end to lower yourself into the water so as to avoid a splash—you know. It could be heard and cause some beastly complication."

He kept silent for a while, then whispered, "I understand."

"I won't be there to see you go," I began with an effort. "The rest . . . I only hope I have understood, too."

"You have. From first to last"—and for the first time there seemed to be a faltering, something strained in his whisper. He caught hold of my arm, but the ringing of the supper bell made me start. He didn't though; he only released his grip.

After supper I didn't come below again till well past eight o'clock. The faint, steady breeze was loaded with dew; and the wet, darkened sails held all there was of propelling power in it. The night, clear and starry, sparkled darkly, and the opaque, lightless patches shifting slowly against the low stars were the drifting islets. On the port bow there was a big one more distant and shadowily imposing by the great space of sky it eclipsed.

On opening the door I had a back view of my very own self looking at a chart. He had come out of the recess and was standing near the table.

"Quite dark enough," I whispered.

He stepped back and leaned against my bed with a level, quiet glance. I sat on the couch. We had nothing to say to each other. Over our heads the officer of the watch moved here and there. Then I heard him move quickly. I knew what that meant. He was making for the companion; and presently his voice was outside my door.

"We are drawing in pretty fast, sir. Land looks rather close."

"Very well," I answered. "I am coming on deck directly."

I waited till he was gone out of the cuddy, then rose. My double moved too. The time had come to exchange our last whispers, for neither of us was ever to hear each other's natural voice.

"Look here!" I opened a drawer and took out three sovereigns. "Take this anyhow. I've got six and I'd give you the lot, only I must keep a little money to buy some fruit and vegetables for the crew from native boats as we go through Sunda Straits."

He shook his head.

"Take it," I urged him, whispering desperately. "No one can tell what——"

He smiled and slapped meaningly the only pocket of the sleeping jacket. It was not safe, certainly. But I produced a large old silk handkerchief of mine, and tying the three pieces of gold in a corner, pressed it on him. He was touched, I supposed, because he took it at last and tied it quickly round his waist under the jacket, on his bare skin.

Our eyes met; several seconds elapsed, till, our glances still mingled, I extended my hand and turned the lamp out. Then I passed through the cuddy, leaving the door of my room wide open. . . . "Steward!"

He was still lingering in the pantry in the greatness of his zeal, giving a rub-up to a plated cruet stand the last thing before going to bed. Being careful not to wake up the mate, whose room was opposite, I spoke in an undertone.

He looked round anxiously, "Sir!"

"Can you get me a little hot water from the galley?"

"I am afraid, sir, the galley fire's been out for some time now."

"Go and see."

He flew up the stairs.

"Now," I whispered, loudly, into the saloon —too loudly, perhaps, but I was afraid I couldn't make a sound. He was by my side in an instant—the double captain slipped past the stairs—through a tiny dark passage . . . a sliding door. We were in the sail locker, scrambling on our knees over the sails. A sudden thought struck me. I saw myself wandering barefooted, bareheaded, the sun beating on my dark poll. I snatched off my floppy hat and tried hurriedly in the dark to ram it on my other self. He dodged and fended off silently. I wonder what he thought had come to me before he understood and suddenly desisted. Our hands met gropingly, lingered united in a steady, motionless clasp for a second. . . . No word was breathed by either of us when they separated.

I was standing quietly by the pantry door when the steward returned.

"Sorry, sir. Kettle barely warm. Shall I light the spirit lamp?"

"Never mind."

I came out on deck slowly. It was now a matter of conscience to shave the land as close as possible—for now he must go overboard whenever the ship was put in stays. Must! There could be no going back for him. After a moment I walked over to leeward and my heart flew into my mouth at the nearness of the land on the bow. Under any other circumstances I would not have held on a minute longer. The second mate had followed me anxiously.

I looked on till I felt I could command my voice.

"She will weather," I said then in a quiet tone.

"Are you going to try that, sir?" he stammered out incredulously.

I took no notice of him and raised my tone just enough to be heard by the helmsman.

"Keep her good full."

"Good full, sir."

The wind fanned my cheek, the sails slept, the world was silent. The strain of watching the dark loom of the land grow bigger and denser was too much for me. I had shut my eyes—because the ship must go closer. She must! The stillness was intolerable. Were we standing still?

When I opened my eyes the second view started my heart with a thump. The black southern hill of Koh-ring seemed to hang right over the ship like a towering fragment of the ever-lasting night. On that enormous mass of blackness there was not a gleam to be seen, not a sound to be heard. It was gliding irresistibly towards us and yet seemed already within reach of the hand. I saw the vague figures of the watch grouped in the waist, gazing in awed silence.

"Are you going on, sir?" inquired an unsteady voice at my elbow.

I ignored it. I had to go on.

"Keep her full. Don't check her way. That won't do now," I said, warningly.

"I can't see the sails very well," the helmsman answered me, in strange, quavering tones.

Was she close enough? Already she was, I won't say in the shadow of the land, but in the very blackness of it, already swallowed up as it were, gone too close to be recalled, gone from me altogether.

"Give the mate a call," I said to the young man who stood at my elbow as still as death. "And turn all hands up."

My tone had a borrowed loudness reverberated from the height of the land. Several voices cried out together: "We are all on deck, sir."

Then stillness again, with the great shadow gliding closer, towering higher, without a light, without a sound. Such a hush had fallen on the ship that she might have been a bark of the dead floating in slowly under the very gates of Erebus.

"My God! Where are we?"

It was the mate moaning at my elbow. He was thunderstruck, and as it were deprived of the moral support of his whiskers. He clapped his hands and absolutely cried out, "Lost!"

"Be quiet," I said, sternly.

He lowered his tone, but I saw the shadowy gesture of his despair. "What are we doing here?"

"Looking for the land wind."

He made as if to tear his hair, and addressed me recklessly.

"She will never get out. You have done it, sir. I knew it'd end in something like this. She will never weather, and you are too close now to stay. She'll drift ashore before she's round. O my God!"

I caught his arm as he was raising it to batter his poor devoted head, and shook it violently.

"She's ashore already," he wailed, trying to tear himself away.

"Is she? . . . Keep good full there!"

"Good full, sir," cried the helmsman in a frightened, thin, childlike voice.

I hadn't let go the mate's arm and went on shaking it. "Ready about, do you hear? You go forward"—shake—"and stop there"—shake—"and hold your noise"—shake—"and see these head-sheets properly overhauled"—shake, shake—shake.

And all the time I dared not look towards the land lest my heart should fail me. I released my grip at last and he ran forward as if fleeing for dear life.

I wondered what my double there in the sail locker thought of this commotion. He was able to hear everything—and perhaps he was able to understand why, on my conscience, it had to be thus close—no less. My first order "Hard alee!" re-echoed ominously under the towering shadow of Koh-ring as if I had shouted in a mountain gorge. And then I watched the land intently. In that smooth water and light wind it was impossible to feel the ship coming-to. No! I could not feel her. And my second self was making now ready to ship out and lower himself overboard. Perhaps he was gone already . . . ?

The great black mass brooding over our very mastheads began to pivot away from the ship's side silently. And now I forgot the secret stranger ready to depart, and remembered only that I was a total stranger to the ship. I did not know her. Would she do it? How was she to be handled?

I swung the mainyard and waited helplessly. She was perhaps stopped, and her very fate hung in the balance, with the black mass of Koh-ring like the gate of the everlasting night towering over her taffrail. What would she do now? Had she way on her yet? I stepped to the side swiftly, and on the shadowy water I could see nothing except a faint phosphorescent flash revealing the glassy smoothness of the sleeping surface. It was impossible to tell—and I had not learned yet the feel of my ship. Was she moving? What I needed was something easily seen, a piece of paper, which I could throw overboard and watch. I had nothing on me. To run down for it I didn't dare. There was no time. All at once my strained, yearning stare distinguished a white object floating within a yard of the ship's side. White on the black water. A phosphorescent flash passed under it. What was that thing? . . . I recognized my own floppy hat. It must have fallen off his head . . . and he didn't bother. Now I had what I wanted—the saving mark for my eyes. But I hardly thought of my other self, now gone from the ship, to be hidden forever from all friendly faces, to be a fugitive and a vagabond on the earth, with no brand of the curse on his sane forehead to stay a slaying hand . . . too proud to explain.

And I watched the hat—the expression of

my sudden pity for his mere flesh. It had been meant to save his homeless head from the dangers of the sun. And now—behold—it was saving the ship, by serving me for a mark to help out the ignorance of my strangeness. Ha! It was drifting forward, warning me just in time that the ship had gathered sternway.

"Shift the helm," I said in a low voice to the seaman standing still like a statue.

The man's eyes glistened wildly in the binnacle light as he jumped round to the other side and spun round the wheel.

I walked to the break of the poop. On the overshadowed deck all hands stood by the forebraces waiting for my order. The stars ahead seemed to be gliding from right to left. And all was so still in the world that I heard the quiet remark, "She's round," passed in a tone of intense relief between two seamen.

"Let go and haul."

The foreyards ran round with a great noise, amidst cheery cries. And now the frightful whiskers made themselves heard giving various orders. Already the ship was drawing ahead. And I was alone with her. Nothing! no one in the world should stand now between us, throwing a shadow on the way of silent knowledge and mute affection, the perfect communion of a seaman with his first command.

Walking to the taffrail, I was in time to make out, on the very edge of a darkness thrown by a towering black mass like the very gateway of Erebus—yes, I was in time to catch an evanescent glimpse of my white hat left behind to mark the spot where the secret sharer of my cabin and of my thoughts, as though he were my second self, had lowered himself into the water to take his punishment: a free man, a proud swimmer striking out for a new destiny.

ANTON CHEKHOV

The Darling

Translated by Constance Garnett

Olenka, the daughter of the retired collegiate assessor, Plemyanniakov, was sitting in her back porch, lost in thought. It was hot, the flies were persistent and teasing, and it was pleasant to reflect that it would soon be evening. Dark rain-clouds were gathering from the east, and bringing from time to time a breath of moisture in the air.

Kukin, who was the manager of an open-air theatre called the Tivoli, and who lived in the lodge, was standing in the middle of the garden looking at the sky.

"Again!" he observed despairingly. "It's going to rain again! Rain every day, as though to spite me! I might as well hang myself! It's ruin! Fearful losses every day."

He flung up his hands, and went on, addressing Olenka: "There! that's the life we lead, Olga Semyonovna. It's enough to make one cry. One works and does one's utmost; one wears oneself out, getting no sleep at night, and racks one's brain what to do for the best. And then what happens? To begin with, one's public is ignorant, boorish. I give them the very best operetta, a dainty masque, first-rate music-hall artists. But do you suppose that's what they want! They don't understand anything of that sort. They want a clown; what they ask for is vulgarity. And then look at the weather! Almost every evening it rains. It started on the tenth of May, and it's kept it up all May and June. It's simply awful! The public doesn't come, but

I've to pay the rent just the same, and pay the artists."

The next evening the clouds would gather again, and Kukin would say with an hysterical laugh:

"Well, rain away, then! Flood the garden, drown me! Damn my luck in this world and the next! Let the artists have me up! Send me to prison!—to Siberia!—the scaffold! Ha, ha, ha!"

And next day the same thing.

Olenka listened to Kukin with silent gravity, and sometimes tears came into her eyes. In the end his misfortunes touched her; she grew to love him. He was a small thin man, with a yellow face, and curls combed forward on his forehead. He spoke in a thin tenor; as he talked his mouth worked on one side, and there was always an expression of despair on his face; yet he aroused a deep and genuine affection in her. She was always fond of someone, and could not exist without loving. In earlier days she had loved her papa, who now sat in a darkened room, breathing with difficulty; she had loved her aunt who used to come every other year from Bryansk; and before that, when she was at school, she had loved her French master. She was a gentle, soft-hearted, compassionate girl, with mild, tender eyes and very good health. At the sight of her full rosy cheeks, her soft white neck with a little dark mole on it, and the kind, naïve smile, which came into her face when she listened to anything pleasant, men thought, "Yes, not half bad," and smiled too, while lady visitors could not refrain from seizing her hand in the middle of a conversation, exclaiming in a gush of delight, "You darling!"

The house in which she had lived from her birth upwards, and which was left her in her father's will, was at the extreme end of the town, not far from the Tivoli. In the evenings and at night she could hear the band playing, and the crackling and banging of fireworks, and it seemed to her that it was Kukin struggling with his destiny, storming the entrenchments of his chief foe, the indifferent public; there was a sweet thrill at her heart, she had no desire to sleep, and when he returned home at daybreak, she tapped softly at her bedroom window, and showing him only her face and one shoulder through the curtain, she gave him a friendly smile. . . .

He proposed to her, and they were married. And when he had a closer view of her neck and her plump, fine shoulders, he threw up his hands, and said:

"You darling!"

He was happy, but as it rained on the day and night of his wedding, his face still retained an expression of despair.

They got on very well together. She used to sit in his office, to look after things in the Tivoli, to put down the accounts and pay the wages. And her rosy cheeks, her sweet, naïve, radiant smile, were to be seen now at the office window, now in the refreshment bar or behind the scenes at the theatre. And already she used to say to her acquaintances that the theatre was the chief and most important thing in life, and that it was only through the drama that one could derive true enjoyment and become cultivated and humane.

"But do you suppose the public understands that?" she used to say. "What they want is a clown. Yesterday we gave 'Faust Inside Out,' and almost all the boxes were empty; but if Vanitchka and I had been producing some vulgar thing, I assure you the theatre would have been packed. To-morrow Vanitchka and I are doing 'Orpheus in Hell.' Do come."

And what Kukin said about the theatre and the actors she repeated. Like him she despised the public for their ignorance and their indifference to art; she took part in the rehearsals, she corrected the actors, she kept an eye on the behaviour of the musicians, and when there was an unfavourable notice in the local paper, she shed tears, and then went to the editor's office to set things right.

The actors were fond of her and used to call her "Vanitchka and I," and "the darling"; she was sorry for them and used to lend them small sums of money, and if they deceived her, she used to shed a few tears in private, but did not complain to her husband.

They got on well in the winter too. They took the theatre in the town for the whole winter, and let it for short terms to a Little Russian company, or to a conjurer, or to a local dramatic society. Olenka grew stouter, and was always beaming with satisfaction, while Kukin grew thinner and yellower, and continually complained of their terrible losses, although he had not done badly all the winter. He used to cough at night, and she used to give him hot raspberry tea or lime-flower water, to rub him with eau-de-Cologne and to wrap him in her warm shawls.

"You're such a sweet pet!" she used to say with perfect sincerity, stroking his hair. "You're such a pretty dear!"

Towards Lent he went to Moscow to collect a new troupe, and without him she could not sleep, but sat all night at her window, looking at the stars, and she compared herself with the hens, who are awake all night and uneasy when the cock is not in the hen-house. Kukin was detained in Moscow, and wrote that he would be back at Easter, adding some instructions about the Tivoli. But on the Sunday before Easter, late in the evening, came a sudden ominous knock at the gate; someone was hammering on the gate as though on a barrel—boom, boom, boom! The drowsy cook went flopping with her bare feet through the puddles, as she ran to open the gate.

"Please open," said someone outside in a thick bass. "There is a telegram for you."

Olenka had received telegrams from her husband before, but this time for some reason she felt numb with terror. With shaking hands she opened the telegram and read as follows:

"Ivan Petrovitch died suddenly to-day. Awaiting immate instructions fufuneral Tuesday."

That was how it was written in the telegram—"fufuneral," and the utterly incomprehensible word "immate." It was signed by the stage manager of the operatic company.

"My darling!" sobbed Olenka. "Vanitchka, my precious, my darling! Why did I ever meet you! Why did I know you and love you! Your poor heart-broken Olenka is all alone without you!"

Kukin's funeral took place on Tuesday in Moscow, Olenka returned home on Wednesday, and as soon as she got indoors she threw herself on her bed and sobbed so loudly that it could be heard next door, and in the street.

"Poor darling!" the neighbours said, as they crossed themselves. "Olga Semyonovna, poor darling! How she does take on!"

Three months later Olenka was coming home from mass, melancholy and in deep mourning. It happened that one of her neighbours, Vassily Andreitch Pustovalov, returning home from church, walked back beside her. He was the manager at Babakayev's, the timber merchant's. He wore a straw hat, a white waistcoat, and a gold watch-chain, and looked more like a country gentleman than a man in trade.

"Everything happens as it is ordained, Olga Semyonovna," he said gravely, with a sympathetic note in his voice; "and if any of our dear ones die, it must be because it is the will of God, so we ought to have fortitude and bear it submissively."

After seeing Olenka to her gate, he said good-bye and went on. All day afterwards she heard his sedately dignified voice, and whenever she shut her eyes she saw his dark beard. She liked him very much. And apparently she had made an impression on him too, for not long afterwards an elderly lady, with whom she was only slightly acquainted, came to drink coffee with her, and as soon as she was seated at table began to talk about Pustovalov, saying that he was an excellent man whom one could thoroughly depend upon, and that any girl would be glad to marry him. Three days later Pustovalov came himself. He did not stay long, only about ten minutes, and he did not say much, but when he left, Olenka loved him—loved him so much that she lay awake all night in a perfect fever, and in the morning she sent for the elderly lady. The match was quickly arranged, and then came the wedding.

Pustovalov and Olenka got on very well together when they were married.

Usually he sat in the office till dinner-time, then he went out on business, while Olenka took his place, and sat in the office till evening, making up accounts and booking orders.

"Timber gets dearer every year; the price rises twenty per cent," she would say to her customers and friends. "Only fancy we used to sell local timber, and now Vassitchka always has to go for wood to the Mogilev district. And the freight!" she would add, covering her cheeks with her hands in horror. "The freight!"

It seemed to her that she had been in the timber trade for ages and ages, and that the most important and necessary thing in life was timber; and there was something intimate and touching to her in the very sound of words such as "baulk," "post," "beam," "pole," "scantling," "batten," "lath," "plank," etc.

At night when she was asleep she dreamed of perfect mountains of planks and boards, and long strings of waggons, carting timber somewhere far away. She dreamed that a whole regiment of six-inch beams forty feet high, standing on end, was marching upon the timber-yard; that logs, beams, and boards knocked together with the resounding crash of dry wood, kept falling and getting up again, piling themselves on each other. Olenka cried out in her sleep, and Pustovalov said to her tenderly: "Olenka, what's the matter, darling? Cross yourself!"

Her husband's ideas were hers. If he thought the room was too hot, or that business was slack, she thought the same. Her husband did not care for entertainments, and on holidays he stayed home. She did likewise.

"You are always at home or in the office," her friends said to her. "You should go to the theatre, darling, or to the circus."

"Vassitchka and I have no time to go to theatres," she would answer sedately. "We have no time for nonsense. What's the use of these theatres?"

On Saturdays Pustovalov and she used to go to the evening service; on holidays to early mass, and they walked side by side with softened faces as they came home from church. There was a pleasant fragrance about them both, and her silk dress rustled agreeably. At home they drank tea, with fancy bread and jams of various kinds, and afterwards they ate pie. Every day at twelve o'clock there was a savoury smell of beet-root soup and of mutton or duck in their yard, and on fast-days of fish, and no one could pass the gate without feeling hungry. In the office the samovar was always boiling, and customers were regaled with tea and cracknels. Once a week the couple went to the baths and returned side by side, both red in the face.

"Yes, we have nothing to complain of, thank God," Olenka used to say to her acquaintances. "I wish everyone were as well off as Vassitchka and I."

When Pustovalov went away to buy wood in the Mogilev district, she missed him dreadfully, lay awake and cried. A young veterinary surgeon in the army, called Smirnin, to whom they had let their lodge, used sometimes to come in in the evening. He used to talk to her and play cards with her, and this entertained her in her husband's absence. She was particularly interested in what he told her of his home life. He was married and had a little boy, but was separated from his wife because she had been unfaithful to him, and now he hated her and used to send her forty roubles a month for the maintenance of their son. And hearing of all this, Olenka sighed and shook her head. She was sorry for him.

"Well, God keep you," she used to say to him at parting, as she lighted him down the stairs with a candle. "Thank you for coming to cheer me up, and may the Mother of God give you health."

And she always expressed herself with the same sedateness and dignity, the same reasonableness, an imitation of her husband. As the veterinary surgeon was disappearing behind the door below, she would say:

"You know, Vladimir Platonitch, you'd better make it up with your wife. You should forgive her for the sake of your son. You may be sure the little fellow understands."

And when Pustovalov came back, she told him in a low voice about the veterinary surgeon and his unhappy home life, and both sighed and shook their heads and talked about the boy, who, no doubt, missed his father, and by some strange connection of ideas, they went up to the holy ikons, bowed to the ground before them and prayed that God would give them children.

And so the Pustovalovs lived for six years quietly and peaceably in love and complete harmony.

But behold! one winter day after drinking hot tea in the office, Vassily Andreitch went out into the yard without his cap on to see about sending off some timber, caught cold and was taken ill. He had the best doctors, but he grew worse and died after four months' illness. And Olenka was a widow once more.

"I've nobody, now you've left me, my darling," she sobbed, after her husband's funeral. "How can I live without you, in wretchedness and misery! Pity me, good people, all alone in the world!"

She went about dressed in black with long "weepers," and gave up wearing hat and gloves for good. She hardly ever went out, except to church, or to her husband's grave, and led the life of a nun. It was not till six months later that she took off the weepers and opened the shutters of the windows. She was sometimes seen in the mornings, going with her cook to market for provisions, but what went on in her house and how she lived now could only be surmised. People guessed, from seeing her drinking tea in her garden with the veterinary surgeon, who read the newspaper aloud to her, and from the fact that, meeting a lady she knew at the post-office, she said to her:

"There is no proper veterinary inspection in our town, and that's the cause of all sorts of epidemics. One is always hearing of people's getting infection from the milk supply, or catching diseases from horses and cows. The health of domestic animals ought to be as well cared for as the health of human beings."

She repeated the veterinary surgeon's words, and was of the same opinion as he about everything. It was evident that she could not live a year without some attachment, and had found new happiness in the lodge. In anyone else this would have been censured, but no one could think ill of Olenka; everything she did was so natural. Neither she nor the veterinary surgeon said anything to other people of the change in their relations, and tried, indeed, to conceal it, but without success, for Olenka could not keep a secret. When he had visitors, men serving in his regiment, and she poured out tea or served the supper, she would begin talking of the cattle plague, of the foot and mouth disease, and of the municipal slaughter-houses. He was dreadfully embarrassed, and when the guests had gone, he would seize her by the hand and hiss angrily:

"I've asked you before not to talk about what you don't understand. When we veterinary surgeons are talking among ourselves, please don't put your word in. It's really annoying."

And she would look at him with astonishment and dismay, and ask him in alarm: "But, Voloditchka, what *am* I to talk about?"

And with tears in her eyes she would embrace him, begging him not to be angry, and they were both happy.

But this happiness did not last long. The veterinary surgeon departed, departed for ever with his regiment, when it was transferred to a distant place—to Siberia, it may be. And Olenka was left alone.

Now she was absolutely alone. Her father had long been dead, and his arm-chair lay in the attic, covered with dust and lame of one leg. She got thinner and plainer, and when people met her in the street they did not look at her as they used to, and did not smile to her; evidently her best years were over and left behind, and now a new sort of life had begun for her, which did not bear thinking about. In the evening Olenka sat in the porch, and heard the band playing and the fireworks popping in the Tivoli, but now the sound stirred no response. She looked into her yard without interest, thought of nothing, wished for nothing, and afterwards, when night came on she went to bed and dreamed of her empty yard. She ate and drank as it were unwillingly.

And what was worst of all, she had no opinions of any sort. She saw the objects about her and understood what she saw, but could not form any opinion about them, and did not know what to talk about. And how awful it is not to have any opinions! One sees a bottle, for instance, or the rain, or a peasant driving in his cart, but what the bottle is for, or the rain, or the peasant, and what is the meaning of it, one can't say, and could not even for a thousand roubles. When she had Kukin, or Pustovalov, or the veterinary surgeon, Olenka could explain everything, and give her opinion about anything you like, but now there was the same emptiness in her brain and in her heart as there was in her yard outside. And it was as harsh and as bitter as wormwood in the mouth.

Little by little the town grew in all directions. The road became a street, and where the Tivoli and the timber-yard had been, there were new turnings and houses. How rapidly time passes! Olenka's house grew dingy, the roof got rusty, the shed sank on one side, and the whole yard was overgrown with docks and stinging-nettles. Olenka herself had grown plain and elderly; in summer she sat in the porch, and her soul, as before, was empty and dreary and full of bitterness. In winter she sat at her window and looked at the snow. When she caught the scent of spring, or heard the chime of the church bells, a sudden rush of memories from the past came over her, there was a tender ache in her heart, and her eyes brimmed over with tears; but this was only for a minute, and then came emptiness again and the sense of the futility of life. The black kitten, Briska, rubbed against her and purred softly, but Olenka was not touched by these feline caresses. That was not what she needed. She wanted a love that would absorb her whole being, her whole soul and reason—that would give her ideas and an object in life, and would warm her old blood. And she would shake the kitten off her skirt and say with vexation:

"Get along; I don't want you!"

And so it was, day after day and year after year, and no joy, and no opinions. Whatever Mavra, the cook, said she accepted.

One hot July day, towards evening, just as the cattle were being driven by, and the whole yard was full of dust, someone suddenly knocked at the gate. Olenka went to open it herself and was dumfounded when she looked out: she saw Smirnin, the veterinary surgeon, grey-headed, and dressed as a civilian. She suddenly remembered everything. She could not help crying and letting her head fall on his breast without uttering a word, and in the violence of her feeling she did not notice how they both walked into the house and sat down to tea.

"My dear Vladimir Platonitch! What fate has brought you?" she muttered, trembling with joy.

"I want to settle here for good, Olga Semyonovna," he told her. "I have resigned my post, and have come to settle down and try my luck on my own account. Besides, it's time for my boy to go to school. He's a big boy. I am reconciled with my wife, you know."

"Where is she?" asked Olenka.

"She's at the hotel with the boy, and I'm looking for lodgings."

"Good gracious, my dear soul! Lodgings! Why not have my house? Why shouldn't that suit you? Why, my goodness, I wouldn't take any rent!" cried Olenka in a flutter, beginning to cry again. "You live here, and the lodge will do nicely for me. Oh dear! how glad I am!"

Next day the roof was painted and the walls were whitewashed, and Olenka, with her arms akimbo, walked about the yard giving directions. Her face was beaming with her old smile, and she was brisk and alert as though she had waked from a long sleep. The veterinary's wife arrived—a thin, plain lady, with short hair and a peevish expression. With her was her little Sasha, a boy of ten, small for his age, blue-eyed, chubby, with dimples in his cheeks. And scarcely had the boy walked into the yard when he ran after the cat, and at once there was the sound of his gay, joyous laugh.

"Is that your puss, auntie?" he asked Olenka. "When she has little ones, do give us a kitten. Mamma is awfully afraid of mice."

Olenka talked to him, and gave him tea. Her heart warmed and there was a sweet ache in her bosom, as though the boy had been her own child. And when he sat at the table in the evening, going over his lessons, she looked at him with deep tenderness and pity as she murmured to herself:

"You pretty pet! . . . my precious! . . . Such a fair little thing, and so clever."

" 'An island is a piece of land which is entirely surrounded by water,' " he read aloud.

"An island is a piece of land," she repeated, and this was the first opinion to which she gave utterance with positive conviction after so many years of silence and dearth of ideas.

Now she had opinions of her own, and at supper she talked to Sasha's parents, saying how difficult the lessons were at the high schools, but that yet the high school was better than a commercial one, since with a high school education all careers were open to one, such as being a doctor or an engineer.

Sasha began going to the high school. His mother departed to Harkov to her sister's and did not return; his father used to go off every day to inspect cattle, and would often be away from home for three days together, and it seemed to Olenka as though Sasha was entirely abandoned, that he was not wanted at home, that he was being starved, and she carried him off to her lodge and gave him a little room there.

And for six months Sasha had lived in the lodge with her. Every morning Olenka came into his bedroom and found him fast asleep, sleeping noiselessly with his hand under his cheek. She was sorry to wake him.

"Sashenka," she would say mournfully, "get up, darling. It's time for school."

He would get up, dress and say his prayers, and then sit down to breakfast, drink three glasses of tea, and eat two large cracknels and half a buttered roll. All this time he was hardly awake and a little ill-humoured in consequence.

"You don't quite know your fable, Sashenka," Olenka would say, looking at him as though he were about to set off on a long journey. "What a lot of trouble I have with you! You must work and do your best, darling, and obey your teachers."

"Oh, do leave me alone!" Sasha would say.

Then he would go down the street to school, a little figure, wearing a big cap and carrying a satchel on his shoulder. Olenka would follow him noiselessly.

"Sashenka!" she would call after him, and she would pop into his hand a date or a caramel. When he reached the street where the school was, he would feel ashamed of being followed by a tall, stout woman; he would turn round and say:

"You'd better go home, auntie. I can go the rest of the way alone."

She would stand still and look after him fixedly till he had disappeared at the school-gate.

Ah, how she loved him! Of her former attachments not one had been so deep; never had her soul surrendered to any feeling so spontaneously, so disinterestedly, and so joyously as now that her maternal instincts were aroused. For this little boy with the dimple in his cheek and the big school cap, she would have given her whole life, she would have given it with joy and tears of tenderness. Why? Who can tell why?

When she had seen the last of Sasha, she returned home, contented and serene, brimming over with love; her face, which had grown younger during the last six months, smiled and beamed; people meeting her looked at her with pleasure.

"Good-morning, Olga Semyonovna, darling. How are you, darling?"

"The lessons at the high school are very difficult now," she would relate at the market. "It's too much; in the first class yesterday they gave him a fable to learn by heart, and a Latin translation and a problem. You know it's too much for a little chap."

And she would begin talking about the teachers, the lessons, and the school books, saying just what Sasha said.

At three o'clock they had dinner together: in the evening they learned their lessons together and cried. When she put him to bed, she would stay a long time making the cross over him and murmuring a prayer; then she would go to bed and dream of that far-away misty future when Sasha would finish his studies and become a doctor or an engineer, would have a big house of his own with horses and a carriage, would get married and have children.... She would fall asleep still thinking of the same thing, and tears would run down her cheeks from her closed eyes, while the black cat lay purring beside her: "Mrr, mrr, mrr."

Suddenly there would come a loud knock at the gate.

Olenka would wake up breathless with alarm, her heart throbbing. Half a minute later would come another knock.

"It must be a telegram from Harkov," she would think, beginning to tremble from head to foot. "Sasha's mother is sending for him from Harkov.... Oh, mercy on us!"

She was in despair. Her head, her hands, and her feet would turn chill, and she would feel that she was the most unhappy woman in the world. But another minute would pass, voices would be heard: it would turn out to be the veterinary surgeon coming home from the club.

"Well, thank God!" she would think.

And gradually the load in her heart would pass off, and she would feel at ease. She would go back to bed thinking of Sasha, who lay sound asleep in the next room, sometimes crying out in his sleep:

"I'll give it you! Get away! Shut up!"

RUDYARD KIPLING

"They"

One view called me to another; one hill top to its fellow, half across the county, and since I could answer at no more trouble than the snapping forward of a lever, I let the country flow under my wheels. The orchid-studded flats of the East gave way to the thyme, ilex, and grey grass of the Downs; these again to the rich cornland and fig-trees of the lower coast, where you carry the beat of the tide on your left hand for fifteen level miles; and when at last I turned inland through a huddle of rounded hills and woods I had run myself clean out of my known marks. Beyond that precise hamlet which stands godmother to the capital of the United States, I found hidden villages where bees, the only things awake, boomed in eight-foot lindens that overhung grey Norman churches; miraculous brooks diving under stone bridges built for heavier traffic than would ever vex them again; tithe-barns larger than their churches, and an old smithy that cried out aloud how it had once been a hall of the Knights of the Temple. Gipsies I found on a common where the gorse, bracken, and heath fought it out together up a mile of Roman road; and a little farther on I disturbed a red fox rolling dog-fashion in the naked sunlight.

As the wooded hills closed about me I stood up in the car to take the bearings of that great Down whose ringed head is a landmark for fifty miles across the low countries. I judged that the lie of the country would bring me across some westward running road that went to his feet, but I did not al-low for the confusing veils of the woods. A quick turn plunged me first into a green cutting brimful of liquid sunshine, next into a gloomy tunnel where last year's dead leaves whispered and scuffled about my tyres. The strong hazel stuff meeting overhead had not been cut for a couple of generations at least, nor had any axe helped the moss-cankered oak and beech to spring above them. Here the road changed frankly into a carpeted ride on whose brown velvet spent primrose-clumps showed like jade, and a few sickly, white-stalked blue-bells nodded together. As the slope favoured I shut off the power and slid over the whirled leaves, expecting every moment to meet a keeper; but I only heard a jay, far off, arguing against the silence under the twilight of the trees.

Still the track descended. I was on the point of reversing and working my way back on the second speed ere I ended in some swamp, when I saw sunshine through the tangle ahead and lifted the brake.

It was down again at once. As the light beat across my face my fore-wheels took the turf of a great still lawn from which sprang horsemen ten feet high with levelled lances, monstrous peacocks, and sleek round-headed maids of honour—blue, black, and glisten-ing—all of clipped yew. Across the lawn—the marshalled woods besieged it on three sides —stood an ancient house of lichened and weather-worn stone, with mullioned windows and roofs of rose-red tile. It was flanked by semi-circular walls, also rose-red, that closed the lawn on the fourth side, and at their feet a box hedge grew man-high. There were doves on the roof about the slim brick chimneys, and I caught a glimpse of an octagonal dove-house behind the screening wall.

Here, then, I stayed; a horseman's green spear laid at my breast; held by the exceeding beauty of that jewel in that setting.

"If I am not packed off for a trespasser, or if this knight does not ride a wallop at me," thought I, "Shakespeare and Queen Elizabeth at least must come out of that half-open garden door and ask me to tea."

A child appeared at an upper window, and I thought the little thing waved a friendly hand. But it was to call a companion, for presently another bright head showed. Then I heard a laugh among the yew-peacocks, and turning to make sure (till then I had been watching the house only) I saw the silver of a fountain behind a hedge thrown up against the sun. The doves on the roof cooed to the cooing water; but between the two notes I caught the utterly happy chuckle of a child absorbed in some light mischief.

The garden door—heavy oak sunk deep in the thickness of the wall—opened further: a woman in a big garden hat set her foot slowly on the time-hollowed stone step and as slowly walked across the turf. I was forming some apology when she lifted up her head and I saw that she was blind.

"I heard you," she said. "Isn't that a motor car?"

"I'm afraid I've made a mistake in my road. I should have turned off up above—I never dreamed"—I began.

"But I'm very glad. Fancy a motor car coming into the garden! It will be such a treat——" She turned and made as though looking about her. "You—you haven't seen any one have you—perhaps?"

"No one to speak to, but the children seemed interested at a distance."

"Which?"

"I saw a couple up at the window just now, and I think I heard a little chap in the grounds."

"Oh, lucky you!" she cried, and her face brightened. "I hear them, of course, but that's all. You've seen them and heard them?"

"Yes," I answered. "And if I know anything of children one of them's having a beautiful time by the fountain yonder. Escaped, I should imagine."

"You're fond of children?"

I gave her one or two reasons why I did not altogether hate them.

"Of course, of course," she cried. "Then you understand. Then you won't think it foolish if I ask you to take your car through the gardens, once or twice—quite slowly. I'm sure they'd like to see it. They see so little, poor things. One tries to make their life pleasant, but——" she threw out her hands towards the woods. "We're so out of the world here."

"That will be splendid," I said. "But I can't cut up your grass."

She faced to the right. "Wait a minute," she said. "We're at the South gate, aren't we? Behind those peacocks there's a flagged path. We call it the Peacock's Walk. You can't see it from here, they tell me, but if you squeeze along by the edge of the wood you can turn at the first peacock and get on to the flags."

It was a sacrilege to wake that dreaming house-front with the clatter of machinery, but I swung the car to clear the turf, brushed along the edge of the wood and turned in on the broad stone path where the fountain-basin lay like one star-sapphire.

"May I come too?" she cried. "No, please don't help me. They'll like it better if they see me."

She felt her way lightly to the front of the car, and with one foot on the step she called: "Children, oh, children! Look and see what's going to happen!"

The voice would have drawn lost souls from the Pit, for the yearning that underlay its sweetness, and I was not surprised to hear an answering shout behind the yews. It must have been the child by the fountain, but he fled at our approach, leaving a little toy boat in the water. I saw the glint of his blue blouse among the still horsemen.

Very disposedly we paraded the length of the walk and at her request backed again. This time the child had got the better of his panic, but stood far off and doubting.

"The little fellow's watching us," I said. "I wonder if he'd like a ride."

"They're very shy still. Very shy. But, oh, lucky you to be able to see them! Let's listen."

I stopped the machine at once, and the humid stillness, heavy with the scent of box, cloaked us deep. Shears I could hear where some gardener was clipping; a mumble of bees and broken voices that might have been the doves.

"Oh, unkind!" she said wearily.

"Perhaps they're only shy of the motor. The little maid at the window looks tremendously interested."

"Yes?" She raised her head. "It was wrong of me to say that. They are really fond of me. It's the only thing that makes life worth living—when they're fond of you, isn't it? I daren't think what the place would be without them. By the way, is it beautiful?"

"I think it is the most beautiful place I have ever seen."

"So they all tell me. I can feel it, of course, but that isn't quite the same thing."

"Then have you never——?" I began, but stopped abashed.

"Not since I can remember. It happened when I was only a few months old, they tell me. And yet I must remember something, else how could I dream about colours. I see light in my dreams, and colours, but I never see *them*. I only hear them just as I do when I'm awake."

"It's difficult to see faces in dreams. Some people can, but most of us haven't the gift," I went on, looking up at the window where the child stood all but hidden.

"I've heard that too," she said. "And they tell me that one never sees a dead person's face in a dream. Is that true?"

"I believe it is—now I come to think of it."

"But how is it with yourself—yourself?" The blind eyes turned towards me.

"I have never seen the faces of my dead in any dream," I answered.

"Then it must be as bad as being blind."

The sun had dipped behind the woods and the long shades were possessing the insolent horsemen one by one. I saw the light die from off the top of a glossy-leaved lance and all the brave hard green turn to soft black. The house, accepting another day at end, as it had accepted an hundred thousand gone, seemed to settle deeper into its rest among the shadows.

"Have you ever wanted to?" she said after the silence.

"Very much sometimes," I replied. The child had left the window as the shadows closed upon it.

"Ah! So've I, but I don't suppose it's allowed.... Where d'you live?"

"Quite the other side of the county—sixty miles and more, and I must be going back. I've come without my big lamp."

"But it's not dark yet. I can feel it."

"I'm afraid it will be by the time I get home. Could you lend me someone to set me on my road at first? I've utterly lost myself."

"I'll send Madden with you to the cross-roads. We are so out of the world, I don't wonder you were lost! I'll guide you round to the front of the house; but you will go slowly, won't you, till you're out of the grounds? It isn't foolish, do you think?"

"I promise you I'll go like this," I said, and let the car start herself down the flagged path.

We skirted the left wing of the house, whose elaborately cast lead guttering alone was worth a day's journey; passed under a great rose-grown gate in the red wall, and so round to the high front of the house which in beauty and stateliness as much excelled the back as that all others I had seen.

"Is it so very beautiful?" she said wistfully when she heard my raptures. "And you like the lead-figures too? There's the old azalea garden behind. They say that this place must have been made for children. Will you help me out, please? I should like to come with you as far as the cross-roads, but I mustn't leave them. Is that you, Madden? I want you to show this gentleman the way to the cross-roads. He has lost his way but—he has seen them."

A butler appeared noiselessly at the miracle of old oak that must be called the front door, and slipped aside to put on his hat. She stood looking at me with open blue eyes in which no sight lay, and I saw for the first time that she was beautiful.

"Remember," she said quietly, "if you are fond of them you will come again," and disappeared within the house.

The butler in the car said nothing till we were nearly at the lodge gates, where catching a glimpse of a blue blouse in a shrubbery I swerved amply lest the devil that leads little boys to play should drag me into child-murder.

"Excuse me," he asked of a sudden, "but why did you do that, Sir?"

"The child yonder."

"Our young gentleman in blue?"

"Of course."

"He runs about a good deal. Did you see him by the fountain, Sir?"

"Oh, yes, several times. Do we turn here?"

"Yes, Sir. And did you 'appen to see them upstairs too?"

"At the upper window? Yes."

"Was that before the mistress come out to speak to you, Sir?"

"A little before that. Why d'you want to know?"

He paused a little. "Only to make sure that —that they had seen the car, Sir, because with children running about, though I'm sure you're driving particularly careful, there might be an accident. That was all, Sir. Here are the cross-roads. You can't miss your way from now on. Thank you, Sir, but that isn't *our* custom, not with——"

"I beg your pardon," I said, and thrust away the British silver.

"Oh, it's quite right with the rest of 'em as a rule. Goodbye, Sir."

He retired into the armour-plated conning tower of his caste and walked away. Evidently a butler solicitous for the honour of his house, and interested, probably through a maid, in the nursery.

Once beyond the signposts at the cross-roads I looked back, but the crumpled hills interlaced so jealously that I could not see where the house had lain. When I asked its name at a cottage along the road, the fat woman who sold sweetmeats there gave me to understand that people with motor cars had small right to live—much less to "go about talking like carriage folk." They were not a pleasant-mannered community.

When I retraced my route on the map that evening I was little wiser. Hawkin's Old Farm appeared to be the survey title of the place, and the old County Gazeteer, generally so ample, did not allude to it. The big house of those parts was Hodnington Hall, Georgian with early Victorian embellishments, as an atrocious steel engraving attested. I carried my difficulty to a neighbour—a deep-rooted tree of that soil—and he gave me a name of a family which conveyed no meaning.

A month or so later—I went again, or it may have been that my car took the road of her own volition. She over-ran the fruitless Downs, threaded every turn of the maze of lanes below the hills, drew through the high-walled woods, impenetrable in their full leaf, came out at the cross-roads where the butler had left me, and a little further on developed an internal trouble which forced me to turn her in on a grass way-waste that cut into a summer-silent hazel wood. So far as I could make sure by the sun and a six-inch Ordnance map, this should be the road flank of that wood which I had first explored from the heights above. I made a mighty serious business of my repairs and a glittering shop of my repair kit, spanners, pump, and the like, which I spread out orderly upon a rug. It was a trap to catch all childhood, for on such a day, I argued, the children would not be far off. When I paused in my work I listened, but the wood was so full of the noises of summer (though the birds had mated) that I could not at first distinguish these from the tread of small cautious feet stealing across the dead leaves. I rang my bell in an alluring manner, but the feet fled, and I repented, for to a child a sudden noise is very real terror. I must have been at work half an hour when I heard in the wood the voice of the blind woman crying: "Children, oh children, where are you?" and the stillness made slow to close on the perfection of that cry. She came towards me, half feeling her way between the tree boles, and though a child it seemed clung to her skirt, it swerved into the leafage like a rabbit as she drew nearer.

"Is that you?" she said, "from the other side of the county?"

"Yes, it's me from the other side of the county."

"Then why didn't you come through the upper woods? They were there just now."

"They were here a few minutes ago. I expect they knew my car had broken down, and came to see the fun."

"Nothing serious, I hope? How do cars break down?"

"In fifty different ways. Only mine has chosen the fifty first."

She laughed merrily at the tiny joke, cooed with delicious laughter, and pushed her hat back.

"Let me hear," she said.

"Wait a moment," I cried, "and I'll get you a cushion."

She set her foot on the rug all covered with spare parts, and stooped above it eagerly. "What delightful things!" The hands

through which she saw glanced in the chequered sunlight. "A box here—another box! Why you've arranged them like playing shop!

"I confess now that I put it out to attract them. I don't need half those things really."

"How nice of you! I heard your bell in the upper wood. You say they were here before that?"

"I'm sure of it. Why are they so shy? That little fellow in blue who was with you just now ought to have got over his fright. He's been watching me like a Red Indian."

"It must have been your bell," she said. "I heard one of them go past me in trouble when I was coming down. They're shy—so shy even with me." She turned her face over her shoulder and cried again: "Children! Oh, children! Look and see!"

"They must have gone off together on their own affairs," I suggested, for there was a murmur behind us of lowered voices broken by the sudden squeaking giggles of childhood. I returned to my tinkerings and she leaned forward, her chin on her hand, listening interestedly.

"How many are they?" I said at last. The work was finished, but I saw no reason to go.

Her forehead puckered a little in thought. "I don't quite know," she said simply. "Sometimes more—sometimes less. They come and stay with me because I love them, you see."

"That must be very jolly," I said, replacing a drawer, and as I spoke I heard the inanity of my answer.

"You—you aren't laughing at me," she cried. "I—I haven't any of my own. I never married. People laugh at me sometimes about them because—because——"

"Because they're savages," I returned. "It's nothing to fret for. That sort laugh at everything that isn't in their own fat lives."

"I don't know. How should I? I only don't like being laughed at about them. It hurts; and when one can't see.... I don't want to seem silly," her chin quivered like a child's as she spoke, "but we blindies have only one skin, I think. Everything outside hits straight at our souls. It's different with you. You've such good defences in your eyes—looking out—before anyone can really pain you in your soul. People forget that with us."

I was silent reviewing that inexhaustible matter—the more than inherited (since it is also carefully taught) brutality of the Christian peoples, beside which the mere heathendom of the West Coast nigger is clean and restrained. It led me a long distance into myself.

"Don't do that!" she said of a sudden, putting her hands before her eyes.

"What?"

She made a gesture with her hand.

"That! It's—it's all purple and black. Don't! That colour hurts."

"But, how in the world do you know about colours?" I exclaimed, for here was a revelation indeed.

"Colours as colours?" she asked.

"No. *Those* Colours which you saw just now."

"You know as well as I do," she laughed, "else you wouldn't have asked that question. They aren't in the world at all. They're in *you*—when you went so angry."

"D'you mean a dull purplish patch, like port-wine mixed with ink?" I said.

"I've never seen ink or port-wine, but the colours aren't mixed. They are separate—all separate."

"Do you mean black streaks and jags across the purple?"

She nodded. "Yes—if they are like this," and zig-zagged her finger again, "but it's more red than purple—that bad colour."

"And what are the colours at the top of the —whatever you see?"

Slowly she leaned forward and traced on the rug the figure of the Egg itself.

"I see them so," she said, pointing with a grass stem, "white, green, yellow, red, purple, and when people are angry or bad, black across the red—as you were just now."

"Who told you anything about it—in the beginning?" I demanded.

"About the colours? No one. I used to ask what colours were when I was little—in table-covers and curtains and carpets, you see—because some colours hurt me and some made me happy. People told me; and when I got older that was how I saw people." Again she traced the outline of the Egg which it is given to very few of us to see.

"All by yourself?" I repeated.

"All by myself. There wasn't anyone else. I only found out afterwards that other people did not see the Colours."

She leaned against the tree-bole plaiting and unplaiting chance-plucked grass stems. The children in the wood had drawn nearer. I could see them with the tail of my eye frolicking like squirrels.

"Now I am sure you will never laugh at me," she went on after a long silence. "Nor at *them*."

"Goodness! No!" I cried, jolted out of my train of thought. "A man who laughs at a child—unless the child is laughing too—is a heathen!"

"I didn't mean that of course. You'd never laugh *at* children, but I thought— I used to think—that perhaps you might laugh about *them*. So now I beg your pardon. . . . What are you going to laugh at?"

I had made no sound, but she knew.

"At the notion of your begging my pardon. If you had done your duty as a pillar of the state and a landed proprietress you ought to have summoned me for trespass when I barged through your woods the other day. It was disgraceful of me—inexcusable."

She looked at me, her head against the tree trunk—long and steadfastly—this woman who could see the naked soul.

"How curious," she half whispered. "How very curious."

"Why, what have I done?"

"You don't understand . . . and yet you understood about the Colours. Don't you understand?"

She spoke with a passion that nothing had justified, and I faced her bewilderedly as she rose. The children had gathered themselves in a roundel behind a bramble bush. One sleek head bent over something smaller, and the set of the little shoulders told me that fingers were on lips. They too, had some child's tremendous secret. I alone was hopelessly astray there in the broad sunlight.

"No," I said, and shook my head as though the dead eyes could note. "Whatever it is, I don't understand yet. Perhaps I shall later —if you'll let me come again."

"You will come again," she answered. "You will surely come again and walk in the wood."

"Perhaps the children will know me well enough by that time to let me play with them—as a favour. You know what children are like."

"It isn't a matter of favour but of right," she replied, and while I wondered what she meant, a dishevelled woman plunged round the bend of the road, loose-haired, purple, almost lowing with agony as she ran. It was my rude, fat friend of the sweetmeat shop. The blind woman heard and stepped forward. "What is it, Mrs. Madehurst?" she asked.

The woman flung her apron over her head and literally grovelled in the dust, crying that her grandchild was sick to death, that the local doctor was away fishing, that Jenny the mother was at her wit's end, and so forth, with repetitions and bellowings.

"Where's the next nearest doctor?" I asked between paroxysms.

"Madden will tell you. Go round to the house and take him with you. I'll attend to this. Be quick!" She half-supported the fat woman into the shade. In two minutes I was blowing all the horns of Jericho under the front of the House Beautiful, and Madden, in the pantry, rose to the crisis like a butler and a man.

A quarter of an hour at illegal speeds caught us a doctor five miles away. Within the half-hour we had decanted him, much interested in motors, at the door of the sweetmeat shop, and drew up the road to await the verdict.

"Useful things cars," said Madden, all man and no butler. "If I'd had one when mine took sick she wouldn't have died."

"How was it?" I asked.

"Croup. Mrs. Madden was away. No one knew what to do. I drove eight miles in a tax cart for the doctor. She was choked when we came back. This car 'd ha' saved her. She'd have been close on ten now."

"I'm sorry," I said. "I thought you were rather fond of children from what you told me going to the cross-roads the other day."

"Have you seen 'em again, Sir—this mornin'?"

"Yes, but they're well broke to cars. I couldn't get any of them within twenty yards of it."

He looked at me carefully as a scout considers a stranger—not as a menial should lift his eyes to his divinely appointed superior.

"I wonder why," he said just above the breath that he drew.

We waited on. A light wind from the sea wandered up and down the long lines of the woods, and the wayside grasses, whitened already with summer dust, rose and bowed in sallow waves.

A woman, wiping the suds off her arms, came out of the cottage next the sweetmeat shop.

"I've be'n listenin' in de back-yard," she said cheerily. "He says Arthur's unaccountable bad. Did ye hear him shruck just now? Unaccountable bad. I reckon t'will come Jenny's turn to walk in de wood nex' week along Mr. Madden."

"Excuse me, Sir, but your lap-robe is slipping," said Madden deferentially. The woman started, dropped a curtsey, and hurried away.

"What does she mean by 'walking in the wood'?" I asked.

"It must be some saying they use hereabouts. I'm from Norfolk myself," said Madden. "They're an independent lot in this country. She took you for a chauffeur, Sir."

I saw the Doctor come out of the cottage followed by a draggle-tailed wench who clung to his arm as though he could make treaty for her with Death. "Dat sort," she wailed—"dey're just as much to us dat has 'em as if dey was lawful born. Just as much—just as much! An' God he'd be just as pleased if you saved 'un, Doctor. Don't take it from me. Miss Florence will tell ye de very same. Don't leave 'im, Doctor!"

"I know. I know," said the man, "but he'll be quiet for a while now. We'll get the nurse and the medicine as fast as we can." He signalled me to come forward with the car, and I strove not to be privy to what followed; but I saw the girl's face, blotched and frozen with grief, and I felt the hand without a ring clutching at my knees when we moved away.

The Doctor was a man of some humour, for I remember he claimed my car under the Oath of Æsculapius, and used it and me without mercy. First we convoyed Mrs. Madehurst and the blind woman to wait by the sick bed till the nurse should come. Next we invaded a neat county town for prescriptions (the Doctor said the trouble was cerebro-spinal meningitis), and when the County Institute, banked and flanked with scared market cattle, reported itself out of nurses for the moment we literally flung ourselves loose upon the county. We conferred with the owners of great houses—magnates at the ends of overarching avenues whose big-boned womenfolk strode away from their tea-tables to listen to the imperious Doctor. At last a whitehaired lady sitting under a cedar of Lebanon and surrounded by a court of magnificent Borzois—all hostile to motors—gave the Doctor, who received them as from a princess, written orders which we bore many miles at top speed, through a park, to a French nunnery, where we took over in exchange a pallid-faced and trembling Sister. She knelt at the bottom of the tonneau telling her beads without pause till, by

short cuts of the Doctor's invention, we had her to the sweetmeat shop once more. It was a long afternoon crowded with mad episodes that rose and dissolved like the dust of our wheels; cross-sections of remote and incomprehensible lives through which we raced at right angles; and I went home in the dusk, wearied out, to dream of the clashing horns of cattle; round-eyed nuns walking in a garden of graves; pleasant tea-parties beneath shaded trees; the carbolic-scented, grey-painted corridors of the County Institute; the steps of shy children in the wood, and the hands that clung to my knees as the motor began to move.

I had intended to return in a day or two, but it pleased Fate to hold me from that side of the county, on many pretexts, till the elder and the wild rose had fruited. There came at last a brilliant day, swept clear from the south-west, that brought the hills within hand's reach—a day of unstable airs and high filmy clouds. Through no merit of my own I was free, and set the car for the third time on that known road. As I reached the crest of the Downs I felt the soft air change, saw it glaze under the sun; and, looking down at the sea, in that instant beheld the blue of the Channel turn through polished silver and dulled steel to dingy pewter. A laden collier hugging the coast steered outward for deeper water and, across copper-coloured haze, I saw sails rise one by one on the anchored fishing-fleet. In a deep dene behind me an eddy of sudden wind drummed through sheltered oaks, and spun aloft the first day sample of autumn leaves. When I reached the beach road the sea-fog fumed over the brickfields, and the side was telling all the groins of the gale beyond Ushant. In less than an hour summer England vanished in chill grey. We were again the shut island of the North, all the ships of the world bellowing at our perilous gates; and between their outcries ran the piping of bewildered gulls. My cap dripped moisture, the folds of the rug held it in pools or sluiced it away in runnels, and the salt-rime stuck to my lips.

Inland the smell of autumn loaded the thickened fog among the trees, and the drip became a continuous shower. Yet the late flowers—mallow of the wayside, scabious of the field, and dahlia of the garden—showed gay in the midst, and beyond the sea's breath there was little sign of decay in the leaf. Yet in the villages the house doors were all open, and bare-legged, bare-headed children sat at ease on the damp doorsteps to shout "pip-pip" at the stranger.

I made bold to call at the sweetmeat shop, where Mrs. Madehurst met me with a fat woman's hospitable tears. Jenny's child, she said, had died two days after the nun had come. It was, she felt, best out of the way, even though insurance offices, for reasons which she did not pretend to follow, would not willingly insure such stray lives. "Not but what Jenny didn't tend to Arthur as though he'd come all proper at de end of de first year—like Jenny herself." Thanks to Miss Florence, the child had been buried with a pomp which, in Mrs. Madehurst's opinion, more than covered the small irregularity of its birth. She described the coffin, within and without, the glass hearse, and the evergreen lining of the grave.

"But how's the mother?" I asked.

"Jenny? Oh, she'll get over it. I've felt dat way with one or two o' my own. She'll get over. She's walkin' in de wood now."

"In this weather?"

Mrs. Madehurst looked at me with narrowed eyes across the counter.

"I dunno but it opens de 'eart like. Yes, it opens de 'eart. Dat's where losin' and bearin' comes so alike in de long run, we do say."

Now the wisdom of the old wives is greater than that of all the Fathers, and this last oracle sent me thinking so extendedly as I went up the road, that I nearly ran over a woman and a child at the wooded corner by the lodge gates of the House Beautiful.

"Awful weather!" I cried, as I slowed dead for the turn.

"Not so bad," she answered placidly out of the fog. "Mine's used to 'un. You'll find yours indoors, I reckon."

Indoors, Madden received me with professional courtesy, and kind inquiries for the health of the motor, which he would put under cover.

I waited in a still, nut-brown hall, pleasant with late flowers and warmed with a delicious wood fire—a place of good influence and great peace. (Men and women may sometimes, after great effort, achieve a creditable lie; but the house, which is their temple, cannot say anything save the truth of those who have lived in it.) A child's cart and a doll lay on the black-and-white floor, where a rug had been kicked back. I felt that the children had only just hurried away—to hide themselves, most like—in the many turns of the great adzed staircase that climbed statelily out of the hall, or to crouch at gaze behind the lions and roses of the carven gallery above. Then I heard her voice above me, singing as the blind sing—from the soul:—

In the pleasant orchard-closes.[1]

And all my early summer came back at the call.

> In the pleasant orchard-closes,
>   God bless all our gains say we—
> But may God bless all our losses,
>   Better suits with our degree.

---

[1] "In . . . orchard-closes": the opening line of "The Lost Bower," by Elizabeth Barrett Browning (1806–1861). The missing fifth line reads: "Listen, gentle—ay, and simple! listen, children on the knee!" The poem relates an incident of the author's childhood when, climbing Malvern Hills, she discovered a beautiful, but secret, bower and there experienced "a sense of music which was rather felt than heard," a moment of mystical ecstasy. She never found the bower again, but believed she would see it only after death, with God.

She dropped the marring fifth line, and repeated—

Better suits with our degree!

I saw her lean over the gallery, her linked hands white as pearl against the oak.

"Is that you—from the other side of the county?" she called.

"Yes, me—from the other side of the county," I answered laughing.

"What a long time before you had to come here again." She ran down the stairs, one hand lightly touching the broad rail. "It's two months and four days. Summer's gone!"

"I meant to come before, but Fate prevented."

"I knew it. Please do something to that fire. They don't let me play with it, but I can feel it's behaving badly. Hit it!"

I looked on either side of the deep fireplace, and found but a half-charred hedgestake with which I punched a black log into flame.

"It never goes out, day or night," she said, as though explaining. "In case any one comes in with cold toes, you see."

"It's even lovelier inside than it was out," I murmured. The red light poured itself along the age-polished dusky panels till the Tudor roses and lions of the gallery took colour and motion. An old eagle-topped convex mirror gathered the picture into its mysterious heart, distorting afresh the distorted shadows, and curving the gallery lines into the curves of a ship. The day was shutting down in half a gale as the fog turned to stringy scud. Through the uncurtained mullions of the broad window I could see valiant horsemen of the lawn rear and recover against the wind that taunted them with legions of dead leaves.

"Yes, it must be beautiful," she said. "Would you like to go over it? There's still light enough upstairs."

I followed her up the unflinching, wagon-wide staircase to the gallery whence opened the thin fluted Elizabethan doors.

"Feel how they put the latch low down for the sake of the children." She swung a light door inward.

"By the way, where are they?" I asked. "I haven't even heard them to-day."

She did not answer at once. Then, "I can only hear them," she replied softly. "This is one of their rooms—everything ready, you see."

She pointed into a heavily-timbered room. There were little low gate tables and children's chairs. A doll's house, its hooked front half open, faced a great dappled rocking-horse, from whose padded saddle it was but a child's scramble to the broad window-seat overlooking the lawn. A toy gun lay in a corner beside a gilt wooden cannon.

"Surely they've only just gone," I whispered. In the failing light a door creaked cautiously. I heard the rustle of a frock and the patter of feet—quick feet through a room beyond.

"I heard that," she cried triumphantly. "Did you? Children, O children, where are you?"

The voice filled the walls that held it lovingly to the last perfect note, but there came no answering shout such as I had heard in the garden. We hurried on from room to oak-floored room; up a step here, down three steps there; among a maze of passages; always mocked by our quarry. One might as well have tried to work an unstopped warren with a single ferret. There were bolt-holes innumerable—recesses in walls, embrasures of deep slitten windows now darkened, whence they could start up behind us; and abandoned fireplaces, six feet deep in the masonry, as well as the tangle of communicating doors. Above all, they had the twilight for their helper in our game. I had caught one or two joyous chuckles of evasion, and once or twice had seen the silhouette of a child's frock against some darkening window at the end of a passage; but we returned empty-handed to the gallery, just as a middle-aged woman was setting a lamp in its niche.

"No, I haven't seen her either this evening, Miss Florence," I heard her say, "but that Turpin he says he wants to see you about his shed."

"Oh, Mr. Turpin must want to see me very badly. Tell him to come to the hall, Mrs. Madden."

I looked down into the hall whose only light was the dulled fire, and deep in the shadow I saw them at last. They must have slipped down while we were in the passages, and now thought themselves perfectly hidden behind an old gilt leather screen. By child's law, my fruitless chase was as good as an introduction, but since I had taken so much trouble I resolved to force them to come forward later by the simple trick, which children detest, of pretending not to notice them. They lay close, in a little huddle, no more than shadows except when a quick flame betrayed an outline.

"And now we'll have some tea," she said. "I believe I ought to have offered it you at first, but one doesn't arrive at manners somehow when one lives alone and is considered —h'm—peculiar." Then with very pretty scorn, "would you like a lamp to see to eat by?"

"The firelight's much pleasanter, I think." We descended into that delicious gloom and Madden brought tea.

I took my chair in the direction of the screen ready to surprise or be surprised as the game should go, and at her permission, since a hearth is always sacred, bent forward to play with the fire.

"Where do you get these beautiful short faggots from?" I asked idly. "Why, they are tallies!"

"Of course," she said. "As I can't read or write I'm driven back on the early English tally for my accounts. Give me one and I'll tell you what it meant."

I passed her an unburned hazel-tally, about a foot long, and she ran her thumb down the nicks.

"This is the milk-record for the home farm for the month of April last year, in gallons," said she. "I don't know what I should have done without tallies. An old forester of mine taught me the system. It's out of date now for every one else; but my tenants respect it. One of them's coming now to see me. Oh, it doesn't matter. He has no business here out of office hours. He's a greedy, ignorant man —very greedy or—he wouldn't come here after dark."

"Have you much land then?"

"Only a couple of hundred acres in hand, thank goodness. The other six hundred are nearly all let to folk who knew my folk before me, but this Turpin is quite a new man—and a highway robber."

"But are you sure I sha'n't be——?"

"Certainly not. You have the right. He hasn't any children."

"Ah, the children!" I said, and slid my low chair back till it nearly touched the screen that hid them. "I wonder whether they'll come out for me."

There was a murmur of voices—Madden's and a deeper note—at the low, dark side door, and a ginger-headed, canvas-gaitered giant of the unmistakable tenant farmer type stumbled or was pushed in.

"Come to the fire, Mr. Turpin," she said.

"If—if you please, Miss, I'll—I'll be quite as well by the door." He clung to the latch as he spoke like a frightened child. Of a sudden I realised that he was in the grip of some almost overpowering fear.

"Well?"

"About that new shed for the young stock —that was all. These first autumn storms settin' in ... but I'll come again, Miss." His teeth did not chatter much more than the door latch.

"I think not," she answered levelly. "The new shed—m'm. What did my agent write you on the 15th?"

"I—fancied p'raps that if I came to see you —ma—man to man like, Miss. But——"

His eyes rolled into every corner of the room wide with horror. He half opened the door through which he had entered, but I noticed it shut again—from without and firmly.

"He wrote what I told him," she went on. "You are overstocked already. Dunnett's Farm never carried more than fifty bullocks —even in Mr. Wright's time. And *he* used cake. You've sixty-seven and you don't cake. You've broken the lease in that respect. You're dragging the heart out of the farm."

"I'm—I'm getting some minerals—super-phosphates—next week. I've as good as ordered a truck-load already. I'll go down to the station to-morrow about 'em. Then I can come and see you man to man like, Miss, in the daylight. . . . That gentleman's not going away, is he?" He almost shrieked.

I had only slid the chair a little further back, reaching behind me to tap on the leather of the screen, but he jumped like a rat.

"No. Please attend to me, Mr. Turpin." She turned in her chair and faced him with his back to the door. It was an old and sordid little piece of scheming that she forced from him—his plea for the new cowshed at his landlady's expense, that he might with the covered manure pay his next year's rent out of the valuation after, as she made clear, he had bled the enriched pastures to the bone. I could not but admire the intensity of his greed, when I saw him out-facing for its sake whatever terror it was that ran wet on his forehead.

I ceased to tap the leather—was, indeed, calculating the cost of the shed—when I felt my relaxed hand taken and turned softly between the soft hands of a child. So at last I had triumphed. In a moment I would turn and acquaint myself with those quick-footed wanderers. . . .

The little brushing kiss fell in the centre of my palm—as a gift on which the fingers were, once, expected to close: as the all faith-ful half-reproachful signal of a waiting child not used to neglect even when grown-ups were busiest—a fragment of the mute code devised very long ago.

Then I knew. And it was as though I had known from the first day when I looked across the lawn at the high window.

I heard the door shut. The woman turned to me in silence, and I felt that she knew.

What time passed after this I cannot say. I was roused by the fall of a log, and mechanically rose to put it back. Then I returned to my place in the chair very close to the screen.

"Now you understand," she whispered, across the packed shadows.

"Yes, I understand—now. Thank you."

"I—I only hear them." She bowed her head in her hands. "I have no right, you know—no other right. I have neither borne nor lost— neither borne nor lost!"

"Be very glad then," said I, for my soul was torn open within me.

"Forgive me!"

She was still, and I went back to my sorrow and my joy.

"It was because I loved them so," she said at last, brokenly. "*That* was why it was, even from the first—even before I knew that they —they were all I should ever have. And I loved them so!"

She stretched out her arms to the shadows and the shadows within the shadow.

"They came because I loved them—because I needed them. I—I must have made them come. Was that wrong, think you?"

"No—no."

"I—I grant you that the toys and—and all that sort of thing were nonsense, but—but I used to so hate empty rooms myself when I was little." She pointed to the gallery. "And the passages all empty. . . . And how could I ever bear the garden door shut? Suppose——"

"Don't! For pity's sake, don't!" I cried. The twilight had brought a cold rain with gusty squalls that plucked at the leaded windows.

"And the same thing with keeping the fire

in all night. *I* don't think it so foolish—do you?"

I looked at the broad brick hearth, saw, through tears I believe, that there was no unpassable iron on or near it, and bowed my head.

"I did all that and lots of other things— just to make believe. Then they came. I heard them, but I didn't know that they were not mine by right till Mrs. Madden told me——"

"The butler's wife? What?"

"One of them—I heard—she saw. And knew. Hers! *Not* for me. I didn't know at first. Perhaps I was jealous. Afterwards, I began to understand that it was only because I loved them, not because—— . . . Oh, you *must* bear or lose," she said piteously. "There is no other way—and yet they love me. They must! Don't they?"

There was no sound in the room except the lapping voices of the fire, but we two listened intently, and she at least took comfort from what she heard. She recovered herself and half rose. I sat still in my chair by the screen.

"Don't think me a wretch to whine about myself like this, but—but I'm all in the dark, you know, and *you* can see."

In truth I could see, and my vision confirmed me in my resolve, though that was like the very parting of spirit and flesh. Yet a little longer I would stay since it was the last time.

"You think it is wrong, then?" she cried sharply, though I had said nothing.

"Not for you. A thousand times no. For you it is right. . . . I am grateful to you beyond words. For me it would be wrong. For me only. . . ."

"Why?" she said, but passed her hand before her face as she had done at our second meeting in the wood. "Oh, I see," she went on simply as a child. "For you it would be wrong." Then with a little indrawn laugh, "and, d'you remember, I called you lucky— once—at first. You who must never come here again!"

She left me to sit a little longer by the screen, and I heard the sound of her feet die out along the gallery above.

SHERWOOD ANDERSON

Loneliness

He was the son of Mrs. Al Robinson who once owned a farm on a side road leading off Trunion Pike, east of Winesburg and two miles beyond the town limits. The farmhouse was painted brown and the blinds to all of the windows facing the road were kept closed. In the road before the house a flock of chickens, accompanied by two guinea hens, lay in the deep dust. Enoch lived in the house with his mother in those days and when he was a young boy went to school at the Winesburg High School. Old citizens remembered him as a quiet, smiling youth inclined to silence. He walked in the middle of the road when he came into town and sometimes read a book. Drivers of teams had to shout and swear to make him realize where he was so that he would turn out of the beaten track and let them pass.

When he was twenty-one years old Enoch went to New York City and was a city man for fifteen years. He studied French and went to an art school, hoping to develop a faculty he had for drawing. In his own mind he planned to go to Paris and to finish his art education among the masters there, but that never turned out.

Nothing ever turned out for Enoch Robinson. He could draw well enough and he had many odd delicate thoughts hidden away in his brain that might have expressed themselves through the brush of a painter, but he was always a child and that was a handicap to his worldly development. He never grew up and of course he couldn't understand people and he couldn't make people understand

him. The child in him kept bumping against things, against actualities like money and sex and opinions. Once he was hit by a street car and thrown against an iron post. That made him lame. It was one of the many things that kept things from turning out for Enoch Robinson.

In New York City, when he first went there to live and before he became confused and disconcerted by the facts of life, Enoch went about a good deal with young men. He got into a group of other young artists, both men and women, and in the evenings they sometimes came to visit him in his room. Once he got drunk and was taken to a police station where a police magistrate frightened him horribly, and once he tried to have an affair with a woman of the town met on the sidewalk before his lodging house. The woman and Enoch walked together three blocks and then the young man grew afraid and ran away. The woman had been drinking and the incident amused her. She leaned against the wall of a building and laughed so heartily that another man stopped and laughed with her. The two went away together, still laughing, and Enoch crept off to his room trembling and vexed.

The room in which young Robinson lived in New York faced Washington Square and was long and narrow like a hallway. It is important to get that fixed in your mind. The story of Enoch is in fact the story of a room almost more than it is the story of a man.

And so into the room in the evening came young Enoch's friends. There was nothing particularly striking about them except that they were artists of the kind that talk. Everyone knows of the talking artists. Throughout all of the known history of the world they have gathered in rooms and talked. They talk of art and are passionately, almost feverishly, in earnest about it. They think it matters much more than it does.

And so these people gathered and smoked cigarettes and talked and Enoch Robinson, the boy from the farm near Winesburg, was there. He stayed in a corner and for the most part said nothing. How his big blue childlike eyes stared about! On the walls were pictures he had made, crude things, half finished. His friends talked of these. Leaning back in their chairs, they talked and talked with their heads rocking from side to side. Words were said about line and values and composition, lots of words, such as are always being said.

Enoch wanted to talk too but he didn't know how. He was too excited to talk coherently. When he tried he sputtered and stammered and his voice sounded strange and squeaky to him. That made him stop talking. He knew what he wanted to say, but he knew also that he could never by any possibility say it. When a picture he had painted was under discussion, he wanted to burst out with something like this: "You don't get the point," he wanted to explain; "the picture you see doesn't consist of the things you see and say words about. There is something else, something you don't see at all, something you aren't intended to see. Look at this one over here, by the door here, where the light from the window falls on it. The dark spot by the road that you might not notice at all is, you see, the beginning of everything. There is a clump of elders there such as used to grow beside the road before our house back in Winesburg, Ohio, and in among the elders there is something hidden. It is a woman, that's what it is. She has been thrown from a horse and the horse has run away out of sight. Do you not see how the old man who drives a cart looks anxiously about? That is

Thad Grayback who has a farm up the road. He is taking corn to Winesburg to be ground into meal at Comstock's mill. He knows there is something in the elders, something hidden away, and yet he doesn't quite know.

"It's a woman you see, that's what it is! It's a woman and, oh, she is lovely! She is hurt and is suffering but she makes no sound. Don't you see how it is? She lies quite still, white and still, and the beauty comes out from her and spreads over everything. It is in the sky back there and all around everywhere. I didn't try to paint the woman, of course. She is too beautiful to be painted. How dull to talk of composition and such things! Why do you not look at the sky and then run away as I used to do when I was a boy back there in Winesburg, Ohio?"

That is the kind of thing young Enoch Robinson trembled to say to the guests who came into his room when he was a young fellow in New York City, but he always ended by saying nothing. Then he began to doubt his own mind. He was afraid the things he felt were not getting expressed in the pictures he painted. In a half indignant mood he stopped inviting people into his room and presently got into the habit of locking the door. He began to think that enough people had visited him, that he did not need people any more. With quick imagination he began to invent his own people to whom he could really talk and to whom he explained the things he had been unable to explain to living people. His room began to be inhabited by the spirits of men and women among whom he went, in his turn saying words. It was as though everyone Enoch Robinson had ever seen had left with him some essence of himself, something he could mould and change to suit his own fancy, something that understood all about such things as the wounded woman behind the elders in the pictures.

The mild, blue-eyed young Ohio boy was a complete egotist, as all children are egotists. He did not want friends for the quite simple reason that no child wants friends. He wanted most of all people of his own mind, people with whom he could really talk, people he could harangue and scold by the hour, servants, you see, to his fancy. Among these people he was always self-confident and bold. They might talk, to be sure, and even have opinions of their own, but always he talked last and best. He was like a writer busy among the figures of his brain, a kind of tiny blue-eyed king he was, in a six-dollar room facing Washington Square in the city of New York.

Then Enoch Robinson got married. He began to get lonely and to want to touch actual flesh-and-bone people with his hands. Days passed when his room seemed empty. Lust visited his body and desire grew in his mind. At night strange fevers, burning within, kept him awake. He married a girl who sat in a chair next to his own in the art school and went to live in an apartment house in Brooklyn. Two children were born to the woman he married, and Enoch got a job in a place where illustrations are made for advertisements.

That began another phase of Enoch's life. He began to play at a new game. For a while he was very proud of himself in the role of producing citizen of the world. He dismissed the essence of things and played with realities. In the fall he voted at an election and he had a newspaper thrown on his porch each morning. When in the evening he came home from work he got off a streetcar and walked sedately along behind some business man, striving to look very substantial and important. As a payer of taxes he thought he should post himself on how things are run. "I'm getting to be of some moment, a real part of things, of the state and the city and all that," he told himself with an amusing miniature air of dignity. Once, coming home from Philadelphia, he had a discussion with a man met on a train. Enoch talked about the advisability of the government's owning and operating the railroads and the man gave him a cigar. It was Enoch's notion that such a move

on the part of the government would be a good thing, and he grew quite excited as he talked. Later he remembered his own words with pleasure. "I gave him something to think about, that fellow," he muttered to himself as he climbed the stairs to his Brooklyn apartment.

To be sure, Enoch's marriage did not turn out. He himself brought it to an end. He began to feel choked and walled in by the life in the apartment, and to feel toward his wife and even toward his children as he had felt concerning the friends who once came to visit him. He began to tell little lies about business engagements that would give him freedom to walk alone in the street at night and, the chance offering, he secretly re-rented the room facing Washington Square. Then Mrs. Al Robinson died on the farm near Winesburg, and he got eight thousand dollars from the bank that acted as trustee of her estate. That took Enoch out of the world of men altogether. He gave the money to his wife and told her he could not live in the apartment any more. She cried and was angry and threatened, but he only stared at her and went his own way. In reality the wife did not care much. She thought Enoch slightly insane and was a little afraid of him. When it was quite sure that he would never come back, she took the two children and went to a village in Connecticut where she had lived as a girl. In the end she married a man who bought and sold real estate and was contented enough.

And so Enoch Robinson stayed in the New York room among the people of his fancy, playing with them, talking to them, happy as a child is happy. They were an odd lot, Enoch's people. They were made, I suppose, out of real people he had seen and who had for some obscure reason made an appeal to him. There was a woman with a sword in her hand, an old man with a long white beard who went about followed by a dog, a young girl whose stockings were always coming down and hanging over her shoe tops.

There must have been two dozen of the shadow people, invented by the child-mind of Enoch Robinson, who lived in the room with him.

And Enoch was happy. Into the room he went and locked the door. With an absurd air of importance he talked aloud, giving instructions, making comments on life. He was happy and satisfied to go on making his living in the advertising place until something happened. Of course something did happen. That is why he went back to live in Winesburg and why we know about him. The thing that happened was a woman. It would be that way. He was too happy. Something had to come into his world. Something had to drive him out of the New York room to live out his life an obscure, jerky little figure, bobbing up and down on the streets of an Ohio town at evening when the sun was going down behind the roof of Wesley Moyer's livery barn.

About the thing that happened. Enoch told George Willard about it one night. He wanted to talk to someone, and he chose the young newspaper reporter because the two happened to be thrown together at a time when the younger man was in a mood to understand.

Youthful sadness, young man's sadness, the sadness of a growing boy in a village at the year's end, opened the lips of the old man. The sadness was in the heart of George Willard and was without meaning, but it appealed to Enoch Robinson.

It rained on the evening when the two met and talked, a drizzly wet October rain. The fruition of the year had come and the night should have been fine with a moon in the sky and the crisp sharp promise of frost in the air, but it wasn't that way. It rained and little puddles of water shone under the street lamps on Main Street. In the woods in the darkness beyond the Fair Ground water dripped from the black trees. Beneath the trees wet leaves were pasted against tree roots that protruded from the ground. In gardens back of houses in Winesburg dry shriveled potato vines lay sprawling on the ground. Men who finished the evening meal and who had planned to go uptown to talk the evening away with other men at the back of some store changed their minds. George Willard tramped about in the rain and was glad that it rained. He felt that way. He was like Enoch Robinson on the evenings when the old man came down out of his room and wandered alone in the streets. He was like that only that George Willard had become a tall young man and did not think it manly to weep and carry on. For a month his mother had been very ill and that had something to do with his sadness, but not much. He thought about himself and to the young that always brings sadness.

Enoch Robinson and George Willard met beneath a wooden awning that extended out over the sidewalk before Voight's wagon shop on Maumee Street just off the main street of Winesburg. They went together from there through the rain-washed streets to the older man's room on the third floor of the Heffner Block. The young reporter went willingly enough. Enoch Robinson asked him to go after the two had talked for ten minutes. The boy was a little afraid but had never been more curious in his life. A hundred times he had heard the old man spoken of as a little off his head and he thought himself rather brave and manly to go at all. From the very beginning, in the street in the rain, the old man talked in a queer way, trying to tell the story of the room in Washington Square and of his life in the room. "You'll understand if you try hard enough," he said conclusively. "I have looked at you when you went past me on the street and I think you can understand. It isn't hard. All you have to do is to believe what I say, just listen and believe, that's all there is to it."

It was past eleven o'clock that evening when old Enoch, talking to George Willard in the room in the Heffner Block, came to the vital thing, the story of the woman and of what drove him out of the city to live out his life alone and defeated in Winesburg. He sat on a cot by the window with his head in his hand and George Willard was in a chair by a table. A kerosene lamp sat on the table and the room, although almost bare of furniture, was scrupulously clean. As the man talked George Willard began to feel that he would like to get out of the chair and sit on the cot also. He wanted to put his arms about the little old man. In the half darkness the man talked and the boy listened, filled with sadness.

"She got to coming in there after there hadn't been anyone in the room for years," said Enoch Robinson. "She saw me in the hallway of the house and we got acquainted. I don't know just what she did in her own room. I never went there. I think she was a musician and played a violin. Every now and then she came and knocked at the door and I opened it. In she came and sat down beside me, just sat and looked about and said nothing. Anyway, she said nothing that mattered."

The old man arose from the cot and moved about the room. The overcoat he wore was wet from the rain and drops of water kept falling with a soft thump on the floor. When he again sat upon the cot George Willard got out of the chair and sat beside him.

"I had a feeling about her. She sat there in the room with me and she was too big for the room. I felt that she was driving everything else away. We just talked of little things, but I couldn't sit still. I wanted to touch her with my fingers and to kiss her. Her hands were so strong and her face was so good and she looked at me all the time."

The trembling voice of the old man became silent and his body shook as from a chill. "I was afraid," he whispered. "I was terribly afraid. I didn't want to let her come in when she knocked at the door but I couldn't sit still. 'No, no,' I said to myself, but I got up and opened the door just the same. She was so grown up, you see. She was a woman. I

thought she would be bigger than I was there in that room."

Enoch Robinson stared at George Willard, his childlike blue eyes shining in the lamplight. Again he shivered. "I wanted her and all the time I didn't want her," he explained. "Then I began to tell her about my people, about everything that meant anything to me. I tried to keep quiet, to keep myself to myself, but I couldn't. I felt just as I did about opening the door. Sometimes I ached to have her go away and never come back any more."

The old man sprang to his feet and his voice shook with excitement. "One night something happened. I became mad to make her understand me and to know what a big thing I was in that room. I wanted her to see how important I was. I told her over and over. When she tried to go away, I ran and locked the door. I followed her about. I talked and talked and then all of a sudden things went to smash. A look came into her eyes and I knew she did understand. Maybe she had understood all the time. I was furious. I couldn't stand it. I wanted her to understand but, don't you see, I couldn't let her understand. I felt that then she would know everything, that I would be submerged, drowned out, you see. That's how it is. I don't know why."

The old man dropped into a chair by the lamp and the boy listened, filled with awe. "Go away, boy," said the man. "Don't stay here with me any more. I thought it might be a good thing to tell you but it isn't. I don't want to talk any more. Go away."

George Willard shook his head and a note of command came into his voice, "Don't stop now. Tell me the rest of it," he commanded sharply. "What happened? Tell me the rest of the story."

Enoch Robinson sprang to his feet and ran to the window that looked down into the deserted main street of Winesburg. George Willard followed. By the window the two stood, the tall awkward boy-man and the little wrinkled man-boy. The childish, eager voice carried forward the tale. "I swore at her," he explained. "I said vile words. I ordered her to go away and not to come back. Oh, I said terrible things. At first she pretended not to understand but I kept at it. I screamed and stamped on the floor. I made the house ring with my curses. I didn't want ever to see her again and I knew, after some of the things I said, that I never would see her again."

The old man's voice broke and he shook his head. "Things went to smash," he said quietly and sadly. "Out she went through the door and all the life there had been in the room followed her out. She took all of my people away. They all went out through the door after her. That's the way it was."

George Willard turned and went out of Enoch Robinson's room. In the darkness by the window, as he went through the door, he could hear the thin old voice whimpering and complaining. "I'm alone, all alone here," said the voice. "It was warm and friendly in my room but now I'm all alone."

JAMES JOYCE

Two Gallants

The grey warm evening of August had descended upon the city and a mild warm air, a memory of summer, circulated in the streets. The streets, shuttered for the repose of Sunday, swarmed with a gaily coloured crowd. Like illumined pearls the lamps shone from the summits of their tall poles upon the living texture below which, changing shape and hue unceasingly, sent up into the warm grey evening air an unchanging, unceasing murmur.

Two young men came down the hill of Rutland Square. One of them was just bringing a long monologue to a close. The other, who walked on the verge of the path and was at times obliged to step on to the road, owing to his companion's rudeness, wore an amused listening face. He was squat and ruddy. A yachting cap was shoved far back from his forehead and the narrative to which he listened made constant waves of expression break forth over his face from the corners of his nose and eyes and mouth. Little jets of wheezing laughter followed one another out of his convulsed body. His eyes, twinkling with cunning enjoyment, glanced at every moment towards his companion's face. Once or twice he rearranged the light waterproof which he had slung over one shoulder in toreador fashion. His breeches, his white rubber shoes and his jauntily slung waterproof expressed youth. But his figure fell into rotundity at the waist, his hair was scant and grey and his face, when the waves of expression had passed over it, had a ravaged look.

When he was quite sure that the narrative had ended he laughed noiselessly for fully half a minute. Then he said:

"Well! . . . That takes the biscuit!"

His voice seemed winnowed of vigour; and to enforce his words he added with humour:

"That takes the solitary, unique, and, if I may so call it, *recherché* biscuit!"

He became serious and silent when he had said this. His tongue was tired for he had been talking all the afternoon in a public-house in Dorset Street. Most people considered Lenehan a leech but, in spite of this reputation, his adroitness and eloquence had always prevented his friends from forming any general policy against him. He had a brave manner of coming up to a party of them in a bar and of holding himself nimbly at the borders of the company until he was included in a round. He was a sporting vagrant armed with a vast stock of stories, limericks and riddles. He was insensitive to all kinds of discourtesy. No one knew how he achieved the stern task of living, but his name was vaguely associated with racing tissues.

"And where did you pick her up, Corley?" he asked.

Corley ran his tongue swiftly along his upper lip.

"One night, man," he said, "I was going along Dame Street and I spotted a fine tart under Waterhouse's clock and said goodnight, you know. So we went for a walk round by the canal and she told me she was a slavey in a house in Baggot Street. I put my arm round her and squeezed her a bit that night. Then next Sunday, man, I met her by appointment. We went out to Donnybrook and I brought her into a field there. She told me she used to go with a dairyman. . . . It was fine, man. Cigarettes every night she'd bring me and paying the tram out and back. And one night she brought me two bloody fine cigars—O, the real cheese, you know, that the old fellow used to smoke. . . . I was afraid, man, she'd get in the family way. But she's up to the dodge."

"Maybe she thinks you'll marry her," said Lenehan.

"I told her I was out of a job," said Corley. "I told her I was in Pim's. She doesn't know my name. I was too hairy to tell her that. But she thinks I'm a bit of class, you know."

Lenehan laughed again, noiselessly.

"Of all the good ones ever I heard," he said, "that emphatically takes the biscuit."

Corley's stride acknowledged the compliment. The swing of his burly body made his friend execute a few light skips from the path to the roadway and back again. Corley was the son of an inspector of police and he had inherited his father's frame and gait. He walked with his hands by his sides, holding himself erect and swaying his head from side to side. His head was large, globular and oily; it sweated in all weathers; and his large round hat, set upon it sideways, looked like a bulb which had grown out of another. He always stared straight before him as if he were on parade and, when he wished to gaze after someone in the street, it was necessary for him to move his body from the hips. At present he was about town. Whenever any job was vacant a friend was always ready to give him the hard word. He was often to be seen walking with policemen in plain clothes, talking earnestly. He knew the inner side of all affairs and was fond of delivering final judgments. He spoke without listening to the speech of his companions. His conversation was mainly about himself: what he had said to such a person and what such a person had

said to him and what he had said to settle the matter. When he reported these dialogues he aspirated the first letter of his name after the manner of Florentines.

Lenehan offered his friend a cigarette. As the two young men walked through the crowd Corley occasionally turned to smile at some of the passing girls but Lenehan's gaze was fixed on the large faint moon circled with a double halo. He watched earnestly the passing of the grey web of twilight across its face. At length he said:

"Well . . . tell me, Corley, I suppose you'll be able to pull it off all right, eh?"

Corley closed one eye expressively as an answer.

"Is she game for that?" asked Lenehan dubiously. "You can never know women."

"She's all right," said Corley. "I know the way to get around her, man. She's a bit gone on me."

"You're what I call a gay Lothario," said Lenehan. "And the proper kind of a Lothario, too!"

A shade of mockery relieved the servility of his manner. To save himself he had the habit of leaving his flattery open to the interpretation of raillery. But Corley had not a subtle mind.

"There's nothing to touch a good slavey," he affirmed. "Take my tip for it."

"By one who has tried them all," said Lenehan.

"First I used to go with girls, you know," said Corley, unbosoming; "girls off the South Circular. I used to take them out, man, on the tram somewhere and pay the tram or take them to a band or a play at the theatre or buy them chocolate and sweets or something that way. I used to spend money on them right enough," he added, in a convincing tone, as if he was conscious of being disbelieved.

But Lenehan could well believe it; he nodded gravely.

"I know that game," he said, "and it's a mug's game."

"And damn the thing I ever got out of it," said Corley.

"Ditto here," said Lenehan.

"Only off of one of them," said Corley.

He moistened his upper lip by running his tongue along it. The recollection brightened his eyes. He too gazed at the pale disc of the moon, now nearly veiled, and seemed to meditate.

"She was . . . a bit of all right," he said regretfully.

He was silent again. Then he added:

"She's on the turf now. I saw her driving down Earl Street one night with two fellows with her on a car."

"I suppose that's your doing," said Lenehan.

"There was others at her before me," said Corley philosophically.

This time Lenehan was inclined to disbelieve. He shook his head to and fro and smiled.

"You know you can't kid me, Corley," he said.

"Honest to God!" said Corley. "Didn't she tell me herself?"

Lenehan made a tragic gesture.

"Base betrayer!" he said.

As they passed along the railings of Trinity College, Lenehan skipped out into the road and peered up at the clock.

"Twenty after," he said.

"Time enough," said Corley. "She'll be there all right. I always let her wait a bit."

Lenehan laughed quietly.

"Ecod! Corley, you know how to take them," he said.

"I'm up to all their little tricks," Corley confessed.

"But tell me," said Lenehan again, "are you sure you can bring it off all right? You know it's a ticklish job. They're damn close on that point. Eh? . . . What?"

His bright, small eyes searched his companion's face for reassurance. Corley swung his head to and fro as if to toss aside an insistent insect, and his brows gathered.

"I'll pull it off," he said. "Leave it to me, can't you?"

Lenehan said no more. He did not wish to ruffle his friend's temper, to be sent to the devil and told that his advice was not wanted. A little tact was necessary. But Corley's brow was soon smooth again. His thoughts were running another way.

"She's a fine decent tart," he said, with appreciation; "that's what she is."

They walked along Nassau Street and then turned into Kildare Street. Not far from the porch of the club a harpist stood in the roadway, playing to a little ring of listeners. He plucked at the wires heedlessly, glancing quickly from time to time at the face of each new-comer and from time to time, wearily also, at the sky. His harp, too, heedless that her coverings had fallen about her knees, seemed weary alike of the eyes of strangers and of her master's hands. One hand played in the bass melody of *Silent, O Moyle*, while the other hand careered in the treble after each group of notes. The notes of the air sounded deep and full.

The two young men walked up the street without speaking, the mournful music following them. When they reached Stephen's Green they crossed the road. Here the noise of trams, the lights and the crowd released them from their silence.

"There she is!" said Corley.

At the corner of Hume Street a young woman was standing. She wore a blue dress and a white sailor hat. She stood on the curbstone, swinging a sunshade in one hand. Lenehan grew lively.

"Let's have a look at her, Corley," he said.

Corley glanced sideways at his friend and an unpleasant grin appeared on his face.

"Are you trying to get inside me?" he asked.

"Damn it!" said Lenehan boldly, "I don't want an introduction. All I want is to have a look at her. I'm not going to eat her."

"O . . . A look at her?" said Corley, more amiably. "Well . . . I'll tell you what. I'll go over and talk to her and you can pass by."

"Right!" said Lenehan.

Corley had already thrown one leg over the chains when Lenehan called out:

"And after? Where will we meet?"

"Half ten," answered Corley, bringing over his other leg.

"Where?"

"Corner of Merrion Street. We'll be coming back."

"Work it all right now," said Lenehan in farewell.

Corley did not answer. He sauntered across the road swaying his head from side to side. His bulk, his easy pace, and the solid sound of his boots had something of the conqueror in them. He approached the young woman and, without saluting, began at once to converse with her. She swung her umbrella more quickly and executed half turns on her heels. Once or twice when he spoke to her at close quarters she laughed and bent her head.

Lenehan observed them for a few minutes. Then he walked rapidly along beside the chains at some distance and crossed the road obliquely. As he approached Hume Street corner he found the air heavily scented and his eyes made a swift anxious scrutiny of the young woman's appearance. She had her Sunday finery on. Her blue serge skirt was held at the waist by a belt of black leather. The great silver buckle of her belt seemed to depress the centre of her body, catching the light stuff of her white blouse like a clip. She wore a short black jacket with mother-of-pearl buttons and a ragged black boa. The ends of her tulle collarette had been carefully disordered and a big bunch of red flowers was pinned in her bosom stems upwards. Lenehan's eyes noted approvingly her stout short muscular body. Frank rude health glowed in her face, on her fat red cheeks and in her unabashed blue eyes. Her features were blunt. She had broad nostrils, a straggling mouth which lay open in a contented leer, and two projecting front teeth. As he passed Lenehan took off his cap and, after about ten seconds, Corley returned a salute to the air. This he did by raising his hand vaguely and pensively changing the angle of position of his hat.

Lenehan walked as far as the Shelbourne Hotel where he halted and waited. After waiting for a little time he saw them coming towards him and, when they turned to the right, he followed them, stepping lightly in his white shoes, down one side of Merrion Square. As he walked on slowly, timing his pace to theirs, he watched Corley's head which turned at every moment towards the young woman's face like a big ball revolving on a pivot. He kept the pair in view until he had seen them climbing the stairs of the Donnybrook tram; then turned about and went back the way he had come.

Now that he was alone his face looked older. His gaiety seemed to forsake him and, as he came by the railings of the Duke's Lawn, he allowed his hand to run along them. The air which the harpist had played began to control his movements. His softly padded feet played the melody while his fingers swept a scale of variations idly along the railings after each group of notes.

He walked listlessly round Stephen's Green and then down Grafton Street. Though his eyes took note of many elements of the crowd through which he passed they did so morosely. He found trivial all that was meant to charm him and did not answer the glances which invited him to be bold. He knew that he would have to speak a great deal, to invent and to amuse, and his brain and throat were too dry for such a task. The problem of how he could pass the hours till he met Corley again troubled him a little. He could think of no way of passing them but to keep on walking. He turned to the left when he came to the corner of Rutland Square and felt more at ease in the dark quiet street, the sombre look of which suited his mood. He paused at last before the window of a poor-looking shop over which the words *Refreshment Bar* were printed in white letters. On the glass of the window were two flying inscriptions: *Ginger Beer* and *Ginger Ale*. A cut ham was exposed on a great blue dish while near it on a plate lay a segment of very light plum-pudding. He eyed this food earnestly for some time and then, after glancing warily up and down the street, went into the shop quickly.

He was hungry for, except some biscuits which he had asked two grudging curates to bring him, he had eaten nothing since breakfast-time. He sat down at an uncovered wooden table opposite two work-girls and a mechanic. A slatternly girl waited on him.

"How much is a plate of peas?" he asked.

"Three halfpence, sir," said the girl.

"Bring me a plate of peas," he said, "and a bottle of ginger beer."

He spoke roughly in order to belie his air of gentility for his entry had been followed by a pause of talk. His face was heated. To appear natural he pushed his cap back on his head and planted his elbows on the table. The mechanic and the two work-girls examined him point by point before resuming their conversation in a subdued voice. The girl brought him a plate of grocer's hot peas, seasoned with pepper and vinegar, a fork and his ginger beer. He ate his food greedily and found it so good that he made a note of the shop mentally. When he had eaten all the peas he sipped his ginger beer and sat for some time thinking of Corley's adventure. In his imagination he beheld the pair of lovers walking along some dark road; he heard Corley's voice in deep energetic gallantries and saw again the leer of the young woman's mouth. This vision made him feel keenly his own poverty of purse and spirit. He was tired of knocking about, of pulling the devil by the tail, of shifts and intrigues. He would be thirty-one in November. Would he never get a good job? Would he never have a home of his own? He thought how pleasant it would be to have a warm fire to sit by and a good dinner to sit down to. He had walked the streets long enough with friends and with girls. He knew what those friends were

worth: he knew the girls too. Experience had embittered his heart against the world. But all hope had not left him. He felt better after having eaten than he had felt before, less weary of his life, less vanquished in spirit. He might yet be able to settle down in some snug corner and live happily if he could only come across some good simple-minded girl with a little of the ready.

He paid twopence halfpenny to the slatternly girl and went out of the shop to begin his wandering again. He went into Capel Street and walked along towards the City Hall. Then he turned into Dame Street. At the corner of George's Street he met two friends of his and stopped to converse with them. He was glad that he could rest from all his walking. His friends asked him had he seen Corley and what was the latest. He replied that he had spent the day with Corley. His friends talked very little. They looked vacantly after some figures in the crowd and sometimes made a critical remark. One said that he had seen Mac an hour before in Westmoreland Street. At this Lenehan said that he had been with Mac the night before in Egan's. The young man who had seen Mac in Westmoreland Street asked was it true that Mac had won a bit over a billiard match. Lenehan did not know: he said that Holohan had stood them drinks in Egan's.

He left his friends at a quarter to ten and went up George's Street. He turned to the left at the City Markets and walked on into Grafton Street. The crowd of girls and young men had thinned and on his way up the street he heard many groups and couples bidding one another good-night. He went as far as the clock of the College of Surgeons: it was on the stroke of ten. He set off briskly along the northern side of the Green hurrying for fear Corley should return too soon. When he reached the corner of Merrion Street he took his stand in the shadow of a lamp and brought out one of the cigarettes which he had reserved and lit it. He leaned against the lamp-post and kept his gaze fixed on the part from which he expected to see Corley and the young woman return.

His mind became active again. He wondered had Corley managed it successfully. He wondered if he had asked her yet or if he would leave it to the last. He suffered all the pangs and thrills of his friend's situation as well as those of his own. But the memory of Corley's slowly revolving head calmed him somewhat: he was sure Corley would pull it off all right. All at once the idea struck him that perhaps Corley had seen her home by another way and given him the slip. His eyes searched the street: there was no sign of them. Yet it was surely half-an-hour since he had seen the clock of the College of Surgeons. Would Corley do a thing like that? He lit his last cigarette and began to smoke it nervously. He strained his eyes as each tram stopped at the far corner of the square. They must have gone home by another way. The paper of his cigarette broke and he flung it into the road with a curse.

Suddenly he saw them coming towards him. He started with delight and keeping close to his lamp-post tried to read the result in their walk. They were walking quickly, the young woman taking quick short steps, while Corley kept beside her with his long stride. They did not seem to be speaking. An intimation of the result pricked him like the point of a sharp instrument. He knew Corley would fail; he knew it was no go.

They turned down Baggot Street and he followed them at once, taking the other footpath. When they stopped he stopped too. They talked for a few moments and then the young woman went down the steps into the area of a house. Corley remained standing at the edge of the path, a little distance from the front steps. Some minutes passed. Then the hall-door was opened slowly and cautiously. A woman came running down the front steps and coughed. Corley turned and went towards her. His broad figure hid hers from view for a few seconds and then she reappeared running up the steps. The door closed on her and Corley began to walk swiftly towards Stephen's Green.

Lenehan hurried on in the same direction. Some drops of light rain fell. He took them as a warning and, glancing back towards the house which the young woman had entered to see that he was not observed, he ran eagerly across the road. Anxiety and his swift run made him pant. He called out:

"Hallo, Corley!"

Corley turned his head to see who had called him, and then continued walking as before. Lenehan ran after him, settling the waterproof on his shoulders with one hand.

"Hallo, Corley!" he cried again.

He came level with his friend and looked keenly in his face. He could see nothing there.

"Well?" he said. "Did it come off?"

They had reached the corner of Ely Place. Still without answering, Corley swerved to the left and went up the side street. His features were composed in stern calm. Lenehan kept up with his friend, breathing uneasily. He was baffled and a note of menace pierced through his voice.

"Can't you tell us?" he said. "Did you try her?"

Corley halted at the first lamp and stared grimly before him. Then with a grave gesture he extended a hand towards the light and, smiling, opened it slowly to the gaze of his disciple. A small gold coin shone in the palm.

FRANZ KAFKA

The Judgment

Translated by Willa and Edwin Muir

It was a Sunday morning in the very height of spring. Georg Bendemann, a young merchant, was sitting in his own room on the first floor of one of a long row of small, ramshackle houses stretching beside the river which were scarcely distinguishable from each other except in height and coloring. He had just finished a letter to an old friend of his who was now living abroad, had put it into its envelope in a slow and dreamy fashion, and with his elbows propped on the writing table was gazing out of the window at the river, the bridge and the hills on the farther bank with their tender green.

He was thinking about his friend, who had actually run away to Russia some years before, being dissatisfied with his prospects at home. Now he was carrying on a business in St. Petersburg, which had flourished to begin with but had long been going downhill, as he always complained on his increasingly rare visits. So he was wearing himself out to no purpose in a foreign country; the unfamiliar full beard he wore did not quite conceal the face Georg had known so well since childhood, and his skin was growing so yellow as to indicate some latent disease. By his own account he had no regular connection with the colony of his fellow countrymen out there and almost no social intercourse with Russian families, so that he was resigning himself to becoming a permanent bachelor.

What could one write to such a man, who had obviously run off the rails, a man one could be sorry for but could not help? Should one advise him to come home, to transplant himself and take up his old friendships again—there was nothing to hinder him—and in general to rely on the help of his friends? But that was as good as telling him, and the more kindly the more offensively, that all his efforts hitherto had miscarried, that he should finally give up, come back home, and be gaped at by everyone as a returned prodigal, that only his friends knew what was what and that he himself was just a big child who should do what his successful and home-keeping friends prescribed. And was it certain, besides, that all the pain one would have to inflict on him would achieve its object? Perhaps it would not even be possible to get him to come home at all —he said himself that he was now out of touch with commerce in his native country— and then he would still be left an alien in a foreign land embittered by his friends' advice and more than ever estranged from them. But if he did follow their advice and then didn't fit in at home—not out of malice, of course, but through force of circumstances—couldn't get on with his friends or without them, felt humiliated, couldn't be said to have either friends or a country of his own any longer, wouldn't it have been better for him to stay abroad just as he was?

Taking all this into account, how could one be sure that he would make a success of life at home?

For such reasons, supposing one wanted to keep up correspondence with him, one could not send him any real news such as could frankly be told to the most distant acquaintance. It was more than three years since his last visit, and for this he offered the lame excuse that the political situation in Russia was too uncertain, which apparently would not permit even the briefest absence of a small business man while it allowed hundreds of thousands of Russians to travel peacefully abroad. But during these three years Georg's own position in life had changed a lot. Two years ago his mother had died, since when he and his father had shared the household together, and his friend had of course been informed of that and had expressed his sympathy in a letter phrased so dryly that the grief caused by such an event, one had to conclude, could not be realized in a distant country. Since that time, however, Georg had applied himself with greater determination to the business as well as to everything else.

Perhaps during his mother's lifetime his father's insistence on having everything his own way in the business had hindered him from developing any real activity of his own, perhaps since her death his father had become less aggressive, although he was still active in the business, perhaps it was mostly due to an accidental run of good fortune—which was very probable indeed—but at any rate during those two years the business had developed in a most unexpected way, the staff had had to be doubled, the turnover was five times as great, no doubt about it, further progress lay just ahead.

But Georg's friend had no inkling of this improvement. In earlier years, perhaps for the last time in that letter of condolence, he had tried to persuade Georg to emigrate to Russia and had enlarged upon the prospects of success for precisely Georg's branch of trade. The figures quoted were microscopic by comparison with the range of Georg's present operations. Yet he shrank from letting his friend know about his business success, and if he were to do it now retrospectively that certainly would look peculiar.

So Georg confined himself to giving his friend unimportant items of gossip such as rise at random in the memory when one is idly thinking things over on a quiet Sunday. All he desired was to leave undisturbed the idea of the home town which his friend must have built up to his own content during the long interval. And so it happened to Georg that three times in three fairly widely separated letters he had told his friend about the engagement of an unimportant man to an equally unimportant girl, until indeed, quite contrary to his intentions, his friend began to show some interest in this notable event.

Yet Georg preferred to write about things like these rather than to confess that he himself had got engaged a month ago to a Fräulein Frieda Brandenfeld, a girl from a well-to-do family. He often discussed this friend of his with his fiancée and the peculiar relationship that had developed between them in their correspondence. "So he won't be coming to our wedding," said she, "and yet I have a right to get to know all your friends." "I don't want to trouble him," answered Georg. "Don't misunderstand me, he would probably come, at least I think so, but he would feel that his hand had been forced and he would be hurt, perhaps he would envy me and certainly he'd be discontented and without being able to do anything about his discontent he'd have to go away again alone. Alone—do you know what that means?" "Yes, but may he not hear about our wedding in some other fashion?" "I can't prevent that, of course, but it's unlikely, considering the way he lives." "Since your friends are like that, Georg, you shouldn't ever have got engaged at all." "Well, we're both to blame for that; but I wouldn't have it any other way now." And when, breathing quickly under his kisses, she still brought out: "All the same, I do feel upset," he thought it could not really involve him in trouble were he to send the news to his friend. "That's the kind of man I am and he'll just have to take me as I am," he said to himself, "I can't cut myself to another pattern that might make a more suitable friend for him."

And in fact he did inform his friend, in the long letter he had been writing that Sunday morning, about his engagement, with these words: "I have saved my best news to the end. I have got engaged to a Fräulein Frieda Brandenfeld, a girl from a well-to-do family, who only came to live here a long time after you went away, so that you're hardly likely to know her. There will be time to tell you more about her later, for today let me just say that I am very happy and as between you and me the only difference in our relationship is that instead of a quite ordinary kind of friend you will now have in me a happy friend. Besides that, you will acquire in my fiancée, who sends her warm greetings and will soon write you herself, a genuine friend of the opposite sex, which is not without importance to a bachelor. I know that there are many reasons why you can't come to see us, but would not my wedding be precisely the right occasion for giving all obstacles the go-by? Still, however that may be, do just as seems good to you without regarding any interests but your own."

With this letter in his hand Georg had been sitting a long time at the writing table, his face turned towards the window. He had barely acknowledged, with an absent smile, a greeting waved to him from the street by a passing acquaintance.

At last he put the letter in his pocket and went out of his room across a small lobby into his father's room, which he had not entered for months. There was in fact no need for him to enter it, since he saw his father daily at business and they took their midday meal together at an eating house; in the evening, it was true, each did as he pleased,

yet even then, unless Georg—as mostly happened—went out with friends or, more recently, visited his fiancée, they always sat for a while, each with his newspaper, in their common sitting room.

It surprised Georg how dark his father's room was even on this sunny morning. So it was overshadowed as much as that by the high wall on the other side of the narrow courtyard. His father was sitting by the window in a corner hung with various mementoes of Georg's dead mother, reading a newspaper which he held to one side before his eyes in an attempt to overcome a defect of vision. On the table stood the remains of his breakfast, not much of which seemed to have been eaten.

"Ah, Georg," said his father, rising at once to meet him. His heavy dressing gown swung open as he walked and the skirts of it fluttered round him.—"My father is still a giant of a man," said Georg to himself.

"It's unbearably dark here," he said aloud.

"Yes, it's dark enough," answered his father.

"And you've shut the window, too?"

"I prefer it like that."

"Well, it's quite warm outside," said Georg, as if continuing his previous remark, and sat down.

His father cleared away the breakfast dishes and set them on a chest.

"I really only wanted to tell you," went on Georg, who had been vacantly following the old man's movements, "that I am now sending the news of my engagement to St. Petersburg." He drew the letter a little way from his pocket and let it drop back again.

"To St. Petersburg?" asked his father.

"To my friend there," said Georg, trying to meet his father's eye.—In business hours he's quite different, he was thinking. How solidly he sits here with his arms crossed.

"Oh, yes. To your friend," said his father, with peculiar emphasis.

"Well, you know, Father, that I wanted not to tell him about my engagement at first.

Out of consideration for him, that was the only reason. You know yourself he's a difficult man. I said to myself that someone else might tell him about my engagement, although he's such a solitary creature that that was hardly likely—I couldn't prevent that—but I wasn't ever going to tell him myself."

"And now you've changed your mind?" asked his father, laying his enormous newspaper on the window sill and on top of it his spectacles, which he covered with one hand.

"Yes, I've been thinking it over. If he's a good friend of mine, I said to myself, my being happily engaged should make him happy too. And so I wouldn't put off telling him any longer. But before I posted the letter I wanted to let you know."

"Georg," said his father, lengthening his toothless mouth, "listen to me! You've come to me about this business, to talk it over with me. No doubt that does you honor. But it's nothing, it's worse than nothing, if you don't tell me the whole truth. I don't want to stir up matters that shouldn't be mentioned here. Since the death of our dear mother certain things have been done that aren't right. Maybe the time will come for mentioning them, and maybe sooner than we think. There's many a thing in the business I'm not aware of, maybe it's not done behind my back—I'm not going to say that it's done behind my back—I'm not equal to things any longer, my memory's failing, I haven't an eye for so many things any longer. That's the course of nature in the first place, and in the second place the death of our dear mother hit me harder than it did you.—But since we're talking about it, about this letter, I beg you, Georg, don't deceive me. It's a trivial affair, it's hardly worth mentioning, so don't deceive me. Do you really have this friend in St. Petersburg?"

Georg rose in embarrassment. "Never mind my friends. A thousand friends wouldn't make up to me for my father. Do you know what I think? You're not taking enough care of yourself. But old age must be taken care of. I can't do without you in the business, you know that very well, but if the business is going to undermine your health, I'm ready to close it down tomorrow forever. And that won't do. We'll have to make a change in your way of living. But a radical change. You sit here in the dark, and in the sitting room you would have plenty of light. You just take a bite of breakfast instead of properly keeping up your strength. You sit by a closed window, and the air would be so good for you. No, Father! I'll get the doctor to come, and we'll follow his orders. We'll change your room, you can move into the front room and I'll move in here. You won't notice the change, all your things will be moved with you. But there's time for all that later. I'll put you to bed now for a little; I'm sure you need to rest. Come, I'll help you take off your things, you'll see I can do it. Or if you would rather go into the front room at once, you can lie down in my bed for the present. That would be the most sensible thing."

Georg stood close beside his father, who had let his head with its unkempt white hair sink on his chest.

"Georg," said his father in a low voice, without moving.

Georg knelt down at once beside his father. In the old man's weary face he saw the pupils, over-large, fixedly looking at him from the corners of the eyes.

"You have no friends in St. Petersburg. You've always been a leg-puller and you haven't even shrunk from pulling my leg. How could you have a friend out there! I can't believe it."

"Just think back a bit, Father," said Georg, lifting his father from the chair and slipping off his dressing gown as he stood feebly enough, "it'll soon be three years since my friend came to see us last. I remember that you used not to like him very much. At least twice I kept you from seeing him, although he was actually sitting with me in my room. I could quite well understand your dislike of him, my friend has his peculiarities. But then, later, you got on with him very well. I was proud because you listened to him and nodded and asked him questions. If you think back you're bound to remember. He used to tell us the most incredible stories of the Russian Revolution. For instance, when he was on a business trip to Kiev and ran into a riot, and saw a priest on a balcony who cut a broad cross in blood on the palm of his hand and held the hand up and appealed to the mob. You've told that story yourself once or twice since."

Meanwhile Georg had succeeded in lowering his father down again and carefully taking off the woollen drawers he wore over his linen underpants and his socks. The not particularly clean appearance of this underwear made him reproach himself for having been neglectful. It should have certainly been his duty to see that his father had clean changes of underwear. He had not yet explicitly discussed with his bride-to-be what arrangements should be made for his father in the future, for they had both of them silently taken it for granted that the old man would go on living alone in the old house. But now he made a quick, firm decision to take him into his own future establishment. It almost looked, on closer inspection, as if the care he meant to lavish there on his father might come too late.

He carried his father to bed in his arms. It gave him a dreadful feeling to notice that while he took the few steps towards the bed the old man on his breast was playing with his watch chain. He could not lay him down on the bed for a moment, so firmly did he hang on to the watch chain.

But as soon as he was laid in bed, all seemed well. He covered himself up and even drew the blankets farther than usual over his shoulders. He looked up at Georg with a not unfriendly eye.

"You begin to remember my friend, don't you?" asked Georg, giving him an encouraging nod.

"Am I well covered up now?" asked his father, as if he were not able to see whether his feet were properly tucked in or not.

"So you find it snug in bed already," said Georg, and tucked the blankets more closely round him.

"Am I well covered up?" asked the father once more, seeming to be strangely intent upon the answer.

"Don't worry, you're well covered up."

"No!" cried his father, cutting short the answer, threw the blankets off with a strength that sent them all flying in a moment and sprang erect in bed. Only one hand lightly touched the ceiling to steady him.

"You wanted to cover me up, I know, my young sprig, but I'm far from being covered up yet. And even if this is the last strength I have, it's enough for you, too much for you. Of course I know your friend. He would have been a son after my own heart. That's why you've been playing him false all these years. Why else? Do you think I haven't been sorry for him? And that's why you had to lock yourself up in your office—the Chief is busy, mustn't be disturbed—just so that you could write your lying little letters to Russia. But thank goodness a father doesn't need to be taught how to see through his son. And now that you thought you'd got him down, so far down that you could set your bottom on him and sit on him and he wouldn't move, then my fine son makes up his mind to get married!"

Georg stared at the bogey conjured up by his father. His friend in St. Petersburg, whom his father suddenly knew too well, touched his imagination as never before. Lost in the vastness of Russia he saw him. At the door of an empty, plundered warehouse he saw him. Among the wreckage of his showcases, the slashed remnants of his wares, the falling gas brackets, he was just standing up. Why did he have to go so far away!

"But attend to me!" cried his father, and Georg, almost distracted, ran towards the bed to take everything in, yet came to a stop halfway.

"Because she lifted up her skirts," his father began to flute, "because she lifted her skirts like this, the nasty creature," and mimicking her he lifted his shirt so high that one could see the scar on his thigh from his war wound, "because she lifted her skirts like this and this you made up to her, and in order to make free with her undisturbed you have disgraced your mother's memory, betrayed your friend and stuck your father into bed so that he can't move. But he can move, or can't he?"

And he stood up quite unsupported and kicked his legs out. His insight made him radiant.

Georg shrank into a corner, as far away from his father as possible. A long time ago he had firmly made up his mind to watch closely every least movement so that he should not be surprised by any indirect attack, a pounce from behind or above. At this moment he recalled this long-forgotten resolve and forgot it again, like a man drawing a short thread through the eye of a needle.

"But your friend hasn't been betrayed after all!" cried his father, emphasizing the point with stabs of his forefinger. "I've been representing him here on the spot."

"You comedian!" Georg could not resist the retort, realized at once the harm done and, his eyes starting in his head, bit his tongue back, only too late, till the pain made his knees give.

"Yes, of course I've been playing a comedy! A comedy! That's a good expression! What other comfort was left to a poor old widower? Tell me—and while you're answering me be you still my living son—what else was left to me, in my back room, plagued by a disloyal staff, old to the marrow of my bones? And my son strutting through the world, finishing off deals that I had prepared for him, bursting with triumphant glee and stalking away from his father with the closed face of a respectable business man!

Do you think I didn't love you, I, from whom you are sprung?"

Now he'll lean forward, thought Georg. What if he topples and smashes himself! These words went hissing through his mind.

His father leaned forward but did not topple. Since Georg did not come any nearer, as he had expected, he straightened himself again.

"Stay where you are, I don't need you! You think you have strength enough to come over here and that you're only hanging back of your own accord. Don't be too sure! I am still much the stronger of us two. All by myself I might have had to give way, but your mother has given me so much of her strength that I've established a fine connection with your friend and I have your customers here in my pocket!"

"He has pockets even in his shirt!" said Georg to himself, and believed that with this remark he could make him an impossible figure for all the world. Only for a moment did he think so, since he kept on forgetting everything.

"Just take your bride on your arm and try getting in my way! I'll sweep her from your very side, you don't know how!"

Georg made a grimace of disbelief. His father only nodded, confirming the truth of his words, towards Georg's corner.

"How you amused me today, coming to ask me if you should tell your friend about your engagement. He knows it already, you stupid boy, he knows it all! I've been writing to him, for you forgot to take my writing things away from me. That's why he hasn't been here for years, he knows everything a hundred times better than you do yourself, in his left hand he crumples your letters unopened while in his right hand he holds up my letters to read through!"

In his enthusiasm he waved his arm over his head. "He knows everything a thousand times better!" he cried.

"Ten thousand times!" said Georg, to make

fun of his father, but in his very mouth the words turned into deadly earnest.

"For years I've been waiting for you to come with some such question! Do you think I concern myself with anything else? Do you think I read my newspapers? Look!" and he threw Georg a newspaper sheet which he had somehow taken to bed with him. An old newspaper, with a name entirely unknown to Georg.

"How long a time you've taken to grow up! Your mother had to die, she couldn't see the happy day, your friend is going to pieces in Russia, even three years ago he was yellow enough to be thrown away, and as for me, you see what condition I'm in. You have eyes in your head for that!"

"So you've been lying in wait for me!" cried Georg.

His father said pityingly, in an offhand manner: "I suppose you wanted to say that sooner. But now it doesn't matter." And in a louder voice: "So now you know what else there was in the world besides yourself, till now you've known only about yourself! An innocent child, yes, that you were, truly, but still more truly have you been a devilish human being!—And therefore take note: I sentence you now to death by drowning!"

Georg felt himself urged from the room. The crash with which his father fell on the bed behind him was still in his ears as he fled. On the staircase, which he rushed down as if its steps were an inclined plane, he ran into his charwoman on her way up to do the morning cleaning of the room. "Jesus!" she cried, and covered her face with her apron, but he was already gone. Out of the front door he rushed, across the roadway, driven towards the water. Already he was grasping at the railings as a starving man clutches food. He swung himself over, like the distinguished gymnast he had once been in his youth, to his parents' pride. With weakening grip he was still holding on when he spied between the railings a motor-bus coming which would easily cover the noise of his fall, called in a low voice: "Dear parents, I have always loved you, all the same," and let himself drop.

At this moment an unending stream of traffic was just going over the bridge.

D. H. LAWRENCE

Second Best

"Oh, I'm tired!" Frances exclaimed petulantly, and in the same instant she dropped down on the turf, near the hedge-bottom. Anne stood a moment surprised, then, accustomed to the vagaries of her beloved Frances, said:

"Well, and aren't you always likely to be tired, after travelling that blessed long way from Liverpool yesterday?" and she plumped down beside her sister. Anne was a wise young body of fourteen, very buxom, brimming with common sense. Frances was much older, about twenty-three, and whimsical, spasmodic. She was the beauty and the clever child of the family. She plucked the goose-grass buttons from her dress in a nervous, desperate fashion. Her beautiful profile, looped above with black hair, warm with the dusky-and-scarlet complexion of a pear, was calm as a mask, her thin brown hand plucked nervously.

"It's not the journey," she said, objecting to Anne's obtuseness. Anne looked inquiringly at her darling. The young girl, in her self-confident, practical way, proceeded to reckon up this whimsical creature. But suddenly she found herself full in the eyes of Frances; felt two dark, hectic eyes flaring challenge at her, and she shrank away. Frances was peculiar for these great, exposed looks, which disconcerted people by their violence and their suddenness.

"What's a matter, poor old duck?" asked Anne, as she folded the slight, wilful form of her sister in her arms. Frances laughed shakily, and nestled down for comfort on the budding breasts of the strong girl.

"Oh, I'm only a bit tired," she murmured, on the point of tears.

"Well, of course you are, what do you expect?" soothed Anne. It was a joke to Frances that Anne should play elder, almost mother to her. But then, Anne was in her unvexed teens; men were like big dogs to her: while Frances, at twenty-three, suffered a good deal.

The country was intensely morning-still. On the common everything shone beside its shadow, and the hill-side gave off heat in silence. The brown turf seemed in a low state of combustion, the leaves of the oaks were scorched brown. Among the blackish foliage in the distance shone the small red and orange of the village.

The willows in the brook-course at the foot zling effect like diamonds. It was a puff of of the common suddenly shook with a daz-wind. Anne resumed her normal position. She spread her knees, and put in her lap a handful of hazel nuts, whity-green leafy things, whose one cheek was tanned between brown and pink. These she began to crack and eat. Frances, with bowed head, mused bitterly.

"Eh, you know Tom Smedley?" began the young girl, as she pulled a tight kernel out of its shell.

"I suppose so," replied Frances sarcastically.

"Well, he gave me a wild rabbit what he'd caught, to keep with my tame one—and it's living."

"That's a good thing," said Frances, very detached and ironic.

"Well, it *is!* He reckoned he'd take me to Ollerton Feast, but he never did. Look here, he took a servant from the rectory; I saw him."

"So he ought," said Frances.

"No, he oughtn't! And I told him so. And I told him I should tell you—an' I have done."

Click and snap went a nut between her teeth. She sorted out the kernel, and chewed complacently.

"It doesn't make much difference," said Frances.

"Well, 'appen it doesn't; but I was mad with him all the same."

"Why?"

"Because I was; he's no right to go with a servant."

"He's a perfect right," persisted Frances, very just and cold.

"No, he hasn't, when he'd said he'd take me."

Frances burst into a laugh of amusement and relief.

"Oh, no; I'd forgot that," she said, adding, "and what did he say when you promised to tell me?"

"He laughed and said, 'She won't fret her fat over that.' "

"And she won't," sniffed Frances.

There was silence. The common, with its sere, blonde-headed thistles, its heaps of silent bramble, its brown-husked gorse in the glare of sunshine, seemed visionary. Across the brook began the immense pattern of agriculture, white chequering of barley stubble, brown squares of wheat, khaki patches of pasture, red stripes of fallow, with the woodland and the tiny village dark like ornaments, leading away to the distance, right to the hills, where the check-pattern grew smaller and smaller, till, in the blackish haze of heat, far off, only the tiny white squares of barley stubble showed distinct.

"Eh, I say, here's a rabbit hole!" cried Anne suddenly. "Should we watch if one comes out? You won't have to fidget, you know."

The two girls sat perfectly still. Frances watched certain objects in her surroundings: they had a peculiar, unfriendly look about them: the weight of greenish elderberries on their purpling stalks; the twinkling of the yellowing crab-apples that clustered high up in the hedge, against the sky: the exhausted, limp leaves of the primroses lying flat in the hedge-bottom: all looked strange to her. Then her eyes caught a movement. A mole was moving silently over the warm, red soil, nosing, shuffling hither and thither, flat, and dark as a shadow, shifting about, and as suddenly brisk, and as silent, like a very ghost of *joie de vivre.* Frances started, from habit was about to call on Anne to kill the little pest. But, to-day her lethargy of unhappiness was too much for her. She watched the little brute paddling, snuffing, touching things to discover them, running in blindness, delighted to ecstasy by the sunlight and the hot, strange things that caressed its belly and its nose. She felt a keen pity for the little creature.

"Eh, our Fran, look there! It's a mole."

Anne was on her feet, standing watching the dark, unconscious beast. Frances frowned with anxiety.

"It doesn't run off, does it?" said the young girl softly. Then she stealthily approached the creature. The mole paddled fumblingly away. In an instant Anne put her foot upon it, not too heavily. Frances could see the struggling, swimming movement of the little pink hands of the brute, the twisting and twitching of its pointed nose, as it wrestled under the sole of the boot.

"It *does* wriggle!" said the bonny girl, knitting her brows in a frown at the eerie sensation. Then she bent down to look at her trap. Frances could now see, beyond the edge of the boot-sole, the heaving of the velvet shoulders, the pitiful turning of the sightless face, the frantic rowing of the flat, pink hands.

"Kill the thing," she said, turning away her face.

"Oh—I'm not," laughed Anne, shrinking.

"You can, if you like."

"I *don't* like," said Frances, with quiet intensity.

After several dabbing attempts, Anne succeeded in picking up the little animal by the scruff of its neck. It threw back its head, flung its long blind snout from side to side, the mouth open in a peculiar oblong, with tiny pinkish teeth at the edge. The blind, frantic mouth gaped and writhed. The body, heavy and clumsy, hung scarcely moving.

"Isn't it a snappy little thing," observed Anne, twisting to avoid the teeth.

"What are you going to do with it?" asked Frances sharply.

"It's got to be killed—look at the damage they do. I s'll take it home and let dadda or somebody kill it. I'm not going to let it go."

She swaddled the creature clumsily in her pocket-handkerchief and sat down beside her sister. There was an interval of silence, during which Anne combated the efforts of the mole.

"You've not had much to say about Jimmy this time. Did you see him often in Liverpool?" Anne asked suddenly.

"Once or twice," replied Frances, giving no sign of how the question troubled her.

"And aren't you sweet on him any more, then?"

"I should think I'm not, seeing that he's engaged."

"Engaged? Jimmy Barrass! Well, of all things! I never thought *he'd* get engaged."

"Why not, he's as much right as anybody else?" snapped Frances.

Anne was fumbling with the mole.

" 'Appen so," she said at length; "but I never thought Jimmy would, though."

"Why not?" snapped Frances.

"*I* don't know—this blessed mole, it'll not keep still!—who's he got engaged to?"

"How should I know?"

"I thought you'd ask him; you've known

him long enough. I s'd think he thought he'd get engaged now he's a Doctor of Chemistry."

Frances laughed in spite of herself.

"What's that got to do with it?" she asked.

"I'm sure it's got a lot. He'll want to feel *somebody* now, so he's got engaged. Hey, stop it; go in!"

But at this juncture the mole almost succeeded in wriggling clear. It wrestled and twisted frantically, waved its pointed blind head, its mouth standing open like a little shaft, its big, wrinkled hands spread out.

"Go in with you!" urged Anne, poking the little creature with her forefinger, trying to get it back into the handkerchief. Suddenly the mouth turned like a spark on her finger.

"Oh!" she cried, "he's bit me."

She dropped him to the floor. Dazed, the blind creature fumbled round. Frances felt like shrieking. She expected him to dart away in a flash, like a mouse, and there he remained groping; she wanted to cry to him to be gone. Anne, in a sudden decision of wrath, caught up her sister's walking-cane. With one blow the mole was dead. Frances was startled and shocked. One moment the little wretch was fussing in the heat, and the next it lay like a little bag, inert and black—not a struggle, scarce a quiver.

"It is dead!" Frances said breathlessly. Anne took her finger from her mouth, looked at the tiny pinpricks, and said:

"Yes, he is, and I'm glad. They're vicious little nuisances, moles are."

With which her wrath vanished. She picked up the dead animal.

"Hasn't it got a beautiful skin," she mused, stroking the fur with her forefinger, then with her cheek.

"Mind," said Frances sharply. "You'll have the blood on your skirt!"

One ruby drop of blood hung on the small snout, ready to fall. Anne shook it off on to some harebells. Frances suddenly became calm; in that moment, grown-up.

"I suppose they have to be killed," she said, and a certain rather dreary indifference succeeded to her grief. The twinkling crab-apples, the glitter of brilliant willows now seemed to her trifling, scarcely worth the notice. Something had died in her, so that things lost their poignancy. She was calm, indifference overlying her quiet sadness. Rising, she walked down to the brook course.

"Here, wait for me," cried Anne, coming tumbling after.

Frances stood on the bridge, looking at the red mud trodden into pockets by the feet of cattle. There was not a drain of water left, but everything smelled green, succulent. Why did she care so little for Anne, who was so fond of her? she asked herself. Why did she care so little for any one? She did not know, but she felt a rather stubborn pride in her isolation and indifference.

They entered a field where stooks of barley stood in rows, the straight, blonde tresses of the corn streaming on to the ground. The stubble was bleached by the intense summer, so that the expanse glared white. The next field was sweet and soft with a second crop of seeds; thin, straggling clover whose little pink knobs rested prettily in the dark green. The scent was faint and sickly. The girls came up in single file, Frances leading.

Near the gate a young man was mowing with the scythe some fodder for the afternoon feed of the cattle. As he saw the girls he left off working and waited in an aimless kind of way. Frances was dressed in white muslin, and she walked with dignity, detached and forgetful. Her lack of agitation, her simple, unheeding advance made him nervous. She had loved the far-off Jimmy for five years, having had in return his half-measures. This man only affected her slightly.

Tom was of medium stature, energetic in build. His smooth, fair-skinned face was burned red, not brown, by the sun, and this ruddiness enhanced his appearance of good humour and easiness. Being a year older than Frances, he would have courted her long ago had she been so inclined. As it was,

he had gone his uneventful way amiably, chatting with many a girl, but remaining unattached, free of trouble for the most part. Only he knew he wanted a woman. He hitched his trousers just a trifle self-consciously as the girls approached. Frances was a rare, delicate kind of being, whom he realized with a queer and delicious stimulation in his veins. She gave him a slight sense of suffocation. Somehow, this morning, she affected him more than usual. She was dressed in white. He, however, being matter-of-fact in his mind, did not realize. His feeling had never become conscious, purposive.

Frances knew what she was about. Tom was ready to love her as soon as she would show him. Now that she could not have Jimmy, she did not poignantly care. Still, she would have something. If she could not have the best—Jimmy, whom she knew to be something of a snob—she would have the second best, Tom. She advanced rather indifferently.

"You are back, then!" said Tom. She marked the touch of uncertainty in his voice.

"No," she laughed, "I'm still in Liverpool," and the undertone of intimacy made him burn.

"This isn't you, then?" he asked.

Her heart leapt up in approval. She looked in his eyes, and for a second was with him.

"Why, what do you think?" she laughed.

He lifted his hat from his head with a distracted little gesture. She liked him, his quaint ways, his humour, his ignorance, and his slow masculinity.

"Here, look here, Tom Smedley," broke in Anne.

"A moudiwarp! Did you find it dead?" he asked.

"No, it bit me," said Anne.

"Oh, aye! An' that got your rag out, did it?"

"No, it didn't!" Anne scolded sharply. "Such language!"

"Oh, what's up wi' it?"

"I can't bear you to talk broad."

"Can't you?"

He glanced at Frances.

"It isn't nice," Frances said. She did not care, really. The vulgar speech jarred on her as a rule; Jimmy was a gentleman. But Tom's manner of speech did not matter to her.

"I like you to talk *nicely*," she added.

"Do you," he replied, tilting his hat, stirred.

"And generally you *do*, you know," she smiled.

"I s'll have to have a try," he said, rather tensely gallant.

"What?" she asked brightly.

"To talk nice to you," he said. Frances coloured furiously, bent her head for a moment, then laughed gaily, as if she liked this clumsy hint.

"Eh now, you mind what you're saying," cried Anne, giving the young man an admonitory pat.

"You wouldn't have to give yon mole many knocks like that," he teased, relieved to get on safe ground, rubbing his arm.

"No indeed, it died in one blow," said Frances, with a flippancy that was hateful to her.

"You're not so good at knockin' 'em?" he said, turning to her.

"I don't know, if I'm cross," she said decisively.

"No?" he replied, with alert attentiveness.

"I could," she added, harder, "if it was necessary."

He was slow to feel her difference.

"And don't you consider it *is* necessary?" he asked, with misgiving.

"W—ell—is it?" she said, looking at him steadily, coldly.

"I reckon it is," he replied, looking away, but standing stubborn.

She laughed quickly.

"But it isn't necessary for *me*," she said, with slight contempt.

"Yes, that's quite true," he answered.

She laughed in a shaky fashion.

"*I know it is*," she said; and there was an awkward pause.

"Why, would you *like* me to kill moles then?" she asked tentatively, after a while.

"They do us a lot of damage," he said, standing firm on his own ground, angered.

"Well, I'll see the next time I come across one," she promised, defiantly. Their eyes met, and she sank before him, her pride troubled. He felt uneasy and triumphant and baffled, as if fate had gripped him. She smiled as she departed.

"Well," said Anne, as the sisters went through the wheat stubble; "I don't know what you two's been jawing about, I'm sure."

"Don't you?" laughed Frances significantly.

"No, I don't. But, at any rate, Tom Smedley's a good deal better to my thinking than Jimmy, so there—and nicer."

"Perhaps he is," said Frances coldly.

And the next day, after a secret, persistent hunt, she found another mole playing in the heat. She killed it, and in the evening, when Tom came to the gate to smoke his pipe after supper, she took him the dead creature.

"Here you are then!" she said.

"Did you catch it?" he replied, taking the velvet corpse into his fingers and examining it minutely. This was to hide his trepidation.

"Did you think I couldn't?" she asked, her face very near his.

"Nay, I didn't know."

She laughed in his face, a strange little laugh that caught her breath, all agitation, and tears, and recklessness of desire. He looked frightened and upset. She put her hand to his arm.

"Shall you go out wi' me?" he asked, in a difficult, troubled tone.

She turned her face away, with a shaky laugh. The blood came up in him, strong, overmastering. He resisted it. But it drove him down, and he was carried away. Seeing the winsome, frail nape of her neck, fierce love came upon him for her, and tenderness.

"We s'll 'ave to tell your mother," he said. And he stood, suffering, resisting his passion for her.

"Yes," she replied, in a dead voice. But there was a thrill of pleasure in this death.

KATHERINE ANNE PORTER

Theft

She had the purse in her hand when she came in. Standing in the middle of the floor, holding her bathrobe around her and trailing a damp towel in one hand, she surveyed the immediate past and remembered everything clearly. Yes, she had opened the flap and spread it out on the bench after she had dried the purse with her handkerchief.

She had intended to take the Elevated, and naturally she looked in her purse to make certain she had the fare, and was pleased to find forty cents in the coin envelope. She was going to pay her own fare, too, even if Camilo did have the habit of seeing her up the steps and dropping a nickel in the machine before he gave the turnstile a little push and sent her through it with a bow. Camilo by a series of compromises had managed to make effective a fairly complete set of smaller courtesies, ignoring the larger and more troublesome ones. She had walked with him to the station in a pouring rain, because she knew he was almost as poor as she was, and when he insisted on a taxi, she was firm and said, "You know it simply will not do." He was wearing a new hat of a pretty biscuit shade, for it never occurred to him to buy anything of a practical color; he had put it on for the first time and the rain was spoiling it. She kept thinking, "But this is dreadful, where will he get another?" She compared it with Eddie's hats that always seemed to be precisely seven years old and as if they had been quite purposely left out in the rain, and yet they sat with a careless and incidental rightness on Eddie. But Camilo was far different; if he wore a shabby hat it would be merely shabby on him, and he would lose his spirits over it. If she had not feared Camilo would take it badly, for he insisted on the practice of his little ceremonies up to the point he had fixed for them, she would have said to him as they left Thora's house, "Do go home. I can surely reach the station by myself."

"It is written that we must be rained upon tonight," said Camilo, "so let it be together."

At the foot of the platform stairway she staggered slightly—they were both nicely set up on Thora's cocktails—and said: "At least, Camilo, do me the favor not to climb these stairs in your present state, since for you it is only a matter of coming down again at once, and you'll certainly break your neck."

He had made three quick bows, he was Spanish, and leaped off through the rainy darkness. She stood watching him, for he was a very graceful young man, thinking that tomorrow morning he would gaze soberly at his spoiled hat and soggy shoes and possibly associate her with his misery. As she watched, he stopped at the far corner and took off his hat and hid it under his overcoat. She felt she had betrayed him by seeing, because he would have been humiliated if he thought she even suspected him of trying to save his hat.

Roger's voice sounded over her shoulder above the clang of the rain falling on the stairway shed, wanting to know what she was doing out in the rain at this time of night, and did she take herself for a duck? His long, imperturbable face was streaming with water, and he tapped a bulging spot on the breast of his buttoned-up overcoat. "Hat," he said. "Come on, let's take a taxi."

She settled back against Roger's arm which he laid around her shoulders, and with the gesture they exchanged a glance full of long amiable associations, then she looked through the window at the rain changing the shapes of everything, and the colors. The taxi dodged in and out between the pillars of the Elevated, skidding slightly on every curve, and she said: "The more it skids the calmer I feel, so I really must be drunk."

"You must be," said Roger. "This bird is a homicidal maniac, and I could do with a cocktail myself this minute."

They waited on the traffic at Fortieth Street and Sixth Avenue, and three boys walked before the nose of the taxi. Under the globes of light they were cheerful scarecrows, all very thin and all wearing very seedy snappy-cut suits and gay neckties. They were not very sober either, and they stood for a moment wobbling in front of the car, and there was an argument going on among them. They leaned toward each other as if they were getting ready to sing, and the first one said: "When I get married it won't be jus' for getting married, I'm gonna marry for *love*, see?" and the second one said, "Aw, gwan and tell that stuff to *her*, why n't yuh?" and the third one gave a kind of hoot, and said, "Hell, dis guy? Wot the hell's he got?" and the first one said: "Aaah, shurrup yuh mush, I got plenty." Then they all squealed and scrambled across the street beating the first one on the back and pushing him around.

"Nuts," commented Roger, "pure nuts."

Two girls went skittering by in short transparent raincoats, one green, one red, their heads tucked against the drive of the rain. One of them was saying to the other, "Yes, I know all about *that*. But what about me? You're always so sorry for *him* . . ." and they ran on with their little pelican legs flashing back and forth.

The taxi backed up suddenly and leaped forward again, and after a while Roger said: "I had a letter from Stella today, and she'll be home on the twenty-sixth, so I suppose she's made up her mind and it's all settled."

"I had a sort of letter today too," she said, "making up my mind for me. I think it is time for you and Stella to do something definite."

When the taxi stopped on the corner of West Fifty-third Street, Roger said, "I've just enough if you'll add ten cents," so she opened her purse and gave him a dime, and he said, "That's beautiful, that purse."

"It's a birthday present," she told him, "and I like it. How's your show coming?"

"Oh, still hanging on, I guess. I don't go near the place. Nothing sold yet. I mean to keep right on the way I'm going and they can take it or leave it. I'm through with the argument."

"It's absolutely a matter of holding out, isn't it?"

"Holding out's the tough part."

"Good night, Roger."

"Good night, you should take aspirin and push yourself into a tub of hot water, you look as though you're catching cold."

"I will."

With the purse under her arm she went upstairs, and on the first landing Bill heard her step and poked his head out with his hair tumbled and his eyes red, and he said: "For Christ's sake, come in and have a drink with me. I've had some bad news."

"You're perfectly sopping," said Bill, looking at her drenched feet. They had two drinks, while Bill told her how the director had thrown his play out after the cast had been picked over twice, and had gone through three rehearsals. "I said to him, 'I didn't say it was a masterpiece, I said it would make a good show.' And he said, 'It just doesn't *play*, do you see? It needs a doctor.' So I'm stuck, absolutely stuck," said Bill, on the edge of weeping again, "I've been crying," he told her, "in my cups." And he went on to ask her if she realized his wife was ruining him with her extravagance. "I send her ten dollars every week of my unhappy life, and I don't really have to. She threatens to jail me if I don't, but she can't do it. God, let her try it after the way she treated me! She's no right to alimony and she knows it. She keeps on saying she's got to have it for the baby and I keep on sending it because I can't bear to see anybody suffer. So I'm way behind on the piano and the victrola, both—"

"Well, this is a pretty rug, anyhow," she said.

Bill stared at it and blew his nose. "I got it at Ricci's for ninety-five dollars," he said. "Ricci told me it once belonged to Marie Dressler, and cost fifteen hundred dollars, but there's a burnt place on it, under the divan. Can you beat that?"

"No," she said. She was thinking about her empty purse and that she could not possibly expect a check for her latest review for another three days, and her arrangement with the basement restaurant could not last much longer if she did not pay something on account. "It's no time to speak of it," she said, "but I've been hoping you would have by now that fifty dollars you promised for my scene in the third act. Even if it doesn't play. You were to pay me for the work anyhow out of your advance."

"Weeping Jesus," said Bill, "you, too?" He gave a loud sob, or hiccough, in his moist handkerchief. "Your stuff was no better than mine, after all. Think of that."

"But you got something for it," she said. "Seven hundred dollars."

Bill said, "Do me a favor, will you?" Have another drink and forget about it. I can't, you know I can't, I would if I could, but you know the fix I'm in."

"Let it go, then," she found herself saying almost in spite of herself. She had meant to be quite firm about it. They drank again without speaking, and she went to her apartment on the floor above.

There, she now remembered distinctly, she

had taken the letter out of the purse before she spread the purse out to dry.

She had sat down and read the letter over again: but there were phrases that insisted on being read many times, they had a life of their own separate from the others, and when she tried to read past and around them, they moved with the movement of her eyes, and she could not escape them . . . "thinking about you more than I mean to . . . yes, I even talk about you . . . why were you so anxious to destroy . . . even if I could see you now I would not . . . not worth all this abominable . . . the end . . ."

Carefully she tore the letter into narrow strips and touched a lighted match to them in the coal grate.

Early the next morning she was in the bathtub when the janitress knocked and then came in, calling out that she wished to examine the radiators before she started the furnace going for the winter. After moving about the room for a few minutes, the janitress went out, closing the door very sharply.

She came out of the bathroom to get a cigarette from the package in the purse. The purse was gone. She dressed and made coffee, and sat by the window while she drank it. Certainly the janitress had taken the purse, and certainly it would be impossible to get it back without a great deal of ridiculous excitement. Then let it go. With this decision of her mind, there rose coincidentally in her blood a deep almost murderous anger. She set the cup carefully in the center of the table, and walked steadily downstairs, three long flights and a short hall and a steep flight into the basement, where the janitress, her face streaked with coal dust, was shaking up the furnace. "Will you please give me back my purse? There isn't any money in it. It was a present, and I don't want to lose it."

The janitress turned without straightening up and peered at her with hot flickering eyes, a red light from the furnace reflected in them. "What do you mean, your purse?"

"The gold cloth purse you took from the wooden bench in my room," she said. "I must have it back."

"Before God I never laid eyes on your purse, and that's the holy truth," said the janitress.

"Oh, well then, keep it," she said, but in a very bitter voice; "keep it if you want it so much." And she walked away.

She remembered how she had never locked a door in her life, on some principle of rejection in her that made her uncomfortable in the ownership of things, and her paradoxical boast before the warnings of her friends, that she had never lost a penny by theft; and she had been pleased with the bleak humility of this concrete example designed to illustrate and justify a certain fixed, otherwise baseless and general faith which ordered the movements of her life without regard to her will in the matter.

In this moment she felt that she had been robbed of an enormous number of valuable things, whether material or intangible: things lost or broken by her own fault, things she had forgotten and left in houses when she moved: books borrowed from her and not returned, journeys she had planned and had not made, words she had waited to hear spoken to her and had not heard, and the words she had meant to answer with; bitter alternatives and intolerable substitutes worse than nothing, and yet inescapable: the long patient suffering of dying friendships and the dark inexplicable death of love—all that she had had, and all that she had missed, were lost together, and were twice lost in this landslide of remembered losses.

The janitress was following her upstairs with the purse in her hand and the same deep red fire flickering in her eyes. The janitress thrust the purse towards her while they were still a half dozen steps apart, and said: "Don't never tell on me. I musta been crazy. I get crazy in the head sometimes, I swear I do. My son can tell you."

She took the purse after a moment, and the janitress went on: "I got a niece who is going on seventeen, and she's a nice girl and I thought I'd give it to her. She needs a pretty purse. I musta been crazy; I thought maybe you wouldn't mind, you leave things around and don't seem to notice much."

She said: "I missed this because it was a present to me from someone . . ."

The janitress said: "He'd get you another if you lost this one. My niece is young and needs pretty things, we oughta give the young ones a chance. She's got young men after her maybe will want to marry her. She oughta have nice things. She needs them bad right now. You're a grown woman, you've had your chance, you ought to know how it is!"

She held the purse out to the janitress saying: "You don't know what you're talking about. Here, take it, I've changed my mind. I really don't want it."

The janitress looked up at her with hatred and said: "I don't want it either now. My niece is young and pretty, she don't need fixin' up to be pretty, she's young and pretty anyhow! I guess you need it worse than she does!"

"It wasn't really yours in the first place," she said, turning away. "You mustn't talk as if I had stolen it from you."

"It's not from me, it's from her you're stealing it," said the janitress, and went back downstairs.

She laid the purse on the table and sat down with the cup of chilled coffee, and thought: I was right not to be afraid of any thief but myself, who will end by leaving me nothing.

RYŪNOSUKE AKUTAGAWA

In a Grove

Translated by Takashi Kojima

The Testimony of a Woodcutter Questioned by a High Police Commissioner

Yes, sir. Certainly, it was I who found the body. This morning, as usual, I went to cut my daily quota of cedars, when I found the body in a grove in a hollow in the mountains. The exact location? About 150 meters off the Yamashina stage road. It's an out-of-the-way grove of bamboo and cedars.

The body was lying flat on its back dressed in a bluish silk kimono and a wrinkled headdress of the Kyoto style. A single sword-stroke had pierced the breast. The fallen bamboo-blades around it were stained with bloody blossoms. No, the blood was no longer running. The wound had dried up, I believe. And also, a gad-fly was stuck fast there, hardly noticing my footsteps.

You ask me if I saw a sword or any such thing?

No, nothing, sir. I found only a rope at the root of a cedar near by. And . . . well, in addition to a rope, I found a comb. That was all. Apparently he must have made a battle of it before he was murdered, because the grass and fallen bamboo-blades had been trampled down all around.

"A horse was near by?"

No, sir. It's hard enough for a man to enter, let alone a horse.

The Testimony of a Traveling Buddhist Priest Questioned by a High Police Commissioner

The time? Certainly, it was about noon yesterday, sir. The unfortunate man was on the road from Sekiyama to Yamashina. He was walking toward Sekiyama with a woman accompanying him on horseback, who I have since learned was his wife. A scarf hanging from her head hid her face from view. All I saw was the color of her clothes, a lilac-colored suit. Her horse was a sorrel with a fine mane. The lady's height? Oh, about four feet five inches. Since I am a Buddhist priest, I took little notice about her details. Well, the man was armed with a sword as well as a bow and arrows. And I remember that he carried some twenty odd arrows in his quiver.

Little did I expect that he would meet such a fate. Truly human life is as evanescent as the morning dew or a flash of lightning. My words are inadequate to express my sympathy for him.

The Testimony of a Policeman Questioned by a High Police Commissioner

The man that I arrested? He is a notorious brigand called Tajomaru. When I arrested him, he had fallen off his horse. He was groaning on the bridge at Awataguchi. The time? It was in the early hours of last night. For the record, I might say that the other day I tried to arrest him, but unfortunately he escaped. He was wearing a dark blue silk kimono and a large plain sword. And, as you see, he got a bow and arrows somewhere. You say that this bow and these arrows look like the ones owned by the dead man? Then

Tajomaru must be the murderer. The bow wound with leather strips, the black lacquered quiver, the seventeen arrows with hawk feathers—these were all in his possession I believe. Yes, sir, the horse is, as you say, a sorrel with a fine mane. A little beyond the stone bridge I found the horse grazing by the roadside, with his long rein dangling. Surely there is some providence in his having been thrown by the horse.

Of all the robbers prowling around Kyoto, this Tajomaru has given the most grief to the women in town. Last autumn a wife who came to the mountain back of the Pindora of the Toribe Temple, presumably to pay a visit, was murdered, along with a girl. It has been suspected that it was his doing. If this criminal murdered the man, you cannot tell what he may have done with the man's wife. May it please your honor to look into this problem as well.

The Testimony of an Old Woman Questioned by a High Police Commissioner

Yes sir, that corpse is the man who married my daughter. He does not come from Kyoto. He was a samurai in the town of Kokufu in the province of Wakasa. His name was Kanazawa no Takehiko, and his age was twenty-six. He was of a gentle disposition, so I am sure he did nothing to provoke the anger of others.

My daughter? Her name is Masago, and her age is nineteen. She is a spirited, fun-loving girl, but I am sure she has never known any man except Takehiko. She has a small, oval, dark-complected face with a mole at the corner of her left eye.

Yesterday Takehiko left for Wakasa with my daughter. What bad luck it is that things should have come to such a sad end! What has become of my daughter? I am resigned to giving up my son-in-law as lost, but the fate of my daughter worries me sick. For heaven's sake leave no stone unturned to find her. I hate that robber Tajomaru, or whatever his name is. Not only my son-in-law, but my daughter . . . (Her later words were drowned in tears.)

Tajomaru's Confession

I killed him, but not her. Where's she gone? I can't tell. Oh, wait a minute. No torture can make me confess what I don't know. Now things have come to such a head, I won't keep anything from you.

Yesterday a little past noon I met that couple. Just then a puff of wind blew, and raised her hanging scarf, so that I caught a glimpse of her face. Instantly it was again covered from my view. That may have been one reason; she looked like a Bodhisattva.[1] At that moment I made up my mind to capture her even if I had to kill her man.

Why? To me killing isn't a matter of such great consequence as you might think. When a woman is captured, her man has to be killed anyway. In killing, I use the sword I wear at my side. Am I the only one who kills people? You, you don't use your swords. You kill people with your power, with your money. Sometimes you kill them on the pretext of working for their good. It's true they don't bleed. They are in the best of health, but all the same you've killed them. It's hard to say who is a greater sinner, you or me. (An ironical smile.)

But it would be good if I could capture a woman without killing her man. So, I made up my mind to capture her, and do my best not to kill him. But it's out of the question on the Yamashina stage road. So I managed to lure the couple into the mountains.

It was quite easy. I became their traveling companion, and I told them there was an old mound in the mountain over there, and that I had dug it open and found many mirrors

---

[1] *Bodhisattva:* in Buddhist theology, applied to one who has attained such perfect knowledge it can be said to be the essence of his being: he must undergo only one more birth before reaching the state of a supreme Buddha.

and swords. I went on to tell them I'd buried the things in a grove behind the mountain, and that I'd like to sell them at a low price to anyone who would care to have them. Then . . . you see, isn't greed terrible? He was beginning to be moved by my talk before he knew it. In less than half an hour they were driving their horse toward the mountain with me.

When he came in front of the grove, I told them that the treasures were buried in it, and I asked them to come and see. The man had no objection—he was blinded by greed. The woman said she would wait on horseback. It was natural for her to say so, at the sight of a thick grove. To tell you the truth, my plan worked just as I wished, so I went into the grove with him, leaving her behind alone.

The grove is only bamboo for some distance. About fifty yards ahead there's a rather open clump of cedars. It was a convenient spot for my purpose. Pushing my way through the grove, I told him a plausible lie that the treasures were buried under the cedars. When I told him this, he pushed his laborious way toward the slender cedar visible through the grove. After a while the bamboo thinned out, and we came to where a number of cedars grew in a row. As soon as we got there, I seized him from behind. Because he was a trained, sword-bearing warrior, he was quite strong, but he was taken by surprise, so there was no help for him. I soon tied him up to the root of a cedar. Where did I get a rope? Thank heaven, being a robber, I had a rope with me, since I might have to scale a wall at any moment. Of course it was easy to stop him from calling out by gagging his mouth with fallen bamboo leaves.

When I disposed of him, I went to his woman and asked her to come and see him, because he seemed to have been suddenly taken sick. It's needless to say that this plan also worked well. The woman, her sedge hat off, came into the depths of the grove, where I led her by the hand. The instant she caught sight of her husband, she drew a small sword. I've never seen a woman of such violent temper. If I'd been off guard, I'd have got a thrust in my side. I dodged, but she kept on slashing at me. She might have wounded me deeply or killed me. But I'm Tajomaru. I managed to strike down her small sword without drawing my own. The most spirited woman is defenseless without a weapon. At least I could satisfy my desire for her without taking her husband's life.

Yes, . . . without taking his life. I had no wish to kill him. I was about to run away from the grove, leaving the woman behind in tears, when she frantically clung to my arm. In broken fragments of words, she asked that either her husband or I die. She said it was more trying than death to have her shame known to two men. She gasped out that she wanted to be the wife of whichever survived. Then a furious desire to kill him seized me. (Gloomy excitement.)

Telling you in this way, no doubt I seem a crueler man than you. But that's because you didn't see her face. Especially her burning eyes at that moment. As I saw her eye to eye, I wanted to make her my wife even if I were to be struck by lightning. I wanted to make her my wife . . . this single desire filled my mind. This was not only lust, as you might think. At that time if I'd had no other desire than lust, I'd surely not have minded knocking her down and running away. Then I wouldn't have stained my sword with his blood. But the moment I gazed at her face in the dark grove, I decided not to leave there without killing him.

But I didn't like to resort to unfair means to kill him. I untied him and told him to cross swords with me. (The rope that was found at the root of the cedar is the rope I dropped at the time.) Furious with anger, he drew his thick sword. And quick as thought, he sprang at me ferociously, without speaking a word. I needn't tell you how our fight turned out. The twenty-third stroke . . . please remember this. I'm impressed with this fact still. Nobody under the sun has ever clashed swords with me twenty strokes. (A cheerful smile.)

When he fell, I turned toward her, lowering my blood-stained sword. But to my great astonishment she was gone. I wondered to where she had run away. I looked for her in the clump of cedars. I listened, but heard only a groaning sound from the throat of the dying man.

As soon as we started to cross swords, she may have run away through the grove to call for help. When I thought of that, I decided it was a matter of life and death to me. So, robbing him of his sword, and bow and arrows, I ran out to the mountain road. There I found her horse still grazing quietly. It would be a mere waste of words to tell you the later details, but before I entered town I had already parted with the sword. That's all my confession. I know that my head will be hung in chains anyway, so put me down for the maximum penalty. (A defiant attitude.)

The Confession of a Woman Who Has Come to the *Shimizu* Temple

That man in the blue silk kimono, after forcing me to yield to him, laughed mockingly as he looked at my bound husband. How horrified my husband must have been! But no matter how hard he struggled in agony, the rope cut into him all the more tightly. In spite of myself I ran stumblingly toward his side. Or rather I tried to run toward him, but the man instantly knocked me down. Just at that moment I saw an indescribable light in my husband's eyes. Something beyond expression . . . his eyes make me shudder even now. That instantaneous look of my husband, who couldn't speak a word, told me all his heart. The flash in his eyes was neither anger nor sorrow . . . only a cold light, a look of loathing. More struck by the look in his eyes than by the blow of the thief, I called out in spite of myself and fell unconscious.

In the course of time I came to, and found that the man in blue silk was gone. I saw only my husband still bound to the root of the cedar. I raised myself from the bamboo-blades with difficulty, and looked into his face; but the expression in his eyes was just the same as before.

Beneath the cold contempt in his eyes, there was hatred. Shame, grief, and anger . . . I didn't know how to express my heart at that time. Reeling to my feet, I went up to my husband.

"Takejiro," I said to him, "since things have come to this pass, I cannot live with you. I'm determined to die, . . . but you must die, too. You saw my shame. I can't leave you alive as you are."

This was all I could say. Still he went on gazing at me with loathing and contempt. My heart breaking, I looked for his sword. It must have been taken by the robber. Neither his sword nor his bow and arrows were to be seen in the grove. But fortunately my small sword was lying at my feet. Raising it over head, once more I said, "Now give me your life. I'll follow you right away."

When he heard these words, he moved his lips with difficulty. Since his mouth was stuffed with leaves, of course his voice could not be heard at all. But at a glance I understood his words. Despising me, his look said only, "Kill me." Neither conscious nor unconscious, I stabbed the small sword through the lilac-colored kimono into his breast.

Again at this time I must have fainted. By the time I managed to look up, he had already breathed his last—still in bonds. A streak of sinking sunlight streamed through the clump of cedars and bamboos, and shone on his pale face. Gulping down my sobs, I untied the rope from his dead body. And . . . and what has become of me since I have no more strength to tell you. Anyway I hadn't the strength to die. I stabbed my own throat with the small sword, I threw myself into a pond at the foot of the mountain, and I tried to kill myself in many ways. Unable to end my life, I am still living in dishonor. (A lonely smile.) Worthless as I am, I must have been forsaken even by the most merciful Kwannon.[2] I killed my own husband. I was violated by the robber. Whatever can I do? Whatever can I . . . I . . . (Gradually, violent sobbing.)

The Story of the Murdered Man, as Told Through a Medium

After violating my wife, the robber, sitting there, began to speak comforting words to her. Of course I couldn't speak. My whole body was tied fast to the root of a cedar. But meanwhile I winked at her many times, as much as to say "Don't believe the robber." I wanted to convey some such meaning to her. But my wife, sitting dejectedly on the bamboo leaves, was looking hard at her lap. To all appearances, she was listening to his words. I was agonized by jealousy. In the meantime the robber went on with his clever talk, from one subject to another. The robber finally made his bold, brazen proposal. "Once your virtue is stained, you won't get along well with your husband, so won't you be my wife instead? It's my love for you that made me be violent toward you."

While the criminal talked, my wife raised her face as if in a trance. She had never looked so beautiful as at that moment. What did my beautiful wife say in answer to him while I was sitting bound there? I am lost in space, but I have never thought of her answer without burning with anger and jealousy. Truly she said, . . . "Then take me away with you wherever you go."

This is not the whole of her sin. If that were all, I would not be tormented so much in the dark. When she was going out of the grove as if in a dream, her hand in the robber's, she suddenly turned pale, and pointed

at me tied to the root of the cedar, and said, "Kill him! I cannot marry you as long as he lives." "Kill him!" she cried many times, as if she had gone crazy. Even now these words threaten to blow me headlong into the bottomless abyss of darkness. Has such a hateful thing come out of a human mouth ever before? Have such cursed words ever struck a human ear, even once? Even once such a . . . (A sudden cry of scorn.) At these words the robber himself turned pale. "Kill him," she cried, clinging to his arms. Looking hard at her, he answered neither yes or no . . . but hardly had I thought about his answer before she had been knocked down into the bamboo leaves. (Again a cry of scorn.) Quietly folding his arms, he looked at me and said, "What will you do with her? Kill her or save her? You have only to nod. Kill her?" For these words alone I would like to pardon his crime.

While I hesitated, she shrieked and ran into the depths of the grove. The robber instantly snatched at her, but he failed even to grasp her sleeve.

After she ran away, he took up my sword, and my bow and arrows. With a single stroke he cut one of my bonds. I remember his mumbling, "My fate is next." Then he disappeared from the grove. All was silent after that. No, I heard someone crying. Untying the rest of my bonds, I listened carefully, and I noticed that it was my own crying. (Long silence.)

I raised my exhausted body from the root of the cedar. In front of me there was shining the small sword which my wife had dropped. I took it up and stabbed my breast. A bloody lump rose to my mouth, but I didn't feel any pain. When my breast grew cold, everything was as silent as the dead in their graves. What profound silence! Not a single bird-note was heard in the sky over this grave in the hollow of the mountains. Only a lonely light lingered on the cedars and mountains. By and by the light gradually grew fainter, till the cedars and bamboo were

---

[2] *Kwannon:* Japanese name of the Buddhist goddess of mercy.

lost to view. Lying there, I was enveloped in deep silence.

Then someone crept up to me. I tried to see who it was. But darkness had already been gathering round me. Someone . . . that someone drew the small sword softly out of my breast in its invisible hand. At the same time once more blood flowed into my mouth. And once and for all I sank down into the darkness of space.

ISAAC BABEL

Di Grasso

A Tale of Odessa

Translated by Walter Morison

I was fourteen, and of the undauntable fellowship of dealers in theater tickets. My boss was a tricky customer with a permanently screwed-up eye and enormous silky handle bars; Nick Schwarz was his name. I came under his sway in that unhappy year when the Italian Opera flopped in Odessa. Taking a lead from the critics on the local paper, our impresario decided not to import Anselmi[1] and Tito Ruffo[2] as guest artistes but to make do with a good stock company. For this he was sorely punished; he went bankrupt, and we with him. We were promised Chaliapin[3] to straighten out our affairs, but Chaliapin wanted three thousand a performance; so instead we had the Sicilian tragedian Di Grasso with his troupe. They arrived at the hotel in peasant carts crammed with children, cats, cages in which Italian birds hopped and skipped. Casting an eye over this gypsy crew, Nick Schwarz opined:

"Children, this stuff won't sell."

When he had settled in, the tragedian made his way to the market with a bag. In the evening he arrived at the theater with another bag. Hardly fifty people had turned up.

We tried selling tickets at half-price, but there were no takers.

That evening they staged a Sicilian folk drama, a tale as commonplace as the change from night to day and vice versa. The daughter of a rich peasant pledges her troth to a shepherd. She is faithful to him till one day there drives out from the city a young slicker in a velvet waistcoat. Passing the time of day with the new arrival, the maiden giggled in all the wrong places and fell silent when she shouldn't have. As he listened to them, the shepherd twisted his head this way and that like a startled bird. During the whole of the first act he kept flattening himself against walls, dashing off somewhere, his pants flapping, and on his return gazing wildly about.

"This stuff stinks," said Nick Schwarz in the intermission. "Only place it might go down is some dump like Kremenchug."

The intermission was designed to give the maiden time to grow ripe for betrayal. In the second act we just couldn't recognize her: she behaved insufferably, her thoughts were clearly elsewhere, and she lost no time in handing the shepherd back his ring. Thereupon he led her over to a poverty-stricken but brightly painted image of the Holy Virgin, and said in his Sicilian patois:

"Signora," said he in a low voice, turning away, "the Holy Virgin desires you to give

[1] *Anselmi:* Giuseppe Anselmi (1876–1929), Italian tenor.
[2] *Tito Ruffo:* or Titta Ruffo (1878–1953), Italian baritone.
[3] *Chaliapin:* Feodor Chaliapin (1873–1938), Russian bass.

me a hearing. To Giovanni, the fellow from the city, the Holy Virgin will grant as many women as he can cope with; but I need none save you. The Virgin Mary, our stainless intercessor, will tell you exactly the same thing if you ask Her."

The maiden stood with her back to the painted wooden image. As she listened she kept impatiently tapping her foot.

In the third act Giovanni, the city slicker, met his fate. He was having a shave at the village barber's, his powerful male legs thrust out all over the front of the stage. Beneath the Sicilian sun the pleats in his waistcoat gleamed. The scene represented a village fair. In a far corner stood the shepherd; silent he stood there amid the carefree crowd. First he hung his head; then he raised it, and beneath the weight of his attentive and burning gaze Giovanni started stirring and fidgeting in his barber chair, till pushing the barber aside he leaped to his feet. In a voice shaking with passion he demanded that the policeman should remove from the village square all persons of a gloomy and suspicious aspect. The shepherd —the part was played by Di Grasso himself— stood there lost in thought; then he gave a smile, soared into the air, sailed across the stage, plunged down on Giovanni's shoulders, and having bitten through the latter's throat, began, growling and squinting, to suck blood from the wound. Giovanni collapsed, and the curtain, falling noiselessly and full of menace, hid from us killed and killer. Waiting for no more, we dashed to the box office in Theater Lane, which was to open next day, Nick Schwarz beating the rest by a short neck. Came the dawn, and with it the *Odessa News* informed the few people who had been at the theater that they had seen the most remarkable actor of the century.

On this visit Di Grasso played *King Lear, Othello, Civil Death,* Turgenev's *The Parasite,* confirming with every word and every gesture that there is more justice in outbursts of noble passion than in all the joyless rules that run the world.

Tickets for these shows were snapped up at five times face value. Scouting round for ticket-traders, would-be purchasers found them at the inn, yelling their heads off, purple, vomiting a harmless sacrilege.

A pink and dusty sultriness was injected into Theater Lane. Shopkeepers in felt slippers bore green bottles of wine and barrels of olives out onto the pavement. In tubs outside the shops macaroni seethed in foaming water, and the steam from it melted in the distant skies. Old women in men's boots dealt in seashells and souvenirs, pursuing hesitant purchasers with loud cries. Moneyed Jews with beards parted down the middle and combed to either side would drive up to the Northern Hotel and tap discreetly on the doors of fat women with raven hair and little mustaches, Di Grasso's actresses. All were happy in Theater Lane; all, that is, save for one person. I was that person. In those days catastrophe was approaching me: at any moment my father might miss the watch I had taken without his permission and pawned to Nick Schwarz. Having had the gold turnip long enough to get use to it, and being a man who replaced tea as his morning drink by Bessarabian wine, Nick Schwarz, even with his money back, could still not bring himself to return the watch to me. Such was his character. And my father's character differed in no wise from his. Hemmed in by these two characters, I sorrowfully watched other people enjoying themselves. Nothing remained for me but to run away to Constantinople. I had made all the arrangements with the second engineer of the S.S. *Duke of Kent,* but before embarking on the deep I decided to say goodbye to Di Grasso. For the last time he was playing the shepherd who is swung aloft by an incomprehensible power. In the audience were all the Italian colony, with the bald but shapely consul at their head. There were fidgety Greeks and bearded externs with their gaze fastened fanatically upon some point invisible to all other mortals; there was the long-armed

Utochkin. Nick Schwarz had even brought his missis, in a violet shawl with a fringe; a woman with all the makings of a grenadier she was, stretching right out to the steppes, and with a sleepy little crumpled face at the far end. When the curtain fell this face was drenched in tears.

"Now you see what love means," she said to Nick as they were leaving the theater.

Stomping ponderously, Madam Schwarz moved along Langeron Street; tears rolled from her fishlike eyes, and the shawl with the fringe shuddered on her obese shoulders. Dragging her mannish soles, rocking her head, she reckoned up, in a voice that made the street re-echo, the women who got on well with their husbands.

" 'Ducky' they're called by their husbands; 'sweetypie' they're called . . ."

The cowed Nick walked along by his wife, quietly blowing on his silky mustaches. From force of habit I followed on behind, sobbing. During a momentary pause Madam Schwarz heard my sobs and turned around.

"See here," she said to her husband, her fisheyes agoggle, "may I not die a beautiful death if you don't give the boy his watch back!"

Nick froze, mouth agape; then came to and, giving me a vicious pinch, thrust the watch at me sideways.

"What can I expect of him," the coarse and tear-muffled voice of Madam Schwarz wailed disconsolately as it moved off into the distance, "what can I expect but beastliness today and beastliness tomorrow? I ask you, how long is a woman supposed to put up with it?

They reached the corner and turned into Pushkin Street. I stood there clutching the watch, alone; and suddenly, with a distinctness such as I had never before experienced, I saw the columns of the Municipal Building soaring up into the heights, the gas-lit foliage of the boulevard, Pushkin's[4] bronze head touched by the dim gleam of the moon; saw for the first time the things surrounding me as they really were: frozen in silence and ineffably beautiful.

---

[4] Pushkin: Alexander Pushkin (1799–1837), Russian writer.

JEAN TOOMER

Theater

Life of nigger alleys, of pool rooms and restaurants and near-beer saloons soaks into the walls of Howard Theater and sets them throbbing jazz songs. Black-skinned, they dance and shout above the tick and trill of white-walled buildings. At night, they open doors to people who come in to stamp their feet and shout. At night, road-shows volley songs into the mass-heart of black people. Songs soak the walls and seep out to the nigger life of alleys and near-beer saloons, of the Poodle Dog and Black Bear cabarets. Afternoons, the house is dark, and the walls are sleeping singers until rehearsal begins. Or until John comes within them. Then they start throbbing to a subtle syncopation. And the space-dark air grows softly luminous.

John is the manager's brother. He is seated at the center of the theater, just before rehearsal. Light streaks down upon him from a window high above. One half his face is orange in it. One half his face is in shadow. The soft glow of the house rushes to, and compacts about, the shaft of light. John's mind coincides with the shaft of light. Thoughts rush to, and compact about it. Life of the house and of the slowly awakening stage swirls to the body of John, and thrills it. John's body is separate from the thoughts that pack his mind.

Stage-lights, soft, as if they shine through clear pink fingers. Beneath them, hid by the shadow of a set, Dorris. Other chorus girls drift in. John feels them in the mass. And as if his own body were the mass-heart of a black audience listening to them singing, he wants to stamp his feet and shout. His mind, contained above desires of his body, singles the girls out, and tries to trace origins and plot destinies.

A pianist slips into the pit and improvises jazz. The walls awake. Arms of the girls, and their limbs, which . . jazz, jazz . . by lifting up their tight street skirts they set free, jab the air and clog the floor in rhythm to the music. (Lift your skirts, Baby, and talk t papa!) Crude, individualized, and yet . . monotonous. . .

John: Soon the director will herd you, my full-lipped, distant beauties, and tame you, and blunt your sharp thrusts in loosely suggestive movements, appropriate to Broadway. (O dance!) Soon the audience will paint your dusk faces white, and call you beautiful. (O dance!) Soon I. . . (O dance!) I'd like. . .

Girls laugh and shout. Sing discordant snatches of other jazz songs. Whirl with loose passion into the arms of passing show-men.

John: Too thick. Too easy. Too monotonous. Her whom I'd love I'd leave before she knew that I was with her. Her? Which? (O dance!) I'd like to. . .

Girls dance and sing. Men clap. The walls sing and press inward. They press the men and girls, they press John towards a center of physical ecstasy. Go to it, Baby! Fan yourself, and feed your papa! Put . . nobody lied . . and take . . when they said I cried over you. No lie! The glitter and color of stacked scenes, the gilt and brass and crimson of the house, converge towards a center of physical ecstasy. John's feet and torso and his blood press in. He wills thought to rid his mind of passion.

"All right, girls. Alaska. Miss Reynolds, please."

The director wants to get the rehearsal through with.

The girls line up. John sees the front row: dancing ponies. The rest are in shadow. The leading lady fits loosely in the front. Lack-life, monotonous. "One, two, three—" Music starts. The song is somewhere where it will not strain the leading lady's throat. The dance is somewhere where it will not strain the girls. Above the staleness, one dancer throws herself into it. Dorris. John sees her. Her hair, crisp-curled, is bobbed. Bushy, black hair bobbing about her lemon-colored face. Her lips are curiously full, and very red. Her limbs in silk purple stockings are lovely. John feels them. Desires her. Holds off.

John: Stage-door johnny; chorus-girl. No, that would be all right. Dictie, educated, stuck-up; show-girl. Yep. Her suspicion would be stronger than her passion. It wouldnt work. Keep her loveliness. Let her go.

Dorris sees John and knows that he is looking at her. Her own glowing is too rich a thing to let her feel the slimness of his diluted passion.

"Who's that?" she asks her dancing partner.

"Th manager's brother. Dictie. Nothin doin, hon."

Dorris tosses her head and dances for him until she feels she has him. Then, withdrawing disdainfully, she flirts with the director.

Dorris: Nothin doin? How come? Aint I as good as him? Couldnt I have got an education if I'd wanted one? Dont I know respectable folks, lots of em, in Philadelphia and New York and Chicago? Aint I had men as good as him? Better. Doctors an lawyers. Whats a manager's brother, anyhow?

Two steps back, and two steps front.

"Say, Mame, where do you get that stuff?"

"Whatshmean, Dorris?"

"If you two girls cant listen to what I'm telling you, I know where I can get some who can. Now listen."

Mame: Go to hell, you black bastard.

Dorris: Whats eatin at him, anyway?

"Now follow me in this, you girls. Its three counts to the right, three counts to the left, and then you shimmy—"

John: —and then you shimmy. I'll bet she can. Some good cabaret, with rooms upstairs. And what in hell do you think you'd get from it? Youre going wrong. Here's right: get her to herself—(Christ, but how she'd bore you after the first five minutes)—not if you get her right she wouldnt. Touch her, I mean. To herself—in some room perhaps. Some cheap, dingy bedroom. Hell no. Cant be done. But the point is, brother John, it can be done. Get her to herself somewhere, anywhere. Go down in yourself—and she'd be calling you all sorts of asses while you were in the process of going down. Hold em, bud. Cant be done. Let her go. (Dance and I'll love you!) And keep her loveliness.

"All right now, Chicken Chaser. Dorris and girls. Where's Dorris? I told you to stay on the stage, didnt I? Well? Now thats enough. All right. All right there, Professor? All right. One, two, three—"

Dorris swings to the front. The line of girls, four deep, blurs within the shadow of suspended scenes. Dorris wants to dance. The director feels that and steps to one side. He smiles, and picks her for a leading lady, one of these days. Odd ends of stage-men emerge from the wings, and stare and clap. A crap game in the alley suddenly ends. Black faces crowd the rear stage doors. The girls, catching joy from Dorris, whip up within the footlights' glow. They forget set steps; they find their own. The director forgets to bawl them out. Dorris dances.

John: Her head bobs to Broadway. Dance from yourself. Dance! O just a little more.

Dorris' eyes burn across the space of seats to him.

Dorris: I bet he can love. Hell, he cant love. He's too skinny. His lips are too skinny. He wouldnt love me anyway, only for that. But

I'd get a pair of silk stockings out of it. Red silk. I got purple. Cut it, kid. You cant win him to respect you that away. He wouldnt anyway. Maybe he would. Maybe he'd love. I've heard em say that men who look like him (what does he look like?) will marry if they love. O will you love me? And give me kids, and a home, and everything? (I'd like to make your nest, and honest, hon, I wouldnt run out on you.) You will if I make you. Just watch me.

Dorris dances. She forgets her tricks. She dances.

Glorious songs are the muscles of her limbs.

And her singing is of canebrake loves and mangrove feastings.

The walls press in, singing. Flesh of a throbbing body, they press close to John and Dorris. They close them in. John's heart beats tensely against her dancing body. Walls press his mind within his heart. And then, the shaft of light goes out the window high above him. John's mind sweeps up to follow it. Mind pulls him upward into dream.   Dorris dances. . . John dreams:

Dorris is dressed in a loose black gown splashed with lemon ribbons. Her feet taper long and slim from trim ankles. She waits for him just inside the stage door. John, collar and tie colorful and flaring, walks towards the stage door. There are no trees in the alley. But his feet feel as though they step on autumn leaves whose rustle has been pressed out of them by the passing of a million satin slippers. The air is sweet with roasting chestnuts, sweet with bonfires of old leaves. John's melancholy is a deep thing that seals all senses but his eyes, and makes him whole.

Dorris knows that he is coming. Just at the right moment she steps from the door, as if there were no door. Her face is tinted like the autumn alley. Of old flowers, or of a southern canefield, her perfume. "Glorious Dorris." So his eyes speak. And their sadness is too deep for sweet untruth. She barely touches his arm. They glide off with footfalls softened on the leaves, the old leaves powdered by a million satin slippers.

They are in a room. John knows nothing of it. Only, that the flesh and blood of Dorris are its walls. Singing walls. Lights, soft, as if they shine through clear pink fingers. Soft lights, and warm.

John reaches for a manuscript of his, and reads. Dorris, who has no eyes, has eyes to understand him. He comes to a dancing scene. The scene is Dorris. She dances. Dorris dances. Glorious Dorris. Dorris whirls, whirls, dances. . .

                Dorris dances.
The pianist crashes a bumper chord. The whole stage claps. Dorris, flushed, looks quick at John. His whole face is in shadow. She seeks for her dance in it. She finds it a dead thing in the shadow which is his dream. She rushes from the stage. Falls down the steps into her dressing-room. Pulls her hair. Her eyes, over a floor of tears, stare at the whitewashed ceiling. (Smell of dry paste, and paint, and soiled clothing.) Her pal comes in. Dorris flings herself into the old safe arms, and cries bitterly.

"I told you nothin doin," is what Mame says to comfort her.

WILLIAM FAULKNER

Wash

Sutpen stood above the pallet bed on which the mother and child lay. Between the shrunken planking of the wall the early sunlight fell in long pencil strokes, breaking upon his straddled legs and upon the riding whip in his hand, and lay across the still shape of the mother, who lay looking up at him from still, inscrutable, sullen eyes, the child at her side wrapped in a piece of dingy though clean cloth. Behind them an old Negro woman squatted beside the rough hearth where a meager fire smoldered.

"Well, Milly," Sutpen said, "too bad you're not a mare. Then I could give you a decent stall in the stable."

Still the girl on the pallet did not move. She merely continued to look up at him without expression, with a young, sullen, inscrutable face still pale from recent travail. Sutpen moved, bringing into the splintered pencils of sunlight the face of a man of sixty. He said quietly to the squatting Negress, "Griselda foaled this morning."

"Horse or mare?" the Negress said.

"A horse. A damned fine colt. . . . What's this?" He indicated the pallet with the hand which held the whip.

"That un's a mare, I reckon."

"Hah," Sutpen said. " A damned fine colt. Going to be the spit and image of old Rob Roy when I rode him North in '61. Do you remember?"

"Yes, Marster."

"Hah." He glanced back towards the pallet. None could have said if the girl still watched him or not. Again his whip hand indicated the pallet. "Do whatever they need with whatever we've got to do it with." He went out, passing out the crazy doorway and stepping down into the rank weeds (there yet leaned rusting against the corner of the porch the scythe which Wash had borrowed from him three months ago to cut them with) where his horse waited, where Wash stood holding the reins.

When Colonel Sutpen rode away to fight the Yankees, Wash did not go. "I'm looking after the Kernel's place and niggers," he would tell all who asked him and some who had not asked—a gaunt, malaria-ridden man with pale, questioning eyes, who looked about thirty-five, though it was known that he had not only a daughter but an eight-year-old granddaughter as well. This was a lie, as most of them—the few remaining men between eighteen and fifty—to whom he told it, knew, though there were some who believed that he himself really believed it, though even these believed that he had better sense than to put it to the test with Mrs. Sutpen or the Sutpen slaves. Knew better or was just too lazy and shiftless to try it, they said, knowing that his sole connection with the Sutpen plantation lay in the fact that for years now Colonel Sutpen had allowed him to squat in a crazy shack on a slough in the river bottom on the Sutpen place, which Sutpen had built for a fishing lodge in his bachelor days and which had since fallen in dilapidation from disuse, so that now it looked like an aged or sick wild beast crawled terrifically there to drink in the act of dying.

The Sutpen slaves themselves heard of his statement. They laughed. It was not the first time they had laughed at him, calling him white trash behind his back. They began to ask him themselves, in groups, meeting him in the faint road which led up from the slough and the old fish camp, "Why ain't you at de war, white man?"

Pausing, he would look about the ring of black faces and white eyes and teeth behind which derision lurked. "Because I got a daughter and family to keep," he said. "Git out of my road, niggers."

"Niggers?" they repeated; "niggers?" laughing now. "Who him, calling us niggers?"

"Yes," he said. "I ain't got no niggers to look after my folks if I was gone."

"Nor nothing else but dat shack down yon dat Cunnel wouldn't *let* none of us live in."

Now he cursed them; sometimes he rushed at them, snatching up a stick from the ground while they scattered before him, yet seeming to surround him still with that black laughing, derisive, evasive, inescapable, leaving him panting and impotent and raging. Once it happened in the very back yard of the big house itself. This was after bitter news had come down from the Tennessee mountains and from Vicksburg, and Sherman had passed through the plantation, and most of the Negroes had followed him. Almost everything else had gone with the Federal troops, and Mrs. Sutpen had sent word to Wash that he could have the scuppernongs ripening in the arbor in the back yard. This time it was a house servant, one of the few Negroes who remained; this time the Negress had to retreat up the kitchen steps, where she turned. "Stop right dar, white man. Stop right whar you is. You ain't never crossed dese steps whilst Cunnel here, and you ain't ghy' do hit now."

This was true. But there was this of a kind of pride: he had never tried to enter the big house, even though he believed that if he had, Sutpen would have received him, permitted him. "But I ain't going to give no black nigger the chance to tell me I can't go nowhere," he said to himself. "I ain't even going to give Kernel the chance to have to cuss a nigger on my account." This, though he and Sutpen had spent more than one afternoon together on those rare Sundays when there would be no company in the house. Perhaps his mind knew that it was because Sutpen had nothing else to do, being a man who could not bear his own company. Yet the fact remained that the two of them would spend whole afternoons in the scuppernong arbor, Sutpen in the hammock and Wash squatting against a post, a pail of cistern water between them, taking drink for drink from the same demijohn. Meanwhile on weekdays he would see the fine figure of the man—they were the same age almost to a day, though neither of them (perhaps because Wash had a grandchild while Sutpen's son was a youth in school) ever thought of himself as being so—on the fine figure of the black stallion, galloping about the plantation. For that moment his heart would be quiet and proud. It would seem to him that that world in which Negroes, whom the Bible told him had been created and cursed by God to be brute and vassal to all men of white skin, were better found and housed and even clothed than he and his; that world in which he sensed always about him mocking echoes of black laughter was but a dream and an illusion, and that the actual world was this one across which his own lonely apotheosis seemed to gallop on the black thoroughbred, thinking how the Book said also that all men were created in the image of God and hence all men made the same image in God's eyes at least; so that he could say, as though speaking of himself, "A fine proud man. If God Himself was to come down and ride the natural earth, that's what He would aim to look like."

Sutpen returned in 1865, on the black stallion. He seemed to have aged ten years. His son had vanished the same winter in which his wife had died. He returned with his citation for gallantry from the hand of General Lee to a ruined plantation, where for a year now his daughter had subsisted partially on the meager bounty of the man to whom fifteen years ago he had granted permission to live in that tumbledown fishing camp whose very existence he had at the time forgotten. Wash was there to meet him, unchanged: still gaunt, still ageless, with his pale, questioning gaze, his air diffident, a little servile, a little familiar. "Well, Kernel," Wash said, "they kilt us but they ain't whupped us yit, air they?"

That was the tenor of their conversation for the next five years. It was inferior whiskey which they drank now together from a stoneware jug, and it was not in the scuppernong arbor. It was in the rear of the little store which Sutpen managed to set up on the high-road: a frame shelved room where, with Wash for clerk and porter, he dispensed kerosene and staple foodstuffs and stale gaudy candy and cheap beads and ribbons to Negroes or poor whites of Wash's own kind, who came afoot or on gaunt mules to haggle tediously for dimes and quarters with a man who at one time could gallop (the black stallion was still alive; the stable in which his jealous get lived was in better repair than the house where the master himself lived) for ten miles across his own fertile land and who had led troops gallantly in battle; until Sutpen in fury would empty the store, close and lock the doors from the inside. Then he and Wash would repair to the rear and the jug. But the talk would not be quiet now, as when Sutpen lay in the hammock, delivering an arrogant monologue while Wash squatted guffawing against his post. They both sat now, though Sutpen had the single chair while Wash used whatever box or keg was handy, and even this for just a little while, because soon Sutpen would reach that stage of impotent and furious undefeat in which he would rise, swaying and plunging, and declare again that he would take his pistol and the black stallion and ride single-handed into Washington and kill Lincoln, dead now, and Sherman, now a private citizen. "Kill them!" he would shout. "Shoot them down like the dogs they are—"

"Sho, Kernel; sho, Kernel," Wash would say, catching Sutpen as he fell. Then he would commandeer the first passing wagon or, lacking that, he would walk the mile to the nearest neighbor and borrow one and return and carry Sutpen home. He entered the house now. He had been doing so for a long time, taking Sutpen home in whatever borrowed wagon might be, talking him into locomotion with cajoling murmurs as though he were a horse, a stallion himself. The daughter would meet them and hold open the door without a word. He would carry his burden through the once white formal entrance, surmounted by a fanlight imported piece by piece from Europe and with a board now nailed over a missing pane, across a velvet carpet from which all nap was now gone, and up a formal stairs, now but a fading ghost of bare boards between two strips of fading paint, and into the bedroom. It would be dusk by now, and he would let his burden sprawl onto the bed and undress it and then he would sit quietly in a chair beside. After a time the daughter would come to the door. "We're all right now," he would tell her. "Don't you worry none, Miss Judith."

Then it would become dark, and after a while he would lie down on the floor beside the bed, though not to sleep, because after a time—sometimes before midnight—the man on the bed would stir and groan and then speak. "Wash?"

"Hyer I am, Kernel. You go back to sleep. We ain't whupped yit, air we? Me and you kin do hit."

Even then he had already seen the ribbon about his granddaughter's waist. She was now fifteen, already mature, after the early way of her kind. He knew where the ribbon came from; he had been seeing it and its kind daily for three years, even if she had lied about where she got it, which she did not, at once bold, sullen, and fearful.

"Sho now," he said. "Ef Kernel wants to give hit to you, I hope you minded to thank him."

His heart was quiet, even when he saw the dress, watching her secret, defiant, frightened face when she told him that Miss Judith, the daughter, had helped her to make it. But he was quite grave when he approached Sutpen after they closed the store that afternoon, following the other to the rear.

"Get the jug," Sutpen directed.

"Wait," Wash said. "Not yit for a minute."

Neither did Sutpen deny the dress. "What about it?" he said.

But Wash met his arrogant stare; he spoke quietly. "I've knowed you for going on twenty years. I ain't never yit denied to do what you told me to do. And I'm a man nigh sixty. And she ain't nothing but a fifteen-year-old gal."

"Meaning that I'd harm a girl? I, a man as old as you are?"

"If you was ara other man, I'd say you was as old as me. And old or no old, I wouldn't let her keep that dress nor nothing else that come from your hand. But you are different."

"How different?" But Wash merely looked at him with his pale, questioning, sober eyes. "So that's why you are afraid of me?"

Now Wash's gaze no longer questioned. It was tranquil, serene. "I ain't afraid. Because you air brave. It ain't that you were a brave man at one minute or day of your life and got a paper to show hit from General Lee. But you air brave, the same as you air alive and breathing. That's where hit's different. Hit don't need no ticket from nobody to tell me that. And I know that whatever you handle or tech, whether hit's a regiment of men or a ignorant gal or just a hound dog, that you will make hit right."

Now it was Sutpen who looked away, turning suddenly, brusquely. "Get the jug," he said sharply.

"Sho, Kernel," Wash said.

So on that Sunday dawn two years later, having watched the Negro midwife, whom he had walked three miles to fetch, enter the crazy door beyond which his granddaughter lay wailing, his heart was still quiet though concerned. He knew what they had been saying—the Negroes in cabins about the land, the white men who loafed all day long about the store, watching quietiy the three of them: Sutpen, himself, his granddaughter with her air of brazen and shrinking defiance as her condition become daily more and more obvious, like three actors that came and went upon a stage. "I know what they say to one another," he thought. "I can almost hyear them: *Wash Jones has fixed old Sutpen at last. Hit taken him twenty years, but he has done hit at last.*"

It would be dawn after a while, though not yet. From the house, where the lamp shone dim beyond the warped door frame, his granddaughter's voice came steadily as though run by a clock, while thinking went slowly and terrifically, fumbling, involved somehow with a sound of galloping hooves, until there broke suddenly free in mid-gallop the fine proud figure of the man on the fine proud stallion, galloping; and then that at which thinking fumbled, broke free too and quite clear, not in justification nor even explanation, but as the apotheosis, lonely, explicable, beyond all fouling by human touch: "He is bigger than all them Yankees that kilt his son and his wife and taken his niggers and ruined his land, bigger than this hyer durn country that he fit for and that has denied him into keeping a little country store; bigger than the denial which hit helt to his lips like the bitter cup in the Book. And how could I have lived this nigh to him for twenty years without being teched and changed by him? Maybe I ain't as big as him and maybe I ain't done none of the galloping. But at least I done been drug along. Me and him kin do hit, if so be he will show me what he aims for me to do."

Then it was dawn. Suddenly he could see the house, and the old Negress in the door looking at him. Then he realized that his granddaughter's voice had ceased. "It's a girl," the Negress said. "You can go tell him if you want to." She reëntered the house.

"A girl," he repeated; "a girl"; in astonishment, hearing the galloping hooves, seeing the proud galloping figure emerge again. He seemed to watch it pass, galloping through avatars which marked the accumulation of years, time, to the climax where it galloped beneath a brandished sabre and a shot-torn flag rushing down a sky in color like thunderous sulphur, thinking for the first time in his life that perhaps Sutpen was on old man like himself. "Gittin a gal," he thought in that astonishment; then he thought with the pleased surprise of a child: "Yes, sir. Be dawg if I ain't lived to be a great-grandpaw after all."

He entered the house. He moved clumsily, on tiptoe, as if he no longer lived there, as if the infant which had just drawn breath and cried in light had dispossessed him, be it of his own blood too though it might. But even above the pallet he could see little save the blur of his granddaughter's exhausted face. Then the Negress squatting at the hearth spoke, "You better gawn tell him if you going to. Hit's daylight now."

But this was not necessary. He had no more than turned the corner of the porch where the scythe leaned which he had borrowed three months ago to clear away the weeds through which he walked, when Sutpen himself rode up on the old stallion. He did not wonder how Sutpen had got the word. He took it for granted that this was what had brought the other out at this hour on Sunday morning, and he stood while the other dismounted, and he took the reins from Sutpen's hand, an expression on his gaunt face almost imbecile with a kind of weary triumph, saying, "Hit's a gal, Kernel. I be dawg if you ain't as old as I am —" until Sutpen passed him and entered the house. He stood there with the reins in his hand and heard Sutpen cross the floor to the pallet. He heard what Sutpen said, and something seemed to stop dead in him before going on.

The sun was now up, the swift sun of Mississippi latitudes, and it seemed to him that he stood beneath a strange sky, in a strange scene, familiar only as things are familiar in dream, like the dreams of falling to one who has never climbed. "I kain't have heard what I thought I heard," he thought quietly. "I know I kain't." Yet the voice, the familiar voice which had said the words was still speaking, talking now to the old Negress about a colt foaled that morning. "That's why he was up so early," he thought. "That was hit. Hit ain't me and mine. Hit ain't even hisn that got him outen bed."

Sutpen emerged. He descended into the weeds, moving with that heavy deliberation which would have been haste when he was younger. He had not yet looked full at Wash. He said, "Dicey will stay and tend to her. You better—" Then he seemed to see Wash facing him and paused. "What?" he said.

"You said—" To his own ears Wash's voice sounded flat and ducklike, like a deaf man's. "You said if she was a mare, you could give her a good stall in the stable."

"Well?" Sutpen said. His eyes widened and narrowed, almost like a man's fists flexing and shutting, as Wash began to advance towards him, stooping a little. Very astonishment kept Sutpen still for the moment, watching that man whom in twenty years he had no more known to make any motion save at command than he had the horse which he rode. Again his eyes narrowed and widened; without moving he seemed to rear suddenly upright. "Stand back," he said suddenly and sharply. "Don't you touch me."

"I'm going to tech you, Kernel," Wash said in that flat, quiet, almost soft voice, advancing.

Sutpen raised the hand which held the riding whip; the old Negress peered around the crazy door with her black gargoyle face of a worn gnome. "Stand back, Wash," Sutpen said. Then he struck. The old Negress leaped down into the weeds with the agility of a goat and fled. Sutpen slashed Wash again across the face with the whip, striking him to his knees. When Wash rose and advanced once more he held in his hands the scythe which he had borrowed from Sutpen three months ago and which Sutpen would never need again.

When he reëntered the house his granddaughter stirred on the pallet bed and called his name fretfully. "What was that?" she said.

"What was what, honey?"

"That ere racket out there."

" 'Twarn't nothing," he said gently. He knelt and touched her hot forehead clumsily. "Do you want ara thing?"

"I want a sup of water," she said querulously. "I been laying here wanting a sup of water a long time but don't nobody care enough to pay me no mind."

"Sho now," he said soothingly. He rose stiffly and fetched the dipper of water and raised her head to drink and laid her back and watched her turn to the child with an absolutely stonelike face. But a moment later he saw that she was crying quietly. "Now, now," he said, "I wouldn't do that. Old Dicey says hit's a right fine gal. Hit's all right now. Hit's all over now. Hit ain't no need to cry now."

But she continued to cry quietly, almost sullenly, and he rose again and stood uncomfortably above the pallet for a time, thinking as he had thought when his own wife lay so and then his daughter in turn: "Women. Hit's a mystry to me. They seem to want em, and yit when they git em they cry about hit. Hit's a mystry to me. To ara man." Then he moved away and drew a chair up to the window and sat down.

Through all that long, bright, sunny forenoon he sat at the window, waiting. Now and then he rose and tiptoed to the pallet. But his granddaughter slept now, her face sullen and calm and weary, the child in the crook of her arm. Then he returned to the chair and sat again, waiting, wondering why it took them so long, until he remembered that it was Sunday. He was sitting there at mid-afternoon when a half-grown white boy came around the corner of the house upon the body and

gave a choked cry and looked up and glared for a mesmerized instant at Wash in the window before he turned and fled. Then Wash rose and tiptoed again to the pallet.

The granddaughter was awake now, wakened perhaps by the boy's cry without hearing it. "Milly," he said, "air you hungry?" She didn't answer, turning her face away. He built up the fire on the hearth and cooked the food which he had brought home the day before: fatback it was, and cold corn pone; he poured water into the stale coffee pot and heated it. But she would not eat when he carried the plate to her, so he ate himself, quietly, alone, and left the dishes as they were and returned to the window.

Now he seemed to sense, feel, the men who would be gathering with horses and guns and dogs—the curious, and the vengeful: men of Sutpen's own kind, who had made the company about Sutpen's table in the time when Wash himself had yet to approach nearer to the house than the scuppernong arbor—men who had also shown the lesser ones how to fight in battle, who maybe also had signed papers from the generals saying that they were among the first of the brave; who had also galloped in the old days arrogant and proud on the fine horses across the fine plantations—symbols also of admiration and hope; instruments too of despair and grief.

That was who they would expect him to run from. It seemed to him that he had no more to run from than he had to run to. If he ran, he would merely be fleeing one set of bragging and evil shadows for another just like them, since they were all of a kind throughout all the earth which he knew, and he old, too old to flee far even if he were to flee. He could never escape them, no matter how much or how far he ran: a man going on sixty could not run that far. Not far enough to escape beyond the boundaries of earth where such men lived, set the order and the rule of living. It seemed to him that he now saw for the first time, after five years, how it was that Yankees or any other living armies had managed to whip them: the gallant, the proud, the brave; the acknowledged and chosen best among them all to carry courage and honor and pride. Maybe if he had gone to the war with them he would have discovered them soonor. But if he had discovered them sooner, what would he have done with his life since? How could he have borne to remember for five years what his life had been before?

Now it was getting toward sunset. The child had been crying; when he went to the pallet he saw his granddaughter nursing it, her face still bemused, sullen, inscrutable. "Air you hungry yit?" he said.

"I don't want nothing."

"You ought to eat."

This time she did not answer at all, looking down at the child. He returned to his chair and found that the sun had set. "Hit kain't be much longer," he thought. He could feel them quite near now, the curious and the vengeful. He could even seem to hear what they were saying about him, the undercurrent of believing beyond the immediate fury: *Old Wash Jones he come a tumble at last. He thought he had Sutpen, but Sutpen fooled him. He thought he had Kernel where he would have to marry the gal or pay up. And Kernel refused.* "But I never expected that, Kernel!" he cried aloud, catching himself at the sound of his own voice, glancing quickly back to find his granddaughter watching him.

"Who you talking to now?" she said.

"Hit ain't nothing. I was just thinking and talked out before I knowed hit."

Her face was becoming indistinct again, again a sullen blur in the twilight. "I reckon so. I reckon you'll have to holler louder than that before he'll hear you, up yonder at that house. And I reckon you'll need to do more than holler before you get him down here too."

"Sho now," he said. "Don't you worry none." But already thinking was going smoothly on: "You know I never. You know how I ain't never expected or asked nothing from ara living man but what I expected from you. And

I never asked that. I didn't think hit would need. I said, *I don't need to. What need has a fellow like Wash Jones to question or doubt the man that General Lee himself says in a handwrote ticket that he was brave?* Brave," he thought. "Better if nara one of them had never rid back home in '65"; thinking *Better if his kind and mine too had never drawn the breath of life on this earth. Better that all who remain of us be blasted from the face of earth than that another Wash Jones should see his whole life shredded from him and shrivel away like a dried shuck thrown onto the fire.*

He ceased, became still. He heard the horses, suddenly and plainly; presently he saw the lantern and the movement of men, the glint of gun barrels, in its moving light. Yet he did not stir. It was quite dark now, and he listened to the voices and the sounds of underbrush as they surrounded the house. The lantern itself came on; its light fell upon the quiet body in the weeds and stopped, the horses tall and shadowy. A man descended and stooped in the lantern light, above the body. He held a pistol; he rose and faced the house. "Jones," he said.

"I'm here," Wash said quietly from the window. "That you, Major?"

"Come out."

"Sho," he said quietly. "I just want to see my granddaughter."

"We'll see to her. Come on out."

"Sho, Major. Just a minute."

"Show a light. Light your lamp."

"Sho. In just a minute." They could hear his voice retreat into the house, though they could not see him as he went swiftly to the crack in the chimney where he kept the butcher knife: the one thing in his slovenly life and house in which he took pride, since it was razor sharp. He approached the pallet, his granddaughter's voice:

"Who is it? Light the lamp, grandpaw."

"Hit won't need no light, honey. Hit won't take but a minute," he said, kneeling, fumbling toward her voice, whispering now.

"Where air you?"

"Right here," she said fretfully. "Where would I be? What is. . . ." His hand touched her face. "What is. . . . Grandpaw! Grand. . . ."

"Jones!" the sheriff said. "Come out of there!"

"In just a minute, Major," he said. Now he rose and moved swiftly. He knew where in the dark the can of kerosene was, just as he knew that it was full, since it was not two days ago that he had filled it at the store and held it there until he got a ride home with it, since the five gallons were heavy. There were still coals on the hearth; besides the crazy building itself was like tinder: the coals, the hearth, the walls exploding in a single blue glare. Against it the waiting men saw him in a wild instant springing toward them with the lifted scythe before the horses reared and whirled. They checked the horses and turned them back toward the glare, yet still in wild relief against it the gaunt figure ran toward them with lifted scythe.

"Jones!" the sheriff shouted. "Stop! Stop, or I'll shoot. Jones! *Jones!*" Yet still the gaunt, furious figure came on against the glare and roar of the flames. With the scythe lifted, it bore down upon them, upon the wild glaring eyes of the horses and the swinging glints of gun barrels, without any cry, any sound.

JORGE LUIS BORGES

The Lottery in Babylon

Translated by John M. Fein

Like all men in Babylon, I have been proconsul; like all, a slave. I have also known omnipotence, opprobrium, imprisonment. Look: the index finger on my right hand is missing. Look: through the rip in my cape you can see a vermilion tattoo on my stomach. It is the second symbol, Beth. This letter, on nights when the moon is full, gives me power over men whose mark is Gimmel, but it subordinates me to the men of Aleph, who on moonless nights owe obedience to those marked with Gimmel. In the half light of dawn, in a cellar, I have cut the jugular vein of sacred bulls before a black stone. During a lunar year I have been declared invisible. I shouted and they did not answer me; I stole bread and they did not behead me. I have known what the Greeks do not know, incertitude. In a bronze chamber, before the silent handkerchief of the strangler, hope has been faithful to me, as has panic in the river of pleasure. Heraclides Ponticus tells with amazement that Pythagoras remembered having been Pyrrhus and before that Euphorbus and before that some other mortal. In order to remember similar vicissitudes I do not need to have recourse to death or even to deception.

I owe this almost atrocious variety to an institution which other republics do not know or which operates in them in an imperfect and secret manner: the lottery. I have not looked into its history; I know that the wise men cannot agree. I know of its powerful purposes what a man who is not versed in astrology can know about the moon. I come from a dizzy land where the lottery is the basis of reality. Until today I have thought as little about it as I have about the conduct of indecipherable divinities or about my heart. Now, far from Babylon and its beloved customs, I think with a certain amount of amazement about the lottery and about the blasphemous conjectures which veiled men murmur in the twilight.

My father used to say that formerly—a matter of centuries, of years?—the lottery in Babylon was a game of plebeian character. He recounted (I don't know whether rightly) that barbers sold, in exchange for copper coins, squares of bone or of parchment adorned with symbols. In broad daylight a drawing took place. Those who won received silver coins without any other test of luck. The system was elementary, as you can see.

Naturally these "lotteries" failed. Their moral virtue was nil. They were not directed at all of man's faculties, but only at hope. In the face of public indifference, the merchants who founded these venal lotteries began to lose money. Someone tried a reform: The interpolation of a few unfavorable tickets in the list of favorable numbers. By means of this reform, the buyers of numbered squares ran the double risk of winning a sum and of paying a fine that could be considerable. This slight danger (for every thirty favorable numbers there was one unlucky one) awoke, as is natural, the interest of the public. The Babylonians threw themselves into the game. Those who did not acquire chances were considered pusillanimous, cowardly. In time, that justified disdain was doubled. Those who did not play were scorned, but also the losers who paid the fine were scorned. The Company (as it came to be known then) had to take care of the winners, who could not cash in their prizes if almost the total amount of the fines was unpaid. It started a lawsuit against the losers. The judge condemned them to pay the original fine and costs or spend several days in jail. All chose jail in order to defraud the Company. The bravado of a few is the source of the omnipotence of the Company and of its metaphysical and ecclesiastical power.

A little while afterward the lottery lists omitted the amounts of fines and limited themselves to publishing the days of imprisonment that each unfavorable number indicated. That laconic spirit, almost unnoticed at the time, was of capital importance. *It was the first appearance in the lottery of nonmonetary elements.* The success was tremendous. Urged by the clientele, the Company was obliged to increase the unfavorable numbers.

Everyone knows that the people of Babylon are fond of logic and even of symmetry. It was illogical for the lucky numbers to be computed in round coins and the unlucky ones in days and nights of imprisonment. Some moralists reasoned that the possession of money does not always determine happiness and that other forms of happiness are perhaps more direct.

Another concern swept the quarters of the poorer classes. The members of the college of priests multiplied their stakes and enjoyed all the vicissitudes of terror and hope; the poor (with reasonable or unavoidable envy) knew that they were excluded from that notoriously delicious rhythm. The just desire that all, rich and poor, should participate equally in the lottery, inspired an indignant agitation, the memory of which the years have not erased. Some obstinate people did not understand (or pretended not to understand) that it was a question of a new order, of a necessary historical stage. A slave stole a crimson ticket, which in the drawing credited him with the burning of his tongue. The legal code fixed that same penalty for the one who stole a ticket. Some Babylonians argued that he deserved the burning irons in his status of a thief; others, generously, that the executioner should apply it to him because chance had determined it that way. There were disturbances, there were lamentable drawings of blood, but the masses of Babylon finally imposed their will against the opposition of the rich. The people achieved amply its generous purposes. In the first place, it caused the Company to accept total power. (That unification was necessary, given the vastness and complexity of the new operations.) In the second place, it made the lottery secret, free and general. The mercenary sale of chances was abolished. Once initiated in the mysteries of Baal, every free man automatically participated in the sacred drawings, which took place in the labyrinths of the god every sixty nights and which determined his destiny until the next drawing. The consequences were incalculable. A fortunate play could bring about his promotion to the council of wise men or the imprisonment of an enemy (public or private) or finding, in the peaceful darkness of his room, the woman who begins to excite him and whom he never expected to see again. A bad play: mutilation, different kinds of infamy, death. At times one single fact—the vulgar murder of C, the mysterious apotheosis of B—was the happy solution of thirty or forty drawings. To combine the plays was difficult, but one must remember that the individuals of the Company were (and are) omnipotent and astute. In many cases the knowledge that certain happinesses were the simple product of chance would have diminished their virtue. To avoid that obstacle, the agents of the Company made use of the power of suggestion and magic. Their steps, their maneuverings, were secret. To find out about the intimate hopes and terrors of each individual, they had astrologists and spies. There were certain stone lions, there was a sacred latrine called Qaphqa, there were fissures in a dusty aqueduct which, according to general opinion, *led to the Company;* malignant or benevolent persons deposited information in these places. An alphabetical file collected these items of varying truthfulness.

Incredibly, there were complaints. The Company, with its usual discretion, did not answer directly. It preferred to scrawl in the rubbish of a mask factory a brief statement which now figures in the sacred scriptures. This doctrinal item observed that the lottery is an interpolation of chance in the order of the world and that to accept errors is not to contradict chance: it is to corroborate it. It likewise observed that those lions and that sacred receptacle, although not disavowed by the Company (which did not abandon the right to consult them), functioned without official guarantee.

This declaration pacified the public's restlessness. It also produced other effects, perhaps unforeseen by its writer. It deeply modified the spirit and the operations of the Company. I don't have much time left; they tell us that the ship is about to weigh anchor. But I shall try to explain it.

However unlikely it might seem, no one had tried out before then a general theory of chance. Babylonians are not very speculative. They revere the judgments of fate, they deliver to them their lives, their hopes, their panic, but it does not occur to them to investigate fate's labyrinthine laws nor the gyratory spheres which reveal it. Nevertheless, the *unofficial* declaration that I have mentioned inspired many discussions of judicial-mathematical character. From some one of them the following conjecture was born: If the lottery is an intensification of chance, a periodical infusion of chaos in the cosmos, would it not be right for chance to intervene in all stages of the drawing and not in one alone? Is it not ridiculous for chance to dictate someone's death and have the circumstances of that death—secrecy, publicity, the fixed time of an hour or a century—not subject to chance? These just scruples finally caused a considerable reform, whose complexities (aggravated by centuries' practice) only a few specialists understand, but which I shall try to summarize, at least in a symbolic way.

Let us imagine a first drawing, which decrees the death of a man. For its fulfillment one proceeds to another drawing, which proposes (let us say) nine possible executors. Of these executors, four can initiate a third drawing which will tell the name of the executioner, two can replace the adverse order with a fortunate one (finding a treasure, let us say), another will intensify the death penalty (that is, will make it infamous or enrich it with tortures), others can refuse to fulfill it. This is the symbolic scheme. In reality *the number of drawings is infinite.* No decision is final, all branch into others. Ignorant people suppose that infinite drawings require an infinite time; actually it is sufficient for time to be infinitely subdivisible, as the famous parable of the contest with the tortoise teaches. This infinity harmonizes admirably with the sinuous numbers of Chance and with the Celestial Archetype of the Lottery, which the Platonists adore. Some warped echo of our rites seems to have resounded on the Tiber: Ellus Lampridius, in the *Life of Antoninus Heliogabalus,* tells that this emperor wrote on shells the lots that were destined for his guests, so that one received ten pounds of gold and another ten flies, ten dormice, ten bears. It is permissible to recall that Heliogabalus was brought up in Asia Minor, among the priests of the eponymous god.

There are also impersonal drawings, with an indefinite purpose. One decrees that a sapphire of Taprobana be thrown into the waters of the Euphrates; another, that a bird be released from the roof of a tower; another, that each century there be withdrawn (or added) a grain of sand from the innumerable ones on the beach. The consequences are, at times, terrible.

Under the beneficent influence of the Company, our customs are saturated with chance. The buyer of a dozen amphoras of Damascene wine will not be surprised if one of them contains a talisman or a snake. The scribe who writes a contract almost never fails to introduce some erroneous information. I myself, in this hasty declaration, have falsified some splendor, some atrocity. Perhaps, also, some mysterious monotony . . . Our historians, who are the most penetrating on the globe, have invented a method to correct chance. It is well known that the operations of this method are (in general) reliable, although, naturally, they are not divulged without some portion of deceit. Furthermore, there is nothing so contaminated with fiction as the history of the Company. A paleographic document, exhumed in a temple, can be the result of yesterday's lottery or of an age-old lottery. No book is published without some discrepancy in each one of the copies. Scribes take a secret oath to omit, to interpolate, to change. The indirect lie is also cultivated.

The Company, with divine modesty, avoids all publicity. Its agents, as is natural, are secret. The orders which it issues continually (perhaps incessantly) do not differ from those lavished by impostors. Moreover, who can brag about being a mere impostor? The drunkard who improvises an absurd order, the dreamer who awakens suddenly and strangles the woman who sleeps at his side, do they not execute, perhaps, a secret decision of the Company? That silent functioning, comparable to God's, gives rise to all sorts of conjectures. One abominably insinuates that the Company has not existed for centuries and that the sacred disorder of our lives is purely hereditary, traditional. Another judges it eternal and teaches that it will last until the last night, when the last god annihilates the world. Another declares that the Company is omnipotent, but that it only has influence in tiny things: in a bird's call, in the shadings of rust and of dust, in the half dreams of dawn. Another, in the words of masked heresiarchs, *that it has never existed and will not exist*. Another, no less vile, reasons that it is indifferent to affirm or deny the reality of the shadowy corporation, because Babylon is nothing else than an infinite game of chance.

ELIZABETH BOWEN

Mysterious Kôr

Full moonlight drenched the city and searched it; there was not a niche left to stand in. The effect was remorseless: London looked like the moon's capital—shallow, cratered, extinct. It was late, but not yet midnight; now the buses had stopped the polished roads and streets in this region sent for minutes together a ghostly unbroken reflection up. The soaring new flats and the crouching old shops and houses looked equally brittle under the moon, which blazed in windows that looked its way. The futility of the black-out became laughable: from the sky, presumably, you could see every slate in the roofs, every whited kerb, every contour of the naked winter flowerbeds in the park; and the lake, with its shining twists and tree-darkened islands would be a landmark for miles, yes, miles, overhead.

However, the sky, in whose glassiness floated no clouds but only opaque balloons, remained glassy-silent. The Germans no longer came by the full moon. Something more immaterial seemed to threaten, and to be keeping people at home. This day between days, this extra tax, was perhaps more than senses and nerves could bear. People stayed indoors with a fervour that could be felt: the buildings strained with battened-down human life, but not a beam, not a voice, not a note from a radio escaped. Now and then under streets and buildings the earth rumbled: the Underground sounded loudest at this time.

Outside the now gateless gates of the park, the road coming downhill from the north-west turned south and became a street, down whose perspective the traffic lights went through their unmeaning performance of changing colour. From the promontory of pavement outside the gates you saw at once up the road and down the street: from behind where you stood, between the gateposts, appeared the lesser strangeness of grass and water and trees. At this point, at this moment, three French soldiers, directed to a hostel they could not find, stopped singing to listen derisively to the waterbirds wakened up by the moon. Next, two wardens coming off duty emerged from their post and crossed the road diagonally, each with an elbow cupped inside a slung-on tin hat. The wardens turned their faces, mauve in the moonlight, towards the Frenchmen with no expression at all. The two sets of steps died in opposite directions, and, the birds subsiding, nothing was heard or seen until, a little way down the street, a trickle of people came out of the Underground, around the anti-panic brick wall. These all disappeared quickly, in an abashed way, or as though dissolved in the street by some white acid, but for a girl and a soldier who, by their way of walking, seemed to have no destination but each other and to be not quite certain even of that. Blotted into one shadow, he tall, she little, these two proceeded towards the park. They looked in, but did not go in; they stood there debating without speaking. Then, as though a command from the street behind them had been received by their synchronized bodies, they faced round to look back the way they had come.

His look up the height of a building made his head drop back, and she saw his eyeballs glitter. She slid her hand from his sleeve, stepped to the edge of the pavement and said: 'Mysterious Kôr.'

'What is?' he said, not quite collecting himself.

'This is—

"Mysterious Kôr thy walls forsaken stand,
Thy lonely towers beneath a lonely moon—"
—this is Kôr.'

'Why,' he said, 'it's years since I've thought of that.'

She said: 'I think of it all the time—

"Not in the waste beyond the swamps and sand,
Thy fever-haunted forest and lagoon,
Mysterious Kôr thy walls—"

—a completely forsaken city, as high as cliffs and as white as bones, with no history——'

'But something must once have happened: why had it been forsaken?'

'How could anyone tell you when there's nobody there?'

'Nobody there since how long?'

'Thousands of years.'

'In that case, it would have fallen down.'

'No, not Kôr,' she said with immediate authority. 'Kôr's altogether different; it's very strong; there is not a crack in it anywhere for a weed to grow in; the corners of stones and the monuments might have been cut yesterday, and the stairs and arches are built to support themselves.'

'You know all about it,' he said, looking at her.

'I know, I know all about it.'

'What, since you read that book?'

'Oh, I didn't get much from that; I just got the name. I knew that must be the right name; it's like a cry.'

'Most like the cry of a crow to me.' He reflected, then said: 'But the poem begins with "Not"—"*Not in the waste beyond the swamps and sand——*" And it goes on, as I remember, to prove Kôr's not really anywhere. When even a poem says there's no such place——'

'What it tries to say doesn't matter: I see what it makes me see. Anyhow, that was written some time ago, at that time when they thought they had got everything taped, because the whole world had been explored, even the middle of Africa. Every thing and place had been found and marked on some map; so what wasn't marked on any map couldn't be there at all. So *they* thought: that was why he wrote the poem. "*The world is disenchanted,*" it goes on. That was what set me off hating civilization.'

'Well, cheer up,' he said; 'there isn't much of it left.'

'Oh, yes, I cheered up some time ago. This war shows we've by no means come to the end. If you can blow whole places out of existence, you can blow whole places into it. I don't see why not. They say we can't say what's come out since the bombing started. By the time we've come to the end, Kôr may be the one city left: the abiding city. I should laugh.'

'No, you wouldn't,' he said sharply. '*You* wouldn't—at least, I hope not. I hope you don't know what you're saying—does the moon make you funny?'

'Don't be cross about Kôr; please don't Arthur,' she said.

'I thought girls thought about people.'

'What, these days?' she said. 'Think about people? How can anyone think about people if they've got any heart? I don't know how other girls manage: I always think about Kôr.'

'Not about me?' he said. When she did not at once answer, he turned her hand over, in anguish, inside his grasp. 'Because I'm not there when you want me—is that my fault?'

'But to think about Kôr *is* to think about you and me.'

'In that dead place?'

'No, ours—we'd be alone there.'

Tightening his thumb on her palm while he thought this over, he looked behind them,

165   Elizabeth Bowen

around them, above them—even up at the sky. He said finally: 'But we're alone here.'

'That was why I said "Mysterious Kôr".'

'What, you mean we're there now, that here's there, that now's then? . . . *I* don't mind,' he added, letting out as a laugh the sigh he had been holding in for some time. 'You ought to know the place, and for all I could tell you we might be anywhere: I often do have it, this funny feeling, the first minute or two when I've come up out of the Underground. Well, well: join the Army and see the world.' He nodded towards the perspective of traffic lights and said, a shade craftily: 'What are those, then?'

Having caught the quickest possible breath, she replied: 'Inexhaustible gases; they bored through to them and lit them as they came up; by changing colour they show the changing of minutes; in Kôr there is no sort of other time.'

'You've got the moon, though: that can't help making months.'

'Oh, and the sun, of course; but those two could do what they liked; we should not have to calculate when they'd come or go.'

'We might not have to,' he said, 'but I bet I should.'

'I should not mind what you did, so long as you never said, "What next?" '

'I don't know about "next", but I do know what we'd do first.'

'What, Arthur?'

'Populate Kôr.'

She said: 'I suppose it would be all right if our children were to marry each other?'

But her voice faded out; she had been reminded that they were homeless on this his first night of leave. They were, that was to say, in London without any hope of any place of their own. Pepita shared a two-roomed flatlet with a girl friend, in a by-street off the Regent's Park Road, and towards this they must make their half-hearted way. Arthur was to have the sitting-room divan, usually occupied by Pepita, while she herself had half of her girl friend's bed. There was really no room for a third, and least of all for a man, in those small rooms packed with furniture and the two girls' belongings: Pepita tried to be grateful for her friend Callie's forbearance —but how could she be, when it had not occurred to Callie that she would do better to be away to-night? She was more slow-witted than narrow-minded—but Pepita felt she owed a kind of ruin to her. Callie, not yet known to be home later than ten, would be now waiting up, in her house-coat, to welcome Arthur. That would mean three-sided chat, drinking cocoa, then turning in: that would be that, and that would be all. That was London, this war—they were lucky to have a roof —London, full enough before the Americans came. Not a place: they would even grudge you sharing a grave—that was what even married couples complained. Whereas in Kôr . . .

In Kôr . . . Like glass, the illusion shattered: a car hummed like a hornet towards them, veered, showed its scarlet taillight, streaked away up the road. A woman edged round a front door and along the area railings timidly called her cat; meanwhile a clock near, then another set further back in the dazzling distance, set about striking midnight. Pepita, feeling Arthur release her arm with an abruptness that was the inverse of passion, shivered; whereat he asked brusquely: 'Cold? Well, which way?—we'd better be getting on.'

Callie was no longer waiting up. Hours ago she had set out the three cups and saucers, the tins of cocoa and household milk and, on the gas-ring, brought the kettle to just short of the boil. She had turned open Arthur's bed, the living-room divan, in the neat inviting way she had learnt at home—then, with a modest impulse, replaced the cover. She had, as Pepita foresaw, been wearing her cretonne housecoat, the nearest thing to a hostess gown that she had; she had already brushed her hair for the night, rebraided it, bound the braids in a coronet round her head. Both lights and the wireless had been on, to make the room both look and sound gay: all alone, she had come to that peak moment at which company should arrive—but so seldom does. From then on she felt welcome beginning to wither in her, a flower of the heart that had bloomed too early. There she had sat like an image, facing the three cold cups, on the edge of the bed to be occupied by an unknown man.

Callie's innocence and her still unsought-out state had brought her to take a proprietary pride in Arthur; this was all the stronger, perhaps, because they had not yet met. Sharing the flat with Pepita, this last year, she had been content with reflecting the heat of love. It was not, surprisingly, that Pepita seemed very happy—there were times when she was palpably on the rack, and this was not what Callie could understand. 'Surely you owe it to Arthur,' she would then say, 'to keep cheerful? So long as you love each other——' Callie's calm brow glowed—one might say that it glowed in place of her friend's; she became the guardian of that ideality which for Pepita was constantly lost to view. It was true, with the sudden prospect of Arthur's leave, things had come nearer to earth: he became a proposition, and she would have been as glad if he could have slept somewhere else. Physically shy, a brotherless virgin, Callie shrank from sharing this flat with a young man. In this flat you could hear everything: what was once a three-windowed Victorian drawing-room had been partitioned, by very thin walls, into kitchenette, living-room, Callie's bedroom. The living-room was in the centre; the two others open off it. What was once the conservatory, half a flight down, was now converted into a draughty bathroom, shared with somebody else on the girls' floor. The flat, for these days, was cheap —even so, it was Callie, earning more than Pepita, who paid the greater part of the rent: it thus became up to her, more or less, to express goodwill as to Arthur's making a third. 'Why, it will be lovely to have him here,' Callie said. Pepita accepted the good

will without much grace—but then, had she ever much grace to spare?—she was as restlessly secretive, as self-centred, as a little half-grown black cat. Next came a puzzling moment: Pepita seemed to be hinting that Callie should fix herself up somewhere else. 'But where would I go?' Callie marvelled when this was at last borne in on her. 'You know what London's like now. And, anyway' —here she laughed, but hers was a forehead that coloured as easily as it glowed—'it wouldn't be proper, would it, me going off and leaving just you and Arthur; I don't know what your mother would say to me. No, we may be a little squashed, but we'll make things ever so homey. I shall not mind playing gooseberry, really, dear.'

But the hominess by now was evaporating, as Pepita and Arthur still and still did not come. At half-past ten, in obedience to the rule of the house, Callie was obliged to turn off the wireless, whereupon silence out of the stepless street began seeping into the slighted room. Callie recollected the fuel target and turned off her dear little table lamp, gaily painted with spots to make it look like a toadstool, thereby leaving only the hanging light. She laid her hand on the kettle, to find it gone cold again and sigh for the wasted gas if not for her wasted thought. Where are they? Cold crept up her out of the kettle; she went to bed.

Callie's bed lay along the wall under the window: she did not like sleeping so close up under glass, but the clearance that must be left for the opening of door and cupboards made this the only possible place. Now she got in and lay rigidly on the bed's inner side, under the hanging hems of the window curtains, training her limbs not to stray to what would be Pepita's half. This sharing of her bed with another body would not be the least of her sacrifice to the lovers' love; tonight would be the first night—or at least, since she was an infant—that Callie had slept with anyone. Child of a sheltered middle-class household, she had kept physical distances all her life. Already repugnance and shyness ran through her limbs; she was preyed upon by some more obscure trouble than the expectation that she might not sleep. As to *that*, Pepita was restless; her tossings on the divan, her broken-off exclamations and blurred pleas had been to be heard, most nights, through the dividing wall.

Callie knew, as though from a vision, that Arthur would sleep soundly, with assurance and majesty. Did they not all say, too, that a soldier sleeps like a log? With awe she pictured, asleep, the face that she had not yet, awake, seen—Arthur's man's eyelids, cheekbones and set mouth turned up to the darkened ceiling. Wanting to savour darkness herself, Callie reached out and put off her bedside lamp.

At once she knew that something was happening—outdoors, in the street, the whole of London, the world. An advance, an extraordinary movement was silently taking place; blue-white beams overflowed from it, silting, dropping round the edges of the muffling black-out curtains. When, starting up, she knocked a fold of the curtain, a beam like a mouse ran across her bed. A searchlight, the most powerful of all time, might have been turned full and steady upon her defended window; finding flaws in the black-out stuff, it made veins and stars. Once gained by this idea of pressure she could not lie down again; she sat tautly, drawn-up knees touching her breasts, and asked herself if there were anything she should do. She parted the curtains, opened them slowly wider, looked out—and was face to face with the moon.

Below the moon, the houses opposite her window blazed black in transparent shadow; and something—was it a coin or a ring?—glittered half-way across the chalk-white street. Light marched in past her face, and she turned to see where it went: out stood the curves and garlands of the great white marble Victorian mantelpiece of that lost drawing-room; out stood, in the photographs turned her way, the thoughts with which her

parents had faced the camera, and the humble puzzlement of her two dogs at home. Of silver brocade, just faintly purpled with roses, became her house-coat hanging over the chair. And the moon did more: it exonerated and beautified the lateness of the lovers' return. No wonder, she said to herself, no wonder—if this was the world they walked in, if this was whom they were with. Having drunk in the white explanation, Callie lay down again. Her half of the bed was in shadow, but she allowed one hand to lie, blanched, in what would be Pepita's place. She lay and looked at the hand until it was no longer her own.

Callie woke to the sound of Pepita's key in the latch. But no voices? What had happened? Then she heard Arthur's step. She heard his unslung equipment dropped with a weary, dull sound, and the plonk of his tin hat on a wooden chair. 'Sssh-sssh!' Pepita exclaimed, 'she *might* be asleep!'

Then at last Arthur's voice: 'But I thought you said——'

'I'm not asleep: I'm just coming!' Callie called out with rapture, leaping out from her form in shadow into the moonlight, zipping on her enchanted house-coat over her nightdress, kicking her shoes on, and pinning in place, with a trembling firmness, her plaits in their coronet round her head. Between these movements of hers she heard not another sound. Had she only dreamed they were there? Her heart beat: she stepped through the living-room, shutting her door behind her.

Pepita and Arthur stood the other side of the table; they gave the impression of being lined up. Their faces, at different levels—for Pepita's rough, dark head came only an inch above Arthur's khaki shoulder—were alike in abstention from any kind of expression; as though, spiritually, they both still refused to be here. Their features looked faint, weathered—was this the work of the moon? Pepita said at once: 'I suppose we are very late?'

'I don't wonder,' Callie said, 'on this lovely night.'

Arthur had not raised his eyes; he was looking at the three cups. Pepita now suddenly jogged his elbow, saying, 'Arthur, wake up; say something; this is Callie—well, Callie, this is Arthur, of course.'

'Why, yes, of course this is Arthur,' returned Callie, whose candid eyes since she entered had not left Arthur's face. Perceiving that Arthur did not know what to do, she advanced round the table to shake hands with him. He looked up, she looked down, for the first time: she rather beheld than felt his red-brown grip on what still seemed her glove of moonlight. 'Welcome, Arthur,' she said. 'I'm so glad to meet you at last. I hope you will be comfortable in the flat.'

'It's been kind of you,' he said after consideration.

'Please do not feel that,' said Callie. 'This is Pepita's home, too, and we both hope—don't we, Pepita—that you'll regard it as yours. Please feel free to do just as you like. I am sorry it is so small.'

'Oh, I don't know,' Arthur said, as though hypnotized; 'it seems a nice little place.'

Pepita, meanwhile, glowered and turned away.

Arthur continued to wonder, though he had once been told, how these two unalike girls had come to set up together—Pepita so small, except for her too-big head, compact of childish brusqueness and of unchildish passion, and Callie, so sedate, waxy and tall—an unlit candle. Yes, she was like one of those candles on sale outside a church; there could be something votive even in her demeanour. She was unconscious that her good manners, those of and old-fashioned country doctor's daughter, were putting the other two at a disadvantage. He found himself touched by the grave good faith with which Callie was wearing that tartish house-coat, above which her face kept the glaze of sleep; and, as she knelt to re-light the gas-ring under the kettle, he marked the strong, delicate arch of one bare foot, disappearing into the arty green shoe. Pepita was now too near him ever again to be seen

as he now saw Callie—in a sense, he never *had* seen Pepita for the first time: she had not been, and still sometimes was not, his type. No, he had not thought of her twice; he had not remembered her until he began to remember her with passion. You might say he had not seen Pepita coming: their love had been a collision in the dark.

Callie, determined to get this over with, knelt back and said: 'Would Arthur like to wash his hands?' When they had heard him stumble down the half-flight of stairs, she said to Pepita: 'Yes, I was so glad you had the moon.'

'Why?' said Pepita. She added: 'There was too much of it.'

'You're tired. Arthur looks tired, too.'

'How would you know? He's used to marching about. But it's all this having no place to go.'

'But, Pepita, you——'

But at this point Arthur came back: from the door he noticed the wireless, and went direct to it. 'Nothing much on now, I suppose?' he doubtfully said.

'No, you see it's past midnight; we're off the air. And, anyway, in this house they don't like the wireless late. By the same token,' went on Callie, friendly smiling, 'I'm afraid I must ask you, Arthur, to take your boots off, unless, of course, you mean to stay sitting down. The people below us——'

Pepita flung off, saying something under her breath, but Arthur, remarking, 'No, I don't mind,' both sat down and began to take off his boots. Pausing, glancing to left and right at the divan's fresh cotton spread, he said: 'It's all right is it, for me to sit on this?'

'That's my bed,' said Pepita. 'You are to sleep in it.'

Callie then made the cocoa, after which they turned in. Preliminary trips to the bathroom having been worked out, Callie was first to retire, shutting the door behind her so that Pepita and Arthur might kiss each other good night. When Pepita joined her, it was without knocking: Pepita stood still in the moon and began to tug off her clothes. Glancing with hate at the bed, she asked: 'Which side?'

'I expected you'd like the outside.'

'What are you standing about for?'

'I don't really know: as I'm inside I'd better get in first.'

'Then why not get in?'

When they had settled rigidly, side by side, Callie asked: 'Do you think Arthur's got all he wants?'

Pepita jerked her head up. 'We can't sleep in all this moon.'

'Why, you don't believe the moon does things, actually?'

'Well, it couldn't hope to make some of us *much* more screwy.'

Callie closed the curtains, then said: 'What do you mean? And—didn't you hear?—I asked if Arthur's got all he wants.'

'That's what I meant—have you got a screw loose, really?'

'Pepita, I won't stay here if you're going to be like this.'

'In that case, you had better go in with Arthur.'

'What about me?' Arthur loudly said through the wall. 'I can hear practically all you girls are saying.'

They were both startled—rather that than abashed. Arthur, alone in there, had thrown off the ligatures of his social manner: his voice held the whole authority of his sex—he was impatient, sleepy, and he belonged to no one.

'Sorry,' the girls said in unison. Then Pepita laughed soundlessly, making their bed shake, till to stop herself she bit the back of her hand, and this movement made her elbow strike Callie's cheek. 'Sorry,' she had to whisper. No answer: Pepita fingered her elbow and found, yes, it was quite true, it was wet. 'Look, shut up crying, Callie: what have I done?'

Callie rolled right round, in order to press her forehead closely under the window, into the curtains, against the wall. Her weeping continued to be soundless: now and then, un-

able to reach her handkerchief, she staunched her eyes with a curtain, disturbing slivers of moon. Pepita gave up marvelling, and soon slept: at least there is something in being dog-tired.

A clock struck four as Callie woke up again —but something else had made her open her swollen eyelids. Arthur, stumbling about on his padded feet, could be heard next door attempting to make no noise. Inevitably, he bumped the edge of the table. Callie sat up: by her side Pepita lay like a mummy rolled half over, in forbidding, tenacious sleep. Arthur groaned. Callie caught a breath, climbed lightly over Pepita, felt for her torch on the mantelpiece, stopped to listen again. Arthur groaned again: Callie, with movements soundless as they were certain, opened the door and slipped through to the living-room. 'What's the matter?' she whispered. 'Are you ill?'

'No; I just got a cigarette. Did I wake you up?'

'But you groaned.'

'I'm sorry; I'd no idea.'

'But do you often?'

'I've no idea, really, I tell you,' Arthur repeated. The air of the room was dense with his presence, overhung by tobacco. He must be sitting on the edge of his bed, wrapped up in his overcoat—she could smell the coat, and each time he pulled on the cigarette his features appeared down there, in the fleeting, dull reddish glow. 'Where are you?' he asked. 'Show a light.'

Her nervous touch on her torch, like a reflex to what he said, made it flicker up for a second. 'I am just by the door; Pepita's asleep; I'd better go back to bed.'

'Listen. Do you two get on each other's nerves?'

'Not till to-night,' said Callie, watching the uncertain swoops of the cigarette as he reached across to the ash-tray on the edge of the table. Shifting her bare feet patiently, she added: 'You don't see us as we usually are.'

'She's a girl who shows things in funny ways—I expect she feels bad at our putting you out like this—I know I do. But then we'd got no choice, had we?'

'It is really I who am putting you out,' said Callie.

'Well, that can't be helped either, can it? You had the right to stay in your own place. If there'd been more time, we might have gone to the country, though I still don't see where we'd have gone there. It's one harder when you're not married, unless you've got the money. Smoke?'

'No, thank you. Well, if you're all right, I'll go back to bed.'

'I'm glad she's asleep—funny the way she sleeps, isn't it? You can't help wondering where she is. You haven't got a boy, have you, just at present?'

'No. I've never had one.'

'I'm not sure in one way that you're not better off. I can see there's not so much in it for a girl these days. It makes me feel cruel the way I unsettle her: I don't know how much it's me myself or how much it's something the matter that I can't help. How are any of us to know how things could have been? They forget war's not just only war; it's years out of people's lives that they've never had before and won't have again. Do you think she's fanciful?'

'Who, Pepita?'

'It's enough to make her—to-night was the pay-off. We couldn't get near any movie or any place for sitting; you had to fight into the bars, and she hates the staring in bars, and with all that milling about, every street we went, they kept on knocking her even off my arm. So then we took the tube to that park down there, but the place was as bad as day-light, let alone it was cold. We hadn't the nerve—well, that's nothing to do with you.'

'I don't mind.'

'Or else you don't understand. So we began to play—we were off in Kôr.'

'Core of what?'

'Mysterious Kôr—ghost city.'

'Where?'

'You may ask. But I could have sworn she saw it, and from the way she saw it I saw it, too. A game's a game, but what's a hallucination? You begin by laughing, then it gets in you and you can't laugh it off. I tell you, I woke up just now not knowing where I'd been; and I had to get up and feel round this table before I even knew where I was. It wasn't till then that I thought of a cigarette. Now I see why she sleeps like that, if that's where she goes.'

'But she is just as often restless; I often hear her.'

'Then she doesn't always make it. Perhaps it takes me, in some way—— Well, I can't see any harm: when two people have got no place, why not Kôr, as a start? There are no restrictions on wanting, at any rate.'

'But, oh, Arthur, can't wanting want what's human?'

He yawned. 'To be human's to be at a dead loss.' Stopping yawning, he ground out his cigarette: the china tray skidded at the edge of the table. 'Bring that light here a moment —that is, will you? I think I've messed ash all over these sheets of hers.'

Callie advanced with the torch alight, but at arm's length: now and then her thumb made the beam wobble. She watched the lit-up inside of Arthur's hand as he brushed the sheet; and once he looked up to see her white-nightgowned figure curving above and away from him, behind the arc of light. 'What's that swinging?'

'One of my plaits of hair. Shall I open the window wider?'

'What, to let the smoke get out? Go on. And how's your moon?'

'Mine?' Marvelling over this, as the first sign that Arthur remembered that she was Callie, she uncovered the window, pushed up the sash, then after a minute said: 'Not so strong.'

Indeed, the moon's power over London and the imagination had now declined. The siege of light had relaxed; the search was over; the street had a look of survival and no more. Whatever had glittered there, coin or ring, was now invisible or had gone. To Callie it seemed likely that there would never be such a moon again; and on the whole she felt this was for the best. Feeling air reach in like a tired arm round her body, she dropped the curtains against it and returned to her own room.

Back by her bed, she listened: Pepita's breathing still had the regular sound of sleep. At the other side of the wall the divan creaked as Arthur stretched himself out again. Having felt ahead of her lightly, to make sure her half was empty, Callie climbed over Pepita and got in. A certain amount of warmth had travelled between the sheets from Pepita's flank, and in this Callie extended her sword-cold body: she tried to compose her limbs; even they quivered after Arthur's words in the dark, words *to* the dark. The loss of her own mysterious expectation, of her love for love, was a small thing beside the war's total of unlived lives. Suddenly Pepita flung out one hand: its back knocked Callie lightly across the face.

Pepita had now turned over and lay with her face up. The hand that had struck Callie must have lain over the other, which grasped the pyjama collar. Her eyes, in the dark, might have been either shut or open, but nothing made her frown more or less steadily: it became certain, after another moment, that Pepita's act of justice had been unconscious. She still lay, as she had lain, in an avid dream, of which Arthur had been the source, of which Arthur was not the end. With him she looked this way, that way, down the wide, void, pure streets, between statues, pillars and shadows, through archways and colonnades. With him she went up the stairs down which nothing but moon came; with him trod the ermine dust of the endless halls, stood on terraces, mounted the extreme tower, looked down on the statued squares, the wide, void, pure streets. He was the password, but not the answer: it was to Kôr's finality that she turned.

ERNEST HEMINGWAY

A Natural History of the Dead

It has always seemed to me that the war has been omitted as a field for the observations of the naturalist. We have charming and sound accounts of the flora and fauna of Patagonia by the late W. H. Hudson,[1] the Reverend Gilbert White[2] has written most interestingly of the Hoopoe on its occasional and not at all common visits to Selborne, and Bishop Stanley[3] has given up a valuable, although popular, *Familiar History of Birds*. Can we not hope to furnish the reader with a few rational and interesting facts about the dead? I hope so.

When that persevering traveller, Mungo Park,[4] was at one period of his course fainting in the vast wilderness of an African desert, naked and alone, considering his days as numbered and nothing appearing to remain for him to do but to lie down and die, a small moss-flower of extraordinary beauty caught his eye. 'Though the whole plant,' says he, 'was no larger than one of my fingers, I could not contemplate the delicate formation of its roots, leaves and capsules without admiration. Can that Being who planted, watered and brought to perfection, in this obscure part of the world, a thing which appears of so small importance, look with unconcern upon the situation and suffering of

creatures formed after his own image? Surely not. Reflections like these would not allow me to despair; I started up and, disregarding both hunger and fatigue, travelled forward, assured that relief was at hand: and I was not disappointed.'

With a disposition to wonder and adore in like manner, as Bishop Stanley says, can any branch of Natural History be studied without increasing that faith, love and hope which we also, every one of us, need in our journey through the wilderness of life? Let us therefore see what inspiration we may derive from the dead.

In war the dead are usually the male of the human species, although this does not hold true with animals, and I have frequently seen dead mares among the horses. An interesting aspect of war, too, is that it is only there that the naturalist has an opportunity to observe the dead of mules. In twenty years of observation in civil life I had never seen a dead mule and had begun to entertain doubts as to whether these animals were really mortal. On rare occasions I had seen what I took to be dead mules, but on close approach these always proved to be living creatures who seemed to be dead through their quality of complete repose. But in war these animals succumb in much the same manner as the more common and less hardy horse.

Most of the mules that I saw dead were along mountain roads or lying at the foot of steep declivities whence they had been pushed to rid the road of their encumbrance. They seemed a fitting enough sight in the

---

[1] *W. H. Hudson:* (1841–1922), English naturalist and author.

[2] *Gilbert White:* (1720–1793), English naturalist.

[3] *Bishop Stanley:* Edward Stanley (1779–1849), Bishop or Norwich.

[4] *Mungo Park:* (1771–1806), Scottish explorer in Africa.

mountains where one was accustomed to their presence, and looked less incongruous there than they did later, at Smyrna, where the Greeks broke the legs of all their baggage animals and pushed them off the quay into the shallow water to drown. The numbers of broken-legged mules and horses drowning in the shallow water called for a Goya to depict them. Although, speaking literally, one can hardly say that they called for a Goya since there has only been one Goya, long dead, and it is extremely doubtful if these animals, were they able to call, would call for pictorial representation of their plight but, more likely, would, if they were articulate, call for someone to alleviate their condition.

Regarding the sex of the dead it is a fact that one becomes so accustomed to the sight of all the dead being men that the sight of a dead woman is quite shocking. I first saw inversion of the usual sex of the dead after the explosion of a munition factory which had been situated in the countryside near Milan, Italy. We drove to the scene of the disaster in trucks along poplar-shaded roads, bordered with ditches containing much minute animal life, which I could not clearly observe because of the great clouds of dust raised by the trucks. Arriving where the munition plant had been, some of us were put to patrolling about those large stocks of munitions which for some reason had not exploded, while others were put at extinguishing a fire which had gotten into the grass of an adjacent field; which task being concluded, we were ordered to search the immediate vicinity and surrounding fields for bodies. We found and carried to an improvised mortuary a good number of these and, I must admit, frankly, the shock it was to find these dead were women rather than men. In those days women had not yet commenced to wear their hair cut short, as they did later for several years in Europe and America, and the most disturbing thing, perhaps because it was the most unaccus-

tomed, was the presence, and even more disturbing, the occasional absence of this long hair. I remember that after we had searched quite thoroughly for the complete dead we collected fragments. Many of these were detached from a heavy, barbed-wire fence which had surrounded the position of the factory and from the still existent portions of which we picked many of these detached bits which illustrated only too well the tremendous energy of high explosive. Many fragments we found a considerable distance away in the fields, they being carried farther by their own weight.

On our return to Milan I recall one or two of us discussing the occurrence and agreeing that the quality of unreality and the fact that there were no wounded did much to rob the disaster of a horror which might have been much greater. Also the fact that it had been so immediate and that the dead were in consequence still as little unpleasant as possible to carry and deal with made it quite removed from the usual battlefield experience. The pleasant, though dusty, ride through the beautiful Lombard countryside also was a compensation for the unpleasantness of the duty and on our return, while we exchanged impressions, we all agreed that it was indeed fortunate that the fire which broke out just before we arrived had been brought under control as rapidly as it had and before it had attained any of the seemingly huge stocks of unexploded munitions. We agreed too that the picking up of the fragments had been an extraordinary business; it being amazing that the human body should be blown into pieces which exploded along no anatomical lines, but rather divided as capriciously as the fragmentation in the burst of a high explosive shell.

A naturalist, to obtain accuracy of observation, may confine himself in his observations to one limited period and I will take first that following the Austrian offensive of June 1918 in Italy as one in which the dead were present in their greatest numbers, a withdrawal having been forced and an advance later made to recover the ground lost so that the positions after the battle were the same as before except for the presence of the dead. Until the dead are buried they change somewhat in appearance each day. The colour change in Caucasian races is from white to yellow, to yellow-green, to black. If left long enough in the heat the flesh comes to resemble coal-tar, especially where it has been broken or torn, and it has quite a visible tar-like iridescence. The dead grow larger each day until sometimes they become quite too big for their uniforms, filling these until they seem blown tight enough to burst. The individual members may increase in girth to an unbelievable extent and faces fill as taut and globular as balloons. The surprising thing, next to their progressive corpulence, is the amount of paper that is scattered about the dead. Their ultimate position, before there is any question of burial, depends on the location of the pockets in the uniform. In the Austrian army these pockets were in the back of the breeches and the dead, after a short time, all consequently lay on their faces, the two hip pockets pulled out and, scattered around them in the grass, all those papers their pockets contained. The heat, the flies, the indicative positions of the bodies in the grass, and the amount of paper scattered are the impressions one retains. The smell of battlefield in hot weather one cannot recall. You can remember that there was such a smell, but nothing ever happens to you to bring it back. It is unlike the smell of a regiment, which may come to you suddenly while riding in the street car and you will look across and see the man who has brought it to you. But the other thing is gone as completely as when you have been in love; you remember things that happened, but the sensation cannot be recalled.

One wonders what that persevering traveller, Mungo Park, would have seen on a battlefield in hot weather to restore his confidence. There were always poppies in the wheat in the end of June, and in July, and the mulberry trees were in full leaf and one could see the heat waves rise from the barrels of the guns where the sun struck them through the screens of leaves; the earth was turned a bright yellow at the edge of holes where mustard gas shells had been and the average broken house is finer to see than one that has been shelled, but few travellers would take a good full breath of that early summer air and have any such thoughts as Mungo Park about those formed in His own image.

The first thing that you found about the dead was that, hit badly enough, they died like animals. Some quickly from a little wound you would not think would kill a rabbit. They died from little wounds as rabbits die sometimes from three or four small grains of shot that hardly seem to break the skin. Others would die like cats; a skull broken in and iron in the brain, they lie alive two days like cats that crawl into the coal bin with a bullet in the brain and will not die until you cut their heads off. Maybe cats do not die then, they say they have nine lives. I do not know, but most men die like animals, not men. I'd never seen a natural death, so called, and so I blamed it on the war and like the persevering traveller, Mungo Park, knew that here was something else, that always absent something else, and then I saw one.

The only natural death I've ever seen, outside of loss of blood, which isn't bad, was death from Spanish influenza. In this you drown in mucus, choking and how you know the patient's dead is: at the end he turns to be a little child again, though with his manly force, and fills the sheets as full as any diaper with one vast, final, yellow cataract that flows and dribbles on after he's gone. So now I want to see the death of any self-called Humanist[5] because a persevering traveller

---

[5] The Reader's indulgence is requested for this mention of an extinct phenomenon. The reference, like all references to fashions, dates the story, but it is retained because of its mild historical interest and because its omission would spoil the rhythm. [Hemingway's note.]

like Mungo Park or me lives on and maybe yet will live to see the actual death of members of this literary sect and watch the noble exits that they make. In my musings as a naturalist it has occurred to me that while decorum is an excellent thing some must be indecorous if the race is to be carried on since the position prescribed for procreation is indecorous, highly indecorous, and it occurred to me that perhaps that is what these people are, or were: the children of decorous cohabitation. But regardless of how they started I hope to see the finish of a few, and speculate how worms will try that long preserved sterility; with their quaint pamphlets gone to bust and into footnotes all their lust.

While it is, perhaps, legitimate to deal with these self-designated citizens in a natural history of the dead, even though the designation may mean nothing by the time this work is published, yet it is unfair to the other dead, who were not dead in their youth of choice, who owned no magazines, many of whom had doubtless never even read a review, that one has seen in the hot weather with a half-pint of maggots working where their mouths have been. It was not always hot weather for the dead, much of the time it was the rain that washed them clean when they lay in it and made the earth soft when they were buried in it and sometimes then kept on until the earth was mud and washed them out and you had to bury them again. Or in the winter in the mountains you had to put them in the snow and when the snow melted in the spring someone else had to bury them. They had beautiful burying grounds in the mountains, war in the mountains is the most beautiful of all war, and in one of them, at a place called Pocol, they buried a general who was shot through the head by a sniper. This is where those writers are mistaken who write books called *Generals Die in Bed*, because this general died in a trench dug in snow, high in the mountains, wearing an Alpini hat with an eagle feather in it and a hole in front

you couldn't put your little finger in and a hole in back you could put your fist in, if it were a small fist and you wanted to put it there, and much blood in the snow. He was a damned fine general, and so was General von Behr who commanded the Bavarian Alpenkorps troops at the battle of Caporetto and was killed in his staff car by the Italian rearguard as he drove into Udine ahead of his troops, and the titles of all such books should be *Generals Usually Die in Bed*, if we are to have any sort of accuracy in such things.

In the mountains, too, sometimes, the snow fell on the dead outside the dressing station on the side that was protected by the mountain from any shelling. They carried them into a cave that had been dug into the mountainside before the earth froze. It was in this cave that a man whose head was broken as a flower-pot may be broken, although it was all held together by membranes and a skilfully applied bandage now soaked and hardened, with the structure of his brain disturbed by a piece of broken steel in it, lay a day, a night, and a day. The stretcher-bearers asked the doctor to go in and have a look at him. They saw him each time they made a trip and even when they did not look at him they heard him breathing. The doctor's eyes were red and the lids swollen, almost shut from tear gas. He looked at the man twice; once in daylight, once with a flashlight. That too would have made a good etching for Goya, the visit with the flashlight, I mean. After looking at him the second time the doctor believed the stretcher-bearers when they said the soldier was still alive.

'What do you want me to do about it?' he asked.

There was nothing they wanted done. But after a while they asked permission to carry him out and lay him with the badly wounded.

'No. No. No!' said the doctor, who was busy. 'What's the matter? Are you afraid of him?'

'We don't like to hear him in there with the dead.'

'Don't listen to him. If you take him out of there you will have to carry him right back in.'

'We wouldn't mind that, Captain Doctor.'

'No,' said the doctor. 'No. Didn't you hear me say no?'

'Why don't you give him an overdose of morphine?' asked an artillery officer who was waiting to have a wound in his arm dressed.

'Do you think that is the only use I have for morphine? Would you like me to have to operate without morphine? You have a pistol, go out and shoot him yourself.'

'He's been shot already,' said the officer. 'If some of you doctors were shot you'd be different.'

'Thank you very much,' said the doctor, waving a forceps in the air. 'Thank you a thousand times. What about these eyes?' He pointed the forceps at them. 'How would you like these?'

'Tear gas. We call it lucky if it's tear gas.'

'Because you leave the line,' said the doctor. 'Because you come running here with your tear gas to be evacuated. You rub onions in your eyes.'

'You are beside yourself. I do not notice your insults. You are crazy.'

The stretcher-bearers came in.

'Captain Doctor,' one of them said.

'Get out of here!' said the doctor.

They went out.

'I will shoot the poor fellow,' the artillery officer said. 'I am a humane man. I will not let him suffer.'

'Shoot him then,' said the doctor. 'Shoot him. Assume the responsibility. I will make a report. Wounded shot by lieutenant of artillery in first curing post. Shoot him. Go ahead, shoot him.'

'You are not a human being.'

'My business is to care for the wounded, not to kill them. That is for gentlemen of the artillery.'

'Why don't you care for him then?'

'I have done so. I have done all that can be done.'

'Why don't you send him down on the cable railway?'

'Who are you to ask me questions? Are you my superior officer? Are you in command of this dressing-post? Do me the courtesy to answer.'

The lieutenant of artillery said nothing. The others in the room were all soldiers and there were no other officers present.

'Answer me,' said the doctor, holding a needle up in his forceps. 'Give me a response.'

'F— yourself,' said the artillery officer.

'So,' said the doctor. 'So, you said that. All right. All right. We shall see.'

The lieutenant of artillery stood up and walked toward him.

'F— yourself,' he said. 'F— yourself. F— your mother. F— your sister. . . .'

The doctor tossed the saucer full of iodine in his face. As he came toward him, blinded, the lieutenant fumbled for his pistol. The doctor skipped quickly behind him, tripped him and, as he fell to the floor, kicked him several times and picked up the pistol in his rubber gloves. The lieutenant sat on the floor holding his good hand to his eyes.

'I'll kill you!' he said. 'I'll kill you as soon as I can see.'

'I am the boss,' said the doctor. 'All is forgiven since you know I am the boss. You cannot kill me because I have your pistol. Sergeant! Adjutant! Adjutant!'

'The adjutant is at the cable railway,' said the sergeant.

'Wipe out this officer's eyes with alcohol and water. He has got iodine in them. Bring me the basin to wash my hands. I will take this officer next.'

'You won't touch me.'

'Hold him tight. He is a little delirious.'

One of the stretcher-bearers came in.

'Captain Doctor.'

'What do you want?'

'The man in the dead-house—'

'Get out of here.'

'Is dead, Captain Doctor. I thought you would be glad to know.'

'See, my poor Lieutenant? We dispute about nothing. In time of war we dispute about nothin.'

'F— you,' said the lieutenant of artillery. He still could not see. 'You've blinded me.'

'It is nothing,' said the doctor. 'Your eyes will be all right. It is nothing. A dispute about nothing.'

'Ayee! Ayee! Ayee!' suddenly screamed the lieutenant. 'You have blinded me! You have blinded me!'

'Hold him tight,' said the doctor. 'He is in much pain. Hold him very tight.'

SAMUEL BECKETT

Stones (an extract from *Molloy*)

There are people the sea doesn't suit, who prefer the mountains or the plain. Personally I feel no worse there than anywhere else. Much of my life has ebbed away before this shivering expanse, to the sound of the waves in storm and calm, and the claws of the surf. Before, no, more than before, one with, spread on the sand, or in a cave. In the sand I was in my element, letting it trickle between my fingers, scooping holes that I filled in a moment later or that filled themselves in, flinging it in the air by handfuls, rolling in it. And in the cave, lit by the beacons at night, I knew what to do in order to be no worse off than elsewhere. And that my land went no further, in one direction at least, did not displease me. And to feel there was one direction at least in which I could go no further, without first getting wet, then drowned, was a blessing. For I have always said, First learn to walk, then you can take swimming lessons. But don't imagine my region ended at the coast, that would be a grave mistake. For it was this sea too, its reefs and distant islands, and its hidden depths. And I too once went forth on it, in a sort of oarless skiff, but I paddled with an old bit of driftwood. And I sometimes wonder if I ever came back, from that voyage. For if I see myself putting to sea, and the long hours without landfall, I do not see the return, the tossing on the breakers, and I do not hear the frail keel grating on the shore. I took advantage of being at the seaside to lay in a store of sucking-stones. They were pebbles but I call them stones. Yes, on this occasion I laid in a considerable store. I distributed them equally among my four pockets, and sucked them turn and turn about. This raised a problem which I first solved in the following way. I had say sixteen stones, four in each of my four pockets these being the two pockets of my trousers and the two pockets of my greatcoat. Taking a stone from the right pocket of my greatcoat, and putting it in my mouth, I replaced it in the right pocket of my greatcoat by a stone from the right pocket of my trousers, which I replaced by a stone from the left pocket of my trousers, which I replaced by a stone from the left pocket of my greatcoat, which I replaced by the stone which was in my mouth, as soon as I had finished sucking it. Thus there were still four stones in each of my four pockets, but not quite the same stones. And when the desire to suck took hold of me again, I drew again on the right pocket of my greatcoat, certain of not taking the same stone as the last time. And while I sucked it I rearranged the other stones in the way I have just described. And so on. But this solution did not satisfy me fully. For it did not escape me that, by an extraordinary hazard, the four stones circulating thus might always be the same four. In which case, far from sucking the sixteen stones turn and turn about, I was really only sucking four, always the same, turn and turn about. But I shuffled them well in my pockets, before I began to suck, and again, while I sucked, before transferring them, in the hope of obtaining a more general circulation of the stones from pocket to pocket. But this was only a makeshift that could not long content a man like me. So I began to look for something else. And the first thing I hit upon was that I might do better to transfer the stones four by four, instead of one by one, that is to say, during the sucking, to take the three stones remaining in the right pocket of my greatcoat and replace them by the four in the right pocket of my trousers, and these by the four in the left pocket of my trousers, and these by the four in the left pocket of my greatcoat, and finally these by the three from the right pocket of my greatcoat, plus the one, as soon as I had finished sucking it, which was in my mouth. Yes, it seemed to me at first that by so doing I would arrive at a better result. But on further reflection I had to change my mind and confess that the circulation of the stones four by four came to exactly the same thing as their circulation one by one. For if I was certain of finding each time, in the right pocket of my greatcoat, four stones totally different from their immediate predecessors, the possibility nevertheless remained of my always chancing on the same stone, within each group of four, and consequently of my sucking, not the sixteen turn and turn about as I wished, but in fact four only, always the same, turn and turn about. So I had to seek elsewhere than in the mode of circulation. For no matter how I caused the stones to circulate, I always ran the same risk. It was obvious that by increasing the number of my pockets I was bound to increase my chances of enjoying my stones in the way I planned, that is to say one after the other until their number was exhausted. Had I had eight pockets, for example, instead of the four I did have, then even the most diabolical hazard could not have prevented me from sucking at least eight of my sixteen stones, turn and turn about. The truth is I should have needed sixteen pockets in order to be quite easy in my mind. And for a long time I could see no other conclusion than this, that short of having sixteen pockets, each with its stone, I could never reach the goal I had set myself, short of an extraordi-

nary hazard. And if at a pitch I could double the number of my pockets, were it only by dividing each pocket in two, with the help of a few safety-pins let us say, to quadruple them seemed to be more than I could manage. And I did not feel inclined to take all that trouble for a half-measure. For I was beginning to lose all sense of measure, after all this wrestling and wrangling, and to say, All or nothing. And if I was tempted for an instant to establish a more equitable proportion between my stones and my pockets, by reducing the former to the number of the latter, it was only for an instant. For it would have been an admission of defeat. And sitting on the shore, before the sea, the sixteen stones spread out before my eyes, I gazed at them in anger and perplexity. For just as I had difficulty in sitting on a chair, or in an arm-chair, because of my stiff leg you understand, so I had none in sitting on the ground, because of my stiff leg, for it was about this time that my good leg, good in the sense that it was not stiff, began to stiffen. I needed a prop under the ham you understand, and even under the whole length of the leg, the prop of the earth. And while I gazed thus at my stones, revolving interminable martingales all equally defective, and crushing handfuls of sand, so that the sand ran through my fingers and fell back on the strand, yes, while thus I lulled my mind and part of my body, one day suddenly it dawned on the former, dimly, that I might perhaps achieve my purpose without increasing the number of my pockets, or reducing the number of my stones, but simply by sacrificing the principle of trim. The meaning of this illumination, which suddenly began to sing within me, like a verse of Isaiah, or of Jeremiah, I did not penetrate at once, and notably the word trim, which I had never met with, in this sense, long remained obscure. Finally I seemed to grasp that this word trim could not here mean anything else, anything better, than the distribution of the sixteen stones in four groups of four, one group in each pocket, and that it was my refusal to consider any distribution other than this that had vitiated my calculations until then and rendered the problem literally insoluble. And it was on the basis of this interpretation, whether right or wrong, that I finally reached a solution, inelegant assuredly, but sound, sound. Now I am willing to believe, indeed I firmly believe, that other solutions to this problem might have been found, and indeed may still be found, no less sound, but much more elegant, than the one I shall now describe, if I can. And I believe too that had I been a little more insistent, a little more resistant, I could have found them myself. But I was tired, but I was tired, and I contented myself ingloriously with the first solution that was a solution, to this problem. But not to go over the heartbreaking stages through which I passed before I came to it, here it is, in all its hideousness. All (all!) that was necessary was to put for example, to begin with, six stones in the right pocket of my greatcoat, or supply-pocket, five in the right pocket of my trousers, and five in the left pocket of my trousers, that makes the lot, twice five ten plus six sixteen, and none, for none remained, in the left pocket of my greatcoat, which for the time being remained empty, empty of stones that is, for its usual contents remained, as well as occasional objects. For where do you think I hid my vegetable knife, my silver, my horn and the other things that I have not yet named, perhaps shall never name. Good. Now I can begin to suck. Watch me closely. I take a stone from the right pocket of my greatcoat, suck it, stop sucking it, put it in the left pocket of my greatcoat, the one empty (of stones). I take a second stone from the right pocket of my greatcoat, suck it, put it in the left pocket of my greatcoat. And so on until the right pocket of my greatcoat is empty (apart from its usual and casual contents) and the six stones I have just sucked, one after the other, are all in the left pocket of my greatcoat. Pausing then, and concentrating, so as not to make a balls of it, I transfer to the right pocket of my greatcoat, in which there are no stones left, the five stones in the right pocket of my trousers, which I replace by the five stones in the left pocket of my trousers, which I replace by the six stones in the left pocket of my greatcoat. At this stage then the left pocket of my greatcoat is again empty of stones, while the right pocket of my greatcoat is again supplied, and in the right way, that is to say with other stones than those I have just sucked. These other stones I then begin to suck, one after the other, and to transfer as I go along to the left pocket of my greatcoat, being absolutely certain, as far as one can be in an affair of this kind, that I am not sucking the same stones as a moment before, but others. And when the right pocket of my greatcoat is again empty (of stones), and the five I have just sucked are all without exception in the left pocket of my greatcoat, then I proceed to the same redistribution as a moment before, or a similar redistribution, that is to say I transfer to the right pocket of my greatcoat, now again available, the five stones in the right pocket of my trousers, which I replace by the six stones in the left pocket of my trousers, which I replace by the five stones in the left pocket of my greatcoat. And there I am ready to begin again. Do I have to go on? No, for it is clear that after the next series, of sucks and transfers, I shall be back where I started, that is to say with the first six stones back in the supply-pocket, the next five in the right pocket of my stinking old trousers and finally the last five in left pocket of same, and my sixteen stones will have been sucked once at least in impeccable succession, not one sucked twice, not one left unsucked. It is true that the next time I could scarcely hope to suck my stones in the same order as the first time and that the first, seventh and twelfth for example of the first cycle might very well be the sixth, eleventh and sixteenth respectively of the second, if the worst came to the worst. But that was a drawback I could not avoid. And if in the cycles taken together utter confusion was bound to reign, at least within each cycle taken separately I could be easy in my mind, at least as easy as one can be, in a proceeding of this kind. For in order for each cycle to be identical, as to the succession of stones in my mouth, and God knows I had set my heart on it, the only means were numbered stones or sixteen pockets. And rather than make twelve more pockets or number my stones, I preferred to make the best of the comparative peace of mind I enjoyed within each cycle taken separately. For it was not enough to number the stones, but I would have had to remember, every time I put a stone in my mouth, the number I needed and look for it in my pocket. Which would have put me off stone for ever, in a very short time. For I would never have been sure of not making a mistake, unless of course I had kept a kind of register, in which to tick off the stones one by one, as I sucked them. And of this I believed myself incapable. No, the only perfect solution would have been the sixteen pockets, symmetrically disposed, each one with its stone. Then I would have needed neither to number nor to think, but merely, as I sucked a given stone, to move on the fifteen others, each to the next pocket, a delicate business admittedly, but within my power, and to call always on the same pocket when I felt like a suck. This would have freed me from all anxiety, not only within each cycle taken separately, but also for the sum of all cycles, though they went on forever. But however imperfect my own solution was, I was pleased at having found it all alone, yes, quite pleased. And if it was perhaps less sound than I had thought in the first flush of discovery, its inelegance never diminished. And it was above all inelegant in this, to my mind, that the uneven distribution was painful to me, bodily. It is true that a kind of equilibrium was reached, at a given moment, in the early stages of each cycle, namely after the third suck and before the fourth, but it did not last long, and the rest of the time I felt the weight of the stones dragging me now to one side, now to the other. So it was something more than a principle I abandoned, when I abandoned the equal distribution, it was a bodily need. But to suck the stones in the way I have described, not haphazard, but with method, was also I think a bodily need. Here then were two incompatible bodily needs, at loggerheads. Such things happen. But deep down I didn't give a tinker's curse about being off my balance, dragged to the right hand and the left, backwards and forwards. And deep down it was all the same to me whether I sucked a different stone each time or always the same stone, until the end of time. For they all tasted exactly the same. And if I had collected sixteen, it was not in order to ballast myself in such and such a way, or to suck them turn about, but simply to have a little store, so as never to be without. But deep down I didn't give a fiddler's curse about being without, when they were all gone they would be all gone, I wouldn't be any the worse off, or hardly any. And the solution to which I rallied in the end was to throw away all the stones but one, which I kept now in one pocket, now in another, and which of course I soon lost, or threw away, or gave away, or swallowed. It was a wild part of the coast. I don't remember having been seriously molested. The black speck I was, in the great pale stretch of sand, who could wish it harm? Some came near, to see what it was, whether it wasn't something of value from a wreck, washed up by the storm. But when they saw the jetsam was alive, decently if wretchedly clothed, they turned away. Old women and young ones, yes, too, come to gather wood, came and stared, in the early days. But they were always the same and it was in vain I moved from one place to another, in the end they all knew what I was and kept their distance. I think one of them one day, detaching herself from her companions, came and offered me something to eat and that I looked at her in silence, until she went away. Yes, it seems to me some such incident occurred about this time. But perhaps I am thinking of another stay, at an earlier time, for this will be my last, my last but one, or two, there is never a last, by the sea. However that may be I see a young woman coming towards me and stopping from time to time to look back at her companions. Huddled together like sheep they watch her recede, urging her on, and laughing no doubt, I seem to hear laughter, far away. Then it is her back I see, as she goes away, now it is towards me she looks back, but without stopping. But perhaps I am merging two times in one, and two women, one coming towards me, shyly, urged on by the cries and laughter of her companions, and the other going away from me, unhesitatingly. For those who came towards me I saw coming from afar, most of the time, that is one of the advantages of the seaside. Black specks in the distance I saw them coming, I could follow all their manoeuvres, saying, It's getting smaller, or, it's getting bigger. Yes, to be taken unawares was so to speak impossible, for I turned often towards the land too. Let me tell you something, my sight was better at the seaside! Yes, ranging far and wide over these vast flats, where nothing lay, nothing stood, my good eye saw more clearly and there were even days when the bad one too had to look away. And not only did I see more clearly, but I had less difficulty in saddling with a name the rare things I saw. These are some of the advantages and disadvantages of the seaside. Or perhaps it was I who was changing, why not? And in the morning, in my cave, and even sometimes at night, when the storm raged, I felt reasonably secure from the elements and mankind. But there too there is a price to pay. In your box, in your caves, there too there is a price to pay. And which you pay willingly, for a time, but which you cannot go on paying forever. For you cannot go on buying the same thing forever, with your little pittance. And unfortunately there are other needs than that of rotting in peace, it's not the word, I mean of course my mother whose image, blunted for

some time past, was beginning now to harrow me again. So I went back inland, for my town was not strictly speaking on the sea, whatever may have been said to the contrary. And to get to it you had to go inland, I at least knew of no other way. For between my town and the sea there was a kind of swamp which, as far back as I can remember, and some of my memories have their roots deep in the immediate past, there was always talk of draining, by means of canals I suppose, or of transforming into a vast port and docks, or into a city on piles for the workers, in a word of redeeming somehow or other. And with the same stone they would have killed the scandal, at the gates of their metropolis, of a stinking steaming swamp in which an incalculable number of human lives were yearly engulfed, the statistics escape me for the moment and doubtless always will, so complete is my indifference to this aspect of the question. It is true they actually began to work and that work is still going on in certain areas in the teeth of adversity, setbacks, epidemics and the apathy of the Public Works Department, far from me to deny it. But from this to proclaiming that the sea came lapping at the ramparts of my town, there was a far cry. And I for my part will never lend myself to such a perversion (of the truth), until such time as I am compelled or find it convenient to do so. And I knew this swamp a little, having risked my life in it, cautiously, on several occasions, at a period of my life richer in illusions than the one I am trying to patch together here, I mean richer in certain illusions, in others poorer. So there was no way of coming at my town directly, by sea, but you had to disembark well to the north or the south and take to the roads, just imagine that, for they had never heard of Watt,[1] just imagine that too. And now my progress, slow and painful at all times, was more so than ever, because of my short stiff leg, the

---

[1] *Watt:* title character of a novel by Beckett.

same which I thought had long been as stiff as a leg could be, but damn the bit of it, for it was growing stiffer than ever, a thing I would not have thought possible, and at the same time, shorter every day, but above all because of the other leg, supple hitherto and now growing rapidly stiff in its turn but not yet shortening, unhappily. For when the two legs shorten at the same time, and at the same speed, then all is not lost, no. But when one shortens, and the other not, then you begin to be worried. Oh not that I was exactly worried, but it was a nuisance, yes, a nuisance. For I didn't know which foot to land on, when I came down. Let us try and get this dilemma clear. Follow me carefully. The stiff leg hurt me, admittedly, I mean the old stiff leg, and it was the other which I normally used as a pivot, or prop. But now this latter, as a result of its stiffening I suppose, and the ensuing commotion among nerves and sinews, was beginning to hurt me even more than the other. What a story, God send I don't make a balls of it. For the old pain, do you follow me, I had got used to it, in a way, yes, in a kind of way. Whereas to the new pain, though of the same family exactly, I had not yet had time to adjust myself. Nor should it be forgotten that having one bad leg plus another more or less good, I was able to nurse the former exclusively, with the help of my crutches. But I no longer had this resource! For I no longer had one bad leg plus another more or less good, but now both were equally bad. And the worse, to my mind, was that which till now had been good, at least comparatively good, and whose change for the worse I had not yet got used to. So in a way, if you like, I had still one bad leg and one good, or rather less bad, with this difference however, that the less bad now was the less good of heretofore. It was therefore on the old bad leg that I often longed to lean, between one crutch-stroke and the next. For while still extremely sensitive, it was less so than the other, or it was equally so, if you like, but it did not seem so, to me, because

of its seniority. But I couldn't! What? Lean on it. For it was shortening, don't forget, whereas the other, though stiffening, was not yet shortening, or so far behind its fellow that to all intents and purposes, I'm lost, no matter. If I could even have bent it, at the knee, or even at the hip, I could have made it seem as short as the other, long enough to land on the true short one, before taking off again. But I couldn't. What? Bend it. For how could I bend it, when it was stiff? I was therefore compelled to work the same old leg as heretofore, in spite of its having become, at least as far as the pain was concerned, the worse of the two and the more in need of nursing. Sometimes to be sure, when I was lucky enough to chance on a road conveniently cambered, or by taking advantage of a not too deep ditch or any other breach of surface, I managed to lengthen my short leg, for a short time. But it had done no work for so long that it did not know how to go about it. And I think a pile of dishes would have better supported me than it, which had so well supported me, when I was a tiny tot. And another factor of disequilibrium was here involved, I mean when I thus made the best of the lie of the land, I mean my crutches, which would have needed to be unequal, one short and one long, if I was to remain vertical. No? I don't know. In any case the ways I went were for the most part little forest paths, that's understandable, where differences of level, though abounding, were too confused and too erratic to be of any help to me. But did it make such a difference after all, as far as the pain was concerned, whether my leg was free to rest or whether it had to work? I think not. For the suffering of the leg at rest was constant and monotonous. Whereas the leg condemned to the increase of pain inflicted by work knew the decrease of pain dispensed by work suspended, the space of an instant. But I am human, I fancy, and my progress suffered, from this state of affairs, and from the slow and painful progress it had always been, whatever may have been said to the contrary, was changed, saving your presence, to a veritable calvary, with no limit to its stations and no hope of crucifixion, though I say it myself, and no Simon, and reduced me to frequent halts. Yes, my progress reduced me to stopping more and more often, it was the only way to progress, to stop. And though it is no part of my tottering intentions to treat here in full, as they deserve, these brief moments of the immemorial expiation, I shall nevertheless deal with them briefly, out of the goodness of my heart, so that my story, so clear till now, may not end in darkness, the darkness of these towering forests, these giant fronds, where I hobble, listen, fall, rise, listen and hobble on, wondering sometimes, need I say, if I shall ever see again the hated light, at least unloved, stretched palely between the last boles, and my mother, to settle with her, and if I would not do better, at least just as well, to hang myself from a bough, with a liane.

RICHARD WRIGHT

Big Boy Leaves Home

I

Yo mama don wear no drawers . . .

Clearly, the voice rose out of the woods, and died away. Like an echo another voice caught it up:

Ah seena when she pulled em off . . .

Another, shrill, cracking, adolescent:

N she washed 'em in alcohol . . .

Then a quartet of voices, blending in harmony, floated high above the tree tops:

N she hung 'em out in the hall . . .

Laughing easily, four black boys came out of the woods into cleared pasture. They walked lollingly in bare feet, beating tangled vines and bushes with long sticks.

"Ah wished Ah knowed some mo lines t tha song."

"Me too."

"Yeah, when yuh gits t where she hangs em out in the hall yuh has t stop."

"Shucks, whut goes wid *hall*?"

"*Call*."

"*Fall*."

"*Wall*."

"*Quall*."

They threw themselves on the grass, laughing.

"Big Boy?"

"Huh?"

"Yuh know one thing?"

"Whut?"

"Yuh sho is crazy!"

"Crazy?"

"Yeah, yuh crazys a bed-bug!"

"Crazy bout whut?"

"Man, whoever hearda *quall*?"

"Yuh said yuh wanted something t go wid *hall*, didnt yuh?"

"Yeah, but whuts a *quall*?"

"Nigger, a *qualls* a *quall*."

They laughed easily, catching and pulling long green blades of grass with their toes.

"Waal, ef a *qualls* a *quall*, whut IS a *quall*?"

"Oh, Ah know."

"Whut?"

"Tha ol song goes something like this:

Yo mama don wear no drawers,
  Ah seena when she pulled em off,
N she washed em in alcohol,
  N she hung em out in the hall,
  N then she put em back on her QUALL!"

They laughed again. Their shoulders were flat to the earth, their knees propped up, and their faces square to the sun.

"Big Boy, yuhs CRAZY!"

"Don ax me nothin else."

"Nigger, yuhs CRAZY!"

They fell silent, smiling, drooping the lids of their eyes softly against the sunlight.

"Man, don the groun feel warm?"

"Jus lika bed."

"Jeeesus, Ah could stay here ferever."

"Me too."

"Ah kin feel tha ol sun goin all thu me."

"Feels like mah bones is warm."

In the distance a train whistled mournfully.

"There goes number fo!"

"Hittin on all six!"

"Highballin it down the line!"

"Boun fer up Noth, Lawd, boun fer up Noth!"

They began to chant, pounding bare heels in the grass.

> Dis train boun fo Glory
> Dis train, Oh Hallelujah
> Dis train boun fo Glory
> Dis train, Oh Hallelujah
> Dis train boun fo Glory
> Ef yuh ride no need fer fret er worry
> Dis train, Oh Hallelujah
> Dis train . . .
>
> Dis train don carry no gambler
> Dis train, Oh Hallelujah
> Dis train don carry no gambler
> Dis train, Oh Hallelujah
> Dis train don carry no gambler
> No fo day creeper er midnight rambler
> Dis train, Oh Hallelujah
> Dis train . . .

When the song ended they burst out laughing, thinking of a train bound for Glory.

"Gee, thas a good ol song!"

"Huuuuummmmmmmmman . . ."

"Whut?"

"Geeee whiiiiiiz . . ."

"Whut?"

"Somebody don let win! Das whut!"

Buck, Bobo and Lester jumped up. Big Boy stayed on the ground, feigning sleep.

"Jeeesus, tha sho stinks!"

"Big Boy!"

Big Boy feigned to snore.

"Big Boy!"

Big Boy stirred as though in sleep.

"Big Boy!"

"Hunh?"

"Yuh rotten inside!"

"Rotten?"

"Lawd, cant yuh smell it?"

"Smell whut?"

"Nigger, yuh mus gotta bad col!"

"*Smell whut?*"

"NIGGER, YUH BROKE WIN!"

Big Boy laughed and fell back on the grass, closing his eyes.

"The hen whut cackles is the hen whut laid the egg."

"We ain no hens."

"Yuh cackled, didnt yuh?"

The three moved off with noses turned up.

"C mon!"

"Where yuh-all goin?"

"T the creek fer a swim."

"Yeah, les swim."

"Naw buddy naw!" said Big Boy, slapping the air with a scornful palm.

"Aw, c mon! Don be a heel!"

"N git *lynched*? Hell naw!"

"He ain gonna see us."

"How yuh know?"

"Cause he ain."

"Yuh-all go on. Ahma stay right here," said Big Boy.

"Hell, let im stay! C mon, les go," said Buck.

The three walked off, swishing at grass and bushes with sticks. Big Boy looked lazily at their backs.

"Hey!"

Walking on, they glanced over their shoulders.

"Hey, niggers!"

"C mon!"

Big Boy grunted, picked up his stick, pulled to his feet, and stumbled off.

"Wait!"

"C mon!"

He ran, caught up with them, leaped upon their backs, bearing them to the ground.

"Quit, Big Boy!"

"Gawddam, nigger!"

"Git t hell offa me!"

Big Boy sprawled in the grass beside them, laughing and pounding his heels in the ground.

"Nigger, whut yuh think we is, hosses?"

"How come yuh always hoppin on us?"

"Lissen, wes gonna double-team on yuh one of these days n beat yo ol ass good."

Big Boy smiled.

"Sho nough?"

"Yeah, don yuh like it?"

"We gonna beat yuh sos yuh cant walk!"

"N dare yuh t do nothin erbout it!"

Big Boy bared his teeth.

"C mon! Try it now!"

The three circled around him.

"Say, Buck, yuh grab his feets!"

"N yuh git his head, Lester!"

"N Bobo, yuh git berhin n grab his arms!"

Keeping more than arm's length, they circled round and round Big Boy.

"C mon!" said Big Boy, feinting at one and then the other.

Round and round they circled, but could not seem to get any closer. Big Boy stopped and braced his hands on his hips.

"Is all three of yuh-all scareda me?"

"Les git im some other time," said Bobo, grinning.

"Yeah, we kin ketch yuh when yuh ain thinkin," said Lester.

"We kin trick yuh," said Buck.

They laughed and walked together.

Big Boy belched.

"Ahm hongry," he said.

"Me too."

"Ah wished Ah hada big hot pota bellybusters!"

"Cooked wid some good ol salty ribs . . ."

"N some good ol egg cornbread . . ."

"N some buttermilk . . ."

"N some hot peach cobbler swimmin in juice . . ."

"Nigger, hush!"

They began to chant, emphasizing the rhythm by cutting at grass with sticks.

Bye n bye
Ah wanna piece of pie
Pies too sweet
Ah wanna piece of meat
Meats too red
Ah wanna piece of bread
Breads too brown
Ah wanna go t town
Towns too far
Ah wanna ketch a car
Cars too fas
Ah fall n break mah ass
Ahll understan it better bye n bye . . .

They climbed over a barbed-wire fence and entered a stretch of thick woods. Big Boy was whistling softly, his eyes half-closed.

"LES GIT IM!"

Buck, Lester, and Bobo whirled, grabbed Big Boy about the neck, arms, and legs, bearing him to the ground. He grunted and kicked wildly as he went back into weeds.

"Hol im tight!"

"Git his arms! Git his arms!"

"Set on his legs so he cant kick!"

Big Boy puffed heavily, trying to get loose.

"WE GOT YUH NOW, GAWDDAMMIT, WE GOT YUH NOW!"

"Thas a Gawddam lie!" said Big Boy. He kicked, twisted, and clutched for a hold on one and then the other.

"Say, yuh-all hep me hol his arms!" said Bobo.

"Aw, we got this bastard now!" said Lester.

"Thas a Gawddam lie!" said Big Boy again.

"Say, yuh-all hep me hol his arms!" called Bobo.

Big Boy managed to encircle the neck of Bobo with his left arm. He tightened his elbow scissorslike and hissed through his teeth:

"Yuh got me, ain yuh?"

"Hol im!"

"Les beat this bastard's ass!"

"Say, hep me hol his *arms*! Hes got aholda mah *neck*!" cried Bobo.

Big Boy squeezed Bobo's neck and twisted his head to the ground.

"Yuh got me, ain yuh?"

"Quit, Big Boy, yuh chokin me; yuh hurtin mah neck!" cried Bobo.

"Turn me loose!" said Big Boy.

"Ah ain got yuh! Its the others whut got yuh!" pleaded Bobo.

"Tell them others t git t hell offa me or Ahma break yo neck," said Big Boy.

"Ssssay, yyyuh-all gggit ooooffa Bbig Boy. Hhhes got me," gurgled Bobo.

"Cant yuh hol im?"

"Nnaw, hhes ggot mmah nneck . . ."

Big Boy squeezed tighter.

"N Ahma break it too less yuh tell em t git t hell offa me!"

"Ttturn mmmeee llloose," panted Bobo, tears gushing.

"Cant yuh hol im, Bobo?" asked Buck.

"Nnaw, yuh-all tturn im lloose; hhhes got mah nnneck . . ."

"Grab his neck, Bobo . . ."

"Ah cant; yugurgur . . ."

To save Bobo, Lester and Buck got up and ran to a safe distance. Big Boy released Bobo, who staggered to his feet, slobbering and trying to stretch a crick out of his neck.

"Shucks, nigger, yuh almos broke mah neck," whimpered Bobo.

"Ahm gonna break yo ass nex time," said Big Boy.

"Ef Bobo coulda hel yuh we woulda had yuh," yelled Lester.

"Ah wuznt gonna let im do that," said Big Boy.

They walked together again, swishing sticks.

"Yuh see," began Big Boy, "when a ganga guys jump on yuh, all yuh gotta do is jus put the heat on one of them n make im tell the others t let up, see?"

"Gee, thas a good idee!"

"Yeah, thas a good idee!"

"But yuh almos broke mah neck, man," said Bobo.

"Ahma smart nigger," said Big Boy, thrusting out his chest.

II

They came to the swimming hole.

"Ah ain goin in," said Bobo.

"Done got scared?" asked Big Boy.

"Naw, Ah ain scared . . ."

"How come yuh ain goin in?"

"Yuh know ol man Harvey don errlow no niggers t swim in this hole."

"N jus las year he took a shot at Bob fer swimmin in here," said Lester.

"Shucks, ol man Harvey ain studyin bout us niggers," said Big Boy.

"Hes at home thinkin about his jelly-roll," said Buck.

They laughed.

"Buck, yo mins lowern a snakes belly," said Lester.

"Ol man Harveys too doggone ol t think erbout jelly-roll," said Big Boy.

"Hes dried up; all the saps done lef im," said Bobo.

"C mon, les go!" said Big Boy.

Bobo pointed.

"See tha sign over yonder?"

"Yeah."

"Whut it say?"

"NO TRESPASSIN," read Lester.

"Know whut tha mean?"

"Mean ain no dogs n niggers errlowed," said Buck.

"Waal, wes here now," said Big Boy. "Ef he ketched us even like this thered be trouble, so we just as waal go in . . ."

"Ahm wid the nex one!"

"Ahll go ef anybody else goes!"

Big Boy looked carefully in all directions. Seeing nobody, he began jerking off his overalls.

"LAS ONE INS A OL DEAD DOG!"

"THAS YO MA!"

"THAS YO PA!"

"THAS BOTH YO MA N YO PA!"

They jerked off their clothes and threw them in a pile under a tree. Thirty seconds later they stood, black and naked, on the edge of the hole under a sloping embankment. Gingerly Big Boy touched the water with his foot.

"Man, this waters col," he said.

"Ahm gonna put mah cloes back on," said Bobo, withdrawing his foot.

Big Boy grabbed him about the waist.

"Like hell yuh is!"

"Git outta the way, nigger!" Bobo yelled.

"Throw im in!" said Lester.

"Duck im!"

Bobo crouched, spread his legs, and braced himself against Big Boy's body. Locked in each other's arms, they tussled on the edge of the hole, neither able to throw the other.

"C mon, les me n yuh push em in."

"O.K."

Laughing, Lester and Buck gave the two locked bodies a running push. Big Boy and Bobo splashed, sending up silver spray in the sunlight. When Big Boy's head came up he yelled:

"Yuh bastard!"

"Tha wuz yo ma yuh pushed!" said Bobo, shaking his head to clear the water from his eyes.

They did a surface dive, came up and struck out across the creek. The muddy water foamed. They swam back, waded into shallow water, breathing heavily and blinking eyes.

"C mon in!"

"Man, the waters fine!"

Lester and Buck hesitated.

"Les wet em," Big Boy whispered to Bobo.

Before Lester and Buck could back away, they were dripping wet from handsful of scooped water.

"Hey, quit!"

"Gawddam, nigger! Tha waters col!"

"C mon in!" called Big Boy.

"We jus as waal go on in now," said Buck.

"Look n see ef anybodys comin."

Kneeling, they squinted among the trees.

"Ain nobody."

"C mon, les go."

They waded in slowly, pausing each few steps to catch their breath. A desperate water battle began. Closing eyes and backing away, they shunted water into one another's faces with the flat palms of hands.

"Hey, cut it out!"

"Yeah, Ahm bout drownin!"

They came together in water up to their navels, blowing and blinking. Big Boy ducked, upsetting Bobo.

"Look out, nigger!"

"Don holler so loud!"

"Yeah, they kin hear yo ol big mouth a mile erway."

"This waters too col fer me."

"Thas cause it rained yistiddy."

They swam across and back again.

"Ah wish we hada bigger place t swim in."

"The white folks got plenty swimmin pools n we ain got none."

"Ah useta swim in the ol Missippi when we lived in Vicksburg."

Big Boy put his head under the water and blew his breath. A sound came like that of a hippopotamus.

"C mon, les be hippos."

Each went to a corner of the creek and put his mouth just below the surface and blew like a hippopotamus. Tiring, they came and sat under the embankment.

"Look like Ah gotta chill."

"Me too."

"Les stay here n dry off."

"Jeeesus, Ahm col!"

They kept still in the sun, suppressing shivers. After some of the water had dried off their bodies they began to talk through clattering teeth.

"Whut would yuh do ef ol man Harveyd come erlong right now?"

"Run like hell!"

"Man, Ahd run so fas hed thinka black streaka lightnin shot pass im."

"But spose he hada gun?"

"Aw, nigger, shut up!"

They were silent, They ran their hands over wet, trembling legs, brushing water away. Then their eyes watched the sun sparkling on the restless creek.

Far away a train whistled.

"There goes number seven!"

"Headin fer up Noth!"

"Blazin it down the line!"

"Lawd, Ahm goin Noth some day."

"Me too, man."

"They say colored folks up Noth is got ekual rights."

They grew pensive. A black winged butterfly hovered at the water's edge. A bee droned. From somewhere came the sweet scent of honeysuckles. Dimly they could hear sparrows twittering in the woods. They rolled from side to side, letting sunshine dry their skins and warm their blood. They plucked blades of grass and chewed them.

"Oh!"

They looked up, their lips parting.

"Oh!"

A white woman, poised on the edge of the opposite embankment, stood directly in front of them, her hat in her hand and her hair lit by the sun.

"Its a woman!" whispered Big Boy in an underbreath, "A *white* woman!"

They stared, their hands instinctively covering their groins. Then they scrambled to their feet. The white woman backed slowly out of sight. They stood for a moment, looking at one another.

"Les git outta here!" Big Boy whispered.

"Wait till she goes erway."

"Les run, theyll ketch us here naked like this!"

"Mabbe theres a man wid her."

"C mon, les git our cloes," said Big Boy.

They waited a moment longer, listening.

"Whut t hell! Ahma git mah cloes," said Big Boy.

Grabbing at short tufts of grass, he climbed the embankment.

"Don run out there now!"

"C mon back, fool!"

Bobo hesitated. He looked at Big Boy, and then at Buck and Lester.

"Ahm goin wid Big Boy n git mah cloes," he said.

"Don run out there naked like tha, fool!" said Buck. "Yuh don know whos out there!"

Big Boy was climbing over the edge of the embankment.

"C mon," he whispered.

Bobo climbed after. Twenty-five feet away the woman stood. She had one hand over her mouth. Hanging by fingers, Buck and Lester peeped over the edge.

"C mon back; that womans scared," said Lester.

Big Boy stopped, puzzled. He looked at the woman. He looked at the bundle of clothes. Then he looked at Buck and Lester.

"C mon, les git our cloes!"

He made a step.

"Jim!" the woman screamed.

Big Boy stopped and looked around. His hands hung loosely at his sides. The woman, her eyes wide, her hand over her mouth, backed away to the tree where their clothes lay in a heap.

"Big Boy, come back n wait till shes gone!"

Bobo ran to Big Boy's side.

"Les go home! Theyll ketch us here," he urged.

Big Boy's throat felt tight.

"Lady, we wanna git our cloes," he said.

Buck and Lester climbed the embankment and stood indecisively. Big Boy ran toward the tree.

"Jim!" the woman screamed. "Jim! Jim!"

Black and naked, Big Boy stopped three feet from her.

"We wanna git our cloes," he said again, his words coming mechanically.

He made a motion.

"You go away! You go away! I tell you, you go away!"

Big Boy stopped again, afraid. Bobo ran and snatched the clothes. Buck and Lester tried to grab theirs out of his hands.

"You go away! You go away! You go away!" the woman screamed.

"Les go!" said Bobo, running toward the woods.

CRACK!

Lester grunted, stiffened, and pitched forward. His forehead struck a toe of the woman's shoes.

Bobo stopped, clutching the clothes. Buck whirled. Big Boy stared at Lester, his lips moving.

"Hes gotta gun; hes gotta gun!" yelled Buck, running wildly.

CRACK!

Buck stopped at the edge of the embankment, his head jerked backward, his body arched stiffly to one side; he toppled headlong, sending up a shower of bright spray to the sunlight. The creek bubbled.

Big Boy and Bobo backed away, their eyes fastened fearfully on a white man who was running toward them. He had a rifle and wore an army officer's uniform. He ran to the woman's side and grabbed her hand.

"You hurt, Bertha, you hurt?"

She stared at him and did not answer.

The man turned quickly. His face was red. He raised the rifle and pointed it at Bobo. Bobo ran back, holding the clothes in front of his chest.

"Don shoot me, Mistah, don shoot me . . ."

Big Boy lunged for the rifle, grabbing the barrel.

"You black sonofabitch!"

Big Boy clung desperately.

"Let go, you black bastard!"

The barrel pointed skyward.

CRACK!

The white man, taller and heavier, flung Big Boy to the ground. Bobo dropped the clothes, ran up, and jumped onto the white man's back.

"You black sonsofbitches!"

The white man released the rifle, jerked Bobo to the ground, and began to batter the naked boy with his fists. Then Big Boy swung, striking the man in the mouth with the barrel. His teeth caved in, and he fell, dazed. Bobo was on his feet.

"C mon, Big Boy, les go!"

Breathing hard, the white man got up and faced Big Boy. His lips were trembling, his neck and chin wet with blood. He spoke quietly.

"Give me that gun, boy!"

Big Boy leveled the rifle and backed away. The white man advanced.

"Boy, I say give me that gun!"

Bobo had the clothes in his arms.

"Run, Big Boy, run!"

The man came at Big Boy.

"Ahll kill yuh; Ahll kill yuh!" said Big Boy.

His fingers fumbled for the trigger.

The man stopped, blinked, spat blood. His eyes were bewildered. His face whitened. Suddenly, he lunged for the rifle, his hands outstretched.

CRACK!

He fell forward on his face.

"Jim!"

Big Boy and Bobo turned in surprise to look at the woman.

"Jim!" she screamed again, and fell weakly at the foot of the tree.

Big Boy dropped the rifle, his eyes wide. He looked around. Bobo was crying and clutching the clothes.

"Big Boy, Big Boy . . ."

Big Boy looked at the rifle, started to pick it up, but didn't. He seemed at a loss. He looked at Lester, then at the white man; his eyes followed a thin stream of blood that seeped to the ground.

"Yuh done killed im," mumbled Bobo.

"Les go home!"

Naked, they turned and ran toward the woods. When they reached the barbed-wire fence they stopped.

"Les git our cloes on," said Big Boy.

They slipped quickly into overalls. Bobo held Lester's and Buck's clothes.

"Whut we gonna do wid these?"

Big Boy stared. His hands twitched.

"Leave em."

They climbed the fence and ran through the woods. Vines and leaves switched their faces. Once Bobo tripped and fell.

"C mon!" said Big Boy.

Bobo started crying, blood streaming from his scratches.

"Ahm scared!"

"C mon! Don cry! We wanna git home fo they ketches us!"

"Ahm scared!" said Bobo again, his eyes full of tears.

Big Boy grabbed his hand and dragged him along.

"C mon!"

III

They stopped when they got to the end of the woods. They could see the open road leading home, home to ma and pa. But they hung back, afraid. The thick shadows cast from the trees were friendly and sheltering. But the wide glare of sun stretching out over the fields was pitiless. They crouched behind an old log.

"We gotta git home," said Big Boy.

"Theys gonna lynch us," said Bobo, half-questioningly.

Big Boy did not answer.

"Theys gonna lynch us," said Bobo again.

Big Boy shuddered.

"Hush!" he said. He did not want to think of it. He could not think of it; there was but one thought, and he clung to that one blindly. He had to get home, home to ma and pa.

Their heads jerked up. Their ears had caught the rhythmic jingle of a wagon. They fell to the ground and clung flat to the side of a log. Over the crest of the hill came the top of a hat. A white face. Then shoulders in a blue shirt. A wagon drawn by two horses pulled into full view.

Big Boy and Bobo held their breath, waiting. Their eyes followed the wagon till it was lost in dust around a bend of the road.

"We gotta git home," said Big Boy.

"Ahm scared," said Bobo.

"C mon! Les keep t the fields."

They ran till they came to the cornfields. Then they went slower, for last year's corn stubbles bruised their feet.

They came in sight of a brickyard.

"Wait a minute," gasped Big Boy.

They stopped.

"Ahm goin on t mah home n yuh better go on t yos."

Bobo's eyes grew round.

"Ahm scared!"

"Yuh better go on!"

"Lemme go wid yuh; theyll ketch me . . ."

"Ef yuh kin git home mabbe yo folks kin hep yuh t git erway."

Big Boy started off. Bobo grabbed him.

"Lemme go wid yuh!"

Big Boy shook free.

"Ef yuh stay here theys gonna lynch yuh!" he yelled, running.

After he had gone about twenty-five yards he turned and looked; Bobo was flying through the woods like the wind.

Big Boy slowed when he came to the railroad. He wondered if he ought to go through the streets or down the track. He decided on the tracks. He could dodge a train better than a mob.

He trotted along the ties, looking ahead and back. His cheek itched, and he felt it. His hand came away smeared with blood. He wiped it nervously on his overalls.

When he came to his back fence he heaved himself over. He landed among a flock of startled chickens. A bantam rooster tried to spur him. He slipped and fell in front of the kitchen steps, grunting heavily. The ground was slick with greasy dishwater.

Panting, he stumbled through the doorway.

"Lawd, Big Boy, whuts wrong wid yuh?"

His mother stood gaping in the middle of the floor. Big Boy flopped wordlessly onto a stool, almost toppling over. Pots simmered on the stove. The kitchen smelled of food cooking.

"Whuts the matter, Big Boy?"

Mutely, he looked at her. Then he burst into tears. She came and felt the scratches on his face.

"Whut happened t yuh, Big Boy? Somebody been botherin yuh?"

"They after me, Ma! They after me . . ."

"Who!"

"Ah . . . Ah . . . We . . ."

"Big Boy, whuts wrong wid yuh?"

"He killed Lester n Buck," he muttered simply.

"Killed!"

"Yessum."

"Lester n Buck!"

"Yessum, Ma!"

"How killed?"

"He shot em, Ma!"

"Lawd Gawd in Heaven, have mercy on us all! This is mo trouble, mo trouble," she moaned, wringing her hands.

"N Ah killed im, Ma . . ."

She stared, trying to understand.

"Whut happened, Big Boy?"

"We tried t git our cloes from the tree . . ."

"Whut tree?"

"We wuz swimmin, Ma. N the white woman . . ."

"*White* woman? . . ."

"Yessum. She wuz at the swimmin hole . . ."

"Lawd have mercy! Ah knowed yuh boys wuz gonna keep on till yuh got into somethin like this!"

She ran into the hall.

"Lucy!"

"Mam?"

"C mere!"

"Mam?"

"C mere, Ah say!"

"Whutcha wan, Ma? Ahm sewin."

"Chile, will yuh c mere like Ah ast yuh?"

Lucy came to the door holding an unfinished apron in her hands. When she saw Big Boy's face she looked wildly at her mother.

"Whuts the matter?"

"Wheres Pa?"

"Hes out front, Ah reckon."

"Git im, quick!"

"Whuts the matter, Ma?"

"Go git yo Pa, Ah say!"

Lucy ran out. The mother sank into a chair, holding a dish rag. Suddenly, she sat up.

"Big Boy, Ah thought yuh wuz at school?"

Big Boy looked at the floor.

"How come yuh didnt go t school?"

"We went t the woods."

She sighed.

"Ah done done all Ah kin fer yuh, Big Boy. Only Gawd kin hep yuh now."

"Ma, don let em git me; don let em git me . . ."

His father came into the doorway. He stared at Big Boy, then at his wife.

"Whuts Big Boy inter now?" he asked sternly.

"Saul, Big Boys done gone n got inter trouble wid the white folks."

The old man's mouth dropped, and he looked from one to the other.

"Saul, we gotta git im erway from here."

"Open yo mouth n talk! Whut yuh been doin?" The old man gripped Big Boy's shoulders and peered at the scratches on his face.

"Me n Lester n Buck n Bobo wuz out on ol man Harveys place swimmin . . ."

"Saul, its a *white* woman!"

Big Boy winced. The old man compressed his lips and stared at his wife. Lucy gaped at her brother as though she had never seen him before.

"Whut happened? Cant yuh-all talk?" the old man thundered, with a certain helplessness in his voice.

"We wuz swimmin," Big Boy began, "n then a white woman comes up t the hole. We got up right erway t git our cloes sos we could git erway, n she started screamin. Our cloes wuz right by the tree where she wuz standin, n when we started to git em she jus screamed. We tol her we wanted our cloes . . . Yuh see, Pa, she wuz standin right *by* our cloes; n when we went t git em she jus screamed . . . Bobo got the cloes, n then he shot Lester . . ."

"*Who* shot Lester?"

"The white man."

"Whut white man?"

"Ah dunno, Pa. He wuz a soljer, n he had a rifle."

"A soljer?"

"Yessuh."

"A *soljer*?"

"Yessuh, Pa. A soljer."

The old man frowned.

"N then whut yuh-all do?"

"Waal, Buck said, 'Hes gotta gun!' N we started runnin. N then he shot Buck, n he fell in the swimmin hole. We didnt see im no mo . . . He wuz close on us then. He looked at the white woman n then he started t shoot Bobo. Ah grabbed the gun, n we started fightin. Bobo jumped on his back. He started beatin Bobo. Then Ah hit im wid the gun. Then he started at me n Ah shot im. Then we run . . ."

"Who seen?"

"Nobody."

"Wheres Bobo?"

"He went home."

"Anybody run after yuh-all?"

"Nawsuh."

"Yuh see anybody?"

"Nawsuh. Nobody but a white man. But he didnt see us."

"How long fo yuh-all lef the swimmin hole?"

"Little while ergo."

The old man nervously brushed his hand across his eyes and walked to the door. His lips moved, but no words came.

"Saul, whut we gonna do?"

"Lucy," began the old man, "go t Brother Sanders n tell im Ah said c mere; n go t Brother Jenkins n tell im Ah said c mere; n go t Elder Peters n tell im Ah said c mere. N don say nothin t nobody but whut Ah tol yuh. N when yuh git thu come straight back. Now go!"

Lucy dropped her apron across the back of a chair and ran down the steps. The mother bent over, crying and praying. The old man walked slowly over to Big Boy.

"Big Boy?"

Big Boy swallowed.

"Ahm talkin t yuh!"

"Yessuh."

"How come yuh didnt go t school this mawnin?"

"We went t the woods."

"Didnt yo ma send yuh t school?"

"Yessuh."

"How come yuh didnt go?"

"We went t the woods."

"Don yuh know thas wrong?"

"Yessuh."

"How come yuh go?"

Big Boy looked at his fingers, knotted them, and squirmed in his seat.

"AHM TALKIN T YUH!"

His wife straightened up and said reprovingly:

"Saul!"

The old man desisted, yanking nervously at the shoulder straps of his overalls.

"How long wuz the woman there?"

"Not long."

"Wuz she young?"

"Yessuh. Lika gal."

"Did yuh-all say anythin t her?"

"Nawsuh. We jus said we wanted our cloes."

"N whut she say?"

"Nothin, Pa. She jus backed erway t the tree n screamed."

The old man stared, his lips trying to form a question.

"Big Boy, did yuh-all bother her?"

"Nawsuh, Pa. We didnt *touch* her."

"How long fo the white man come up?"

"Right erway."

"Whut he say?"

"Nothin. He jus cussed us."

Abruptly the old man left the kitchen.

"Ma, cant Ah go fo they ketches me?"

"Sauls doin whut he kin."

"Ma, Ma, Ah don wan em t ketch me . . ."

"Sauls doin whut he kin. Nobody but the good Lawd kin hep us now."

The old man came back with a shotgun and leaned it in a corner. Fascinatedly, Big Boy looked at it.

There was a knock at the front door.

"Liza, see whos there."

She went. They were silent, listening. They could hear her talking.

"Whos there?"

"Me."

"Who?"

"Me, Brother Sanders."

"C mon in. Sauls waitin fer yuh."

Sanders paused in the doorway, smiling.

"Yuh sent fer me, Brother Morrison?"

"Brother Sanders, wes in deep trouble here."

Sanders came all the way into the kitchen.

"Yeah?"

"Big Boy done gone n killed a white man."

Sanders stopped short, then came forward, his face thrust out, his mouth open. His lips moved several times before he could speak.

"A *white* man?"

"They gonna kill me; they gonna kill me!" Big Boy cried, running to the old man.

"Saul, cant we git im erway somewhere?"

"Here now, take it easy; take it easy," said Sanders, holding Big Boy's wrists.

"They gonna kill me; they gonna lynch me!"

Big Boy slipped to the floor. They lifted him to a stool. His mother held him closely, pressing his head to her bosom.

"Whut we gonna do?" asked Sanders.

"Ah done sent fer Brother Jenkins n Elder Peters."

Sanders leaned his shoulders against the wall. Then as the full meaning of it all came to him, he exclaimed:

"Theys gonna git a mob! . . ." His voice broke off and his eyes fell on the shotgun.

Feet came pounding on the steps. They turned toward the door. Lucy ran in crying. Jenkins followed. The old man met him in the middle of the room, taking his hand.

"Wes in bad trouble here, Brother Jenkins. Big Boy's done gone n killed a white man. Yuh-alls gotta hep me . . ."

Jenkins looked hard at Big Boy.

"Elder Peters says hes comin," said Lucy.

"When all this happen?" asked Jenkins.

"Near bout a hour ergo, now," said the old man.

"Whut we gonna do?" asked Jenkins.

"Ah wanna wait till Elder Peters come," said the old man helplessly.

"But we gotta work fas ef we gonna do anythin," said Sanders. "Well git in trouble jus standin here like this."

Big Boy pulled away from his mother.

"Pa, lemme go now! Lemme me go now!"

"Be still, Big Boy!"

"Where kin yuh go?"

"Ah could ketch a freight!"

"Thas *sho* death!" said Jenkins. "Theyll be watchin em all!"

"Kin yuh-all hep me wid some money?" the old man asked.

They shook their heads.

"Saul, whut kin we do? Big Boy cant stay here."

There was another knock at the door.

The old man backed stealthily to the shotgun.

"Lucy go!"

Lucy looked at him, hesitating.

"Ah better go," said Jenkins.

It was Elder Peters. He came in hurriedly.

"Good evenin, everbody!"

"How yuh, Elder?"

"Good evenin."

"How yuh today?"

Peters looked around the crowded kitchen.

"Whuts the matter?"

"Elder, wes in deep trouble," began the old man. "Big Boy n some mo boys . . ."

". . . Lester n Buck n Bobo . . ."

". . . wuz over on ol man Harveys place swimmin . . ."

"N he don like us niggers *none*," said Peters emphatically. He widened his legs and put his thumbs in the armholes of his vest.

". . . n some white woman . . ."

"Yeah?" said Peters, coming closer.

". . . comes erlong n the boys tries t git their cloes where they done lef em under a tree. Waál, she started screamin n all, see? Reckon she thought the boys wuz after her. Then a white man in a soljer suit shoots two of em . . ."

". . . Lester n Buck . . ."

"Huummm," said Peters. "Tha wuz ol man Harveys son."

"Harveys son?"

"Yuh mean the one tha wuz in the Army?"

"Yuh mean Jim?"

"Yeah," said Peters. "The papers said he wuz here fer a vacation from his regiment. N tha woman the boys saw wuz jus erbout his wife . . ."

They stared at Peters. Now that they knew what white person had been killed, their fears became definite.

"N whut else happened?"

"Big Boy shot the man . . ."

"Harveys *son*?"

"He had t, Elder. He wuz gonna shoot im ef he didnt . . ."

"Lawd!" said Peters. He looked around and put his hat back on.

"How long ergo wuz this?"

"Mighty near an hour now, Ah reckon."

"Do the white folks know yit?"

"Don know, Elder."

"Yuh-all better git this boy outta here right now," said Peters. "Cause ef yuh don theres gonna be a lynchin . . ."

"Where kin Ah go, Elder?" Big Boy ran up to him.

They crowded around Peters. He stood with his legs wide apart, looking up at the ceiling.

"Mabbe we kin hide im in the church till he kin git erway," said Jenkins.

Peters' lips flexed.

"Naw, Brother, thall never do! Theyll git im there sho. N anyhow, ef they ketch im there itll ruin us all. We gotta git the boy outta town . . ."

Sanders went up to the old man.

"Lissen," he said in a whisper. "Mah son, Will, the one whut drives fer the Magnolia Express Comny, is taking a truck o goods t Chicawgo in the mawnin. If we kin hide Big Boy somewhere till then, we kin put im on the truck . . ."

"Pa, please, lemme go wid Will when he goes in the mawnin," Big Boy begged.

The old man stared at Sanders.

"Yuh reckon thas safe?"

"Its the only thing yuh *kin* do," said Peters.

"But where we gonna hide im till then?"

"Whut time you boy leavin out in the mawnin?"

"At six."

They were quiet, thinking. The water kettle on the stove sang.

"Pa, Ah knows where Will passes erlong wid the truck out on Bullards Road. Ah kin hide in one of them ol kilns . . ."

"Where?"

"In one of them kilns we built . . ."

"But theyll git yuh there," wailed the mother.

"But there ain no place else fer im t go."

"Theres some holes big ernough fer me t git

in n stay till Will comes erlong," said Big Boy. "Please Pa. lemme go fo they ketches me . . ."

"Let im go!"

"Please, Pa . . ."

The old man breathed heavily.

"Lucy, git his things!"

"Saul, theyll git im out there!" wailed the mother, grabbing Big Boy.

Peters pulled her away.

"Sister Morrison, ef yuh don let im go n git erway from here hes gonna be caught shos theres a Gawd in Heaven!"

Lucy came running with Big Boy's shoes and pulled them on his feet. The old man thrust a battered hat on his head. The mother went to the stove and dumped the skillet of corn pone into her apron. She wrapped it, and unbuttoning Big Boy's overalls, pushed it into his bosom.

"Heres somethin fer yuh t eat; n pray, Big Boy, cause thas all anybody kin do now . . ."

Big Boy pulled to the door, his mother clinging to him.

"Let im go, Sister Morrison!"

"Run fas, Big Boy!"

Big Boy raced across the yard, scattering the chickens. He paused at the fence and hollered back:

"Tell Bobo where Ahm hidin n tell im t c mon!"

IV

He made for the railroad, running straight toward the sunset. He held his left hand tightly over his heart, holding the hot pone of corn bread there. At times he stumbled over the ties, for his shoes were tight and hurt his feet. His throat burned from thirst; he had had no water since noon.

He veered off the track and trotted over the crest of a hill, following Bullard's Road. His feet slipped and slid in the dust. He kept his eyes straight ahead, fearing every clump of shrubbery, every tree. He wished it were night. If he could only get to the kilns without meeting anyone. Suddenly a thought came to him like a blow. He recalled hearing the old folks tell tales of blood-hounds, and fear made him run slower. None of them had thought of that. Spose blood-houns wuz put on his trail? Lawd! Spose a whole pack of em, foamin n howlin, tore im t pieces? He went limp and his feet dragged. Yeah, thas whut they wuz gonna send after im, bloodhouns! N then thered be no way fer im t dodge! Why hadnt Pa let him take tha shotgun? He stopped. He oughta go back n git tha shotgun. And then when the mob came he would take some with him.

In the distance he heard the approach of a train. It jarred him back to a sharp sense of danger. He ran again, his big shoes sopping up and down in the dust. He was tired and his lungs were bursting from running. He wet his lips, wanting water. As he turned from the road across a plowed field he heard the train roaring at his heels. He ran faster, gripped in terror.

He was nearly there now. He could see the black clay on the sloping hillside. Once inside a kiln he would be safe. For a little while, at least. He thought of the shotgun again. If he only had something! Someone to talk to . . . Thas right! Bobo! Bobod be wid im. Hed almost fergot Bobo. Bobod bringa gun; he knowed he would. N tergether they could kill the whole mob. Then in the mawning theyd git inter Will's truck n go far erway, t Chicawgo . . .

He slowed to a walk, looking back and ahead. A light wind skipped over the grass. A beetle lit on his cheek and he brushed it off. Behind the dark pines hung a red sun. Two bats flapped against that sun. He shivered, for he was growing cold; the sweat on his body was drying.

He stopped at the foot of the hill, trying to choose between two patches of black kilns high above him. He went to the left, for there lay the ones he, Bobo, Lester, and Buck had dug only last week. He looked around again; the landscape was bare. He climbed the embankment and stood before a row of black

pits sinking four and five feet deep into the earth. He went to the largest and peered in. He stiffened when his ears caught the sound of a whir. He ran back a few steps and poised on his toes. Six foot of snake slid out of the pit and went into coil. Big Boy looked around wildly for a stick. He ran down the slope, peering into the grass. He stumbled over a tree limb. He picked it up and tested it by striking it against the ground.

Warily, he crept back up the slope, his stick poised. When about seven feet from the snake he stopped and waved the stick. The coil grew tighter, the whir sounded louder, and a flat head reared to strike. He went to the right, and the flat head followed him, the blue-black tongue darting forth; he went to the left, and the flat head followed him there too.

He stopped, teeth clenched. He had to kill this snake. Jus had t kill im! This wuz the safest pit on the hillside. He waved the stick again, looking at the snake before, thinking of a mob behind. The flat head reared higher. With stick over shoulder, he jumped in, swinging. The stick sang through the air, catching the snake on the side of the head, sweeping him out of coil. There was a brown writhing mass. Then Big Boy was upon him, pounding blows home, one on top of the other. He fought viciously, his eyes red, his teeth bared in a snarl. He beat till the snake lay still; then he stomped it with his heel, grinding its head into the dirt.

He stopped, limp, wet. The corners of his lips were white with spittle. He spat and shuddered.

Cautiously, he went to the hole and peered. He longed for a match. He imagined whole nests of them in there waiting. He put the stick into the hole and waved it around. Stooping, he peered again. It mus be awright. He looked over the hillside, his eyes coming back to the dead snake. Then he got to his knees and backed slowly into the hole.

When inside he felt there must be snakes all about him, ready to strike. It seemed he could see and feel them there, waiting tensely in coil. In the dark he imagined long white fangs ready to sink into his neck, his side, his legs. He wanted to come out, but kept still. Shucks, he told himself, ef there wuz any snakes in here they sho woulda done bit me by now. Some of his fear left, and he relaxed.

With elbows on the ground and chin on palms, he settled. The clay was cold to his knees and thighs, but his bosom was kept warm by the hot pone of corn bread. His thirst returned and he longed for a drink. He was hungry, too. But he did not want to eat the corn pone. Naw, not now. Mabbe after erwhile, after Bobod came. Then theyd both eat the corn pone.

The view from his hole was fringed by the long tufts of grass. He could see all the way to Bullard's Road, and even beyond. The wind was blowing, and in the east the first touch of dusk was rising. Every now and then a bird floated past, a spot of wheeling black printed against the sky. Big Boy sighed, shifted his weight, and chewed at a blade of grass. A wasp droned. He heard number nine, far away and mournful.

The train made him remember how they had dug these kilns on long hot summer days, how they had made boilers out of big tin cans, filled them with water, fixed stoppers for steam, cemented them in holes with wet clay, and built fires under them. He recalled how they had danced and yelled when a stopper blew out of a boiler, letting out a big spout of steam and a shrill whistle. There were times when they had the whole hillside blazing and smoking. Yeah, yuh see, Big Boy wuz Casey Jones n wuz speedin it down the gleamin rails of the Southern Pacific. Bobo had number two on the Santa Fe. Buck wuz on the Illinoy Central. Lester the Nickel Plate. Lawd, how they shelved the wood in! The boiling water would almost jar the cans loose from the clay. More and more pine-knots and dry leaves would be piled under the cans. Flames would grow so tall they would have to shield their eyes. Sweat would pour off their faces. Then, suddenly, a peg would shoot high into

the air, and

Pssseeeezzzzzzzzzzzzzzzzzzzzzz . . .

Big Boy sighed and stretched out his arm, quenching the flames and scattering the smoke. Why didnt Bobo c mon? He looked over the fields; there was nothing but dying sunlight. His mind drifted back to the kilns. He remembered the day when Buck, jealous of his winning, had tried to smash his kiln. Yeah, that ol sonofabitch! Naw, Lawd! He didnt go t say tha! Whut wuz he thinkin erbout? Cussin the dead! Yeah, po ol Buck wuz dead now. N Lester too. Yeah, it wuz awright fer Buck t smash his kiln. Sho. N he wished he hadnt socked ol Buck so hard tha day. He wuz sorry fer Buck now. N he sho wished he hadnt cussed po ol Bucks ma, neither. Tha wuz sinful! Mabbe Gawd would git im fer tha? But he didnt go t do it! Po Buck! Po Lester! Hed never treat anybody like tha ergin, never . . .

Dusk was slowly deepening. Somewhere, he could not tell exactly where, a cricket took up a fitful song. The air was growing soft and heavy. He looked over the fields, longing for Bobo . . .

He shifted his body to ease the cold damp of the ground, and thought back over the day. Yeah, hed been dam right erbout not wantin t go swimmin. N ef hed followed his right min hed neverve gone n got inter all this trouble. At first hed said naw. But shucks, somehow hed just went on wid the res. Yeah, he shoulda went on t school tha mawnin, like Ma told im t do. But, hell, who wouldnt git tireda awways drivin a guy t school! Tha wuz the big trou awways drivin a guy t school. He wouldnt be in all this trouble now ef it wuznt fer that Gawddam school! Impatiently, he took the grass out of his mouth and threw it away, demolishing the little red school house . . .

Yeah, ef they had all kept still n quiet when tha ol white woman showed-up, mabbe shedve went on off. But yuh never kin tell erbout these white folks. Mabbe she wouldntve went. Mabbe tha white man woulda killed all of em! All *fo* of em! Yeah, yuh never kin tell erbout white folks. Then, ergin, mabbe tha white woman woulda went on off n laffed. Yeah, mabbe tha white man woulda said: *Yuh nigger bastards git t hell outta here! Yuh know Gawddam well yuh don berlong here!* N then they woulda grabbed their cloes n run like all hell . . . He blinked the white man away. Where wuz Bobo? Why didnt he hurry up n c mon?

He jerked another blade and chewed. Yeah, ef pa had only let im have tha shotgun! He could stan off a whole mob wid a shotgun. He looked at the ground as he turned a shotgun over in his hands. Then he leveled it at an advancing white man. *Boooom!* The man curled up. Another came. He reloaded quickly, and let him have what the other had got. He too curled up. Then another came. He got the same medicine. Then the whole mob swirled around him, and he blazed away, getting as many as he could. They closed in; but, by Gawd, he had done his part, hadnt he? N the newspapersd say: NIGGER KILLS DOZEN OF MOB BEFO LYNCHED! Er mabbe theyd say: TRAPPED NIGGER SLAYS TWENTY BEFO KILLED! He smiled a little. Tha wouldnt be so bad, would it? Blinking the newspaper away, he looked over the fields. Where wuz Bobo? Why didnt he hurry up n c mon?

He shifted, trying to get a crick out of his legs. Shucks, he wuz gittin tireda this. N it wuz almos dark now. Yeah, there wuz a little bittie star way over yonder in the eas. Mabbe tha white man wuznt dead? Mabbe they wuznt even lookin fer im? Mabbe he could go back home now? Naw, better wait erwhile. Thad be bes. But, Lawd, ef he only had some water! He could hardly swallow, his throat was so dry. Gawddam them white folks! Thas all they wuz good fer, t run a nigger down lika rabbit! Yeah, they git yuh in a corner n then they let yuh have it. A thousan of em! He shivered, for the cold of the clay was chilling his bones. Lawd, spose they foun im here in this hole? N wid nobody t hep im? . . . But

ain no use thinkin erbout tha; wait till trouble come fo yuh start fightin it. But ef tha mob came one by one hed wipe em all out. Clean up the whole bunch. He caught one by the neck and choked him long and hard, choked him till his tongue and eyes popped out. Then he jumped upon his chest and stomped him like he had stomped that snake. When he had finished with one, another came. He choked him too. Choked till he sank slowly to the ground, gasping . . .

"Hoalo!"

Big Boy snatched his fingers from the white man's neck and looked over the fields. He saw nobody. Had someone spied him? He was sure that somebody had hollered. His heart pounded. But, shucks, nobody couldnt see im here in this hole . . . But mabbe they seen im when he wuz comin n had laid low n wuz now closin in on im! Praps they wuz signalin fer the others? Yeah, they wuz creepin up on im! Mabbe he oughta git up n run . . . Oh! Mabbe tha wuz Bobo! Yeah, Bobo! He oughta clim out n see ef Bobo wuz lookin fer im . . . He stiffened.

"Hoalo!"

"Hoalo!"

"Wheres yuh?"

"Over here on Bullards Road!"

"C mon over!"

"Awright!"

He heard footsteps. Then voices came again, low and far away this time.

"Seen anybody?"

"Naw. Yuh?"

"Naw."

"Yuh reckon they got erway?"

"Ah dunno. Its hard t tell."

"Gawddam them sonofabitchin niggers!"

"We oughta kill ever black bastard in this country!"

"Waal, Jim got two of em, anyhow."

"But Bertha said there wuz *fo*!"

"Where in hell they hidin?"

"She said one of em wuz named Big Boy, or somethin like tha."

"We went t his shack lookin fer im."

"Yeah?"

"But we didnt fin im."

"These niggers stick tergether; they don never tell on each other."

"We looked all thu the shack n couldnt fin hide ner hair of im. Then we drove the ol woman n man out n set the shack on fire . . ."

"Jeesus! Ah wished Ah coulda been there!"

"Yuh shoulda heard the ol nigger woman howl . . ."

"Hoalo!"

"C mon over!"

Big Boy eased to the edge and peeped. He saw a white man with a gun slung over his shoulder running down the slope. Wuz they gonna search the hill? Lawd, there wuz no way fer im t git erway now; he wuz caught! He shoulda knowed theyd git im here. N he didnt hava thing, notta thing t fight wid. Yeah, soon as the blood-houns came theyd fin im. Lawd, have mercy! Theyd lynch im right here on the hill . . . Theyd git im n tie im t a stake n burn im erlive! Lawd! Nobody but the good Lawd could hep im now, nobody . . .

He heard more feet running. He nestled deeper. His chest ached. Nobody but the good Lawd could hep now. They wuz crowdin all round im n when they hada big crowd theyd close in on im. Then itd be over . . . The good Lawd would have t hep im, cause nobody could hep im now, nobody . . .

And then he went numb when he remembered Bobo. Spose Bobod come now? Hed be caught sho! Both of em would be caught! They'd make Bobo tell where he wuz! Bobo oughta not try to come now. Somebody oughta tell im . . . But there wuz nobody; there wuz no way . . .

He eased slowly back to the opening. There was a large group of men. More were coming. Many had guns. Some had coils of rope slung over shoulders.

"Ah tell yuh they still here, somewhere . . ."

"But we looked all over!"

"What t hell! Wouldnt do t let em git erway!"

"Naw. Ef they git erway notta woman in this town would be safe."

"Say, whuts tha yuh got?"

"Er pillar."

"Fer whut?"

"Feathers, fool!"

"Chris! Thisll be hot ef we kin ketch them niggers!"

"Ol Anderson said he wuz gonna bringa barrela tar!"

"Ah got some gasoline in mah car ef yuh need it."

Big Boy had no feelings now. He was waiting. He did not wonder if they were coming after him. He just waited. He did not wonder about Bobo. He rested his cheek against the cold clay, waiting.

A dog barked. He stiffened. It barked again. He balled himself into a knot at the bottom of the hole, waiting. Then he heard the patter of dog feet.

"Look!"

"Whuts he got?"

"Its a snake!"

"Yeah, the dogs foun a snake!"

"Gee, its a big one!"

"Shucks, Ah wish he could fin one of them sonofabitchin niggers!"

The voices sank to low murmurs. Then he heard number twelve, its bell tolling and whistle crying as it slid along the rails. He flattened himself against the clay. Someone was singing:

"We'll hang ever nigger t a sour apple tree . . ."

When the song ended there was hard laughter. From the other side of the hill he heard the dog barking furiously. He listened. There was more than one dog now. There were many and they were barking their throats out.

"Hush, Ah hear them dogs!"

"When theys barkin like tha theys foun somethin!"

"Here they come over the hill!"

"WE GOT IM! WE GOT IM!"

There came a roar. Tha mus be Bobo! tha mus be Bobo . . . In spite of his fear, Big Boy looked. The road, and half of the hillside across the road, were covered with men. A few were at the top of the hill, stenciled against the sky. He could see dark forms moving up the slopes. They were yelling.

"By Gawd, we got im!"

"C mon!"

"Where is he?"

"Theyre bringin im over the hill!"

"Ah got a rope fer im!"

"Say, somebody go n git the others!"

"Where is he? Cant we see im, Mister?"

"They say Berthas comin, too."

"Jack! Jack! Don leave me! Ah wanna see im!"

"Theyre bringin im over the hill, sweetheart!"

"AH WANNA BE THE FIRS T PUT A ROPE ON THA BLACK BASTARDS NECK!"

"Les start the fire!"

"Heat the tar!"

"Ah got some chains t chain im."

"Bring im over this way!"

"Chris, Ah wished Ah hada drink . . ."

Big Boy saw men moving over the hill. Among them was a long dark spot. Tha mus be Bobo; tha mus be Bobo theys carryin . . . They'll git im here. He oughta git up n run. He clamped his teeth and ran his hand across his forehead, bringing it away wet. He tried to swallow, but could not; his throat was dry.

They had started the song again:

"We'll hang ever nigger t a sour apple tree . . ."

There were women singing now. Their voices made the song round and full. Song waves rolled over the top of pine trees. The sky sagged low, heavy with clouds. Wind was rising. Sometimes cricket cries cut surprisingly across the mob song. A dog had gone to the utmost top of the hill. At each lull of the song his howl floated full into the night.

Big Boy shrank when he saw the first tall flame light the hillside. Would they see im here? Then he remembered you could not see into the dark if you were standing in the light. As flames leaped higher he saw two men rolling a barrel up the slope.

"Say, gimme a han here, will yuh?"

"Awright, heave!"

"C mon! Straight up! Git t the other end!"

"Ah got the feathers here in this pillar!"

"BRING SOME MO WOOD!"

Big Boy could see the barrel surrounded by flames. The mob fell back, forming a dark circle. Theyd fin im here! He had a wild impulse to climb out and fly across the hills. But his legs would not move. He stared hard, trying to find Bobo. His eyes played over a long dark spot near the fire. Fanned by wind, flames leaped higher. He jumped. That dark spot had moved. Lawd, thas Bobo; thas Bobo . . .

He smelt the scent of tar, faint at first, then stronger. The wind brought it full into his face, then blew it away. His eyes burned and he rubbed them with his knuckles. He sneezed.

"LES GIT SOURVINEERS!"

He saw the mob close in around the fire. Their faces were hard and sharp in the light of the flames. More men and women were coming over the hill. The long dark spot was smudged out.

"Everbody git back!"

"Look! Hes gotta finger!"

"C MON! GIT THE GALS BACK FROM THE FIRE!"

"Hes got one of his ears, see?"

"Whuts the matter!"

"A woman fell out! Fainted, Ah reckon . . ."

The stench of tar permeated the hillside. The sky was black and the wind was blowing hard.

"HURRY UP N BURN THE NIGGER FO IT RAINS!"

Big Boy saw the mob fall back, leaving a small knot of men about the fire. Then, for the first time, he had a full glimpse of Bobo.

A black body flashed in the light. Bobo was

struggling, twisting; they were binding his arms and legs.

When he saw them tilt the barrel he stiffened. A scream quivered. He knew the tar was on Bobo. The mob fell back. He saw a tar-drenched body glistening and turning.

"THE BASTARDS GOT IT!"

There was a sudden quiet. Then he shrank violently as the wind carried, like a flurry of snow, a widening spiral of white feathers into the night. The flames leaped tall as the trees. The scream came again. Big Boy trembled and looked. The mob was running down the slopes, leaving the fire clear. Then he saw a writhing white mass cradled in yellow flame, and heard screams, one on top of the other, each shriller and shorter than the last. The mob was quiet now, standing still, looking up the slopes at the writhing white mass gradually growing black, growing black in a cradle of yellow flame.

"PO ON MO GAS!"

"Gimme a lif, will yuh!"

Two men were struggling, carrying between them a heavy can. They set it down, tilted it, leaving it so that the gas would trickle down to the hollowed earth around the fire.

Big Boy slid back into the hole, his face buried in clay. He had no feelings now, no fears. He was numb, empty, as though all blood had been drawn from him. Then his muscles flexed taut when he heard a faint patter. A tiny stream of cold water seeped to his knees, making him push back to a drier spot. He looked up; rain was beating in the grass.

"Its rainin!"

"C mon, les git t town!"

". . . don worry, when the fire git thu wid im hell be gone . . ."

"Wait, Charles! Don leave me; its slippery here . . ."

"Ahll take some of yuh ladies back in mah car . . ."

Big Boy heard the dogs barking again, this time closer. Running feet pounded past. Cold water chilled his ankles. He could hear rain-drops steadily hissing.

Now a dog was barking at the mouth of the hole, barking furiously, sensing a presence there. He balled himself into a knot and clung to the bottom, his knees and shins buried in water. The bark came louder. He heard paws scraping and felt the hot scent of dog breath on his face. Green eyes glowed and drew nearer as the barking, muffled by the closeness of the hole, beat upon his eardrums. Backing till his shoulders pressed against the clay, he held his breath. He pushed out his hands, his fingers stiff. The dog yawped louder, advancing, his bark rising sharp and thin. Big Boy rose to his knees, his hands before him. Then he flattened out still more against the bottom, breathing lungsful of hot dog scent, breathing it slowly, hard, but evenly. The dog came closer, bringing hotter dog scent. Big Boy could go back no more. His knees were slipping and slopping in the water. He braced himself, ready. Then, he never exactly knew how—he never knew whether he had lunged or the dog had lunged—they were together, rolling in the water. The green eyes were beneath him, between his legs. Dognails bit into his arms. His knees slipped backward and he landed full on the dog; the dog's breath left in a heavy gasp. Instinctively, he fumbled for the throat as he felt the dog twisting between his knees. The dog snarled, long and low, as though gathering strength. Big Boy's hands traveled swiftly over the dog's back, groping for the throat. He felt dognails again and saw green eyes, but his fingers had found the throat. He choked, feeling his fingers sink; he choked, throwing back his head and stiffening his arms. He felt the dog's body heave, felt dognails digging into his loins. With strength flowing from fear, he closed his fingers, pushing his full weight on the dog's throat. The dog heaved again, and lay still . . . Big Boy heard the sound of his own breathing filling the hole, and heard shouts and footsteps above him going past.

For a long, long time he held the dog, held it long after the last footstep had died out, long after the rain had stopped.

V

Morning found him still on his knees in a puddle of rainwater, staring at the stiff body of a dog. As the air brightened he came to himself slowly. He held still for a long time, as though waking from a dream, as though trying to remember.

The chug of a truck came over the hill. He tried to crawl to the opening. His knees were stiff and a thousand needle-like pains shot from the bottom of his feet to the calves of his legs. Giddiness made his eyes blur. He pulled up and looked. Through brackish light he saw Will's truck standing some twenty-five yards away, the engine running. Will stood on the runningboard, looking over the slopes of the hill.

Big Boy scuffled out, falling weakly in the wet grass. He tried to call to Will, but his dry throat would make no sound. He tried again.

"Will!"

Will heard, answering:

"Big Boy, c mon!"

He tried to run, and fell. Will came, meeting him in the tall grass.

"C mon," Will said, catching his arm.

They struggled to the truck.

"Hurry up!" said Will, pushing him onto the runningboard.

Will pushed back a square trapdoor which swung above the back of the driver's seat. Big Boy pulled through, landing with a thud on the bottom. On hands and knees he looked around in the semi-darkness.

"Wheres Bobo?"

Big Boy stared.

"Wheres Bobo?"

"They got im."

"When?"

"Las night."

"The mob?"

Big Boy pointed in the direction of a charred sapling on the slope of the opposite hill. Will looked. The trapdoor fell. The engine purred, the gears whined, and the truck lurched forward over the muddy road, sending Big Boy on his side.

For a while he lay as he had fallen, on his side, too weak to move. As he felt the truck swing around a curve he straightened up and rested his back against a stack of wooden boxes. Slowly, he began to make out objects in the darkness. Through two long cracks fell thin blades of daylight. The floor was of smooth steel, and cold to his thighs. Splinters and bits of sawdust danced with the rumble of the truck. Each time they swung around a curve he was pulled over the floor; he grabbed at corners of boxes to steady himself. Once he heard the crow of a rooster. It made him think of home, of ma and pa. He thought he remembered hearing somewhere that the house had burned, but could not remember where . . . It all seemed unreal now.

He was tired. He dozed, swaying with the lurch. Then he jumped awake. The truck was running smoothly, on gravel. Far away he heard two short blasts from the Buckeye Lumber Mill. Unconsciously, the thought sang through his mind: It six erclock . . .

The trapdoor swung in. Will spoke through a corner of his mouth.

"How yuh comin?"

"Awright."

"How they git Bobo?"

"He wuz comin over the hill."

"Whut they do?"

"They burnt im . . . Will, Ah wan some water; mah throats like fire . . ."

"Well git some when we pass a fillin station."

Big Boy leaned back and dozed. He jerked awake when the truck stopped. He heard Will get out. He wanted to peep through the trapdoor, but was afraid. For a moment, the wild fear he had known in the hole came back. Spose theyd search n fin im? He quieted when he heard Will's footstep on the running-board. The trapdoor pushed in. Will's hat came through, dripping.

"Take it, quick!"

Big Boy grabbed, spilling water into his face. The truck lurched. He drank. Hard cold lumps of brick rolled into his hot stomach. A dull pain made him bend over. His intestines seemed to be drawing into a tight knot. After a bit it eased, and he sat up, breathing softly.

The truck swerved. He blinked his eyes. The blades of daylight had turned brightly golden. The sun had risen.

The truck sped over the asphalt miles, sped northward, jolting him, shaking out of his bosom the crumbs of corn bread, making them dance with the splinters and sawdust in the golden blades of sunshine.

He turned on his side and slept.

ALBERT CAMUS

The Guest

Translated by Justin O'Brien

The schoolmaster was watching the two men climb towards him. One was on horseback, the other on foot. They had not yet tackled the abrupt rise leading to the schoolhouse built on the hillside. They were toiling onwards, making slow progress in the snow, among the stones, on the vast expanse of the high, deserted plateau. From time to time the horse stumbled. Without hearing anything yet, he could see the breath issuing from the horse's nostrils. One of the men, at least, knew the region. They were following the trail although it had disappeared days ago under a layer of dirty white snow. The schoolmaster calculated that it would take them half an hour to get on to the hill. It was cold; he went back into the school to get a sweater.

He crossed the empty, frigid classroom. On the blackboard the four rivers of France, drawn with four different coloured chalks, had been flowing towards their estuaries for the past three days. Snow had suddenly fallen in mid October after eight months of drought without the transition of rain, and the twenty pupils, more or less, who lived in the villages scattered over the plateau had stopped coming. With fair weather they would return. Daru now heated only the single room that was his lodging, adjoining the classroom and giving also on to the plateau to the east. Like the class windows, his window looked to the south too. On that side the school was a few kilometres from the point where the plateau began to slope towards the south. In clear weather could be seen the purple mass of the mountain range where the gap opened on to the desert.

Somewhat warmed, Daru returned to the window from which he had first seen the two men. They were no longer visible. Hence they must have tackled the rise. The sky was not so dark, for the snow had stopped falling during the night. The morning had opened with a dirty light which had scarcely become brighter as the ceiling of clouds lifted. At two in the afternoon it seemed as if the day were merely beginning. But still this was better than those three days when the thick snow was falling amidst unbroken darkness with little gusts of wind that rattled the double door of the classroom. Then Daru had spent long hours in his room, leaving it only to go to the shed and feed the chickens or get some coal. Fortunately the delivery truck from Tadjid, the nearest village to the north, had brought his supplies two days before the blizzard. It would return in forty-eight hours.

Besides, he had enough to resist a siege, for the little room was cluttered with bags of wheat that the administration left as a stock to distribute to those of his pupils whose families had suffered from the drought. Actually they had all been victims because they were all poor. Every day Daru would distribute a ration to the children. They had missed it, he knew, during these bad days. Possibly one of the fathers or big brothers would come this afternoon and he could supply them with grain. It was just a matter of carrying them over to the next harvest. Now shiploads of wheat were arriving from France and the worst was over. But it would be hard to forget that poverty, that army of ragged ghosts wandering in the sunlight, the plateaux burned to a cinder month after month, the earth shrivelled up little by little, literally scorched, every stone bursting into dust under one's foot. The sheep had died then by thousands and even a few men, here and there, sometimes without anyone's knowing.

In contrast with such poverty, he who lived almost like a monk in his remote schoolhouse, none the less satisfied with the little he had and with the rough life, had felt like a lord with his whitewashed walls, his narrow couch, his unpainted shelves, his well, and his weekly provision of water and food. And suddenly this snow, without warning, without the foretaste of rain. This is the way the region was, cruel to live in, even without men—who didn't help matters either. But Daru had been born here. Everywhere else, he felt exiled.

He stepped out on to the terrace in front of the schoolhouse. The two men were now halfway up the slope. He recognized the horseman as Balducci, the old gendarme he had known for a long time. Balducci was holding on the end of a rope an Arab who was walking behind him with hands bound and head lowered. The gendarme waved a greeting to which Daru did not reply, lost as he was in contemplation of the Arab dressed in a faded blue jellaba, his feet in sandals but covered with socks of heavy raw wool, his head surmounted by a narrow, short *chéche*. They were approaching. Balducci was holding back his horse in order not to hurt the Arab, and the group was advancing slowly.

Within earshot, Balducci shouted: 'One hour to do the three kilometres from El Ameur!' Daru did not answer. Short and square in his thick sweater, he watched them climb. Not once had the Arab raised his head.

'Hello,' said Daru when they got up on to the terrace. 'Come in and warm up.' Balducci painfully got down from his horse without letting go the rope. From under his bristling moustache he smiled at the schoolmaster, His little dark eyes, deep-set under a tanned forehead, and his mouth surrounded with wrinkles made him look attentive and studious. Daru took the bridle, led the horse to the shed, and came back to the two men, who were now waiting for him in the school. He led them into his room. 'I am going to heat up the classroom,' he said. 'We'll be more comfortable there.' When he entered the room again, Balducci was on the couch. He had undone the rope tying him to the Arab, who had squatted near the stove. His hands still bound, the *chéche* pushed back on his head, he was looking towards the window. At first Daru noticed only his huge lips, fat, smooth, almost negroid; yet his nose was straight, his eyes were dark and full of fever. The *chéche* revealed an obstinate forehead and, under the weathered skin now rather discoloured by the cold, the whole face had a restless and rebellious look that struck Daru when the Arab, turning his face towards him, looked him straight in the eyes. 'Go into the other room,' said the schoolmaster, 'and I'll make you some mint tea.' 'Thanks,' Balducci said. 'What a nuisance! How I long for retirement.' And addressing his prisoner in Arabic: 'Come on, you.' The Arab got up and, slowly, holding his bound wrists in front of him, went into the classroom.

With the tea, Daru brought a chair. But Balducci was already enthroned on the nearest pupil's desk and the Arab had squatted against the teacher's platform facing the stove, which stood between the desk and the window. When he held out the glass of tea to the prisoner, Daru hesitated at the sight of his bound hands. 'He might perhaps be untied.' 'Certainly,' said Balducci. 'That was for the journey.' He started to get to his feet. But Daru, setting the glass on the floor, had knelt beside the Arab. Without saying anything, the

Arab watched him with his feverish eyes. Once his hands were free, he rubbed his swollen wrists against each other, took the glass of tea, and sucked up the burning liquid in swift little sips.

'Good,' said Daru. 'And where are you headed for?'

Balducci withdrew his moustache from the tea. 'Here, my boy.'

'Odd pupils! And you're spending the night?'

'No. I'm going back to El Ameur. And you will deliver this fellow to Tinguit. He is expected at police headquarters.'

Balducci was looking at Daru with a friendly little smile.

'What's this story?' asked the schoolmaster. 'Are you pulling my leg?'

'No, my boy. Those are the orders.'

'The orders? I'm not . . .' Daru hesitated not wanting to hurt the old Corsican. 'I mean, that's not my job.'

'What! What's the meaning of that? In wartime people do all kinds of jobs.'

'Then I'll wait for the declaration of war!' Balducci nodded.

'O.K. But the orders exist and they concern you too. Things are brewing, it appears. There is talk of a forthcoming revolt. We are mobilized, in a way.'

Daru still had his obstinate look.

'Listen, my boy,' Balducci said. 'I like you and you must understand. There's only a dozen of us at El Ameur to patrol throughout the whole territory of a small department and I must get back in a hurry. I was told to hand this man over to you and return without delay. He couldn't be kept there. His village was beginning to stir; they wanted to take him back. You must take him to Tinguit tomorrow before the day is over. Twenty kilometres shouldn't worry a husky fellow like you. After that, all will be over. You'll come back to your pupils and your comfortable life.'

Behind the wall the horse could be heard snorting and pawing the earth. Daru was looking out of the window. Decidedly, the weather was clearing and the light was increasing over the snowy plateau. When all the snow was melted, the sun would take over again and once more would burn the fields of stone. For days, still, the unchanging sky would shed its dry light on the solitary expanse where nothing had any connexion with man.

'After all,' he said, turning around towards Balducci, 'what did he do?' And, before the gendarme had opened his mouth, he asked: 'Does he speak French?'

'No, not a word. We had been looking for him for a month, but they were hiding him. He killed his cousin.'

'Is he against us?'

'I don't think so. But you can never be sure.'

'Why did he kill?'

'A family squabble, I think. One owed the other grain, it seems. It's not at all clear. In short, he killed his cousin with a billhook. You know, like a sheep, *kreezk!*'

Balducci made the gesture of drawing a blade across his throat and the Arab, his attention attracted, watched him with a sort of anxiety. Daru felt a sudden wrath against the man, against all men with their rotten spite, their tireless hates, their blood lust.

But the kettle was singing on the stove. He served Balducci more tea, hesitated, then served the Arab again, who, a second time, drank avidly. His raised arms made the jellaba fall open and the schoolmaster saw his thin, muscular chest.

'Thanks, my boy,' Balducci said. 'And now, I'm off.'

He got up and went towards the Arab, taking a small rope from his pocket.

'What are you doing?' Daru asked dryly.

Balducci, disconcerted, showed him the rope.

'Don't bother.'

The old gendarme hesitated. 'It's up to you. Of course, you are armed?'

'I have my shot gun.'

'Where?'

'In the trunk.'

'You ought to have it near your bed.'

'Why? I have nothing to fear.'

'You're mad. If there's an uprising, no one is safe, we're all in the same boat.'

'I'll defend myself. I'll have time to see them coming.'

Balducci began to laugh, then suddenly the moustache covered the white teeth.

'You'll have time? O.K. That's just what I was saying. You have always been a little cracked. That's why I like you, my son was like that.'

At the same time he took out his revolver and put it on the desk.

'Keep it; I don't need two weapons from here to El Ameur.'

The revolver shone against the black paint of the table. When the gendarme turned towards him, the schoolmaster caught the smell of leather and horseflesh.

'Listen, Balducci,' Daru said suddenly, 'every bit of this disgusts me, and most of all your fellow here. But I won't hand him over. Fight, yes, if I have to. But not that.'

The old gendarme stood in front of him and looked at him severely.

'You're being a fool,' he said slowly. 'I don't like it either. You don't get used to putting a rope on a man even after years of it, and you're even ashamed—yes, ashamed. But you can't let them have their way.'

'I won't hand him over,' Daru said again.

'It's an order, my boy, and I repeat it.'

'That's right. Repeat to them what I've said to you: I won't hand him over.'

Balducci made a visible effort to reflect. He looked at the Arab and at Daru. At last he decided.

'No, I won't tell them anything. If you want to drop us, go ahead; I'll not denounce you. I have an order to deliver the prisoner and I'm doing so. And now you'll just sign this paper for me.'

'There's no need. I'll not deny that you left him with me.'

'Don't be mean with me. I know you'll tell the truth. You're from hereabouts and you are a man. But you must sign, that's the rule.'

Daru opened his drawer, took out a little square bottle of purple ink, the red wooden penholder with the 'sergeant-major' pen he used for making models of penmanship, and signed. The gendarme carefully folded the paper and put it into his wallet. Then he moved towards the door.

'I'll see you off,' Daru said.

'No,' said Balducci. 'There's no use being polite. You insulted me.'

He looked at the Arab, motionless in the same spot, sniffed peevishly, and turned away towards the door. 'Good-bye son,' he said. The door shut behind him. Balducci appeared suddenly outside the window and then disappeared. His footsteps were muffled by the snow. The horse stirred on the other side of the wall and several chickens fluttered in fright. A moment later Balducci reappeared outside the window leading the horse by the bridle. He walked towards the little rise without turning round and disappeared from sight with the horse following him. A big stone could be heard bouncing down. Daru walked back towards the prisoner, who, without stirring, never took his eyes off him. 'Wait,' the schoolmaster said in Arabic and went towards the bedroom. As he was going through the door, he had a second thought, went to the desk, took the revolver, and stuck it in his pocket. Then, without looking back, he went into his room.

For some time he lay on his couch watching the sky gradually close over, listening to the silence. It was this silence that had seemed painful to him during the first days here, after the war. He had requested a post in the little town at the base of the foothills separating the upper plateaux from the desert. There, rocky walls, green and black to the north, pink and lavender to the south, marked the frontier of eternal summer. He had been named to a post farther north, on the plateau itself. In the beginning, the solitude and the silence had been hard for him on these wastelands peopled only by stones. Occasionally, furrows suggested cultivation, but they had been dug to uncover a certain kind of stone good for building. The only ploughing here was to harvest rocks. Elsewhere a thin layer of soil accumulated in the hollows would be scraped out to enrich paltry village gardens. This is the way it was: bare rock covered three-quarters of the region. Towns sprang up, flourished, then disappeared; men came by, loved one another or fought bitterly, then died. No one in this desert, neither he nor his guest, mattered. And yet, outside this desert neither of them, Daru knew, could have really lived.

When he got up, no noise came from the classroom. He was amazed at the unmixed joy he derived from the mere thought that the Arab might have fled and that he would be alone with no decision to make. But the prisoner was there. He had merely stretched out between the stove and the desk. With eyes open, he was staring at the ceiling. In that position, his thick lips were particularly noticeable, giving him a pouting look. 'Come,' said Daru. The Arab got up and followed him. In the bedroom, the schoolmaster pointed to a chair near the table under the window. The Arab sat down without taking his eyes off Daru.

'Are you hungry?'

'Yes,' the prisoner said.

Daru set the table for two. He took flour and oil, shaped a cake in a frying-pan, and lighted the little stove that functioned on bottled gas. While the cake was cooking, he went out to the shed to get cheese, eggs, dates, and condensed milk. When the cake was done he set it on the window sill to cool, heated some condensed milk diluted with water, and beat up the eggs into an omelet. In one of his motions he knocked against the revolver stuck in his right pocket. He set the bowl down, went into the classroom, and put the revolver in his desk drawer. When he came back to the room, night was falling. He put on the light and served the Arab. 'Eat,' he said. The Arab took a piece of the cake, lifted it eagerly to his mouth, and stopped short.

'And you?' he asked.

'After you. I'll eat too.'

The thick lips opened slightly. The Arab hesitated, then bit into the cake determinedly.

The meal over, the Arab looked at the schoolmaster. 'Are you the judge?'

'No, I'm simply keeping you until tomorrow.'

'Why do you eat with me?'

'I'm hungry.'

The Arab fell silent. Daru got up and went out. He brought back a folding bed from the shed, set it up between the table and the stove, at right-angles to his own bed. From a large suitcase which, upright in a corner, served as a shelf for papers, he took two blankets and arranged them on the camp bed. Then he stopped, felt useless, and sat down on his bed. There was nothing more to do or to get ready. He had to look at this man. He looked at him, therefore, trying to imagine his face bursting with rage. He couldn't do so. He could see nothing but the dark yet shining eyes and the animal mouth.

'Why did you kill him?' he asked in a voice whose hostile tone surprised him.

The Arab looked away.

'He ran away. I ran after him.'

He raised his eyes to Daru again and they were full of a sort of woeful interrogation. 'Now what will they do to me?'

'Are you afraid?'

He stiffened, turning his eyes away.

'Are you sorry?'

The Arab stared at him open-mouthed. Obviously he did not understand. Daru's annoyance was growing. At the same time he felt awkward and self-conscious with his big body wedged between the two beds.

'Lie down there,' he said impatiently. 'That's your bed.'

The Arab didn't move. He called to Daru: 'Tell me!'

The schoolmaster looked at him.

'Is the gendarme coming back tomorrow?'

'I don't know.'

'Are you coming with us?'

'I don't know. Why?'

The prisoner got up and stretched out on top of the blankets, his feet towards the window. The light from the electric bulb shone straight into his eyes and he closed them at once.

'Why?' Daru repeated, standing beside the bed.

The Arab opened his eyes under the blinding light and looked at him, trying not to blink.

'Come with us,' he said.

In the middle of the night, Daru was still not asleep. He had gone to bed after undressing completely; he generally slept naked. But, when he suddenly realized that he had nothing on, he hesitated. He felt vulnerable and the temptation came to him to put on his clothes again. Then he shrugged his shoulders; after all, he wasn't a child and, if need be, he could break his adversary in two. From his bed he could observe him, lying on his back, still motionless with his eyes closed under the harsh light. When Daru turned out the light, the darkness seemed to coagulate all of a sudden. Little by little, the night came back to life in the window where the starless sky was stirring gently. The schoolmaster soon made out the body lying at his feet. The Arab still did not move, but his eyes seemed open. A faint wind was prowling around the schoolhouse. Perhaps it would drive away the clouds and the sun would reappear.

During the night the wind increased. The hens fluttered a little and then were silent. The Arab turned over on his side with his back to Daru, who thought he heard him moan. Then he listened for his guest's breathing, become heavier and more regular. He listened to that breath so close to him and mused without being able to go to sleep. In this room where he had been sleeping alone for a year, this presence bothered him. But it bothered him also by imposing on him a sort of brotherhood he knew well but refused to accept in the present circumstances. Men who share the same rooms, soldiers or prisoners, develop a strange alliance as if, having cast off their armour with their clothing, they fraternized every evening, over and above their differences, in the ancient community of dream and fatigue. But Daru shook himself; he didn't like such musings, and it was essential to sleep.

A little later, however, when the Arab stirred slightly, the schoolmaster was still not asleep. When the prisoner made a second move, he stiffened, on the alert. The Arab was lifting himself slowly on his arms with almost the motion of a sleepwalker. Seated upright in bed, he waited motionless without turning his head towards Daru, as if he were listening attentively. Daru did not stir; it had just occurred to him that the revolver was still in the drawer of his desk. It was better to act at once. Yet he continued to observe the prisoner, who, with the same slithery motion, put his feet on the ground, waited again, then began to stand up slowly. Daru was about to call out to him when the Arab began to walk, in a quite natural but extraordinarily silent way. He was heading towards the door at the end of the room that opened into the shed. He lifted the latch with precaution and went out, pushing the door behind him but without shutting it. Daru had not stirred. 'He is running away,' he merely thought. 'Good riddance!' Yet he listened attentively. The hens were not fluttering; the guest must be on the plateau. A faint sound of water reached him, and he didn't know what it was until the Arab again stood framed in the doorway, closed the door carefully, and came back to bed without a sound. Then Daru turned his back on him and fell asleep. Still later he seemed, from the depths of his sleep, to hear furtive steps around the schoolhouse. 'I'm dreaming! I'm dreaming!' he repeated to himself. And he went on sleeping.

When he awoke, the sky was clear; the loose window let in a cold, pure air. The Arab was asleep, hunched up under the blankets now, his mouth open, utterly relaxed. But when Daru shook him, he started dreadfully, staring at Daru with wild eyes as if he had never seen him and such a frightened expression that the schoolmaster stepped back. 'Don't be afraid. It's me. You must eat.' The Arab nodded his head and said yes. Calm had returned to his face, but his expression was vacant and listless.

The coffee was ready. They drank it seated together on the folding bed as they munched their pieces of the cake. Then Daru led the Arab under the shed and showed him the tap where he washed. He went back into the room, folded the blankets and the bed, made his own bed and put the room in order. Then he went through the classroom and out on to the terrace. The sun was already rising in the blue sky; a soft, bright light was bathing the deserted plateau. On the ridge the snow was melting in spots. The stones were about to reappear. Crouched on the edge of the plateau, the schoolmaster looked at the deserted expanse. He thought of Balducci. He had hurt him, for he had sent him off in a way as if he didn't want to be associated with him. He could still hear the gendarme's farewell and, without knowing why, he felt strangely empty and vulnerable. At that moment, from the other side of the schoolhouse, the prisoner coughed. Daru listened to him almost despite himself and then, furious, threw a pebble that whistled through the air before sinking into the snow. That man's stupid crime revolted him, but to hand him over was contrary to honour. Merely thinking of it made him smart with humiliation. And he cursed at one and the same time his own people who had sent him this Arab and the Arab too who had dared to kill and not managed to get away. Daru got up, walked in a circle on the terrace, waited motionless, and then went back into the schoolhouse.

The Arab, leaning over the cement floor of the shed, was washing his teeth with two fingers. Daru looked at him and said: 'Come.' He went back into the room ahead of the prisoner. He slipped a hunting-jacket on over his sweater and put on walking-shoes. Standing, he waited until the Arab had put on his *chéche* and sandals. They went into the classroom and the schoolmaster pointed to the exit, saying: 'Go ahead.' The fellow didn't budge. 'I'm coming,' said Daru. The Arab went out. Daru went back into the room and made a package of pieces of rusk, dates, and sugar. In the classroom, before going out, he hesitated a second in front of his desk, then crossed the threshold and locked the door. 'That's the way,' he said. He started towards the east, followed by the prisoner. But, a short distance from the schoolhouse, he thought he heard a slight sound behind them. He retraced his steps and examined the surroundings of the house; there was no one there. The Arab watched him without seeming to understand. 'Come on,' said Daru.

They walked for an hour and rested beside a sharp peak of limestone. The snow was melting faster and faster and the sun was drinking up the puddles at once, rapidly cleaning the plateau, which gradually dried and vibrated like the air itself. When they resumed walking, the ground rang under their feet. From time to time a bird rent the space in front of them with a joyful cry. Daru breathed in deeply the fresh morning light. He felt a sort of rapture before the vast familiar expanse, now almost entirely yellow under its dome of blue sky. They walked an hour more, descending towards the south. They reached a level height made up of crumbly rocks. From there on, the plateau sloped down, eastward, towards a low plain where there were a few spindly trees and, to the south, towards outcroppings of rock that gave the landscape a chaotic look.

Daru surveyed the two directions. There was nothing but the sky on the horizon. Not a man could be seen. He turned towards the Arab, who was looking at him blankly. Daru held out the package to him. 'Take it,' he said. 'There are dates, bread, and sugar. You can hold out for two days. Here are a thousand francs too.' The Arab took the package and the money but kept his full hands at chest level as if he didn't know what to do with what was being given him. 'Now look,' the schoolmaster said as he pointed in the direction of the east, 'there's the way to Tinguit. You have a two-hour walk. At Tinguit you'll find the administration and the police. They are expecting you.' The Arab looked towards the east, still holding the package and the money against his chest. Daru took his elbow and turned him rather roughly towards the south. At the foot of the height on which they stood could be seen a faint path. 'That's the trail across the plateau. In a day's walk from here you'll find pasture lands and the first nomads. They'll take you in and shelter you according to their law.' The Arab had now turned towards Daru and a sort of panic was visible in his expression. 'Listen,' he said. Daru shook his head: 'No, be quiet. Now I'm leaving you.' He turned his back on him, took two long steps in the direction of the school, looked hesitantly at the motionless Arab, and started off again. For a few minutes he heard nothing but his own step resounding on the cold ground and did not turn his head. A moment later, however, he turned around. The Arab was still there on the edge of the hill, his arms hanging now, and he was looking at the schoolmaster. Daru felt something rise in his throat. But he swore with impatience, waved vaguely, and started off again. He had already gone some distance when he again stopped and looked. There was no longer anyone on the hill.

Daru hesitated. The sun was now rather high in the sky and was beginning to beat down on his head. The schoolmaster retraced his steps, at first somewhat uncertainly, then with decision. When he reached the little hill, he was bathed in sweat. He climbed it as fast as he could and stopped, out of breath, at the top. The rock-fields to the south stood out sharply against the blue sky, but on the plain to the east a steamy heat was already rising. And in that slight haze, Daru, with heavy heart, made out the Arab walking slowly on the road to prison.

A little later, standing before the window of the classroom, the schoolmaster was watching the clear light bathing the whole surface of the plateau, but he hardly saw it. Behind him on the blackboard, among the winding French rivers, sprawled the clumsily chalked-up words he had just read: 'You handed over our brother. You will pay for this.' Daru looked at the sky, the plateau, and, beyond, the invisible lands stretching all the way to the sea. In this vast landscape he had loved so much, he was alone.

SHIRLEY JACKSON

The Renegade

It was eight-twenty in the morning. The twins were loitering over their cereal, and Mrs. Walpole, with one eye on the clock and the other on the kitchen window past which the school bus would come in a matter of minutes, felt the unreasonable irritation that comes with being late on a school morning, the wading-through-molasses feeling of trying to hurry children.

"You'll have to walk," she said ominously, for perhaps the third time. "The bus won't wait."

"I'm hurrying," Judy said. She regarded her full glass of milk smugly. "I'm closer to through than Jack."

Jack pushed his glass across the table and they measured meticulously, precisely. "No," he said. "Look how much more you have than me."

"It doesn't *matter*," Mrs. Walpole said, "it doesn't *matter*. Jack, *eat* your cereal."

"She didn't have any more than me to start with," Jack said. "Did she have any more than me, Mom?"

The alarm clock had not gone off at seven as it should. Mrs. Walpole heard the sound of the shower upstairs and calculated rapidly; the coffee was slower than usual this morning, the boiled eggs a shade too soft. She had only had time to pour herself a glass of fruit juice and no time to drink it. *Someone*—Judy or Jack or Mr. Walpole—was going to be late.

"*Judy*," Mrs. Walpole said mechanically, "*Jack*."

Judy's hair was not accurately braided. Jack would get off without his handkerchief.

Mr. Walpole would certainly be irritable.

The yellow-and-red bulk of the school bus filled the road outside the kitchen window, and Judy and Jack streaked for the door, cereal uneaten, books most likely forgotten. Mrs. Walpole followed them to the kitchen door, calling, "Jack, your milk money; come straight home at noon." She watched them climb into the school bus and then went briskly to work clearing their dishes from the table and setting a place for Mr. Walpole. She would have to have breakfast herself later, in the breathing-spell that came after nine o'clock. That meant her wash would be late getting on the line, and if it rained that afternoon, as it certainly might, nothing would be dry. Mrs. Walpole made an effort, and said, "Good morning, dear," as her husband came into the kitchen. He said, "Morning," without glancing up and Mrs. Walpole, her mind full of unfinished sentences that began, "Don't you think other people ever have any feelings or—" started patiently to set his breakfast before him. The soft-boiled eggs in their dish, the toast, the coffee. Mr. Walpole devoted himself to his paper, and Mrs. Walpole, who wanted desperately also to say, "I don't suppose you notice that I haven't had a chance to eat—" set the dishes down as softly as she could.

Everything was going smoothly, although half-an-hour late, when the telephone rang. The Walpoles were on a party line, and Mrs. Walpole usually let the phone ring her number twice before concluding that it was really their number; this morning, before nine o'clock, with Mr. Walpole not half-through his breakfast, it was an unbearable intrusion, and Mrs. Walpole went reluctantly to answer it. "Hello," she said forbiddingly.

"Mrs. Walpole," the voice said, and Mrs. Walpole said, "Yes?" The voice—it was a woman—said, "I'm sorry to bother you, but this is—" and gave an unrecognizable name. Mrs. Walpole said, "Yes?" again. She could hear Mr. Walpole taking the coffeepot off the stove to pour himself a second cup.

"Do you have a dog? Brown-and-black hound?" the voice continued. With the word *dog* Mrs. Walpole, in the second before she answered, "Yes," comprehended the innumerable aspects of owning a dog in the country (six dollars for spaying, the rude barking late at night, the watchful security of the dark shape sleeping on the rug beside the double-decker beds in the twins' room, the inevitability of a dog in the house, as important as a stove, or a front porch, or a subscription to the local paper; more, and above any of these things, the dog herself, known among the neighbors as Lady Walpole, on an exact par with Jack Walpole or Judy Walpole; quiet, competent, exceedingly tolerant), and found in none of them a reason for such an early morning call from a voice which she realized now was as irritable as her own.

"Yes," Mrs. Walpole said shortly, "I own a dog. Why?"

"Big brown-and-black hound?"

Lady's pretty markings, her odd face. "Yes," Mrs. Walpole said, her voice a little more impatient, "yes, that is certainly my dog. Why?"

"He's been killing my chickens." The voice sounded satisfied now; Mrs. Walpole had been cornered.

For several seconds Mrs. Walpole was quiet, so that the voice said, "Hello?"

"That's perfectly ridiculous," Mrs. Walpole said.

"This morning," the voice said with relish, "your dog was chasing our chickens. We heard the chickens at about eight o'clock, and my husband went out to see what was the matter and found two chickens dead and he saw a big brown-and-black hound down with the chickens and he took a stick and chased the dog away and then he found two more dead ones. He says," the voice went on flatly, "that it's lucky he didn't think to take his shotgun out with him because you wouldn't have any more dog. Most awful mess you ever saw," the voice said, "blood and feathers everywhere."

"What makes you think it's *my* dog?" Mrs. Walpole said weakly.

"Joe White—he's a neighbor of yours—was passing at the time and saw my husband chasing the dog. Said it was your dog."

Old man White lived in the next house but one to the Walpoles. Mrs. Walpole had always made a point of being courteous to him, inquired amiably about his health when she saw him on the porch as she passed, had regarded respectfully the pictures of his grandchildren in Albany.

"I see," Mrs. Walpole said, suddenly shifting her ground. "Well, if you're absolutely *sure*. I just can't believe it of Lady. She's so gentle."

The other voice softened, in response to Mrs. Walpole's concern. "It *is* a shame," the other woman said. "I can't tell you how sorry I am that it happened. But . . ." her voice trailed off significantly.

"Of *course* we'll take care of the damage," Mrs. Walpole said quickly.

"No, no," the woman said, almost apologetically. "Don't even *think* about it."

"But of *course*—" Mrs. Walpole began, bewildered.

"The dog," the voice said. "You'll have to do something about the dog."

A sudden unalterable terror took hold of Mrs. Walpole. Her morning had gone badly, she had not yet had her coffee, she was faced with an evil situation she had never known before, and now the voice, its tone, its inflection, had managed to frighten Mrs. Walpole with a word like "something."

"How?" Mrs. Walpole said finally. "I mean, what do you want me to do?"

There was a brief silence on the other end of the wire, and then the voice said briskly, "I'm sure I don't know, missus. I've always heard that there's no way to stop a chicken-killing dog. As I say, there was no damage to speak of. As a matter of fact, the chickens the dog killed are plucked and in the oven now."

Mrs. Walpole's throat tightened and she closed her eyes for a minute, but the voice went inflexibly on. "We wouldn't ask you to do anything except take care of the dog. Naturally, you understand that we can't have a dog killing our chickens?"

Realizing that she was expected to answer, Mrs. Walpole said, "Certainly."

"So . . ." the voice said.

Mrs. Walpole saw over the top of the phone that Mr. Walpole was passing her on his way to the door. He waved briefly to her and she nodded at him. He was late; she had intended to ask him to stop at the library in the city. Now she would have to call him later. Mrs. Walpole said sharply into the phone, "First of all, of course, I'll have to make sure it's my dog. If it *is* my dog I can promise you you'll have no more trouble."

"It's your dog all right." The voice had assumed the country flatness; if Mrs. Walpole wanted to fight, the voice implied, she had picked just the right people.

"Good-bye," Mrs. Walpole said, knowing that she was making a mistake in parting from this woman angrily; knowing that she should stay on the phone for an interminable apologetic conversation, try to beg her dog's life back from this stupid inflexible woman who cared so much for *her* stupid chickens.

Mrs. Walpole put the phone down and went out into the kitchen. She poured herself a cup of coffee and made herself some toast.

I am not going to let this bother me until after I have had my coffee, Mrs. Walpole told herself firmly. She put extra butter on her toast and tried to relax, moving her back against the chair, letting her shoulders sag. Feeling like this at nine-thirty in the morning, she thought, it's a feeling that belongs with eleven o'clock at night. The bright sun outside was not as cheerful as it might be; Mrs. Walpole decided suddenly to put her wash off until tomorrow. They had not lived in the country town long enough for Mrs. Walpole to feel the disgrace of washing on Tuesday as mortal; they were still city folk and would probably always be city folk, people who owned a chicken-killing dog, people who washed on Tuesday, people who were not able to fend for themselves against the limited world of earth and food and weather that the country folk took so much for granted. In this situation as in all such others—the disposal of rubbish, the weather stripping, the baking of angel-food cake—Mrs. Walpole was forced to look for advice. In the country it is extremely difficult to "get a man" to do things for you, and Mr. and Mrs. Walpole had early fallen into the habit of consulting their neighbors for information which in the city would have belonged properly to the superintendent, or the janitor, or the man from the gas company. When Mrs. Walpole's glance fell on Lady's water dish under the sink, and she realized that she was indescribably depressed, she got up and put on her jacket and a scarf over her head and went next door.

Mrs. Nash, her next-door neighbor, was frying doughnuts, and she waved a fork at Mrs. Walpole at the open door and called, "Come in, can't leave the stove." Mrs. Walpole, stepping into Mrs. Nash's kitchen, was painfully aware of her own kitchen with the dirty dishes in the sink. Mrs. Nash was wearing a shockingly clean house dress and her kitchen was freshly washed; Mrs. Nash was able to fry doughnuts without making any sort of a mess.

"The men do like fresh doughnuts with their lunch," Mrs. Nash remarked without any more preamble than her nod and invitation to Mrs. Walpole. "I always try to get enough made ahead, but I never do."

"I wish I could make doughnuts," Mrs. Walpole said. Mrs. Nash waved the fork hospitality at the stack of still-warm doughnuts on the table and Mrs. Walpole helped herself to one, thinking: This will give me indigestion.

"Seems like they all get eaten by the time I finish making them," Mrs. Nash said. She surveyed the cooking doughnuts and then, satisfied that she could look away for a minute, took one herself and began to eat it standing by the stove. "What's wrong with you?" she asked. "You look sort of peaked this morning."

"To tell you the truth," Mrs. Walpole said, "it's our dog. Someone called me this morning that she's been killing chickens."

Mrs. Nash nodded. "Up to Harris's," she said. "I know."

Of course she'd know by now, Mrs. Walpole thought.

"You know," Mrs. Nash said, turning again to the doughnuts, "they do say there's nothing to do with a dog kills chickens. My brother had a dog once killed sheep, and I don't know *what* they didn't do to break that dog, but of course nothing would do it. Once they get the taste of blood." Mrs. Nash lifted a golden doughnut delicately out of the frying kettle, and set it down on a piece of brown paper to drain. "They get so's they'd rather kill than eat, hardly."

"But what can I *do*?" Mrs. Walpole asked. "Isn't there *anything*?"

"You can try, of course," Mrs. Nash said. "Best thing to do first is tie her up. Keep her tied, with a good stout chain. Then at least she won't go chasing no more chickens for a while, save you getting her killed *for* you."

Mrs. Walpole got up reluctantly and began to put her scarf on again. "I guess I'd better get a chain down at the store," she said.

"You going downstreet?"

"I want to do my shopping before the kids come home for lunch."

"Don't buy any store doughnuts," Mrs. Nash said. "I'll run up later with a dishful for you. You get a good stout chain for that dog."

"Thank you," Mrs. Walpole said. The bright sunlight across Mrs. Nash's kitchen doorway, the solid table bearing its plates of doughnuts, the pleasant smell of the frying, were all symbols somehow of Mrs. Nash's safety, her confidence in a way of life and a security that had no traffic with chicken-killing, no city fears, an assurance and cleanliness so great that she was willing to bestow its overflow on the Walpoles, bring them doughnuts and overlook Mrs. Walpole's dirty kitchen. "Thank you," Mrs. Walpole said again, inadequately.

"You tell Tom Kittredge I'll be down for a pork roast later this morning," Mrs. Nash said. "Tell him to save it for me."

"I shall." Mrs. Walpole hesitated in the doorway and Mrs. Nash waved the fork at her.

"See you later," Mrs. Nash said.

Old man White was sitting on his front porch in the sun. When he saw Mrs. Walpole he grinned broadly and shouted to her, "Guess you're not going to have any more dog."

I've got to be nice to him, Mrs. Walpole thought, he's not a traitor or a bad man by country standards; anyone would tell on a chicken-killing dog; but he doesn't have to be so pleased about it, she thought, and tried to make her voice pleasant when she said, "Good morning, Mr. White."

"Gonna have her shot?" Mr. White asked. "Your man got a gun?"

"I'm so worried about it," Mrs. Walpole said. She stood on the walk below the front porch and tried not to let her hatred show in her face as she looked up at Mr. White.

"It's too bad about a dog like that," Mr. White said.

At least he doesn't blame *me*, Mrs. Walpole thought. "Is there anything I can do?" she said.

Mr. White thought. "Believe you might be able to cure a chicken-killer," he said. "You get a dead chicken and tie it around the dog's neck, so he can't shake it loose, see?"

"Around her neck?" Mrs. Walpole asked, and Mr. White nodded, grinning toothlessly.

"See, when he can't shake it loose at first he tries to play with it and then it starts to bother him, see, and then he tries to roll it off and it won't come and then he tries to bite it off and it won't come and then when he sees it won't come he thinks he's never gonna get rid of it, see, and he gets scared. And then you'll have him coming around with his tail between his legs and this thing hanging around his neck and it gets worse and worse."

Mrs. Walpole put one hand on the porch railing to steady herself. "What do you do then?" she asked.

"Well," Mr. White said, "the way I heard it, see, the chicken gets riper and riper and the more the dog sees it and feels it and smells it, see, the more he gets to hate chicken. And he can't ever get rid of it, see?"

"But the dog," Mrs. Walpole said. "Lady, I mean. How long do we have to leave it around her neck?"

"Well," Mr. White said with enthusiasm, "I guess you leave it on until it gets ripe enough to fall off by itself. See, the head...."

"I see," Mrs. Walpole said. "Would it work?"

"Can't say," Mr. White said. "Never tried it myself." His voice said that *he* had never had a chicken-killing dog.

Mrs. Walpole left him abruptly; she could not shake the feeling that if it were not for Mr. White, Lady would not have been identified as the dog killing the chickens; she wondered briefly if Mr. White had maliciously blamed Lady because they were city folk, and then thought, No, no man around here would bear false witness against a dog.

When she entered the grocery it was almost empty; there was a man at the hardware counter and another man leaning against the meat counter talking to Mr. Kittredge, the grocer. When Mr. Kittredge saw Mrs. Walpole come in he called across the store, "Morning, Mrs. Walpole. Fine day."

"Lovely," Mrs. Walpole said, and the grocer said, "Bad luck about the dog."

"I don't know what to do about it," Mrs. Walpole said, and the man talking to the grocer looked at her reflectively, and then back at the grocer.

"Killed three chickens up to Harris's this morning," the grocer said to the man and the man nodded solemnly and said, "Heard about that."

Mrs. Walpole came across to the meat counter and said, "Mrs. Nash said would you save her a roast of pork. She'll be down later to get it."

"Going up that way," the man standing with the grocer said. "Drop it off."

"Right," the grocer said.

The man looked at Mrs. Walpole and said, "Gonna have to shoot him, I guess?"

"I hope not," Mrs. Walpole said earnestly. "We're all so fond of the dog."

The man and the grocer looked at one another for a minute, and then the grocer said reasonably, "Won't do to have a dog going around killing chickens, Mrs. Walpole."

"First thing you know," the man said, "someone'll put a load of buckshot into him, he won't come home no more." He and the grocer both laughed.

"Isn't there any way to cure the dog?" Mrs. Walpole asked.

"Sure," the man said. "Shoot him."

"Tie a dead chicken around his neck," the grocer suggested. "That might do it."

"Heard of a man did that," the other man said.

"Did it help?" Mrs. Walpole asked eagerly.

The man shook his head slowly and with determination.

"You know," the grocer said. He leaned his elbow on the meat counter; he was a great talker. "You know," he said again, "my father had a dog once used to eat eggs. Got into the chicken-house and used to break the eggs open and lick them up. Used to eat maybe half the eggs we got."

"That's a bad business," the other man said. "Dog eating eggs."

"Bad business," the grocer said in confirmation. Mrs. Walpole found herself nodding. "Last, my father couldn't stand it no more. Here half his eggs were getting eaten," the grocer said. "So he took an egg once, set it on the back of the stove for two, three days, till the egg got good and ripe, good and hot through, and that egg smelled pretty bad. Then—I was there, boy twelve, thirteen years old—he called the dog one day, and the dog come running. So I held the dog, and my daddy opened the dog's mouth and put in the egg, red-hot and smelling to heaven, and then he held the dog's mouth closed so's the dog couldn't get rid of the egg anyway except swallow it." The grocer laughed and shook his head reminiscently.

"Bet that dog never ate another egg," the man said.

"Never touched another egg," the grocer said firmly. "You put an egg down in front of that dog, he'd run's though the devil was after him."

"But how did he feel about you?" Mrs. Walpole asked. "Did he ever come near *you* again?"

The grocer and the other man both looked at her. "How do you mean?" the grocer said.

"Did he ever *like* you again?"

"Well," the grocer said, and thought. "No," he said finally, "I don't believe you could say's he ever did. Not much of a dog, though."

"There's one thing you ought to try," the other man said suddenly to Mrs. Walpole, "you really want to cure that dog, there's one thing you ought to try."

"What's that?" Mrs. Walpole said.

"You want to take that dog," the man said, leaning forward and gesturing with one hand, "take him and put him in a pen with a mother hen's got chicks to protect. Time she's through with him he won't never chase another chicken."

The grocer began to laugh and Mrs. Walpole looked, bewildered, from the grocer to the other man, who was looking at her without a smile, his eyes wide and yellow, like a cat's.

"What would happen?" she asked uncertainly.

"Scratch his eyes out," the grocer said succinctly. "He wouldn't ever be able to *see* another chicken."

Mrs. Walpole realized that she felt faint. Smiling over her shoulder, in order not to seem discourteous, she moved quickly away from the meat counter and down to the other end of the store. The grocer continued talking to the man behind the meat counter and after a minute Mrs. Walpole went outside, into the air. She decided that she would go home and lie down until nearly lunchtime, and do her shopping later in the day.

At home she found that she could not lie down until the breakfast table was cleared and the dishes washed, and by the time she had done that it was almost time to start lunch. She was standing by the pantry shelves, debating, when a dark shape crossed the sunlight in the doorway and she realized that Lady was home. For a minute she stood still, watching Lady. The dog came in quietly, harmlessly, as though she had spent the morning frolicking on the grass with her friends, but there were spots of blood on her legs and she drank her water eagerly. Mrs. Walpole's first impulse was to scold her, to hold her down and beat her for the deliberate, malicious pain she had inflicted, the murderous brutality a pretty dog like Lady could keep so well hidden in their home; then Mrs. Walpole, watching Lady go quietly and settle down in her usual spot by the stove, turned helplessly and took the first cans she found from the pantry shelves and brought them to the kitchen table.

Lady sat quietly by the stove until the children came in noisily for lunch, and then she leaped up and jumped on them, welcoming them as though they were the aliens and she the native to the house. Judy, pulling Lady's ears, said, "Hello, Mom, do you know what Lady did? You're a bad bad dog," she said to Lady, "you're going to get shot."

Mrs. Walpole felt faint again and set a dish down hastily on the table. "Judy Walpole," she said.

"She *is*, Mom," Judy said. "She's going to get shot."

Children don't realize, Mrs. Walpole told herself, death is never real to them. Try to be sensible, she told herself. "Sit down to lunch, children," she said quietly.

"But, *Mother*," Judy said, and Jack said, "She *is*, Mom."

They sat down noisily, unfolding their napkins and attacking their food without looking at it, eager to talk.

"You *know* what Mr. Shepherd said, Mom?" Jack demanded, his mouth full.

"Listen," Judy said, "we'll tell you what he said."

Mr. Shepherd was a genial man who lived near the Walpoles and gave the children nickels and took the boys fishing. "He says Lady's going to get shot," Jack said.

"But the spikes," Judy said. "Tell about the spikes."

"The *spikes*," Jack said. "Listen, Mommy. He says you got to get a collar for Lady...."

"A strong collar," Judy said.

"And you get big thick nails, like spikes, and you hammer them into the collar."

"All around," Judy said. "Let *me* tell it, Jack! You hammer these nails all around so's they make spikes inside the collar."

"But it's loose," Jack said. "Let *me* tell this part. It's loose and you put it around Lady's neck...."

"And—" Judy put her hand on her throat and made a strangling noise.

"Not *yet*," Jack said. "Not *yet*, dopey. First you get a long long long long rope."

"A *real* long rope," Judy amplified.

"And you fasten it to the collar and then we put the collar on Lady," Jack said. Lady was sitting next to him and he leaned over and said, "Then we put this real sharp spiky collar around your neck," and kissed the top of her head while Lady regarded him affectionately.

"And then we take her where there are chickens," Judy said, "and we show her the chickens, and we turn her loose."

"And make her chase the chickens," Jack said. "And *then*, and then, when she gets right up close to the chickens, we puuuuuuull on the rope—"

"And—" Judy made her strangling noise again.

"The spikes cut her head off," Jack finished dramatically.

They both began to laugh and Lady, looking from one to the other, panted as though she were laughing too.

Mrs. Walpole looked at them, at her two children with their hard hands and their sunburned faces laughing together, their dog with blood still on her legs laughing with them. She went to the kitchen doorway to look outside at the cool green hills, the motion of the apple tree in the soft afternoon breeze.

"Cut your head right off," Jack was saying.

Everything was quiet and lovely in the sunlight, the peaceful sky, the gentle line of the hills. Mrs. Walpole closed her eyes, suddenly feeling the harsh hands pulling her down, the sharp points closing in on her throat.

TRUMAN CAPOTE

My Side of the Matter

I know what is being said about me and you can take my side or theirs, that's your own business. It's my word against Eunice's and Olivia-Ann's, and it should be plain enough to anyone with two good eyes which one of us has their wits about them. I just want the citizens of the U.S.A. to know the facts, that's all.

The facts: On Sunday, August 12, this year of our Lord, Eunice tried to kill me with her papa's Civil War sword and Olivia-Ann cut up all over the place with a fourteen-inch hog knife. This is not even to mention lots of other things.

It began six months ago when I married Marge. That was the first thing I did wrong. We were married in Mobile after an acquaintance of only four days. We were both sixteen and she was visiting my cousin Georgia. Now that I've had plenty of time to think it over, I can't for the life of me figure how I fell for the likes of her. She has no looks, no body, and no brains whatsoever. But Marge is a natural blonde and maybe that's the answer. Well, we were married going on three months when Marge ups and gets pregnant; the second thing I did wrong. Then she starts hollering that she's got to go home to Mama —only she hasn't got no mama, just these two aunts. Eunice and Olivia-Ann. So she makes me quit my perfectly swell position clerking at the Cash'n' Carry and move here to Admiral's Mill which is nothing but a damn gap in the road any way you care to consider it.

The day Marge and I got off the train at the L&N depot it was raining cats and dogs and do you think anyone came to meet us? I'd shelled out forty-one cents for a telegram, too! Here my wife's pregnant and we have to tramp seven miles in a downpour. It was bad on Marge and I couldn't carry hardly any of our stuff on account of I have terrible trouble with my back. When I first caught sight of this house I must say I was impressed. It's big and yellow and has real columns out in front and japonica trees, both red and white, lining the yard.

Eunice and Olivia-Ann had seen us coming and were waiting in the hall. I swear I wish you could get a look at these two. Honest, you'd die! Eunice is this big old fat thing with a behind that must weigh a tenth of a ton. She troops around the house, rain or shine, in this real old-fashioned nighty, calls it a kimono, but it isn't anything in this world but a dirty flannel nighty. Furthermore she chews tobacco and tries to pretend so ladylike, spitting on the sly. She keeps gabbing about what a fine education she had, which is her way of attempting to make me feel bad, although, personally, it never bothers me so much as one whit as I know for a fact she can't even read the funnies without she spells out every single, solitary word. You've got to hand her one thing, though—she can add and subtract money so fast that there's no doubt but what she could be up in Washington, D.C., working where they make the stuff. Not that she hasn't got plenty of money! Naturally she says she hasn't but I know she has because one day, accidentally, I happened to find close to a thousand dollars hidden in a flower pot on the side porch. I didn't touch one cent, only Eunice says I stole a hundred-dollar bill which is a venomous lie from start to finish. Of course anything Eunice says is an order from headquarters as not a breathing soul in Admiral's Mill can stand up and say he doesn't owe her money and if she said Charlie Carson (a blind, ninety-year-old invalid who hasn't taken a step since 1896) threw her on her back and raped her everybody in this county would swear the same on a stack of Bibles.

Now Olivia-Ann is worse, and that's the truth! Only she's not so bad on the nerves as Eunice, for she is a natural-born half-wit and ought to be kept in somebody's attic. She's real pale and skinny and has a mustache. She squats around most of the time whittling on a stick with her fourteen-inch hog knife, otherwise she's up to some devilment, like what she did to Mrs. Harry Steller Smith. I swore not ever to tell anyone that, but when a vicious attempt has been made on a person's life, I say the hell with promises.

Mrs. Harry Steller Smith was Eunice's canary named after a woman from Pensacola who makes home-made cure-all that Eunice takes for the gout. One day I heard this terrible racket in the parlor and upon investigating, what did I find but Olivia-Ann shooing Mrs. Harry Steller Smith out an open window with a broom and the door to the bird cage wide. If I hadn't walked in at exactly that moment she might never have been caught. She got scared that I would tell Eunice and blurted out the whole thing, said it wasn't fair to keep one of God's creatures locked up that way, besides which she couldn't stand Mrs. Harry Steller Smith's singing. Well, I felt kind of sorry for her and she gave me two dollars, so I helped her cook up a story for Eunice. Of course I wouldn't have taken the money except I thought it would ease her conscience.

The very *first* words Eunice said when I stepped inside this house were, "So this is what you ran off behind our back and married, Marge?"

Marge says, "Isn't he the best-looking thing, Aunt Eunice?"

Eunice eyes me u-p and d-o-w-n and says, "Tell him to turn around."

While my back is turned, Eunice says, "You sure must've picked the runt of the litter. Why, this isn't any sort of man at all."

I've never been so taken back in my life! True, I'm slightly stocky, but then I haven't got my full growth yet.

"He is too," says Marge.

Olivia-Ann, who's been standing there with her mouth so wide the flies could buzz in and out, says, "You heard what Sister said. He's not any sort of a man whatsoever. The very idea of this little runt running around claiming to be a man! Why, he isn't even of the male sex!"

Marge says, "You seem to forget, Aunt Olivia-Ann, that this is my husband, the father of my unborn child."

Eunice made a nasty sound like only she can and said, "Well, all I can say is I most certainly wouldn't be bragging about it."

Isn't that a nice welcome? And after I gave up my perfectly swell position clerking at the Cash 'n' Carry.

But it's not a drop in the bucket to what came later that same evening. After Bluebell cleared away the supper dishes, Marge asked, just as nice as she could, if we could borrow the car and drive over to the picture show at Phoenix City.

"You must be clear out of your head," says Eunice, and, honest, you'd think we'd asked for the kimono off her back.

"You must be clear out of your head," says Olivia-Ann.

"It's six o'clock," says Eunice, "and if you think I'd let that runt drive my just-as-good-as-brand-new 1934 Chevrolet as far as the privy and back you must've gone clear out of your head."

Naturally such language makes Marge cry.

"Never you mind, honey," I said, "I've driven pulenty of Cadillacs in my time."

"Humf," says Eunice.

"Yeah," says I.

Eunice says, "If he's ever so much as driven a plow I'll eat a dozen gophers fried in turpentine."

"I won't have you refer to my husband in any such manner," says Marge. "You're acting simply outlandish! Why, you'd think I'd picked up some absolutely strange man in some absolutely strange place."

"If the shoe fits, wear it!" says Eunice.

"Don't think you can pull the sheep over our eyes," says Olivia-Ann in that braying voice of hers so much like the mating call of a jackass you can't rightly tell the difference.

"We weren't born just around the corner, you know," says Eunice.

Marge says, "I'll give you to understand that I'm legally wed till death do us part to this man by a certified justice of the peace as of three and one-half months ago. Ask anybody. Furthermore, Aunt Eunice, he is free, white and sixteen. Furthermore, George Far Sylvester does not appreciate hearing his father referred to in any such manner."

George Far Sylvester is the name we've planned for the baby. Has a strong sound, don't you think? Only the way things stand I have positively no feelings in the matter now whatsoever.

"How can a girl have a baby with a girl?" says Olivia-Ann, which was a calculated attack on my manhood. "I do declare there's something new every day."

"Oh, shush up," says Eunice. "Let us hear no more about the picture show in Phoenix City."

Marge sobs, "Oh-h-h, but it's Judy Garland."

"Never mind, honey," I said, "I most likely saw the show in Mobile ten years ago."

"That's a deliberate falsehood," shouts Olivia-Ann. "Oh, you are a scoundrel, you are. Judy hasn't been in the pictures ten years." Olivia-Ann's never seen not even one picture show in her entire fifty-two years (she won't tell anybody how old she is but I dropped a card to the capitol in Montgomery and they were very nice about answering), but she sub-

scribes to eight movie books. According to Postmistress Delancey, it's the only mail she ever gets outside of the Sears & Roebuck. She has this positively morbid crush on Gary Cooper and has one trunk and two suitcases full of his photos.

So we got up from the table and Eunice lumbers over to the window and looks out to the chinaberry tree and says, "Birds settling in their roost—time we went to bed. You have your old room, Marge, and I've fixed a cot for this gentleman on the back porch."

It took a solid minute for that to sink in.

I said, "And what, if I'm not too bold to ask, is the objection to my sleeping with my lawful wife?"

Then they both started yelling at me.

So Marge threw a conniption fit right then and there. "Stop it, stop it, stop it! I can't stand any more. Go on, babydoll—go on and sleep wherever they say. Tomorrow we'll see. . . ."

Eunice says, "I swanee if the child hasn't got a grain of sense, after all."

"Poor dear," says Olivia-Ann, wrapping her arm around Marge's waist and herding her off, "poor dear, so young, so innocent. Let's us just go and have a good cry on Olivia-Ann's shoulder."

May, June, and July and the best part of August I've squatted and sweltered on that damn back porch without an ounce of screening. And Marge—she hasn't opened her mouth in protest, not once! This part of Alabama is swampy, with mosquitoes that could murder a buffalo, given half a chance, not to mention dangerous flying roaches and a posse of local rats big enough to haul a wagon train from here to Timbuctoo. Oh, if it wasn't for that little unborn George I would've been making dust tracks on the road, way before now. I mean to say I haven't had five seconds alone with Marge since that first night. One or the other is always chaperoning and last week they like to have blown their tops when Marge locked herself in her room and they couldn't find me nowhere. The truth is I'd been down watching the niggers bale cotton but just for spite I let on to Eunice like Marge and I'd been up to no good. After that they added Bluebell to the shift.

And all this time I haven't even had cigarette change.

Eunice has hounded me day in and day out about getting a job. "Why don't the little heathen go out and get some honest work?" says she. As you've probably noticed, she never speaks to me directly, though more often than not I am the only one in her royal presence. "If he was any sort of man you could call a man he'd be trying to put a crust of bread in that girl's mouth instead of stuffing his own off my vittles." I think you should know that I've been living almost exclusively on cold yams and leftover grits for three months and thirteen days and I've been down to consult Dr. A. N. Carter twice. He's not exactly sure whether I have the scurvy or not.

And as for my not working, I'd like to know what a man of my abilities, a man who held a perfectly swell position with the Cash'n' Carry would find to do in a flea-bag like Admiral's Mill? There is all of one store here and Mr. Tubberville, the proprietor, is actually so lazy it's painful for him to have to sell anything. Then we have the Morning Star Baptist Church but they already have a preacher, an awful old turd named Shell whom Eunice drug over one day to see about the salvation of my soul. I heard him with my own ears tell her I was too far gone.

But it's what Eunice has done to Marge that really takes the cake. She has turned that girl against me in the most villainous fashion that words could not describe. Why, she even reached the point when she was sassing me back, but I provided her with a couple of good slaps and put a stop to that. No wife of mine is ever going to be disrespectful to me, not on your life!

The enemy lines are stretched tight: Bluebell, Olivia-Ann, Eunice, Marge, and the whole rest of Admiral's Mill (pop. 342). Allies: none.

Such was the situation as of Sunday, August 12, when the attempt was made upon my very life.

Yesterday was quiet and hot enough to melt rock. The trouble began at exactly two o'clock. I know because Eunice has one of those fool cuckoo contraptions and its scares the daylights out of me. I was minding my own personal business in the parlor, composing a song on the upright piano which Eunice bought for Olivia-Ann and hired her a teacher to come all the way from Columbus, Georgia, once a week. Postmistress Delancey, who was my friend till she decided that it was maybe not so wise, says that the fancy teacher tore out of this house one afternoon like old Adolf Hitler was on his tail and leaped in his Ford coupé, never to be heard from again. Like I say, I'm trying to keep cool in the parlor not bothering a living soul when Olivia-Ann trots in with her hair all twisted up in curlers and shrieks, "Cease that infernal racket this very instant! Can't you give a body a minute's rest? And get off my piano right smart. It's not your piano, it's my piano and if you don't get off it right smart I'll have you in court like a shot the first Monday in September."

She's not anything in this world but jealous on account of I'm a natural-born musician and the songs I make up out of my own head are absolutely marvelous.

"And just look what you've done to my genuine ivory keys, Mr. Sylvester," says she, trotting over to piano, "torn nearly every one of them off right at the roots for purentee meanness, that's what you've done."

She knows good and well that the piano was ready for the junk heap the moment I entered this house.

I said, "Seeing as you're such a know-it-all, Miss Olivia-Ann, maybe it would interest you to know that I'm in the possession of a few interesting tales myself. A few things that maybe other people would be very grateful to know. Like what happened to Mrs. Harry Steller Smith, as for instance."

Remember Mrs. Harry Steller Smith?

She paused and looked at the empty bird cage. "You gave me your oath," says she and turned the most terrifying shade of purple.

"Maybe I did and again maybe I didn't," says I. "You did an evil thing when you betrayed Eunice that way but if some people will leave other people alone then maybe I can overlook it."

Well, sir, she walked out of there just as *nice* and *quiet* as you please. So I went and stretched out on the sofa which is the most horrible piece of furniture I've ever seen and is part of a matched set Eunice bought in Atlanta in 1912 and paid two thousand dollars for, cash—or so she claims. This set is black and olive plush and smells like wet chicken feathers on a damp day. There is a big table in one corner of the parlor which supports two pictures of Miss E and O-A's mama and papa. Papa is kind of handsome but just between you and me I'm convinced he has black blood in him from somewhere. He was a captain in the Civil War and that is one thing that I'll never forget on account of his sword which is displayed over the mantel and figures prominently in the action yet to come. Mama has that hang-dog, half-wit look like Olivia-Ann, though I must say Mama carries it better.

So I had just dozed off when I heard Eunice bellowing, "Where is he? Where is he?" And the next thing I know she's framed in the doorway with her hands planted plumb on those hippo hips and the whole pack scrunched up behind her: Bluebell, Olivia-Ann and Marge.

Several seconds passed with Eunice tapping her big old bare foot just as fast and furious as she could and fanning her fat face with this cardboard picture of Niagara Falls.

"Where is it?" says she. "Where's my hundred dollars that he made away with while my trusting back was turned?"

"*This* is the straw that broke the camel's back," says I, but I was too hot and tired to get up.

"That's not the only back that's going to be broke," says she, her bug eyes about to pop clear out of their sockets. "That was my funeral money and I want it back. Wouldn't you know he'd steal from the dead?"

"Maybe he didn't take it," says Marge.

"You keep your mouth out of this, missy," says Olivia-Ann.

"He stole my money sure as shooting," says Eunice. "Why, look at his eyes—black with guilt!"

I yawned and said, "Like they say in the courts—if the party of the first part falsely accuses the party of the second part then the party of the first part can be locked away in jail even if the State Home is where they rightfully belong for the protection of all concerned."

"God will punish him," says Eunice.

"Oh, Sister," says Olivia-Ann, "let us not wait for God."

Whereupon Eunice advances on me with this most peculiar look, her dirty flannel nighty jerking along the floor. And Olivia-Ann leeches after her and Bluebell lets forth this moan that must have been heard clear to Eufala and back while Marge stands there wringing her hands and whimpering.

"Oh-h-h," sobs Marge, "please give her back that money, babydoll."

I said, "et tu Brute?" which is from William Shakespeare.

"Look at the likes of him," says Eunice, "lying around all day not doing so much as licking a postage stamp."

"Pitiful," clucks Olivia-Ann.

"You'd think he was having a baby instead of that poor child." Eunice speaking.

Bluebell tosses in her two cents, "Ain't it the truth?"

"Well, if it isn't the old pots calling the kettle black," says I.

"After loafing here for three months does this runt have the audacity to cast aspersions in my direction?" says Eunice.

I merely flicked a bit of ash from my sleeve and not the least bit fazed said, "Dr. A. N.

Carter has informed me that I am in a dangerous scurvy condition and can't stand the least excitement whatsoever—otherwise I'm liable to foam at the mouth and bite somebody."

Then Bluebell says, "Why don't he go back to that trash in Mobile, Miss Eunice? I'se sick and tired of carryin' his ol' slop jar."

Naturally that coal-black nigger made me so mad I couldn't see straight.

So just as calm as a cucumber I arose and picked up this umbrella off the hat tree and rapped her across the head with it until it cracked smack in two.

"My real Japanese silk parasol!" shrieks Olivia-Ann.

Marge cries, "You've killed Bluebell, you've killed poor old Bluebell!"

Eunice shoves Olivia-Ann and says, "He's gone clear out of his head, Sister! Run! Run and get Mr. Tubberville!"

"I don't like Mr. Tubberville," says Olivia-Ann staunchly. "I'll go get my hog knife." And she makes a dash for the door but seeing as I care nothing for death I brought her down with a sort of tackle. It wrenched my back something terrible.

"He's going to kill her!" hollers Eunice loud enough to bring the house down. "He's going to murder us all! I warned you, Marge. Quick, child, get Papa's sword!"

So Marge gets Papa's sword and hands it to Eunice. Talk about wifely devotion! And, if that's not bad enough, Olivia-Ann gives me this terrific knee punch and I had to let go. The next thing you know we hear her out in the yard bellowing hymns.

> Mine eyes have seen the glory of the
>   coming of the Lord;
> He is trampling out the vintage where
>   the grapes of wrath are stored . . .

Meanwhile Eunice is sashaying all over the place wildly thrashing Papa's sword and somehow I've managed to clamber atop the piano. Then Eunice climbs up on the piano stool and how that rickety contraption survived a monster like her I'll never be the one to tell.

"Come down from there, you yellow coward, before I run you through," says she and takes a whack and I've got a half-inch cut to prove it.

By this time Bluebell has recovered and skittered away to join Olivia-Ann holding services in the front yard. I guess they were expecting my body and God knows it would've been theirs if Marge hadn't passed out cold.

That's the only good thing I've got to say for Marge.

What happened after that I can't rightly remember except for Olivia-Ann reappearing with her fourteen-inch hog knife and a bunch of the neighbors. But suddenly Marge was the star attraction and I suppose they carried her to her room. Anyway, as soon as they left I barricaded the parlor door.

I've got all those black and olive plush chairs pushed against it and that big mahogany table that must weigh a couple of tons and the hat tree and lots of other stuff. I've locked the windows and pulled down the shades. Also I've found a five-pound box of Sweet Love candy and this very minute I'm munching a juicy, creamy, chocolate cherry. Sometimes they come to the door and knock and yell and plead. Oh, yes, they've started singing a song of a very different color. But as for me—I give them a tune on the piano every now and then just to let them know I'm cheerful.

PHILIP ROTH

Novotny's Pain

In the early months of the Korean War, a young man who had been studying to be a television cameraman in a night school just west of the Loop in Chicago was drafted into the Army and almost immediately fell ill. He awoke one morning with a pain on the right side of his body, directly above the buttock. When he rolled over, it was as though whatever bones came together inside him there were not meeting as they should. The pain, however, was not what had awakened him; his eyes always opened themselves five minutes before the appearance in the barracks of the Charge of Quarters. Though there was much of Army life that he had to grit his teeth to endure, he did not have to work at getting up on time; it simply happened to him. When it was necessary to grit his teeth, he gritted them and did what he was told. In that way, he was like a good many young men who suffered military life alongside him or had suffered it before him. His sense of shame was strong, as was his sense of necessity; the two made him dutiful.

Also, he was of foreign extraction, and though his hard-working family had not as yet grown fat off the fat of the land, it was nevertheless in their grain to feel indebted to this country. Perhaps if they had been a little fatter they would have felt less indebted. As it was, Novotny believed in fighting for freedom, but because what he himself wanted most from any government was that it should let him alone to live his life. His patriotism, then—his commitment to wearing this republic's uniform and carrying this republic's gun —was seriously qualified by his feeling of confinement and his feeling of loss, both of which were profound.

When the C.Q. got around to Novotny's bed that morning, he did not shine his flashlight into the soldier's eyes; he simply put a hand to his arm and said, "You better get yourself up, young trooper." Novotny was appreciative of this gentleness, and though, as he stepped from his bunk, the pain across his back was momentarily quite sharp, he met the day with his usual decision. Some mornings, making the decision required that he swallow hard and close his eyes, but he never failed to make it: *I am willing.* He did not know if any of those around him had equivalent decisions to make, because he did not ask. He did not mull much over motive. People were honest or dishonest, good or bad, himself included.

After dressing, he moved off with four others to the mess hall, where it was their turn to work for the day. It was still dark, and in the barracks the other recruits slept on. The previous day the entire company had marched fifteen miserable miles with full packs, and then, when it was dark, they had dropped down on their stomachs and fired at pinpoints of light that flickered five hundred yards away and were supposed to be the gunfire of the enemy. Before they had climbed into trucks at midnight, they were ordered to attention and told in a high, whiny voice by their captain, a National Guardsman recently and unhappily called back to duty, that only one out of every fifty rounds they had fired had hit the targets. This news had had a strong effect upon the weary recruits, and the trucks had been silent all the way to the barracks, where it had been necessary for them to clean their rifles and scrape the mud from their boots before they flung themselves onto the springs of their bunks for a few hours' rest.

At the mess hall, the K.P.s were each served two large spoonfuls of Army eggs and a portion of potatoes. The potatoes had not been cooked long enough, and the taste they left on the palate was especially disheartening at such an early hour, with no light outdoors and a cold wind blowing. But Novotny did not complain. For one thing, he was occupied with finding a comfortable position in which to sit and eat—he had the pain only when he twisted the wrong way. Besides, the food was on his tray to give him strength, not pleasure. Novotny did not skip meals, no matter how ill-prepared they were, for he did not want to lose weight and be unequal to the tasks assigned him.

Before entering the Army, Novotny had worked for several years as an apprentice printer with a company that manufactured telephone books in Chicago. It had turned out to be dull work, and because he considered himself a bright and ambitious young man, he had looked around for a night school where he might learn a job with a future. He had settled on television, and for over a year he had been attending classes two evenings a week. He had a girl friend and a mother, to both of whom he had a strong attachment; his girl friend he loved, his mother he took care of. Novotny did not want to cause any trouble. On the other hand, he did not want to be killed. With his girl friend, he had been a man of passion; he dreamed of her often. He was thrifty, and had four hundred dollars in a savings account in the First Continental Bank on LaSalle Street in Chicago. He knew for a fact that he had been more adept at his work than anyone else in his television course. He hated the Army because nothing he did there was for himself.

The labors of the K.P.s began at dawn, and at midnight—light having come and gone—they were still at it. The cooks had ordered the men around all day until five in the afternoon, when the Negro mess sergeant showed up. He hung his Eisenhower jacket on a hook, rolled up the sleeves of his shirt, and said, "As there is a regimental inspection tomorrow morning, we will now get ourselves down to the fine points of housecleaning, gentlemens." The K.P.s had then proceeded to scrub the mess hall from floor to ceiling, inside and out.

A little after midnight, while Novotny was working away at the inside of a potato bin with a stiff brush and a bucket of hot, soapy water, the man working beside him began to cry. He said the sergeant was never going to let them go to sleep. The sergeant would be court-martialed for keeping them up like this. They would all get weak and sick. All Novotny knew of the fellow beside him was that his name was Reynolds and that he had been to college. Apparently, the mess sergeant only knew half that much, but that was enough; he came into the storeroom and saw Reynolds weeping into the empty potato bins. "College boy," he said, "wait'll they get you over in Korea." The sergeant delivered his words standing over them, looking down, and for the moment Novotny stopped feeling sorry for himself.

When the scrubbing was finished, Novotny and Reynolds had to carry back the potatoes, which were in garbage cans, and dump them into the bins. Reynolds began to explain to Novotny that he had a girl friend whom he was supposed to have called at ten-thirty. For some reason, Reynolds said, his not having been able to get to a phone had made him lose control. Novotny had, till then, been feeling superior to Reynolds. For all his resenting of the stupidity that had made them scrub out bins one minute so as to dump dirty potatoes back into them the next, he had been feeling somewhat in league with the sergeant. Now Reynolds' words broke through to his own unhappiness, and he was about to say a kind word to his companion when the fellow suddenly started crying again. Reynolds threw his hand up to cover his wet cheeks and dropped his end of the can. Novotny's body stiffened; with a great effort he yanked up on the can so that it wouldn't come down on Reynolds' toes. Pain cut deep across the base of Novotny's spine.

Later, he limped back to the barracks. He got into bed and counted up the number of hours he had spent scrubbing out what hadn't even needed to be scrubbed. At a dollar and a quarter an hour, he would have made over twenty dollars. Nineteen hours was as much night-school time as he had been able to squeeze into three weeks. He had known Rose Anne, his girl, for almost a year, but never had he spent nineteen consecutive hours in her company. Though once they had had twelve hours. . . . He had driven in his Hudson down to Champaign, where she was a freshman at the University of Illinois, and they had stayed together, in the motel room he had rented, from noon to midnight, not even going out for meals. He had driven her back to her dormitory, his shoelaces untied and wearing no socks. Never in his life had he been so excited.

The following week, he had been drafted.

After completing his eight weeks of basic training, Novotny was given a week's leave. His first evening home, his mother prepared a large meal and then sat down opposite him at the table and watched him eat it. After dinner, he stood under the hot shower for twenty minutes, letting the water roll over him. In his bedroom, he carefully removed the pins from a new white-on-white shirt and laid it out on the bedspread, along with a pair of Argyles, a silver tie clasp, cufflinks, and his blue suit. He polished his shoes—not for the captain's pleasure, but for his own—and chose a tie. Then he dressed for his date as he had learned to dress for a date from an article he had read in a Sunday picture magazine, while in high school, that he kept taped

to the inside of his closet door. He had always collected articles having to do with how to act at parties, or dances, or on the job; his mother had never had any reason not to be proud of Novotny's behavior. She kissed him when he left the house, told him how handsome he looked, and then tears moved over her eyes as she thanked him for the government checks—for always having been a good son.

Novotny went to a movie with Rose Anne, and afterward he drove to the forest preserve where they remained until 2 A.M. In bed, later, he cursed the Army. He awoke the following morning to find that the pain, which had not troubled him for some weeks, had returned. It came and went through the next day and the following night, when once again he saw Rose Anne. Two days later, he visited the family doctor, who said Novotny had strained a muscle, and gave him a diathermy treatment. On their last night together, Rose Anne said that if writing would help, she would write not just twice a day, as was her habit, but three times a day, even four. In the dark of the forest preserve, she told Novotny that she dreamed about his body; in the dark, he told her that he dreamed of hers.

He left her weeping into a Kleenex in her dim front hallway, and drove home in a mood darker than any he had ever known. He would be killed in Korea and never see Rose Anne again, or his mother. And how unfair—for he *had* been a good son. Following his father's death, he had worked every day after school, plus Wednesday nights and Saturdays. When he had been drafted, he had vowed he would do whatever they told him to do, no matter how much he might resent it. He had kept his mouth shut and become proficient at soldiering. The better he was at soldiering, the better chance he had of coming out alive and in one piece. But that night when he left Rose Anne, he felt he had no chance at all. He would leave some part of his body on the battlefield, or come home to Rose Anne in a box. Good as he had been—industrious, devoted, stern, sacrificing—he would never have the pleasure of being a husband, or a television cameraman, or a comfort to his mother in her old age.

Five days after his return to the post—where he was to receive eight weeks of advanced infantry training, preparatory to being shipped out—he went on sick call. He sat on a long bench in the barren waiting room, and while two sullen prisoners from the stockade mopped the floor around his feet, he had his temperature taken. There were thirteen men on sick call, and they all watched the floor being washed and held thermometers under their tongues. When Novotny got to see the medic, who sat outside the doctor's office, he told him that every time he twisted or turned or stepped down on his right foot, he felt a sharp pain just above the buttock on the right side of his body. Novotny was sent back to duty with three inches of tape across his back, and a packet of APC pills.

At mail call the following morning, Novotny received a letter from Rose Anne unlike any he had ever received from her before. It was not only that her hand was larger and less controlled than usual; it was what she said. She had written down, for his very eyes to see, all those things she dreamed about when she dreamed about his body. He saw, suddenly, scenes of passion that he and she were yet to enact, moments that would not merely repeat the past but would be even deeper, even more thrilling. Oh Rose Anne—how had he found her?

Novotny's company spent the afternoon charging around with fixed bayonets—crawling, jumping up, racing ahead, through fences, over housetops, down into trenches—screaming murderously all the while. At one point, leaping from a high wall, Novotny almost took his eye out with his own bayonet; he had been dreaming of his beautiful future.

The next morning, he walked stiffly to sick call and asked to see the doctor. When, in response to a question, he said it was his back

that hurt him, the medic who was interviewing him replied sourly, "Everybody's back hurts." The medic told Novotny to take off his shirt so that he could lay on a few more inches of tape. Novotny asked if he could please see the doctor for just a minute. He was informed that the doctor was only seeing men with temperatures of a hundred or more. Novotny had no temperature, and he returned to his unit, as directed.

On the seventh weekend, with only one more week of training left, Novotny was given a seventy-two-hour pass. He caught a plane to Chicago and a bus to Champaign, carrying with him only a small ditty bag and Rose Anne's impassioned letter. Most of Friday, most of Saturday, and all day Sunday, Rose Anne wept, until Novotny was more miserable than he had ever imagined a man could be. On Sunday night, she held him in her arms and he proceeded to tell her at last of how he had been mistreated by the medic; till then he had not wanted to cause her more grief than she already felt. She stroked his hair while he told how he had not even been allowed to see a doctor. Rose Anne wept and said the medic should be shot. They had no right to send Novotny to Korea if they wouldn't even look after his health here at home. What would happen to him if his back started to act up in the middle of a battle? How could he take care of himself? She raised many questions—rational ones, irrational ones, but none that Novotny had not already considered himself.

Novotny traveled all night by train so as to be back at the base by reveille. He spent most of the next day firing a Browning automatic, and the following morning, when he was to go on K.P., he could not even lift himself from his bed, so cruel was the pain in his back.

In the hospital, the fellow opposite Novotny had been in a wheelchair for two years with osteomyelitis. Every few months, they shortened his legs; nevertheless, the disease continued its slow ascent. The man on Novotny's right had dropped a hand grenade in basic training and blown bits of both his feet off. Down at the end of Novotny's aisle lay a man who had had a crate full of ammunition tip off a truck onto him, and the rest of the men in the ward, many of whom were in the hospital to learn to use prosthetic devices, had been in Korea.

The day after Novotny was assigned to the ward, the man the crate had fallen on was wheeled away to be given a myelogram. He came back to the ward holding his head in his hands. As soon as Novotny was able to leave his bed, he made his way over to this fellow's bed, and because he had heard that the man's condition had been diagnosed as a back injury, he asked him how he was feeling. He got around to asking what a myelogram was, and why he had come back to the ward holding his head. The fellow was talkative enough, and told him that they had injected a white fluid directly into his spine and then X-rayed him as the fluid moved down along the vertebrae, so as to see if the spinal discs were damaged. He told Novotny that apparently it was the stuff injected into him that had given him the headache, but then he added that, lousy as he had felt, he considered himself pretty lucky. He had heard of cases, he said, where the needle had slipped. Novotny had himself heard of instances where doctors had left towels and sponges inside patients, so he could believe it. The man said that all the needle had to do was go off by a hairbreadth and it would wind up in the tangle of nerves leading into the spine. Two days later, two damaged discs were cut out of the man with the injured back, and three of his vertebrae were fused together. All through the following week he lay motionless in his bed.

One evening earlier, while Novotny was still restricted to bed, he had been visited by Reynolds. Reynolds had come around to say good-bye; the entire outfit was to be flown out the next day. Since Reynolds and Novotny hardly knew each other, they had been silent after Reynolds spoke of what was to happen to him and the others the following day. Then Reynolds had said that Novotny was lucky to have developed back trouble when he did; he wouldn't have minded a touch of it himself. Then he left.

When Novotny was out of bed and walking around, X-rays were taken of his back, and the doctors told him they showed no sign of injury or disease; there was a slight narrowing of the intervertebral space between what they referred to on the pictures as L-1 and L-2, but nothing to suggest damage to the disc —which was what Novotny had worked up courage to ask them about. The doctors took him into the examination room and bent him forward and backward. They ran a pin along his thigh and calf and asked if he felt any sensation. They laid him down on a table and, while they slowly raised his leg, asked if he felt any pain. When his leg was almost at a ninety-degree angle with his body, Novotny thought that he did feel his pain—he did, most certainly, remember the pain, and remembered the misery of no one's taking it seriously but himself. Then he thought of all the men around him who hobbled on artificial limbs during the day and moaned in their beds at night, and he said nothing. Consequently, they sent him back to duty.

He was shunted into an infantry company that was in its seventh week of advanced training. Two days before the company was to be shipped out, he awoke in the morning to discover that the pain had returned. He was able to limp to sick call, where he found on duty the unsympathetic medic, who, almost immediately upon seeing Novotny, began to unwind a roll of three-inch tape. Novotny raised an objection, and an argument ensued, which was settled when the doctor emerged from behind his door. He ordered Novotny into his office and had him strip. He told him to bend forward and touch his toes. Novotny tried, but could come only to within a few inches of them. The doctor looked over Novotny's medical record and then asked if he expected the Army to stand on its head because one soldier couldn't touch his toes. He asked him what he expected the Army to do for him. The doctor said there were plenty of G.I.s with sore backs in Korea. And with worse. Plenty worse.

Though the pain diminished somewhat during the day, it returned the next morning with increased severity. Novotny could by this time visualize his own insides—he saw the bone as white, and the spot where the pain was located as black. At breakfast, he changed his mind three times over, then went off to the first sergeant to ask permission to go on sick call. He had decided finally that if he did not go and have the condition taken care of within the next few days it would simply get worse and worse; surely there would be no time for medical attention, no proper facilities, while they were in transit to Korea. And, once in Korea, those in charge would surely be even more deaf to his complaints than they were here; there they would be deafened by the roar of cannons. The first sergeant asked Novotny what the matter was this time, and he answered that his back hurt. The first sergeant said what the medic had said the first day: "Everybody's back hurts." But he let him go.

At sick call, the doctor sat Novotny down and asked him what *he* thought was wrong with him. What the suffering soldier had begun to think was that perhaps he had cancer or leukemia. It was really in an effort to minimize his complaint that he said that maybe he had a slipped disc. The doctor said that if Novotny had slipped a disc he wouldn't even be able to walk around. Novotny suddenly found it difficult to breathe. What had he done in life to deserve this? What had he done, from the day he had grown out of short pants, but everything that was asked of him? He told the doctor that all he knew was that he had a pain. He tried to explain that taping it up didn't seem to work; the pain wasn't on the surface but deep inside his back. The doctor said it was deep inside his head. When the doctor told him to go back to duty like a man, Novotny refused.

Novotny was taken to the hospital, and to the office of the colonel in charge of orthopedics. He was a bald man with weighty circles under his eyes and a very erect carriage, who looked to have lived through a good deal. The colonel asked Novotny to sit down and tell him about the pain. Novotny, responding to a long-suffering quality in the man that seemed to him to demand respect, told him the truth: he had rolled over one morning during his basic training, and there it had been, deep and sharp. The colonel asked Novotny if he could think of anything at all that might have caused the pain. Novotny recounted what had happened on K.P. with Reynolds. The doctor asked if that had occurred before the morning he had awakened with the pain, or after it. Novotny admitted that it was after. But surely, he added, that must have aggravated the pain. The doctor said that that did not clear up the problem of where the pain had come from in the first place. He reminded Novotny that the X-rays showed nothing. He ordered Novotny to take off his hospital blues and stretch out on the examination table. By this time, of course, Novotny knew all the tests by heart; once, in fact, he anticipated what he was about to be asked to do, and the colonel gave him a strange look.

When the doctor was finished, he told Novotny that he had a lumbosacral strain with some accompanying muscle spasm. Nothing more. It was what they used to call a touch of lumbago. Novotny stood up to leave, and the colonel informed him that when he was released from the hospital he would have to appear at a summary court-martial for having refused to obey the doctor's order to return to duty. Novotny felt weak enough to faint. He was suddenly sorry he had ever opened his mouth. He was ashamed. He heard himself explaining to the colonel that he had refused to obey only because he had felt too sick to go back to duty. The colonel said it was for a trained doctor to decide how sick or well Novotny was. But, answered Novotny —hearing the gates to the stockade slamming shut behind him, imagining prison scenes so nasty even he couldn't endure them—but the doctor had made a mistake. As the colonel said, he *did* have a lumbosacral strain, and muscle spasm, too. In a steely voice, the colonel told him that there were men in Korea who had much worse. That was the statement to which Novotny had no answer; it was the statement that everyone finally made to him.

When they put him in traction, he had further premonitions of his court-martial and his subsequent internment in the stockade. He, Novotny, who had never broken a law in his life. What was happening? Each morning, he awoke at the foot of the bed, pulled there by the weights tied to his ankles and hanging to the floor. His limbs and joints ached day in and day out from being stretched. More than once, he had the illusion of being tortured for a crime he had not committed, although he knew that the traction was therapeutic. At the end of a week, the weights were removed and he was sent to the physical-therapy clinic, where he received heat treatments and was given a series of exercises to perform. Some days, the pain lessened almost to the point of disappearing. Other days, it was as severe as it had ever been. Then he believed that they would have to cut him open, and it would be the doctor at sick call who would be court-martialed instead of himself. When the pain was at its worst, he felt vindicated; but then, too, when it was at its worst he was most miserable.

He was only alone when he was in the bathroom, and it was there that he would try to bend over and touch his toes. He repeated and repeated this, as though it were a key to something. One day, thinking himself alone, he had begun to strain toward his toes when

he was turned around by the voice of the osteomyelitis victim, who was sitting in the doorway in his wheelchair. "How's your backache, buddy?" he said, and wheeled sharply away. Everybody in the ward somehow knew bits of Novotny's history; nobody, nobody knew the whole story.

Nobody he didn't know liked him; and he stopped liking those he did know. His mother appeared at the hospital two weeks after his admittance. She treated him like a hero, leaving with him a shoebox full of baked goods and a Polish sausage. He could not bring himself to tell her about his court-martial; he could not disappoint her—and that made him angry. He was even glad to see her go, lonely as he was. Then, the following weekend, Rose Anne arrived. Everybody whistled when she walked down the ward. And he was furious at her—but for what? For being so desirable? So perfect? They argued, and Rose Anne went back to Champaign, bewildered. That night, the Negro fellow next to Novotny, who had lost his right leg in the battle of Seoul, leaned over the side of his bed and said to him, with a note in his voice more dreamy than malicious, "Hey, man, you got it made."

The next day, very early, Novotny went to the hospital library and searched the shelves until he found a medical encyclopedia. He looked up "slipped disc." Just as he had suspected, many of his own symptoms were recorded there. His heart beat wildly as he read of the difficulties of diagnosing a slipped disc, even with X-rays. Ah yes, only the myelogram was certain. He read on and on, over and over, symptoms, treatments, and drugs. One symptom he read of was a tingling sensation that ran down the back of the leg and into the foot, caused by pressure of the herniated disc on a nerve. The following morning, he awoke with a tingling sensation that ran down the back of his right leg and into his foot. Only momentarily was he elated; then it hurt.

On his weekly ward rounds, the colonel, followed by the nurse and the resident, walked up to each bed and talked to the patient; everyone waited his turn silently, as in formation. The colonel examined stumps, incisions, casts, prosthetic devices, and then asked each man how he felt. When he reached Novotny, he asked him to step out of bed and into the aisle, and there he had him reach down and touch his toes. Novotny tried, bending and bending. Someone in the ward called out, "Come on, Daddy, you can do it." Another voice called, "Push, Polack, *push*"—and then it seemed to him that all the patients in the ward were shouting and laughing, and the colonel was doing nothing to restrain them. "Ah, wait'll they get you in Korea"—and then suddenly the ward was silent, for Novotny was straightening up, his face a brilliant red. "I can't do it, sir," he said. "Does your back feel better?" the colonel asked. "Yes, sir." "Do you think we should send you back to duty?" "I've had a tingling sensation down the back of my right leg," Novotny said. "So?" the colonel asked. The ward was silent; Novotny decided not to answer.

In the afternoon, Novotny was called to the colonel's office. He walked there without too much difficulty—but then it was not unusual for the pain to come and go and come back again, with varying degrees of severity. Sometimes the cycle took hours, sometimes days, sometimes only minutes. It was enough to drive a man crazy.

In the colonel's office, Novotny was told that he was going to get another chance. Novotny was too young, the colonel said, not to be extended a little forgiveness for his self-concern. If he went back to duty, the charges against him would be dismissed and there would be no court-martial. The colonel said that with a war on there was nothing to be gained by putting a good soldier behind bars. The colonel let Novotny know that he was impressed by his marksmanship record, which he had taken the trouble to look up in the company files.

When it was Novotny's turn to speak, he could only think to ask if the colonel believed

the tingling sensation in his leg meant nothing at all. The colonel, making it obvious that it was patience he was displaying, asked Novotny what *he* thought it meant. Novotny said he understood it to be a symptom of a slipped disc. The colonel asked him how he knew that, and Novotny—hesitating only a moment, then going on with the truth, on and on with it—said that he had read it in a book. The colonel, his mouth turning down in disgust, asked Novotny if he was that afraid of going to Korea. Novotny did not know what to answer; he truly had not thought of it that way before. The colonel then asked him if he ever broke out in a cold sweat at night. Novotny said no—the only new symptom he had was the tingling in the leg. The colonel brought a fist down on his desk and told Novotny that the following day he was sending him over to see the psychiatrist. He could sit out the rest of the war in the nuthouse.

What to do? Novotny did not know. It was not a cold but a hot sweat that he was in all through dinner. In the evening, he walked to the Coke machine in the hospital basement, as lonely as he had ever been. A nurse passed him in the hall and smiled. She thought he was sick. He drank his Coke, but when he saw two wheelchairs headed his way he turned and moved up the stairs to the hospital library. He began to perspire again, and then he set about looking through the shelves for a book on psychology. Since he knew as little about psychology as he did about medicine, he had to look for a very long time. He did not want to ask for the help of the librarian, even though she was a civilian. At last he was able to pick out two books, and he sat down on the floor between the stacks, where nobody could see him.

Much of what he read he did not completely follow, but once in a while he came upon an anecdote, and in his frustration with the rest of the book, he would read that feverishly. He read of a woman in a European country who had imagined that she was pregnant. She had swelled up, and then, after nine months, she had had labor pains—but no baby. Because it had all been in her imagination. *Her imagination had made her swell up!* Novotny read this over several times. He was respectful of facts, and believed what he found in books. He did not believe that a man would take the time to sit down and write a book so as to tell other people lies.

When he walked back to the ward, his back seemed engulfed in flames. It was then that he became absorbed in the fantasy of reaching inside himself and cutting out of his body the offending circle of pain. He saw himself standing over his own naked back and twisting down on an instrument that resembled the little utensil that is sold in dime stores to remove the core of a grapefruit. In his bed, he could not find a position in which the pain could be forgotten or ignored. He got up and went to the phone booth, where he called long distance to Rose Anne. He could barely prevent himself from begging her to get on a plane and fly down to him that very night. And yet—the darkness, his fright, his fatigue were taking their toll—if it wasn't his back that was causing the pain, was it Rose Anne? Was he being punished for being so happy with her? Were they being punished for all that sex? Unlike his mother, he was not the kind of Catholic who believed in Hell; he was not the kind who was afraid of sex. All he wanted was his chance at life. That was all.

In the washroom, before he returned to bed, he tried to touch his toes. He forced himself down and down and down until his eyes were cloudy from pain and his fingers had moved to within an inch of the floor. But he could not keep his brain from working, and he did not know what to think. If a woman could imagine herself to be in labor, then for him, too, anything was possible. He leaned over the sink and looked into the mirror. With the aid of every truthful cell in his pained body, he admitted to his own face that he was—yes, he was—frightened of going to Korea. Terribly frightened. But wasn't

everybody? He wondered if nothing could be wrong with him. He wondered if nothing he knew was so.

The next day, the psychiatrist asked Novotny if he felt nervous. He said he didn't. The psychiatrist asked if he had felt nervous before he had come into the Army. Novotny said no, that he had been happy. He asked if Novotny was afraid of high places, and if he minded being in crowds; he asked if he had any brothers and sisters, and which he liked better, his mother or his father. Novotny answered that his father was dead. He asked which Novotny had liked better before his father died. Novotny did not really care to talk about this subject, particularly to someone he didn't even know, but he had decided to be as frank and truthful with the psychiatrist as it was still possible for him to be—at least, he meant to tell him what he *thought* was the truth. Novotny answered that his father had been lazy and incompetent, and the family was finally better off with him gone. The psychiatrist then asked Novotny about Rose Anne. Novotny was frank. He asked Novotny if his back hurt when he was being intimate with Rose Anne. Novotny answered that sometimes it did and sometimes it didn't. He asked Novotny if, when it did hurt, they ceased being intimate. Novotny dropped his head. It was with a searing sense that some secret had been uncovered, something he himself had not even known, that he admitted that they did not. He simply could not bring himself, however, to tell the psychiatrist what exactly they did do when Novotny's back was at its worst. He said quickly that he planned to marry Rose Anne—that he had always known he would marry her. The psychiatrist asked where the couple would live and Novotny said with his mother. When he asked Novotny why, Novotny said because he had to take care of her, too.

The psychiatrist made Novotny stand up, close his eyes, and try to touch the tips of his index fingers together. While Novotny's eyes were closed, the psychiatrist leaned forward and, in a whisper, asked if Novotny was afraid of dying. The weight of all that he had been put through in the past weeks came down upon the shoulders of the young soldier. He broke down and admitted to a fear of death. He began to weep and to say that he didn't want to die. The psychiatrist asked him if he hated the Army, and he admitted that he did.

The psychiatrist's office was across the street from the main hospital, in the building the colonel had called the nuthouse. Novotny, full of shame, was led out of the building by an attendant with a large ring of keys hooked to his belt; he had to unlock three doors before Novotny got out to the street. He went out the rear door, just in sight of a volleyball game that was being played within a wire enclosure at the back of the building. To pull himself together before returning to the hostile cripples in the ward, Novotny watched the teams bat the ball back and forth over the net, and then he realized that they were patients who spent their days and nights inside the building from which he had just emerged. It occurred to him that the doctors were going to put him into the psychiatric hospital. Not because he was making believe he had a pain in his back—which, he had come to think, was really why they had been going to put him in the stockade—but precisely because he was *not* making believe. He was feeling a pain for which there was no cause. He had a terrible vision of Rose Anne having to come here to visit him. She was only a young girl, and he knew that it would frighten her so much to be led through three locked doors that he would lose her. He was about to begin to lose things.

He pulled himself straight up—he had been stooping—and clenched his teeth and told himself that in a certain number of seconds the pain would be gone for good. He counted to thirty, and then took a step. He came down upon his right foot with only half his weight, but the pain was still there, so sharp that it made his eyes water. The volleyball smashed against the fence through which he was peering, and, trying to walk as he remembered himself walking when he was a perfectly healthy young man, a man with nothing to fear—a man, he thought, who had not even begun to know of all the confusion growing up inside him—he walked away.

The colonel had Novotny called to his office the following day. The night before, Novotny had got little sleep, but by dawn he had reached a decision. Now, though he feared the worst, he marched to the colonel's office with a plan of action held firmly in mind. When Novotny entered, the colonel asked him to sit down, and proceeded to tell him of his own experiences in the Second World War. He had flown with an airborne division at a time when he was only a little more than Novotny's age. He had jumped from a plane over Normandy and broken both his legs, and then been shot in the chest by a French farmer for a reason he still did not understand. The colonel said that he had returned from Korea only a week before Novotny had entered the hospital. He wished that Novotny could see what the men there were going through—he wished Novotny could be a witness to the bravery and the courage and the comradery, and, too, to the misery and suffering. The misery of our soldiers and of those poor Koreans! He was not angry with Novotny personally; he was only trying to tell him something for his own good. Novotny was too young to make a decision that might disgrace him for the rest of his life. He told the young soldier that if he walked around with that back of his for a few weeks, if he just stopped *thinking* about it all the time, it would be as good as new. That, in actual fact, it was almost as good as new right now. He said that Novotny's trouble was that he was a passive-aggressive.

Novotny's voice was very thin when he asked the colonel what he meant. The colonel read to him what the psychiatrist had written. It was mostly the answers that Novotny had given to the psychiatrist's questions; some of it had to do with the way Novotny had sat, and the tone of his voice, and certain words he had apparently used. In the end, the report said that Novotny was a passive-aggressive and recommended he be given an administrative separation from the Army, and the appropriate discharge. Novotny asked what that meant. The colonel replied that the appropriate discharge as far as he was concerned was "plain and simple"; he took down a book of regulations from a shelf behind him, and after flipping past several pages read to Novotny in a loud voice. " 'An undesirable discharge is an administrative separation from the service under conditions other than honorable. It is issued for unfitness, misconduct, or security reasons.' " He looked up, got no response, and, fiery-eyed, read further. " 'It is recognized that all enlisted personnel with behavior problems cannot be rehabilitated by proper leadership and/or psychiatric assistance. It is inevitable that a certain percentage of individuals entering the service subsequently will demonstrate defective moral habits, irresponsibility, inability to profit by experience—' " He paused to read the last phrase again, and then went on— " 'untrustworthiness, lack of regard for the rights of others, and inability to put off pleasures and impulses of the moment.' " He engaged Novotny's eye. " 'Often,' " he said, returning to the regulation, " 'these individuals show poor performance despite intelligence, superficial charm, and a readiness to promise improvement. The effective leader is able to rehabilitate only the percentage of persons with behavior problems who are amenable to leadership.' " He stopped. "You can say that again," he mumbled, and pushed the book forward on his desk so that it faced Novotny. "Unfitness, soldier," he said, tapping his finger on the page. "It's what we use to get the crackpots out—bed-wetters, homos, petty thieves, malingerers, and so on." He waited for Novotny to take in the page's contents, and while he did, the colonel made

it clear that such a discharge followed a man through life. Novotny, raising his head slightly, asked again what a passive-aggressive was. The colonel looked into his eyes and said, "Just another kind of coward."

What Novotny had decided in bed the night before was to request a myelogram. Of course, there lived still in his imagination the man who said that all the needle had to do was be off by a hairbreadth; he was convinced, in fact, that something like that was just what would happen to him, given the way things had begun to go in his life. But though such a prospect frightened him, he did not see that he had any choice. The truth had to be known, one way or the other. But when the colonel finished and waited for him to speak, he remained silent.

"What do you have against the Army, Novotny?" the colonel asked. "What makes you so special?"

Novotny did not mention the myelogram. Why *should* he? Why should he have to take so much from people when he had an honest-to-God pain in his back? He was not imagining it, he was not making it up. He had practically ruptured himself when Reynolds had dropped the end of the can of potatoes. Maybe he had only awakened with a simple strain that first morning, but trying to keep the can from dropping on Reynolds' toes, he had done something serious to his back. That all the doctors were unable to give a satisfactory diagnosis did not make his pain any less real.

"You are a God-damned passive-aggressive, young man, what do you think of that?" the colonel said.

Novotny did not speak.

"You know how many people in America have low back pain?" the colonel demanded. "Something like fifteen per cent of the adult population of this country has low back pain —and what do you think they do, quit? Lay down on the job? What do you think a man does who has a family and responsibilities— stop supporting them? You know what your trouble is, my friend? You think life owes you something. You think something's coming to you. I spotted you right off, Novotny. You're going to get your way in this world. Everybody else can go to hell, just so long as you have your way. Imagine if all those men in Korea, if they all gave in to every little ache and pain. Imagine if that was what our troops had done at Valley Forge, or Okinawa. Then where would we all be? Haven't you ever heard of self-sacrifice? The average man, if you threatened him with this kind of discharge, would do just about anything he could to avoid it. But not you. Even if you have a pain, haven't you got the guts to go ahead and serve like everybody else? Well, answer me, yes or no?"

But Novotny would not answer. All he had done was answer people and tell them the truth, and what had it got him? What good was it, being good? What good was it, especially if at bottom you were bad anyway? What good was it, acting strong, if at bottom you were weak and couldn't *be* strong if you wanted to? With the colonel glaring across at him, the only solace Novotny had was to think that nobody knew any more about him than he himself did. Whatever anybody chose to call him didn't really mean a thing.

"Ah, get out of my sight," the colonel said. "People like you make me sick. Go ahead, join the bed-wetters and the queers. Get the hell out of here."

Within six days, the Army had rid itself of Novotny. It took Novotny, however, a good deal more than six days to rid himself of infirmity, if he can be said ever to have rid himself of infirmity—or, at least, the threat of infirmity. During the next year, he missed days of work and evenings of night school, and spent numerous weekends on a mattress supported by a bed board, where he rested and nursed away his pain. He went to one doctor who prescribed a set of exercises, and another who prescribed a steel brace, which Novotny bought but found so uncomfortable that he finally had to stick it away in the attic, though it had cost forty-five dollars. Another doctor, who had been recommended to him, listened to his story, then simply shrugged his shoulders; and still another told Novotny what the colonel had—that many Americans had low back ailments, that they were frequently of unknown origin, and that he would have to learn to live with it.

That, finally was what he tried to do. Gradually, over the years, the pain diminished in severity and frequency, though even today he has an occasional bad week, and gets a twinge if he bends the wrong way or picks up something he shouldn't. He is married to Rose Anne and is employed as a television cameraman by an educational channel in Chicago. His mother lives with him and his wife in Park Forest. For the most part, he leads a quiet, ordinary sort of life, though his attachment to Rose Anne is still marked by an unusual passion. When the other men in Park Forest go bowling on Friday nights, Novotny stays home, for he tries not to put strains upon his body to which he has decided it is not equal. In a way, all the awfulness of those Army days has boiled down to that—no bowling. There are nights, of course, when Novotny awakens from a dead sleep to worry in the dark about the future. What will happen to him? What won't? But surely those are questions he shares with all men, sufferers of low back pain and non-sufferers alike. Nobody has ever yet asked to see his discharge papers, so about that the colonel was wrong.

About the Authors

Nathaniel Hawthorne (1804–1864), on graduating from Bowdoin College, entered a twelve-year writing apprenticeship. This period culminated in his first masterpiece, *Twice-Told Tales* (1837), the short-story collection in which "Wakefield" appeared. Fame and success, however, did not come until the publication of *The Scarlet Letter* (1850). In these works, as in those that followed (*The House of the Seven Gables*, 1851; *The Blithedale Romance*, 1852), Hawthorne typically drew on the Puritan history of his native New England and the devices of the Gothic tale, a story of horror usually written for horror's sake, well-known for its haunted houses, bloodstained tapestries, eerie noises, and smiling apparitions. But in Hawthorne's hands these devices become symbols, woven into allegories of psychological subtlety that reveal the division between reason and emotion and the influence of sin on the individual and his society. In the twice-told story of Wakefield—once from a "journalistic" account, then from Hawthorne's imagination—the smiling real protagonist makes himself over into the unreal Outcast of the Universe. For further biographical, critical, or historical information, consult: Frederick C. Crews, *The Sins of the Fathers: Hawthorne's Psychological Themes* (New York, 1966); Richard H. Fogle, *Hawthorne's Fiction: The Light and the Dark*, revised edition (Norman, Okla., 1964); Julian Hawthorne, *Nathaniel Hawthorne and His Wife*, two volumes (Boston, 1884); A. N. Kaul, *Hawthorne: A Collection of Critical Essays* (Englewood Cliffs, 1966); Andrew Schiller, "The Moment and the Endless Voyage: A Study of Hawthorne's 'Wakefield,'" *Diameter*, I (March 1951), 7–12; Randall Stewart, *Nathaniel Hawthorne* (New Haven, 1948); Hyatt H. Waggoner, *Hawthorne: A Critical Study*, revised edition (Cambridge, Mass., 1963); and Yvor Winters, *Maule's Curse* (Norfolk, Conn., 1938).

Feodor Dostoevsky (1821–1881) believed passionately in man's need to expiate his sins through suffering, a conviction that grew as Dostoevsky underwent violent personal experiences. A congenital epileptic, Dostoevsky lived to see his father savagely murdered, and fellow revolutionaries and himself face a firing squad, then suddenly be reprieved and sentenced to hard labor in Siberia. Despite these experiences, the ability not only to endure and understand but also to transcend personal degradation and tragedy informs even the grimmest of Dostoevsky's subjects: the struggle between good and evil in a dual personality (*The Double*, 1846), the Siberian experiences of *The House of the Dead* (1862), the psychology of a murderer (*Crime and Punishment*, 1866), the suicidal searcher after immortality (*The Possessed*, 1871), and the contradictions in complex human personalities (*The Brothers Karamazov*, 1880). To sufferers and scoffers alike the Ridiculous Man proclaims the meaning of his dream-vision: "I will not and I cannot believe that evil is the normal condition among men." For further biographical, critical, or historical information, consult: Edward H. Carr, *Dostoevsky (1821–1881): A New Biography* (London, 1949); Jessie Coulson, *Dostoevsky: A Self-Portrait* (London and New York, 1962); David Magarshack, *Dostoevsky* (New York, 1962); Ernest

J. Simmons, *Dostoevsky: The Making of a Novelist* (London and New York, 1940); Elizabeth W. Trahan, "The Golden Age—Dream of a Ridiculous Man?" *Slavic and East European Journal*, XVII (1959), 349–71; Edward Wasiolek, *Dostoevsky: The Major Fiction* (Cambridge, Mass., 1964); René Wellek, *Dostoevsky: A Collection of Critical Essays* (Englewood Cliffs, 1962); and Avrahm Yarmolinsky, *Dostoevsky: His Life and Art*, second edition, completely revised (New York, 1957).

Gustave Flaubert (1821–1880), after studying law in Paris, contracted a nervous disorder from which he sought relief first through travel and then in semiretirement. A perfectionist, he wrote little but exquisitely; discounting a satire left fragmentary at his death, Flaubert's achievement rests on *Madame Bovary* (1857), *Salammbô* (1862), *L'Education sentimentale* (1869), *The Temptation of St. Anthony* (1848–1849; published complete in 1874), and *Three Tales* (in which "The Legend of St. Julian the Hospitaler" appeared, 1877). Flaubert's work is characterized by restraint, economy, and incisiveness of detail; he searched deliberately and painstakingly for what is called *le mot juste* (precisely the right word in the right place) to achieve simplicity, objectivity, and unity of tone and texture. One does not, however, read far into "St. Julian" before realizing that Flaubert's simplicity is deceptive. The form on which the tale is based—the ancient "life of a saint"—is easy enough, but the eye of the biographer seizes on startling juxtapositions: for example, Julian's mother "heard the voices of angels and her head fell back on her pillow over which hung a martyr's bone in a frame of carbuncles." Simplicity is deliberately exaggerated to produce its opposite, becoming pregnant with ironic implications. For further biographical, critical, or historical information, consult: Benjamin F. Bart, *Flaubert* (Syracuse, N. Y., 1967); Benjamin F. Bart, "The Moral of Flaubert's 'Saint Julien,'"

Romanic Review, XXXVIII (1947), 23–33; Victor Brombert, "Flaubert's 'Saint Julien': The Sin of Existing," *Publications of the Modern Language Association*, LXXXI (1966), 297–302; Raymond D. Giraud, *Flaubert: A Collection of Critical Essays* (Englewood Cliffs, 1964); Hugh Kenner, *Flaubert, Joyce and Beckett: The Stoic Comedians* (Boston, 1962); Philip Spencer, *Flaubert: A Biography* (New York, 1952); Enid Starkie, *Flaubert: The Making of the Master* (London, 1967); Lionel Trilling, "Flaubert's Last Testament," *Partisan Review*, XX (1953), 627–30; repeated in *The Opposing Self: Nine Essays in Criticism* (New York, 1955), pp. 201–5.

Henry James (1843–1916) once characterized the goal of fiction as "catching the very note and trick, the strange irregular rhythm of life" (in "The Art of Fiction," 1884). To this end he applied his early studies in law and painting, his copious self-communions in notebooks, extensive travel through Europe, and his omnivorous mind and alert eye. If the different terrains he covered seem large, the object on which he focused in each is just as formidable; for James was intent upon rendering the every "note and trick" of his characters' minds, through either metaphors or images clustered about a common center. His own mind was particularly sparked when this intention was united with one of his two favorite themes: the collision of American naïveté with Old World suavity (as in *The American*, 1877; *Daisy Miller*, 1878; *The Portrait of a Lady*, 1881; *The Wings of the Dove*, 1902; *The Ambassadors*, 1903; *The Golden Bowl*, 1904) or the sudden sense of life unlived or unfulfilled (as in "The Beast in the Jungle," 1903; "The Jolly Corner," 1909; "The Bench of Desolation," 1910). "The Altar of the Dead" (1895) is one of the seminal works elaborating the latter theme, and its constant references to jewelry, gold, and general richness reveal as much about its protagonist's psychology as about his milieu. For further biographical, critical, or historical information, consult: Joseph Warren Beach, *The Method of Henry James*, enlarged edition with corrections (Philadelphia, 1954); R. P. Blackmur, "The Sacred Fount," *Kenyon Review*, IV (1942), 338–40; Van Wyck Brooks, *The Pilgrimage of Henry James* (New York, 1925); F. W. Dupee, *Henry James*, revised edition (New York, 1956); Leon Edel, *Henry James* (Minneapolis, 1960); Leon Edel, *Henry James: A Collection of Critical Essays* (Englewood Cliffs, 1963); Edwin Honig, "The Merciful Fraud in Three Stories of Henry James," *Tiger's Eye*, I (October 1949), 91–5; Henry James, *The Art of the Novel: Critical Prefaces* (New York, 1946), especially pp. 241–45; repeated by F. O. Matthiessen and Kenneth B. Murdock, in *The Notebooks of Henry James* (New York, 1947), pp. 164–67.

Joseph Conrad (1857–1924), born to Polish aristocrats who were murdered for their revolutionary activities, went to sea at sixteen, and at twenty taught himself English from newspapers. After two decades of seafaring, he retired and wrote his first novel, *Almayer's Folly* (1895). This was followed by a long list of works: to name but a few, *The Nigger of the "Narcissus"* (1898), *Lord Jim* (1900), *Heart of Darkness* and *Youth* (1902), *Typhoon* (1903), *The Secret Agent* (1907), *Chance* (1914), and *Victory* (1917). These works are characterized by foreign settings, adventures, and oscillating or complex points of view; but pervading even the most exotic setting or fantastic adventure is the mind of the author: introspective, inclined toward gloom, uncertain that man may ever possess the whole truth, desiring association with other men, but often finding only isolation. "The Secret Sharer" is an exploration and symbolization of growing self-knowledge, with its paradoxes and ambivalences. The progress of the story is initiated as the young captain glimpses Leggatt first as "complete but for the head," then makes him the double of his thoughts, and is finally forced to view him, as before "the very gateway of Erebus . . . a proud

swimmer striking out for a new destiny." For further biographical, critical, or historical information, consult: Jocelyn Baines, *Joseph Conrad: A Critical Biography* (New York, 1960); A. J. Guerard, *Joseph Conrad* (New York, 1947); Bruce Harkness, *Conrad's "The Secret Sharer" and the Critics* (Belmont, Cal., 1962); Marvin Mudrick, *Conrad: A Collection of Critical Essays* (Englewood Cliffs, 1966); Claire Rosenfield, "The Shadow Within," *Daedalus*, XCII (1963), 333; J. L. Simmons, "The Dual Morality in Conrad's 'The Secret Sharer,'" *Studies in Short Fiction*, II (1965), 209–20; Oliver Warner, *Joseph Conrad* (London, 1951); Porter Williams, "The Brand of Cain in 'The Secret Sharer,'" *Modern Fiction Studies*, X (1964), 27–30; John H. Wills, "Conrad's 'The Secret Sharer,'" *University of Kansas City Review*, XXVIII (1961), 115–26; and Morton D. Zabel, "Conrad: 'The Secret Sharer,'" *New Republic*, CIV (1941), 567–68, 570–74.

Anton Chekhov (1860–1904) began to write stories in 1880 to support his medical studies. He wrote under various pen names, his favorite being a most apt "The Man Without a Spleen." For, in both fiction and drama, the Chekhovian tone—if it can be defined at all—is customarily simple, gentle, sympathetic, and delicate (as opposed to the legendary wrath, temper, or melancholy attributed to spleen) despite the tragic circumstances it overlays. It is not, however, either passive or quiescent, as a careful reading of "The Darling" quickly reveals. Chekhov's heroine here, as does his hero in the short novel *Ward No. 6* (1892) and almost all his best stories (as, for example, "The Kiss," "On the Road," and "Happiness," 1886–1887; "The Betrothed," 1903) or plays, engages in a battle between the suppression of life through stagnation and life's fulfillment through action and indomitable will. The battle in "The Darling" falls, it should be noted, into four repetitive parts, comparable to, if less complex than, the usual four-act structure of Chekhov's plays. For further biographical, critical, or historical information, see the biography in the section on drama in this book, and consult: Anton Chekhov, *The Selected Letters,* translated by Sidonie K. Lederer (New York, 1965); Robert Jackson, *Chekhov: A Collection of Critical Essays* (Englewood Cliffs, 1967); Seymour Lainoff, "Chekhov's 'The Darling,' " *Explicator,* XIII (1955), Item 24; Ernest J. Simmons, *Chekhov* (Boston, 1962); Leo Tolstoy, "The Darling," *The Works of Leo Tolstoy,* translated by Aylmer Maude (London, 1929), XVIII, 65–9; and Thomas Winner, *Chekhov and His Prose* (New York, 1966).

Rudyard Kipling (1865–1936), the first English writer to receive a Nobel Prize (in 1907), was born in Bombay and educated at the United Services College, Westward Ho! His career parallels that of British imperialism, with its rise in the late nineteenth century and its decline in the early twentieth; today it is the Kipling of the former period that most readers recognize, the man of the latter having been largely forgotten. The Kipling of " 'They' " (1904) is not precisely the same as the "brassy" balladeer of *Departmental Ditties* (1886) or *Barrack-Room Ballads* (1892), the sea-jungle-war popular storyteller of *Plain Tales from the Hills* (1887), *The Light That Failed* (1890), the Jungle Books (1894–1895), *Captains Courageous* (1897), and *Kim* (1901). " 'They' " is a mystical fantasy in which the protagonist, a man "from the other side of the county" grieving for a dead daughter, wanders into a yew-studded estate. What he learns there about death is communicated obliquely through symbols or symbolic action: the yew tree shaped into a soldier holding a lance, children whose laughter may be heard though they cannot be seen, a blind lady who knows all colors and traces an occult egg in dust, a misquoted passage of verse by Elizabeth Barrett Browning, and a final moment of illumination pitted against a terrifying debate. For further biographical, critical, or historical information, consult: C. A. Bodelson, *Aspects of Kipling's Art* (New York, 1964); C. E. Car-

rington, *The Life of Rudyard Kipling* (Garden City, 1955); Walter M. Hart, *Kipling: The Story Writer* (Berkeley, 1918); R. Thurston Hopkins, *Rudyard Kipling: A Literary Appreciation* (London, 1915); Peter Penzoldt, *The Supernatural in Fiction* (London, 1952), especially pp. 134–42; Andrew Rutherford, *Kipling's Mind and Art: Selected Critical Essays* (Stanford, 1964); Edward Shanks, *Rudyard Kipling: A Study in Literary and Political Ideas* (London, 1940); and J. M. S. Tompkins, *The Art of Rudyard Kipling* (London, 1959).

Sherwood Anderson (1876–1941) was, in his lifetime, a factory hand, a painter, a stable boy, a soldier in the Spanish-American War, an advertising man, and the owner-manager of a paint factory in his native Ohio. The sense of drifting implied by this catalogue, coupled with a sense of the utter desolation surrounding him, moved Anderson, in middle life, to articulate his concern over mechanized man and his hypocritical industrial society. Such concerns fill his novels and short stories —to cite but a few: *Windy McPherson's Son* (1916), *Marching Men* (1917), *Winesburg, Ohio* (1919), *Poor White* (1920), *The Triumph of the Egg* (1921), and *Dark Laughter* (1925). *Winesburg* (in which "Loneliness" appeared) is perhaps Anderson's best-known and best-loved work. He called it his "book of the grotesque," indicating his obsession with inarticulate, repressed characters who retreat into illusion, inaction, or hallucination. The static, repetitive, self-conscious style of the stories, and their subordination of plot motion—both well exemplified by "Loneliness"—perfectly underscore Anderson's vision of life fixed and frozen. For further biographical, critical, or historical information, consult: Rex Burbank, *Sherwood Anderson* (New York, 1964); Herbert Gold, "The Purity and Cunning of Sherwood Anderson," *Hudson Review,* X (1957), 551–2; Irving Howe, *Sherwood Anderson* (New York, 1951); Ray L. White, *The Achievement of Sherwood Anderson: Essays in Criticism* (Chapel Hill, 1966); and James Schevill,

Sherwood Anderson: His Life and Work (Denver, 1951).

James Joyce (1882–1941), when told that his final work, *Finnegans Wake* (1939), required a lifetime to read, replied that so it should be, since the book had required a lifetime to write. If this complaint had been registered about his relatively less complex earlier works, the same response would still have been applicable: for Joyce's few but influential works—a volume of verse, a play, and four books of fiction—were the distillation, each at its time of publication, of his total experience, experimentation, and devotion to art. His short stories, *Dubliners* (in which "Two Gallants" appeared, 1914), he called epiphanies, designating his belief in the holiness of all life and the illumination of the divine that marks the true artist's insight into life. In "Two Gallants" that insight occurs when Corley, one of the almost vaudevillian Mutt-and-Jeff team, reveals to Lenehan, "his disciple," the provocative, symbolic gold coin in the palm of an outstretched hand. In *A Portrait of the Artist as a Young Man* (1916) and *Ulysses* (1922) the concept of the epiphany is expanded as it unites with the stream-of-consciousness technique. For further biographical, critical, or historical information, consult: Robert Boyle, " 'Two Gallants' and 'Ivy Day in the Committee Room,' " *James Joyce Quarterly*, I (1963), 3–9; Richard Ellmann, *James Joyce* (New York, 1959); Brewster Ghiselin, "The Unity of Joyce's *Dubliners*," *Accent*, XVI (1956), 201–2; Richard Levin and Charles Shattuck, "First Flight to Ithaca: A New Reading of Joyce's *Dubliners*," *Accent*, IV (1944), 84–5; William T. Noon, *Joyce and Aquinas* (New Haven, 1957), especially pp. 83–4; William Y. Tindall, *A Reader's Guide to James Joyce* (New York, 1959); Florence L. Walzl, "Symbols in Joyce's 'Two Gallants,' " *James Joyce Quarterly*, II (Winter 1965), 73–81.

Franz Kafka (1883–1924) was a German Jew whose works, for the most part, were published posthumously. He wrote logically and lucidly of a world in which logic and lucidity were momentary, ambiguity and nightmare of longer and harsher duration: Gregor Samsa of "The Metamorphosis" awakens one morning to find "himself transformed in his bed into a gigantic insect"; the hero of "The Judgment"—Kafka's very first story, written in a single evening in 1913—goes to tell his invalid father of a friend's marriage and enters upon a cross-examination of his ambivalent motives, resulting in death. An overwhelming sense of guilt, an impulse to admit guilt contradicted by an impulse to rebel against some unproven accusation, a vision of the world ensnarled by governmental red tape and incomprehensible man-made institutions— these problems are typically found in Kafka's short works, and elaborated at greater length in the novels, *The Trial* (1925) and *The Castle* (1926). For further biographical, critical, or historical information, consult: Kate Flores, "Franz Kafka and the Nameless Guilt: An Analysis of 'The Judgment,' " *Quarterly Review of Literature*, III (1947), 382–405; Ronald Gray, *Kafka: A Collection of Critical Essays* (Englewood Cliffs, 1962); Claude-Edmonde Magny, "The Objective Depiction of Absurdity," *Quarterly Review of Literature*, II (1945), 214–18; Charles Neider, *The Frozen Sea: A Study of Franz Kafka* (New York, 1948); Nathan A. Scott, *Rehearsals of Discomposure* (New York, 1952); Erwin R. Steinberg, "The Judgment in Kafka's 'The Judgment,' " *Modern Fiction Studies*, VIII (1962), 23–30; and Herbert Tauber, *Franz Kafka* (New Haven, 1948).

D. H. Lawrence (1885–1930), though not a follower of Freud's theories, was vitally interested in the exploration of man's unconscious. He believed that the rational had been, to man's detriment, emphasized over the instinctual; for him, the body, with its eruptive life force, was man's soul. Lawrence's beliefs, as well as his antimilitarist position and his marriage to a German during World War I, led to the suppression of his novel *The Rainbow* (1915); and as a result, he left his native England to wander from one country to the next. The wandering increased and enhanced Lawrence's output as a host of travel books and new novels followed: to the early *Sons and Lovers* (1913) he now added, among others, *Women in Love* (1921), *Aaron's Rod* (1922), and the then-controversial *Lady Chatterley's Lover* (1929). In "Second Best" the physical contrast between the fourteen-year-old Anne and the twenty-three-year-old Frances (particularly their skin tones) and their different reactions to the mole come together concisely to state one of Lawrence's major themes and concerns: the surfacing of the unconscious, the eruption of sexual instinct. For further biographical, critical, or historical information, consult: George H. Ford, *Double Measure: A Study of the Novels and Stories of D. H. Lawrence* (New York, 1965); Graham Hough, *The Dark Sun: A Study of D. H. Lawrence* (London, 1956); Keith Sagar, *The Art of D. H. Lawrence* (Cambridge, Eng., 1966); Mark Spilka, *D. H. Lawrence: A Collection of Critical Essays* (Englewood Cliffs, 1963); E. W. Tedlock, *D. H. Lawrence: Artist and Rebel* (Albuquerque, 1963); Daniel A. Weiss, *Oedipus in Nottingham: D. H. Lawrence* (Seattle, 1962); and Kingsley Widmer, *The Art of Perversity* (Seattle, 1962).

Katherine Anne Porter (b. 1890) did not begin to publish her work until she was thirty, and recognition did not come until the appearance of *Flowering Judas* (1930; a volume of six stories expanded to ten in 1935). Her reputation rests on several books of essays and translations, five novelettes (among them *Noon Wine*, 1937, and *Pale Horse, Pale Rider*, 1939), three collections of stories, and one novel (*Ship of Fools*, 1962). As small as her output may be, Miss Porter's works cover a large and diverse number of geographical areas: Mexico, Europe, the American Southwest and East. In all her works the spareness of her style emphasizes an unsparing honesty with herself and her subjects. In "Theft" quick snatches of overheard conversation and brief encounters act to suggest rather than fully state the heroine's environment; the fact that her name is not mentioned once throughout the story adds weight of meaning to the purse, its loss and recovery, and the heroine's final stark thought. For further biographical, critical, or historical information, consult: George Greene, "Brimstone and Roses: Notes on Katherine Anne Porter," *Thought*, XXXVI (1961), 430–31; George Hendrick, *Katherine Anne Porter* (New York, 1965); William L. Nance, *Katherine Anne Porter and the Art of Rejection* (Chapel Hill, 1964); Leonard Prager, "Getting and Spending: Porter's 'Theft,'" *Perspective*, XI (1960), 230–34; and William B. Stein, "'Theft': Porter's Politics of Modern Love," *Perspective*, XI (1960), 223–8.

Ryūnosuke Akutagawa (1892–1927) was born in Tokyo to middle-class parents; his mother died of insanity shortly after his birth, and at thirty-five he committed suicide with an overdose of barbiturates, An art collector, an avid reader, an experimenter in several genres, Akutagawa was influenced by the Western "confessional" novel, a form that, despite being alien and offensive to the general Oriental taste for more objective art, was just being introduced to the East, through translation, in his lifetime. Yet as "In a Grove" demonstrates, the "confessional" form ideally suits Akutagawa's anatomy of objectivity—or rather the impossibility of being objective: a common crime evokes from the seven people involved in it seven different stories. The fascination of the tale lies, then, in its manipulation of many different points of view. Who, the author would seem to query, is telling the "truth"? One and/or all of them? How can we ever know any "truth" detached from the persons who perceive it? There is almost no criticism written in English for a student interested in pursuing the study of Akutagawa further; he should, however, see Takashi Kojima's translation, *Rash-ōmon and Other Stories* (New York, 1952), and possibly a microfilm of Kinya Tsuruta's doctoral dissertation, "Akutagawa Ryūno-suke: His Concepts of Life and Art" (unpublished dissertation, University of Washington, 1968).

Isaac Babel (1894–1939–41?) was born to a middle-class Russian–Jewish family in Odessa. Up to 1923 he had published only a few stories, having held minor posts during the Russian Revolution and ensuing civil war, fought with the cavalry, and run a printing press. His fame rests on two volumes of stories, *Tales of Odessa* (1923–1924) and *Red Cavalry* (1926), although the exact amount of work Babel wrote, like his fate, is uncertain. Babel was arrested during the purges of the 1930s and died in a concentration camp sometime between 1939 and 1941 (recent authority says March 17, 1941) either of typhoid fever or by shooting. "Di Grasso" belongs to neither of his famous books; Babel published the story in a magazine. It represents, nevertheless, the underpinning of all we know of Babel's art: for in Di Grasso's "leap," as in the reactions of the persona, Nick, and his wife, we recognize a symbol of the relationships between the artist and his audience. For further biographical, critical, or historical information, consult: Isaac Babel, *Collected Stories*, translated by Walter Morison, with an introduction by Lionel Trilling (New York, 1955); Isaac Babel, *The Lonely Years, 1925–1939* (New York, 1964); Steven Marcus, "The Stories of Isaac Babel," *Partisan Review*, XII (1955), 410–11; and Frank O'Connor, *The Lonely Voice: A Study of the Short Story* (Cleveland, 1963).

Jean Toomer (1894–1967) once observed: "We do not have states of being; we have states of dreaming." And a sense of dreaming pervades the content and structure of his best-known work, *Cane* (1923), a book combining realistic detail with a tone of rhapsodic mysti-cism and merging character sketches, short stories, and verse. "Theater," Toomer's story-sketch of frustrated lovers from that volume, pits John's "dream" against that of Dorris, deliberately treating both as separate musical themes that counterpoint one another, yet are incapable of reaching final harmony. For further biographical, critical, or historical information, consult: Arna Bontemps, "The Harlem Renaissance," *Saturday Review of Literature*, XXX (March 22, 1947), 12–13, 44; Arna Bontemps, "The Negro Renaissance: Jean Toomer and the Harlem Writers of the 1920's," *Anger, and Beyond: The Negro Writer in the United States*, Herbert Hill, ed. (New York, 1966); Eugene Holmes, "Jean Toomer, Apostle of Beauty," *Opportunity*, III (August 1925), 252–4, 260; Paul Rosenfeld, "Jean Toomer," *Men Seen* (New York, 1925); and Darwin T. Turner, "And Another Passing," *Negro American Literature Forum*, I (Fall 1967).

William Faulkner (1897–1962), accepting the Nobel Prize in 1950, characterized good writing as that which pursues "the problems of the human heart in conflict with itself . . . because only that is worth writing about, worth the agony and the sweat." Speaking nearly two decades after creating and peopling his mythical Yoknapatawpha County and exploring the conflict between honor and passion in such works as *The Sound and the Fury* (1929), *Light in August* (1932), *Absalom, Absalom!* (1936), and *The Unvanquished* (1938), Faulkner went on to enunciate his belief in man's immortality, not because man "has an inexhaustible voice, but because he has a soul, a spirit capable of comparison and sacrifice and endurance." The terrifying concluding scene of "Wash," with its hero alone, bearing down, with a scythe, upon unconquerable forces, attests eloquently to the integrity of Faulkner's vision and conviction. For further biographical, critical, or historical information, consult: Melvin Backman, *Faulkner: The Major Years: A Critical Study* (Bloomington, Ind., 1966); Dale G. Breaden

"William Faulkner and the Land," *American Quarterly*, X (1958), 355–6; Frederick J. Hoffman, *William Faulkner*, second edition, revised (New York, 1966); Irving Howe, *William Faulkner: A Critical Study*, second edition (New York, 1962); Neil D. Isaacs, "Götterdämmerung in Yoknapatawpha," *Tennessee Studies in Literature*, VIII (1963), 47–55; Ward L. Miner, *The World of William Faulkner* (Durham, N. C., 1952); and Charles H. Nilon, *Faulkner and the Negro* (New York, 1965).

Jorge Luis Borges (b. 1899), an Argentinian educated in Europe, has worked with equal success in verse (*Luna de enfrente*, 1925), the essay (*Inquisiones*, 1925), and fiction (*Ficciones*, 1944, and *El Aleph*, 1949). Though he would be the first to object to such a label, his stories are fantasies of the intellect, devoid of plot, general in characterization, but rich in tone of voice. They dwell on attempts of men to impose rational constructions upon a labyrinthine universe and to seek out their destinies within their visions. The best features of the essay—the "subjective" pursuit of an idea—and verse—precise but suggestive symbols—merge in Borgés' fiction. The resulting works may be viewed equally as essays containing story elements or stories containing essayistic comment on their intellectual composition. There is no dichotomy in the structure—rather a unified double vision extending to the characterization that is offered and projected in the stories' titles: in "The Lottery in Babylon" the protagonist has been both "proconsul" and "slave," and knows "omnipotence" as well as "opprobrium"; no little importance is attached to the setting, for Babylon, by tradition, has been a symbol both for high civilization and for vice and decadence. For further biographical, critical, or historical information, consult: Ana M. Barrenechea, *Borgés, the Labyrinth Maker*, edited and translated by Robert Lima (New York, 1965); Jorge Luis Borges, *Labyrinths: Selected Stories & Other Writings*, edited by Donald A. Yates and James E. Irby (New York, 1964); Richard Burgin, *Conversations with Jorge Luis Borges* (New York, 1969); and Miguel Enguínados, "Image and Escape in the Short Stories of Jorge Luis Borges," *Texas Quarterly*, IV (Winter 1961), 118–27.

Elizabeth Bowen (b. 1899), speaking of E. M. Forster, an author influential upon her own work, commends his fusing of the banal and inexplicable, his irony that holds "mockery in curb," his feeling for place, and his dialogue in which speakers precipitate action and illustrate "the striking-power of the thing said." While Miss Bowen's world is smaller than Forster's and her subjects narrowed to "affairs of the heart," the qualities of the two authors are not dissimilar. From her first collection of stories (*Encounters*, 1923) through *The Demon Lover* (in which "Mysterious Kôr" appeared, in 1946) and the greatly acclaimed *The Heat of the Day* (1949), she has demonstrated the power to evoke a sense of setting in which every detail tensely fits. "Mysterious Kôr," in essence a love story of the usual triangular dimensions, achieves tensity as the author, noted for her clear patterns, views the pattern-breaking effects of war on three individuals' behavior. For further biographical, critical, or historical information, consult: Jocelyn Brooke, *Elizabeth Bowen* (London and New York, 1952); William W. Heath, *Elizabeth Bowen: An Introduction to Her Novels* (Madison, Wis., 1961); and Edward Mitchell, "Themes in Elizabeth Bowen's Short Stories," *Critique*, VIII (Spring–Summer 1966), 48–9.

Ernest Hemingway (1899–1961) served in World War I as an ambulance driver and infantryman with the Italian army. After the war, working in Paris as a correspondent for the *Toronto Star*, he began to write his first stories (now collected in *The Fifth Column and the First Forty-Nine Stories*). His first substantial novel, *The Sun Also Rises* (1926), introduced the hero Hemingway was to develop in various guises: the maimed man struggling silently or actively against fate, who appears not only in *To Have and Have Not* (1937), but also in Hemingway's last major work, *The Old Man and the Sea* (1953), as the old fisherman whose luck seems to have turned against him. In "A Natural History of the Dead" Hemingway turns his training in journalism to good account: the ironic essayistic beginning provides a panoramic context for the brief story to follow. The tension and coherence of the story depend primarily on dialogue—rapid, terse, and "true." "All you have to do," Hemingway told himself as a young man in Paris (*A Moveable Feast*, 1964), "is write one true sentence." He "would write one true sentence, and then go on from there." He was awarded the Nobel Prize in 1954. For further biographical, critical, or historical information, consult: Sheridan Baker, *Ernest Hemingway: An Introduction and Interpretation* (New York, 1967); Carlos Baker, *Hemingway: The Writer as Artist*, third edition (Princeton, 1966); Joseph De Falco, *The Hero in Hemingway's Short Stories* (Pittsburgh, 1963); John Portz, "Allusion and Structure in Hemingway's 'A Natural History of the Dead,'" *Tennessee Studies in Literature*, X (1965), 27–41; and Robert Penn Warren, "Hemingway," *Kenyon Review*, IX (1947), 4–5.

Samuel Beckett (b. 1906), once approached about writing a libretto for an opera, replied that if he did, it would be composed entirely of sighs. An Irishman who now writes mostly in French, and for whom mime has grown increasingly important, Beckett presents worlds, whether in drama or fiction, in which men attempt to communicate with themselves or others from their separate garbage cans, or buried to their chins in earth, or lying solitary on barren beaches. In the Beckett world there is absurdity, madness, boredom, cruelty, and suffering, but there is nothing to do, nothing to expect, nothing to desire. Silence alone is real if it reveals consciousness, continuity, self, and anguish; for the concern

of man is self-definition; and that can only be achieved, if at all, by rejecting all notions of the ready-made in one's environment and language. "Who am I?" is the continual question struggling toward that silence through every deliberately deranged, rhapsodic syllable of "Stones," an extract, previously published as a story, from the novel *Molloy* (1947–1949; translated 1951). Sequels, *Malone Dies* and *The Unnamable*, as well as the plays *Waiting for Godot* (1958) and *Endgame* (1958), develop, in differing ways, Beckett's pursuit of identity and language of self. Beckett was awarded the Nobel Prize in 1969. For further biographical, critical, or historical information, consult: *Beckett at 60: A Festschrift* (London, 1967); Richard N. Coe, *Beckett* (Edinburgh, 1964); Martin Esslin, *Samuel Beckett: A Collection of Critical Essays* Englewood Cliffs, 1965); John Fletcher, *The Novels of Samuel Beckett* (London, 1964); Frederick J. Hoffman, *Samuel Beckett: The Language of Self* (New York, 1964); and Hugh Kenner, *Samuel Beckett: A Critical Study* (New York, 1961).

Richard Wright (1908–1960), as has been frequently noted, was the first modern writer to concentrate on the problems of the American Negro in the ghetto. *Native Son* (1940) protests the victimization of the Negro by white society, and *Black Boy* (1945), Wright's autobiography, recounts the personal experiences on which Wright's stories, novels, and essays are based—experiences of alienation, distrust, and suffering. "Big Boy Leaves Home" is the first story in Wright's first important book, *Uncle Tom's Children* (1938). Though placed in a rural rather than an urban setting, its initial pastoral-like quality of song and horseplay ironically heightens the violent confrontation between black and white to come. For further biographical or critical information, consult: Keneth Kinnamon, "The Pastoral Impulse in Richard Wright," *Midcontinent American Studies Journal*, X (Spring 1969), 41–7; Nathan F. Scott, "Search for Beliefs:

The Fiction of Richard Wright," *University of Kansas City Review,* XXIII (1956), 19–24; Nathan A. Scott, "The Dark and Haunted Tower of Richard Wright," *Graduate Comment,* VII (July 1964), 93–9; and Constance Webb, *Richard Wright: A Biography* (New York, 1968).

Albert Camus (1913–1960), according to one critic, wrote his essays, fiction, and drama like a "condemned man": death and its various instruments haunted him. But the death that concerned Camus was not only physical: rather it was moral or psychological—occurring at that moment when a man, pursuing truth and detachment, confronts a situation in which he must choose not between right and wrong but between two "wrongs." In one form or another this situation presents itself in the works *The Stranger* (1942), *The Plague* (1947), *The Rebel* (1953), and *The Fall* (1956). In "The Guest" the "neutral" schoolteacher finds himself forced to choose a principle on which to act or not when any choice means involvement and "death." Camus was awarded the Nobel Prize in 1957. For further biographical, critical, or historical information, consult: Germaine Brée, *Albert Camus* (New York, 1964); Germaine Brée, *Camus: A Collection of Critical Essays* (Englewood Cliffs, 1962); Philip Thody, *Albert Camus, 1913–1960* (New York, 1961); and Philip Thody, *Albert Camus: A Study of His Work* (London, 1957).

Shirley Jackson (1919–1965) attracted wide attention through the story that also named the first half-title of her collection, *The Lottery; or the Adventures of James Harris* (1949). In subsequent works, such as the novels *The Haunting of Hill House* (1959) and *We Have Always Lived in the Castle* (1962), she displays the same singular characteristics apparent in her first collection and in the story "The Renegade": a depiction of commonplace events under a gathering eerie overcast of Gothic tone, if not of Gothic devices. The sinister qualities of Miss Jackson's characters and situations lie not in mysterious smiles or unexplained bloodstains but, as in "The Renegade," in a very real chicken-killing dog, real neighbors with blunt "advice," and real children, naïve in their cruelty. Miss Jackson's work has been extensively reviewed, but little substantial criticism now exists. Those interested in examining her work would do well to read the books mentioned directly above, as well as her *The Road Through the Wall* (1948), *Hangsaman* (1951), and *The Bird's Nest* (1954).

Truman Capote (b. 1924) boasts of having written speeches for a politician, danced on a river boat, painted flowers on glass, and studied fortunetelling. He need not boast of having written his first novel at the age of twenty-three, since the publication of *Other Voices, Other Rooms* (1948) was greeted with a fanfare that made this fact as well as almost every other of his life public knowledge. Capote's talent continued to make itself felt in *A Tree of Night and Other Stories* (1949) and *The Grass Harp*, and reasserted itself still later in the study of a Kansas murder, *In Cold Blood* (1965). More often than not he writes of twentieth-century Southern America, its decaying mansions and dwindling patriarchal society. Capote's characters and situations, like Shirley Jackson's, evoke a sense of the Gothic, but usually through the point of view of a child or adolescent. In "My Side of the Matter," through an uncanny balance between the grotesque and the hilarious, Gothic fantasy becomes, in Capote's hands, Gothic extravaganza. Though his books have been widely reviewed, little general criticism of Capote's works now exists.

Philip Roth (b. 1933) shares with Chekhov the ability to combine the pathetic and the humorous in such a way as to produce tragic and comic effects simultaneously. His first book (*Goodbye, Columbus,* 1959) and his latest (*Portnoy's Complaint,* 1969), as well as

"Novotny's Pain," anthologized here, illustrate Roth's instinct for dealing with the seemingly commonplace, for wringing from it all its potential irony, then compounding the irony by dismissing his subject as less important than it is. For further biographical or critical information, consult: Joseph E. Brewer, "The Anti-Hero in Contemporary Literature," *Iowa English Yearbook*, XII (1967), 55–60; Irving and Harriet Deer, "Philip Roth and the Crisis in American Fiction," *Minnesota Review*, VI (1966), 353–60; Alfred Kazin, "Tough-minded Mr. Roth," *Contemporaries* (Boston, 1962), pp. 258–62.

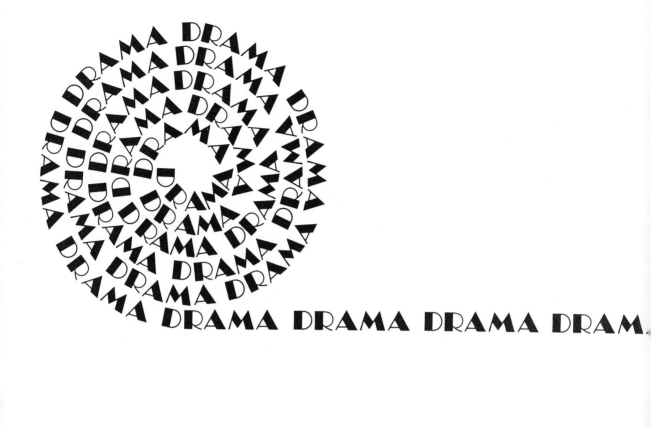

PENTHEUS *(to the guards):* Get hold of him. He is laughing at me and the whole city.

DIONYSUS *(to the guards):* I warn you not to bind me . . . *(To Pentheus.)* I am sane, you are mad.

PENTHEUS *(to Dionysus):* My orders overrule yours. *(To the guards.)* Bind him, I tell you.

DIONYSUS: You do not know what life you live, or what you do, or who you are.

Given these few lines of a Greek tragedy, *The Bacchae,* let us see what can be deduced from them about the character of any play. They are a conversation, a rapid give-and-take that reveals an obvious conflict of wills. As in a court report of legal proceedings, the two opposing speakers ask and answer questions or hurl accusations at each other. And, indeed, the essence of any play is its *agon,* a passionate physical or psychological battle, much like the presentation of a court case, with its attempts to reach the truth through examination, cross-examination, summations, and pleas. But a court record reports everything: repetitions, irrelevancies, purely worthless information. For the playwright there can be no worthless information: repetitions must serve to point a direction, and seeming irrelevancies must at some later time underscore that direction. The playwright's task is one of economy, concentration, and above all, intensification. He selects his data as carefully as his words. Data and words reflect his own vision and weight the case given to the audience in favor of one combatant.

One of the author's ways to shade the issues is through connotation. For most words, in addition to their denotative (exact or precise) meanings, share connotative (associated or accrued) meanings, which a writer subtly maneuvers. In Dionysus' first speech, the words "sane" and "mad" connote far more than personal or factual conclusions; they encompass the fundamental oppositions of the play as well as its attempts to arrive at a definition of "wisdom" and "god." Finally, to enhance these broader meanings, Euripides has shaped his words and sentences into verse: in the Greek they are consciously patterned both spatially and rhythmically, specifically for the best manipulation of his thought or, in this case, narrative.

The printed narrative conveys only a small part of Euripides' intention, however, for it was created for performance: to be read aloud, and, manifestly, to be *acted*. The total effect of a play depends upon its several particular voices; when any play is read rather than watched, there will be a drop in transferred meaning; the reader should try to compensate for this loss by imagining stage settings and stage directions. If he is successful, his two-dimensional characters will move on this imaginary set, talking *with* each other, and, by implication, *to* the audience. The play can reach its third dimension only in performance.

The characters, in speaking to each other, define the conflict of the play. The terms of this conflict are dictated to a large degree by the physical theatre the author writes for, by the conventions of that theatre, and by the members of its audience. Euripides' plays, for example, had a vast popular audience. Twice a year the citizens of Athens held festivals honoring the god Dionysus, in which authors entered their plays in competition for prizes from a jury chosen by lot as representative of the audience. The fifth-century theatre was huge; spectators sat on steps carved out of stone or on wooden benches, often built into a hillside, but in any case banked steeply in a semicircle about the orchestra (a circular dancing space) where the chorus performed. Slightly behind this space was the stage proper, raised a few steps and backed by an all-purpose building that faced the center rows of seats. This building (skene) provided a place to change costumes and to make entrances and exits; it served as the backdrop, or static scenery, for fifth-century Greek plays. Eventually the skene became stylized, with three doors that could represent entrances to a palace, rooms within it, or, in comedy, the front doors of next-door neighbors. For *The Bacchae*, therefore, all the set designer had to do was place a small shrine stage left (audience right), and the play was ready to begin with Dionysus' entrance.

The characters were as starkly stylized as their setting. The Greek chorus, ten to twenty men, spoke or sang their lines to the accompaniment of music and their own dancing, translating through combined vocal and choreographed rhythms the ideas as well as the emotions contained in their odes; they reflected the playwright's, or the society's, point of view on the action of the play. Behind the chorus, on the raised stage, the tragic actors in their high, painted masks and sculptured, brilliant robes moved majestically through their parts. In order to be seen and heard by such a large audience, an actor was provided with special equipment: built-up shoes, intended both to make the figure more visible and to give the illusion of a "man greater than other men," and a huge, helmet-like mask, which acted as a megaphone and was molded to convey traditional character types (king, mother, god) and the required emotions (fear, love, joy). Oedipus, Sophocles' doomed king, having gouged out his eyes, is delineated on his last entrance as a stumbling old man, his beard torn, his fixed black eye sockets streaming glittering red blood/paint. And Dionysus, the ambiguous god of *The Bacchae*, wears a smiling mask, painted perhaps with the beautiful impassive smile of the imbecile. These built-up figures were, obviously, clumsy; Greek tragedy relied on formal conversation and ritual confrontations, unlike Greek comedy, whose middle-class slaves and carping owners had more freedom of movement in simple contemporary dress. The tragic actor conveyed his meanings almost completely through his intonations and a few large gestures.

By Molière's time, the theatre had moved indoors. His stage looked much like our present one, raised above the level of the seated audience and raked back (slanted at an angle highest to the back of the stage), with a pit area directly in front, where the holders of the cheapest tickets stood. French spectators, like their English contemporaries, came to the theatre to gossip, eavesdrop, make assignations, play a game of cards, comment on the ladies, criticize the author, and even, on occasion, to watch the play. The pit was filled with apprentices to various trades, old soldiers, gorgeous fops, pimps, prostitutes, and children selling oranges and carrying notes from one interested spectator to another. Higher seats and boxes accommodated people with more money and slightly more discretion, who played a stationary role in this lightly boisterous, gleefully critical audience. Indeed, some nobles were not content to play in the audience, but took seats on stage, causing actors to complain of seated marquises where the trees should be. Eventually, Molière's company came under the patronage of the King, Louis XIV himself, and performed often at Versailles, Louis' sumptuous country palace, which included a complete theatre for productions.

In spite of his audience's static tastes, Molière's subject matter varied a great deal, as did his characters and settings. He wrote elaborate masques (allegories with much music and dancing) and ballets for court entertainment in addition to his well-known comedies. Masques required fantastic "machines"—apparatuses propelling winged gods and chariots—adapted for spectacular effects. In step with his century's desire for a return to Classical values, however, Molière wrote his comedies for one set, generally the Greek three doors, or perhaps a drawing room. The actors wore fashionable clothes, as dictated by their characters: in *Tartuffe*, Elmire and Mariane would glisten in tiers of silver lace on taffeta, satin and brocade, iridescent colors—lavender, turquoise, magenta—pieced together or embroidered over each other, with diamonds, pearls, or rubies scattered artfully over all. Head-dresses were no less extravagant: feathers, ribbons, and ropes of precious jewels were entwined in towering, curled, powdered wigs. Cosmetics were precisely those of the court ladies: no stage makeup was necessary. In contrast, Orgon and Tartuffe would enter in drab black. But Valère would counterpoint the ladies' theme in foppish overstatement, with cascading lace at his throat and cuffs, feathers and bows in his hat, red silk hose, and a brightly jeweled snuffbox.

Because he was writing comedy, Molière was exempt from the more rigorous Neoclassical "rules" of time, place, and action; his comedies of manners were divided into the prescribed five acts, but the dialogue and action —as, for instance, in Orgon's slapstick scenes with the chattering maid who refuses to be silenced—are much freer than those of the formal verse tragedies of the time. This contemporary quality, in fact, precipitated censorship troubles in the case of *Tartuffe:* a modern religious hypocrite is far more insulting than one safely labeled as "Greek" or "Roman"—or even "last year's."

In revolt against the popular theatre, Henrik Ibsen often wrote in defiance of a possible audience, contemptuous of its patronage. In *Ghosts* he dared to discuss hereditary syphilis; in *A Doll's House*, to reflect the emerging modern woman's dilemma and the growing feminist movement. His approach to, and attitude toward, these topics were never what his audience wanted to entertain; rather, they were what Ibsen thought and felt he was personally compelled to convey. While he had close ties to a growing realistic movement (whose leaders were intent upon applying objective, photographic techniques to common subjects), Ibsen developed from the movement the "well-made" play in serious drama, a play in which each episode in a definite sequence contributes to the inexorable climax and end of the action.

Cause and effect—results grounded in thoroughly comprehensible beginnings and ideas—are essential to, indeed taken for granted in, the realistic theatre. Almost concurrent with the development of the realistic approach to drama, theatre designers began to replace the old system of highly artificial painted flats with more and more accurate representations, culminating in the box set, an exact and enclosed replica of a room or an outdoors scene. The set designated by Ibsen and built for *The Master Builder*—the workroom, the porch, Solness' home—is no less precise than the characters inhabiting these spaces. Actors developed new techniques of identifying with, and trying to understand, the characters they played, as the characters were drawn in closer conjunction to their actual surroundings and the objects within those surroundings.

Anton Chekhov disagreed with the extent of Ibsen's "realism": he is reported to have observed that people didn't act or talk as he saw Ibsen's characters behave. Modern skepticism, for Chekhov, had destroyed normal progressions and political or religious idealism. "We have," he wrote, "neither near nor remote aims and our souls are as flat and bare as a billiard table." Thus Chekhov's entire orientation is *away* from the significant action and causal relationship that Ibsen relied on as a means of exploring the world. Nothing ever "happens" in a Chekhov play: usually the characters, clutching at the properties of their lives—notebooks, newspapers, prizes—as if they *were* their lives, have a sense of impending action, of possible change; but it is never satisfied. The characters in *The Three Sisters* hope to move to Moscow, yet never build up the necessary impetus, or they see the impetus stifled in the very moment of its emergence. Significant action is subverted, or thrown away offstage; the characters rhapsodize on details that seem to have lost their context, recalling snatches of songs and speaking in mournful fragments to themselves or beyond others. In Chekhov's four-act structure (a deliberate avoidance of the five-act structure, which requires a climax and exact symmetry), comedy balances tragedy, irony negates romance, and the characters continue, rather than live, their lives, illustrating the absurdity of the world by their own unbreakable habits.

Luigi Pirandello and Jean-Claude van Itallie, representatives of the "modern" and "contemporary" threatre respectively, are direct inheritors of Chekhov's view of the world as irrational. To continue the breakup of the realistic tradition, Pirandello set out to explore the nature of truth *within* the structure of the realistic theatre; at the same time he evolved a completely new form of his own. Within a conventional box set, his characters create the most amazing situations from the most commonplace beginnings; they carry causation to its ultimate and logical conclusions and force reality to distort itself. He transforms the theatre proper, its costumes, makeup, and settings, cutting through their pretense of mirroring and projecting life. They become, simultaneously and paradoxically, life itself and a repeated metaphor. *Henry IV* is a presentation of the problems of madness and sanity through the medium of an elaborate, historically accurate play invented to keep a madman happy. In another of Pirandello's masterpieces, six characters invade a theatre and insist that someone write a play about them. They claim to be a normal happy family who may, or may not, commit a murder; actually, they hate and contradict one another. The actors to whom they speak do not believe their story and cannot perform properly. In Pirandello's hands, then, stage artifice exposes the artifice of reality, and vice versa.

More recently, a host of playwrights has attempted to reduce theatre to its essentials, again in the antirealistic tradition. "Antiestablishment," "third theatre," "total theatre," "the theatre of cruelty," "the theatre of the absurd," "underground"—these are only a few of the descriptive tags attached to the work of playwrights such as Samuel Beckett, Jean Genet, Eugène Ionesco, Harold Pinter, and Jean-Claude van Itallie. Although the tags do not all mean the same thing, and although there are striking differences in the attitudes and techniques of these men, they are united in their efforts to make their work an *event* rather than a *show*. Rejecting the logic of traditional dramatic formulas, they embrace the frankly fantastic, intuitive, free, and improvisational. Cabarets, cellars, church lofts, coffee houses, and store windows are, for them, more suitable platforms than established commercial stages. The plays themselves concentrate on mood rather than on action, rendering symbolic states of being rather than moving in any given plot direction. Stage dynamics tend to be relatively constant: the lighting is spare, frequently unchanging in intensity or color; the setting is stripped bare; characters are few; and the dialogue is terse, fragmentary, and repetitive, delivered at the same tempo, pitch, and volume. The relationship between the actors and audience is altered from performers and spectators (as in van Itallie's first playlet, *Interview*, from *America Hurrah*) to a merging of personality in which each acquires the identity of the other and undergoes the same experience.

Modern plays, then, are pared down to dialogue. Dialogue remains the basic tool of the dramatist, for only through it can he develop the plot (simple or complex), which illustrates the theme of his play, and the characters who bring it to life. Necessarily, as in any story, each character reveals himself to the audience through his own words and actions as well as through what he says about another character. The two main characters in the plot are generally termed the protagonist (with whom the audience sympathizes) and the antagonist (who tries to block the protagonist from success). Thus in *Tartuffe* Elmire and Tartuffe are opposed and gradually defined as protagonist and antagonist through their successive encounters. Occasionally, an author can play on, or reverse, the feelings of his audience about his characters: Chekhov never presents an antagonist to his three sisters, and they may seem to grow steadily less sympathetic as the play goes on. Henry IV, like many other tragic heroes, is his own antagonist; society is against him, but, essentially, he defeats himself.

In our quotation from *The Bacchae,* Dionysus and Pentheus illustrate the plot, or the conflict, of the play; Dionysus seems the protagonist, Pentheus his adversary, in the given situation of power and a threat of imprisonment.

But as the same characters meet in succeeding episodes, the definition of their conflict becomes deeper and more complex, playing on the paired and contrasted meanings of "mad" and "sane," "reality" and "illusion," "wisdom" and "ignorance"; correspondingly, the simple identification of characters as sympathetic or unsympathetic becomes increasingly doubtful.

This inevitable doubt is built into a good play through its character development. Each character enters the play with a defined goal; he seeks something. But as he mets and reacts to other characters, his purpose will be constantly explored, clarified, and reshaped, both by himself and by the others surrounding him. It takes Elmire, Damis, and the rest of the conspirators against Tartuffe almost three acts to form a workable plan for his downfall; Hilde and Solness may be adversaries at the end of *The Master Builder*, but in two out of the three acts she gives strength and purpose to his fading life.

Emerging around these opposing characters and defined through their conflict is the society the author specifies for his play. The list of *dramatis personae* is polarized as supplementary characters (second leads) attach themselves to one of the two main characters as helpers. Finally, a middle group of characters remains: those courtiers, soldiers, neighbors, who are largely indifferent to the goals disputed by the main characters. Rather, they view both extremes presented as unworkable and therefore undesirable. Their inertia actually operates against both sides, for they will be most interested in the *status quo*.

As the plot progresses with the help and clarification of all these characters, the pattern of development and definition mentioned above takes place over and over again, in episode after episode of the play. Francis Fergusson, in his book *The Idea of a Theatre*, sees this pattern as involving the three steps of purpose, passion, and perception. A character enters each new situation or confrontation with a defined purpose or goal in mind, and then undergoes some suffering, doubt, or confusion that alters his aim into a new perception. Dialogues join together to form movements or episodes, in which the character learns something that changes him (as, for example, when Dionysus learns that he must attack Pentheus and therefore must be more ruthless). Eventually these episodes force the audience as well as the characters to a final, sometimes painful, perception.

We have been speaking of plot as containing, or being built upon, a seeking after some goal by the protagonist that is frustrated by circumstances and by other characters. This conflict is usually viewed in terms of a ritual: both classic genres of drama, tragedy and comedy, as well as the subsidiary forms of romance and satire, are said to depict a quest, the main characters' desire of something: an unattainable new world or lover, a necessary revenge or justice. Although the goals and pathways of their protagonists differ, both tragedy and comedy demand fulfillment of the hero's quest and frustration of his adversary's.

Essentially, the tragic protagonist seeks the ideal in a world that is all too real. He wants ideal justice, perfect love, or complete peace; he thinks in absolutes and becomes obsessed by them. Because his society is pragmatic and therefore more interested in the useful than the imaginable, the tragic hero is never able to succeed in his quest without making some great sacrifice, often even his life. In a true tragedy, this sacrifice will shock the play's society into motion, resulting in the protagonist's fulfillment: his father will be avenged, his name cleared, or the antagonist finally recognized as "evil" by the society. As the tragic form shades toward irony or satire, however, the protagonist's passion makes less and less impression on his society and therefore on his antagonist. He struggles to force society into change; but in his conflict, his alternatives become ever more limited until he is left with no choice but his own destruction. Tragedy always leaves the audience a final question: Was the goal worth the sacrifice? And if so, why?

Comedy, satire, and sometimes romance are presently the more popular forms of drama, and indeed of fiction in general. Perhaps because we belong to such a society-conscious age, we prefer the social ambience of comedy to the individual searchings of tragedy. The comic protagonist almost always has as his antagonist an active representative of society; he is confronted by a blocking character who is a part of the inert mass the protagonist tries to move. In order to reach his goal, the comic protagonist must somehow force the removal of his antagonist; most often, he manages to demonstrate to society that his aims are practical and should be implemented, whereas his adversary's aims will actually be harmful to the state. *Tartuffe* is a classic example of this progression: Elmire convinces Orgon that Tartuffe is evil; Tartuffe's subsequent actions against Orgon convince society (the King) that he is harmful and must be stopped. And he is.

Confronted with such an antagonist, the protagonist has three choices: he can form a new society of his own that permits the fulfillment of his goals; he can persuade society to expel the blocking character(s); or he can convert his antagonist to the acceptance of his goals. In any of these cases, the play ends "happily"; the protagonist does not have to make any of the important sacrifices, since he is a practical man in a practical society that will be converted by at least some forms of reason. When he demonstrates that his aims are useful while his adversary simply impedes the operation of society, he has won.

Romance concentrates on the winning more than on any comic aspect; the hero will always slay the barbarian, giant, or dragon, and win his distant fair maiden, challenge and exorcise the uninvited ghost, journey to and colonize exotic territories in or beyond this world. Indeed, no one in the story, though he may be seriously concerned about the hero's well-being, is ever doubtful about his ultimate victory. Satire, by contrast, concentrates on the faults of society that the protagonist seeks to correct or the flaws in the blocking characters that he wants to remove. If the protagonist eventually succeeds, the play is a satiric comedy, like *Tartuffe*. But if he makes no impression and cannot accomplish his goals even through his own death, then he is an ironic or satiric protagonist. Henry IV may be thought either tragic or ironic, since he does not manage to move or impress society. But his final imprisonment, his inevitable choice of madness with its connotations of self-destruction, make him, in the end, more tragic than ironic.

But whether the character is tragic, comic, satiric, or a figure of romance, whether nothing seems to happen or event seems to pile onto event, whether the spectacle is viewed from wooden benches banked into a hillside, armchairs within a palace, abandoned depots or barns, churches or living rooms—sumptuously set and lit or dismantled of all but dialogue and movement—drama's progression is from purpose to passion to perception. In all the various forms of drama there can be no substitute for intensity. Words, data, and their rhythms, mood, spectacle, and movement must subserve, work toward, and accomplish that end. Pirandello once boasted that in his plays he had succeeded in "convert[ing] intellect into passion." Such a conversion is actually the goal of any playwright, ancient or modern. A play, it has been observed, is like a "magnifying glass that focuses the full heat of the sun on the head of a pin."

EURIPIDES

The Bacchae

Translated by Philip Vellacott

Characters

DIONYSUS

CHORUS *of Oriental women, devotees of Dionysus*

TEIRESIAS, *a blind Seer*

CADMUS, *founder of Thebes, and formerly king*

PENTHEUS, *his grandson, now king of Thebes*

A GUARD *attending Pentheus*

A HERDSMAN

A MESSENGER

AGAUË, *daughter of Cadmus and mother of Pentheus*

Scene: *Before the palace of Pentheus in Thebes. At one side of the stage is the monument of Semele; above it burns a low flame, and around it are the remains of ruined and blackened masonry.*

DIONYSUS *enters on stage right. He has a crown of ivy, a* thyrsus[1] *in his hand, and a fawnskin draped over his body. He has long flowing hair and a youthful, almost feminine beauty.*

DIONYSUS: I am Dionysus, son of Zeus. My mother was Semele,[2] daughter of Cadmus;

I was delivered from her womb by the fire of a lightning-flash. To-day I have laid aside the appearance of a god, and have come disguised as a mortal man to this city of Thebes, where flow the two rivers, Dirce and Ismenus. Here by the palace I see the monument recording my mother's death by lightning; here are the smouldering ruins of her house, which bear the still living flame of Zeus's fire—the undying token of Hera's cruelty to my mother. Cadmus does well to keep this ground untrodden, a precinct consecrated to his daughter; and I now have decked it round with sprays of young vine-leaves.

From the fields of Lydia and Phrygia, fertile in gold, I came to the sun-beaten Persian plains, the walled towns of Bactria, harsh Media, wealthy Arabia, and the whole of that Asian sea-board where Greeks and Orientals live side by side in crowded magnificent cities; and before reaching this, the first city

---

[1] *Thyrsus:* a light stick of reed or fennel, with fresh strands of ivy twined round it. It was carried by every devotee of Dionysus; and the action of the play illustrates the supernatural power that was held to reside in it. [Tr.]

[2] *Semele:* She desired to see Zeus as he appeared to other gods and was consequently destroyed by his lightning.

of Hellas I have seen, I had already, in all those regions of the East, danced my dance and established my ritual, to make my godhead manifest to mortal men.

And the reason why Thebes is the first place in Hellas where, at my command, women have raised the Bacchic shout, put on the fawnskin cloak, and taken my weapon in their hands, the thyrsus wreathed with ivy—the reason is this: my mother's sisters said—what they should have been the last to say—that I, Dionysus, was not the progeny of Zeus; but that Semele, being with child by some mortal, at her father's suggestion ascribed to Zeus the loss of her virginity; and they loudly insisted that this lie about the fatherhood of her child was the sin for which Zeus had struck her dead.

Therefore I have plagued these same sisters with madness, and driven them all frantic out of doors; now their home is the mountains, and their wits are gone. And I made them carry the emblems of my mysteries; and the whole female population of Thebes, every woman there was in the town, I drove raving from their homes; now they have joined the daughters of Cadmus, and there they are, sitting roofless on the rocks under the silver fir-trees. Thebes must learn, unwilling though she is, that my Bacchic revels are something beyond her present knowledge and understanding; and I must vindicate the honour of my mother Semele, by manifesting myself before the human race as the god whom she bore to Zeus.

Now Cadmus has handed over his kingly honours and his throne to his daughter's son Pentheus. And this Pentheus is a fighter against God—he defies me, excludes me from libations, never names me in prayer. Therefore I will demonstrate to him, and to all Thebes, that I am a god.

When I have set all in order here, I will pass on to some other place, and manifest myself. Meanwhile, if the Theban city in anger tries to bring the Bacchae home from the mountains by force, I will join that army of women possessed and lead them to battle. And this is why I have changed my divine form to human, and appear in the likeness of a man.

Come, my holy band of revellers, women I have brought from lands of the East, from the slopes of Tmolus, bastion of Lydia, to be with me and share my travels! Raise the music of your Phrygian home, the timbrels invented by Rhea the Great Mother and by me; surround the palace of Pentheus and strike up such a peal of sound as shall make Thebes turn to look! I will go to the glens of Cithaeron where my Bacchae are, and join their dances.

DIONYSUS *goes out towards the mountain; the* CHORUS *enter where* DIONYSUS *entered, from the road by which they have travelled.*

CHORUS:

From far-off lands of Asia,   [*Strophe 1*
From Tmolus the holy mountain,
We run with the god of laughter;
Labour is joy and weariness is sweet,
And our song resounds to Bacchus!

Beware of the interloper!   [*Antistrophe 1*
Indoors or out, who listens?
Let every lip be holy;
Stand well aloof, be silent, while we sing
The appointed hymn to Bacchus!

Blest is the happy man   [*Strophe 2*
Who knows the mysteries the gods ordain,
And sanctifies his life,
Joins soul with soul in mystic unity,
And, by due ritual made pure,
Enters the ecstasy of mountain solitudes;
Who observes the mystic rites
Made lawful by Cybele the Great Mother;
Who crowns his head with ivy,
And shakes aloft his wand in worship
   of Dionysus.

On, on! Run, dance, delirious, possessed!

Dionysus comes to his own;
Bring from the Phrygian hills to the broad
    streets of Hellas
The god, child of a god,
Spirit of revel and rapture, Dionysus!

Once, on the womb that held
    him   [*Antistrophe 2*
The fire-bolt flew from the hand of Zeus;
And pains of child-birth bound his mother
    fast,
And she cast him forth untimely,
And under the lightning's lash relinquished
    life;
And Zeus the son of Cronos
Ensconced him instantly in a secret womb
Chambered within his thigh,
And with golden pins closed him from
    Hera's sight.

So, when the Fates had made him ripe for
    birth,
Zeus bore the bull-horned god
And wreathed his head with wreaths of
    writhing snakes;
Which is why the Maenads catch
Wild snakes, nurse them and twine them
    round their hair.

O Thebes, old nurse that cradled
        Semele,   [*Strophe 3*
Be ivy-garlanded, burst into flower
With wreaths of lush bright-berried bryony,
Bring sprays of fir, green branches torn
    from oaks,
Fill soul and flesh with Bacchus' mystic
    power;
Fringe and bedeck your dappled fawnskin
    cloaks
With woolly tufts and locks of purest white.
There's a brute wildness in the
    fennel-wands—
Reverence it well. Soon the whole land will
    dance
    When the god with ecstatic shout
    Leads his companies out
    To the mountain's mounting height

Swarming with riotous bands
Of Theban women leaving
Their spinning and their weaving
Stung with the maddening trance
    Of Dionysus!

O secret chamber the Curetes[3]
    knew!   [*Antistrophe 3*
O holy cavern in the Cretan glade
Where Zeus was cradled, where for our
    delight
The triple-crested Corybantes[4] drew
Tight the round drum-skin, till its wild beat
    made
Rapturous rhythm to the breathing
    sweetness
Of Phrygian flutes! Then divine Rhea found
The drum could give her Bacchic airs
    completeness;
    From her, the Mother of all,
    The crazy Satyrs soon,
    In their dancing festival
    When the second year comes round,
    Seized on the timbrel's tune
    To play the leading part
    In feasts that delight the heart
        Of Dionysus.

O what delight is in the mountains!   [*Epode*
There the celebrant,[5] wrapped in his sacred
    fawnskin,
Flings himself on the ground surrendered,
While the swift-footed company streams on;
There he hunts for blood, and rapturously
Eats the raw flesh of the slaughtered goat,
Hurrying on to the Phrygian or Lydian

---

[3] *Curetes:* mythical people of Crete to whom the infant
Zeus was entrusted by his mother, Rhea.

[4] *Corybantes:* priests of Cybele whose worship was celebrated with orgiastic dances and music.

[5] *The celebrant:* Dionysus and the Chorus comprise the
typical group of Bacchic worshippers, a male leader
with a devoted band of women and girls. The leader
flings himself on the ground in the climax of ecstacy,
when the power of the god enters into him and he becomes possessed. [Tr.]

mountain heights.
Possessed, ecstatic, he leads their happy
    cries;
The earth flows with milk, flows with wine,
Flows with nectar of bees;
The air is thick with a scent of Syrian myrrh.
The celebrant runs entranced, whirling the
    torch
That blazes red from the fennel-wand in his
    grasp,
And with shouts he rouses the scattered
    bands,
Sets their feet dancing,
As he shakes his delicate locks to the wild
    wind.
And amidst the frenzy of song he shouts
    like thunder:
'On, on! Run, dance, delirious, possessed!
You, the beauty and grace of golden Tmolus,
Sing to the rattle of thunderous drums,
Sing for joy,
Praise Dionysus, god of joy!
Shout like Phrygians, sing out the tunes you
    know,
While the sacred pure-toned flute
Vibrates the air with holy merriment,
In time with the pulse of the feet that flock
To the mountains, to the mountains!'
And, like a foal with its mother at pasture,
Runs and leaps for joy every daughter of
    Bacchus.

Enter TEIRESIAS. *Though blind, he makes his
way unaided to the door, and knocks.*

TEIRESIAS: Who keeps the gate? (*A servant is
heard answering from inside.*) Call out Cadmus, the son of Agenor, who came from
Sidonia to build these walls of Thebes. Go,
someone, tell him Teiresias is looking for
him. He knows why I have come—the agreement I made with him—old as I am, and he
older still—to get myself a Bacchic wand,
put on the fawnskin cloak, and wear a garland of young ivy-shoots.

Enter CADMUS.

CADMUS: O my dear friend, I knew your voice,
although I was indoors, as soon as I heard
it —the wise voice of a wise man. Look, I am
ready, I have everything the god prescribes.
Dionysus is my own daughter's son; and
now he has shown himself to the world as a
god, it is right that I should do all I can to
exalt him. Where should we go to dance,
and take our stand with the rest, tossing our
old grey beards? You must guide me in this,
Teiresias—you're nearly as old as I am, and
you understand such matters. No, it won't
be too much for me; I can beat time with
my thyrsus night and day! It's a happy thing
to forget one's age.

TEIRESIAS: Then you feel just as I do. I am
young too; I'll make an attempt at the dance.

CADMUS: You don't think we should make our
way to the mountains in a carriage?

TEIRESIAS: No, no, that would not show the
same respect for the god.

CADMUS: I'll be your guide then—two old men
together.

TEIRESIAS: The god will guide us there, and
without weariness.

CADMUS: Shall we be the only men in Thebes
who dance to Bacchus?

TEIRESIAS: We are the only men right-minded;
the rest are perverse.

CADMUS: We are wasting time. Now, take my
hand.

TEIRESIAS: There; hold firmly, with a good grip.

CADMUS: Mortals must not make light of the
gods—I would never do so.

TEIRESIAS: We entertain no theories or speculations in divine matters. The beliefs we have
received from our ancestors—beliefs as old
as time—cannot be destroyed by any argument, nor by any ingenuity the mind can
invent. No doubt I shall be criticized for
wearing an ivy-wreath and setting off for the
dance; they will say I have no sense of what
befits my age. They will be wrong: the god
has drawn no distinction between young and
old, which should dance and which should
not. He wishes to receive honour alike from
all; he will not have his worship made a mat-

ter of nice calculation.

CADMUS: Teiresias, since you are blind I must be your prophet. I see Pentheus the son of Echion, to whom I have resigned my rule in Thebes, hurrying towards the palace. He looks thoroughly upset! What is he going to tell us?

Enter PENTHEUS. *He addresses the audience, without at first noticing* CADMUS *and* TEIRESIAS, *who stand at the opposite side of the stage.*

PENTHEUS: I've been away from Thebes, as it happens; but I've heard the news—this extraordinary scandal in the city. Our women, I discover, have abandoned their homes on some pretence of Bacchic worship, and go gadding about in the woods on the mountain side, dancing in honour of this upstart god Dionysus, whoever he may be. They tell me, in the midst of each group of revellers stands a bowl full of wine; and the women go creeping off this way and that to lonely places and there give themselves to lecherous men, under the excuse that they are Maenad priestesses; though in their ritual Aphrodite comes before Bacchus.

Well, those that I've caught, my guards are keeping safe; we've tied their hands, and lodged them at State expense. Those still at large on the mountain I am going to hunt out; and that includes my own mother Agaüe, and her sisters Ino and Autonoe. Once I have them secure in iron chains I shall soon put a stop to this outrageous Bacchism.

I understand too that some Oriental magician or conjurer has arrived from Lydia, a fellow with golden hair flowing in scented ringlets, the flush of wine in his face and the charm of Aphrodite in his eyes; and that he entices our young girls with his Bacchic mysteries, and spends day and night in their company. Only let me get that fellow inside my walls—I'll cut his head from his shoulders; that will finish his thyrsus-waving and hair-tossing. *He* is the one—this foreigner—

who has spread stories about Dionysus, that he is a god, that he was sewn up in Zeus's thigh. The truth about Dionysus is that he's dead, burnt to a cinder by lightning along with his mother, because she lied about Zeus —said that Zeus had lain with her. But whoever this man may be, does not his insufferable behaviour merit the worst of punishments, hanging?

He turns to go, and sees CADMUS *and* TEIRESIAS.

Why, look! Another miracle! Here's the prophet Teiresias, and my mother's father, playing the Bacchant, in dappled fawnskin and carrying fennel-wands! Well, there's a sight for laughter! (*But he is raging, not laughing.*) Sir, I am ashamed to see two men of your age with so little sense of decency. Come, you are my grandfather: throw away your garland, get rid of that thyrsus. *You* persuaded him into this, Teiresias. No doubt you hope that, when you have introduced this new god to the people, you will be his appointed seer, you will collect the fees for sacrifices. Your grey hairs are your protection; otherwise you should sit with all these crazy females in prison, for encouraging such pernicious performances.

As for women, my opinion is this: when the sparkle of sweet wine appears at their feasts, no good can be expected from their ceremonies.

CHORUS: What profanity! Sir, do you not revere the gods, or Cadmus, who sowed the seed of the earth-born men? Echion your father was one of them—will you shame your own blood?

TEIRESIAS: When a clever man has a plausible theme to argue, to be eloquent is no great feat. But though you seem, by your glib tongue, to be intelligent, yet your words are foolish. Power and eloquence in a headstrong man can only lead to folly; and such a man is a danger to the state.

This new divinity whom you ridicule—no words of mine could adequately express the ascendancy he is destined to achieve through the length and breadth of Hellas. There are two powers, young man, which are supreme in human affairs: first, the goddess Demeter; she is the Earth—call her by what name you will; and she supplies mankind with solid food. Second, Dionysus, the son of Semele; the blessing he provides is the counterpart to the blessing of bread; he discovered and bestowed on men the service of drink, the juice that streams from the vine-clusters; men have but to take their fill of wine, and the sufferings of an unhappy race are banished, each day's troubles are forgotten in sleep—indeed this is our only cure for the weariness of life. Dionysus, himself a god, is poured out in offering to the gods; so that through him mankind receives blessing.

Now for the legend that he was sewn up in Zeus's thigh—do you mock at it? Then I will explain to you the truth that lies in the legend. When Zeus snatched the infant Dionysus away from the fire of the lightning, and brought him to Olympus as a god, Hera wanted to cast him out of heaven; so, to prevent her, Zeus—as you would expect—devised a plan. He broke off a piece of the sky that envelops the earth, made it into the likeness of a child, and gave it to Hera as a pledge, to soothe her jealousy. He entrusted the true Dionysus to others to bring up. Now the ancient word for a *pledge*[6] is very similar to our word 'thigh'; and so in time the word was mistaken, and men said Dionysus was saved by Zeus's *thigh*, instead of by Zeus's *pledge*, because a pledge was given to Hera in his likeness.

And this god is a prophet; for the Bacchic ecstasy and frenzy contain a strong element of prophecy. When Dionysus enters in power into a human body, he endows the possessed person with power to foretell the future. He also in some degree shares the function of Ares, god of war. It has happened that an army, equipped and stationed for battle, has fled in panic before a spear has been raised. This too is a madness sent by Dionysus.

Ay, and the day will come when you shall see him on the very rocks of Delphi, amidst flaring torches bounding over the twin-peaked ridge, hurling and brandishing his Bacchic staff, honoured by all Hellas.

Come, Pentheus, listen to me. You rely on force; but it is not force that governs human affairs. If you think otherwise—beware of mistaking your perverse opinion for wisdom. Welcome Dionysus to Thebes; pour libations to him, garland your head and celebrate his rites. Dionysus will not compel women to control their lusts. Self-control in all things depends on our own natures. This is a fact you should consider; for a chaste-minded woman will come to no harm in the rites of Bacchus. And think of this too: when crowds stand at the city gates, and the people glorify the name of Pentheus, you are filled with pleasure; so, I think, Dionysus is glad to receive honour.

So then I, and Cadmus, whom you mock, will wear the ivy-wreath and join in the dancing—we are both old men, but this is our duty; and no words of yours shall persuade me to fight against the gods. For your mind is most pitifully diseased; and there is no medicine that can heal you. Yet . . . there is one remedy[7] for your madness.

CHORUS: What you have said, Teiresias, means no dishonour to Phoebus, whose prophet you are; and shows your wisdom in honouring Dionysus as a great god.

CADMUS: My son, Teiresias has advised you well. Do not venture outside the customary pieties; stay with us. Just now your wits are scattered; you think you are talking sense, but it is not sense at all. And even if you are right, and this god is not a god, at least let

---

[6] *The ancient word for a* pledge: the translation necessarily expands the original. *Homeros* means 'pledge', and *meros* 'thigh'. [Tr.]

[7] *There is one remedy:* the prophet hints at Pentheus' approaching death. [Tr.]

him have your word of acknowledgment; lie for a good purpose, so that Semele may be honoured as mother of a god, and I and our whole family may gain in dignity. Remember Actaeon—his tragic end; he boasted, out in these valleys, that he was a better hunter than Artemis, and was torn to pieces and devoured by the very hounds he had bred. Don't invite the same fate! Come, let me put this ivy-wreath on your head. Join us in worshipping Dionysus.

PENTHEUS: Keep your hands off! Go to your Bacchic rites; and don't wipe off your crazy folly on me! But I will punish this man who has taught you your lunacy. Go, one of you, immediately to the place of augury where Teiresias practises, smash it with crowbars, knock down the walls, turn everything upside down, fling out his holy fripperies to the winds. That will sting him more than anything else. The rest of you, comb the city and find this effeminate foreigner, who plagues our women with this strange disease and turns them into whores. If you catch him, bring him here in chains, and I'll have him stoned to death. He shall be sorry he ever came revelling in Thebes.

Exit PENTHEUS.

TEIRESIAS: Foolhardy man, you don't know what you are saying. You were out of your mind before; now you are raving mad.

Come, Cadmus; let us go and pray both for this man, brutish as he is, and for Thebes, and entreat Dionysus to be forbearing. Come, take your thyrsus and follow. Try to support me—there, we will help each other. It would be a pity for us both to fall; but never mind that. We must pay our service to Dionysus the son of Zeus. Cadmus: the name *Pentheus* means *grief.* Let us hope he is not going to bring grief on your house. I am not speaking by inspiration; I judge by his conduct. The things he has said reveal the depth of his folly.

Exeunt TIERESIAS *and* CADMUS.

CHORUS:
Holiness, Queen of heaven,   [*Strophe 1*
Holiness, golden-winged ranging the earth,
Do you hear his blasphemy?
Pentheus dares—do you hear?—to revile
   the god of joy,
The son of Semele, who when the
   gay-crowned feast is set
Is named among gods the chief;
Whose gifts are joy and union of soul
   in dancing,
Joy in music of flutes,
Joy when sparkling wine at feasts of the
   gods
Soothes the sore regret,
Banishes every grief,
When the reveller rests, enfolded deep
In the cool shade of ivy-shoots,
On wine's soft pillow of sleep.

The brash, unbridled
   tongue,   [*Antistrophe 1*
The lawless folly of fools, will end in pain.
But the life of wise content
Is blest with quietness, escapes the storm
And keeps its house secure.
Though blessed gods dwell in the distant
   skies,
They watch the ways of men.
To know much is not to be wise.
Pride more than mortal hastens life to
   its end;
And they who in pride pretend
Beyond man's limit, will lose what lay
Close to their hand and sure.
I count it madness, and know no cure
   can mend
The evil man and his evil way.

O to set foot on Aphrodite's
   island,   [*Strophe 2*
On Cyprus, haunted by the Loves, who
   enchant
Brief life with sweetness; or in that strange
   land

Whose fertile river carves a hundred
   channels
To enrich her rainless sand;
Or where the sacred pastures of Olympus
   slant
Down to Pieria, where the Muses dwell—
Take me, O Bromius, take me and inspire
Laughter and worship! There our holy spell
And ecstasy are welcome; there the gentle
   band
Of Graces have their home, and sweet Desire.

Dionysus, son of Zeus, delights in
   banquets;   [*Antistrophe 2*
And his dear love is Peace, giver of wealth,
Saviour of young men's lives—a goddess
   rare!
In wine, his gift that charms all griefs away,
Alike both rich and poor may have their
   part.
His enemy is the man who has no care
To pass his years in happiness and health,
His days in quiet and his nights in joy,
Watchful to keep aloof both mind and heart
From men whose pride claims more than
   mortals may.
The life that wins the poor man's common
   voice,
His creed, his practice—this shall be my
   choice.

Some of the guards whom PENTHEUS *sent to
arrest* DIONYSUS *now enter with their prisoner.*
PENTHEUS *enters from the palace.*

GUARD: Well, sir, we went after this lion you
told us to hunt, and we have been successful.
But—we found the lion was tame! He made
no attempt to escape, but freely held out his
hands to be bound. He didn't even turn pale,
but kept the fresh colour you see in his face
now, smiling, and telling us to tie him up
and run him in; waited for me, in fact—
gave us no trouble at all. Naturally I felt a
bit awkward. 'You'll excuse me, sir,' I said,
'I don't want to arrest you, but it's the king's
orders.'

And there's another thing, sir. Those
women you rounded up and put in fetters
and in prison, those religious maniacs—
why, they're all gone, let loose to the glens;
and there they are, dancing and calling on
Bacchus. The fetters simply fell from their
limbs, the bolts flew back without the touch
of any mortal hand, and let the doors open.
Master, this man has come to our city of
Thebes with a load of miracles. What is
going to happen next is your concern, not
mine.

PENTHEUS: Untie his hands.[8] (*The guard does
so.*) He is in the trap, and he's not nimble
enough to escape me now.

Well, my man: you have a not unhand-
some figure—for attracting women, which
is your object in coming to Thebes. Those
long curls of yours show that you're no
wrestler—cascading close over your cheeks,
most seductively. Your complexion, too,
shows a carefully-preserved whiteness; you
keep out of the sun and walk in the shade,
to use your lovely face for courting Aphrodite. . . .

Ah, well; tell me first what country you
were born in.

DIONYSUS: That is easily told without boasting.
Doubtless you have heard of the flowery
mountain, Tmolus.

PENTHEUS: Yes, the range that curves round
the city of Sardis.

DIONYSUS: That was my home; I am a Lydian.

PENTHEUS: And why do you bring these rituals
to Hellas?

DIONYSUS: Dionysus the son of Zeus instructed
me.

PENTHEUS: Is there a Lydian Zeus, then, who
begets new gods?

DIONYSUS: No; I speak of your Zeus, who made
Semele his bride here in Thebes.

PENTHEUS: And when Dionysus took possession of you, did he appear in a dream by

---

[8] *Untie his hands:* the text is uncertain. A very slight
alteration gives a completely different meaning: 'You
are more mad than he is'–addressed to the guard and
his fellows. [Tr.]

night, or visible before your eyes?

DIONYSUS: I saw him face to face; and he entrusted to me these mysteries.

PENTHEUS: What form do these mysteries of yours take?

DIONYSUS: That cannot be told to the uninitiated.

PENTHEUS: What do the worshippers gain from it?

DIONYSUS: That is not lawful for you to hear—yet it is worth hearing.

PENTHEUS: A clever answer, baited to rouse my curiosity.

DIONYSUS: Curiosity will be useless; the rites of the god abhor an impious man.

PENTHEUS: If you say you saw Dionysus clearly—what was his appearance?

DIONYSUS: It was what he wished it to be. I had no say in that.

PENTHEUS: Another clever evasion, telling nothing.

DIONYSUS: *A wise speech sleeps in a foolish ear.*

PENTHEUS: Is this the first place where you have introduced Dionysus?

DIONYSUS: No; every Eastern land dances these mysteries.

PENTHEUS: I believe it. Oriental standards are altogether inferior to ours.

DIONYSUS: In this point they are superior. But their customs are different.

PENTHEUS: Do you celebrate your mysteries by night or by day?

DIONYSUS: Chiefly by night. Darkness induces religious awe.

PENTHEUS: For women darkness is treacherous and impure.

DIONYSUS: Impurity can be practised by daylight too.

PENTHEUS: It is time you were punished for your foul, slippery tongue.

DIONYSUS: And you for your crass impieties.

PENTHEUS: How bold his Bacchic inspiration makes him! He knows how to argue too.

DIONYSUS: Tell me my sentence. What punishment are you going to inflict?

PENTHEUS: First I'll cut off your scented silky hair.

DIONYSUS: My hair I keep for the god; it is sacred to him.

PENTHEUS: Next, hand over that thyrsus.

DIONYSUS: Take it from me yourself. I carry it for Dionysus, whose it is.

PENTHEUS: And I shall keep you safe in prison.

DIONYSUS: The god himself will set me free whenever I wish.

PENTHEUS: Set you free? When you stand among those frenzied women and pray to him—no doubt!

DIONYSUS: He is here, close by me, and sees what is being done to me.

PENTHEUS: Oh, indeed? Where? To my eyes he is quite invisible.

DIONYSUS: Here at my side. You, being a blasphemer, cannot see him.

PENTHEUS (*to the guards*): Get hold of him. He is laughing at me and the whole city.

DIONYSUS (*to the guards*): I warn you not to bind me.... (*To* PENTHEUS.) I am sane, you are mad.

PENTHEUS (*to* DIONYSUS): My orders overrule yours. (*To the guards.*) Bind him, I tell you.

DIONYSUS: You do not know what life you live, or what you do, or who you are.

PENTHEUS: Who I am? Pentheus, son of Echion and Agauë.

DIONYSUS: *Pentheus* means 'sorrow'. The name fits you well.

PENTHEUS: Take him away. Imprison him over there in the stables; he'll have all the darkness he wants—You can dance in there! As for these women you've brought to aid and abet you, I shall either send them to the slave market, or retain them in my own household to work at the looms; that will keep their hands from drumming on tambourines!

DIONYSUS: I will go. Nothing can happen to me that is not my destiny. But Dionysus, who you say is dead, will pursue you and take his revenge for this sacrilege. You are putting *him* in prison, when you lay hands on me.

Guards take DIONYSUS *away to the stables;* PENTHEUS *follows.*

CHORUS:

Dirce, sweet and holy maid,   [*Strophe*
Acheloüs' Theban daughter,
Once the child of Zeus was made
Welcome in your welling water,
When the lord of earth and sky
Snatched him from the undying flame,
Laid him safe within his thigh,
Calling loud the infant's name:
'Twice-born Dithyrambus! Come,
Enter here your father's womb;
Bacchic child, I now proclaim
This in Thebes shall be your name.'
Now, divine Dirce, when my head is
     crowned
And my feet dance in Bacchus' revelry—
Now you reject me from your holy
     ground.
Why should you fear me? By the purple
     fruit.
That glows in glory on Dionysus' tree,
His dread name yet shall haunt your
     memory!

O what anger lies beneath [*Antistrophe*
Pentheus' voice and sullen face—
Offspring of the dragon's teeth,
And Echion's earth-born race,
Brute with bloody jaws agape,
God-defying, gross and grim,
Slander of his human shape!
Soon he'll chain us limb to limb—
Bacchus' servants! Yes, and more:
Even now our comrade lies
Deep on his dark prison floor.
Dionysus! do your eyes
See us? O son of Zeus, the oppressor's rod
Falls on your worshippers; come, mighty
     god,
Brandish your golden thyrsus and
     descend
From great Olympus; touch this
     murderous man,
And bring his violence to a sudden end!

Where are you, Dionysus? Leading your
     dancing bands   [*Epode*

Over the mountain slopes, past many a
     wild beast's lair,
Or upon rocky crags, with the thyrsus in
     their hands?
Or in the wooded coverts, maybe, of
     Olympus, where
Orpheus once gathered the trees and
     mountain beasts,
Gathered them with his lyre, and sang an
     enchanting air.
Happy vale of Pieria! Bacchus delights in
     you;
He will cross the flood and foam of the
     Axius river, and there
He will bring his whirling Maenads, with
     dancing and with feasts,—
Cross the father of waters, Lydias, generous
     giver
Of wealth and luck, they say, to the land he
     wanders through,
Whose famous horses graze by the rich and
     lovely river.

*Suddenly a shout is heard from inside the
building—the voice of* DIONYSUS.

DIONYSUS:

Io, Io! Do you know my voice, do you
     hear?
Worshippers of Bacchus! Io, Io!
CHORUS: Who is that? Where is he? The voice
of Dionysus calling to us!
DIONYSUS: Io, Io! Hear me again: I am the son
of Semele, the son of Zeus!
CHORUS:

Io, Io, our lord, our lord!
Come, then, come to our company,
     lord of joy!
DIONYSUS: O dreadful earthquake, shake the
floor of the world!
CHORUS (*with a scream of terror*):
Pentheus' palace is falling, crumbling in
     pieces! (*They continue severally.*)
Dionysus stands in the palace; bow before
     him!
We bow before him. See how the roof and
     pillars

Plunge to the ground! God from the
    inner prison
Will shout the shout of victory.

*The flame on Semele's tomb grows and
brightens.*

DIONYSUS:
    Fan to a blaze the flame the lightning lit;
    Kindle the conflagration of Pentheus'
      palace!
CHORUS:
    Look, look, look!
    Do you see, do you see the flame of Semele's
      tomb,
    The flame that remained when she died of
      the lightning stroke?

A noise of crashing masonry is heard.

    Down, trembling Maenads! Hurl yourselves
      to the ground!
    Your god is wrecking the palace, roof to
      floor;
    He heard our cry—he is coming, the son of
      Zeus!

The doors open and DIONYSUS *appears.*

DIONYSUS: Women of Asia, why are you cower-
    ing terrified on the ground? You heard
    Bacchus himself shattering Pentheus' pal-
    ace; come, stand up! Stop this trembling!
    Courage!
CHORUS: Oh, what a joy to hear your Bacchic
    shout! You have saved us. We were de-
    serted and alone: how happy we are to see
    you!
DIONYSUS: Were you plunged in despair, when
    I was sent inside to be thrown into Pen-
    theus' dark dungeon?
CHORUS: How could we help it? Who was there
    to protect us, if you were taken? But tell us
    how you escaped from the clutches of this
    wicked man.
DIONYSUS: I alone with effortless ease deliv-
    ered myself.

CHORUS: But did he not bind your arms with
    knotted ropes?
DIONYSUS: Ha, ha! There I made a mockery
    of him. He thought he was binding me; but
    he fed himself on delusion—he neither took
    hold of me nor even touched me. Near the
    stall where he took me to shut me in, he
    found a bull; and he was tying his rope
    round the bull's knees and hooves, panting
    with rage, dripping sweat, and biting his
    lips; while I sat quietly by and watched
    him. And it was then that Bacchus came and
    shook the building and made the flame on
    his mother's tomb flare up. When Pentheus
    saw this, he imagined the place was on fire,
    and went rushing this way and that, calling
    to the servants to bring water, till the whole
    household was in commotion—all for noth-
    ing.

    Then he thought I had escaped. He left
    throwing water, snatched up his murderous
    sword and darted into the palace. There-
    upon Dionysus—or so it seemed to me; I
    tell what I thought—made a phantom figure
    appear in the palace courtyard; and Pen-
    theus flew at it, and kept stabbing at the
    sunny air, imagining he was killing *me*.

    But the god had further humiliation in
    store for him: he laid the stable-buildings in
    ruins on the ground—there they lie, a heap
    of rubble, to break his heart as he looks at
    my prison. Now he is helpless with exhaus-
    tion. He has dropped his sword. He, a mor-
    tal man, dared to take arms against a god. I
    walked quietly out of the palace, and here I
    am. Pentheus does not disturb me. But I
    hear his heavy tread indoors; I think he
    will be out here in a moment. What will he
    say after this? For all his rage, he shall not
    ruffle me. The wise man preserves a smooth-
    tempered self-control.

Enter PENTHEUS.

PENTHEUS: This is outrageous. That foreigner
    was locked up and in chains a little while
    ago; now he has escaped me. (*He sees*

DIONYSUS *and gives an excited shout*.) That's the man! What's going on? How did you get out? How dare you show yourself here before my very doors?

DIONYSUS: Stay where you are. You are angry. Now control yourself.

PENTHEUS: You were bound and locked in: how did you escape?

DIONYSUS: Did you not hear me say that I should be set free by—

PENTHEUS: By whom? Everything you say is strange.

DIONYSUS: By him who plants for mortals the rich-clustered vine.

PENTHEUS: The god who makes men fools and women mad.[9]

DIONYSUS: A splendid insult, that, to Dionysus!

PENTHEUS (*to attendant guards*): Close the gates all round—every gate in the city wall.

DIONYSUS: And why? Cannot gods pass even over walls?

PENTHEUS: Oh, you know everything—except the things you ought to know.

DIONYSUS: The things one ought to know most of all, those things I know.

But first listen to what this man has to tell you; he comes from the mountains with news.—I will stay here; I promise not to run away.

Enter a HERDSMAN.

HERDSMAN: Pentheus, ruler of Thebes! I come from Cithaeron, where the ground is never free from dazzling shafts of snow.

PENTHEUS: And what urgent news do you bring me?

HERDSMAN: I have seen the holy Bacchae, who in madness went streaming bare-limbed out of the city gates. I have come with the intention of telling you, my lord, and the city, of their strange and terrible doings—things past all wonder. But I would like to know first if I may speak freely of what is going on there, or if I should trim my words. I am afraid of your hastiness, my lord, your hot temper; you are too much like a king.

PENTHEUS: Say all that you have to say; fear nothing from me. The more terrible your story about the Bacchae, the more certainly will I execute justice upon this man, the instigator of their wickedness.

HERDSMAN: Just when the sun's rays first beamed out to warm the earth, I was pasturing my cattle and working up towards the high ground; when I saw three groups of women who had been dancing together. The leader of one group was Autonoe; your mother Agauë was at the head of the second, and Ino of the third. They were all sleeping, stretched out and quiet. Some rested on beds of pine-needles, some had pillows of oak-leaves; they lay just as they had thrown themselves down on the ground,—but with modesty in their posture; they were not drunk with wine, as you told us, or with music of flutes; nor was there any love-making there in the loveliness of the woods.

As soon as your mother Agauë heard the lowing of the horned cattle, she stood up among the Bacchae and called loudly to them to rouse themselves from sleep. And they threw off the strong sleep from their eyes and leapt to their feet. They were a sight to marvel at for modesty and comeliness—women old and young, and girls still unmarried. First they let down their hair over their shoulders; those whose fawnskins had come loose from their fastenings tied them up; and they girdled the dappled fur with snakes which licked their cheeks. And some would have in their arms a young gazelle, or wild wolf-cubs, and give them their own white milk—those who had infants at home recently born, so that their breasts were still full. And they wreathed their heads with garlands of ivy and oak and flowering bryony.

And one of them took her thyrsus and struck it on the rock; and from the rock

---

[9] *The god who makes* . . . : this is conjecturally supplied in place of a missing line. [Tr.]

there gushed a spring of limpid water; another struck her wand down into the earth, and there the god made a fountain of wine spring up; and any who wanted milk had only to scratch the earth with the tip of her fingers, and there was the white stream flowing for her to drink; and from the ivy-bound thyrsus a sweet ooze of honey dripped. Oh! if you had been there and seen all this, you would have entreated with prayers this god whom you now accuse.

Well, we herdsmen and shepherds gathered and stood talking together, and arguing about these strange and extraordinary doings. And one fellow, a gadder up to town, and a good speaker, addressed the rest of us. 'You who live on the holy mountain heights,' he said, 'how if we should hunt down the king's mother, Agauë, bring her away from these orgies, and do the king a service?' We thought it was a good suggestion; so we hid ourselves among the leafy bushes and waited our chance.

When the set time came, the women began brandishing their wands and preparing to dance, calling in unison on the son of Zeus, 'Iacchus! Bromius!' And the whole mountain, and the wild beasts too, became a part of their joyful dance—there was nothing that was not roused to leap and run.

Now Agauë as she ran happened to pass close to me; so I sprang out of the ambush where we lay hidden, meaning to capture her. But she cried out, 'Oh, my swift hounds, we are being hunted by these men. Come, then, and follow; arm yourselves with the thyrsus, and follow me!'

So we fled, and escaped being torn in pieces by these possessed women. But our cattle were feeding there on the fresh grass; and the Bacchae attacked them, with their bare hands. You could see Agauë take up a bellowing young heifer with full udders, and hold it by the legs with her two arms stretched wide. Others were tearing our cows limb from limb, and you could see perhaps some ribs or a cleft hoof being tossed high and low; and pieces of bloody flesh hung dripping on the pine-branches. And bulls, which one moment were savagely looking along their horns, the next were thrown bodily to the ground, dragged down by the soft hands of girls—thousands of them; and they stripped the flesh off their bodies faster than you could wink your royal eyes.

Then, like birds, skimming the ground as they ran, they scoured the plain which stretches by the river Asopus and produces a rich harvest for Thebes; and like an enemy army they bore down on the villages of Hysiae and Erythrae, which lie on the low slopes of Cithaeron, and ransacked them. They snatched up children out of the houses; all the plunder they laid on their shoulders stayed safely there without any fastening; nothing fell to the dark earth, not bronze or iron even; they carried fire on their heads, and their hair was not burnt.

The villagers, of course, were furious at being plundered by the Bacchae, and they resisted with weapons; and then, my lord, was an astonishing sight to behold. The spears cast by the villagers drew no blood; but the women, hurling the thyrsus like a spear, dealt wounds; those women turned the men to flight. There was the power of a god in that.

Then they went back to the place they had started from, to those fountains the god had made flow for them. And they washed off the blood, and the snakes licked the stains clean from their cheeks.

So, master, whoever this god may be, receive him in our city. He has great power in many ways; but especially, as I hear, it was he who gave men the gift of the vine as a cure for sorrow. And if there were no more wine, why, there's an end of love, and of every other pleasure in life.

CHORUS: I hesitate to speak freely before the king; yet I will say it: there is no greater god than Dionysus.

PENTHEUS: This outrageous Bacchism advances on us like a spreading fire, disgracing us before all Hellas. We must waste no time. (*To the* HERDSMAN.) Go at once to the Electran gate; tell all my men who bear shields, heavy or light, all who ride fast horses or twang the bowstring, to meet me there in readiness for an assault on the Bacchae. This is past all bearing, if we are to let women so defy us.

DIONYSUS: You refuse, Pentheus, to listen to what I say or to alter your behaviour. Yet, in spite of all I have suffered at your hands, I warn you to stay where you are and not to take arms against a god. Dionysus will not stand quietly by and see you drive his Bacchae from their mountain rites.

PENTHEUS: I want no instruction from you. You have escaped from your fetters—be content; or I will punish you again.

DIONYSUS: You are a mortal, he is a god. If I were you I would control my rage and sacrifice to him, rather than kick against the pricks.

PENTHEUS: Sacrifice! I will indeed—an offering of women's blood, slaughtered as they deserve in the glens of Cithaeron.

DIONYSUS: You will all be put to flight. It would be disgraceful for the wands of Bacchic women to rout your brazen shields.

PENTHEUS: This foreigner is an impossible man to deal with; in prison or out, he will not hold his tongue.

DIONYSUS: My friend! A happy settlement may still be found.

PENTHEUS: How? By making me a slave to my own slaves?

DIONYSUS: I will bring those women here, without use of weapons.

PENTHEUS: Heaven help us, you are plotting some trick.

DIONYSUS: A trick? If I use my power to save you?

PENTHEUS: This is something you have arranged with the women, so that the revelling may continue.

DIONYSUS: This is something, certainly, that I have arranged—not with them, but with the god.

PENTHEUS: That is enough from you.—Bring out my armour, there!

DIONYSUS (*with an authoritative shout*): Wait! (*Then, quietly.*) Would you like to *see* those women, sitting together, there in the mountains?

PENTHEUS: Yes, indeed; I would give a large sum of gold to see them.

From now on DIONYSUS *gradually establishes a complete ascendancy over* PENTHEUS.

DIONYSUS: And what has betrayed you into this great eagerness?

PENTHEUS: I am not eager to see them drunk; that would be a painful sight.

DIONYSUS: Yet you would be glad to see a sight that would pain you?

PENTHEUS: I would, yes; if I could sit quietly under the pine-trees and watch.

DIONYSUS: However secretly you go they will track you down.

PENTHEUS: You are quite right. I will go openly.

DIONYSUS: Shall I show you the way, then? You will venture on this?

PENTHEUS: Lead me there at once; I am impatient.

DIONYSUS: Then, first dress yourself in a fine linen gown.

PENTHEUS: Why a linen gown? Must I change my sex?

DIONYSUS: They will kill you if you are seen there dressed as a man.

PENTHEUS: You are quite right; you think of everything!

DIONYSUS: It was Dionysus who inspired me with that thought.

PENTHEUS: How can your suggestion best be carried out?

DIONYSUS: I will come indoors with you and dress you.

PENTHEUS: Dress me? Not in woman's clothes? I would be ashamed.

DIONYSUS: You have lost your enthusiasm for watching the Maenads.

PENTHEUS: What kind of dress do you say you will put on me?

DIONYSUS: I will cover your head with long, flowing hair.

PENTHEUS: And after that? What will my costume look like?

DIONYSUS: A robe falling to your feet; and a snood on your head.

PENTHEUS: Anything else?

DIONYSUS: A thyrsus in your hand, and a dappled fawnskin round you.

PENTHEUS: I could never wear woman's clothes.

DIONYSUS: If you join battle with the Bacchae there will be bloodshed.

PENTHEUS: You are right; I must first go to spy on them.

DIONYSUS: That is wiser than inviting violence by using it.

PENTHEUS: And how shall I get through the streets of Thebes without being seen?

DIONYSUS: We will go by lonely ways; I will guide you.

PENTHEUS: I must not be laughed at by the Bacchae—anything rather than that. Now I will go in, and decide how best to act.

DIONYSUS: You may. My own preparations are all made.

PENTHEUS: I will go, then; and I will either visit the mountains armed—or else I will follow your advice.

Exit PENTHEUS.

DIONYSUS: Women, this man is walking into the net. He will visit the Bacchae; and there he shall be punished with death.

Dionysus (for you are not far away), all is now in your hands. Let us be revenged on him! And—first assail him with fantastic madness and drive him out of his mind; for while he is sane he will never consent to put on a woman's clothes; but once he has broken from the rein of reason he will put them on. I long to set Thebes laughing at him, as I lead him dressed like a woman through the streets; to humble him from the arrogance with which he threatened me at first.

Now I will go, to array Pentheus in the dress which he will take down with him to the world of the dead, slaughtered by his own mother's hands. And he shall know the son of Zeus, Dionysus; who, though most gentle to mankind, can prove a god of terror irresistible.

DIONYSUS *follows* PENTHEUS *into the palace.*

CHORUS:

O for long nights of worship, gay [*Strophe*
With the pale gleam of dancing feet,
With head tossed high to the dewey air—
Pleasure mysterious and sweet!
O for the joy of a fawn at play
In the fragrant meadow's green delight,
Who has leapt out free from the woven
    snare,
Away from the terror of chase and flight,
And the huntsman's shout, and the
    straining pack,
And skims the sand by the river's brim
With the speed of wind in each aching
    limb,
To the blessed lonely forest where
The soil's unmarked by a human track,
And leaves hang thick and the shades are
    dim.

What prayer should we call wise?   [*Refrain*
What gift of Heaven should man
Count a more noble prize,
A prayer more prudent, than
To stretch a conquering arm
Over the fallen crest
Of those who wished us harm?
And what is noble every heart loves best.

Slow, yet unfailing, move the
    Powers   [*Antistrophe*
Of heaven with the moving hours.
When mind runs mad, dishonours God,

And worships self and senseless pride,
Then Law eternal wields the rod.
Still Heaven hunts down the impious man,
Though divine subtlety may hide
Time's creeping foot. No mortal ought
To challenge Time—to overbear
Custom in act, or age in thought.
All men, at little cost, may share
The blessing of a pious creed;
Truths more than mortal, which began
In the beginning, and belong
To very nature—these indeed
Reign in our world, are fixed and strong.

What prayer should we call wise? [*Refrain*
What gift of heaven should man
Count a more noble prize,
A prayer more prudent, than
To stretch a conquering arm
Over the fallen crest
Of those who wished us harm?
And what is noble every heart loves best.

Blest is the man who cheats the stormy
    sea   [*Epode*
And safely moors beside the sheltering
    quay;
So, blest is he who triumphs over trial.
One man, by various means, in wealth or
    strength
Outdoes his neighbour; hope in a thousand
    hearts
Colours a thousand different dreams;
    at length
Some find a dear fulfilment, some denial.
  But this I say,
  That he who best
  Enjoys each passing day
  Is truly blest.

Enter DIONYSUS. *He turns to call* PENTHEUS.

DIONYSUS: Come, perverse man, greedy for
sights you should not see, impatient for
deeds you should not do—Pentheus! Come
out of the palace and show yourself to me,
wearing the garb of a frenzied Bacchic
woman, ready to spy on your mother and
all her company!

Enter PENTHEUS *dressed as a Bacchic devotee. He is dazed, and entirely subservient to*
DIONYSUS.

Ah! You look exactly like one of Cadmus'
daughters.
PENTHEUS: Why—I seem to see two suns; I
see a double Thebes, and the city wall with
its seven gates—double! I see you leading
me forward—you are like a bull, you have
horns growing on your head. Tell me, were
you an animal a little while ago? You have
certainly become a bull.
DIONYSUS: The god did not favour us before;
now he is with us, and we have made our
peace with him. Now you see as you ought
to see.
PENTHEUS: Well, how do I look? Do you think
I stand like Ino or like my mother Agauë?
DIONYSUS: I think you are their very image.
Wait—this curl of hair is out of place, not as
I arranged it under your snood.
PENTHEUS: I must have shaken it loose in-
doors, tossing my head up and down like a
Bacchic reveller.
DIONYSUS: Come, it is for me to look after you;
I will set it straight. Now, lift your head.
PENTHEUS: There, *you* put it right. I depend
entirely on you.
DIONYSUS: And your girdle is loose; and the
folds of your gown are not hanging straight
to your ankles.
PENTHEUS: I agree, they are not—at least, here
by the right foot. But on the other side the
gown hangs well to the heel.
DIONYSUS: I think you will reckon me the
chief of your friends, when you see the
Bacchae and find to your surprise how well
they are behaving—will you not?

But PENTHEUS *is not listening.*

PENTHEUS: Ought I to hold my thyrsus in this
hand or in the right, to look more like a
Bacchanal?

DIONYSUS: Hold it in your right hand, and raise it at the same time as you raise your right foot. (PENTHEUS *attempts it.*) I am glad you are so—changed in mind.

PENTHEUS: Do you think I could lift up on my shoulders the glens of Cithaeron, with all the women revelling there?

DIONYSUS: You could, if you wished. Before, your mind was diseased; now, it is as it should be.

PENTHEUS: Shall we take crowbars? Or shall I simply set my shoulder, or my arm, against the mountain peaks, and tear them up with my hands?

DIONYSUS: No, you must not destroy the homes of the Nymphs, and the haunts where Pan sits piping.

PENTHEUS: You are right. Women are not to be subdued by brute force. I will hide among the pine-trees.

DIONYSUS: Hide? Yes! You shall find the right hiding-place to hide you—coming like a crafty spy to watch the Maenads!

PENTHEUS: Yes, I can picture them—like birds in the thickets, wrapped in the sweet snare of love.

DIONYSUS: That is the very thing you are going to look for; and perhaps you will catch them—if you are not first caught yourself.

PENTHEUS: Now lead me through the central streets of Thebes. There is no one dares to do this—I am the only *man* among them.

DIONYSUS: You alone suffer for the whole city —you alone; and the struggle that awaits you is your destined ordeal. Come; I will see you safely there; another shall bring you home.

PENTHEUS: You mean my mother?

DIONYSUS: A sight for all to see.

PENTHEUS: It is for that I am going.

DIONYSUS: You will be carried home—

PENTHEUS: What splendour that will be!

DIONYSUS: —in your mother's arms.

PENTHEUS: Why, you make a weakling of me!

DIONYSUS: That is—one way of putting it.

PENTHEUS: Yet it is what I deserve

Exit PENTHEUS.

DIONYSUS: Pentheus, you are a man to make men fear; and fearful will be your end—an end that shall raise your fame to the height of heaven. Stretch out your hands, Agaue, and you her sisters, daughters of Cadmus! I am bringing the young man to his battle; and I and Dionysus shall be victors. (*Then he adds quietly*) What more shall happen, the event will show.

Exit DIONYSUS.

CHORUS:
Hounds of Madness, fly to the mountain,
   fly   [*Strophe*
Where Cadmus' daughters are dancing in
   ecstasy!
Madden them like a frenzied herd
   stampeding,
Against the madman hiding in woman's
   clothes
To spy on the Maenad's rapture!
First his mother shall see him craning his
   neck
Down from a rounded rock or a withered
   trunk,
And shout to the Maenads, 'Who is the
   man, you Bacchae,
Who has come to the mountain, come to the
   mountain spying
On the swift wild mountain-dances of
   Cadmus' daughters?
Which of you is his mother?
No, that lad never lay in a woman's
   womb;
A lioness gave him suck, or a Libyan
   Gorgon!'

Justice, now be revealed! Now let your
   sword
Thrust—through and through—to sever
   the throat
Of the godless, lawless, shameless son of
   Echion,
Who sprang from the womb of Earth!

See! With contempt of right, with a
reckless rage   [*Antistrophe*
To combat your and your mother's
mysteries, Bacchus,
With maniac fury out he goes, stark mad,
For a trial of strength against *your*
invincible arm!
The sober and humble heart
That accords the gods their due without
carp or cavil,
And knows that his days are as dust,
shall live untouched.
I have no wish to grudge the wise their
wisdom;
But the joys *I* seek are greater, outshine
all others,
And lead our life to goodness and
loveliness:
The joy of the holy heart
That night and day is bent to honour the
gods
And disown all custom that breaks the
bounds of right.

Justice, now be revealed! Now let your
sword
Thrust—through and through—to sever the
throat
Of the godless, lawless, shameless son of
Echion,
Who sprang from the womb of Earth!

*Then with growing excitement, shouting in
unison, and dancing to the rhythm of their
words.*

Come, Dionysus!   [*Epode*
Come, and appear to us!
Come like a bull or a
Hundred-headed serpent,
Come like a lion snorting
Flame from your nostrils!
Swoop down, Bacchus, on the
Hunter of the Bacchae;
Smile at him and snare him;
Then let the stampeding
Herd of the Maenads

Throw him and throttle him,
Catch, trip, trample him to death!

Enter a MESSENGER.

MESSENGER: O house once glorious throughout Hellas, house of the old Sidonian king who sowed in this soil the dragon's earth-born crop! How I weep for you! I am a slave; but a good slave feels the blow that strikes his master.

CHORUS: What has happened? Have you news from the mountains?

MESSENGER: Pentheus, the son of Echion, is dead.

CHORUS: Dionysus, god of rapture! Your power is revealed!

MESSENGER: What? What did you say? Do you even exult at the cruel end that has overtaken my master?

CHORUS: I am no Greek; I sing for joy in a foreign tune. Now I've no need to cower in terror of prison.

MESSENGER: Do you suppose Thebes has no men left to take command?

CHORUS: Dionysus commands *me*; not Thebes, but Dionysus.

MESSENGER: Allowance must be made for you; yet, when irreparable wrong has been done, it is shameful to rejoice.

CHORUS: Tell me what happened; tell me, how did he die—this tyrant pursuing his tyranny?

MESSENGER: When we had left the houses of Thebes behind, and crossed the river Asopus, we began climbing the foothills of Cithaeron, Pentheus and I—I was attending my master—, and that foreigner who was showing us the way to what we were to see.

Well, first we sat down in a grassy glade; we kept our footsteps and our talk as quiet as possible, so as to see without being seen. We were in a valley full of streams, with cliffs on either side; and there, under the close shade of pine-trees, the Maenads were sitting, their hands busy at their happy tasks. Some of them were twining with fresh leaves a thyrsus that had lost its ivy; others, like foals let loose from the painted yokes, were singing holy songs[10] to each other in turn.

But the ill-fated Pentheus did not see these women; and he said, 'From where we are standing, my friend, I cannot clearly make out these pretended worshippers, these Maenads; if I climbed a towering pine-tree on the cliff-side I could have a proper view of their shameful behaviour.'

And then—I saw that foreigner do an amazing thing. He took hold of the topmost skiey branch of a pine and dragged it down, down, down to the dark earth. It was bent in a circle as a bow is bent, as the curve of of wheel,[11] drawn with peg and line, bends the running rim to its own shape; so the foreigner took that mountain-pine in his hands and bent it to the ground—a thing no mortal man could do. Then he set Pentheus on the top branches, and began letting the tree spring upright, slipping it steadily through his grip, and taking care not to unseat him; and the pine-trunk straightened itself and soared into the soaring sky with the king sitting astride; so that he was more plainly visible to the women than they were to him.

And he was just coming into view on his lofty perch,—the foreigner was nowhere to be seen—when a voice—I suppose it was Dionysus—pealed out from heaven: 'Women! I bring you the man who made a mockery of you, and of me, and of my holy rites. Now punish him.' And in the very moment the voice spoke, a flash of unearthly fire stretched between the sky and the ground.

The whole air fell silent. The wooded glade held every leaf silent. You could hear no cry of any beast. The women had not caught distinctly what the voice said; they stood up and gazed around. Then came a second word of command. As soon as Cadmus' daughters recognized the clear bidding of Bacchus, they darted forward with the speed of doves on the wing, and all the Bacchae after them. Up the valley, along by the stream, over the rocks they went leaping on, possessed with the very breath of the god. When they saw the king sitting in the tree, first they climbed the cliff where it rose up like a battlement, and with all their strength pelted him with pieces of rock, or aimed pine-branches at him like javelins. Some were hurling the thyrsus at their pitiable target; but the shots fell short—the height was too great for all their efforts; while the wretched man sat there trapped and helpless.

At last, with a force like lightning, they tore down branches of oak, and used these as levers, trying to tear out the tree's roots. All their struggles were useless. Then Agaüe spoke to them: 'Come, you Maenads, stand round the tree and grip it. We must catch this climbing beast, or he will reveal the secret dances of Dionysus.' A thousand hands grasped the tree; and they tore it from the earth. Then from his high perch plunging and crashing to the ground came Pentheus, with one incessant scream as he understood what end was near.

First his mother, as priestess, began the ritual of death, and fell upon him. He tore off the headband from his hair, that his wretched mother might recognize him and not kill him. 'Mother!' he cried, touching her cheek, 'it is I, your son, Pentheus, whom you bore to Echion. O mother, have

---

[10] *Were singing holy songs:* the Greek word is *Bacchic* songs. In English this adjective is too often associated with the 'profane' drinking of wine, whereas in this play it always has a religious or at least a ritualistic meaning. In translation I have been deliberately inconsistent, using both *Bacchic* and *holy* for the sake of keeping both ideas operative. [Tr.]

[11] *As the curve of a wheel* . . . : a difficult passage of which no satisfactory translation can be made. An emended text gives: 'As a bow by which an untrue wheel, chiselled on a lathe, is swiftly rotated.' This would refer to the use of a bent pole or tree as a source of power. [Tr.]

mercy on me; I have sinned, but I am your son: do not kill me!'

Agaüe was foaming at the mouth, her eyes were rolling wildly. She was not in her right mind; she was under the power of Dionysus; and she would not listen to him. She gripped his right arm between wrist and elbow; she set her foot against his ribs; and she tore his arm off by the shoulder. It was no strength of hers that did it; the god was in her fingers and made it easy. Ino was at him on the other side, tearing at his flesh; and now Autonoe joined them, and the whole pack of raving women. There was a single continuous yell—Pentheus shrieking as long as life was left in him, the women howling in triumph. One of them was carrying an arm, another had a foot with the shoe still on it; the ribs were stripped—clawed clean. Every hand was thick red with blood; and they were tossing and catching, to and fro, like a ball, the flesh of Pentheus.

His body lies scattered, some under hard rocks, some in the deep green woods; it will not be easy to find. His poor head—his mother is holding it; she has fixed it on the point of her thyrsus, and carries it openly over the mountain-side, leaving her sisters dancing with the Maenads. And she is coming here to the palace, exulting in her fearful and horrible prey, shouting to Bacchus as her fellow-hunter, calling him her partner in the kill, her comrade in victory. But Bacchus gives her tears for her reward.

I am going; I want to be far away from this horror before Agaüe comes.

The noblest thing a man can have is a humble and quiet heart that reveres the gods. I think that is also the wisest thing for a man to possess, if he will but use it.

Exit.

CHORUS:
Let us dance a dance to Bacchus, shout and
    sing

For the fall of Pentheus, heir of the
    dragon's seed,
Who hid his beard in a woman's gown,
And sealed his death with the holy sign
Of ivy wreathing a fennel-reed,
When bull led man to the ritual
    slaughter-ring.
Frenzied daughters of Cadmus, what
    renown
Your victory wins you—such a song
As groans must stifle, tears must drown!
Emblem of conquest, brave and fine!—
A mother's hand, defiled
With blood and dripping red
Caresses the torn head
Of her own murdered child!

But look! I see Pentheus' mother, Agaüe, running towards the palace, with eyes wildly rolling. Welcome the worshipping company of Dionysus!

AGAÜE *appears, frenzied and panting, with* PENTHEUS' *head held in her hand. The rest of her band of devotees, whom the* CHORUS *saw approaching with her, do not enter; but a few are seen standing by the entrance, where they wait until the end of the play.*

AGAÜE: Women of Asia! Worshippers of Bacchus!

AGAÜE *tries to show them* PENTHEUS' *head; they shrink from it.*

CHORUS:
    Why do you urge me? Oh!
AGAÜE:
    I am bringing home from the mountains
    A vine-branch freshly cut,
    For the gods have blessed our hunting.
CHORUS:
    We see it . . . and welcome you in
        fellowship.
AGAÜE:
    I caught him without a trap,
    A lion-cub, young and wild.
    Look, you may see him: there!

CHORUS:
> Where was it?

AGAUË:
> On Cithaeron;
> The wild and empty mountain—

CHORUS:
> Cithaeron!

AGAUË:
> . . . spilt his life-blood.

CHORUS:
> Who shot him?

AGAUË:
> I was first;
> All the women are singing,
> 'Honour to great Agauë!'

CHORUS:
> And then—who next?

AGAUË:
> Why, Cadmus' . . .

CHORUS:
> What—Cadmus?

AGAUË:
> Yes, his daughters—
> But after me, after me—
> Laid their hands to the kill.
> To-day was a splendid hunt!
> Come now, join in the feast!

CHORUS:
> What, wretched woman? *Feast?*

AGAUË (*tenderly stroking the head as she holds it*):
> This calf is young: how thickly
> The new-grown hair goes crisping
> Up to his delicate crest!

CHORUS:
> Indeed, his long hair makes him
> Look like some wild creature.

AGAUË:
> The god is a skilled hunter;
> And he poised his hunting women,
> And hurled them at the quarry.

CHORUS:
> True, our god is a hunter.

AGAUË:
> Do you praise me?

CHORUS:
> Yes, we praise you.

AGAUË:
> So will the sons of Cadmus . . .

CHORUS:
> And Pentheus too, Agauë?[12]

AGAUË:
> Yes, he will praise his mother
> For the lion-cub she killed.

CHORUS:
> Oh, fearful!

AGAUË:
> Ay, fearful!

CHORUS:
> You are happy?

AGAUË:
> I am enraptured;
> Great in the eyes of the world,[13]
> Great are the deeds I've done,
> And the hunt that I hunted there!

CHORUS: Then, poor Agauë, show this triumphant spoil of yours that you've carried home—show it to the people of Thebes.

AGAUË: Come, then, all you Thebans who live in this lofty and lovely city, come and see the beast we have caught and killed—we, Cadmus' daughters; caught not with nets or thonged Thessalian javelins, but with our own white arms and fingers. After this, should huntsmen boast, who buy their paltry tools from the armourer? We with our bare hands caught this quarry, then tore it limb from limb.

Where is my father? Let him come here! And my son Pentheus, where is he? Let him

---

12 *And Pentheus too, Agauë?*: the Chorus are physically shocked by the sight of Agauë and her prey, but their attitude does not change to pity. Agauë has been (in their view, justly) punished for her blasphemy against Dionysus, by being tricked into performing the usual Bacchic rite of slaughter, not upon the usual victim, a beast, but upon a man, and that her own son. She is now an abhorred and polluted creature, unfit for the company of the 'pure' Bacchae. Hence, though they welcome the punishment of Pentheus, their tone towards Agauë is one not of admiration but of contempt. This line in particular indicates the complete absence of pity. [Tr.]

13 *Great in the eyes of the world*: another hint of the 'manifestation' of the nature of the god. [Tr.]

get a strong ladder, and take this head, and climb up and nail it to the top of the palace wall, this lion that I hunted and brought home!

Enter CADMUS *with attendants bearing the body of* PENTHEUS.

CADMUS: Come, men. Bring your sad burden that was Pentheus; bring him to his home. I found the fragments of his body scattered in a thousand places, no two together, about the glens of Cithaeron, or hidden in thick woods; and with weary search I gathered them, and have brought them here.

I had already returned with old Teiresias from the Bacchic dance, and was inside the walls of the city, when news was brought me of my daughters' terrible deed. I turned straight back to the mountain; and here I bring my son, killed by the Maenads. I saw Autonoe, who bore Acteon to Aristaeus, and her sister Ino, there among the copses, still in their unhappy frenzy; but I understand that Agaue came raving towards the palace —it is true, there she is! Oh, what a terrible sight!

AGAUË: Father! You may boast as loudly as you will, that no man living is so blest in his daughters; I mean all three, but myself especially. I have left weaving at the loom for greater things—for hunting wild beasts with my bare hands. See here what I carry in my arms; this is the prize I won; I have brought it to hang on your palace wall. Take it, Father; hold it. Be proud of my hunting, and call your friends to a banquet; let them all envy and congratulate you, for the splendour of my deed.

CADMUS: O anguish unmeasured, intolerable! O pitiful hands—your splendid deed is murder! What victim is this you would lay at the gods' feet, calling Thebes, and me, to a banquet? Your suffering is worst, but mine is next. Dionysus, god of joy, has been just, but too cruel. He was born of my blood,

and he has destroyed my house.

AGAUË: How ill-humoured old age makes a man! How he scowls at me! I wish that my son were a great hunter, like his mother, pursuing wild beasts with all the young men of Thebes; but he can only fight against gods. Father, you must reason with him. Let someone call him here before me, to see my good fortune.

CADMUS: Oh, my daughters! If you come to understand what you have done, how terrible your suffering will be! But if you remain always as you are now, though you could not be called happy, at least you will not know your own misery.

AGAUË: Misery? What is wrong? Where is my cause for misery?

CADMUS: First, turn your eyes this way—look at the sky.

AGAUË: I am looking. Why do you tell me to look at it?

CADMUS: Is it still the same, or does it seem to you to have changed?

AGAUË: It is brighter than before—more luminous.

CADMUS: And this madness you suffered from —is it still with you?

AGAUË: I do not know what you mean. But I feel a change in my mind; my thoughts are somehow clearer.

CADMUS: Can you now hear and answer clearly?

AGAUË: Yes . . . I have forgotten what we said just now, Father.

CADMUS: When you were married, whose house did you come to?

AGAUË: You gave me to Echion, who was said to have been sown in the ground.

CADMUS: Then, Echion had a son born to him —who was he?

AGAUË: Pentheus—my son and his father's.

CADMUS: Yes: and whose head is that you hold in your arms?

AGAUË: A lion's—or so the women said who hunted it.

CADMUS: Now look straight at it; it is not much trouble to look.

AGAUË *looks at the head in silence; then cries out.*

AGAUË: Oh! What am I looking at? What am I holding?

CADMUS: Look at it steadily, and understand more clearly.

AGAUË: I see—O gods, what horror! What torture!

CADMUS: Does this seem to you like a lion?

AGAUË: No, it is Pentheus' head I hold in my accursed hand.

CADMUS: Tears have been shed for him already —before you knew it was he.

AGAUË: Who killed him? How did he come into my hands?

CADMUS: O bitter truth, revealed in a cruel hour!

AGAUË: Tell me—my heart is bursting—I must know the rest.

CADMUS: You killed him—you and your sisters.

AGAUË: Where was it done? At home? Or where else?

CADMUS: Where Actaeon was torn by hounds.

AGAUË: Cithaeron? What evil fate brought Pentheus there?

CADMUS: He went in scorn of Dionysus and your frenzied worship.

AGAUË: But how was it we were all there?

CADMUS: You were mad; the whole city was possessed by Dionysus.

AGAUË: Now I understand: Dionysus has destroyed us.

CADMUS: He was insulted and abused. You did not acknowledge his godhead.

AGAUË: Where is the dear body of my son, Father?

CADMUS: It is here. I searched long for it, and brought it.

AGAUË: Is it decently composed, limb to limb?

CADMUS: Not yet; we came here as quickly as possible.[14]

AGAUË: I will do it myself, if I may be allowed to touch him.

CADMUS: You will be allowed; your guilt is not greater than his.

AGAUË: But what part had Pentheus in my madness?

CADMUS: He was like you in not reverencing Dionysus. Therefore the god has joined all in one destruction, you and your sisters, and Pentheus, to strike down my house and me. I have no son; and now I see the child of your womb, my unhappy daughter, cut off by a shameful and horrible death. Pentheus, dear boy, my daughter's child, this house looked to you as its head; you were its bond of strength; and Thebes feared you. No man would slight your old grandfather if he saw you near; you would give him his deserts. Now I, Cadmus the Great, who sowed in the ground the seed of the Theban race, and reaped a glorious harvest, shall live, a dishonoured exile, far from my home.

O dearest son—yes, even in death you shall be held most dear to me—never again will you touch my beard, and call me Grandfather, and put your arm round me and say, 'Who has wronged you, or insulted you? Who is unkind to you or vexes you? Tell me, Grandfather, that I may punish him.' . . . Never again. Now there is only misery for me, suffering for you, tears for your mother, torment for all our family.

If there be any man who derides the unseen world, let him consider the death of Pentheus, and acknowledge the gods.[15]

---

[14] *Not yet; we came here . . . :* this and the following two lines are missing in the text, and here conjecturally supplied. [Tr.]

[15] *. . . and acknowledge the gods:* the climax of the play's irony. . . . *has shattered my whole life:* after these words there is a long gap in the MS. From quotations found in ancient writers editors have collected a considerable number of fragments probably belonging to this gap; and the lines here printed are pieced together from these, in a form something like that we may expect Euripides to have used. The MS text begins again with the words, *You shall change your form to a serpent,* on p. [287]. The puzzling prophecy that follows thereafter raises too many questions to be dealt with here; see the excellent note on this passage in Professor Dodd's edition. [Tr.] [Second edition published in 1960 by the Clarendon Press—eds.]

CHORUS: Cadmus, I grieve for you. Your grandson suffered justly, but you most cruelly.

AGAUË: Father, you see how one terrible hour has shattered my whole life, and turned my pride to shame, my happiness to horror. Now I long only to compose my son's body for burial, and lament for him; and then to go away and die. But I do not know if this is lawful; my hands are filthy with a pollution of their own making. When I have spilt the blood that is my own, torn the flesh that grew in my own womb, how can I, without offence to the gods, clasp him to my breast, or chant his ritual dirge? Yet I beg you, if you think it not blasphemous, let me touch my son, and say farewell to that dear body which I loved, and destroyed unknowing. It is right that you should pity, for you suffer too, although you have not sinned.

CADMUS: My daughter, you and I and our whole house are crushed and broken by the anger of Dionysus. It is not for me to keep you from your son. Only I would warn you to steel your heart against a sight that must be fearful to any eyes, but most of all to a mother's. (*To his attendants*) Lay your burden here before her, and remove the covering, that Agaué may see her son.

The coffin is laid on the ground before AGAUË, *who kneels beside it.*

AGAUË: O dearest child, how unnatural are these tears, that should have fallen from your eyes upon my dead face. Now I shall die with none to weep for me. I am justly punished; for in pride I blasphemed the god Dionysus, and did not understand the things I ought to have understood. You too are punished for the same sin; and I cannot tell whether your fate or mine is the more terrible. But since you have suffered with me, you will forgive me both for what I did, not knowing what I did, and for what I do now, touching you with unholy hands—at once your cruellest enemy and your dearest lover.

Now I place your limbs as they should lie; I kiss the flesh that my own body fed, my own care reared to manhood. Come, father, help me; lay his poor head here; as far as we can, make all exact and seemly.

O dearest face, O young fresh cheek; O kingly eyes, your light now darkened! O my son! See, with this veil I now cover your head, your torn and bloodstained limbs.

Now take him up and carry him to burial—a king lured to a shameful death by the anger of a god.

DIONYSUS *appears above the wall of the palace.*

CHORUS: But look! What is this? It is he, our lord Dionysus himself, no longer disguised as mortal, but in the glory of his godhead!

DIONYSUS: Behold me, a god great and powerful, Dionysus, immortal son of Zeus and Semele!

I come to the City of Seven Gates, to Thebes, whose men and women mocked me, denied my divinity, and refused to receive my holy rites. Now they see clearly the result of impious folly. The royal house is overthrown; the city's streets are full of guilty fear, as every Theban repents too late for his blindness and blasphemy. First and chief in sin was this man Pentheus, who not only rejected my just claims, but put me in fetters and insulted me. Therefore death came to him in the most shameful way of all, at the hands of his own mother. This fate he has justly suffered; for no god can see his worship scorned, and hear his name profaned, and not pursue vengeance to the utmost limit; that mortal men may know that the gods are greater than they.

Now listen further, while I reveal what is destined for the people of Thebes. The day will come when they will be driven from their city to wander East and West over the earth; for Zeus will not suffer a godless city to remain.

Agaué and her sisters must leave Thebes this very day; their exile will prove a full and just penance for the foul pollution they have incurred in this bloodshed. Never again shall they see their native land; for it is an offence to piety that hands so defiled should remain to take part in the city's sacrifices.

Now, Cadmus, I will tell you what suffering you yourself are destined to fulfil. You shall change your form to a serpent; and your wife Harmonia, whom you, though mortal, received from her divine father Ares, shall likewise change to a beast of the earth, and become a snake. Thus says the oracle of Zeus: You, at the head of a barbaric army, shall with your wife drive a pair of oxen yoked to a wagon; with your innumerable host you shall destroy many cities; but when they plunder the temple of Apollo's oracle, their reward shall be sorrow at their home-coming. But you yourself and Harmonia shall be saved by Ares, who shall bestow on you immortal life among the blessed ones.

I, who tell you this, am Dionysus, son of no mortal father, but of Zeus. If you all had chosen wisdom, when you would not, you would have found the son of Zeus your friend, and you would now be happy.

CADMUS: Dionysus, have mercy on us; we have sinned.

DIONYSUS: You recognize me too late; when you should have known me, you did not.

CADMUS: All this we have realized; but your vengeance is too heavy.

DIONYSUS: I am a god; and you insulted me.

CADMUS: Gods should not be like men, keeping anger for ever.

DIONYSUS: Zeus my father ordained this from the beginning.

AGAUË: All hope is gone, Father. Our sentence is passed: we are exiles.

DIONYSUS: Why then put off what is inevitable?

Exit DIONYSUS.

CADMUS: O my daughter, what utter misery and horror has overtaken us all—you, and your sisters, and me your unhappy father. In my old age I must leave my home and travel to strange lands. Further than that, it is foretold that I shall lead a mixed barbarian horde against Hellas. Both I and my wife, Harmonia, child of Ares, must take the brute form of serpents, and thus I am to lead her, at the head of an armed force, to desecrate the altars and tombs of the Hellenes. And I am to find no respite from suffering; I may not even cross the deep-flowing stream of Acheron to find peace in death.

AGAUË: And I shall live in exile, separated from you, Father.

CADMUS: Poor child! Why do you throw your arms round me, cherishing my white hair as a swan cares for its old helpless ones?

AGAUË: Where am I to turn, driven from my home and country?

CADMUS: I do not know, child; your father is little help to you.

AGAUË:
Farewell, my home; farewell the land I know.
Exiled, accursed and wretched, now I go
Forth from this door where first I came a bride.

CADMUS:
Go, daughter; find some secret place to hide
Your shame and sorrow.

AGAUË: Father, I weep for you.

CADMUS: I for your suffering, and your sisters' too.

AGAUË:
There is strange tyranny in the god who sent
Against your house this cruel punishment.

CADMUS:
Not strange: our citizens despised his claim,
And you, and they, put him to open shame.

AGAUË: Father, farewell.

CADMUS:
                Poor child! I cannot tell

How you can *fare well;* yet I say, Fare-
    well.

AGAUË:

I go to lead my sisters by the hand
To share my wretchedness in a foreign
    land.

*She turns to the Theban women who have
been waiting at the edge of the stage.*

Come, see me forth.
                Gods, lead me to some place
Where loath'd Cithaeron may not see my
    face,
Nor I Cithaeron. I have had my fill
Of mountain-ecstasy; now take who will

My holy ivy-wreath, my thyrsus-rod,
All that reminds me how I served this
    god!

Exit, followed by CADMUS.

CHORUS:

Gods manifest themselves in many forms,
Bring many matters to surprising ends;
The things we thought would happen do
    not happen;
The unexpected God makes possible:
And that is what has happened here
    to-day.

Exeunt.

MOLIÈRE

Tartuffe

Translated by Renée Waldinger

Characters

MADAME PERNELLE, *Orgon's mother*
ORGON, *Elmire's husband*
ELMIRE, *Orgon's wife*
DAMIS, *Orgon's son*
MARIANE, *Orgon's daughter*
VALÈRE, *Mariane's admirer*
CLÉANTE, *Orgon's brother-in-law*
TARTUFFE, *a hypocrite*
DORINE, *Mariane's maid*
MONSIEUR LOYAL, *a sergeant*
AN OFFICER
FLIPOTE, *Madame Pernelle's maid*

Scene: *The action takes place in Paris.*

ACT I

Scene 1 (MADAME PERNELLE, FLIPOTE, *her maid,* ELMIRE, MARIANE, DORINE, DAMIS, CLÉANTE)

MADAME PERNELLE: Come, Flipote, come, let's get rid of them.

ELMIRE: You are walking so fast that I can hardly follow you.

MADAME PERNELLE: Don't bother, daughter, don't bother; don't go any further; there is no need for all this ceremony.

ELMIRE: We are only doing what is due to you. But, mother, what makes you leave so quickly?

MADAME PERNELLE: Because I cannot bear to see such goings on, and no one tries to please me. Yes, I leave your house, very little impressed; all my instructions are contradicted here; nothing is respected, everyone has his say, and it's just like a circus.

DORINE: If . . .

MADAME PERNELLE: You are, my girl, somewhat of a loud-mouth and very fresh; you're mighty free with your advice.

DAMIS: But . . .

MADAME PERNELLE: You are a fool, my boy, to put it bluntly. I, your own grandmother, tell you so, and I have told my son, your father, a hundred times, that you were fast becoming a good-for-nothing, and that you would not give him anything but trouble.

MARIANE: I think . . .

MADAME PERNELLE: My goodness, granddaughter, you seem so modest, and to look at you, butter would not melt in your mouth. But, as they say, still waters run deep, and you do secretly things I dislike very much.

ELMIRE: But, mother . . .

MADAME PERNELLE: If you don't mind, daughter, your behavior is completely wrong: you should set them a good example and their late mother managed them much better. You are extravagant and it offends me to see you dressed like a princess. The woman who wants to please her husband only, daughter, does not need so much finery.

CLÉANTE: But after all, Madame . . .

MADAME PERNELLE: As for you, sir, who are her brother, I esteem you very much, I like you and respect you; nevertheless, if I were my son, her husband, I would entreat you not to come into our house. You are always advocating a way of life that should not be followed by decent people. I am speaking very frankly, but that's the way I am, and I do not mince words when I have something on my mind.

DAMIS: Your Mr. Tartuffe is a blessed soul, no doubt.

MADAME PERNELLE: He is a very worthy man to whom one ought to pay attention, and I cannot allow, without getting angry, to have him attacked by a fool like you.

DAMIS: What! should I allow a censorious bigot to usurp an absolute authority in this house? And shall we not be permitted the least amusement unless that dear gentleman gives us his consent?

DORINE: If we were to listen to him and believe in his maxims, we could not do anything without committing a sin; for he controls everything, this zealous critic.

MADAME PERNELLE: And whatever he controls is very well controlled. He wishes to show you the way to Heaven, and my son ought to make all of you love him.

DAMIS: No, really, grandmother, neither father nor anything else will ever induce me to look kindly upon him. I would betray my heart were I to speak differently. His manner constantly enrages me; I can foresee that, at one time or another, I shall come to a real quarrel with that boor.

DORINE: To be sure, it's downright scandalous to see a stranger take over such authority in this house; to see a beggar, who had no shoes when he came, and whose clothes were not worth sixpence, so far forget himself that he contradicts everything and plays the master.

MADAME PERNELLE: Mercy on me! Matters would be far better if everything were managed according to his pious directions.

DORINE: He passes for a saint in your imagination. Believe me, all he does is nothing but hypocrisy.

MADAME PERNELLE: What a tongue!

DORINE: I would not trust him without good security, any more than I would his man Laurent.

MADAME PERNELLE: I do not know what the servant may be at heart, but I shall vouch that the master is a worthy man. You bear him ill-will and reject him only because he tells you the truth. It's against sin that his heart rises in anger, and he does everything in the interests of Heaven.

DORINE: Yes, but why, especially lately, can't he endure that anyone come into this house? In what way does an honest visit offend Heaven to such an extent that we must have such a fuss about it that our ears are splitting? Among ourselves, do you want me to be frank? Upon my word I believe him to be jealous of my mistress.

MADAME PERNELLE: Hold your tongue and mind what you are saying. He is not the only one who condemns these visits. All the bustle that attends the people you frequent, these carriages forever stationed at the door, the noisy company of so many footmen, cause a great disturbance in the whole neighborhood. I am willing to believe that there is really no harm; but then people do talk of it, and that is not right.

CLÉANTE: Alas, Madame, will you prevent people from talking? It would be a very unhappy thing in life, if, for the foolish stories that can be told about us, we had to renounce our best friends, and even if we could resolve to do so, do you think we would oblige everyone to keep his tongue? There is no protection against slander. Let us therefore pay no attention to all that silly chatter, let us endeavor to live innocently and leave the gossips to say what they please.

DORINE: May not Daphné, our neighbor, and her little husband, be the persons who speak ill of us? Those whose own conduct is most ridiculous are always the first to slander others. They never fail to catch eagerly the slightest rumor of a love-affair, to spread the news of it with the greatest joy and to give it the turn they want. By coloring other people's actions like their own, they think they can justify their own to society; and in the false hope of some resemblance, give an air of innocence to their own intrigues; or shift elsewhere part of the public blame with which they are too heavily burdened.

MADAME PERNELLE: All these arguments have nothing to do with this. Everyone knows that Orante leads an exemplary life; all her cares tend to Heaven; and I have heard it said that she strongly condemns the company that comes here.

DORINE: An admirable example, indeed, and this lady is very kind! It is true that she lives very austerely; but it is age that has put this ardent zeal into her heart, and everyone knows that she is a prude against her true wishes. As long as she was able to make conquests she enjoyed her advantages well enough. But seeing the lustre of her eyes diminish, she wishes to renounce the world which is on the point of leaving her; and under the pompous cloak of lofty wisdom conceals the decay of her worn-out charms. These are the vicissitudes of former coquettes. It is hard for them to see their admirers desert them. Thus, forsaken, their gloomy anxiety sees no other recourse but that of prudery; and the severity of these good women censures everything and forgives nothing. Loudly they find fault with everyone's life, not through charity, but through envy which cannot bear that another enjoy those pleasures for which their age makes them no longer yearn.

MADAME PERNELLE: These are the fancy stories that are told to please you, daughter. We all have to keep quiet in your house for my lady keeps chattering all day. But I intend to have my say in my turn. Let me tell you that my son never did anything wiser than to take this devout man into his family; that Heaven, as a matter of fact, has sent him here to reclaim your lost souls; that for your salvation you ought to listen to him; and that he censures nothing that is not censurable. These visits, these balls, these conversations are all inventions of the wicked spirit. Pious words are never heard at any of them; only idle chatter, songs and nonsense. Quite often your neighbor comes in for his share of it and everyone knows how to slander right and left. In short, sensible people become completely mixed up by the confusion of such get-togethers. A thousand different idle stories are started in no time and, as a certain preacher said so well the other day, it's a perfect tower of Babel, for everyone chatters away without interruption. And to tell you the story which brought this up . . . (Pointing to CLÉANTE.) But here is this young man giggling already. Go and look for the fools that make you laugh, and without . . . goodbye, daughter, I will say no more. Let me tell you that I have lost a good deal of my respect for your home and that it will be a long time before I set foot in it again. (Slapping FLIPOTE's face.) Let's go, you! You're dreaming and your head is lost in the clouds. By my word, I'll know how to warm your ears. Let's go, you slut, let's go!

Scene 2 (CLÉANTE, DORINE)

CLÉANTE: I don't want to go there, for fear she should start arguing again; that this old lady . . .

DORINE: Ah! It is too bad she does not hear you talk this way; she would soon tell you that you have some nerve and that she is not old enough to be called that.

CLÉANTE: How excited she got with us for nothing, and how infatuated she seems with her Tartuffe!

DORINE: Oh! really, all this is nothing compared with the son; and if you had seen him you would say: "It's much worse." During our troubles[1] he acted like a man of sense and showed courage in the service of the king, but he has become a perfect dolt since he got so fond of his Tartuffe. He calls him brother and loves him in his heart a hundred times more than his mother, his son, his daughter or his wife. He is the sole confidant of all his secrets and the wise director of all his actions. He caresses him, embraces him; and it seems to me, he couldn't show more tenderness to a mistress. He wants him to be seated at the head of the table; he is delighted to see him eat more than half a dozen men; the choicest morsels of everything must be given to him, and if he happens to belch, he tells him: "May God preserve you!" In short he is crazy about him; he means everything to him, he's his hero; he admires all he does, quotes him on all occasions; he looks upon his most trifling actions as miracles, and every word he utters is considered an oracle. The other who knows his dupe and wishes to make the most of him, understands the art of dazzling him by a hundred deceitful tricks. His pretended devotions draw constantly large sums from our master and he assumes the right of commenting upon the conduct of every one of us. Even the conceited ass who is his valet takes it upon himself to lecture us; he comes preaching to us with fierce looks and throws away our ribbons, our rouge and beauty patches. The rascal, the other day, tore with his own hands a fine handkerchief he had found in a prayer book, saying that it was a dreadful sin to mix the finery of the devil with holy things.

Scene 3 (ELMIRE, MARIANE, DAMIS, CLÉANTE, DORINE)

ELMIRE: You are very fortunate not to have been present at the speech she made at the door. But I just saw my husband; since he didn't see me I want to go upstairs to await his coming.

CLÉANTE: I'll wait for him here to waste less time, and merely to say hello.

DAMIS: Hint something about my sister's marriage. I suspect that Tartuffe is opposed to it and that he is forcing my father to make so many evasions; and you are not unaware of the great interest I take in it. If one passion fills my sister's and Valére's heart, his sister, as you know, is dear to me; and if it were necessary . . .

DORINE: He is coming.

Scene 4 (ORGON, CLÉANTE, DORINE)

ORGON: Ah! brother, good day.

CLÉANTE: I was leaving and I am glad to see you back. The country is not very cheerful at present.

ORGON: Dorine . . . (*To* CLÉANTE.) Brother, pray, stay. Allow me to inquire what news there is here, to ease my mind. (*To* DORINE.) Has everything gone on well these two days? What has happened here? How is everyone?

DORINE: The day before yesterday, my mistress was feverish the whole day and had a terrible headache.

ORGON: And Tartuffe?

---

[1] *Troubles:* a reference to the troubles of the Fronde, when members of the nobility opposed King Louis XIV and the court party. Orgon was loyal to the King.

DORINE: Tartuffe? He's fine, stout and fat, with a good complexion and a rosy mouth.

ORGON: Poor man!

DORINE: The whole night she did not close her eyes for a moment; she was so feverish that she could not sleep and we had to sit up with her till the morning.

ORGON: And Tartuffe?

DORINE: Feeling pleasantly sleepy, he went to his room when he left the table, and jumped into his warm bed where he slept undisturbed till the next day.

ORGON: Poor man!

DORINE: Finally, giving in to our arguments, she resolved to let herself be bled,[2] and she was immediately relieved.

ORGON: And Tartuffe?

DORINE: He revived his courage, as he should, and fortifying his soul against all misfortunes, drank four large cups of wine to make up for the blood that our mistress had lost.

ORGON: Poor man!

DORINE: At present both are fine; I shall go and inform our mistress how glad you are of her recovery.

Scene 5 (ORGON, CLÉANTE)

CLÉANTE: She is laughing at you, to your face, brother, and without wishing to make you angry I shall tell you quite frankly that she is right. Have you ever heard of such a whim? And can it be that a man has such magic power in our day to make you forget everything for him? That after having relieved his indigence in your house, you should go so far as to . . .

ORGON: Stop right there, brother; you do not know the man of whom you are speaking.

CLÉANTE: I do not know him, if you like; but, after all, to know what kind of man he must be . . .

ORGON: Brother, you would be delighted to know him and there would be no end to your raptures. He is a man . . . who . . . ha! . . . a man . . . in short, a man. Whoever follows his precepts enjoys a deep peace and looks at everyone as so much dirt. Yes, I am becoming quite different since I am in contact with him. He teaches not to be attached to anything, he detaches my soul from all friendships, and were I to see my brother, children, mother, and wife die, it wouldn't bother me any more than that.

CLÉANTE: Humane sentiments, these, my brother!

ORGON: Ah! if you had seen how I met him you would have liked him as much as I do. Every day he came to church, looking so gentle, and kneeled right opposite me. He attracted the eyes of the whole congregation by the fervor with which he sent his prayers to Heaven; he sighed, was enraptured, and humbly kissed the ground every few moments. And, when I went out, he swiftly ran before me to offer me holy water at the door. Informed by his servant, who imitated him in everything, of his poverty and his station in life, I made him some presents; but, with great modesty, he always wanted to return some of them. "It's too much," he said to me, "it's too much by half. I do not deserve to arouse your pity." And when I refused to take them back, he would go and give them to the poor, right in my presence. Finally the Heavens moved me to bring him into my house and, since then, everything seems to prosper here. I see that he corrects everything and that, for my sake, he even takes a great interest in my wife; he warns me about the people who flirt with her and he is far more jealous of her than I am. But you won't believe how far his religious zeal goes; he considers a sin every little trifle in himself; a mere nothing is all that is needed to shock him; so much so that the other day he accused himself of having caught a flea, while praying, and having killed it in anger.

---

[2] *Bled:* a reference to bloodletting, a common remedy of the time.

CLÉANTE: My goodness! I believe you are mad, brother. Are you making fun of me with such a speech? And what do you mean with all that foolishness? . . .

ORGON: Brother, these words have the tone of free-thinking. You are somewhat tainted with it, and, as I have told you several times, you will get yourself into some unpleasant business.

CLÉANTE: This is the usual speech of people like you. They want everyone to be blind as they are. To be clear-sighted is to be a free-thinker; and whoever does not worship these empty affectations has neither respect nor faith for sacred things. Come, all your speeches do not frighten me; I know what I am saying and the Heavens see my heart. We are not slaves of all your affected demonstrations; there are hypocrites in religion as well as in courage; and, as we never see truly brave men make a lot of noise wherever honor leads them, so the good and truly pious whom we ought to imitate are not the ones who make such demonstrations. What! won't you make any distinction between hypocrisy and true devotion. You want to treat in the same way and give the same honor to the mask as to the face; put artifice on a level with sincerity, confound appearance with reality, value the shadow as much as the person, and counterfeit money as much as good money? Men, for the most part, are strange creatures! They never keep the golden mean. The bounds of reason are too narrow for them; in every characteristic they go beyond its limitations and they often spoil the noblest action because they want to exaggerate it and push it too far. These are just a few comments I am making, brother.

ORGON: Yes, you are no doubt a revered doctor of theology; you possess all the knowledge in the world; you are the only wise man and the only enlightened one; the oracle, the Cato, of the present age, and compared to you all men are fools.

CLÉANTE: I am not, brother, a revered doctor of theology and I do not possess all the wisdom in the world; but, to make it short, I know enough to differentiate between truth and falsehood. And just as I see no type of person more worthy of praise than the truly devout, for nothing in the world is nobler and more beautiful than true devotion; so I see nothing more hateful than the put-on expression of a pretended zeal, than those downright charlatans, those public devotees, whose sacrilegious and deceitful grimace abuse with impunity, and according to their fancy, make a jest of what is most venerable and sacred among men; those people who, motivated by self-interest, make a trade of piety, and want to buy honor and reputation at the cost of hypocritical looks to Heaven and affected raptures; these people, let me tell you, whom we see show an uncommon zeal for the next world in order to make their fortunes in this; who, with great affectation and much prayer, daily beg for and preach ,solitude, whole remaining in the midst of the court; who know how to reconcile their zeal with their vices; who are passionate, revengeful, faithless and full of artifice, and who, in order to destroy a man, insolently cover their private resentment under the cloak of Heaven's interests. They are the more dangerous in their wrath because they use against us the weapons we revere and because their passion, for which they are commended, prompts them to assassinate us with a consecrated blade. There are too many of this vile character. But the sincerely devout are easily recognized. Our age has shown us some, brother, who may serve as glorious examples. Look at Ariston, look at Périandre, Oronte, Alcidamas, Polydore, Clitandre: no one contests their title. They are not at all braggarts of virtue; we see none of this insufferable ostentation in them and their devotion is humane and manageable. They do not censure all our actions; they think there is too much pride in all these corrections; and leaving big words to others, reprove our actions by their own. They do not consider something evil just because it seems so, and they are always ready to judge others favorably. They have no cabals, no intrigues to carry on; all their desire is to live well themselves. They never persecute a sinner, they hate sin only, nor do they exert a keener zeal for the interests of Heaven, than Heaven itself does. These are the men for me; this is the way to act, this is, in short, the example to be followed. Your man is indeed not of that type. You vaunt his zeal with the best intention, but I believe you are dazzled by a false lustre.

ORGON: My dear brother-in-law, have you had your say?

CLÉANTE: Yes.

ORGON: Then I am your humble servant. (*He tries to leave.*)

CLÉANTE: Pray, one word more, brother. Let's stop this discussion. You know you promised to take Valère for your son-in-law.

ORGON: Yes.

CLÉANTE: You had chosen a date for this wedding.

ORGON: That is true.

CLÉANTE: Why then postpone the ceremony?

ORGON: I don't know.

CLÉANTE: Could you have some other intention?

ORGON: Perhaps.

CLÉANTE: Will you break your word?

ORGON: I am not saying that.

CLÉANTE: There is no obstacle, I think, to prevent you from fulfilling your promise.

ORGON: That depends.

CLÉANTE: Why so much fuss about a single word. Valère sent me to ask you about it.

ORGON: Heaven be praised!

CLÉANTE: But what shall I tell him?

ORGON: Anything you wish.

CLÉANTE: But I have to know your intentions. What are they?

ORGON: To do what Heaven ordains.

CLÉANTE: But to the point. Valère has your

word. Will you keep it, or not?

ORGON: Good-bye.

CLÉANTE: (*Alone*): I fear some misfortune for his love. I must warn him of what is going on.

ACT II

Scene 1 (ORGON, MARIANE)

ORGON: Mariane.

MARIANE: Father.

ORGON: Come here. I have something to tell you in secret.

MARIANE: What are you looking for?

ORGON (*Who is looking into a closet*): I want to see whether there is anyone who could overhear us because this little place is fit for such a purpose. Now we are all right. I have always, Mariane, found you of sweet disposition, and you have always been very dear to me.

MARIANE: I am very much obliged to you for this fatherly affection.

ORGON: That is well said, daughter; and to deserve it, your only care should be to please me.

MARIANE: That is indeed the height of my ambition.

ORGON: Very well. What do you think of Tartuffe, our guest?

MARIANE: Who, I?

ORGON: You. Take care how you answer.

MARIANE: Alas! I'll say whatever you wish.

ORGON: That is sensibly spoken. Tell me then, daughter, that he is a man of the highest merit, that he touches your heart, and that it would be pleasant to you to have him, with my consent, become your husband. Eh?

MARIANE (*Drawing back in surprise*): What?

ORGON: What is the matter?

MARIANE: Excuse me?

ORGON: What?

MARIANE: I must have misunderstood?

ORGON: How?

MARIANE: Who, would you have me say,

touches my heart, and whom would it be pleasant to have for a husband with your consent?

ORGON: Tartuffe.

MARIANE: That is not so, father, I assure you. Why do you wish me to tell you such a falsehood?

ORGON: But I want it to be the truth; and it is sufficient for you that I have resolved it.

MARIANE: What! You wish, father . . .

ORGON: Yes, daughter, I intend to join Tartuffe to my family through your marriage. He will be your husband. I have decided that I have a right to . . .

Scene 2 (DORINE, ORGON, MARIANE)

ORGON: What are you doing here? Your curiosity is very great, my girl, to bring you to listen in such a way.

DORINE: In truth, I do not know whether it is a rumor which arises from some conjecture or from chance, but I have heard the news of this marriage and I treated it as a pure joke.

ORGON: Why, is the thing so incredible?

DORINE: So much so, sir, that I don't even believe you when you say it.

ORGON: I know how to make you believe it.

DORINE: Oh, come, sir, you are telling us a funny story.

ORGON: I'm only telling you what you will soon see.

DORINE: Nonsense!

ORGON: What I say, daughter, is no joke.

DORINE: Come, don't believe your father! he is joking.

ORGON: I am telling you . . .

DORINE: No, it's in vain, we won't believe you.

ORGON: At last, my anger . . .

DORINE: Well, then, we'll believe you and it's too bad for you. What, can it be, sir, what with that air of common sense and this beard in the middle of the face, you are mad enough to want . . .

ORGON: Listen here: you have taken certain liberties here that quite displease me; I am telling you that, my girl.

DORINE: Let's talk without getting angry, I beg you, sir. Are you making fun of us, sir, in making this scheme? Your daughter is not cut out for a bigot, he has other things to think about. And besides, what will such an alliance bring you? Why should you, with all your wealth, go and choose a beggar for a son-in-law . . .

ORGON: Hold your tongue. If he has nothing, know that we ought to esteem him for it. His poverty is no doubt an honest poverty. It ought to raise him above all honors because he has allowed himself to be deprived of his wealth by his little care of things temporal and his great attachment to things eternal. But my help will give him the means of getting out of his troubles and of recovering his property. His lands are well-known in his province and, as poor as he is, he is indeed a nobleman.

DORINE: Yes, he says so, and this vanity does not agree very well with piety. Whoever embraces the innocence of a holy life should not boast so much of his name and his lineage; and the humble ways of piety cannot endure the glare of that ambition. What is the good of this pride? . . . But this talk offends you. Let us speak of his person and let's leave his lineage alone. Would you, without any compunction, give a girl like her to a man like him? Shouldn't you think of propriety and foresee the consequences of such a marriage? Remember that a girl's virtue is in danger when her wishes are thwarted in her marriage; that her intention of living virtuously depends upon the qualities of the husband who has been chosen for her, and those men who are always pointed at for having unfaithful wives, often make their wives what they are. In short it's very difficult to be faithful to certain types of husbands and whoever gives his daughter to a man she hates is responsible to Heaven for the mistakes she makes. Consider to what perils your plan exposes you.

ORGON: I can tell you that I need her to teach me how to live!

DORINE: You cannot do better but follow my advice.

ORGON: Let's not waste any more time with this nonsense, daughter. I know what you need and I am your father. I had promised you to Valère; but besides his liking to gamble, or so I heard, I suspect him of being somewhat of a free-thinker. I don't notice that he goes to church very much.

DORINE: Do you want him to run there just when you go, like those who go there only to be seen?

ORGON: I am not asking your advice about this. In short, the other one is on the best terms with Heaven, and that is a treasure second to none. This union will gratify your wishes to the full; it will be replete with sweetness and delight. You will live together, faithful in your love, really like two children, like turtle-doves. There will never be any unhappy fights between you and you will do with him whatever you may wish.

DORINE: She? She won't make anything but a fool out of him, I assure you.

ORGON: Hey! What language!

DORINE: I say that he has the look of one and that his destiny, sir, will be stronger than all your daughter's virtue.

ORGON: Stop interrupting me and try to hold your tongue without poking your nose into what does not concern you.

DORINE: I am only talking, sir, in your interest. (*She always interrupts him when he turns around to talk to his daughter.*)

ORGON: You take too much interest; hold your tongue, if you please.

DORINE: If I didn't care for you . . .

ORGON: I don't want you to care for me.

DORINE: But I wish to care for you, sir, in spite of yourself!

ORGON: Ah!

DORINE: I have your reputation much at heart and I cannot bear to have you made the subject of everyone's gossip.

ORGON: Won't you keep quiet?

DORINE: It's against my conscience to let you make such an alliance.

ORGON: Will you hold your tongue, you serpent, whose impudence . . .

DORINE: Ah! you are so pious and yet you fly into a rage!

ORGON: Yes, I get very angry at all that impertinence and I am resolved that you shall hold your tongue.

DORINE: Be it so. But even though I do not say a word, I still think so.

ORGON: Think, if you wish; but take care not to talk to me about it, or . . . Enough. (*Turning to his daughter.*) As a wise man I have carefully weighed everything.

DORINE (*Aside*): I am so furious that I can't talk.

ORGON: Without being a fop, Tartuffe looks like . . .

DORINE: Yes, he has some mug!

ORGON: That even if you have no relish for his other gifts . . . (*He turns to* DORINE *and looks at her.*)

DORINE: She has some bargain! If I were in her shoes, a man would surely not marry me against my will without impunity. I would show him, soon after the ceremony, that a wife has a revenge always at hand.

ORGON: Then you won't pay any attention to what I say?

DORINE: What are you complaining about? I am not talking to you.

ORGON: Then what are you doing?

DORINE: I am talking to myself.

ORGON: Very well. To punish her extreme insolence, I'll have to give her a slap in the face. (*He gets into position to give her a slap; and every time he looks around,* DORINE *stands straight without talking.*) You must approve my plan, daughter . . . You must believe that the husband . . . whom I have chosen for you . . . (*To* DORINE.) Why aren't you talking to yourself?

DORINE: I have nothing to say to myself.

ORGON: Just another little word.

DORINE: I don't feel like it.

ORGON: Of course, I was watching you.

DORINE: I am not such a fool.

ORGON: In short, daughter, you must obey and show a complete deference for my choice.

DORINE (*As she runs away*): I would scorn to take such a husband. (*He wants to slap her, but misses.*)

ORGON: You have a cursed hussy with you, daughter, with whom I couldn't live any longer without forgetting myself. I am not in a condition to continue this conversation; her insolent remarks have made me boiling mad and I am going to take some air to recover a little.

Scene 3 (DORINE, MARIANE)

DORINE: Pray tell me, have you lost your tongue? And must I act your part in this affair? Will you allow such a senseless proposal to be made to you without saying the least word against it?

MARIANE: What do you want me to do against a tyrannical father?

DORINE: What you have to do to ward off such a menace.

MARIANE: What?

DORINE: Tell him that a heart cannot love by proxy; that you are getting married for yourself, not for him; that since you are the one for whom the whole transaction is made, it is you, not he, who must like the husband; and that if he finds his Tartuffe so charming, he can marry him without any interference.

MARIANE: A father, I confess, has so much authority over us that I never had the strength to answer him.

DORINE: But let's talk about this. Valère has made advances to you; do you love him, pray, or don't you?

MARIANE: Ah! you do great injustice to my love, Dorine! Do you have to ask me that? Haven't I opened my heart to you a hundred times about that, and don't you know how much in love I am with him?

DORINE: How do I know whether your lips have spoken of the true feelings of your heart and whether you are really taken with this admirer?

MARIANE: You do me great wrong, Dorine, when you doubt it, and my true feelings have but been shown too clearly.

DORINE: You really love him, then?

MARIANE: Yes, passionately.

DORINE: And, to all appearance, he loves you as well?

MARIANE: I think so.

DORINE: And you are equally anxious to be married to each other?

MARIANE: Of course.

DORINE: What do you expect from this other match, then?

MARIANE: To kill myself if they force me to do it.

DORINE: Very well. That's a recourse that hadn't occurred to me. You only have to die to get out of trouble. No doubt this remedy is marvelous. I get furious when I hear that kind of language.

MARIANE: My goodness, Dorine, how angry you are getting! You don't sympathize at all with anyone's unhappiness.

DORINE: I do not sympathize with anyone who talks nonsense, and gives in as you do at a decisive moment.

MARIANE: But what do you want? If I am timid . . .

DORINE: Love requires firmness.

MARIANE: But have I wavered in my affection for Valère? And isn't it his business to obtain my father's consent?

DORINE: But what! If your father is a churlish fool who is entirely bewitched by his Tartuffe, and will break up a match he had agreed on, is that your lover's fault?

MARIANE: But shall I, by a flat refusal and scornful disdain, show everyone how much in love I am? However great my love may be, shall I, for Valère's sake, forget the modesty of my sex and my filial duty? And do you want me to display my passion to everyone . . .

DORINE: No, no, I don't want anything. I see

that you want to belong to Monsieur Tartuffe; and now I think of it, I would be in the wrong to turn you away from such a union. Why should I oppose your wishes? The match in itself is very advantageous. Monsieur Tartuffe! Oh! oh! is this a trifling offer? Certainly Monsieur Tartuffe, all things considered, is not a man to be sneezed at, and it's no small honor to be his better half. Everyone is already crowning him with glory. He belongs to the nobility in his part of the country, he is good-looking. He has red ears and a florid complexion; you'll be only too happy with such a husband.

MARIANE: Good gracious . . .

DORINE: You can't imagine how happy you will be when you are the wife of such a handsome husband!

MARIANE: Ah! stop such talk, I beg you, and give me your help against this match. I give up. I am ready to do anything.

DORINE: No; a daughter has to obey her father, were he to give her an ape for a husband. Yours is an enviable fate, what are you complaining of? You will drive in a stage-coach to his provincial town which will abound in uncles and cousins, and you will enjoy entertaining them. First you will be introduced to the best society. You will go and visit, by way of welcome, the bailiff's lady and the magistrate's wife, who will do you the honor of giving you a folding-chair. There, at carnival time, you may expect a ball, with a large band, to wit, two bagpipes, and sometimes you may see Fagotin and his marionettes. If your husband, however . . .

MARIANE: Ah, you are killing me! Try rather to help with your advice.

DORINE: I am your servant.

MARIANE: Ah! Dorine, have pity . . .

DORINE: To punish you, this match must take place.

MARIANE: Dear girl, please!

DORINE: No.

MARIANE: If I declare to you that . . .

DORINE: No. Tartuffe is your man and you shall have a taste of him.

MARIANE: You know that I have always confided in you. Do me . . .

DORINE: No. You shall be Tartuffed.

MARIANE: Well! since my fate cannot move you, leave me from now on entirely to my despair. My heart will seek help there and I know an infallible remedy for all my suffering. (*She wants to leave.*)

DORINE: Hey there! come back, I'll forget my anger. After all, I must take pity on you.

MARIANE: Look here, if they expose me to this cruel torment, let me tell you, Dorine, I shall die.

DORINE: Don't worry; it can cleverly be prevented . . . But here comes Valère, your beloved.

Scene 4 (VALÈRE, MARIANE, DORINE)

VALÈRE: I have just been told some news, my dear, that I didn't know and which is certainly very pretty.

MARIANE: What's that?

VALÈRE: That you are marrying Tartuffe.

MARIANE: There is no doubt that my father has taken this idea into his head.

VALÈRE: Your father, my dear . . .

MARIANE: Has altered his mind. He has just proposed this to me.

VALÈRE: What! Seriously?

MARIANE: Yes, seriously; he has openly declared himself for this match.

VALÈRE: And what, my dear, are your intentions?

MARIANE: I don't know.

VALÈRE: The answer is honest. You don't know?

MARIANE: No.

VALÈRE: No?

MARIANE: What would you advise me?

VALÈRE: I? I'll advise you to take this husband.

MARIANE: That is your advice?

VALÈRE: Yes.

MARIANE: Seriously?

VALÈRE: Of course. The choice is glorious and well worth consideration.

MARIANE: Well, sir, this is an advice that I shall accept.

VALÈRE: You will have no trouble in following it, it seems to me.

MARIANE: No more than it cost you to give it.

VALÈRE: I? I gave it to you to please you.

MARIANE: And I shall take it to please you.

DORINE (*Aside*): Let's see what this will come to.

VALÈRE: This, then, is how you love? And it was all deceit when you . . .

MARIANE: Let us not speak of that, pray. You have told me frankly that I should accept the husband selected for me; and I declare that I intend to do it since you give me this wholesome advice.

VALÈRE: Don't use my advice as your excuse. You had already made your decision, and you are grasping any frivolous pretext to justify the breaking of your word.

MARIANE: That is true, and it's well said.

VALÈRE: No doubt about it; and you have never had any real love for me.

MARIANE: Alas! you may think so, if you please.

VALÈRE: Yes, yes; I may think so; but my offended feelings will perhaps forestall you in such a design; and I know where to offer both my heart and my hand.

MARIANE: Ah! I don't doubt it; the love that merit arouses . . .

VALÈRE: For Heaven's sake, let's drop merit. No doubt I have very little of that and you prove it. But I hope much from the kindness another will show me; and I know someone who will welcome me and will not be ashamed to consent to repair my loss.

MARIANE: The loss is not so great, and you easily enough console yourself of this change . . .

VALÈRE: I'll do my best, you may depend on that. A heart that forgets us wounds our reputation; we must do our best to forget it also. If we do not succeed we must at least pretend to do so; for the cowardice of continuing to love the one who aban-doned us is never forgiven.

MARIANE: This sentiment is certainly noble and sublime.

VALÈRE: It is so; and everyone must approve it. What! would you have me keep my love for you forever and see you before my very eyes pass into the arms of another without bestowing elsewhere a heart which you reject?

MARIANE: On the contrary; as for me, that is what I hope for and I wish it were already done.

VALÈRE: You wish it?

MARIANE: Yes.

VALÈRE: You have insulted me enough, madam; and I am going to satisfy you this very instant. (*He is about to leave, but comes back.*)

MARIANE: Very well.

VALÈRE: Remember, at least, that you yourself drive me to this extremity.

MARIANE: Yes.

VALÈRE: And that my intention only follows your example.

MARIANE: Very well, my example.

VALÈRE: Enough; you will be obeyed on the spot.

MARIANE: So much the better.

VALÈRE: This is the last time you will ever see me.

MARIANE: So much the better.

VALÈRE (*Leaves, but turns back at the door*): Hey?

MARIANE: What?

VALÈRE: Didn't you call me?

MARIANE: I? You are dreaming.

VALÈRE: Well then, I'll keep on going. Farewell, madam.

MARIANE: Farewell, sir.

DORINE: I think that you are losing your senses with all that folly, and I let you quarrel so long to see how far you would go. Come here, Monsieur Valère. (*She takes hold of his arm and* VALÈRE *makes a show of resistance.*)

VALÈRE: Hey! What do you want, Dorine?

DORINE: Come here.

VALÈRE: No, no; I am too indignant. Don't hinder me from what she wants.

DORINE: Stop.

VALÈRE: No, look here, I have made up my mind.

DORINE: Ah!

MARIANE: He cannot bear to see me, my presence drives him away; I would do much better to leave him here alone.

DORINE (*Leaving* VALÈRE *and running to* MARIANE): Now the other. Where are you going?

MARIANE: Leave me.

DORINE: You must come back.

MARIANE: No, no, Dorine; you are trying to detain me in vain.

VALÈRE: I see indeed that the sight of me is a torture to her; and I had no doubt better free her from it.

DORINE (*Leaving* MARIANE *and running to* VALÈRE): Again? The devil take you! Stop this nonsense and come here both of you. (*She holds them both.*)

VALÈRE: But what are your intentions?

MARIANE: What do you want to do?

DORINE: To get you together again and rescue you. (*To* VALÈRE.) Are you mad to have such an argument?

VALÈRE: Didn't you hear how she spoke to me?

DORINE: Are you out of your senses to get so angry?

MARIANE: Didn't you see the whole thing, and how he treated me?

DORINE (*To* VALÈRE): Nonsense on both sides. She has no other wish than to remain yours, I can vouch for that. (*To* MARIANE.) He loves no one but you, and has no other desire but to be your husband, I answer for it upon my life.

MARIANE: Why give me such advice, then?

VALÈRE: Why ask me for advice on such a subject?

DORINE: You are a couple of fools. Come, give me your hand, both of you. (*To* VALÈRE.) Come, you.

VALÈRE (*Giving his hand to* DORINE): What's the good of my hand?

DORINE (*To* MARIANE): Come now, yours.

MARIANE (*Also giving her hand*): What's the use of all that?

DORINE: Goodness me! Come here, quickly. You love each other more than you may think.

VALÈRE (*To* MARIANE): Don't do things with such bad grace and try to look at me without anger. (MARIANE *looks at* VALÈRE *and smiles faintly.*)

DORINE: To tell the truth, lovers are all crazy.

VALÈRE: Now really! have I no cause for complaint? And, not wanting to lie, weren't you mean to take pleasure in telling me such painful things.

MARIANE: But aren't you the most ungrateful man . . .

DORINE: Let's leave this whole discussion for another time and let us think about averting this confounded marriage.

MARIANE: Tell us what we should do.

DORINE: We shall do all kinds of things. Your father is making fun of us, and all of this is nonsense. But, as for you, it would be better that you pretend to comply quietly with his extravagance so that, in case of need, it will be easier for you to delay this proposed marriage. In gaining time we shall remedy everything. Sometimes you'll pretend an illness which will overcome you suddenly and will require delay; sometimes you'll pretend some ill omen; you, unluckily, met a corpse, broke a mirror, or dreamed of muddy water. In short, the best of this is that they cannot unite you to anyone else but him unless you say yes. But, the better to succeed, it would be wise, it seems to me, that we are not seen talking together. (*To* VALÈRE.) Leave now, and without delay urge your friends to make Orgon keep his promise. We are going to interest her brother and enlist her stepmother on our side. Farewell.

VALÈRE (*To* MARIANE): Whatever efforts we may be all making, my greatest hope, to tell the truth, lies in you.

MARIANE (*To* VALÈRE): I cannot answer for

wishes of a father, but I shall belong to no one but to Valère.

VALÈRE: How happy you make me! and whatever they may try . . .

DORINE: Ah! lovers never get tired of talking. Go, I tell you.

VALÈRE (*Takes a step and comes back*): Finally . . .

DORINE: What chattering! (*Pushing each of them by the shoulder.*) Go this way, and you, the other.

ACT III

Scene 1 (DAMIS, DORINE)

DAMIS: May lightning strike me dead this very instant, may everyone treat me as the greatest of scoundrels, if any respect or authority shall stop me from doing something rash.

DORINE: For pity's sake, curb this temper. Your father has only talked about it. We do not always carry out what we propose and the road is long between the plan and the deed.

DAMIS: I must stop the plots of this conceited ass and whisper a few words into his ear.

DORINE: Gently, pray! Let your mother-in-law deal with him as well as with your father. She has some influence with Tartuffe; he agrees to all that she says and he could even have some tender feelings for her. Would to Heaven that this were true! A pretty thing it would be! In short, the interest she takes in you forces her to send for him; she wants to sound him out about this marriage that troubles you, to know his intentions, and to acquaint him with the sad consequences which it may cause, if he entertains any hope on this subject. His servant told me that he was praying and I wasn't able to see him; but he also told me that he was coming down. Leave then, if you please, and let me wait for him.

DAMIS: I may be present at this interview.

DORINE: No: they must be alone.

DAMIS: I shall not say anything to him.

DORINE: You are joking; we know your usual outbursts and that's the perfect way to spoil everything. Go.

DAMIS: No, I want to see without getting angry.

DORINE: How annoying you are! He is coming; go away.

Scene 2 (TARTUFFE, LAURENT, DORINE)

TARTUFFE (*Noticing* DORINE): Laurent, put away my hair shirt and my scourge and pray that Heaven may ever enlighten you. If anyone comes to see me tell them that I have gone to the prisoners to share the alms that I have received.

DORINE: What affectation and what boasting!

TARTUFFE: What do you want?

DORINE: To tell you . . .

TARTUFFE (*Taking a handkerchief from his pocket*): Ah! For Heaven's sake! Before you say anything, take this handkerchief, I beg you.

DORINE: What?

TARTUFFE: Cover this bosom which I cannot bear to see. The soul is offended by such sights and they give rise to sinful thoughts.

DORINE: You are, then, very susceptible to temptation, and the flesh makes a strong impression on your senses! Of course I do not know what heat inflames you, but my desires are not so quickly aroused; and I could see you naked from head to toe without being tempted in the least by that whole hide of yours.

TARTUFFE: Show a little modesty in your conversation or I shall leave you on the spot.

DORINE: No, no, I am the one who will leave you alone. I have only two words to say to you. My mistress is going to come down to this room and she wishes the favor of a moment's conversation.

TARTUFFE: Alas! with pleasure.

DORINE: (*Aside*): How he softens up! Upon my word, I stick to what I've said of him.

TARTUFFE: Is she coming soon?

DORINE: I think I hear her. Yes, it is she, and I leave you together.

Scene 3 (ELMIRE, TARTUFFE)

TARTUFFE: May Heaven, with its great kindness, forever give you health, both of soul and body; and bless your days as much as the humblest of its votaries desires!

ELMIRE: I am much obliged for this pious wish; but let us take a seat to be more comfortable.

TARTUFFE: Are you completely recovered from your illness?

ELMIRE: Completely; my fever soon left me.

TARTUFFE: My prayers have not sufficient merit to have brought about this grace from above; but I did not make any vows to Heaven that did not concern your recovery.

ELMIRE: Your zeal for me has been too solicitous.

TARTUFFE: Your dear health cannot be overrated and I would have given mine to make it well again.

ELMIRE: That is carrying Christian charity very far, and I am much indebted to you for all this kindness.

TARTUFFE: I do far less for you than you deserve.

ELMIRE: I wanted to talk to you in private about a certain matter, and I am very glad that no one is here to observe us.

TARTUFFE: I am also overjoyed at it, and you may be sure that it is very pleasant to me, Madam, to find myself alone with you. It is an opportunity that I have often requested from Heaven without having it granted before this.

ELMIRE: What I wish is a few words with you in which you bare your heart and conceal nothing from me.

TARTUFFE: And I too, as a rare favor, wish only to show you my entire soul, and to swear to you that the criticisms I have made about the visits you receive in homage of your charms, do not come from any hatred towards you, but rather from a passionate zeal that carries me away, and from a pure motive . . .

ELMIRE: That is how I understand it; and I believe that it is my salvation that gives you this concern.

TARTUFFE: (*Pressing her fingertips*): Yes, Madam, without doubt; and my fervor is such . . .

ELMIRE: Ow! you squeeze me too hard.

TARTUFFE: It's from excessive zeal. I never had any intention of hurting you, and I would much rather . . . (*He puts his hand on her knee.*)

ELMIRE: What is your hand doing there?

TARTUFFE: I am feeling your dress; its material is very soft.

ELMIRE: Ah! I beg you, let go of me! I am very ticklish. (*She pulls back her chair and* TARTUFFE *draws nearer with his.*)

TARTUFFE: Gracious me! How marvellous is the workmanship of this lace! They work in a miraculous way today; never has anything been so beautifully made.

ELMIRE: That is true. But let us talk a little of what concerns us. I have heard that my husband wants to retract his promise and give his daughter to you. Tell me, is that true?

TARTUFFE: He has briefly mentioned it to me; but to tell you the truth, Madam, that is not the happiness for which I am sighing, and I behold elsewhere the marvellous attractions of the felicity which would satisfy all my wishes.

ELMIRE: That is because you have no love for earthly things.

TARTUFFE: My breast does not contain a heart of stone.

ELMIRE: As for me, I believe that all your sighs tend towards Heaven and that nothing here below rouses your desires.

TARTUFFE: The love which attaches us to eternal beauties does not extinguish in us the love of temporal ones. Our senses can easily be charmed with the perfect works that Heaven has created. Its reflected charms shine forth in such as you; but in your person it displays its rarest wonders. It has poured out on your face such beauty that eyes are dazzled and the heart enraptured; and I could not look at you, perfect creature, without admiring in you the author of nature, and without feeling my heart touched with an ardent love at the sight of the fairest of portraits in which he painted himself. At first I feared that this secret ardor was a clever snare of the dark spirit, and my heart even resolved to flee from your eyes, thinking that you might be an obstacle to my salvation. But finally I perceived, oh most charming beauty, that my passion could be not guilty; that I could reconcile it with modesty, and that is what has made me give in to it. It is, I confess, a great presumption on my part to dare to offer you this heart; but I expect, in my hopes, everything from your kindness, and nothing from the vain efforts of my weakness. In you are my hope, my happiness, my peace; on you depend my torment or beatitude. And it is by your decision solely, that I shall be happy, if you wish it, or miserable, if it pleases you.

ELMIRE: The declaration is extremely gallant; but it is, to tell the truth, somewhat surprising. It seems to me that you should protect your heart better, and reflect upon a design of this nature. A pious man like you, whom everyone speaks of as . . .

TARTUFFE: Ah! although I am a pious man, I am not the less a man; and when it beholds your celestial charms, a heart lets itself be conquered and reasons not. I know that such words coming from me seem strange; but after all, Madam, I am no angel, and if you condemn the declaration I make, you must lay the blame upon your bewitching charms. From the moment I first set eyes upon your more than human splendor, you became the queen of my being. The ineffable sweetness of your divine glances broke down the resistance of my obstinate heart; it surmounted everything, fastings,

prayers, tears, and turned all my desires to your charms. My eyes and my sighs have told you so a thousand times; and to explain myself better, I am now using my voice. If you should look with some kindness upon the tribulations of your unworthy slave, if your goodness will console me, and will condescend to stoop to my nothingness, I shall always have for you, oh sweet miracle, a devotion, which nothing can equal. Your honor does not run any risk with me and need fear no disgrace on my part. All these court gallants whom women idolize are noisy in their doings and vain in their talk; they are constantly boasting of their successes and they receive no favors without divulging them; and their indiscreet tongues, in which people confide, desecrate the altar on which their hearts offer sacrifice. But people like us burn with a discreet flame and with them a secret is always kept. The care we take of our own reputation is a complete guarantee for the person beloved, and it is only with us, when our heart is accepted, that love is found without scandal and pleasure without fear.

ELMIRE: I am listening to what you say, and your rhetoric explains in rather strong terms to me. But aren't you afraid that I might feel like telling my husband of this gallant ardor; and that the prompt knowledge of that kind of love might well alter the friendship he has for you?

TARTUFFE: I know that you are too kind and that you will forgive my temerity; that you will excuse, under the score of human frailty, the violent outbursts of a love that offends you; and will consider, by looking at yourself, that I am not blind, and that a man is made of flesh and blood.

ELMIRE: Some might, perhaps, take this in another manner; but I shall show my discretion. I shall not tell the matter to my husband; but in return I want something from you; that is to forward honestly and without any quibbling the marriage of Valère and Mariane; to renounce the unjust power which would enrich you with what belongs to another; and . . .

Scene 4 (ELMIRE, DAMIS, TARTUFFE)

DAMIS: (*Emerging from a closet in which he had hidden*): No, Madam, no; this must be made public. I was in there and I heard everything; and Providence seems to have led me there to confound the pride of a traitor who wrongs me; to show me a way of taking my revenge of his hypocrisy and insolence; to undeceive my father and bare fully the heart of a villain who talks to you of love.

ELMIRE: No, Damis, it is enough that he reforms and tries to deserve my forgiveness. Since I have promised it, do not make me break my word. I do not feel like provoking a scandal; a woman laughs at such foolishness and never troubles her husband's ears with it.

DAMIS: You have your reasons for acting in this manner, and I have mine too for acting otherwise. To wish to spare him is ridiculous; and the insolent pride of his bigotry has already triumphed too much over my rightful anger and created too many disorders among us. The scoundrel has governed my father too long and has plotted against my affections as well as Valère's. My father must be undeceived about this perfidious scoundrel; and Heaven offers me an easy means. I am indebted to It for this opportunity and it is too favorable a one to be neglected. I would deserve to have it taken from me if, having it in hand, I did not make use of it.

ELMIRE: Damis . . .

DAMIS: No, if you please, I must do what I think best. My heart is filled with joy now, and whatever you may say will never dissuade me from the pleasure of taking my revenge. Without going any further I shall make an end to the affair; and here is just the perfect opportunity.

Scene 5 (ORGON, DAMIS, TARTUFFE, ELMIRE)

DAMIS: We are going to entertain you, father, with a completely fresh incident which will surprise you greatly. You are well repaid for all your caresses and this gentleman rewards your tenderness handsomely. His great zeal for you has just come to light. He aims at nothing less than at dishonoring you; and I have surprised him here making to your wife the insulting confession of a guilty passion. She has a sweet disposition and her too-discreet heart wanted absolutely to keep this secret from you; but I cannot encourage such impudence and think that to have been silent about it would have been to do you an injury.

ELMIRE: Yes, I believe that we should never break in upon a husband's peace with such foolish stories; that our honor does not depend upon that and that it is enough for us to know how to defend ourselves. These are my feelings; and you would have said nothing, Damis, if I had any credit with you.

Scene 6 (ORGON, DAMIS, TARTUFFE)

ORGON: What have I just heard, oh Heavens! is it credible?

TARTUFFE: Yes, brother, I am a wicked, guilty, unhappy sinner, full of iniquity, the greatest villain that ever breathed. Every moment of my life is filled with blemishes; it is only a mass of crimes and corruption and I see that Heaven, in order to punish me, wants to mortify me on this occasion. Whatever great offence may be levelled at me, I will not dare to have the pride to deny it. Believe what you are told, arm your resentment, and like a criminal, drive me from your house. No shame could be great enough that I would not deserve more.

ORGON (*To his son*): Ah, traitor, do you dare, by this falsehood, try to tarnish the purity of his virtue?

DAMIS: What! the feigned meekness of this hypocrite will make you deny . . .

ORGON: Hold your tongue, accursed plague!

TARTUFFE: Ah! Let him talk; you accuse him wrongly, and you had much better believe what he tells you. Why be so favorable to me after hearing such a fact? Are you aware, after all, of what I am capable? Do you trust my outward appearance, brother? And because of what you see, believe me to be better? No, no, you let appearances deceive you, and I am nothing less, alas, than what they think of me. Everyone takes me for a respectable man; but the truth is that I am worthless. (*Turning to* DAMIS.) Yes, my dear son, speak up, call me a treacherous infamous lost scoundrel, a thief, a murderer; crush me with even more hateful names; I am not contradicting you, I have deserved them; and am willing to endure disgrace on my knees, as shame brought about by the crimes of my life.

ORGON (*To* TARTUFFE): Brother, that is too much. (*To his son.*) Doesn't your heart relent, traitor?

DAMIS: What? His words beguile you so far as to . . .

ORGON: Hold your tongue, rascal! (*To* TARTUFFE.) Brother, hey! Rise, I beg you. (*To his son.*) Infamous scoundrel!

DAMIS: He can . . .

ORGON: Hold your tongue!

DAMIS: I am beside myself! What! I pass . . .

ORGON: If you say one more word, I'll break your arm.

TARTUFFE: Brother, in the name of Heaven, do not forget yourself. I would much rather suffer the greatest hardship than have him receive the slightest scratch because of me.

ORGON (*To his son*): Ungrateful monster!

TARTUFFE: Leave him be. If I have to ask you, on both knees, to forgive him . . .

ORGON (*To* TARTUFFE): Alas! you must be jesting? (*To his son.*) Behold his kindness, scoundrel.

DAMIS: Then . . .

ORGON: Peace!

DAMIS: What, I . . .

ORGON: Peace, I tell you! I know well what motive goads you to attack him. All of you hate him and I now see wife, children and servants all let loose against him. Every trick is impudently used to remove this pious person from my house; but the more you strive to get him out, the greater care I shall take to keep him here; and I shall hasten to give him my daughter to confound the pride of my whole family.

DAMIS: Do you mean to compel her to accept him?

ORGON: Yes, traitor, and this very evening to make you really furious. Ah! I defy you all and shall let you know that I must be obeyed and that I am the master. Come, retract; and right now, scoundrel, throw yourself at his feet to ask his forgiveness.

DAMIS: Who, I? forgiveness of this rascal who, by his impostures . . .

ORGON: Ah! you resist, you tramp, and insult him to boot? A stick, a stick! (*To* TARTUFFE.) Don't hold me back. (*To his son.*) Out of my house, this very instant, and never dare set foot into it again.

DAMIS: Yes, I shall leave, but . . .

ORGON: Quickly, leave this place. I deprive you of your inheritance, rascal, and give you my curse, besides.

Scene 7 (ORGON, TARTUFFE)

ORGON: To offend a holy person that way!

TARTUFFE: Oh Heaven! forgive him the anguish he has given me. (*To* ORGON.) If you could understand my grief at seeing myself blackened in my brother's sight . . .

ORGON: Alas!

TARTUFFE: The very thought of this ingratitude wounds me so terribly . . . The horror I conceive of it . . . My heart is so oppressed that I cannot speak and think that it will be my death.

ORGON (*Running, in tears, towards the door through which he has sent away his son*): Scoundrel! I am sorry that my hand has spared you and that I have not knocked you down on the spot. Compose yourself, brother, and don't be troubled.

TARTUFFE: Let us put an end to these unhappy discussions. I realize what uneasiness I have brought into this house and I think, brother, that I have to leave it.

ORGON: What? Are you jesting?

TARTUFFE: They hate me and I see that they are trying to make you suspect my integrity.

ORGON: What does it matter? Do you see me listening to them?

TARTUFFE: They will not fail to continue, you may be sure, and these same stories, which you are rejecting now, will perhaps be listened to another time.

ORGON: No, brother, never.

TARTUFFE: Ah! brother, a wife can easily deceive a husband.

ORGON: No, no.

TARTUFFE: Allow me, by removing myself from here promptly, to deprive them of any cause for attacking me thus.

ORGON: No, you will stay; my life depends on it.

TARTUFFE: Well, then I shall have to mortify myself. However, if you would . . .

ORGON: Ah!

TARTUFFE: So be it, let us not talk about it any more. But I know how I must behave on this occasion. Honor is a delicate thing and friendship obliges me to prevent rumors and not to give any room for suspicion. I shall avoid your wife and you will not see me . . .

ORGON: No, in spite of everybody, you will see her often. To drive everyone mad is my greatest joy, and I want you to be seen with her at all times. And that isn't all; the better to brave them all, I wish to have no other heir but you, and I am going right now to sign you a deed of gift for my whole estate. A true and honest friend whom I take for my son-in-law is far dearer to me than son, wife, and relatives. Wouldn't you accept what I propose?

TARTUFFE: The will of Heaven be done in all things!

ORGON: Poor man! Let us quickly have a draft drawn up and let all envy burst with spite!

ACT IV

Scene 1 (CLÉANTE, TARTUFFE)

CLÉANTE: Yes, everyone talks about it, and you can believe me, the scandal caused by this news is not to your credit. And I have met you, sir, quite opportunely, to tell you my opinion in two words. I am not examining these reports very thoroughly; I shall pass over that and take the thing at its worst. Let us suppose that Damis has not acted well and that you have been wrongly accused; is it not the part of a good Christian to forgive the offense to smother all desire of vengeance in your heart? And should you allow that, because of a quarrel with you, a son be driven from his father's house? I am telling you again and I am talking frankly, that great and small are scandalized by it; and if you will take my advice you will make peace and not push matters to extremes. Make a sacrifice of your anger to God, and restore a son to his father's favor.

TARTUFFE: Alas! as far as I am concerned I would like that with all my heart. I, sir, do not bear him any ill-will; I forgive him everything, I blame him for nothing and I should like to serve him with my best capacities. But the interests of Heaven could not consent to that, and if he returns into this house, I shall have to leave. After his unparalleled action any relationship between us would give rise to scandal. Heaven knows what everyone would immediately think of it. They would ascribe it to shrewd policy, and they would say everywhere that, feeling guilty, I pretend a charitable zeal for my accuser; that I am afraid and wish to conciliate him in order to bribe him, in a sly manner, into silence.

CLÉANTE: You put us off here with sham excuses and all your reasons, sir, are too far-fetched. Why do you take into your hands the interests of Heaven? Does It need us to punish the guilty? Leave the care of Its own vengeance to itself; think only of the forgiveness of all offenses It prescribes, and do not consider the judgment of men when you follow the sovereign orders of Heaven. What! the trivial regard for what men may think will hinder the glory of a good action? No, no, let us always do what Heaven prescribes and let us not perplex our heads with any other cares.

TARTUFFE: I have told you already that in my heart I forgive him; and that, sir, is doing what Heaven ordains; but after the scandal and the affront of today, Heaven does not require me to live with him.

CLÉANTE: And does it require you, sir, to lend an ear to what mere caprice dictates to his father; and to accept the gift of an estate to which, in justice, you have no claim whatever?

TARTUFFE: Those who know me will not think that this proceeds from self-interest. All the riches of this world have little attraction for me; I am not dazzled by their false glare; and if I should decide to accept from his father this donation that he wished to make me, it is only, to tell the truth, because I fear that all that wealth might fall into wicked hands; lest it may be divided among people who would make a bad use of it in this world and would not use it, as I intend to do, for the glory of Heaven and the good of my fellow-men.

CLÉANTE: Hey, sir, you need not have such delicate scruples which may occasion the complaints of a rightful heir. Allow him, without worrying about anything, to become the owner of his estate at his own perils, and consider that it is even better that he misuses it than that you should be accused of defrauding him of it. I am only surprised that you could have accepted such a proposal without embarrassment; for, after all, has true piety any maxim which shows how to rob a legitimate heir

of his property? And, if it is true that Heaven has put into your heart an invincible obstacle to your living with Damis, wouldn't it be better that, as a discreet person, you should make a civil retreat from this house, than to allow that, contrary to all reason, the son be turned away from it because of you. Believe me, sir, this would be giving a proof of your probity...

TARTUFFE: It is half past three, sir; certain pious duties call me upstairs, and you will excuse my leaving you so soon.

CLÉANTE: Ah!

Scene 2 (ELMIRE, MARIANE, DORINE, CLÉANTE)

DORINE: For Heaven's sake, sir, try to help her as we do. She is in mortal grief; and the marriage contract that her father resolved upon for tonight drives her every moment to despair. He is just coming. Pray let us unite our efforts and try, by force or cunning, to frustrate this unfortunate design that has caused us all so much trouble.

Scene 3 (ORGON, ELMIRE, MARIANE, CLÉANTE, DORINE)

ORGON: Ah! I am glad to see you all assembled. (*To* MARIANE.) There is something in this contract to make you laugh and you know already what that means.

MARIANE (*On her knees*): Father, in the name of Heaven that is a witness to my grief and by everything that can move your heart, forego somewhat your paternal rights and dispense my true desires from obedience. Do not compel me, by this harsh rule, to complain to Heaven for what I owe you; and this life, alas, that you have given me, do not make it wretched, father. If, contrary to the tender hopes that I have formed, you forbid me to belong to the one I dared love, at least out of your kindness that I implore on my knees, save me from the torment of belonging to the man I abhor; and do not drive me to despair by exerting your full power over me.

ORGON (*Touched*): Come, be firm, my heart! Let there be no human weakness!

MARIANE: Your kindness for him does not hurt me: show it to its full extent; give him your estate and should it not be enough, add all of mine to it. I consent with all my heart and I leave you to dispose of it. But at least do not go as far as my own person, and allow me to end, in the austerity of a convent, the sad days that Heaven has allotted to me.

ORGON: Ah! there we have it! All girls want to become nuns when their father opposes their love affairs. Get up. The more repugnance you feel in accepting it, the greater will be your merit. Mortify your senses by this marriage and do not bother me any further.

DORINE: But what! . . .

ORGON: Hold your tongue, you. Meddle only in what concerns you. I absolutely forbid you to say another word.

CLÉANTE: If you allow me to answer you and give you some advice . . .

ORGON: Brother, your advice is the best in the world: it is very rational and I set great store by it. But you will allow me not to avail myself of it.

ELMIRE (*To her husband*): Upon seeing what I see, I no longer know what to say, and I quite admire your blindness. You must be very bewitched, and prepossessed in his favor to deny to us the incident of today.

ORGON: I am your servant and judge by appearances. I know your indulgence for my rascal of a son, and you were afraid to disavow the nasty trick he wanted to play on that poor man. For you were too unexcited to be believed and you would have appeared much more upset.

ELMIRE: Must our honor bluster so vehemently at the simple confession of an amorous outburst? And can we reply to all that concerns it only with fury in our eyes and insults in our mouth? As for me, I simply laugh at such talk, and scandal about this does not please me in the least. I like to show my discreetness quietly and am not at all in favor of these savage prudes, whose honor is armed with claws and teeth, and who, at the least word, would disfigure a man's face. Heaven preserve me from such good discretion! I prefer a virtue that is not diabolical, and believe that a discreet and cold refusal is not less effective in discouraging an admirer.

ORGON: Well, I know the whole affair and will not alter my course of action.

ELMIRE: Once more I am surprised at your strange weakness. But what answer would your credulity make if I should let you see that you have been told the truth?

ORGON: See?

ELMIRE: Yes.

ORGON: Nonsense!

ELMIRE: But if I found the means to let you see it clearly? . . .

ORGON: Idle stories!

ELMIRE: What a man! Answer me at least. I am not asking you to believe us; but suppose that a place could be found where you might see and overhear everything; what would you say then of your honest man?

ORGON: In that case, I would say that . . . I wouldn't say anything, because this couldn't be.

ELMIRE: Your delusion has lasted long enough and I have been accused too much of imposture. I must, for my gratification, and without going any further, make you a witness to all I have told you.

ORGON: So be it; I take you at your word. We shall see your dexterity and how you will make good this promise.

ELMIRE: (*To* DORINE): Ask him to see me.

DORINE: He is crafty and perhaps it will be difficult to catch him.

ELMIRE: No; we are easily duped by those we love, and conceit drives us to deceive ourselves. Ask him to come down. (*Turning to* CLÉANTE *and to* MARIANE.) And you, go now.

Scene 4 (ELMIRE, ORGON)

ELMIRE: Come over to this table and hide under it.

ORGON: What!

ELMIRE: It's essential that you be well concealed.

ORGON: Why under this table!

ELMIRE: For Heaven's sake! let me do what I want. I have thought about my plan, and you will judge. Get under there, I tell you, and when you are there, be careful that you are neither seen nor heard.

ORGON: I confess that I am very complaisant; but I want to see the end of your enterprise.

ELMIRE: I believe that you will have nothing to reply to me. (*To her husband who is hidden under the table.*) Mind! I am going to touch upon a strange subject of conversation; do not be shocked in any way. I must be permitted to say whatever I may like, for it is to convince you as I have promised. Since I am reduced to it, I am going to make this hypocrite drop his mask by addressing sweet words to him, by flattering the shameless desires of his passion and giving him full scope for his boldness. As it is for your sake alone, and the better to confound him, that I pretend to yield to his wishes, I shall cease as soon as you show yourself, and things will go only as far as you wish. It is for you to stop his mad passion when you think matters have gone far enough, to spare your wife, and not to expose me any more than is necessary to disabuse you. It is your concern, you can control it, and . . . He is coming. Keep still and take care not to come out.

Scene 5 (TARTUFFE, ELMIRE, ORGON [*under the table*])

TARTUFFE: I have been told that you wish to speak to me here.

ELMIRE: Yes. I have secrets to reveal to you. But close this door before I tell them to you and look everywhere for fear of being overheard. A scene like the one we had before is surely not one we want here. I was never so startled in my life. Damis frightened me terribly for you, and you saw indeed that I did my utmost to change his intentions and moderate his outbursts. My confusion, it is true, was so great that I did not have the idea of contradicting him; but thank Heaven, because of that, everything has turned out for the best and is upon a much surer footing. The esteem in which you are held has dispelled the storm and my husband cannot take offense at you. The better to brave the scandal of people's nasty comments he wants us to be together at all times; and that is why I can, without fear of incurring blame, be together alone with you; and this justifies me in opening to you my heart, a little too ready, perhaps, to listen to your passion.

TARTUFFE: This language is somewhat difficult to understand, Madam, and a little while ago, you spoke in a quite different manner.

ELMIRE: Ah! if such a refusal makes you angry, how little you know the heart of a woman! How little you understand what it tries to convey when it defends itself so feebly. Our modesty will always combat, in these moments, those tender sentiments with which we may be inspired. Whatever reason we may find for the passion that subdued us, we shall always feel a little ashamed to confess it. We deny it at first, but in such a way as to give you sufficiently to understand that our heart surrenders; that for the sake of honor, words oppose our wishes, and that such refusals promise everything. Without doubt, this is making a rather daring confession to you, and showing little regard for our modesty; but since these words have at last escaped me, would I have tried so hard to restrain Damis? Would I, pray, have so complacently listened, for such a long time, to the offer of your heart? Would I have taken the matter as I have done, if the offer of your heart had had nothing in it to please me? And when I myself tried to force you to refuse the match which had just been proposed, what should such insistence have given you to understand, but the interest I was inclined to take in you, and the vexation it would have given me that this marriage should in the least divide a heart that I wish all to myself.

TARTUFFE: It is indeed an extreme pleasure, Madam, to hear these words from the lips one loves; their honey plentifully diffuses throughout every sense a sweetness I have never before tasted. The happiness of pleasing you is my supreme study, and my heart will find its beatitude in fulfilling your wishes; but, you must excuse this heart if it dares still to have some doubt in its own felicity. I may look upon these words as a sort of stratagem to compel me to break off a match that is on the point of being concluded; and if I may explain myself frankly to you, I shall not rely upon these tender words, until some of your favors, for which I sigh, have assured me of the sincerity they have expressed, and fixed in my heart a firm belief in the bewitching kindness that you have for me.

ELMIRE (*Coughs to warn her husband*): What! Would you proceed so fast and exhaust the tenderness of a heart at once? We take the greatest pains to make the sweetest declarations; meanwhile that is not enough for you, and we cannot go so far as to satisfy you, unless we push the affair to the ultimate favors?

TARTUFFE: The less we deserve a blessing, the less we dare hope for it. Our love can hardly rely upon words. We suspect easily a fate filled with happiness and we wish to enjoy it before believing in it. As for me, who knows I deserve your favors so little, I doubt the success of my rashness; and shall believe nothing, Madam, until you have convinced my passion by tangible proof.

ELMIRE: Good Heavens! how tyrannically your love acts! And into what strange confusion it throws me! With what a fierce sway it governs our hearts, and with what violence it pushes for what it desires! What! Can I find not protection from your pursuit, and will you hardly give me time to breathe? Is it decent to persist with such rigor and to insist upon your demands being satisfied immediately; and to take advantage thus, by your pressing efforts, of the weakness, which you see one has for you?

TARTUFFE: But if you look upon my addresses with a favorable eye, why do you refuse me convincing proofs?

ELMIRE: But how can I consent to what you wish without offending the Heaven of which you are always speaking?

TARTUFFE: If it is only Heaven that is opposed to my desires, it is a trifle for me to remove such an obstacle; and that need be no restraint upon your love.

ELMIRE: But they terrify us so with the judgment of Heaven!

TARTUFFE: I can dissipate these ridiculous fears for you, Madam, and I know the art of easing scruples. Heaven forbids, it is true, certain gratifications (*a scoundrel is speaking*), but there are ways of compounding those matters. According to different wants, there is a science which stretches the strings of our conscience, and which rectifies the immorality of our action with the purity of our intentions. We shall be able to initiate you into these secrets, Madam; you have only to let yourself be led by me. Satisfy my desires and have no fear; I shall be responsible for everything and shall take the sin upon myself. (ELMIRE *coughs hard.*) You are coughing very much, Madam.

ELMIRE: Yes, I am very uncomfortable.

TARTUFFE: Would you like a piece of this licorice?

ELMIRE: It's an obstinate cold, no doubt; and I know that all the licorice in the world will do nothing for it.

TARTUFFE: That is, to be sure, very annoying.

ELMIRE: Yes, more than I can say.

TARTUFFE: In short, your scruples are easily overcome. You may be sure of complete secrecy with me and the harm lies only in the stir it arouses. The scandal it creates is what constitutes the offense, and sinning in secret is not sinning at all.

ELMIRE (*After having coughed once more*): In short I see that I must resolve to yield, that I must consent to grant you everything; and that with less than this I should not expect that you be satisfied and give in. It is indeed very hard to go to that extreme and it is quite against my will that I venture this far; but since you are obstinately bent upon reducing me to this, since you will not believe anything I say, but ask for more convincing proofs, I must resolve to do it and satisfy you. If this gratification offends, so much the worse for those who force me to it: the fault certainly ought not to be mine.

TARTUFFE: Yes, Madam; I take it upon myself; and the thing in itself . . .

ELMIRE: Open the door a little and look, pray, if my husband is not in that gallery.

TARTUFFE: What need is there to take so much care about him? Between ourselves, he is a man to be led by the nose. He is likely to take pride in all our conversations and I have brought him so far that he will see everything without believing anything.

ELMIRE: It does not matter. Go out, pray, for a moment, and look carefully everywhere outside.

Scene 6 (ORGON, ELMIRE)

ORGON (*Coming from under the table*): This is, I admit to you, an abominable man! I can't get over it, and all of this stuns me completely.

ELMIRE: What! You come out so soon? You must be jesting. Get under the tablecloth again; it isn't time yet. Stay to the end to make sure of everything and do not trust mere conjectures.

ORGON: No, nothing more wicked ever came out of hell.

ELMIRE: Good Heavens! You should not believe too lightly; let yourself be fully convinced before giving in; and don't be hasty for fear of making a mistake. (*She pushes her husband behind her.*)

Scene 7 (TARTUFFE, ELMIRE, ORGON)

TARTUFFE: Everything conspires, Madam, to my satisfaction. I have surveyed this whole apartment; no one is there, and my delighted soul . . .

ORGON (*Stopping him*): Gently! you are too eager in your amorous desires, and you should not abandon yourself to your passion. Ah! ah! my good man, you wished to deceive me! How your soul gives in to temptation! You would marry my daughter and covet my wife! I have doubted for a long time that all of this was really true and I always expected that you would change your tone; but this is pushing the proof far enough: I am satisfied and wish for no more.

ELMIRE (*To* TARTUFFE): It is against my inclinations that I have done all this; but I have been reduced to the necessity of treating you thus.

TARTUFFE: What! you believe . . .

ORGON: Come, pray, no protests; get out of here; and without more ado.

TARTUFFE: My intention . . .

ORGON: These speeches are no longer of any use, you must get out of this house this very instant.

TARTUFFE: It's for you to get out, you who speak as if you were the master. The house belongs to me, I will make you realize it, and will show you plainly that it is useless to have recourse to these base tricks to pick a quarrel with me; that you are not as safe as you may think when you insult me; that I have the means of confounding and punishing imposture, of avenging offended Heaven and making those repent, who talk of turning me out of here.

Scene 8 (ELMIRE, ORGON)

ELMIRE: What kind of language is this, and what does he mean?

ORGON: To tell you the truth I am very embarrassed and this is no laughing matter.

ELMIRE: How so?

ORGON: I see my fault by what he says and the deed of gift troubles my mind.

ELMIRE: The deed of gift? . . .

ORGON: Yes, the thing is done. But I have something else that disturbs me too.

ELMIRE: What is that?

ORGON: You will know everything; but first let us see whether a certain casket is still upstairs.

ACT V

Scene 1 (ORGON, CLÉANTE)

CLÉANTE: Where would you run?

ORGON: Alas! how would I know?

CLÉANTE: It seems to me that we should begin by consulting together what can be done in this emergency.

ORGON: This casket troubles me terribly; it makes me despair more than all the rest.

CLÉANTE: This casket is then an important mystery?

ORGON: It is a deposit that Argas, this friend for whom I feel so sorry, has himself put into my hands in the greatest secrecy. He selected me for this when he fled; and from what he told me these are the papers upon which his life and fortune depend.

CLÉANTE: Why then did you entrust it into other hands?

ORGON: Merely out of a scruple of my conscience. I went straight to confide the secret to my traitor; and his arguments persuaded me to give him this casket to keep, so that, in case of any inquiry, I might be able to deny it by a ready subterfuge, whereby my conscience might be fully secure, when taking an oath contrary to the truth.

CLÉANTE: This is very bad, at least to judge from appearances; and the deed of gift and this confidence have been, to tell you my sentiments, steps which you have taken too inconsiderately. You can be carried far with such pledges; and this fellow having these advantages over you, it is a great imprudence on your part to drive him to extremities; and you ought to seek some gentler method.

ORGON: What! Under the fair appearance of such touching zeal to hide such a double-dealing heart and so wicked a soul! And I, who received him in my house poor and indigent . . . It is all over. I renounce all pious people . . . I shall henceforth hold them in utter abhorrence and shall become worse towards them, than the very devil.

CLÉANTE: Well! now you exaggerate again! You never preserve a moderate temper in anything; you never keep within reason's bounds, and always rush from one extreme to another. You see your error and realize that you have been imposed upon by a hypocritical zeal. But, in order to reform, what reason is there that you should be guilty of a worse mistake, and that you should make no difference between the heart of that perfidious rascal and those of all pious people? What! because a rascal has audaciously deceived you, under the pompous show of apparent austerity, will you insist that everyone is like him and that there is no really pious man to be found nowadays? Leave these foolish deductions to free-thinkers, distinguish between real virtue and the appearance of it; never bestow your esteem too hastily and keep it in the necessary middle course. Beware, if possible, of doing honor to imposture; but at the same time, do not attack true piety; and if you must fall into an extreme, rather offend again on the other side.

Scene 2 (DAMIS, ORGON, CLÉANTE)

DAMIS: What! father, is it true that this scoundrel threatens you, that he has forgotten all the favors that he has received and that his cowardly and too-contemptible pride turns your kindness for him against yourself?

ORGON: Yes, my son; and it causes me inconceivable grief.

DAMIS: Leave him to me, I want to cut off both his ears. Such insolence must not be tolerated; I must free you from him at once; and, to put an end to this affair, I have to strike him down.

CLÉANTE: That is spoken just like a young fellow; moderate, if you please, these violent outbursts; we live under a government, and in an age, in which violence only makes matters worse.

Scene 3 (MADAME PERNELLE, MARIANE, ELMIRE, DORINE, DAMIS, ORGON, CLÉANTE)

MADAME PERNELLE: What is this? What dreadful things do I hear?

ORGON: Some news that my own eyes have witnessed, and you see how I am repaid for my care. I harbor piously a man in his misery; I shelter him and treat him as my own brother; daily I heap favors on him; I give him my daughter and my whole fortune; and at that very moment, the perfidious, infamous wretch forms the wicked design of seducing my wife; and, not content even with these base attempts, he dares to threaten me with my own favors; and to ruin me, wants to use the advantages that my indiscreet good nature have given him; to turn me out of my estate which I have made over to him and reduce me to that condition from which I rescued him.

DORINE: Poor man!

MADAME PERNELLE: I can never believe, my son, that he wanted to commit such a black deed.

ORGON: What!

MADAME PERNELLE: Good people are always envied.

ORGON: What do you mean by this talk, mother?

MADAME PERNELLE: That there are strange doings in your house and that we know but too-well the hatred they bear him.

ORGON: What has this hatred to do with what I have told you?

MADAME PERNELLE: I have told you a hundred times when you were a little boy: virtue is always persecuted in this world; the envious will die, but envy never.

ORGON: But in what way does this bear on today's events?

MADAME PERNELLE: They may have made up a hundred idle stories against him.

ORGON: I have already told you that I saw everything myself.

MADAME PERNELLE: The malice of slanderers is very great.

ORGON: You will make me swear, mother. I have already told you that I saw this audacious crime with my own eyes.

MADAME PERNELLE: Evil tongues have always venom to scatter about, and nothing here below can guard against it.

ORGON: This is a very senseless argument. I have seen it, I tell you, seen it with my own eyes, seen, what you call seen. Must I din it a hundred times into your ears and shout like four people.

MADAME PERNELLE: My goodness! most of the time, appearances deceive; you must not always judge by what you see.

ORGON: I am getting furious.

MADAME PERNELLE: Human nature is liable to false suspicions and good is often construed as evil.

ORGON: Must I construe as a charitable design the desire to kiss my wife?

MADAME PERNELLE: It is necessary to have good reasons when you accuse people; and you should have waited until you were quite certain of the thing.

ORGON: How the devil could I be more certain? Should I have waited, mother, till before my very eyes, he had...You will make me say some foolish thing.

MADAME PERNELLE: In short his soul burns with too-pure a flame, and I cannot conceive at all that he would have attempted the things that have been mentioned.

ORGON: Come, I am so angry that if you were not my mother, I don't know what I might say to you.

DORINE: A just punishment, sir, for what happens in this world; you would not believe anyone and now no one will believe you.

CLÉANTE: We are wasting in mere trifles the time that should be spent in taking other measures. One must not sleep while a scoundrel threatens.

DAMIS: What! would his impudence go to that extreme?

ELMIRE: As for me, I do not believe that this is possible, and his ingratitude is too visible here.

CLÉANTE: Do not depend on that; he will be cunning enough to justify his doings against you, and for less than this, a powerful clique has involved people in a dismal maze. I tell you once more that armed with what he has you should never have urged him that far.

ORGON: That is true; but what could I do? At the presumption of that traitor, I was unable to master my resentment.

CLÉANTE: I wish with all my heart that we could patch up even an appearance of peace between you two.

ELMIRE: If I had known how he was armed against us I would have avoided bringing things to such a crisis, and my . . .

ORGON (To DORINE): What does this man want? Go and see quickly. I am in a fine condition to have someone come to see me.

Scene 4 (MONSIEUR LOYAL, MADAME PERNELLE, ORGON, DAMIS, MARIANE, DORINE, ELMIRE, CLÉANTE)

MONSIEUR LOYAL: Good morning, dear sister. Pray, let me speak to your master.

DORINE: He is busy, and I doubt whether he can see anyone at present.

MONSIEUR LOYAL: I have no intention of intruding in this house. I believe that my visit will have nothing to displease him, and I have come about a matter of which he will be very glad.

DORINE: Your name?

MONSIEUR LOYAL: Tell him only that I come on the part of Monsieur Tartuffe, for his good.

DORINE (To ORGON): This is a man who comes, in a civil way, from Monsieur Tartuffe, for some business about which, he says, you will be very glad.

CLÉANTE: You must see who this man is and what he wants.

ORGON: Perhaps he comes to reconcile us. How shall I behave towards him?

CLÉANTE: Your anger must not burst out; and if he speaks of an agreement, you must listen to him.

MONSIEUR LOYAL: Good day, sir. May Heaven punish those who would wrong you, and may it be as favorable to you as I wish!

ORGON: This mild beginning confirms my conjecture and already foretells some reconciliation.

MONSIEUR LOYAL: Your whole family has always been dear to me and I was servant to your father.

ORGON: Sir, I am very ashamed, and beg your pardon for not knowing your name.

MONSIEUR LOYAL: My name is Loyal, I am a native of Normandy; I am a bailiff of the upper court, in spite of envy. For forty years, thank Heaven, I have had the good fortune to fill that office with great honor; and I have come, with your leave, sir, to serve you with the writ of a certain decree.

ORGON: What! you are here . . .

MONSIEUR LOYAL: Please, no excitement, sir. This is nothing but a summons, an order to leave this house, you and yours, to take out your furniture and make room for others, without delay or remission, as required hereby.

ORGON: I! Leave this house.

MONSIEUR LOYAL: Yes, sir, if you please. The house at present, as you well know, belongs incontestably to good Monsieur Tartuffe. He is henceforth lord and master of your whole estate, by virtue of a contract of which I am the bearer. It is in due form, and cannot be contested.

DAMIS: This impudence is certainly enormous, and I admire it.

MONSIEUR LOYAL: Sir, my business is not with you; it is with this gentleman; he is both reasonable and mild; and he knows too well the duty of an honest man to oppose the law in any way.

ORGON: But . . .

MONSIEUR LOYAL: Yes, sir, I know that you would not rebel for a million in gold, and that, like a gentleman, you will allow me to execute here the orders I have received.

DAMIS: Mister bailiff, you could easily get the feel of a stick on your black gown here.

MONSIEUR LOYAL: Sir, either make your son hold his tongue or leave the room; I should be very sorry to be obliged to write this down and to see your name figure in my official report.

DORINE (*Aside*): This Mister Loyal looks very disloyal.

MONSIEUR LOYAL: I have great sympathy, sir, for all honest people, and I have charged myself with these writs only to oblige and please you, only to prevent the choice of those who, not having the same consideration for you that inspires me, might have proceeded in a less gentle way.

ORGON: And what can be worse than to order people to leave their own house?

MONSIEUR LOYAL: You are given time and I shall suspend until tomorrow the execution of the warrant, sir. I shall only come to spend the night here with ten of my helpers without a scandal and without noise. As a formality you will have to bring me the keys to your door before you go to bed, please. I shall take care not to disturb your rest and to permit nothing improper. But early tomorrow morning you must do your best to clear the house of even the least utensil. My helpers will assist you and I have picked out strong fellows to help you

remove everything. One cannot act better than I do, I think; and as I am treating you with great indulgence, I beg you also, sir, to make good use of it, so that I may not be annoyed in the execution of my duty.

ORGON (*Aside*): I would willingly give just now the best hundred gold pieces I have left for the pleasure of striking on his snout the soundest blow that ever was dealt.

CLÉANTE (*Softly to* ORGON): Leave well alone. Let us not spoil anything further.

DAMIS: I can hardly restrain myself at this strange impertinence, and my hand is itching.

DORINE: Upon my word, Monsieur Loyal, with such a broad back, a few blows of a strong stick would do you no harm.

MONSIEUR LOYAL: We might easily punish these infamous words, my girl; and there are laws against women too.

CLÉANTE: Let's stop all this, sir; we've had enough. Give us this paper right now, pray, and leave us.

MONSIEUR LOYAL: Till we see you again. May Heaven bless you all!

ORGON: And may it confound you, and the one who sent you.

Scene 5 (ORGON, CLÉANTE, MARIANE, ELMIRE, MADAME PERNELLE, DORINE, DAMIS)

ORGON: Well! mother, do you see now whether I am right; and you may judge of the rest from this performance. Do you at last see his treacheries?

MADAME PERNELLE: I am stunned and feel as if dropped from the clouds.

DORINE: You are wrong to complain, you are wrong to blame him, and his pious intentions are confirmed by this. His virtue is made perfect in the love for his neighbor. He knows that riches often corrupt man, and, out of true charity, he wants to take everything away from you that might become an obstacle to your salvation.

ORGON: Hold your tongue! these are the words I must always repeat to you.

CLÉANTE: Let's go and see what course of action you should choose.

ELMIRE: Go and expose the audacity of this ungrateful wretch. This proceeding invalidates the contract; and his treachery will appear too black to allow him to have the success which we surmise.

Scene 6 (VALERE, ORGON, CLÉANTE, ELMIRE, MARIANE)

VALÈRE: It is with great regret, sir, that I come to bother you; but I am constrained to it by a pressing danger. A very intimate and faithful friend of mine, who knows the interest which I take in what concerns you, has for my sake, by a most delicate step, violated the secrecy due to the affairs of State, and has just sent me advice, the consequence of which reduces you to the expedient of sudden flight. The scoundrel who has long imposed upon you, has accused you to the King an hour ago, and among other charges which he brings against you, has put into his hands the important casket of a state criminal, of which, he says, contrary to the duty of a subject, you have kept the guilty secret. I do not know the details of the crime laid to your charge; but a warrant has been issued against you; and to execute it better, he himself is to accompany the person who is to arrest you.

CLÉANTE: Now his rights are armed; and this is how the traitor seeks to make himself master of your estate.

ORGON: The man is, I confess, a wicked beast.

VALÈRE: The least delay may be fatal to you. I have my coach at the door to carry you off with a thousand louis which I bring you. Let us not waste any time, the blow is terrible, and is one of those that are best parried by flight. I offer myself to conduct you to a place of safety, and will accompany you to the end of your flight.

ORGON: Alas! what do I not owe to your obliging care! To thank you I must wait for another time; and I ask Heaven to be so propitious to me that I may one day acknowledge this generous service. Farewell; be careful, the rest of you.

CLÉANTE: Go quickly. We will try, brother, to do what is proper.

Scene 7 (A POLICE OFFICER, TARTUFFE, VALÈRE, ORGON, ELMIRE, MARIANE, *etc.*)

TARTUFFE: Slowly, sir, slowly, do not run so fast. You will not have to go far to find a lodging; we take you prisoner in the King's name.

ORGON: Traitor! You have reserved this blow for the last! That is the stroke, villain, by which you ruin me completely; and this crowns all your perfidies.

TARTUFFE: Your insults cannot make me angry; Heaven has taught me to suffer everything.

CLÉANTE: Your moderation is great, I confess!

DAMIS: How impudently the villain makes fun of Heaven!

TARTUFFE: All your outbursts cannot move me in the least; and I think of nothing but my duty.

MARIANE: You may glorify yourself very much upon this; and this task is very honorable for you to undertake.

TARTUFFE: A task cannot but be glorious when it proceeds from the power that sends me here.

ORGON: But did you remember, ungrateful scoundrel, that my charitable hand rescued you from a wretched condition?

TARTUFFE: Yes, I know what help I received from you; but the King's interest is my first duty. The just obligation of this sacred duty stifles all gratitude in my heart; and I would sacrifice to such a powerful consideration, friends, wife, relatives, and myself with them.

ELMIRE: The hypocrite!

DORINE: How well he knows how to make himself a cloak of all that is sacred!

CLÉANTE: But if it is as perfect as you say, this zeal which inspires you and upon which you pride yourself, why hasn't it shown itself until Orgon caught you trying to seduce his wife; and why did you not think of denouncing him until his honor obliged him to drive you from his house. I am not saying that the gift of his whole estate which he had made to you should have turned you from your duty; but, intending to treat him as a criminal today, why did you consent to take anything from him?

TARTUFFE (*To the officer*): Pray, sir, free me from this clamor, and be good enough to execute your orders.

OFFICER: Yes, we have indeed delayed too long to discharge them; your words remind me of this just in time; and to execute them, follow me at once to the prison which is destined to be your abode.

TARTUFFE: Who? I, sir?

OFFICER: Yes, you.

TARTUFFE: Why to prison?

OFFICER: I have no intention of giving you the reason. (*To* ORGON.) Compose yourself, sir, after so great an alarm. We live under a King[3] who is an enemy of fraud, a King whose eyes penetrate into the heart and whom the art of impostors cannot deceive. His great soul is blessed with sharp discernment, and always looks clearly at things; it is never betrayed by exaggeration, and his solid reason falls into no excess. He bestows lasting glory on men of worth; but he shows this zeal without blindness, and his love for sincerity does not foreclose his heart to the horror which falsehood must inspire. Even this person was not able to deceive him and he has kept clear of more artful snares. From the very beginning he has perceived, because of his great enlightenment, all the vileness concealed within his heart. In coming to accuse you, he betrayed himself, and by a just stroke of supreme justice, has shown himself to the King as a notorious rogue against whom he had received information under another

name; and his life is a long series of wicked actions, of which whole volumes might be written. Our monarch, in short, has defeated his vile ingratitude and disloyalty towards you; he has added this affair to his other misdeeds, and has placed me under his orders, only to see his impertinence carried out to the end, and to oblige him to give you full satisfaction. Yes, he wishes me to strip this traitor of all your papers which he claims to possess, and to give them to you. By his sovereign power he annuls the obligation of the contract which gave him all your estate and lastly, he forgives you this secret offense in which the flight of a friend has involved you; and this is the reward of your former zeal in upholding his rights; to show that his heart knows how to recompense a good action when you least expect it; that merit with him is never lost; and that he remembers good much better than evil.

DORINE: Heaven be praised!

MADAME PERNELLE: Now I can breathe.

ELMIRE: Happy ending!

MARIANE: Who would have dared say so?

ORGON (*To* TARTUFFE): Well, there you are, traitor . . .

CLÉANTE: Ah! brother, stop; and do not descend to indignities. Leave the wretch to his unhappy fate and do not add to the remorse that overwhelms him. Rather wish that his heart, on this day, may return to virtue; and that he may reform his life, by detesting his vice, and may soften the justice of our great King; while you throw yourself at his knees to render thanks for his kindness, which has treated you so leniently.

ORGON: Yes, this is well said. Let us throw ourselves joyfully at his feet, to praise the kindness which his heart displays to us. Then, having acquitted ourselves of this first duty, we must apply ourselves to the just cares of another, and by a sweet union crown in Valère the flame of a generous and sincere lover.

---

[3] *King:* Louis XIV (1643–1715).

HENRIK IBSEN

The Master Builder

Translated by James Walter McFarlane

Characters

HALVARD SOLNESS, *master builder*
MRS. ALINE SOLNESS, *his wife*
DR. HERDAL, *the family doctor*
KNUT BROVIK, *sometime architect, now working for Solness*
RAGNAR BROVIK, *his son, a draughtsman*
KAJA FOSLI, *his niece, a book-keeper*
HILDE WANGEL
Other women
People in the street

The action takes place in Solness's house

ACT I

A plainly furnished office in SOLNESS's *house. In the left wall, double doors lead out to the hall. On the right is the door to the inner rooms of the house. In the back wall, an open door to the drawing office. Downstage, left, a desk with books, papers, and writing materials. Upstage from the door, a stove. In the corner, right, a sofa with a table and a couple of chairs. On the table, a water carafe and glasses. Downstage, right, a smaller table with a rocking-chair and an armchair. Shaded lamps are burning on the table in the office, on the table in the corner, and on the desk.*

Within the drawing office sit KNUT BROVIK *and his son* RAGNAR, *busy with plans and calculations.* KAJA FOSLI *is standing at the desk in the office, writing in the ledger.* KNUT BROVIK *is a thin old man, with white hair and beard. He is dressed in a rather threadbare but well preserved black coat. He wears spectacles and a white cravat which has gone rather yellow.* RAGNAR BROVIK *is in his thirties, well dressed, fair-haired, with a slight stoop.* KAJA FOSLI *is a slightly-built girl in her early twenties, neatly dressed but rather delicate looking. She is wearing a green eye-shade. All three work for a while in silence.*

KNUT BROVIK (*suddenly gets up from the drawing table as though in distress and comes forward into the doorway, breathing heavily and with difficulty*): Oh, I can't stand this much longer!

KAJA (*goes across to him*): You must be feeling pretty bad tonight, are you, Uncle?

BROVIK: Oh, I think it gets worse every day.

RAGNAR (*has risen and comes over*): You'd better go home, Father. Try and get some sleep. . . .

BROVIK (*impatiently*): Go to bed, you mean? Do you want me to suffocate?

KAJA: Well, take a little walk, then.

RAGNAR: Yes, do that. I'll come with you.

BROVIK (*vehemently*): I'm not leaving before he gets back. Tonight there's going to be some plain speaking with . . . (*With suppressed bitterness.*) . . . with him . . . with the boss.

KAJA (*fearfully*): Oh no, Uncle! . . . Please let that wait!

RAGNAR: Yes, better wait, Father!

BROVIK (*struggling for breath*): Ah . . . ah . . . ! I doubt if I've got much time for waiting.

KAJA (*listening*): Sh! I can hear him coming up the steps.

All three go back to their work again. Short silence. HALVARD SOLNESS, *master builder, enters by the hall door. He is a man of mature years, strong and vigorous, with close-cut curly hair, dark moustache, and dark bushy eyebrows. He wears a grey-green jacket, buttoned-up, with a high collar and broad revers. On his head he has a soft grey felt hat, and he has a couple of folders under his arm.*

SOLNESS (*by the door, points towards the drawing office and asks in a whisper*): Have they gone?

KAJA (*in a low voice, shaking her head*): No.

She takes off her eye-shade. SOLNESS *walks across the room, throws his hat on a chair, lays the folders on the table by the sofa, and comes over towards the desk again.* KAJA *continues to write but seems nervous and uneasy.*

SOLNESS (*aloud*): What's that you are entering up, Miss Fosli?

KAJA (*starts*): Oh, it's just something that . . .

SOLNESS: Let me see. (*He bends over her, pretending to look at the ledger, and whispers.*) Kaja?

KAJA (*in a low voice, still writing*): Yes?

SOLNESS: Why do you always take that eye-shade off when I come in?

KAJA (*as before*): Because I look so awful with it on.

SOLNESS (*with a smile*): And that's something you don't want, eh, Kaja?

KAJA (*half glancing up at him*): Not for anything in the world. Not in *your* eyes.

SOLNESS (*gently stroking her hair*): Poor, poor little Kaja. . . .

KAJA (*moving her head away*): Sh! . . . They can hear you!

Solness strolls across the room to the right, turns and stops by the door into the drawing office.

SOLNESS: Has anybody been here asking for me?

RAGNAR (*gets up*): Yes, the young couple who want that villa built out at Løvstrand.

SOLNESS (*growling*): Oh, them? Well, *they'll* have to wait. I haven't got the plans straight in my mind yet.

RAGNAR (*comes closer, rather hesitantly*): They were rather anxious to have the drawings soon.

SOLNESS (*as before*): Oh Lord, yes! That's what they always want!

BROVIK (*looks up*): Because they're just dying to move into a place of their own, they said.

SOLNESS: Yes, yes! We know *that*. They're prepared to make do with anything. Find themselves . . . somewhere to live. Any kind of place to move into, that's all. But not a *home*. No thank you! If that's how it is, let them go to somebody else. Tell them *that* the next time they come.

BROVIK (*pushes his spectacles up on to his forehead and looks at him aghast*): To somebody else? Would you turn down a commission like that?

SOLNESS (*impatiently*): Yes, damn it, yes! If that's the way it is. . . . Rather that than go and build any old thing. (*Bursts out.*) Anyway, I don't know anything about these people!

BROVIK: They're substantial enough. Ragnar knows them. He's a friend of the family. Thoroughly substantial people.

SOLNESS: Oh, substantial . . . substantial! That isn't what I mean at all. Good Lord . . . don't *you* understand me now, either? (*Angrily.*) I don't want anything to do with these strangers. They can go to somebody else—anybody they like—I don't care.

BROVIK (*gets up*): Do you seriously mean that?

SOLNESS (*sulkily*): Yes, I do . . . For once.

He walks across the room. BROVIK *exchanges a glance with* RAGNAR *who makes a warning gesture, and then comes forward into the other room.*

BROVIK: I'd like a few words with you, if I may?

SOLNESS: Certainly.

BROVIK (*to* KAJA): Go along in there for a moment, Kaja.

KAJA (*uneasily*): But, Uncle . . .

BROVIK: Do as I say, child. And shut the door after you.

KAJA *goes reluctantly into the drawing office, glancing anxiously and imploringly at* SOLNESS, *and shuts the door.*

BROVIK (*lowers his voice*): I don't want these poor children to know how bad I am.

SOLNESS: Yes, you are not looking too well these days.

BROVIK: I won't last much longer. I get weaker and weaker every day.

SOLNESS: Sit down a moment.

BROVIK: Thank you, may I?

SOLNESS (*moves the armchair a little for him*): Here you are. Well?

BROVIK (*after sitting down with difficulty*): Well, it's this question of Ragnar. This is what's worrying me most. What's to become of him?

SOLNESS: Your son will of course remain with me—as long as he wants to, that is.

BROVIK: But that's just the point. He doesn't want to. He doesn't feel he can any longer.

SOLNESS: Well, he's making pretty good money, I'd have thought. But if he feels he wants more, I wouldn't say 'no' to . . .

BROVIK: No, no! It's not that at all! (*Impatiently.*) It's about time he had the chance of doing some independent work.

SOLNESS (*without looking at him*): Do you think Ragnar has the ability necessary for that?

BROVIK: That's what's so terrible. The fact is I've begun to have doubts about the boy. Because you've never once said a single encouraging word about him. All the same, I can't help feeling there *is* something there. He *must* have some ability.

SOLNESS: But he hasn't really learnt anything . . . thoroughly, I mean. Except how to draw.

BROVIK (*looks at him with suppressed hatred and says hoarsely*): You hadn't learnt much about the business either, when you were working for me. But that didn't stop you from launching out. (*Breathing with difficulty.*) Or from getting on. You went and left me standing . . . and a lot of other people as well.

SOLNESS: Well, things just ran my way.

BROVIK: You're right. Everything ran your way. So surely you haven't the heart to let me die . . . without seeing something of what Ragnar can do. And I also very much want to see them married . . . before I go.

SOLNESS (*sharply*): Does *she* want that?

BROVIK: Not Kaja so much. But Ragnar talks about it every day. (*Pleads.*) You must . . . you *must* let him try doing something on his own! I *must* see something the boy has done himself! Do you hear?

SOLNESS (*irritably*): But, damn it, commissions like that don't just grow on trees!

BROVIK: He could have a very nice commission right now. Quite a big job.

SOLNESS (*startled and uneasy*): Could he?

BROVIK: If you would give your approval.

SOLNESS: What sort of job is it?

BROVIK (*a little hesitantly*): He could get the job building that villa at Løvstrand.

SOLNESS: *That*! But I'm going to build that myself!

BROVIK: But *you're* not particularly interested in it.

SOLNESS (*flares up*): Not interested! Who says I'm not?

BROVIK: You said so yourself, just now.

SOLNESS: Oh, you shouldn't pay any attention to what I . . . *say*. Could Ragnar get the job of building that villa?

BROVIK: Yes. He knows the family, you see. And then—just for the fun of it more or less—he's drawn up plans and estimates and such like. . . .

SOLNESS: And these plans, are they pleased with them? The people who are going to live there?

BROVIK: Yes. As long as you're ready to look them over and approve them. . . .

SOLNESS: And then they would get Ragnar to build their home for them?

BROVIK: They liked his ideas very much indeed. They felt they were getting something quite new, they said.

SOLNESSS Aha! *New*! Not the sort of old-fashioned rubbish *I* generally build!

BROVIK: They thought it was somehow different.

SOLNESS (*with suppressed bitterness*): So it was Ragnar they came to see—while I was out!

BROVIK: They came to talk to you. To ask if you might be willing to withdraw . . .

SOLNESS (*flaring up*): Withdraw! Me!

BROVIK: As long as you felt that Ragnar's drawings . . .

SOLNESS: I!—Withdraw in favor of your son!

BROVIK: Withdraw from the agreement, they meant.

SOLNESS: It comes to the same thing! (*Laughs bitterly.*) So that's it! Halvard Solness—he's to start backing down now, eh? Making way for younger men. Much younger men, maybe? Just get out of the way! Out of the way!

BROVIK: Good Heavens, surely there's room here for more than just one . . . ?

SOLNESS: Oh, there isn't all that much room to spare round here. Well, that's as may be. But I'm never going to back down! I'll never give way to anybody! Never of my own free will. Never in this world will I do *that*!

BROVIK (*rises with difficulty*): Have I to die like this? An unhappy man, without any proof that I was right to have faith and confidence in Ragnar? Without ever seeing a single example of his work? Must I do this?

SOLNESS (*half turns to one side and mutters*): H'm! Stop asking me these things now.

BROVIK: I won't! Answer me! Must I die so miserably?

SOLNESS (*seems to battle with himself, then says in a low but firm voice*): You must die as best you can.

BROVIK: So be it.

He walks across the room.

SOLNESS (*follows him, half in desperation*): Don't you understand? There's nothing else *I* can do! I am what I am! And I can't change myself!

BROVIK: No, no! I suppose you can't. (*He sways and stops beside the sofa table.*) Could I have a glass of water?

SOLNESS: Of course. (*Pours a glass and hands it to him.*)

BROVIK: Thanks.

He drinks and puts the glass down. SOLNESS *walks across to the door into the drawing office and opens it.*

SOLNESS: Ragnar! You'd better come and take your father home.

RAGNAR *gets up quickly. He and* KAJA *come into the office.*

RAGNAR: What is it, Father?

BROVIK: Take my arm. Now let's go.

RAGNAR: All right. Get your things, Kaja.

SOLNESS: Miss Fosli is to stay behind. Just for a moment. There's a letter I want written.

BROVIK (*looks at* SOLNESS): Good night. Sleep well—if you can.

SOLNESS: Good night.

BROVIK *and* RAGNAR *go out by the door into the hall.* KAJA *walks over to the desk.* SOLNESS *stands with bowed head by the armchair, right.*

KAJA (*uncertainly*): Is it some letter...?

SOLNESS (*shortly*): No, of course it isn't. (*Looks sternly at her.*) Kaja!

KAJA (*frightened, in a low voice*): Yes?

SOLNESS (*points with a commanding finger at the floor*): Come over here! At once!

KAJA (*hesitating*): Yes.

SOLNESS (*as before*): Closer!

KAJA (*obeying*): What do you want me for?

SOLNESS (*looks at her for a moment*): Is it you I'm to thank for all this?

KAJA: No, no! You mustn't think that!

SOLNESS: So now you want to go and get married.

KAJA (*in a low voice*): Ragnar and I have been engaged four or five years now, and . . .

SOLNESS: And now you think it's time you did something about it. Isn't that so?

KAJA: Ragnar and Uncle say I must. So I suppose I'll have to.

SOLNESS (*more gently*): And you're also really quite fond of Ragnar, aren't you, Kaja?

KAJA: I was very fond of Ragnar once. . . . Before I came here to work for you.

SOLNESS: But not any longer? Not at all?

KAJA (*passionately clasps her hands and holds them out to him*): Oh, you know very well there's only one person I care about now! There's nobody else in the whole wide world! I'll never care for anybody else!

SOLNESS: That's what you say. Yet you are going to leave me. Leave me sitting here, alone with everything.

KAJA: But couldn't I stay on here with you, even if Ragnar . . . ?

SOLNESS (*with a deprecating gesture*): No, no, that certainly can't be done. If Ragnar goes off and starts up on his own account, he'll be needing you himself.

KAJA (*wringing her hands*): Oh, I don't see how I *can* be separated from you. It seems so utterly impossible!

SOLNESS: Then see if you can't get Ragnar to drop these stupid ideas. Go and marry him as much as you like . . . (*Changes his tune.*) Well, what I mean is—get him to stay on in this good job he's got with me. Because then I'll be able to keep you too, Kaja my dear.

KAJA: Oh yes, how lovely it would be if things worked out like that!

SOLNESS (*takes her head in his hands and whispers*): You see, I can't do without you. I must have you here near me every single day.

KAJA (*in rapture*): Oh God! Oh God!

SOLNESS (*kisses her hair*): Kaja! Kaja!

KAJA (*sinks at his feet*): Oh, how good you are to me! How incredibly good you are!

SOLNESS (*urgently*): Get up! Get up, for Heaven's sake! I think I hear somebody coming!

He helps her up. She staggers over to the desk. MRS. SOLNESS *enters by the door, right. She looks thin and drawn, with traces of former beauty. Fair hair in ringlets. Elegantly dressed, all in black. She speaks rather slowly and with a plaintive voice.*

MRS. SOLNESS (*in the doorway*): Halvard!

SOLNESS (*turns*): Oh, is that you, my dear?

MRS. SOLNESS (*with a glance at* KAJA): I'm afraid I am intruding.

SOLNESS: Not at all. Miss Fosli only has a short letter to write.

MRS. SOLNESS: So I see.

SOLNESS: What did you want me for, Aline?

MRS. SOLNESS: I just wanted to say that Dr. Herdal is in the drawing-room. Perhaps you'll join us, Halvard?

SOLNESS (*looks at her suspiciously*): H'm! Does the doctor specially want to talk to me?

MRS. SOLNESS: No, not specially. He called in to see me, but he'd like to say 'hello' to you at the same time.

SOLNESS (*laughs quietly*): I imagine he would. Well, please ask him to wait a moment.

MRS. SOLNESS: Then you'll look in and see him later?

SOLNESS: Perhaps. Later . . . later, my dear. In a little while.

MRS. SOLNESS (*with another glance at* KAJA): Well, don't forget, now, Halvard.

She withdraws, closing the door behind her.

KAJA (*in a low voice*): Oh God! Oh God! I'm sure Mrs. Solness thinks badly of me!

SOLNESS: Not at all. Not more than usual, anyway. But you'd better go now, Kaja, all the same.

KAJA: Yes, yes. I *must* go now.

SOLNESS (*sternly*): And mind you get that other matter settled for me! Do you hear!

KAJA: Oh, if it only depended on me . . .

SOLNESS: I'm telling you I want it settled. And by tomorrow at latest!

KAJA (*fearfully*): If it can't be done any other way, I'd gladly break it off with him.

SOLNESS (*flaring up*): Break it off! Have you gone mad! You'd break it off?

KAJA (*desperately*): Yes, rather that than. . . . I *must* . . . I *must* stay here with you. I can't leave you! It's utterly . . . utterly impossible!

SOLNESS (*bursting out*): But, damn it, what about Ragnar! It's Ragnar I'm . . .

KAJA (*looks at him with terror in her eyes*): Is it mainly because of Ragnar that you . . . ?

SOLNESS (*controlling himself*): No, no, of course not! You just don't understand.

(*Gently and quietly.*) It's you I want, of course. You above all, Kaja. But that's just why you've got to get Ragnar to stay in his job. There, there . . . off you go home now.

KAJA: Yes, yes. Good night.

SOLNESS: Good night. (*As she turns to go.*) Oh, by the way. Are Ragnar's drawings in there?

KAJA: Yes, I didn't see him take them.

SOLNESS: Go in and find them for me, please. I might just glance over them.

KAJA (*happily*): Oh yes, please do.

SOLNESS: For your sake, Kaja my dear. Well, do hurry up and get them for me, won't you?

KAJA *hurries into the drawing office, rummages anxiously in the table drawer, takes out a folder and brings it out.*

KAJA: Here are all the drawings.

SOLNESS: Good. Put them over there on the table.

KAJA (*putting down the folder*): Good night then. (*Pleads.*) And think kindly of me.

SOLNESS: I always do. Good night, my dear little Kaja. (*Glances to the right.*) Off you go now!

MRS. SOLNESS *and* DR. HERDAL *come in through the door, right. He is a stout, elderly man, with a round, good-humoured face, clean-shaven, with thinning fair hair and gold-rimmed spectacles.*

MRS. SOLNESS (*in the doorway*): Halvard, I can't keep the doctor waiting any longer.

SOLNESS: Well, come in, then.

MRS. SOLNESS (*to* KAJA, *who is turning down the lamp on the desk*): Finished the letter, Miss Fosli?

KAJA (*in confusion*): The letter . . . ?

SOLNESS: Yes, it was quite a short one.

MRS. SOLNESS: It must have been very short.

SOLNESS: You can go now, Miss Fosli. And see you are in good time in the morning.

KAJA: I will. Good night, Mrs. Solness.

She goes out through the hall door.

MRS. SOLNESS: How nice for you, Halvard, that you managed to find that girl.

SOLNESS: It is rather. She's useful in all sorts of ways.

MRS. SOLNESS: She seems to be.

DR. HERDAL: Good at book-keeping, too?

SOLNESS: Well . . . at least she's had a fair amount of training over the last two years. She's also pleasant and willing in every way.

MRS. SOLNESS: Yes, *that* must be very agreeable. . . .

SOLNESS: It is. Especially when one doesn't exactly enjoy a glut of that kind of thing.

MRS. SOLNESS (*mildly reproachful*): How can you say that, Halvard?

SOLNESS: Oh no, no, Aline dear. You must forgive me.

MRS. SOLNESS: It's nothing.—Well, Doctor, you'll look in again later and have tea with us?

DR. HERDAL: As soon as I've made my call, I'll be back.

MRS. SOLNESS: Thank you.

She goes out through the door, right.

SOLNESS: Are you in a hurry, Doctor?

DR. HERDAL: No, not at all.

SOLNESS: Could I have a word with you?

DR. HERDAL: With pleasure.

SOLNESS: Let's sit down. (*He beckons to the doctor to take the rocking-chair, and himself takes the armchair. Looks searchingly at him.*) Tell me. . . . Did you notice anything about Aline?

DR. HERDAL: Just now, while she was in here, you mean?

SOLNESS: Yes. In her manner towards me. Did you notice anything?

DR. HERDAL (*smiles*): Well, dash it . . . one couldn't very well help noticing that your wife . . . hm! . . .

SOLNESS: Well?

DR. HERDAL: . . . That your wife isn't particu-

larly enamoured of this Miss Fosli.

SOLNESS: Is that all? I've noticed that myself.

DR. HERDAL: Not that that's so very surprising.

SOLNESS: What?

DR. HERDAL: That she doesn't exactly like your having another woman beside you all day long.

SOLNESS: No, no, you may be right. Aline, too. But that's something that just cannot be helped.

DR. HERDAL: Couldn't you get yourself a male clerk?

SOLNESS: Grab the first man who came along? No, thank you—I wouldn't want that.

DR. HERDAL: But if your wife . . . ? Being so frail . . . What if she can't face up to this situation?

SOLNESS: Then, by God, that's just too bad! That's what I feel like saying, at least. I *must* keep Kaja Fosli. Nobody else will do, but her.

DR. HERDAL: Nobody else?

SOLNESS (*shortly*): No, nobody.

DR. HERDAL (*pulling his chair closer*): Listen to me, Mr. Solness. May I ask you a question about a rather confidential matter?

SOLNESS: Certainly.

DR. HERDAL: You know . . . women have a damn keen intuition about certain things. . . .

SOLNESS: They have. That's very true. But . . . ?

DR. HERDAL: Well, now listen. If your wife can't stand this Kaja Fosli at any price . . .

SOLNESS: Well, what of it?

DR. HERDAL: . . . Might she not in some way have certain . . . certain slight grounds for this instinctive dislike?

SOLNESS (*looks at him and rises*): Aha!

DR. HERDAL: Don't take offence! But hasn't she?

SOLNESS (*curtly and firmly*): No.

DR. HERDAL: No grounds whatsoever?

SOLNESS: None, apart from her own suspicious nature.

DR. HERDAL: I know you've known a good many women in your life.

SOLNESS: Yes, I have.

DR. HERDAL: And been pretty fond of some of them?

SOLNESS: Yes, I have that.

DR. HERDAL: But in the case of Miss Fosli...? Nothing of that sort enters into it?

SOLNESS: No, nothing at all—not on *my* side.

DR. HERDAL: And on hers?

SOLNESS: I don't think you've any right to ask that, Dr. Herdal.

DR. HERDAL: We began by talking about your wife's intuition.

SOLNESS: That's true. And for that matter... (*Drops his voice.*) In one sense, Aline's intuition, as you call it... in fact hasn't let her down.

DR. HERDAL: Well—there we are!

SOLNESS (*sits*): Dr. Herdal... I am now going to tell you a strange story. If you would care to listen to it?

DR. HERDAL: I like listening to strange stories.

SOLNESS: Very well. I dare say you remember that I took Knut Brovik and his son into my employ just after the old man had completely failed in business.

DR. HERDAL: I remember something of the kind, yes.

SOLNESS: Because actually they are both pretty clever, you know. They both have ability, in their different ways. But then the son took it into his head to get engaged. And then, of course, he began thinking of getting married ... and of setting up on his own as a builder. They all get ideas like that, young people nowadays.

DR. HERDAL (*laughs*): Yes, it's an obsession with them—this wanting to be together.

SOLNESS: Well. But that didn't suit *my* book at all. I needed Ragnar myself. And the old man, too. He's so extraordinarily clever at working out stresses and strains and cubic contents ... and all that damned rigmarole, you know.

DR. HERDAL: I dare say that's also all part of the job.

SOLNESS: It is, indeed. But Ragnar—he was absolutely intent on setting up on his own. There was no arguing with him.

DR. HERDAL: Yet he's stayed with you all the same.

SOLNESS: Yes, and I'll tell you why. One day this girl, Kaja Fosli, called in to see them for something. She'd never been here before. And when I saw how completely infatuated with each other those two were, I had an idea: if I could somehow get her into the office here, maybe Ragnar would stay, too.

DR. HERDAL: That was a fair assumption.

SOLNESS: Yes, but I never dropped the slightest hint of this at the time. I just stood and looked at her—wishing with all my soul that I had her here. Then I made one or two pleasant little remarks to her, about one thing and another. Then off she went.

DR. HERDAL: Well?

SOLNESS: Well then, the next day, in the evening after old Brovik and Ragnar had gone home, she came back here to me, and acted as though I had come to some sort of arrangement with her.

DR. HERDAL: Arrangement? What about?

SOLNESS: About the very thing I'd been wishing for. But about which I hadn't said a single word.

DR. HERDAL: Very odd.

SOLNESS: Yes, wasn't it? And then she wanted to be told what work she would be doing. Whether she could start straight away the next morning. Things like that.

DR. HERDAL: Don't you think she did it so that she could be near her young man?

SOLNESS: That also occurred to me at first. But no, that wasn't it. She seemed to drift right away from him—once she was here working for me.

DR. HERDAL: Drifted over to you?

SOLNESS: Yes, completely. I can tell she can feel me looking at her, even when her back's turned. I've only got to go near her, and at once she is all shaking and trembling. What do you make of that?

DR. HERDAL: H'm! I dare say that could be explained.

SOLNESS: Well, but what about that other matter? Her believing I'd *spoken* to her of things I'd only wished for—silently? Inwardly? To myself? Can you explain that to me, Dr. Herdal?

DR. HERDAL: No, that I can't offer to do.

SOLNESS: I might have guessed. That's why I've never felt like talking about it before. —But now, you see, it's becoming such a damned nuisance. Day after day I've got to walk about here pretending I.... And it's not fair on her, poor thing. (*Vehemently.*) But there's nothing else I *can* do! Because if she runs away from me—then away goes Ragnar, too.

DR. HERDAL: You've said nothing of all this to your wife?

SOLNESS: No.

DR. HERDAL: Why on earth don't you?

SOLNESS (*looking intently at him, and speaking in a low voice*): Because I somehow ... enjoy the mortification of letting Aline do me an injustice.

DR. HERDAL (*shaking his head*): I don't understand a single, blessed word of all this.

SOLNESS: Oh, yes. You see it's rather like paying off a tiny instalment on a huge immeasurable debt....

DR. HERDAL: To your wife?

SOLNESS: Yes. And that always eases one's mind a little. One can breathe more freely for a while, you understand.

DR. HERDAL: No, I'm damned if I understand a word....

SOLNESS (*breaks off and gets up again*): Well, well—then let's not talk any more about it. (*He wanders across the room, comes back and stops beside the table, and looks at the doctor with a sly smile.*) You must be thinking that you've got me nicely launched now, eh, Doctor?

DR. HERDAL (*rather crossly*): Nicely launched? I still don't understand you in the slightest, Mr. Solness.

SOLNESS: Oh, come now, why not admit it? I see it all too clearly.

DR. HERDAL: *What* do you see?

SOLNESS (*slowly and quietly*): That you come snooping round here to keep an eye on me.

DR. HERDAL: *I* do! Why on earth should I want to do that?

SOLNESS: Because you think I'm ... (*Flaring up.*) Well, damn it, you think the same about me as Aline does.

DR. HERDAL: And what does *she* think about you, then?

SOLNESS (*controlling himself again*): She's begun to think I'm ... so to speak ... ill.

DR. HERDAL: Ill! You! She's never said a single word about that to me. What's supposed to be wrong with you, my dear fellow?

SOLNESS (*leans over the back of the chair and whispers*): Aline thinks I'm mad. That's what she thinks.

DR. HERDAL (*rising*): But my dear Mr. Solness ...!

SOLNESS: Yes, she does, by thunder! That's how it is. And she's got you to believe it, too. Oh, I assure you, Doctor, it's quite plain to me you do ... quite plain. I'm not so easily fooled, let me tell you.

DR. HERDAL (*looks at him astounded*): Never, Mr. Solness ... never once has such a thought occurred to me.

SOLNESS (*with an incredulous smile*): Indeed? Really not?

DR. HERDAL: No, never! Nor to your wife either, I'm sure. I think I could almost swear to that.

SOLNESS: Well, perhaps you'd better not. You see, in a way ... she might have good grounds for thinking so.

DR. HERDAL: Well, now, really I must say ...!

SOLNESS (*with a gesture of his hand, interrupts*): All right, my dear Doctor ... let's not pursue this any further. It's best we agree to differ. (*Switches to a mood of quiet amusement.*) But tell me, Doctor ... hm! ...

DR. HERDAL: Yes?

SOLNESS: Since you don't think I'm ... as you might say ... ill—or crazy—or mad, or anything like that....

DR. HERDAL: You mean, what then?

SOLNESS: Then you probably imagine I'm a very happy man?

DR. HERDAL: And would that be *only* imagination?

SOLNESS (*laughs*): No, no! Of course not! Heaven forbid! Think what it is to be Solness, the master builder! Halvard Solness! Oh yes, I'm grateful all right!

DR. HERDAL: Well, I must say *I* reckon you've had quite incredible luck on your side.

SOLNESS (*suppressing a sad smile*): Yes, I have. I can't complain.

DR. HERDAL: First, that ghastly old fortress of a house of yours went and burnt down. That was a real bit of luck.

SOLNESS (*seriously*): It was Aline's family home that burnt down. Remember that.

DR. HERDAL: Yes, it must have been a sad loss to her.

SOLNESS: She's never got over it, not to this very day. Not in all these twelve or thirteen years.

DR. HERDAL: The thing that followed must have been the worst blow of all for her.

SOLNESS: The two things together.

DR. HERDAL: But you yourself . . . you saw your chance and took it. Started out as a poor country lad, and now look at you—at the top of your profession. Yes indeed, Mr. Solness, you certainly have had all the luck.

SOLNESS (*glances nervously at him*): Yes. That's what makes me feel so horribly afraid.

DR. HERDAL: Afraid? Because you have all the luck?

SOLNESS: Night and day it terrifies me . . . terrifies me. Some day, you see, that luck must change.

DR. HERDAL: Nonsense! What is going to change it?

SOLNESS (*firmly and definitely*): Youth is.

DR. HERDAL: Puh! Youth! I wouldn't have said you were exactly decrepit yet. Oh no! I'd say you were more firmly established here now than you've ever been.

SOLNESS: The turn is coming. I can sense it. I feel it getting nearer. Somebody or other is going to demand: Make way for me! And then all the others will come storming up,

threatening and shouting: Get out of the way! Get out of the way! Yes, just you watch, Doctor! One of these days, youth is going to come here beating on the door. . . .

DR. HERDAL (*laughs*): Well, good Lord, what of it?

SOLNESS: What of it? Just that that will mean the end of Master Builder Solness. (*There is a knock on the door, left. He starts.*) What's that! Did you hear something?

DR. HERDAL: Somebody's knocking.

SOLNESS (*loudly*): Come in!

HILDE WANGEL *comes in by the door from the hall. She is of medium height, lithe, of slim build. Slightly tanned by the sun. She wears walking clothes, with her skirt hitched up, a sailor's collar open at the neck, and a small sailor hat on her head. She has a rucksack on her back, a plaid in a strap, and a long alpenstock.*

HILDE WANGEL (*walks across to* SOLNESS, *her eyes shining and happy*): Good evening!

SOLNESS (*looks uncertainly at her*): Good evening. . . .

HILDE (*laughing*): I do believe you don't recognize me.

SOLNESS: Well . . . in actual fact . . . just for the moment. . . .

DR. HERDAL (*approaches her*): But I recognize you, young lady. . . .

HILDE (*delighted*): Well, if it isn't . . .

DR. HERDAL: It most certainly is. (*To* SOLNESS.) We met earlier this summer at one of those hostels up in the mountains. (*To* HILDE.) What happened to the other ladies?

HILDE: Oh, they went further west.

DR. HERDAL: I don't think they liked us making all that noise in the evening.

HILDE: No, I'm sure they didn't.

DR. HERDAL (*wagging his finger*): Moreover, it cannot be denied that you *did* rather flirt with us a little.

HILDE: Well, it was much more fun than sitting knitting socks with all those old ladies.

DR. HERDAL (*laughs*): I entirely agree.

SOLNESS: Have you just come to town this evening?

HILDE: Yes, I've just arrived.

DR. HERDAL: All alone, Miss Wangel?

HILDE: Certainly!

SOLNESS: Wangel? Is your name Wangel?

HILDE (*looks at him with amused surprise*): Of course it is.

SOLNESS: Could you by any chance be the daughter of the doctor up at Lysanger?

HILDE (*as before*): Yes. Who else would I be the daughter of?

SOLNESS: Well, so that's where we met each other. The summer I was up there building a tower on the old church.

HILDE (*more seriously*): Yes, that was the occasion.

SOLNESS: Well, that's a long time ago.

HILDE (*looking steadily at him*): Ten years ago exactly.

SOLNESS: I imagine you were only a child at the time.

HILDE (*casually*): About twelve or thirteen, at any rate.

DR. HERDAL: Is this the first time you've been to town, Miss Wangel?

HILDE: Yes, it is.

SOLNESS: And perhaps you don't know anybody here?

HILDE: Nobody but you. Oh, and your wife.

SOLNESS: So you know *her*, too?

HILDE: Only slightly. I met her when she was spending a few days up in the mountains for her health. . . .

SOLNESS: Ah, up *there*.

HILDE: She said I must be sure to call on her if ever I was in town. (*Smiles.*) Not that that was necessary.

SOLNESS: Odd that she never mentioned it. . . .

HILDE *puts her stick down by the stove, takes off her rucksack and puts it and the plaid on the sofa.* DR. HERDAL *moves across to help her.* SOLNESS *stands looking at her.*

HILDE (*going up to him*): May I ask if I can stay the night?

SOLNESS: I'm sure that can be arranged.

HILDE: Because I haven't any other clothes apart from what I've got on. Oh, and a set of underclothes in my rucksack. But they'll need washing—they're filthy.

SOLNESS: That's easily managed. I'll just tell my wife. . . .

DR. HERDAL: Meanwhile I'll go and see my patient.

SOLNESS: Yes, do that. And you'll be looking in again later.

DR. HERDAL (*merrily, with a glance at* HILDE): You're damned right I shall. (*Laughs.*) So you were right in your forecast after all, Mr. Solness!

SOLNESS: In what way?

DR. HERDAL: Youth *has* come knocking at your door.

SOLNESS (*cheerfully*): Yes, but in rather a different way.

DR. HERDAL: It is indeed! No doubt about it!

He goes out through the hall door. SOLNESS *opens the door, right, and speaks into the side room.*

SOLNESS: Aline! Could you come in, please? There's a Miss Wangel here, whom I believe you know.

MRS. SOLNESS (*appears in the doorway*): Who is it, do you say? (*Sees* HILDE.) Oh, is it you? (*Goes across to shake hands.*) So you did come to town after all.

SOLNESS: Miss Wangel has just arrived. She is wondering if she can stay the night.

MRS. SOLNESS: Here with us? Yes, with pleasure.

SOLNESS: To get herself tidied up a little, you understand.

MRS. SOLNESS: I shall do what I can for you. It's no more than my duty. Your luggage will be coming along later, I suppose?

HILDE: I have no luggage.

MRS. SOLNESS: Well, I'm sure everything will be all right, nevertheless. Now, if you don't mind being left here with my husband for a moment, I'll see about getting a room ready for you.

SOLNESS: Can't we use one of the nurseries? They're all ready.

MRS. SOLNESS: Oh, yes. We've plenty of room *there.* (*To* HILDE.) You sit down and rest a little.

She goes out, right. HILDE *wanders about the room, her hands behind her back, looking at this and that.* SOLNESS *stands down by the table, also with his hands behind his back, following her with his eyes.*

HILDE (*stops and looks at him*): Do you have more than one nursery, then?

SOLNESS: There are three nurseries in the house.

HILDE: That's a lot. You must have many children.

SOLNESS: No, we have no children. But now *you* can be the child while you're here.

HILDE: For tonight, yes. I won't cry. I'm going to try and sleep like a log, if I can.

SOLNESS: Yes, I imagine you must be very tired.

HILDE: No, I'm not! But it makes no difference. . . . Because it's absolutely marvellous to lie in bed like that and dream.

SOLNESS: Do you often dream at night?

HILDE: Yes, I do! Almost always.

SOLNESS: What do you dream about mostly?

HILDE: I'm not saying tonight. Some other time—perhaps.

She again wanders about the room, stops by the desk, and turns over some of the books and papers.

SOLNESS (*walks over to her*): Looking for something?

HILDE: No, I'm just looking at all these things. (*Turns.*) Perhaps I mustn't?

SOLNESS: Please do.

HILDE: Is it you who writes in this big ledger?

SOLNESS: No, it's my book-keeper.

HILDE: A woman?

SOLNESS (*smiles*): Yes, of course.

HILDE: And she belongs to the office?

SOLNESS: Yes.

HILDE: Is she married?

SOLNESS: No, she's single.

HILDE: I see.

SOLNESS: But I think she's getting married soon.

HILDE: That's nice for *her.*

SOLNESS: But it's not so nice for *me.* Because then I'll have nobody to help me.

HILDE: Can't you find somebody else just as good?

SOLNESS: Perhaps you'd like to stay here—and write things in the ledger?

HILDE (*looks scornfully at him*): Not likely! No, thank you—we're not having anything of that! (*She again walks about the room and sits in the rocking-chair.* SOLNESS *also walks across to the table.* HILDE *continues as before.*) . . . There must be better things to do around here than that! (*Looks at him with a smile.*) Don't you agree?

SOLNESS: Of course. First of all you'll be wanting to go round the shops and get yourself all rigged out.

HILDE (*gaily*): No, I rather think I'll give *that* a miss!

SOLNESS: Oh?

HILDE: Yes. You see, I've spent all my money.

SOLNESS (*laughs*): No luggage and no money, eh?

HILDE: Neither. But, hell! What's it matter?

SOLNESS: You know, I like you for that!

HILDE: Only for *that*?

SOLNESS: That—and other things. (*Sits down in the armchair.*) Is your father still alive?

HILDE: Yes, he's alive.

SOLNESS: And now perhaps you are thinking of studying here?

HILDE: That hadn't occurred to me.

SOLNESS: But you'll be staying here some time, I dare say?

HILDE: All depends how things go. (*She sits for a moment rocking herself, looking at him half-seriously, half-smiling. Then she takes off her hat and puts it on the table in front of her.*) Mr. Solness?

SOLNESS: Yes?

HILDE: Are you very forgetful?

SOLNESS: Forgetful? Not as far as I know.

HILDE: Don't you want to talk to me at all about what happened up there?

SOLNESS (*momentarily startled*): Up at Lysanger? (*Casually.*) Well, there wasn't all that much to talk about, I don't think.

HILDE (*looks reproachfully at him*): How can you sit there and say a thing like that!

SOLNESS: Well, suppose *you* talk to me about it, then.

HILDE: When the tower was finished, there were great goings-on in town.

SOLNESS: Yes, I shan't forget that day so easily.

HILDE: Won't you? That *is* nice of you!

SOLNESS: Nice?

HILDE: There was a band in the churchyard. And hundreds and hundreds of people. We schoolgirls were dressed in white. And all of us had flags.

SOLNESS: Ah yes, those flags! Those I do remember.

HILDE: Then you climbed straight up the scaffolding. Right to the very top. And you had a big wreath with you. And you hung that wreath right on the top of the weathercock.

SOLNESS (*curtly interrupting*): I used to do that in those days. It's an old custom.

HILDE: It was wonderfully exciting, standing down there and looking up at you. Imagine now—if he were to fall! The master builder himself!

SOLNESS (*as though dismissing the matter*): Yes, yes, and it might very easily have happened. Because one of those little devils in white was shouting and yelling at me so much. . . .

HILDE (*her eyes sparkling with joy*): 'Hurrah for Mr. Solness!' 'Hurrah for the master builder!' Yes!

SOLNESS: . . . And waving and flapping her flag so much that I . . . that I almost grew dizzy at the sight of it.

HILDE (*more quietly, seriously*): That little

devil—was *me*.

SOLNESS (*looking fixedly at her*): I can see it was now. It *must* have been you.

HILDE (*once more animated*): It was marvellous—terribly exciting! I couldn't believe any builder in the world could have built such an enormously high tower. And then you yourself went and stood right at the very top! As large as life! And not even the slightest bit dizzy. The very thought of it made me sort of . . . dizzy.

SOLNESS: What made you so sure that I wasn't . . . ?

HILDE (*dismissing the idea*): Oh, don't be silly! I felt it inside me. For otherwise you couldn't have stood up there singing.

SOLNESS (*looks at her in amazement*): Singing? I sang?

HILDE: You most certainly did.

SOLNESS (*shaking his head*): I've never sung a note in my life.

HILDE: Yes, you have. You sang then. It sounded like harps in the air.

SOLNESS (*thoughtfully*): There's something very strange about this.

HILDE (*is silent a moment, looks at him, and says in a low voice*): But it was then—afterwards—that the real thing happened.

SOLNESS: The real thing?

HILDE (*sparkling and animated*): Surely I don't have to remind you about *that*?

SOLNESS: Yes, please! Remind me a little about that, too.

HILDE: Don't you remember they gave a big dinner for you at the club?

SOLNESS: Ah, yes. That must have been the same evening. Because I left the next morning.

HILDE: And after the club you were invited home to us.

SOLNESS: That's quite right, Miss Wangel. It's amazing how well you have remembered all these little details.

HILDE: Little details! I like that! Was it merely a little detail that I happened to be alone in the room when you arrived?

SOLNESS: Were you?

HILDE (*without answering him*): You didn't call me a little devil that time.

SOLNESS: I don't suppose I did.

HILDE: You said that I looked lovely in my white dress. That I looked like a little princess.

SOLNESS: And I'm sure you did, Miss Wangel. Added to the fact that . . . I felt so light and free that day.

HILDE: And then you said that when I grew up I should be *your* princess.

SOLNESS (*laughs a little*): Well, well. . . . Did I say that, too?

HILDE: Yes, you did. And when I asked how long I had to wait, you said you'd come back in ten years—like a troll—and carry me off. To Spain or somewhere. And there you promised you'd buy me a kingdom.

SOLNESS (*as before*): Well, after a good dinner you're not always in a mood to count your coppers. But did I really say all this?

HILDE (*laughing quietly*): Yes. And you also said what this kingdom would be called.

SOLNESS: Well?

HILDE: It was to be called the Kingdom of Orangia, you said.

SOLNESS: Well, that's an appetizing sort of name.

HILDE: I didn't like it a bit. It sounded as if you were trying to make fun of me.

SOLNESS: I'm sure that wasn't my intention.

HILDE: Indeed I should hope not. Considering what you did after that. . . .

SOLNESS: What on earth did I do after that?

HILDE: Oh, I might have known you'd say you'd forgotten that, too! Surely one couldn't help remembering a thing like that!

SOLNESS: Well, just give me a little hint, and I might. . . . Well?

HILDE (*looks steadily at him*): You went and kissed me, Mr. Solness.

SOLNESS (*open-mouthed, rises from his chair*): I *did*!

HILDE: Yes, you did. You took me in your arms and bent me backwards and kissed me. Many times.

SOLNESS: Really now, my dear Miss Wangel . . . !

HILDE (*getting up*): You're not going to deny it!

SOLNESS: I certainly do deny it!

HILDE (*looks scornfully at him*): Well, well!

She turns and walks slowly across to the stove, where she remains standing, motionless, her back turned, and her hands clasped behind her. Short pause.

SOLNESS (*walks warily up behind her*): Miss Wangel . . . ? (HILDE *remains silent and motionless.*) Don't stand there like a statue. All this you've just told me—it must be something you've dreamt. (*Puts his hand on her arm.*) Listen, now . . . (HILDE *makes an impatient gesture with her arm.* SOLNESS *speaks as though a thought suddenly strikes him.*) Or . . . wait a moment! There's more in this than meets the eye, I tell you. (HILDE *does not move.* SOLNESS *speaks quietly but emphatically.*) I must have *thought* it all. I must have willed it . . . wished it . . . desired it. And then. . . . Mightn't that be the explanation? (HILDE *remains silent.* SOLNESS *speaks impatiently.*) All right, damn it . . . ! So I *did* do it then!

HILDE (*turns her head a little without actually looking at him*): Then you admit it?

SOLNESS: Yes, anything you like.

HILDE: That you put your arms round me?

SOLNESS: Yes.

HILDE: And bent me back?

SOLNESS: Right back.

HILDE: And kissed me?

SOLNESS: Yes, I did.

HILDE: Many times?

SOLNESS: As many as you like.

HILDE (*quickly turns to face him, her eyes once again shining with happiness*): There, you see! I finally got it out of you!

SOLNESS (*with a faint smile*): Yes. Imagine me forgetting a thing like that.

HILDE (*walks away from him, again a little*

sulky): Oh, I suppose you must have kissed many women in your time.

SOLNESS: No, you mustn't believe that of me. (HILDE *sits in the armchair, while* SOLNESS *stands leaning against the rocking-chair, watching her intently.*) Miss Wangel?

HILDE: Yes?

SOLNESS: What happened then? What followed . . . between you and me?

HILDE: Nothing followed. You know that very well. Because then all the other guests arrived, and . . . Pah!

SOLNESS: That's right. The others arrived. Fancy me forgetting *that* as well.

HILDE: Oh, you haven't forgotten anything. You just felt a bit ashamed. One doesn't forget a thing like that, I know.

SOLNESS: No, one wouldn't think so.

HILDE (*looks at him vivaciously again*): Or maybe you've also forgotten what date it was?

SOLNESS: What date . . . ?

HILDE: Yes, what date was it when you hung the wreath on the tower? Well? Tell me— quickly!

SOLNESS: Hm! The actual date I'm afraid I've forgotten. All I know is it was ten years ago. Some time in the autumn.

HILDE (*nods slowly several times*): It was ten years ago. The nineteenth of September.

SOLNESS: Yes, it must have been about then. Fancy you remembering that as well! (*Stops.*) But wait a moment . . . ! Today's the nineteenth of September.

HILDE: It is indeed. And the ten years are up. And you didn't come . . . as you promised me you would.

SOLNESS: Promised you? Threatened you, you mean probably?

HILDE: I didn't think of it as a threat.

SOLNESS: Well then, I was probably fooling.

HILDE: Was that all you wanted to do? Make a fool of me?

SOLNESS: Or joking, probably. Heavens above, I can't remember now. But it must have been something like that. After all, you were only a child at the time.

HILDE: Ah, maybe I wasn't such a child as all that! Not such a babe as you think.

SOLNESS (*looks searchingly at her*): Did you honestly think in all seriousness that I'd come back?

HILDE (*with a half-suppressed roguish smile*): Of course! I expected *that* much of you.

SOLNESS: That I'd come to your home and carry you off with me?

HILDE: Just like a troll—yes!

SOLNESS: And make you a princess?

HILDE: That's what you promised.

SOLNESS: And give you a kingdom too?

HILDE (*looks up at the ceiling*): Why not? It didn't actually have to be an ordinary, real kingdom.

SOLNESS: But something else just as good?

HILDE: Yes, at least as good. (*Looks at him for a moment.*) If you could build the highest church tower in the world, I thought to myself, then surely you'd be able to arrange some kind of kingdom or other.

SOLNESS (*shaking his head*): I don't really follow you, Miss Wangel.

HILDE: Don't you? It seems simple enough to me.

SOLNESS: No, I just can't make out if you mean all you say. Or whether you are just joking. . . .

HILDE (*smiles*): My turn to make a fool of you, perhaps?

SOLNESS: Exactly. To make . . . fools of us both. (*Looks at her.*) Did you know that I was married?

HILDE: Yes, I've known it all along. Why do you ask that?

SOLNESS (*casually*): Oh, I was just wondering. (*Looks earnestly at her and says quietly.*) Why have you come?

HILDE: Because I want my kingdom. The time's up.

SOLNESS (*with an involuntary laugh*): Ha! That's good!

HILDE (*gaily*): Bring out my kingdom, master builder! (*Raps with her finger.*) My kingdom on the table!

SOLNESS (*pushes the rocking-chair closer and sits down*): Seriously—why have you come? What in fact do you want here?

HILDE: Oh, first I want to go round and look at all the things you've built.

SOLNESS: That's going to keep you pretty busy.

HILDE: Yes, I know you've built an awful lot.

SOLNESS: I have. Especially in recent years.

HILDE: Many church towers, too? Great high ones, I mean?

SOLNESS: No, I don't build church towers any more. Nor churches either.

HILDE: What do you build now, then?

SOLNESS: Homes for people.

HILDE (*pensively*): Couldn't you . . . try putting some kind of tower on them too?

SOLNESS (*starts*): What do you mean by that?

HILDE: I mean . . . something pointing . . . right up into the air. With a weathercock on top at a great dizzy height.

SOLNESS (*muses a little*): Strange you should say that. That's what I want to do more than anything.

HILDE (*impatiently*): Then why don't you?

SOLNESS (*shakes his head*): Because people don't want that.

HILDE: Fancy not wanting it!

SOLNESS (*in a lighter vein*): But now I'm building a new house for myself. Just across the way here.

HILDE: For yourself?

SOLNESS: Yes. It's just about ready. And *it's* got a tower.

HILDE: A high tower?

SOLNESS: Yes.

HILDE: Very high?

SOLNESS: People are sure to say it's too high. For a house.

HILDE: I'll be out first thing in the morning to see that tower.

SOLNESS (*sits with his hand on his cheek gazing at her*): Tell me, Miss Wangel . . . what's your name? Your first name, I mean?

HILDE: My name's Hilde, of course.

SOLNESS (*as before*): Hilde? Really?

HILDE: Don't you remember? You called me Hilde yourself. The day you—misbehaved.

SOLNESS: Did I also do that?

HILDE: But that time you said 'Little Hilde'. And that I didn't like.

SOLNESS: So you didn't like that, Miss Hilde?

HILDE: No. Not on an occasion like that. But 'Princess Hilde', however. . . . That will sound rather well, I think.

SOLNESS: Yes, indeed. Princess Hilde of . . . of . . . What was to be the name of that kingdom?

HILDE: Pah! I don't want to hear any more about *that* stupid kingdom. I'm going to want a very different sort.

SOLNESS (*has leant back in the chair, still gazing at her*): Isn't it strange. . . . The more I think about it, the more I seem to have been tormenting myself for years . . . hm!

HILDE: How?

SOLNESS: . . . Trying to identify . . . some experience I felt I must have forgotten. But I never discovered what it could have been.

HILDE: You should have tied a knot in your handkerchief, master builder.

SOLNESS: Then I'd only have gone about worrying what the knot was for.

HILDE: Ah yes, I dare say you find trolls of *that* sort, too.

SOLNESS (*getting up slowly*): How very good it is that you've come to me now.

HILDE (*looks deep into his eyes*): Is it good?

SOLNESS: I've been so alone here. Staring at everything, so utterly helpless. (*Lowers his voice.*) I tell you—I have begun to be so afraid, so terribly afraid, of youth.

HILDE (*snorting*): Pah! Is youth anything to be afraid of!

SOLNESS: Yes, it is. That's why I've locked and barred myself in. (*Secretively.*) I tell you, youth will come here and beat on my door, and force its way in!

HILDE: Then I think you'd better go out and open up for youth.

SOLNESS: Open up?

HILDE: Yes. And let youth in. On friendly terms.

SOLNESS: No, no, no! Can't you see! Youth brings retribution. It is in the vanguard of change. . . . Marching under a new banner.

HILDE (*rises and looks at him and says, her mouth trembling*): Can you use *me*, master builder.

SOLNESS: Yes, I can indeed! For you too seem to be marching under a new banner. Youth against youth . . . !

DR. HERDAL *comes in through the hall door.*

DR. HERDAL: Ah. . . . You and Miss Wangel still here?

SOLNESS: Yes. We have had many things to talk about, we two.

HILDE: Things old and new.

DR. HERDAL: Have you now!

HILDE: And it's been such fun. Mr. Solness has a quite incredible memory. He remembers everything, right down to the final detail.

MRS. SOLNESS *comes in by the door, right.*

MRS. SOLNESS: There we are now, Miss Wangel. Your room is ready.

HILDE: Oh, how very kind of you!

SOLNESS (*to his wife*): The nursery?

MRS. SOLNESS: Yes. The middle one. But we must have something to eat first.

SOLNESS (*nods to* HILDE): So Hilde sleeps in the nursery.

MRS. SOLNESS (*looks at him*): Hilde?

SOLNESS: Yes, Miss Wangel is called Hilde. I used to know her when she was a child.

MRS. SOLNESS: Did you now, Halvard! Well, come along in. Supper's ready.

She takes DR. HERDAL'*s arm and goes out with him, right. Meanwhile* HILDE *has gathered her things together.*

HILDE (*softly and quickly to* SOLNESS): Was it true what you said? Can you use me in some way?

SOLNESS (*taking her things from her*): You are the very one I have needed most.

HILDE (*looks at him in joy and wonder and clasps her hands*): Oh, praise be . . . !

SOLNESS (*tense*): Well?

HILDE: Then I *have* my kingdom!

SOLNESS (*involuntarily*): Hilde . . . !

HILDE (*again her mouth trembling*): Almost— I was going to say.

She goes out, right. SOLNESS *follows her.*

ACT II

One of the smaller sitting-rooms in SOLNESS'*s house; pleasantly furnished. In the back wall is a glass door giving out on to the verandah and the garden. Across the right corner is a large bay window, in which stand plant-holders. Corresponding to this, in the left corner, is a bay containing a small door papered like the wall. In each of the side walls is an ordinary door. Downstage right, a console table with a large mirror. Flowers and plants in rich profusion. Downstage left, a sofa with a table and chairs. Further back, a bookcase. Well out into the room, in front of the bay window, a small table and a couple of chairs. It is early in the day.*

SOLNESS *is sitting at the small table, with* RAGNAR BROVIK'*s folder open in front of him. He turns over the drawings, and looks closely at some of them.* MRS. SOLNESS *walks noiselessly about with a little watering-can, watering the flowers. She is dressed in black, as before. Her hat, coat, and parasol are lying on a chair by the mirror.* SOLNESS *follows her occasionally with his eyes without her noticing. Neither of them speaks.*

KAJA FOSLI *quietly enters by the door on the left.*

SOLNESS (*turning his head and speaking casually*): Oh, it's you, is it?

KAJA: I just wanted to let you know I'd arrived.

SOLNESS: Yes, yes, very good. Isn't Ragnar there too?

KAJA: No, not yet. He had to stay and wait

for the doctor. But he's coming along later to ask you about . . .

SOLNESS: How is the old man today?

KAJA: Bad. He says he's very sorry but he'll have to stay in bed today.

SOLNESS: Of course he must. But you'd better get on with your work now.

KAJA: Yes. (*Stops by the door.*) Will you be wanting to speak to Ragnar when he comes?

SOLNESS: No—not particularly.

KAJA *goes out again, left.* SOLNESS *remains sitting, looking through the drawings.*

MRS. SOLNESS (*over by the plants*): I shouldn't wonder if he, too, died.

SOLNESS (*looks at her*): He too? Who else do you mean?

MRS. SOLNESS: Ah yes. Old Mr. Brovik—he's also going to die now, Halvard. You'll see.

SOLNESS: Aline dear, don't you think you should go for a little walk?

MRS. SOLNESS: Yes, I suppose I should.

She carries on attending to the flowers.

SOLNESS (*bent over the drawings*): Is she still asleep?

MRS. SOLNESS (*looks at him*): Is it Miss Wangel you are sitting there thinking about.

SOLNESS (*carelessly*): I just happened to think of her.

MRS. SOLNESS: Miss Wangel was up long ago.

SOLNESS: Was she indeed?

MRS. SOLNESS: When I looked in, she was sitting there seeing to her things.

She steps in front of the mirror and begins slowly to put her hat on.

SOLNESS (*after a short pause*): So we did find a use for one of the nurseries after all, Aline.

MRS. SOLNESS: Yes, we did.

SOLNESS: And I think it's better that way than having everything standing empty.

MRS. SOLNESS: The emptiness is dreadful. You are right.

SOLNESS (*closes the folder, rises and walks over to her*): You'll see, Aline—from now on things are going to be better. Much nicer. Life's going to be easier—especially for *you.*

MRS. SOLNESS (*looks at him*): From now on?

SOLNESS: Yes. Believe me, Aline . . .

MRS. SOLNESS: You mean—because *she's* come?

SOLNESS (*controlling himself*): What I mean of course is . . . once we've moved into the new house.

MRS. SOLNESS (*taking her coat*): You think so, Halvard? That things will be any better *then?*

SOLNESS: I can't honestly see why not. Surely you believe they will, too?

MRS. SOLNESS: Where that new house is concerned, I can't believe anything.

SOLNESS (*displeased*): I am very sorry to hear it. Because it's mainly for your sake I've built it.

He goes to help her on with her coat.

MRS. SOLNESS (*moves away*): You already do far too much for my sake.

SOLNESS (*with some vehemence*): Now, now, you mustn't say things like that, Aline! I can't bear to hear you say things like that.

MRS. SOLNESS: Very well, Halvard, I won't say them.

SOLNESS: But I meant what I said. You'll see —you are going to find everything very nice over in the new place.

MRS. SOLNESS: Oh, God! Nice . . . for me!

SOLNESS (*eagerly*): Yes, yes, you will! I am sure you will. You know . . . all sorts of things there are going to remind you of what was once your . . .

MRS. SOLNESS: Of what had once been Father's and Mother's. And which was all burnt down.

SOLNESS (*in a low voice*): Yes, yes, poor Aline. That was a dreadful blow for you.

MRS. SOLNESS (*cries out in grief*): Build as

much as you will, Halvard—you can never build another real home for me!

SOLNESS (*walks across the room*): Then for God's sake let's say no more about it.

MRS. SOLNESS: We never do talk about it, generally. You just avoid the subject . . .

SOLNESS (*halts abruptly and looks at her*): I do? And why should I do that? Avoid the subject?

MRS. SOLNESS: Oh, Halvard, I understand you so well. It's because you want to spare me. And to show me you forgive me—as far as you ever can.

SOLNESS (*stares in astonishment*): Forgive *you*! You really mean you yourself, Aline!

MRS. SOLNESS: Of course it's myself I mean.

SOLNESS (*involuntarily to himself*): That too!

MRS. SOLNESS: As for the old house—what happened was meant to be. Heavens, when fate strikes . . .

SOLNESS: Yes, you are right. There's no escaping fate—as they say.

MRS. SOLNESS: But the terrible things that followed the fire . . . ! *That's* something I can never . . . never . . . never . . .

SOLNESS (*vehemently*): Don't think about it, Aline!

MRS. SOLNESS: I must think about it. And talk about it sometimes, too. Because I don't think I can bear it any longer. Knowing I can never forgive myself . . .

SOLNESS (*exclaiming*): Yourself!

MRS. SOLNESS: Yes, because really I had two loyalties. One to you, and one to the children. I should have been hard. Not let the horror of it overwhelm me. Or grief either, because my home was burnt down. (*Wrings her hands.*) Oh, if only I *could* have, Halvard!

SOLNESS (*gently, moved, comes towards her*): Aline . . . you must promise me you'll never again think these thoughts. . . . Please, promise me that, my dear!

MRS. SOLNESS: Oh, God! . . . Promise! promise! Anybody can promise anything. . . .

SOLNESS (*clenches his hands and walks across the room*): Oh, this is hopeless! Never so much as a glint of the sun! Not a glimmer of light ever enters this home!

MRS. SOLNESS: This is no home, Halvard.

SOLNESS: Ah, no, you're right there. And God knows, perhaps you're right to think it's not going to be any better for us in the new house either.

MRS. SOLNESS: It never will. Just as empty . . . just as desolate there as it is here.

SOLNESS (*vehemently*): Then why on earth have we built it? Can you tell me that?

MRS. SOLNESS: No, that you must answer yourself.

SOLNESS (*glances at her suspiciously*): What do you mean by *that*, Aline?

MRS. SOLNESS: What do I mean?

SOLNESS: Yes, damn it! You said it so strangely. As though you were insinuating something.

MRS. SOLNESS: No, I assure you . . .

SOLNESS (*goes closer*): Oh, I know how things are, thank you very much. I've got eyes *and* I've got ears, Aline! Believe you me!

MRS. SOLNESS: But what is all this? What is it?

SOLNESS (*stands in front of her*): You always manage to find some sly, hidden meaning even in my most innocent remarks, don't you?

MRS. SOLNESS: Do I? Do *I* do that?

SOLNESS (*laughs*): Ha! ha! ha! But that's only natural, Aline! When you've got to cope with a sick man in the house. . . .

MRS. SOLNESS (*alarmed*): Sick? Are you sick, Halvard?

SOLNESS (*shouts*): A madman then! A lunatic! Call me what you will.

MRS. SOLNESS (*fumbles for the back of the chair and sits down*): Halvard . . . for God's sake . . . !

SOLNESS: But you're wrong, both of you. Both you and the doctor. There's nothing like that wrong with me. (*He walks up and down the room.* MRS. SOLNESS *follows him anxiously with her eyes. Then he walks across to her and says calmly.*) Actually, there's absolutely nothing wrong with me.

MRS. SOLNESS: No, of course not. But what's troubling you, then?

SOLNESS: Just that sometimes I feel as if I'm cracking up under this terrible burden of debt. . . .

MRS. SOLNESS: Debt, you say? But you're not in debt to anyone, Halvard!

SOLNESS (*quietly, with emotion*): Endlessly in debt to you . . . to you . . . to you, Aline.

MRS. SOLNESS (*slowly rising*): What is behind all this? You might as well tell me at once.

SOLNESS: There's nothing behind it. I've never done you any wrong. Never knowingly, never deliberately, that is. And yet—I feel weighed down by a great crushing sense of guilt.

MRS. SOLNESS: Guilt . . . on my account?

SOLNESS: Mainly on your account.

MRS. SOLNESS: Then you are . . . sick after all, Halvard.

SOLNESS (*heavily*): I suppose I must be. Or something of the kind. (*He looks towards the door, right, which opens.*) Ah! Now things look brighter.

HILDE WANGEL *comes in. She has made one or two changes in her dress and let down her skirt.*

HILDE: Good morning, master builder!

SOLNESS (*nods*): Slept well?

HILDE: Marvellously well! Like a child in a cradle. Oh, I lay there and stretched myself like . . . like a princess!

SOLNESS (*smiling a little*): Quite comfortable, then.

HILDE: I should say so!

SOLNESS: And I imagine you dreamt, too.

HILDE: Yes. But that was horrid.

SOLNESS: Oh?

HILDE: Yes, because I dreamt I was falling over a terribly high, steep cliff. Don't you ever have that dream yourself?

SOLNESS: Why yes . . . now and then . . .

HILDE: It's very exciting . . . as you go falling, falling . . .

SOLNESS: It makes me feel as if my blood is running cold.

HILDE: Do you tuck your knees up under you as you fall?

SOLNESS: Yes, as high as I possibly can.

HILDE: So do I.

MRS. SOLNESS (*picks up her parasol*): I think I must go to town now, Halvard. (*To* HILDE.) And I'll try and bring you back a few things you might need.

HILDE (*goes to throw her arms round her neck*): Oh my dearest, sweetest Mrs. Solness! Really this is too kind of you! Frightfully kind . . .

MRS. SOLNESS (*deprecatingly, as she frees herself*): Not at all. It's no more than my duty. I'm very glad to do it.

HILDE (*offended, pouts*): Actually, I don't see why I can't go into town as I am—now that I've got my things looking smart again. Or maybe you think I can't?

MRS. SOLNESS: To tell you the truth, I fancy one or two people might stare at you a little.

HILDE (*snorting*): Pooh! Is that all! I think that'd be fun!

SOLNESS (*with ill-concealed irritability*): Yes, but people might start thinking *you* were mad too, you see.

HILDE: Mad? Are there such a lot of mad people in this town?

SOLNESS (*points to his forehead*): Here you see one, at any rate.

HILDE: You—master builder!

MRS. SOLNESS: Oh, really now, my dear Halvard!

SOLNESS: Haven't you realized that yet?

HILDE: No, I haven't actually. (*Thinks a moment, then gives a little laugh.*) Well, maybe there was one little thing, in fact.

SOLNESS: There you are, you see, Aline!

MRS. SOLNESS: And what sort of thing might that be, Miss Wangel?

HILDE: I'm not telling.

SOLNESS: Oh, please do!

HILDE: No, thank you—I'm not as mad as all that!

MRS. SOLNESS: When you and Miss Wangel are alone, she'll probably tell you, Halvard.

SOLNESS: Oh, you think so?

MRS. SOLNESS: Yes, of course. Because you've known her so long. Ever since she was a child . . . you say.

She goes out by the door, left.

HILDE (*after a moment*): Can't your wife bring herself to like me just a little.

SOLNESS: Did she give you that impression?

HILDE: Couldn't you see it?

SOLNESS (*evasively*): Aline's become rather withdrawn these last few years.

HILDE: Has she?

SOLNESS: If only you could get to know her properly . . . Because really she's so kind . . . and so good . . . and fundamentally such a fine person. . . .

HILDE (*impatiently*): But if she's all these things—why did she have to say all that about duty?

SOLNESS: About duty?

HILDE: Yes, she said she'd go out and buy some things for me. Because it was her *duty*, she said. Oh, I can't stand that nasty, horrid word!

SOLNESS: Why not?

HILDE: Because it sounds so cold and sharp and prickly. Duty, duty, duty! Don't you think so, too? That it seems to sting you?

SOLNESS: Hm! I haven't really thought about it.

HILDE: It does! And if she's as nice as you say she is—why should she say a thing like that?

SOLNESS: But, good Lord, what should she have said?

HILDE: She could have said she wanted to do it because she liked me such a frightful lot. She might have said something along those lines. Something that was really warm and sincere, don't you see?

SOLNESS (*looking at her*): Is that the way you want things?

HILDE: Yes, I do. (*She walks about the room, stops by the bookcase and looks at the books.*) What a lot of books you have.

SOLNESS: Oh, I've collected quite a few.

HILDE: Do you read all these books?

SOLNESS: There was a time when I used to try. Do you read?

HILDE: No! Never! Not any more. I can't really see any point in it.

SOLNESS: That's precisely how I feel, too.

HILDE *wanders about a little, stops by the small table, opens the folder and turns over some of the paper.*

HILDE: Did you do all these plans?

SOLNESS: No, they were done by a young assistant of mine.

HILDE: Somebody you have trained yourself?

SOLNESS: Oh yes, I dare say he's learnt a thing or two from me.

HILDE (*sits down*): Then he's probably very clever? (*Looks for a moment at a drawing.*) Isn't he?

SOLNESS: Oh, not too bad. I can use him. . . .

HILDE: Yes, indeed! He must be frightfully clever.

SOLNESS: You mean you can tell that from his drawings?

HILDE: What? From these bits and pieces? No. But if he's been a pupil of *yours* . . .

SOLNESS: Oh, *that*! Plenty of people have been pupils of mine. But that didn't necessarily make them anything very much.

HILDE (*looks at him and shakes her head*): Honestly, I can't understand how you can be so stupid.

SOLNESS: Stupid? Do you think I'm so very stupid?

HILDE: I certainly do. If you're to go and let yourself train all these people. . . .

SOLNESS (*starts*): Well? And why not?

HILDE (*gets up, half in earnest, half laughingly*): Oh, no, master builder! What's the point of that! Nobody but you should be allowed to build. You should do it all alone. Do everything yourself. Now you know.

SOLNESS (*involuntarily*): Hilde . . . !

HILDE: Well?

SOLNESS: What on earth made you say that?

HILDE: Why? Do you think I'm completely mad to think that?

SOLNESS: No, that's not what I meant. But now I'll tell you something.

HILDE: Well?

SOLNESS: Here alone . . . in my own secret thoughts . . . I am myself obsessed by that very same idea.

HILDE: Well, I should say that's pretty natural.

SOLNESS (*watching her rather closely*): And doubtless you'd already noticed it?

HILDE: As a matter of fact I hadn't.

SOLNESS: But just now . . . when you said you thought I was . . . a bit queer? There was one thing, you said. . . .

HILDE: Oh, I was thinking of something quite different.

SOLNESS: What were you thinking?

HILDE: Never you mind.

SOLNESS (*walks across the room*): All right . . . as you wish. (*Halts by the bay.*) Come over here. I want to show you something.

HILDE (*goes closer*): What?

SOLNESS: See there? Over in the garden . . . ?

HILDE: Yes?

SOLNESS (*pointing*): Just beyond where they've been quarrying . . .

HILDE: That new house, you mean.

SOLNESS: The one being built, yes. It's nearly finished.

HILDE: That's a very high tower it's got, isn't it?

SOLNESS: The scaffolding's still up.

HILDE: Is that your new house?

SOLNESS: Yes.

HILDE: The house you are going to move into soon?

SOLNESS: Yes.

HILDE (*looks at him*): Are there nurseries in that house too?

SOLNESS: Three, like here.

HILDE: And no children.

SOLNESS: No, and never will be.

HILDE (*with a half smile*): Well, isn't it like I said, then . . . ?

SOLNESS: What do you mean?

HILDE: That you are a little . . . mad, after all.

SOLNESS: Was that what you had in mind?

HILDE: Yes. All those empty nurseries where I was sleeping.

SOLNESS (*drops his voice*): We did have children . . . Aline and I.

HILDE (*looks intently at him*): Did you?

SOLNESS: Two little boys. Both the same age.

HILDE: Twins.

SOLNESS: Yes, twins. It's about eleven or twelve years ago now.

HILDE (*cautiously*): And they are both . . . ? You don't have the twins any longer?

SOLNESS (*with quiet emotion*): We only had them about three weeks. Scarcely that. (*Bursts out.*) Oh, Hilde, you don't know how glad I am that you've come! At last I have somebody I can talk to.

HILDE: Can't you talk to . . . to *her*?

SOLNESS: Not about this. Not as I want to . . . and need to. (*Sadly.*) And not about much else, either.

HILDE (*in a low voice*): Was that all you meant when you said you needed me?

SOLNESS: Mainly that. Yesterday, at least. Today I'm not so certain . . . (*Breaking off.*) Let's sit down over here, Hilde. You sit there on the sofa . . . then you can see the garden. (HILDE *sits down in the corner of the sofa.* SOLNESS *pulls up a chair.*) Would you like to hear about it?

HILDE: Yes, I'd love to sit and listen to you.

SOLNESS (*sits down*): Then I'll tell you all about it.

HILDE: Now I can look at both you and the garden, master builder. So tell me! Now!

SOLNESS (*points to the bay window*): Over there, on that high ground . . . where you can see the new house . . .

HILDE: Yes?

SOLNESS: . . . That was where Aline and I lived for the first few years. In those days there was an old house up there that had belonged to her mother. And which we inherited. Along with the whole of that enormous garden, too.

HILDE: Was there a tower on that house as well?

SOLNESS: No, nothing like that. It was a great, ugly, dark barn of a place to look at. But it was pretty cosy and comfortable inside.

HILDE: What did you do, then? Pull the whole thing down?

SOLNESS: No. It burnt down.

HILDE: All of it?

SOLNESS: Yes.

HILDE: Was it a great blow to you?

SOLNESS: It depends how you look at it. That fire was the making of me as a builder . . .

HILDE: Well, but . . . ?

SOLNESS: We had only just got our two little boys . . .

HILDE: The poor little twins.

SOLNESS: They were so sturdy and healthy when they were born. You could positively see them growing from one day to the next.

HILDE: Babies grow fast the first few days.

SOLNESS: A prettier sight you couldn't wish to see—Aline lying there with the two of them. But then came the night of the fire . . .

HILDE (tense): What happened? Tell me! Was anyone burnt?

SOLNESS: No, that wasn't it. They got everybody safely out of the house. . . .

HILDE: Well, what then . . . ?

SOLNESS: Aline suffered a terrible shock. The alarm . . . the scramble to get out . . . the pandemonium . . . and on top of it all the freezing night air. . . . For they had to be carried out just as they were. Both she and the children.

HILDE: And this was too much for them?

SOLNESS: No, not for them. But Aline started running a fever. And that affected her milk. She insisted on feeding them herself. It was her duty, she said. And both our little boys . . . (Clenches his hands.) . . . They both . . .

HILDE: They didn't survive that?

SOLNESS: No, that they didn't survive. That was what took them from us.

HILDE: That must have been terribly hard for you.

SOLNESS: Hard enough for me. But ten times harder for Aline. (Clenches his hands in silent fury.) Ah, why do such things happen in this world! (Curtly and firmly.) From the day I lost them I've never wanted to build another church.

HILDE: Perhaps not even that church tower of ours, either.

SOLNESS: Not really. I know I was glad and relieved when that tower was finished.

HILDE: I know that, too.

SOLNESS: And now I never build anything of that sort any more—never! No churches, and no church towers!

HILDE (nods slowly): Only houses for people to live in.

SOLNESS: Homes for human beings, Hilde.

HILDE: But homes with high towers and spires.

SOLNESS: Those for preference. (On a ligther note.) So you see—as I said before—that fire was the thing that made me. As a master builder, I mean.

HILDE: Why don't you call yourself an architect, like the rest?

SOLNESS: I never really had the proper training. Most of what I know I've taught myself.

HILDE: But you made your way to the top, all the same, master builder.

SOLNESS: Yes, thanks to that fire. I divided up most of the grounds into building sites. And there I could build exactly the way I wanted. From then on I never looked back.

HILDE (looks searchingly at him): You must surely be a very happy man. The way things have gone for you.

SOLNESS (darkly): Happy? You say that, too? Just like all the others.

HILDE: Well, I feel you must be. If only you could stop thinking about those two little boys. . . .

SOLNESS (slowly): Those two little boys . . . they are not so easily forgotten, Hilde.

HILDE (a little uncertainly): Do they still weigh so heavily on you—after all these years?

SOLNESS (*looking steadily at her, without answering*): A happy man, you said . . .

HILDE: Well, *aren't* you? Apart from that?

SOLNESS (*still looking at her*): When I was telling you all that business about the fire . . .

HILDE: Well?

SOLNESS: Wasn't there one particular thought that struck you?

HILDE (*tries hard to think*): No. What have you got in mind?

SOLNESS (*with quiet emphasis*): That fire, and that alone, was the thing that gave me the chance to build homes. Warm, cheerful, comfortable homes, where fathers and mothers and their children could live together, secure and happy, and feeling that it's good to be alive. And more than anything to belong to each other—in great things and in small.

HILDE (*eagerly*): Well then, doesn't it make you very happy knowing you can make such lovely homes?

SOLNESS: But the price, Hilde! The terrible price I've had to pay that this might be so.

HILDE: But isn't that also something you can surmount?

SOLNESS: No. To be able to build homes for other people, I have had to renounce . . . for ever renounce . . . any hope of having a home of my own. I mean a home with children. Or even with a father and mother.

HILDE (*cautiously*): But did you *have* to? For ever, did you say?

SOLNESS (*nods slowly*): That was the price of 'happiness' people are always talking about. (*With a heavy sigh.*) That happiness . . . hm . . . that happiness wasn't to be got any cheaper, Hilde.

HILDE (*as before*): But couldn't things still turn out all right?

SOLNESS: Never in this world. Never. That's another consequence of the fire. And of Aline's illness afterwards.

HILDE (*looks at him with an indefinable expression*): Yet you still go on building all these nurseries.

SOLNESS (*earnestly*): Haven't you ever noticed, Hilde, how seductive, how inviting . . . the impossible is?

HILDE (*ponders*): The impossible? (*Eagerly.*) Why yes! Do you feel that too?

SOLNESS: Yes, I do.

HILDE: So you've also something of the troll in you?

SOLNESS: What do you mean—troll?

HILDE: Well, what would *you* call a thing like that?

SOLNESS (*gets up*): All right, just as you say. (*Vehemently.*) But is it any wonder I'm becoming like a troll . . . the way things are going for me! The way *everything* is . . . everlastingly!

HILDE: How do you mean?

SOLNESS (*in a low voice with inward emotion*): Mark well what I'm telling you, Hilde. Everything I've managed to achieve, everything I've built and created . . . all the beauty and security, the comfort and the good cheer . . . all the magnificence, even . . . (*Clenches his hands.*) Oh, the very thought of it is terrible . . . !

HILDE: What is so terrible?

SOLNESS: All this I somehow have to make up for. Pay for. Not in money. But in human happiness. And not with my own happiness alone. But also with others'. Don't you see that, Hilde! That's the price my status as an artist has cost me—and others. And every single day I have to stand by and watch this price being paid for me anew. Over and over again—endlessly!

HILDE (*rises and looks fixedly at him*): You must be thinking of . . . of *her!*

SOLNESS: Yes. Above all of Aline. You see Aline had her vocation in life, too. Quite as much as I had mine. (*His voice trembles.*) But her vocation had to be ruined . . . crushed, smashed to pieces . . . so that mine could go marching on to . . . to some kind of great victory. Because, you know, Aline . . . had a talent for building, too.

HILDE: She had! For building?

SOLNESS (*shakes his head*): Not houses and

towers and spires . . . Not the kind of thing I play about with . . .

HILDE: What, then?

SOLNESS (*softly, with emotion*): A talent for building children's souls, Hilde. So building their souls that they might grow straight and fine, nobly and beautifully formed, to their full human stature. That was where Aline's talent lay. And look now where it lies. Unused . . . and for ever unusable. No earthly use for anything. . . . Like a charred heap of ruins.

HILDE: Yes, but even if this is true . . . ?

SOLNESS: It is true. It is. I know it is.

HILDE: Well, even so, you aren't in any way to blame.

SOLNESS (*fixes his eyes on her and nods slowly*): Ah, that is precisely the great and terrible question. That is the doubt that nags me, day and night.

HILDE: That!

SOLNESS: Well, let's suppose I *was* to blame. In a sort of way.

HILDE: You! For the fire!

SOLNESS: For the whole thing. For everything . . . And yet . . . I may also be completely innocent.

HILDE (*looks at him with troubled eyes*): Oh, master builder! If you can say things like that, you must be . . . ill, after all.

SOLNESS: Hm! . . . Don't suppose I'll ever be exactly bursting with health in *that* respect.

RAGNAR BROVIK *cautiously opens the small door in the corner, left.* HILDE *walks across the room.*

RAGNAR (*as he sees* HILDE): Oh, I beg your pardon, Mr. Solness.

He is about to withdraw.

SOLNESS: No, no, please don't go. Let's get it settled.

RAGNAR: Ah yes . . . if we could!

SOLNESS: Your father's no better, I hear.

RAGNAR: Father is sinking fast now. That's why I beg of you . . . please write something nice on one of my drawings. Something for Father to read before he . . .

SOLNESS (*vehemently*): I don't want to hear any more about these drawings of yours!

RAGNAR: Have you looked at them?

SOLNESS: Yes, I have.

RAGNAR: And they're no good? And *I'm* no good either?

SOLNESS (*evasively*): Stay on here with me, Ragnar. You can have everything just the way you want it. Then you can marry Kaja. Live without a care. Perhaps even happily. Only don't think of building on your own.

RAGNAR: Ah, well . . . then I'd better go home and tell Father this. I promised him I would. *Shall* I tell Father this . . . before he dies?

SOLNESS (*with a moan*): Oh, tell him . . . tell him what you like. What do I care! Best say nothing at all! (*Bursts out.*) There's nothing else I *can* do, Ragnar!

RAGNAR: Then can I take the drawings with me?

SOLNESS: Yes, take them . . . take them away. They're on the table there.

RAGNAR (*walks across*): Thanks.

HILDE (*placing her hand on the folder*): No, leave them.

SOLNESS: Why?

HILDE: Because I want to look at them, too.

SOLNESS: But you *have*. (*To* RAGNAR.) Well then, leave them there.

RAGNAR: All right.

SOLNESS: And now straight home to your father.

RAGNAR: Yes, I suppose I'd better.

SOLNESS (*as if in desperation*): Ragnar, you *mustn't* ask me to do things I *can't* do. Do you hear me, Ragnar! You mustn't.

RAGNAR: No, no. Excuse me. . . .

He bows and goes out by the corner door. HILDE *walks across and sits on a chair by the mirror.*

HILDE (*looks angrily at* SOLNESS): That was a nasty thing to do.

SOLNESS: You think so, too?

HILDE: Really very nasty indeed. And hard and wicked and cruel.

SOLNESS: Oh, you don't understand my position.

HILDE: All the same . . . No, you shouldn't be like that.

SOLNESS: You said yourself just now that I was the only one who should be allowed to build.

HILDE: *I* can say things like that. But not *you.*

SOLNESS: Who better than I? Considering the price I've had to pay to get where I am.

HILDE: Oh yes . . . you mean your domestic bliss . . . or whatever you call it.

SOLNESS: And with it my peace of mind.

HILDE (*rises*): Peace of mind! (*Feelingly.*) Ah yes, you're right! . . . Poor master builder! . . . You must be thinking that . . .

SOLNESS (*with a quiet chuckle*): You just sit down again, Hilde, and I'll tell you something funny.

HILDE (*expectantly, sits down*): Well?

SOLNESS: It all sounds so absurdly trivial. You see, the whole thing comes down in the end to a crack in the chimney.

HILDE: Is that all?

SOLNESS: Yes, to begin with.

He moves a chair closer to HILDE'*s and sits down.*

HILDE (*impatiently slapping her knee*): So there was this crack in the chimney?

SOLNESS: Long, long before the fire, I had noticed the crack in the flue. Every time I was in the loft, I looked to see if it was still there.

HILDE: And it was?

SOLNESS: Yes. Because nobody else knew about it.

HILDE: And you didn't say anything?

SOLNESS: No, I didn't.

HILDE: Never thought about repairing it?

SOLNESS: I thought about it . . . but it never got any further than that. Every time I thought I'd get on with it, a hand seemed to reach out and stop me. Not today, I'd think. Tomorrow. So nothing ever got done.

HILDE: Yes, but why did you always keep putting it off?

SOLNESS: Because I'd got an idea. (*Slowly, and in a low voice.*) Through that little black crack in the chimney I might perhaps make my way—to success as a builder.

HILDE (*staring into space*): That must have been exciting.

SOLNESS: Irresistible almost. Utterly irresistible. At that time, the whole thing seemed so simple, so trivial. I wanted it to happen in winter some time. Just before dinner. I would be out for a drive in the sleigh with Aline. The people at home would have had great fires going in the stoves . . .

HILDE: Of course, it would be fearfully cold that day, wouldn't it?

SOLNESS: Fairly bitter, yes. And they would want the place nice and warm for Aline to come back to.

HILDE: I imagine she feels the cold, rather.

SOLNESS: She does. And then on our way home we would see the smoke.

HILDE: Just the smoke?

SOLNESS: First the smoke. But when we reached the front gates, the whole of that great wooden box would be a roaring mass of flames. . . . That's how I wanted it to be, you see.

HILDE: Oh, why in Heaven's name couldn't it have happened like that!

SOLNESS: Ah, you may well ask, Hilde.

HILDE: But tell me, master builder. Are you absolutely certain the fire was caused by the crack in the chimney?

SOLNESS: On the contrary, I am quite sure the crack in the chimney had nothing to do with the fire.

HILDE: What!

SOLNESS: It has been clearly established that the fire broke out in a cupboard—in an entirely different part of the house.

HILDE: Then why all this moaning about the crack in the chimney?

SOLNESS: May I go on talking to you a little longer, Hilde?

HILDE: Yes, if only you'll try and talk sensibly. . . .

SOLNESS: I'll try.

He moves his chair closer.

HILDE: Come on! Out with it, master builder.

SOLNESS (*confidentially*): Don't you believe too, Hilde, that you find certain people have been singled out, specially chosen, gifted with the power and the ability to *want* something, to *desire* something, to *will* something . . . so insistently . . . and so ruthlessly . . . that they inevitably get it in the end? Don't you believe that?

HILDE (*with an inscrutable expression in her eyes*): If that is so, we'll see some day . . . if I am one of the chosen.

SOLNESS: One doesn't achieve such great things *alone*. Oh, no. One has to have . . . helpers and servants . . . if anything's to come of it. But they never come of their own accord. One has to summon them imperiously, inwardly, you understand.

HILDE: Who are these helpers and servants?

SOLNESS: Oh, we can talk about that some other time. Let's keep to the matter of the fire for the present.

HILDE: Don't you think that fire would have occurred anyway—even if you hadn't wished for it?

SOLNESS: If old Knut Brovik had owned the house, it would never have burnt down quite so conveniently for *him*. I'm quite certain of that. He doesn't know how to call upon these helpers . . . nor upon the servants, either. (*Gets up restlessly.*) You see, Hilde . . . I *am* actually the one who's to blame for those two little boys having to pay with their lives. And perhaps I'm to blame too for Aline never becoming what she could and should have been. And what she most of all wanted to be.

HILDE: Yes, but if it's only these helpers and servants who . . . ?

SOLNESS: Who called on the helpers and servants? *I* did! And they came and did my bidding. (*In rising excitement.*) That's what people call being lucky. But let me tell you what that sort of luck feels like! It feels as if my breast were a great expanse of raw flesh. And these helpers and servants go flaying off skin from other people's bodies to patch *my* wound. Yet the wound never heals . . . never! Oh, if only you knew how it sometimes burns and throbs.

HILDE (*looks attentively at him*): You *are* ill, master builder. Very ill, I rather think.

SOLNESS: Say *mad*. For that's what you mean.

HILDE: No, I don't think there's anything much wrong with your reason.

SOLNESS: What, then? Out with it!

HILDE: What I'm wondering is whether you weren't born with rather a fragile conscience.

SOLNESS: Fragile conscience? What the devil's that?

HILDE: I mean your conscience is actually very fragile. Sort of delicate. Won't stand up to things. Can't bear much weight.

SOLNESS (*growling*): H'm. What should one's conscience be like then, may I ask?

HILDE: In your case I should want to see a conscience that was . . . well, thoroughly robust.

SOLNESS: Robust, eh? Well. Have *you* a robust conscience, I wonder?

HILDE: Yes, I think so. I've never noticed it wasn't.

SOLNESS: Probably hasn't been particularly tested, I imagine.

HILDE (*with a trembling of the lips*): Oh, leaving Father wasn't all that easy. I'm terribly fond of him.

SOLNESS: Oh, come! When it's just for a month or two . . .

HILDE: I'll probably never go back home again.

SOLNESS: Never? Why did you leave him, then?

HILDE (*half serious, half in jest*): Aren't you

forgetting again that the ten years are up?

SOLNESS: Oh, nonsense! Was there something wrong at home? Eh?

HILDE (*utterly serious*): Something inside me forced me, drove me here. Drew me, tempted me, too.

SOLNESS (*eagerly*): There you are! There you are, Hilde! There's a troll in you, too. Just as in me. And it's the troll in us, you see, that calls on the powers outside. Then we *have* to give in—whether we like it or not.

HILDE: I rather think you are right, master builder.

SOLNESS (*walking about the room*): It's fantastic the number of devils there are in the world you never even *see*, Hilde!

HILDE: Devils, too?

SOLNESS (*stops*): Good devils and bad devils. Blond devils and dark devils! If only you could be sure which kind had hold of you —the light ones or the dark! (*Walks about.*) Ha! There'd be no bother then.

HILDE (*follows him with her eyes*): Or if one had a really tough and vigorous conscience. So that one *dared* to do what one *wanted*.

SOLNESS (*halts by the console table*): I think in this respect most people are just as cowardly as I am.

HILDE: Could be.

SOLNESS (*leans against the table*): In the sagas ... Have you read any of these old sagas?

HILDE: Oh, yes! In the days when I used to read books, I ...

SOLNESS: The sagas are all about the vikings who sailed to foreign lands and plundered and burned and killed ...

HILDE: And carried off women ...

SOLNESS: And held them captive ...

HILDE: Took them home with them in their ships ...

SOLNESS: And behaved towards them like ... like the worst of trolls.

HILDE (*staring straight ahead with half-veiled eyes*): I think that must be exciting.

SOLNESS (*with a short, gruff laugh*): Taking women, you mean?

HILDE: *Being* taken.

SOLNESS (*looks at her for a moment*): Indeed.

HILDE (*as though breaking off her thoughts*): But you were saying about these vikings, master builder ... ?

SOLNESS: Ah, yes. Those fellows now—they had robust consciences all right. They hadn't lost any of their appetite when they got home. Happy as children they were, too. As for the women—very often they wouldn't hear tell of leaving them. Can you understand that sort of thing, Hilde?

HILDE: I understand these women perfectly.

SOLNESS: Aha! Perhaps you'd do the same yourself?

HILDE: Why not?

SOLNESS: Live ... of your own free will ... with a wild brute like that?

HILDE: If he was a brute I'd grown really fond of, I ...

SOLNESS: Could you grow fond of a man like that?

HILDE: Good Lord, you can't always help whom you get fond of, can you?

SOLNESS (*looks thoughtfully at her*): No ... I dare say it's the troll within us decides *that*.

HILDE (*with a half laugh*): Along with all those other blessed devils you know so well. The fair ones and the dark ones.

SOLNESS (*warmly and quietly*): I hope the devils choose kindly for you, Hilde.

HILDE: They have chosen for me, already. Once and for all.

SOLNESS (*looks intently at her*): Hilde ... you are like some wild forest bird.

HILDE: Far from it. I don't hide myself away in the bushes.

SOLNESS: No, no. There's maybe more of the bird of prey in you.

HILDE: Yes ... perhaps. (*With great vehemence.*) And why not a bird of prey! Why shouldn't I go hunting, too? Take the prey I want? If I can get my claws into it. And hold it firm.

SOLNESS: Hilde ... do you know what you are?

HILDE: Yes, I'm some strange kind of bird.

SOLNESS: No. You are like the early dawn. When I look at you, it's as though I were looking at the sunrise.

HILDE: Tell me, master builder—are you sure you have never called to me? Inwardly, I mean?

SOLNESS (*quietly and slowly*): I rather think I must have.

HILDE: What do want of me?

SOLNESS: You are youth, Hilde.

HILDE (*smiling*): That youth you are so afraid of?

SOLNESS (*nods slowly*): And to which in my heart I am drawn so sorely.

HILDE *rises, walks over to the little table and picks up* RAGNAR BROVIK's *folder.*

HILDE (*holding the folder out to him*): Now what about these drawings. . . .

SOLNESS (*curtly, waving it aside*): Put those things away! I've seen enough of them.

HILDE: Yes, but you're going to endorse them for him, aren't you?

SOLNESS: Endorse them! Never in this world.

HILDE: With that poor old man lying at death's door! Can't you do him and his son this one kindness before they are parted? Then perhaps he might get the commission to build it, too.

SOLNESS: Yes, that's precisely what he would do. He'll have made sure of that all right, our fine young friend.

HILDE: But, good Lord, even if he has, couldn't you tell a white lie for once—just a little one?

SOLNESS: Lie? (*Furious.*) Hilde—get those damn drawings out of my sight!

HILDE (*withdraws the folder a little*): Now, now—don't bite me. You talk about trolls. I think you are behaving a bit like a troll yourself. (*Looks round.*) Where do you keep your pen and ink?

SOLNESS: Don't keep any in here.

HILDE (*walks to the door*): But that girl will have some out here. . . .

SOLNESS: Stay where you are, Hilde! . . . You wanted me to tell a lie, you said. Well, I suppose I might, for his poor old father's sake. Because . . . I broke him once. Smashed him.

HILDE: Him, too?

SOLNESS: I needed room for myself. But this Ragnar . . . he must never on any account be allowed to get ahead.

HILDE: Poor boy, he's not likely to, is he? If he isn't much good, then . . .

SOLNESS (*comes closer, looks at her and whispers*): Once Ragnar Brovik gets started, he'll have me down in the dust. He'll break me . . . just as I broke his father.

HILDE: Break *you*? So he *is* good?

SOLNESS: He's good all right, don't you worry! He represents youth standing there ready to beat upon my door. Ready to finish off Master Builder Solness.

HILDE (*looks at him with quiet reproach*): And yet you wanted to shut him out. For shame, master builder!

SOLNESS: It's cost me enough already, this battle I've fought. Besides, I'm afraid the helpers and servants might not obey me any more.

HILDE: Then you'll just have to manage on your own. Nothing else for it.

SOLNESS: Hopeless, Hilde. My luck will turn. Sooner or later. Retribution is inexorable.

HILDE (*fearfully, holding her hands over her ears*): Don't say things like that! Do you want to kill me! Do you want to rob me of more than life itself?

SOLNESS: And what is that?

HILDE: To see you great. See you with a garland in your hand. High, high up on a church tower. (*Calm again.*) So get out your pencil. You must surely have a pencil on you?

SOLNESS (*takes out his notebook*): I have one here.

HILDE (*putting the folder on the table*): Good. Now we'll both sit down here, master builder. (SOLNESS *sits at the table.* HILDE, *behind him, leans over the back of the chair.*) And now we'll write on the drawings. Something really nice and really kind we'll write. For this nasty old Roar, or whatever his name is.

SOLNESS (*writes a few words, turns his head and looks up at her*): Tell me one thing, Hilde.

HILDE: Yes?

SOLNESS: If you've in fact been waiting for me all these ten years . . .

HILDE: Well?

SOLNESS: Why didn't you write to me? Then I could have answered you.

HILDE (*swiftly*): No, no, no! That's just what I didn't want.

SOLNESS: Why not?

HILDE: I was afraid that might spoil everything. . . . But we were going to write something on the drawings, master builder.

SOLNESS: So we were.

HILDE (*leaning over him and watching as he writes*): Very kind and generous. Oh, how I hate . . . how I hate this . . . Roald.

SOLNESS (*writing*): Have you never really *cared* for anyone, Hilde?

HILDE (*in a hard voice*): What did you say?

SOLNESS: I asked whether you'd ever really cared for anyone.

HILDE: Anyone else, I suppose you mean?

SOLNESS (*looks up at her*): For anyone else, yes. Haven't you ever? All these ten years? Never?

HILDE: Oh yes, now and again. When I was really furious with you for not coming.

SOLNESS: So you have taken an interest in other people?

HILDE: A little. For a week or so. Good Lord, master builder, you know how things are.

SOLNESS: Hilde . . . what have you come here for?

HILDE: Don't waste time on chattering. All this time that poor old man might be dying.

SOLNESS: Answer me, Hilde. What do you want of me?

HILDE: I want my kingdom.

SOLNESS: H'm. . . .

He glances quickly at the door, left, and then

goes on writing on the drawings. MRS. SOLNESS *comes in at that moment; she is carrying some parcels.*

MRS. SOLNESS: I've brought a few of the things for you myself, Miss Wangel. The larger parcels are being delivered later.

HILDE: Oh, really how extremely kind of you!

MRS. SOLNESS: No more than my duty. Nothing else.

SOLNESS (*reading through what he has written*): Aline!

MRS. SOLNESS: Yes?

SOLNESS: Did you notice whether the girl—the book-keeper was out there?

MRS. SOLNESS: Yes, of course she was.

SOLNESS (*puts the drawings in the folder*): H'm. . . .

MRS. SOLNESS: She was standing by the desk—as she always is when I walk through the room.

SOLNESS (*gets up*): Then I'll just give this to her. And tell her that . . .

HILDE (*takes the folder from him*): Oh, no! That pleasure is mine! (*She walks towards the door but turns.*) What's she called?

SOLNESS: She's called Miss Fosli.

HILDE: Ugh, that sounds so cold! Her first name, I mean?

SOLNESS: Kaja—I think.

HILDE (*opens the door and shouts out*): Kaja! Come in here! Hurry! The master builder wants to speak to you.

KAJA FOSLI *appears at the door.*

KAJA (*looks at him, terrified*): Here I am. . . .

HILDE (*hands her the folder*): Look, Kaja! You can take these now. The master builder has written something on them.

KAJA: Oh, at last!

SOLNESS: Take them to the old man as quickly as you can.

KAJA: I'll take them home at once.

SOLNESS: Yes, do that. And this means Ragnar can do the building.

KAJA: Oh, please can he come and thank you

for everything...?

SOLNESS (*hard*): I want no thanks. You can tell him that from me.

KAJA: Yes, I'll...

SOLNESS: And tell him at the same time that from now on I've no more use for him. Or for you either.

KAJA (*softly, tremulously*): Not for me either!

SOLNESS: You'll have other things to think about now. And to look after. And isn't that just as it should be? Now, off home you go with those drawings, Miss Fosli. Quickly! Do you hear!

KAJA (*as before*): Yes, Mr. Solness.

She goes out.

MRS. SOLNESS: Heavens, what shifty eyes that girl has.

SOLNESS: What? That poor little creature?

MRS. SOLNESS: Ah, I've got eyes to see, Halvard. . . . Are you really giving them notice?

SOLNESS: Yes.

MRS. SOLNESS: The girl, too?

SOLNESS: Isn't that what you wanted?

MRS. SOLNESS: But how will you manage without *her*...? Ah, yes! You've probably somebody else up your sleeve, Halvard.

HILDE (*gaily*): Well, I wouldn't be much good behind a desk, anyway.

SOLNESS: Now, now...things will work out somehow, Aline. You just give your mind now to the business of moving into the new house, as soon as possible. This evening we'll have the topping-out...(*Turns to* HILDE.) We'll put the wreath right high up on the very top of the tower. What do you say to *that*, Miss Hilde?

HILDE (*looks at him with glistening eyes*): It'll be absolutely marvellous to see you so high up again!

SOLNESS: Me!

MRS. SOLNESS: Dear God, Miss Wangel, put that out of your mind! My husband...! When he gets so dizzy?

HILDE: Dizzy! No, surely not!

MRS. SOLNESS: Oh, he does.

HILDE: But I've seen him myself right at the top of a high church tower.

MRS. SOLNESS: Yes, I've heard people say that. But it's quite impossible....

SOLNESS (*vehemently*): Impossible . . . yes, impossible! But I did it, all the same.

MRS. SOLNESS: How can you say that, Halvard? You can't even bear to go out on to the first floor balcony here. You've always been like that.

SOLNESS: You might see something different tonight.

MRS. SOLNESS (*in alarm*): No, no, no! Please God, don't let me ever see such a thing! I'll send for the doctor immediately. He'll put a stop to it.

SOLNESS: But, Aline . . . !

MRS. SOLNESS: I will. Because you're ill, Halvard. There's no other explanation! Oh, God! Oh, God!

She goes quickly out, right.

HILDE (*looks intently at him*): *Is* it true, or isn't it?

SOLNESS: That I get dizzy?

HILDE: That *my* master builder dare not . . . cannot climb as high as he builds?

SOLNESS: Is that the way you see it?

HILDE: Yes.

SOLNESS: I'm beginning to think no part of me is safe from you.

HILDE (*looks towards the bay window*): Up there. Right up there....

SOLNESS: You could live in the topmost room in the tower, Hilde. . . . Could live there like a princess.

HILDE (*flatly, between earnest and jest*): Yes, that's what you promised me.

SOLNESS: *Did* I, in fact?

HILDE: For shame, master builder! You said I was to be a princess. That you would give me a kingdom. And then you took me and . . . Well!

SOLNESS (*cautiously*): Are you quite sure it

isn't some kind of dream . . . some fantasy that's taken hold of you.

HILDE (*sharply*): You mean you didn't do it?

SOLNESS: Don't really know . . . (*More quietly.*) But one thing I do know now, and that is that I . . .

HILDE: That you . . . ? Say it!

SOLNESS: . . . That I ought to have done it.

HILDE (*bursts out gaily*): You could never be dizzy!

SOLNESS: Tonight we'll put up the wreath . . . Princess Hilde.

HILDE (*with a bitter grimace*): Over your new home . . . yes.

SOLNESS: Over the new house. Which will never be a home for me.

He goes out through the garden door.

HILDE (*stares straight ahead with half-closed eyes and whispers to herself; the only words heard are*): . . . terribly exciting. . . .

ACT III

A large broad verandah belonging to SOLNESS's *house. Left, part of the house can be seen, with a door leading out on to the verandah. Right, the railings of the verandah. At the back, a flight of steps leads down from the narrow end of the verandah to the garden below. Tall old trees in the garden extend their branches over the verandah and towards the house. Extreme right, in among the trees, a glimpse is caught of the lower part of the new villa, with scaffolding round the tower section. In the background, the garden is bounded by an old wooden fence. Beyond the fence is a street with mean dilapidated cottages.*

Sunlit clouds against the evening sky. On the verandah by the wall of the house stands a garden bench, in front of which is a long table. On the other side of the table an armchair and some stools. All the furniture is wickerwork.

MRS. SOLNESS, *wrapped in a large white crêpe shawl, sits resting in the armchair gazing out to the right.*

After a moment HILDE WANGEL *comes up the steps from the garden. She is dressed as before and is wearing her hat. On her breast she wears a little bunch of small garden flowers.*

MRS. SOLNESS (*turning her head slightly*): Been for a walk in the garden, Miss Wangel?

HILDE: Yes, I've been down there having a look round.

MRS. SOLNESS: And found some flowers too, I see.

HILDE: Yes, I have! There are lots and lots of them, down in among the bushes.

MRS. SOLNESS: Oh, *are* there? Still? I hardly ever go down there.

HILDE (*approaching*): What? I imagined you rushing down there every day.

MRS. SOLNESS (*with a faint smile*): I don't 'rush' anywhere. Not any more.

HILDE: But don't you go every so often, just to look in on all the lovely things down there?

MRS. SOLNESS: It's all become so remote. I am almost afraid to look at it again.

HILDE: Your own garden?

MRS. SOLNESS: I don't feel it *is* mine any more.

HILDE: Oh, come now . . . ?

MRS. SOLNESS. No, no it isn't. Not like it was in Mother's and Father's day. They've taken such an awful lot of the garden away, Miss Wangel. Do you know, they've split it all up and gone and built houses on it, for a lot of strangers! People I don't even know. And they sit there in their windows looking at me.

HILDE (*brightly*): Mrs. Solness?

MRS. SOLNESS: Yes?

HILDE: May I stay here beside you for a little while?

MRS. SOLNESS: Certainly, if you would like to.

HILDE *moves a stool across to the armchair and sits down.*

HILDE: Ah! Here you can really sit and sun yourself. Like a cat.

MRS. SOLNESS (*places her hand gently on* HILDE's *neck*): How nice you wanting to sit beside *me*. I thought you were going in to see my husband.

HILDE: What would I want with him?

MRS. SOLNESS: To help him, I suppose.

HILDE: No, thank you. Anyway he isn't in. He's over there with the workmen. But he looked so fierce that I didn't dare speak to him.

MRS. SOLNESS: Oh, he's very mild and gentle, really.

HILDE: *He* is!

MRS. SOLNESS: You still don't know him properly yet, Miss Wangel.

HILDE (*looks affectionately at her*): Are you glad you're moving into the new house?

MRS. SOLNESS: I should be glad, really. It's what Halvard wants. . . .

HILDE: Oh, not just for that, surely.

MRS. SOLNESS: Oh yes, Miss Wangel. After all it's my duty—doing what *he* wants. Just that it's often rather hard to make oneself fit in.

HILDE: Yes, that must be hard.

MRS. SOLNESS: Believe me, it is. And when you're only a poor creature like myself. . . .

HILDE: When you have gone through as much as you have, you mean. . . .

MRS. SOLNESS: How do you know about that?

HILDE: Your husband told me.

MRS. SOLNESS: He rarely talks about these things to me. Yes, indeed, I've been through a great deal in my lifetime, Miss Wangel.

HILDE (*looks at her sympathetically and nods slowly*): Poor Mrs. Solness. First there was that fire . . .

MRS. SOLNESS (*with a sigh*): Yes, I lost everything.

HILDE: Then worse was to follow.

MRS. SOLNESS (*looks questioningly at her*): Worse?

HILDE: The worst thing of all.

MRS. SOLNESS: What do you mean?

HILDE (*softly*): You lost your two little boys.

MRS. SOLNESS: Oh, them, yes. Well, you know, that was something else again. That was an act of destiny. One must learn to accept such things and be thankful.

HILDE: Do you do that?

MRS. SOLNESS: Not always, I'm afraid. I know very well that it's my duty. But I can't.

HILDE: Ah, well. I think that's understandable.

MRS. SOLNESS: Time and time again I have to tell myself that it was a just punishment . . .

HILDE: How?

MRS. SOLNESS: Because I wasn't resolute enough in misfortune.

HILDE: But I don't understand. . . .

MRS. SOLNESS: No, no, Miss Wangel. . . . Don't talk to me any more about my two little boys. We need not be sad about them. They are happy where they are—so happy now. No, it's the small losses in life that cut deep into the heart. Losing things that other people think nothing of.

HILDE (*puts her arms on* MRS. SOLNESS's *knee and looks affectionately up at her*): Dear Mrs. Solness, tell me! What things?

MRS. SOLNESS: Just little things. Like I said. All the old portraits on the walls were burnt. And all the old silk dresses were burnt. Things that had been in the family for years and years. And all Mother's and Grandmother's lace—that was burnt too. And even the jewels! (*Sadly.*) And all the dolls.

HILDE: The dolls?

MRS. SOLNESS (*choking with tears*): I had nine lovely dolls.

HILDE: And they were burnt too?

MRS. SOLNESS: All of them. Oh, I found that hard—so hard.

HILDE: Had you put them all away, then? From when you were little?

MRS. SOLNESS: Not put away. The dolls and I had gone on living together.

HILDE: After you had grown up?

MRS. SOLNESS: Yes, long after that.

HILDE: And after you were married, too?

MRS. SOLNESS: Oh, yes. As long as he didn't see, it was . . . But then they all got burnt, poor things. Nobody thought of saving *them*. Oh, it's so sad when you think about it. Now, you mustn't laugh at me, Miss Wangel.

HILDE: I'm not laughing.

MRS. SOLNESS: Because in a way they too were living things, you know. I carried them under my heart. Like little unborn children.

DR. HERDAL, *hat in hand, comes out through the door and catches sight of* MRS. SOLNESS *and* HILDE.

DR. HERDAL: You'll catch cold sitting out here, Mrs. Solness.

MRS. SOLNESS: It seems nice and warm out here today.

DR. HERDAL: Ah, well. But is there something the matter? You sent me a note.

MRS. SOLNESS (*gets up*): There's something I must talk to you about.

DR. HERDAL: Very well. Then perhaps we'd better go inside. (*To* HILDE.) In your mountaineering kit again today, Miss Wangel?

HILDE (*gaily, as she rises*): Rather! In full regalia! But there's no climbing and breaking my neck for me today. We two will sit nicely down below and watch, Doctor.

DR. HERDAL: What are we supposed to watch?

MRS. SOLNESS (*in a low and terrified voice, to* HILDE): Hush, hush, for Heaven's sake! He's coming! Try and persuade him to give up this idea. And do let us be friends, Miss Wangel. Can't we?

HILDE (*throws her arms impetuously round* MRS. SOLNESS'*s neck*): Oh, if only we could.

MRS. SOLNESS (*freeing herself gently*): There, there! Here he is, Doctor! I'd like a word with you.

DR. HERDAL: Is it about him?

MRS. SOLNESS: Yes, it's about him. Come inside.

She and the doctor go into the house. A moment later SOLNESS *comes up the steps from the garden.* HILDE'*s face takes on a serious expression.*

SOLNESS (*glances towards the door of the house, which is cautiously closed from inside*): Have you noticed, Hilde, that as soon as I come, she goes.

HILDE: I have noticed that your coming makes her go.

SOLNESS: Perhaps. But I can't help that. (*Looks attentively at her.*) Are you cold, Hilde? You look as if you are.

HILDE: I've just emerged from a tomb.

SOLNESS: What do you mean?

HILDE: That the frost has seized my bones, master builder.

SOLNESS (*slowly*): I think I understand. . . .

HILDE: What are you doing up here?

SOLNESS: I saw you from over there.

HILDE: Then you must have seen her too?

SOLNESS: I knew she'd go the moment I came.

HILDE: Does it hurt you very much—the way she avoids you?

SOLNESS: In one way it's a kind of relief.

HILDE: That you don't have to face her?

SOLNESS: Yes.

HILDE: That you're not constantly being reminded how hard she's taking it—this about the two boys.

SOLNESS: Yes. Chiefly that.

HILDE *walks across the verandah with her hands clasped behind her back, stands by the railing and looks out over the garden.*

SOLNESS (*after a short pause*): Were you talking with her for long?

HILDE *stands motionless and does not answer.*

SOLNESS: I said, was it for long?

HILDE *is silent as before.*

SOLNESS: What did she talk about, Hilde?

HILDE *remains silent.*

SOLNESS: Poor Aline! It was probably about the boys.

HILDE *shudders nervously, then she nods rapidly several times.*

SOLNESS: She'll never get over it. Never, never

get over it. (*He comes closer.*) Now you're standing there like a statue again. You also stood like that last night.

HILDE (*turns and looks at him with large serious eyes*): I want to leave.

SOLNESS (*sharply*): Leave!

HILDE: Yes.

SOLNESS: But I won't let you!

HILDE: What is there for me to do here now?

SOLNESS: Just stay here, Hilde!

HILDE (*looks him up and down*): Oh yes, thank you very much. But it wouldn't stop at *that.*

SOLNESS (*impulsively*): So much the better!

HILDE (*vehemently*): I can't hurt someone I *know*! Can't take what belongs to her.

SOLNESS: Who says you will?

HILDE (*continuing*): A stranger, yes! That's something quite different! Somebody I'd never set eyes on. But anybody I'd been close to . . . ! No! No! Ugh!

SOLNESS: But I've never suggested anything else!

HILDE: Oh, master builder, you know very well what would happen. And that's why I'm leaving.

SOLNESS: And what will happen to me when you are gone? What will I have to live for? Afterwards?

HILDE (*with the enigmatic expression in her eyes*): There's no need to worry about *you.* You have your duty towards her. Live for that duty.

SOLNESS: Too late. These powers . . . these . . . these . . .

HILDE: . . . Devils . . .

SOLNESS: Yes, devils! And the troll in me too. They have drained her of all her life's blood. (*Laughs despairingly.*) And it was for my sake they did it! Yes! (*Heavily.*) And now she is dead—on my account. And here I am, chained alive to this dead woman. (*In wild anguish.*) Me . . . a man who *cannot* live a joyless life!

HILDE (*walks round the table and sits down on the bench, her elbows on the table and her head in her hands; she sits a moment looking at him*): What are you going to build next?

SOLNESS (*shakes his head*): I don't think I'll be building very much more.

HILDE: No more cheerful family homes? For mother and father and the children.

SOLNESS: God knows if there'll be any call for that kind of thing from now on.

HILDE: Poor master builder! When for ten years you've given your whole life to that very thing.

SOLNESS: Yes, you may well say that, Hilde.

HILDE (*breaking out*): Oh, this whole business is so stupid, so absolutely stupid!

SOLNESS: What is?

HILDE: This not daring to reach out and lay hold on happiness. On life! Just because standing in the way happens to be somebody one knows!

SOLNESS: Somebody one has no right to push aside.

HILDE: I only wonder if one really does have the right, in fact? Yet even so. . . . Oh, if only one could fall asleep and leave the whole sorry business behind!

She lays her arms flat down upon the table, rests the left side of her head on her hands and shuts her eyes.

SOLNESS (*turns the armchair round and sits down by the table*): Did you have a cheerful happy home—in your father's house, Hilde?

HILDE (*motionless and answering as though half asleep*): All I had was a cage.

SOLNESS: And you don't want to go back there again?

HILDE (*as before*): A forest bird never wants a cage.

SOLNESS: Preferring to swoop through the empty sky . . .

HILDE (*continuing as before*): To swoop upon its prey . . .

SOLNESS (*resting his gaze upon her*): Ah, any man with a bit of viking spirit . . .

HILDE (*in an ordinary voice, opening her eyes but not moving*): And what else? Tell me that!

SOLNESS: A robust conscience.

HILDE *sits up animatedly on the bench. Her eyes again glisten happily.*

HILDE (*nods to him*): I know what you'll build next time!

SOLNESS: Then you know more than I do, Hilde.

HILDE: Yes. But these master builders— they're so stupid, you know.

SOLNESS: So what will it be?

HILDE (*nods again*): The castle.

SOLNESS: What castle?

HILDE: *My* castle, of course.

SOLNESS: You want a castle now?

HILDE: You owe me a kingdom, don't you?

SOLNESS: That's what you keep telling me.

HILDE: Well then! You owe me this kingdom. And surely any kingdom carries a castle with it, doesn't it?

SOLNESS (*more and more animatedly*): Yes, that's generally the way.

HILDE: Good! Then build it for me! Quickly!

SOLNESS (*laughs*): This very minute, eh?

HILDE: Of course! Time's up! Ten years. And I'm not waiting any longer. So—bring out the castle, master builder!

SOLNESS: It's no easy matter owing *you* anything, Hilde.

HILDE: You should have thought of that before. Now it's too late. So! (*Beating on the table.*) Out with the castle! It's *my* castle! I want it at once!

SOLNESS (*more seriously, leans over towards her with his arms on the table*): How do you picture this castle, Hilde?

Her expression slowly changes, and she seems to be gazing deep into her own soul.

HILDE (*slowly*): My castle shall stand on high ground. Very high it must stand. And open to all sides. So I can see into the far, far distance.

SOLNESS: With a high tower, I suppose?

HILDE: A tremendously high tower. And at the very top of the tower there's to be a balcony. And out up there I shall stand . . .

SOLNESS (*involuntarily clutches at his forehead*): How you can enjoy standing at such a dizzy height . . .

HILDE: But of course! That's where I shall stand looking at the others—at those who build churches. And homes for father and mother and the children. And you can also come up and have a look.

SOLNESS (*in a low voice*): Will the master builder be allowed to come up to his princess?

HILDE: If the master builder wishes it.

SOLNESS (*more softly*): Then I think the master builder will come.

HILDE (*nods*): The master builder—he will come.

SOLNESS: But he'll never build again. Poor old master builder!

HILDE (*animatedly*): Yes, he will! We two will do it together. And we'll build the loveliest . . . quite the loveliest thing in all the world.

SOLNESS (*tense*): Hilde! Tell me what that is!

HILDE (*looks at him with a smile, shakes her head a little, pouts, and speaks to him as though to a child*): These master builders— what very, very stupid people they are.

SOLNESS: Yes, of course they're stupid. But tell me what it is! What is it that's quite the loveliest thing in all the world. Which we two are to build together?

HILDE (*is silent for a moment and then says with an enigmatic expression in her eyes*): Castles in the air.

SOLNESS: Castles in the air?

HILDE (*nods*): Yes, castles in the air! Do you know what a castle in the air is?

SOLNESS: From what you say, it's the loveliest thing in the world.

HILDE (*rises abruptly and makes a gesture of repudiation with her hand*): Yes, yes, of course! Castles in the air—they're so easy to take refuge in. So easy to build, too . . . (*Looks scornfully at him.*) Particularly for master builders with . . . weak nerves.

SOLNESS (*rises*): After today we two will build together, Hilde.

HILDE (*with a doubting smile*): A *proper* castle in the air?

SOLNESS: Yes, with a real foundation.

RAGNAR BROVIK *comes out of the house. He is carrying a large green wreath with flowers and silk ribbons.*

HILDE (*with a cry of joy*): The wreath! Oh, how absolutely marvellous this is going to be!

SOLNESS (*surprised*): How is it *you* are bringing the wreath, Ragnar?

RAGNAR: I promised the foreman I would.

SOLNESS (*relieved*): Then your father must be a little better?

RAGNAR: No.

SOLNESS: Didn't what I wrote make him feel any better?

RAGNAR: It came too late.

SOLNESS: Too late!

RAGNAR: He was no longer conscious when she got back with it. He had had a stroke.

SOLNESS: Then you must go home to him. You must look after your father!

RAGNAR: He doesn't need me any more.

SOLNESS: But surely you ought to be with him.

RAGNAR: She's sitting by the bed.

SOLNESS (*somewhat uncertainly*): Kaja?

RAGNAR (*looks darkly at him*): Yes, Kaja.

SOLNESS: Go home, Ragnar. Be with him and with her. Let *me* have the wreath.

RAGNAR (*suppressing a mocking smile*): You're not thinking of doing it yourself . . . ?

SOLNESS: I want to take it down there myself. (*Takes the wreath from him.*) Now go home. We don't need you today.

RAGNAR: I know you don't need me after this. But today I'm staying.

SOLNESS: All right, stay, if you really want to.

HILDE (*by the railings*): Master builder! I'm going to stand here and watch you.

SOLNESS: Watch me!

HILDE: It's going to be terribly exciting.

SOLNESS (*in a low voice*): We'll talk about that later, Hilde.

He takes the wreath and goes down the steps and across the garden.

HILDE (*looks after him and then turns to RAGNAR*): I think you might at least have thanked him.

RAGNAR: Thanked him? Me thank *him*?

HILDE: Yes, you really should!

RAGNAR: More likely you are the one I ought to thank.

HILDE: How can you say a thing like that?

RAGNAR (*without answering her*): But just you beware! You don't know him properly yet.

HILDE (*fierily*): I know him better than anybody!

RAGNAR (*laughs bitterly*): Thank him! The man who held me down year after year! The man who undermined my father's faith in me. Who made me lose faith in myself. . . . And all that just to . . . !

HILDE (*as though suspecting something*): To what . . . ? Tell me! Quickly!

RAGNAR: Just to be able to keep her for himself.

HILDE (*with a sudden movement towards him*): That girl at the desk!

RAGNAR: Yes.

HILDE (*threateningly, with clenched hands*): It's not true! You're lying!

RAGNAR: I wouldn't have believed it either, until today—when she told me herself.

HILDE (*as though beside herself*): What did she say? I want to know! Now! This minute!

RAGNAR: She said that he has taken control of her mind—utterly and completely. Taken possession of all her thoughts. She says she can never escape him. That she wants to stay here where *he* is. . . .

HILDE (*with flashing eyes*): She won't get the chance!

RAGNAR (*inquiringly*): Who says she won't?

HILDE (*quickly*): He'll say she won't!

RAGNAR: Ah, yes—I understand everything now. After this she'd be nothing but a nuisance.

HILDE: You don't understand anything—if you can say a thing like that! No! I'll tell you why he held on to her.

RAGNAR: Why?

HILDE: To keep *you.*

RAGNAR: Did he tell you this?

HILDE: No, but it's true! It must be true. (*Wildly.*) I want it to be true! I *want* it to be!

RAGNAR: And as soon as you came, he let her go.

HILDE: It was *you* he let go! You! Why should he bother himself about girls like her?

RAGNAR (*reflecting*): Could he really have been afraid of me all this time?

HILDE: *He* afraid! I think you flatter yourself.

RAGNAR: He must have realized long ago that I had something. Anyway, don't you see that's precisely what he is—*afraid*!

HILDE: Him! Don't make me laugh!

RAGNAR: In his own way he *is* afraid. The great master builder! Things like spoiling other people's lives—the way he spoilt my father's and mine—he's not afraid of *that.* But a little thing like climbing up a bit of scaffolding —you watch him steer well clear of that!

HILDE: Ah, you should have seen him way up high, high as I once saw him—so high it left your senses reeling!

RAGNAR: Did you see that?

HILDE: I certainly did. Free and proud he stood there, tying the wreath to the weathercock!

RAGNAR: I knew he'd risked it *once* in his life. One solitary occasion. We've often talked about it among ourselves. But no power on earth would get him to do it again.

HILDE: He'll do it again today!

RAGNAR (*scornfully*): That's what you think!

HILDE: We'll see him!

RAGNAR: We won't! Neither of us will ever live to see that!

HILDE (*vehemently, beside herself*): I *will*! I *will* see it! I *must* see it!

RAGNAR: He won't do it. He simply *daren't* do it. Because he's now got this fatal flaw—this great master builder of ours!

MRS. SOLNESS *comes out of the house on to the verandah.*

MRS. SOLNESS (*looking around her*): Isn't he here? Where's he gone?

RAGNAR: Mr. Solness is over there with the workmen.

HILDE: He took the wreath.

MRS. SOLNESS (*in terror*): He took the wreath! Oh God! Oh God! Brovik—you must go down to him! Get him to come back here!

RAGNAR: Shall I tell him you want to speak to him?

MRS. SOLNESS: Oh yes, please do! No, no! Don't say *I* want him! Tell him there's somebody here. Say he must come at once.

RAGNAR: Very well. I'll do that, Mrs. Solness.

He goes down the steps and away through the garden.

MRS. SOLNESS: Oh, Miss Wangel, you can't imagine the dread I go through on his account.

HILDE: But what's so frightening about this?

MRS. SOLNESS: Oh, surely you see. Suppose he meant it! Suppose he takes it into his head to climb the scaffolding!

HILDE (*excitedly*): Do you think he will?

MRS. SOLNESS: Oh, you never know what he's going to do. He's capable of doing absolutely anything!

HILDE: Ah! So you too think he's possibly a bit—er . . . ?

MRS. SOLNESS: I no longer know what to think. The doctor has told me so many different things, and when I remember some of the other things I've heard him say, and put two and two together . . .

DR. HERDAL *puts his head in through the doorway.*)

DR. HERDAL: Isn't he coming soon?

MRS. SOLNESS: Yes, I think so. He's been sent for.

DR. HERDAL (*approaches*): But hadn't you better go inside, Mrs. Solness. . . .

MRS. SOLNESS: No, no! I'll stay out here and wait for Halvard.

DR. HERDAL: But there are some ladies here to see you . . .

MRS. SOLNESS: Oh, my God! Why must it be now!

DR. HERDAL: They say they want to watch the ceremony.

MRS. SOLNESS: Ah, well, I suppose I'd better go in and see them. It's my duty.

HILDE: Can't you ask these ladies to go away?

MRS. SOLNESS: No, I couldn't possibly do that. Now they've come, it's my duty to receive them. You wait out here, though . . . so you can be here when he comes.

DR. HERDAL: And try to keep him talking as long as possible. . . .

MRS. SOLNESS: Yes, please do, dear Miss Wangel. Hold on to him as tightly as you can.

HILDE: Wouldn't it be best if you did this yourself?

MRS. SOLNESS: Oh dear, yes! It is *my* duty, really. But when one is so beset by duties . . .

DR. HERDAL (*looking towards the garden*): He's coming!

MRS. SOLNESS: And here am I, having to go in.

DR. HERDAL (*to* HILDE): Don't say anything about my being here.

HILDE: Oh, no! I think I can find other things to talk to Mr. Solness about.

MRS. SOLNESS: And do please hold tight on to him. I think *you* can do that best.

MRS. SOLNESS *and* DR. HERDAL *go into the house.* HILDE *remains behind, standing on the verandah.* SOLNESS *comes up the steps from the garden.*

SOLNESS: They tell me somebody wants me.

HILDE: Yes, master builder. Me.

SOLNESS: Oh, it's you, Hilde. I was afraid it might be Aline and the doctor.

HILDE: You seem pretty afraid altogether!

SOLNESS: You think so?

HILDE: Yes. People are saying that you are afraid of climbing . . . up the scaffolding, for instance.

SOLNESS: Well, that's a different matter.

HILDE: Then you are afraid to do it?

SOLNESS: Yes, I am.

HILDE: Afraid you might fall and dash yourself to pieces?

SOLNESS: No, not that.

HILDE: What, then?

SOLNESS: I am afraid of retribution, Hilde.

HILDE: Retribution? (*Shakes her head.*) I don't understand.

SOLNESS: Sit down. And I'll tell you something.

HILDE: Yes, do! Quickly!

She sits down on a stool by the railing and looks expectantly at him.

SOLNESS (*throwing his hat on the table*): You know that I first began by building churches.

HILDE (*nods*): I know that.

SOLNESS: You see, I was brought up in a God-fearing home out in the country. That's why I thought building churches was the worthiest thing I could do.

HILDE: Yes, yes.

SOLNESS: And I think I can say that I built those humble little churches with such honesty and sincerity and devotion that . . .

HILDE: Well?

SOLNESS: Well . . . that I think He should have been pleased with me.

HILDE: He? Which he?

SOLNESS: He for whom the churches were intended, of course! He, whose honour and glory they were meant to serve.

HILDE: I see! But are you so sure that . . . He wasn't . . . pleased with you?

SOLNESS (*scornfully*): He pleased with *me*! How can you say things like that, Hilde? He who has let loose this troll within me to rampage about as it will? He who bade them all be ready night and day to minister to me . . . all these . . . these . . .

HILDE: Devils . . .

SOLNESS: Yes, of both kinds. Oh no, I was soon made to realize that He wasn't pleased with me. (*Mysteriously.*) In fact, you know, that's why He let the old house burn down.

HILDE: Was that the reason?

SOLNESS: Yes, don't you see? He wanted to give me the chance of becoming a complete master of my craft, so that I could build ever more splendid churches for Him. At first I didn't understand what He was getting at. Then suddenly I realized.

HILDE: When was that?

SOLNESS: It was when I built that church tower up at Lysanger.

HILDE: That's what I thought.

SOLNESS: You see, Hilde, up there in a strange place where I had time to think, I was able to turn things over in my mind. It was then I realized why He had taken my little children from me. It was so that I should have nothing else to cling to. No love or happiness or anything like that, you see. I was to be a master builder, and that was all. I was to spend my whole life building for Him. (*Laughs.*) But that idea didn't come to much.

HILDE: What did you do then?

SOLNESS: First, I scrutinized myself . . . examined myself . . .

HILDE: And then?

SOLNESS: Then—just as He had—I did the *impossible.*

HILDE: The impossible?

SOLNESS: Never before had I been able to stand heights. But that day I could.

HILDE (*leaps up*): Yes, yes, you could!

SOLNESS: And as I stood there on high, at the very top, and as I hung the wreath on the weathercock, I spoke to Him: Listen to me, Almighty One! From this day forward, I too will be free. A master builder free in his own field, as you are in yours. Never again will I build churches for you. Only homes for the people.

HILDE (*with wide glistening eyes*): *That* was the song I heard in the air!

SOLNESS: But He got His own back later on.

HILDE: What do you mean by that?

SOLNESS (*looks at her despondently*): Building homes for the people isn't worth a brass farthing, Hilde.

HILDE: What makes you say that now?

SOLNESS: Because now I see that people have no use for these homes of theirs. It doesn't help them to be happy. And I probably wouldn't have had any use for a home like that, either. Even if I'd owned one. (*Laughs quietly and bitterly.*) And now, looking back, what does it all add up to? In fact, I've built nothing. Nor did I really sacrifice anything for the chance to build. Nothing! Absolutely nothing!

HILDE: You're not going to build anything else after this?

SOLNESS (*animatedly*): Oh yes, I am! I am just about to begin!

HILDE: What's it to be? Tell me quickly!

SOLNESS: The one thing I think can contain human happiness—that's what I'm going to build now.

HILDE (*looks fixedly at him*): Master builder, you mean our castles in the air.

SOLNESS: Yes. Castles in the air.

HILDE: I'm afraid your mind would reel before we got half-way.

SOLNESS: Not if I can go hand in hand with *you,* Hilde.

HILDE (*with suppressed venom*): Only me? Won't there be several of us?

SOLNESS: Who else?

HILDE: Oh, that Kaja out of the office. Poor thing, aren't you going to take her along with you, too?

SOLNESS: Ah! So that's what Aline was sitting here talking to you about.

HILDE: *Is* it true, or isn't it?

SOLNESS (*angrily*): I won't answer that! You must believe in me, implicitly!

HILDE: For ten years I have believed in you, utterly and completely.

SOLNESS: You must go on believing!

HILDE: Then let me see you standing on high again!

SOLNESS (*sadly*): Oh, Hilde . . . I can't do a thing like that every day.

HILDE (*passionately*): I want you to! (*Pleadingly.*) Just once more, master builder! Do the *impossible* once more!

SOLNESS (*stands and looks deep into her eyes*): *If* I try it, Hilde, I shall stand up there and speak to Him as I did last time.

HILDE (*with rising excitement*): What will you say to Him?

SOLNESS: I shall say to him: Hear me, Great and Mighty Lord! Judge me as you will. But henceforth I shall build one thing only, quite the loveliest thing in the whole world . . .

HILDE (*carried away*): Yes . . . Yes . . . Yes!

SOLNESS: . . . Build it together with the princess I love . . .

HILDE: Yes, tell Him that! Tell Him that!

SOLNESS: Yes. And then I shall say to Him: Now I go down to take her in my arms and kiss her . . .

HILDE: . . . Many times! Say that!

SOLNESS: . . . Many, many times, I shall say.

HILDE: And then . . . ?

SOLNESS: Then I shall wave my hat and come down to earth . . . and do as I told Him.

HILDE (*with arms outstretched*): Now I see you again as you were when there was a song in the air!

SOLNESS (*looks at her with bowed head*): How did you become as you are, Hilde?

HILDE: How did you make me as I am?

SOLNESS (*abruptly and firmly*): The princess shall have her castle.

HILDE (*joyfully clapping her hands*): Oh, master builder . . . ! My lovely, lovely castle! Our castle in the air!

SOLNESS: On its firm foundation.

In the street a crowd of people have gathered; they can be glimpsed indistinctly through the trees. The sound of a brass band can be heard in the distance behind the new house. MRS. SOLNESS, *wearing a fur round her neck,* DR. HERDAL, *with her white shawl over his arm, and several ladies come out on to the verandah.* RAGNAR BROVIK *comes up at that moment from the garden.*

MRS. SOLNESS (*to* RAGNAR): Is there going to be a band?

RAGNAR: Yes. The band of the builders' union! (*To* SOLNESS.) The foreman asked me to tell you he's ready to go up with the wreath.

SOLNESS (*takes his hat*): Good. I'll go down myself.

MRS. SOLNESS (*anxiously*): What do you want down there, Halvard?

SOLNESS (*curtly*): I must be down there among the men.

MRS. SOLNESS: Yes, down there. Down below.

SOLNESS: That's where I generally am, aren't I? In the ordinary way.

He goes down the steps and across the garden.

MRS. SOLNESS (*calls after him over the railing*): But tell the man to be careful as he's climbing up! Promise me, Halvard!

DR. HERDAL (*to* MRS. SOLNESS): There, I was right, you see. He's given up those wild ideas.

MRS. SOLNESS: Oh, what a relief! Twice we've had workmen falling down. Both of them dashed to pieces instantly. (*Turns to* HILDE.) Thank you, Miss Wangel, for keeping such a tight hold on him. I'm sure *I'd* never have managed him.

DR. HERDAL (*gaily*): Yes, yes, Miss Wangel! You know how to hold tight on to somebody when you set your mind to it!

MRS. SOLNESS *and* DR. HERDAL *walk over to the ladies, who stand by the steps looking out over the garden.* HILDE *remains standing by the railing in the foreground.* RAGNAR *walks over to her.*

RAGNAR (*with suppressed laughter, in a low voice*): Miss Wangel. . . . Do you see all those young people down in the street?

HILDE: Yes.

RAGNAR: They are all the other builders in training, come to watch the master.

HILDE: What do they want to watch him for?

RAGNAR: They want to see him too scared to climb his own building.

HILDE: So that's what the lads want, is it?

RAGNAR (*venomously and scornfully*): He's kept us down too long. Now we want to watch him having to stay down, too.

HILDE: That's something you won't see. Not this time.

RAGNAR (*smiles*): Oh? Where will we see him, then?

HILDE: Right up high! High up by the weathercock is where you'll see him!

RAGNAR (*laughs*): Him! Don't you believe it!

HILDE: He means to get to the top. And that's where you'll see him.

RAGNAR: He means to, yes! I'm prepared to believe that. But he just *can't* do it. He'll be dizzy long before he's got half-way. He'll have to crawl down again on his hands and knees!

DR. HERDAL (*pointing*): Look! There goes the foreman up the ladder.

MRS. SOLNESS: And he's got the wreath to carry as well. Oh, let's hope he takes care!

RAGNAR (*stares incredulously and cries out*): But surely that's . . .

HILDE (*with a shout of joy*): It's the master builder himself!

MRS. SOLNESS (*shouts out in terror*): Yes, it's Halvard! Oh my God . . . ! Halvard! Halvard!

DR. HERDAL: Shh! Don't shout to him!

MRS. SOLNESS (*almost beside herself*): I must go to him! I must get him down again!

DR. HERDAL (*holding her back*): Everybody keep still! Not a sound!

HILDE (*motionless, following* SOLNESS *with her eyes*): Climbing, climbing. Higher and higher! Look! Just look!

RAGNAR (*breathlessly*): He *must* turn back now! There's no other way.

HILDE: Climbing, climbing. He's nearly at the top.

MRS. SOLNESS: Oh, I shall die of terror. I can't bear to watch!

DR. HERDAL: Don't look at him then.

HILDE: There he is, standing on the very top plank! Right at the top!

DR. HERDAL: Nobody move! Do you hear!

HILDE (*in quiet jubilation*): At last! At last! Now I see him great and free again!

RAGNAR (*almost speechless*): But this is . . .

HILDE: This is the way I've seen him all these ten years. How confident he looks standing there! Terribly exciting, all the same! Look at him! Now he's hanging the wreath over the spire!

RAGNAR: I feel as though I am witnessing something utterly impossible.

HILDE: Yes! What he is doing now *is* impossible! (*With that enigmatic expression in her eyes.*) Can you see anybody else up there with him?

RAGNAR: There is nobody else.

HILDE: Yes, there is. He is disputing with someone.

RAGNAR: You are wrong.

HILDE: Don't you hear a song in the air, either?

RAGNAR: It must be the wind in the tree-tops.

HILDE: *I* hear a song. A mighty song! (*Cries in wild jubilation.*) Look! Look! Now he's waving his hat! He's waving to us down here! Oh, let's wave back to him! Now, now he's done it! (*Snatches the white shawl from the doctor, waves it about and shouts up in the air.*) Hurrah for the master builder!

DR. HERDAL: Stop it! Stop it! For God's sake . . . !

The ladies on the verandah wave their handkerchiefs, and the people in the street join in the cheering. There is a sudden silence, and then there is a cry of terror from the crowd. A human body and some planks and poles can be indistinctly glimpsed plunging down among the trees.

MRS. SOLNESS AND THE LADIES (*together*): He is falling! He is falling!

MRS. SOLNESS *sways and falls back in a faint; amid cries and confusion, the ladies catch her. The crowd in the street breaks down the fence and rushes into the garden.* DR. HERDAL *also hurries down there. Short pause.*

HILDE (*continues to stare upwards, as though turned to stone*): *My* master builder!

RAGNAR (*supporting himself trembling against the railing*): He must have been dashed to pieces. Killed instantaneously.

ONE OF THE LADIES (*as* MRS. SOLNESS *is carried into the house*): Run to the doctor . . .

RAGNAR: I can't move . . .

ANOTHER LADY: Then shout to somebody!

RAGNAR (*tries to shout*): How is it? Is he alive?

A VOICE (*down in the garden*): The master builder is dead!

OTHER VOICES (*nearer*): His head is all smashed in. . . . He fell right into the quarry.

HILDE (*turns to* RAGNAR *and says quietly*): I can't see him up there now.

RAGNAR: This is terrible. So in fact he couldn't do it.

HILDE (*with a kind of quiet, bewildered triumph*): But he got right to the top. And I heard harps in the air. (*Waves the shawl upwards and shouts with a wild intensity.*) My . . . my . . . master builder!

ANTON CHEKHOV

Three Sisters

Translated by Elizaveta Fen

Characters

PROZOROV, *Andrey Serghyeevich*
NATASHA (*Natalia Ivanovna*), *his fiancée, afterwards his wife*
OLGA (*Olga Serghyeevna, Olia*)
MASHA (*Maria Serghyeevna*) } *his sisters*
IRENA (*Irena Serghyeevna*)
KOOLYGHIN, *Fiodor Ilyich, master at the High School for boys, husband of Masha*
VERSHININ, *Alexandr Ignatyevich, Lieutenant-Colonel, Battery Commander*
TOOZENBACH, *Nikolai Lvovich, Baron, Lieutenant in the Army*
SOLIONY, *Vassily Vassilich, Captain*
CHEBUTYKIN, *Ivan Romanych, Army Doctor*
FEDOTIK, *Aleksey Petrovich, Second Lieutenant*
RODÉ, *Vladimir Karlovich, Second Lieutenant*
FERAPONT (*Ferapont Spiridonych*), *an old porter from the County Office*
ANFISA, *the Prozorovs' former nurse, an old woman of 80*

Scene: *The action takes place in a county town.*

ACT I

A drawing-room in the Prozorovs' house; it is separated from a large ballroom at the back by a row of columns. It is midday; there is cheerful sunshine outside. In the ballroom the table is being laid for lunch. OLGA, *wearing the regulation dark-blue dress of a secondary school mistress, is correcting her pupils' work, standing or walking about as she does so.* MASHA, *in a black dress, is sitting reading a book, her hat on her lap.* IRENA, *in white, stands lost in thought.*

OLGA: It's exactly a year ago that Father died, isn't it? This very day, the fifth of May— your Saint's day,[1] Irena. I remember it was very cold and it was snowing. I felt then as if I should never survive his death; and you had fainted and were lying quite still, as if you were dead. And now—a year's gone by,

---

[1] *Saint's day:* The feast day of the saint after whom Irena was named; a day celebrated like a birthday in many European countries.

and we talk about it so easily. You're wearing white, and your face is positively radiant. . . .

A clock strikes twelve.

The clock struck twelve then, too. (*A pause.*) I remember when Father was being taken to the cemetery there was a military band, and a salute with rifle fire. That was because he was a general, in command of a brigade. And yet there weren't many people at the funeral. Of course, it was raining hard, raining and snowing.

IRENA: Need we bring up all these memories?

Baron TOOZENBACH, CHEBUTYKIN *and* SOLIONY *appear behind the columns by the table in the ballroom.*

OLGA: It's so warm to-day that we can keep the windows wide open, and yet there aren't any leaves showing on the birch trees. Father was made a brigadier eleven years ago, and then he left Moscow and took us with him. I remember so well how everything in Moscow was in blossom by now, everything was soaked in sunlight and warmth. Eleven years have gone by, yet I remember everything about it, as if we'd only left yesterday. Oh, Heavens! When I woke up this morning and saw this flood of sunshine, all this spring sunshine, I felt so moved and so happy! I felt such a longing to get back home to Moscow!

CHEBUTYKIN (*to* TOOZENBACH): The devil you have!

TOOZENBACH: It's nonsense, I agree.

MASHA (*absorbed in her book, whistles a tune under her breath*).

OLGA: Masha, do stop whistling! How can you? (*A pause.*) I suppose I must get this continual headache because I have to go to school every day and go on teaching right into the evening. I seem to have the thoughts of someone quite old. Honestly, I've been feeling as if my strength and youth were running out of me drop by drop, day after day. Day after day, all these four years that I've been working at the school. . . . I just have one longing and it seems to grow stronger and stronger. . . .

IRENA: If only we could go back to Moscow! Sell the house, finish with our life here, and go back to Moscow.

OLGA: Yes, Moscow! As soon as we possibly can.

CHEBUTYKIN *and* TOOZENBACH *laugh.*

IRENA: I suppose Andrey will soon get a professorship. He isn't likely to go on living here. The only problem is our poor Masha.

OLGA: Masha can come and stay the whole summer with us every year in Moscow.

MASHA (*whistles a tune under her breath*).

IRENA: Everything will settle itself, with God's help. (*Looks through the window.*) What lovely weather it is to-day! Really, I don't know why there's such joy in my heart. I remembered this morning that it was my Saint's day, and suddenly I felt so happy, and I thought of the time when we were children, and Mother was still alive. And then such wonderful thoughts came to me, such wonderful stirring thoughts!

OLGA: You're so lovely to-day, you really do look most attractive. Masha looks pretty to-day, too. Andrey could be good-looking, but he's grown so stout. It doesn't suit him. As for me, I've just aged and grown a lot thinner. I suppose it's through getting so irritated with the girls at school. But to-day I'm at home, I'm free, and my headache's gone, and I feel much younger than I did yesterday. I'm only twenty-eight, after all. . . . I suppose everything that God wills must be right and good, but I can't help thinking sometimes that if I'd got married and stayed at home, it would have been a better thing for me. (*A pause.*) I would have been very fond of my husband.

TOOZENBACH (*to* SOLIONY): Really, you talk such a lot of nonsense, I'm tired of listening to you. (*Comes into the drawing-room.*) I forgot to tell you: Vershinin, our new battery commander, is going to call on you to-day. (*Sits down by the piano.*)

OLGA: I'm very glad to hear it.

IRENA: Is he old?

TOOZENBACH: No, not particularly. Forty, forty-five at the most. (*Plays quietly.*) He seems a nice fellow. Certainly not a fool. His only weakness is that he talks too much.

IRENA: Is he interesting?

TOOZENBACH: He's all right, only he's got a wife, a mother-in-law and two little girls. What's more, she's his second wife. He calls on everybody and tells them that he's got a wife and two little girls. He'll tell you about it, too, I'm sure of that. His wife seems to be a bit soft in the head. She wears a long plait like a girl, she is always philosophizing and talking in high-flown language, and then she often tries to commit suicide, apparently just to annoy her husband. I would have run away from a wife like that years ago, but he puts up with it, and just grumbles about it.

SOLIONY (*enters the drawing-room with* CHEBUTYKIN): Now I can only lift sixty pounds with one hand, but with two I can lift two hundred pounds, or even two hundred and forty. So I conclude from that that two men are not just twice as strong as one, but three times as strong, if not more.

CHEBUTYKIN (*reads the paper as he comes in*): Here's a recipe for falling hair . . . two ounces of naphthaline, half-a-bottle of methylated spirit . . . dissolve and apply once a day.... (*Writes it down in a notebook.*) Must make a note of it. (*To* SOLIONY.) Well, as I was trying to explain to you, you cork the bottle and pass a glass tube through the cork. Then you take a pinch of ordinary powdered alum, and . . .

IRENA: Ivan Romanych, dear Ivan Romanych!

CHEBUTYKIN: What is it, my child, what is it?

IRENA: Tell me, why is it I'm so happy to-day? Just as if I were sailing along in a boat with big white sails, and above me the wide, blue sky, and in the sky great white birds floating around?

CHEBUTYKIN (*kisses both her hands, tenderly*): My little white bird!

IRENA: You know, when I woke up this morning, and after I'd got up and washed, I suddenly felt as if everything in the world had become clear to me, and I knew the way I ought to live. I know it all now, my dear Ivan Romanych. Man must work by the sweat of his brow whatever his class, and that should make up the whole meaning and purpose of his life and happiness and contentment. Oh, how good it must be to be a workman, getting up with the sun and breaking stones by the roadside—or a shepherd—or a schoolmaster teaching the children—or an engine-driver on the railway. Good Heavens! it's better to be a mere ox or horse, and work, than the sort of young woman who wakes up at twelve, and drinks her coffee in bed, and then takes two hours dressing. . . . How dreadful! You know how you long for a cool drink in hot weather? Well, that's the way I long for work. And if I don't get up early from now on and really work, you can refuse to be friends with me any more, Ivan Romanych.

CHEBUTYKIN (*tenderly*): So I will, so I will....

OLGA: Father taught us to get up at seven o'clock and so Irena always wakes up at seven—but then she stays in bed till at least nine, thinking about something or other. And with such a serious expression on her face, too! (*Laughs.*)

IRENA: You think it's strange when I look serious because you always think of me as a little girl. I'm twenty, you know!

TOOZENBACH: All this longing for work. . . . Heavens! how well I can understand it! I've never done a stroke of work in my life. I was born in Petersburg, an unfriendly, idle city—born into a family where work and worries were simply unknown. I remember a valet pulling off my boots for me when I came home from the cadet school. . . . I grumbled at the way he did it, and my mother looked on in admiration. She was quite surprised when other people looked at me in any other way. I was so carefully protected from work! But I doubt whether they succeeded in protecting me for good and all—yes, I doubt it very much! The time's come: there's a terrific thunder-cloud advancing upon us, a mighty storm is coming to freshen us up! Yes, it's coming all right, it's quite near already, and it's going to blow away all this idleness and indifference, and prejudice against work, this rot of boredom that our society is suffering from. I'm going to work, and in twenty-five or thirty years' time every man and woman will be working. Every one of us!

CHEBUTYKIN: I'm not going to work.

TOOZENBACH: You don't count.

SOLIONY: In twenty-five years' time you won't be alive, thank goodness. In a couple of years you'll die from a stroke—or I'll lose my temper with you and put a bullet in your head, my good fellow. (*Takes a scent bottle from his pocket and sprinkles the scent over his chest and hands.*)

CHEBUTYKIN (*laughs*): It's quite true that I never have done any work. Not a stroke since I left the university. I haven't even read a book, only newspapers. (*Takes another newspaper out of his pocket.*) For instance, here. . . . I know from the paper that there was a person called Dobroliubov,[2] but what he wrote about I've not the faintest idea. . . . God alone knows. . . . (*Someone knocks on the floor from downstairs.*) There! They're calling me to come down: there's someone come to see me. I'll be back in a moment. . . . (*Goes out hurriedly, stroking his beard.*)

IRENA: He's up to one of his little games.

TOOZENBACH: Yes. He looked very solemn as he left. He's obviously going to give you a present.

IRENA: I do dislike this sort of thing. . . .

OLGA: Yes, isn't it dreadful? He's always doing something silly.

MASHA: "A green oak grows by a curving shore, And round that oak hangs a golden chain"[3] . . . (*Gets up as she sings under her breath.*)

OLGA: You're sad to-day, Masha.

MASHA (*puts on her hat, singing*).

OLGA: Where are you going?

MASHA: Home.

IRENA: What a strange thing to do.

TOOZENBACH: What! Going away from your sister's party?

MASHA: What does it matter? I'll be back this evening. Good-bye, my darling. (*Kisses IRENA.*) And once again—I wish you all the happiness in the world. In the old days when Father was alive we used to have thirty or forty officers at our parties. What gay parties we had! And to-day—what have we got to-day? A man and a half, and the place is as quiet as a tomb. I'm going home. I'm depressed to-day, I'm sad, so don't listen to me. (*Laughs through her tears.*) We'll have a talk later, but good-bye for now, my dear. I'll go somewhere or other. . . .

IRENA (*displeased*): Really, you are a . . .

OLGA (*tearfully*): I understand you, Masha.

SOLIONY: If a man starts philosophizing, you call that philosophy, or possibly just sophistry, but if a woman or a couple of women start philosophizing you call that . . . what would you call it, now? Ask me another!

MASHA: What are you talking about? You are a disconcerting person!

SOLIONY: Nothing.
"He had no time to say 'Oh, oh!'
Before that bear had struck him low" . . .[4]

A pause.

---

2 *Dobroliubov:* Nikolay Alexandrovich (1836–1861), Russian critic who believed that literature reflects, but cannot change, reality.

3 *"A green oak . . . chain":* from the Introduction to *Russlan and Ludmila,* a poem by A. S. Pushkin (1799–1837).

4 *"He had . . . low":* from "The Peasant and the Laborer," a fable by I. A. Krylov (c. 1769–1844).

MASHA (*to* OLGA, *crossly*): Do stop snivelling!

Enter ANFISA *and* FERAPONT, *the latter carrying a large cake.*

ANFISA: Come along, my dear, this way. Come in, your boots are quite clean. (*To* IRENA.) A cake from Protopopov, at the Council Office.

IRENA: Thank you. Tell him I'm very grateful to him. (*Takes the cake.*)

FERAPONT: What's that?

IRENA (*louder*): Tell him I sent my thanks.

OLGA: Nanny, will you give him a piece of cake? Go along, Ferapont, they'll give you some cake.

FERAPONT: What's that?

ANFISA: Come along with me, Ferapont Spiridonych, my dear. Come along. (*Goes out with* FERAPONT.)

MASHA: I don't like that Protopopov fellow, Mihail Potapych, or Ivanych, or whatever it is. It's best not to invite him here.

IRENA: I haven't invited him.

MASHA: Thank goodness.

Enter CHEBUTYKIN, *followed by a soldier carrying a silver samovar. Murmurs of astonishment and displeasure.*

OLGA (*covering her face with her hands*): A samovar! But this is dreadful![5] (*Goes through to the ballroom and stands by the table.*)

IRENA: My dear Ivan Romanych, what are you thinking about?

TOOZENBACH (*laughs*): Didn't I tell you?

MASHA: Ivan Romanych, you really ought to be ashamed of yourself!

CHEBUTYKIN: My dear, sweet girls, I've no one in the world but you. You're dearer to me than anything in the world! I'm nearly sixty, I'm an old man, a lonely, utterly unimportant old man. The only thing that's worth

anything in me is my love for you, and if it weren't for you, really I would have been dead long ago. (*To* IRENA.) My dear, my sweet little girl, haven't I known you since the very day you were born? Didn't I carry you about in my arms? . . . didn't I love your dear mother?

IRENA: But why do you get such expensive presents?

CHEBUTYKIN (*tearfully and crossly*): Expensive presents! . . . Get along with you! (*To the orderly.*) Put the samovar over there. (*Mimics* IRENA.) Expensive presents!

The orderly takes the samovar to the ballroom.

ANFISA (*crosses the drawing-room*): My dears, there's a strange colonel just arrived. He's taken off his coat and he's coming up now. Irenushka, do be nice and polite to him, won't you? (*In the doorway.*) And it's high time we had lunch, too. . . . Oh, dear! (*Goes out.*)

TOOZENBACH: It's Vershinin, I suppose.

Enter VERSHININ.

TOOZENBACH: Lieutenant-Colonel Vershinin!

VERSHININ (*to* MASHA *and* IRENA): Allow me to introduce myself—Lieutenant-Colonel Vershinin. I's so glad, so very glad to be here at last. How you've changed! Dear, dear, how you've changed!

IRENA: Please, do sit down. We're very pleased to see you, I'm sure.

VERSHININ (*gaily*): I'm so glad to see you, so glad! But there were three of you, weren't there?—three sisters. I remember there were three little girls. I don't remember their faces, but I knew your father, Colonel Prozorov, and I remember he had three little girls. Oh, yes, I saw them myself. I remember them quite well. How time flies! Dear, dear, how it flies!

TOOZENBACH: Alexandr Ignatyevich comes from Moscow.

---

[5] *Dreadful:* In Russia, a silver samovar is the traditional gift for a twenty-fifth wedding anniversary.

IRENA: From Moscow? You come from Moscow?

VERSHININ: Yes, from Moscow. Your father was a battery commander there, and I was an officer in the same brigade. (*To* MASHA.) I seem to remember your face a little.

MASHA: I don't remember you at all.

IRENA: Olia, Olia! (*Calls toward the ballroom.*) Olia, do come!

OLGA *enters from the ballroom.*

IRENA: It seems that Lieutenant-Colonel Vershinin comes from Moscow.

VERSHININ: You must be Olga Serghyeevna, the eldest. And you are Maria. . . . And you are Irena, the youngest. . . .

OLGA: You come from Moscow?

VERSHININ: Yes. I studied in Moscow and entered the service there. I stayed there quite a long time, but then I was put in charge of a battery here—so I moved out here, you see. I don't really remember you, you know, I only remember that there were three sisters. I remember your father, though, I remember him very well. All I need to do is to close my eyes and I can see him standing there as if he were alive. I used to visit you in Moscow.

OLGA: I thought I remembered everybody, and yet . . .

VERSHININ: My Christian names are Alexandr Ignatyevich.

IRENA: Alexandr Ignatyevich, and you come from Moscow! Well, what a surprise!

OLGA: We're going to live there, you know.

IRENA: We hope to be there by the autumn. It's our home town, we were born there. . . . In Staraya Basmannaya Street.

Both laugh happily.

MASHA: Fancy meeting a fellow townsman so unexpectedly! (*Eagerly.*) I remember now. Do you remember, Olga, there was someone they used to call "the lovesick Major"? You were a Lieutenant then, weren't you, and you were in love with someone or other, and everyone used to tease you about it. They called you "Major" for some reason or other.

VERSHININ (*laughs*): That's it, that's it. . . . "The lovesick Major," that's what they called me.

MASHA: In those days you only had a moustache. . . . Oh, dear, how much older you look! (*Tearfully.*) How much older!

VERSHININ: Yes, I was still a young man in the days when they called me "the lovesick Major." I was in love then. It's different now.

OLGA: But you haven't got a single grey hair! You've aged, yes, but you're certainly not an old man.

VERSHININ: Nevertheless, I'm turned forty-two. Is it long since you've left Moscow?

IRENA: Eleven years. Now what are you crying for, Masha, you funny girl? . . . (*Tearfully.*) You'll make me cry, too.

MASHA: I'm not crying. What was the street you lived in?

VERSHININ: In the Staraya Basmannaya.

OLGA: We did, too.

VERSHININ: At one time I lived in the Niemietzkaya Street. I used to walk from there to the Krasny Barracks, and I remember there was such a gloomy bridge I had to cross. I used to hear the noise of the water rushing under it. I remember how lonely and sad I felt there. (*A pause.*) But what a magnificently wide river you have here! It's a marvellous river!

OLGA: Yes, but this is a cold place. It's cold here, and there are too many mosquitoes.

VERSHININ: Really? I should have said you had a really good healthy climate here, a real Russian climate. Forest, river . . . birch-trees, too. The dear, unpretentious birch-trees—I love them more than any of the other trees. It's nice living here. But there's one rather strange thing, the station is fifteen miles from the town. And no one knows why.

SOLIONY: I know why it is. (*Everyone looks at him.*) Because if the station were nearer, it wouldn't be so far away, and as it is so far away, it can't be nearer. (*An awkward silence.*)

TOOZENBACH: You like your little joke, Vassily Vassilich.

OLGA: I'm sure I remember you now. I know I do.

VERSHININ: I knew your mother.

CHEBUTYKIN: She was a good woman, God bless her memory!

IRENA: Mamma was buried in Moscow.

OLGA: At the convent of Novo-Dievichye.

MASHA: You know, I'm even beginning to forget what she looked like. I suppose people will lose all memory of us in just the same way. We'll be forgotten.

VERSHININ: Yes, we shall all be forgotten. Such is our fate, and we can't do anything about it. And all the things that seem serious, important and full of meaning to us now will be forgotten one day—or anyway they won't seem important any more. (*A pause.*) It's strange to think that we're utterly unable to tell what will be regarded as great and important in the future and what will be thought of as just paltry and ridiculous. Didn't the great discoveries of Copernicus—or of Columbus, if you like—appear useless and unimportant to begin with?— whereas some rubbish, written up by an eccentric fool, was regarded as a revelation of great truth? It may well be that in time to come the life we live to-day will seem strange and uncomfortable and stupid and not too clean, either, and perhaps even wicked. . . .

TOOZENBACH: Who can tell? It's just as possible that future generations will think that we lived our lives on a very high plane and remember us with respect. After all, we no longer have tortures and public executions and invasions, though there's still a great deal of suffering!

SOLIONY (*in a high-pitched voice as if calling to chickens*): Cluck, cluck, cluck! There's nothing our good Baron loves as much as a nice bit of philosophizing.

TOOZENBACH: Vassily Vassilich, will you kindly leave me alone? (*Moves to another chair.*) It's becoming tiresome.

SOLIONY (*as before*): Cluck, cluck, cluck! . . .

TOOZENBACH (*to* VERSHININ): The suffering that we see around us—and there's so much of it—itself proves that our society has at least achieved a level of morality which is higher. . . .

VERSHININ: Yes, yes, of course.

CHEBUTYKIN: You said just now, Baron, that our age will be called great; but people are small all the same. . . . (*Gets up.*) Look how small I am.

A violin is played off stage.

MASHA: That's Andrey playing the violin; he's our brother, you know.

IRENA: We've got quite a clever brother. . . . We're expecting him to be a professor. Papa was a military man, but Andrey chose an academic career.

OLGA: We've been teasing him to-day. We think he's in love, just a little.

IRENA: With a girl who lives down here. She'll be calling in to-day most likely.

MASHA: The way she dresses herself is awful! It's not that her clothes are just ugly and old-fashioned, they're simply pathetic. She'll put on some weird-looking, bright yellow skirt with a crude sort of fringe affair, and then a red blouse to go with it. And her cheeks look as though they've been scrubbed, they're so shiny! Andrey's not in love with her—I can't believe it; after all, he has got some taste. I think he's just playing the fool, just to annoy us. I heard yesterday that she's going to get married to Protopopov, the chairman of the local council. I thought it was an excellent idea. (*Calls through the side door.*) Andrey, come here, will you? Just for a moment, dear.

Enter ANDREY.

OLGA: This is my brother, Andrey Serghyee-vich.

VERSHININ: Vershinin.

ANDREY: Prozorov. (*Wipes the perspiration from his face.*) I believe you've been appointed battery commander here?

OLGA: What do you think, dear? Alexandr Ignatyevich comes from Moscow.

ANDREY: Do you, really? Congratulations! You'll get no peace from my sisters now.

VERSHININ: I'm afraid your sisters must be getting tired of me already.

IRENA: Just look, Andrey gave me this little picture frame to-day. (*Shows him the frame.*) He made it himself.

VERSHININ (*looks at the frame, not knowing what to say*): Yes, it's . . . it's very nice indeed. . . .

IRENA: Do you see that little frame over the piano? He made that one, too.

ANDREY *waves his hand impatiently and walks off.*

OLGA: He's awfully clever, and he plays the violin, and he makes all sorts of things, too. In fact, he's very gifted all round. Andrey, please, don't go. He's got such a bad habit—always going off like this. Come here!

MASHA *and* IRENA *take him by the arms and lead him back, laughing.*

MASHA: Now just you come here!

ANDREY: Do leave me alone, please do!

MASHA: You are a silly! They used to call Alexandr Ignatyevich "the lovesick Major," and he didn't get annoyed.

VERSHININ: Not in the least.

MASHA: I feel like calling you a "lovesick fiddler."

IRENA: Or a "lovesick professor."

OLGA: He's fallen in love! Our Andriusha's in love!

IRENA (*clapping her hands*): Three cheers for Andriusha! Andriusha's in love!

CHEBUTYKIN (*comes up behind* ANDREY *and*

puts his arms round his waist*): "Nature created us for love alone." . . . (*Laughs loudly, still holding his paper in his hand.*)

ANDREY: That's enough of it, that's enough. . . . (*Wipes his face.*) I couldn't get to sleep all night, and I'm not feeling too grand just now. I read till four o'clock, and then I went to bed, but nothing happened. I kept thinking about one thing and another . . . and it gets light so early; the sun just pours into my room. I'd like to translate a book from the English while I'm here during the summer.

VERSHININ: You read English, then?

ANDREY: Yes. My father—God bless his memory—used to simply wear us out with learning. It sounds silly, I know, but I must confess that since he died I've begun to grow stout, as if I'd been physically relieved of the strain. I've grown quite stout in a year. Yes, thanks to Father, my sisters and I know French and German and English, and Irena here knows Italian, too. But what an effort it all cost us!

MASHA: Knowing three languages in a town like this is an unnecessary luxury. In fact, not even a luxury, but just a sort of useless encumbrance . . . it's rather like having a sixth finger on your hand. We know a lot of stuff that's just useless.

VERSHININ: Really! (*Laughs.*) You know a lot of stuff that's useless! It seems to me that there's no place on earth, however dull and depressing it may be, where intelligence and education can be useless. Let us suppose that among the hundred thousand people in this town, all of them, no doubt, very backward and uncultured, there are just three people like yourselves. Obviously, you can't hope to triumph over all the mass of ignorance around you; as your life goes by, you'll have to keep giving in little by little until you get lost in the crowd, in the hundred thousand. Life will swallow you up, but you'll not quite disappear, you'll make some impression on it. After you've gone, perhaps six more people like you will turn up, then twelve, and so on, until in the end most people will have become like you. So in two or three hundred years life on this old earth of ours will have become marvellously beautiful. Man longs for a life like that, and if it isn't here yet, he must imagine it, wait for it, dream about it, prepare for it, he must know and see more than his father and his grandfather did. (*Laughs.*) And you're complaining because you know a lot of stuff that's useless.

MASHA (*takes off her hat*): I'll be staying to lunch.

IRENA (*with a sigh*): Really, someone should have written all that down.

ANDREY *has left the room, unnoticed.*

TOOZENBACH: You say that in time to come life will be marvellously beautiful. That's probably true. But in order to share in it now, at a distance so to speak, we must prepare for it and work for it.

VERSHININ (*gets up*): Yes. . . . What a lot of flowers you've got here! (*Looks round.*) And what a marvellous house! I do envy you! All my life I seem to have been pigging it in small flats, with two chairs and a sofa and a stove which always smokes. It's the flowers that I've missed in my life, flowers like these! . . . (*Rubs his hands.*) Oh, well, never mind!

TOOZENBACH: Yes, we must work. I suppose you're thinking I'm a sentimental German. But I assure you I'm not—I'm Russian. I don't speak a word of German. My father was brought up in the Greek Orthodox faith. (*A pause.*)

VERSHININ (*walks up and down the room*): You know, I often wonder what it would be like if you could start your life over again—deliberately, I mean, consciously. . . . Suppose you could put aside the life you'd lived already, as though it was just a sort of rough draft, and then start another one like a fair copy. If that happened, I think the thing you'd want most of all would be not to repeat yourself. You'd try

at least to create a new environment for yourself, a flat like this one, for instance, with some flowers and plenty of light. . . . I have a wife, you know, and two little girls; and my wife's not very well, and all that. . . . Well, if I had to start my life all over again, I wouldn't marry. . . . No, no!

Enter KOOLYGHIN, *in the uniform of a teacher.*

KOOLYGHIN (*approaches* IRENA): Congratulations, dear sister—from the bottom of my heart, congratulations on your Saint's day. I wish you good health and everything a girl of your age ought to have! And allow me to present you with this little book. . . . (*Hands her a book.*) It's the history of our school covering the whole fifty years of its existence. I wrote it myself. Quite a trifle, of course—I wrote it in my spare time when I had nothing better to do—but I hope you'll read it nevertheless. Good morning to you all! (*To* VERSHININ.) Allow me to introduce myself. Koolyghin's the name; I'm a master at the secondary school here. And a town councillor. (*To* IRENA.) You'll find a list in the book of all the pupils who have completed their studies at our school during the last fifty years. *Feci quod potui, faciant meliora potentes.*[6] (*Kisses* MASHA.)

IRENA: But you gave me this book last Easter!

KOOLYGHIN (*laughs*): Did I really? In that case, give it me back—or no, better give it to the Colonel. Please do take it, Colonel. Maybe you'll read it some time when you've nothing better to do.

VERSHININ: Thank you very much. (*Prepares to leave.*) I'm so very glad to have made your acquaintance. . . .

OLGA: You aren't going are you? . . . Really, you mustn't.

IRENA: But you'll stay and have lunch with us! Please do.

---

[6] *Feci . . . potentes*: "I did what I could, let those who are more able do better."

OLGA: Please do.

VERSHININ (*bows*): I see I've intruded on your Saint's day party. I didn't know. Forgive me for not offering you my congratulations. (*Goes into the ballroom with* OLGA.)

KOOLYGHIN: To-day is Sunday, my friends, a day of rest; let us rest and enjoy it, each according to his age and position in life! We shall have to roll up the carpets and put them away till the winter. . . . We must remember to put some naphthaline on them, or Persian powder. . . . The Romans enjoyed good health because they knew how to work *and* how to rest. They had *mens sana in corpore sano.*[7] Their life had a definite shape, a form. . . . The director of the school says that the most important thing about life is form. . . . A thing that loses its form is finished—that's just as true of our ordinary, everyday lives. (*Takes* MASHA *by the waist and laughs.*) Masha loves me. My wife loves me. Yes, and the curtains will have to be put away with the carpets, too. . . . I'm cheerful to-day, I'm in quite excellent spirits. . . . Masha, we're invited to the director's at four o'clock to-day. A country walk has been arranged for the teachers and their families.

MASHA: I'm not going.

KOOLYGHIN (*distressed*): Masha, darling, why not?

MASHA: I'll tell you later. . . . (*Crossly.*) All right, I'll come, only leave me alone now. . . . (*Walks off.*)

KOOLYGHIN: And after the walk we shall all spend the evening at the director's house. In spite of weak health, that man is certainly sparing no pains to be sociable. A first-rate, thoroughly enlightened man! A most excellent person! After the conference yesterday he said to me: "I'm tired, Fiodor Ilyich. I'm tired!" (*Looks at the clock, then at his watch.*) Your clock is seven minutes fast. Yes, "I'm tired," he said.

---

7 *Mens . . . sano:* "a sound mind in a sound body."

The sound of the violin is heard off stage.

OLGA: Will you all come and sit down, please! Lunch is ready. There's a pie.

KOOLYGHIN: Ah, Olga, my dear girl! Last night I worked up to eleven o'clock, and I felt tired, but to-day I'm quite happy. (*Goes to the table in the ballroom.*) My dear Olga!

CHEBUTYKIN (*puts the newspaper in his pocket and combs his beard*): A pie? Excellent!

MASHA (*sternly to* CHEBUTYKIN): Remember, you mustn't take anything to drink to-day. Do you hear? It's bad for you.

CHEBUTYKIN: Never mind. I've got over that weakness long ago! I haven't done any heavy drinking for two years. (*Impatiently.*) Anyway, my dear, what does it matter?

MASHA: All the same, don't you dare to drink anything. Mind you don't now! (*Crossly, but taking care that her husband does not hear.*) So now I've got to spend another of these damnably boring evenings at the director's!

TOOZENBACH: I wouldn't go if I were you, and that's that.

CHEBUTYKIN: Don't you go, my dear.

MASHA: Don't go, indeed! Oh, what a damnable life! It's intolerable. . . . (*Goes into the ballroom.*)

CHEBUTYKIN (*follows her*): Well, well! . . .

SOLIONY (*as he passes* TOOZENBACH *on the way to the ballroom*): Cluck, cluck, cluck!

TOOZENBACH: Do stop it, Vassily Vassilich. I've really had enough of it. . . .

SOLIONY: Cluck, cluck, cluck! . . .

KOOLYGHIN (*gaily*): Your health, Colonel! I'm a schoolmaster . . . and I'm quite one of the family here, as it were. I'm Masha's husband. She's got a sweet nature, such a very sweet nature!

VERSHININ: I think I'll have a little of this dark vodka. (*Drinks.*) Your health! (*To* OLGA.) I do feel so happy with you people!

Only IRENA *and* TOOZENBACH *remain in the drawing-room.*

IRENA: Masha's a bit out of humour to-day.

You know, she got married when she was eighteen, and then her husband seemed the cleverest man in the world to her. It's different now. He's the kindest of men, but not the cleverest.

OLGA (*impatiently*): Andrey, will you please come?

ANDREY (*off stage*): Just coming. (*Enters and goes to the table.*)

TOOZENBACH: What are you thinking about?

IRENA: Oh, nothing special. You know, I don't like this man Soliony, I'm quite afraid of him. Whenever he opens his mouth he says something silly.

TOOZENBACH: He's a strange fellow. I'm sorry for him, even though he irritates me. In fact, I feel more sorry for him than irritated. I think he's shy. When he's alone with me, he can be quite sensible and friendly, but in company he's offensive and bullying. Don't go over there just yet, let them get settled down at the table. Let me stay beside you for a bit. Tell me what you're thinking about. (*A pause.*) You're twenty . . . and I'm not thirty yet myself. What years and years we still have ahead of us, a whole long succession of years, all full of my love for you! . . .

IRENA: Don't talk to me about love, Nikolai Lvovich.

TOOZENBACH (*not listening*): Oh, I long so passionately for life, I long to work and strive so much, and all this longing is somehow mingled with my love for you, Irena. And just because you happen to be beautiful, life appears beautiful to me! What are you thinking about?

IRENA: You say that life is beautiful. Maybe it is—but what if it only seems to be beautiful? Our lives, I mean the lives of us three sisters, haven't been beautiful up to now. The truth is that life has been stifling us, like weeds in a garden. I'm afraid I'm crying. . . . So unnecessary. . . . (*Quickly dries her eyes and smiles.*) We must work, work! The reason we feel depressed and take such a gloomy view of life is that we've never known what it is to make a real effort.

We're the children of parents who despised work. . . .

Enter NATALIA IVANOVNA. *She is wearing a pink dress with a green belt.*

NATASHA: They've gone in to lunch already. . . . I'm late. . . . (*Glances at herself in a mirror, adjusts her dress.*) My hair seems to be all right. . . . (*Catches sight of* IRENA.) My dear Irena Serghyeevna, congratulations! (*Gives her a vigorous and prolonged kiss.*) You've got such a lot of visitors. . . . I feel quite shy. . . . How do you do, Baron?

OLGA (*enters the drawing-room*): Oh, there you are, Natalia Ivanovna! How are you, my dear?

They kiss each other.

NATASHA: Congratulations! You've such a lot of people here. I feel dreadfully shy. . . .

OLGA: It's all right, they're all old friends. (*Alarmed, dropping her voice.*) You've got a green belt on! My dear, that's surely a mistake!

NATASHA: Why, is it a bad omen, or what?

OLGA: No, but it just doesn't go with your dress . . . it looks so strange. . . .

NATASHA (*tearfully*): Really? But it isn't really green, you know, it's a sort of dull colour. . . . (*Follows* OLGA *to the ballroom.*)

All are now seated at the table; the drawing-room is empty.

KOOLYGHIN: Irena, you know, I do wish you'd find yourself a good husband. In my view it's high time you got married.

CHEBUTYKIN: You ought to get yourself a nice little husband, too, Natalia Ivanovna.

KOOLYGHIN: Natalia Ivanovna already has a husband in view.

MASHA (*strikes her plate with her fork*): A glass of wine for me, please! Three cheers for our jolly old life! We keep our end up, we do!

KOOLYGHIN: Masha, you won't get more than five out of ten for good conduct!

VERSHININ: I say, this liqueur's very nice. What is it made of?

SOLIONY: Black beetles!

IRENA: Ugh! ugh! How disgusting!

OLGA: We're having roast turkey for dinner to-night, and then apple tart. Thank goodness, I'll be here all day to-day . . . this evening, too. You must all come this evening.

VERSHININ: May I come in the evening, too?

IRENA: Yes, please do.

NATASHA: They don't stand on ceremony here.

CHEBUTYKIN: "Nature created us for love alone." . . . (*Laughs.*)

ANDREY (*crossly*): Will you stop it, please? Aren't you tired of it yet?

FEDOTIK and RODÉ come in with a large basket of flowers.

FEDOTIK: Just look here, they're having lunch already!

RODÉ (*in a loud voice*): Having their lunch? So they are, they're having lunch already.

FEDOTIK: Wait half a minute. (*Takes a snapshot.*) One! Just one minute more! . . . (*Takes another snapshot.*) Two! All over now.

They pick up the basket and go into the ballroom where they are greeted uproariously.

RODÉ (*loudly*): Congratulations, Irena Serghyeevna! I wish you all the best, everything you'd wish for yourself! Gorgeous weather to-day, absolutely marvellous. I've been out walking the whole morning with the boys. You do know that I teach gym at the high school, don't you? . . .

FEDOTIK: You may move now, Irena Serghyeevna, that is, if you want to. (*Takes a snapshot.*) You do look attractive to-day. (*Takes a top out of his pocket.*) By the way, look at this top. It's got a wonderful hum.

IRENA: What a sweet little thing!

MASHA: "A green oak grows by a curving shore, And round that oak hangs a golden chain." . . . A green chain around that oak. . . . (*Peevishly.*) Why do I keep on saying that? Those lines have been worrying me all day long!

KOOLYGHIN: Do you know, we're thirteen at table?

RODÉ (*loudly*): You don't really believe in these old superstitions, do you? (*Laughter.*)

KOOLYGHIN: When thirteen people sit down to table, it means that some of them are in love. Is it you, by any chance, Ivan Romanych?

CHEBUTYKIN: Oh, I'm just an old sinner. . . . But what I can't make out is why Natalia Ivanovna looks so embarrassed.

Loud laughter. NATASHA runs out into the drawing-room, ANDREY follows her.

ANDREY: Please, Natasha, don't take any notice of them! Stop . . . wait a moment. . . . Please!

NATASHA: I feel so ashamed. . . . I don't know what's the matter with me, and they're all laughing at me. It's awful of me to leave the table like that, but I couldn't help it. . . . I just couldn't. . . . (*Covers her face with her hands.*)

ANDREY: My dear girl, please, please don't get upset. Honestly, they don't mean any harm, they're just teasing. My dear, sweet girl, they're really good-natured folks, they all are, and they're fond of us both. Come over to the window, they can't see us there. . . . (*Looks round.*)

NATASHA: You see, I'm not used to being with a lot of people.

ANDREY: Oh, how young you are, Natasha, how wonderfully, beautifully young! My dear, sweet girl, don't get so upset! Do believe me, believe me. . . . I'm so happy, so full of love, of joy. . . . No, they can't see us here! They can't see us! How did I come to love you, when was it? . . . I don't understand anything. My precious, my sweet, my innocent girl, please—I want you to marry me!

I love you, I love you as I've never loved anybody.... (*Kisses her.*)

Enter two officers and, seeing NATASHA *and* ANDREY *kissing, stand and stare in amazement.*

ACT II

The scene is the same as in Act I. It is eight o'clock in the evening. The faint sound of an accordion is heard coming from the street.
The stage is unlit. Enter NATALIA IVANOVNA *in a dressing-gown, carrying a candle. She crosses the stage and stops by the door leading to* ANDREY'S *room.*

NATASHA: What are you doing, Andriusha? Reading? It's all right, I only wanted to know.... (*Goes to another door, opens it, looks inside and shuts it again.*) No one's left a light anywhere....

ANDREY (*enters with a book in his hand*): What is it, Natasha?

NATASHA: I was just going round to see if anyone had left a light anywhere. It's carnival week, and the servants are so excited about it . . . anything might happen! You've got to watch them. Last night about twelve o'clock I happened to go into the dining-room, and—would you believe it?—there was a candle alight on the table. I've not found out who lit it. (*Puts the candle down.*) What time is it?

ANDREY (*glances at his watch*): Quarter past eight.

NATASHA: And Olga and Irena still out. They aren't back from work yet, poor things! Olga's still at some teachers' conference, and Irena's at the post office. (*Sighs.*) This morning I said to Irena: "Do take care of yourself, my dear." But she won't listen. Did you say it was a quarter past eight? I'm afraid Bobik is not at all well. Why does he get so cold? Yesterday he had a temperature, but to-day he feels quite cold when you touch him.... I'm so afraid!

ANDREY: It's all right, Natasha. The boy's well enough.

NATASHA: Still, I think he ought to have a special diet. I'm so anxious about him. By the way, they tell me that some carnival party's supposed to be coming here soon after nine. I'd rather they didn't come, Andriusha.

ANDREY: Well, I really don't know what I can do. They've been asked to come.

NATASHA: This morning the dear little fellow woke up and looked at me, and then suddenly he smiled. He recognized me, you see. "Good morning, Bobik," I said, "good morning, darling precious!" And then he laughed. Babies understand everything, you know, they understand us perfectly well. Anyway, Andriusha, I'll tell the servants not to let that carnival party in.

ANDREY (*irresolutely*): Well . . . it's really for my sisters to decide, isn't it? It's their house, after all.

NATASHA: Yes, it's their house as well. I'll tell them, too.... They're so kind.... (*Walks off.*) I've ordered sour milk for supper. The doctor says you ought to eat nothing but sour milk, or you'll never get any thinner. (*Stops.*) Bobik feels cold. I'm afraid his room is too cold for him. He ought to move into a warmer room, at least until the warm weather comes. Irena's room, for instance—that's just a perfect room for a baby: it's dry, and it gets the sun all day long. We must tell her: perhaps she'd share Olga's room for a bit.... In any case, she's never at home during the day, she only sleeps there.... (*A pause.*) Andriusha, why don't you say anything?

ANDREY: I was just day-dreaming.... There's nothing to say, anyway....

NATASHA: Well.... What was it I was going to tell you? Oh, yes! Ferapont from the Council Office wants to see you about something.

ANDREY (*yawns*): Tell him to come up.

NATASHA *goes out.* ANDREY, *bending over the candle which she has left behind, begins to read his book. Enter* FERAPONT *in an old shabby overcoat, his collar turned up, his ears muffled in a scarf.*

ANDREY: Hello, old chap! What did you want to see me about?

FERAPONT: The chairman's sent you the register and a letter or something. Here they are. (*Hands him the book and the letter.*)

ANDREY: Thanks. That's all right. Incidentally, why have you come so late? It's gone eight already.

FERAPONT: What's that?

ANDREY (*raising his voice*): I said, why have you come so late? It's gone eight already.

FERAPONT: That's right. It was still daylight when I came first, but they wouldn't let me see you. The master's engaged, they said. Well, if you're engaged, you're engaged. I'm not in a hurry. (*Thinking that* ANDREY *has said something.*) What's that?

ANDREY: Nothing. (*Turns over the pages of the register.*) Tomorrow's Friday, there's no meeting, but I'll go to the office just the same . . . do some work. I'm so bored at home! . . . (*A pause.*) Yes, my dear fellow, how things do change, what a fraud life is! So strange! To-day I picked up this book, just out of boredom, because I hadn't anything to do. It's a copy of some lectures I attended at the University. . . . Good Heavens! Just think—I'm secretary of the local council now, and Protopopov's chairman, and the most I can ever hope for is to become a member of the council myself! I—a member of the local council! I, who dream every night that I'm a professor in Moscow University, a famous academician, the pride of all Russia!

FERAPONT: I'm sorry, I can't tell you. I don't hear very well.

ANDREY: If you could hear properly I don't think I'd be talking to you like this. I must talk to someone, but my wife doesn't seem to understand me, and as for my sisters . . . I'm afraid of them for some reason or other, I'm afraid of them laughing at me

and pulling my leg. . . . I don't drink and I don't like going to pubs, but my word! how I'd enjoy an hour or so at Tyestov's, or the Great Moscow Restaurant! Yes, my dear fellow, I would indeed!

FERAPONT: The other day at the office a contractor was telling me about some business men who were eating pancakes in Moscow. One of them ate forty pancakes and died. It was either forty or fifty, I can't remember exactly.

ANDREY: You can sit in some huge restaurant in Moscow without knowing anyone, and no one knowing you; yet somehow you don't feel that you don't belong there. . . . Whereas here you know everybody, and everybody knows you, and yet you don't feel you belong here, you feel you don't belong at all. . . . You're lonely and you feel a stranger.

FERAPONT: What's that? (*A pause.*) It was the same man that told me—of course, he may have been lying—he said that there's an enormous rope stretched right across Moscow.

ANDREY: Whatever for?

FERAPONT: I'm sorry, I can't tell you. That's what he said.

ANDREY: What nonsense! (*Reads the book.*) Have you ever been to Moscow?

FERAPONT (*after a pause*): No. It wasn't God's wish. (*A pause.*) Shall I go now?

ANDREY: Yes, you may go. Good-bye. (FERAPONT *goes out.*) Good-bye. (*Reading.*) Come in the morning to take some letters. . . . You can go now. (*A pause.*) He's gone. (*A bell rings.*) Yes, that's how it is. . . . (*Stretches and slowly goes to his room.*)

Singing is heard off stage; a nurse is putting a baby to sleep. Enter MASHA *and* VERSHININ. *While they talk together, a maid lights a lamp and candles in the ballroom.*

MASHA: I don't know. (*A pause.*) I don't know. Habit's very important, of course. For instance, after Father died, for a long time we couldn't get accustomed to the idea that we hadn't any orderlies to wait on us. But, habit apart, I think it's quite right what I was saying. Perhaps it's different in other places, but in this town the military certainly do seem to be the nicest and most generous and best-mannered people.

VERSHININ: I'm thirsty. I could do with a nice glass of tea.

MASHA (*glances at her watch*): They'll bring it in presently. You see, they married me off when I was eighteen. I was afraid of my husband because he was a school-master, and I had only just left school myself. He seemed terribly learned then, very clever and important. Now it's quite different, unfortunately.

VERSHININ: Yes.... I see....

MASHA: I don't say anything against my husband—I'm used to him now—but there are such a lot of vulgar and unpleasant and offensive people among the other civilians. Vulgarity upsets me, it makes me feel insulted, I actually suffer when I meet someone who lacks refinement and gentle manners, and courtesy. When I'm with the other teachers, my husband's friends, I just suffer.

VERSHININ: Yes, of course. But I should have thought that in a town like this the civilians and the army people were equally uninteresting. There's nothing to choose between them. If you talk to any educated person here, civilian or military, he'll generally tell you that he's just worn out. It's either his wife, or his house, or his estate, or his horse, or something. . . . We Russians are capable of such elevated thoughts—then why do we have such low ideals in practical life? Why is it, why?

MASHA: Why?

VERSHININ: Yes, why does his wife wear him out, why do his children wear him out? And what about *him* wearing out his wife and children?

MASHA: You're a bit low-spirited to-day, aren't you?

VERSHININ: Perhaps. I haven't had any dinner to-day. I've had nothing to eat since morning. One of my daughters is a bit off colour, and when the children are ill, I get so worried. I feel utterly conscience-stricken at having given them a mother like theirs. Oh, if only you could have seen her this morning! What a despicable woman! We started quarrelling at seven o'clock, and at nine I just walked out and slammed the door. (*A pause.*) I never talk about these things in the ordinary way. It's a strange thing, but you're the only person I feel I dare complain to. (*Kisses her hand.*) Don't be angry with me. I've nobody, nobody but you.... (*A pause.*)

MASHA: What a noise the wind's making in the stove! Just before Father died the wind howled in the chimney just like that.

VERSHININ: Are you superstitious?

MASHA: Yes.

VERSHININ: How strange. (*Kisses her hand.*) You really are a wonderful creature, a marvellous creature! Wonderful, marvellous! It's quite dark here, but I can see your eyes shining.

MASHA (*Moves to another chair*): There's more light over here.

VERSHININ: I love you, I love you, I love you. . . . I love your eyes, I love your movements. . . . I dream about them. A wonderful, marvellous being!

MASHA (*Laughing softly*): When you talk to me like that, somehow I can't help laughing, although I'm afraid at the same time. Don't say it again, please. (*Half-audibly.*) Well, no . . . go on. I don't mind. . . . (*Covers her face with her hands.*) I don't mind. . . . Someone's coming. . . . Let's talk about something else. . . .

Enter IRENA *and* TOOZENBACH *through the ballroom.*

TOOZENBACH: I have a triple-barrelled name —Baron Toozenbach-Krone-Alschauer—but actually I'm a Russian. I was baptized in the Greek-Orthodox faith, just like yourself. I haven't really got any German characteristics, except maybe the obstinate patient way I keep on pestering you. Look how I bring you home every evening.

IRENA: How tired I am!

TOOZENBACH: And I'll go on fetching you from the post office and bringing you home every evening for the next twenty years—unless you send me away.... (*Noticing* MASHA *and* VERSHININ, *with pleasure.*) Oh, it's you! How are you?

IRENA: Well, here I am, home at last! (*To* MASHA.) A woman came into the post office just before I left. She wanted to send a wire to her brother in Saratov to tell him her son had just died, but she couldn't remember the address. So we had to send the wire without an address, just to Saratov. She was crying and I was rude to her, for no reason at all. "I've not time to waste," I told her. So stupid of me. We're having the carnival crowd to-day, aren't we?

MASHA: Yes.

IRENA (*sits down*): How nice it is to rest! I am tired!

TOOZENBACH (*smiling*): When you come back from work, you look so young, so pathetic, somehow.... (*A pause.*)

IRENA: I'm tired. No, I don't like working at the post office, I don't like it at all.

MASHA: You've got thinner. . . . (*Whistles.*) You look younger, too, and your face looks quite boyish.

TOOZENBACH: It's the way she does her hair.

IRENA: I must look for another job. This one doesn't suit me. It hasn't got what I always longed for and dreamed about. It's the sort of work you do without inspiration, without even thinking.

Someone knocks at the floor from below.

That's the Doctor knocking. (*To* TOOZENBACH.) Will you answer him, dear? . . . I can't.... I'm so tired.

TOOZENBACH (*knocks on the floor.*)

IRENA: He'll be up in a moment. We must do something about all this. Andrey and the Doctor went to the club last night and lost at cards again. They say Andrey lost two hundred roubles.

MASHA (*with indifference*): Well, what are we to do about it?

IRENA: He lost a fortnight ago, and he lost in December, too. I wish to goodness he'd lose everything we've got, and soon, too, and then perhaps we'd move out of this place. Good Heavens, I dream of Moscow every night. Sometimes I feel as if I were going mad. (*Laughs.*) We're going to Moscow in June. How many months are there till June? . . . February, March, April, May . . . nearly half-a-year!

MASHA: We must take care that Natasha doesn't get to know about him losing at cards.

IRENA: I don't think she cares.

Enter CHEBUTYKIN. *He has been resting on his bed since dinner and has only just got up. He combs his beard, then sits down at the table and takes out a newspaper.*

MASHA: There he is. Has he paid his rent yet?

IRENA (*laughs*): No. Not a penny for the last eight months. I suppose he's forgotten.

MASHA (*laughs*): How solemn he looks sitting there!

They all laugh. A pause.

IRENA: Why don't you say something, Alexandr Ignatyevich?

VERSHININ: I don't know. I'm just longing for some tea. I'd give my life for a glass of tea! I've had nothing to eat since morning. . . .

CHEBUTYKIN: Irena Serghyeevna!

IRENA: What is it?

CHEBUTYKIN: Please come here. *Venez ici!* (IRENA *goes over to him and sits down at the table.*) I can't do without you.

IRENA *lays out the cards for a game of patience.*

VERSHININ: Well, if we can't have any tea, let's do a bit of philosophizing, anyway.

TOOZENBACH: Yes, let's. What about?

VERSHININ: What about? Well . . . let's try to imagine what life will be like after we're dead, say in two or three hundred years.

TOOZENBACH: All right, then. . . . After we're dead, people will fly about in balloons, the cut of their coats will be different, the sixth sense will be discovered, and possibly even developed and used, for all I know. . . . But I believe, life itself will remain the same; it will still be difficult and full of mystery and full of happiness. And in a thousand years' time people will still be sighing and complaining: "How hard this business of living is!"—and yet they'll still be scared of death and unwilling to die, just as they are now.

VERSHININ (after a moment's thought): Well, you know . . . how shall I put it? I think everything in the world is bound to change gradually—in fact, it's changing before our very eyes. In two or three hundred years, or maybe in a thousand years—it doesn't matter how long exactly—life will be different. It will be happy. Of course, we shan't be able to enjoy that future life, but all the same, what we're living for now is to create it, we work and . . . yes, we suffer in order to create it. That's the goal of our life, and you might say that's the only happiness we shall ever achieve.

MASHA (laughs quietly.)

TOOZENBACH: Why are you laughing?

MASHA: I don't know. I've been laughing all day to-day.

VERSHININ (to TOOZENBACH): I went to the same cadet school as you did but I never went on to the Military Academy. I read a great deal, of course, but I never know what books I ought to choose, and probably I read a lot of stuff that's not worth anything. But the longer I live the more I seem to long for knowledge. My hair's going grey and I'm getting on in years, and yet how little I know, how little! All the same, I think I do know one thing which is not only true but also most important. I'm sure of it. Oh, if only I could convince you that there's not going to be any happiness for our own generation, that there mustn't be and won't be. . . . We've just got to work and work. All the happiness is reserved for our descendants, our remote descendants. (A pause.) Anyway, if I'm not to be happy, then at least my children's children will be.

FEDOTIK and RODÉ enter the ballroom; they sit down and sing quietly, one of them playing on a guitar.

TOOZENBACH: So you won't even allow us to dream of happiness! But what if I am happy?

VERSHININ: You're not.

TOOZENBACH (flinging up his hands and laughing): We don't understand one another, that's obvious. How can I convince you?

MASHA (laughs quietly.)

TOOZENBACH (holds up a finger to her): Show a finger to her and she'll laugh! (To VERSHININ.) And life will be just the same as ever not merely in a couple of hundred years' time, but in a million years. Life doesn't change, it always goes on the same; it follows its own laws, which don't concern us, which we can't discover anyway. Think of the birds that migrate in the autumn, the cranes, for instance: they just fly on and on. It doesn't matter what sort of thoughts they've got in their heads, great thoughts or little thoughts, they just fly on and on, not knowing where or why. And they'll go on flying no matter how many philosophers they happen to have flying with them. Let them philosophize as much as they like, as long as they go on flying.

MASHA: Isn't there some meaning?

TOOZENBACH: Meaning? . . . Look out there, it's snowing. What's the meaning of that? (A pause.)

MASHA: I think a human being has got to have some faith, or at least he's got to seek faith.

Otherwise his life will be empty, empty. . . . How can you live and not know why the cranes fly, why children are born, why the stars shine in the sky! . . . You must either know why you live, or else . . . nothing matters . . . everything's just wild grass. . . . (*A pause.*)

VERSHININ: All the same, I'm sorry my youth's over.

MASHA: "It's a bore to be alive in this world, friends," that's what Gogol[8] says.

TOOZENBACH: And I feel like saying: it's hopeless arguing with you, friends! I give you up.

CHEBUTYKIN (*reads out of the paper*): Balsac's[9] marriage took place at Berdichev.

IRENA (*sings softly to herself.*)

CHEBUTYKIN: Must write this down in my notebook. (*Writes.*) Balsac's marriage took place at Berdichev. (*Reads on.*)

IRENA (*playing patience, pensively*): Balsac's marriage took place at Berdichev.

TOOZENBACH: Well, I've thrown in my hand. Did you know that I'd sent in my resignation, Maria Serghyeevna?

MASHA: Yes, I heard about it. I don't see anything good in it, either. I don't like civilians.

TOOZENBACH: Never mind. (*Gets up.*) What sort of a soldier do I make, anyway? I'm not even good-looking. Well, what does it matter? I'll work. I'd like to do such a hard day's work that when I came home in the evening I'd fall on my bed exhausted and go to sleep at once. (*Goes to the ballroom.*) I should think working men sleep well at night!

FEDOTIK (*to* IRENA): I've got you some coloured crayons at Pyzhikov's, in Moscow Street. And this little penknife, too. . . .

IRENA: You still treat me as if I were a little girl. I wish you'd remember I'm grown up now. (*Takes the crayons and the penknife, joyfully.*) They're awfully nice!

---

8 *Gogol:* Nikolay V. (1809–1852), Russian novelist and playwright.

9 *Balsac:* or [Honoré] de Balzac (1799–1850), French novelist.

FEDOTIK: Look, I bought a knife for myself, too. You see, it's got another blade here, and then another . . . this thing's for cleaning your ears, and these are nail-scissors, and this is for cleaning your nails. . . .

RODÉ (*in a loud voice*): Doctor, how old are you?

CHEBUTYKIN: I? Thirty-two.

Laughter.

FEDOTIK: I'll show you another kind of patience. (*Sets out the cards.*)

The samovar is brought in, and ANFISA *attends to it. Shortly afterwards* NATASHA *comes in and begins to fuss around the table.*

SOLIONY (*enters, bows to the company and sits down at the table.*)

VERSHININ: What a wind, though!

MASHA: Yes. I'm tired of winter! I've almost forgotten what summer is like.

IRENA (*playing patience*): I'm going to go out. We'll get to Moscow!

FEDOTIK: No, it's not going out. You see, the eight has to go on the two of spades. (*Laughs.*) That means you won't go to Moscow.

CHEBUTYKIN (*reads the paper*): Tzitzikar. Smallpox is raging. . . .

ANFISA (*goes up to* MASHA): Masha, the tea's ready, dear. (*To* VERSHININ.) Will you please come to the table, your Excellency? Forgive me, your name's slipped my memory. . . .

MASHA: Bring it here, Nanny. I'm not coming over there.

IRENA: Nanny!

ANFISA: Comi-ing!

NATASHA (*to* SOLIONY): You know, even tiny babies understand what we say perfectly well! "Good morning, Bobik," I said to him only to-day, "Good morning, my precious!" —and then he looked at me in such a special sort of way. You may say it's only a mother's imagination, but it isn't, I do assure you. No, no! He really is an extraordinary child!

SOLIONY: If that child were mine, I'd cook him up in a frying pan and eat him. (*Picks up his glass, goes into the drawing-room and sits down in a corner.*)

NATASHA (*covers her face with her hands*): What a rude, ill-mannered person!

MASHA: People who don't even notice whether it's summer or winter are lucky! I think I'd be indifferent to the weather if I were living in Moscow.

VERSHININ: I've just been reading the diary of some French cabinet minister—he wrote it in prison. He got sent to prison in connection with the Panama affair. He writes with such a passionate delight about the birds he can see through the prison window—the birds he never even noticed when he was a cabinet minister. Of course, now he's released he won't notice them any more. . . . And in the same way, you won't notice Moscow once you live there again. We're not happy and we can't be happy: we only want happiness.

TOOZENBACH (*picks up a box from the table*): I say, where are all the chocolates?

IRENA: Soliony's eaten them.

TOOZENBACH: All of them?

ANFISA (*serving* VERSHININ *with tea*): Here's a letter for you, Sir.

VERSHININ: For me? (*Takes the letter.*) From my daughter. (*Reads it.*) Yes, of course. . . . Forgive me, Maria Serghyeevna, I'll just leave quietly. I won't have any tea. (*Gets up, agitated.*) Always the same thing. . . .

MASHA: What is it? Secret?

VERSHININ (*in a low voice*): My wife's taken poison again. I must go. I'll get away without them seeing me. All this is so dreadfully unpleasant. (*Kisses* MASHA's *hand.*) My dear, good, sweet girl. . . . I'll go out this way, quietly. . . . (*Goes out.*)

ANFISA: Where's he off to? And I've just brought him some tea! What a queer fellow!

MASHA (*flaring up*): Leave me alone! Why do you keep worrying me? Why don't you leave me in peace? (*Goes to the table, cup in hand.*) I'm sick and tired of you, silly old woman!

ANFISA: Why. . . . I didn't mean to offend you, dear.

ANDREY'S VOICE (*off stage*): Anfisa!

ANFISA (*mimics him*): Anfisa! Sitting there in his den! . . . (*Goes out.*)

MASHA (*by the table in the ballroom, crossly*): Do let me sit down somewhere! (*Jumbles up the cards laid out on the table.*) You take up the whole table with your cards! Why don't you get on with your tea?

IRENA: How bad-tempered you are, Masha!

MASHA: Well, if I'm bad-tempered, don't talk to me, then. Don't touch me!

CHEBUTYKIN (*laughs*): Don't touch her! . . . Take care you don't touch her!

MASHA: You may be sixty, but you're always gabbling some damn nonsense or other, just like a child. . . .

NATASHA (*sighs*): My dear Masha, need you use such expressions? You know, with your good looks you'd be thought so charming, even by the best people—yes, I honestly mean it—if only you wouldn't use these expressions of yours! Je vous prie, pardonnez moi, Marie, mais vous avez des manières un peu grossières.[10]

TOOZENBACH (*with suppressed laughter*): Pass me . . . I say, will you please pass me. . . . Is that cognac over there, or what? . . .

NATASHA: Il parait que mon Bobik déjà ne dort pas.[11] . . . I think he's awake. He's not been too well to-day. I must go and see him . . . excuse me. (*Goes out.*)

IRENA: I say, where has Alexandr Ignatyevich gone to?

MASHA: He's gone home. His wife's done something queer again.

---

[10] *Je vous prie . . . grossières:* "I beg you, pardon me, Marie, but your manners are a bit coarse."

[11] *Il parait . . . pas:* "It seems that my Bobik already isn't asleep"; unidiomatic.

TOOZENBACH (*goes over to* SOLIONY *with a decanter of cognac*): You always sit alone brooding over something or other—though what it's all about nobody knows. Well, let's make it up. Let's have cognac together. (*They drink.*) I suppose I'll have to play the piano all night to-night—a lot of rubbishy tunes, of course. . . . Never mind!

SOLIONY: Why did you say "let's make it up"? We haven't quarrelled.

TOOZENBACH: You always give me the feeling that there's something wrong between us. You're a strange character, no doubt about it.

SOLIONY (*recites*): "I am strange, but who's not so? Don't be angry, Aleko!"[12]

TOOZENBACH: What's Aleko got to do with it? . . . (*A pause.*)

SOLIONY: When I'm alone with somebody I'm all right, I'm just like other people. But in company, I get depressed and shy, and . . . I talk all sorts of nonsense. All the same, I'm a good deal more honest and well-intentioned than plenty of others. I can prove I am.

TOOZENBACH: You often make me angry because you keep on pestering me when we're in company—but all the same, I do like you for some reason. . . . I'm going to get drunk to-night, whatever happens! Let's have another drink!

SOLIONY: Yes, let's. (*A pause.*) I've never had anything against you personally, Baron. But my temperament's rather like Lermontov's. (*In a low voice.*) I even look a little like Lermontov, I've been told. . . . (*Takes a scent bottle from his pocket and sprinkles some scent on his hands.*)

TOOZENBACH: I have sent in my resignation! Finished! I've been considering it for five years, and now I've made up my mind at last. I'm going to work.

SOLIONY (*recites*): "Don't be angry, Aleko. . . . Away, away with all your dreams!"

During the conversation ANDREY *enters quietly*

[12] "*I am strange . . . Aleko*": from *The Gypsies*, a poem by M. Y. Lermontov (1814–1841).

with a book in his hand and sits down by the candle.

TOOZENBACH: I'm going to work!

CHEBUTYKIN (*comes into the drawing-room with* IRENA): And the food they treated me to was the genuine Caucasian stuff: onion soup, followed by chehartma—that's a meat dish, you know.

SOLIONY: Chereshma isn't meat at all; it's a plant, something like an onion.

CHEBUTYKIN: No-o, my dear friend. Chehartma isn't an onion, it's roast mutton.

SOLIONY: I tell you chereshma is a kind of onion.

CHEBUTYKIN: Well, why should I argue about it with you? You've never been to the Caucasus and you've never tasted chehartma.

SOLIONY: I haven't tasted it because I can't stand the smell of it. Chereshma stinks just like garlic.

ANDREY (*imploringly*): Do stop it, friends! Please stop it!

TOOZENBACH: When's the carnival crowd coming along?

IRENA: They promised to be here by nine—that means any moment now.

TOOZENBACH (*embraces* ANDREY *and sings*): "Ah, my beautiful porch, my lovely new porch, my . . ."

ANDREY (*dances and sings*): "My new porch all made of maple-wood. . . ."

CHEBUTYKIN (*dances*): "With fancy carving over the door. . . ." (*Laughter.*)

TOOZENBACH (*kisses* ANDREY): Let's have a drink, the devil take it! Andriusha, let's drink to eternal friendship. I'll come with you when you go back to Moscow University.

SOLIONY: Which university? There are two universities in Moscow.

ANDREY: There's only one.

SOLIONY: I tell you there are two.

ANDREY: Never mind, make it three. The more the merrier.

SOLIONY: There are two universities in Moscow.

Murmurs of protest and cries of "Hush!"

There are two universities in Moscow, an old one and a new one. But if you don't want to listen to what I'm saying, if my conversation irritates you, I can keep silent. In fact I can go to another room.... (*Goes out through one of the doors.*)

TOOZENBACH: Bravo, bravo! (*Laughs.*) Let's get started, my friends, I'll play for you. What a funny creature that Soliony is! ... (*Sits down at the piano and plays a waltz.*)

MASHA (*dances alone*): The Baron is drunk, the Baron is drunk, the Baron is drunk....

Enter NATASHA.

NATASHA (*to* CHEBUTYKIN): Ivan Romanych! (*Speaks to him, then goes out quietly.* CHEBUTYKIN *touches* TOOZENBACH *on the shoulder and whispers to him.*)

IRENA: What is it?

CHEBUTYKIN: It's time we were going. Goodnight.

IRENA: But really.... What about the carnival party?

ANDREY (*embarrassed*): The carnival party's not coming. You see, my dear, Natasha says that Bobik isn't very well, and so ... Anyway, I don't know ... and certainly don't care....

IRENA (*shrugs her shoulders*): Bobik's not very well! ...

MASHA: Never mind, we'll keep our end up! If they turn us out, out we must go! (*To* IRENA.) It isn't Bobik who's not well, it's her.... There! ... (*Taps her forehead with her finger.*) Petty little bourgeois housewife!

ANDREY *goes to his room on the right.* CHEBUTYKIN *follows him. The guests say good-bye in the ballroom.*

FEDOTIK: What a pity! I'd been hoping to spend the evening here, but of course, if the baby's ill.... I'll bring him some toys to-morrow.

RODÉ (*in a loud voice*): I had a good long sleep after lunch to-day on purpose, I thought I'd be dancing all night. I mean to say, it's only just nine o'clock.

MASHA: Let's go outside and talk it over. We can decide what to do then.

Voices are heard saying "Good-bye! God bless you!" and TOOZENBACH *is heard laughing gaily. Everyone goes out.* ANFISA *and a maid clear the table and put out the lights. The nurse sings to the baby off stage. Enter* ANDREY, *wearing an overcoat and hat, followed by* CHEBUTYKIN. *They move quietly.*

CHEBUTYKIN: I've never found time to get married, somehow ... partly because my life's just flashed past me like lightning, and partly because I was always madly in love with your mother and she was married....

ANDREY: One shouldn't marry. One shouldn't marry because it's so boring.

CHEBUTYKIN: That may be so, but what about loneliness? You can philosophize as much as you like, dear boy, but loneliness is a dreadful thing. Although, really ... well, it doesn't matter a damn, of course! ...

ANDREY: Let's get along quickly.

CHEBUTYKIN: What's the hurry? There's plenty of time.

ANDREY: I'm afraid my wife may try to stop me.

CHEBUTYKIN: Ah!

ANDREY: I won't play cards to-night, I'll just sit and watch. I'm not feeling too well. ... What ought I to do for this breathlessness, Ivan Romanych?

CHEBUTYKIN: Why ask me, dear boy? I can't remember—I simply don't know.

ANDREY: Let's go through the kitchen.

They go out. A bell rings. The ring is repeated, then voices and laughter are heard.

IRENA (*coming in*): What's that?

ANFISA (*in a whisper*): The carnival party.

The bell rings again.

IRENA: Tell them there's no one at home, Nanny. Apologize to them.

ANFISA *goes out.* IRENE *walks up and down the room, lost in thought. She seems agitated. Enter* SOLIONY.

SOLIONY (*puzzled*): There's no one here. . . . Where is everybody?

IRENA: They've gone home.

SOLIONY: How strange! Then you're alone here?

IRENA: Yes, alone. (*A pause.*) Well . . . good-night.

SOLIONY: I know I behaved tactlessly just now, I lost control of myself. But you're different from the others, you stand out high above them—you're pure, you can see where the truth lies. . . . You're the only person in the world who can possibly understand me. I love you. . . . I love you with a deep, in-finite . . .

IRENA: Do please go away. Good-night!

SOLIONY: I can't live without you. (*Follows her.*) Oh, it's such a delight just to look at you! (*With tears.*) Oh, my happiness! Your glorious, marvellous, entrancing eyes—eyes like no other woman's I've ever seen. . . .

IRENA (*coldly*): Please stop it, Vassily Vassilich!

SOLIONY: I've never spoken to you of my love before . . . it makes me feel as if I were living on a different planet. . . . (*Rubs his forehead.*) Never mind! I can't force you to love me, obviously. But I don't intend to have any rivals—successful rivals, I mean. . . . No, no! I swear to you by everything I hold sacred that if there's anyone else, I'll kill him. Oh, how wonderful you are!

Enter NATASHA *carrying a candle.*

NATASHA (*pokes her head into one room, then into another, but passes the door leading to her husband's room*): Andrey's reading in there. Better let him read. Forgive me, Vassily Vassilich, I didn't know you were here.

I'm afraid I'm not properly dressed.

SOLIONY: I don't care. Good-bye. (*Goes out.*)

NATASHA: You must be tired, my poor dear girl. (*Kisses* IRENA.) You ought to go to bed earlier.

IRENA: Is Bobik asleep?

NATASHA: Yes, he's asleep. But he's not sleeping peacefully. By the way, my dear, I've been meaning to speak to you for some time but there's always been something . . . either you're not here, or I'm too busy. . . . You see, I think that Bobik's nursery is so cold and damp. . . . And your room is just ideal for a baby. Darling, do you think you could move into Olga's room?

IRENA (*not understanding her*): Where to?

The sound of bells is heard outside, as a "troika" is driven up to the house.

NATASHA: You can share a room with Olia for the time being, and Bobik can have your room. He is such a darling! This morning I said to him: "Bobik, you're my very own! My very own!" And he just gazed at me with his dear little eyes. (*The door bell rings.*) That must be Olga. How late she is!

A maid comes up to NATASHA *and whispers in her ear.*

NATASHA: Protopopov! What a funny fellow! Protopopov's come to ask me to go for a drive with him. In a troika! (*Laughs.*) Aren't these men strange creatures! . . .

The door bell rings again.

Someone's ringing. Shall I go for a short drive? Just for a quarter of an hour? (*To the maid.*) Tell him I'll be down in a minute. (*The door bell rings.*) That's the bell again. I suppose it's Olga. (*Goes out.*)

The maid runs out; IRENA *sits lost in thought. Enter* KOOLYGHIN *and* OLGA, *followed by* VERSHININ.

KOOLYGHIN: Well! What's the meaning of this? You said you were going to have a party.

VERSHININ: It's a strange thing. I left here about half an hour ago, and they were expecting a carnival party then.

IRENA: They've all gone.

KOOLYGHIN: Masha's gone, too? Where has she gone to? And why is Protopopov waiting outside in a troika? Who's he waiting for?

IRENA: Please don't ask me questions. I'm tired.

KOOLYGHIN: You . . . spoilt child!

OLGA: The conference has only just ended. I'm quite worn out. The headmistress is ill and I'm deputizing for her. My head's aching, oh, my head, my head. . . . (*Sits down.*) Andrey lost two hundred roubles at cards last night. The whole town's talking about it. . . .

KOOLYGHIN: Yes, the conference exhausted me, too. (*Sits down.*)

VERSHININ: So now my wife's taken it into her head to try to frighten me. She tried to poison herself. However, everything's all right now, so I can relax, thank goodness. . . . So we've got to go away? Well, good-night to you, all the best. Fiodor Illych, would you care to come along with me somewhere or other? I can't stay at home to-night, I really can't. . . . Do come!

KOOLYGHIN: I'm tired. I don't think I'll come. (*Gets up.*) I'm tired. Has my wife gone home?

IRENA: I think so.

KOOLYGHIN (*kisses IRENA's hand*): Good-night. We can rest to-morrow and the day after to-morrow, two whole days! Well, I wish you all the best. (*Going out.*) How I long for some tea! I reckoned on spending the evening in congenial company, but—*o, falla-cem hominum spem!*[13] Always use the accusative case in exclamations.

VERSHININ: Well, it looks as if I'll have to go somewhere by myself. (*Goes out with KOO-LYGHIN, whistling.*)

---

[13] *O, fallacem . . . spem:* "oh, the futile hopes of men."

OLGA: My head aches, oh, my head. . . . Andrey lost at cards . . . the whole town's talking. . . . I'll go and lie down. (*Going out.*) To-morrow I'm free. Heavens, what a joy! To-morrow I'm free, and the day after to-morrow I'm free. . . . My head's aching, oh, my poor head. . . .

IRENA (*alone*): They've all gone. No one's left.

Someone is playing an accordion in the street. The nurse sings in the next room.

NATASHA (*crosses the ballroom, wearing a fur coat and cap. She is followed by the maid*): I'll be back in half an hour. I'm just going for a little drive. (*Goes out.*)

IRENA (*alone, with intense longing*): Moscow! Moscow! Moscow!

ACT III

A bedroom now shared by OLGA and IRENA. There are two beds, one on the right, the other on the left, each screened off from the center of the room. It is past two o'clock in the morning. Off stage the alarm is being sounded on account of a fire which has been raging for some time. The inmates of the house have not yet been to bed. MASHA is lying on a couch, dressed, as usual, in black. OLGA and ANFISA come in.

ANFISA: Now they're sitting down there, under the stairs. . . . I keep telling them to come upstairs, that they shouldn't sit down there, but they just cry. "We don't know where our Papa is," they say, "perhaps he's got burned in the fire." What an idea! And there are people in the yard, too . . . half dressed. . . .

OLGA (*takes a dress out of a wardrobe*): Take this grey frock, Nanny. . . . And this one. . . . This blouse, too. . . . And this skirt. Oh, Heavens! what is happening! Apparently the whole of the Kirsanovsky Street's been burnt down. . . . Take this . . . and this, too. . . . (*Throws the clothes into ANFISA's arms.*) The poor Vershinins had a fright. Their house only just escaped being burnt down. They'll have to spend the night here . . . we mustn't let them go home. Poor Fedotik's lost everything, he's got nothing left. . . .

ANFISA: I'd better call Ferapont, Oliushka, I can't carry all this.

OLGA (*rings*): No one takes any notice when I ring. (*Calls through the door.*) Is anyone there? Will someone come up, please!

A window, red with the glow of fire, can be seen through the open door. The sound of a passing fire engine is heard.

How dreadful it all is! And how tired of it I am! (*Enter* FERAPONT.) Take this downstairs please. . . . The Kolotilin girls are sitting under the stairs . . . give it to them. And this, too. . . .

FERAPONT: Very good, Madam. Moscow was burned down in 1812 just the same. Mercy on us! . . . Yes, the French were surprised all right.

OLGA: Go along now, take this down.

FERAPONT: Very good. (*Goes out.*)

OLGA: Give it all away, Nanny, dear. We won't keep anything, give it all away. . . . I'm so tired, I can hardly keep on my feet. We mustn't let the Vershinins go home. The little girls can sleep in the drawing-room, and Alexandr Ignatyevich can share the downstairs room with the Baron. Fedotik can go in with the Baron, too, or maybe he'd better sleep in the ballroom. The doctor's gone and got drunk—you'd think he'd done it on purpose; he's so hopelessly drunk that we can't let anyone go into his room. Vershinin's wife will have to go into the drawing-room, too.

ANFISA (*wearily*): Don't send me away, Oliushka, darling! Don't send me away!

OLGA: What nonsense you're talking, Nanny! No one's sending you away.

ANFISA (*leans her head against* OLGA's *breast*): My dearest girl! I do work, you know, I work as hard as I can. . . . I suppose now I'm getting weaker, I'll be told to go. But where can I go? Where? I'm eighty years old. I'm over eighty-one!

OLGA: You sit down for a while, Nanny. . . . You're tired, you poor dear. . . . (*Makes her sit down.*) Just rest a bit. You've turned quite pale.

Enter NATASHA.

NATASHA: They're saying we ought to start a subscription in aid of the victims of the fire. You know—form a society or something for the purpose. Well, why not? It's an excellent idea! In any case it's up to us to help the poor as best we can. Bobik and Sofochka are fast asleep as if nothing had happened. We've got such a crowd of people in the house; the place seems full of people whichever way you turn. There's 'flu about in the town. . . . I'm so afraid the children might catch it.

OLGA (*without listening to her*): You can't see the fire from this room; it's quiet in here.

NATASHA: Yes. . . . I suppose my hair is all over the place. (*Stands in front of the mirror.*) They say I've got stouter, but it's not true! I'm not a bit stouter. Masha's asleep . . . she's tired, poor girl. . . . (*To* ANFISA, *coldly.*) How dare you sit down in my presence? Get up! Get out of here! (ANFISA *goes out. A pause.*) I can't understand why you keep that old woman in the house.

OLGA (*taken aback*): Forgive me for saying it, but I can't understand how you . . .

NATASHA: She's quite useless here. She's just a peasant woman, her right place is in the country. You're spoiling her. I do like order in the home, I don't like having useless people about. (*Strokes* OLGA's *cheek*). You're tired, my poor dear! Our headmistress is tired! You know, when my Sofochka grows up and goes to school, I'll be frightened of you.

OLGA: I'm not going to be a headmistress.

NATASHA: You'll be asked to, Olechka. It's settled.

OLGA: I'll refuse. I couldn't do it. . . . I wouldn't be strong enough. (*Drinks water.*) You spoke so harshly to Nanny just now. . . . You must forgive me for saying so, but I just can't stand that sort of thing . . . it made me feel quite faint. . . .

NATASHA (*agitated*): Forgive me, Olia, forgive me. I didn't mean to upset you.

MASHA *gets up, picks up a pillow and goes out in a huff.*

OLGA: Please try to understand me, dear. . . . It may be that we've been brought up in a peculiar way, but anyway I just can't bear it. When people are treated like that, it gets me down, I feel quite ill. . . . I simply get unnerved. . . .

NATASHA: Forgive me, dear, forgive me! . . . (*Kisses her.*)

OLGA: Any cruel or tactless remark, even the slightest discourtesy, upsets me. . . .

NATASHA: It's quite true, I know I often say things which would be better left unsaid— but you must agree with me, dear, that she'd be better in the country somewhere.

OLGA: She's been with us for thirty years.

NATASHA: But she can't do any work now, can she? Either I don't understand you, or you don't want to understand me. She can't work, she just sleeps or sits about.

OLGA: Well, let her sit about.

NATASHA (*in surprise*): What do you mean, let her sit about? Surely she is a servant! (*Tearfully.*) No, I don't understand you, Olia! I have a nurse for the children and a wet nurse and we share a maid and a cook. Whatever do we want this old woman for? What for?

The alarm is sounded again.

OLGA: I've aged ten years to-night.

NATASHA: We must sort things out, Olia. You're working at your school, and I'm working at home. You're teaching and I'm running the house. And when I say anything about the servants, I know what I'm talking about. . . . That old thief, that old witch must get out of this house to-morrow! . . . (*Stamps her feet.*) How dare you vex me so? How dare you? (*Recovering her self-control.*) Really, if you don't move downstairs, we'll always be quarrelling. This is quite dreadful!

Enter KOOLYGHIN.

KOOLYGHIN: Where's Masha? It's time we went home. They say the fire's getting less fierce. (*Stretches.*) Only one block got burnt down, but to begin with it looked as if the whole town was going to be set on fire by that wind. (*Sits down.*) I'm so tired, Olechka, my dear. You know, I've often thought that if I hadn't married Masha, I'd have married you, Olechka. You're so kind. I'm worn out. (*Listens.*)

OLGA: What is it?

KOOLYGHIN: The doctor's got drunk just as if he'd done it on purpose. Hopelessly drunk. . . . As if he'd done it on purpose. (*Gets up.*) I think he's coming up here. . . . Can you hear him? Yes, he's coming up. (*Laughs.*) What a fellow, really! . . . I'm going to hide myself. (*Goes to the wardrobe and stands between it and the wall.*) What a scoundrel!

OLGA: He's been off drinking for two years, and now suddenly he goes and gets drunk. . . . (*Walks with* NATASHA *towards the back of the room.*)

CHEBUTYKIN *enters; walking firmly and soberly he crosses the room, stops, looks round, then goes to the wash-stand and begins to wash his hands.*

CHEBUTYKIN (*glumly*): The devil take them all . . . all the lot of them! They think I can treat anything just because I'm a doctor, but I know positively nothing at all. I've forgotten everything I used to know. I remember nothing, positively nothing. . . . (OLGA *and* NATASHA *leave the room without* his noticing.) The devil take them! Last Wednesday I attended a woman at Zasyp. She died, and it's all my fault that she did die. Yes. . . . I used to know a thing or two twenty-five years ago, but now I don't remember anything. Not a thing! Perhaps I'm not a man at all, but I just imagine that I've got hands and feet and a head. Perhaps I don't exist at all, and I only imagine that I'm walking about and eating and sleeping. (Weeps.) Oh, if only I could simply stop existing! (Stops crying, glumly.) God knows. . . . The other day they were talking about Shakespeare and Voltaire at the club. . . . I haven't read either, never read a single line of either, but I tried to make out by my expression that I had. The others did the same. How petty it all is! How despicable! And then suddenly I thought of the woman I killed on Wednesday. It all came back to me, and I felt such a swine, so sick of myself that I went and got drunk. . . .

Enter IRENA, VERSHININ *and* TOOZENBACH. TOO- ZENBACH *is wearing a fashionable new civilian suit.*

IRENA: Let's sit down here for a while. No one will come in here.

VERSHININ: The whole town would have been burnt down but for the soldiers. They're a fine lot of fellows! (*Rubs his hands with pleasure.*) Excellent fellows! Yes, they're a fine lot!

KOOLYGHIN (*approaches them*): What's the time?

TOOZENBACH: It's gone three. It's beginning to get light.

IRENA: Everyone's sitting in the ballroom and nobody thinks of leaving. That man Soliony there, too. . . . (*To* CHEBUTYKIN.) You ought to go to bed, Doctor.

CHEBUTYKIN: I'm all right. . . . Thanks. . . . (*Combs his beard.*)

KOOLYGHIN (*laughs*): Half seas over,[14] Ivan Romanych! (*Slaps him on the shoulder.*) You're a fine one! *In vino veritas*,[15] as they used to say in Rome.

TOOZENBACH: Everyone keeps asking me to arrange a concert in aid of the victims of the fire.

IRENA: Well, who'd you get to perform in it?

TOOZENBACH: It could be done if we wanted to. Maria Serghyeevna plays the piano wonderfully well, in my opinion.

KOOLYGHIN: Yes, wonderfully well!

IRENA: She's forgotten how to. She hasn't played for three years. . . . or maybe it's four.

TOOZENBACH: Nobody understands music in this town, not a single person. But I do—I really do—and I assure you quite definitely that Maria Serghyeevna plays magnificently. She's almost a genius for it.

KOOLYGHIN: You're right, Baron. I'm very fond of Masha. She's such a nice girl.

TOOZENBACH: Fancy being able to play so exquisitely, and yet having nobody, nobody at all, to appreciate it!

KOOLYGHIN (*sighs*): Yes. . . . But would it be quite proper for her to play in a concert? (*A pause.*) I don't know anything about these matters, my friends. Perhaps it'll be perfectly all right. But you know, although our director is a good man, a very good man indeed, and most intelligent, I know that he does hold certain views. . . . Of course, this doesn't really concern him, but I'll have a word with him about it, all the same, if you like.

CHEBUTYKIN (*picks up a china clock and examines it.*)

VERSHININ: I've got my clothes in such a mess helping to put out the fire, I must look like nothing on earth. (*A pause.*) I believe they were saying yesterday that our brigade might be transferred to somewhere a long way away. Some said it was to be Poland, and some said it was Cheeta, in Siberia.

---

[14] *Half seas over:* British colloquialism meaning "drunk."

[15] *In vino veritas:* "In wine, the truth."

TOOZENBACH: I heard that, too. Well, the town will seem quite deserted.

IRENA: We'll go away, too!

CHEBUTYKIN (drops clock and breaks it): Smashed to smithereens!

A pause. Everyone looks upset and embarrassed.

KOOLYGHIN (picks up the pieces): Fancy breaking such a valuable thing! Ah, Ivan Romanych, Ivan Romanych! You'll get a bad mark for that!

IRENA: It was my mother's clock.

CHEBUTYKIN: Well, supposing it was. If it was your mother's, then it was your mother's. Perhaps I didn't smash it. Perhaps it only appears that I did. Perhaps it only appears to us that we exist, whereas in reality we don't exist at all. I don't know anything, no one knows anything. (Stops at the door.) Why are you staring at me? Natasha's having a nice little affair with Protopopov, and you don't see it. You sit here seeing nothing, and meanwhile Natasha's having a nice little affair with Protopopov. . . . (Sings.) Would you like a date? . . . (Goes out.)

VERSHININ: So. . . . (Laughs.) How odd it all is, really. (A pause.) When the fire started, I ran home as fast as I could. When I got near, I could see that our house was all right and out of danger, but the two little girls were standing there, in the doorway in their night clothes. Their mother wasn't there. People were rushing about, horses, dogs . . . and in the kiddies' faces I saw a frightened, anxious, appealing look, I don't know what! . . . My heart sank when I saw their faces. My God, I thought, what will these children have to go through in the course of their poor lives? And they may live a long time, too! I picked them up and ran back here with them, and all the time I was running, I was thinking the same thing: what will they have to go through?

(The alarm is sounded. A pause.) When I got here, my wife was here already . . . angry, shouting!

Enter MASHA carrying a pillow; she sits down on the couch.

VERSHININ: And when my little girls were standing in the doorway with nothing on but their night clothes, and the street was red with the glow of the fire and full of terrifying noises, it struck me that the same sort of thing used to happen years ago, when armies used to make sudden raids on towns, and plunder them and set them on fire. . . . Anyway, is there any essential difference between things as they were and as they are now? And before very long, say, in another two or three hundred years, people may be looking at our present life just as we look at the past now, with horror and scorn. Our own times may seem uncouth to them, boring and frightfully uncomfortable and strange. . . . Oh, what a great life it'll be then, what a life! (Laughs.) Forgive me, I'm philosophizing my head off again . . . but may I go on, please? I'm bursting to philosophize just at the moment. I'm in the mood for it. (A pause.) You seem as if you've all gone to sleep. As I was saying: what a great life it will be in the future! Just try to imagine it. . . . At the present time there are only three people of your intellectual calibre in the whole of this town, but future generations will be more productive of people like you. They'll go on producing more and more of the same sort until at last the time will come when everything will be just as you'd wish it yourselves. People will live their lives in your way, and then even you may be outmoded, and a new lot will come along who will be even better than you are. . . . (Laughs.) I'm in quite a special mood to-day. I feel full of a tremendous urge to live. . . . (Sings.)

"To Love all ages are in fee,
The passion's good for you and me.". . .[16]

(*Laughs.*)

MASHA (*sings*): Tara-tara-tara. . . .
VERSHININ: Tum-tum. . . .
MASHA: Tara-tara . . .
VERSHININ: Tum-tum, tum-tum. . . . (*Laughs.*)

Enter FEDOTIK.

FEDOTIK (*dancing about*): Burnt, burnt! Everything I've got burnt!

All laugh.

IRENA: It's hardly a joking matter. Has everything really been burnt?
FEDOTIK (*laughs*): Everything, completely. I've got nothing left. My guitar's burnt, my photographs are burnt, all my letters are burnt. Even the little note-book I was going to give you has been burnt.

Enter SOLIONY.

IRENA: No, please go away, Vassily Vassilich. You can't come in here.
SOLIONY: Can't I? Why can the Baron come in here if I can't?
VERSHININ: We really must go, all of us. What's the fire doing?
SOLIONY: It's dying down, they say. Well, I must say it's a peculiar thing that the Baron can come in here, and I can't. (*Takes a scent bottle from his pocket and sprinkles himself with scent.*)
VERSHININ: Tara-tara.
MASHA: Tum-tum, tum-tum.
VERSHININ (*laughs, to* SOLIONY): Let's go to the ballroom.
SOLIONY: Very well, we'll make a note of this.

"I hardly need to make my moral yet more clear: That might be teasing geese, I fear!"[17] (*Looks at* TOOZENBACH.) Cluck, cluck, cluck! (*Goes out with* VERSHININ *and* FEDOTIK.)
IRENA: That Soliony has smoked the room out. . . . (*Puzzled.*) The Baron's asleep. Baron! Baron!
TOOZENBACH (*waking out of his doze*): I must be tired. The brick-works. . . . No, I'm not talking in my sleep. I really do intend to go to the brick-works and start working there quite soon. I've had a talk with the manager. (*To* IRENA, *tenderly.*) You are so pale, so beautiful, so fascinating. . . . Your pallor seems to light up the darkness around you, as if it were luminous, somehow. . . . You're sad, you're dissatisfied with the life you have to live. . . . Oh, come away with me, let's go away and work together!
MASHA: Nikolai Lvovich, I wish you'd go away.
TOOZENBACH (*laughs*): Oh, you're here, are you? I didn't see you. (*Kisses* IRENA's *hand.*) Goodbye, I'm going. You know as I look at you now, I keep thinking of the day—it was a long time ago, your Saint's day—when you talked to us about the joy of work. . . . You were so gay and high-spirited then. . . . And what a happy life I saw ahead of me! Where is it all now? (*Kisses her hand.*) There are tears in your eyes. You should go to bed, it's beginning to get light . . . it's almost morning. . . . Oh, if only I could give my life for you!
MASHA: Nikolai Lvovich, please go away! Really now. . . .
TOOZENBACH: I'm going. (*Goes out.*)
MASHA (*lies down*): Are you asleep, Fiodor?
KOOLYGHIN: Eh?
MASHA: Why don't you go home?
KOOLYGHIN: My darling Masha, my sweet, my precious Masha. . . .
IRENA: She's tired. Let her rest a while, Fyedia.
KOOLYGHIN: I'll go in a moment. My wife, my dear, good wife! . . . How I love you! . . . only you!

---

[16] *"To Love . . . me":* from the opera *Eugene Onegin* by P. I. Tchaikovsky (1840–1893).

[17] *"I hardly . . . fear":* from *Geese,* a fable by I. A. Krylov.

MASHA (*crossly*): *Amo, amas, amat, amamus, amatis, amant!*[18]

KOOLYGHIN (*laughs*): Really, she's an amazing woman!—I've been married to you for seven years, but I feel as if we were only married yesterday. Yes, on my word of honour, I do! You really are amazing! Oh, I'm so happy, happy, happy!

MASHA: And I'm so bored, bored, bored! (*Sits up.*) I can't get it out of my head. . . . It's simply disgusting. It's like having a nail driven into my head. No, I can't keep silent about it any more. It's about Andrey. . . . He's actually mortgaged his house to a bank, and his wife's got hold of all the money—and yet the house doesn't belong to him, it belongs to all four of us! Surely, he must realize that, if he's got any honesty.

KOOLYGHIN: Why bring all this up, Masha? Why bother about it now? Andriusha owes money all round. . . . Leave him alone.

MASHA: Anyway, it's disgusting. (*Lies down.*)

KOOLYGHIN: Well, we aren't poor, Masha. I've got work, I teach at the county school, I give private lessons in my spare time. . . . I'm just a plain, honest man. . . . *Omnia mea mecum porto,*[19] as they say.

MASHA: I don't ask for anything, but I'm just disgusted by injustice. (*A pause.*) Why don't you go home, Fiodor?

KOOLYGHIN (*kisses her*): You're tired. Just rest here for a while. . . . I'll go home and wait for you. . . . Go to sleep. (*Goes to the door.*) I'm happy, happy, happy! (*Goes out.*)

IRENA: The truth is that Andrey is getting **to** be shallow-minded. He's aging and since he's been living with that woman he's lost all the inspiration he used to have! Not long ago he was working for a professorship, and yet yesterday he boasted of having at last been elected a member of the County Council. Fancy him a member, with Protopopov as chairman! They say the whole town's laughing at him, he's the only one who doesn't know anything or see anything. And now, you see, everyone's at the fire, while he's just sitting in his room, not taking the slightest notice of it. Just playing his violin. (*Agitated.*) Oh, how dreadful it is, how dreadful, how dreadful! I can't bear it any longer, I can't, I really can't! . . .

Enter OLGA. *She starts arranging things on her bedside table.*

IRENA (*sobs loudly*): You must turn me out of here! Turn me out; I can't stand it any more!

OLGA (*alarmed*): What is it? What is it, darling?

IRENA (*sobbing*): Where. . . . Where has it all gone to? Where is it? Oh, God! I've forgotten. . . . I've forgotten everything . . . there's nothing but a muddle in my head. . . . I don't remember what the Italian for "window" is, or for "ceiling.". . . Every day I'm forgetting more and more, and life's slipping by, and it will never, never come back. . . . We shall never go to Moscow. . . . I can see that we shall never go. . . .

OLGA: Don't, my dear, don't. . . .

IRENA (*trying to control herself*): Oh, I'm so miserable! . . . I can't work, I won't work! I've had enough of it, enough! . . . First I worked on the telegraph, now I'm in the County Council office, and I hate and despise everything they give me to do there. . . . I'm twenty-three years old, I've been working all this time, and I feel as if my brain's dried up. I know I've got thinner and uglier and older, and I find no kind of satisfaction in anything, none at all. And the time's passing . . . and I feel as if I'm moving away from any hope of a genuine, fine life, I'm moving further and further away and sinking into a kind of abyss. I feel in despair, and I don't know why I'm still alive, why I haven't killed myself. . . .

OLGA: Don't cry, my dear child, don't cry. . . . It hurts me.

---

[18] *Amo . . . amant:* variations on the Latin verb "to love."

[19] *Omnia . . . porto:* "Everything I have I carry with me."

IRENA: I'm not crying any more. That's enough of it. Look, I'm not crying now. Enough of it, enough! . . .

OLGA: Darling, let me tell you something. . . . I just want to speak as your sister, as your friend. . . . That is, if you want my advice. . . . Why don't you marry the Baron?

IRENA (weeps quietly.)

OLGA: After all, you do respect him, you think a lot of him. . . . It's true, he's not good-looking, but he's such a decent, clean-minded sort of man. . . . After all, one doesn't marry for love, but to fulfil a duty. At least, I think so, and I'd marry even if I weren't in love. I'd marry anyone that proposed to me, as long as he was a decent man. I'd even marry an old man.

IRENA: I've been waiting all this time, imagining that we'd be moving to Moscow, and I'd meet the man I'm meant for there. I've dreamt about him and I've loved him in my dreams. . . . But it's all turned out to be nonsense . . . nonsense. . . .

OLGA (embracing her): My darling sweetheart, I understand everything perfectly. When the Baron resigned his commission and came to see us in his civilian clothes, I thought he looked so plain that I actually started to cry. . . . He asked me why I was crying. . . . How could I tell him? But, of course, if it were God's will that he should marry you, I'd feel perfectly happy about it. That's quite a different matter, quite different!

NATASHA, carrying a candle, comes out of the door on the right, crosses the stage and goes out through the door on the left without saying anything.

MASHA (sits up): She goes about looking as if she'd started the fire.

OLGA: You're silly, Masha. You're the stupidest person in our family. Forgive me for saying so.

A pause.

MASHA: My dear sisters, I've got something to confess to you. I must get some relief, I feel the need of it in my heart. I'll confess it to you two alone, and then never again, never to anybody! I'll tell you in a minute. (In a low voice.) It's a secret, but you'll have to know everything. I can't keep silent any more. (A pause.) I'm in love, in love. . . . I love that man. . . . You saw him here just now. . . . Well, what's the good? . . . I love Vershinin. . . .

OLGA (goes behind her screen): Don't say it. I don't want to hear it.

MASHA: Well, what's to be done? (Holding her head.) I thought he was queer at first, then I started to pity him . . . then I began to love him . . . love everything about him—his voice, his talk, his misfortunes, his two little girls. . . .

OLGA: Nevertheless, I don't want to hear it. You can say any nonsense you like, I'm not listening.

MASHA: Oh, you're stupid, Olia! If I love him, well—that's my fate! That's my destiny. . . . He loves me, too. It's all rather frightening, isn't it? Not a good thing, is it? (Takes IRENA by the hand and draws her to her.) Oh, my dear! . . . How are we going to live through the rest of our lives? What's going to become of us? When you read a novel, everything in it seems so old and obvious, but when you fall in love yourself, you suddenly discover that you don't really know anything, and you've got to make your own decisions. . . . My dear sisters, my dear sisters! . . . I've confessed it all to you, and now I'll keep quiet. . . . I'll be like that madman in the story by Gogol—silence . . . silence! . . .

Enter ANDREY followed by FERAPONT.

ANDREY (crossly): What do you want? I don't understand you.

FERAPONT (stopping in the doorway, impatiently): I've asked you about ten times already, Andrey Serghyeevich.

ANDREY: In the first place, you're not to call

me Andrey Serghyeevich—call me "Your Honour."

FERAPONT: The firemen are asking Your Honour if they may drive through your garden to get to the river. They've been going a long way round all this time—it's a terrible business!

ANDREY: All right. Tell them it's all right. (FERAPONT *goes out.*) They keep on plaguing me. Where's Olga? (OLGA *comes from behind the screen.*) I wanted to see you. Will you give me the key to the cupboard? I've lost mine. You know the key I mean, the small one you've got....

OLGA *silently hands him the key.* IRENA *goes behind the screen on her side of the room.*

ANDREY: What a terrific fire! It's going down though. That Ferapont annoyed me, the devil take him! Silly thing he made me say.... Telling him to call me "Your Honour"! ... (*A pause.*) Why don't you say anything, Olia? (*A pause.*) It's about time you stopped this nonsense ... sulking like this for no reason whatever. . . . You here, Masha? And Irena's here, too. That's excellent! We can talk it over then, frankly and once for all. What have you got against me? What is it?

OLGA: Drop it now, Andriusha. Let's talk it over to-morrow. (*Agitated.*) What a dreadful night!

ANDREY (*in great embarrassment*): Don't get upset. I'm asking you quite calmly, what have you got against me? Tell me frankly.

VERSHININ'S VOICE (*off stage*): Tum-tum-tum!

MASHA (*in a loud voice, getting up*): Tara-tara-tara! (*To* OLGA.) Good-bye, Olia, God bless you! (*Goes behind the screen and kisses* IRENA.) Sleep well.... Good-bye, Andrey. I should leave them now, they're tired ... talk it over to-morrow.... (*Goes out.*)

OLGA: Really, Andriusha, let's leave it till to-morrow.... (*Goes behind the screen on her side of the room.*) It's time to go to bed.

ANDREY: I only want to say one thing, then I'll go. In a moment.... First of all, you've got something against my wife, against Natasha. I've always been conscious of it from the day we got married. Natasha is a fine woman, she's honest and straightforward and high-principled.... That's my opinion. I love and respect my wife. You understand that I respect her, and I expect others to respect her, too. I repeat: she's an honest, high-principled woman, and all your grievances against her—if you don't mind my saying so—are just imagination, and nothing more.... (*A pause.*) Secondly, you seem to be annoyed with me for not making myself a professor, and not doing any academic work. But I'm working in the Council Office, I'm a member of the County Council, and I feel my service there is just as fine and valuable as any academic work I might do. I'm a member of the County Council, and if you want to know, I'm proud of it! (*A pause.*) Thirdly ... there's something else I must tell you.... I know I mortgaged the house without asking your permission.... That was wrong, I admit it, and I ask you to forgive me.... I was driven to it by my debts.... I'm in debt for about thirty-five thousand roubles. I don't play cards any more, I've given it up long ago.... The only thing I can say to justify myself is that you girls get an annuity, while I don't get anything ... no income, I mean.... (*A pause.*)

KOOLYGHIN (*calling through the door*): Is Masha there? She's not there? (*Alarmed.*) Where can she be then? It's very strange.... (*Goes away.*)

ANDREY: So you won't listen? Natasha is a good, honest woman, I tell you. (*Walks up and down the stage, then stops.*) When I married her, I thought we were going to be happy, I thought we should all be happy.... But ... oh, my God! ... (*Weeps.*) My dear sisters, my dear, good sisters, don't believe what I've been saying, don't believe it.... (*Goes out.*)

KOOLYGHIN (*through the door, agitated*): Where's Masha? Isn't Masha here? Extraordinary! (*Goes away.*)

The alarm is heard again. The stage is empty.

IRENA (*speaking from behind the screen*): Olia! Who's that knocking on the floor?

OLGA: It's the doctor, Ivan Romanych. He's drunk.

IRENA: It's been one thing after another all night. (*A pause.*) Olia! (*Peeps out from behind the screen.*) Have you heard? The troops are being moved from the district ... they're being sent somewhere a long way off.

OLGA: That's only a rumour.

IRENA: We'll be left quite alone then.... Olia!

OLGA: Well?

IRENA: Olia, darling, I do respect the Baron. ... I think a lot of him, he's a very good man.... I'll marry him, Olia, I'll agree to marry him, if only we can go to Moscow! Let's go, please do let's go! There's nowhere in all the world like Moscow. Let's go, Olia! Let's go!

ACT IV

The old garden belonging to the Prozorovs' house. A river is seen at the end of a long avenue of fir-trees, and on the far bank of the river a forest. On the right of the stage there is a verandah with a table on which champagne bottles and glasses have been left. It is midday. From time to time people from the street pass through the garden to get to the river. Five or six soldiers march through quickly.

CHEBUTYKIN, radiating a mood of benevolence which does not leave him throughout the act, is sitting in a chair in the garden. He is wearing his army cap and is holding a walking stick, as if ready to be called away at any moment. KOOLYGHIN, with a decoration round his neck and with his moustache shaved off, TOOZENBACH and IRENA are standing on the verandah saying good-bye to FEDOTIK and RODÉ, who are coming down the steps. Both officers are in marching uniform.

TOOZENBACH (*embracing FEDOTIK*): You're a good fellow, Fedotik; we've been good friends! (*Embraces RODÉ.*) Once more, then. ... Good-bye, my dear friends!

IRENA: Au revoir!

FEDOTIK: It's not "au revoir." It's good-bye. We shall never meet again!

KOOLYGHIN: Who knows? (*Wipes his eyes, smiling.*) There! you've made me cry.

IRENA: We'll meet some time.

FEDOTIK: Perhaps in ten or fifteen years' time. But then we'll hardly know one another.... We shall just meet and say, "How are you?" coldly.... (*Takes a snapshot.*) Wait a moment.... Just one more, for the last time.

RODÉ (*embraces TOOZENBACH*): We're not likely to meet again.... (*Kisses IRENA's hand.*) Thank you for everything ... everything!

FEDOTIK (*annoyed*): Do just wait a second!

TOOZENBACH: We'll meet again if we're fated to meet. Do write to us. Be sure to write.

RODÉ (*glancing round the garden*): Good-bye, trees! (*Shouts.*) Heigh-ho! (*A pause.*) Good-bye, echo!

KOOLYGHIN: I wouldn't be surprised if you got married out there, in Poland.... You'll get a Polish wife, and she'll put her arms round you and say: Kohane![20] (*Laughs.*)

FEDOTIK (*glances at his watch*): There's less than an hour to go. Soliony is the only one from our battery who's going down the river on the barge. All the others are marching with the division. Three batteries are leaving to-day by road and three more to-morrow—then the town will be quite peaceful.

TOOZENBACH: Yes, and dreadfully dull, too.

RODÉ: By the way, where's Maria Serghyeevna?

---

[20] *Kohane:* Polish for "beloved."

KOOLYGHIN: She's somewhere in the garden.

FEDOTIK: We must say good-bye to her.

RODÉ: Good-bye. I really must go, or I'll burst into tears. (*Quickly embraces* TOOZENBACH *and* KOOLYGHIN, *kisses* IRENA's *hand.*) Life's been very pleasant here....

FEDOTIK (*to* KOOLYGHIN): Here's something for a souvenir for you—a note-book with a pencil. . . . We'll go down to the river through here. (*They go off, glancing back.*)

RODÉ (*shouts*): Heigh-ho!

KOOLYGHIN (*shouts*): Good-bye!

At the back of the stage FEDOTIK *and* RODÉ *meet* MASHA, *and say good-bye to her; she goes off with them.*

IRENA: They've gone.... (*Sits down on the bottom step of the verandah.*)

CHEBUTYKIN: They forgot to say good-bye to me.

IRENA: Well, what about you?

CHEBUTYKIN: That's true, I forgot, too. Never mind, I'll be seeing them again quite soon. I'll be leaving to-morrow. Yes...only one more day. And then, in a year's time I'll be retiring. I'll come back here and finish the rest of my life near you. There's just one more year to go and then I get my pension. ...(*Puts a newspaper in his pocket and takes out another.*) I'll come back here and lead a reformed life. I'll be a nice, quiet, well-behaved little man.

IRENA: Yes, it's really time you reformed, my dear friend. You ought to live a different sort of life, somehow.

CHEBUTYKIN: Yes.... I think so, too. (*Sings quietly.*) Tarara-boom-di-ay. . . . I'm sitting on a tomb-di-ay....

KOOLYGHIN: Ivan Romanych is incorrigible! Incorrigible!

CHEBUTYKIN: Yes, you ought to have taken me in hand. You'd have reformed me!

IRENA: Fiodor's shaved his moustache off. I can't bear to look at him.

KOOLYGHIN: Why not?

CHEBUTYKIN: If I could just tell you what your face looks like now—but I daren't.

KOOLYGHIN: Well! Such are the conventions of life! *Modus vivendi,*[21] you know. The director shaved his moustache off, so I shaved mine off when they gave me an inspectorship. No one likes it, but personally I'm quite indifferent. I'm content. Whether I've got a moustache or not, it's all the same to me. (*Sits down.*)

ANDREY (*passes across the back of the stage pushing a pram with a child asleep in it.*)

IRENA: Ivan Romanych, my dear friend, I'm awfully worried about something. You were out in the town garden last night—tell me what happened there?

CHEBUTYKIN: What happened? Nothing. Just a trifling thing. (*Reads his paper.*) It doesn't matter anyway.

KOOLYGHIN: They say that Soliony and the Baron met in the town garden outside the theatre last night and . . .

TOOZENBACH: Don't please! What's the good? ...(*Waves his hand at him deprecatingly and goes into the house.*)

KOOLYGHIN: It was outside the theatre.... Soliony started badgering the Baron, and he lost patience and said something that offended him.

CHEBUTYKIN: I don't know anything about it. It's all nonsense.

KOOLYGHIN: A school-master once wrote "nonsense" in Russian over a pupil's essay, and the pupil puzzled over it, thinking it was a Latin word. (*Laughs.*) Frightfully funny, you know! They say that Soliony's in love with Irena and that he got to hate the Baron more and more.... Well, that's understandable. Irena's a very nice girl. She's a bit like Masha, she tends to get wrapped up in her own thoughts. (*To* IRENA.) But your disposition is more easy-going than Masha's. And yet Masha has a very nice disposition, too. I love her, I love my Masha.

From the back of the stage comes a shout: "Heigh-ho!"

---

21 *Modus vivendi:* "manner of living."

IRENA (*starts*): Anything seems to startle me to-day. (*A pause.*) I've got everything ready, too. I'm sending my luggage off after lunch. The Baron and I are going to get married to-morrow, and directly afterwards we're moving to the brick-works, and the day after to-morrow I'm starting work at the school. So our new life will begin, God willing! When I was sitting for my teacher's diploma, I suddenly started crying for sheer joy, with a sort of feeling of blessedness.... (*A pause.*) The carrier will be coming for my luggage in a minute....

KOOLYGHIN: That's all very well, but somehow I can't feel that it's meant to be serious. All ideas and theories, but nothing really serious. Anyway, I wish you luck from the bottom of my heart.

CHEBUTYKIN (*moved*): My dearest girl, my precious child! You've gone on so far ahead of me, I'll never catch up with you now. I've got left behind like a bird which has grown too old and can't keep up with the rest of the flock. Fly away, my dears, fly away, and God be with you! (*A pause.*) It's a pity you've shaved your moustache off, Fiodor Illyich.

KOOLYGHIN: Don't keep on about it, please! (*Sighs.*) Well, the soldiers will be leaving to-day, and everything will go back to what it was before. Anyway, whatever they say, Masha is a good, loyal wife. Yes, I love her dearly and I'm thankful for what God has given me. Fate treats people so differently. For instance, there's an excise clerk here called Kozyrev. He was at school with me and he was expelled in his fifth year because he just couldn't grasp the *ut consecutivum*.[22] He's dreadfully hard up now, and in bad health, too, and whenever I meet him, I just say to him: "Hullo, *ut consecutivum!*" "Yes," he replies, "that's just the trouble—*consecutivum*" . . . and he starts coughing. Whereas I—I've been lucky all my life. I'm happy, I've actually been awarded

the order of Saint Stanislav, second class—and now I'm teaching the children the same old *ut consecutivum*. Of course, I'm clever, cleverer than plenty of other people, but happiness does not consist of merely being clever....

In the house someone plays "The Maiden's Prayer."

IRENA: To-morrow night I shan't have to listen to "The Maiden's Prayer." I shan't have to meet Protopopov.... (*A pause.*) By the way, he's in the sitting-room. He's come again.

KOOLYGHIN: Hasn't our headmistress arrived yet?

IRENA: No, we've sent for her. If you only knew how difficult it is for me to live here by myself, without Olia! She lives at the school now; she's the headmistress and she's busy the whole day. And I'm here alone, bored, with nothing to do, and I hate the very room I live in. So I've just made up my mind—if I'm really not going to be able to live in Moscow, that's that. It's my fate, that's all. Nothing can be done about it. It's God's will, everything that happens, and that's the truth. Nikolai Lvovich proposed to me.... Well, I thought it over, and I made up my mind. He's such a nice man, it's really extraordinary how nice he is.... And then suddenly I felt as though my soul had grown wings, I felt more cheerful and so relieved somehow that I wanted to work again. Just to start work!...Only something happened yesterday, and now I feel as though something mysterious is hanging over me....

CHEBUTYKIN: Nonsense!

NATASHA (*speaking through the window*): Our headmistress!

KOOLYGHIN: Our headmistress has arrived! Let's go indoors.

Goes indoors with IRENA.

CHEBUTYKIN (*reads his paper and sings*

---

[22] *Ut consecutivum:* "and so it follows."

quietly to himself): Tarara-boom-di-ay.... I'm sitting on a tomb-di-ay....

MASHA *walks up to him;* ANDREY *passes across the back of the stage pushing the pram.*

MASHA: You look very comfortable sitting here....

CHEBUTYKIN: Well, why not? Anything happening?

MASHA (*sits down*): No, nothing. (*A pause.*) Tell me something. Were you in love with my mother?

CHEBUTYKIN: Yes, very much in love.

MASHA: Did she love you?

CHEBUTYKIN (*after a pause*): I can't remember now.

MASHA: Is my man here? Our cook Marfa always used to call her policeman "my man." Is he here?

CHEBUTYKIN: Not yet.

MASHA: When you have to take your happiness in snatches, in little bits, as I do, and then lose it, as I've lost it, you gradually get hardened and bad-tempered. (*Points at her breast.*) Something's boiling over inside me, here. (*Looking at* ANDREY, *who again crosses the stage with the pram.*) There's Andrey, our dear brother.... All our hopes are gone. It's the same as when thousands of people haul a huge bell up into a tower. Untold labour and money is spent on it, and then suddenly it falls and gets smashed. Suddenly, without rhyme or reason. It was the same with Andrey....

ANDREY: When are they going to settle down in the house? They're making such a row.

CHEBUTYKIN: They will soon. (*Looks at his watch.*) This is an old-fashioned watch: it strikes.... (*Winds his watch which then strikes.*) The first, second and fifth batteries will be leaving punctually at one o'clock. (*A pause.*) And I shall leave to-morrow.

ANDREY: For good?

CHEBUTYKIN: I don't know. I may return in about a year. Although, God knows... it's

all the same....

The sounds of a harp and a violin are heard.

ANDREY: The town will seem quite empty. Life will be snuffed out like a candle. (*A pause.*) Something happened yesterday outside the theatre; everybody's talking about it. I'm the only one that doesn't seem to know about it.

CHEBUTYKIN: It was nothing. A lot of nonsense. Soliony started badgering the Baron, or something. The Baron lost his temper and insulted him, and in the end Soliony had to challenge him to a duel. (*Looks at his watch.*) I think it's time to go....At half-past twelve, in the forest over there, on the other side of the river.... Bang-bang! (*Laughs.*) Soliony imagines he's like Lermontov. He actually writes poems. But, joking apart, this is his third duel.

MASHA: Whose third duel?

CHEBUTYKIN: Soliony's.

MASHA: What about the Baron?

CHEBUTYKIN: Well, what about him? (*A pause.*)

MASHA: My thoughts are all in a muddle.... But what I mean to say is that they shouldn't be allowed to fight. He might wound the Baron or even kill him.

CHEBUTYKIN: The Baron's a good enough fellow, but what does it really matter if there's one Baron more or less in the world? Well, let it be! It's all the same. (*The shouts of "Ah-oo!" and "Heigh-ho!" are heard from beyond the garden.*) That's Skvortsov, the second, shouting from the boat. He can wait.

ANDREY: I think it's simply immoral to fight a duel, or even to be present at one as a doctor.

CHEBUTYKIN: That's only how it seems. . . . We don't exist, nothing exists, it only seems to us that we do.... And what difference does it make?

MASHA: Talk, talk, nothing but talk all day long!... (*Starts to go.*) Having to live in this awful climate with the snow threatening to fall at any moment, and then on the top of it having to listen to all this sort of talk.... (*Stops.*) I won't go into the house, I can't bear going in there.... Will you let me know when Vershinin comes?... (*Walks off along the avenue.*) Look, the birds are beginning to fly away already! (*Looks up.*) Swans or geese.... Dear birds, happy birds. ... (*Goes off.*)

ANDREY: Our house will seem quite deserted. The officers will go, you'll go, my sister will get married, and I'll be left alone in the house.

CHEBUTYKIN: What about your wife?

Enter FERAPONT *with some papers.*

ANDREY: My wife is my wife. She's a good, decent sort of woman.... she's really very kind, too, but there's something about her which pulls her down to the level of an animal . . . a sort of mean, blind, thick-skinned animal—anyway, not a human being. I'm telling you this as a friend, the only person I can talk openly to. I love Natasha, it's true. But at times she appears to me so utterly vulgar, that I feel quite bewildered by it, and then I can't understand why, for what reasons I love her—or, anyway, did love her.

CHEBUTYKIN (*gets up*): Well, dear boy, I'm going away to-morrow and it may be we shall never see each other again. So I'll give you a bit of advice. Put on your hat, take a walking stick, and go away.... Go away, and don't ever look back. And the further you go, the better.

SOLIONY *passes across the back of the stage accompanied by two officers. Seeing* CHEBUTY-KIN, *he turns towards him, while the officers walk on.*

SOLIONY: It's time, Doctor. Half past twelve already. (*Shakes hands with* ANDREY.)

CHEBUTYKIN: In a moment. Oh, I'm tired of you all. (*To* ANDREY.) Andriusha, if anyone asks for me, tell them I'll be back presently. (*Sighs.*) Oh-ho-ho!

SOLIONY:
"He had no time to say 'Oh, oh!'
Before that bear had struck him low."...

(*Walks off with him.*) What are you groaning about, old man?

CHEBUTYKIN: Oh, well!

SOLIONY: How do you feel?

CHEBUTYKIN (*crossly*): Like a last year's bird's-nest.

SOLIONY: You needn't be so agitated about it, old boy. I shan't indulge in anything much, I'll just scorch his wings a little, like a woodcock's. (*Takes out a scent bottle and sprinkles scent over his hands.*) I've used up a whole bottle to-day, but my hands still smell. They smell like a corpse. (*A pause.*) Yes.... Do you remember that poem of Lermontov's?

"And he, rebellious, seeks a storm,
As if in storms there were tranquillity."...

CHEBUTYKIN: Yes.

"He had no time to say 'Oh, oh!'
Before that bear had struck him low."

Goes out with SOLIONY. *Shouts of "Heigh-ho!" and "Ah-oo!" are heard. Enter* ANDREY *and* FERAPONT.

FERAPONT: Will you sign these papers, please?

ANDREY (*with irritation*): Leave me alone! Leave me alone, for Heaven's sake. (*Goes off with the pram.*)

FERAPONT: Well, what am I supposed to do with the papers then? They are meant to be signed, aren't they? (*Goes to back of stage.*)

Enter IRENA *and* TOOZENBACH, *the latter wearing a straw hat.* KOOLYGHIN *crosses the stage, calling: "Ah-oo! Masha! Ah-oo!"*

TOOZENBACH: I think he's the only person in the whole town who's glad that the army is leaving.

IRENA: That's quite understandable, really. (*A pause.*) The town will look quite empty.

TOOZENBACH: My dear, I'll be back in a moment.

IRENA: Where are you going?

TOOZENBACH: I must slip back to the town, and then . . . I want to see some of my colleagues off.

IRENA: It's not true. . . . Nikolai, why are you so absent-minded to-day? (*A pause.*) What happened outside the theatre last night?

TOOZENBACH (*with a movement of impatience*): I'll be back in an hour. . . . I'll be back with you again. (*Kisses her hands.*) My treasure! . . . (*Gazes into her eyes.*) It's five years since I first began to love you, and still I can't get used to it, and you seem more beautiful every day. What wonderful, lovely hair! What marvellous eyes! I'll take you away to-morrow. We'll work, we'll be rich, my dreams will come to life again. And you'll be happy! But—there's only one "but," only one—you don't love me!

IRENA: I can't help that! I'll be your wife, I'll be loyal and obedient to you, but I can't love you. . . . What's to be done? (*Weeps.*) I've never loved anyone in my life. Oh, I've had such dreams about being in love! I've been dreaming about it for ever so long, day and night . . . but somehow my soul seems like an expensive piano which someone has locked up and the key's got lost. (*A pause.*) Your eyes are so restless.

TOOZENBACH: I was awake all night. Not that there's anything to be afraid of in my life, nothing threatening. . . . Only the thought of that lost key torments me and keeps me awake. Say something to me. . . . (*A pause.*) Say something!

IRENA: What? What am I to say? What?

TOOZENBACH: Anything.

IRENA: Don't, my dear, don't. . . . (*A pause.*)

TOOZENBACH: Such trifles, such silly things sometimes become so important suddenly, for no apparent reason! You laugh at them, just as you always have done, you still regard them as trifles, and yet you suddenly find they're in control, and you haven't the power to stop them. But don't let us talk about all that! Really, I feel quite elated. I feel as if I was seeing those fir-trees and maples and birches for the first time in my life. They all seem to be looking at me with a sort of inquisitive look and waiting for something. What beautiful trees—and how beautiful, when you think of it, life ought to be with trees like these! (*Shouts of "Ah-oo! Heigh-ho!" are heard.*) I must go, it's time. . . . Look at that dead tree, it's all dried-up, but it's still swaying in the wind along with the others. And in the same way, it seems to me that, if I die, I shall still have a share in life somehow or other. Good-bye, my dear. . . . (*Kisses her hands.*) Your papers, the ones you gave me, are on my desk, under the calendar.

IRENA: I'm coming with you.

TOOZENBACH (*alarmed*): No, no! (*Goes off quickly, then stops in the avenue.*) Irena!

IRENA: What?

TOOZENBACH (*not knowing what to say*): I didn't have any coffee this morning. Will you tell them to get some ready for me? (*Goes off quickly.*)

IRENA *stands, lost in thought, then goes to the back of the stage and sits down on a swing. Enter* ANDREY *with the pram;* FERAPONT *appears.*

FERAPONT: Andrey Serghyeevich, the papers aren't mine, you know, they're the office papers. I didn't make them up.

ANDREY: Oh, where has all my past life gone to?—the time when I was young and gay and clever, when I used to have fine dreams and great thoughts, and the present and the future were bright with hope? Why do we become so dull and commonplace and uninteresting almost before we've begun to live? Why do we get lazy, indifferent, useless, unhappy?...This town's been in existence for two hundred years; a hundred thousand people live in it, but there's not one who's any different from all the others! There's never been a scholar or an artist or a saint in this place, never a single man sufficiently outstanding to make you feel passionately that you wanted to emulate him. People here do nothing but eat, drink and sleep....Then they die and some more take their places, and they eat, drink and sleep, too,—and just to introduce a bit of variety into their lives, so as to avoid getting completely stupid with boredom, they indulge in their disgusting gossip and vodka and gambling and law-suits. The wives deceive their husbands, and the husbands lie to their wives, and pretend they don't see anything and don't hear anything....And all this overwhelming vulgarity and pettiness crushes the children and puts out any spark they might have in them, so that they, too, become miserable, half-dead creatures, just like one another and just like their parents!...(*To* FERAPONT, *crossly.*) What do you want?

FERAPONT: What? Here are the papers to sign.

ANDREY: What a nuisance you are!

FERAPONT (*hands him the papers*): The porter at the finance department told me just now ...he said last winter they had two hundred degrees of frost in Petersburg.

ANDREY: I hate the life I live at present, but oh! the sense of elation when I think of the future! Then I feel so light-hearted, such a sense of release! I seem to see light ahead, light and freedom. I see myself free, and my children, too,—free from idleness, free from *kvass*,[23] free from eternal meals of goose and cabbage, free from after-dinner naps, free from all this degrading parasitism!...

FERAPONT: They say two thousand people were frozen to death. They say everyone was scared stiff. It was either in Petersburg or

in Moscow, I can't remember exactly.

ANDREY (*with sudden emotion, tenderly*): My dear sisters, my dear good sisters! (*Tearfully.*) Masha, my dear sister!...

NATASHA (*through the window*): Who's that talking so loudly there? Is that you, Andriusha? You'll wake Sofochka. *Il ne faut pas faire du bruit, la Sophie est dormie déjà. Vous êtes un ours.*[24] (*Getting angry.*) If you want to talk, give the pram to someone else. Ferapont, take the pram from the master.

FERAPONT: Yes, Madam. (*Takes the pram.*)

ANDREY (*shamefacedly*): I was talking quietly.

NATASHA (*in the window, caressing her small son*): Bobik! Naughty Bobik! Aren't you a naughty boy!

ANDREY (*glancing through the papers*): All right, I'll go through them and sign them if they need it. You can take them back to the office later. (*Goes into the house, reading the papers.*)

FERAPONT *wheels the pram into the garden.*

NATASHA (*in the window*): What's Mummy's name, Bobik? You darling! And who's that lady? Auntie Olia. Say: "Hullo, Auntie Olia."

Two street musicians, a man and a girl, enter and begin to play on a violin and a harp; VERSHININ, OLGA *and* ANFISA *come out of the house and listen in silence for a few moments; then* IRENA *approaches them.*

OLGA: Our garden's like a public road; everybody goes through it. Nanny, give something to the musicians.

ANFISA (*giving them money*): Go along now, God bless you, good people! (*The musicians bow and go away.*) Poor, homeless folk! Whoever would go dragging round the streets playing tunes if he had enough to eat? (*To* IRENA.) How are you, Irenushka? (*Kisses her.*) Ah, my child, what a life I'm

---

[23] *Kvass:* a thin sour beer made from rye or barley.

[24] *Il ne faut . . . ours:* "You must not make any noise, Sophie is asleep already. You're a bear."

having! Such comfort! In a large flat at the school with Oliushka—and no rent to pay, either! The Lord's been kind to me in my old age. I've never had such a comfortable time in my life, old sinner that I am! A big flat, and no rent to pay, and a whole room to myself, with my own bed. All free. Sometimes when I wake up in the night I begin to think, and then—Oh, Lord! Oh, Holy Mother of God!—there's no one happier in the world than me!

VERSHININ (*glances at his watch*): We shall be starting in a moment, Olga Serghyeevna. It's time I went. (*A pause.*) I wish you all the happiness in the world . . . everything. . . . Where's Maria Serghyeevna?

IRENA: She's somewhere in the garden. I'll go and look for her.

VERSHININ: That's kind of you. I really must hurry.

ANFISA: I'll come and help to look for her. (*Calls out.*) Mashenka, ah-oo! (*Goes with* IRENA *towards the far end of the garden.*) Ah-oo! Ah-oo!

VERSHININ: Everything comes to an end. Well, here we are—and now it's going to be "good-bye." (*Looks at his watch.*) The city gave us a sort of farewell lunch. There was champagne, and the mayor made a speech, and I ate and listened, but in spirit I was with you here.... (*Glances round the garden.*) I've grown so...so accustomed to you.

OLGA: Shall we meet again some day, I wonder?

VERSHININ: Most likely not! (*A pause.*) My wife and the two little girls will be staying on here for a month or two. Please, if anything happens, if they need anything....

OLGA: Yes, yes, of course. You needn't worry about that. (*A pause.*) To-morrow there won't be a single officer or soldier in the town.... All that will be just a memory, and, of course, a new life will begin for us here.... (*A pause.*) Nothing ever happens as we'd like it to. I didn't want to be a headmistress, and yet now I am one. It means

we shan't be going to live in Moscow....

VERSHININ: Well.... Thank you for everything. Forgive me if ever I've done anything.... I've talked a lot too much, far too much.... Forgive me for that, don't think too unkindly of me.

OLGA (*wipes her eyes*): Now...why is Masha so long coming?

VERSHININ: What else can I tell you now it's time to say "good-bye"? What shall I philosophize about now?... (*Laughs.*) Yes, life is difficult. It seems quite hopeless for a lot of us, just a kind of impasse.... And yet you must admit that it is gradually getting easier and brighter, and it's clear that the time isn't far off when the light will spread everywhere. (*Looks at his watch.*) Time, it's time for me to go.... In the old days the human race was always making war, its entire existence was taken up with campaigns, advances, retreats, victories.... But now all that's out of date, and in its place there's a huge vacuum, clamouring to be filled. Humanity is passionately seeking something to fill it with and, of course, it will find something some day. Oh! If only it would happen soon! (*A pause.*) If only we could educate the industrious people and make the educated people industrious.... (*Looks at his watch.*) I really must go....

OLGA: Here she comes!

Enter MASHA.

VERSHININ: I've come to say good-bye....

OLGA *walks off and stands a little to one side so as not to interfere with their leave-taking.*

MASHA (*looking into his face*): Good-bye! ... (*A long kiss.*)

OLGA: That'll do, that'll do.

MASHA (*sobs loudly.*)

VERSHININ: Write to me.... Don't forget me! Let me go...it's time. Olga Serghyeevna, please take her away...I must go...I'm late already. . . . (*Deeply moved, kisses* OLGA's *hands, then embraces* MASHA *once again and goes out quickly.*)

OLGA: That'll do, Masha! Don't, my dear, don't. . . .

Enter KOOLYGHIN.

KOOLYGHIN (*embarrassed*): Never mind, let her cry, let her. . . . My dear Masha, my dear, sweet Masha. . . . You're my wife, and I'm happy in spite of everything. . . . I'm not complaining, I've no reproach to make—not a single one. . . . Olga here is my witness. . . . We'll start our life over again in the same old way, and you won't hear a word from me . . . not a hint. . . .

MASHA (*suppressing her sobs*): "A green oak grows by a curving shore, And round that oak hangs a golden chain." . . . "A golden chain round that oak." . . . Oh, I'm going mad. . . . By a curving shore . . . a green oak. . . .

OLGA: Calm yourself, Masha, calm yourself. . . . Give her some water.

MASHA: I'm not crying any more. . . .

KOOLYGHIN: She's not crying any more . . . she's a good girl.

The hollow sound of a gun-shot is heard in the distance.

MASHA: "A green oak grows by a curving shore, And round that oak hangs a golden chain." . . . A green cat . . . a green oak . . . I've got it all mixed up. . . . (*Drinks water.*) My life's messed up. . . . I don't want anything now. . . . I'll calm down in a moment. . . . it doesn't matter. . . . What *is* "the curving shore"? Why does it keep coming into my head all the time? My thoughts are all mixed up.

Enter IRENA.

OLGA: Calm down, Masha. That's right . . . good girl! . . . Let's go indoors.

MASHA (*irritably*): I'm not going in there! (*Sobs, but immediately checks herself.*) I don't go into that house now, and I'm not going to. . . .

IRENA: Let's sit down together for a moment, and not talk about anything. I'm going away to-morrow, you know. . . .

A pause.

KOOLYGHIN: Yesterday I took away a false beard and a moustache from a boy in the third form. I've got them here. (*Puts them on.*) Do I look like our German teacher? . . . (*Laughs.*) I do, don't I? The boys are funny.

MASHA: It's true, you do look like that German of yours.

OLGA (*laughs*): Yes, he does.

MASHA *cries.*

IRENA: That's enough, Masha!

KOOLYGHIN: Very much like him, I think!

Enter NATASHA.

NATASHA (*to the maid*): What? Oh, yes. Mr. Protopopov is going to keep an eye on Sofochka, and Andrey Serghyeevich is going to take Bobik out in the pram. What a lot of work these children make! . . . (*To* IRENA.) Irena, you're really leaving to-morrow? What a pity! Do stay just another week, won't you? (*Catching sight of* KOOLYGHIN, *shrieks; he laughs and takes off the false beard and moustache.*) Get away with you! How you scared me! (*To* IRENA.) I've grown so accustomed to you being here. . . . You mustn't think it's going to be easy for me to be without you. I'll get Andrey and his old violin to move into your room: he can saw away at it as much as he likes there. And then we'll move Sofochka into his room. She's such a wonderful child, really! Such a lovely little girl! This morning she looked at me with such a sweet expression, and then she said: "Ma-mma!"

KOOLYGHIN: It's quite true, she is a beautiful child.

NATASHA: So to-morrow I'll be alone here. (*Sighs.*) I'll have this fir-tree avenue cut down first, then that maple tree over there. It looks so awful in the evenings.... (*To* IRENA.) My dear, that belt you're wearing doesn't suit you at all. Not at all in good taste. You want something brighter to go with that dress.... I'll tell them to put flowers all round here, lots of flowers, so that we get plenty of scent from them.... (*Sternly.*) Why is there a fork lying on this seat? (*Going into the house, to the maid.*) Why is that fork left on the seat there? (*Shouts.*) Don't answer me back!

KOOLYGHIN: There she goes again.

A band plays a military march off stage; all listen.

OLGA: They're going.

Enter CHEBUTYKIN.

MASHA: The soldiers are going. Well.... Happy journey to them! (*To her husband.*) We must go home.... Where's my hat and cape?...

KOOLYGHIN: I took them indoors. I'll bring them at once.

OLGA: Yes, we can go home now. It's time.

CHEBUTYKIN: Olga Serghyeevna!

OLGA: What is it? (*A pause.*) What?

CHEBUTYKIN: Nothing.... I don't know quite how to tell you.... (*Whispers into her ear.*)

OLGA (*frightened*): It can't be true!

CHEBUTYKIN: Yes... a bad business.... I'm so tired... quite worn out.... I don't want to say another word.... (*With annoyance.*) Anyway, nothing matters!...

MASHA: What's happened?

OLGA (*puts her arms round* IRENA): What a dreadful day!... I don't know how to tell you, dear....

IRENA: What is it? Tell me quickly, what is it? For Heaven's sake!... (*Cries.*)

CHEBUTYKIN: The Baron's just been killed in a duel.

IRENA (*cries quietly*): I knew it, I knew it....

CHEBUTYKIN (*goes to the back of the stage and sits down*): I'm tired.... (*Takes a newspaper out of his pocket.*) Let them cry for a bit.... (*Sings quietly to himself.*) Tararaboom-di-ay, I'm sitting on a tomb-di-ay.... What difference does it make?...

The three sisters stand huddled together.

MASHA: Oh, listen to that band! They're leaving us...one of them's gone for good...for ever! We're left alone...to start our lives all over again. We must go on living...we must go on living....

IRENA (*puts her head on* OLGA's *breast*): Some day people will know why such things happen, and what the purpose of all this suffering is.... Then there won't be any more riddles.... Meanwhile we must go on living ...and working. Yes, we must just go on working! To-morrow I'll go away alone and teach in a school somewhere; I'll give my life to people who need it.... It's autumn now, winter will soon be here, and the snow will cover everything...but I'll go on working and working!...

OLGA (*puts her arms round both her sisters*): How cheerfully and jauntily that band's playing—really I feel as if I wanted to live! Merciful God! The years will pass, and we shall all be gone for good and quite forgotten.... Our faces and our voices will be forgotten and people won't even know that there were once three of us here.... But our sufferings may mean happiness for the people who come after us.... There'll be a time when peace and happiness reign in the world, and then we shall be remembered kindly and blessed. No, my dear sisters, life isn't finished for us yet! We're going to live! The band is playing so cheerfully and joyfully—maybe, if we wait a little longer, we shall find out why we live, why we suffer. ...Oh, if we only knew, if only we knew!

The music grows fainter and fainter. KOOLY-GHIN, *smiling happily, brings out the hat and the cape.* ANDREY *enters; he is pushing the pram with* BOBIK *sitting in it.*

CHEBUTYKIN (*sings quietly to himself*): Tarara-boom-di-ay. . . . I'm sitting on a tomb-di-ay. . . . (*Reads the paper.*) What does it matter? Nothing matters!

OLGA: If only we knew, if only we knew! . . .

LUIGI PIRANDELLO

Henry IV

Translated by Edward Storer

Characters

HENRY IV[1]
THE MARCHIONESS MATILDA SPINA
FRIDA, *her daughter*
CHARLES DI NOLLI, *the young Marquis*
BARON TITO BELCREDI
DOCTOR DIONYSIUS GENONI
HAROLD (FRANK)
LANDOLPH (LOLO)   *The four private counsellors (The*
ORDULPH (MOMO)   *names in brackets are nicknames)*
BERTHOLD (FINO)
JOHN, *the old waiter*
THE TWO VALETS IN COSTUME

A Solitary Villa in Italy in Our Own Time

ACT I

Salon in the villa, furnished and decorated so as to look exactly like the throne room of Henry IV in the royal residence at Goslar.[2] Among the antique decorations there are two modern life-size portraits in oil painting. They are placed against the back wall, and mounted in a wooden stand that runs the whole length of the wall. (It is wide and protrudes, so that it is like a large bench.) One of the paintings is on the right; the other on the left of the throne, which is in the middle of the wall and divides the stand.

The Imperial chair and Baldachin.

The two portraits represent a lady and a gentleman, both young, dressed up in carnival costumes: one as "Henry IV," the other as the "Marchioness Matilda of Tuscany."[3] Exits to right and left.

---

[1] *Henry IV:* (1050–1106), German king from 1054 to 1077, emperor from 1084 of the Salian dynasty. Because of his extreme youth, Henry's first decade as ruler was overseen by a series of regents. His attempt to strengthen royal power and maintain a united German kingdom led him into conflicts with Saxon nobles (preeminently, Otto of Nordheim, Duke of Bavaria, and Godfrey of Lorraine), Pope Gregory VII, and his rebellious sins Conrad and Henry.

[2] *Goslar:* Henry's permanent capital.

[3] *"Marchioness Matilda of Tuscany":* Henry's lifelong enemy, at whose castle in Canossa he humbled himself before Pope Gregory VII. She gave refuge to Henry's second wife, Praxedis, when Praxedis was suspected of marital infidelity, and she urged Conrad, Henry's son, to revolt.

When the curtain goes up, the two valets jump down, as if surprised, from the stand on which they have been lying, and go and take their positions, as rigid as statues, on either side below the throne with their halberds in their hands. Soon after, from the second exit, right, enter HAROLD, LANDOLPH *and* BERTHOLD, *young men employed by the* MARQUIS CHARLES DI NOLLI *to play the part of "Secret Counsellors" at the court of "Henry IV." They are, therefore, dressed like German knights of the XIth century.* BERTHOLD, *nicknamed Fino, is just entering on his duties for the first time. His companions are telling him what he has to do and amusing themselves at his expense. The scene is to be played rapidly and vivaciously.*

LANDOLPH (*to* BERTHOLD *as if explaining*): And this is the throne room.

HAROLD: At Goslar.

ORDULPH: Or at the castle in the Hartz,[4] if you prefer.

HAROLD: Or at Wurms.

LANDOLPH: According as to what's doing, it jumps about with us, now here, now there.

ORDULPH: In Saxony.

HAROLD: In Lombardy.

LANDOLPH: On the Rhine.

ONE OF THE VALETS (*without moving, just opening his lips*): I say . . .

HAROLD (*turning round*): What is it?

FIRST VALET (*like a statue*): Is he coming in or not? (*He alludes to* HENRY IV.)

ORDULPH: No, no, he's asleep. You needn't worry.

SECOND VALET (*releasing his pose, taking a long breath and going to lie down again on the stand*): You might have told us at once.

FIRST VALET (*going over to* HAROLD): Have you got a match, please?

LANDOLPH: What? You can't smoke a pipe here, you know.

FIRST VALET (*while* HAROLD *offers him a light*):

No; a cigarette. (*Lights his cigarette and lies down again on the stand.*)

BERTHOLD (*who has been looking on in amazement, walking round the room, regarding the costumes of the others*): I say . . . this room . . . these costumes . . . Which Henry IV is it? I don't quite get it. Is he Henry IV of France or not? (*At this* LANDOLPH, HAROLD, *and* ORDULPH, *burst out laughing.*)

LANDOLPH (*still laughing; and pointing to* BERTHOLD *as if inviting the others to make fun of him*): Henry of France he says: ha! ha!

ORDULPH: He thought it was the king of France!

HAROLD: Henry IV of Germany, my boy: the Salian dynasty![5]

ORDULPH: The great and tragic Emperor!

LANDOLPH: He of Canossa. Every day we carry on here the terrible war between Church and State, by Jove.

ORDULPH: The Empire against the Papacy!

HAROLD: Anti-popes against the Pope!

LANDOLPH: Kings against anti-kings!

ORDULPH: War on the Saxons!

HAROLD: And all the rebels Princes!

LANDOLPH: Against the Emperor's own sons!

BERTHOLD (*covering his head with his hands to protect himself against this avalanche of information*): I understand! I understand! Naturally, I didn't get the idea at first. I'm right then: these aren't costumes of the XVIth century?

HAROLD: XVIth century be hanged!

ORDULPH: We're somewhere between a thousand and eleven hundred.

LANDOLPH: Work it out for yourself: if we are before Canossa on the 25th of January, 1071 . . . [6]

BERTHOLD (*more confused than ever*): Oh my God! What a mess I've made of it!

---

[4] *Hartz:* one of the many castles Henry constructed in order to strengthen royal power.

[5] *Salian dynasty:* comprising the line of German emperors Conrad II, Henry III, Henry IV, Henry V, from 1024 to 1125.

[6] *Canossa on the 25th of January, 1071:* the year was actually 1077.

ORDULPH: Well, just slightly, if you supposed you were at the French court.

BERTHOLD: All that historical stuff I've swatted up!

LANDOLPH: My dear boy, it's four hundred years earlier.

BERTHOLD (*getting angry*): Good Heavens! You ought to have told me it was Germany and not France. I can't tell you how many books I've read in the last fifteen days.

HAROLD: But I say, surely you knew that poor Tito was Adalbert of Bremen,[7] here?

BERTHOLD: Not a damned bit!

LANDOLPH: Well, don't you see how it is? When Tito died, the Marquis Di Nolli . . .

BERTHOLD: Oh, it was he, was it? He might have told me.

HAROLD: Perhaps he thought you knew.

LANDOLPH: He didn't want to engage anyone else in substitution. He thought the remaining three of us would do. But *he* began to cry out: "With Adalbert driven away . . .":[8] because, you see, he didn't imagine poor Tito was dead; but that, as Bishop Adalbert, the rival bishops of Cologne and Mayence had driven him off . . .

BERTHOLD (*taking his head in his hand*): But I don't know a word of what you're talking about.

ORDULPH: So much the worse for you, my boy!

HAROLD: But the trouble is that not even we know who you are.

BERTHOLD: What? Not even you? You don't know who I'm supposed to be?

ORDULPH: Hum! "Berthold."

BERTHOLD: But which Berthold? And why Berthold?

LANDOLPH (*solemnly imitating* HENRY IV): "They've driven Adalbert away from me. Well then, I want Berthold! I want Berthold!" That's what he said.

HAROLD: We three looked one another in the eyes: who's got to be Berthold?

ORDULPH: And so here you are, "Berthold," my dear fellow!

LANDOLPH: I'm afraid you will make a bit of a mess of it.

BERTHOLD (*indignant, getting ready to go*): Ah, no! Thanks very much, but I'm off! I'm out of this!

HAROLD (*restraining him with the other two, amid laughter*): Steady now! Don't get excited!

LANDOLPH: Cheer up, my dear fellow! We don't any of us know who we are really. He's Harold; he's Ordulph! I'm Landolph! That's the way he calls us. We've got used to it. But who are we? Names of the period! Yours, too, is a name of the period: Berthold! Only one of us, poor Tito, had got a really decent part, as you can read in history: that of the Bishop of Bremen. He was just like a real bishop. Tito did it awfully well, poor chap!

HAROLD: Look at the study he put into it!

LANDOLPH: Why, he even ordered his Majesty about, opposed his views, guided and counselled him. We're "secret counsellors"—in a manner of speaking only; because it is written in history that Henry IV was hated by the upper aristocracy for surrounding himself at court with young men of the bourgeoisie.

ORDULPH: Us, that is.

LANDOLPH: Yes, small devoted vassals, a bit dissolute and very gay . . .

BERTHOLD: So I've got to be gay as well?

HAROLD: I should say so! Same as we are!

ORDULPH: And it isn't too easy, you know.

LANDOLPH: It's a pity; because the way we're got up, we could do a fine historical reconstruction. There's any amount of material in the story of Henry IV. But, as a matter of fact, we do nothing. We have the form without the content. We're worse than the real secret counsellors of Henry IV; because certainly no one had given them a part to play—at any rate, they didn't feel they had a part to play. It was their life. They looked after their own interests at the

---

7 *Adalbert of Bremen*: one of Henry's regents and his ally against the rebellious nobles.

8 *"With Adalbert driven away . . ."*: Henry was forced, in 1066, by Adalbert's enemies to dismiss him.

expense of others, sold investitures and—what not! We stop here in this magnificent court—for what?—Just doing nothing. We're like so many puppets hung on the wall, waiting for someone to come and move us or make us talk.

HAROLD: Ah, no, old sport, not quite that! We've got to give the proper answer, you know. There's trouble if he asks you something and you don't chip in with the cue.

LANDOLPH: Yes, that's true.

BERTHOLD: Don't rub it in too hard! How the devil am I to give him the proper answer, if I've swatted up Henry IV of France, and now he turns out to be Henry IV of Germany? (*The other three laugh.*)

HAROLD: You'd better start and prepare yourself at once.

ORDULPH: We'll help you out.

HAROLD: We've got any amount of books on the subject. A brief run through the main points will do to begin with.

ORDULPH: At any rate, you must have got some sort of general idea.

HAROLD: Look here! (*Turns him around and shows him the portrait of the Marchioness Matilda on the wall.*) Who's that?

BERTHOLD (*looking at it*): That? Well, the thing seems to me somewhat out of place, anyway: two modern paintings in the midst of all this respectable antiquity!

HAROLD: You're right! They weren't there in the beginning. There are two niches there behind the pictures. They were going to put up two statues in the style of the period. Then the places were covered with those canvases there.

LANDOLPH (*interrupting and continuing*): They would certainly be out of place if they really were paintings!

BERTHOLD: What are they, if they aren't paintings?

LANDOLPH: Go and touch them! Pictures all right ... but for him! (*Makes a mysterious gesture to the right, alluding to* HENRY IV.) ... who never touches them! ...

BERTHOLD: No? What are they for him?

LANDOLPH: Well, I'm only supposing, you know; but I imagine I'm about right. They're images such as ... well—such as a mirror might throw back. Do you understand? That one there represents himself, as he is in this throne room, which is all in the style of the period. What's there to marvel at? If we put you before a mirror, won't you see yourself, alive, but dressed up in ancient costume? Well, it's as if there were two mirrors there, which cast back living images in the midst of a world which, as you well see, when you have lived with us, comes to life too.

BERTHOLD: I say, look here ... I've no particular desire to go mad here.

HAROLD: Go mad, be hanged! You'll have a fine time!

BERTHOLD: Tell me this: how have you all managed to become so learned?

LANDOLPH: My dear fellow, you can't go back over 800 years of history without picking up a bit of experience.

HAROLD: Come on! Come on! You'll see how quickly you get into it!

ORDULPH: You'll learn wisdom, too, at this school.

BERTHOLD: Well, for Heaven's sake, help me a bit! Give me the main lines, anyway.

HAROLD: Leave it to us. We'll do it all between us.

LANDOLPH: We'll put your wires on you and fix you up like a first-class marionette. Come along! (THEY *take him by the arm to lead him away.*)

BERTHOLD (*stopping and looking at the portrait on the wall*): Wait a minute! You haven't told me who that is. The Emperor's wife?

HAROLD: No! The Emperor's wife is Bertha of Susa, the sister of Amadeus II of Savoy.

ORDULPH: And the Emperor, who wants to be young with us, can't stand her, and wants to put her away.

LANDOLPH: That is his most ferocious enemy: Matilda, Marchioness of Tuscany.

BERTHOLD: Ah, I've got it: the one who gave hospitality to the Pope!

LANDOLPH: Exactly: at Canossa!

ORDULPH: Pope Gregory VII!

HAROLD: Our *bête noir!*[9] Come on! come on! (*All four move toward the right to go out, when, from the left, the old servant* JOHN *enters in evening dress.*)

JOHN (*quickly, anxiously*): Hss! Hss! Frank! Lolo!

HAROLD (*turning round*): What is it?

BERTHOLD (*marvelling at seeing a man in modern clothes enter the throne room*): Oh! I say, this is a bit too much, this chap here!

LANDOLPH: A man of the XXth century, here! Oh, go away! (THEY *run over to him, pretending to menace him and throw him out.*)

ORDULPH (*heroically*): Messenger of Gregory VII, away!

HAROLD: Away! Away!

JOHN (*annoyed, defending himself*): Oh, stop it! Stop it, I tell you!

ORDULPH: No, you can't set foot here!

HAROLD: Out with him!

LANDOLPH (*to* BERTHOLD): Magic, you know! He's a demon conjured up by the Wizard of Rome! Out with your swords! (*Makes as if to draw a sword.*)

JOHN (*shouting*): Stop it, will you? Don't play the fool with me! The Marquis has arrived with some friends . . .

LANDOLPH: Good! Good! Are there ladies too?

ORDULPH: Old or young?

JOHN: There are two gentlemen.

HAROLD: But the ladies, the ladies, who are they?

JOHN: The Marchioness and her daughter.

LANDOLPH (*surprised*): What do you say?

ORDULPH: The Marchioness?

JOHN: The Marchioness! The Marchioness!

HAROLD: Who are the gentlemen?

JOHN: I don't know.

HAROLD (*to* BERTHOLD): They're coming to bring us a message from the Pope, do you see?

ORDULPH: All messengers of Gregory VII! What fun!

JOHN: Will you let me speak, or not?

ORDULPH: Come on then!

JOHN: One of the two gentlemen is a doctor, I fancy.

LANDOLPH: Oh, I see, one of the usual doctors.

HAROLD: Bravo Berthold, you'll bring us luck!

LANDOLPH: You wait and see how we'll manage this doctor!

BERTHOLD: It looks as if I were going to get into a nice mess right away.

JOHN: If the gentlemen would allow me to speak . . . they want to come here into the throne room.

LANDOLPH (*surprised*): What? She? The Marchioness here?

HAROLD: Then this is something quite different! No play-acting this time!

LANDOLPH: We'll have a real tragedy: that's what!

BERTHOLD (*curious*): Why? Why?

ORDULPH (*pointing to the portrait*): She is that person there, don't you understand?

LANDOLPH: The daughter is the fiancée of the Marquis. But what have they come for, I should like to know?

ORDULPH: If he sees her, there'll be trouble.

LANDOLPH: Perhaps he won't recognize her any more.

JOHN: You must keep him there, if he should wake up . . .

ORDULPH: Easier said than done, by Jove!

HAROLD: You know what he's like!

JOHN:—even by force, if necessary! Those are my orders. Go on! Go on!

HAROLD: Yes, because who knows if he hasn't already wakened up?

ORDULPH: Come on then!

LANDOLPH (*going towards* JOHN *with the others*): You'll tell us later what it all means.

JOHN (*shouting after them*): Close the door there, and hide the key! That other door too. (*Pointing to the other door on right.*)

JOHN (*to the* TWO VALETS): Be off, you two! There! (*Pointing to exit right.*) Close the door after you, and hide the key!

---

9 *Bête noir:* literally, a black beast; an object of aversion or detestation.

The TWO VALETS *go out by the first door on right.* JOHN *moves over to the left to show in:* DONNA MATILDA SPINA, *the young* MARCHIONESS FRIDA, DR. DIONYSIUS GENONI, *the* BARON TITO BELCREDI *and the young* MARQUIS CHARLES DI NOLLI, *who, as master of the house, enters last.*

DONNA MATILDA SPINA *is about 45, still handsome, although there are too patent signs of her attempts to remedy the ravages of time with make-up. Her head is thus rather like a Walkyrie.*[10] *This facial make-up contrasts with her beautiful sad mouth. A widow for many years, she now has as her friend the* BARON TITO BELCREDI, *whom neither she nor anyone else takes seriously—at least so it would appear.*

What TITO BELCREDI *really is for her at bottom, he alone knows; and he is, therefore, entitled to laugh, if his friend feels the need of pretending not to know. He can always laugh at the jests which the beautiful Marchioness makes with others at his expense. He is slim, prematurely gray, and younger than she is. His head is bird-like in shape. He would be a very vivacious person, if his ductile agility (which among other things makes him a redoubtable swordsman) were not enclosed in a sheath of Arab-like laziness, which is revealed in his strange, nasal drawn-out voice.*

FRIDA, *the daughter of the Marchioness, is 19. She is sad; because her imperious and too beautiful mother puts her in the shade, and provokes facile gossip against her daughter as well as against herself. Fortunately for her, she is engaged to the* MARQUIS CHARLES DI NOLLI.

CHARLES DI NOLLI *is a stiff young man, very indulgent towards others, but sure of himself for what he amounts to in the world. He is worried about all the responsibilities which he believes weigh on him. He is dressed in* deep mourning for the recent death of his mother.

DR. DIONYSIUS GENONI *has a bold rubicund Satyr-like face, prominent eyes, a pointed beard (which is silvery and shiny) and elegant manners. He is nearly bald. All enter in a state of perturbation, almost as if afraid, and all (except* DI NOLLI) *looking curiously about the room. At first, they speak sotto voce.*

DI NOLLI (*to* JOHN): Have you given the orders properly?

JOHN: Yes, my Lord; don't be anxious about that.

BELCREDI: Ah, magnificent! magnificent!

DOCTOR: How extremely interesting! Even in the surroundings his raving madness—is perfectly taken into account!

DONNA MATILDA (*glancing round for her portrait, discovers it, and goes up close to it*): Ah! Here it is! (*Going back to admire it, while mixed emotions stir within her.*) Yes ...yes ... (*Calls her daughter* FRIDA.)

FRIDA: Ah, your portrait!

DONNA MATILDA: No, no ... look again, it's you, not I, there!

DI NOLLI: Yes, it's quite true. I told you so. I ...

DONNA MATILDA: But I would never have believed it! (*Shaking as if with a chill.*) What a strange feeling it gives one! (*Then looking at her daughter.*) Frida, what's the matter? (*She pulls her to her side, and slips an arm round her waist.*) Come: don't you see yourself in me there?

FRIDA: Well, I really ...

DONNA MATILDA: Don't you think so? Don't you, really? (*Turning to* BELCREDI.) Look at it, Tito! Speak up, man!

BELCREDI (*without looking*): Ah, no! I shan't look at it. For me, *a priori*, certainly not!

DONNA MATILDA: Stupid! You think you are paying me a compliment! (*Turning to* DOCTOR GENONI.) What do you say, Doctor? Do say something, please!

DOCTOR (*makes a movement to go near to the picture*).

---

[10] *Walkyrie:* In German mythology a divine female messenger of Odin or Wotan, who rides over battlefields gathering the spirits of dead heroes.

BELCREDI (*with his back turned, pretending to attract his attention secretly*):—Hss! No, Doctor! For the love of Heaven, have nothing to do with it!

DOCTOR (*getting bewildered and smiling*): And why shouldn't I?

DONNA MATILDA: Don't listen to him! Come here! He's insufferable!

FRIDA: He acts the fool by profession, didn't you know that?

BELCREDI (*to the* DOCTOR, *seeing him go over*): Look at your feet, Doctor! Mind where you're going!

DOCTOR: Why?

BELCREDI: Be careful you don't put your foot in it!

DOCTOR (*laughing feebly*): No, no. After all, it seems to me there's no reason to be astonished at the fact that a daughter should resemble her mother!

BELCREDI: Hullo! Hullo! He's done it now; he's said it.

DONNA MATILDA (*with exaggerated anger, advancing towards* BELCREDI): What's the matter? What has he said? What has he done?

DOCTOR (*candidly*): Well, isn't it so?

BELCREDI (*answering the* MARCHIONESS): I said there was nothing to be astounded at—and you are astounded! And why so, then, if the thing is so simple and natural for you now?

DONNA MATILDA (*still more angry*): Fool! fool! It's just because it is so natural! Just because it isn't my daughter who is there. (*Pointing to the canvas.*) That is my portrait; and to find my daughter there instead of me fills me with astonishment, an astonishment which, I beg you to believe, is sincere. I forbid you to cast doubts on it.

FRIDA (*slowly and wearily*): My God! It's always like this . . . rows over nothing . . .

BELCREDI (*also slowly, looking dejected, in accents of apology*): I cast no doubt on anything! I noticed from the beginning that you haven't shared your mother's astonishment; or, if something did astonish you, it was because the likeness between you and the portrait seemed so strong.

DONNA MATILDA: Naturally! She cannot recognize herself in me as I was at her age; while I, there, can very well recognize myself in her as she is now!

DOCTOR: Quite right! Because a portrait is always there fixed in the twinkling of an eye: for the young lady something far away and without memories, while, for the Marchioness, it can bring back everything: movements, gestures, looks, smiles, a whole heap of things . . .

DONNA MATILDA: Exactly!

DOCTOR (*continuing, turning towards her*): Naturally enough, you can live all these old sensations again in your daughter.

DONNA MATILDA: He always spoils every innocent pleasure for me, every touch I have of spontaneous sentiment! He does it merely to annoy me.

DOCTOR (*frightened at the disturbance he has caused, adopts a professorial tone*): Likeness, dear Baron, is often the result of imponderable things. So one explains that . . .

BELCREDI (*interrupting the discourse*): Somebody will soon be finding a likeness between you and me, my dear Professor!

DI NOLLI: Oh! let's finish with this, please! (*Points to the two doors on the right, as a warning that there is someone there who may be listening.*) We've wasted too much time as it is!

FRIDA: As one might expect when *he's* present. (*Alludes to* BELCREDI.)

DI NOLLI: Enough! The Doctor is here; and we have come for a very serious purpose which you all know is important for me.

DOCTOR: Yes, that is so! But now, first of all, let's try to get some points down exactly. Excuse me, Marchioness, will you tell me why your portrait is here? Did you present it to him then?

DONNA MATILDA: No, not at all. How could I have given it to him? I was just like Frida then—and not even engaged. I gave it to him three or four years after the accident. I gave it to him because his mother wished it so much . . . (*Points to* DI NOLLI.)

DOCTOR: She was his sister? (*Alludes to* HENRY IV.)

DI NOLLI: Yes, Doctor; and our coming here is a debt we pay to my mother who has been dead for more than a month. Instead of being here, she and I (*Indicating Frida.*) ought to be traveling together...

DOCTOR: ...taking a cure of quite a different kind!

DI NOLLI:—Hum! Mother died in the firm conviction that her adored brother was just about to be cured.

DOCTOR: And can't you tell me, if you please, how she inferred this?

DI NOLLI: The conviction would appear to have derived from certain strange remarks which he made, a little before mother died.

DOCTOR: Oh, remarks!...Ah!...It would be extremely useful for me to have those remarks, word for word, if possible.

DI NOLLI: I can't remember them. I know that mother returned awfully upset from her last visit with him. On her death-bed, she made me promise that I would never neglect him, that I would have doctors see him, and examine him.

DOCTOR: Um! Um! Let me see! let me see! Sometimes very small reasons determine ...and this portrait here then?...

DONNA MATILDA: For Heaven's sake, Doctor, don't attach excessive importance to this. It made an impression on me because I had not seen it for so many years!

DOCTOR: If you please, quietly, quietly...

DI NOLLI:—Well, yes, it must be about fifteen years ago.

DONNA MATILDA: More, more: eighteen!

DOCTOR: Forgive me, but you don't quite know what I'm trying to get at. I attach a very great importance to these two portraits... They were painted, naturally, prior to the famous—and most regrettable pageant, weren't they?

DONNA MATILDA: Of course!

DOCTOR: That is...when he was quite in his right mind—that's what I've been trying to say. Was it his suggestion that they should be painted?

DONNA MATILDA: Lots of the people who took part in the pageant had theirs done as a souvenir...

BELCREDI: I had mine done—as "Charles of Anjou!"[11]

DONNA MATILDA: ...as soon as the costumes were ready.

BELCREDI: As a matter of fact, it was proposed that the whole lot of us should be hung together in a gallery of the villa where the pageant took place. But in the end, everybody wanted to keep his own portrait.

DONNA MATILDA: And I gave him this portrait of me without very much regret...since his mother... (*Indicates* DI NOLLI.)

DOCTOR: You don't remember if it was he who asked for it?

DONNA MATILDA: Ah, that I don't remember... Maybe it was his sister, wanting to help out...

DOCTOR: One other thing: was it his idea, this pageant?

BELCREDI (*at once*): No, no, it was mine!

DOCTOR: If you please...

DONNA MATILDA: Don't listen to him! It was poor Belassi's idea.

BELCREDI: Belassi! What had he got to do with it?

DONNA MATILDA: Count Belassi, who died, poor fellow, two or three months after...

BELCREDI: But if Belassi wasn't there when...

DI NOLLI: Excuse me, Doctor; but is it really necessary to establish whose the original idea was?

DOCTOR: It would help me, certainly!

BELCREDI: I tell you the idea was mine! There's nothing to be proud of in it, seeing what the result's been. Look here, Doctor, it was like this. One evening, in the first days of November, I was looking at an illustrated German review in the club. I

---

11 "*Charles of Anjou*": (1246–1285), founder of the House of Anjou.

was merely glancing at the pictures, because I can't read German. There was a picture of the Kaiser, at some University town where he had been a student ... I don't remember which.

DOCTOR: Bonn, Bonn!

BELCREDI:—You are right: Bonn! He was on horseback, dressed up in one of those ancient German student guild-costumes, followed by a procession of noble students, also in costume. The picture gave me the idea. Already someone at the club had spoken of a pageant for the forthcoming carnival. So I had the notion that each of us should choose for this Tower of Babel pageant to represent some character: a king, an emperor, a prince, with his queen, empress, or lady, alongside of him—and all on horseback. The suggestion was at once accepted.

DONNA MATILDA: I had my invitation from Belassi.

BELCREDI: Well, he wasn't speaking the truth! That's all I can say, if he told you the idea was his. He wasn't even at the club the evening I made the suggestion, just as he (*Meaning* HENRY IV.) wasn't there either.

DOCTOR: So he chose the character of Henry IV?

DONNA MATILDA: Because I ... thinking of my name, and not giving the choice any importance, said I would be the Marchioness Matilda of Tuscany.

DOCTOR: I ... don't understand the relation between the two.

DONNA MATILDA:—Neither did I, to begin with, when he said that in that case he would be at my feet like Henry IV at Canossa. I had heard of Canossa of course; but to tell the truth, I'd forgotten most of the story; and I remember I received a curious impression when I had to get up my part, and found that I was the faithful and zealous friend of Pope Gregory VII in deadly enmity with the Emperor of Germany. Then I understood why, since I had chosen to represent his implacable enemy, he wanted

to be near me in the pageant as Henry IV.

DOCTOR: Ah, perhaps because ...

BELCREDI:—Good Heavens, Doctor, because he was then paying furious court to her! (*Indicates the* MARCHIONESS.) And she, naturally ...

DONNA MATILDA: Naturally? Not naturally at all ...

BELCREDI (*pointing to her*): She shouldn't stand him ...

DONNA MATILDA:—No, that isn't true! I didn't dislike him. Not at all! But for me, when a man begins to want to be taken seriously, well ...

BELCREDI (*continuing for her*): He gives you the clearest proof of his stupidity.

DONNA MATILDA: No, dear; not in this case; because he was never a fool like you.

BELCREDI: Anyway, I've never asked you to take me seriously.

DONNA MATILDA: Yes, I know. But with him one couldn't joke. (*Changing her tone and speaking to the* DOCTOR.) One of the many misfortunes which happen to us women, Doctor, is to see before us every now and again a pair of eyes glaring at us with a contained intense promise of eternal devotion. (*Bursts out laughing.*) There is nothing quite so funny. If men could only see themselves with that eternal look of fidelity in their faces! I've always thought it comic; then more even than now. But I want to make a confession—I can do so after twenty years or more. When I laughed at him then, it was partly out of fear. One might have almost believed a promise from those eyes of his. But it would have been very dangerous.

DOCTOR (*with lively interest*): Ah! ah! This is most interesting! Very dangerous, you say?

DONNA MATILDA: Yes, because he was very different from the others. And then, I am ... well ... what shall I say? ... a little impatient of all that is pondered, or tedious. But I was too young then, and a woman. I had the bit between my teeth. It would have required more courage than I felt I possessed. So I laughed at him too—with re-morse, to spite myself, indeed; since I saw that my own laugh mingled with those of all the others—the other fools—who made fun of him.

BELCREDI: My own case, more or less!

DONNA MATILDA: You make people laugh at you, my dear, with your trick of always humiliating yourself. It was quite a differ-ent affair with him. There's a vast differ-ence. And you—you know—people laugh in your face!

BELCREDI: Well, that's better than behind one's back!

DOCTOR: Let's get to the facts. He was then already somewhat exalted, if I understand rightly.

BELCREDI: Yes, but in a curious fashion, Doctor.

DOCTOR: How?

BELCREDI: Well, cold-bloodedly so to speak.

DONNA MATILDA: Not at all! It was like this, Doctor! He was a bit strange, certainly; but only because he was fond of life: eccentric, there!

BELCREDI: I don't say he simulated exaltation. On the contrary, he was often genuinely exalted. But I could swear, Doctor, that he saw himself at once in his own exaltation. Moreover, I'm certain it made him suffer. Sometimes he had the most comical fits of rage against himself.

DOCTOR: Yes?

DONNA MATILDA: That is true.

BELCREDI (to DONNA MATILDA): And why? (To the DOCTOR.) Evidently, because that im-mediate lucidity that comes from acting, assuming a part, at once put him out of key with his own feelings, which seemed to him not exactly false, but like something he was obliged to give the value there and then of—what shall I say—of an act of intelligence, to make up for that sincere cordial warmth he felt lacking. So he im-provised, exaggerated, let himself go, so as to distract and forget himself. He appeared inconstant, fatuous, and—yes—even ridicu-lous, sometimes.

DOCTOR: And may we say unsociable?

BELCREDI: No, not at all. He was famous for getting up things: *tableaux vivants*,[12] dances, theatrical performances for char-ity: all for the fun of the thing, of course. He was a jolly good actor, you know!

DI NOLLI: Madness has made a superb actor of him.

BELCREDI: —Why, so he was even in the old days. When the accident happened, after the horse fell . . .

DOCTOR: Hit the back of his head, didn't he?

DONNA MATILDA: Oh, it was horrible! He was beside me! I saw him between the horse's hoofs! It was rearing!

BELCREDI: None of us thought it was anything serious at first. There was a stop in the pageant, a bit of disorder. People wanted to know what had happened. But they'd al-ready taken him off to the villa.

DONNA MATILDA: There wasn't the least sign of a wound, not a drop of blood.

BELCREDI: We thought he had merely fainted.

DONNA MATILDA: But two hours afterwards . . .

BELCREDI: He reappeared in the drawing-room of the villa . . . that is what I wanted to say . . .

DONNA MATILDA: My God! What a face he had. I saw the whole thing at once!

BELCREDI: No, no! that isn't true. Nobody saw it, Doctor, believe me!

DONNA MATILDA: Doubtless, because you were all like mad folk.

BELCREDI: Everybody was pretending to act his part for a joke. It was a regular Babel.

DONNA MATILDA: And you can imagine, Doctor, what terror struck into us when we under-stood that he, on the contrary, was playing his part in deadly earnest . . .

DOCTOR: Oh, he was there too, was he?

BELCREDI: Of course! He came straight into the midst of us. We thought he'd quite re-covered, and was pretending, fooling, like all the rest of us . . . only doing it rather

---

12 *Tableaux vivants:* pictures depicting famous scenes and composed of living, costumed performers.

better; because, as I say, he knew how to act.

DONNA MATILDA: Some of them began to hit him with their whips and fans and sticks.

BELCREDI: And then—as a king, he was armed, of course—he drew out his sword and menaced two or three of us . . . It was a terrible moment, I can assure you!

DONNA MATILDA: I shall never forget that scene —all our masked faces hideous and terrified gazing at him, at that terrible mask of his face, which was no longer a mask, but madness, madness personified.

BELCREDI: He was Henry IV, Henry IV in person, in a moment of fury.

DONNA MATILDA: He'd got into it all the detail and minute preparation of a month's careful study. And it all burned and blazed there in the terrible obsession which lit his face.

DOCTOR: Yes, that is quite natural, of course. The momentary obsession of a dilettante became fixed, owing to the fall and the damage to the brain.

BELCREDI (*to* FRIDA *and* DI NOLLI): You see the kind of jokes life can play on us. (*To* DI NOLLI.) You were four or five years old. (*To* FRIDA.) Your mother imagines you've taken her place there in that portrait; when, at the time, she had not the remotest idea that she would bring you into the world. My hair is already grey; and he— look at him—(*Points to portrait*)—ha! A smack on the head, and he never moves again: Henry IV for ever!

DOCTOR (*seeking to draw the attention of the others, looking learned and imposing*):— Well, well, then it comes, we may say, to this . . .

Suddenly the first exit to right, the one nearest footlights, opens, and BERTHOLD *enters all excited.*

BERTHOLD (*rushing in*): I say! I say! (*Stops for a moment, arrested by the astonishment which his appearance has caused in the others.*)

FRIDA (*running away terrified*): Oh dear! oh dear! it's he, it's . . .

DONNA MATILDA (*covering her face with her hands so as not to see*): Is it, is it he?

DI NOLLI: No, no, what are you talking about? Be calm!

DOCTOR: Who is it then?

BELCREDI: One of our masqueraders.

DI NOLLI: He is one of the four youths we keep here to help him out in his madness . . .

BERTHOLD: I beg your pardon, Marquis . . .

DI NOLLI: Pardon be damned! I gave orders that the doors were to be closed, and that nobody should be allowed to enter.

BERTHOLD: Yes, sir, but I can't stand it any longer, and I ask you to let me go away this very minute.

DI NOLLI: Oh, you're the new valet, are you? You were supposed to begin this morning, weren't you?

BERTHOLD: Yes, sir, and I can't stand it, I can't bear it.

DONNA MATILDA (*to* DI NOLLI *excitedly*): What? Then he's not so calm as you said?

BERTHOLD (*quickly*):—No, no, my lady, it isn't he; it's my companions. You say "help him out with his madness," Marquis; but they don't do anything of the kind. They're the real madmen. I come here for the first time, and instead of helping me . . .

LANDOLPH *and* HAROLD *come in from the same door, but hesitate on the threshold.*

LANDOLPH: Excuse me?

HAROLD: May I come in, my Lord?

DI NOLLI: Come in! What's the matter? What are you all doing?

FRIDA: Oh God! I'm frightened! I'm going to run away. (*Makes towards exit at left.*)

DI NOLLI (*restraining her at once*): No, no, Frida!

LANDOLPH: My Lord, this fool here . . . (*Indicates* BERTHOLD.)

BERTHOLD (*protesting*): Ah, no thanks, my friends, no thanks! I'm not stopping here! I'm off!

LANDOLPH: What do you mean—you're not stopping here?

HAROLD: He's ruined everything, my Lord, running away in here!

LANDOLPH: He's made him quite mad. We can't keep him in there any longer. He's given orders that he's to be arrested; and he wants to "judge" him at once from the throne: What is to be done?

DI NOLLI: Shut the door, man! Shut the door! Go and close that door! (LANDOLPH *goes over to close it.*)

HAROLD: Ordulph, alone, won't be able to keep him there.

LANDOLPH:—My Lord, perhaps if we could announce the visitors at once, it would turn his thoughts. Have the gentlemen thought under what pretext they will present themselves to him?

DI NOLLI:—It's all been arranged! (*To the* DOCTOR.) If you, Doctor, think it well to see him at once....

FRIDA: I'm not coming! I'm not coming! I'll keep out of this. You too, mother, for Heaven's sake, come away with me!

DOCTOR:—I say...I suppose he's not armed, is he?

DI NOLLI:—Nonsense! Of course not. (*To* FRIDA.) Frida, you know this is childish of you. You wanted to come!

FRIDA: I didn't at all. It was mother's idea.

DONNA MATILDA: And I'm quite ready to see him. What are we going to do?

BELCREDI: Must we absolutely dress up in some fashion or other?

LANDOLPH:—Absolutely essential, indispensable, sir. Alas! as you see...(*Shows his costume*), there'd be awful trouble if he saw you gentlemen in modern dress.

HAROLD: He would think it was some diabolical masquerade.

DI NOLLI: As these men seem to be in costume to you, so we appear to be in costume to him, in these modern clothes of ours.

LANDOLPH: It wouldn't matter so much if he wouldn't suppose it to be the work of his mortal enemy.

BELCREDI: Pope Gregory VII?

LANDOLPH: Precisely. He calls him "a pagan."

BELCREDI: The Pope a pagan? Not bad that!

LANDOLPH:—Yes, sir,—and a man who calls up the dead! He accuses him of all the diabolical arts. He's terribly afraid of him.

DOCTOR: Persecution mania!

HAROLD: He'd be simply furious.

DI NOLLI (*to* BELCREDI): But there's no need for you to be there, you know. It's sufficient for the Doctor to see him.

DOCTOR:—What do you mean?...I? Alone?

DI NOLLI:—But they are there. (*Indicates the three young men.*)

DOCTOR: I don't mean that...I mean if the Marchioness...

DONNA MATILDA: Of course. I mean to see him too, naturally. I want to see him again.

FRIDA: Oh, why, mother, why? Do come away with me, I implore you!

DONNA MATILDA (*imperiously*): Let me do as I wish! I came here for this purpose! (*To* LANDOLPH.) I shall be "Adelaide," the mother.

LANDOLPH: Excellent! The mother of the Empress Bertha. Good! It will be enough if her Ladyship wears the ducal crown and puts on a mantel that will hide her other clothes entirely. (*To* HAROLD.) Off you go, Harold!

HAROLD: Wait a moment! And this gentleman here?...(*Alludes to the* DOCTOR.)

DOCTOR:—Ah yes...we decided I was to be... the Bishop of Cluny, Hugh of Cluny![13]

HAROLD: The gentleman means the Abbot. Very good! Hugh of Cluny.

LANDOLPH:—He's often been here before!

DOCTOR (*amazed*):—What? Been here before?

LANDOLPH:—Don't be alarmed! I mean that it's an easily prepared disguise...

HAROLD: We've made use of it on other occasions, you see!

DOCTOR: But ...

---

[13] *Hugh of Cluny:* Henry's godfather, who interceded for him at Canossa.

LANDOLPH: Oh, no there's no risk of his remembering. He pays more attention to the dress than to the person.

DONNA MATILDA: That's fortunate for me too then.

DI NOLLI: Frida, you and I'll get along. Come on, Tito!

BELCREDI: Ah no. If she (*Indicates the* MARCHIONESS.) stops here, so do I!

DONNA MATILDA: But I don't need you at all.

BELCREDI: You may not need me, but I should like to see him again myself. Mayn't I?

LANDOLPH: Well, perhaps it would be better if there were three.

HAROLD: How is the gentleman to be dressed then?

BELCREDI: Oh, try and find some easy costume for me.

LANDOLPH (*to* HAROLD): Hum! Yes . . . he'd better be from Cluny too.

BELCREDI: What do you mean—from Cluny?

LANDOLPH: A Benedictine's habit of the Abbey of Cluny. He can be in attendance on Monsignor. (*To* HAROLD.) Off you go! (*To* BERTHOLD.) And you too get away and keep out of sight all today. No, wait a bit! (*To* BERTHOLD.) You bring here the costumes he will give you. (*To* HAROLD.) You go at once and announce the visit of the "Duchess Adelaide" and "Monsignor Hugh of Cluny." Do you understand? (HAROLD *and* BERTHOLD *go off by the first door on the right.*)

DI NOLLI: We'll retire now. (*Goes off with* FRIDA, *left.*)

DOCTOR: Shall I be a *persona grata*[14] to him, as Hugh of Cluny?

LANDOLPH: Oh, rather! Don't worry about that! Monsignor has always been received here with great respect. You too, my Lady, he will be glad to see. He never forgets that it was owing to the intercession of you that he was admitted to the Castle of Canossa and the presence of Gregory VII, who didn't want to receive him.

BELCREDI: And what do I do?

---

14 *Persona grata:* "acceptable person."

LANDOLPH: You stand a little apart, respectfully: that's all.

DONNA MATILDA (*irritated, nervous*): You would do well to go away, you know.

BELCREDI (*slowly, spitefully*): How upset you seem! . . .

DONNA MATILDA (*proudly*): I am as I am. Leave me alone!

BERTHOLD *comes in with the costumes.*

LANDOLPH (*seeing him enter*): Ah, the costumes: here they are. This mantle is for the Marchioness . . .

DONNA MATILDA: Wait a minute! I'll take off my hat. (*Does so and gives it to* BERTHOLD.)

LANDOLPH: Put it down there! (*Then to the* MARCHIONESS, *while he offers to put the ducal crown on her head.*) Allow me!

DONNA MATILDA: Dear, dear! Isn't there a mirror here?

LANDOLPH: Yes, there's one there. (*Points to the door on the left.*) If the Marchioness would rather put it on herself . . .

DONNA MATILDA: Yes, yes, that will be better. Give it to me! (*Takes up her hat and goes off with* BERTHOLD, *who carries the cloak and the crown.*)

BELCREDI: Well, I must say, I never thought I should be a Benedictine monk! By the way, this business must cost an awful lot of money.

THE DOCTOR: Like any other fantasy, naturally!

BELCREDI: Well, there's a fortune to go upon.

LANDOLPH: We have got there a whole wardrobe of costumes of the period, copied to perfection from old models. This is my special job. I get them from the best theatrical costumers. They cost lots of money. (DONNA MATILDA *re-enters, wearing mantle and crown.*)

BELCREDI (*at once, in admiration*): Oh magnificent! Oh, truly regal!

DONNA MATILDA (*looking at* BELCREDI *and bursting out into laughter*): Oh no, no! Take it off! You're impossible. You look like an ostrich dressed up as a monk.

BELCREDI: Well, how about the Doctor?

THE DOCTOR: I don't think I looked so bad, do I?

DONNA MATILDA: No; the Doctor's all right ... but you are too funny for words.

THE DOCTOR: Do you have many receptions here then?

LANDOLPH: It depends. He often gives orders that such and such a person appear before him. Then we have to find someone who will take the part. Women too ...

DONNA MATILDA (*hurt, but trying to hide the fact*): Ah, women too?

LANDOLPH: Oh, yes; many at first.

BELCREDI (*laughing*): Oh, that's great! In costume, like the Marchioness?

LANDOLPH: Oh well, you know, women of the kind that lend themselves to ...

BELCREDI: Ah, I see! (*Perfidiously to the MARCHIONESS.*) Look out, you know he's becoming dangerous for you.

The second door on the right opens, and HAROLD *appears making first of all a discreet sign that all conversation should cease.*

HAROLD: His Majesty, the Emperor!

The TWO VALETS *enter first, and go and stand on either side of the throne. Then* HENRY IV *comes in between* ORDULPH *and* HAROLD, *who keep a little in the rear respectfully.*

HENRY IV *is about 50 and very pale. The hair on the back of his head is already grey; over the temples and forehead it appears blond, owing to its having been tinted in an evident and puerile fashion. On his cheek bones he has two small, doll-like dabs of color, that stand out prominently against the rest of his tragic pallor. He is wearing a penitent's sack over his regal habit, as at Canossa. His eyes have a fixed look which is dreadful to see, and this expression is in strained contrast with the sackcloth.* ORDULPH *carries the Imperial crown;* HAROLD, *the sceptre with eagle, and the globe with the cross.*

HENRY IV (*bowing first to* DONNA MATILDA *and afterwards to the* DOCTOR): My lady ... Monsignor ... (*Then he looks at* BELCREDI *and seems about to greet him too; when, suddenly, he turns to* LANDOLPH, *who has approached him, and asks him sotto voce and with diffidence.*) Is that Peter Damiani?[15]

LANDOLPH: No, Sire. He is a monk from Cluny who is accompanying the Abbot.

HENRY IV (*looks again at* BELCREDI *with increasing mistrust, and then noticing that he appears embarrassed and keeps glancing at* DONNA MATILDA *and the* DOCTOR, *stands upright and cries out*): No, it's Peter Damiani! It's no use, father, your looking at the Duchess. (*Then turning quickly to* DONNA MATILDA *and the* DOCTOR *as though to ward off a danger.*) I swear it! I swear that my heart is changed towards your daughter. I confess that if he (*Indicates* BELCREDI.) hadn't come to forbid it in the name of Pope Alexander, I'd have repudiated her. Yes, yes, there were people ready to favour the repudiation: the Bishop of Mayence would have done it for a matter of one hundred and twenty farms. (*Looks at* LANDOLPH *a little perplexed and adds.*) But I mustn't speak ill of the bishops at this moment! (*More humbly to* BELCREDI.) I am grateful to you, believe me, I am grateful to you for the hindrance you put in my way!—God knows, my life's been all made of humiliations: my mother, Adalbert, Tribur,[16] Goslar! And now this sackcloth you see me wearing! (*Changes tone suddenly and speaks like one who goes over his part in a parenthesis of astuteness.*) It doesn't matter: clarity of ideas, perspicacity, firmness and patience under adversity that's the

---

[15] *Peter Damiani:* Cardinal-Bishop of Ostia, who led churchmen holding positions between that of Henry and Pope Gregory VII, and who interfered with Henry's attempt to divorce his first wife, Bertha.

[16] *Tribur:* At Tribur, October 1076, the Saxon nobles and clergy forced Henry to free himself of Pope Gregory VII's order of excommunication.

thing. (*Then turning to all and speaking solemnly.*) I know how to make amends for the mistakes I have made; and I can humiliate myself even before you, Peter Damiani. (*Bows profoundly to him and remains curved. Then a suspicion is born in him which he is obliged to utter in menacing tones, almost against his will.*) Was it not perhaps you who started that obscene rumor that my holy mother had illicit relations with the Bishop of Augusta?

BELCREDI (*since* HENRY IV *has his finger pointed at him*): No, no, it wasn't I . . .

HENRY IV (*straightening up*): Not true, not true? Infamy! (*Looks at him and then adds.*) I didn't think you capable of it! (*Goes to the* DOCTOR *and plucks his sleeve, while winking at him knowingly.*) Always the same, Monsignor, those bishops, always the same!

HAROLD (*softly, whispering as if to help out the doctor*): Yes, yes, the rapacious bishops!

THE DOCTOR (*to* HAROLD, *trying to keep it up*): Ah, yes, those fellows . . . ah yes . . .

HENRY IV: Nothing satisfies them! I was a little boy, Monsignor . . . One passes the time, playing even, when, without knowing it, one is a king.—I was six years old; and they tore me away from my mother, and made use of me against her without my knowing anything about it . . . always profaning, always stealing, stealing! . . . One greedier than the other . . . Hanno worse than Stephen! Stephen worse than Hanno![17]

LANDOLPH (*sotto voce, persuasively, to call his attention*): Majesty!

HENRY IV (*turning round quickly*): Ah yes . . . this isn't the moment to speak ill of the bishops. But this infamy against my mother, Monsignor, is too much. (*Looks at the* MARCHIONESS *and grows tender.*) And I can't even weep for her, Lady . . . I appeal to you who have a mother's heart! She came

here to see me from her convent a month ago . . . They had told me she was dead! (*Sustained pause full of feeling. Then smiling sadly.*) I can't weep for her; because if you are here now, and I am like this (*Shows the sackcloth he is wearing.*) it means I am twenty-six years old!

HAROLD: And that she is therefore alive, Majesty! . . .

ORDULPH: Still in her convent!

HENRY IV (*looking at them*): Ah yes! And I can postpone my grief to another time. (*Shows the* MARCHIONESS *almost with coquetry the tint he has given to his hair.*) Look! I am still fair . . . (*Then slowly as if in confidence.*) For you . . . there's no need! But little exterior details do help! A matter of time, Monsignor, do you understand me? (*Turns to the* MARCHIONESS *and notices her hair.*) Ah, but I see that you too, Duchess . . . Italian, eh? (*As much as to say "false"; but without any indignation, indeed rather with malicious admiration.*) Heaven forbid that I should show disgust or surprise! Nobody cares to recognize that obscure and fatal power which sets limits to our will. But I say, if one is born and one dies . . . Did you want to be born, Monsignor? I didn't! And in both cases, independently of our wills, so many things happen we would wish didn't happen, and to which we resign ourselves as best we can! . . .

DOCTOR (*merely to make a remark, while studying* HENRY IV *carefully*): Alas! Yes, alas!

HENRY IV: It's like this: When we are not resigned, out come our desires. A woman wants to be a man . . . an old man would be young again. Desires, ridiculous fixed ideas of course—But reflect! Monsignor, those other desires are not ridiculous: I mean, those desires where the will is kept within the limits of the possible. Not one of us can lie or pretend. We're all fixed in good faith in a certain concept of ourselves. However, Monsignor, while you keep yourself in order, holding on with both your hands to your holy habit, there slips down from your

---

[17] *Hanno . . . Stephen:* Hanno, Archbishop of Cologne, was one of Henry's regents. Stephen, probably Pope Stephen IX. Hanno was an ally of Godfrey of Lorraine; Stephen, of Godfrey's brother.

sleeves, there peels off from you like . . . like a serpent . . . something you don't notice: life, Monsignor! (*Turns to the* MARCHIONESS.) Has it never happened to you, my Lady, to find a different self in yourself? Have you always been the same? My God! One day . . . how was it, how was it you were able to commit this or that action? (*Fixes her so intently in the eyes as almost to make her blanch.*) Yes, that particular action, that very one: we understand each other! But don't be afraid: I shall reveal it to none. And you, Peter Damiani, how could you be a friend of that man? . . .

LANDOLPH: Majesty!

HENRY IV (*at once*): No, I won't name him! (*Turning to* BELCREDI.) What did you think of him? But we all of us cling tight to our conceptions of ourselves, just as he who is growing old dyes his hair. What does it matter that this dyed hair of mine isn't a reality for you, if it *is*, to some extent, for me?— you, you, my Lady, certainly don't dye your hair to deceive the others, nor even yourself; but only to cheat your own image a little before the looking-glass. I do it for a joke! You do it seriously! But I assure you that you too, Madam, are in masquerade, though it be in all seriousness; and I am not speaking of the venerable crown on your brows or the ducal mantle. I am speaking only of the memory you wish to fix in yourself of your fair complexion one day when it pleased you—or of your dark complexion, if you were dark: the fading image of your youth! For you, Peter Damiani, on the contrary, the memory of what you have been, of what you have done, seems to you a recognition of past realities that remain within you like a dream. I'm in the same case too: with so many inexplicable memories—like dreams! Ah! . . . There's nothing to marvel at in it, Peter Damiani! Tomorrow it will be the same thing with our life of today! (*Suddenly getting excited and taking hold of his sackcloth.*) This sackcloth here . . . (*Beginning to take it off with a gesture*

of almost ferocious joy while the THREE VALETS *run over to him, frightened, as if to prevent his doing so.*) Ah, my God! (*Draws back and throws off sackcloth.*) Tomorrow, at Bressanone, twenty-seven German and Lombard bishops will sign with me the act of deposition of Gregory VII! No Pope at all! Just a false monk!

ORDULPH (*with the other three*): Majesty! Majesty! In God's name! . . .

HAROLD (*inviting him to put on the sackcloth again*): Listen to what he says, Majesty!

LANDOLPH: Monsignor is here with the Duchess to intercede in your favor. (*Makes secret signs to the* DOCTOR *to say something at once.*)

DOCTOR (*foolishly*): Ah yes . . . yes . . . we are here to intercede . . .

HENRY IV (*repenting at once, almost terrified, allowing the three to put on the sackcloth again, and pulling it down over him with his own hands*): Pardon . . . yes . . . pardon, Monsignor: forgive me, my Lady . . . I swear to you I feel the whole weight of the anathema. (*Bends himself, takes his face between his hands, as though waiting for something to crush him. Then changing tone, but without moving, says softly to* LANDOLPH, HAROLD *and* ORDULPH.) But I don't know why I cannot be humble before that man there! (*Indicates* BELCREDI.)

LANDOLPH (*sotto voce*): But why, Majesty, do you insist on believing he is Peter Damiani, when he isn't, at all?

HENRY IV (*looking at him timorously*): He isn't Peter Damiani?

HAROLD: No, no, he is a poor monk, Majesty.

HENRY IV (*sadly with a touch of exasperation*): Ah! None of us can estimate what we do when we do it from instinct . . . You perhaps, Madam, can understand me better than the others, since you are a woman and a Duchess. This is a solemn and decisive moment. I could, you know, accept the assistance of the Lombard bishops, arrest the Pope, lock him up here in the castle, run to Rome and elect an anti-Pope; offer alliance to Robert Guiscard[18]—and Gregory VII would be lost! I resist the temptation; and, believe me, I am wise in doing so. I feel the atmosphere of our times and the majesty of one who knows how to be what he ought to be! a Pope! Do you feel inclined to laugh at me, seeing me like this? You would be foolish to do so; for you don't understand the political wisdom which makes this penitent's sack advisable. The parts may be changed tomorrow. What would you do then? Would you laugh to see the Pope a prisoner? No! It would come to the same thing: I dressed as a penitent, today; he, as prisoner tomorrow! But woe to him who doesn't know how to wear his mask, be he king or Pope!—Perhaps he is a bit too cruel! No! Yes, yes, maybe!—You remember, my Lady, how your daughter Bertha, for whom, I repeat, my feelings have changed (*Turns to* BELCREDI *and shouts to his face as if he were being contradicted by him.*)—Yes, changed on account of the affection and devotion she showed me in that terrible moment ... (*Then once again to the* MARCHIONESS.) ... you remember how she came with me, my Lady, followed me like a beggar and passed two nights out in the open, in the snow? You are her mother! Doesn't this touch your mother's heart? Doesn't this urge you to pity, so that you will beg His Holiness for pardon, beg him to receive us?

DONNA MATILDA (*trembling, with feeble voice*): Yes, yes, at once ...

DOCTOR: It shall be done!

HENRY IV: And one thing more! (*Draws them in to listen to him.*) It isn't enough that he should receive me! You know he can do *everything*—everything. I tell you! He can even call up the dead. (*Touches his chest.*) Behold me! Do you see me? There is no magic art unknown to him. Well, Monsig-

nor, my Lady, my torment is really this: that whether here or there (*Pointing to his portrait almost in fear.*) I can't free myself from this magic. I am a penitent now, you see; and I swear to you I shall remain so until he receives me. But you two, when the excommunication is taken off, must ask the Pope to do this thing he can so easily do: to take me away from that; (*Indicating the portrait again.*) and let me live wholly and freely my miserable life. A man can't always be twenty-six, my Lady. I ask this of you for your daughter's sake too; that I may love her as she deserves to be loved, well disposed as I am now, all tender towards her for her pity. There: it's all there! I am in your hands! (*Bows.*) My Lady! Monsignor!

He goes off, bowing grandly, through the door by which he entered, leaving everyone stupefied, and the MARCHIONESS *so profoundly touched, that no sooner has he gone than she breaks out into sobs and sits down almost fainting.*

CURTAIN

ACT II

Another room of the villa, adjoining the throne room. Its furniture is antique and severe. Principal exit at rear in the background. To the left, two windows looking on the garden. To the right, a door opening into the throne room.

Late afternoon of the same day.

DONNA MATILDA, *the* DOCTOR *and* BELCREDI *are on the stage engaged in conversation; but* DONNA MATILDA *stands to one side, evidently annoyed at what the other two are saying; although she cannot help listening, because, in her agitated state, everything interests her in spite of herself. The talk of the other two attracts her attention, because she instinctively feels the need for calm at the moment.*

---

[18] *Robert Guiscard:* a Norman prince and ally of Pope Gregory VII, who drove Henry out of Rome after Henry had forced the Pope to take refuge.

BELCREDI: It may be as you say, Doctor, but that was my impression.

DOCTOR: I won't contradict you; but, believe me, it is only . . . an impression.

BELCREDI: Pardon me, but he even said so, and quite clearly. (*Turning to the* MARCHIONESS.) Didn't he, Marchioness?

DONNA MATILDA (*turning round*): What did he say? . . . (*Then not agreeing.*) Oh yes . . . but not for the reason you think!

DOCTOR: He was alluding to the costumes we had slipped on . . . Your cloak (*Indicating the* MARCHIONESS.) our Benedictine habits . . . But all this is childish!

DONNA MATILDA (*turning quickly, indignant*): Childish? What do you mean, Doctor?

DOCTOR: From one point of view, it is—I beg you to let me say so, Marchioness! Yet, on the other hand, it is much more complicated than you can imagine.

DONNA MATILDA: To me, on the contrary, it is perfectly clear!

DOCTOR (*with a smile of pity of the competent person towards those who do not understand*): We must take into account the peculiar psychology of madmen; which, you must know, enables us to be certain that they observe things and can, for instance, easily detect people who are disguised; can in fact recognize the disguise and yet believe in it; just as children do, for whom disguise is both play and reality. That is why I used the word childish. But the thing is extremely complicated, inasmuch as he must be perfectly aware of being an image to himself and for himself—that image there, in fact! (*Alluding to the portrait in the throne room, and pointing to the left.*)

BELCREDI: That's what he said!

DOCTOR: Very well then—An image before which other images, ours, have appeared: understand? Now he, in his acute and perfectly lucid delirium, was able to detect at once a difference between his image and ours: that is, he saw that ours were make-believes. So he suspected us; because all madmen are armed with a special diffidence. But that's all there is to it! Our make-believe, built up all round his, did not seem pitiful to him. While his seemed all the more tragic to us, in that he, as if in defiance—understand?—and induced by his suspicion, wanted to show us up merely as a joke. That was also partly the case with him, in coming before us with painted cheeks and hair, and saying he had done it on purpose for a jest.

DONNA MATILDA (*impatiently*): No, it's not that, Doctor. It's not like that! It's not like that!

DOCTOR: Why isn't it, may I ask?

DONNA MATILDA (*with decision but trembling*): I am perfectly certain he recognized me!

DOCTOR: It's not possible . . . it's not possible!

BELCREDI (*at the same time*): Of course not!

DONNA MATILDA (*more than ever determined, almost convulsively*): I tell you, he recognized me! When he came close up to speak to me—looking in my eyes, right into my eyes—he recognized me!

BELCREDI: But he was talking of your daughter!

DONNA MATILDA: That's not true! He was talking of me! Of me!

BELCREDI: Yes, perhaps, when he said . . .

DONNA MATILDA (*letting herself go*): About my dyed hair! But didn't you notice that he added at once: "or the memory of your dark hair, if you were dark"? He remembered perfectly well that I was dark—then!

BELCREDI: Nonsense! nonsense!

DONNA MATILDA (*not listening to him, turning to the* DOCTOR): My hair, Doctor, is really dark—like my daughter's! That's why he spoke of her.

BELCREDI: But he doesn't even know your daughter! He's never seen her!

DONNA MATILDA: Exactly! Oh, you never understand anything! By my daughter, stupid, he meant me—as I was then!

BELCREDI: Oh, this is catching! This is catching, this madness!

DONNA MATILDA (*softly, with contempt*): Fool!

BELCREDI: Excuse me, were you ever his wife?

Your daughter is his wife—in his delirium: Bertha of Susa.

DONNA MATILDA: Exactly! Because I, no longer dark—as he remembered me—but *fair*, introduced myself as "Adelaide," the mother. My daughter doesn't exist for him: he's never seen her—you said so yourself! So how can he know whether she's fair or dark?

BELCREDI: But he said dark, speaking generally, just as anyone who wants to recall, whether fair or dark, a memory of youth in the color of the hair! And you, as usual, begin to imagine things! Doctor, you said I ought not to have come! It's she who ought not to have come!

DONNA MATILDA (*upset for a moment by* BELCREDI's *remark, recovers herself. Then with a touch of anger, because doubtful*): No, no...he spoke of me...He spoke all the time to me, with me, of me...

BELCREDI: That's not bad! He didn't leave me a moment's breathing space and you say he was talking all the time to you? Unless you think he was alluding to you too, when he was talking to Peter Damiani!

DONNA MATILDA (*defiantly, almost exceeding the limits of courteous discussion*): Who knows? Can you tell me why, from the outset, he showed a strong dislike for you, for you alone? (*From the tone of the question, the expected answer must almost explicitly be: "because he understands you are my lover."* BELCREDI *feels this so well that he remains silent and can say nothing.*)

DOCTOR: The reason may also be found in the fact that only the visit of the Duchess Adelaide and the Abbot of Cluny was announced to him. Finding a third person present, who had not been announced, at once his suspicions...

BELCREDI: Yes, exactly! His suspicion made him see an enemy in me: Peter Damiani! But she's got it into her head, that he recognized her...

DONNA MATILDA: There's no doubt about it! I could see it from his eyes, Doctor. You know, there's a way of looking that leaves no doubt whatever...Perhaps it was only for an instant, but I am sure!

DOCTOR: It is not impossible: a lucid moment...

DONNA MATILDA: Yes, perhaps...And then his speech seemed to me full of regret for his and my youth—for the horrible thing that happened to him, that has held him in that disguise from which he has never been able to free himself, and from which he longs to be free—he said so himself!

BELCREDI: Yes, so as to be able to make love to your daughter, or you, as you believe—having been touched by your pity.

DONNA MATILDA: Which is very great, I would ask you to believe.

BELCREDI: As one can see, Marchioness; so much so that a mircle-worker might expect a miracle from it!

DOCTOR: Will you let me speak? I don't work miracles, because I am a doctor and not a miracle-worker. I listened very intently to all he said; and I repeat that that certain analogical elasticity, common to all systematized delirium, is evidently with him much... what shall I say?—much relaxed! The elements, that is, of his delirium no longer hold together. It seems to me he has lost the equilibrium of his second personality and sudden recollections drag him—and this is very comforting—not from a state of incipient apathy, but rather from a morbid inclination to reflective melancholy, which shows a...a very considerable cerebral activity. Very comforting, I repeat! Now if, by this violent trick we've planned...

DONNA MATILDA (*turning to the window, in the tone of a sick person complaining*): But how is it that the motor has not returned? It's three hours and a half since...

DOCTOR: What do you say?

DONNA MATILDA: The motor, Doctor! It's more than three hours and a half...

DOCTOR (*taking out his watch and looking at it*): Yes, more than four hours, by this!

DONNA MATILDA: It could have reached here an hour ago at least! But, as usual . . .

BELCREDI: Perhaps they can't find the dress . . .

DONNA MATILDA: But I explained exactly where it was! (*Impatiently.*) And Frida . . . where is Frida?

BELCREDI (*looking out of the window*): Perhaps she is in the garden with Charles . . .

DOCTOR: He'll talk her out of her fright.

BELCREDI: She's not afraid, Doctor; don't you believe it: the thing bores her rather . . .

DONNA MATILDA: Just don't ask anything of her! I know what she's like.

DOCTOR: Let's wait patiently. Anyhow, it will soon be over, and it has to be in the evening . . . It will only be the matter of a moment! If we can succeed in rousing him, as I was saying, and in breaking at one go the threads—already slack—which still bind him to this fiction of his, giving him back what he himself asks for—you remember, he said: "one cannot always be twenty-six years old, madam!" if we can give him freedom from this torment, which even *he* feels is a torment, then if he is able to recover at one bound the sensation of the distance of time . . .

BELCREDI (*quickly*): He'll be cured! (*Then emphatically with irony.*) We'll pull him out of it all!

DOCTOR: Yes, we may hope to set him going again, like a watch which has stopped at a certain hour . . . just as if we had our watches in our hands and were waiting for that other watch to go again.—A shake—so—and let's hope it'll tell the time again after its long stop. (*At this point the* MARQUIS CHARLES DI NOLLI *enters from the principal entrance.*)

DONNA MATILDA: Oh, Charles! . . . And Frida? Where is she?

DI NOLLI: She'll be here in a moment.

DOCTOR: Has the motor arrived?

DI NOLLI: Yes.

DONNA MATILDA: Yes? Has the dress come?

DI NOLLI: It's been here some time.

DOCTOR: Good! Good!

DONNA MATILDA (*trembling*): Where is she? Where's Frida?

DI NOLLI (*shrugging his shoulders and smiling sadly, like one lending himself unwillingly to an untimely joke*): You'll see, you'll see! . . . (*Pointing towards the hall.*) Here she is! . . . (BERTHOLD *appears at the threshold of the hall, and announces with solemnity.*)

BERTHOLD: Her Highness the Countess Matilda of Canossa! (FRIDA *enters, magnificent and beautiful, arrayed in the robes of her mother as "Countess Matilda of Tuscany," so that she is a living copy of the portrait in the throne room.*)

FRIDA (*passing* BERTHOLD, *who is bowing, says to him with disdain*): Of Tuscany, of Tuscany! Canossa is just one of my castles!

BELCREDI (*in admiration*): Look! Look! She seems another person . . .

DONNA MATILDA: One would say it were I! Look!—Why, Frida, look! She's exactly my portrait, alive!

DOCTOR: Yes, yes . . . Perfect! Perfect! The portrait, to the life.

BELCREDI: Yes, there's no question about it. She *is* the portrait! Magnificent!

FRIDA: Don't make me laugh, or I shall burst! I say, mother, what a tiny waist you had? I had to squeeze so to get into this!

DONNA MATILDA (*arranging her dress a little*): Wait! . . . Keep still! . . . These pleats . . . is it really so tight?

FRIDA: I'm suffocating! I implore you, to be quick! . . .

DOCTOR: But we must wait till it's evening!

FRIDA: No, no, I can't hold out till evening!

DONNA MATILDA: Why did you put it on so soon?

FRIDA: The moment I saw it, the temptation was irresistible . . .

DONNA MATILDA: At least you could have called me, or have had someone help you! It's still all crumpled.

FRIDA: So I saw, mother; but they are old creases; they won't come out.

DOCTOR: It doesn't matter, Marchioness! The illusion is perfect. (*Then coming nearer and asking her to come in front of her daughter, without hiding her.*) If you please, stay there, there ... at a certain distance ... now a little more forward ...

BELCREDI: For the feeling of the distance of time ...

DONNA MATILDA (*slightly turning to him*): Twenty years after! A disaster! A tragedy!

BELCREDI: Now don't let's exaggerate!

DOCTOR (*embarrassed, trying to save the situation*): No, no! I meant the dress ... so as to see ... You know ...

BELCREDI (*laughing*): Oh, as for the dress, Doctor, it isn't a matter of twenty years! It's eight hundred! An abyss! Do you really want to shove him across it (*Pointing first to* FRIDA *and then to* MARCHIONESS.) from there to here? But you'll have to pick him up in pieces with a basket! Just think now: for us it is a matter of twenty years, a couple of dresses, and a masquerade. But, if, as you say, Doctor, time has stopped for and around him: if he lives there (*Pointing to* FRIDA.) with her, eight hundred years ago ... I repeat: the giddiness of the jump will be such, that finding himself suddenly among us ... (*The* DOCTOR *shakes his head in dissent.*) You don't think so?

DOCTOR: No, because life, my dear Baron, can take up its rhythms. This—our life—will at once become real also to him; and will pull him up directly, wresting from him suddenly the illusion, and showing him that the eight hundred years, as you say, are only twenty! It will be like one of those tricks, such as the leap into space, for instance, of the Masonic rite, which appears to be heaven knows how far, and is only a step down the stairs.

BELCREDI: Ah! An idea! Yes! Look at Frida and the Marchioness, Doctor! Which is more advanced in time? We old people, Doctor! The young ones think they are more ahead; but it isn't true: we are more ahead, because time belongs to us more than to them.

DOCTOR: If the past didn't alienate us ...

BELCREDI: It doesn't matter at all! How does it alienate us? They (*Pointing to* FRIDA *and* DI NOLLI.) have still to do what we have accomplished, Doctor: to grow old, doing the same foolish things, more or less, as we did ... This is the illusion: that one comes forward through a door to life. It isn't so! As soon as one is born, one starts dying; therefore, he who started first is the most advanced of all. The youngest of us is father Adam! Look there: (*Pointing to* FRIDA.) eight hundred years younger than all of us—the Countess Matilda of Tuscany. (*He makes her a deep bow.*)

DI NOLLI: I say, Tito, don't start joking.

BELCREDI: Oh, you think I am joking? ...

DI NOLLI: Of course, of course ... all the time.

BELCREDI: Impossible! I've even dressed up as a Benedictine ...

DI NOLLI: Yes, but for a serious purpose.

BELCREDI: Well, exactly. If it has been serious for the others ... for Frida, now, for instance. (*Then turning to the* DOCTOR.) I swear, Doctor, I don't yet understand what you want to do.

DOCTOR (*annoyed*): You'll see! Let me do as I wish ... At present you see the Marchioness still dressed as ...

BELCREDI: Oh, she also ... has to masquerade?

DOCTOR: Of course! of course! In another dress that's in there ready to be used when it comes into his head he sees the Countess Matilda of Canossa before him.

FRIDA (*while talking quietly to* DI NOLLI *notices the* DOCTOR's *mistake*): Of Tuscany, of Tuscany!

DOCTOR: It's all the same!

BELCREDI: Oh, I see! He'll be faced by two of them ...

DOCTOR: Two, precisely! And then ...

FRIDA (*calling him aside*): Come here, Doctor! Listen!

DOCTOR: Here I am! (*Goes near the two young people and pretends to give some explanations to them.*)

BELCREDI (*softly to* DONNA MATILDA): I say, this is getting rather strong, you know!

DONNA MATILDA (*looking him firmly in the*

face): What?

BELCREDI: Does it really interest you as much as all that—to make you willing to take part in...? For a woman this is simply enormous!...

DONNA MATILDA: Yes, for an ordinary woman.

BELCREDI: Oh, no, my dear, for all women,—in a question like this! It's an abnegation.

DONNA MATILDA: I owe it to him.

BELCREDI: Don't lie! You know well enough it's not hurting you!

DONNA MATILDA: Well, then, where does the abnegation come in?

BELCREDI: Just enough to prevent you losing caste in other people's eyes—and just enough to offend me!...

DONNA MATILDA: But who is worrying about you now?

DI NOLLI (*coming forward*): It's all right. It's all right. That's what we'll do! (*Turning toward* BERTHOLD.) Here you, go and call one of those fellows!

BERTHOLD: At once! (*Exit.*)

DONNA MATILDA: But first of all we've got to pretend that we are going away.

DI NOLLI: Exactly! I'll see to that... (*To* BELCREDI.) You don't mind staying here?

BELCREDI (*ironically*): Oh, no, I don't mind, I don't mind!...

DI NOLLI: We must look out not to make him suspicious again, you know.

BELCREDI: Oh, Lord! *He* doesn't amount to anything!

DOCTOR: He must believe absolutely that we've gone away. (LANDOLPH *followed by* BERTHOLD *enters from the right.*)

LANDOLPH: May I come in?

DI NOLLI: Come in! Come in! I say—your name's Lolo, isn't it?

LANDOLPH: Lolo, or Landolph, just as you like!

DI NOLLI: Well, look here: the Doctor and the Marchioness are leaving, at once.

LANDOLPH: Very well. All we've got to say is that they have been able to obtain the permission for the reception from His Holiness. He's in there in his own apartments repenting of all he said—and in an awful state to have the pardon! Would you mind coming a minute?... If you would, just for a minute... put on the dress again...

DOCTOR: Why, of course, with pleasure...

LANDOLPH: Might I be allowed to make a suggestion? Why not add that the Marchioness of Tuscany has interceded with the Pope that he should be received?

DONNA MATILDA: You see, he has recognized me!

LANDOLPH: Forgive me...I don't know my history very well. I am sure you gentlemen know it much better! But I thought it was believed that Henry IV had a secret passion for the Marchioness of Tuscany.

DONNA MATILDA (*at once*): Nothing of the kind! Nothing of the kind!

LANDOLPH: That's what I thought! But he says he's loved her...he's always saying it... And now he fears that her indignation for this secret love of his will work him harm with the Pope.

BELCREDI: We must let him understand that this aversion no longer exists.

LANDOLPH: Exactly! Of course!

DONNA MATILDA (*to* BELCREDI): History says—I don't know whether you know it or not—that the Pope gave way to the supplications of the Marchioness Matilda and the Abbot of Cluny. And I may say, my dear Belcredi, that I intended to take advantage of this fact—at the time of the pageant—to show him my feelings were not so hostile to him as he supposed.

BELCREDI: You are most faithful to history, Marchioness...

LANDOLPH: Well then, the Marchioness could spare herself a double disguise and present herself with Monsignor (*Indicating the* DOCTOR.) as the Marchioness of Tuscany.

DOCTOR (*quickly, energetically*): No, no! That won't do at all. It would ruin everything. The impression from the confrontation must be a sudden one, give a shock! No, no, Marchioness, you will appear again as the Duchess Adelaide, the mother of the Empress. And then we'll go away. This is most necessary: that he should know we've gone away. Come on! Don't let's waste any more time! There's a lot to prepare.

Exeunt the DOCTOR, DONNA MATILDA, *and* LANDOLPH, *right.*

FRIDA: I am beginning to feel afraid again.

DI NOLLI: Again, Frida?

FRIDA: It would have been better if I had seen him before.

DI NOLLI: There's nothing to be frightened of, really.

FRIDA: He isn't furious, is he?

DI NOLLI: Of course not! he's quite calm.

BELCREDI (*with ironic sentimental affectation*): Melancholy! Didn't you hear that he loves you?

FRIDA: Thanks! That's just why I am afraid.

BELCREDI: He won't do you any harm.

DI NOLLI: It'll only last a minute . . .

FRIDA: Yes, but there in the dark with him . . .

DI NOLLI: Only for a moment; and I will be near you, and all the others behind the door ready to run in. As soon as you see your mother, your part will be finished . . .

BELCREDI: I'm afraid of a different thing: that we're wasting our time . . .

DI NOLLI: Don't begin again! The remedy seems a sound one to me.

FRIDA: I think so too! I feel it! I'm all trembling!

BELCREDI: But, mad people, my dear friends—though they don't know it, alas—have this felicity which we don't take into account . . .

DI NOLLI (*interrupting, annoyed*): What felicity? Nonsense!

BELCREDI (*forcefully*): They don't reason!

DI NOLLI: What's reasoning got to do with it, anyway?

BELCREDI: Don't you call it reasoning that he will have to do—according to us—when he sees her (*Indicates* FRIDA.) and her mother? We've reasoned it all out, surely!

DI NOLLI: Nothing of the kind: no reasoning at all! We put before him a double image of his own fantasy, or fiction, as the Doctor says.

BELCREDI (*suddenly*): I say, I've never understood why they take degrees in medicine.

DI NOLLI (*amazed*): Who?

BELCREDI: The alienists![19]

DI NOLLI: What ought they to take degrees in, then?

FRIDA: If they are alienists, in what else should they take degrees?

BELCREDI: In law, of course! All a matter of talk! The more they talk, the more highly they are considered. "Analogous elasticity," "the sensation of distance in time!" And the first thing they tell you is that they don't work miracles—when a miracle's just what is wanted! But they know that the more they say they are not miracle-workers, the more folk believe in their seriousness!

BERTHOLD (*who has been looking through the keyhole of the door on right*): There they are! There they are! They're coming in here.

DI NOLLI: Are they?

BERTHOLD: He wants to come with them . . . Yes! . . . He's coming too!

DI NOLLI: Let's get away, then! Let's get away, at once! (*To* BERTHOLD.) You stop here!

BERTHOLD: Must I?

Without answering him, DI NOLLI, FRIDA, *and* BELCREDI *go out by the main exit, leaving* BERTHOLD *surprised. The door on the right opens, and* LANDOLPH *enters first, bowing. Then* DONNA MATILDA *comes in, with mantle and ducal crown as in the first act; also the* DOCTOR *as the* ABBOT OF CLUNY. HENRY IV *is among them in royal dress.* ORDULPH *and* HAROLD *enter last of all.*

HENRY IV (*following up what he has been saying in the other room*): And now I will ask you a question: how can I be astute, if you think me obstinate?

DOCTOR: No, no, not obstinate!

HENRY IV (*smiling, pleased*): Then you think me really astute?

DOCTOR: No, no, neither obstinate, nor astute.

---

[19] *Alienists:* early name for psychiatrists.

HENRY IV (*with benevolent irony*): Monsignor, if obstinacy is not a vice which can go with astuteness, I hoped that in denying me the former, you would at least allow me a little of the latter. I can assure you I have great need of it. But if you want to keep it all for yourself . . .

DOCTOR: I? I? Do I seem astute to you?

HENRY IV: No. Monsignor! What do you say? Not in the least! Perhaps in this case, I may seem a little obstinate to you. (*Cutting short to speak to* DONNA MATILDA.) With your permission: a word in confidence to the Duchess. (*Leads her aside and asks her very earnestly.*) Is your daughter really dear to you?

DONNA MATILDA (*dismayed*): Why, yes, certainly . . .

HENRY IV: Do you wish me to compensate her with all my love, with all my devotion, for the grave wrongs I have done her—though you must not believe all the stories my enemies tell about my dissoluteness!

DONNA MATILDA: No, no, I don't believe them. I never have believed such stories.

HENRY IV: Well, then are you willing?

DONNA MATILDA (*confused*): What?

HENRY IV: That I return to love your daughter again? (*Looks at her and adds, in a mysterious tone of warning.*) You mustn't be a friend of the Marchioness of Tuscany!

DONNA MATILDA: I tell you again that she has begged and tried not less than ourselves to obtain your pardon . . .

HENRY IV (*softly, but excitedly*): Don't tell me that! Don't say that to me! Don't you see the effect it has on me, my Lady?

DONNA MATILDA (*looks at him; then very softly as if in confidence*): You love her still?

HENRY IV (*puzzled*): Still? Still, you say? You know, then? But nobody knows! Nobody must know!

DONNA MATILDA: But perhaps she knows, if she has begged so hard for you!

HENRY IV (*looks at her and says*): And you love your daughter? (*Brief pause. He turns to the* DOCTOR *with laughing accents.*) Ah, Monsignor, it's strange how little I think of my wife! It may be a sin, but I swear to you that I hardly feel her at all in my heart. What is stranger is that her own mother scarcely feels her in her heart. Confess, my Lady, that she amounts to very little for you. (*Turning to the* DOCTOR.) She talks to me of that other woman, insistently, insistently, I don't know why! . . .

LANDOLPH (*humbly*): Maybe, Majesty, it is to disabuse you of some ideas you have had about the Marchioness of Tuscany. (*Then, dismayed at having allowed himself this observation, adds.*) I mean just now, of course . . .

HENRY IV: You too maintain that she has been friendly to me?

LANDOLPH: Yes, at the moment, Majesty.

DONNA MATILDA: Exactly! Exactly! . . .

HENRY IV: I understand. That is to say, you don't believe I love her. I see! I see! Nobody's ever believed it, nobody's ever thought it. Better so, then! But enough, enough! (*Turns to the* DOCTOR *with changed expression.*) Monsignor, you see? The reasons the Pope has had for revoking the excommunication have got nothing at all to do with the reasons for which he excommunicated me originally. Tell Pope Gregory we shall meet again at Brixen. And you, Madame, should you chance to meet your daughter in the courtyard of the castle of your friend the Marchioness, ask her to visit me. We shall see if I succeed in keeping her close beside me as wife and Empress. Many women have presented themselves here already assuring me that they were she. And I thought to have her—yes, I tried sometimes—there's no shame in it, with one's wife!—But when they said they were Bertha, and they were from Susa, all of them—I can't think why—started laughing! (*Confidentially.*) Understand?—in bed— I undressed—so did she—yes, by God, undressed—a man and a woman—it's natural after all! Like that, we don't bother much about who we are. And one's dress is like a phantom that hovers always near one. Oh, Monsignor, phantoms in general are nothing more than trifling disorders of the spirit: images we cannot contain within the bounds of sleep. They reveal themselves even when we are awake, and they frighten us. I . . . ah . . . I am always afraid when, at night time, I see disordered images before me. Sometimes I am even afraid of my own blood pulsing loudly in my arteries in the silence of night, like the sound of a distant step in a lonely corridor! . . . But, forgive me! I have kept you standing too long already. I thank you, my Lady, I thank you, Monsignor. (DONNA MATILDA *and the* DOCTOR *go off bowing. As soon as they have gone,* HENRY IV *suddenly changes his tone.*) Buffoons, buffoons! One can play any tune on them! And that other fellow . . . Pietro Damiani! . . . Caught him out perfectly! He's afraid to appear before me again. (*Moves up and down excitedly while saying this; then sees* BERTHOLD, *and points him out to the other three valets.*) Oh, look at this imbecile watching me with his mouth wide open! (*Shakes him.*) Don't you understand? Don't you see, idiot, how I treat them, how I play the fool with them, make them appear before me just as I wish? Miserable, frightened clowns that they are! And you (*Addressing the* VALETS.) are amazed that I tear off their ridiculous masks now, just as if it wasn't I who had made them mask themselves to satisfy this taste of mine for playing the madman!

LANDOLPH — HAROLD — ORDULPH (*bewildered, looking at one another*): What? What does he say? What?

HENRY IV (*answers them imperiously*): Enough! enough! Let's stop it. I'm tired of it. (*Then as if the thought left him no peace.*) By God! The impudence! To come here along with her lover! . . . And pretending to do it out of pity! So as not to infuriate a poor devil already out of the world, out of time, out of life! If it hadn't been supposed to be done out of pity, one can well imagine

that fellow wouldn't have allowed it. Those people expect others to behave as they wish all the time. And, of course, there's nothing arrogant in that! Oh, no! Oh, no! It's merely their way of thinking, of feeling, of seeing. Everybody has his own way of thinking; you fellows, too. Yours is that of a flock of sheep —miserable, feeble, uncertain . . . But those others take advantage of this and make you accept their way of thinking; or, at least, they suppose they do; because, after all, what do they succeed in imposing on you? Words, words which anyone can interpret in his own manner! That's the way public opinion is formed! And it's a bad look out for a man who finds himself labelled one day with one of these words which everyone repeats; for example "madman," or "imbecile." Don't you think it is rather hard for a man to keep quiet, when he knows that there is a fellow going about trying to persuade everybody that he is as he sees him, trying to fix him in other people's opinion as a "madman"—according to him? Now I am talking seriously! Before I hurt my head, falling from my horse . . . (*Stops suddenly, noticing the dismay of the four young men.*) What's the matter with you? (*Imitates their amazed looks.*) What? Am I, or am I not, mad? Oh, yes! I'm mad all right! (*He becomes terrible.*) Well, then, by God, down on your knees, down on your knees! (*Makes them go down on their knees one by one.*) I order you to go down on your knees before me! And touch the ground three times with your foreheads! Down, down! That's the way you've got to be before madmen! (*Then annoyed with their facile humiliation.*) Get up, sheep! You obeyed me, didn't you? You might have put the strait jacket on me! . . . Crush a man with the weight of a word—it's nothing—a fly! all our life is crushed by the weight of words: the weight of the dead. Look at me here: can you really suppose that Henry IV is still alive? All the same, I speak, and order you live men about! Do you think it's a joke that the dead continue to live?—Yes, *here* it's a joke! But get out into the live world!—Ah, you say: what a beautiful sunrise—for us! All time is before us!—Dawn! We will do what we like with this day— Ah, yes! To Hell with tradition, the old conventions! Well, go on! You will do nothing but repeat the old, old words, while you imagine you are living! (*Goes up to* BERTHOLD *who has now become quite stupid.*) You don't understand a word of this do you? What's your name?

BERTHOLD: I? . . . What? . . . Berthold . . .

HENRY IV: Poor Berthold! What's your name here?

BERTHOLD: I . . . I . . . my name is Fino.

HENRY IV (*feeling the warning and critical glances of the others, turns to them to reduce them to silence*): Fino?

BERTHOLD: Fino Pagliuca, sire.

HENRY IV (*turning to* LANDOLPH): I've heard you call each other by your nick-names often enough! Your name is Lolo isn't it?

LANDOLPH: Yes, sire . . . (*Then with a sense of immense joy.*) Oh Lord! Oh Lord! Then he is not mad . . .

HENRY IV (*brusquely*): What?

LANDOLPH (*hesitating*): No . . . I said . . .

HENRY IV: Not mad, any more. No. Don't you see? We're having a joke on those that think I am mad! (*To* HAROLD.) I say, boy your name's Franco . . . (*To* ORDULPH.) And yours . . .

ORDULPH: Momo.

HENRY IV: Momo, Momo . . . A nice name that!

LANDOLPH: So he isn't . . .

HENRY IV: What are you talking about? Of course not! Let's have a jolly, good laugh! . . . (*Laughs.*) Ah! . . . Ah! . . . Ah! . . .

LANDOLPH—HAROLD—ORDULPH (*looking at each other half happy and half dismayed*): Then he's cured! . . . he's all right! . . .

HENRY IV: Silence! Silence! . . . (*To* BERTHOLD.) Why don't you laugh? Are you offended? I didn't mean it especially for you. It's convenient for everybody to insist that certain people are mad, so they can be shut up. Do you know why? Because it's impossible to hear them speak! What shall I say of these people who've just gone away? That one is a whore, another a libertine, another a swindler . . . don't you think so? You can't believe a word he says . . . don't you think so?—By the way, they all listen to me terrified. And why are they terrified, if what I say isn't true? Of course, you can't believe what madmen say—yet, at the same time, they stand there with their eyes wide open with terror!—Why? Tell me, tell me, why?— You see I'm quite calm now!

BERTHOLD: But perhaps, they think that . . .

HENRY IV: No, no, my dear fellow! Look me well in the eyes! . . . I don't say that it's true—nothing is true, Berthold! But . . . look me in the eyes!

BERTHOLD: Well . . .

HENRY IV: You see? You see? . . . You have terror in your own eyes now because I seem mad to you! There's the proof of it! (*Laughs.*)

LANDOLPH (*coming forward in the name of the others, exasperated*): What proof?

HENRY IV: Your being so dismayed because now I seem again mad to you. You have thought me mad up to now, haven't you? You feel that this dismay of yours can become terror too—something to dash away the ground from under your feet and deprive you of the air you breathe! Do you know what it means to find yourselves face to face with a madman—with one who shakes the foundations of all you have built up in yourselves, your logic, the logic of all your constructions? Madmen, lucky folk! construct without logic, or rather with a logic that flies like a feather. Voluble! Voluble! Today like this and tomorrow—who knows? You say: "This cannot be"; but for them everything can be. You say: "This isn't true!" And why? Because it doesn't seem true to you, or you, or you . . . (*Indicates the three of them in succession.*) . . . and to a hundred thousand others! One must see what seems true to these hundred thousand others who are not supposed to be mad! What a magnificent spectacle they afford, when they reason! What flowers of logic they scatter! I know that when I was a child, I thought the moon in the pond was real. How many things I thought real! I believed everything I was told—and I was happy! Because it's a terrible thing if you don't hold on to that which seems true to you today—to that which will seem true to you tomorrow, even if it is the opposite of that which seemed true to you yesterday. I would never wish you to think, as I have done, on this horrible thing which really drives one mad: that if you were beside another and looking into his eyes—as I one day looked into somebody's eyes — you might as well be a beggar before a door never to be opened to you; for he who does enter there will never be you, but someone unknown to you with his own different and impenetrable world . . . (*Long pause. Darkness gathers in the room, increasing the sense of strangeness and consternation in which the four young men are involved.* HENRY IV *remains aloof, pondering on the misery which is not only his, but everybody's. Then he pulls himself up, and says in an ordinary tone.*) It's getting dark here . . .

ORDULPH: Shall I go for a lamp?

HENRY IV (*ironically*): The lamp, yes the lamp! . . . Do you suppose I don't know that as soon as I turn my back with my oil lamp to go to bed, you turn on the electric light for yourselves, here, and even there, in the throne room? I pretend not to see it!

ORDULPH: Well, then, shall I turn it on now?

HENRY IV: No, it would blind me! I want my lamp!

ORDULPH: It's ready here behind the door. (*Goes to the main exit, opens the door, goes out for a moment, and returns with an ancient lamp which is held by a ring at the top.*)

HENRY IV: Ah, a little light! Sit there around the table, no, not like that; in an elegant,

easy, manner! . . . (*To* HAROLD.) Yes, you, like that! (*Poses him.*) (*Then to* BERTHOLD.) You, so! . . . and I, here! (*Sits opposite them.*) We could do with a little decorative moonlight. It's very useful for us, the moonlight. I feel a real necessity for it, and pass a lot of time looking up at the moon from my window. Who would think, to look at her that she knows that eight hundred years have passed, and that I, seated at the window, cannot really be Henry IV gazing at the moon like any poor devil? But, look, look! See what a magnificent night scene we have here: the emperor surrounded by his faithful counsellors! . . . How do you like it?

LANDOLPH (*softly to* HAROLD, *so as not to break the enchantment*): And to think it wasn't true!

HENRY IV: True? What wasn't true?

LANDOLPH (*timidly as if to excuse himself*): No . . . I mean . . . I was saying this morning to him (*Indicates* BERTHOLD.)—he has just entered on service here—I was saying: what a pity that dressed like this and with so many beautiful costumes in the wardrobe . . . and with a room like that . . . (*Indicates the throne room.*)

HENRY IV: Well? what's the pity?

LANDOLPH: Well . . . that we didn't know . . .

HENRY IV: That it was all done in jest, this comedy?

LANDOLPH: Because we thought that . . .

HAROLD (*coming to his assistance*): Yes . . . that it was done seriously!

HENRY IV: What do you say? Doesn't it seem serious to you?

LANDOLPH: But if you say that . . .

HENRY IV: I say that—you are fools! You ought to have known how to create a fantasy for yourselves, not to act it for me, or anyone coming to see me; but naturally, simply, day by day, before nobody, feeling yourselves alive in the history of the eleventh century, here at the court of your emperor, Henry IV! You, Ordulph (*Taking him by the arm.*), alive in the castle of Goslar, waking up in the morning, getting out of bed, and entering straightway into the dream, clothing yourself in the dream that would be no more a dream, because you would have lived it, felt it all alive in you. You would have drunk it in with the air you breathed; yet knowing all the time that it was a dream, so you could better enjoy the privilege afforded you of having to do nothing else but live this dream, this far off and yet actual dream! And to think that at a distance of eight centuries from this remote age of ours, so colored and so sepulchral, the men of the twentieth century are torturing themselves in ceaseless anxiety to know how their fates and fortunes will work out! Whereas you are already in history with me . . .

LANDOLPH: Yes, yes, very good!

HENRY IV: . . . Everything determined, everything settled!

ORDULPH: Yes, yes!

HENRY IV: And sad as is my lot, hideous as some of the events are, bitter the struggles and troublous the time—still all history! All history that cannot change, understand? All fixed for ever! And you could have admired at your ease how every effect followed obediently its cause with perfect logic, how every event took place precisely and coherently in each minute particular! The pleasure, the pleasure of history, in fact, which is so great, was yours.

LANDOLPH: Beautiful, beautiful!

HENRY IV: Beautiful, but it's finished! Now that you know, I could not do it any more! (*Takes his lamp to go to bed.*) Neither could you, if up to now you haven't understood the reason of it! I am sick of it now. (*Almost to himself with violent contained rage.*) By God, I'll make her sorry she came here! Dressed herself up as a mother-in-law for me . . . ! And he as an abbot . . . ! And they bring a doctor with them to study me . . . ! Who knows if they don't hope to cure me? . . . Clowns . . . ! I'd like to smack one of them at least in the face: yes, that one— a famous swordsman, they say! . . . He'll kill

me . . . Well, we'll see, we'll see! . . . (*A knock at the door.*) Who is it?

THE VOICE OF JOHN: Deo Gratias!

HAROLD (*very pleased at the chance for another joke*): Oh, it's John, it's old John, who comes every night to play the monk.

ORDULPH (*rubbing his hands*): Yes, yes! Let's make him do it!

HENRY IV (*at once, severely*): Fool, why? Just to play a joke on a poor old man who does it for love of me?

LANDOLPH (*to* ORDULPH): It has to be as if it were true.

HENRY IV: Exactly, as if true! Because, only so, truth is not a jest. (*Opens the door and admits* JOHN *dressed as a humble friar with a roll of parchment under his arm.*) Come in, come in, father! (*Then assuming a tone of tragic gravity and deep resentment.*) All the documents of my life and reign favorable to me were destroyed deliberately by my enemies. One only has escaped destruction, this, my life, written by a humble monk who is devoted to me. And you would laugh at him! (*Turns affectionately to* JOHN, *and invites him to sit down at the table.*) Sit down, father, sit down! Have the lamp near you! (*Puts the lamp near him.*) Write! Write!

JOHN (*opens the parchment and prepares to write from dictation*): I am ready, your Majesty!

HENRY IV (*dictating*): "The decree of peace proclaimed at Mayence helped the poor and the good, while it damaged the powerful and the bad. (*Curtain begins to fall.*) It brought wealth to the former, hunger and misery to the latter . . ."

CURTAIN

ACT III

The throne room so dark that the wall at the bottom is hardly seen. The canvases of the two portraits have been taken away; and, within their frames, FRIDA, *dressed as the*

"*Marchioness of Tuscany*" *and* CHARLES DI NOLLI, *as "Henry IV," have taken the exact positions of the portraits.*

For a moment, after the raising of curtain, the stage is empty. Then the door on the left opens; and HENRY IV, *holding the lamp by the ring on top of it, enters. He looks back to speak to the four young men, who, with* JOHN, *are presumedly in the adjoining hall, as at the end of the second act.*

HENRY IV: No, stay where you are, stay where you are. I shall manage all right by myself. Good night! (*Closes the door and walks, very sad and tired, across the hall towards the second door on the right, which leads into his apartments.*)

FRIDA (*as soon as she sees that he has just passed the throne, whispers from the niche like one who is on the point of fainting away with fright*): Henry . . .

HENRY IV (*stopping at the voice, as if someone had stabbed him traitorously in the back, turns a terror-stricken face towards the wall at the bottom of the room; raising an arm instinctively, as if to defend himself and ward off a blow*): Who is calling me? (*It is not a question, but an exclamation vibrating with terror, which does not expect a reply from the darkness and the terrible silence of the hall, which suddenly fills him with the suspicion that he is really mad.*)

FRIDA (*at his shudder of terror, is herself not less frightened at the part she is playing, and repeats a little more loudly*): Henry! . . . (*But, although she wishes to act the part as they have given it to her, she stretches her head a little out of frame towards the other frame.*)

HENRY IV (*gives a dreadful cry; lets the lamp fall from his hands to cover his head with his arms, and makes a movement as if to run away*).

FRIDA (*jumping from the frame on to the stand and shouting like a mad woman*): Henry! . . . Henry! . . . I'm afraid! . . . I'm terrified! . . .

And while DI NOLLI *jumps in turn on to the stand and thence to the floor and runs to* FRIDA *who, on the verge of fainting, continues to cry out, the* DOCTOR, DONNA MATILDA, *also dressed as "Matilda of Tuscany,"* TITO BELCREDI, LANDOLPH, BERTHOLD *and* JOHN *enter the hall from the doors on the right and on the left. One of them turns on the light: a strange light coming from lamps hidden in the ceiling so that only the upper part of the stage is well lighted. The others without taking notice of* HENRY IV, *who looks on astonished by the unexpected inrush, after the moment of terror which still causes him to tremble, run anxiously to support and comfort the still shaking* FRIDA, *who is moaning in the arms of her fiancé. All are speaking at the same time.*

DI NOLLI: No, no, Frida . . . Here I am . . . I am beside you!

DOCTOR (*coming with the others*): Enough! Enough! There's nothing more to be done! . . .

DONNA MATILDA: He is cured, Frida. Look! He is cured! Don't you see?

DI NOLLI (*astonished*): Cured?

BELCREDI: It was only for fun! Be calm!

FRIDA: No! I am afraid! I am afraid!

DONNA MATILDA: Afraid of what? Look at him! He was never mad at all! . . .

DI NOLLI: That isn't true! What are you saying? Cured?

DOCTOR: It appears so. I should say so . . .

BELCREDI: Yes, yes! They have told us so. (*Pointing to the four young men.*)

DONNA MATILDA: Yes, for a long time! He has confided in them, told them the truth!

DI NOLLI (*now more indignant than astonished*): But what does it mean? If, up to a short time ago . . . ?

BELCREDI: Hum! He was acting, to take you in and also us, who in good faith . . .

DI NOLLI: Is it possible? To deceive his sister, also, right up to the time of her death?

HENRY IV (*remains apart, peering at one and now at the other under the accusation and the mockery of what all believe to be a cruel* joke of his, which is now revealed. He has shown by the flashing of his eyes that he is meditating a revenge, which his violent contempt prevents him from defining clearly, as yet. Stung to the quick and with a clear idea of accepting the fiction they have insidiously worked up as true, he bursts forth at this point): Go on, I say! Go on!

DI NOLLI (astonished at the cry): Go on! What do you mean?

HENRY IV: It isn't *your* sister only that is dead!

DI NOLLI: My sister? Yours, I say, whom you compelled up to the last moment, to present herself here as your mother Agnes!

HENRY IV: And was she not *your* mother?

DI NOLLI: My mother? Certainly my mother!

HENRY IV: But your mother is dead for me, *old and far away!* You have just got down now from there. (*Pointing to the frame from which he jumped down.*) And how do you know whether I have not wept her long in secret, dressed even as I am?

DONNA MATILDA (*dismayed, looking at the others*): What does he say? (*Much impressed, observing him.*) Quietly! quietly, for Heaven's sake!

HENRY IV: What do I say? I ask all of you if Agnes was not the mother of Henry IV? (*Turns to* FRIDA *as if she were really the "Marchioness of Tuscany."*) You, Marchioness, it seems to me, ought to know.

FRIDA (*still frightened, draws closer to* DI NOLLI): No, no, I don't know. Not I!

DOCTOR: It's the madness returning.... Quiet now, everybody!

BELCREDI (*indignant*): Madness indeed, Doctor! He's acting again! ...

HENRY IV (*suddenly*): I? You have emptied those two frames over there, and he stands before my eyes as Henry IV ...

BELCREDI: We've had enough of this joke now.

HENRY IV: Who said joke?

DOCTOR (*loudly to* BELCREDI): Don't excite him, for the love of God!

BELCREDI (*without lending an ear to him, but speaking louder*): But they have said so

(*Pointing again to the four young men.*), they, they!

HENRY IV (*turning around and looking at them*): You? Did you say it was all a joke?

LANDOLPH (*timid and embarrassed*): No ... really we said that you were cured.

BELCREDI: Look here! Enough of this! (*To* DONNA MATILDA.) Doesn't it seem to you that the sight of him (*Pointing to* DI NOLLI.), Marchioness, and that of your daughter dressed so, is becoming an intolerable puerility?

DONNA MATILDA: Oh, be quiet! What does the dress matter, if he is cured?

HENRY IV: Cured, yes! I am cured! (*To* BELCREDI.) ah, but not to let it end this way all at once, as you suppose! (*Attacks him.*) Do you know that for twenty years nobody has ever dared to appear before me here like you and that gentleman? (*Pointing to the* DOCTOR.)

BELCREDI: Of course I know it. As a matter of fact, I too appeared before you this morning dressed ...

HENRY IV: As a monk, yes!

BELCREDI: And you took me for Peter Damiani! And I didn't even laugh, believing, in fact, that ...

HENRY IV: That I was mad! Does it make you laugh seeing her like that, now that I am cured? And yet you might have remembered that in my eyes her appearance now ... (*Interrupts himself with a gesture of contempt.*) Ah! (*Suddenly turns to the* DOCTOR.) You are a doctor, aren't you?

DOCTOR: Yes.

HENRY IV: And you also took part in dressing her up as the Marchioness of Tuscany? To prepare a counter-joke for me here, eh?

DONNA MATILDA (*impetuously*): No, no! What do you say? It was done for you! I did it for your sake.

DOCTOR (*quickly*): To attempt, to try, not knowing ...

HENRY IV (*cutting him short*): I understand. I say counter-joke, in his case (*Indicates*

BELCREDI.) because he believes that I have been carrying on a jest . . .

BELCREDI: But excuse me, what do you mean? You say yourself you are cursed.

HENRY IV: Let me speak! (*To the* DOCTOR.) Do you know, Doctor, that for a moment you ran the risk of making me mad again? By God, to make the portraits speak; to make them jump alive out of their frames . . .

DOCTOR: But you saw that all of us ran in at once, as soon as they told us . . .

HENRY IV: Certainly! (*Contemplates* FRIDA *and* DI NOLLI, *and then looks at the* MARCHIONESS, *and finally at his own costume.*) The combination is very beautiful . . . Two couples . . . Very good, very good, Doctor! For a madman, not bad! . . . (*With a slight wave of his hand to* BELCREDI.) It seems to him now to be a carnival out of season, eh? (*Turns to look at him.*) We'll get rid now of this masquerade costume of mine, so that I may come away with you. What do you say?

BELCREDI: With me? With us?

HENRY IV: Where shall we go? To the Club? In dress coats and with white ties? Or shall both of us go to the Marchioness' house?

BELCREDI: Wherever you like! Do you want to remain here still, to continue—alone—what was nothing but the unfortunate joke of a day of carnival? It is really incredible, incredible how you have been able to do all this, freed from the disaster that befell you!

HENRY IV: Yes, you see how it was! The fact is that falling from my horse and striking my head as I did, I was really mad for I know not how long . . .

DOCTOR: Ah! Did it last long?

HENRY IV (*very quickly to the* DOCTOR): Yes, Doctor, a long time! I think it must have been about twelve years. (*Then suddenly turning to speak to* BELCREDI.) Thus I saw nothing, my dear fellow, of all that, after that day of carnival, happened for you but not for me: how things changed, how my friends deceived me, how my place was taken by another, and all the rest of it! And suppose my place had been taken in the

heart of the woman I loved? . . . And how should I know who was dead or who had disappeared? . . . All this, you know, wasn't exactly a jest for me, as it seems to you . . .

BELCREDI: No, no! I don't mean that if you please. I mean after . . .

HENRY IV: Ah, yes? After? One day—(*Stops and addresses the* DOCTOR.)—A most interesting case, Doctor! Study me well! Study me carefully! (*Trembles while speaking.*) All by itself, who knows how, one day the trouble here (*Touches his forehead.*) mended. Little by little, I open my eyes, and at first I don't know whether I am asleep or awake. Then I know I am awake. I touch this thing and that; I see clearly again . . . Ah!—then, as *he* says (*Alludes to* BELCREDI.) away, away with this masquerade, this incubus! Let's open the windows, breathe life once again! Away! Away! Let's run out! (*Suddenly pulling himself up.*) But where? And to do what? To show myself to all, secretly, as Henry IV, not like this, but arm in arm with you, among my dear friends?

BELCREDI: What are you saying?

DONNA MATILDA: Who could think it? It's not to be imagined. It was an accident.

HENRY IV: They all said I was mad before. (*To* BELCREDI.) And you know it! You were more ferocious than any one against those who tried to defend me.

BELCREDI: Oh, that was only a joke!

HENRY IV: Look at my hair! (*Shows him the hair on the nape of his neck.*)

BELCREDI: But mine is grey too!

HENRY IV: Yes, with this difference: that mine went grey here, as Henry IV, do you understand? And I never knew it! I perceived it all of a sudden, one day, when I opened my eyes; and I was terrified because I understood at once that not only had my hair gone grey, but that I was all grey, inside; that everything had fallen to pieces, that everything was finished; and I was going to arrive hungry as a wolf, at a banquet which had already been cleared away . . .

BELCREDI: Yes, but, what about the others?...

HENRY IV (*quickly*): Ah, yes, I know! They couldn't wait until I was cured, not even those, who, behind my back, pricked my saddled horse till it bled....

DI NOLLI (*agitated*): What, what?

HENRY IV: Yes, treacherously, to make it rear and cause me to fall.

DONNA MATILDA (*quickly, in horror*): This is the first time I knew that.

HENRY IV: That was also a joke, probably!

DONNA MATILDA: But who did it? Who was behind us, then?

HENRY IV: It doesn't matter who it was. All those that went on feasting and were ready to leave me their scrapings, Marchioness, of miserable pity, or some dirty remnant of remorse in the filthy plate! Thanks! (*Turning quickly to the* DOCTOR.) Now, Doctor, the case must be absolutely new in the history of madness; I preferred to remain mad—since I found everything ready and at my disposal for this new exquisite fantasy. I would live it—this madness of mine —with the most lucid consciousness; and thus revenge myself on the brutality of a stone which had dented my head. The solitude—this solitude—squalid and empty as it appeared to me when I opened my eyes again—I determined to deck it out with all the colors and splendors of that far off day of carnival, when you (*Looks at* DONNA MATILDA *and points* FRIDA *out to her.*)—when you, Marchioness, triumphed. So I would oblige all those who were around me to follow, by God, at my orders that famous pageant which had been—for you and not for me—the jest of a day. I would make it become—for ever—no more a joke but a reality, the reality of a real madness: here, all in masquerade, with throne room, and these my four secret counsellors: secret and, of course, traitors. (*He turns quickly towards them.*) I should like to know what you have gained by revealing the fact that I was cured! If I am cured, there's no longer any need of you, and you will be discharged!

To give anyone one's confidence...that is really the act of a madman. But now I accuse you in my turn. (*Turning to the others.*) Do you know? They thought (*Alludes to the* VALETS.) they could make fun of me too with you. (*Bursts out laughing. The others laugh, but shamefacedly, except* DONNA MATILDA.)

BELCREDI (*to* DI NOLLI): Well, imagine that... That's not bad...

DI NOLLI (*to the* FOUR YOUNG MEN): You?

HENRY IV: We must pardon them. This dress (*Plucking his dress.*) which is for me the evident, involuntary caricature of that other continuous, everlasting masquerade, of which we are the involuntary puppets (*Indicates* BELCREDI.), when, without knowing it, we mask ourselves with that which we appear to be...ah, that dress of theirs, this masquerade of theirs, of course, we must forgive it them, since they do not yet see it is identical with themselves . . . (*Turning again to* BELCREDI.) You know, it is quite easy to get accustomed to it. One walks about as a tragic character, just as if it were nothing...(*Imitates the tragic manner.*) in a room like this...Look here, Doctor! I remember a priest, certainly Irish, a nice-looking priest, who was sleeping in the sun one November day, with his arm on the corner of the bench of a public garden. He was lost in the golden delight of the mild sunny air which must have seemed for him almost summery. One may be sure that in that moment he did not know any more that he was a priest, or even where he was. He was dreaming...A little boy passed with a flower in his hand. He touched the priest with it here on the neck. I saw him open his laughing eyes, while all his mouth smiled with the beauty of his dream. He was forgetful of everything...But all at once, he pulled himself together, and stretched out his priest's cassock; and there came back to his eyes the same seriousness which you have seen in mine; because the Irish priests defend the seriousness of their

Catholic faith with the same zeal with which I defend the sacred rights of hereditary monarchy! I am cured, gentlemen: because I can act the madman to perfection, here; and I do it very quietly, I'm only sorry for you that have to live your madness so agitatedly, without knowing it or seeing it.

BELCREDI: It comes to this, then, that it is we who are mad. That's what it is!

HENRY IV (*containing his irritation*): But if you weren't mad, both you and she (*Indicating the* MARCHIONESS.), would you have come here to see me?

BELCREDI: To tell the truth, I came here believing that you were the madman.

HENRY IV (*suddenly indicating the* MARCHIONESS): And she?

BELCREDI: Ah, as for her . . . I can't say. I see she is all fascinated by your words, by this *conscious* madness of yours. (*Turns to her.*) Dressed as you are (*Speaking to her.*), you could even remain here to live it out, Marchioness.

DONNA MATILDA: You are insolent!

HENRY IV (*conciliatingly*): No, Marchioness, what he means to say is that the miracle would be complete, according to him, with you here, who—as the Marchioness of Tuscany, you well know,—could not be my friend, save, as at Canossa, to give me a little pity . . .

BELCREDI: Or even more than a little! She said so herself!

HENRY IV (*to the* MARCHIONESS, *continuing*): And even, shall we say, a little remorse! . . .

BELCREDI: Yes, that too she has admitted.

DONNA MATILDA (*angry*): Now look here . . .

HENRY IV (*quickly, to placate her*): Don't bother about him! Don't mind him! Let him go on infuriating me—though the Doctor's told him not to. (*Turns to* BELCREDI.) But do you suppose I am going to trouble myself any more about what happened between us—the share you had in my misfortune with her (*Indicates the* MARCHIONESS *to him and pointing* BELCREDI *out to her.*), the part he has now in your life? This is my life!

Quite a different thing from your life! Your life, the life in which you have grown old—I have not lived that life. (*To* DONNA MATILDA.) Was this what you wanted to show me with this sacrifice of yours, dressing yourself up like this, according to the Doctor's idea? Excellently done, Doctor! Oh, an excellent idea:—"As we were then, eh? and as we are now?" But I am not a madman according to your way of thinking, Doctor. I know very well that that man there (*Indicates* DI NOLLI.) cannot be me; because I am Henry IV, and have been, these twenty years, cast in this eternal masquerade. She has lived these years! (*Indicates the* MARCHIONESS.) She has enjoyed them and has become—look at her!—a woman I can no longer recognize. It is so that I knew her! (*Points to* FRIDA *and draws near her.*) This is the Marchioness I know, always this one! . . . You seem a lot of children to be so easily frightened by me . . . (*To* FRIDA.) And you're frightened too, little girl, aren't you, by the jest that they made you take part in —though they didn't understand it wouldn't be the jest they meant it to be, for me? Oh miracle of miracles! Prodigy of prodigies! The dream alive in you! More than alive in you! It was an image that wavered there and they've made you come to life! Oh, mine! You're mine, mine, mine, in my own right! (HE *holds her in his arms, laughing like a madman, while all stand still terrified. Then as they advance to tear* FRIDA *from his arms, he becomes furious, terrible and cries imperiously to his* VALETS.) Hold them! Hold them! I order you to hold them!

The FOUR YOUNG MEN *amazed, yet fascinated, move to execute his orders, automatically, and seize* DI NOLLI, *the* DOCTOR, *and* BELCREDI.

BELCREDI (*freeing himself*): Leave her alone! Leave her alone! You're no madman!

HENRY IV (*in a flash draws the sword from the side of* LANDOLPH, *who is close to him*): I'm not mad, eh! Take that, you! . . . (*Drives sword into him. A cry of horror goes up. All rush over to assist* BELCREDI, *crying out together.*)

DI NOLLI: Has he wounded you?

BERTHOLD: Yes, yes, seriously!

DOCTOR: I told you so!

FRIDA: Oh God, oh God!

DI NOLLI: Frida, come here!

DONNA MATILDA: He's mad, mad!

DI NOLLI: Hold him!

BELCREDI (*while* THEY *take him away by the left exit,* HE *protests as he is borne out*): No, no, you're not mad! You're not mad. He's not mad!

THEY *go out by the left amid cries and excitement. After a moment, one hears a still sharper, more piercing cry from* DONNA MATILDA, *and then, silence.*

HENRY IV (*who has remained on the stage between* LANDOLPH, HAROLD *and* ORDULPH, *with his eyes almost starting out of his head, terrified by the life of his own masquerade which has driven him to crime.*) Now, yes . . . we'll have to (*Calls his* VALETS *around him as if to protect him.*) here we are . . . together . . . for ever!

CURTAIN

JEAN-CLAUDE VAN ITALLIE

America Hurrah

Interview: A Fugue for Eight Actors

Characters

FIRST INTERVIEWER
FIRST APPLICANT
SECOND APPLICANT
THIRD APPLICANT
FOURTH APPLICANT
SECOND INTERVIEWER
THIRD INTERVIEWER
FOURTH INTERVIEWER

The set is white and impersonal.

Two subway stairs are at the back of the stage. On the sides there is one entrance for Applicants and another entrance for Interviewers.

The only furniture or props needed are eight grey blocks.

The actors, four men and four women, are dressed in black-and-white street clothes. During the employment agency section only, Interviewers wear translucent plastic masks.

There is an intermittent harpsichord accompaniment: dance variations (minuet, Virginia reel, twist) on a familiar American tune. But much of the music (singing, whistling, humming) is provided by the actors on stage. It is suggested, moreover, that as a company

of actors and a director approach the play they find their own variations in rhythmic expression. The successful transition from one setting to the next depends on the actors' ability to play together as a company and to drop character instantaneously and completely in order to assume another character, or for a group effect.

The FIRST INTERVIEWER *for an employment agency, a young woman, sits on stage as the* FIRST APPLICANT, *a Housepainter, enters.*

FIRST INTERVIEWER (*standing*): How do you do?

FIRST APPLICANT (*sitting*): Thank you, I said, not knowing where to sit.

The characters will often include the audience in what they say, as if they were being interviewed by the audience.

FIRST INTERVIEWER (*pointedly*): Won't you sit down?

FIRST APPLICANT (*standing again quickly, afraid to displease*): I'm sorry.

FIRST INTERVIEWER (*busy with imaginary papers, pointing to a particular seat*): There. Name, please?

FIRST APPLICANT: Jack Smith.

FIRST INTERVIEWER: Jack what Smith?

FIRST APPLICANT: Beg pardon?

FIRST INTERVIEWER: Fill in the blank space, please. Jack blank space Smith.

FIRST APPLICANT: I don't have any.

FIRST INTERVIEWER: I asked you to sit down. (*pointing*) There.

FIRST APPLICANT (*sitting*): I'm sorry.

FIRST INTERVIEWER: Name, please?

FIRST APPLICANT: Jack Smith.

FIRST INTERVIEWER: You haven't told me your MIDDLE name.

FIRST APPLICANT: I haven't got one.

FIRST INTERVIEWER (*suspicious but writing it down*): No middle name.

SECOND APPLICANT, *a woman, a Floorwasher, enters.*

FIRST INTERVIEWER: How do you do?

SECOND APPLICANT (*sitting*): Thank you, I said, not knowing what.

FIRST INTERVIEWER: Won't you sit down?

SECOND APPLICANT (*standing*): I'm sorry.

FIRST APPLICANT: I am sitting.

FIRST INTERVIEWER (*pointing*): There. Name, please?

SECOND APPLICANT (*sitting*): Jane Smith.

FIRST APPLICANT: Jack Smith.

FIRST INTERVIEWER: What blank space Smith?

SECOND APPLICANT: Ellen.

FIRST APPLICANT: Haven't got one.

FIRST INTERVIEWER: What job are you applying for?

FIRST APPLICANT: Housepainter.

SECOND APPLICANT: Floorwasher.

FIRST INTERVIEWER: We haven't many vacancies in that. What experience have you had?

FIRST APPLICANT: A lot.

SECOND APPLICANT: Who needs experience for floorwashing?

FIRST INTERVIEWER: You will help me by making your answers clear.

FIRST APPLICANT: Eight years.

SECOND APPLICANT: Twenty years.

THIRD APPLICANT, *a Banker, enters.*

FIRST INTERVIEWER: How do you do?

SECOND APPLICANT: I'm good at it.

FIRST APPLICANT: Very well.

THIRD APPLICANT (*sitting*): Thank you, I said, as casually as I could.

FIRST INTERVIEWER: Won't you sit down?

THIRD APPLICANT (*standing again*): I'm sorry.

SECOND APPLICANT: I am sitting.

FIRST APPLICANT (*standing again*): I'm sorry.

FIRST INTERVIEWER (*pointing to a particular seat*): There. Name, please?

FIRST APPLICANT: Jack Smith.

SECOND APPLICANT: Jane Smith.

THIRD APPLICANT: Richard Smith.

FIRST INTERVIEWER: What EXACTLY Smith, please?

THIRD APPLICANT: Richard F.

SECOND APPLICANT: Jane Ellen.

FIRST APPLICANT: Jack None.

FIRST INTERVIEWER: What are you applying for?

FIRST APPLICANT: Housepainter.

SECOND APPLICANT: I need money.

THIRD APPLICANT: Bank president.

FIRST INTERVIEWER: How many years have you been in your present job?

THIRD APPLICANT: Three.

SECOND APPLICANT: Twenty.

FIRST APPLICANT: Eight.

FOURTH APPLICANT, *a Lady's Maid, enters.*

FIRST INTERVIEWER: How do you do?

FOURTH APPLICANT: I said thank you, not knowing where to sit.

THIRD APPLICANT: I'm fine.

SECOND APPLICANT: Do I have to tell you?

FIRST APPLICANT: Very well.

FIRST INTERVIEWER: Won't you sit down?

FOURTH APPLICANT: I'm sorry.

THIRD APPLICANT (*sitting again*): Thank you.

SECOND APPLICANT (*standing again*): I'm sorry.

FIRST APPLICANT (*sitting*): Thanks.

FIRST INTERVIEWER (*pointing to a particular seat*): There. Name, please?

FOURTH APPLICANT *sits*.

ALL APPLICANTS: Smith.

FIRST INTERVIEWER: What Smith?

FOURTH APPLICANT: Mary Victoria.

THIRD APPLICANT: Richard F.

SECOND APPLICANT: Jane Ellen.

FIRST APPLICANT: Jack None.

FIRST INTERVIEWER: How many years' experience have you had?

FOURTH APPLICANT: Eight years.

SECOND APPLICANT: Twenty years.

FIRST APPLICANT: Eight years.

THIRD APPLICANT: Three years four months and nine days not counting vacations and sick leave and the time both my daughters and my wife had the whooping cough.

FIRST INTERVIEWER: Just answer the questions, please.

FOURTH APPLICANT: Yes, sir.

THIRD APPLICANT: Sure.

SECOND APPLICANT: I'm sorry.

FIRST APPLICANT: That's what I'm doing.

SECOND INTERVIEWER, *a young man, enters and goes to inspect Applicants. With the entrance of each Interviewer, the speed of the action accelerates.*

SECOND INTERVIEWER: How do you do?

FIRST APPLICANT (*standing*): I'm sorry.

SECOND APPLICANT (*sitting*): Thank you.

THIRD APPLICANT (*standing*): I'm sorry.

FOURTH APPLICANT (*sitting*): Thank you.

SECOND INTERVIEWER: What's your name?

FIRST INTERVIEWER: Your middle name, please.

FIRST APPLICANT: Smith.

SECOND APPLICANT: Ellen.

THIRD APPLICANT: Smith, Richard F.

FOURTH APPLICANT: Mary Victoria Smith.

FIRST INTERVIEWER: What is your exact age?

SECOND INTERVIEWER: Have you any children?

FIRST APPLICANT: I'm thirty-two years old.

SECOND APPLICANT: One son.

THIRD APPLICANT: I have two daughters.

FOURTH APPLICANT: Do I have to tell you that?

FIRST INTERVIEWER: Are you married, single, or other?

SECOND INTERVIEWER: Have you ever earned more than that?

FIRST APPLICANT: No.

SECOND APPLICANT: Never.

THIRD APPLICANT: Married.

FOURTH APPLICANT: Single, NOW.

THIRD INTERVIEWER, *a woman, enters.*

THIRD INTERVIEWER: How do you do?

FIRST APPLICANT (*sitting*): Thank you.

SECOND APPLICANT (*standing*): I'm sorry.

THIRD APPLICANT (*sitting*): Thank you.

FOURTH APPLICANT (*standing*): I'm sorry.

FOURTH INTERVIEWER, *a man, appears on the heels of* THIRD INTERVIEWER.

FOURTH INTERVIEWER: How do you do?

FIRST APPLICANT (*standing*): I'm sorry.

SECOND APPLICANT (*sitting*): Thank you.

THIRD APPLICANT (*standing*): I'm sorry.

FOURTH APPLICANT (*sitting*): Thank you.

ALL INTERVIEWERS: What is your Social Security Number, please?

Applicants do the next four speeches simultaneously.

FIRST APPLICANT: 333 dash 6598 dash 5590765439 dash 003.

SECOND APPLICANT: 999 dash 5733 dash 699075432 dash 11.

THIRD APPLICANT (*sitting*): I'm sorry. I left it home. I can call if you let me use the phone.

FOURTH APPLICANT: I always get it confused with my Checking Account Number.

Interviewers do the next four speeches in a round.

FIRST INTERVIEWER: Will you be so kind as to tell me a little about yourself?

SECOND INTERVIEWER: Can you fill me in on something about your background please?

THIRD INTERVIEWER: It'd be a help to our employers if you'd give me a little for our files.

FOURTH INTERVIEWER: Now what would you say, say, to a prospective employer about yourself?

Applicants address parts of the following four speeches, in particular, directly to the audience.

FIRST APPLICANT: I've been a Union member twenty years, I said to them, if that's the kind of thing you want to know. Good health, I said. Veteran of two wars. Three kids. Wife's dead. Wife's sister, she takes care of them. I don't know why I'm telling you this, I said smiling. (*sits*)

SECOND APPLICANT (*standing*): So what do you want to know, I told the guy. I've been washin' floors for twenty years. Nobody's ever complained. I don't loiter after hours, I said to him. Just because my boy's been in trouble is no reason, I said, no reason—I go right home, I said to him. Right home. (*sits*)

THIRD APPLICANT (*standing*): I said that I was a Republican and we could start right there. And then I said that I spend most of my free time watching television or playing in the garden of my four-bedroom house with our two lovely daughters, aged nine and eleven. I mentioned that my wife plays with us too, and that her name is Katherine, although, I said casually, her good friends call her Kitty. I wasn't at all nervous. (*sits*)

FOURTH APPLICANT (*standing*): Just because I'm here, sir, I told him, is no reason for you to patronize me. I've been a lady's maid, I said, in houses you would not be allowed into. My father was a gentleman of leisure, AND what's more, I said, my references are unimpeachable.

FIRST INTERVIEWER: I see.

SECOND INTERVIEWER: All right.

THIRD INTERVIEWER: That's fine.

FOURTH INTERVIEWER: Of course.

Applicants do the following four speeches simultaneously.

FIRST APPLICANT: Just you call anybody at the Union and ask them. They'll hand me a clean bill of health.

SECOND APPLICANT: I haven't been to jail if that's what you mean. Not me. I'm clean.

THIRD APPLICANT: My record is impeccable. There's not a stain on it.

FOURTH APPLICANT: My references would permit me to be a governess, that's what.

FIRST INTERVIEWER (*going to* FIRST APPLICANT *and inspecting under his arms*): When did you last have a job housepainting?

SECOND INTERVIEWER (*going to* SECOND APPLICANT *and inspecting her teeth*): Where was the last place you worked?

THIRD INTERVIEWER (*going to* THIRD APPLICANT *and inspecting him*): What was your last position in a bank?

FOURTH INTERVIEWER (*going to* FOURTH APPLICANT *and inspecting her*): Have you got your references with you?

Applicants do the following four speeches simultaneously, with music under.

FIRST APPLICANT: I've already told you I worked right along till I quit.

SECOND APPLICANT: Howard Johnson's on Fifty-first Street all last month.

THIRD APPLICANT: First Greenfield International and Franklin Banking Corporation Banking and Stone Incorporated.

FOURTH APPLICANT: I've got a letter right here in my bag. Mrs. Muggintwat only let me go because she died.

Interviewers do the next four speeches in a round.

FIRST INTERVIEWER (*stepping around and speaking to* SECOND APPLICANT): Nothing terminated your job at Howard Johnson's? No franks, say, missing at the end of the day, I suppose?

SECOND INTERVIEWER (*stepping around and speaking to* THIRD APPLICANT): It goes without saying, I suppose, that you could stand an FBI Security Test?

THIRD INTERVIEWER (*stepping around and speaking to* FOURTH APPLICANT): I suppose there are no records of minor thefts or, shall we say, borrowings from your late employer?

FOURTH INTERVIEWER (*stepping around and speaking to* FIRST APPLICANT): Nothing political in your Union dealings? Nothing Leftist, I suppose? Nothing Rightist either, I hope.

Applicants and Interviewers line up for a square dance. Music under the following.

FIRST APPLICANT (*bowing to* FIRST INTERVIEWER): What's it to you, buddy?

SECOND APPLICANT (*bowing to* SECOND INTERVIEWER): Eleanor Roosevelt wasn't more honest.

THIRD APPLICANT (*bowing to* THIRD INTERVIEWER): My record is lily-white, sir!

FOURTH APPLICANT (*bowing to* FOURTH INTERVIEWER): Mrs. Thumbletwat used to take me to the bank and I'd watch her open her box!

Each Interviewer, during his next speech, goes upstage to form another line.

FIRST INTERVIEWER: Good!
SECOND INTERVIEWER: Fine!
THIRD INTERVIEWER: Swell!
FOURTH INTERVIEWER: Fine!

Applicants come downstage together; they do the next four speeches simultaneously and directly to the audience.

FIRST APPLICANT: I know my rights. As a veteran. AND a citizen. I know my rights. AND my cousin is very well-known in certain circles, if you get what I mean. In the back room of a certain candy store in the Italian district of this city my cousin is VERY well known, if you get what I mean. I know my rights. And I know my cousin.

SECOND APPLICANT (*putting on a pious act, looking up to heaven*): Holy Mary Mother of God, must I endure all the sinners of this earth? Must I go on a poor washerwoman in this City of Sin? Help me, oh my God, to leave this earthly crust, and damn your silly impudence, young man, if you think you can treat an old woman like this. You've got another thought coming, you have.

THIRD APPLICANT: I have an excellent notion to report you to the Junior Chamber of Commerce of this city of which I am the Secretary and was in line to be elected Vice President and still will be if you are able to find me gainful and respectable employ!

FOURTH APPLICANT: Miss Thumblebottom married into the Twiths and if you start insulting me, young man, you'll have to start in insulting the Twiths as well. A Twith isn't a nobody, you know, as good as a Thumbletwat, AND they all call me their loving Mary, you know.

ALL INTERVIEWERS (*in a loud raucous voice*): Do you smoke?

Each Applicant, during his next speech, turns upstage.

FIRST APPLICANT: No thanks.
SECOND APPLICANT: Not now.
THIRD APPLICANT: No thanks.
FOURTH APPLICANT: Not now.
ALL INTERVIEWERS (*again in a harsh voice and bowing or curtsying*): Do you mind if I do?
FIRST APPLICANT: I don't care.
SECOND APPLICANT: Who cares?
THIRD APPLICANT: Course not.
FOURTH APPLICANT: Go ahead.

Interviewers form a little group off to themselves.

FIRST INTERVIEWER: I tried to quit but couldn't manage.

SECOND INTERVIEWER: I'm a three-pack-a-day man, I guess.

THIRD INTERVIEWER: If I'm gonna go I'd rather go smoking.

FOURTH INTERVIEWER: I'm down to five a day.

Applicants all start to sneeze.

FIRST APPLICANT: Excuse me, I'm gonna sneeze.

SECOND APPLICANT: Have you got a hanky?

THIRD APPLICANT: I have a cold coming on.

FOURTH APPLICANT: I thought I had some tissues in my bag.

Applicants all sneeze.

FIRST INTERVIEWER: Gezundheit.

SECOND INTERVIEWER: God bless you.

THIRD INTERVIEWER: Gezundheit.

FOURTH INTERVIEWER: God bless you.

Applicants all sneeze simultaneously.

FIRST INTERVIEWER: God bless you.

SECOND INTERVIEWER: Gezundheit.

THIRD INTERVIEWER: God bless you.

FOURTH INTERVIEWER: Gezundheit.

Applicants return to their seats.

FIRST APPLICANT: Thanks, I said.

SECOND APPLICANT: I said thanks.

THIRD APPLICANT: Thank you, I said.

FOURTH APPLICANT: I said thank you.

Interviewers stand on their seats and say the following as if one person were speaking.

FIRST INTERVIEWER: Do you

SECOND INTERVIEWER: speak any

THIRD INTERVIEWER: foreign

FOURTH INTERVIEWER: languages?

FIRST INTERVIEWER: Have you

SECOND INTERVIEWER: got a

THIRD INTERVIEWER: college

FOURTH INTERVIEWER: education?

FIRST INTERVIEWER: Do you

SECOND INTERVIEWER: take

THIRD INTERVIEWER: shorthand?

FOURTH INTERVIEWER: Have you

FIRST INTERVIEWER: any

SECOND INTERVIEWER: special

THIRD INTERVIEWER: qualifications?

FIRST INTERVIEWER: Yes?

FIRST APPLICANT (*stepping up to Interviewers*): Sure, I can speak Italian, I said. My whole family is Italian so I oughta be able to, and I can match colors, like green to green, so that even your own mother couldn't tell the difference, begging your pardon, I said, I went through the eighth grade. (*steps back*)

SECOND INTERVIEWER: Next.

SECOND APPLICANT (*stepping up to Interviewers*): My grandmother taught me some Gaelic, I told the guy. And my old man could rattle off in Yiddish when he had a load on. I never went to school at all excepting church school, but I can write my name good and clear. Also, I said, I can smell an Irishman or a Yid a hundred miles off. (*steps back*)

THIRD INTERVIEWER: Next.

THIRD APPLICANT (*stepping up to Interviewers*): I've never had any need to take shorthand in my position, I said to him. I've a Z.A. in business administration from Philadelphia, and a Z.Z.A. from M.Y.U. night school. I mentioned that I speak a little Spanish, of course, and that I'm a whiz at model frigates and warships. (*steps back*)

FOURTH INTERVIEWER: Next.

FOURTH APPLICANT (*stepping up to Interviewers*): I can sew a straight seam, I said, hand or machine, and I have been exclusively a lady's maid although I CAN cook and will too if I have someone to assist me, I said. Unfortunately, aside from self-education, grammar school is as far as I have progressed. (*steps back*)

Each Interviewer, during his next speech, bows or curtsies to the Applicant nearest him.

FIRST INTERVIEWER: Good.
SECOND INTERVIEWER: Fine.
THIRD INTERVIEWER: Very helpful.
FOURTH INTERVIEWER: Thank you.

Each Applicant, during his next speech, jumps on the back of the Interviewer nearest him.

FOURTH APPLICANT: You're welcome, I'm sure.
THIRD APPLICANT: Anything you want to know.
SECOND APPLICANT: Just ask me.
FIRST APPLICANT: Fire away, fire away.

The next eight speeches are spoken simultaneously, with Applicants on Interviewers' backs.

FIRST INTERVIEWER: Well unless there's anything special you want to tell me, I think—
SECOND INTERVIEWER: Is there anything more you think I should know about before you—
THIRD INTERVIEWER: I wonder if we've left anything out of this questionnaire or if you—
FOURTH INTERVIEWER: I suppose I've got all the information down here unless you can—
FIRST APPLICANT: I've got kids to support, you know, and I need a job real quick—
SECOND APPLICANT: Do you think you could try and get me something today because I—
THIRD APPLICANT: How soon do you suppose I can expect to hear from your agency? Do you—
FOURTH APPLICANT: I don't like to sound pressureful, but you know I'm currently on unemploy—

Each Applicant, during his next speech, jumps off Interviewer's back.

FIRST APPLICANT: Beggin' your pardon.
SECOND APPLICANT: So sorry.
THIRD APPLICANT: Excuse me.

FOURTH APPLICANT: Go ahead.

Each Interviewer, during his next speech, bows or curtsies and remains in that position.

FIRST INTERVIEWER: That's quite all right.
SECOND INTERVIEWER: I'm sorry.
THIRD INTERVIEWER: I'm sorry.
FOURTH INTERVIEWER: My fault.

Each Applicant, during his next speech, begins leap-frogging over Interviewers' backs.

FIRST APPLICANT: My fault.
SECOND APPLICANT: My fault.
THIRD APPLICANT: I'm sorry.
FOURTH APPLICANT: My fault.

Each Interviewer, during his next speech, begins leap-frogging too.

FIRST INTERVIEWER: That's all right.
SECOND INTERVIEWER: My fault.
THIRD INTERVIEWER: I'm sorry.
FOURTH INTERVIEWER: Excuse me.

The leap-frogging continues as the preceding eight lines are repeated simultaneously. Then the Interviewers confer in a huddle and come out of it.

FIRST INTERVIEWER: Do you enjoy your work?
FIRST APPLICANT: Sure, I said, I'm proud. Why not? Sure I know I'm no Rembrandt, I said, but I'm proud of my work, I said to him.
SECOND APPLICANT: I told him it stinks. But what am I supposed to do, sit home and rot?
THIRD APPLICANT: Do I like my work, he asked me. Well, I said, to gain time, do I like my work? Well, I said, I don't know.
FOURTH APPLICANT: I told him right straight out: for a sensible person, a lady's maid is the ONLY POSSIBLE way of life.
SECOND INTERVIEWER: Do you think you're irreplaceable?

ALL APPLICANTS: Oh, yes indeed.

ALL INTERVIEWERS: Irreplaceable?

ALL APPLICANTS: Yes, yes indeed.

THIRD INTERVIEWER: Do you like me?

FIRST APPLICANT: You're a nice man.

SECOND APPLICANT: Huh?

THIRD APPLICANT: Why do you ask?

FOURTH APPLICANT: It's not a question of LIKE.

FIRST INTERVIEWER: Well, we'll be in touch with you.

This is the beginning of leaving the agency. Soft music under. Applicants and Interviewers push their seats into two masses of four boxes, one on each side of the stage. Applicants leave first, joining hands to form a revolving door.

All are now leaving the agency, not in any orderly fashion. Interviewers start down one of the subway stairs at the back of the stage and Applicants start down the other. The following speeches overlap and are heard indistinctly as crowd noise.

FOURTH INTERVIEWER: What sort of day will it be?

FIRST APPLICANT: I bet we'll have rain.

SECOND APPLICANT: Cloudy, clearing in the afternoon.

THIRD APPLICANT: Mild, I think, with some snow.

FOURTH APPLICANT: Precisely the same as yesterday.

SECOND APPLICANT: Can you get me one?

FIRST INTERVIEWER: See you tomorrow.

THIRD APPLICANT: When will I hear from you?

SECOND INTERVIEWER: We'll let you know.

FOURTH APPLICANT: Where's my umbrella?

THIRD INTERVIEWER: I'm going to a movie.

FIRST APPLICANT: So how about it?

FOURTH INTERVIEWER: Good night.

THIRD APPLICANT: Can you help me, Doctor, I asked.

When all of the actors are offstage, the FOURTH INTERVIEWER *makes a siren sound and the following speeches continue from downstairs as a loud crowd noise for a few moments; they overlap so that the stage is empty only briefly.*

FIRST INTERVIEWER: It'll take a lot of work on your part.

SECOND INTERVIEWER: I'll do what I can for you.

THIRD INTERVIEWER: Of course I'll do my best.

FIRST INTERVIEWER: God helps those who help themselves.

FIRST APPLICANT: I have sinned deeply, Father, I said.

FIRST INTERVIEWER: You certainly have. I hope you truly repent.

SECOND INTERVIEWER: In the name of the Father, etcetera, and the Holy Ghost.

THIRD INTERVIEWER: Jesus saves.

FOURTH APPLICANT: I said can you direct me to Fourteenth Street, please?

FIRST INTERVIEWER: Just walk down that way a bit and then turn left.

SECOND INTERVIEWER: Just walk down that way a bit and then turn right.

THIRD INTERVIEWER: Take a cab!

FOURTH APPLICANT: Do you hear a siren?

ALL INTERVIEWERS: What time is it?

FIRST APPLICANT: Half-past three.

SECOND APPLICANT: It must be about four.

THIRD APPLICANT: Half-past five.

FOURTH APPLICANT: My watch has stopped.

FIRST INTERVIEWER: Do you enjoy your work?

SECOND INTERVIEWER: Do you think you're irreplaceable?

THIRD INTERVIEWER: Do you like me?

The actor who played the FOURTH INTERVIEWER *comes on stage while continuing to make the loud siren noise. The actress who played the* FOURTH APPLICANT *comes on stage and speaks directly to the audience.*

FOURTH APPLICANT: Can you direct me to Fourteenth Street, please, I said. I seem to have lost my—I started to say, and then I was nearly run down.

The remaining actors return to the stage to play various people on Fourteenth Street: ladies shopping, a panhandler, a man in a sandwich board, a peddler of "franks and orange," a snooty German couple, a lecher, a pair of sighing lovers, and so on. The actors walk straight forward toward the audience and then walk backwards to the rear of the stage. Each time they approach the audience, they do so as a different character. The actor will need to find the essential vocal and physical mannerisms of each character, play them, and drop them immediately to assume another character. The FOURTH APPLICANT *continues to address the audience directly, to involve them in her hysteria, going up the aisle and back.*

FOURTH APPLICANT: I haven't got my Social Security—I started to say, I saw someone right in front of me and I said, could you direct me please to Fourteenth Street, I have to get to Fourteenth Street, please, to get a bargain, I explained, although I could hardly remember what it was I wanted to buy. I read about it in the paper today, I said, only they weren't listening and I said to myself, my purpose for today is to get to—and I couldn't remember, I've set myself the task of—I've got to have—it's that I can save, I remembered, I can save if I can get that bargain at—and I couldn't remember where it was so I started to look for my wallet which I seem to have mislaid in my purse, and a man—please watch where you're going, I shouted with my purse half-open, and I seemed to forget—Fourteenth Street, I remembered, and you'd think with all these numbered streets and avenues a person wouldn't get lost—you'd think a person would HELP a person, you'd think so. So I asked the most respectable looking man I could find, I asked him, please can you direct me to Fourteenth Street. He wouldn't answer. Just wouldn't. I'm lost, I said to myself. The paper said—the television said—they said, I couldn't remember what they

said. I turned for help: "Jesus Saves" the sign said, and a man was carrying it, both sides of his body, staring straight ahead. "Jesus Saves" the sign said.

The passers-by jostle her more and more.

FOURTH APPLICANT: I couldn't remember where I was going. "Come and be saved" it said, so I asked the man with the sign, please, sir, won't you tell me how to, dear Lord, I thought, anywhere, please, sir, won't you tell me how to—can you direct me to Fourteenth Street, PLEASE!

The passers-by have covered the FOURTH APPLICANT. *All actors mill about until they reach designated positions on the stage where they face the audience, a line of women and a line of men, students in a gym class. The* SECOND INTERVIEWER *has stayed coolly out of the crowd during this last; now he is the* GYM INSTRUCTOR.

GYM INSTRUCTOR: I took my last puff and strode resolutely into the room. Ready men, I asked brightly. And one and two and three and four and one and two and keep it up.

The GYM INSTRUCTOR *is trying to help his students mold themselves into the kind of people seen in advertisements and the movies. As he counts to four the students puff out their chests, smile, and look perfectly charming. As he counts to four again, the students relax and look ordinary.*

GYM INSTRUCTOR: You wanna look like the guys in the movies, don't you, I said to the fellahs. Keep it up then. You wanna radiate that kinda charm and confidence they have in the movies, don't you, I said to the girls. Keep it up then, stick 'em out, that's what you got 'em for. Don't be ashamed. All of you, tuck in your butts, I said loudly. That's the ticket, I said, wishing to hell I had a cigarette. You're selling, selling all the time, that right, miss? Keep on selling, I said. And one and two and three and four and ever see that guy on TV, I said. What's his name, I asked them. What's his name? Aw, you know his name, I said, forgetting his name. Never mind, it'll come to you, I said. He comes in here too. See that, I said, grabbing a guy out of line and showing 'em his muscle. See that line, I said, making the guy feel good, know what that is? It's boyishness, I said. You come here, I said, throwing him back into the line, and it'll renew your youthfulness, I said, taking a deep breath. And one and two and three and four and smile, I said, smiling. Not so big, I said, smiling less. You look like creeps, I said, when you smile that big. When you smile, hold something back. Make like you're holding back something big, I said, a secret, I said. That's the ticket. And one and two and three and four and... (*accelerating the rhythm to a double count*) Anybody got a cigarette, I said suddenly, without thinking. I was just kidding, I said then, sheepishly. One and two and three and four, I said, wishing I had a cigarette. And one and two and three and four...

The rapid movements of the gym class become the vibrations of passengers on a moving subway train. The actors rush to the boxes stage left, continuing to vibrate. Two of the actors stand on the boxes and smile like subway advertisements while the others, directly in front of them, are pushed against each other on the crowded train. They make an appropriate soft subway noise, a kind of rhythmic hiss and, as the subway passengers, form their faces into frozen masks of indifference.

SECOND APPLICANT (*squeezing her way to an uncomfortable front seat and speaking half to herself*): God forgive me... you no-good chump, I said to him, I used to love you... not now. Not now... God forgive me...

God forgive me for being old. Not now, I said. I wouldn't wipe the smell off your uncle's bottom now, not for turnips, no. God forgive me... Remember how we used to ride the roller coaster out at Coney Island, you and me? Remember? Holding hands in the cold and I'd get so scared and you'd get so scared and we'd hug each other and buy another ticket... Remember?... Look now, I said. Look at me now! God forgive you for leaving me with nothing... God forgive you for being dead... God forgive me for being alive...

The actress who played the THIRD INTERVIEWER *slips out of the subway as though it were her stop and sits on a box, stage right, as a* TELEPHONE OPERATOR. *The other actors form a telephone circuit by holding hands in two concentric circles around the boxes, stage left; they change the hissing sound of the subway into the whistling of telephone circuits.*

TELEPHONE OPERATOR: Just one moment and I will connect you with Information.

The TELEPHONE OPERATOR *alternates her official voice with her ordinary voice; she uses the latter when she talks to her friend Roberta, another operator whom she reaches by flipping a switch. When she is talking to Roberta, the whistling of the telephone circuit changes into a different rhythm and the arms of the actors, which are forming the circuit, move into a different position.*

TELEPHONE OPERATOR: Just one moment and I will connect you with Information. Ow! Listen, Roberta, I said, I've got this terrible cramp. Hang up and dial again, please; we find nothing wrong with that number at all. You know what I ate, I said to her, you were there. Baked macaroni, Wednesday special, maple-nut fudge, I said. I'm sorry but the number you have reached is not—I can feel it gnawing at me at the bottom of my belly, I told her. Do you think it's serious, Roberta? Appendicitis? I asked. Thank you for giving us the area code but the number you have reached is not in this area. Roberta, I asked her, do you think I have cancer? One moment, please, I'm sorry the number you have reached—ow! Well, if it's lunch, Roberta, I said to her, you know what they can do with it tomorrow. Ow! One moment, please, I said. Ow, I said, Roberta, I said, it really hurts.

The TELEPHONE OPERATOR *falls off her seat in pain. The whistling of the telephone circuit becomes a siren. Three actors carry the* TELEPHONE OPERATOR *over to the boxes, stage left, which now serve as an operating table. Three actors imitate the* TELEPHONE OPERATOR'S *breathing pattern while four actors behind her make stylized sounds and movements as surgeons and nurses in the midst of an operation. The* TELEPHONE OPERATOR'S *breathing accelerates, then stops. After a moment the actors begin spreading over the stage and making the muted sounds of a cocktail party: music, laughter, talk. The actors find a position and remain there, playing various aspects of a party in slow motion and muted tones. They completely ignore the* FIRST INTERVIEWER *who, as a* GIRL AT THE PARTY, *goes from person to person as if she were in a garden of living statues.*

GIRL AT THE PARTY (*rapidly and excitedly*): And then after the ambulance took off I went up in the elevator and into the party. Did you see the accident, I asked, and they said they did, and what did he look like, and I said he wore a brown coat and had straight brown hair. He stepped off the curb right in front of me. We had been walking up the same block, he a few feet ahead of me, this block right here, I said, but she wasn't listening. Hi, my name is Jill, I said to somebody sitting down and they looked at me and smiled so I said his arm was torn out of its socket and his face was on the pavement gasping but I didn't touch him and she smiled and walked away and I said after her, you aren't supposed to touch someone before—I WANTED to help, I said, but she wasn't listening. When a man came up and said was it someone you knew and I said yes, it was someone I knew slightly, someone I knew, yes, and he offered me a drink and I said no thanks, I didn't want one, and he said well how well did I know him, and I said I knew him well, yes, I knew him very well. You were coming together to the party, he said. Yes, I said, excuse me. Hi, my name is Jill, did you hear a siren, and they said oh you're the one who saw it, was he killed? (*becoming resigned to the fact that no one is listening*) And I said yes I was, excuse me, and went back across the room but couldn't find another face to talk to until I deliberately bumped into somebody because I had to tell them one of us couldn't come because of the accident. It was Jill. Jill couldn't come. I'm awfully sorry, I said, because of the accident. She had straight brown hair, I said, and was wearing a brown coat, and two or three people looked at me strangely and moved off. I'm sorry, I said to a man, and I laughed, and moved off. I'm dead, I said to several people and started to push them over, I'm dead, thank you, I said, thank you, please, I said, I'm dead, until two or three of them got hold of my arms and hustled me out. I'm sorry, I said, I couldn't come because of the accident. I'm sorry. Excuse me.

The GIRL AT THE PARTY *is lowered to the floor by two of the men and then all fall down except the actor who played the Fourth Interviewer. He remains seated as a* PSYCHIATRIST. *The* THIRD APPLICANT, *on the floor, props his head up on his elbow and speaks to the audience.*

THIRD APPLICANT: Can you help me, Doctor, I asked him.

The PSYCHIATRIST *crosses his legs and assumes a professional expression.*

THIRD APPLICANT: Well, it started, well it started, I said, when I was sitting in front of the television set with my feet on the coffee table. Now I've sat there hundreds of times, thousands maybe, with a can of beer in my hand. I like to have a can of beer in my hand when I watch the beer ads. But now for no reason I can think of, the ad was making me sick. So I used the remote control to get to another channel, but each channel made me just as sick. The television was one thing and I was a person, and I was going to be sick. So I turned it off and had a panicky moment. I smelled the beer in my hand and as I vomited I looked around the living room for something to grab on to, something to look at, but there was just our new furniture. I tried to get a hold of myself. I tried to stare straight ahead above the television set, at a little spot on the wall I know. I've had little moments like that before, Doctor, I said, panicky little moments like that when the earth seems to slip out from under, and everything whirls around and you try to hold onto something, some object, some thought, but I couldn't think of anything. Later the panic went away, I told him, it went away, and I'm much better now. But I don't feel like doing anything anymore, except sit and stare at the wall. I've lost my job. Katherine thought I should come and see you. Can you help me, Doctor, I asked him.
PSYCHIATRIST:
Blah, blah, blah, blah, blah, blah, HOSTILE.
Blah, blah, blah, blah, blah, blah, PENIS.
Blah, blah, blah, blah, blah, blah, MOTHER.
   (*holding out his hand*)
Blah, blah, blah, blah, blah, blah, MONEY.

The THIRD APPLICANT *takes the* PSYCHIATRIST's *hand and gets up, extending his left hand to the next actor. This begins a grand right and left with all the actors all over the stage.*

ALL (*chanting as they do the grand right and left*):

Blah, blah, blah, blah, blah, blah, HOSTILE.
Blah, blah, blah, blah, blah, blah, PENIS.
Blah, blah, blah, blah, blah, blah, MOTHER.
Blah, blah, blah, blah, blah, blah, MONEY.
Blah, blah, blah, blah, blah, blah, HOSTILE.
Blah, blah, blah, blah, blah, blah, PENIS.
Blah, blah, blah, blah, blah, blah, MOTHER.
Blah, blah, blah, blah, blah, blah, MONEY.
   (*forming couples and locking hands with arms crossed, continuing to move, but in a smaller circle*)
Blah, blah, blah, blah, blah, blah, blah.
Blah, blah, blah, blah, blah, blah, blah.

Now they slow down to the speed of a church procession. The women bow their heads, letting their hair fall forward over their faces. The "blah, blah, blah" continues, but much more slowly while some of the women accompany it with a descant of "Kyrie Eleison." After they have gone around in a circle once this way, the actor who played the FOURTH INTERVIEWER *sits with his back to the audience as a* PRIEST. *The* FIRST APPLICANT *kneels next to him, facing the audience as if in a confessional booth. The other six actors are at the back of the stage in two lines, swaying slightly, heads down. The women are in front with their hair still down over their faces.*

FIRST APPLICANT (*crossing himself perfunctorily and starting to speak; his manner is not impassioned; it is clear that he comes regularly to repeat this always fruitless ritual*): Can you help me, Father, I said, as I usually do, and he said, as usual, nothing. I'm your friend, the housepainter, I said, the good housepainter. Remember me, Father? He continued, as usual, to say nothing. Almost the only color you get to paint these days, Father, I said, is white. Only white, Father, I said, not expecting any more from him than usual, but going on anyway. The color

I really like to paint, Father, is red, I said. Pure brick red. Now there's a confession, Father. He said nothing. I'd like to take a trip to the country, Father, I said, and paint a barn door red, thinking that would get a rise out of him, but it didn't. God, I said then, deliberately taking the Lord's name in vain, the result of taking a three-inch brush and lightly kissing a coat of red paint on a barn door is something stunning and beautiful to behold. He still said nothing. Father, I said, springing it on him, Father, I'd like to join a monastery. My wife's sister, she could take care of the kids. Still nothing. Father, I said again, I'd like to join a monastery. Can you help me, Father? Nothing. Father, I said, I've tried lots of things in my life, I've gone in a lot of different directions, Father, and none of them seems any better than any other, Father, I said. Can you help me, Father, I said. But he said nothing as usual, and then, as usual, I went away.

The FIRST APPLICANT *and the* FOURTH INTERVIEWER, *who haven't moved at all during the confession, move upstage to join the others as the music starts up violently in a rock beat. The actors do a rock version of the Virginia reel.*

SECOND INTERVIEWER (*loudly*): My

All bow to partners.

FOURTH APPLICANT (*loudly*): fault.

All dos-á-dos.

SECOND APPLICANT (*loudly*): Excuse

All circle around.

FOURTH INTERVIEWER (*loudly*): me.

All peel off.

FIRST INTERVIEWER (*loudly*): Can you
SECOND APPLICANT (*loudly*): help
FIRST APPLICANT (*loudly*): me?
FOURTH INTERVIEWER (*loudly*): Next.

All continue dancing, joining hands at the center to form a revolving door again. They repeat the preceding eight speeches. Then the SECOND INTERVIEWER *speaks rapidly, as a* SQUARE DANCE CALLER.

SQUARE DANCE CALLER: Step right up, ladies and gents, and shake the hand of the next governor of this state. Shake his hand and say hello. Tell your friends you shook the hand of the next governor of the state. Step right up and shake his hand. Ask him questions. Tell him problems. Say hello. Step right up, shake his hand, shake the hand, ladies and gents, of the next governor of the state. Tell your folks: I shook his hand. When he's famous you'll be proud. Step right up, ladies and gents, and shake his hand. Ask him questions. Tell him problems. Say hello. Step right up, ladies and gents. Don't be shy. Shake the hand of the next governor of this state.

The actors have formed a crowd, downstage right, facing the audience. They give the impression of being but a few of a great number of people, all trying to squeeze to the front to see and speak to the political candidate. The FOURTH INTERVIEWER, *now playing a* POLITICIAN, *stands on a box, stage left, facing the audience. The* SECOND INTERVIEWER *stands by the crowd and keeps it in order.*

POLITICIAN: Thank you very much, I said cheerfully, and good luck to you, I said, turning my smile to the next one.

The FIRST INTERVIEWER, *panting as the* GIRL AT THE PARTY, *squeezes out of the crowd and rushes up to the* POLITICIAN, *who smiles at her benignly.*

POLITICIAN: Our children ARE our most important asset, I agreed earnestly. Yes they are, I said solemnly. Children, I said, with a long pause, are our most important asset. I only wish I could, madame, I said earnestly, standing tall, but rats, I said regretfully, are a city matter.

The FIRST INTERVIEWER *returns to the crowd while the* THIRD INTERVIEWER, *as the* TELEPHONE OPERATOR, *rushes up to the* POLITICIAN. *She appeals to him, making the same noise she made when her stomach hurt her.*

POLITICIAN: Nobody knows more about red tape than I do, I said knowingly, and I wish you luck, I said, turning my smile to the next one.

The THIRD INTERVIEWER *returns to the crowd and the* FOURTH APPLICANT *goes up to the* POLITICIAN.

POLITICIAN: I certainly will, I said, with my eyes sparkling, taking a pencil out of my pocket. And what's your name, I said, looking at her sweetly and signing my name at the same time. That's a lovely name, I said.

The FOURTH APPLICANT *returns to the crowd while the* THIRD APPLICANT, *as an* OLDER MAN, *shakes the* POLITICIAN's *hand.*

POLITICIAN: Yes sir, I said, those were the days. And good luck to you, sir, I said respectfully but heartily, and look out for the curb, I said, turning my smile to the next one.

The THIRD APPLICANT *returns to the crowd and the* SECOND APPLICANT *approaches the* POLITICIAN.

POLITICIAN: Indeed yes, the air we breathe IS foul, I said indignantly. I agree with you entirely, I said wholeheartedly. And if my opponent wins it's going to get worse, I said with conviction. We'd all die within ten years, I said. And good luck to you, madame, I said politely, and turned my smile to the next one.

The FIRST APPLICANT *approaches him, his cap in his hand.*

POLITICIAN: Well, I said confidingly, getting a bill through the legislature is easier said than done, and answering violence, I said warningly, with violence, I said earnestly, is not the answer, and how do you do, I said, turning my smile to the next one.

Next, two SIGHING LOVERS—*we saw them on Fourteenth Street*—*played by the* FIRST *and* SECOND INTERVIEWERS, *approach the* POLITICIAN.

POLITICIAN: No, I said, I never said my opponent would kill us all. No, I said, I never said that. May the best man win, I said manfully.

Half-hearted cheers. The FIRST *and* SECOND INTERVIEWERS *return to the crowd.*

POLITICIAN: I do feel, I said without false modesty, that I'm better qualified in the field of foreign affairs than my opponents are, yes, I said, BUT, I said, with a pause for emphasis, foreign policy is the business of the President, not the Governor, therefore I will say nothing about the war, I said with finality.

The crowd makes a restive sound, then freezes.

POLITICIAN: Do you want us shaking hands, I asked the photographer, turning my profile to the left. Goodbye, I said cheerfully, and good luck to you too.

The crowd makes a louder protest, then freezes.

POLITICIAN: I'm sorry, I said seriously, but I'll have to study that question a good deal more before I can answer it.

The crowd makes an angry noise, then freezes.

POLITICIAN: Of course, I said frowning, we must all support the President, I said as I turned concernedly to the next one.

The crowd makes a very angry sound, then freezes.

POLITICIAN: I'm sorry about the war, I said. Nobody could be sorrier than I am, I said sorrowfully. But I'm afraid, I said gravely, that there are no easy answers. (*smiles, pleased with himself*) Good luck to you too, I said cheerfully, and turned my smile to the next one.

The POLITICIAN *topples from his box, beginning his speech all over again. Simultaneously, all the other actors lurch about the stage, speaking again in character: the* SHOPPER ON FOURTEENTH STREET, *the* GYM INSTRUCTOR, *the* SUBWAY RIDER, *the* TELEPHONE OPERATOR, *the* GIRL AT THE PARTY, *the* ANALYSAND, *and the* HOUSE-PAINTER. *Simultaneously, they all stop and freeze, continue again, freeze again, then continue with music under. The* SECOND INTERVIEWER, *acting as policeman, begins to line them up in a diagonal line, like marching dolls, one behind the other. As they are put into line they begin to move their mouths without sound, like fish in a tank. The music stops. When all are in line the* SECOND INTERVIEWER *joins them.*

SECOND INTERVIEWER: My
FOURTH APPLICANT: fault.
SECOND APPLICANT: Excuse
FOURTH INTERVIEWER: me.
FIRST INTERVIEWER: Can you
SECOND APPLICANT: help
FIRST APPLICANT: me?
FOURTH INTERVIEWER: Next.

All continue marching in place, moving their mouths, and shouting their lines as the lights come slowly down.

SECOND INTERVIEWER: My
FOURTH APPLICANT: fault.
SECOND APPLICANT: Excuse
FOURTH INTERVIEWER: me.
FIRST INTERVIEWER: Can you
SECOND APPLICANT: help
FIRST APPLICANT: me?
FOURTH INTERVIEWER: Next.

TV

The youth Narcissus mistook his own reflection in the water for another person . . . He was numb. He had adapted to his extension of himself and had become a closed system.

Marshall McLuhan

Characters

HAL

SUSAN

GEORGE

HELEN FARGIS, THE PRESIDENT'S WIFE, A UGP RESEARCHER, A MEMBER OF THE ROCK AND ROLL GROUP, A PEACE MARCHER, LILY HEAVEN, THE HEADACHE SUFFERER, A SINGER IN THE EVANGELIST CHOIR, AND MOTHER IN "MY FAVORITE TEENAGER," *played by one actress*

HARRY FARGIS, FIRST NEWS ANNOUNCER, STEVE, THE PRESIDENT, A UGP RESEARCHER, A MEMBER OF THE ROCK AND ROLL GROUP, WEATHER ANNOUNCER, HE IN THE BILLION DOLLAR MOVIE, EVANGELIST, AND FATHER IN "MY FAVORITE TEENAGER," *played by one actor*

WONDERBOY, SECOND NEWS ANNOUNCER, THE MAN IN THE CIGARETTE COMMERCIAL, BILL, UGP ANNOUNCER, A MEMBER OF THE ROCK AND ROLL GROUP, ONE YOUNG MAN FROM NEW YORK CITY, LILY HEAVEN'S ANNOUNCER, RON CAMPBELL, JOHNNY HOLLAND, AND A SINGER IN THE EVANGELIST CHOIR, *played by one actor*

THE WOMAN IN THE CIGARETTE COMMERCIAL, THE PRESIDENT'S OLDER DAUGHTER, A UGP RESEARCHER, A MEMBER OF THE ROCK AND ROLL GROUP, A PEACE MARCHER, FAMOUS TELEVISION PERSONALITY, CAROL, SHE IN THE BILLION DOLLAR MOVIE, AND A SINGER IN THE EVANGELIST CHOIR, *played by one actress*

SALLY, THE PRESIDENT'S YOUNGER DAUGHTER, THE SPANISH TEACHER, A UGP RESEARCHER, A MEMBER OF THE ROCK AND ROLL GROUP, ANNIE KAPPELHOFF, LADY ANNOUNCER, LUCI, A SINGER IN THE EVANGELIST CHOIR, AND DAUGHTER IN "MY FAVORITE TEENAGER," *played by one actress*

The set is white and impersonal. There are two doors on the stage right wall: one leads to the rest rooms, the other to the hall.

Downstage right is the control console in a television viewing room. It faces the audience.

Above the console, also facing the audience, is a screen. Projected on it, from the rear, is the logo of a television station.

Downstage left is a water cooler, a closet for coats, and a telephone. Downstage right is a bulletin board. Upstage center is a table with a coffee maker on it.

HAL and SUSAN are seated at the console, SUSAN in the middle chair. They are both in their twenties. HAL is playing, as he often will, with his penknife: whittling pencils, paring his nails, or throwing it at the bulletin board. SUSAN is involved with the papers on the console, with sharpening pencils, and so forth.

At the back of the stage, on the left, are the five actors who will portray what will appear on television. For the moment they have no light on them and their backs are to the audience.

To indicate the correlation of the events and dialogue on television with those which occur in the viewing room, the play is printed in two columns.

HAL

So what do you say?

SUSAN

I don't know.

HAL

That doesn't get us very far, does it?

SUSAN

Well, it's such a surprise your asking. I was planning to work on my apartment.

HAL

I'll help you, after the movie.

SUSAN

That's too late. One thing I have to have is eight hours' sleep. I really have to have that.

GEORGE *enters; he is older than* HAL *and* SUSAN, *and is in charge of the viewing room.*

HAL

Hi, George.

SUSAN

Hello, George.

GEORGE (*to* SUSAN)

Is that a new dress?

SUSAN (*nodding toward* HAL)

HE didn't even notice.

GEORGE *puts his coat and jacket in the closet and puts on a cardigan sweater.*

GEORGE

How many check marks have you made, Hal?

HAL

I don't know, George. I don't count.

SUSAN

I got it on Fourteenth Street. I love going into places like that because they're so cheap.

GEORGE

If you don't make at least a hundred check marks, they'll dock you. That's what the totals count column is for.

SUSAN *(looking at herself in a mirror)*

Have I lost any weight?

GEORGE

Where would you lose it from?

HAL

George, how come they haven't asked us for a detailed report in nearly three weeks?

GEORGE

How should I know?

HAL

Think they're forgetting about us, George?

SUSAN

I was trying to tell in the Ladies, but the fluorescent light in there just burns your eyes.

HAL

I've never been to the Ladies. You think I'd like it?

GEORGE

This viewing room is the backbone of the rating system.

HAL

He said that to you LAST month, George. Things move fast.

GEORGE

Are you trying to make me nervous?

HAL

Maybe.

GEORGE

Well don't, because my stomach is not very good this morning.

SUSAN

  I want to know seriously, and I mean seriously, do you think I've lost any weight?

GEORGE

  Where from?

HAL

  Why don't you let yourself go?

SUSAN

  What do you mean?

HAL

  Just let nature take its course.

SUSAN

  What if nature wants you to be a big fat
slob?

HAL

  Then be a big fat slob.

SUSAN

  Thanks.

HAL, SUSAN, *and* GEORGE *sit down and get ready for the day's work.*
GEORGE *turns a dial on the console which turns on TV. Two of the*
PEOPLE ON TELEVISION *turn around to play* HELEN *and* HARRY FARGIS.

All of the PEOPLE ON TELEVISION *are dressed in shades of gray. They
make no costume changes and use no real props. Their faces are
made up with thin horizontal black lines to suggest the way they
might appear to a viewer. They are playing television images. Their
style of acting is cool, not pushy. As television characters, they have
only a few facial masks, such as "cute," "charming," or "serious,"
which they use infallibly, like signals, in the course of each television
segment.*

After each television segment, the PEOPLE *involved in it will freeze
where they are until it is time for them to become another character.*

As the play progresses, the PEOPLE ON TELEVISION *will use more and
more of the stage. The impression should be that of a slow invasion
of the viewing room.* HAL, SUSAN, *and* GEORGE *will simply move around
the* PEOPLE ON TELEVISION *when that becomes necessary. Ultimately,
the control console itself will be taken over by television characters,
so that the distinction between what is on television and what is
occurring in the viewing room will be lost completely.*

*The attention of the audience should be focused not on a parody of
television, but on the relationship of the life that appears on television to the life that goes on in the viewing room.*

All of the actors will need to be constantly aware of what is happening on all parts of the stage, in order to give and take the attention of the audience to and from each other, and also in order to demonstrate the influence of the style of certain television segments on the behavior of HAL, SUSAN, *and* GEORGE.

(*Slide on screen: Wonderboy's face.*)

HAL
Why try to look like somebody else?

HELEN *and* HARRY FARGIS *are at home.* HELEN *is baking cookies.*

HELEN
Harry, what are you working on in the garage?

SUSAN
I'm trying to look like myself, thin. Very thin.

HARRY
If I succeed in my experiment, nobody in the world will be hungry for love. Ever again.

HAL (*offering him one*)
Want a cigarette, George?
GEORGE
No, thanks.

HELEN
Hungry for love? Harry, you make me nervous.
HELEN
You really do.

HAL
Just one?
GEORGE
No.

HARRY
Men will put down their arms.

SUSAN
Hal, why don't you try to help George instead of being so cruel?

HELEN
You haven't been to work for a week now. You'll lose your job.

HAL
I'm just offering him a cigarette.

HARRY
You don't understand. This is more important.
HELEN
Oh, Harry. I don't understand you at all any more. I really don't.

GEORGE (*as* HAL *takes the cigarette away*)
Give me one.
SUSAN
Hal, that's utter torture for George.

GEORGE
Give me one.

SUSAN
Don't, George. He's just playing cat and mouse.

HAL
That's right, George. Don't have one. I'm just playing cat and mouse. (*lights a cigarette*)

GEORGE
Just give it to me, will you?

SUSAN
Try to control yourself for just another half hour, George.
GEORGE
No.
SUSAN
Why not?
GEORGE
Because I don't wanna control myself for just another half hour.
HAL
Whatever you want, George. (*hands a cigarette to George*)

HARRY *goes back to the garage.* HELEN *mumbles to herself as she cleans up the kitchen.*

HELEN
I don't know.

HELEN
I just don't know. He used to be so docile.

HELEN
And now I just don't know—
HARRY (*calling from garage*)
Helen!
HELEN
Harry?'

HARRY
Helen, my experiments.
HELEN
Harry, what?

HARRY
A terrible mistake.
HELEN
Harry, your voice—

HARRY (*his voice getting lower and gruffer*)
For the love of heaven, Helen, keep away from me.

HELEN
What happened?

HARRY

I can't restrain myself anymore. I'm coming through the garage door. (*comes through the garage door, wearing a monster mask; his voice is now very deep and gruff*) I'm irresistibly attracted to you, Helen, irresistibly.

HELEN

Eeeeeeeeeeeeeeeeeeeek!

HARRY (*stepping toward her*)

Helen, I love you. (*goes to embrace her*)

HELEN

Harry, you're hideous. Eeeeek! Eeeeeeeeeeeek! Eeeeeeeeeeeek!

As HELEN *screams*, WONDERBOY *is discovered, in mufti, doing his homework.*

SUSAN

What was the point of that, Hal?

HAL

No point.

WONDERBOY

Two superquantums plus five uranium neutrons, and I've got the mini-sub fuel. Hooray. Boy, will my friends in the U.S. Navy be pleased. Hey, what's that? Better use my wonder-vision. Helen Fargis seems to be in trouble. Better change to Wonderboy. (*as if throwing open his shirt*) And fly over there in a flash. (*jumping as if flying*) I guess I'm in the nick of time. (*with one super-powerful punch in the jaw he subdues* HARRY, *the monster*)

HELEN

Oh, Wonderboy, what would have happened if you hadn't come? But what will happen to IT?

WONDERBOY

I'll fly him to a distant zoo where they'll take good care of him.

HELEN

Oh, Wonderboy, how can I ever repay you?

WONDERBOY

Are those home-baked cookies I smell?

HELEN *smiles at* WONDERBOY *through her tears; he puts his arm around her shoulders.*

SUSAN

The president of the company has an Eames chair.

GEORGE
How do you know that?

SUSAN
Jennifer showed it to me.
GEORGE
You asked to see it?

SUSAN
Don't worry George. He wasn't there. I just had this crazy wild impulse as I was passing his office. I wanted to see what it looked like. Isn't that wild?

HAL
Did you sit in it?

SUSAN
I didn't dare. What would I have said if he'd come in?

GEORGE *goes to the rest room.*

HAL
I love you, Mr. President of my great big company, and that's why I'm sitting in your nice warm leather arm chair.
SUSAN
You're perverted. I don't want to be a person working in a company who's never seen her president.

WONDERBOY
Tune in tomorrow, boys and girls, when I'll subdue a whole country full of monsters.

(*Slide: "Winners Eat Wondrex."*)

WONDERBOY
And in the meantime, remember: winners eat Wondrex. (*smiles and jumps in the air, as if flying away*)

(*Slide: little girls with shopping bags.*)

FIRST NEWS ANNOUNCER
Little girls with big shopping bags means back to school season is here again. Among the many shoppers in downtown New York were Darlene, nine, Lila, four, and Lucy Gladden, seven, of Lynbrook, Long Island.

(*Slide: the Vice President.*)

FIRST NEWS ANNOUNCER
In Washington, D.C., as he left John Foster Dulles Airport, as President Johnson's favorite

(*Slide: second view of the Vice President.*)

FIRST NEWS ANNOUNCER
representative, the Vice President said he was bursting with confidence.

(*Slide: first view of Vietnamese mourners.*)

SUSAN (*to* HAL, *who has gotten up*)
While you're up—
HAL
What?
SUSAN
You know. Get me a Coke. (*titters at her own joke*)

HAL *goes out through the hall door.* GEORGE *returns from the rest room.*

GEORGE (*turning TV sound off*)
Can I come over tonight?

SUSAN
Not tonight. (*goes to bulletin board*)

GEORGE (*following her*)
Why not tonight?
SUSAN
Because I don't feel like it.
GEORGE
You have a date?
SUSAN
What business is that of yours? Don't think because—
GEORGE
Who with?

SECOND NEWS ANNOUNCER
U.S. spokesmen in Saigon said families would be given adequate shelter and compensation. Our planes are under strict orders not to return to base with any bombs. The United States regrets that a friendly village was hit. The native toll was estimated at sixty.

(*Slide: second view of Vietnamese mourners.*)

SECOND NEWS ANNOUNCER
This was high, explained spokesmen, in answer to questions, because of the type of bomb dropped. These are known as Lazy Dogs. Each Lazy Dog bomb contains ten thousand slivers of razor-sharp steel.

(*Slide: third view of Vietnamese mourners.*)

Volume off.

(*Slide: a pack of Longford cigarettes superimposed on a lake.*)

Two PEOPLE ON TELEVISION *do a silent commercial for Longford cigarettes: a man lights a woman's cigarette and she looks pleased.*

SUSAN

None of your business.

GEORGE

What about late, after you get back, like one o'clock?

SUSAN

That's too late. I need lots of sleep.

GEORGE

I'll call first.

SUSAN

You'd better.

Whenever HAL, SUSAN, *and* GEORGE *have nothing else to do, they stare straight ahead, as if at a television screen.* GEORGE *and* SUSAN *do this now.* HAL *comes back with two Cokes.* GEORGE *goes to the telephone and dials it.*

GEORGE

Hello, dear. Yes, I'm here. Listen, I'm afraid I have to take the midnight to three shift.

HAL *turns TV volume on.*

GEORGE

I've got to. The night supervisor is out.

GEORGE

And I've already said I would.

GEORGE

Listen, let's talk about it over dinner, huh? I'll be out after you go to sleep and in before you wake up so what's the difference? Listen, let's talk about it over dinner, I said. Listen, I love you. Goodbye. (*hangs up*)

HAL (*watching TV intently but talking to George*)

You have to take the midnight to three shift, George? That's really too bad.

(Slide on the screen: "The Endless Frontier.")

SALLY *and* BILL *are two characters in the Western.*

SALLY

Don't go, Bill.

BILL

I've got to.

SALLY

Oh, Bill.

BILL *leaves.*

SALLY

Oh, Bill.

SALLY *fixes her hair in the mirrow.*

SALLY *is surprised by* STEVE, *the villain, who has just been waiting for* BILL *to ride off.*

SALLY

Steve!

HAL

Got a call while I was out?

GEORGE (*snapping TV volume off*)

Do either of you want to take on some evening overtime this week?

SUSAN

Which?

GEORGE

Five to midnight Tuesday and Thursday.

HAL

Thursday.

SUSAN

Oh, all right, I'll take Tuesday.

HAL

Did you want Thursday?

SUSAN

I'd like to get the apartment finished.

HAL

Then give me Tuesday.

SUSAN

Not if you HAVE something on Thursday.

HAL

No sweat.

SUSAN

Oh, I know. It was that talk with that man.

HAL *turns TV volume on.*

GEORGE (*snapping TV volume off*)

What talk with what man?

SUSAN

A man he has to talk to.

GEORGE

About a job?

HAL

I probably won't even see him.

GEORGE

What kind of job?

HAL

For the government. I tell you I probably won't see him.

STEVE

Bill's dead, Sally.

SALLY

I don't believe you.

Volume off.

STEVE *tries to embrace* SALLY. *She slaps him hard as he approaches her. He tries it again. She slaps him again. He tries it a third time. She gets him a third time. Then he grabs and kisses her despite her terrible struggling.*

BILL, *his arm wounded, appears again. Seeing* STEVE *with* SALLY, *he draws and aims.*

BILL

Sally, duck!

Volume off.

SALLY *ducks.* BILL *shoots* STEVE, *then goes to* SALLY *to make sure she's all right.* STEVE, *however, is not badly wounded and he reaches for* BILL's *gun. The gun falls to the floor and they fight.* SALLY *tries to get into the fight but is pushed away.*

GEORGE

If you quit, Hal, I'll need three weeks' notice. If you care about severance pay.

HAL (*turning TV volume on*)

I haven't seen him yet, even.

GEORGE

Or about me.

HAL

I wasn't going to mention it.

SUSAN

I'm sorry. It was my fault.

GEORGE (*turning volume off*)

Just don't spring anything on me. If you don't like the job, leave. But don't spring anything on me because I can't take it, you know that.

HAL

George, I'm NOT quitting.

SUSAN

He likes this job too much, George.

HAL

I love it more than my own life. I wouldn't leave it for all the world. Honest Injun, George. (*turns volume on*)

GEORGE

Can you imagine what I'd have to go through to train another person? Can you?

SUSAN

Listen, I just remembered a joke. There's this writing on the subway. "I love grills" it says on the wall. So somebody crosses out "grills" and writes in "girls." "I love

BILL *is losing his fight with* STEVE *because of his wounded arm.* STEVE *is about to get the gun.*

SALLY (*warningly*)

Bill!

Volume off.

In the nick of time, SALLY *shoots* STEVE *in the back with a rifle. As he falls he makes a mute appeal to her. He is dead now and she is appalled at what she's done.*

SALLY (*embracing* BILL)

Oh, Bill!

BILL

I love you, Sally.

SALLY (*touched*)

Oh, Bill.

BILL

Let's move to another town.

SALLY (*delighted*)

Oh Bill.

BILL *and* SALLY *ride off together into the dusk.*

girls" it says now. And then somebody else writes in, "What about us grills?" (*laughs and laughs over this*)

SUSAN

What about us grills? Isn't that fantastic?

HAL

What's the matter with you?

SUSAN (*still laughing*)

I think that's the funniest thing I ever heard.

HAL

Shhhh.

SUSAN *continues laughing.*

HAL

Shhhhh. Stop it.

SUSAN

I can't.

SUSAN

I can't stop. Get the water.

GEORGE *gets up to get some water.* HAL *wants to watch TV and can't hear it at all because of* SUSAN'S *laughter.*

HAL

This is easier. (*slaps* SUSAN *very hard on the face*)

(*Slide: the President and his family.*)

SECOND NEWS ANNOUNCER

The President is accompanied by his wife, Lady Bird Johnson, and by his two daughters, Lynda Bird Johnson and Luci Baines Johnson Nugent, who lives in nearby Austin with her husband Patrick Nugent, President Johnson's son-in-law.

(*Slide: second view of the* PRESIDENT *and his family.*)

The PRESIDENT *appears at a podium reading a speech. He is indeed accompanied by his wife and daughters.*

(*Slide: the* PRESIDENT *alone.*)

PRESIDENT

We will stamp out aggression wherever and whenever.

PRESIDENT

We will tighten our defenses and fight, to guarantee the peace of our children, our children's children, and their children.

PRESIDENT

That all men are not well-intentioned or well-informed or even basically good, is unfortunate.

465   Jean-Claude van Itallie

SUSAN
Ow!

SUSAN
Just who do you think you are!

HAL
Are you finished?
SUSAN
I couldn't help it.

SUSAN
Sadist.

SUSAN
Why didn't anyone get water?
GEORGE
Don't look at me.

SUSAN
You don't slap people because they're sick.

HAL
Every day we go through the same thing.
You laugh. We bring you water. You spill
the water all over everybody, and half an
hour later you stop.

SUSAN
Give me the water, George. I'm going to
take a pill.

PRESIDENT
But these people will not be indulged.

Applause by the PRESIDENT's *family. No sound
in this play need be put on tape; all of it can
be provided by the* PEOPLE ON TELEVISION.

PRESIDENT
Those who are our friends will declare
themselves publicly. The others, we will not
tolerate.

(*Slide: second view of the President alone.*)

PRESIDENT
Belief in American success and victory is
the cornerstone of our faith.

PRESIDENT
Whatever else may chance to happen on
far-off shores, nothing, I repeat nothing,
will be allowed to disturb the serenity of
our cities and suburbs, and when we fight
we fight for a safer and more comfortable
America, now and in years to come. Thank
you.

(*Slide: third view of the President and his
family.*)

SECOND NEWS ANNOUNCER
The President and his family will now be
cheered by the cadet corps.

The PRESIDENT *and his family respond to
cheers like mechanical dolls. Turning his
back, the* SECOND NEWS ANNOUNCER *provides*

GEORGE
What makes you laugh like that?

HAL *lowers the volume but does not turn it off.*

SUSAN
I'm a hysteric. I mean I'm not constantly hysterical but sometimes I get that way. I react that way, through my body. You're a compulsive, Hal, a nasty little compulsive.

HAL (*turning volume off*)
How do you know?
SUSAN
I've discussed it with my analyst. Hysterics react through their bodies. Compulsives react compulsively.
GEORGE
What does he say about me?
SUSAN
He doesn't.
GEORGE
Hmph.
HAL
How long have you been going now? Twenty-seven years?
SUSAN
A year, wise guy.
HAL
How long do you expect to be going?
SUSAN
It might take another two or three years.
GEORGE
I know people who have gone for ten or twelve years.
HAL
Don't you think that's a lot?
GEORGE
If you need it, you need it. It's a sickness like any other sickness. It's got to be looked after.

us with one hummed bar of "So Hello Lyndon."

A SPANISH TEACHER *appears.*

(*Slide: the Spanish Teacher's face.*)

Volume low.

SPANISH TEACHER
Buenos dias muchachos and muchachas. Hello, boys and girls. Muchachos. Boys. Muchachas. Girls. Aqui es la casa. Here is the house. Casa. House.

Volume off.

The SPANISH TEACHER *finishes the lesson.*

Efficient Researchers walk back and forth across the stage, checking things, nodding at each other curtly, and so on.

(*Slide: the efficient researchers.*)

HAL
   What did they do in the old days?
GEORGE (*turning volume up*)
   They stayed sick.

Volume up.

UGP ANNOUNCER
   Who are they? They are a community of
   devotion.

(*Slide: "UGP" in very Germanic lettering.*)

UGP ANNOUNCER
   Men and women whose lives are dedicated
   to the researching of more perfect products
   for you. Get the benefit of a community of
   devotion. Look for the letters UGP whenever you buy a car, radio, television set, or
   any of a thousand other products. Their
   tool: devotion. Their goal: perfection.

(*Slide: a civil rights demonstration.*)

SUSAN
   My analyst has been going to HIS analyst
   for twenty-five years.
HAL
   How do you know?
SUSAN
   He told me.

FIRST NEWS ANNOUNCER
   Three men were critically injured during a
   civil rights demonstration in Montgomery,
   Alabama today.

GEORGE
   Can you feel the tranquilizer working?
SUSAN
   A little bit. I think so.

(*Slide: the Vice President.*)

FIRST NEWS ANNOUNCER
   This afternoon the Vice President arrived
   in Honolulu. As he stepped off the plane he
   told newsmen things are looking up.

(*Slide: a map of China.*)

GEORGE
   Maybe I should have one too.

FIRST NEWS ANNOUNCER
   The Defense Department today conceded
   that United States aircraft may have mis-
   takenly flown over Chinese territory last

SUSAN (*turning volume off.*)
Are you upset?

GEORGE
I can feel my stomach.

SUSAN (*reaching into her bag to give him a pill*)
Here.
GEORGE
I'd like some coffee.
HAL
I'd like some lunch.
SUSAN
Lunch! I'll get it. (*dashes into her coat and is almost out the door*)
HAL
Hey!
SUSAN
Rare with onion and a danish. I know. So long, you guys.
HAL (*throwing his penknife into the bulletin board*)
Think she's all right?
GEORGE
People wouldn't say this was a crazy office or anything like that.
HAL
Nope.
GEORGE
She's really a nice girl, isn't she?
HAL (*doing calisthenics*)
Yup.
GEORGE
You like her, don't you?
HAL
Yup.
GEORGE
I mean you don't just think she's a good lay, do you?
HAL
What makes you think I lay her?
GEORGE
Well, don't you?
HAL
George, that's an old trick.

month. It regrets the incident.

Volume off.

(*Slide: a rock and roll group.*)

A ROCK AND ROLL GROUP *is seen singing and playing.*

GEORGE
I'm just trying to find out if you really like her.

HAL
Why do you care?

GEORGE
I feel protective.

HAL
That's right. She's half your age, isn't she?

GEORGE
Not exactly half.

HAL
How old are you, George, exactly?

GEORGE
Forty-three.

HAL (*crossing to water cooler*)
Humph.

GEORGE
What's that mean?

HAL
I was just wondering what it was like to be forty-three.

GEORGE
It stinks.

HAL
That's what I thought.

GEORGE
You'll be forty-three sooner than you think.

HAL
I'll never be forty-three.

GEORGE
Why not?

HAL
I don't intend to live that long.

The ROCK AND ROLL GROUP *bows.*

GEORGE
You have something?

(*Slide: a group of peace marchers.*)

HAL
No. I just don't intend to live that long. (*returns to console and turns volume on*)

A group of PEACE MARCHERS *appears.*

FIRST NEWS ANNOUNCER
A group of so-called peaceniks marched down the center mall of the capital today, singing:

GEORGE (*sits*)
You're probably a socialist.

The PEACE MARCHERS *sing "We Shall Overcome."*

HAL
   A socialist?
GEORGE
   A socialist at twenty and a Republican at
forty. Everybody goes through that cycle.

FIRST NEWS ANNOUNCER
   One young man from New York City pre-
dicted:
ONE YOUNG MAN FROM NEW YORK CITY
   The Washington Monument's going to burst
into bloom and—

*It is as if the sound were cut off on the word
he was going to say, but we can read "Fuck"
on his lips.*

(Slide: Annie Kappelhoff.)

GEORGE
   It's healthy.

FIRST NEWS ANNOUNCER
   A little girl, Annie Kappelhoff, had her own
opinion:
ANNIE (*as if leading a cheer*)
   Burn yourselves, not your draft cards, burn
yourselves, not your draft cards—

The sound is cut off on ANNIE, *too, as she
continues the same cheer.*

FIRST NEWS ANNOUNCER
   Later in the day Annie was the star of her
own parade. She's head-cheerleader of Wilu-
met High School in Maryland. Today Annie
cheered her team on to victory, thirty to
nothing, over neighboring South Dearing.
Annie is also an ardent supporter of the
young American Nazi party, and hopes
to become a model. And now, a message.

(Slide: a jar of K-F soap-cream.)

HAL
   Are you a Republican, George?

FAMOUS TV PERSONALITY
   Are you one of those lucky women who has
all the time in the world?

GEORGE
   That's right.
HAL
   You know I have a lot of friends who won't
even speak to Republicans.

GEORGE
  I'd rather not discuss politics.
HAL
  Why not?
GEORGE
  Because we probably don't see eye to eye.
HAL
  So?
GEORGE
  So I'd rather not discuss it. And my stomach's upset.

FAMOUS TV PERSONALITY
  Or are you like most of us: busy, busy, busy all day long with home or job so that when evening comes you hardly have time to wash your face, much less transform yourself into the living doll he loves.

FAMOUS TV PERSONALITY
  Well then, K-F is for you. More than a soap. More than a cream. It's a soap-cream. You apply it in less time than it takes to wash your face and it leaves your skin tingling with loveliness. Try it. And for an extra super thrill, use it in the shower.

(*Slide: Lily Heaven.*)

LILY HEAVEN'S ANNOUNCER
  The Lily Heaven Show, ladies and gentlemen, starring that great star of stage, screen, and television: Lily Heaven.

Out through imaginary curtains comes LILY HEAVEN, *very starlike. She greets her audience in her own inimitable way. She sings a line from a popular American love song.*

There is a special knock on the viewing room door.

HAL
  What's that?
GEORGE
  Nothing.

GEORGE *turns volume off.*

Volume off.

HAL
  What do you mean, nothing?
GEORGE (*calling*)
  One minute.
HAL (*getting panicky*)
  One minute until what?

(*Slide: a second view of Lily Heaven.*)

GEORGE *turns out the lights in the viewing room.*

HAL
   I knew it. What's going on?
GEORGE (*calling*)
   Okay.
HAL
   Okay what? What? What?
SUSAN (*coming through the door with a cake with lighted candles on it*)
   Okay this, stupid.
HAL
   Oh my God, you're crazy.
SUSAN AND GEORGE
   One, two, three.
      (*singing*)
   Happy Birthday to you,
   Happy Birthday to you,
   Happy Birthday dear Ha-al,
   Happy Birthday to you.

SUSAN *kisses* HAL *on the lips.*

SUSAN
   Happy Birthday. You had no idea, did you?
HAL
   No.
GEORGE
   Happy Birthday.
HAL
   Thanks a lot.
SUSAN
   Make a wish and blow.

HAL *blows on the candles but doesn't get them all.*

SUSAN
   Well, almost.

GEORGE *turns the viewing room lights on again, and* SUSAN *gets two presents from the closet.*

SUSAN
   People thought I was crazy walking down

the hall with this cake and this lunch in a paper bag. And I was petrified one of you would swing the door open while I was waiting in the corridor and knock me down and the cake and everything. I was almost sure you'd guessed, Hal, when I put the presents in my locker this morning.

HAL

I hadn't.

SUSAN

I love birthdays. I know it's childish but I really do. Look at the card on George's.

HAL

It's cute.

SUSAN

Open it.

HAL *opens the package. It's a tie.*

HAL

Well thanks, George. I can use this. (*makes a mock noose of it around his neck*)

GEORGE

You're welcome.

SUSAN (*looking at the label as if she hadn't seen it before*)

It's a good tie.

GEORGE

What'd you expect?

GEORGE *is biting into an egg salad sandwich.* HAL *starts to open the second present.*

SUSAN (*stopping* HAL)

Save mine for when we eat the cake, so the birthday will last longer.

HAL

George, there's egg salad all over the dials.

GEORGE (*turning volume on*)

Sorry.

SUSAN

Here's a napkin. I'll make some coffee.

GEORGE

Good.

LILY HEAVEN *finishes singing and bows.*

LILY HEAVEN

So long, everybody.

LILY HEAVEN

This is Lily Heaven saying so long.

Applause from part of LILY HEAVEN's *audience, played by the* PEOPLE ON TELEVISION, *who stand behind her.*

GEORGE *and* HAL *are mesmerized by* LILY HEAVEN. SUSAN *is paying no attention but is fussing with the coffee things and putting paper bags, as party hats, on* HAL *and* GEORGE.

GEORGE
Give me another of those tranquilizers, please. The first one doesn't seem to have done a thing.

HAL *turns the volume off.* SUSAN *has plugged in the hot plate and coffee maker. She also has some real coffee and a jar of dried cream, some sugar and sugar substitute in little bags stolen from a luncheonette, napkins and little wooden stick-stirrers.*

HAL (*who has been opening his present*)
Say, this is nice.
SUSAN
It's an art book.
HAL
I can see that.
GEORGE
Hal especially interested in art?
SUSAN
A person doesn't have to be especially interested in art to like it.
HAL
It must have cost a lot, Susan. Here, George.

LILY HEAVEN (*as if each sentence were her last*)
Here's wishing you a good week before we meet again. From all of us here to all of you out there: so long. Thanks a lot and God bless you. This is Lily signing off. I only hope that you enjoyed watching us as much as we enjoyed being here. So long. It's been wonderful being with you. Really grand, and I hope you'll invite us into your living room again next week. I only wish we could go on but I'm afraid it's time to say so long, so from the actors and myself, from the staff here, I want to wish you all a very very good week. This is your Lily saying so long to you. So long. So long. So long. So long. Have a happy, and so long. Till next week. Bye. So long. Bye. So long.

(*Slide: a weather map.*)

WEATHER ANNOUNCER
And now, the weather.

Volume off.

(*passes* GEORGE *a piece of cake*)

SUSAN

Well, as a matter of fact, I got it on sale at Marboro.

HAL

If I had a place for it everything would be fine. Cake, Susan?

SUSAN (*to* GEORGE)

Hal still doesn't have a place.

GEORGE

What kind of place are you looking for?

HAL

I'd like to find an apartment with more than one small room for under a hundred dollars.

SUSAN

Do you want to live in the Village?

HAL

Makes no difference.

GEORGE

Don't live down there.

SUSAN

Why not?

GEORGE

It's too crowded.

SUSAN

It's not so crowded, and in the Village you can see a lot of wonderful faces.

GEORGE

Yes, well frankly I've been working for a living for twenty-one years and I resent having to support a lot of bums on relief.

SUSAN

That's not the Village. That's the Bowery.

GEORGE

Let's not talk about it.

SUSAN

Why not?

GEORGE

I already told Hal that people with differing points of view shouldn't talk about politics. And I shouldn't be eating this cake either. (*snaps volume on*)

(*Slide: Miracle Headache Pills.*)

Still without volume, an advertisement for Miracle Headache Pills: a woman is seen before and after taking the pills.

LADY ANNOUNCER *begins to speak, still without volume.*

(*Slide: First Federal Savings Bank.*)

LADY ANNOUNCER

And now First Federal Savings and Kennel-Heart Dog Food present Luncheon With Carol, a program especially designed for the up-to-date woman. Our topic for today: I Quit. And here's Carol.

(Slide: Carol and Ron Campbell.)

CAROL

Hello, ladies. This is Carol. I have as my guest today Mr. Ron Campbell just back from an eighteen month tour of duty in Vietnam. Mr. Campbell was a member of the famed Green Berets. He is a holder of the Bronze Star and the South Vietnamese Order of Merit; he has been nominated for the U.S. Silver Star. A few weeks ago he was offered a field commission as captain. But instead of accepting, what did you do, Ron?

RON

I quit.

CAROL

That's right, you quit. Tell us why you quit, Ron, when you were obviously doing so well.

RON

I didn't like being there.

CAROL

You didn't?

RON

No.

CAROL (*cheerfully*)

I see.

RON

We're committing mass murder.

CAROL (*interested*)

Yes?

RON

We're trying to take over a people that don't want to be taken over by anybody.

CAROL

Now, Ron, American boys are out there dying so somebody must be doing something wrong somewhere.

RON

Whoever in Hanoi or Peking or Washington is sending men out to be killed, THEY'RE doing something wrong.

CAROL (*interested in his opinion, tolerant*)

I see.

RON

You do? Well I was there for a year and a

half and every day I saw things that would make you sick. Heads broken, babies smashed against walls—

CAROL (*deeply sympathetic*)
I KNOW.

RON
You know?

CAROL
War is horrible.

RON
Listen—

CAROL
Thank you, Ron. We've been talking this afternoon, ladies, with Ron Campbell, war hero.

RON
Will you let me say something, please?

CAROL (*tolerating him, kindly*)
And a fascinating talk it's been, Ron, but I'm afraid our time is up.

RON
One—

CAROL (*with her special smile for the ladies*)
Ladies, see you all tomorrow.

SUSAN (*dreamily*)
I think I'm floating further and further left.

GEORGE
You don't know a thing about it.

SUSAN
I was listening to Norman Thomas last night—

LADY ANNOUNCER
This program was brought to you by First Federal Savings and Kennel-Heart Dog Food. The opinions expressed on this program are not necessarily those of anyone connected with it. A dog in the home means a dog with a heart.

(*Slide: Kennel-Heart Dog Food.*)

LADY ANNOUNCER
Kennel-Heart. Bow-wow. Wow.

(*Slide: "Billion Dollar Movie."*)

GEORGE
I'm going to the Men's Room.

SUSAN
Poor George.

HAL
You still haven't told me about tonight.

SUSAN

Told you what about tonight?

HAL

Are we going to the movies or are we not going to the movies?

SUSAN

I don't know. I can't make up my mind.

HAL

That's just fine.

SUSAN

I want to work on my apartment.

HAL

Okay.

SUSAN

I should really get it done.

HAL

You're right.

SUSAN

Suppose I let you know by the end of the afternoon?

HAL

Suppose we forget I ever suggested it.

A very English man and a very English woman appear in the movie.

HE

Sarah.

SHE

Yes, Richard.

HE

Our old apartment.

SHE

Yes, Richard. It's still here.

HE

It seems very small to me.

SHE

It does to me, too.

HE

Do you think we can live in it again?

SHE

Not in the old way.

HE

In a better way.

SHE

You've changed too, Richard, for the better.

HE

So have you, darling, for the better.

SHE

I've learned a lot.

HE

Maybe that's what war is for.

479 Jean-Claude van Itallie

SUSAN

Oh, all right, I'll go. Happy?

HAL

I'm so happy I could put a bullet through my brain.

SUSAN

Sugar?

HAL

You're like my grandmother.

SUSAN

How?

HAL

She asked me if I took sugar every day we lived together. It was very comforting.

HAL

Hal, she used to say to me, my grandmother, you're going to be a big man.

HAL

Everybody's going to love you. She used to sing that song to me: "Poppa's gonna buy you a dog named Rover, and if that dog don't bark, Poppa's gonna buy you a looking glass, and if that looking glass should

The PEOPLE ON TELEVISION *hum "White Cliffs of Dover" under the following.*

SHE

The brick wall in front of the window is gone.

HE

We'll rebuild for the future.

SHE

I hope there is never any more war. Ever, ever again.

HE

Amen.

(*Slide: "The End."*)

The PEOPLE ON TELEVISION *sing, meaningfully, the last line of "White Cliffs of Dover": "To-morrow, just you wait and see."*

FIRST NEWS ANNOUNCER *appears.*

(*Slide: baseball player.*)

FIRST NEWS ANNOUNCER

Baseball's Greg Pironelli, fifty-six, died to-day of a heart attack in St. Petersburg, Florida. He hit a total of four hundred and eighty home runs and had a lifetime batting average of three forty-one.

(*Slide: a baseball game.*)

FIRST NEWS ANNOUNCER

In 1963, the year he was elected to base-ball's hall of fame in Cooperstown, New York, Pironelli suffered his first stroke. Pi-

break, you're still the sweetest little boy in town."

SUSAN
That's nice.

GEORGE *enters and goes directly to telephone.*

GEORGE
Hello, darling? Listen, I've gotten out of it. Isn't that good news? The midnight shift.

GEORGE
I'm looking forward to being home nice and comfy with you.

GEORGE
You know my stomach is killing me. Sure I will. Wait a minute.

GEORGE *takes out a pencil.*

GEORGE
Toothpaste. Cauliflower. That's a good idea.

GEORGE
Large face cream. Why large? No, I don't care. I was just asking.

GEORGE
Okay. Listen, I'm really looking forward to seeing you.

ronelli owned a Florida-wide chain of laundries.

(*Slide: "Johnny Holland Show."*)

JOHNNY
We're back.

(*Slide: Johnny and Luci.*)

JOHNNY
That's a very pretty dress you've got on, Luci.
LUCI
Thank you, Johnny.

JOHNNY
How does it feel living in Austin after all the excitement of the big wedding?
LUCI
It feels fine.

JOHNNY
Do you miss your father?

LUCI
Oh sure, I miss him.

JOHNNY (*awkward pause*)
I guess your heart belongs to Daddy, huh?
LUCI
That's right.

JOHNNY (*awkward pause*)
Is your father hard to get along with?

GEORGE

No, I haven't been drinking, and it's rotten
of you to ask.

GEORGE

Okay, okay. Bye. (*hangs up telephone*)

SUSAN

Have a little coffee, George.

GEORGE

No, thanks.

HAL

Oh, come on, George, have a little coffee.

GEORGE

A sip.

SUSAN

Sugar or superine?

LUCI

Oh, no. When I want something I just
march right in, cuddle up in his lap, and
give him a great big kiss.

(*Slide: a second view of Johnny and Luci.*)

JOHNNY (*awkward pause*)

So you'd say your father is affectionate?

LUCI

Very affectionate.

JOHNNY (*awkward pause*)

Does he ever ask your advice about important matters?

LUCI

Well, one day I told him what I thought,
good and proper, about all those nervous
nellies interfering with my Daddy's war.

JOHNNY *does a double take of scandalized
amusement to the audience.*

(*Slide: Johnny doing double take.*)

JOHNNY

And what did he say?

LUCI

He laughed.

JOHNNY

It's lovely talking to you, Luci.

GEORGE
Sugar.

SUSAN
George.
GEORGE
Don't take care of me. I said sugar.
SUSAN
Whatever you want, George.

SUSAN
George, what are you eating now?
GEORGE
Chicken sandwich.
SUSAN
Give me a bite.

HAL *plays with his penknife.* SUSAN *eats another piece of cake.* GEORGE *eats his chicken sandwich.*

GEORGE *starts to cough.*

SUSAN
What's the matter, George?

GEORGE *motions her away and continues to cough.*

LUCI
It's nice talking to you too, Johnny.
JOHNNY
We'll be back.

(*Slide: "Johnny Holland Show."*)

An EVANGELIST *appears with his choir, which is singing "Onward Christian Soldiers."*

(*Slide: the Evangelist.*)

EVANGELIST
If we could look through the ceiling of this wonderful new air-conditioned stadium we could see the stars. Nonetheless I have heard them in faraway countries, I have heard them criticize, criticize us and the leaders we know and love.

EVANGELIST
Why? Well I will tell you why. They criticize us because we are rich, as if money itself were evil. Money, the Bible says, is the root of evil, not evil itself. I have seen a roomful of men and women, powerful Hollywood celebrities at four o'clock A.M. in the morning, listening to me with tears streaming down their faces crying out to me that they had lost touch with God.

EVANGELIST
"In God We Trust" is on our coins, ladies and gentlemen—

(*Slide: a second view of the Evangelist.*)

The EVANGELIST CHOIR *sings "Onward Christian Soldiers."*

483 Jean-Claude van Itallie

HAL (*turning volume off*)   *Volume off.*

  Spit it out, George.

SUSAN

  Hal, leave him alone.

HAL

  George, spit it out. (*thumps* GEORGE *on the back*)

SUSAN

  Hal! George, is it epilepsy?

HAL

  It's something in his throat.

SUSAN

  Try to tell us what it is, George.

HAL AND GEORGE

  Chicken!

HAL

  He has a chicken bone stuck in his throat.

SUSAN

  Oh my God. Well give him some water.

GEORGE's *choking is getting worse.*

HAL

  Water will wash right by it. Let me look. (*holds* GEORGE'S *head and looks into his mouth*) Don't move, George. I want to take a look. (*looks in* GEORGE'S *mouth*) There it is.

SUSAN (*also looking*)

  Ugh, it's stuck in his throat. I'll get some water.

HAL *and* SUSAN *let go of* GEORGE, *who falls to the floor.*

HAL

  Not water.

SUSAN

  Why not?

HAL

  Because water will wash right past the thing. It needs something to push it out.

SUSAN

  Like what?

HAL

  Like bread.

SUSAN

  Bread? Bread will get stuck on the bone and

he'll choke.

HAL

You're wrong.

SUSAN

I'm right.

HAL

Bread will push it right down.

SUSAN

Water will do that.

HAL

You're wrong.

SUSAN

It's you that's wrong and won't admit it.

HAL

I'm going to give him some bread.

SUSAN

I won't allow it.

HAL

YOU won't allow it?

SUSAN

It'll kill him.

HAL

He's choking right now and I'm going to give him some of this bread.

SUSAN

Give him water.

HAL

I said bread.

SUSAN (*starting to walk past* HAL)

And I said water.

HAL (*grabbing her arm*)

Bread.

SUSAN

Water. Ow, you're hurting me.

GEORGE *is having a very bad time.* HAL *and* SUSAN *turn to look at him, speaking softly.*

SUSAN

Let's call the operator.

HAL

It would take too long.

SUSAN

And he wouldn't like anyone to see him.

HAL

Why not?

SUSAN

I don't know.

At this point GEORGE *finally coughs the thing up, and his cough subsides into an animal pant.*

SUSAN (*going to him, patting him*)

Poor George.

HAL

It's over.

SUSAN

No thanks to you.

HAL

Nor you.

SUSAN (*putting* GEORGE'S *head on her breast*)

He might have choked. Poor George.

GEORGE (*pushing her away*)

Fuck!

GEORGE *lurches against the console on his way to the bathroom, accidentally turning on the volume.*

EVANGELIST CHOIR (*still singing "Onward Christian Soldiers."*)

"With the cross of Jesus—"

(*Slide: Mother, Father, and Daughter in "My Favorite Teenager."*)

HAL *changes channels from the* EVANGELIST'S *meeting to "My Favorite Teenager."*

SUSAN (*sitting in her chair*)

Poor George.

MOTHER

Why aren't you going?

DAUGHTER (*sitting in* GEORGE'S *chair at the control console*)

Because I told Harold Sternpepper he could take me.

MOTHER

Yes, and—

DAUGHTER

Well, Harold Sternpepper is a creep. Everybody knows that.

The remaining PEOPLE ON TELEVISION *make the sound of canned laughter.*

HAL (*sitting in his chair*)

What movie are we going to?

So, why—

DAUGHTER

Oh, because I was mad at Gail.

Canned laughter.

MOTHER

What about Johnny Beaumont?

SUSAN

I don't know.

DAUGHTER

What about him?

HAL

What about George?

MOTHER

Well, guess it's none of my business.

SUSAN

What about him?

FATHER

What's the matter?

HAL

Well, I guess it's none of my business.

GEORGE (*returning*)

What's the matter?

(*Slide: second view of Mother, Father, and Daughter in "My Favorite Teenager."*)

DAUGHTER

Nothing.

FATHER

Why aren't you dressed for the prom?

DAUGHTER

I'm not going to the prom.

SUSAN

Nothing.

GEORGE

Going somewhere?

FATHER

Why not? Why isn't she going, Grace?

MOTHER

Don't ask me. I just live here.

SUSAN

We're going to the movies.

Canned laughter.

FATHER

Why doesn't anybody tell me anything around here?

HAL *and* SUSAN *and* GEORGE *are slowing down because they are mesmerized by "My Favorite Teenager."*

Canned laughter.

DAUGHTER (*getting up from* GEORGE's *chair*)

Oh, why don't you two leave me alone? I'm not going because nobody's taking me.

GEORGE

What movie are you going to?

GEORGE
Mind if I come along?

SUSAN
Oh, George, you don't really want to.

GEORGE
I'd be pleased as punch.

SUSAN
Hal, say something.

HAL (*to* GEORGE)
You look bushed to me, George.

GEORGE
Who's bushed?

GEORGE *sits in his chair.*

HAL, SUSAN, *and* GEORGE *are completely mesmerized by the TV show.*

FATHER (*sitting on* GEORGE'S *chair*)
Nobody's taking my little girl to the junior prom? I'll take her myself.

DAUGHTER (*stifling a yelp of horror*)
Oh no, Daddy, don't bother. I mean how would it look, I mean—

FATHER
I'd be pleased as punch.

DAUGHTER (*aside to* MOTHER)
Help.

Canned laughter.

MOTHER (*to* FATHER)
Now, dear, don't you think for your age—

Canned laughter.

FATHER
My age?

Canned laughter.

FATHER (*standing and doing a two-step*)
I'd like to see anybody laugh at my two-step.

Canned laughter.

DAUGHTER (*in despair*)
Oh, Daddy. Mother, DO something.

Canned laughter.

MOTHER (*putting her arm around* GEORGE'S *shoulders*)
I think it's a very nice idea. And maybe I'll go with Harold Sternpepper.

Canned laughter.

DAUGHTER (*loudly, sitting on* HAL'S *knee*)
Oh, Mother, oh, Daddy, oh no!

The canned laughter mounts. Music.

(Slide: "My Favorite Teenager.")

Now they all speak like situation-comedy characters.

HAL
What movie shall we go to?

GEORGE
Let's talk about it over dinner.

HAL
Who said anything about dinner?

All of the PEOPLE ON TELEVISION *do canned laughter now. They are crowded around the control console.*

SUSAN
Isn't anybody going to ask me what I want to do?

Canned laughter.

GEORGE
Sure, what do you want, Susan?

HAL
It's up to you.

(Slide: Hal, Susan, and George with the same facial expressions they now have on the stage.)

SUSAN
Well, have I got a surprise for you two. I'M going home to fix up my apartment and you two can have dinner TOGETHER.

> HAL, SUSAN, *and* GEORGE *join in the canned laughter. Then, lights off. Slide off. Curtain call: all are in the same position, silent, their faces frozen into laughing masks.*

Motel: A Masque for Three Dolls

... after all our subtle colour and nervous rhythm, after the faint mixed tints of Conder, what more is possible? After us the Savage God.

W. B. Yeats

Characters

MOTEL-KEEPER

MAN

WOMAN

Lights come up on the MOTEL-KEEPER *doll. The intensity of the light will increase as the play continues.*

The MOTEL-KEEPER *doll is large, much larger than human size, but the impression of hugeness can come mainly from the fact that her head is at least three times larger than would be normal in proportion to her body. She is all gray. She has a large full skirt which reaches to the floor. She has squarish breasts. The hair curlers on her head suggest electronic receivers.*

The MOTEL-KEEPER *doll has eyeglasses which are mirrors. It doesn't matter what these mirrors reflect at any given moment. The audience may occasionally catch a glimpse of itself, or be bothered by reflections of light in the mirrors. It doesn't matter; the sensory nerves of the audience are not to be spared.*

The motel room in which the MOTEL-KEEPER *doll stands is anonymously modern, except for certain "homey" touches. A neon light blinks outside the window. The colors in the room, like the colors in the clothes on the* MAN *and* WOMAN *dolls, are violent combinations of oranges, pinks, and reds against a reflective plastic background.*

The MOTEL-KEEPER'S VOICE, *which never stops, comes from a loudspeaker, or from several loudspeakers in the theatre. The* VOICE *will be, at first, mellow and husky and then, as the light grows harsher and brighter, the* VOICE *will grow harsher too, more set in its pattern, hard finally, and patronizing and petty.*

An actor on platform shoes works the MOTEL-KEEPER *doll from inside it. The actor can move only the doll's arms or its entire body. As the* VOICE *begins, the arms move, and then the* MOTEL-KEEPER *doll fusses about the room in little circles.*

MOTEL-KEEPER'S VOICE: I am old. I am an old idea: the walls; that from which it springs forth. I enclose the nothing, making then a place in which it happens. I am the room: a Roman theatre where cheers break loose the lion; a railroad carriage in the forest at Compiègne, in 1918, and in 1941. I have been rooms of marble and rooms of cork, all letting forth an avalanche. Rooms of mud and rooms of silk. This room will be slashed too, as if by a scimitar, its contents spewed and yawned out. That is what happens. It is almost happening, in fact. I am this room.

As the MOTEL-KEEPER'S VOICE *continues, the doors at the back of the room open and headlights shine into the eyes of the audience; passing in front of the headlights, in silhouette, we see two more huge dolls, the* MAN *and the* WOMAN.

MOTEL-KEEPER'S VOICE: It's nice; not so fancy as some, but with all the conveniences. And a touch of home. The antimacassar comes from my mother's house in Boise. Boise, Idaho. Sits kind of nice, I think, on the Swedish swing. That's my own idea, you know. All modern, up-to-date, that's it—no motel on this route is more up-to-date. Or cleaner. Go look, then talk me a thing or two.

The WOMAN *doll enters. Her shoulders are thrown way back, like a girl posing for a calendar. Her breasts are particularly large and perfect, wiggleable if possible. She has a cherry-lipstick smile, blond hair, and a garish patterned dress.*

Both the MAN *and the* WOMAN *dolls are the same size as the* MOTEL-KEEPER *doll, with heads at least three times larger than would be* normal for their bodies. The MAN *and the* WOMAN *dolls, however, are flesh-colored and have more mobility. The actors inside these dolls are also on platform shoes. There is absolutely no rapport between the* MOTEL-KEEPER *and the* MAN *and* WOMAN. All of the MOTEL-KEEPER'S *remarks are addressed generally. She is never directly motivated by the actions of the* MAN *and* WOMAN *dolls.*

As the WOMAN *doll enters, she puts down her purse and inspects the room. Then she takes off her dress, revealing lace panties and bra.*

MOTEL-KEEPER'S VOICE: All modern here but, as I say, with the tang of home. Do you understand? When folks are fatigued, in a strange place? Not that it's old-fashioned. No. Not in the wrong way. There's a push-button here for TV. The toilet flushes of its own accord. All you've got to do is get off. Pardon my mentioning it, but you'll have to go far before you see a thing like that on this route. Oh, it's quite a room. Yes. And reasonable. Sign here. Pardon the pen leak. I can see you're fatigued.

The WOMAN *doll goes into the bathroom.*

MOTEL-KEEPER'S VOICE: Any children? Well, that's nice. Children don't appreciate travel. And rooms don't appreciate children. As it happens it's the last one I've got left. I'll just flip my vacancy switch. Twelve dollars, please. In advance that'll be. That way you can go any time you want to go, you know, get an early start. On a trip to see sights, are you? That's nice. You just get your luggage while I unlock the room. You can see the light.

The MAN *doll enters carrying a suitcase. He*

has a cigar and a loud Florida shirt. He closes the door, inspects the room, and takes off his clothes, except for his loudly patterned shorts.

MOTEL-KEEPER'S VOICE: There now. What I say doesn't matter. You can see. It speaks for itself. The room speaks for itself. You can see it's a perfect 1966 room. But a taste of home. I've seen to that. A taste of home. Comfy, cozy, nice, but a taste of newness. That's what. You can see it. The best stop on route Six Sixty-Six. Well, there might be others like it, but this is the best stop. You've arrived at the right place. This place. And a hooked rug. I don't care what, but I've said no room is without a hooked rug.

Sound of the toilet flushing.

MOTEL-KEEPER'S VOICE: No complaints yet. Never. Modern people like modern places. Oh yes. I can tell. They tell me. And reasonable. Very very reasonable rates. No cheaper rates on the route, not for this. You receive what you pay for.

Sound of the toilet flushing again.

MOTEL-KEEPER'S VOICE: All that driving and driving and driving. Fatigued. You must be. I would be. Miles and miles and miles.

The MAN doll begins an inspection of the bed. He pulls at the bedspread, testing its strength.

MOTEL-KEEPER'S VOICE: Fancy. Fancy your ending up right here. You didn't know and I didn't know. But you did. End up right here. Respectable and decent and homelike. Right here.

The WOMAN doll comes back from the bathroom to get her negligee from her purse. She returns to the bathroom.

MOTEL-KEEPER'S VOICE: All folks everywhere sitting in the very palm of God. Waiting, whither, whence.

The MAN doll pulls the bedspread, blankets, and sheets off the bed, tearing them apart. He jumps hard on the bed.

MOTEL-KEEPER'S VOICE: Any motel you might have come to on Six Sixty-Six. Any motel. On that vast network of roads. Whizzing by, whizzing by. Trucks too. And cars from everywhere. Full up with folks, all sitting in the very palm of God. I can tell proper folks when I get a look at them. All folks.

The MAN doll rummages through the suitcase, throwing clothes about the room.

MOTEL-KEEPER'S VOICE: Country roads, state roads, United States roads. It's a big world and here you are. I noticed you got a license plate. I've not been to there myself. I've not been to anywhere myself, excepting town for supplies, and Boise. Boise, Idaho.

Toilet articles and bathroom fixtures, including toilet paper and the toilet seat, are thrown out of the bathroom. The MAN doll casually tears pages out of the Bible.

MOTEL-KEEPER'S VOICE: The world arrives to me, you'd say. It's a small world. These plastic flowers here: "Made in Japan" on the label. You noticed? Got them from the catalogue. Cat-al-ogue. Every product in this room is ordered.

The MAN doll pulls down some of the curtains. Objects continue to be thrown from the bathroom.

MOTEL-KEEPER'S VOICE: Ordered from the catalogue. Excepting the antimacassars and the hooked rug. Made the hooked rug myself. Tang of home. No room is a room without. Course the bedspread, hand-hooked, hooked near here at town. Mrs. Harritt. Betsy Harritt gets materials through another catalogue. Cat-al-ogue.

The WOMAN *doll comes out of the bathroom wearing her negligee over her panties and bra. When the* MAN *doll notices her, he stops his other activities and goes to her.*

MOTEL-KEEPER'S VOICE: Myself, I know it from the catalogue: bottles, bras, breakfasts, refrigerators, cast iron gates, plastic posies,

The WOMAN *doll opens her negligee and the* MAN *doll pulls off her bra. The* MAN *and* WOMAN *dolls embrace. The* WOMAN *doll puts lipstick on her nipples.*

MOTEL-KEEPER'S VOICE: paper subscriptions, Buick trucks, blankets, forks, clitter-clack darning hooks, transistors and antimacassar, vinyl plastics,

The MAN *doll turns on the TV. It glares viciously and plays loud rock and roll music.*

MOTEL-KEEPER'S VOICE: crazy quilts, paper hair-pins, cats, catnip, club feet, canisters, banisters, holy books, tattooed toilet articles, tables, tea cozies,

The MAN *doll writes simple obscene words on the wall. The* WOMAN *doll does the same with her lipstick.*

MOTEL-KEEPER'S VOICE: pickles, bayberry candles, South Dakotan Kewpie Dolls, fiberglass hair, polished milk, amiable grand-pappies, colts, Galsworthy books, cribs, cabinets, teeter-totters,

The WOMAN *doll has turned to picture-making. She draws a crude cock and coyly adds pubic hair and drops of come.*

MOTEL-KEEPER'S VOICE: and television sets.

Oh I tell you it, I do. It's a wonder. Full with things, the world, full up. Shall I tell you my thought? Next year there's a shelter to be built by me, yes. Shelter motel. Everything to be placed under the ground. Signs up in every direction up and down Six Sixty-Six.

The MAN *and* WOMAN *dolls twist.*

MOTEL-KEEPER'S VOICE: Complete Security, Security While You Sleep Tight, Bury Your Troubles At This Motel, Homelike, Very Comfy, and Encased In Lead, Every Room Its Own Set, Fourteen Day Emergency Supplies $5.00 Extra,

The rock and roll music gets louder and louder. A civil-defense siren, one long wail, begins to build. The MAN *and* WOMAN *dolls proceed methodically to greater and greater violence. They smash the TV screen and picture frames. They pull down the remaining curtains, smash the window, throw bits of clothing and bedding around, and finally tear off the arms of the* MOTEL-KEEPER *doll.*

MOTEL-KEEPER'S VOICE: Self-Contained Latrine Waters, Filters, Counters, Periscopes and Mechanical Doves, Hooked Rugs, Dearest Little Picture Frames for Loved Ones— Made in Japan—through the catalogue. Cat-a-logue. You can pick items and products: cablecackles—so nice—cuticles, twice-twisted combs with corrugated calisthenics, meat-beaters, fish-tackles, bug bombs, toasted terra-cotta'd Tanganyikan switch blades, ochre closets, ping-pong balls, didies, Capricorn and Cancer prognostics, crackers, total uppers, stick pins, basting tacks . . .

The MOTEL-KEEPER'S VOICE *is drowned out by the other sounds—siren and music—which have built to a deafening pitch and come from all parts of the theatre. The door opens again and headlights shine into the eyes of the audience.*

The actor inside the MOTEL-KEEPER doll has slipped out of it. The MAN and WOMAN dolls tear off the head of the MOTEL-KEEPER doll, then throw her body aside.

Then, one by one, the MAN and WOMAN dolls leave the motel room and walk down the aisle. Fans blow air through the debacle on stage onto the audience.

After an instant more of excruciatingly loud noise: blackout and silence.

It is preferable that the actors take no bow after this play.

About the Authors

Euripides (c. 480–407 B.C.) lived and wrote during the Peloponnesian War (431–404), the period of decline after Athens' Golden Age that culminated in its eventual defeat by Sparta. Reflecting the growing sense of loss and disillusionment prevalent in Athens, Euripides' tragedies are at once allegories of political decay and explorations into the forces, good and evil, that make up life. The greatly acclaimed *Medea* (431) and the *Hippolytus* (428) dramatize the struggles between human loyalties and chance, and the effect of chance on life; both *The Suppliants* (421) and the *Trojan Women* (415) depict the brutality of war. In the *Orestes* (408) and his last play, the *Bacchae* (407), Euripides probes the conflict between man's mind and his soul, the responsibility of man for his own fate. The question he poses would seem to be: Is there such a thing as fate—or God? For further biographical, critical, or historical information, consult: William Nickerson Bates, *Euripides: A Student of Human Nature* (New York, 1961); Paul Decharme, *Euripides and the Spirit of His Dramas*, translated by James Loeb (New York, 1968); L. H. G. Greenwood, *Aspects of Euripidean Tragedy* (Cambridge, Eng., 1953); G. M. A. Grube, *The Drama of Euripides* (London, 1941); G. G. A. Murray, *Euripides and His Age* (London, 1965); and Gilbert Norwood, *Essays on Euripidean Drama* (Berkeley, 1954).

Molière (or **Jean Baptiste Poquelin**, 1622–1673) wrote and acted for his own company, under the patronage of King Louis XIV, from 1660 until his death. In his plays, action or plot is dominated by a comic character with an *idée fixe*, or obsession, that threatens to upset, if not to ruin, the lives of the other characters. Only by uniting against him to reveal his obsession, and thereby his hypocrisy, do the characters bring the play to a happy ending. The action of *Tartuffe* (1664, publicly performed 1669) is patterned along these lines: the other members of the household must form a league against the religious hypocrite to outwit him. *Don Juan* (1665), *The Misanthrope* (1666), *The Miser* (1668), *The Would-Be Gentleman* (1670), and *The Imaginary Invalid* (1673), whose titles describe their domineering main characters and their obsessions, are all comedies in the same vein, all explorations of hypocrisy and self-deception. For further biographical, critical, or historical information, consult: Hobart Chatfield Chatfield-Taylor, *Molière* (New York, 1906); Lionel Gossman, *Men and Masks: A Study of Molière* (Baltimore, 1963); Jacques Guicharnaud, *Molière: A Collection of Critical Essays* (Englewood Cliffs, 1964); David Herbert Judd, *Molière and the Comedy of Intellect* (Berkeley; 1962); D. B. W. Lewis, *Molière: The Comic Mask* (London, 1959); and Arthur A. Tilley, *Molière* (New York, 1968).

Henrik Ibsen (1828–1906) gained his extensive knowledge of stagecraft in his native Norway, successively as a stage manager (in Bergen, 1851–1857) and as a theatre director (in Oslo, 1857–1862). But it was only after 1864, when he accepted a traveling scholarship through Europe and exiled himself from a country he felt stifled his creativity, that Ibsen began to write his first best-known plays: the tragic *Brand* (1866) and the gay but profound *Peer Gynt* (1867); both are in verse and, despite their differing tones, totally Scandinavian in theme, conception, and background. Perhaps more familiar to modern audiences, though, are the realistic prose plays of social protest that followed: *Pillars of Society* (1877), *A Doll's House* (1879), *Ghosts* (1881), *An Enemy of the People* (1882), and *The Wild Duck* (1884). In these Ibsen continued to dramatize the social problems raised in his earliest efforts, but now in terms of recognizable individuals, their inner conflicts, and the consequences of their actions on their own souls rather than on society. Ibsen's last plays, beginning with *Rosmersholm* (1886) and *Hedda Gabler* (1890), represent the consummation of all his former tendencies: these focus more on mental states than on action or even character, and combine suggestive symbols with semiautobiographical materials to probe the effects of relentless idealism or selfish individuality. In *The Master Builder* (1892), through a burned house and a looming church steeple as much as through Solness' mind, Ibsen unflinchingly depicts the relation of an artist to his craft—his greed, egotism, and fear of youth, his instinct for simultaneous creativeness and self-destruction. For further biographical, critical, or historical information, consult: M. C. Bradbrook, *Ibsen, The Norwegian: A Revaluation* (Hamden, Conn., 1966); Robert Brustein, *The Theatre of Revolt* (Boston, 1964), especially pp. 37–83; F. Bull, *Ibsen: The Man and the Dramatist* (Oxford, Eng., 1954); B. W. Downs, *Ibsen: The Intellectual Background* (Cambridge, Eng., 1946); Rolf Fjelde, *Ibsen: A Collection of Critical Essays* (Englewood Cliffs, 1965); Henrik B. Jaeger, *Henrik Ibsen: A Critical Biography*, translated by William Morton Payne, second edition (Chicago, 1901); G. B. Shaw, *The Quintessence of Ibsenism* (London, 1891); and A. E. Zucker, *Ibsen: The Master Builder* (New York, 1929).

Anton Chekhov (1860–1904) sought, in his plays as in his stories, to present life indirectly, impersonally, without obtrusive rearrangement. There were, he claimed, no heroes or villains in his drama. Whether Chekhov's characters are nobles, servants, doctors, businessmen, idealistic scholars, military men, they all eat, smoke, drink, play games or music; they all complain of the weather, their physical ailments, boredom or frustration, clinging to lost hopes as to physical objects that become the symbols of their smothered desires and regrets. Whatever the play, the same characters revolve in the same plot in the same four-act structure that reduces all actions to the same level of importance. Chekhov espoused no particular philosophy, and pretenders to prophecy—like Vershinin of *The Three Sisters* (1901) or Trofimov of *The Cherry Orchard* (1904)—either repeat themselves into absurdity or cannot minister to their own needs, much less the needs of others. Beneath the continual half-gloom of life "as it is," broken by buffoonery that underscores the sense of death-in-life all the more, however, there sounds the note that life is not "as it should be." But Chekhov lays the blame on no one individual or group: if he derides the inertia of provincial nobles, the vulgarity, ignorance, and officiousness of servants and the *nouveaux riches* do not escape his irony either. The earlier plays, *The Sea Gull* (1896) and *Uncle Vanya* (1899), are similar in tone and intentions. For further biographical, critical, or historical information, consult: Robert Brustein, *The Theatre of Revolt* (Boston, 1964), especially pp. 137–79; and the works listed under Chekhov's name in the section on fiction in this book.

Luigi Pirandello (1867–1936) was awarded a Nobel Prize in 1934. He taught literature in Rome most of his life, while writing novels and plays. Because of his obsession with the relation of appearance to reality, he is said to be the author of *one* play with *one-hundred different acts*. The typical Pirandellian three-act play generally revolves about the thesis that reality is a flux, and man, because of his reason, abhors change and so creates a role to give meaning to a reality that essentially has none. The result is that man lives in illusion, like an actor behind a mask. Pirandello is no exception; thus, in his mind, actors, plays, and writers become multiple metaphors as they comment, through an illusion, on men creating still further illusions. *Henry IV* (1922) is not only man acting on reality but an actor portraying an actor, and a madman-dramatist creating history who has become so aware of changing reality that he possesses a lucidity none of the "sane" around him comprehends. The test of that lucidity is Henry's ability to shift his roles with the shifts of reality, one second to the next, act by act. The borderlines between reality and appearance are further examined in *Right You Are If You Think You Are* (1917), *Six Characters in Search of an Author* (1921), *Each in His Own Way* (1924), *Tonight We Improvise* (1930), and *When One Is Somebody* (1933). For further biographical, critical, or historical information, consult: Robert Brustein, *The Theatre of Revolt* (Boston, 1964), especially pp. 281–317; Glauco Cambon, *Pirandello: A Collection of Critical Essays* (Englewood Cliffs, 1967); Walter F. Starkie, *Luigi Pirandello*, third edition (Berkeley, 1965); and Domenico Vittorini, *The Drama of Luigi Pirandello* (New York, 1957).

Jean-Claude van Itallie (b. 1936) came from Belgium to the United States during the Second World War. A graduate of Harvard (1958), he has written several plays, but the best known and most widely acclaimed is the trilogy, *America Hurrah* (1966), which includes *Interview, TV,* and *Motel*. While many critics have noted flaws in these three playlets, almost all have conceded the freshness of their experimental nature. The freshness is evident in van Itallie's merging of theatrical conventions and other media: the "plots" of all flick by with the quick movement of cinematic frames, and television (in *TV*) and tape (in *Motel*) figure prominently in van Itallie's technique. Divisions between "actors" and "spectators"—indeed, between one dramatic character and another—are broken down through the treatment of voices as in a fugue: the voices are used like orchestral instruments, or groups of them, which state and develop an idea contrapuntally, the idea gradually building in complexity to an overpowering climax. That "fugue" signifies, in psychiatry, a type of amnesia and recovery is just as important to van Itallie's intentions as the term's musical meaning: as one character completes another's sentence or dissolves into another character or the audience, the effect is, in Robert Brustein's words, to "suggest a nation's nightmares and afflictions. . . . to relax frustration and loneliness by showing that it is still possible for men to share a common humanity. . . ." For further critical information, consult: Robert Brustein, "Theatre: Three Views of America," *New Republic*, CLV (December 3, 1966), 31–33; Harold Clurman, "Theatre," *Nation*, CCIII (November 28, 1966), 586–588; Richard Gilman, "Experiments in Theatre," *Newsweek*, LXVIII (November 21, 1966), 114; Robert J. Schroeder, ed., *The New Underground Theatre* (New York, 1968); and "The Theatre: Air-Conditioned Blightmare," *Time*, LXXXVIII (November 18, 1966), 79–80.

POETRY POETRY

ASSIGNMENT: Read Sir Thomas Wyatt's poem
               "They Flee from Me,"
               and, in a three-page paper,
               relate to, and interpret,
               the poem. Due Monday.

They Flee from Me

They flee from me that sometime did me seek,
   With naked foot stalking in my chamber.
I have seen them gentle, tame, and meek,
   That now are wild and do not remember
   That sometime they put themselves in danger
      To take bread at my hand; and now they range
      Busily seeking with a continual change.

Thankt be fortune, it hath been otherwise
   Twenty times better; but once, in special,
In thin array, after a pleasant guise,
   When her loose gown from her shoulders did fall,
   And she me caught in her arms long and small,
      Therewith all sweetly did me kiss,
      And softly said: "Dear heart, how like you this?"

It was no dream; I lay broad waking:
   But all is turned thorough my gentleness
Into a strange fashion of forsaking;
   And I have leave to go of her goodness;
   And she also to use new-fangleness.
      But since that I so kindely am served,
      I fain would know what she hath deserved.

*"Relate to, and interpret, the poem." But it's poetry—so I won't know what
it's about. (Reads the poem.) It breaks up into pieces, and they don't go
together. The first part talks about "they"—animals?—fleeing, the second
part's sex, and the third is flat out about the way she's treated him. "They"
are wild and used to be tame: cat, tiger, a bird or a rabbit maybe, but it's
really women he's lost . . .*

The CADillac PULLed up ahead of the FORD,
The FORD got HOT and wouldn't DO no MORE,
It then got CLOUdy and STARted to RAIN,
I TOOted my HORN for a PASsing LANE,
The RAINwater blowin' all UNder my HOOD
I KNOW that I was DOin' my MOtor GOOD.
MAbelLEENE, why can't YOU be TRUE?
Oh MAbelLEENE, why CAN'T you be TRUE?
You've STARted back doin' the THINGS you USED to DO . . .*

But he doesn't really care too much about them cutting out, because he's really concerned about one woman who went after him, but now she's "forsaken" him, and for some reason she shouldn't have, even if they did . . . But why does he keep rapping about it in the last part—does he still love her? . . .

The BELL HOP'S tears keep FLOOwing,
The DESK CLERK'S dressed in BLACK.
They've BEEN so LOONG on LOOnely Street,
They NEver WILL go BACK.
And they're so LOOnely,
Oh, they're so LOOnely,
They're so LOOnely,
They PRAY to DIE . . .†

hate her? . . .

TAKE a—TAKE another LITtle PIECE
        of my HEART now baby,
BREAK a—Break another LITle bit
        of my HEART oh darling now,
You know you've GOT IT,
        if it MAKES you FEEL GOOD . . .††

care at all? (Pause, turns off radio.) *I don't see any way to tell. I'd better look it up.* (Longer pause, while student looks up Wyatt, Sir Thomas, sonnet, and poetry, English, history of, in encyclopedia, finding one reference to "They Flee from Me"—it's described as a poem about lost love.) *Right.*

Wyatt introduced the sonnet form into English, only according to them, this isn't a sonnet. I see that! *It doesn't have fourteen lines. He used Italian models, only they don't think this had a model, and he wrote using conventional descriptions and situations, but what does that mean? Maybe I could start the paper "This is a* very *tender poem"? But I'm not sure it is—he doesn't love her, only he does. I can't understand those last two lines . . .*

Maybe a consideration of the rest of the poem would help. The student has tried, superficially, to figure out the poem. But, jumping from line to line and from tentative idea to vague association, he hasn't given enough attention to any one thought to develop it, probably because he doesn't have much faith in his own ideas. Finally he gives up on instantly deciphering the whole poem, and settles on the last two lines as being clear enough clues to spur the beginning of a paper. In other words, the student has seen the problems but is afraid to ask himself the obvious questions: he's put "them"—the authorities—in the way of his understanding "them" in the poem. But "answers" to poems should come from *inside*—which is why we all "relate to, and interpret," poems differently.

Poems are wholes, and when a reader feels an intellectual, emotional "connection" with a poem, it should be with the *total* poem. The student certainly sees the major question in "They Flee from Me"—he is puzzled by the poet's *tone* (the attitude of the speaker toward his subject)—but stifles this concern and cuts off his instinctive exploration of the entire poem because he feels his questions are too subjective, too associational in technique. In declining the challenge of the poem he is simply refusing to use his imagination, for fear that it may mislead him. A subjective approach to any puzzle requires courage: the imaginative person is one who is sometimes seized by an answer before his mind can formulate the process by which it leaped to the answer. He must be patient—momentarily suspending the gratification of his impulses, tolerating disorder. Often he is not even able to articulate the terms of the problem when he first confronts it. Although he cannot define either the limits of the project or his own technique, he will hold on until both take shape and can be supported, and until he begins to progress toward his goal. He will build his own bridges.

So this student has at least begun the process. He is intrigued at first, then discouraged when he loses faith (almost immediately after a rich spurt of ideas) in his own ability to solve the puzzle. But, as far as he goes, he's right: the poem obviously does break into sections (or *stanzas*, units of lines forming a division of a poem and recurring in the same pattern or in recognizable variations of the pattern), as well as attitudes; there *is* a discrepancy between "they" and "she"; and there *is* a difference in situation between the second and third stanzas. Having gotten this far, however, he refuses to try to answer "Why," even though these perceptions are on the same level as his knowing that the poem is not a sonnet. In the latter case he could count lines and use models; in the former the "facts" are vague, less black and white. But in both cases the perceptions are tools. If all of the above facts about the poem were accepted, and authority—which has told him nothing useful—ignored, where does he then turn?

Inward. The first stanza uses "they," "them," "they," indefinite pronouns to describe an indefinite subject that "stalks," was once "gentle, tame, and meek" enough to "take bread" at the speaker's hand, but now is "wild," and "flees." Certainly the stanza makes a vivid impression: its constant polarization, the careful time oppositions of "now" and "sometime" as part of a definition through contrasts, puts the reader in a frame, forces him to a visualization of *something* animal. But the impact of this implicit *image* (in poetry, a description that has a special meaning for its writer, or a word or cluster of words evoking sensory experiences of hearing, sight, smell, taste, or touch) should initiate some speculation on what animal the poet has in mind. Here *connotation* (an idea suggested by, or associated with, a word, distinct from its specific meaning) helps. The meaning of "stalking" (moving stealthily or haughtily) should eliminate rabbits, and bread doesn't normally appeal to any kind of cat.

But is it vital to know precisely what the poet had in mind? Perhaps, perhaps not. For the subjective method, in its application, involves an acceptance of doubt, a recognition of ambivalence. One alternative may eventually be discarded, or both may be retained: opposites do not necessarily cancel each other out. Wyatt manipulates his reader by means of this perception of ambivalence. He sets limits to the reader's imagination, but he never dictates specific terms. For the specific term here, we choose deer —largely because "stalking" connotes a deer's walk for us, and we remember feeding bread and popcorn to deer in zoos. A good case could be made for birds, if you think of them strutting around on their stemlike legs. Any others?

Always implicitly, the first stanza of "They Flee from Me" states that these animals are really women, women who used to seek the speaker out but now have gone on to "greener pastures." If this indirect construction gives you a sense that the poem breaks into fragments, notice that probably the largest rupture occurs between the first and second stanzas, when Wyatt moves his implicit image of woman/animal to the explicit, and therefore more "realistic," description of a specific event and a specific "animal."

But why does he use the imagery in the first stanza, then discard it in the second, at the same time shifting from "they" to "she"? Apparently "they" once sought him as "she" does in the second stanza: the speaker seems to be describing a succession of mistresses, all of whom eventually left him, since their "ranging" can be equated with her "new-fangleness" and "strange fashion of forsaking." Thus these experiences, even the best-remembered one, were somewhat alike. But changes in imagery often reflect changes in tone or attitude. Is such a change taking place here?

Perhaps the first stanza is describing a general trend, or a change in fashionable behavior that Wyatt simply observes. There's no problem about his tone in the first stanza: it's fairly objective, presenting empirical information that results from observation. Only when we reach the second stanza do we get a value judgment in "Twenty times better," indicating that a specific event (the loss of a certain person or a certain pleasure), is his concern. Then the next question should be, "Is the speaker actually making a further contrast?" Is he saying that the woman he loves is different in quality from the women he has known . . . and therefore should act differently? Is she represented as a human being to contrast her to (or set her above?) the other, "animal" natures of most women? And can she, in fact, be so removed?

In the second stanza, Wyatt presents as striking—and as simple—a picture of his mistress as he did of his wandering animals. And yet the poet's image leaves room for the reader's imagination. Wyatt's sixteenth-century lady probably differs greatly from the woman the reader (having his own remembered loves and disappointments) has in mind. Any reader could see her as the Venus of the fifteenth-century Florentine painter Botticelli, disembodied, remote, self-absorbed, blown shoreward by the allegorical, carefully sculptured nymphs and breezes that gently accompany her. Shell-tinted, ethereal, this Venus represents heavenly love; she is almost two-dimensional in her detachment from a world etched as delicately pastel as herself. Or Wyatt's lady could resemble La Bella, the model for the Venus of Urbino by the sixteenth-century Venetian painter Titian, a woman triumphantly of this world, serenely waiting while her maids gather up her clothing. Voluptuous, warm and glowing, she is contrasted with the inanimate colors around her, the pink and white of her bed and the green velvet hangings in the background. If Botticelli's Venus looks through the spectator, Titian's appraises him; but, different as these paintings are, either of them, or many others, could illustrate Wyatt's poem, for Wyatt provides only a basic charcoal sketch: each reader fills in his own images and details.

Such a concept of poem as artifact, as "made object," goes back to the

Greek definition of *poema*. Each reader—including the poet—invests the artifact with special meanings through special associations. Here the point is, once more, the resulting concreteness of the image: since we all daydream, we all create images in this mode. The "finished" (that is, "read") poem becomes a joint enterprise between writer and reader.

The filmic quality of the speaker's memory in "They Flee from Me" furthers this association: since the poet frames his memory as a dream sequence, he opens the reader's mind to such a world, a world where things suddenly, inexplicably but inevitably, change. How often do our memories of incidents or actions take on the choreography of a dream?

You might have seen me RUNning
THROUGH the LONG abandoned RUINS
Of the DREAMS you LEFT behind.
If you reMEMber someTHING THERE
That glided PAST YOU . . .

Don't be CONcerned, it WILL not HARM you.
It's only ME pursuing SOMEthing I'm not SURE of.
ACROSS my DREAM, with NETS of WONder,
I CHASE the BRIGHT eLUsive BUTterfly of LOVE.*

As in a ballet, every action is slowed down, more heavily emphasized, until a simple embrace ("she me caught in her arms") seems to contain all the meaning, all the melodramatic importance of the universe itself. Here Wyatt, step by cautious step, is moving his reader through his own experiences, giving new insight rather than telling new facts. The importance of the remembered embrace overshadows, erases, the momentary importance of other "gentle" creatures—and the reader *knows* it. He is not told.

This dream imagery provides a necessary sense of continuity in the first two stanzas for poet and reader. But the poet's new reaction in stanza three begins another movement: "It was no dream; I lay broad waking" shifts to present reality. If his memories are real, so is his present sense of loss. The bleak statement of fact breaks into the stream of reminiscences, brings his imagination to a halt, and redirects both himself and the reader. Why? Perhaps because he must live in the present, "now" rather than "sometime."

We have found the underlying thematic unity of the poem. But the shifts, Wyatt's divisions of thought into near-musical movements, are still more obvious than the unbroken theme. Like the musician constructing a symphony, Wyatt reinforces these movements by writing stanzas in *rime royal* (seven-line units rhyming *ababbcc*), self-contained rhymes, and taut rhythm.

None of the rhymes carries over to a succeeding stanza, but Wyatt loosens the rhythm, changing the beat as he changes the vowels, from the full slowness of "Therewith all sweetly did me kiss,/And softly said: 'Dear heart, how like you this?' " to the emphatic flatness of "And I have leave to go of her goodness;/And she also to use new-fangleness." The second stanza flows: even the words take longer to pronounce than the relatively more commonplace vocabulary of the third stanza, where there is no description, no embellishment, no luxury—just fact.

For other examples, look at the elongated syllables, the correspondingly slow tempo of Axton-Durden-Presley's "Heartbreak Hotel" (the second popular song earlier cited), as opposed to the hammering flat tones of Ragovoy-Burns's "Piece of My Heart" (the third). Then read the light, floating tones of Lind's "Elusive Butterfly" (the fourth). In these songs, as well as in poems, time and sound changes are obviously meant to reflect changing thoughts, helping and influencing the reader. In Wyatt's case, how does the sound of the first stanza differ from either of the other two? What sorts of words and vowel sounds does Wyatt use—long, as in the second stanza; or staccato, as in the third? Or is there another possibility?

Poems reflect thought through sound; they should be read aloud, for the reader's first clue to meaning may well be a change in sound, rhythm, or *rhyme* (the identity or correspondence of sound patterns). Rhyme is especially useful in determining tone: in "The Love Song of J. Alfred Prufrock," the speaker's *perfect terminal* rhyming of

Should I, after tea and cakes and *ices*,
Have the strength to force the moment to its *crisis?*

reflects his own view of his strength and the world's likely opinion. Another use of rhyme for tone is evident in John Crowe Ransom's "Judith of Bethulia," when the speaker employs the *consonantal, slant,* or *imperfect* rhyme of "clergy" and "orgy" to sustain an ironic tone. Tension mounts in Coleridge's "Rime of the Ancient Mariner" with each succeeding *leonine* or *internal* sound pattern:

And through the *drifts* the snowy *clifts* . . .
Nor shapes of *men* nor beast we *ken* . . .
The ice was *here*, the ice was *there* . . .
It cracked and *growled*, and roared and *howled*.

When X. J. Kennedy rhymes "Andromache" and "Schenectady" (in "Inscriptions after Fact"), it is probably impossible for the reader to keep a straight face.

Rhythm (a basically regular recurrence of grouped, stressed, and unstressed syllables), through its allocation of emphasis, is another clear indication of tone and, therefore, of meaning. As in all art, poetry intends to build the audience's expectations: having set up a regular pattern of rhythm or rhyme, a poet will either fulfill the anticipation he has created by continuing the pattern, or will frustrate the reader by change. In the same way, the rock singer traditionally stresses a song's built-in beat, while a jazz singer just as traditionally departs from it. In "Mabellene," Chuck Berry follows a regular rhythm, an *anapest* (two unstressed syllables followed by a stressed one) for the first several lines. Then he departs from this pattern in the *refrain* (a line or lines repeated at regular intervals), and more syllables are stressed in the *iambic* pattern (two syllables, the first unstressed, the second stressed), as the basis of the singer's complaint, "You've started back doin' the things you used to do," is reached.

In a song, the music helps the listener to determine stressed words or syllables, so that when we speak of a new "arrangement" of a song, we are talking about a singer's reinterpretation of the writer's idea, often obviously different from the composer's intended rhythm. In a poem, the only guideline is the individual reader's interpretation of the poet's thought.

There would seem to be an infinite number of readings possible for any poem; but, just as with his imagery, so too with his rhythm: the poet actually sets limits for the reader. The first stanza of "They Flee from Me" is obviously governed by the "now"–"sometime" contrast. So in the first line, "They flee from me that sometime did me seek," the contrasting words "flee" and "seek" must carry the heaviest emphasis. The *scansion* (determination of rhythm, more fully discussed in this book's Glossary) for the rest of the line, however, depends on the reader.

Having considered all these elements, we now have the background to take up the final question: What *is* the tone of the last stanza?

An interpretation of tone proceeds from the reader's idea of the main character presented by the poet, the (fictitious) narrator imagined by the poet to speak the words of a poem—in other words, the *persona* speaking. So when we ask "What's he like?" we are asking "What's his tone of voice?" as well. Sometimes the persona is an obvious put-on, like a comedian's *shtick*, trademark, or gimmick (Jack Benny's age, stinginess, and so on) or a stripper's name (Candy Barr or Tempus Fugit). Other gimmicks would include the Beatles' haircuts, Linus' blanket, Schroeder's piano (♪ ♩ 𝅝), Snoopy's airplane ("Here's the World War I flying ace . . ."), Alabama governor George Wallace's rhetoric, Norman Mailer's ego (!), and Presley's pelvis.

Sometimes, however, the persona speaks and acts with such sincerity that the reader cannot distinguish him from his creator. Generally this confusion results from a reader's *stock response:* the persona is expressing the idea that the reader has a built-in reaction to. One reader may react favorably to a persona who rhymes moon and June, dove and love. Another may enjoy the exposition of rape, blood, and murder. Such responses form the basis of most advertising strategies: "Come on and take it off. Take it all off." "The Mini-Brute." "Is it true blondes have more fun?" "All my men wear ————, or they wear nothing at all." By more subtle variations on this technique, the reader is lured into some reaction to the author's masquerade.

Skillfully portrayed personas can be very real indeed. Robert Frost's pose as a simple farmer or George Herbert's representation of himself as a country parson solidifying his faith both seem true personalities to their readers. To convey other impressions, the poet may choose to picture himself in an unworldly guise: his persona may be godlike, possessed of special knowledge or superior perception. Whitman makes perhaps the most obvious use of this character, but certainly Wordsworth, Coleridge, and many others use the same device. Finally, the poet can move from real to unreal persona in the course of one poem to intensify the reader's sharing of a specific perception. Yeats, Dylan Thomas, and D. H. Lawrence shift personas as well as rhythm, rhyme, diction, and imagery, to guide their readers with just such effects.

But one might ask, "Why have a persona at all?" The poet may indeed feel, at least partially, just as his persona does. However, unless he is able to look at the problem objectively, to find a way of detaching himself, his dissertation on his own problems or joys will have little, or possibly the wrong, effect on the reader. The use of persona permits this detachment. In "Skunk Hour," Robert Lowell uses a persona who is a voyeur. Writers to Ann Landers describe the same sort of sexual frustration and may have a similar feeling of hopelessness. But Lowell molds these sensations, forms all the textbook indications—"I watched for love-cars," "My mind's not right"—into a carefully governed, thoroughly artistic "I." The detailed descriptions of the town, and, later, the scavenging skunk, lend realism to the poem. But the author's planting of just the right song ("Love, O careless love . . .") and a quotation from Satan's speeches in *Paradise Lost* ("I myself am hell") underscore Lowell's detachment, his use of his creation. Further, the persona naïvely notices the skunks, focusing the reader's attention on the title: he himself sees no parallel, but Lowell and the reader recognize a kinship between the only two creatures "here," a voyeur's "ill-spirit" and a mother skunk "swilling the garbage pail." By imposing on us such a hyperawareness of his persona, any poet can impress us, influence us, force us to recognize how our experiences parallel, touch, or oppose his.

If "They Flee from Me" forces such a recognition, we may assume that Wyatt's persona *is different* from Wyatt. *How* different they are, however, is a question we cannot answer; but an analysis of the whole poem should say something about the persona. We are back to the student's questions: Is the persona in "They Flee from Me" bitter, amused, or detached? Does he still love the girl? Hate her? Even care?

We cannot answer the questions; even as omniscient authors we can only answer them for ourselves, because the experiences we bring to the poem are different from everyone else's. The student associates "Mabellene," "Heartbreak Hotel," and "Piece of My Heart" with "They Flee from Me." We associate deer, Botticelli and Titian, "Elusive Butterfly," and "From Both Sides Now."

MOONS and JUNES and FERris WHEELS
The DIZzy dancing WAY you FEEL
When every FAIry TALE comes REAL,
I've LOOKED at LOVE that WAY.
But now it's JUST anOTHer show
You LEAVE 'em LAUGHing when you GO.
And if you CARE don't LET them KNOW,
Don't GIVE yourSELF aWAY.
I've LOOKED at love from BOTH SIDES now
From WIN and LOSE and STILL someHOW
It's LOVE'S ilLUsions I reCALL
I really DON'T know LOVE at ALL.*

Just as we realize that every outside connection tells us something, but not everything, about the poem, we know also that our final interpretations of the poem must be different. Of course, Wyatt has "looked at love from both sides now," though his conclusions may not be Joni Mitchell's or Judy Collins'. Nor ours. But finally our conclusions will be based on these associations, because our perceptions result from our individual experiences. A reaction to a poem is not a value judgment—"This is a *very* tender poem." Rather, it is an impression and a description of a unique event colored and motivated by previous experience. You bring yourself to poems. Poems must happen to you—and you change each other.

ANONYMOUS ballads of the middle ages

Sir Patrick Spens

The king sits in Dumferling toune,
   Drinking the blude-reid wine:
"O whar will I get guid sailor,
   To sail this schip of mine?"

Up and spak an eldern knicht,
   Sat at the kings richt kne:
"Sir Patrick Spens is the best sailor
   That sails upon the se."

The king has written a braid letter,
   And signd it wi his hand,
And sent it to Sir Patrick Spens,
   Was walking on the sand.

The first line that Sir Patrick red,
   A loud lauch lauched he;
The next line that Sir Patrick red,
   The teir blinded his ee.

"O wha is this has don this deid,
   This ill deid don to me,
To send me out this time o' the yeir,
   To sail upon the se!   20

"Mak hast, mak haste, my mirry men all,
   Our guid schip sails the morne:"
"O say na sae, my master deir,
   For I feir a deadlie storme.

"Late late yestreen I saw the new moone,
   Wi the auld moone in hir arme,
And I feir, I feir, my deir master,
   That we will cum to harme."

---

l. 9. *braid:* plain, clear.

O our Scots nobles wer richt laith
   To weet their cork-heild schoone;   30
Bot lang owre a' the play wer playd,
   Their hats they swam aboone.

O lang, lang may their ladies sit,
   Wi thair fans into their hand,
Or eir they se Sir Patrick Spens
   Cum sailing to the land.

O lang, lang may the ladies stand,
   Wi thair gold kems in their hair,
Waiting for thair ain deir lords,
   For they'll se thame na mair.   40

Haf owre, haf owre to Aberdour,
   It's fiftie fadom deip,
And thair lies guid Sir Patrick Spens,
   Wi the Scots lords at his feit.

---

l. 29. *laith:* loathe.
l. 32. *aboone:* above.

The Daemon Lover

"O where have you been, my long, long love,
   This long seven years and mair?"
"O I'm come to seek my former vows
   Ye granted me before."

"O hold your tongue of your former vows,
   For they will breed sad strife;
O hold your tongue of your former vows,
   For I am become a wife."

He turned him right and round about,
   And the tear blinded his ee: 10
"I wad never hae trodden on Irish ground,
   If it had not been for thee.

"I might hae had a king's daughter,
   Far, far beyond the sea;
I might have had a king's daughter,
   Had it not been for love o thee."

"If ye might have had a king's daughter,
    Yer sel ye had to blame;
Ye might have taken the king's daughter,
    For ye kend that I was nane.   20

"If I was to leave my husband dear,
    And my two babes also,
O what have you to take me to,
    If with you I should go?"

"I hae seven ships upon the sea—
    The eighth brought me to land—
With four-and-twenty bold mariners,
    And music on every hand."

She has taken up her two little babes,
    Kissd them baith cheek and chin: 30
"O fair ye weel, my ain two babes,
    For I'll never see you again."

She set her foot upon the ship,
    No mariners could she behold;
But the sails were o the taffetie,
    And the masts o the beaten gold.

She had not sailed a league, a league,
    A league but barely three,
When dismal grew his countenance,
    And drumlie grew his ee.   40

They had not saild a league, a league,
    A league but barely three,
Until she espied his cloven foot,
    And she wept right bitterlie.

"O hold your tongue of your weeping,"
        says he,
    "Of your weeping now let me be;
I will shew you how the lilies grow
    On the banks of Italy."

"O what hills are yon, yon pleasant hills,
    That the sun shines sweetly on?"   50

"O yon are the hills of heaven," he said,
    "Where you will never win."

"O whaten a mountain is yon," she said,
    "All so dreary wi frost and snow?"
"O yon is the mountain of hell," he cried,
    "Where you and I will go."

He strack the tap-mast wi his hand,
    The fore-mast wi his knee,
And he brake that gallant ship in twain,
    And sank her in the sea.   60

Edward

"Why dois your brand sae drap wi bluid,
                Edward, Edward,
Why dois your brand sae drap wi bluid,
    And why sae sad gang yee O?"
"O I hae killed my hauke sae guid,
                Mither, mither,
O I hae killed my hauke sae guid,
    And I had nae mair bot hee O."

"Your haukis bluid was nevir sae reid,
                Edward, Edward,   10
Your haukis bluid was nevir sae reid,
    My deir son I tell thee O."
"O I hae killed my reid-roan steid,
                Mither, mither,
O I hae killed my reid-roan steid,
    That erst was sae fair and frie O."

"Your steid was auld, and ye hae gat mair,
                Edward, Edward,
Your steid was auld, and ye hae gat mair,
    Sum other dule ye drie O."   20
"O I hae killed my fadir deir,
                Mither, mither,

---

l. 20. *kend:* knew.
l. 40. *drumlie:* gloomy.

l. 1. *brand:* sword.
l. 20. *dule:* sorrow.

O I hae killed my fadir deir,
    Alas, and wae is mee O!"

"And whatten penance wul ye drie for that,
             Edward, Edward?
And whatten penance will ye drie for that?
    My deir son, now tell me O."
"Ile set my feit in yonder boat,
             Mither, mither,   30
Ile set my feit in yonder boat,
    And Ile fare ovir the sea O."

"And what wul ye doe wi your towirs and
    your ha,
             Edward, Edward?
And what wul ye doe wi your towirs and
    your ha,
    That were sae fair to see O?"
"Ile let thame stand tul they doun fa,
             Mither, mither.
Ile let thame stand tul they doun fa,
    For here nevir mair maun I bee O."   40

"And what wul ye leive to your bairns and
    your wife,
             Edward, Edward?
And what wul ye leive to your bairns and
    your wife,
    Whan ye gang ovir the sea O?"
"The warldis room, late them beg thrae life,
             Mither, mither,
The warldis room, late them beg thrae life,
    For thame nevir mair wul I see O."

"And what wul ye leive to your ain mither
    deir,
             Edward, Edward?   50
And what wul ye leive to your ain mither
    deir?
    My deir son, now tell me O."
"The curse of hell frae me sall ye beir,
             Mither, mither,
The curse of hell frae me sall ye beir,
    Sic counseils ye gave to me O."

ANONYMOUS LYRICS of THE MIDDLE AGES

Sumer Is Icumen In

Sing! cuccu, nu. Sing! cuccu.
Sing! cuccu. Sing! cuccu, nu.

Sumer is icumen in—
Lhude sing! cuccu.
Groweth sed and bloweth med
And springth the wude nu—
Sing! cuccu.

Awe bleteth after lomb,
Lhouth after calve cu,
Bulluc sterteth, bucke verteth,   10
Murie sing! cuccu.
Cuccu, cuccu,
Well singes thu, cuccu—
Ne swik thu naver nu!

---

l. 4. *Lhude:* loud.
l. 5. *med:* meadow.
l. 6. *wude:* wood.
l. 14. *Ne swik thu naver nu!:* Now don't ever stop!

Western Wind

Westron winde, when will thou blow,
The smalle raine downe can raine?
Christ if my love were in my armes,
And I in my bed againe.

The Corpus Christi Carol

Lully, lulley, lully, lulley,
  The fawcon hath born my mak away.

He bare him up, he bare him down,
He bare him into an orchard brown.

In that orchard ther was an hall,
That was hanged with purpill and pall.

And in that hall ther was a bed:
It was hanged with gold so red.

And in that bed ther lythe a knight,
His woundes bleding day and night.   10

By that bedes side ther kneleth a may,
And she wepeth both night and day.

And by that bedes side ther stondeth a ston,
'Corpus Christi' wreten theron.

---

l. 2. *mak:* mate.
l. 11. *may:* maiden.

Sir Thomas Wyatt

My Galley Charged with Forgetfulness

My galley, chargèd with forgetfulness,
Thorough sharp seas, in winter nights doth
  pass,

---

l. 2. *Thorough:* through.

'Tween rock and rock; and eke mine enemy,
  alas,
That is my lord, steereth with cruelness;
And every oar, a thought in readiness,
As though that death were light in such a
  case;
An endless wind doth tear the sail apace
Of forcèd sighs and trusty fearfulness;
A rain of tears, a cloud of dark disdain,
Hath done the wearied cords great
  hinderance,   10
Wreathèd with error and eke with ignorance;
The stars be hid that led me to this pain:
Drowned is Reason, that should me consort;
And I remain, despairing of the port.

---

l. 3. *eke:* also.

They Flee from Me

They flee from me that sometime did me seek,
  With naked foot stalking in my chamber.
I have seen them gentle, tame, and meek,
  That now are wild and do not remember
  That sometime they put themselves in
    danger
    To take bread at my hand; and now
     they range
    Busily seeking with a continual change.

Thankt be fortune, it hath been otherwise
  Twenty times better; but once, in special,
In thin array, after a pleasant guise,   10
  When her loose gown from her shoulders
    did fall,
  And she me caught in her arms long and
    small,
    Therewith all sweetly did me kiss,
    And softly said: "Dear heart, how like
    you this?"

It was no dream; I lay broad waking:
  But all is turned thorough my gentleness

Into a strange fashion of forsaking;
  And I have leave to go of her goodness;
  And she also to use new-fangleness.
    But since that I so kindely am served, 20
    I fain would know what she hath
      deserved.

My Lute, Awake

My lute, awake, perform the last
Labor that thou and I shall waste,
And end that I have now begun,
For when this song is sung and past,
My lute, be still, for I have done.

As to be heard where ear is none,
As lead to grave in marble stone,
My song may pierce her heart as soon.
Should we then sigh, or sing, or moan?
No, no, my lute, for I have done.   10

The rocks do not so cruelly
Repulse the waves continually,
As she my suit and affection;
So that I am past remedy,
Whereby my lute and I have done.

Proud of the spoil that thou hast got
Of simple hearts thorough Love's shot,
By whom unkind thou hast them won,
Think not he hath his bow forgot,
Although my lute and I have done.   20

Vengeance shall fall on thy disdain
That makest but game on earnest pain.
Think not alone under the sun
Unquit to cause thy lovers plain,
Although my lute and I have done.

Perchance thee lie withered and old
The winter nights that are so cold,

Plaining in vain unto the moon;
Thy wishes then dare not be told,
Care then who list, for I have done.   30

And then may chance thee to repent
The time that thou has lost and spent
To cause thy lovers sigh and swoon;
Then shalt thou know beauty but lent,
And wish and want, as I have done.

Now cease, my lute, this is the last
Labor that thou and I shall waste,
And ended is that we begun.
Now is the song both sung and past.
My lute, be still, for I have done.   40

SiR WalTeR RaleigH

Nature, That Washed Her Hands in Milk

Nature, that washed her hands in milk,
And had forgot to dry them,
Instead of earth took snow and silk,
At Love's request to try them,
If she a mistress could compose
To please Love's fancy out of those.

Her eyes he would should be of light,
A violet breath, and lips of jelly;
Her hair not black, nor overbright,
And of the softest down her belly;   10
As for her inside he'd have it
Only of wantonness and wit.

At Love's entreaty such a one
Nature made, but with her beauty
She hath framed a heart of stone;
So as Love, by ill destiny,

Must die for her whom Nature gave him,
Because her darling would not save him.

But Time (which Nature doth despise,
And rudely gives her Love the lie,   20
Makes Hope a fool, and Sorrow wise)
His hands doth neither wash nor dry;
But being made of steel and rust,
Turns snow and silk and milk to dust.

The light, the belly, lips, and breath,
He dims, discolors, and destroys;
With those he feeds but fills not death,
Which sometimes were the food of joys.
Yea, Time doth dull each lively wit,
And dries all wantonness with it.   30

Oh, cruel Time! which takes in trust
Our youth, our joys, and all we have,
And pays us but with age and dust;
Who in the dark and silent grave
When we have wandered all our ways
Shuts up the story of our days.

EdMUNd SPENSER

Sonnet LXXVII

Was it a dreame, or did I see it playne,
A goodly table of pure yvory;
All spred with iuncats, fit to entertayne
The greatest Prince with pompous roialty.
Mongst which there in a siluer dish did ly
Twoo golden apples of vnualewd price:
Far passing those which Hercules came by,

---

l. 3. *iuncats:* sweetmeats, delicacies.
l. 7. *Hercules:* in Greek and Roman mythology, son of
Zeus, renowned for physical strength.

Or those which Atalanta did entice.
Exceeding sweet, yet voyd of sinfull vice,
That many sought yet none could euer taste,   10
Sweet fruit of pleasure brought from paradice
By loue himselfe, and in his garden plaste.
Her brest that table was so richly spredd,
My thoughts the guests, which would thereon
    haue fedd.

[from *Amoretti*]

---

l. 8. *Atalanta:* in Greek legend, a maiden who offered
to marry any man able to defeat her in a race; Hip-
pomenes won by dropping three golden apples, which
she stopped to pick up, along the way.

Epithalamion

Ye learnèd sisters, which have oftentimes
Beene to me ayding, others to adorne,
Whom ye thought worthy of your gracefull
    rymes,
That even the greatest did not greatly scorne
To heare theyr names sung in your simple
    layes,
But joyèd in theyr praise;
And when ye list your owne mishaps to
    mourne,
Which death, or love, or fortunes wreck did
    rayse,
Your string could soone to sadder tenor turne,
And teach the woods and waters to lament   10
Your dolefull dreriment:
Now lay those sorrowful complaints aside,
And having all your heads with girland
    crownd,
Helpe me mine owne loves prayses to
    resound;
Ne let the same of any be envide:

---

l. 7. *ye list:* [it] pleases you.

So Orpheus did for his owne bride:
So I unto my selfe alone will sing;
The woods shall to me answer, and my eccho
    ring.

Early, before the worlds light giving lampe
His golden beame upon the hils doth spred, 20
Having disperst the nights unchearefull
    dampe,
Doe ye awake, and, with fresh lustyhed,
Go to the bowre of my belovèd love,
    My truest turtle dove:
Bid her awake; for Hymen is awake,
And long since ready forth his maske to move,
With his bright tead that flames with many a
    flake,
And many a bachelor to waite on him,
    In theyr fresh garments trim.
Bid her awake therefore, and soone her
    dight,   30
For lo! the wishèd day is come at last,
That shall, for al the paynes and sorrowes
    past,
Pay to her usury of long delight:
    And whylest she doth her dight,
Doe ye to her of joy and solace sing,
That all the woods may answer, and your
    eccho ring.

Bring with you all the nymphes that you can
    heare,
Both of the rivers and the forrests greene,
And of the sea that neighbours to her neare,
Al with gay girlands goodly wel beseene. 40
And let them also with them bring in hand
    Another gay girland,
For my fayre love, of lillyes and of roses,
Bound truelove wize with a blew silke riband.

And let them make great store of bridale
    poses,
And let them eeke bring store of other
    flowers,
    To deck the bridale bowers.
And let the ground whereas her foot shall
    tread,
For feare the stones her tender foot should
    wrong,
Be strewed with fragrant flowers all along, 50
And diapred lyke the discolored mead.
Which done, doe at her chamber dore awayt,
    For she will waken strayt;
The whiles doe ye this song unto her sing
The woods shall to you answer, and your
    eccho ring.

Ye nymphes of Mulla, which with careful
    heed
The silver scaly trouts doe tend full well,
And greedy pikes which use therein to feed,
(Those trouts and pikes all others doo excel)
And ye likewise which keepe the rushy
    lake,   60
    Where none doo fishes take,
Bynd up the locks the which hang scatterd
    light,
And in his waters, which your mirror make,
Behold your faces as the christall bright,
That when you come whereas my love
    doth lie,
    No blemish she may spie.
And eke ye lightfoot mayds which keepe the
    dere
That on the hoary mountayne use to towre,
And the wylde wolves, which seeke them to
    devoure,
With your steele darts doo chase from coming
    neer,   70
    Be also present heere,
To helpe to decke her, and to help to sing,
That all the woods may answer, and your
    eccho ring.

---

l. 16. *Orpheus:* in Greek mythology, musician whose magic ability on the lyre affected beasts, rocks, and trees; when his wife Eurydice died, he obtained her release from the underworld on the condition that he would not look at her until they had reached the upper world, but he failed at the last moment.
l. 25. *Hymen:* god of marriage.
l. 27. *tead:* torch.
l. 34. *dight:* deck, adorn.

l. 51. *diapred lyke the discolored mead:* diversely adorned like the varicolored meadows.
l. 56. *Mulla:* name for an Irish river.

517 Edmund Spenser

Wake now, my love, awake! for it is time:
The rosy Morne long since left Tithones bed,
All ready to her silver coche to clyme,
And Phœbus gins to shew his glorious hed.
Hark how the cheerfull birds do chaunt theyr
    laies,
    And carroll of loves praise!
The merry larke hir mattins sings aloft,   80
The thrush replyes, the mavis descant playes,
The ouzell shrills, the ruddock warbles soft,
So goodly all agree, with sweet consent,
    To this dayes merriment.
Ah! my deere love, why doe ye sleepe thus
    long,
When meeter were that ye should now awake,
T'awayt the comming of your joyous make,
And hearken to the birds love-learnèd song,
    The deawy leaves among?
For they of joy and pleasance to you sing,   90
That all the woods them answer, and theyr
    eccho ring.

My love is now awake out of her dreame,
And her fayre eyes, like stars that dimmèd
    were
With darksome cloud, now shew theyr goodly
    beams
More bright then Hesperus his head doth
    rere.
Come now, ye damzels, daughters of delight,
    Helpe quickly her to dight.
But first come ye, fayre Houres, which were
    begot,
In Joves sweet paradice, of Day and Night,
Which doe the seasons of the year allot,   100
And al that ever in this world is fayre
    Do make and still repayre.
And ye three handmayds of the Cyprian
    Queene,
The which doe still adorne her beauties pride,
Helpe to addorne my beautifullest bride:

I. 75. *Tithones:* husband of Aurora, goddess of dawn.
I. 77. *Phœbus:* in Greek mythology, god of sun.
I. 82. *ouzell:* blackbird.
I. 82. *ruddock:* robin.
I. 95. *Hesperus:* Venus, the evening star.
I. 103. *Cyprian Queene:* Venus.

And as ye her array, still throw betweene
    Some graces to be seene:
And as ye use to Venus, to her sing,
The whiles the woods shal answer, and your
    eccho ring.

Now is my love all ready forth to come: 110
Let all the virgins therefore well awayt,
And ye fresh boyes, that tend upon her
    groome,
Prepare your selves, for he is comming strayt.
Set all your things in seemely good aray,
    Fit for so joyfull day,
The joyfulst day that ever sunne did see.
Faire Sun, shew forth thy favourable ray,
And let thy lifull heat not fervent be,
For feare of burning her sunshyny face,
    Her beauty to disgrace.   120
O fayrest Phœbus, father of the Muse,
If ever I did honour thee aright,
Or sing the thing that mote thy mind delight,
Doe not thy servants simple boone refuse,
But let this day, let this one day be myne,
    Let all the rest be thine.
Then I thy soverayne prayses loud wil sing,
That all the woods shal answer, and theyr
    eccho ring.

Harke how the minstrels gin to shrill aloud
Their merry musick that resounds from
    far,   130
The pipe, the tabor, and the trembling croud,
That well agree withouten breach or jar.
But most of all the damzels doe delite,
    When they their tymbrels smyte,
And thereunto doe daunce and carrol sweet,
That all the sences they doe ravish quite,
The whyles the boyes run up and downe the
    street,
Crying aloud with strong confusèd noyce,
    As if it were one voyce.
"Hymen, Iö Hymen, Hymen," they do
    shout,   140
That even to the heavens theyr shouting shrill
Doth reach, and all the firmament doth fill;

I. 131. *croud:* fiddle.

To which the people, standing all about,
As in approvance doe thereto applaud,
  And loud advaunce her laud,
And evermore they "Hymen, Hymen" sing,
That al the woods them answer, and theyr
    eccho ring.

Loe! where she comes along with portly pace,
Lyke Phœbe, from her chamber of the east,
Arysing forth to run her mighty race,   150
Clad all in white, that seemes a virgin best.
So well it her beseemes, that ye would weene
  Some angell she had beene.
Her long loose yellow locks lyke golden wyre,
Sprinckled with perle, and perling flowres
    atweene,
Doe lyke a golden mantle her attyre,
And being crownèd with a girland greene,
  Seeme lyke some mayden queene.
Her modest eyes, abashéd to behold
So many gazers as on her do stare,   160
Upon the lowly ground affixèd are;
Ne dare lift up her countenance too bold,
But blush to heare her prayses sung so loud,
  So farre from being proud.
Nathlesse doe ye still loud her prayses sing,
That all the woods may answer, and your
    eccho ring.

Tell me, ye merchants daughters, did ye see
So fayre a creature in your towne before,
So sweet, so lovely, and so mild as she,
Adorned with beautyes grace and vertues
    store?   170
Her goodly eyes lyke saphyres shining bright,
  Her forehead yvory white,
Her cheekes lyke apples which the sun hath
    rudded,
Her lips lyke cherryes charming men to byte,
Her breast like to a bowle of creame
    uncrudded,
  Her paps lyke lyllies budded,
Her snowie necke lyke to a marble towre,
And all her body like a pallace fayre,

Ascending uppe, with many a stately stayre,
To honors seat and chastities sweet bowre. 180
Why stand ye still, ye virgins, in amaze,
  Upon her so to gaze,
Whiles ye forget your former lay to sing,
To which the woods did answer, and your
    eccho ring.

But if ye saw that which no eyes can see,
The inward beauty of her lively spright,
Garnisht with heavenly guifts of high degree,
Much more then would ye wonder at that
    sight,
And stand astonisht lyke to those which red
    Medusaes mazeful hed.   190
There dwels sweet Love and constant
    Chastity,
Unspotted Fayth, and comely Womanhood,
Regard of Honour, and mild Modesty;
There Vertue raynes as queene in royal
    throne,
  And giveth lawes alone,
The which the base affections doe obay.
And yeeld theyr services unto her will;
Ne thought of thing uncomely ever may
Thereto approch to tempt her mind to ill.
Had ye once seene these her celestial
    threasures,   200
  And unrevealèd pleasures,
Then would ye wonder, and her prayses sing,
That al the woods should answer, and your
    echo ring.

Open the temple gates unto my love,
Open them wide that she may enter in,
And all the postes adorne as doth behove,
And all the pillours deck with girlands trim,
For to receyve this saynt with honour dew,
  That commeth in to you.
With trembling steps and humble
    reverence,   210
She commeth in before th' Almighties view:
Of her, ye virgins, learne obedience,

---

l. 175. *uncrudded:* uncurdled.

l. 190. *Medusa:* in Greek mythology, a monster with snakes for hair and a gaze that turned anyone who looked at her into stone.

When so ye come into those holy places,
    To humble your proud faces.
Bring her up to th' high altar, that she may
The sacred ceremonies there partake,
The which do endlesse matrimony make;
And let the roring organs loudly play
The praises of the Lord in lively notes,
    The whiles with hollow throates   220
The choristers the joyous antheme sing,
That al the woods may answere, and their
        eccho ring.

Behold, whiles she before the altar stands,
Hearing the holy priest that to her speakes,
And blesseth her with his two happy hands,
How the red roses flush in her cheekes,
And the pure snow with goodly vermill stayne,
    Like crimson dyde in grayne:
That even th' angels, which continually
About the sacred altare doe remaine,   230
Forget their service and about her fly,
Ofte peeping in her face, that seemes more
        fayre,
The more they on it stare.
But her sad eyes, still fastened on the ground,
Are governèd with goodly modesty,
That suffers not one looke to glaunce awry,
Which may let in a little thought unsownd.
Why blush ye, love, to give to me your hand,
The pledge of all our band?
Sing, ye sweet angels, Alleluya sing,   240
That all the woods may answere, and your
        eccho ring.

Now al is done; bring home the bridge againe,
Bring home the triumph of our victory,
Bring home with you the glory of her gaine,
With joyance bring her and with jollity.
Never had man more joyfull day then this,
Whom heaven would heape with blis.
Make feast therefore now all this live long
        day;
This day for ever to me holy is;
Poure out the wine without restraint or
        stay,   250
Poure not by cups, but by the belly full,
Poure out to all that wull,

And sprinkle all the postes and wals with
        wine,
That they may sweat, and drunken be withall.
Crowne ye God Bacchus with a coronall.
And Hymen also crowne with wreathes of
        vine;
And let the Graces daunce unto the rest,
For they can doo it best:
The whiles the maydens doe theyr carroll
        sing,
The which the woods shal answer, and theyr
        eccho ring.   260

Ring ye the bels, ye yong men of the towne,
And leave your wonted labors for this day:
This day is holy; doe ye write it downe,
That ye for ever it remember may.
This day the sunne is in his chiefest hight,
With Barnaby the bright,
From whence declining daily by degrees,
He somewhat loseth of his heat and light,
When once the Crab behind his back he sees.
But for this time it ill ordainèd was,   270
To chose the longest day in all the yeare,
And shortest night, when longest fitter weare:
Yet never day so long, but late would passe.
Ring ye the bels, to make it weare away,
And bonefires make all day,
And daunce about them, and about them sing:
That all the woods may answer, and your
        eccho ring.

Ah! when will this long weary day have end,
And lende me leave to come unto my love?
How slowly do the houres theyr numbers
        spend!   280
How slowly does sad Time his feathers move!
Hast thee, O fayrest planet, to thy home
Within the westerne foame:
Thy tyrèd steedes long since have need of rest.
Long though it be, at last I see it gloome,
And the bright evening star with golden creast

---

l. 255. *Bacchus:* god of wine.
l. 266. *Barnaby:* Saint Barnabus, whose day (June 11) coincided under the old calendar with the summer solstice (June 22).

Appeare out of the east.
Fayre childe of beauty, glorious lampe of
    love,
That all the host of heaven in rankes doost
    lead,
And guydest lovers through the nightes
    dread,   **290**
How chearefully thou lookest from above,
And seemst to laugh atweene thy twinkling
    light,
As joying in the sight
Of these glad many, which for joy doe sing,
That all the woods them answer, and their
    echo ring!

Now ceasse, ye damsels, your delights
    forepast;
Enough is it that all the day was youres:
Now day is doen, and night is nighing fast:
Now bring the bryde into the brydall boures
The night is come, now soone her disaray, **300**
And in her bed her lay;
Lay her in lillies and in violets,
And silken courteins over her display,
And odoured sheetes, and Arras coverlets.
Behold how goodly my faire love does ly,
In proud humility!
Like unto Maia, when as Jove her tooke
In Tempe, lying on the flowry gras,
Twixt sleepe and wake, after she weary was
With bathing in the Acidalian brooke.   **310**
Now it is night, ye damsels may be gon,
And leave my love alone.
And leave likewise your former lay to sing:
The woods no more shal answere, nor your
    echo ring.

Now welcome, night! thou night so long
    expected,
That long daies labour doest at last defray,
And all my cares, which cruell Love collected,
Hast sumd in one, and cancellèd for aye:
Spread thy broad wing over my love and me,
That no man may us see,   **320**
And in thy sable mantle us enwrap,
From feare of perrill and foule horror free.
Let no false treason seeke us to entrap,

Nor any dread disquiet once annoy
The safety of our joy:
But let the night be calme and quietsome,
Without tempestuous storms or sad afray:
Lyke as when Jove with fayre Alcmena lay,
When he begot the great Tirynthian groome:
Or lyke as when he with thy selfe did lie,   **330**
And begot Majesty.
And let the mayds and yongmen cease to sing:
Ne let the woods them answer, nor theyr
    eccho ring.

Let no lamenting cryes, nor dolefull teares,
Be heard all night within, nor yet without:
Ne let false whispers, breeding hidden feares,
Breake gentle sleepe with misconceivèd dout.
Let no deluding dreames, nor dreadful sights,
Make sudden sad affrights;
Ne let house-fyres, nor lightnings helplesse
    harmes,   **340**
Ne let the Pouke, nor other evill sprights,
Ne let mischivous witches with theyr
    charmes,
Ne let hob goblins, names whose sense we see
    not,
Fray us with things that be not.
Let not the shriech oule, nor the storke be
    heard
Nor the night raven that still deadly yels,
Nor damnèd ghosts cald up with mighty spels,
Nor griesly vultures make us once affeard:
Ne let th' unpleasant quyre of frogs still
    croking
Make us to wish theyr choking.   **350**
Let none of these theyr drery accents sing;
Ne let the woods them answer, nor theyr
    eccho ring.

But let stil Silence trew night watches keepe,
That sacred Peace may in assurance rayne,
And tymely Sleep, when it is tyme to sleepe,
May poure his limbs forth on your pleasant
    playne,

---

l. 329. *Tirynthian groome:* Hercules, born at Tiryus,
who cleaned the stables of King Augeas.

The whiles an hundred little wingèd loves,
　Like divers fethered doves,
Shall fly and flutter round about our bed,
And in the secret darke, that none
　　reproves,　　　　　　　　　　　　360
Their prety stealthes shall worke, and snares
　shal spread
To filch away sweet snatches of delight,
　Conceald through covert night.
Ye sonnes of Venus, play your sports at will:
For greedy Pleasure, careless of your toyes,
Thinks more upon her paradise of joyes,
Then what ye do, albe it good or ill.
All night therefore attend your merry play,
　For it will soone be day:
Now none doth hinder you, that say or
　　sing,　　　　　　　　　　　　　　370
Ne will the woods now answer, nor your
　eccho ring.

Who is the same which at my window peepes?
Or whose is that faire face that shines so
　　bright?
Is it not Cinthia, she that never sleepes,
But walkes about high heaven al the night?
O fayrest goddesse, do thou not envy
　My love with me to spy:
For thou likewise didst love, though now
　　unthought,
And for a fleece of woll, which privily
The Latmian shephard once unto thee
　　brought,　　　　　　　　　　　　380
　His pleasures with thee wrought.
Therefore to us be favorable now;
And sith of wemens labours thou hast charge,
And generation goodly dost enlarge,
Encline thy will t' effect our wishful vow,
And the chast wombe informe with timely
　seed,
　That may our comfort breed:
Till which we cease our hopefull hap to sing,
Ne let the woods us answere, nor our eccho
　ring.

_____
l. 380. *Latmian shephard:* Endymion, beloved of the
moon goddess.

And thou, great Juno, which with awful
　　might　　　　　　　　　　　　　390
The lawes of wedlock still dost patronize,
And the religion of the faith first plight
With sacred rites hast taught to solemnize,
And eeke for comfort often callèd art
　Of women in their smart,
Eternally bind thou this lovely band,
And all thy blessings unto us impart.
And thou, glad Genius, in whose gentle hand
The bridale bowre and geniall bed remaine,
　Without blemish or staine,　　　　400
And the sweet pleasures of theyr loves delight
With secret ayde doest succour and supply,
Till they bring forth the fruitfull progeny,
Send us the timely fruit of this same night.
And thou, fayre Hebe, and thou, Hymen free,
　Grant that it may so be.
Til which we cease your further prayse to
　sing,
Ne any woods shal answer, nor your eccho
　ring.

And ye high heavens, the temple of the gods,
In which a thousand torches flaming
　　bright　　　　　　　　　　　　410
Doe burne, that to us wretched earthly clods
In dreadful darknesse lend desirèd light,
And all ye powers which in the same remayne,
　More then we men can fayne,
Poure out your blessing on us plentiously,
And happy influence upon us raine,
That we may raise a large posterity,
Which from the earth, which they may long
　possesse
　With lasting happinesse,
Up to your haughty pallaces may mount,　420
And for the guerdon of theyr glorious merit,
May heavenly tabernacles there inherit,
Of blessed saints for to increase the count.
So let us rest, sweet love, in hope of this,
And cease till then our tymely joyes to sing:
The woods no more us answer, nor our eccho
　ring.

Song, made in lieu of many ornaments

With which my love should duly have bene
    dect,
Which cutting off through hasty accidents,
Ye would not stay your dew time to
    expect,   **430**
  But promist both to recompens,
Be unto her a goodly ornament,
And for short time an endlesse moniment.

sir philip sidney

Sonnet I

Loving in truth, and faine in verse my love to
    show,
That the deare She might take some pleasure
    of my paine:
Pleasure might cause her reade, reading might
    make her know,
Knowledge might pitie winne, and pitie grace
    obtaine,
  I sought fit words to paint the blackest face
    of woe,
Studying inventions fine, her wits to
    entertaine:
Oft turning others' leaves, to see if thence
    would flow
Some fresh and fruitfull showers upon my
    sunne-burn'd braine.
  But words came halting forth, wanting
    Invention's stay,
Invention, Nature's child, fled step-dame
    Studie's blowes,   **10**
And others' feete still seem'd but strangers in
    my way.

Thus great with child to speake, and helplesse
    in my throwes,

l. 1. *faine:* desirous.
l. 10. *Invention:* imagination.

Biting my trewand pen, beating my selfe for
    spite,
  'Foole,' said my Muse to me, 'looke in thy
    heart and write.'

          [from *Astrophel and Stella*]

l. 13. *trewand:* truant.

Sonnet XX

Flie, fly, my friends, I have my death wound;
    fly,
See there that boy, that murthring boy I say,
Who like a theefe, hid in darke bush doth ly,
Till bloudie bullet get him wrongfull pray.
  So Tyran he no fitter place could spie,
Nor so faire levell in so secret stay,
As that sweete blacke which vailes the
    heav'nly eye:
There himselfe with his shot he close doth lay.
  Poore passenger, passe now thereby I did,
And staid pleasd with the prospect of the
    place,   **10**
While that blacke hue from me the bad guest
    hid:
But straight I saw motions of lightning'
    grace,
  And then descried the glistring of his dart:
  But ere I could flie thence, it pierc'd my
    heart.

          [from *Astrophel and Stella*]

Ring Out Your Belles, Let Mourning Shewes Be Spread

Ring out your belles, let mourning shewes
    be spread,
  For love is dead:

All Love is dead, infected
With plague of deepe disdaine:
Worth as nought worth rejected,
And Faith faire scorne doth gaine.
   From so ungratefull fancie,
   From such a femall franzie,
   From them that use men thus,
   Good Lord deliver us.   10

Weepe neighbours, weepe, do you not heare it
    said,
  That Love is dead?
   His death-bed peacock's follie,
   His winding sheete is shame,
   His will false-seeming holie,
   His sole exec'tour blame.
     From so ungratefull fancie,
     From such a femall franzie,
     From them that use men thus,
     Good Lord deliver us.   20

Let Dirge be sung, and Trentals rightly read,
  For Love is dead:
   Sir wrong his tombe ordaineth,
   My mistresse' Marble hart,
   Which Epitaph containeth,
   'Her eyes were once his dart'.
     From so ungratefull fancie,
     From such a femall franzie,
     From them that use men thus,
     Good Lord deliver us.   30

Alas, I lie: rage hath this errour bred,
  Love is not dead.
   Love is not dead, but sleepeth
   In her unmatched mind:
   Where she his counsell keepeth,
   Till due desert she find.
     Therefore from so vile fancie,
     To call such wit a franzie,
     Who love can temper thus,
     Good Lord deliver us.   40

---

l. 21. *Trentals:* literally, thirty masses; masses for the dead.

william shakespeare

When Daisies Pied and Violets Blue

When daisies pied and violets blue
   And lady-smocks all silver-white
And cuckoo-buds of yellow hue
   Do paint the meadows with delight,
The cuckoo then, on every tree,
Mocks married men; for thus sings he,
    Cuckoo,
Cuckoo, cuckoo! O word of fear
Unpleasing to a married ear!

When shepherds pipe on oaten straws,   10
   And merry larks are ploughmen's clocks,
When turtles tread, and rooks, and daws,
   And maidens bleach their summer
     smocks,
The cuckoo then, on every tree,
Mocks married men; for thus sings he,
    Cuckoo,
Cuckoo, cuckoo! O word of fear,
Unpleasing to a married ear!

[from *Love's Labour's Lost*]

---

l. 9. *Unpleasing . . . ear:* Because of her habit of laying eggs in others' nests, the cuckoo was a popular symbol for marital infidelity.

When Icicles Hang by the Wall

When icicles hang by the wall,
   And Dick the shepherd blows his nail,
And Tom bears logs into the hall,

---

l. 2. *nail:* fingernail.

And milk comes frozen home in pail,
When blood is nipp'd, and ways be foul,
Then nightly sings the staring owl,
    Tu-whit, to-who,
    A merry note,
While greasy Joan doth keel the pot.

When all aloud the wind doth blow,   10
    And coughing drowns the parson's saw,
And birds sit brooding in the snow,
    And Marian's nose looks red and raw,
When roasted crabs hiss in the bowl,
Then nightly sings the staring owl,
    Tu-whit, to-who,
    A merry note,
While greasy Joan doth keel the pot.

        [from *Love's Labour's Lost*]

Take, O Take Those Lips Away

Take, O take those lips away,
    That so sweetly were forsworn;
And those eyes, the break of day,
    Lights that do mislead the morn:
But my kisses bring again,
    Bring again,
Seals of love, but seal'd in vain,
    Seal'd in vain.

        [from *Measure for Measure*]

Full Fadom Five Thy Father Lies

Full fadom five thy father lies,
    Of his bones are coral made:
Those are pearls that were his eyes;
    Nothing of him that doth fade
But doth suffer a sea-change

Into something rich and strange:
Sea nymphs hourly ring his knell:
    Ding, dong.
Hark, now I hear them—ding-dong bell.

        [from *The Tempest*]

Sonnet XXIX

When, in disgrace with Fortune and men's
    eyes,
I all alone beweep my outcast state,
And trouble deaf heaven with my bootless
    cries,
And look upon myself and curse my fate,
Wishing me like to one more rich in hope,
Featured like him, like him with friends
    possessed,
Desiring this man's art, and that man's
    scope,
With what I most enjoy contented least;
Yet in these thoughts myself almost
    despising,
Haply I think on thee, and then my state,   10
Like to the lark at break of day arising
From sullen earth, sings hymns at heaven's
    gate;
    For thy sweet love rem3mb'red such wealth
    brings
    That then I scorn to change my state with
    kings.

l. 3. *bootless:* profitless.
l. 6. *Featured like him:* physically handsome.

Sonnet LXXIII

That time of year thou mayst in me behold
When yellow leaves, or none, or few, do hang
Upon those boughs which shake against the
    cold,

Bare ruined choirs where late the sweet
    birds sang.
In me thou see'st the twilight of such day
As after sunset fadeth in the west,
Which by-and-by black night doth take away,
Death's second self, that seals up all in rest.
In me thou see'st the glowing of such fire
That on the ashes of his youth doth lie,   10
As the deathbed whereon it must expire,
Consumed with that which it was
    nourished by.
  This thou perceiv'st, which makes thy love
    more strong,
  To love that well which thou must leave
    ere long.

Sonnet XCIV

They that have pow'r to hurt and will do
    none,
That do not do the thing they most do show,
Who, moving others, are themselves as stone,
Unmovèd, cold, and to temptation slow—
They rightly do inherit heaven's graces
And husband nature's riches from expense;
They are the lords and owners of their faces,
Others but stewards of their excellence.
The summer's flow'r is to the summer sweet,
Though to itself it only live and die;   10
But if that flow'r with base infection meet,
The basest weed outbraves his dignity:
  For sweetest things turn sourest by their
    deeds;
  Lilies that fester smell far worse than
    weeds.

Sonnet CXVIII

Like as, to make our appetites more keen,
With eager compounds we our palate urge;

As, to prevent our maladies unseen,
We sicken to shun sickness when we purge:
Even so, being full of your ne'er-cloying
    sweetness,
To bitter sauces did I frame my feeding;
And, sick of welfare, found a kind of
    meetness
To be diseased ere that there was true
    needing.
Thus policy in love, t' anticipate
The ills that were not, grew to faults
    assured,   10
And brought to medicine a healthful state,
Which, rank of goodness, would by ill be
    cured.
  But thence I learn, and find the lesson true,
  Drugs poison him that so fell sick of you.

Sonnet CXXXVIII

When my love swears that she is made of
    truth
I do believe her, though I know she lies,
That she might think me some untutored
    youth,
Unlearnèd in the world's false subtilties.
Thus vainly thinking that she thinks me
    young,
Although she knows my days are past the
    best,
Simply I credit her false-speaking tongue:
On both sides thus is simple truth
    suppressed.
But wherefore says she not she is unjust?
And wherefore say not I that I am old?   10
O, love's best habit is in seeming trust,
And age in love loves not to have years told.
  Therefore I lie with her and she with me,
  And in our faults by lies we flattered be.

Sonnet CXLVI

Poor soul, the center of my sinful earth,
My sinful earth these rebel pow'rs that thee
    array,
Why dost thou pine within and suffer dearth,
Painting thy outward walls so costly gay?
Why so large cost, having so short a lease,
Dost thou upon thy fading mansion spend?
Shall worms, inheritors of this excess,
Eat up thy charge? Is this thy body's end?
Then, soul, live thou upon thy servant's loss,
And let that pine to aggravate thy store;   **10**
Buy terms divine in selling hours of dross;
Within be fed, without be rich no more.
  So shalt thou feed on Death, that feeds on
    men,
  And Death once dead, there's no more dying
    then.

Sonnet CLI

Love is too young to know what conscience is;
Yet who knows not conscience is born of love?
Then, gentle cheater, urge not my amiss,
Lest guilty of my faults thy sweet self prove.
For, thou betraying me, I do betray
My nobler part to my gross body's treason;
My soul doth tell my body that he may
Triumph in love; flesh stays no farther
    reason,
But, rising at thy name, doth point out thee
As his triumphant prize. Proud of this
    pride,   **10**
He is contented thy poor drudge to be,
To stand in thy affairs, fall by thy side.
  No want of conscience hold it that I call
  Her "love" for whose dear love I rise and
    fall.

BEN JONSON

On My First Sonne

Farewell, thou child of my right hand, and
    joy;
My sinne was too much hope of thee, lov'd
    boy;
Seven yeeres tho'wert lent to me, and I thee
    pay,
Exacted by thy fate, on the just day.
O, could I loose all father, now. For why
Will man lament the state he should envie?
To have so soone scap'd worlds, and fleshes
    rage,
And, if no other miseries, yet age?
Rest in soft peace, and, ask'd, say here doth
    lye
Ben. Jonson his best piece of poetrie.   **10**
For whose sake, hence-forth, all his vowes be
    such,
As what he loves may never like too much.

---

l. 1. *child . . . right hand:* the Hebrew signification of the name Benjamin.

Inviting a Friend to Supper

To night, grave sir, both my poore house,
    and I
Doe equally desire your companie:
Not that we thinke us worthy such a ghest,
But that your worth will dignifie our feast,
With those that come; whose grace may
    make that seeme
Something, which, else, could hope for no
    esteeme.
It is the faire acceptance, Sir, creates

The entertaynment perfect: not the cates.
Yet shall you have, to rectifie your palate,
An olive, capers, or some better sallade   10
Ushring the mutton; with a short-leg'd hen,
If we can get her, full of egs, and then,
Limons, and wine for sauce: to these, a coney
Is not to be despair'd of, for our money;
And, though fowle, now, be scarce, yet there
    are clarkes,
The skie not falling, thinke we may have
    larkes.
Ile tell you more, and lye, so you will come:
Of partrich, pheasant, wood-cock, of which
    some
May yet be there; and godwit, if we can:
Knat, raile, and ruffe too. How so ere, my
    man   20
Shall reade a piece of *Virgil, Tacitus,*
Livie, or of some better booke to us,
Of which wee'll speake our minds, amidst
    our meate;
And Ile professe no verses to repeate:
To this, if ought appeare, which I not know of,
That will the pastrie, not my paper, show of.
Digestive cheese, and fruit there sure will bee;
But that, which most doth take my Muse,
    and mee,
Is a pure cup of rich Canary-wine,
Which is the Mermaids, now, but shall be
    mine: 30
Of which had *Horace,* or *Anacreon* tasted,
Their lives, as doe their lines, till now had
    lasted.
Tabacco, Nectar, or the Thespian spring,
Are all but *Luthers* beere, to this I sing.

---

l. 8. *cates:* delicacies.
l. 13. *coney:* rabbit.
l. 15. *clarkes:* clerks.
l. 19. *godwit:* a marsh bird.
l. 20. *Knat . . . ruffe:* two birds and a fish.
l. 21. *Virgil:* a Roman poet (70–19 B.C.).
l. 21. *Tacitus:* a Roman historian (A.D. 55?–117?).
l. 22. *Livie:* a Roman historian (59 B.C.–A.D. 17).
l. 30. *Mermaid:* a tavern.
l. 31. *Horace:* a Roman poet (65–8 B.C.).
l. 31. *Anacreon:* a Greek poet (572?–488? B.C.).
l. 33. *Thespian spring:* waters sacred to Thespis, reputed founder of the Greek drama.

Of this we will sup free, but moderately,
And we will have no Pooly', or Parrot by;
Nor shall our cups make any guiltie men:
But, at our parting, we will be, as when
We innocently met. No simple word,
That shall be utter'd at our mirthfull
    boord,   40
Shall make us sad next morning: or affright
The libertie, that wee'll enjoy to night.

---

l. 36. *Pooly', or Parrot:* supposed to be men who once
attacked Jonson.

Song. To Celia

Drinke to me, onely, with thine eyes,
    And I will pledge with mine;
Or leave a kisse but in the cup,
    And Ile not looke for wine.
The thirst, that from the soule doth rise,
    Doth aske a drinke divine:
But might I of *Jove's* Nectar sup,
    I would not change for thine.
I sent thee, late, a rosie wreath,
    Not so much honoring thee,   10
As giving it a hope, that there
    It could not withered bee.
But thou thereon did'st onely breath,
    And sent'st it backe to mee:
Since when it growes, and smells, I sweare,
    Not of it selfe, but thee.

Ode to Himselfe

    Come leave the loathed Stage,
    And the more loathsome Age,
Where pride and impudence in faction knit,
    Usurpe the Chaire of wit:

Inditing and arraigning every day,
　　Something they call a Play.
　　Let their fastidious vaine
　　Commission of the braine,
Runne on, and rage, sweat, censure, and
　　condemn,
They were not made for thee, lesse thou for
　　them.　　　　　　　　　　　　　　　10

　　Say that thou pour'st'hem wheat,
　　And they would Akornes eat:
'Twere simple fury, still thy selfe to wast
　　On such as have no taste:
To offer them a surfeit of pure bread,
　　Whose appetites are dead:
　　No, give them Graines their fill,
　　Huskes, Draffe to drinke, and swill:
If they love Lees, and leave the lusty Wine,
Envy them not, their pallat's with the
　　Swine.　　　　　　　　　　　　　　20

　　No doubt a mouldy Tale,
　　Like *Pericles*, and stale
As the Shrives crusts, and nasty as his Fish,
　　Scraps out of every Dish,
Throwne forth and rak'd into the common
　　Tub,
　　May keep up the Play Club.
　　Broomes sweepings doe as well
　　There, as his Masters meale:
For who the relish of these guests will fit,
Needs set them but the Almes-basket of wit. 30

　　And much good do't yee then,
　　Brave Plush and Velvet men
Can feed on Orts; and safe in your scoene
　　cloaths,
　　Dare quit upon your Oathes
The Stagers, and the stage-writes too; your
　　Peers,
　　Of stuffing your large eares
　　With rage of Commicke socks,
　　Wrought upon twenty Blocks;
Which, if they're torne, and foule, and
　　patch'd enough,

The Gamsters share your gilt, and you
　　their stuffe.　　　　　　　　　　　40

　　Leave things so prostitute,
　　And take th'*Alcaike* Lute;
Or thine owne *Horace*, or *Anacreons* Lyre;
　　Warme thee by *Pindars* fire:
And though thy Nerves be shrunke, and
　　blood be cold,
　　Ere years have made thee old,
　　Strike that disdainfull heat
　　Throughout, to their defeat:
As curious fooles, and envious of thy straine,
May blushing sweare, no Palsi's in thy
　　braine.　　　　　　　　　　　　　50

　　But when they heare thee sing
　　The glories of thy King;
His zeale to God, and his just awe of men,
　　They may be blood-shaken, then
Feele such a flesh-quake to possesse their
　　powers,
　　That no tun'd Harpe like ours,
　　In sound of Peace or Warres,
　　Shall truely hit the Starres
When they shall read the Acts of *Charles*
　　his Reigne,
And see his Chariot triumph 'bove his
　　Waine.　　　　　　　　　　　　　60

---

l. 42. *Alcaike:* characteristic of Alcaeus, Greek poet
(620–580 B.C.), who wrote four-stanza odes with four
lines to a stanza and four feet to a line.
l. 44. *Pindar:* Greek poet (522?–443 B.C.).
l. 59. *Charles:* King Charles I of England (1600–1649).

---

l. 33. *Orts:* scraps of food left from a meal.

john donne

Air and Angels

Twice or thrice had I loved thee,
Before I knew thy face or name;
So in a voice, so in a shapeless flame
Angels affect us oft, and worshiped be;
    Still when, to where thou wert, I came,
Some lovely glorious nothing I did see.
      But since my soul, whose child love is,
Takes limbs of flesh, and else could nothing
        do,
    More subtle than the parent is
Love must not be, but take a body too;   10
    And therefore what thou wert, and who,
      I bid Love ask, and now
That it assume thy body, I allow,
And fix itself in thy lip, eye, and brow.

Whilst thus to ballast love, I thought,
And so more steadily to have gone,
With wares which would sink admiration
I saw I had love's pinnace overfraught;
    Every thy hair for love to work upon
Is much too much, some fitter must be
      sought;   20
    For, nor in nothing, nor in things
Extreme, and scatt'ring bright, can love
      inhere;
    Then as an angel, face, and wings
Of air, not pure as it, yet pure doth wear,
    So thy love may be my love's sphere;
      Just such disparity
As is 'twixt air and angels' purity,
'Twixt women's love and men's will ever be.

---

l. 19. *Every thy hair:* each of your hairs and even your least hair.
l. 22. *scatt'ring:* dazzlingly.
l. 24. *Of air . . . wear:* According to scholastic doctrine, angels, in order to appear to men, assumed bodies of air, less pure than angelic essence.
l. 25. *sphere:* Each celestial sphere was said to be governed by an angel.

The Relic

When my grave is broke up again
Some second guest to entertain
(For graves have learned that
    woman-head,
  To be to more than one a bed)
    And he that digs it spies
A bracelet of bright hair about the bone,
    Will he not let us alone,
And think that there a loving couple lies,
Who thought that this device might be some
    way
To make their souls, at the last busy day,   10
Meet at this grave, and make a little stay?

    If this fall in a time, or land,
    Where mis-devotion doth command,
    Then he that digs us up will bring
    Us to the Bishop and the King
      To make us relics; then
Thou shalt be a Mary Magdalen, and I
    A something else thereby;
All women shall adore us, and some men;
And, since at such time miracles are sought, 20
I would have that age by this paper taught
What miracles we harmless lovers wrought.

    First, we loved well and faithfully,
    Yet knew not what we loved, nor why;
    Difference of sex no more we knew,
    Than our guardian angels do;
      Coming and going, we
Perchance might kiss, but not between those
    meals;
    Our hands ne'er touched the seals
Which nature, injured by late law, sets free. 30
These miracles we did; but now, alas,
All measure, and all language, I should pass,
Should I tell what a miracle she was.

---

l. 2. *Some . . . entertain:* referring to the reuse of burial ground.

Elegy XIX. To His Mistress Going to Bed

Come, madam, come, all rest my powers defy,
Until labor, I in labor lie.
The foe oft-times having the foe in sight,
Is tired with standing though he never fight.
Off with that girdle, like heaven's zone
    glistering,
But a far fairer world encompassing.
Unpin that spangled breastplate which you
    wear,
That the eyes of busy fools may be stopped
    there.
Unlace yourself, for that harmonious chime
Tells me from you that now 'tis your bed
    time.   10
Off with that happy busk, which I envy,
That still can be, and still can stand so nigh.
Your gown, going off, such beauteous state
    reveals,
As when from flowry meads the hill's shadow
    steals.
Off with that wiry coronet and show
The hairy diadem which on you doth grow:
Now off with those shoes, and then
    safely tread
In this love's hallowed temple, this soft bed.
In such white robes, heaven's angels used
    to be
Received by men; thou, Angel, bring'st with
    thee   20
A heaven like Mahomet's Paradise; and
    though
Ill spirits walk in white, we easily know
By this these angels from an evil sprite:
Those set our hairs, but these our flesh
    upright.
    License my roving hands, and let them go
Before, behind, between, above, below.
O my America! my new-found-land,
My kingdom, safeliest when with one man
    manned,

My mine of precious stones, my empery,
How blest am I in this discovering thee!   30
To enter in these bonds is to be free;
Then where my hand is set, my seal shall be.
    Full nakedness! All joys are due to thee,
As souls unbodied, bodies unclothed must be
To taste whole joys. Gems which you women
    use
Are like Atlanta's balls, cast in men's views,
That when a fool's eye lighteth on a gem,
His earthly soul may covet theirs, not them.
Like pictures, or like books' gay coverings
    made
For lay-men, are all women thus arrayed;   40
Themselves are mystic books, which only we
(Whom their imputed grace will dignify)
Must see revealed. Then, since that I may
    know,
As liberally as to a midwife, show
Thyself: cast all, yea, this white linen hence,
Here is no penance, much less innocence.
    To teach thee, I am naked first; why than,
What needst thou have more covering than
    a man.

---

l. 47. *than:* then.

Sonnet XIV

Batter my heart, three-personed God; for
    You
As yet but knock, breathe, shine, and seek to
    mend;
That I may rise and stand, o'erthrow me,
    and bend
Your force, to break, blow, burn, and make
    me new.
I, like an usurped town, to another due,
Labor to admit You, but Oh, to no end!
Reason, Your viceroy in me, me should
    defend,

---

l. 11. *busk:* corset.
l. 15. *coronet:* part of a woman's headdress.

But is captived, and proves weak or untrue.
Yet dearly I love You, and would be loved
   fain,
But am betrothed unto Your enemy: 10
Divorce me, untie or break that knot again,
Take me to You, imprison me, for I,
Except You enthrall me, never shall be free,
Nor ever chaste, except You ravish me.

[from *Holy Sonnets*]

Good Friday, 1613. Riding Westward

Let man's soul be a sphere, and then, in this,
The intelligence that moves, devotion is,
And as the other spheres, by being grown
Subject to foreign motions, lose their own,
And being by others hurried every day,
Scarce in a year their natural form obey,
Pleasure or business, so our souls admit
For their first mover, and are whirled by it.
Hence is 't that I am carried towards the
   West
This day, when my soul's form bends toward
   the East.   10
There I should see a Sun, by rising, set,
And by that setting endless day beget;
But that Christ on this cross did rise and fall,
Sin had eternally benighted all.
Yet dare I almost be glad I do not see
That spectacle of too much weight for me.
Who sees God's face, that is self life, must die;
What a death were it then to see God die?
It made His own lieutenant, Nature, shrink;
It made His footstool crack, and the sun
   wink.   20
Could I behold those hands which span the
   poles,
And tune all spheres at once, pierced with
   those holes?

Could I behold that endless height which is
Zenith to us, and our antipodes,
Humbled below us? or that blood which is
The seat of all our souls, if not of His,
Make dirt of dust, or that flesh which was
   worn
By God, for His apparel, ragg'd and torn?
If on these things I durst not look, durst I
Upon his miserable mother cast mine eye,   30
Who was God's partner here, and furnished
   thus
Half of that sacrifice which ransomed us?
Though these things, as I ride, be from mine
   eye,
They're present yet unto my memory,
For that looks towards them; and Thou
   look'st towards me,
O Saviour, as Thou hang'st upon the tree;
I turn my back to Thee but to receive
Corrections, till Thy mercies Thee leave.
O think me worth Thine anger, punish me,
Burn off my rusts and my deformity,   40
Restore Thine image so much, by Thy grace,
That Thou may'st know me, and I'll turn my
   face.

ROBERT HERRICK

Love What It Is

Love is a circle that doth restlesse move
In the same sweet eternity of love.

---

l. 2. *intelligence:* Each sphere was thought to have a
guiding intelligence.

The Carkanet

Instead of Orient Pearls, of Jet,
I sent my Love a Karkanet:
About her spotlesse neck she knit
The lace, to honour me, or it:
Then think how wrapt was I to see
My Jet t'enthrall such Ivorie.

Delight in Disorder

A sweet disorder in the dresse
Kindles in cloathes a wantonnesse:
A Lawne about the shoulders thrown
Into a fine distraction:
An erring Lace, which here and there
Enthralls the Crimson Stomacher:
A Cuffe neglectfull, and thereby
Ribbands to flow confusedly:
A winning wave (deserving Note)
In the tempestuous petticote: 10
A carelesse shooe-string, in whose tye
I see a wilde civility:
Doe more bewitch me, then when Art
Is too precise in every part.

---

l.3. *Lawne:* fine linen scarf.

Upon Julia's Clothes

When as in silks my *Julia* goes,
Then, then (me thinks) how sweetly flowes
That liquefaction of her clothes.

Next, when I cast mine eyes and see
That brave Vibration each way free;
O how that glittering taketh me!

Corinna's Going a Maying

Get up, get up for shame, the Blooming
       Morne
Upon her wings presents the god unshorne.
    See how *Aurora* throwes her faire
    Fresh-quilted colours through the aire:
    Get up, sweet-Slug-a-bed, and see
    The Dew-bespangling Herbe and Tree.
Each Flower has wept, and bow'd toward
       the East,
Above an houre since; yet you not drest,
       Nay! not so much as out of bed?
       When all the Birds have Mattens seyd, 10
       And sung their thankfull Hymnes: 'tis sin,
       Nay, profanation to keep in,
When as a thousand Virgins on this day,
Spring, sooner then the Lark, to fetch in May.

Rise; and put on your Foliage, and be seene
To come forth, like the Spring-time, fresh
       and greene;
    And sweet as *Flora*. Take no care
    For Jewels for your Gowne, or Haire:
    Feare not; the leaves will strew
    Gemms in abundance upon you: 20
Besides, the childhood of the Day has kept,
Against you come, some *Orient Pearls* unwept:
    Come, and receive them while the light
    Hangs on the Dew-locks of the night:
    And *Titan* on the Eastern hill
    Retires himselfe, or else stands still
Till you come forth. Wash, dresse, be briefe
       in praying:
Few Beads are best, when once we goe a
       Maying.

Come, my *Corinna*, come; and comming,
       marke
How each field turns a street; each street a
       Parke   30

---

l. 10. *Mattens:* matins, or morning prayers.
l. 17. *Flora:* flower goddess.
l. 25. *Titan:* the sun god, Helios.

Made green, and trimm'd with trees: see
   how
Devotion gives each House a Bough,
Or Branch: Each Porch, each doore, ere
   this,
   An Arke a Tabernacle is
Made up of white-thorn neatly enterwove;
As if here were those cooler shades of love.
   Can such delights be in the street,
   And open fields, and we not see't?
   Come, we'll abroad; and let's obay
   The Proclamation made for May: 40
And sin no more, as we have done, by staying;
But my *Corinna*, come, let's goe a Maying.

There's not a budding Boy, or Girle, this day,
But is got up, and gone to bring in May.
   A deale of Youth, ere this, is come
   Back, and with *White-thorn* laden home.
   Some have dispatcht their Cakes and
      Creame,
   Before that we have left to dreame:
And some have wept, and woo'd, and plighted
   Troth,
And chose their Priest, ere we can cast off
   sloth: 50
   Many a green-gown has been given;
   Many a kisse, both odde and even:
   Many a glance too has been sent
   From out the eye, Loves Firmament:
Many a jest told of the Keyes betraying
This night, and Locks pickt, yet w'are not a
   Maying.

Come, let us goe, while we are in our prime;
And take the harmlesse follie of the time.
   We shall grow old apace, and die
   Before we know our liberty.   60
   Our life is short; and our dayes run
   As fast away as do's the Sunne:
And as a vapour, or a drop of raine
Once lost, can ne'r be found againe:
   So when or you or I are made
   A fable, song, or fleeting shade;
   All love, all liking, all delight
   Lies drown'd with us in endlesse night.

Then while time serves, and we are but
   decaying;
Come, my *Corinna*, come, let's goe a
   Maying.   70

GEORGE HERBERT

Redemption

Having been tenant long to a rich Lord,
   Not thriving, I resolved to be bold,
   And make a suit unto him, to afford
A new small-rented lease, and cancel th' old.

In heaven at his manour I him sought:
   They told me there, that he was lately
      gone
   About some land, which he had dearly
      bought
Long since on earth, to take possession.

I straight returned, and knowing his great
   birth,
   Sought him accordingly in great
      resorts;   10
   In cities, theatres, gardens, parks, and
      courts:
At length I heard a ragged noise and mirth

Of thieves and murderers: there I him
   espied,
   Who straight, "Your suit is granted,"
      said, and died.

The Collar

I struck the board, and cried "No more;
    I will abroad.
  What, shall I ever sigh and pine?
My lines and life are free; free as the road,
    Loose as the wind, as large as store.
      Shall I be still in suit?
Have I no harvest but a thorn
    To let me blood, and not restore
What I have lost with cordial fruit?
    Sure there was wine   10
Before my sighs did dry it; there was corn
    Before my tears did drown it;
Is the year only lost to me?
    Have I no bays to crown it,
No flowers, no garlands gay? all blasted,
    All wasted?
Not so, my heart; but there is fruit,
    And thou hast hands.
  Recover all thy sigh-blown age
On double pleasures; leave thy cold dispute 20
    Of what is fit and not; forsake thy cage,
    Thy rope of sands
Which petty thoughts have made; and made
      to thee
    Good cable, to enforce and draw,
    And be thy law,
While thou didst wink and wouldst not see.
    Away! take heed;
    I will abroad.
  Call in thy death's-head there, tie up thy
      fears;
    He that forbears   30
  To suit and serve his need
    Deserves his load."
But as I rav'd and grew more fierce and wild
    At every word,
  Methought I heard one calling "Child,"
    And I replied, "My Lord."

The Pulley

  When God at first made man,
Having a glass of blessings standing by,
Let us, said he, pour on him all we can.
Let the world's riches, which dispersëd lie,
  Contract into a span.

  So strength first made a way,
Then beauty flowed, then wisdom, honor,
    pleasure.
When almost all was out, God made a stay,
Perceiving that alone of all his treasure
  Rest in the bottom lay.   10

  For if I should, said he,
Bestow this jewel also on my creature,
He would adore my gifts instead of me,
And rest in nature, not the God of nature;
  So both should losers be.

  Yet let him keep the rest,
But keep them with repining restlessness.
Let him be rich and weary, that at least,
If goodness lead him not, yet weariness
  May toss him to my breast.   20

Love (III)

Love bade me welcome, yet my soul drew
      back,
    Guilty of dust and sin.
But quick-eyed Love, observing me grow slack
    From my first entrance in,
Drew nearer to me, sweetly questioning
    If I lacked anything.

"A guest," I answered, "worthy to be here."
    Love said, "You shall be he."
"I, the unkind, ungrateful? Ah, my dear,
    I cannot look on thee."   10

Love took my hand, and smiling did reply,
    "Who made the eyes but I?"

"Truth, Lord, but I have marred them;
      let my shame
    Go where it doth deserve."
"And know you not," says Love, "who bore
    the blame?"
      "My dear, then I will serve."
"You must sit down," says Love, "and taste
    my meat."
    So I did sit and eat.

john milton

Lycidas

*In this monody the author bewails a learned
friend, unfortunately drowned in his passage
from Chester on the Irish Seas, 1637. And by
occasion foretells the ruin of our corrupted
clergy then in their height.*

Yet once more, O ye laurels, and once more
Ye myrtles brown, with ivy never sere,
I come to pluck your berries harsh and
    crude,
And with forced fingers rude,
Shatter your leaves before the mellowing
    year.
Bitter constraint, and sad occasion dear,
Compels me to disturb your season due:
For Lycidas is dead, dead ere his prime,

Young Lycidas, and hath not left his peer.
Who would not sing for Lycidas? He knew 10
Himself to sing, and build the lofty rhyme.
He must not float upon his watery bier
Unwept, and welter to the parching wind,
Without the meed of some melodious tear.
   Begin then, sisters of the sacred well,
That from beneath the seat of Jove doth
    spring,
Begin, and somewhat loudly sweep the string.
Hence with denial vain and coy excuse;
So may some gentle muse
With lucky words favor my destined urn,   20
And as he passes turn,
And bid fair peace be to my sable shroud.
For we were nursed upon the self-same hill,
Fed the same flock, by fountain, shade, and
    rill.
   Together both, ere the high lawns appeared
Under the opening eyelids of the morn,
We drove afield, and both together heard
What time the gray-fly winds her sultry horn,
Battening our flocks with the fresh dews of
    night,
Oft till the star that rose, at evening,
    bright,   30
Toward heaven's descent had sloped his
    westering wheel.
Meanwhile the rural ditties were not mute,
Tempered to the oaten flute;
Rough satyrs danced, and fauns with cloven
    heel,
From the glad sound would not be absent
    long,
And old Damaetas loved to hear our song.
   But O the heavy change, now thou art gone,
Now thou art gone, and never must return!
Thee, shepherd, thee the woods and desert
    caves,
With wild thyme and the gadding vine
    o'ergrown,   40
And all their echoes mourn.

---

friend: Edward King, a classmate of Milton's at Cambridge.
ll. 1–2. *laurels, myrtles, ivy:* evergreens traditionally associated with poetry.
l. 6. *dear:* dire.
l. 8. *Lycidas:* a stock pastoral name given Edward King in this poem.

l. 15. *sisters:* the Muses of poetic inspiration.
l. 36. *Damaetas:* a stock pastoral name.

The willows and the hazel copses green
Shall now no more be seen,
Fanning their joyous leaves to thy soft lays.
As killing as the canker to the rose,
Or taint-worm to the weanling herds that
    graze,
Or frost to flowers, that their gay wardrobe
    wear,
When first the white-thorn blows:
Such, Lycidas, thy loss to shepherd's ear.
   Where were ye, nymphs, when the
    remorseless deep   50
Closed o'er the head of your loved Lycidas?
For neither were ye playing on the steep,
Where your old bards, the famous druids,
    lie,
Nor on the shaggy top of Mona high,
Nor yet where Deva spreads her wizard
    stream:
Ay me, I fondly dream!
"Had ye been there"—for what could that
    have done?
What could the Muse herself that Orpheus
    bore,
The Muse herself for her enchanting son
Whom universal nature did lament,   60
When by the rout that made the hideous roar,
His gory visage down the stream was sent,
Down the swift Hebrus to the Lesbian shore?
   Alas! What boots it with uncessant care
To tend the homely slighted shepherd's trade,
And strictly meditate the thankless Muse?
Were it not better done, as others use,
To sport with Amaryllis in the shade,
Or with the tangles of Neaera's hair?
Fame is the spur that the clear spirit doth
    raise   70
(That last infirmity of noble mind)
To scorn delights, and live laborious days;
But the fair guerdon when we hope to find,
And think to burst out into sudden blaze,

Comes the blind Fury with the abhorrèd
    shears,
And slits the thin-spun life. "But not the
    praise,"
Phoebus replied, and touched my trembling
    ears:
"Fame is no plant that grows on mortal soil,
Nor in the glistering foil
Set off to the world, nor in broad rumor
    lies,   80
But lives and spreads aloft by those pure eyes
And perfect witness of all-judging Jove;
As he pronounces lastly on each deed,
Of so much fame in heaven expect thy meed."
   O fountain Arethuse, and thou honored
    flood,
Smooth-sliding Mincius, crowned with vocal
    reeds,
That strain I heard was of a higher mood.
But now my oat proceeds,
And listens to the herald of the sea,
That came in Neptune's plea.   90
He asked the waves and asked the
    felon-winds,
What hard mishap hath doomed this gentle
    swain,
And questioned every gust of rugged wings
That blows from off each beakèd promontory.
They knew not of his story,
And sage Hippotades their answer brings:
That not a blast was from his dungeon
    strayed;
The air was calm, and on the level brine,
Sleek Panopë with all her sisters played.
It was that fatal and perfidious bark   100
Built in the eclipse, and rigged with curses
    dark,

---

l. 58. *Orpheus:* the mythical Greek poet dismembered
by a "rout" of Thracian women.
l. 64. *boots:* profits.
ll. 68–69. *Amaryllis, Neaera:* stock pastoral names for
girls.

l. 75. *Fury:* Atropos, one of the three Fates, who cuts
the thread of life.
l. 77. *Phoebus:* god of poetic inspiration.
l. 85. *Arethuse:* a fountain associated with the pastoral
poetry of Theocritus.
l. 86. *Mincius:* a river associated with the pastoral
poetry of Virgil.
l. 89. *herald:* Triton.
l. 96. *Hippotades:* god of the winds.
l. 99. *Panopë:* chief of the sea nymphs.

That sunk so low that sacred head of thine.
  Next Camus, reverend sire, went footing
    slow,
His mantle hairy, and his bonnet sedge,
Inwrought with figures dim, and on the edge
Like to that sanguine flower inscribed with
    woe.
"Ah, who hath reft," quoth he, "my dearest
    pledge?"
Last came, and last did go,
The pilot of the Galilean Lake;
Two massy keys he bore of metals twain   110
(The golden opes, the iron shuts amain).
He shook his mitered locks, and stern
    bespake:
"How well could I have spared for thee,
    young swain,
Enow of such as for their bellies' sake
Creep, and intrude, and climb into the fold!
Of other care they little reckoning make,
Than how to scramble at the shearers' feast,
And shove away the worthy bidden guest.
Blind mouths, that scarce themselves know
    how to hold
A sheep hook, or have learned aught else the
    least   120
That to the faithful herdman's art belongs!
What recks it them? What need they? They are
    sped,
And when they list, their lean and flashy
    songs
Grate on their scrannel pipes of wretched
    straw.
The hungry sheep look up and are not fed,
But swollen with wind, and the rank mist
    they draw,
Rot inwardly, and foul contagion spread;
Besides what the grim wolf with privy paw
Daily devours apace, and nothing said;

But that two-handed engine at the door   130
Stands ready to smite once, and smite no
    more."
  Return, Alpheus, the dread voice is past,
That shrunk thy streams; return, Sicilian
    Muse,
And call the vales, and bid them hither cast
Their bells and flowerets of a thousand hues.
Ye valleys low, where the mild whispers use
Of shades and wanton winds and gushing
    brooks,
On whose fresh lap the swart star sparely
    looks,
Throw hither all your quaint enameled eyes,
That on the green turf suck the honeyed
    showers,   140
And purple all the ground with vernal flowers.
Bring the rathe primrose that forsaken dies,
The tufted crow-toe, and pale jessamine,
The white pink, and the pansy freaked with
    jet,
The glowing violet,
The musk-rose, and the well-attired woodbine,
With cowslips wan that hang the pensive head,
And every flower that sad embroidery wears.
Bid amaranthus all his beauty shed,
And daffodillies fill their cups with tears,   150
To strew the laureate hearse where Lycid lies.
For so to interpose a little ease,
Let our frail thoughts dally with false
    surmise.
Ay me! Whilst thee the shores and sounding
    seas
Wash far away, where'er thy bones are
    hurled,
Whether beyond the stormy Hebrides,
Where thou perhaps under the whelming tide

---

l. 132. *Alpheus:* a river in love with the nymph-turned-fountain, Arethusa.
l. 133. *Sicilian Muse:* Theocritus, Greek pastoral poet, third century B.C.
l. 138. *swart star:* Sirius, the dog star, which was supposed to wither vegetation in late summer.
l. 142. *rathe:* early.
l. 144. *freaked:* speckled.
l. 156. *Hebrides:* islands to the north of where King died.

l. 103. *Camus:* the river Cam, which flows through Cambridge.
l. 106. *sanguine flower:* the hyacinth, bearing in its cup the word "Alas!" because the flower had sprung from the blood of a boy accidentally killed by Phoebus.
l. 109. *pilot:* Saint Peter, a fisherman, supposedly the first Bishop of Rome.
l. 114. *Enow:* enough.

Visitest the bottom of the monstrous world;
Or whether thou to our moist vows denied,
Sleepest by the fable of Bellerus old,   160
Where the great vision of the guarded mount
Looks toward Namancos and Bayona's hold;
Look homeward, Angel, now, and melt with
    ruth.
And, O ye dolphins, waft the hapless youth.
    Weep no more, woeful shepherds, weep no
        more,
For Lycidas your sorrow is not dead,
Sunk though he be beneath the watery floor,
So sinks the day-star in the ocean bed,
And yet anon repairs his drooping head,
And tricks his beams, and with new-spangled
    ore   170
Flames in the forehead of the morning sky:
So Lycidas sunk low, but mounted high,
Through the dear might of him that walked
    the waves
Where, other groves and other streams along,
With nectar pure his oozy locks he laves,
And hears the unexpressive nuptial song,
In the blest kingdoms meek of joy and love.
There entertain him all the saints above
In solemn troops and sweet societies
That sing, and singing in their glory move,   180
And wipe the tears forever from his eyes.
Now, Lycidas, the shepherds weep no more;
Henceforth thou art the genius of the shore,
In thy large recompense, and shalt be good
To all that wander in that perilous flood.
    Thus sang the uncouth swain to the oaks
        and rills,
While the still morn went out with sandals
    gray;
He touched the tender stops of various quills,
With eager thought warbling his Doric lay.
And now the sun had stretched out all the
    hills,   190

---

l. 160. *Bellerus:* a giant, supposed to be buried in the sea far south.
l. 163. *Angel:* Saint Michael, archangel and warrior, who judges souls justly.
l. 186. *uncouth:* simple.
l. 189. *Doric:* the Greek dialect of the earliest pastoral poets.

And now was dropped into the western bay.
At last he rose, and twitched his mantle blue:
Tomorrow to fresh woods, and pastures new.

On the Late Massacre in Piedmont

Avenge, O Lord, thy slaughtered saints,
    whose bones
Lie scattered on the Alpine mountains cold;
Even them who kept thy truth so pure of old,
When all our fathers worshipped stocks and
    stones,
Forget not: in thy book record their groans
Who were thy sheep, and in their ancient fold
Slain by the bloody Piedmontese, that rolled
Mother with infant down the rocks. Their
    moans
The vales redoubled to the hills, and they
To heaven. Their martyred blood and ashes
    sow   10
O'er all the Italian fields, where still doth
    sway
The triple tyrant; that from these may grow
A hundredfold, who, having learnt thy way,
Early may fly the Babylonian woe.

Piedmont: In 1665 the Waldensians, a sect with beliefs resembling Protestant ones, were partly massacred by Catholics in northern Italy (Piedmont) and southern France.
l. 12. *triple tyrant:* referring to the Pope's tiara with three crowns, one above the other.
l. 14. *Babylonian:* Protestants referred to the Church of Rome as the "whore of Babylon."

Methought I Saw My Late Espoused Saint

Methought I saw my late espousèd saint
Brought to me like Alcestis from the grave

---

l. 2. *Alcestis:* rescued from the underworld by Hercules and restored to her husband, for whose sake she had died.

Whom Jove's great son to her glad husband
   gave,
Rescued from Death by force, though pale
   and faint.
Mine, as whom washed from spot of childbed
   taint
Purification in the old law did save,
And such as yet once more I trust to have
Full sight of her in Heaven without restraint,
Came vested all in white, pure as her mind.
Her face was veiled; yet to my fancied sight 10
Love, sweetness, goodness, in her person
   shined
So clear as in no face with more delight.
But, oh! as to embrace me she inclined,
I waked, she fled, and day brought back my
   night.

Andrew Marvell

To His Coy Mistress

Had we but world enough, and time,
This coyness, lady, were no crime.
We would sit down and think which way
To walk, and pass our long love's day;
Thou by the Indian Ganges' side
Shouldst rubies find; I by the tide
Of Humber would complain. I would
Love you ten years before the Flood;
And you should, if you please, refuse
Till the conversion of the Jews.   10
My vegetable love should grow
Vaster than empires, and more slow.
An hundred years should go to praise
Thine eyes, and on thy forehead gaze;
Two hundred to adore each breast,
But thirty thousand to the rest;
An age at least to every part,

And the last age should show your heart.
For, lady, you deserve this state,
Nor would I love at lower rate.   20
   But at my back I always hear
Time's wingèd chariot hurrying near;
And yonder all before us lie
Deserts of vast eternity.
Thy beauty shall no more be found,
Nor in thy marble vault shall sound
My echoing song; then worms shall try
That long preserved virginity,
And your quaint honor turn to dust,
And into ashes all my lust.   30
The grave's a fine and private place,
But none, I think, do there embrace.
   Now therefore, while the youthful hue
Sits on thy skin like morning dew,
And while thy willing soul transpires
At every pore with instant fires,
Now let us sport us while we may;
And now, like am'rous birds of prey,
Rather at once our time devour,
Than languish in his slow-chapped power. 40
Let us roll all our strength, and all
Our sweetness, up into one ball;
And tear our pleasures with rough strife
Thorough the iron gates of life.
Thus, though we cannot make our sun
Stand still, yet we will make him run.

The Definition of Love

My Love is of a birth as rare
As 'tis for object strange and high:
It was begotten by Despair
Upon Impossibility.

Magnanimous Despair alone
Could show me so divine a thing,
Where feeble Hope could ne'er have flown
But vainly flapt its tinsel wing.

And yet I quickly might arrive
Where my extended soul is fixt,   10

But Fate does iron wedges drive,
And always crowds itself betwixt.

For Fate with jealous eye does see
Two perfect loves; nor lets them close:
Their union would her ruin be,
And her tyrannic power depose.

And therefore her decrees of steel
Us as the distant poles have placed
(Though Love's whole world on us doth
   wheel),
Not by themselves to be embraced: 20

Unless the giddy heaven fall,
And earth some new convulsion tear;
And, us to join, the world should all
Be cramped into a planisphere.

As lines so loves oblique may well
Themselves in every angle greet:
But ours so truly parallel,
Though infinite can never meet.

Therefore the Love which us doth bind,
But Fate so enviously debars,   30
Is the conjunction of the mind,
And opposition of the stars.

---

l.24. *planisphere:* a polar projection, or map, here of both the heavens and the earth.

The Garden

How vainly men themselves amaze
To win the palm, the oak, or bays,
And their uncessant labors see
Crowned from some single herb or tree,
Whose short and narrow vergèd shade
Does prudently their toils upbraid;

---

l. 1. *amaze:* perplex.
l. 2. *palm, oak, bays:* symbols of victory in games, battle, and poetry contests.

While all flowers and all trees do close
To weave the garlands of repose.

Fair quiet, have I found thee here,
And innocence, thy sister dear!   10
Mistaken long, I sought you then
In busy companies of men;
Your sacred plants, if here below,
Only among the plants will grow.
Society is all but rude,
To this delicious solitude.

No white nor red was ever seen
So am'rous as this lovely green.
Fond lovers, cruel as their flame,
Cut in these trees their mistress' name;   20
Little, alas, they know or heed
How far these beauties hers exceed!
Fair trees! wheres'e'r your barks I wound,
No name shall but your own be found.

When we have run our passion's heat,
Love hither makes his best retreat.
The gods that mortal beauty chase,
Still in a tree did end their race:
Apollo hunted Daphne so,
Only that she might laurel grow;   30
And Pan did after Syrinx speed,
Not as a nymph, but for a reed.

What wondrous life is this I lead!
Ripe apples drop about my head;
The luscious clusters of the vine
Upon my mouth do crush their wine;
The nectarine and curious peach
Into my hands themselves do reach;
Stumbling on melons as I pass,
Ensnared with flowers, I fall on grass.   40

Meanwhile the mind from pleasure less
Withdraws into its happiness;

---

l. 29. *Daphne:* Pursued by Apollo, Daphne asked the gods to save her and was changed into a laurel. Apollo wreathed his head with its leaves and proclaimed the tree sacred to him.
l. 31. *Syrinx:* Pursued by Pan, Syrinx was changed into reeds, from which Pan made his pipes.

The mind, that ocean where each kind
Does straight its own resemblance find,
Yet it creates, transcending these,
Far other worlds and other seas,
Annihilating all that's made
To a green thought in a green shade.

Here at the fountain's sliding foot,
Or at some fruit tree's mossy root,   50
Casting the body's vest aside,
My soul into the boughs does glide;
There like a bird it sits and sings,
Then whets, then combs its silver wings;
And till prepared for longer flight,
Waves in its plumes the various light.

Such was that happy garden-state,
While man there walked without a mate;
After a place so pure and sweet,
What other help could yet be meet!   60
But 'twas beyond a mortal's share
To wander solitary there;
Two paradises 'twere, in one,
To live in paradise alone.

How well the skillful gard'ner drew
Of flowers and herbs this dial new,
Where, from above, the milder sun
Does through a fragrant zodiac run;
And as it works, th' industrious bee
Computes its time as well as we.   70
How could such sweet and wholesome hours
Be reckoned but with herbs and flowers?

---

l. 54. *whets:* preens.
l. 60. *meet:* suitable.
l. 66. *dial:* flowers and herbs planted to resemble a sundial complete with the signs of the zodiac.

johN dRydEN

Alexander's Feast

Or, The Power of Music;
An Ode in Honor of St. Cecilia's Day

I

'T was at the royal feast, for Persia won
    By Philip's warlike son:
    Aloft in awful state
    The godlike hero sate
        On his imperial throne:
    His valiant peers were plac'd around;
Their brows with roses and with myrtles
        bound:
    (So should desert in arms be crown'd.)
The lovely Thais, by his side,
Sate like a blooming Eastern bride   10
In flow'r of youth and beauty's pride.
    Happy, happy, happy pair!
    None but the brave,
    None but the brave,
    None but the brave deserves the fair.

Chorus

Happy, happy, happy pair!
None but the brave,
None but the brave,
None but the brave deserves the fair.

II

Timotheus, plac'd on high   20
    Amid the tuneful choir,
    With flying fingers touch'd the lyre:

---

ll. 1–2. *Persia won . . . son:* Alexander the Great (356–323 B.C.), son of Philip of Macedonia, invaded and conquered Persia and its king, Darius, 334–330 B.C.
l. 9. *Thais:* a courtesan.
l. 20. *Timotheus:* a musician.

The trembling notes ascend the sky,
              And heav'nly joys inspire.
The song began from Jove,
Who left his blissful seats above,
(Such is the pow'r of mighty love.)
A dragon's fiery form belied the god:
Sublime on radiant spires he rode,
    When he to fair Olympia press'd;   30
    And while he sought her snowy breast:
Then, round her slender waist he curl'd,
And stamp'd an image of himself, a sov'reign
          of the world.
The list'ning crowd admire the lofty sound;
"A present deity," they shout around;
"A present deity," the vaulted roofs rebound:
    With ravish'd ears
    The monarch hears,
    Assumes the god,
    Affects to nod,   40
And seems to shake the spheres.

Chorus

With ravish'd ears
The monarch hears,
Assumes the god,
Affects to nod,
And seems to shake the spheres.

III

The praise of Bacchus then the sweet
          musician sung,
Of Bacchus ever fair and ever young:
    "The jolly god in triumph comes;
    Sound the trumpets; beat the drums;   50
      Flush'd with a purple grace
      He shews his honest face:
Now give the hautboys breath; he comes,
          he comes.
    Bacchus, ever fair and young,
    Drinking joys did first ordain;

---

l. 25. *Jove:* Jupiter, who visited Alexander's mother, Olympia, in the form of a serpent.
l. 47. *Bacchus:* god of wine.
l. 53. *hautboys:* oboes.

Bacchus' blessings are a treasure,
Drinking is the soldier's pleasure:
    Rich the treasure,
    Sweet the pleasure,
Sweet is pleasure after pain."   60

Chorus

Bacchus' blessings are a treasure,
Drinking is the soldier's pleasure:
    Rich the treasure,
    Sweet the pleasure,
Sweet is pleasure after pain.

IV

    Sooth'd with the sound, the king grew vain;
      Fought all his battles o'er again;
And thrice he routed all his foes; and thrice
          he slew the slain.
The master saw the madness rise;
His glowing cheeks, his ardent eyes;   70
And, while he heav'n and earth defied,
Chang'd his hand, and check'd his pride.
    He chose a mournful Muse,
      Soft pity to infuse:
He sung Darius great and good,
      By too severe a fate,
Fallen, fallen, fallen, fallen,
      Fallen from his high estate,
        And welt'ring in his blood;
Deserted, at his utmost need,   80
By those his former bounty fed;
On the bare earth expos'd he lies,
With not a friend to close his eyes.

With downcast looks the joyless victor sate,
    Revolving in his alter'd soul
      The various turns of chance below;
    And, now and then, a sigh he stole;
      And tears began to flow.

Chorus

Revolving in his alter'd soul
The various turns of chance below;   90

543   John Dryden

And, now and then, a sigh he stole;
And tears began to flow.

V

The mighty master smil'd, to see
That love was in the next degree:
'T was but a kindred sound to move,
For pity melts the mind to love.
   Softly sweet, in Lydian measures,
   Soon he sooth'd his soul to pleasures.
   "War," he sung, "is toil and trouble;
   Honor, but an empty bubble;   100
     Never ending, still beginning,
   Fighting still, and still destroying:
     If the world be worth thy winning,
   Think, O think it worth enjoying;
     Lovely Thais sits beside thee,
     Take the good the gods provide thee."
The many rend the skies with loud applause;
So Love was crown'd, but Music won the
       cause.
   The prince, unable to conceal his pain,
     Gaz'd on the fair   110
      Who caus'd his care,
    And sigh'd and look'd, sigh'd and look'd,
   Sigh'd and look'd, and sigh'd again:
At length, with love and wine at once
       oppress'd,
The vanquish'd victor sunk upon her breast.

Chorus

*   The prince, unable to conceal his pain,*
*   Gaz'd on the fair*
*   Who caus'd his care,*
*   And sigh'd and look'd, sigh'd and look'd,*
*   Sigh'd and look'd, and sigh'd again:*   120
At length, with love and wine at once
*   oppress'd,*
The vanquish'd victor sunk upon her breast.

VI

Now strike the golden lyre again:

I. 97. *Lydian measures:* soft, enervating music.

A louder yet, and yet a louder strain.
Break his bands of sleep asunder,
And rouse him, like a rattling peal of thunder.
    Hark, hark, the horrid sound
      Has rais'd up his head:
      As awak'd from the dead,
      And amaz'd, he stares around.   130
"Revenge, revenge!" Timotheus cries,
   "See the Furies arise!
   See the snakes that they rear,
   How they hiss in their hair,
  And the sparkles that flash from their eyes!
    Behold a ghastly band,
    Each a torch in his hand!
Those are Grecian ghosts, that in battle were
     slain,
     And unburied remain
     Inglorious on the plain: 140
    Give the vengeance due
    To the valiant crew.
Behold how they toss their torches on high,
    How they point to the Persian abodes,
And glitt'ring temples of their hostile gods!"
The princes applaud, with a furious joy;
And the king seiz'd a flambeau with zeal to
      destroy;
    Thais led the way,
    To light him to his prey,
And, like another Helen, fir'd another Troy. 150

Chorus

And the king seiz'd a flambeau with zeal to
*   destroy;*
*   Thais led the way,*
*   To light him to his prey,*
And, like another Helen, fir'd another Troy.

VII

   Thus, long ago,
   Ere heaving bellows learn'd to blow,
    While organs yet were mute;
   Timotheus, to his breathing flute,
    And sounding lyre,
Could swell the soul to rage, or kindle soft
    desire.   160

At last, divine Cecilia came,
   Inventress of the vocal frame;
The sweet enthusiast, from her sacred store,
   Enlarg'd the former narrow bounds,
   And added length to solemn sounds,
With nature's mother wit, and arts unknown
     before.
   Let old Timotheus yield the prize,
     Or both divide the crown;
   He rais'd a mortal to the skies;
     She drew an angel down.   170

Grand Chorus

At last, divine Cecilia came,
   Inventress of the vocal frame;
The sweet enthusiast, from her sacred store,
   Enlarg'd the former narrow bounds,
   And added length to solemn sounds,
With nature's mother wit, and arts unknown
     before.
   Let old Timotheus yield the prize,
     Or both divide the crown;
   He rais'd a mortal to the skies;
     She drew an angel down.   180

Alexander Pope

Epistle II. To a Lady
Of the Characters of Women

Nothing so true as what you once let fall,
'Most Women have no Characters at all'.
Matter too soft a lasting mark to bear,
And best distinguish'd by black, brown,
   or fair.

To a Lady: Pope's acquaintance, Martha Blount.

How many pictures of one Nymph we view,
All how unlike each other, all how true!
Arcadia's Countess, here, in ermin'd pride,
Is there, Pastora by a fountain side:
Here Fannia, leering on her own good man,
Is there, a naked Leda with a Swan.   10
Let then the Fair one beautifully cry,
In Magdalen's loose hair and lifted eye,
Or drest in smiles of sweet Cecilia shine,
With simp'ring Angels, Palms, and Harps
   divine;
Whether the Charmer sinner it, or saint it,
If Folly grows romantic, I must paint it.
   Come then, the colours and the ground
     prepare!
Dip in the Rainbow, trick her off in Air,
Chuse a firm Cloud, before it fall, and in it
Catch, ere she change, the Cynthia of this
   minute.   20
   Rufa, whose eye quick-glancing o'er the
   Park,
Attracts each light gay meteor of a Spark,
Agrees as ill with Rufa studying Locke,
As Sappho's diamonds with her dirty smock,
Or Sappho at her toilet's greasy task,
With Sappho fragrant at an ev'ning Mask:
So morning Insects that in muck begun,
Shine, buzz, and fly-blow in the setting-sun.
   How soft is Silia! fearful to offend,
The Frail one's advocate, the Weak one's
   friend: 30
To her, Calista prov'd her conduct nice,
And good Simplicius asks of her advice.
Sudden, she storms! she raves! You tip the
   wink,
But spare your censure; Silia does not drink.
All eyes may see from what the change arose,
All eyes may see—a Pimple on her nose.

---

l. 7. *Arcadia's Countess:* like "Pastora by a fountain," "Leda with a Swan," "Magdalen," and "Cecilia," which follow, an attitude in which ladies posed for paintings.
l. 18. *Dip:* immerse in a coloring solution.
l. 18. *trick:* sketch in outline.
l. 21. *Rufa:* in Latin, "red-head."
l. 23. *Locke:* John Locke (1632–1704), English philosopher.

Papillia, wedded to her doating spark,
Sighs for the shades—'How charming is a
    Park!'
A Park is purchas'd, but the Fair he sees
All bath'd in tears—'Oh odious, odious
    Trees!'   40
    Ladies, like variegated Tulips, show,
'Tis to their Changes that their charms we
    owe;
Their happy Spots the nice admirer take,
Fine by defect, and delicately weak.
'Twas thus Calypso once each heart alarm'd,
Aw'd without Virtue, without Beauty
    charm'd;
Her Tongue bewitch'd as odly as her Eyes,
Less Wit than Mimic, more a Wit than wise:
Strange graces still, and stranger flights she
    had,
Was just not ugly, and was just not mad;   50
Yet ne'er so sure our passion to create,
As when she touch'd the brink of all we hate.
    Narcissa's nature, tolerably mild,
To make a wash, would hardly stew a child,
Has ev'n been prov'd to grant a Lover's pray'r,
And paid a Tradesman once to make him
    stare,
Gave alms at Easter, in a Christian trim,
And made a Widow happy, for a whim.
Why then declare Good-nature is her scorn,
When 'tis by that alone she can be born?   60
Why pique all mortals, yet affect a name?
A fool to Pleasure, and a slave to Fame:
Now deep in Taylor and the Book of Martyrs,
Now drinking citron with his Grace and
    Chartres.
Now Conscience chills her, and now Passion
    burns;
And Atheism and Religion take their turns;
A very Heathen in the carnal part,

Yet still a sad, good Christian at her heart.
    See Sin in State, majestically drunk,
Proud as a Peeress, prouder as a Punk;   70
Chaste to her Husband, frank to all beside,
A teeming Mistress, but a barren Bride.
What then? let Blood and Body bear the fault,
Her Head's untouch'd, that noble Seat of
    Thought:
Such this day's doctrine—in another fit
She sins with Poets thro' pure Love of Wit.
What has not fir'd her bosom or her brain?
Cæsar and Tall-boy, Charles and Charlema'ne.
As Helluo, late Dictator of the Feast,
The Nose of Hautgout, and the Tip of Taste,   80
Critick'd your wine, and analyz'd your meat,
Yet on plain Pudding deign'd at-home to eat;
So Philomedé, lect'ring all mankind
On the soft Passion, and the Taste refin'd,
Th' Address, the Delicacy—stoops at once,
And makes her hearty meal upon a Dunce.
    Flavia's a Wit, has too much sense to Pray,
To Toast our wants and wishes, is her way;
Nor asks of God, but of her Stars to give
The mighty blessing, 'while we live, to live.' 90
Then all for Death, that Opiate of the soul!
Lucretia's dagger, Rosamonda's bowl.
Say, what can cause such impotence of mind?
A Spark too fickle, or a Spouse too kind.
Wise Wretch! with Pleasures too refin'd to
    please,
With too much Spirit to be e'er at ease,
With too much Quickness ever to be taught,
With too much Thinking to have common
    Thought:
Who purchase Pain with all that Joy can give,
And die of nothing but a Rage to live.   100

---

l. 37. *Papillia:* in Latin, "butterfly."
l. 54. *Wash:* for the hair or skin.
l. 63. *Taylor:* Jeremy Taylor, author of *Holy Living and Holy Dying.*
l. 63. *Book of Martyrs:* a book by John Foxe.
l. 64. *his Grace:* Philip, Duke of Wharton, who died in a Franciscan convent attired in the habit of the order.
l. 64. *Chartres:* Francis Chartres, who, according to Pope, was "a man infamous for all manner of vices."

l. 78. *Tall-boy:* a gullible young lover, after a character in an eighteenth-century play.
l. 78. *Charles:* used generically for the typical footman.
l. 79. *Helluo:* in Latin, "glutton."
l. 80. *Hautgout:* anything with a strong relish or strong scent.
l. 92. *Lucretia's dagger:* Lucretia, or Lucrece, a Roman lady who stabbed herself after being violated by Sextus, son of a Roman king.
l. 92. *Rosamonda:* mistress of Henry II, poisoned by Henry's queen, Eleanor.

Turn then from Wits; and look on Simo's
	Mate,
No Ass so meek, no Ass so obstinate:
Or her, that owns her Faults, but never
	mends,
Because she's honest, and the best of Friends:
Or her, whose life the Church and Scandal
	share,
For ever in a Passion, or a Pray'r:
Or her, who laughs at Hell, but (like her
	Grace)
Cries, 'Ah! how charming if there's no such
	place!'
Or who in sweet vicissitude appears
Of Mirth and Opium, Ratafie and Tears,   110
The daily Anodyne, and nightly Draught,
To kill those foes to Fair ones, Time and
	Thought.
Woman and Fool are two hard things to hit,
For true No-meaning puzzles more than Wit.
	But what are these to great Atossa's mind?
Scarce once herself, by turns all Womankind!
Who, with herself, or others, from her birth
Finds all her life one warfare upon earth:
Shines, in exposing Knaves, and painting
	Fools,
Yet is, whate'er she hates and ridicules.   120
No Thought advances, but her Eddy Brain
Whisks it about, and down it goes again.
Full sixty years the World has been her Trade,
The wisest Fool much Time has ever made.
From loveless youth to unrespected age,
No Passion gratify'd except her Rage.
So much the Fury still out-ran the Wit,
The Pleasure miss'd her, and the Scandal hit.
Who breaks with her, provokes Revenge from
	Hell,
But he's a bolder man who dares be well: 130
Her ev'ry turn with Violence pursu'd,
Nor more a storm her Hate than Gratitude.
To that each Passion turns, or soon or late;
Love, if it makes her yield, must make her
	hate:
Superiors? death! and Equals? what a curse!

But an Inferior not dependant? worse.
Offend her, and she knows not to forgive;
Oblige her, and she'll hate you while you live:
But die, and she'll adore you—Then the Bust
And Temple rise—then fall again to dust.   140
Last night, her Lord was all that's good and
	great,
A Knave this morning, and his Will a Cheat.
Strange! by the Means defeated of the Ends,
By Spirit robb'd of Pow'r, by Warmth of
	Friends,
By Wealth of Follow'rs! without one distress
Sick of herself thro' very selfishness!
Atossa, curs'd with ev'ry granted pray'r,
Childless with all her Children, wants an Heir.
To Heirs unknown descends th' unguarded
	store
Or wanders, Heav'n-directed, to the Poor.   150
	Pictures like these, dear Madam, to design,
Asks no firm hand, and no unerring line;
Some wand'ring touch, or some reflected light,
Some flying stroke alone can hit 'em right:
For how should equal Colours do the knack?
Chameleons who can paint in white and
	black?
	'Yet Cloe sure was form'd without a spot—'
Nature in her then err'd not, but forgot.
'With ev'ry pleasing, ev'ry prudent part,
Say, what can Cloe want?'—she wants a
	Heart. 160
She speaks, behaves, and acts just as she
	ought;
But never, never, reach'd one gen'rous
	Thought.
Virtue she finds too painful an endeavour,
Content to dwell in Decencies for ever.
So very reasonable, so unmov'd,
As never yet to love, or to be lov'd.
She, while her Lover pants upon her breast,
Can mark the figures on an Indian chest;
And when she sees her Friend in deep despair,
Observes how much a Chintz exceeds
	Mohair. 170
Forbid it Heav'n, a Favour or a Debt
She e'er should cancel—but she may forget.
Safe is your Secret still in Cloe's ear;
But none of Cloe's shall you ever hear.

---

l. 110. *Ratafie:* a brandy made with peach and apricot
stones.

Of all her Dears she never slander'd one,
But cares not if a thousand are undone.
Would Cloe know if you're alive or dead?
She bids her Footman put it in her head.
Cloe is prudent—would you too be wise?
Then never break your heart when Cloe
    dies.   180
    One certain Portrait may (I grant) be seen,
Which Heav'n has varnish'd out, and made a
    Queen:
The same for ever! and describ'd by all
With Truth and Goodness, as with Crown and
    Ball:
Poets heap Virtues, Painters Gems at will,
And show their zeal, and hide their want of
    skill.
'Tis well—but, Artists! who can paint or write,
To draw the Naked is your true delight:
That Robe of Quality so struts and swells,
None see what Parts of Nature it conceals. 190
Th' exactest traits of Body or of Mind,
We owe to models of an humble kind.
If QUEENSBURY to strip there's no compelling,
'Tis from a Handmaid we must take a Helen.
From Peer or Bishop 'tis no easy thing
To draw the man who loves his God, or King:
Alas! I copy (or my draught would fail)
From honest Mah'met, or plain Parson Hale.
    But grant, in Public Men sometimes are
    shown,
A Woman's seen in Private life alone: 200
Our bolder Talents in full light display'd,
Your Virtues open fairest in the shade.
Bred to disguise, in Public 'tis you hide;
There, none distinguish 'twixt your Shame
    or Pride,
Weakness or Delicacy; all so nice,
That each may seem a Virtue, or a Vice.
    In Men, we various Ruling Passions find,
In Women, two almost divide the kind;
Those, only fix'd, they first or last obey,

I. 182. *Queen:* Queen Caroline (1683–1737).
I. 193. *Queensberry:* Catherine Hyde, Duchess of Queensberry (1700–1777).
I. 198. *Parson Hale:* Dr. Stephen Hales (1677–1761), a famous physiologist whose vivisections distressed Pope.

The Love of Pleasure, and the Love of
    Sway.   210
    That, Nature gives; and where the lesson
    taught
Is but to please, can Pleasure seem a fault?
Experience, this; by Man's oppression curst,
They seek the second not to lose the first.
    Men, some to Bus'ness, some to Pleasure
    take;
But ev'ry Woman is at heart a Rake:
Men, some to Quiet, some to public Strife;
But ev'ry Lady would be Queen for life.
    Yet mark the fate of a whole Sex of Queens!
Pow'r all their end, but Beauty all the
    means.   220
In Youth they conquer, with so wild a rage,
As leaves them scarce a Subject in their Age:
For foreign glory, foreign joy, they roam;
No thought of Peace or Happiness at home.
But Wisdom's Triumph is well-tim'd Retreat,
As hard a science to the Fair as Great!
Beauties, like Tyrants, old and friendless
    grown,
Yet hate to rest, and dread to be alone,
Worn out in public, weary ev'ry eye,
Nor leave one sigh behind them when they
    die.   230
    Pleasures the sex, as children Birds, pursue,
Still out of reach, yet never out of view,
Sure, if they catch, to spoil the Toy at most,
To covet flying, and regret when lost:
At last, to follies Youth could scarce defend,
'Tis half their Age's prudence to pretend;
Asham'd to own they gave delight before,
Reduc'd to feign it, when they give no more:
As Hags hold Sabbaths, less for joy than
    spight,
So these their merry, miserable Night;   240
Still round and round the Ghosts of Beauty
    glide,
And haunt the places where their Honour
    dy'd.
    See how the World its Veterans rewards!
A Youth of frolicks, an old Age of Cards,
Fair to no purpose, artful to no end,
Young without Lovers, old without a Friend,
A Fop their Passion, but their Prize a Sot,

Alive, ridiculous, and dead, forgot!
    Ah Friend! to dazzle let the Vain design,
To raise the Thought and touch the Heart, be
        thine!   250
That Charm shall grow, while what fatigues
        the Ring
Flaunts and goes down, an unregarded thing.
So when the Sun's broad beam has tir'd the
        sight,
All mild ascends the Moon's more sober light,
Serene in Virgin Modesty she shines,
And unobserv'd the glaring Orb declines.
    Oh! blest with Temper, whose unclouded
        ray
Can make to morrow chearful as to day;
She, who can love a Sister's charms, or hear
Sighs for a Daughter with unwounded ear; 260
She, who ne'er answers till a Husband cools,
Or, if she rules him, never shows she rules;
Charms by accepting, by submitting sways,
Yet has her humour most, when she obeys;
Lets Fops or Fortune fly which way they will;
Disdains all loss of Tickets, or Codille;
Spleen, Vapours, or Small-pox, above them all,
And Mistress of herself, tho' China fall.
    And yet, believe me, good as well as ill,
Woman's at best a Contradiction still.   270
Heav'n, when it strives to polish all it can
Its last best work, but forms a softer Man;
Picks from each sex, to make its Fav'rite
        blest,
Your love of Pleasure, our desire of Rest,
Blends, in exception to all gen'ral rules,
Your Taste of Follies, with our Scorn of
        Fools,
Reserve with Frankness, Art with Truth ally'd,
Courage with Softness, Modesty with Pride,
Fix'd Principles, with Fancy ever new;
Shakes all together, and produces—You.   280
    Be this a Woman's Fame: with this unblest,
Toasts live a scorn, and Queens may die a jest.
This Phœbus promis'd (I forget the year)

---

l. 251. *Ring:* clump of trees in Hyde Park, around which
carriages of fashionable people drove.
l. 266. *Codille:* a term in the fashionable card game
omber.

When those blue eyes first open'd on the
        sphere;
Ascendant Phœbus watch'd that hour with
        care,
Averted half your Parents simple Pray'r,
And gave you Beauty, but deny'd the Pelf
Which buys your sex a Tyrant o'er itself.
The gen'rous God, who Wit and Gold refines,
And ripens Spirits as he ripens Mines,   290
Kept Dross for Duchesses, the world shall
        know it,
To you gave Sense, Good-humour, and a Poet.

[from *Moral Essays*]

william blake

The Lamb

    Little Lamb, who made thee?
        Dost thou know who made thee?
Gave thee life, & bid thee feed
By the stream & o'er the mead;
Gave thee clothing of delight,
Softest clothing, wooly, bright;
Gave thee such a tender voice,
Making all the vales rejoice?
    Little Lamb, who made thee?
        Dost thou know who made thee?   10

    Little Lamb, I'll tell thee,
    Little Lamb, I'll tell thee:
He is called by thy name,
For he calls himself a Lamb.
He is meek, & he is mild;
He became a little child.
I a child, & thou a lamb,
We are called by his name.
    Little Lamb, God bless thee!
    Little Lamb, God bless thee!   20

[from *Songs of Innocence*]

The Divine Image

To Mercy, Pity, Peace, and Love
All pray in their distress;
And to these virtues of delight
Return their thankfulness.

For Mercy, Pity, Peace, and Love
Is God, our father dear,
And Mercy, Pity, Peace, and Love
Is Man, his child and care.

For Mercy has a human heart,
Pity a human face,   10
And Love, the human form divine,
And Peace, the human dress.

Then every man, of every clime,
That prays in his distress,
Prays to the human form divine,
Love, Mercy, Pity, Peace.

And all must love the human form,
In heathen, turk, or jew;
Where Mercy, Love, & Pity dwell
There God is dwelling too.   20

[from *Songs of Innocence*]

The Clod and the Pebble

"Love seeketh not Itself to please,
Nor for itself hath any care,
But for another gives its ease,
And builds a Heaven in Hell's despair."

So sung a little Clod of Clay
Trodden with the cattle's feet,
But a Pebble of the brook
Warbled out these metres meet:

"Love seeketh only Self to please,
To bind another to Its delight,   10

Joys in another's loss of ease,
And builds a Hell in Heaven's despite."

[from *Songs of Experience*]

The Tyger

Tyger! Tyger! burning bright
In the forests of the night,
What immortal hand or eye
Could frame thy fearful symmetry?

In what distant deeps or skies
Burnt the fire of thine eyes?
On what wings dare he aspire?
What the hand dare seize the fire?

And what shoulder, & what art,
Could twist the sinews of thy heart?   10
And when thy heart began to beat,
What dread hand? & what dread feet?

What the hammer? what the chain?
In what furnace was thy brain?
What the anvil? what dread grasp
Dare its deadly terrors clasp?

When the stars threw down their spears,
And water'd heaven with their tears,
Did he smile his work to see?
Did he who made the Lamb make thee?   20

Tyger! Tyger! burning bright
In the forests of the night,
What immortal hand or eye,
Dare frame thy fearful symmetry?

[from *Songs of Experience*]

London

I wander thro' each charter'd street,
Near where the charter'd Thames does flow,
And mark in every face I meet
Marks of weakness, marks of woe.

In every cry of every Man,
In every Infant's cry of fear,
In every voice, in every ban,
The mind-forg'd manacles I hear.

How the Chimney-sweeper's cry
Every black'ning Church appalls;   10
And the hapless Soldier's sigh
Runs in blood down Palace walls.

But most thro' midnight streets I hear
How the youthful Harlot's curse
Blasts the new born Infant's tear,
And blights with plagues the Marriage hearse.

[from *Songs of Experience*]

---

l. 1. *charter'd:* mapped.
l. 10. *appalls:* accuses.

A Poison Tree

I was angry with my friend:
I told my wrath, my wrath did end.
I was angry with my foe:
I told it not, my wrath did grow.

And I water'd it in fears,
Night and morning with my tears;
And I sunnèd it with smiles,
And with soft deceitful wiles.

And it grew both day and night,
Till it bore an apple bright;   10
And my foe beheld it shine,
And he knew that it was mine,

And into my garden stole
When the night had veil'd the pole:
In the morning glad I see
My foe outstretch'd beneath the tree.

[from *Songs of Experience*]

The Human Abstract

Pity would be no more
If we did not make somebody Poor;
And Mercy no more could be
If all were as happy as we.

And mutual fear brings peace,
Till the selfish loves increase:
Then Cruelty knits a snare,
And spreads his baits with care.

He sits down with holy fears,
And waters the ground with tears;   10
Then Humility takes its root
Underneath his foot.

Soon spreads the dismal shade
Of Mystery over his head;
And the Catterpiller and Fly
Feed on the Mystery.

And it bears the fruit of Deceit,
Ruddy and sweet to eat;
And the Raven his nest has made
In its thickest shade.   20

The Gods of the earth and sea
Sought thro' Nature to find this Tree;
But their search was all in vain:
There grows one in the Human Brain.

[from *Songs of Experience*]

ROBERT bURNS

Holy Willie's Prayer

O Thou, wha in the Heavens dost dwell,
Wha, as it pleases best thysel',
Sends ane to heaven and ten to hell,
    A' for thy glory,
And no for ony guid or ill
    They've done afore thee!

I bless and praise thy matchless might,
Whan thousands thou has left in night,
That I am here afore thy sight,
    For gifts an' grace 10
A burnin' an' a shinin' light,
    To a' this place.

What was I, or my generation,
That I should get sic exaltation?
I, wha deserve most just damnation,
    For broken laws,
Sax thousand years 'fore my creation,
    Thro' Adam's cause.

When frae my mither's womb I fell,
Thou might hae plunged me in hell, 20
To gnash my gums, to weep and wail,
    In burnin' lakes,
Where damnèd devils roar and yell,
    Chain'd to their stakes;

Yet I am here a chosen sample,
To show thy grace is great and ample;
I'm here a pillar in thy temple,
    Strong as a rock,
A guide, a buckler, an example
    To a' thy flock. 30

O Lord, thou kens what zeal I bear,
When drinkers drink, and swearers swear,
And singin' there and dancin' here,
    Wi' great an' sma':
For I am keepit by thy fear
    Free frae them a'.

But yet, O Lord! confess I must
At times I'm fash'd wi' fleshy lust;
An' sometimes too, in warldly trust,
    Vile self gets in; 40
But thou remembers we are dust,
    Defil'd in sin.

O Lord! yestreen, thou kens, wi' Meg—
Thy pardon I sincerely beg;
O! may't ne'er be a livin' plague
    To my dishonour,
An' I'll ne'er lift a lawless leg
    Again upon her.

Besides I farther maun allow,
Wi' Lizzie's lass, three times I trow— 50
But, Lord, that Friday I was fou,
    When I cam near her,
Or else thou kens thy servant true
    Wad never steer her.

May be thou lets this fleshly thorn
Beset thy servant e'en and morn
Lest he owre high and proud should turn,
    That he's sae gifted;
If sae, thy hand maun e'en be borne,
    Until thou lift it. 60

Lord, bless thy chosen in this place,
For here thou hast a chosen race;
But God confound their stubborn face,
    And blast their name,
Wha bring thy elders to disgrace
    An' public shame.

---

l. 1. *wha:* who.
l. 3. *ane:* one.
l. 5. *no . . . ill:* not for any good or ill.
l. 19. *frae:* from.

l. 31. *kens:* know.
l. 38. *fash'd:* vexed.
l. 49. *maun:* must.
l. 50. *trow:* believe.
l. 51. *fou:* drunk.
l. 54. *steer:* touch.
l. 58. *sae:* so.

Lord, mind Gawn Hamilton's deserts,
He drinks, an' swears, an' plays at cartes,
Yet has sae mony takin' arts
           Wi' grit an' sma',   70
Frae God's ain priest the people's hearts
           He steals awa'.

An' when we chasten'd him therefor,
Thou kens how he bred sic a splore
As set the warld in a roar
           O' laughin' at us;
Curse thou his basket and his store,
           Kail and potatoes.

Lord, hear my earnest cry an' pray'r,
Against that presbyt'ry o' Ayr;   80
Thy strong right hand, Lord, make it bare
           Upo' their heads;
Lord, weigh it down, and dinna spare,
           For their misdeeds.

O Lord my God, that glib-tongu'd Aiken,
My very heart and soul are quakin',
To think how we stood sweatin', shakin',
           An' piss'd wi' dread,
While he, wi' hingin' lips and snakin',
           Held up his head.   90

Lord, in the day of vengeance try him;
Lord, visit them wha did employ him,
And pass not in thy mercy by them,
           Nor hear their pray'r:
But, for thy people's sake, destroy them,
           And dinna spare.

But, Lord, remember me and mine
Wi' mercies temp'ral and divine,
That I for gear and grace may shine
           Excell'd by nane,   100
And a' the glory shall be thine,
           Amen, Amen!

---

l. 74. *splore:* disturbance.

My Love Is Like a Red Red Rose

My love is like a red red rose
    That's newly sprung in June:
My love is like the melodie
    That's sweetly play'd in tune.

So fair art thou, my bonnie lass,
    So deep in love am I:
And I will love thee still, my dear,
    Till a' the seas gang dry.

Till a' the seas gang dry, my dear,
    And the rocks melt wi' the sun: 10
And I will love thee still, my dear,
    While the sands o' life shall run.

And fare thee weel, my only love,
    And fare thee weel awhile!
And I will come again, my love,
    Tho' it were ten thousand mile.

Go Fetch to Me a Pint o' Wine

Go fetch to me a pint o' wine,
    An' fill it in a silver tassie;
That I may drink, before I go,
    A service to my bonnie lassie.
The boat rocks at the pier o' Leith,
    Fu' loud the wind blaws frae the ferry,
The ship rides by the Berwick-law,
    And I maun leave my bonnie Mary.

The trumpets sound, the banners fly,
    The glittering spears are rankèd ready;   10
The shouts o' war are heard afar,
    The battle closes thick and bloody;
But it's no the roar o' sea or shore
    Wad mak me langer wish to tarry;
Nor shout o' war that's heard afar,
    It's leaving thee, my bonnie Mary.

william wordsworth

Lines Composed a Few Miles Above Tintern Abbey On Revisiting the Banks of the Wye During a Tour. July 13, 1798

Five years have past; five summers, with the
    length
Of five long winters! and again I hear
These waters, rolling from their mountain-
    springs
With a soft inland murmur.—Once again
Do I behold these steep and lofty cliffs,
That on a wild secluded scene impress
Thoughts of more deep seclusion; and
    connect
The landscape with the quiet of the sky.
The day is come when I again repose
Here, under this dark sycamore, and view   10
These plots of cottage-ground, these orchard-
    tufts,
Which at this season, with their unripe fruits,
Are clad in one green hue, and lose
    themselves
'Mid groves and copses. Once again I see
These hedge-rows, hardly hedge-rows, little
    lines
Of sportive wood run wild: these pastoral
    farms,
Green to the very door; and wreaths of
    smoke
Sent up, in silence from among the trees!
With some uncertain notice, as might seem
Of vagrant dwellers in the houseless woods, 20
Or of some Hermit's cave, where by his fire
The Hermit sits alone.
                 These beauteous forms
Through a long absence, have not been to me
As is a landscape to a blind man's eye:
But oft, in lonely rooms, and 'mid the din

Of towns and cities, I have owed to them
In hours of weariness, sensations sweet,
Felt in the blood, and felt along the heart;
And passing even into my purer mind,   30
With tranquil restoration:—feelings too
Of unremembered pleasure: such, perhaps,
As have no slight or trivial influence
On that best portion of a good man's life,
His little, nameless, unremembered acts
Of kindness and of love. Nor less, I trust,
To them I may have owed another gift,
Of aspect more sublime; that blessed mood,
In which the burthen of the mystery,
In which the heavy and the weary weight   40
Of all this unintelligible world,
Is lightened:—that serene and blessed mood,
In which the affections gently lead us on,—
Until, the breath of this corporeal frame
And even the motion of our human blood
Almost suspended, we are laid asleep
In body, and become a living soul:
While with an eye made quiet by the power
Of harmony, and the deep power of joy,
We see into the life of things.   50
                     If this
Be but a vain belief, yet, oh! how oft—
In darkness and amid the many shapes
Of joyless daylight; when the fretful stir
Unprofitable, and the fever of the world,
Have hung upon the beatings of my heart—
How oft, in spirit, have I turned to thee,
O sylvan Wye! thou wanderer thro' the
    woods,
How often has my spirit turned to thee!

  And now, with gleams of half-extinguished
    thought,   60
With many recognitions dim and faint,
And somewhat of a sad perplexity,
The picture of the mind revives again:
While here I stand, not only with the sense
Of present pleasure, but with pleasing
    thoughts
That in this moment there is life and food
For future years. And so I dare to hope,
Though changed, no doubt, from what I was
    when first

I came among these hills; when like a roe
I bounded o'er the mountains, by the sides 70
Of the deep rivers, and the lonely streams,
Wherever nature led: more like a man
Flying from something that he dreads, than
    one
Who sought the thing he loved. For nature
    then
(The coarser pleasures of my boyish days,
And their glad animal movements all gone by)
To me was all in all.—I cannot paint
What then I was. The sounding cataract
Haunted me like a passion: the tall rock,
The mountain, and the deep and gloomy
    wood,   80
Their colours and their forms, were then to
    me
An appetite; a feeling and a love,
That had no need of a remoter charm,
By thought supplied, nor any interest
Unborrowed from the eye.—That time is past,
And all its aching joys are now no more,
And all its dizzy raptures. Not for this
Faint I, nor mourn nor murmur; other gifts
Have followed; for such loss, I would believe,
Abundant recompense. For I have learned 90
To look on nature, not as in the hour
Of thoughtless youth; but hearing oftentimes
The still, sad music of humanity,
Nor harsh nor grating, though of ample
    power
To chasten and subdue. And I have felt
A presence that disturbs me with the joy
Of elevated thoughts; a sense sublime
Of something far more deeply interfused,
Whose dwelling is the light of setting suns,
And the round ocean and the living air,   100
And the blue sky, and in the mind of man:
A motion and a spirit, that impels
All thinking things, all objects of all thought,
And rolls through all things. Therefore am
    I still
A lover of the meadows and the woods,
And mountains; and of all that we behold
From this green earth; of all the mighty
    world
Of eye, and ear,—both what they half create,

And what perceive; well pleased to
    recognise
In nature and the language of the sense,   110
The anchor of my purest thoughts, the nurse,
The guide, the guardian of my heart, and soul
Of all my moral being.
                          Nor perchance,
If I were not thus taught, should I the more
Suffer my genial spirits to decay:
For thou art with me here upon the banks
Of this fair river; thou my dearest Friend,
My dear, dear Friend; and in thy voice
    I catch
The language of my former heart, and
    read   120
My former pleasures in the shooting lights
Of thy wild eyes. Oh! yet a little while
May I behold in thee what I was once,
My dear, dear Sister! and this prayer I make,
Knowing that Nature never did betray
The heart that loved her; 'tis her privilege,
Through all the years of this our life, to lead
From joy to joy: for she can so inform
The mind that is within us, so impress
With quietness and beauty, and so feed   130
With lofty thoughts, that neither evil tongues,
Rash judgments, nor the sneers of selfish
    men,
Nor greetings where no kindness is, nor all
The dreary intercourse of daily life,
Shall e'er prevail against us, or disturb
Our cheerful faith, that all which we behold
Is full of blessings. Therefore let the moon
Shine on thee in thy solitary walk;
And let the misty mountain-winds be free
To blow against thee: and, in after years, 140
When these wild ecstasies shall be matured
Into a sober pleasure; when thy mind
Shall be a mansion for all lovely forms,
Thy memory be as a dwelling-place
For all sweet sounds and harmonies; oh! then,
If solitude, or fear, or pain, or grief,
Should be thy portion, with what healing
    thoughts
Of tender joy wilt thou remember me,

---

l. 118. *Friend:* Wordsworth's sister, Dorothy.

And these my exhortations! Nor, perchance—
If I should be where I no more can hear   150
Thy voice, nor catch from thy wild eyes these
    gleams
Of past existence—wilt thou then forget
That on the banks of this delightful stream
We stood together, and that I, so long
A worshipper of Nature, hither came
Unwearied in that service: rather say
With warmer love—oh! with far deeper zeal
Of holier love. Nor wilt thou then forget,
That after many wanderings, many years
Of absence, these steep woods and lofty
    cliffs,   160
And this green pastoral landscape, were to me
More dear, both for themselves and for thy
    sake!

A Slumber Did My Spirit Seal

A slumber did my spirit seal;
  I had no human fears:
She seemed a thing that could not feel
  The touch of earthly years.

No motion has she now, no force;
  She neither hears nor sees;
Rolled round in earth's diurnal course,
  With rocks, and stones, and trees.

Composed upon Westminster Bridge

September 3, 1802

Earth has not anything to show more fair:
Dull would he be of soul who could pass by
A sight so touching in its majesty:
This City now doth, like a garment, wear
The beauty of the morning; silent, bare,
Ships, towers, domes, theatres, and
  temples lie

Open unto the fields, and to the sky;
All bright and glittering in the smokeless air.
Never did sun more beautifully steep
In his first splendour, valley, rock, or hill;   10
Ne'er saw I, never felt, a calm so deep!
The river glideth at his own sweet will:
Dear God! the very houses seem asleep;
And all that mighty heart is lying still!

It Is a Beauteous Evening, Calm and Free

It is a beauteous evening, calm and free,
The holy time is quiet as a Nun
Breathless with adoration; the broad sun
Is sinking down in its tranquillity;
The gentleness of heaven broods o'er the Sea:
Listen! the mighty Being is awake,
And doth with his eternal motion make
A sound like thunder—everlastingly.
Dear Child! dear Girl! that walkest with
  me here,
If thou appear untouched by solemn
  thought,   10
Thy nature is not therefore less divine:
Thou liest in Abraham's bosom all the year;
And worshipp'st at the Temple's inner shrine,
God being with thee when we know it not.

l. 9. *Child:* Wordsworth's natural daughter, Caroline, by his French sweetheart, Annette Vallon.

Elegiac Stanzas

Suggested by a Picture of Peele Castle, in a Storm, Painted by Sir George Beaumont

I was thy neighbour once, thou rugged Pile!
Four summer weeks I dwelt in sight of thee:

l. 2. *Four summer weeks:* a reference to a visit paid by Wordsworth during a college vacation.

I saw thee every day; and all the while
Thy Form was sleeping on a glassy sea.

So pure the sky, so quiet was the air!
So like, so very like, was day to day!
Whene'er I look, thy Image still was there;
It trembled, but it never passed away.

How perfect was the calm! it seemed no
   sleep;
No mood, which season takes away, or
   brings: 10
I could have fancied that the mighty Deep
Was even the gentlest of all gentle Things.

Ah! then, if mine had been the Painter's hand,
To express what then I saw; and add the
   gleam,
The light that never was, on sea or land,
The consecration, and the Poet's dream;

I would have planted thee, thou hoary Pile
Amid a world how different from this!
Beside a sea that could not cease to smile;
On tranquil land, beneath a sky of bliss.   20

Thou shouldst have seemed a treasure-house
   divine
Of peaceful years; a chronicle of heaven;—
Of all the sunbeams that did ever shine
The very sweetest had to thee been given.

A Picture had it been of lasting ease,
Elysian quiet, without toil or strife;
No motion but the moving tide, a breeze,
Or merely silent Nature's breathing life.

Such, in the fond illusion of my heart,
Such Picture would I at that time have
   made: 30
And seen the soul of truth in every part,
A steadfast peace that might not be betrayed.

So once it would have been,—'tis so no more;
I have submitted to a new control:
A power is gone, which nothing can restore;

A deep distress hath humanised my Soul.

Not for a moment could I now behold
A smiling sea, and be what I have been:
The feeling of my loss will ne'er be old;
This, which I know, I speak with mind
   serene.   40

Then, Beaumont, Friend! who would have
   been the Friend,
If he had lived, of Him whom I deplore,
This work of thine I blame not, but
   commend;
This sea in anger, and that dismal shore.

O 'tis a passionate Work!—yet wise and well,
Well chosen is the spirit that is here;
That Hulk which labours in the deadly swell,
This rueful sky, this pageantry of fear!

And this huge Castle, standing here sublime,
I love to see the look with which it braves,   50
Cased in the unfeeling armour of old time,
The lightning, the fierce wind, and trampling
   waves.

Farewell, farewell the heart that lives alone,
Housed in a dream, at distance from the
   Kind!
Such happiness, wherever it be known,
Is to be pitied; for 'tis surely blind.

But welcome fortitude, and patient cheer,
And frequent sights of what is to be borne!
Such sights, or worse, as are before me
   here.—
Not without hope we suffer and we mourn.   60

---

l. 36. *A deep distress:* Wordsworth's brother, John, went
down with his ship off the Bill of Portland, February 5,
1805.

Ode: Intimations of Immortality from Recollections of Early Childhood

The Child is father of the Man;
And I could wish my days to be
Bound each to each by natural piety.

I

There was a time when meadow, grove,
        and stream,
The earth, and every common sight,
    To me did seem
    Apparelled in celestial light,
The glory and the freshness of a dream.
It is not now as it hath been of yore;—
    Turn whereso'er I may,
      By night or day,
The things which I have seen I now can see
      no more.

II

    The Rainbow comes and goes,   10
    And lovely is the Rose,
    The Moon doth with delight
Look round her when the heavens are bare;
    Waters on a starry night
    Are beautiful and fair;
    The sunshine is a glorious birth;
    But yet I know, where'er I go,
That there hath past away a glory from
      the earth.

III

Now, while the birds thus sing a joyous song,
    And while the young lambs bound   20
      As to the tabor's sound,
To me alone there came a thought of grief:

A timely utterance gave that thought relief,
    And I again am strong:
The cataracts blow their trumpets from
      the steep;
No more shall grief of mine the season wrong;
I hear the Echoes through the mountains
      throng,
The Winds come to me from the fields of
      sleep,
    And all the earth is gay;
      Land and sea   30
    Give themselves up to jollity,
    And with the heart of May
    Doth every Beast keep holiday;—
      Thou Child of Joy,
Shout round me, let me hear thy shouts,
      thou happy
      Shepherd-boy!

IV

Ye blessed Creatures, I have heard the call
    Ye to each other make; I see
The heavens laugh with you in your jubilee;
    My heart is at your festival,   40
    My head hath its coronal,
The fulness of your bliss, I feel—I feel it all.
      Oh evil day! if I were sullen
      While Earth herself is adorning,
        This sweet May-morning,
      And the Children are culling
        On every side,
      In a thousand valleys far and wide,
      Fresh flowers; while the sun shines
        warm,
And the Babe leaps up on his Mother's
      arm:—   50
      I hear, I hear, with joy I hear!
      —But there's a Tree, of many, one,
A single Field which I have looked upon,
Both of them speak of something that
      is gone:
      The Pansy at my feet
      Doth the same tale repeat:
Whither is fled the visionary gleam?
Where is it now, the glory and the dream?

The Child . . . piety: the last three lines of Words-worth's lyric, "My Heart Leaps Up."
l. 21. *tabor:* a small tambourine-like drum.

l. 41. *coronal:* garland.

V

Our birth is but a sleep and a forgetting:
The Soul that rises with us, our life's Star,   60
   Hath had elsewhere its setting,
    And cometh from afar:
   Not in entire forgetfulness,
   And not in utter nakedness,
But trailing clouds of glory do we come
   From God, who is our home:
Heaven lies about us in our infancy!
Shades of the prison-house begin to close
   Upon the growing Boy,
But He beholds the light, and whence it
      flows,   70
   He sees it in his joy;
The Youth, who daily farther from the east
   Must travel, still is Nature's Priest,
   And by the vision splendid
   Is on his way attended;
At length the Man perceives it die away,
And fade into the light of common day.

VI

Earth fills her lap with pleasures of her own;
Yearnings she hath in her own natural kind,
And, even with something of a Mother's
      mind,   80
   And no unworthy aim,
   The homely Nurse doth all she can
To make her Foster-child, her Inmate Man,
   Forget the glories he hath known,
And that imperial palace whence he came.

VII

Behold the Child among his new-born blisses,
A six years' Darling of a pigmy size!
See, where 'mid work of his own hand he lies,
Fretted by sallies of his mother's kisses,
With light upon him from his father's eyes!   90
See, at his feet, some little plan or chart,
Some fragment from his dream of human life,
Shaped by himself with newly-learned art;
   A wedding or a festival,
   A mourning or a funeral;

And this hath now his heart,
And unto this he frames his song:
   Then will he fit his tongue
To dialogues of business, love, or strife;
   But it will not be long   100
   Ere this be thrown aside,
   And with new joy and pride
The little Actor cons another part;
Filling from time to time his "humorous
      stage"
With all the Persons, down to palsied Age,
That Life brings with her in her equipage;
   As if his whole vocation
   Were endless imitation.

VIII

Thou, whose exterior semblance doth belie
   Thy Soul's immensity;   110
Thou best Philosopher, who yet dost keep
Thy heritage, thou Eye among the blind,
That, deaf and silent, read'st the eternal deep,
Haunted forever by the eternal mind,—
   Mighty Prophet! Seer blest!
   On whom those truths do rest,
Which we are toiling all our lives to find,
In darkness lost, the darkness of the grave;
Thou, over whom thy Immortality
Broods like the Day, a Master o'er a Slave,   120
A Presence which is not to be put by;
Thou little Child, yet glorious in the might
Of heaven-born freedom on thy being's height,
Why with such earnest pains dost thou
      provoke
The years to bring the inevitable yoke,
Thus blindly with thy blessedness at strife?
Full soon thy Soul shall have her earthly
      freight,
And custom lie upon thee with a weight,
Heavy as frost, and deep almost as life!

IX

   O joy! that in our embers   130
   Is something that doth live,
   That Nature yet remembers
   What was so fugitive!

The thought of our past years in me doth
        breed
Perpetual benediction: not indeed
For that which is most worthy to be blest;
Delight and liberty, the simple creed
Of Childhood, whether busy or at rest,
With new-fledged hope still fluttering in
        his breast:—
    Not for these I raise   140
      The song of thanks and praise;
    But for those obstinate questionings
    Of sense and outward things,
    Fallings from us, vanishings;
    Blank misgivings of a Creature
Moving about in worlds not realized,
High instincts before which our moral Nature
Did tremble like a guilty Thing surprised:
    But for those first affections,
    Those shadowy recollections,   150
    Which, be they what they may,
Are yet the fountain light of all our day,
Are yet a master light of all our seeing;
    Uphold us, cherish, and have power
      to make
Our noisy years seem moments in the being
Of the eternal Silence: truths that wake,
    To perish never;
Which neither listlessness, nor mad endeavor,
    Nor Man nor Boy,
Nor all that is at enmity with joy,   160
Can utterly abolish or destroy!
    Hence in a season of calm weather
    Though inland far we be,
Our Souls have sight of that immortal sea
    Which brought us hither,
    Can in a moment travel thither,
And see the Children sport upon the shore,
And hear the mighty waters rolling evermore.

X

Then sing, ye Birds, sing, sing a joyous song!
    And let the young Lambs bound   170
    As to the tabor's sound!
We in thought will join your throng,
    Ye that pipe and ye that play,
    Ye that through your hearts to-day

    Feel the gladness of the May!
What though the radiance which was once
      so bright
Be now for ever taken from my sight,
    Though nothing can bring back the hour
Of splendor in the grass, of glory in the
      flower;
    We will grieve not, rather find   180
    Strength in what remains behind;
    In the primal sympathy
    Which having been must ever be;
    In the soothing thoughts that spring
    Out of human suffering;
    In the faith that looks through death,
In years that bring the philosophic mind.

XI

And O, ye Fountains, Meadows, Hills, and
      Groves,
Forbode not any severing of our loves!
Yet in my heart of hearts I feel your
      might;   190
I only have relinquished one delight
To live beneath your more habitual sway.
I love the Brooks which down their channels
    fret,
Even more than when I tripped lightly as
    they;
The innocent brightness of a new-born Day
    Is lovely yet;
The Clouds that gather round the setting sun
Do take a sober coloring from an eye
That hath kept watch o'er man's mortality;
Another race hath been, and other palms are
    won.   200
Thanks to the human heart by which we live,
Thanks to its tenderness, its joys, and fears,
To me the meanest flower that blows can give
Thoughts that do often lie too deep for tears.

SAMUEL TAYLOR COLERIDGE

The Rime of the Ancient Mariner

Part I

An ancient Mariner meeteth three Gallants bidden to a wedding-feast, and detaineth one.

It is an ancient Mariner,
And he stoppeth one of three.
"By thy long grey beard and glittering eye,
Now wherefore stopp'st thou me?

The Bridegroom's doors are opened wide,
And I am next of kin;
The guests are met, the feast is set:
May'st hear the merry din."

He holds him with his skinny hand,
"There was a ship," quoth he.   10
"Hold off! unhand me, grey-beard loon!"
Eftsoons his hand dropt he.

The Wedding-Guest is spellbound by the eye of the old seafaring man, and constrained to hear his tale.

He holds him with his glittering eye—
The Wedding-Guest stood still,
And listens like a three years' child:
The Mariner hath' his will.

The Wedding-Guest sat on a stone:
He cannot choose but hear;
And thus spake on that ancient man,
The bright-eyed Mariner.   20

The Mariner tells how the ship sailed southward with a good wind and fair weather, till it reached the line.

"The ship was cheered, the harbour cleared,
Merrily did we drop
Below the kirk, below the hill,
Below the lighthouse top.

The Sun came up upon the left,
Out of the sea came he!
And he shone bright, and on the right
Went down into the sea.

---

l. 12. *Eftsoons:* at once.

Higher and higher every day,
Till over the mast at noon—"   30
The Wedding-Guest here beat his breast,
For he heard the loud bassoon.

The Wedding-Guest heareth the bridal music; but the Mariner continueth his tale.

The bride hath paced into the hall,
Red as a rose is she;
Nodding their heads before her goes
The merry minstrelsy.

The Wedding-Guest he beat his breast,
Yet he cannot choose but hear;
And thus spake on that ancient man,
The bright-eyed Mariner.   40

The ship driven by a storm toward the south pole.

"And now the STORM-BLAST came, and he
Was tyrannous and strong:
He struck with his o'ertaking wings,
And chased us south along.

With sloping masts and dipping prow,
As who pursued with yell and blow
Still treads the shadow of his foe,
And forward bends his head,
The ship drove fast, loud roared the blast,
And southward aye we fled.   50

And now there came both mist and snow,
And it grew wondrous cold:
And ice, mast-high, came floating by,
As green as emerald.

The land of ice, and of fearful sounds where no living thing was to be seen.

And through the drifts the snowy clifts
Did send a dismal sheen:
Nor shapes of men nor beasts we ken—
The ice was all between.

The ice was here, the ice was there,
The ice was all around: 60
It cracked and growled, and roared and howled,
Like noises in a swound!

Till a great sea-bird, called the Albatross, came through the snow-fog, and was received with great joy and hospitality.

At length did cross an Albatross,
Thorough the fog it came;

l. 57. *ken:* discerned.
l. 62. *swound:* swoon.
l. 64. *Thorough:* through.

As if it had been a Christian soul,
We hailed it in God's name.

It ate the food it ne'er had eat,
And round and round it flew.
The ice did split with a thunder-fit;
The helmsman steered us through!   70

And a good south wind sprung up behind;
The Albatross did follow,
And every day, for food or play,
Came to the mariners' hollo!

In mist or cloud, on mast or shroud,
It perched for vespers nine;
Whiles all the night, through fog-smoke white,
Glimmered the white Moon-shine."

"God save thee, ancient Mariner!
From the fiends, that plague thee thus!—   80
Why look'st thou so?"—With my cross-bow
I shot the ALBATROSS.

Part II

The Sun now rose upon the right:
Out of the sea came he,
Still hid in mist, and on the left
Went down into the sea.

And the good south wind still blew behind,
But no sweet bird did follow,
Nor any day for food or play
Came to the mariners' hollo!   90

And I had done a hellish thing,
And it would work 'em woe:
For all averred, I had killed the bird
That made the breeze to blow.
Ah wretch! said they, the bird to slay,
That made the breeze to blow!

Nor dim nor red, like God's own head,
The glorious Sun uprist:

---

l. 76. *vespers:* evening.

Then all averred, I had killed the bird
That brought the fog and mist.   100
'Twas right, said they, such birds to slay,
That bring the fog and mist.

The fair breeze continues; the ship enters the Pacific Ocean, and sails northward, even till it reaches the Line.

The fair breeze blew, the white foam flew,
The furrow followed free;
We were the first that ever burst
Into that silent sea.

Down dropt the breeze, the sails dropt down,
'Twas sad as sad could be;
And we did speak only to break
The silence of the sea!   110

The ship hath been suddenly becalmed.

All in a hot and copper sky,
The bloody Sun, at noon,
Right up above the mast did stand,
No bigger than the Moon.

Day after day, day after day,
We stuck, nor breath nor motion;
As idle as a painted ship
Upon a painted ocean.

And the Albatross begins to be avenged.

Water, water, every where,
And all the boards did shrink;   120
Water, water, every where,
Nor any drop to drink.

The very deep did rot: O Christ!
That ever this should be!
Yea, slimy things did crawl with legs
Upon the slimy sea.

About, about, in reel and rout
The death-fires danced at night;
The water, like a witch's oils,
Burnt green, and blue and white.   130

A Spirit had followed them; one of the invisible inhabitants of this planet, neither departed souls nor angels; concerning whom the learned Jew, Josephus, and the Platonic Constantinopolitan, Michael Psellus, may be consulted. They are very numerous, and there is no climate or element without one or more.

And some in dreams assurèd were
Of the Spirit that plagued us so;
Nine fathom deep he had followed us
From the land of mist and snow.

And every tongue, through utter drought,
Was withered at the root;

We could not speak, no more than if
We had been choked with soot.

Ah! well a-day! what evil looks
Had I from old and young!   140
Instead of the cross, the Albatross
About my neck was hung.

The shipmates, in their sore distress, would fain throw the whole
guilt on the ancient Mariner: in
sign whereof they hang the dead
sea-bird round his neck.

Part III

There passed a weary time. Each throat
Was parched, and glazed each eye.
A weary time! a weary time!
How glazed each weary eye,
When looking westward, I beheld
A something in the sky.

The ancient Mariner beholdeth a
sign in the element afar off.

At first it seemed a little speck,
And then it seemed a mist;   150
It moved and moved, and took at last
A certain shape, I wist.

A speck, a mist, a shape, I wist!
And still it neared and neared:
As if it dodged a water-sprite,
It plunged and tacked and veered.

With throats unslaked, with black lips baked,
We could nor laugh nor wail;
Through utter drought all dumb we stood!
I bit my arm, I sucked the blood,   160
And cried, A sail! a sail!

At its nearer approach, it seemeth
him to be a ship; and at a dear
ransom he freeth his speech from
the bonds of thirst.

With throats unslaked, with black lips baked,
Agape they heard me call:
Gramercy! they for joy did grin,
And all at once their breath drew in,
As they were drinking all.

A flash of joy;

See! see! (I cried) she tacks no more!
Hither to work us weal;
Without a breeze, without a tide,
She steadies with upright keel!   170

And horror follows. For can it be a
ship that comes onward without
wind or tide?

---

l. 152. *wist:* knew.
l. 164. *Gramercy: grand-merci,* or "mercy on us."

The western wave was all a-flame.
The day was well nigh done!
Almost upon the western wave
Rested the broad bright Sun;
When that strange shape drove suddenly
Betwixt us and the Sun.

And straight the Sun was flecked with bars,
(Heaven's Mother send us grace!)
As if through a dungeon-grate he peered
With broad and burning face.

180

Alas! (thought I, and my heart beat loud)
How fast she nears and nears!
Are those *her* sails that glance in the Sun,
Like restless gossameres?

Are those *her* ribs through which the Sun
Did peer, as through a grate?
And is that Woman all her crew?
Is that a DEATH? and are there two?
Is DEATH that woman's mate?

190

Her lips were red, *her* looks were free,
Her locks were yellow as gold:
Her skin was as white as leprosy,
The Night-mare LIFE-IN-DEATH was she,
Who thicks man's blood with cold.

The naked hulk alongside came,
And the twain were casting dice;
"The game is done! I've won! I've won!"
Quoth she, and whistles thrice.

The Sun's rim dips; the stars rush out:
At one stride comes the dark;
With far-heard whisper, o'er the sea,
Off shot the spectre-bark.

200

We listened and looked sideways up!
Fear at my heart, as at a cup,
My life-blood seemed to sip!
The stars were dim, and thick the night,
The steersman's face by his lamp gleamed white;
From the sails the dew did drip—
Till clomb above the eastern bar

The hornèd Moon, with one bright star   210
Within the nether tip.

One after another,

One after one, by the star-dogged Moon,
Too quick for groan or sigh,
Each turned his face with a ghastly pang,
And cursed me with his eye.

His shipmates drop down dead.

Four times fifty living men,
(And I heard nor sigh nor groan)
With heavy thump, a lifeless lump,
They dropped down one by one.

But Life-in-Death begins her work
on the ancient Mariner.

The souls did from their bodies fly,—   220
They fled to bliss or woe!
And every soul, it passed me by,
Like the whizz of my cross-bow!

Part IV

The Wedding-Guest feareth that a
Spirit is talking to him;

"I fear thee, ancient Mariner!
I fear thy skinny hand!
And thou art long, and lank, and brown,
As is the ribbed sea-sand.

I fear thee and thy glittering eye,
And thy skinny hand, so brown."—

But the ancient Mariner assureth
him of his bodily life, and pro-
ceedeth to relate his horrible penance.

Fear not, fear not, thou Wedding-Guest!   230
This body dropt not down.

Alone, alone, all, all alone,
Alone on a wide wide sea!
And never a saint took pity on
My soul in agony.

He despiseth the creatures of the
calm.

The many men, so beautiful!
And they all dead did lie:
And a thousand thousand slimy things
Lived on; and so did I.

And envieth that they should live,
and so many lie dead.

I looked upon the rotting sea,   240
And drew my eyes away;
I looked upon the rotting deck,
And there the dead men lay.

I looked to heaven, and tried to pray;
But or ever a prayer had gusht,
A wicked whisper came, and made
My heart as dry as dust.

I closed my lids, and kept them close,
And the balls like pulses beat;
For the sky and the sea, and the sea and the sky   250
Lay like a load on my weary eye,
And the dead were at my feet.

The cold sweat melted from their limbs,
Nor rot nor reek did they:
The look with which they looked on me
Had never passed away.

An orphan's curse would drag to hell
A spirit from on high;
But oh! more horrible than that
Is the curse in a dead man's eye!   260
Seven days, seven nights, I saw that curse,
And yet I could not die.

The moving Moon went up the sky,
And no where did abide:
Softly she was going up,
And a star or two beside—

Her beams bemocked the sultry main,
Like April hoar-frost spread;
But where the ship's huge shadow lay,
The charmèd water burnt alway   270
A still and awful red.

Beyond the shadow of the ship,
I watched the water-snakes:
They moved in tracks of shining white,
And when they reared, the elfish light
Fell off in hoary flakes.

Within the shadow of the ship
I watched their rich attire:
Blue, glossy green, and velvet black,
They coiled and swam; and every track   280
Was a flash of golden fire.

O happy living things! no tongue
Their beauty might declare:
A spring of love gushed from my heart,
And I blessed them unaware:
Sure my kind saint took pity on me,
And I blessed them unaware.

He blesseth them in his heart.

The spell begins to break.

The self-same moment I could pray;
And from my neck so free
The Albatross fell off, and sank   290
Like lead into the sea.

Part V

Oh sleep! it is a gentle thing,
Beloved from pole to pole!
To Mary Queen the praise be given!
She sent the gentle sleep from Heaven,
That slid into my soul.

By the grace of the holy Mother,
the ancient Mariner is refreshed
with rain.

The silly buckets on the deck,
That had so long remained,
I dreamt that they were filled with dew;
And when I awoke, it rained.   300

My lips were wet, my throat was cold,
My garments all were dank;
Sure I had drunken in my dreams,
And still my body drank.

I moved, and could not feel my limbs:
I was so light—almost
I thought that I had died in sleep,
And was a blessèd ghost.

He heareth sounds and seeth
strange sights and commotions in
the sky and the element.

And soon I heard a roaring wind:
It did not come anear;   310
But with its sound it shook the sails,
That were so thin and sere.

The upper air burst into life!
And a hundred fire-flags sheen,
To and fro they were hurried about!
And to and fro, and in and out,
The wan stars danced between.

And the coming wind did roar more loud,
And the sails did sigh like sedge;
And the rain poured down from one black cloud;   320
The Moon was at its edge.

The thick black cloud was cleft, and still
The Moon was at its side:
Like waters shot from some high crag,
The lightning fell with never a jag,
A river steep and wide.

The bodies of the ship's crew are
inspired and the ship moves on;
The loud wind never reached the ship,
Yet now the ship moved on!
Beneath the lightning and the Moon
The dead men gave a groan.   330

They groaned, they stirred, they all uprose,
Nor spake, nor moved their eyes;
It had been strange, even in a dream,
To have seen those dead men rise.

The helmsman steered, the ship moved on;
Yet never a breeze up-blew;
The mariners all 'gan work the ropes,
Where they were wont to do;
They raised their limbs like lifeless tools—
We were a ghastly crew.   340

The body of my brother's son
Stood by me, knee to knee:
The body and I pulled at one rope,
But he said nought to me.

But not by the souls of the men,
nor by dæmons of earth or middle
air, but by a blessed troop of an-
gelic spirits, sent down by the invo-
cation of the guardian saint.
"I fear thee, ancient Mariner!"
Be calm, thou Wedding-Guest!
'Twas not those souls that fled in pain,
Which to their corses came again,
But a troop of spirits blest:

For when it dawned—they dropped their arms,   350
And clustered round the mast;
Sweet sounds rose slowly through their mouths,
And from their bodies passed.

Around, around, flew each sweet sound,
Then darted to the Sun;

Slowly the sounds came back again,
Now mixed, now one by one.

Sometimes a-dropping from the sky
I heard the sky-lark sing;
Sometimes all little birds that are,   360
How they seemed to fill the sea and air
With their sweet jargoning!

And now 'twas like all instruments,
Now like a lonely flute;
And now it is an angel's song,
That makes the heavens be mute.

It ceased; yet still the sails made on
A pleasant noise till noon,
A noise like of a hidden brook
In the leafy month of June,   370
That to the sleeping woods all night
Singeth a quiet tune.

Till noon we quietly sailed on,
Yet never a breeze did breathe:
Slowly and smoothly went the ship,
Moved onward from beneath.

The lonesome Spirit from the south-pole carries on the ship as far as the Line, in obedience to the angelic troop, but still requireth vengeance.

Under the keel nine fathom deep,
From the land of mist and snow,
The spirit slid: and it was he
That made the ship to go.   380
The sails at noon left off their tune,
And the ship stood still also.

The Sun, right up above the mast,
Had fixed her to the ocean:
But in a minute she 'gan stir,
With a short uneasy motion—
Backwards and forwards half her length
With a short uneasy motion.

Then like a pawing horse let go,
She made a sudden bound: 390
It flung the blood into my head,
And I fell down in a swound.

---

l. 362. *jargoning:* twittering.

The Polar Spirit's fellow-dæmons, the invisible inhabitants of the element, take part in his wrong; and two of them relate, one to the other, that penance long and heavy for the ancient Mariner hath been accorded to the Polar Spirit, who returneth southward.

How long in that same fit I lay,
I have not to declare;
But ere my living life returned,
I heard and in my soul discerned
Two voices in the air.

"Is it he?" quoth one, "Is this the man?
By him who died on cross,
With his cruel bow he laid full low   400
The harmless Albatross.

The spirit who bideth by himself
In the land of mist and snow,
He loved the bird that loved the man
Who shot him with his bow."

The other was a softer voice,
As soft as honey-dew:
Quoth he, "The man hath penance done,
And penance more will do."

Part VI

First Voice

"But tell me, tell me! speak again,   410
Thy soft response renewing—
What makes that ship drive on so fast?
What is the ocean doing?"

Second Voice

"Still as a slave before his lord,
The ocean hath no blast;
His great bright eye most silently
Up to the Moon is cast—

If he may know which way to go;
For she guides him smooth or grim.
See, brother, see! how graciously   420
She looketh down on him."

First Voice

The Mariner hath been cast into a trance; for the angelic power causeth the vessel to drive north-ward faster than human life could endure.

"But why drives on that ship so fast,
Without or wave or wind?"

Second Voice

"The air is cut away before,
And closes from behind.

Fly, brother, fly! more high, more high!
Or we shall be belated:
For slow and slow that ship will go,
When the Mariner's trance is abated."

The supernatural motion is retarded; the Mariner awakes, and his penance begins anew.

I woke, and we were sailing on   430
As in a gentle weather:
'Twas night, calm night, the moon was high;
The dead men stood together.

All stood together on the deck,
For a charnel-dungeon fitter:
All fixed on me their stony eyes,
That in the Moon did glitter.

The pang, the curse, with which they died,
Had never passed away:
I could not draw my eyes from theirs,   440
Nor turn them up to pray.

The curse is finally expiated.

And now this spell was snapt: once more
I viewed the ocean green,
And looked far forth, yet little saw
Of what had else been seen—

Like one, that on a lonesome road
Doth walk in fear and dread,
And having once turned round walks on,
And turns no more his head;
Because he knows, a frightful fiend   450
Doth close behind him tread.

But soon there breathed a wind on me,
Nor sound nor motion made:
Its path was not upon the sea,
In ripple or in shade.

It raised my hair, it fanned my cheek
Like a meadow-gale of spring—
It mingled strangely with my fears,
Yet it felt like a welcoming.

Swiftly, swiftly flew the ship,   460
Yet she sailed softly too:
Sweetly, sweetly blew the breeze—
On me alone it blew.

Oh! dream of joy! is this indeed
The light-house top I see?
Is this the hill? is this the kirk?
Is this mine own countree?

And the ancient Mariner beholdeth his native country.

We drifted o'er the harbour-bar,
And I with sobs did pray—
O let me be awake, my God!   470
Or let me sleep alway.

The harbour-bay was clear as glass,
So smoothly it was strewn!
And on the bay the moonlight lay,
And the shadow of the Moon.

The rock shone bright, the kirk no less,
That stands above the rock:
The moonlight steeped in silentness
The steady weathercock.

And the bay was white with silent light,   480
Till rising from the same,
Full many shapes, that shadows were,
In crimson colours came.

The angelic spirits leave the dead bodies,

A little distance from the prow
Those crimson shadows were:
I turned my eyes upon the deck—
Oh, Christ! what saw I there!

And appear in their own forms of light.

Each corse lay flat, lifeless and flat,
And, by the holy rood!
A man all light, a seraph-man,   490
On every corse there stood.

This seraph-band, each waved his hand:
It was a heavenly sight!
They stood as signals to the land,
Each one a lovely light;

---

l. 489. *rood:* cross.

This seraph-band, each waved his hand,
No voice did they impart—
No voice; but oh! the silence sank
Like music on my heart.

But soon I heard the dash of oars,   500
I heard the Pilot's cheer;
My head was turned perforce away
And I saw a boat appear.

The Pilot and the Pilot's boy,
I heard them coming fast:
Dear Lord in Heaven! it was a joy
The dead men could not blast.

I saw a third—I heard his voice:
It is the Hermit good!
He singeth loud his godly hymns   510
That he makes in the wood.
He'll shrieve my soul, he'll wash away
The Albatross's blood.

Part VII

This Hermit good lives in that wood
Which slopes down to the sea.
How loudly his sweet voice he rears!
He loves to talk with marineres
That come from a far countree.

He kneels at morn, and noon, and eve—
He hath a cushion plump: 520
It is the moss that wholly hides
The rotted old oak-stump.

The skiff-boat neared: I heard them talk,
"Why, this is strange, I trow!
Where are those lights so many and fair,
That signal made but now?"

"Strange, by my faith!" the Hermit said—
"And they answered not our cheer!
The planks looked warped! and see those sails,
How thin they are and sere!   530
I never saw aught like to them,
Unless perchance it were

l. 512. *shrieve:* shrive; hear confession and give absolution.

Brown skeletons of leaves that lag
My forest-brook along;
When the ivy-tod is heavy with snow,
And the owlet whoops to the wolf below,
That eats the she-wolf's young."

"Dear Lord! it hath a fiendish look—
(The Pilot made reply)
I am a-feared"—"Push on, push on!"   540
Said the Hermit cheerily.

The boat came closer to the ship,
But I nor spake nor stirred;
The boat came close beneath the ship,
And straight a sound was heard.

The ship suddenly sinketh.
Under the water it rumbled on,
Still louder and more dread:
It reached the ship, it split the bay;
The ship went down like lead.

The ancient Mariner is saved in the Pilot's boat.
Stunned by that loud and dreadful sound,   550
Which sky and ocean smote,
Like one that hath been seven days drowned
My body lay afloat;
But swift as dreams, myself I found
Within the Pilot's boat.

Upon the whirl, where sank the ship,
The boat spun round and round;
And all was still, save that the hill
Was telling of the sound.

I moved my lips—the Pilot shrieked   560
And fell down in a fit;
The holy Hermit raised his eyes,
And prayed where he did sit.

I took the oars: the Pilot's boy,
Who now doth crazy go,
Laughed loud and long, and all the while
His eyes went to and fro.
"Ha! ha!" quoth he, "full plain I see,
The Devil knows how to row."

---

l. 535. *tod:* bush.

And now, all in my own countree,   570
I stood on the firm land!
The Hermit stepped forth from the boat,
And scarcely he could stand.

The ancient Mariner earnestly en-
treateth the Hermit to shrieve him;
and the penance of Life falls on
him.

"O shrieve me, shrieve me, holy man!"
The Hermit crossed his brow.
"Say quick," quoth he, "I bid thee say—
What manner of man art thou?"

Forthwith this frame of mine was wrenched
With a woful agony,
Which forced me to begin my tale;   580
And then it left me free.

And ever anon throughout his fu-
ture life an agony constraineth him
to travel from land to land;

Since then, at an uncertain hour,
That agony returns:
And till my ghastly tale is told,
This heart within me burns.

I pass, like night, from land to land;
I have strange power of speech;
That moment that his face I see,
I know the man that must hear me:
To him my tale I teach.   590

What loud uproar bursts from that door!
The wedding-guests are there:
But in the garden-bower the bride
And bride-maids singing are:
And hark the little vesper bell,
Which biddeth me to prayer!

O Wedding-Guest! this soul hath been
Alone on a wide wide sea:
So lonely 'twas, that God himself
Scarce seemèd there to be.   600

O sweeter than the marriage-feast,
'Tis sweeter far to me,
To walk together to the kirk
With a goodly company!—

To walk together to the kirk,
And all together pray,
While each to his great Father bends,
Old men, and babes, and loving friends
And youths and maidens gay!

Farewell, farewell! but this I tell   610
To thee, thou Wedding-Guest!
He prayeth well, who loveth well
Both man and bird and beast.

He prayeth best, who loveth best
All things both great and small;
For the dear God who loveth us,
He made and loveth all.

The Mariner, whose eye is bright,
Whose beard with age is hoar,
Is gone: and now the Wedding-Guest   620
Turned from the bridegroom's door.

He went like one that hath been stunned,
And is of sense forlorn:
A sadder and a wiser man,
He rose the morrow morn.

Frost at Midnight

The Frost performs its secret ministry,
Unhelped by any wind. The owlet's cry
Came loud—and hard, again! loud as before.
The inmates of my cottage, all at rest,
Have left me to that solitude, which suits
Abstruser musings: save that at my side
My cradled infant slumbers peacefully.
'Tis calm indeed! so calm, that it disturbs
And vexes meditation with its strange
And extreme silentness. Sea, hill, and wood, 10
This populous village! Sea, and hill, and wood,
With all the numberless goings-on of life,
Inaudible as dreams! the thin blue flame
Lies on my low-burnt fire, and quivers not;
Only that film, which fluttered on the grate,
Still flutters there, the sole unquiet thing.

Methinks, its motion in this hush of nature
Gives it dim sympathies with me who live,
Making it a companionable form,
Whose puny flaps and freaks the idling
    Spirit   20
By its own moods interprets, every where
Echo or mirror seeking of itself,
And makes a toy of Thought.

                                  But O! how oft,
How oft, at school, with most believing mind,
Presageful, have I gazed upon the bars,
To watch that fluttering *stranger!* and as oft
With unclosed lids, already had I dreamt
Of my sweet birth-place, and the old church-
    tower,
Whose bells, the poor man's only music,
    rang   30
From morn to evening, all the hot Fair-day,
So sweetly, that they stirred and haunted me
With a wild pleasure, falling on mine ear
Most like articulate sounds of things to come!

---

l. 7. *infant:* Coleridge's son, Hartley.
l. 15. *film:* "In all parts of the kingdom these films are called *strangers* and supposed to portend the arrival of some absent friend" [Coleridge].

---

l. 20. *freaks:* sudden, prankish changes.

So gazed I, till the soothing things, I dreamt,
Lulled me to sleep, and sleep prolonged my
    dreams!
And so I brooded all the following morn,
Awed by the stern preceptor's face, mine eye
Fixed with mock study on my swimming
    book:
Save if the door half opened, and I snatched **40**
A hasty glance, and still my heart leaped up,
For still I hoped to see the *stranger's* face,
Townsman, or aunt, or sister more beloved,
My play-mate when we both were clothed
    alike!

    Dear Babe, that sleepest cradled by my side,
Whose gentle breathings, heard in this deep
    calm,
Fill up the interpersèd vacancies
And momentary pauses of the thought!
My babe so beautiful! it thrills my heart
With tender gladness, thus to look at thee, **50**
And think that thou shalt learn far other lore,
And in far other scenes! For I was reared
In the great city, pent 'mid cloisters dim,
And saw nought lovely but the sky and stars.
But *thou*, my babe! shalt wander like a breeze
By lakes and sandy shores, beneath the crags
Of ancient mountain, and beneath the clouds,
Which image in their bulk both lakes and
    shores
And mountain crags: so shalt thou see and
    hear
The lovely shapes and sounds intelligible **60**
Of that eternal language, which thy God
Utters, who from eternity doth teach
Himself in all, and all things in himself.
Great universal Teacher! he shall mould
Thy spirit, and by giving make it ask.

    Therefore all seasons shall be sweet to thee,
Whether the summer clothe the general earth
With greenness, or the redbreast sit and sing
Betwixt the tufts of snow on the bare branch
Of mossy apple-tree, while the nigh thatch **70**
Smokes in the sun-thaw; whether the eave-
    drops fall

Heard only in the trances of the blast,
Or if the secret ministry of frost
Shall hang them up in silent icicles,
Quietly shining to the quiet Moon.

Kubla Khan

In Xanadu did Kubla Khan
A stately pleasure-dome decree:
Where Alph, the sacred river, ran
Through caverns measureless to man
    Down to a sunless sea.
So twice five miles of fertile ground
With walls and towers were girdled round:
And there were gardens bright with sinuous
    rills,
Where blossomed many an incense-bearing
    tree;
And here were forests ancient as the hills, **10**
Enfolding sunny spots of greenery.

But oh! that deep romantic chasm which
    slanted
Down the green hill athwart a cedarn cover!
A savage place! as holy and enchanted
As e'er beneath a waning moon was haunted
By woman wailing for her demon-lover!
And from this chasm, with ceaseless turmoil
    seething,
As if this earth in fast thick pants were
    breathing,
A mighty fountain momently was forced:
Amid whose swift half-intermitted burst **20**
Huge fragments vaulted like rebounding hail,
Or chaffy grain beneath the thresher's flail:
And 'mid these dancing rocks at once and ever
It flung up momently the sacred river.
Five miles meandering with a mazy motion
Through wood and dale the sacred river ran,
Then reached the caverns measureless to man,
And sank in tumult to a lifeless ocean:
And 'mid this tumult Kubla heard from far
Ancestral voices prophesying war! **30**

The shadow of the dome of pleasure
Floated midway on the waves;
Where was heard the mingled measure
From the fountain and the caves.
It was a miracle of rare device,
A sunny pleasure-dome with caves of ice!

A damsel with a dulcimer
In a vision once I saw:
It was an Abyssinian maid,
And on her dulcimer she played,   40
Singing of Mount Abora.
Could I revive within me
Her symphony and song,
To such a deep delight 'twould win me,
That with music loud and long,
I would build that dome in air,
That sunny dome! those caves of ice!
And all who heard should see them there,
And all should cry, Beware! Beware!
His flashing eyes, his floating hair!   50
Weave a circle round him thrice,
And close your eyes with holy dread,
For he on honey-dew hath fed,
And drunk the milk of Paradise.

---

l. 37. *dulcimer:* musical instrument made of wires
stretched over a sounding board and played with two
light hammers.

percy bysshe shelley

Hymn to Intellectual Beauty

1

The awful shadow of some unseen Power
    Floats tho' unseen among us; visiting
    This various world with as inconstant
        wing
As summer winds that creep from flower to
        flower;
Like moonbeams that behind some piny
        mountain shower,
    It visits with inconstant glance
    Each human heart and countenance;
Like hues and harmonies of evening,
    Like clouds in starlight widely spread,
    Like memory of music fled,   10
    Like aught that for its grace may be
Dear, and yet dearer for its mystery.

2

Spirit of BEAUTY, that dost consecrate
    With thine own hues all thou dost shine
        upon
    Of human thought or form, where art thou
        gone?
Why dost thou pass away and leave our state,
This dim vast vale of tears, vacant and
        desolate?
    Ask why the sunlight not for ever
    Weaves rainbows o'er yon mountain river,
Why aught should fail and fade that once is
        shown;   20
    Why fear and dream and death and birth
    Cast on the daylight of this earth
    Such gloom, why man has such a scope
For love and hate, despondency and hope?

3

No voice from some sublimer world hath ever
  To sage or poet these responses given:
  Therefore the names of Demon, Ghost, and
    Heaven,
Remain the records of their vain endeavour:
Frail spells, whose uttered charm might not
    avail to sever,
    From all we hear and all we see,   30
    Doubt, chance, and mutability.
Thy light alone, like mist o'er mountains
    driven,
    Or music by the night wind sent
    Thro' strings of some still instrument,
    Or moonlight on a midnight stream,
Gives grace and truth to life's unquiet dream.

4

Love, Hope, and Self-esteem, like clouds,
    depart
  And come, for some uncertain moments
    lent.
  Man were immortal and omnipotent,
Didst thou, unknown and awful as thou art, 40
Keep with thy glorious train firm state
    within his heart.
    Thou messenger of sympathies
    That wax and wane in lovers' eyes;
Thou, that to human thought art nourishment,
    Like darkness to a dying flame!
    Depart not as thy shadow came:
    Depart not, lest the grave should be,
Like life and fear, a dark reality.

5

While yet a boy I sought for ghosts, and sped
  Thro' many a listening chamber, cave and
    ruin,   50
  And starlight wood, with fearful steps
    pursuing
Hopes of high talk with the departed dead.

I called on poisonous names with which our
    youth is fed:
    I was not heard: I saw them not:
    When musing deeply on the lot
Of life, at that sweet time when winds are
    wooing
    All vital things that wake to bring
    News of birds and blossoming,
    Sudden, thy shadow fell on me;
I shrieked, and clasped my hands in
    ecstacy!   60

6

I vowed that I would dedicate my powers
  To thee and thine: have I not kept the vow?
  With beating heart and streaming eyes,
    even now
I call the phantoms of a thousands hours
Each from his voiceless grave: they have in
    visioned bowers
    Of studious zeal or love's delight
    Outwatched with me the envious night:
They know that never joy illumed my brow,
    Unlinked with hope that thou wouldst
    free
    This world from its dark slavery,   70
    That thou, O awful LOVELINESS,
Wouldst give whate'er these words cannot
    express.

7

The day becomes more solemn and serene
  When noon is past: there is a harmony
  In autumn, and a lustre in its sky,
Which thro' the summer is not heard or seen,
As if it could not be, as if it had not been!
    Thus let thy power, which like the truth
    Of nature on my passive youth
Descended, to my onward life supply   80
    Its calm, to one who worships thee,
    And every form containing thee,
    Whom, SPIRIT fair, thy spells did bind
To fear himself, and love all human kind.

Ode to the West Wind

1

O wild West Wind, thou breath of Autumn's
   being,
Thou, from whose unseen presence the leaves
   dead
Are driven, like ghosts from an enchanter
   fleeing,

Yellow, and black, and pale, and hectic red,
Pestilence-stricken multitudes: O thou,
Who chariotest to their dark wintry bed

The winged seeds, where they lie cold and
   low,
Each like a corpse within its grave, until
Thine azure sister of the spring shall blow

Her clarion o'er the dreaming earth, and fill 10
(Driving sweet buds like flocks to feed in air)
With living hues and odours plain and hill:

Wild Spirit, which art moving every where;
Destroyer and preserver; hear, O, hear!

2

Thou on whose stream, 'mid the steep sky's
   commotion,
Loose clouds like earth's decaying leaves
   are shed,
Shook from the tangled boughs of Heaven
   and Ocean,

Angels of rain and lightning: there are spread
On the blue surface of thine airy surge,
Like the bright hair uplifted from the head 20

Of some fierce Mænad, even from the dim
   verge
Of the horizon to the zenith's height

The locks of the approaching storm. Thou
   dirge

Of the dying year, to which this closing night
Will be the dome of a vast sepulchre,
Vaulted with all thy congregated might

Of vapours, from whose solid atmosphere
Black rain, and fire, and hail will burst: O,
   hear!

3

Thou who didst waken from his summer
   dreams
The blue Mediterranean, where he lay,   30
Lulled by the coil of his crystalline streams,

Beside a pumice isle in Baiæ's bay,
And saw in sleep dim old palaces and towers
Quivering within the wave's intenser day,

All overgrown with azure moss and flowers
So sweet, the sense faints picturing them!
   Thou
For whose path the Atlantic's level powers

Cleave themselves into chasms, while far
   below
The sea-blooms and the oozy woods which
   wear
The sapless foliage of the ocean, know   40

Thy voice, and suddenly grow grey with fear,
And tremble and despoil themselves: O, hear!

4

If I were a dead leaf thou mightest bear;
If I were a swift cloud to fly with thee;
A wave to pant beneath thy power, and share

The impulse of thy strength, only less free
Than thou, O uncontrollable! If even
I were as in my boyhood, and could be

---

l. 21. *Mænad:* female attendant of Bacchus.

l. 32. *Baiæ's bay:* in Campania, Italy.

The comrade of thy wanderings over heaven,
As then, when to outstrip thy skiey speed   **50**
Scarce seemed a vision; I would ne'er have
    striven

As thus with thee in prayer in my sore need.
Oh! lift me as a wave, a leaf, a cloud!
I fall upon the thorns of life! I bleed!

A heavy weight of hours has chained and
    bowed
One too like thee: tameless, and swift, and
    proud.

5

Make me thy lyre, even as the forest is:
What if my leaves are falling like its own!
The tumult of thy mighty harmonies

Will take from both a deep, autumnal tone, **60**
Sweet though in sadness. Be thou, spirit
    fierce,
My spirit! Be thou me, impetuous one!

Drive my dead thoughts over the universe
Like withered leaves to quicken a new birth!
And, by the incantation of this verse,

Scatter, as from an unextinguished hearth
Ashes and sparks, my words among
    mankind!
Be through my lips to unawakened earth

The trumpet of a prophecy! O, Wind,
If Winter comes, can Spring be far behind? **70**

joHn kEATS

The Eve of St. Agnes

1

St. Agnes' Eve—Ah, bitter chill it was!
The owl, for all his feathers, was a-cold;
The hare limped trembling through the
    frozen grass,
And silent was the flock in woolly fold:
Numb were the Beadsman's fingers, while
    he told
His rosary, and while his frosted breath,
Like pious incense from a censer old,
Seemed taking flight for heaven, without a
    death,
Past the sweet Virgin's picture, while his
    prayer he saith.

2

His prayer he saith, this patient, holy
    man;   **10**
Then takes his lamp, and riseth from his
    knees,
And back returneth, meagre, barefoot, wan,
Along the chapel aisle by slow degrees:
The sculptured dead, on each side, seem to
    freeze,
Emprisoned in black, purgatorial rails:
Knights, ladies, praying in dumb orat'ries,
He passeth by; and his weak spirit fails
To think how they may ache in icy hoods and
    mails.

The Eve of St. Agnes: Saint Agnes' Eve is January 20;
according to superstition, a girl who fasted on Saint
Agnes' Eve would dream of her future husband.
l. 5. *Beadsman:* a man paid to pray for his benefactor.

3

Northward he turneth through a little door,
And scarce three steps, ere Music's golden
    tongue   20
Flattered to tears this agèd man and poor;
But no—already had his deathbell rung;
The joys of all his life were said and sung:
His was harsh penance on St. Agnes' Eve:
Another way he went, and soon among
Rough ashes sat he for his soul's reprieve,
And all night kept awake, for sinners' sake to
    grieve.

4

That ancient Beadsman heard the prelude
    soft;
And so it chanced, for many a door was
    wide,
From hurry to and fro. Soon, up aloft,   30
The silver, snarling trumpets 'gan to chide:
The level chambers, ready with their pride,
Were glowing to receive a thousand guests:
The carvèd angels, ever eager-eyed,
Stared, where upon their heads the cornice
    rests,
With hair blown back, and wings put cross-wise
    on their breasts.

5

At length burst in the argent revelry,
With plume, tiara, and all rich array,
Numerous as shadows, haunting faerily
The brain, new stuffed, in youth, with
    triumphs gay   40
Of old romance. These let us wish away,
And turn, sole-thoughted, to one Lady there,
Whose heart had brooded, all that wintry
    day,
On love, and winged St. Agnes' saintly care,
As she had heard old dames full many times
    declare.

6

They told her how, upon St. Agnes' Eve,
Young virgins might have visions of delight,
And soft adorings from their loves receive
Upon the honeyed middle of the night,
If ceremonies due they did aright;   50
As, supperless to bed they must retire,
And couch supine their beauties, lily white;
Nor look behind, nor sideways, but require
Of Heaven with upward eyes for all that
    they desire.

7

Full of this whim was thoughtful Madeline:
The music, yearning like a God in pain,
She scarcely heard: her maiden eyes divine,
Fixed on the floor, saw many a sweeping
    train
Pass by—she heeded not at all: in vain
Came many a tiptoe, amorous cavalier,   60
And back retired; not cooled by high
    disdain,
But she saw not: her heart was otherwhere:
She sighed for Agnes' dreams, the sweetest
    of the year.

8

She danced along with vague, regardless
    eyes,
Anxious her lips, her breathing quick and
    short:
The hallowed hour was near at hand: she
    sighs
Amid the timbrels, and the thronged resort
Of whisperers in anger, or in sport;
'Mid looks of love, defiance, hate, and
    scorn,
Hoodwinked with faery fancy; all amort,   70

---

l. 53. *require:* request.
l. 70. *amort:* deadened.

Save to St. Agnes and her lambs unshorn,
And all the bliss to be before tomorrow morn.

9

So, purposing each moment to retire,
She lingered still. Meantime, across the
    moors,
Had come young Porphyro, with heart on
    fire
For Madeline. Beside the portal doors,
Buttressed from moonlight, stands he,
    and implores
All saints to give him sight of Madeline,
But for one moment in the tedious hours,
That he might gaze and worship all
    unseen;   80
Perchance speak, kneel, touch, kiss—in
    sooth such things have been.

10

He ventures in: let no buzzed whisper tell:
All eyes be muffled, or a hundred swords
Will storm his heart, Love's fev'rous citadel:
For him, those chambers held barbarian
    hordes,
Hyena foemen, and hot-blooded lords,
Whose very dogs would execrations howl
Against his lineage: not one breast affords
Him any mercy in that mansion foul,
Save one old beldame, weak in body and in
    soul.   90

11

Ah, happy chance! the agèd creature came,
Shuffling along with ivory-headed wand,
To where he stood, hid from the torch's
    flame,
Behind a broad hall-pillar, far beyond
The sound of merriment and chorus bland:

He startled her; but soon she knew his face,
And grasped his fingers in her palsied hand,
Saying, "Mercy, Porphyro! hie thee from
    this place;
"They are all here to-night, the whole blood-
    thirsty race!

12

"Get hence! get hence! there's dwarfish
    Hildebrand;   100
"He had a fever late, and in the fit
"He cursèd thee and thine, both house
    and land:
"Then there's that old Lord Maurice, not a
    whit
"More tame for his grey hairs—Alas me! flit!
"Flit like a ghost away."—"Ah, Gossip dear,
"We're safe enough; here in this arm-chair
    sit,
"And tell me how"—"Good Saints! not here,
    not here;
"Follow me, child, or else these stones will be
    thy bier."

13

He followed through a lowly archèd way,
Brushing the cobwebs with his lofty
    plume,   110
And as she muttered "Well-a—well-a-day!"
He found him in a little moonlight room,
Pale, latticed, chill, and silent as a tomb.
"Now tell me where is Madeline," said he,
"O tell me, Angela, by the holy loom
"Which none but secret sisterhood may see,
"When they St. Agnes' wool are weaving
    piously."

14

"St. Agnes! Ah! it is St. Agnes' Eve—
"Yet men will murder upon holy days:
"Thou must hold water in a witch's sieve, 120
"And be liege lord of all the Elves and Fays,
"To venture so: it fills me with amaze
"To see thee, Porphyro!—St. Agnes' Eve!

---

l. 71. *unshorn:* Saint Agnes was always pictured with
lambs. On the anniversary of her martyrdom two lambs
are blessed and shorn; the wool is spun and woven by
nuns.

"God's help! my lady fair the conjuror plays
"This very night: good angels her deceive!
"But let me laugh awhile, I've mickle time to
    grieve."

15

Feebly she laugheth in the languid moon,
While Porphyro upon her face doth look,
Like puzzled urchin on an agèd crone
Who keepeth closed a wondrous riddle-
    book,   130
As spectacled she sits in chimney nook.
But soon his eyes grew brilliant, when
    she told
His lady's purpose; and he scarce could
    brook
Tears, at the thought of those enchantments
    cold,
And Madeline asleep in lap of legends old.

16

Sudden a thought came like a full-blown
    rose,
Flushing his brow, and in his painèd heart
Made purple riot: then doth he propose
A stratagem, that makes the beldame start:
"A cruel man and impious thou art: 140
"Sweet lady, let her pray, and sleep, and
    dream
"Alone with her good angels, far apart
"From wicked men like thee. Go, go!—
    I deem
"Thou canst not surely be the same that thou
    didst seem."

17

"I will not harm her, by all saints I swear,"
Quoth Porphyro: "O may I ne'er find grace
"When my weak voice shall whisper its
    last prayer,
"If one of her soft ringlets I displace,
"Or look with ruffian passion in her face:

"Good Angela, believe me by these tears; 150
"Or I will, even in a moment's space,
"Awake, with horrid shout, my foemen's
    ears,
"And beard them, though they be more fanged
    than wolves and bears."

18

"Ah! why wilt thou affright a feeble soul?
"A poor, weak, palsy-stricken, churchyard
    thing,
"Whose passing-bell may ere the midnight
    toll;
"Whose prayers for thee, each morn and
    evening,
"Were never missed."—Thus plaining, doth
    she bring
A gentler speech from burning Porphyro;
So woeful, and of such deep sorrowing,   160
That Angela gives promise she will do
Whatever he shall wish, betide her weal or
    woe.

19

Which was, to lead him, in close secrecy,
Even to Madeline's chamber, and there
    hide
Him in a closet, of such privacy
That he might see her beauty unespied,
And win perhaps that night a peerless
    bride,
While legioned faeries paced the coverlet,
And pale enchantment held her sleepy-eyed.
Never on such a night have lovers met,   170
Since Merlin paid his Demon all the
    monstrous debt.

20

"It shall be as thou wishest," said the Dame:

II. 171–72. *Merlin . . . debt:* According to a legend, Merlin's father was a demon. Vivien destroyed Merlin through a spell he, himself, had taught her.

I. 126. *mickle:* much.

"All cates and dainties shall be storèd there
"Quickly on this feast night: by the
     tambour frame
"Her own lute thou wilt see: no time to
     spare,
"For I am slow and feeble, and scarce dare
"On such a catering trust my dizzy head.
"Wait here, my child, with patience; kneel
     in prayer
"The while: Ah! thou must needs the lady
     wed,
"Or may I never leave my grave among the
     dead."   180

21

So saying, she hobbled off with busy fear.
The lover's endless minutes slowly passed;
The Dame returned, and whispered in his
     ear
To follow her; with agèd eyes aghast
From fright of dim espial. Safe at last,
Through many a dusky gallery, they gain
The maiden's chamber, silken, hushed, and
     chaste;
Where Porphyro took covert, pleased amain.
His poor guide hurried back with agues in her
     brain.

22

Her falt'ring hand upon the balustrade, 190
Old Angela was feeling for the stair,
When Madeline, St. Agnes' charmèd maid,
Rose, like a missioned spirit, unaware:
With silver taper's light, and pious care,
She turned, and down the agèd gossip led
To a safe level matting. Now prepare,
Young Porphyro, for gazing on that bed;
She comes, she comes again, like ring-dove
     frayed and fled.

---

l. 173. *cates:* provisions.
l. 174. *tambour frame:* double hoops for holding embroidery.
l. 198. *frayed:* frightened.

23

Out went the taper as she hurried in;
Its little smoke, in pallid moonshine,
     died: 200
She closed the door, she panted, all akin
To spirits of the air, and visions wide:
No uttered syllable, or, woe betide!
But to her heart, her heart was voluble,
Paining with eloquence her balmy side;
As though a tongueless nightingale should
     swell
Her throat in vain, and die, heart-stifled, in
     her dell.

24

A casement high and triple-arched there
     was,
All garlanded with carven imag'ries
Of fruit, and flowers, and bunches of
     knot-grass,   210
And diamonded with panes of quaint device,
Innumerable of stains and splendid dyes,
As are the tiger-moth's deep-damasked
     wings;
And in the midst, 'mong thousand
     heraldries,
And twilight saints, and dim emblazonings,
A shielded scutcheon blushed with blood of
     queens and kings.

25

Full on this casement shone the wintry
     moon,
And threw warm gules on Madeline's fair
     breast,
As down she knelt for heaven's grace and
     boon;
Rose-bloom fell on her hands, together
     pressed,   220
And on her silver cross soft amethyst,
And on her hair a glory, like a saint:

---

l. 218. *gules:* blood red.

She seemed a splendid angel, newly
    dressed,
Save wings, for heaven:—Porphyro
    grew faint:
She knelt, so pure a thing, so free from
    mortal taint.

26

Anon his heart revives: her vespers done,
Of all its wreathèd pearls her hair she
    frees;
Unclasps her warmèd jewels one by one;
Loosens her fragrant bodice; by degrees
Her rich attire creeps rustling to her
    knees: 230
Half-hidden, like a mermaid in seaweed,
Pensive awhile she dreams awake, and
    sees,
In fancy, fair St. Agnes in her bed,
But dares not look behind, or all the charm
    is fled.

27

Soon, trembling in her soft and chilly nest,
In sort of wakeful swoon, perplexed she
    lay,
Until the poppied warmth of sleep
    oppressed
Her soothèd limbs, and soul fatigued away;
Flown, like a thought, until the morrow-day;
Blissfully havened both from joy and
    pain;   240
Clasped like a missal where swart Paynims
    pray;
Blinded alike from sunshine and from
    rain,
As though a rose should shut, and be a bud
    again.

28

Stolen to this paradise, and so entranced,
    Porphyro gazed upon her empty dress,

---

l. 241. *Paynims:* pagans.

And listened to her breathing, if it chanced
To wake into a slumberous tenderness:
Which when he heard, that minute did he
    bless,
And breathed himself: then from the
    closet crept,
Noiseless as fear in a wide wilderness,   250
And over the hushed carpet, silent, stepped,
And 'tween the curtains peeped, where, lo!—
    how fast she slept.

29

Then by the bedside, where the faded moon
Made a dim, silver twilight, soft he set
A table and, half anguished, threw thereon
A cloth of woven crimson, gold, and jet:—
O for some drowsy Morphean amulet!
The boisterous midnight, festive clarion,
The kettledrum, and far-heard clarinet,
Affray his ears, though but in dying
    tone:—   260
The hall door shuts again, and all the noise
    is gone.

30

And still she slept an azure-lidded sleep,
In blanchèd linen, smooth, and lavendered,
While he from forth the closet brought
    a heap
Of candied apple, quince, and plum, and
    gourd;
With jellies soother than the creamy curd,
And lucent syrops, tinct with cinnamon;
Manna and dates, in argosy transferred
From Fez; and spicèd dainties, every one,
From silken Samarcand to cedared
    Lebanon.   270

---

l. 257. *Morphean amulet:* a charm. Morpheus was the
god of sleep.
l. 266. *soother:* softer.
l. 267. *tinct:* flavored.
l. 268. *argosy:* merchant ship.

31

These delicates he heaped with glowing
    hand
On golden dishes and in baskets bright
Of wreathèd silver: sumptuous they stand
In the retired quiet of the night,
Filling the chilly room with perfume light.—
"And now, my love, my seraph fair, awake!
"Thou art my heaven, and I thine eremite:
"Open thine eyes, for meek St. Agnes' sake,
"Or I shall drowse beside thee, so my soul
    doth ache."

32

Thus whispering, his warm unnervèd
    arm   280
Sank in her pillow. Shaded was her dream
By the dusk curtains:—'twas a midnight
    charm
Impossible to melt as icèd stream:
The lustrous salvers in the moonlight
    gleam;
Broad golden fringe upon the carpet lies:
It seemed he never, never could redeem
From such a steadfast spell his lady's eyes;
So mused awhile, entoiled in woofèd
    fantasies.

33

Awakening up, he took her hollow lute,—
Tumultuous,—and, in chords that
    tenderest be,   290
He played an ancient ditty, long since mute,
In Provence called, "La belle dame sans
    merci:"
Close to her ear touching the melody;—
Wherewith disturbed, she uttered a soft
    moan:
He ceased—she panted quick—and
    suddenly

---

l. 277. *eremite:* hermit.

Her blue affrayèd eyes wide open shone:
Upon his knees he sank, pale as smooth-
    sculptured stone.

34

Her eyes were open, but she still beheld,
Now wide awake, the vision of her sleep:
There was a painful change, that nigh
    expelled   300
The blisses of her dream so pure and deep,
At which fair Madeline began to weep,
And moan forth witless words with many
    a sigh;
While still her gaze on Porphyro would
    keep;
Who knelt, with joinèd hands and piteous
    eye,
Fearing to move or speak, she looked so
    dreamingly.

35

"Ah, Porphyro!" said she, "but even now
"Thy voice was at sweet tremble in mine
    ear,
"Made tuneable with every sweetest vow;
"And those sad eyes were spiritual and
    clear: 310
"How changed thou art! how pallid, chill,
    and drear!
"Give me that voice again, my Porphyro,
"Those looks immortal, those complainings
    dear!
"Oh, leave me not in this eternal woe,
"For if thou diest, my Love, I know not where
    to go."

36

Beyond a mortal man impassioned far
At these voluptuous accents, he arose,
Ethereal, flushed, and like a throbbing star
Seen mid the sapphire heaven's deep
    repose;
Into her dream he melted, as the rose   320
Blendeth its odor with the violet,—

Solution sweet: meantime the frost-wind
blows
Like Love's alarum pattering the sharp
sleet
Against the windowpanes; St. Agnes' moon
hath set.

37

'Tis dark: quick pattereth the flaw-blown
sleet.
"This is no dream, my bride, my Madeline!"
'Tis dark: the icèd gusts still rave and
beat:
"No dream, alas! alas! and woe is mine!
"Porphyro will leave me here to fade and
pine.—
"Cruel! what traitor could thee hither
bring?   330
"I curse not, for my heart is lost in thine,
"Though thou forsakest a deceivèd thing;—
"A dove forlorn and lost with sick unprunèd
wing."

38

"My Madeline! sweet dreamer! lovely bride!
"Say, may I be for aye thy vassal blest?
"Thy beauty's shield, heart-shaped and
vermeil dyed?
"Ah, silver shrine, here will I take my rest
"After so many hours of toil and quest,
"A famished pilgrim,—saved by miracle.
"Though I have found, I will not rob thy
nest   340
"Saving of thy sweet self; if thou think'st
well
"To trust, fair Madeline, to no rude infidel.

39

"Hark! 'tis an elfin-storm from faery land,
"Of haggard seeming, but a boon indeed:
"Arise—arise! the morning is at hand;—
"The bloated wassailers will never heed:—
"Let us away, my love, with happy speed;

"There are no ears to hear, or eyes to
see,—
"Drowned all in Rhenish and the sleepy
mead:
"Awake! arise! my love, and fearless be, 350
"For o'er the southern moors I have a home
for thee."

40

She hurried at his words, beset with fears,
For there were sleeping dragons all around,
At glaring watch, perhaps, with ready
spears—
Down the wide stairs a darkling way they
found.—
In all the house was heard no human sound.
A chain-drooped lamp was flickering by
each door;
The arras, rich with horseman, hawk,
and hound,
Fluttered in the besieging wind's uproar;
And the long carpets rose along the gusty
floor.   360

41

They glide, like phantoms, into the wide
hall;
Like phantoms, to the iron porch, they
glide;
Where lay the Porter, in uneasy sprawl,
With a huge empty flagon by his side:
The wakeful bloodhound rose, and shook
his hide,
But his sagacious eye an inmate owns:
By one, and one, the bolts full easy slide:—
The chains lie silent on the footworn
stones;—
The key turns, and the door upon its hinges
groans.

42

And they are gone: aye, ages long ago   370
These lovers fled away into the storm.

That night the Baron dreamt of many a woe,
And all his warrior-guests, with shade and form
Of witch, and demon, and large coffin-worm,
Were long be-nightmared. Angela the old
Died palsy-twitched, with meagre face deform;
The Beadsman, after thousand aves told,
For aye unsought-for slept among his ashes cold.

Ode to a Nightingale

My heart aches, and a drowsy numbness pains
  My sense, as though of hemlock I had drunk,
Or emptied some dull opiate to the drains
  One minute past, and Lethe-wards had sunk:
'Tis not through envy of thy happy lot,
  But being too happy in thine happiness,—
    That thou, light-wingèd Dryad of the trees,
      In some melodious plot
  Of beechen green, and shadows numberless,
    Singest of summer in full-throated ease.   10

O, for a draught of vintage! that hath been
  Cooled a long age in the deep-delvèd earth,
Tasting of Flora and the country green,
  Dance, and Provençal song, and sunburnt mirth!
O for a beaker full of the warm South,
  Full of the true, the blushful Hippocrene,

With beaded bubbles winking at the brim,
  And purple-stainèd mouth;
That I might drink, and leave the world unseen,
  And with thee fade away into the forest dim: 20

Fade far away, dissolve, and quite forget
  What thou among the leaves hast never known,
The weariness, the fever, and the fret
  Here, where men sit and hear each other groan;
Where palsy shakes a few, sad, last gray hairs,
  Where youth grows pale, and spectre-thin, and dies;
    Where but to think is to be full of sorrow
      And leaden-eyed despairs,
  Where Beauty cannot keep her lustrous eyes,
    Or new Love pine at them beyond to-morrow.   30

Away! away! for I will fly to thee,
  Not charioted by Bacchus and his pards,
But on the viewless wings of Poesy,
  Though the dull brain perplexes and retards:
Already with thee! tender is the night,
  And haply the Queen-Moon is on her throne,
    Clustered around by all her starry Fays;
      But here there is no light,
  Save what from heaven is with the breezes blown
    Through verdurous glooms and winding mossy ways.   40

I cannot see what flowers are at my feet,
  Nor what soft incense hangs upon the boughs,
But, in embalmèd darkness, guess each sweet
  Wherewith the seasonable month endows
The grass, the thicket, and the fruit-tree wild;

---

l. 4. *Lethe:* mythological waters which rendered loss of memory in their drinker.
l. 7. *Dryad:* tree nymph.
l. 13. *Flora:* flower goddess.
l. 16. *Hippocrene:* spring of the Muses on Mount Helicon.

l. 32. *pards:* leopards.
l. 37. *Fays:* fairies.

White hawthorn, and the pastoral
    eglantine;
Fast fading violets covered up in leaves;
    And mid-May's eldest child,
The coming musk-rose, full of dewy wine,
    The murmurous haunt of flies on
        summer eves.   50

Darkling I listen; and, for many a time
    I have been half in love with easeful Death,
Called him soft names in many a musèd
        rhyme,
    To take into the air my quiet breath;
Now more than ever seems it rich to die,
    To cease upon the midnight with no pain,
        While thou art pouring forth thy soul
            abroad
            In such an ecstasy!
    Still wouldst thou sing, and I have ears in
        vain—
        To thy high requiem become a sod.   60

Thou wast not born for death, immortal Bird!
    No hungry generations tread thee down;
The voice I hear this passing night was heard
    In ancient days by emperor and clown:
Perhaps the self-same song that found a path
    Through the sad heart of Ruth, when, sick
        for home,
        She stood in tears amid the alien corn;
        The same that oft-times hath
    Charmed magic casements, opening on
        the foam
    Of perilous seas, in faery lands forlorn. 70

Forlorn! the very word is like a bell
    To toll me back from thee to my sole self!
Adieu! the fancy cannot cheat so well
    As she is famed to do, deceiving elf.
Adieu! adieu! thy plaintive anthem fades
    Past the near meadows, over the still
        stream,
        Up the hill-side; and now 'tis buried deep
        In the next valley-glades:
    Was it a vision, or a waking dream?
        Fled is that music:—Do I wake or
            sleep?   80

La Belle Dame sans Merci

(First Version)

"Ah, what can ail thee, knight-at-arms,
    Alone and palely loitering?
The sedge is withered from the lake,
    And no birds sing.

"Ah, what can ail thee, knight-at-arms!
    So haggard and so woe-begone?
The squirrel's granary is full,
    And the harvest's done.

"I see a lily on thy brow,
    With anguish moist and fever dew;   10
And on thy cheek a fading rose
    Fast withereth too."

"I met a lady in the meads
    Full beautiful, a faery's child;
Her hair was long, her foot was light,
    And her eyes were wild.

"I made a garland for her head,
    And bracelets too, and fragrant zone;
She looked at me as she did love,
    And made sweet moan.   20

"I set her on my pacing steed,
    And nothing else saw all day long;
For sideways would she lean, and sing
    A faery's song.

"She found me roots of relish sweet,
    And honey wild, and manna dew;
And sure in language strange she said,
    I love thee true.

"She took me to her elfin grot,
    And there she wept and sighed full sore, 30
And there I shut her wild, wild eyes—
    With kisses four.

"And there she lullèd me asleep,
    And there I dreamed, ah woe betide,

The latest dream I ever dreamed
  On the cold hill's side.

"I saw pale kings, and princes too,
  Pale warriors, death-pale were they all;
They cried—'La belle dame sans merci
  Hath thee in thrall!'   40

"I saw their starved lips in the gloom
  With horrid warning gapèd wide,
And I awoke, and found me here
  On the cold hill's side.

"And this is why I sojourn here
  Alone and palely loitering,
Though the sedge is withered from the lake,
  And no birds sing."

This Living Hand

This living hand, now warm and capable
Of earnest grasping, would, if it were cold
And in the icy silence of the tomb,
So haunt thy days and chill thy dreaming
  nights
That thou wouldst wish thine own heart dry
  of blood
So in my veins red life might stream again,
And thou be conscience-calmed—see here
  it is—
I hold it towards you.

alfred, lord tennyson

from In Memoriam A. H. H.

Obiit MDCCCXXXIII

Strong Son of God, immortal Love,
  Whom we, that have not seen thy face,
  By faith, and faith alone, embrace,
Believing where we cannot prove;

Thine are these orbs of light and shade;
  Thou madest Life in man and brute;
  Thou madest Death; and lo, thy foot
Is on the skull which thou hast made.

Thou wilt not leave us in the dust:
  Thou madest man, he knows not why,   10
  He thinks he was not made to die;
And thou has made him: thou art just.

Thou seemest human and divine,
  The highest, holiest manhood, thou.
  Our wills are ours, we know not how;
Our wills are ours, to make them thine.

Our little systems have their day;
  They have their day and cease to be;
  They are but broken lights of thee,
And thou, O Lord, art more than they.   20

We have but faith: we cannot know,
  For knowledge is of things we see;
  And yet we trust it comes from thee,
A beam in darkness: let it grow.

Let knowledge grow from more to more,
  But more of reverence in us dwell;
  That mind and soul, according well,
May make one music as before,

A. H. H.: Arthur Henry Hallam, who died September 15,
1833.

But vaster. We are fools and slight;
   We mock thee when we do not fear: 30
   But help thy foolish ones to bear;
Help thy vain worlds to bear thy light.

Forgive what seem'd my sin in me,
   What seem'd my worth since I began;
   For merit lives from man to man,
And not from man, O Lord, to thee.

Forgive my grief for one removed,
   Thy creature, whom I found so fair.
   I trust he lives in thee, and there
I find him worthier to be loved.   40

Forgive these wild and wandering cries,
   Confusions of a wasted youth;
   Forgive them where they fail in truth,
And in thy wisdom make me wise.

II

Old yew, which graspest at the stones
   That name the underlying dead,
   Thy fibres net the dreamless head,
Thy roots are wrapt about the bones.

The seasons bring the flower again,
   And bring the firstling to the flock;
   And in the dusk of thee the clock
Beats out the little lives of men.

O, not for thee the glow, the bloom,
   Who changest not in any gale,   10
   Nor branding summer suns avail
To touch thy thousand years of gloom;

And gazing on thee, sullen tree,
   Sick for thy stubborn hardihood,
   I seem to fail from out my blood
And grow incorporate into thee.

XI

Calm is the morn without a sound,
   Calm as to suit a calmer grief,

And only thro' the faded leaf
The chestnut pattering to the ground;

Calm and deep peace on this high wold,
   And on these dews that drench the furze,
   And all the silvery gossamers
That twinkle into green and gold;

Calm and still light on yon great plain
   That sweeps with all its autumn bowers, 10
   And crowded farms and lessening towers,
To mingle with the bounding main;

Calm and deep peace in this wide air,
   These leaves that redden to the fall,
   And in my heart, if calm at all,
If any calm, a calm despair;

Calm on the seas, and silver sleep,
   And waves that sway themselves in rest,
   And dead calm in that noble breast
Which heaves but with the heaving deep. 20

XXVII

I envy not in any moods
   The captive void of noble rage,
   The linnet born within the cage,
That never knew the summer woods;

I envy not the beast that takes
   His license in the field of time,
   Unfetter'd by the sense of crime,
To whom a conscience never wakes;

Nor, what may count itself as blest,
   The heart that never plighted troth   10
   But stagnates in the weeds of sloth:
Nor any want-begotten rest.

I hold it true, whate'er befall;
   I feel it, when I sorrow most;
   'T is better to have loved and lost
Than never to have loved at all.

LIV

O, yet we trust that somehow good
  Will be the final goal of ill,
  To pangs of nature, sins of will,
Defects of doubt, and taints of blood;

That nothing walks with aimless feet;
  That not one life shall be destroy'd,
  Or cast as rubbish to the void,
When God hath made the pile complete;

That not a worm is cloven in vain;
  That not a moth with vain desire   10
  Is shrivell'd in a fruitless fire,
Or but subserves another's gain.

Behold, we know not anything;
  I can but trust that good shall fall
  At last—far off—at last, to all,
And every winter change to spring.

So runs my dream; but what am I?
  An infant crying in the night;
  An infant crying for the light,
And with no language but a cry.   20

LV

The wish, that of the living whole
  No life may fail beyond the grave,
  Derives it not from what we have
The likest God within the soul?

Are God and Nature then at strife,
  That Nature lends such evil dreams?
  So careful of the type she seems,
So careless of the single life,

That I, considering everywhere
  Her secret meaning in her deeds,   10
  And finding that of fifty seeds
She often brings but one to bear,

I falter, where I firmly trod,
  And falling with my weight of cares

Upon the great world's altar-stairs
That slope thro' darkness up to God,

I stretch lame hands of faith, and grope,
  And gather dust and chaff, and call
  To what I feel is Lord of all,
And faintly trust the larger hope.   20

LVI

"So careful of the type?" but no.
  From scarped cliff and quarried stone
  She cries, "A thousand types are gone;
I care for nothing, all shall go.

"Thou makest thine appeal to me.
  I bring to life, I bring to death;
  The spirit does but mean the breath:
I know no more." And he, shall he,

Man, her last work, who seem'd so fair,
  Such splendid purpose in his eyes,   10
  Who roll'd the psalm to wintry skies,
Who built him fanes of fruitless prayer,

Who trusted God was love indeed
  And love Creation's final law—
  Tho' Nature, red in tooth and claw
With ravine, shriek'd against his creed—

Who loved, who suffer'd countless ills,
  Who battled for the True, the Just,
  Be blown about the desert dust,
Or seal'd within the iron hills?   20

No more? A monster then, a dream,
  A discord. Dragons of the prime,
  That tare each other in their slime,
Were mellow music match'd with him.

O life as futile, then, as frail!
  O for thy voice to soothe and bless!
  What hope of answer, or redress?
Behind the veil, behind the veil.

---

l. 22. *Dragons . . . prime*: prehistoric monsters.

LXIV

Dost thou look back on what hath been,
   As some divinely gifted man,
   Whose life in low estate began
And on a simple village green;

Who breaks his birth's invidious bar,
   And grasps the skirts of happy chance,
   And breasts the blows of circumstance,
And grapples with his evil star;

Who makes by force his merit known
   And lives to clutch the golden keys,   10
   To mould a mighty state's decrees,
And shape the whisper of the throne;

And moving up from high to higher,
   Becomes on Fortune's crowning slope
   The pillar of a people's hope,
The centre of a world's desire;

Yet feels, as in a pensive dream,
   When all his active powers are still,
   A distant dearness in the hill,
A secret sweetness in the stream,   20

The limit of his narrower fate,
   While yet beside its vocal springs
   He play'd at counsellors and kings,
With one that was his earliest mate;

Who ploughs with pain his native lea
   And reaps the labor of his hands,
   Or in the furrow musing stands:
"Does my old friend remember me?"

XCV

By night we linger'd on the lawn,
   For underfoot the herb was dry;
   And genial warmth; and o'er the sky
The silvery haze of summer drawn;

And calm that let the tapers burn
   Unwavering: not a cricket chirr'd;

The brook alone far-off was heard,
And on the board the fluttering urn.

And bats went round in fragrant skies,
   And wheel'd or lit the filmy shapes   10
   That haunt the dusk, with ermine capes
And woolly breasts and beaded eyes;

While now we sang old songs that peal'd
   From knoll to knoll, where, couch'd at ease,
   The white kine glimmer'd, and the trees
Laid their dark arms about the field.

But when those others, one by one,
   Withdrew themselves from me and night,
   And in the house light after light
Went out, and I was all alone,   20

A hunger seized my heart; I read
   Of that glad year which once had been,
   In those fallen leaves which kept their
     green,
The noble letters of the dead.

And strangely on the silence broke
   The silent-speaking words, and strange
   Was love's dumb cry defying change
To test his worth; and strangely spoke

The faith, the vigor, bold to dwell
   On doubts that drive the coward back,   30
   And keen thro' wordy snares to track
Suggestion to her inmost cell.

So word by word, and line by line,
   The dead man touch'd me from the past,
   And all at once it seem'd at last
The living soul was flash'd on mine,

And mine in this was wound, and whirl'd
   About empyreal heights of thought,
   And came on that which is, and caught
The deep pulsations of the world,   40

Æonian music measuring out
   The steps of Time—the shocks of
     Chance—

The blows of Death. At length my trance
Was cancell'd, stricken thro' with doubt.

Vague words! but ah, how hard to frame
  In matter-moulded forms of speech,
  Or even for intellect to reach
Thro' memory that which I became;

Till now the doubtful dusk reveal'd
  The knolls once more where, couch'd at
    ease,   50
  The white kine glimmer'd, and the trees
Laid their dark arms about the field;

And suck'd from out the distant gloom
  A breeze began to tremble o'er
  The large leaves of the sycamore,
And fluctuate all the still perfume,

And gathering freshlier overhead,
  Rock'd the full-foliaged elms, and swung
  The heavy-folded rose, and flung
The lilies to and fro, and said,   60

"The dawn, the dawn," and died away;
  And East and West, without a breath,
  Mixt their dim lights, like life and death,
To broaden into boundless day.

CVI

Ring out, wild bells, to the wild sky,
  The flying cloud, the frosty light:
  The year is dying in the night;
Ring out, wild bells, and let him die.

Ring out the old, ring in the new,
  Ring, happy bells, across the snow:
  The year is going, let him go;
Ring out the false, ring in the true.

Ring out the grief that saps the mind,
  For those that here we see no more;   10
  Ring out the feud of rich and poor,
Ring in redress to all mankind.

Ring out a slowly dying cause,
  And ancient forms of party strife;
  Ring in the nobler modes of life,
With sweeter manners, purer laws.

Ring out the want, the care, the sin,
  The faithless coldness of the times;
  Ring out, ring out my mournful rhymes,
But ring the fuller minstrel in.   20

Ring out false pride in place and blood,
  The civic slander and the spite;
  Ring in the love of truth and right,
Ring in the common love of good.

Ring out old shapes of foul disease;
  Ring out the narrowing lust of gold;
  Ring out the thousand wars of old,
Ring in the thousand years of peace.

Ring in the valiant man and free,
  The larger heart, the kindlier hand;   30
  Ring out the darkness of the land,
Ring in the Christ that is to be.

CXVIII

Contemplate all this work of Time,
  The giant laboring in his youth;
  Nor dream of human love and truth,
As dying Nature's earth and lime;

But trust that those we call the dead
  Are breathers of an ampler day
  For ever nobler ends. They say,
The solid earth whereon we tread

In tracts of fluent heat began,
  And grew to seeming-random forms,   10
  The seeming prey of cyclic storms,
Till at the last arose the man;

Who throve and branch'd from clime to
    clime,
  The herald of a higher race,
  And of himself in higher place,
If so he type this work of time

Within himself, from more to more;
  Or, crown'd with attributes of woe
  Like glories, move his course, and show
That life is not as idle ore,   20

But iron dug from central gloom,
  And heated hot with burning fears,
  And dipt in baths of hissing tears,
And batter'd with the shocks of doom

To shape and use. Arise and fly
  The reeling Faun, the sensual feast;
  Move upward, working out the beast,
And let the ape and tiger die.

CXXX

Thy voice is on the rolling air;
  I hear thee where the waters run;
  Thou standest in the rising sun,
And in the setting thou art fair.

What art thou then? I cannot guess;
  But tho' I seem in star and flower
  To feel thee some diffusive power,
I do not therefore love thee less.

My love involves the love before;
  My love is vaster passion now;   10
  Tho' mix'd with God and Nature thou,
I seem to love thee more and more.

Far off thou art, but ever nigh;
  I have thee still, and I rejoice;
  I prosper, circled with thy voice;
I shall not lose thee tho' I die.

CXXXI

O living will that shalt endure
  When all that seems shall suffer shock,
  Rise in the spiritual rock,
Flow thro' our deeds and make them pure,

That we may lift from out of dust
  A voice as unto him that hears,

A cry above the conquer'd years
To one that with us works, and trust,

With faith that comes of self-control,
  The truths that never can be proved   10
  Until we close with all we loved,
And all we flow from, soul in soul.

ROBERT bROWNING

Meeting at Night

I

The grey sea and the long black land;
And the yellow half-moon large and low;
And the startled little waves that leap
In fiery ringlets from their sleep,
As I gain the cove with pushing prow,
And quench its speed i' the slushy sand.

II

Then a mile of warm sea-scented beach;
Three fields to cross till a farm appears;
A tap at the pane, the quick sharp scratch
And blue spurt of a lighted match,   10
And a voice less loud, thro' its joys and fears,
Than the two hearts beating each to each!

Parting at Morning

Round the cape of a sudden came the sea,
And the sun looked over the mountain's rim:
And straight was a path of gold for him,
And the need of a world of men for me.

The Bishop Orders His Tomb at Saint Praxed's Church

Rome, 15—

Vanity, saith the preacher, vanity!
Draw round my bed: is Anselm keeping back?
Nephews—sons mine . . . ah God, I know not!
   Well—
She, men would have to be your mother once,
Old Gandolf envied me, so fair she was!
What's done is done, and she is dead beside,
Dead long ago, and I am Bishop since,
And as she died so must we die ourselves,
And thence ye may perceive the world's a
   dream.
Life, how and what is it? As here I lie   10
In this state-chamber, dying by degrees,
Hours and long hours in the dead night, I ask
"Do I live, am I dead?" Peace, peace seems all.
Saint Praxed's ever was the church for peace;
And so, about this tomb of mine. I fought
With tooth and nail to save my niche, ye
   know:
—Old Gandolf cozened me, despite my care;
Shrewd was that snatch from out the corner
   South
He graced his carrion with, God curse the
   same!
Yet still my niche is not so cramped but
   thence   20
One sees the pulpit o' the epistle-side
And somewhat of the choir, those silent seats,
And up into the aery dome where live
The angels, and a sunbeam's sure to lurk:
And I shall fill my slab of basalt there,
And 'neath my tabernacle take my rest,
With those nine columns round me, two and
   two,
The odd one at my feet where Anselm stands:

Peach-blossom marble all, the rare, the ripe
As fresh-poured red wine of a mighty pulse. 30
—Old Gandolf with his paltry onion-stone,
Put me where I may look at him! True peach,
Rosy and flawless: how I earned the prize!
Draw close: that conflagration of my church
—What then? So much was saved if aught
   were missed!
My sons, ye would not be my death? Go dig
The white-grape vineyard where the oil-press
   stood,
Drop water gently till the surface sink,
And if ye find . . . Ah God, I know not, I! . . .
Bedded in store of rotten fig-leaves soft,   40
And corded up in a tight olive-frail,
Some lump, ah God, of *lapis lazuli*,
Big as a Jew's head cut off at the nape,
Blue as a vein o'er the Madonna's breast . . .
Sons, all have I bequeathed you, villas, all,
That brave Frascati villa with its bath,
So, let the blue lump poise between my knees,
Like God the Father's globe on both his hands
Ye worship in the Jesu Church so gay,
For Gandolf shall not choose but see and
   burst!   50
Swift as a weaver's shuttle fleet our years:
Man goeth to the grave, and where is he?
Did I say basalt for my slab, sons? Black—
'T was ever antique-black I meant! How else
Shall ye contrast my frieze to come beneath?
The bas-relief in bronze ye promised me,
Those Pans and Nymphs ye wot of, and
   perchance
Some tripod, thyrsus, with a vase or so,
The Saviour at his sermon on the mount,
Saint Praxed in a glory, and one Pan   60
Ready to twitch the Nymph's last garment off,
And Moses with the tables . . . but I know
Ye mark me not! What do they whisper thee,
Child of my bowels, Anselm? Ah, ye hope
To revel down my villas while I gasp
Bricked o'er with beggar's mouldy travertine

Saint Praxed's Church: named for Saint Praxedes, a Roman virgin of the second century who gave her wealth to poor Christians.
l. 1. *Vanity . . . preacher:* Ecclesiastes 1:2.
l. 21. *epistle-side:* Epistles of the New Testament are read on the right side of the altar as one faces it.

l. 41. *olive-frail:* woven basket.
l. 46. *Frascati:* resort town near Rome.
l. 49. *Jesu:* Jesuit.
l. 58. *thyrsus:* staff of Bacchus, god of wine.

Which Gandolf from his tomb-top chuckles at!
Nay, boys, ye love me—all of jasper, then!
'T is jasper ye stand pledged to, lest I grieve
My bath must needs be left behind, alas!   70
One block, pure green as a pistachio-nut,
There's plenty jasper somewhere in the
    world—
And have I not Saint Praxed's ear to pray
Horses for ye, and brown Greek manuscripts,
And mistresses with great smooth marbly
    limbs?
—That's if ye carve my epitaph aright,
Choice Latin, picked phrase, Tully's every
    word,
No gaudy ware like Gandolf's second line—
Tully, my masters? Ulpian serves his need!
And then how I shall lie through centuries, 80
And hear the blessed mutter of the mass,
And see God made and eaten all day long,
And feel the steady candle-flame, and taste
Good strong thick stupefying incense-smoke!
For as I lie here, hours of the dead night,
Dying in state and by such slow degrees,
I fold my arms as if they clasped a crook,
And stretch my feet forth straight as stone
    can point,
And let the bedclothes, for a mortcloth, drop
Into great laps and folds of sculptor's-
    work: 90
And as yon tapers dwindle, and strange
    thoughts
Grow, with a certain humming in my ears,
About the life before I lived this life,
And this life too, popes, cardinals and priests,
Saint Praxed at his sermon on the mount,
Your tall pale mother with her talking eyes,
And new-found agate urns as fresh as day,
And marble's language, Latin pure, discreet,
—Aha, ELUCESCEBAT quoth our friend?
No Tully, said I, Ulpian at the best!   100

Evil and brief hath been my pilgrimage.
All *lapis*, all, sons! Else I give the Pope
My villas! Will ye ever eat my heart?
Ever your eyes were as a lizard's quick,
They glitter like your mother's for my soul,
Or ye would heighten my impoverished frieze,
Piece out its starved design, and fill my vase
With grapes, and add a visor and a Term,
And to the tripod ye would tie a lynx
That in his struggle throws the thyrsus
    down,   110
To comfort me on my entablature
Whereon I am to lie till I must ask
"Do I live, am I dead?" There, leave me,
    there!
For ye have stabbed me with ingratitude
To death—ye wish it—God, ye wish it! Stone—
Gritstone, a-crumble! Clammy squares which
    sweat
As if the corpse they keep were oozing
    through—
And no more *lapis* to delight the world!
Well, go! I bless ye. Fewer tapers there,
But in a row: and, going, turn your backs 120
—Ay, like departing altar-ministrants,
And leave me in my church, the church for
    peace,
That I may watch at leisure if he leers—
Old Gandolf, at me, from his onion-stone,
As still he envied me, so fair she was!

l. 108. *Term*: a pillar adorned with a bust.

Andrea del Sarto

(*Called "the Faultless Painter"*)

But do not let us quarrel any more,
No, my Lucrezia; bear with me for once:
Sit down and all shall happen as you wish.
You turn your face, but does it bring your
    heart?

Andrea del Sarto: Florentine painter (1486–1531).

l. 77. *Tully:* Marcus Tullius Cicero, whose prose was a
model of style.
l. 79. *Ulpian:* Domitius Ulpianus, a jurist of the third
century whose Latin style is inferior to Cicero's.
l. 89. *mortcloth:* cloth covering a coffin.
l. 99. *Elucescebat:* "He shone forth," carved on Gandolf's tomb; Cicero would have written "elucebat."

I'll work then for your friend's friend,
    never fear,
Treat his own subject after his own way,
Fix his own time, accept too his own price,
And shut the money into this small hand
When next it takes mine. Will it? tenderly?
Oh, I'll content him,—but to-morrow, love! **10**
I often am much wearier than you think,
This evening more than usual, and it seems
As if—forgive now—should you let me sit
Here by the window with your hand in mine
And look a half hour forth on Fiesole,
Both of one mind, as married people use,
Quietly, quietly the evening through,
I might get up to-morrow to my work
Cheerful and fresh as ever. Let us try.
To-morrow, how you shall be glad for this! **20**
Your soft hand is a woman of itself,
And mine the man's bared breast she curls
    inside.
Don't count the time lost, neither; you must
    serve
For each of the five pictures we require:
It saves a model. So! keep looking so—
My serpentining beauty, rounds on rounds!
—How could you ever prick those perfect
    ears,
Even to put the pearl there! oh, so sweet—
My face, my moon, my everybody's moon,
Which everybody looks on and calls his, **30**
And, I suppose, is looked on by in turn,
While she looks—no one's: very dear, no less.
You smile? why, there's my picture ready made,
There's what we painters call our harmony!
A common greyness silvers everything,—
All in a twilight, you and I alike
—You, at the point of your first pride in me
(That's gone you know),—but I, at every
    point;
My youth, my hope, my art, being all toned
    down
To yonder sober pleasant Fiesole. **40**
There's the bell clinking from the chapel-top;
That length of convent-wall across the way
Holds the trees safer, huddled more inside;

The last monk leaves the garden; days
    decrease,
And autumn grows, autumn in everything.
Eh? the whole seems to fall into a shape
As if I saw alike my works and self
And all that I was born to be and do,
A twilight piece. Love, we are in God's hand.
How strange now, looks the life he makes us
    lead; **50**
So free we seem, so fettered fast we are!
I feel he laid the fetter: let it lie!
This chamber for example—turn your head—
All that's behind us! You don't understand
Nor care to understand about my art,
But you can hear at least when people speak:
And that cartoon, the second from the door
—It is the thing, love! so such things should
    be—
Behold Madonna!—I am bold to say.
I can do with my pencil what I know, **60**
What I see, what at bottom of my heart
I wish for, if I ever wish so deep—
Do easily, too—when I say, perfectly,
I do not boast, perhaps: yourself are judge
Who listened to the Legate's talk last week,
And just as much they used to say in France.
At any rate 'tis easy, all of it!
No sketches first, no studies, that's long past:
I do what many dream of, all their lives,
—Dream? strive to do, and agonize to do, **70**
And fail in doing. I could count twenty such
On twice your fingers, and not leave this
    town,
Who strive—you don't know how the others
    strive
To paint a little thing like that you smeared
Carelessly passing with your robes afloat,—
Yet do much less, so much less, Someone
    says,
(I know his name, no matter)—so much less!
Well, less is more, Lucrezia: I am judged.
There burns a truer light of God in them,
In their vexed beating stuffed and stopped-up
    brain, **80**

---

l. 15. *Fiesole:* suburb of Florence.

l. 57. *cartoon:* a large drawing, a study for a tapestry or fresco.

Heart, or whate'er else, than goes on to
    prompt
This low-pulsed forthright craftsman's hand
    of mine.
Their works drop groundward, but
    themselves, I know,
Reach many a time a heaven that's shut to me,
Enter and take their place there sure enough,
Though they come back and cannot tell the
    world.
My works are nearer heaven, but I sit here.
The sudden blood of these men! at a word—
Praise them, it boils, or blame them, it
    boils too.
I, painting from myself and to myself,   **90**
Know what I do, am unmoved by men's
    blame
Or their praise either. Somebody remarks
Morello's outline there is wrongly traced,
His hue mistaken, what of that? or else,
Rightly traced and well ordered, what of
    that?
Speak as they please, what does the
    mountain care?
Ah, but a man's reach should exceed his grasp,
Or what's a heaven for? all is silver-grey
Placid and perfect with my art: the worse!
I know both what I want and what might
    gain,   **100**
And yet how profitless to know, to sigh
"Had I been two, another and myself,
"Our head would have o'erlooked the world!"
    No doubt.
Yonder's a work now, of that famous youth
The Urbinate who died five years ago.
('Tis copied, George Vasari sent it me.)
Well, I can fancy how he did it all,
Pouring his soul, with kings and popes to see,
Reaching, that Heaven might so replenish
    him,
Above and through his art—for it gives
    way;   **110**

That arm is wrongly put—and there again—
A fault to pardon in the drawing's lines,
Its body, so to speak: its soul is right,
He means right—that, a child may
    understand.
Still, what an arm! and I could alter it;
But all the play, the insight and the stretch
Out of me, out of me! And wherefore out?
Had you enjoined them on me, given me soul,
We might have risen to Rafael, I and you!
Nay, Love, you did give all I asked, I
    think—   **120**
More than I merit, yes, by many times.
But had you—oh, with the same perfect brow,
And perfect eyes, and more than perfect
    mouth,
And the low voice my soul hears, as a bird
The fowler's pipe, and follows to the snare—
Had you, with these the same, but brought a
    mind!
Some women do so. Had the mouth there
    urged
"God and the glory! never care for gain.
The present by the future, what is that?
Live for fame, side by side with Agnolo!   **130**
Rafael is waiting: up to God, all three!"
I might have done it for you. So it seems:
Perhaps not. All is as God overrules.
Beside, incentives come from the soul's self;
The rest avail not. Why do I need you?
What wife had Rafael, or has Agnolo?
In this world, who can do a thing, will not;
And who would do it, cannot, I perceive:
Yet the will's somewhat—somewhat, too,
    the power—
And thus we half-men struggle. At the end,   **140**
God, I conclude, compensates, punishes.
'Tis safer for me, if the award be strict,
That I am something underrated here,
Poor this long while, despised, to speak the
    truth.
I dared not, do you know, leave home all day,

---

l. 93. *Morello:* a mountain near Florence.
l. 105. *Urbinate:* Raphael (1483–1520), Italian painter
born in Urbino.

l. 130. *Agnolo:* Michelangelo (1475–1564), Italian painter
and sculptor.

For fear of chancing on the Paris lords.
The best is when they pass and look aside;
But they speak sometimes; I must bear it all.
Well may they speak! That Francis, that first
    time,
And that long festal year at Fontainebleau! 150
I surely then could sometimes leave the
    ground,
Put on the glory, Rafael's daily wear,
In that humane great monarch's golden
    look,—
One finger in his beard or twisted curl
Over his mouth's good mark that made the
    smile,
One arm about my shoulder, round my neck,
The jingle of his gold chain in my ear,
I painting proudly with his breath on me,
All his court round him, seeing with his eyes,
Such frank French eyes, and such a fire of
    souls   160
Profuse, my hand kept plying by those
    hearts,—
And, best of all, this, this, this face beyond,
This in the background, waiting on my work,
To crown the issue with a last reward!
A good time, was it not, my kingly days?
And had you not grown restless . . . but I
    know—
'Tis done and past; 'twas right, my instinct
    said;
Too live the life grew, golden and not grey,
And I'm the weak-eyed bat no sun should
    tempt
Out of the grange whose four walls make his
    world,   170
How could it end in any other way?
You called me, and I came home to your
    heart.
The triumph was—to reach and stay there;
    since

---

l. 146. *Paris lords:* French nobles who insulted del
Sarto. Invited by Francis I of France to paint at Fontainebleau, del Sarto remained there one year, left
with funds to buy art for Francis I, but supposedly
spent the money on his wife and home instead.

I reached it ere the triumph, what is lost?
Let my hands frame your face in your hair's
    gold,
You beautiful Lucrezia that are mine!
"Rafael did this, Andrea painted that—
The Roman's is the better when you pray,
But still the other's Virgin was his wife—"
Men will excuse me. I am glad to judge   180
Both pictures in your presence; clearer grows
My better fortune, I resolve to think.
For, do you know, Lucrezia, as God lives,
Said one day Agnolo, his very self,
To Rafael . . . I have known it all these
    years . . .
(When the young man was flaming out his
    thoughts
Upon a palace-wall for Rome to see,
Too lifted up in heart because of it)
"Friend, there's a certain sorry little scrub
Goes up and down our Florence, none cares
    how,   190
Who, were he set to plan and execute
As you are, pricked on by your popes and
    kings,
Would bring the sweat into that brow of
    yours!"
To Rafael's!—And indeed the arm is wrong.
I hardly dare . . . yet, only you to see,
Give the chalk here—quick, thus the line
    should go!
Ay, but the soul! he's Rafael! rub it out!
Still, all I care for, if he spoke the truth,
(What he? why, who but Michel Agnolo?
Do you forget already words like those?)   200
If really there was such a chance, so lost,—
Is, whether you're—not grateful—but more
    pleased.
Well, let me think so. And you smile indeed!
This hour has been an hour! Another smile?
If you would sit thus by me every night
I should work better, do you comprehend?
I mean that I should earn more, give you
    more.
See, it is settled dusk now; there's a star;
Morello's gone, the watch-lights show the
    wall,

The cue-owls speak the name we call them
    by.   210
Come from the window, love,—come in, at
    last,
Inside the melancholy little house
We built to be so gay with. God is just.
King Francis may forgive me; oft at nights
When I look up from painting, eyes tired out,
The walls become illumined, brick from brick
Distinct, instead of mortar, fierce bright gold,
That gold of his I did cement them with!
Let us but love each other. Must you go?
That Cousin here again? he waits outside? 220
Must see you—you, and not with me? Those
    loans?
More gaming debts to pay? you smiled for
    that?
Well, let smiles buy me! have you more to
    spend?
While hand and eye and something of a heart
Are left me, work's my ware, and what's it
    worth?
I'll pay my fancy. Only let me sit
The grey remainder of the evening out,
Idle, you call it, and muse perfectly
How I could paint, were I but back in France,
One picture, just one more—the Virgin's
    face,   230
Not yours this time! I want you at my side
To hear them—that is, Michel Agnolo—
Judge all I do and tell you of its worth.
Will you? To-morrow, satisfy your friend.
I take the subjects for his corridor,
Finish the portrait out of hand—there, there,
And throw him in another thing or two
If he demurs; the whole should prove enough
To pay for this same Cousin's freak. Beside,
What's better and what's all I care about, 240
Get you the thirteen scudi for the ruff!
Love, does that please you? Ah, but what does
    he,
The Cousin! what does he to please you more?
    I am grown peaceful as old age to-night.

I regret little, I would change still less.
Since there my past life lies, why alter it?
The very wrong to Francis!—it is true
I took his coin, was tempted and complied,
And built this house and sinned, and all is
    said.
My father and my mother died of want.   250
Well, had I riches of my own? you see
How one gets rich! Let each one bear his lot.
They were born poor, lived poor, and poor
    they died:
And I have laboured somewhat in my time
And not been paid profusely. Some good son
Paint my two hundred pictures—let him try!
No doubt, there's something strikes a balance.
    Yes,
You loved me quite enough, it seems to-night.
This must suffice me here. What would one
    have?
In heaven, perhaps, new chances, one more
    chance—   260
Four great walls in the New Jerusalem
Meted on each side by the angel's reed,
For Leonard, Rafael, Agnolo and me
To cover—the three first without a wife,
While I have mine! So—still they overcome
Because there's still Lucrezia,—as I choose.

Again the Cousin's whistle! Go, my Love.

I. 210. *cue-owls:* horned owls whose cry sounds like the
Italian word *liù*.
I. 241. *scudi:* A scudo is an Italian coin.

I. 262. *Meted . . . reed:* In Revelation 21:15, an angel
measures the walls of the holy city with a golden reed.
I. 263. *Leonard:* Leonardo da Vinci (1452–1519), Italian
painter and sculptor.

"Childe Roland to the Dark Tower Came"

See Edgar's Song in Lear

I

My first thought was: he lied in every word,
   That hoary cripple, with malicious eye
   Askance to watch the working of his lie
On mine, and mouth scarce able to afford
Suppression of the glee, that pursed and
    scored
   Its edge, at one more victim gained thereby.

II

What else should he be set for, with his staff?
   What, save to waylay with his lies, ensnare
   All travellers who might find him posted
    there,
And ask the road? I guessed what skull-like
    laugh   10
Would break, what crutch 'gin write my
    epitaph
   For pastime in the dusty thoroughfare,

III

If at his counsel I should turn aside
   Into that ominous tract which, all agree,
   Hides the Dark Tower. Yet acquiescingly
I did turn as he pointed: neither pride
Nor hope rekindling at the end descried,
   So much as gladness that some end might
    be.

IV

For, what with my whole world-wide
   wandering,

See ... Lear: Shakespeare's *King Lear* (III, iv): "Childe
Rowland to the dark tower came;/His word was still
—'Fie, foh, and fum,/I smell the blood of a British
man.' "

What with my search drawn out thro' years,
   my hope   20
Dwindled into a ghost not fit to cope
With that obstreperous joy success would
    bring,—
I hardly tried now to rebuke the spring
   My heart made, finding failure in its scope.

V

As when a sick man very near to death
   Seems dead indeed, and feels begin and end
   The tears and takes the farewell of each
    friend,
And hears one bid the other go, draw breath
Freelier outside, ("since all is o'er," he saith,
   "And the blow fallen no grieving can
    amend;")   30

VI

While some discuss if near the other graves
   Be room enough for this, and when a day
   Suits best for carrying the corpse away,
With care about the banners, scarves and
    staves:
And still the man hears all, and only craves
   He may not shame such tender love and
    stay.

VII

Thus, I had so long suffered in this quest,
   Heard failure prophesied so oft, been writ
   So many times among "The Band"—to wit,
The knights who to the Dark Tower's search
    addressed   40
Their steps—that just to fail as they, seemed
    best,
   And all the doubt was now—should I be fit?

VIII

So, quiet as despair, I turned from him,
   That hateful cripple, out of his highway
   Into the path he pointed. All the day

Had been a dreary one at best, and dim
Was settling to its close, yet shot one grim
　　Red leer to see the plain catch its estray.

IX

For mark! no sooner was I fairly found
　　Pledged to the plain, after a pace or two, 50
　　Than, pausing to throw backward a last
　　　view
O'er the safe road, 't was gone; grey plain all
　　round:
Nothing but plain to the horizon's bound.
　　I might go on; nought else remained to do.

X

So, on I went. I think I never saw
　　Such starved ignoble nature; nothing
　　　throve:
　　For flowers—as well expect a cedar grove!
But cockle, spurge, according to their law
Might propagate their kind, with none to awe,
　　You'd think; a burr had been a treasure-
　　　trove. 60

XI

No! penury, inertness and grimace,
　　In some strange sort, were the land's
　　　portion. "See
　　Or shut your eyes," said Nature peevishly,
"It nothing skills: I cannot help my case:
'T is the Last Judgment's fire must cure this
　　place,
　　Calcine its clods and set my prisoners free."

XII

If there pushed any ragged thistle-stalk
　　Above its mates, the head was chopped; the
　　　bents
　　Were jealous else. What made those holes
　　　and rents

---

l. 64. *skills:* matters.
l. 68. *bents:* stiff, coarse grass.

In the dock's harsh swarth leaves, bruised as
　　to baulk 70
All hope of greenness? 't is a brute must walk
　　Pashing their life out, with a brute's intents.

XIII

As for the grass, it grew as scant as hair
　　In leprosy; thin dry blades pricked the mud
　　Which underneath looked kneaded up with
　　　blood.
One stiff blind horse, his every bone a-stare,
Stood stupefied, however he came there:
　　Thrust out past service from the devil's
　　　stud!

XIV

Alive? he might be dead for aught I know,
　　With that red gaunt and colloped neck
　　　a-strain, 80
　　And shut eyes underneath the rusty mane;
Seldom went such grotesqueness with such
　　woe;
I never saw a brute I hated so;
　　He must be wicked to deserve such pain.

XV

I shut my eyes and turned them on my heart.
　　As a man calls for wine before he fights,
　　I asked one draught of earlier, happier
　　　sights,
Ere fitly I could hope to play my part.
Think first, fight afterwards—the soldier's
　　art:
　　One taste of the old time sets all to rights. 90

XVI

Not it! I fancied Cuthbert's reddening face
　　Beneath its garniture of curly gold,
　　Dear fellow, till I almost felt him fold
An arm in mine to fix me to the place,

---

l. 72. *Pashing:* smashing.

That way he used. Alas, one night's disgrace!
  Out went my heart's new fire and left it
    cold.

XVII

Giles then, the soul of honour—there he
    stands
  Frank as ten years ago when knighted first.
  What honest man should dare (he said) he
    durst.
Good—but the scene shifts—faugh! what
    hangman hands   100
Pin to his breast a parchment? His own bands
  Read it. Poor traitor, spit upon and curst!

XVIII

Better this present than a past like that;
  Back therefore to my darkening path again!
  No sound, no sight as far as eye could
    strain.
Will the night send a howlet or a bat?
I asked: when something on the dismal flat
  Came to arrest my thoughts and change
    their train.

XIX

A sudden little river crossed my path
  As unexpected as a serpent comes.   110
  No sluggish tide congenial to the glooms;
This, as it frothed by, might have been a bath
For the fiend's glowing hoof—to see the wrath
  Of its black eddy bespate with flakes and
    spumes.

XX

So petty yet so spiteful! All along,
  Low scrubby alders kneeled down over it;
  Drenched willows flung them headlong in a
    fit
Of mute despair, a suicidal throng:
The river which had done them all the wrong,

I. 114. *bespate:* spattered.

Whate'er that was, rolled by, deterred no
  whit.   120

XXI

Which, while I forded,—good saints, how
    I feared
  To set my foot upon a dead man's cheek,
  Each step, or feel the spear I thrust to seek
For hollows, tangled in his hair or beard!
—It may have been a water-rat I speared,
  But, ugh! it sounded like a baby's shriek.

XXII

Glad was I when I reached the other bank.
  Now for a better country. Vain presage!
  Who were the strugglers, what war did they
    wage,
Whose savage trample thus could pad the
    dank   130
Soil to a plash? Toads in a poisoned tank,
  Or wild cats in a red-hot iron cage—

XXIII

The fight must so have seemed in that fell
    cirque.
  What penned them there, with all the plain
    to choose?
  No foot-print leading to that horrid mews,
None out of it. Mad brewage set to work
Their brains, no doubt, like galley-slaves the
    Turk
  Pits for his pastime, Christians against
    Jews.

XXIV

And more than that—a furlong on—why,
    there!
  What bad use was that engine for, that
    wheel.   140

I. 130. *pad:* trample.
I. 131. *plash:* puddle.
I. 133. *fell cirque:* deadly circle.
I. 135. *mews:* cage.

Or brake, not wheel—that harrow fit to reel
Men's bodies out like silk? with all the air
Of Tophet's tool, on earth left unaware,
    Or brought to sharpen its rusty teeth of
      steel.

XXV

Then came a bit of stubbed ground, once a
    wood,
    Next a marsh, it would seem, and now mere
      earth
    Desperate and done with; (so a fool finds
      mirth,
Makes a thing and then mars it, till his mood
Changes and off he goes!) within a rood—
    Bog, clay and rubble, sand and stark black
      dearth.   **150**

XXVI

Now blotches rankling, coloured gay and
    grim,
    Now patches where some leanness of the
      soil's
    Broke into moss or substances like boils;
Then came some palsied oak, a cleft in him
Like a distorted mouth that splits its rim
    Gaping at death, and dies while it recoils.

XXVII

And just as far as ever from the end!
    Naught in the distance but the evening,
      naught
    To point my footstep further! At the
      thought,
A great black bird, Apollyon's bosom-friend, **160**
Sailed past, nor beat his wide wing dragon-
      penned

I. 143. *Tophet:* Hell.
I. 149. *within a rood:* within a quarter acre; a small space.
I. 160. *Apollyon:* the devil; the "angel of the bottom pit" (Revelation 9:11).

That brushed my cap—perchance the guide
    I sought.

XXVIII

For, looking up, aware I somehow grew,
    'Spite of the dusk, the plain had given place
    All round to mountains—with such name to
      grace
Mere ugly heights and heaps now stolen in
    view.
How thus they had surprised me,—solve it,
    you!
    How to get from them was no clearer case.

XXIX

Yet half I seemed to recognize some trick
    Of mischief happened to me, God knows
      when—   **170**
    In a bad dream perhaps. Here ended, then,
Progress this way. When, in the very nick
Of giving up, one time more, came a click
    As when a trap shuts—you're inside the den!

XXX

Burningly it came on me all at once,
    This was the place! those two hills on the
      right,
    Crouched like two bulls locked horn in horn
      in fight;
While to the left, a tall scalped mountain . . .
    Dunce,
Dotard, a-dozing at the very nonce,
    After a life spent training for the sight! **180**

XXXI

What in the midst lay but the Tower itself?
    The round squat turret, blind as the fool's
      heart,
    Built of brown stone, without a counterpart
In the whole world. The tempest's mocking
    elf

I. 179. *nonce:* present moment.

Points to the shipman thus the unseen shelf
   He strikes on, only when the timbers start.

XXXII

Not see? because of night perhaps?—why, day
   Came back again for that! before it left,
   The dying sunset kindled through a cleft:
The hills, like giants at a hunting, lay,   190
Chin upon hand, to see the game at bay,—
   "Now stab and end the creature—to the
      heft!"

XXXIII

Not hear? when noise was everywhere! it
   tolled
   Increasing like a bell. Names in my ears
   Of all the lost adventurers my peers,—
How such a one was strong, and such was
   bold,
And such was fortunate, yet each of old
   Lost, lost! one moment knelled the woe of
    years.

XXXIV

There they stood, ranged along the hill-sides,
   met
   To view the last of me, a living frame   200
For one more picture! in a sheet of flame
I saw them and I knew them all. And yet
Dauntless the slug-horn to my lips I set,
   And blew *Childe Roland to the Dark Tower*
   came."

---

l. 203. *slug-horn:* trumpet.

WALT WHITMAN

When Lilacs Last in the Dooryard Bloom'd

I

When lilacs last in the dooryard bloom'd
And the great star early droop'd in the
   western sky in the night,
I mourn'd, and yet shall mourn with
   ever-returning spring.

Ever-returning spring, trinity sure to me you
   bring,
Lilac blooming perennial and drooping star in
   the west,
And thought of him I love.

II

O powerful western fallen star!
O shades of night—O moody, tearful night!
O great star disappear'd—O the black murk
   that hides the star!
O cruel hands that hold me powerless—O   10
   helpless soul of me!
O harsh surrounding cloud that will not free
   my soul.

III

In the dooryard fronting an old farm-house
   near the white-wash'd palings,
Stands the lilac-bush tall-growing with heart-
   shaped leaves of rich green,
With many a pointed blossom rising delicate,
   with the perfume strong I love,
With every leaf a miracle—and from this bush
   in the dooryard,

---

l. 6. *him:* Abraham Lincoln, assassinated April 14, 1865.
His body was taken to Springfield, Illinois, for burial.
See Part V of this poem.

With delicate-color'd blossom and
   heart-shaped leaves of rich green,
A sprig with its flower I break.

IV

In the swamp in secluded recesses,
A shy and hidden bird is warbling a song.
Solitary the thrush,   20
The hermit withdrawn to himself, avoiding
   the settlements,
Sings by himself a song.

Song of the bleeding throat,
Death's outlet song of life, (for well dear
   brother I know,
If thou wast not granted to sing thou would'st
   surely die.)

V

Over the breast of the spring, the land, amid
   cities,
Amid lanes and through old woods, where
   lately the violets peep'd from the ground,
   spotting the gray debris,
Amid the grass in the fields each side of the
   lanes, passing the endless grass,
Passing the yellow-spear'd wheat, every grain
   from its shroud in the dark-brown fields
   uprisen,
Passing the apple-tree blows of white and
   pink in the orchards,   30
Carrying a corpse to where it shall rest in the
   grave,
Night and day journeys a coffin.

VI

Coffin that passes through lanes and streets,
Through day and night with the great cloud
   darkening the land,
With the pomp of the inloop'd flags with the
   cities draped in black,
With the show of the States themselves as of
   crape-veil'd women standing,

With processions long and winding and the
   flambeaus of the night,
With the countless torches lit, with the silent
   sea of faces and the unbared heads,
With the waiting depot, the arriving coffin,
   and the sombre faces,
With dirges through the night, with the
   thousand voices rising strong and solemn, 40
With all the mournful voices of the dirges
   pour'd around the coffin,
The dim-lit churches and the shuddering
   organs—where amid these you journey,
With the tolling tolling bells' perpetual clang,
Here, coffin that slowly passes,
I give you my sprig of lilac.

VII

(Nor for you, for one alone,
Blossoms and branches green to coffins all
   I bring,
For fresh as the morning, thus would I chant
   a song for you O sane and sacred death.

All over bouquets of roses,
O death, I cover you over with roses and
   early lilies,   50
But mostly and now the lilac that blooms
   the first,
Copious I break, I break the sprigs from the
   bushes,
With loaded arms I come, pouring for you,
For you and the coffins all of you O death.)

VIII

O western orb sailing the heaven,
Now I know what you must have meant as a
   month since I walk'd,
As I walk'd in silence the transparent
   shadowy night,
As I saw you had something to tell as you
   bent to me night after night,
As you drooped from the sky low down as if
   to my side, (while the other stars all look'd
   on,)

As we wander'd together the solemn night,
  (for something I know not what kept me
  from sleep,)   60
As the night advanced, and I saw on the rim
  of the west how full you were of woe,
As I stood on the rising ground in the breeze
  in the cool transparent night,
As I watch'd where you pass'd and was lost in
  the netherward black of the night,
As my soul in its trouble dissatisfied sank, as
  where you, sad orb,
Concluded, dropt in the night, and was gone.

IX

Sing on there in swamp,
O singer bashful and tender, I hear your
  notes, I hear your call,
I hear, I come presently, I understand you,
But a moment I linger, for the lustrous star
  has detain'd me,
The star my departing comrade holds and
  detains me.   70

X

O how shall I warble myself for the dead one
  there I loved?
And how shall I deck my song for the large
  sweet soul that has gone?
And what shall my perfume be for the grave
  of him I love?

Sea-winds blown from east and west,
Blown from the Eastern sea and blown from
  the Western sea, till there on the prairies
  meeting,
These and with these and the breath of my
  chant,
I'll perfume the grave of him I love.

XI

O what shall I hang on the chamber walls?
And what shall the pictures be that I hang
  on the walls,
To adorn the burial-house of him I love?   80

Pictures of growing spring and farms and
  homes,
With the Fourth-month eve at sundown, and
  the gray smoke lucid and bright,
With floods of the yellow gold of the gorgeous,
  indolent, sinking sun, burning, expanding
  the air,
With the fresh sweet herbage under foot, and
  the pale green leaves of the trees prolific,
In the distance the flowing glaze, the breast
  of the river, with a wind-dapple here and
  there,
With ranging hills on the banks, with many
  a line against the sky, and shadows,
And the city at hand with dwellings so dense,
  and stacks of chimneys,
And all the scenes of life and the workshops,
  and the workmen homeward returning.

XII

Lo, body and soul—this land,
My own Manhattan with spires, and the
  sparkling and hurrying tides, and the
  ships,   90
The varied and ample land, the South and the
  North in the light, Ohio's shores and
  flashing Missouri,
And ever the far-spreading prairies cover'd
  with grass and corn.

Lo, the most excellent sun so calm and
  haughty,
The violet and purple morn with just-felt
  breezes,
The gentle soft-born measureless light,
The miracle spreading bathing all, the
  fulfill'd noon,
The coming eve delicious, the welcome night
  and the stars,
Over my cities shining all, enveloping man
  and land.

XIII

Sing on, sing on you gray-brown bird,
Sing from the swamps, the recesses, pour

your chant from the bushes, 100
Limitless out of the dusk, out of the cedars
and pines.

Sing on dearest brother, warble your reedy
song,
Loud human song, with voice of uttermost
woe.
O liquid and free and tender!
O wild and loose to my soul—O wondrous
singer!
You only I hear—yet the star holds me,
(but will soon depart,)
Yet the lilac with mastering odor holds me.

XIV

Now while I sat in the day and look'd forth,
In the close of the day with its light and the
fields of spring, and the farmers preparing
their crops,
In the large unconscious scenery of my land
with its lakes and forests, 110
In the heavenly aerial beauty, (after the
perturb'd winds and the storms,)
Under the arching heavens of the afternoon
swift passing, and the voices of children
and women,
The many-moving sea-tides, and I saw the
ships how they sail'd,
And the summer approaching with richness,
and the fields all busy with labor,
And the infinite separate houses, how they all
went on, each with its meals and minutia of
daily usages,
And the streets how their throbbings
throbb'd, and the cities pent—lo, then and
there,
Falling upon them all and among them all,
enveloping me with the rest,
Appear'd the cloud, appear'd the long black
trail,
And I knew death, its thought, and the sacred
knowledge of death.

Then with the knowledge of death as walking
one side of me, 120

And the thought of death close-walking the
other side of me,
And I in the middle as with companions, and
as holding the hands of companions,
I fled forth to the hiding receiving night that
talks not,
Down to the shores of the water, the path by
the swamp in the dimness,
To the solemn shadowy cedars and ghostly
pines so still.

And the singer so shy to the rest receiv'd me,
The gray-brown bird I know receiv'd us
comrades three,
And he sang the carol of death, and a verse
for him I love.

From deep secluded recesses,
From the fragrant cedars and the ghostly
pines so still, 130
Came the carol of the bird.

And the charm of the carol rapt me,
As I held as if by their hands my comrades
in the night,
And the voice of my spirit tallied the song of
the bird.

Come lovely and soothing death,
Undulate round the world, serenely arriving,
arriving,
In the day, in the night, to all, to each,
Sooner or later delicate death.

Prais'd be the fathomless universe,
For life and joy, and for objects and
knowledge curious, 140
And for love, sweet love—but praise! praise!
praise!
For the sure-enwinding arms of cool-enfolding
death.

Dark mother always gliding near with soft
feet,
Have none chanted for thee a chant of fullest
welcome?

Then I chant it for thee, I glorify thee above
    all,
I bring thee a song that when thou must
    indeed come, come unfalteringly.

Approach strong deliveress,
When it is so, when thou hast taken them
    I joyously sing the dead,
Lost in the loving floating ocean of thee,
Laved in the flood by thy bliss O death.   150

From me to thee glad serenades,
Dances for thee I propose saluting thee,
    adornments and feastings for thee,
And the sights of the open landscape and the
    high-spread sky are fitting,
And life and the fields, and the huge and
    thoughtful night.

The night in silence under many a star,
The ocean shore and the husky whispering
    wave whose voice I know,
And the soul turning to thee O vast and
    well-veil'd death,
And the body gratefully nestling close to thee.

Over the tree-tops I float thee a song,
Over the rising and sinking waves, over the
    myriad fields and the prairies wide,   160
Over the dense-pack'd cities all and the
    teeming wharves and ways,
I float this carol with joy, with joy to thee
    O death.

XV

To the tally of my soul,
Loud and strong kept up the gray-brown bird,
With pure deliberate notes spreading filling
    the night.

Loud in the pines and cedars dim,
Clear in the freshness moist and the swamp-
    perfume,
And I with my comrades there in the night.

While my sight that was bound in my eyes
    unclosed,

As to long panoramas of visions.   170

And I saw askant the armies,
I saw as in noiseless dreams hundreds of
    battle-flags,
Borne through the smoke of the battles and
    pierc'd with missiles I saw them,
And carried hither and yon through the
    smoke, and torn and bloody,
And at last but a few shreds left on the staffs,
    (and all in silence,)
And the staffs all splinter'd and broken.

I saw battle-corpses, myriads of them,
And the white skeletons of young men, I saw
    them,
I saw the debris and debris of all the slain
    soldiers of the war,
But I saw they were not as was thought,   180
They themselves were fully at rest, they
    suffer'd not,
The living remain'd and suffer'd, the mother
    suffer'd,
And the wife and the child and the musing
    comrade suffer'd,
And the armies that remain'd suffer'd.

XVI

Passing the visions, passing the night,
Passing, unloosing the hold of my comrades'
    hands,
Passing the song of the hermit bird and the
    tallying song of my soul,
Victorious song, death's outlet song, yet
    varying ever-altering song,
As low and wailing, yet clear the notes, rising
    and falling, flooding the night,
Sadly sinking and fainting, as warning and
    warning, and yet again bursting with joy,190
Covering the earth and filling the spread of
    the heaven,
As that powerful psalm in the night I heard
    from recesses,
Passing, I leave thee lilac with heart-shaped
    leaves,
I leave thee there in the dooryard, blooming,
    returning with spring.

I cease from my song for thee,
From my gaze on thee in the west, fronting
   the west, communing with thee,
O comrade lustrous with silver face in the
   night.

Yet each to keep and all, retrievements out of
   the night,
The song, the wondrous chant of the gray-
   brown bird,
And the tallying chant, the echo arous'd in
   my soul,   200
With the lustrous and drooping star with the
   countenance full of woe,
With the holders holding my hand nearing
   the call of the bird,
Comrades mine and I in the midst, and their
   memory ever to keep, for the dead I loved
   so well,
For the sweetest, wisest soul of all my days
   and lands—and this for his dear sake,
Lilac and star and bird twined with the chant
   of my soul,
There in the fragrant pines and the cedars
   dusk and dim.

Crossing Brooklyn Ferry

I

Flood-tide below me! I see you face to face!
Clouds of the west—sun there half an hour
   high—I see you also face to face.

Crowds of men and women attired in the
   usual costumes, how curious you are to me!
On the ferry-boats the hundreds and hundreds
   that cross, returning home, are more
   curious to me than you suppose,
And you that shall cross from shore to shore
   years hence are more to me, and more in
   my meditations, than you might suppose.

II

The impalpable sustenance of me from all
   things at all hours of the day,

The simple, compact, well-join'd scheme,
   myself disintegrated, every one
   disintegrated yet part of the scheme,
The similitudes of the past and those of the
   future,
The glories strung like beads on my smallest
   sights and hearings, on the walk in the
   street and the passage over the river,
The current rushing so swiftly and
   swimming with me far away,   10
The others that are to follow me, the ties
   between me and them,
The certainty of others, the life, love, sight,
   hearing of others.

Others will enter the gates of the ferry and
   cross from shore to shore,
Others will watch the run of the flood-tide,
Others will see the shipping of Manhattan
   north and west, and the heights of Brooklyn
   to the south and east,
Others will see the islands large and small;
Fifty years hence, others will see them as they
   cross, the sun half an hour high,
A hundred years hence, or ever so many
   hundred years hence, others will see them,
Will enjoy the sunset, the pouring-in of the
   flood-tide, the falling-back to the sea of
   the ebb-tide.

III

It avails not, time nor place—distance avails
   not,   20
I am with you, you men and women of a
   generation, or ever so many generations
   hence,
Just as you feel when you look on the river
   and sky, so I felt,
Just as any of you is one of a living crowd,
   I was one of a crowd,
Just as you are refresh'd by the gladness of
   the river and the bright flow, I was
   refresh'd,
Just as you stand and lean on the rail, yet
   hurry with the swift current, I stood yet
   was hurried,

Just as you look on the numberless masts of
    ships and the thick-stemm'd pipes of
    steamboats, I look'd.

I too many and many a time cross'd the river
    of old,
Watched the Twelfth-month sea-gulls, saw
    them high in the air floating with
    motionless wings, oscillating their bodies,
Saw how the glistening yellow lit up parts of
    their bodies and left the rest in strong
    shadow,
Saw the slow-wheeling circles and the gradual
    edging toward the south,   30
Saw the reflection of the summer sky in the
    water,
Had my eyes dazzled by the shimmering track
    of beams,
Look'd at the fine centrifugal spokes of light
    round the shape of my head in the sunlit
    water,
Look'd on the haze on the hills southward and
    southwestward,
Look'd on the vapor as it flew in fleeces tinged
    with violet,
Look'd toward the lower bay to notice the
    vessels arriving,
Saw their approach, saw aboard those that
    were near me,
Saw the white sails of schooners and sloops,
    saw the ships at anchor,
The sailors at work in the rigging or out
    astride the spars,
The round masts, the swinging motion of the
    hulls, the slender serpentine pennants,   40
The large and small steamers in motion, the
    pilots in their pilot-houses,
The white wake left by the passage, the quick
    tremulous whirl of the wheels,
The flags of all nations, the falling of them at
    sunset,
The scalloped-edged waves in the twilight,
    the ladled cups, the frolicsome crests and
    glistening,
The stretch afar growing dimmer and
    dimmer, the gray walls of the granite
    storehouses by the docks,

On the river the shadowy group, the big
    steam-tug closely flank'd on each side by
    the barges, the hay-boat, the belated lighter,
On the neighboring shore the fires from the
    foundry chimneys burning high and
    glaringly into the night,
Casting their flicker of black contrasted with
    wild red and yellow light over the tops of
    houses, and down into the clefts of streets.

IV

These and all else were to me the same as
    they are to you,
I loved well those cities, loved well the
    stately and rapid river,   50
The men and women I saw were all near
    to me,
Others the same—others who look back on
    me because I look'd forward to them,
(The time will come, though I stop here
    to-day and to-night.)

V

What is it then between us?
What is the count of the scores or hundreds
    of years between us?

Whatever it is, it avails not—distance avails
    not, and place avails not,
I too lived, Brooklyn of ample hills was mine,
I too walk'd the streets of Manhattan island,
    and bathed in the waters around it,
I too felt the curious abrupt questionings stir
    within me.
In the day among crowds of people
    sometimes they came upon me,   60
In my walks home late at night or as I lay in
    my bed they came upon me,
I too had been struck from the float forever
    held in solution,
I too had receiv'd identity by my body,
That I was I knew was of my body, and what
    I should be I knew I should be of my body.

VI

It is not upon you alone the dark patches fall,
The dark threw its patches down upon me
    also,
The best I had done seem'd to me blank and
    suspicious,
My great thoughts as I supposed them, were
    they not in reality meagre?
Nor is it you alone who know what it is to
    be evil,
I am he who knew what it was to be evil,   70
I too knitted the old knot of contrariety,
Blabb'd, blush'd, resented, lied, stole, grudg'd,
Had guile, anger, lust, hot wishes I dared not
    speak,
Was wayward, vain, greedy, shallow, sly,
    cowardly, malignant,
The wolf, the snake, the hog, not wanting
    in me,
The cheating look, the frivolous word, the
    adulterous wish, not wanting,
Refusals, hates, postponements, meanness,
    laziness, none of these wanting,
Was one with the rest, the days and haps of
    the rest,
Was call'd by my nighest name by clear loud
    voices of young men as they saw me
    approaching or passing,
Felt their arms on my neck as I stood, or the
    negligent leaning of their flesh against me
    as I sat,   80
Saw many I loved in the street or ferry-boat
    or public assembly, yet never told them
    a word,
Lived the same life with the rest, the same
    old laughing, gnawing, sleeping,
Play'd the part that still looks back on the
    actor or actress,
The same old role, the role that is what we
    make it, as great as we like,
Or as small as we like, or both great and
    small.

VII

Closer yet I approach you,
What thought you have of me now, I had as

much of you—I laid in my stores in
    advance,
I consider'd long and seriously of you before
    you were born.

Who was to know what should come home
    to me?
Who knows but I am enjoying this?   90
Who knows, for all the distance, but I am as
    good as looking at you now, for all you
    cannot see me?

VIII

Ah, what can ever be more stately and
    admirable to me than mast-hemm'd
    Manhattan?
River and sunset and scallop-edg'd waves of
    flood-tide?
The sea-gulls oscillating their bodies, the
    hay-boat in the twilight, and the belated
    lighter?
What gods can exceed these that clasp me by
    the hand, and with voices I love call me
    promptly and loudly by my nighest name
    as I approach?

What is more subtle than this which ties me
    to the woman or man that looks in my face?
Which fuses me into you now, and pours my
    meaning into you?

We understand then do we not?
What I promis'd without mentioning it, have
    you not accepted?
What the study could not teach—what the
    preaching could not accomplish is
    accomplish'd, is it not?   100

IX

Flow on, river! flow with the flood-tide, and
    ebb with the ebb-tide!
Frolic on, crested and scallop-edg'd waves!
Gorgeous clouds of the sunset! drench with
    your splendor me, or the men and women
    generations after me!

Cross from shore to shore, countless crowds
of passengers!
Stand up, tall masts of Mannahatta! stand up,
beautiful hills of Brooklyn!
Throb, baffled and curious brain! throw out
questions and answers!
Suspend here and everywhere, eternal float
of solution!
Gaze, loving and thirsting eyes, in the house
or street or public assembly!
Sound out, voices of young men! loudly and
musically call me by my nighest name!
Live, old life! play the part that looks back on
the actor or actress!   110
Play the old role, the role that is great or
small according as one makes it!
Consider, you who peruse me, whether I may
not in unknown ways be looking upon you;
Be firm, rail over the river, to support those
who lean idly, yet haste with the hasting
current;
Fly on, sea-birds! fly sideways, or wheel in
large circles high in the air;
Receive the summer sky, you water, and
faithfully hold it till all downcast eyes have
time to take it from you!
Diverge, fine spokes of light, from the shape
of my head, or any one's head, in the sunlit
water!
Come on, ships from the lower bay! pass up
or down, white-sail'd schooners, sloops,
lighters!

Flaunt away, flags of all nations! be duly
lower'd at sunset!
Burn high your fires, foundry chimneys! cast
black shadows at nightfall! cast red and
yellow light over the tops of the houses!
Appearances, now or henceforth, indicate
what you are,   120
You necessary film, continue to envelop the
soul,
About my body for me, and your body for you,
be hung our divinest aromas,
Thrive, cities—bring your freight, bring your
shows, ample and sufficient rivers,

Expand, being than which none else is
perhaps more spiritual,
Keep your places, objects than which none
else is more lasting.

You have waited, you always wait, you dumb,
beautiful ministers,
We receive you with free sense at last, and
are insatiate henceforward,
Not you any more shall be able to foil us, or
withhold yourselves from us,
We use you, and do not cast you aside—we
plant you permanently within us,
We fathom you not—we love you—there is
perfection in you also,   130
You furnish your parts toward eternity,
Great or small, you furnish your parts toward
the soul.

This Compost

I

Something startles me where I thought I was
safest;
I withdraw from the still woods I loved;
I will not go now on the pastures to walk;
I will not strip the clothes from my body to
meet my lover the sea;
I will not touch my flesh to the earth, as to
other flesh, to renew me.

O how can it be that the ground does not
sicken?
How can you be alive, you growths of spring?
How can you furnish health, you blood of
herbs, roots, orchards, grain?
Are they not continually putting distemper'd
corpses within you?
Is not every continent work'd over and over
with sour dead?   10

Where have you disposed of their carcasses?

Those drunkards and gluttons of so many
   generations;
Where have you drawn off all the foul liquid
   and meat?
I do not see any of it upon you to-day—or
   perhaps I am deceiv'd;
I will run a furrow with my plough—I will
   press my spade through the sod, and turn it
   up underneath;
I am sure I shall expose some of the foul
   meat.

II

Behold this compost! behold it well!
Perhaps every mite has once form'd part of a
   sick person—Yet behold!
The grass of spring covers the prairies,
The bean bursts noiselessly through the
   mould in the garden,   20
The delicate spear of the onion pierces
   upward,
The apple-buds cluster together on the
   apple-branches,
The resurrection of the wheat appears with
   pale visage out of its graves,
The tinge awakes over the willow-tree and
   the mulberry-tree,
The he-birds carol mornings and evenings,
   while the she-birds sit on their nests,
The young of poultry break through the
   hatch'd eggs,
The new-born of animals appear—the calf is
   dropt from the cow, the colt from the mare,
Out of its little hill faithfully rise the potato's
   dark green leaves,
Out of its hill rises the yellow maize-stalk—
   the lilacs bloom in the door-yards;
The summer growth is innocent and
   disdainful above all those strata of sour
   dead.   30

What chemistry!
That the winds are really not infectious,
That this is no cheat, this transparent
   green-wash of the sea, which is so
   amorous after me,

That it is safe to allow it to lick my naked
   body all over with its tongues,
That it will not endanger me with the fevers
   that have deposited themselves in it,
That all is clean, forever and forever.
That the cool drink from the well tastes
   so good,
That blackberries are so flavorous and juicy,
That the fruits of the apple-orchard, and of
   the orange-orchard—that melons, grapes,
   peaches, plums, will none of them
   poison me,
That when I recline on the grass I do not
   catch any disease,   40
Though probably every spear of grass rises
   out of what was once a catching disease.

III

Now I am terrified at the Earth! it is that
   calm and patient,
It grows such sweet things out of such
   corruptions,
It turns harmless and stainless on its axis,
   with such endless successions of diseas'd
   corpses,
It distills such exquisite winds out of such
   infused fetor,
It renews with such unwitting looks, its
   prodigal, annual, sumptuous crops,
It gives such divine materials to men, and
   accepts such leavings from them at last.

MATTHEW ARNOLD

Philomela

Hark! ah, the nightingale—
The tawny-throated!
Hark, from that moonlit cedar what a burst!
What triumph! hark!—what pain!
O wanderer from a Grecian shore,
Still, after many years, in distant lands,
Still nourishing in thy bewilder'd brain
That wild, unquench'd, deep-sunken, old-
    world pain—
Say, will it never heal?
And can this fragrant lawn   10
With its cool trees, and night,
And the sweet, tranquil Thames,
And moonshine, and the dew,
To thy rack'd heart and brain
Afford no balm?

Dost thou to-night behold,
Here, through the moonlight on this English
    grass,
The unfriendly palace in the Thracian wild?
Dost thou again peruse
With hot cheeks and sear'd eyes   20
The too clear web, and thy dumb sister's
    shame?
Dost thou once more assay
Thy flight, and feel come over thee,
Poor fugitive, the feathery change
Once more, and once more seem to make
    resound

Philomela: wife of Tereus, King of Daulis in Phocis, often called King of Thrace. Tereus raped Philomela's sister, Procne, and cut out her tongue so she could not reveal her shame. By means of a tapestry she wove, Procne informed her sister, and together they cooked and served Tereus the flesh of his son, then fled. Pursued by Tereus, they appealed to the gods: Procne became a swallow; Philomela, a nightingale; and Tereus, a hawk.

With love and hate, triumph and agony,
Lone Daulis, and the high Cephissian vale?
Listen, Eugenia—
How thick the bursts come crowding through
    the leaves!
Again—thou hearest?   30
Eternal passion!
Eternal pain!

---

l. 27. *Cephissian:* The Cephissus is the chief river of Phocis.

Stanzas from the Grande Chartreuse

Through Alpine meadows soft-suffused
With rain, where thick the crocus blows,
Past the dark forges long disused,
The mule-track from Saint Laurent goes.
The bridge is cross'd, and slow we ride,
Through forest, up the mountain-side.

The autumnal evening darkens round,
The wind is up, and drives the rain;
While, hark! far down, with strangled sound
Doth the Dead Guier's stream complain,   10
Where that wet smoke, among the woods,
Over his boiling cauldron broods.

Swift rush the spectral vapours white
Past limestone scars with ragged pines,
Showing—then blotting from our sight!—
Halt—through the cloud-drift something
    shines!
High in the valley, wet and drear,
The huts of Courrerie appear.

Strike leftward! cries our guide; and higher
Mounts up the stony forest-way.   20
At last the encircling trees retire;

The Grande Chartreuse: the chief monastery of the Carthusian monks, founded in the eleventh century, situated in the Alps of southeastern France.

Look! through the showery twilight grey
What pointed roofs are these advance?—
A palace of the Kings of France?

Approach, for what we seek is here!
Alight, and sparely sup, and wait
For rest in this outbuilding near;
Then cross the sward and reach that gate.
Knock; pass the wicket! Thou art come
To the Carthusians' world-famed home.   30

'The silent courts, where night and day
Into their stone-carved basins cold
The splashing icy fountains play—
The humid corridors behold!
Where, ghostlike in the deepening night,
Cowl'd forms brush by in gleaming white.

The chapel, where no organ's peal
Invests the stern and naked prayer—
With penitential cries they kneel
And wrestle; rising then, with bare   40
And white uplifted faces stand,
Passing the Host from hand to hand;

Each takes, and then his visage wan
Is buried in his cowl once more.
The cells!—the suffering Son of Man
Upon the wall—the knee-worn floor—
And where they sleep, that wooden bed,
Which shall their coffin be, when dead!

The library, where tract and tome
Not to feed priestly pride are there,   50
To hymn the conquering march of Rome,
Nor yet to amuse, as ours are!
They paint of souls the inner strife,
Their drops of blood, their death in life.

The garden, overgrown—yet mild,
See, fragrant herbs are flowering there!
Strong children of the Alpine wild
Whose culture is the brethren's care;
Of human tasks their only one,
And cheerful works beneath the sun.   60

Those halls, too, destined to contain
Each its own pilgrim-host of old,

From England, Germany, or Spain—
All are before me! I behold
The House, the Brotherhood austere!
—And what am I, that I am here?

For rigorous teachers seized my youth,
And purged its faith, and trimm'd its fire,
Show'd me the high, white star of Truth,
There bade me gaze, and there aspire.   70
Even now their whispers pierce the gloom:
What dost thou in this living tomb?

Forgive me, masters of the mind!
At whose behest I long ago
So much unlearnt, so much resign'd—
I come not here to be your foe!
I seek these anchorites, not in ruth,
To curse and to deny your truth;

Not as their friend, or child, I speak!
But as, on some far northern strand,   80
Thinking of his own Gods, a Greek
In pity and mournful awe might stand
Before some fallen Runic stone—
For both were faiths, and both are gone.

Wandering between two worlds, one dead,
The other powerless to be born,
With nowhere yet to rest my head,
Like these, on earth I wait forlorn.
Their faith, my tears, the world deride—
I come to shed them at their side.   90

Oh, hide me in your gloom profound,
Ye solemn seats of holy pain!
Take me, cowl'd forms, and fence me round,
Till I possess my soul again;
Till free my thoughts before me roll,
Not chafed by hourly false control!

For world cries your faith is now
But a dead time's exploded dream;
My melancholy, sciolists say,
Is a pass'd mode, an outworn theme—   100

---

l. 99. *sciolists:* smatterers; scholars with a superficial
attitude.

As if the world had ever had
A faith, or sciolists been sad!

Ah, if it *be* pass'd, take away,
At least, the restlessness, the pain;
Be man henceforth no more a prey
To these out-dated stings again!
The nobleness of grief is gone—
Ah, leave us not the fret alone!

But—if you cannot give us ease—
Last of the race of them who grieve   110
Here leave us to die out with these
Last of the people who believe!
Silent, while years engrave the brow;
Silent—the best are silent now.

Achilles ponders in his tent,
The kings of modern thought are dumb;
Silent they are, though not content,
And wait to see the future come.
They have the grief men had of yore,
But they contend and cry no more.   120

Our fathers water'd with their tears
This sea of time whereon we sail,
Their voices were in all men's ears
Who pass'd within their puissant hail.
Still the same ocean round us raves,
But we stand mute, and watch the waves.

For what avail'd it, all the noise
And outcry of the former men?—
Say, have their sons achieved more joys,
Say, is life lighter now than then?   130
The sufferers died, they left their pain—
The pangs which tortured them remain.

What helps it now, that Byron bore,
With haughty scorn which mock'd the smart,
Through Europe to the Ætolian shore
The pageant of his bleeding heart?

That thousands counted every groan,
And Europe made his woe her own?

What boots it, Shelley! that the breeze
Carried thy lovely wail away,   140
Musical through Italian trees
Which fringe thy soft blue Spezzian bay?
Inheritors of thy distress
Have restless hearts one throb the less?

Or are we easier, to have read,
O Obermann! the sad, stern page,
Which tells us how thou hidd'st thy head
From the fierce tempest of thine age
In the lone brakes of Fontainebleau,
Or chalets near the Alpine snow?   150

Ye slumber in your silent grave!—
The world, which for an idle day
Grace to your mood of sadness gave,
Long since hath flung her weeds away.
The eternal trifler breaks your spell;
But we—we learnt your lore too well!

Years hence, perhaps, may dawn an age,
More fortunate, alas! than we,
Which without hardness will be sage,
And gay without frivolity.   160
Sons of the world, oh, speed those years;
But, while we wait, allow our tears!

Allow them! We admire with awe
The exulting thunder of your race;
You give the universe your law,
You triumph over time and space!
Your pride of life, your tireless powers,
We laud them, but they are not ours.

We are like children rear'd in shade
Beneath some old-world abbey wall,   170
Forgotten in a forest-glade,

---

l. 139. *Shelley:* Percy Bysshe Shelley, who spent his
last days on the shores of the Gulf of Spezzia, north-
western Italy.
l. 146. *Obermann:* a book by Étienne Pivert de Senan-
cour (1770–1846).

---

l. 115. *Achilles:* hero of Homer's *Iliad.*
l. 133. *Byron:* English poet (1788–1824).
l. 135. *Ætolian:* Grecian.

And secret from the eyes of all.
Deep, deep the greenwood round them waves,
Their abbey, and its close of graves!

But, where the road runs near the stream,
Oft through the trees they catch a glance
Of passing troops in the sun's beam—
Pennon, and plume, and flashing lance!
Forth to the world those soldiers fare,
To life, to cities, and to war!   180

And through the wood, another way,
Faint bugle-notes from far are borne,
Where hunters gather, staghounds bay,
Round some fair forest-lodge at morn.
Gay dames are there, in sylvan green;
Laughter and cries—those notes between!

The banners flashing through the trees
Make their blood dance and chain their eyes;
That bugle-music on the breeze
Arrests them with a charm'd surprise.   190
Banner by turns and bugle woo:
Ye shy recluses, follow too!

O children, what do ye reply?—
"Action and pleasure, will ye roam
Through these secluded dells to cry
And call us?—but too late ye come!
Too late for us your call ye blow,
Whose bent was taken long ago.

"Long since we pace this shadow'd nave;
We watch those yellow tapers shine,   200
Emblems of hope over the grave,
In the high altar's depth divine;
The organ carries to our ear
Its accents of another sphere.

"Fenced early in this cloistral round
Of reverie, of shade, of prayer,
How should we grow in other ground?
How can we flower in foreign air?
—Pass, banners, pass, and bugles, cease;
And leave our desert to its peace!"   210

GEORGE MEREDITH

from **Modern Love**

I

By this he knew she wept with waking eyes:
That, at his hand's light quiver by her head,
The strange low sobs that shook their
   common bed
Were called into her with a sharp surprise,
And strangled mute, like little gaping snakes,
Dreadfully venomous to him. She lay
Stone-still, and the long darkness flowed away
With muffled pulses. Then, as midnight makes
Her giant heart of Memory and Tears
Drink the pale drug of silence, and so beat 10
Sleep's heavy measure, they from head to feet
Were moveless, looking through their dead
   black years,
By vain regret scrawled over the blank wall.
Like sculptured effigies they might be seen
Upon their marriage-tomb, the sword
   between;
Each wishing for the sword that severs all.

XXVI

Love ere he bleeds, an eagle in high skies,
Has earth beneath his wings: from
   reddened eve
He views the rosy dawn. In vain they weave
The fatal web below while far he flies.
But when the arrow strikes him, there's a
   change.
He moves but in the track of his spent pain,
Whose red drops are the links of a harsh
   chain,

---

l. 15. *sword between:* In medieval romances the sword
is often used in this manner to suggest chaste relationships.

Binding him to the ground, with narrow
    range.
A subtle serpent then has Love become.
I had the eagle in my bosom erst: 10
Henceforward with the serpent I am cursed.
I can interpret where the mouth is dumb.
Speak, and I see the side-lie of a truth.
Perchance my heart may pardon you this
    deed:
But be no coward:—you that made Love
    bleed,
You must bear all the venom of his tooth!

XXIX

Am I failing? For no longer can I cast
A glory round about this head of gold.
Glory she wears, but springing from the
    mould;
Not like the consecration of the Past!
Is my soul beggared? Something more than
    earth
I cry for still: I cannot be at peace
In having Love upon a mortal lease.
I cannot take the woman at her worth!
Where is the ancient wealth wherewith
    I clothed
Our human nakedness, and could endow   10
With spiritual splendour a white brow
That else had grinned at me the fact
    I loathed?
A kiss is but a kiss now! and no wave
Of a great flood that whirls me to the sea.
But, as you will! we'll sit contentedly,
And eat our pot of honey on the grave.

XLVII

We saw the swallows gathering in the sky,
And in the osier-isle we heard them noise.
We had not to look back on summer joys,
Or forward to a summer of bright dye:
But in the largeness of the evening earth
Our spirits grew as we went side by side.
The hour became her husband and my bride.
Love, that had robbed us so, thus blessed
    our dearth!

The pilgrims of the year waxed very loud
In multitudinous chatterings, as the flood   10
Full brown came from the West, and like
    pale blood
Expanded to the upper crimson cloud.
Love, that had robbed us of immortal things,
This little moment mercifully gave,
Where I have seen across the twilight wave
The swan sail with her young beneath her
    wings.

XLVIII

Their sense is with their senses all mixed in,
Destroyed by subtleties these women are!
More brain, O Lord, more brain! or we
    shall mar
Utterly this fair garden we might win.
Behold! I looked for peace, and thought it
    near.
Our inmost hearts had opened, each to each.
We drank the pure daylight of honest speech.
Alas! that was the fatal draught, I fear.
For when of my lost Lady came the word,
This woman, O this agony of flesh!   10
Jealous devotion bade her break the mesh,
That I might seek that other like a bird.
I do adore the nobleness! despise
The act! She has gone forth, I know not
    where.
Will the hard world my sentience of her
    share?
I feel the truth; so let the world surmise.

L

Thus piteously Love closed what he begat:
The union of this ever-diverse pair!
These two were rapid falcons in a snare,
Condemned to do the flitting of the bat.
Lovers beneath the singing sky of May,
They wandered once; clear as the dew on
    flowers:
But they fed not on the advancing hours:
Their hearts held cravings for the buried day.
Then each applied to each that fatal knife,

Deep questioning, which probes to endless
    dole.   10
Ah, what a dusty answer gets the soul
When hot for certainties in this our life!—
In tragic hints here see what evermore
Moves dark as yonder midnight ocean's force,
Thundering like ramping hosts of warrior
    horse,
To throw that faint thin line upon the shore!

dANTE GAbRiEL ROSSETTi

Troy Town

Heavenborn Helen, Sparta's queen,
    (*O Troy Town!*)
Had two breasts of heavenly sheen,
The sun and moon of the heart's desire;
All Love's lordship lay between.
    (*O Troy's down,*
    Tall Troy's on fire!)

Helen knelt at Venus' shrine,
    (*O Troy Town!*)
Saying, "A little gift is mine,   10
A little gift for a heart's desire.
Hear me speak and make me a sign!
    (*O Troy's down,*
    Tall Troy's on fire!)

Troy Town: This poem is based on two legends; in
one, Helen, Queen of Sparta, dedicated a goblet
shaped like her own breast to Venus; in another, Eris,
goddess of discord, aroused the jealous rivalry of
Venus, Juno, and Minerva by throwing upon a banquet
table a golden apple inscribed "To the Fairest." Paris,
son of King Priam of Troy, was asked to mediate. He
awarded the apple to Venus and was promised Helen
in return, precipitating the Trojan War.

"Look, I bring thee a carven cup;
    (*O Troy Town!*)
See it here as I hold it up—
Shaped it is to the heart's desire,
Fit to fill when the gods would sup.
    (*O Troy's down,*   20
    Tall Troy's on fire!)

"It was molded like my breast;
    (*O Troy Town!*)
He that sees it may not rest,
Rest at all for his heart's desire.
O give ear to my heart's behest!
    (*O Troy's down,*
    Tall Troy's on fire!)

"See my breast, how like it is;
    (*O Troy Town!*)   30
See it bare for the air to kiss!
Is the cup to thy heart's desire?
O for the breast, O make it his!
    (*O Troy's down,*
    Tall Troy's on fire!)

"Yea, for my bosom here I sue;
    (*O Troy Town!*)
Thou must give it where 'tis due,
Give it there to the heart's desire.
Whom do I give my bosom to?   40
    (*O Troy's down,*
    Tall Troy's on fire!)

"Each twin breast is an apple sweet!
    (*O Troy Town!*)
Once an apple stirred the beat
Of thy heart with the heart's desire;
Say, who brought it then to thy feet?
    (*O Troy's down,*
    Tall Troy's on fire!)

"They that claimed it then were three;   50
    (*O Troy Town!*)
For thy sake two hearts did he
Make forlorn of the heart's desire.
Do for him as he did for thee!
    (*O Troy's down,*
    Tall Troy's on fire!)

"Mine are apples grown to the south,
    (*O Troy Town!*)
Grown to taste in the days of drouth,
Taste and waste to the heart's desire;   60
Mine are apples meet for his mouth!"
    (*O Troy's down,*
    Tall Troy's on fire!)

Venus looked on Helen's gift,
    (*O Troy Town!*)
Looked and smiled with subtle drift,
Saw the work of her heart's desire—
"There thou kneel'st for Love to lift!"
    (*O Troy's down,*
    Tall Troy's on fire!)   70

Venus looked in Helen's face,
    (*O Troy Town!*)
Knew far off an hour and place,
And fire lit from the heart's desire;
Laughed and said, "Thy gift hath grace!"
    (*O Troy's down,*
    Tall Troy's on fire!)

Cupid looked on Helen's breast,
    (*O Troy Town!*)
Saw the heart within its nest,   80
Saw the flame of the heart's desire—
Marked his arrow's burning crest.
    (*O Troy's down,*
    Tall Troy's on fire!)

Cupid took another dart,
    (*O Troy Town!*)
Fledged it for another heart,
Winged the shaft with the heart's desire,
Drew the string and said, "Depart!"
    (*O Troy's down,*   90
    Tall Troy's on fire!)

Paris turned upon his bed,
    (*O Troy Town!*)
Turned upon his bed and said,
Dead at heart with the heart's desire—
"O to clasp her golden head!"
    (*O Troy's down,*
    Tall Troy's on fire!)

Sonnet LXXVIII: Body's Beauty

Of Adam's first wife, Lilith, it is told
(The witch he loved before the gift of Eve)
That, ere the snake's, her sweet tongue could
    deceive,
And her enchanted hair was the first gold.
And still she sits, young while the earth is
    old,
And, subtly of herself contemplative,
Draws men to watch the bright web she can
    weave,
Till heart and body and life are in its hold.
The rose and poppy are her flowers; for where
Is he not found, O Lilith, whom shed scent   10
And soft-shed kisses and soft sleep shall
    snare?
Lo! as that youth's eyes burned at thine, so
    went
Thy spell through him, and left his straight
    neck bent
And round his heart one strangling golden
    hair.

[from *The House of Life*]

Emily dickinson

The Gentian Weaves Her Fringes

The Gentian weaves her fringes—
The Maple's loom is red—
My departing blossoms
        Obviate parade.

A brief, but patient illness—
An hour to prepare,
And one below this morning

Is where the angels are—
It was a short procession,
The Bobolink was there—   10
An aged Bee addressed us—
And then we knelt in prayer—
We trust that she was willing—
We ask that we may be.
Summer—Sister—Seraph!
Let us go with thee!

In the name of the Bee—
And of the Butterfly—
And of the Breeze—Amen!

I Never Lost As Much But Twice

I never lost as much but twice,
And that was in the sod.
Twice have I stood a beggar
Before the door of God!

Angels—twice descending
Reimbursed my store—
Burglar! Banker—Father!
I am poor once more!

I Taste a Liquor Never Brewed

I taste a liquor never brewed—
From Tankards scooped in Pearl—
Not all the Vats upon the Rhine
Yield such an Alcohol!

Inebriate of Air—am I—
And Debauchee of Dew—
Reeling—thro endless summer days—
From inns of Molten Blue—

When "Landlords" turn the drunken Bee
Out of the Foxglove's door—   10

When Butterflies—renounce their "drams"—
I shall but drink the more!

Till Seraphs swing their snowy Hats—
And Saints—to windows run—
To see the little Tippler
Leaning against the—Sun—

I Reason, Earth Is Short

I reason, Earth is short—
And Anguish—absolute—
And many hurt,
But, what of that?

I reason, we could die—
The best Vitality
Cannot excel Decay,
But, what of that?

I reason, that in Heaven—
Somehow, it will be even—   10
Some new Equation, given—
But, what of that?

After Great Pain, a Formal Feeling Comes

After great pain, a formal feeling comes—
The Nerves sit ceremonious, like Tombs—
The stiff Heart questions was it He, that bore,
And Yesterday, or Centuries before?

The Feet, mechanical, go round—
Of Ground, or Air, or Ought—
A Wooden way
Regardless grown,
A Quartz contentment, like a stone—

This is the Hour of Lead—   10
Remembered, if outlived,

As Freezing persons, recollect the Snow—
First—Chill—then Stupor—then the
    letting go—

I Heard a Fly Buzz—When I Died

I heard a Fly buzz—when I died—
The Stillness in the Room
Was like the Stillness in the Air—
Between the Heaves of Storm—

The Eyes around—had wrung them dry—
And Breaths were gathering firm
For that last Onset—when the King
Be witnessed—in the Room—

I willed my Keepsakes—Signed away
What portion of me be   10
Assignable—and then it was
There interposed a Fly—

With Blue—uncertain stumbling Buzz—
Between the light—and me—
And then the Windows failed—and then
I could not see to see—

I Like to See It Lap the Miles

I like to see it lap the Miles—
And lick the Valleys up—
And stop to feed itself at Tanks—
And then—prodigious step

Around a Pile of Mountains—
And supercilious peer
In Shanties—by the sides of Roads—
And then a Quarry pare

To fit its Ribs
And crawl between   10

Complaining all the while
In horrid—hooting stanza—
Then chase itself down Hill—

And neigh like Boanerges—
Then—punctual as a Star
Stop—docile and omnipotent
At its own stable door—

l. 14. *Boanerges:* in Mark 3:17, the name given by
Christ to James and John; literally, "sons of thunder."

Because I Could Not Stop for Death

Because I could not stop for Death—
He kindly stopped for me—
The Carriage held but just Ourselves—
And Immortality.

We slowly drove—He knew no haste
And I had put away
My labor and my leisure too,
For His Civility—

We passed the School, where Children strove
At Recess—in the Ring—   10
We passed the Fields of Gazing Grain—
We passed the Setting Sun—

Or rather—He passed Us—
The Dews drew quivering and chill—
For only Gossamer, my Gown—
My Tippet—only Tulle—

We paused before a House that seemed
A Swelling of the Ground—
The Roof was scarcely visible—
The Cornice—in the Ground—   20

Since then—'tis Centuries—and yet
Feels shorter than the Day
I first surmised the Horses' Heads
Were toward Eternity—

l. 16. *Tippet . . . Tulle:* a scarf of thin material.

A Narrow Fellow in the Grass

A narrow Fellow in the Grass
Occasionally rides—
You may have met Him—did you not—
His notice sudden is—

The Grass divides as with a Comb—
A spotted shaft is seen—
And then it closes at your feet
And opens further on—

He likes a Boggy Acre
A Floor too cool for Corn—   10
Yet when a Boy, and Barefoot—
I more than once at Noon

Have passed, I thought, a Whip lash
Unbraiding in the Sun
When stooping to secure it
It wrinkled, and was gone—

Several of Nature's People
I know, and they know me—
I feel for them a transport
Of cordiality—   20

But never met this Fellow
Attended, or alone
Without a tighter breathing
And Zero at the Bone—

THOMAS HARDY

The Subalterns

I

"Poor wanderer," said the leaden sky,
    "I fain would lighten thee,
But there are laws in force on high
    Which say it must not be."

II

—"I would not freeze thee, shorn one," cried
    The North, "knew I but how
To warm my breath, to slack my stride;
    But I am ruled as thou."

III

—"To-morrow I attack thee, wight,"
    Said Sickness.   "Yet I swear   10
I bear thy little ark no spite,
    But am bid enter there."

IV

—"Come hither, Son," I heard Death say;
    "I did not will a grave
Should end thy pilgrimage to-day,
    But I, too, am a slave!"

V

We smiled upon each other then,
    And life to me had less
Of that fell look it wore ere when
    They owned their passiveness.   20

The Ruined Maid

"O 'Melia, my dear, this does everything
    crown!
Who could have supposed I should meet you
    in Town?
And whence such fair garments, such
    prosperi—ty?"—
"O didn't you know I'd been ruined?" said
    she.

—"You left us in tatters, without shoes or
    socks,
Tired of digging potatoes, and spudding up
    docks;
And now you've gay bracelets and bright
    feathers three!"—
"Yes: that's how we dress when we're
    ruined," said she.

—"At home in the barton you said 'thee'
    and 'thou',
And 'thik oon', and 'theäs oon', and
    't 'other'; but now   10
Your talking quite fits 'ee for high
    compa—ny!"—
"Some polish is gained with one's ruin,"
    said she.

—"Your hands were like paws then, your
    face blue and bleak
But now I'm bewitched by your delicate
    cheek,
And your little gloves fit as on any la—dy!"—
"We never do work when we're ruined,"
    says she.

—"You used to call home-life a hag-ridden
    dream,
And you'd sigh, and you'd sock; but at
    present you seem

To know not of megrims or melancho—ly!"—
"True. One's pretty lively when ruined,"
    said she.   20

—"I wish I had feathers, a fine sweeping
    gown,
And a delicate face, and could strut about
    Town!"—
"My dear—a raw country girl, such as you be,
Cannot quite expect that. You ain't ruined,"
    said she.

---

l. 19. *megrims:* low spirits.

l. 6. *spudding up docks:* digging out dockweed.
l. 9. *barton:* farmyard.
l. 10. *'thik oon' . . . 'theäs oon':* this one . . . that one.
l. 18. *sock:* sigh aloud.

By Her Aunt's Grave

"Sixpence a week," says the girl to her lover,
"Aunt used to bring me, for she could confide
In me alone, she vowed. It was to cover
The cost of her headstone when she died.
And that was a year ago last June;
I've not yet fixed it. But I must soon."

"And where is the money now, my dear?"
"O, snug in my purse. . . . Aunt was *so* slow
In saving it—eighty weeks, or near." . . .
"Let's spend it," he hints. "For she won't
    know.   10
There's a dance tonight at the *Load of Hay*."
She passively nods. And they go that way.

---

l. 11. *Load of Hay:* a tavern.

The Oxen

Christmas Eve, and twelve of the clock.
   'Now they are all on their knees,'
An elder said as we sat in a flock
   By the embers in hearthside ease.

We pictured the meek mild creatures where
    They dwelt in their strawy pen,
Nor did it occur to one of us there
    To doubt they were kneeling then.

So fair a fancy few would weave
    In these years! Yet, I feel,   10
If someone said on Christmas Eve,
    'Come; see the oxen kneel,

'In the lonely barton by yonder coomb
    Our childhood used to know,'
I should go with him in the gloom,
    Hoping it might be so.

---

l. 13. *coomb:* a valley closed at one end.

GERARD MANLEY HOPKINS

The Windhover

To Christ our Lord

I caught this morning morning's minion, king-
    dom of daylight's dauphin, dapple-dawn-
    drawn Falcon, in his riding
    Of the rolling level underneath him steady
    air, and striding
High there, how he rung upon the rein of a
    wimpling wing
In his ecstasy! then off, off forth on swing,
    As a skate's heel sweeps smooth on a bow-
    bend: the hurl and gliding

Windhover: a small European falcon noted for its habit
of hovering in air against the wind.
l. 1. *minion:* favorite.
l. 2. *dauphin:* prince, eldest son and heir of a king.
l. 4. *wimpling:* rippling.
l. 6. *bow-bend:* wide turn.

Rebuffed the big wind. My heart in hiding
Stirred for a bird,—the achieve of, the
    mastery of the thing!

Brute beauty and valour and act, oh, air,
    pride, plume here
Buckle! AND the fire that breaks from thee
    then, a billion   10
Times told lovelier, more dangerous, O my
    chevalier!

    No wonder of it: shéer plód makes plough
    down sillion
Shine, and blue-bleak embers, ah my dear,
    Fall, gall themselves, and gash gold-
    vermilion.

---

l. 8. *achieve:* achievement.
l. 11. *told:* counted.
l. 11. *chevalier:* knight.
l. 12. *plód:* plodding.
l. 12. *sillion:* space between furrows in a plowed field.
l. 14. *gall:* wound.

Spring and Fall:

to a young child

Márgarét, are you gríeving
Over Goldengrove unleaving?
Léaves líke the things of man, you
With your fresh thoughts care for, can you?
Áh! ás the heart grows older
It will come to such sights colder
By and by, nor spare a sigh
Though worlds of wanwood leafmeal lie;
And yet you wíll weep and know why.
Now no matter, child, the name: 10
Sórrow's spríngs áre the same.
Nor mouth had, no nor mind, expressed

---

l. 8. *wanwood leafmeal:* woods that are dark and sorrowful, littered with leaves broken or ground into a
coarse dust.

What heart heard of, ghost guessed:
It ís the blight man was born for,
It is Margaret you mourn for.

I Wake and Feel the Fell of Dark, Not Day

I wake and feel the fell of dark, not day.
What hours, O what black hoùrs we have
    spent
This night! what sights you, heart, saw; ways
    you went!
And more must, in yet longer light's delay.
  With witness I speak this. But where I say
Hours I mean years, mean life. And my
    lament
Is cries countless, cries like dead letters sent
To dearest him that lives alas! away.

  I am gall, I am heartburn. God's most deep
    decree
Bitter would have me taste: my taste was
    me;   10
Bones built in me, flesh filled, blood brimmed
    the curse.
  Selfyeast of spirit a dull dough sours. I see
The lost are like this, and their scourge to be
As I am mine, their sweating selves; but
    worse.

My Own Heart Let Me More Have Pity On

My own heart let me more have pity on; let
Me live to my sad self hereafter kind,
Charitable; not live this tormented mind
With this tormented mind tormenting yet.
  I cast for comfort I can no more get
By groping round my comfortless, than blind
Eyes in their dark can day or thirst can find
Thirst's all-in-all in all a world of wet.

Soul, self; come, poor Jackself, I do advise
You, jaded, let be; call off thoughts awhile   10
Elsewhere; leave comfort root-room; let joy
    size
At God knows when to God knows what;
    whose smile
's not wrung, see you; unforeseen times
    rather—as skies
Betweenpie mountains—lights a lovely mile.

william butleR yeats

The Cap and Bells

The jester walked in the garden:
The garden had fallen still;
He bade his soul rise upward
And stand on her window-sill.

It rose in a straight blue garment,
When owls began to call:
It had grown wise-tongued by thinking
Of a quiet and light footfall;

But the young queen would not listen;
She rose in her pale night-gown;   10
She drew in the heavy casement
And pushed the latches down.

He bade his heart go to her,
When the owls called out no more;
In a red and quivering garment
It sang to her through the door.

It had grown sweet-tongued by dreaming
Of a flutter of flower-like hair;
But she took up her fan from the table
And waved it off on the air.   20

'I have cap and bells,' he pondered,
'I will send them to her and die';
And when the morning whitened
He left them where she went by.

She laid them upon her bosom,
Under a cloud of her hair,
And her red lips sang them a love-song
Till stars grew out of the air.

She opened her door and her window,
And the heart and the soul came through,   30
To her right hand came the red one,
To her left hand came the blue.

They set up a noise like crickets,
A chattering wise and sweet,
And her hair was a folded flower
And the quiet of love in her feet.

The Second Coming

Turning and turning in the widening gyre
The falcon cannot hear the falconer;
Things fall apart; the centre cannot hold;
Mere anarchy is loosed upon the world,
The blood-dimmed tide is loosed, and
   everywhere
The ceremony of innocence is drowned;
The best lack all conviction, while the worst
Are full of passionate intensity.

Surely some revelation is at hand;
Surely the Second Coming is at hand.   10
The Second Coming! Hardly are those words
   out
When a vast image out of *Spiritus Mundi*
Troubles my sight: somewhere in sands of
   the desert
A shape with lion body and the head of a man,

A gaze blank and pitiless as the sun,
Is moving its slow thighs, while all about it
Reel shadows of the indignant desert birds.
The darkness drops again; but now I know
That twenty centuries of stony sleep
Were vexed to nightmare by a rocking
   cradle,   20
And what rough beast, its hour come round
   at last,
Slouches towards Bethlehem to be born?

Adam's Curse

We sat together at one summer's end,
That beautiful mild woman, your close friend,
And you and I, and talked of poetry.
I said: 'A line will take us hours maybe;
Yet if it does not seem a moment's thought,
Our stitching and unstitching has been
   naught.
Better go down upon your marrow-bones
And scrub a kitchen pavement, or break
   stones
Like an old pauper, in all kinds of weather;
For to articulate sweet sounds together   10
Is to work harder than all these, and yet
Be thought an idler by the noisy set
Of bankers, schoolmasters, and clergymen
The martyrs call the world.'

                        And thereupon
That beautiful mild woman for whose sake
There's many a one shall find out all
   heartache
On finding that her voice is sweet and low
Replied: 'To be born woman is to know—
Although they do not talk of it at school—   20
That we must labour to be beautiful.'

I said: 'It's certain there is no fine thing
Since Adam's fall but needs much labouring.

I. 1. *gyre:* literally, the ever-widening spiral of the falcon's flight.
I. 12. *Spiritus Mundi:* World Spirit.

I. 2. *woman:* Maud Gonne, an actress with whom Yeats
was hopelessly in love. See also ''Among School Children'' and ''A Bronze Head.''

There have been lovers who thought love
   should be
So much compounded of high courtesy
That they would sigh and quote with learned
   looks
Precedents out of beautiful old books;
Yet now it seems an idle trade enough.'

We sat grown quiet at the name of love;
We saw the last embers of daylight die,   30
And in the trembling blue-green of the sky
A moon, worn as if it had been a shell
Washed by time's waters as they rose and fell
About the stars and broke in days and years.

I had a thought for no one's but your ears:
That you were beautiful, and that I strove
To love you in the old high way of love;
That it had all seemed happy, and yet we'd
   grown
As weary-hearted as that hollow moon.

Among School Children

I

I walk through the long schoolroom
   questioning;
A kind old nun in a white hood replies;
The children learn to cipher and to sing,
To study reading-books and history,
To cut and sew, be neat in everything
In the best modern way—the children's eyes
In momentary wonder stare upon
A sixty-year-old smiling public man.

II

I dream of a Ledaean body, bent
Above a sinking fire, a tale that she   10

Told of a harsh reproof, or trivial event
That changed some childish day to tragedy—
Told, and it seemed that our two natures blent
Into a sphere from youthful sympathy,
Or else, to alter Plato's parable,
Into the yolk and white of the one shell.

III

And thinking of that fit of grief or rage
I look upon one child or t'other there
And wonder if she stood so at that age—
For even daughters of the swan can share   20
Something of every paddler's heritage—
And had that colour upon cheek or hair,
And thereupon my heart is driven wild:
She stands before me as a living child.

IV

Her present image floats into the mind—
Did Quattrocento finger fashion it
Hollow of cheek as though it drank the wind
And took a mess of shadows for its meat?
And I though never of Ledaean kind
Had pretty plumage once—enough of that,   30
Better to smile on all that smile, and show
There is a comfortable kind of old scarecrow.

V

What youthful mother, a shape upon her lap
Honey of generation had betrayed,
And that must sleep, shriek, struggle to
   escape
As recollection or the drug decide,

---

l. 15. *Plato's parable:* In the *Symposium* love is explained by the parable that human beings were once spherical and autonomous but were later divided into halves, each half longing to be reunited with its original half.
l. 26. *Quattrocento:* fifteenth-century Italian painters, especially Botticelli (1444?–1510) and his "Birth of Venus."
l. 34. *Honey of generation:* variously, the pleasure a soul experiences in coming into being; the drug that destroys the memory of "prenatal freedom"; sexual pleasure of the mother in conceiving the child.

---

l. 9. *Ledaean:* Leda, according to Greek mythology, gave birth to Helen (of Troy) through her union with Zeus disguised as a swan. Yeats also refers to the woman he loved, Maud Gonne. See also "Adam's Curse" and "A Bronze Head."

Would think her son, did she but see that
  shape
With sixty or more winters on its head,
A compensation for the pang of his birth,
Or the uncertainty of his setting forth?   40

VI

Plato thought nature but a spume that plays
Upon a ghostly paradigm of things;
Solider Aristotle played the taws
Upon the bottom of a king of kings;
World-famous golden-thighed Pythagoras
Fingered upon a fiddle-stick or strings
What a star sang and careless Muses heard:
Old clothes upon old sticks to scare a bird.

VII

Both nuns and mothers worship images,
But those the candles light are not as those   50
That animate a mother's reveries,
But keep a marble or a bronze repose.
And yet they too break hearts—O Presences
That passion, piety or affection knows,
And that all heavenly glory symbolise—
O self-born mockers of man's enterprise;

VIII

Labour is blossoming or dancing where
The body is not bruised to pleasure soul,
Nor beauty born out of its own despair,
Nor blear-eyed wisdom out of midnight oil. 60
O chestnut-tree, great-rooted blossomer,

---

ll. 41–42. *Plato ... things:* For Plato nature is a copy of
an ideal reality lying beyond the immediate world.
l. 43. *Solider Aristotle ... taws:* Aristotle believed that
form and matter were not wholly separate; also, he was
a tutor of Alexander the Great ("a king of kings") and
was supposed to have thrashed his student with a
leather strap (taws).
l. 45. *Pythagoras:* Greek philosopher, astronomer, and
religious teacher (born c. 580 B.C.), who discovered
the numerical relation between the length of strings
and the notes they produced and used this relation as
the primordial principle to explain the nature of the
world.

Are you the leaf, the blossom or the bole?
O body swayed to music, O brightening
  glance,
How can we know the dancer from the
  dance?

Crazy Jane Talks with the Bishop

I met the Bishop on the road
And much said he and I.
'Those breasts are flat and fallen now,
Those veins must soon be dry;
Live in a heavenly mansion,
Not in some foul sty.'

'Fair and foul are near of kin,
And fair needs foul,' I cried.
'My friends are gone, but that's a truth
Nor grave nor bed denied,   10
Learned in bodily lowliness
And in the heart's pride.

'A woman can be proud and stiff
When on love intent;
But Love has pitched his mansion in
The place of excrement;
For nothing can be sole or whole
That has not been rent.'

Lapis Lazuli

(*For Harry Clifton*)

I have heard that hysterical women say
They are sick of the palette and fiddle-bow,
Of poets that are always gay,
For everybody knows or else should know
That if nothing drastic is done
Aeroplane and Zeppelin will come out,

Pitch like King Billy bomb-balls in
Until the town lie beaten flat.

All perform their tragic play,
There struts Hamlet, there is Lear,   10
That's Ophelia, that Cordelia;
Yet they, should the last scene be there,
The great stage curtain about to drop,
If worthy their prominent part in the play,
Do not break up their lines to weep.
They know that Hamlet and Lear are gay;
Gaiety transfiguring all that dread.
All men have aimed at, found and lost;
Black out; Heaven blazing into the head:
Tragedy wrought to its uttermost.   20
Though Hamlet rambles and Lear rages,
And all the drop-scenes drop at once
Upon a hundred thousand stages,
It cannot grow by an inch or an ounce.

On their own feet they came, or on
    shipboard,
Camel-back, horse-back, ass-back, mule-back,
Old civilisations put to the sword.
Then they and their wisdom went to rack:
No handiwork of Callimachus,
Who handled marble as if it were bronze,   30
Made draperies that seemed to rise
When sea-wind swept the corner, stands;
His long lamp-chimney shaped like the stem
Of a slender palm, stood but a day;
All things fall and are built again,
And those that build them again are gay.

Two Chinamen, behind them a third,
Are carved in lapis lazuli,
Over them flies a long-legged bird,
A symbol of longevity;   40

The third, doubtless a serving-man,
Carries a musical instrument.

Every discoloration of the stone,
Every accidental crack or dent,
Seems a water-course or an avalanche,
Or lofty slope where it still snows
Though doubtless plum or cherry-branch
Sweetens the little half-way house
Those Chinamen climb towards, and I
Delight to imagine them seated there;   50
There, on the mountain and the sky,
On all the tragic scene they stare.
One asks for mournful melodies;
Accomplished fingers begin to play.
Their eyes mid many wrinkles, their eyes,
Their ancient, glittering eyes, are gay.

A Bronze Head

Here at right of the entrance this bronze head,
Human, superhuman, a bird's round eye,
Everything else withered and mummy-dead.
What great tomb-haunter sweeps the distant
    sky
(Something may linger there though all else
die;)
And finds there nothing to make its terror less
Hysterica passio of its own emptiness?

No dark tomb-haunter once; her form all full
As though with magnanimity of light,
Yet a most gentle woman; who can tell   10
Which of her forms has shown her substance
    right?
Or maybe substance can be composite,
Profound McTaggart thought so, and in a
    breath

l. 7. *King Billy:* King William III, who subdued Ireland
in the nineteenth century.
ll. 10–11. *Hamlet . . . Lear:* title characters of two of
Shakespeare's tragedies; Ophelia appears in *Hamlet,*
Cordelia in *King Lear.*
l. 29. *Callimachus:* Athenian sculptor (fifth century B.C.),
none of whose works survive, though they were renowned for polished technical skill.

l. 1. *head:* a statue of Maud Gonne.
l. 7. *Hysterica passio:* hysteria. See *King Lear* (II, ii).
l. 13. *McTaggart:* John McT. E. McTaggart (1866–1925),
philosopher and atheist, who believed in immortality,
arguing that substance was divisible.

A mouthful held the extreme of life and
    death.

But even at the starting-post, all sleek and
    new,
I saw the wildness in her and I thought
A vision of terror that it must live through
Had shattered her soul. Propinquity had
    brought
Imagination to that pitch where it casts out
All that is not itself: I had grown wild   20
And wandered murmuring everywhere,
    'My child, my child!'

Or else I thought her supernatural;
As though a sterner eye looked through her
    eye
On this foul world in its decline and fall;
On gangling stocks grown great, great stocks
    run dry,
Ancestral pearls all pitched into a sty,
Heroic reverie mocked by clown and knave,
And wondered what was left for massacre to
    save.

EdwiN ArliNqToN RobiNsoN

The Man Against the Sky

Between me and the sunset, like a dome
Against the glory of a world on fire,
Now burned a sudden hill,
Bleak, round, and high, by flame-lit height
    made higher,
With nothing on it for the flame to kill
Save one who moved and was alone up there
To loom before the chaos and the glare
As if he were the last god going home
Unto his last desire.

Dark, marvelous, and inscrutable he moved
    on   10
Till down the fiery distance he was gone,
Like one of those eternal, remote things
That range across a man's imaginings
When a sure music fills him and he knows
What he may say thereafter to few men,—
The touch of ages having wrought
An echo and a glimpse of what he thought
A phantom or a legend until then;
For whether lighted over ways that save,
Or lured from all repose,   20
If he go on too far to find a grave,
Mostly alone he goes.

Even he, who stood where I had found him,
On high with fire all round him,
Who moved along the molten west,
And over the round hill's crest
That seemed half ready with him to go down,
Flame-bitten and flame-cleft,
As if there were to be no last thing left
Of a nameless unimaginable town,—   30
Even he who climbed and vanished may have
    taken
Down to the perils of a depth not known,
From death defended though by men
    forsaken,
The bread that every man must eat alone;
He may have walked while others hardly
    dared
Look on to see him stand where many fell;
And upward out of that, as out of hell,
He may have sung and striven
To mount where more of him shall yet be
    given,
Bereft of all retreat,   40
To sevenfold heat,—
As on a day when three in Dura shared
The furnace, and were spared
For glory by that king of Babylon

---

l. 42. *three in Dura:* In Daniel 3–4, King Nebuchadnezzar condemned to death in a "fiery furnace" three
Jews who refused to worship Babylonion idols; they
survived and Nebuchadnezzar was punished by God,
who "Covered him with long feathers, like a bird."

Who made himself so great that God, who
    heard,
Covered him with long feathers, like a bird.

Again, he may have gone down easily,
By comfortable altitudes, and found,
As always, underneath him solid ground
Whereon to be sufficient and to stand   50
Possessed already of the promised land,
Far stretched and fair to see:
A good sight, verily,
And one to make the eyes of her who bore
    him
Shine glad with hidden tears.
Why question of his ease of who before him,
In one place or another where they left
Their names as far behind them as their
    bones,
And yet by dint of slaughter toil and theft,
And shrewdly sharpened stones,   60
Carved hard the way for his ascendency
Through deserts of lost years?
Why trouble him now who sees and hears
No more than what his innocence requires,
And therefore to no other height aspires
Than one at which he neither quails nor
    tires?
He may do more by seeing what he sees
Than others eager for iniquities;
He may, by seeing all things for the best,
Incite futurity to do the rest.   70

Or with an even likelihood,
He may have met with atrabilious eyes
The fires of time on equal terms and passed
Indifferently down, until at last
His only kind of grandeur would have been,
Apparently, in being seen.
He may have had for evil or for good
No argument; he may have had no care
For what without himself went anywhere
To failure or to glory, and least of all   80
For such a stale, flamboyant miracle;
He may have been the prophet of an art
Immovable to old idolatries;
He may have been a player without a part,

Annoyed that even the sun should have the
    skies
For such a flaming way to advertise;
He may have been a painter sick at heart
With Nature's toiling for a new surprise;
He may have been a cynic, who now, for all
Of anything divine that his effete   90
Negation may have tasted,
Saw truth in his own image, rather small,
Forbore to fever the ephemeral,
Found any barren height a good retreat
From any swarming street,
And in the sun saw power superbly wasted:
And when the primitive old-fashioned stars
Came out again to shine on joys and wars
More primitive, and all arrayed for doom,
He may have proved a world a sorry thing 100
In his imagining,
And life a lighted highway to the tomb.

Or, mounting with infirm unsearching tread,
His hopes to chaos led,
He may have stumbled up there from
    the past,
And with an aching strangeness viewed
    the last
Abysmal conflagration of his dreams,—
A flame where nothing seems
To burn but flame itself, by nothing fed;
And while it all went out,   110
Not even the faint anodyne of doubt
May then have eased a painful going down
From pictured heights of power and lost
    renown,
Revealed at length to his outlived endeavor
Remote and unapproachable forever;
And at his heart there may have gnawed
Sick memories of a dead faith foiled and
    flawed
And long dishonored by the living death
Assigned alike by chance
To brutes and hierophants;   120
And anguish fallen on those he loved around
    him
May once have dealt the last blow to
    confound him,
And so have left him as death leaves a child,

Who see it all too near;
And he who knows no young way to forget
May struggle to the tomb unreconciled.
Whatever suns may rise or set
There may be nothing kinder for him here
Than shafts and agonies;
And under these   130
He may cry out and stay on horribly;
Or, seeing in death too small a thing to fear,
He may go forward like a stoic Roman
Where pangs and terrors in his pathway lie,—
Or, seizing the swift logic of a woman,
Curse God and die.

Or maybe there, like many another one
Who might have stood aloft and looked ahead,
Black-drawn against wild red,
He may have built, unawed by fiery gules   140
That in him no commotion stirred,
A living reason out of molecules
Why molecules occurred,
And one for smiling when he might have
   sighed
Had he seen far enough,
And in the same inevitable stuff
Discovered an odd reason too for pride
In being what he must have been by laws
Infrangible and for no kind of cause.
Deterred by no confusion or surprise   150
He may have seen with his mechanic eyes
A world without a meaning, and had room,
Alone amid magnificence and doom,
To build himself an airy monument
That should, or fail him in his vague intent,
Outlast an accidental universe—
To call it nothing worse—
Or, by the burrowing guile
Of Time disintegrated and effaced,
Like once-remembered mighty trees go
   down   160
To ruin, of which by man may now be traced
No part sufficient even to be rotten,
And in the book of things that are forgotten
Is entered as a thing not quite worth while.

I. 136. Curse . . . die: In Job 2:9, Job's wife advised him
in his affliction to curse God.

He may have been so great
That satraps would have shivered at his
   frown,
And all he prized alive may rule a state
No larger than a grave that holds a clown;
He may have been a master of his fate,
And of his atoms,—ready as another   170
In his emergence to exonerate
His father and his mother;
He may have been a captain of a host,
Self-eloquent and ripe for prodigies,
Doomed here to swell by dangerous degrees,
And then give up the ghost.
Nahum's great grasshoppers were such as
   these,
Sun-scattered and soon lost.

Whatever the dark road he may have taken,
This man who stood on high   180
And faced alone the sky,
Whatever drove or lured or guided him,—
A vision answering a faith unshaken,
An easy trust assumed of easy trials,
A sick negation born of weak denials,
A crazed abhorrence of an old condition,
A blind attendance on a brief ambition,—
Whatever stayed him or derided him,
His way was even as ours;
And we, with all our wounds and all our
   powers,   190
Must each await alone at his own height
Another darkness or another light;
And there, of our poor self dominion reft,
If inference and reason shun
Hell, Heaven, and Oblivion,
May thwarted will (perforce precarious,
But for our conservation better thus)
Have no misgiving left
Of doing yet what here we leave undone?
Or if unto the last of these we cleave,   200
Believing or protesting we believe
In such an idle and ephemeral

I. 166. satraps: petty tyrants.
I. 177. Nahum's great grasshoppers: In Nahum 3:17, the
prophet, condemning the corruption of Nineveh, calls
her captains "great grasshoppers . . . when the sun
arises they flee away."

Florescence of the diabolical,—
If, robbed of two fond old enormities,
Our being had no onward auguries,
What then were this great love of ours to say
For launching other lives to voyage again
A little farther into time and pain,
A little faster in a futile chase
For a kingdom and a power and a Race   210
That would have still in sight
A manifest end of ashes and eternal night?
Is this the music of the toys we shake
So loud,—as if there might be no mistake
Somewhere in our indomitable will?
Are we no greater than the noise we make
Along one blind atomic pilgrimage
Whereon by crass chance billeted we go
Because our brains and bones and cartilage
Will have it so?   220
If this we say, then let us all be still
About our share in it, and live and die
More quietly thereby.

Where was he going, this man against the sky?
You know not, nor do I.
But this we know, if we know anything:
That we may laugh and fight and sing
And of our transience here make offering
To an orient Word that will not be erased,
Or, save in incommunicable gleams   230
Too permanent for dreams,
Be found or known.
No tonic and ambitious irritant
Of increase or of want
Has made an otherwise insensate waste
Of ages overthrown
A ruthless, veiled, implacable foretaste
Of other ages that are still to be
Depleted and rewarded variously
Because a few, by fate's economy,   240
Shall seem to move the world the way it goes;
No soft evangel of equality,
Safe-cradled in a communal repose
That huddles into death and may at last
Be covered well with equatorial snows—
And all for what, the devil only knows—
Will aggregate an inkling to confirm
The credit of a sage or of a worm,

Or tell us why one man in five
Should have a care to stay alive   250
While in his heart he feels no violence
Laid on his humor and intelligence
When infant Science makes a pleasant face
And waves again that hollow toy, the Race;
No planetary trap where souls are wrought
For nothing but the sake of being caught
And sent again to nothing will attune
Itself to any key of any reason
Why man should hunger through another
    season
To find out why 'twere better late than
    soon   260
To go away and let the sun and moon
And all the silly stars illuminate
A place for creeping things,
And those that root and trumpet and have
    wings,
And herd and ruminate,
Or dive and flash and poise in rivers and seas,
Or by their loyal tails in lofty trees
Hang screeching lewd victorious derision
Of man's immortal vision.

Shall we, because Eternity records   270
Too vast an answer for the time-born words
We spell, whereof so many are dead that once
In our capricious lexicons
Were so alive and final, hear no more
The Word itself, the living word
That none alive has ever heard
Or ever spelt,
And few have ever felt
Without the fears and old surrenderings
And terrors that began   280
When Death let fall a feather from his wings
And humbled the first man?
Because the weight of our humility,
Wherefrom we gain
A little wisdom and much pain,
Falls here too sore and there too tedious,
Are we in anguish or complacency,
Not looking far enough ahead
To see by what mad couriers we are led
Along the roads of the ridiculous,   290
To pity ourselves and laugh at faith

And while we curse life bear it?
And if we see the soul's dead end in death,
Are we to fear it?
What folly is here that has not yet a name
Unless we say outright that we are liars?
What have we seen beyond our sunset fires
That lights again the way by which we came?
Why pay we such a price, and one we give
So clamoringly, for each racked empty day **300**
That leads one more last human hope away,
As quiet fiends would lead past our crazed
   eyes
Our children to an unseen sacrifice?
If after all that we have lived and thought,
All comes to Nought,—
If there be nothing after Now,
And we be nothing anyhow,
And we know that,—why live?
'Twere sure but weaklings' vain distress
To suffer dungeons where so many doors   **310**
Will open on the cold eternal shores
That look sheer down
To the dark tideless floods of Nothingness
Where all who know may drown.

The Clerks

I did not think that I should find them there
When I came back again; but there they
   stood,
As in the days they dreamed of when young
   blood
Was in their cheeks and women called them
   fair.
Be sure they met me with ancient air,—
And yes, there was a shop-worn brotherhood
About them; but the men were just as good,
And just as human as they ever were.

And you that ache so much to be sublime,
And you that feed yourselves with your
   descent,   **10**
What comes of all your visions and your
   fears?

Poets and kings are but the clerks of Time,
Tiering the same dull webs of discontent
Clipping the same sad alnage of the years.

The Sheaves

Where long the shadows of the wind had
   rolled,
Green wheat was yielding to the change
   assigned;
And as by some vast magic undivined
The world was turning slowly into gold.
Like nothing that was ever bought or sold
It waited there, the body and the mind;
And with a mighty meaning of a kind
That tells the more the more it is not told.

So in a land where all days are not fair,
Fair days went on till on another day   **10**
A thousand golden sheaves were lying there,
Shining and still, but not for long to stay—
As if a thousand girls with golden hair
Might rise from where they slept and go
   away.

ROBERT FROST

'Out, Out—'

The buzz saw snarled and rattled in the yard
And made dust and dropped stove-length
   sticks of wood,
Sweet-scented stuff when the breeze drew
   across it.

'*Out, Out*—': See Shakespeare's *Macbeth* (V, v).

And from there those that lifted eyes could
    count
Five mountain ranges one behind the other
Under the sunset far into Vermont.
And the saw snarled and rattled, snarled and
    rattled,
As it ran light, or had to bear a load.
And nothing happened: day was all but done.
Call it a day, I wish they might have said   10
To please the boy by giving him the half hour
That a boy counts so much when saved from
    work.
His sister stood beside them in her apron
To tell them 'Supper.' At the word, the saw,
As if to prove saws knew what supper meant,
Leaped out at the boy's hand, or seemed to
    leap—
He must have given the hand. However it was,
Neither refused the meeting. But the hand!
The boy's first outcry was a rueful laugh,
As he swung toward them holding up the
    hand   20
Half in appeal, but half as if to keep
The life from spilling. Then the boy saw all—
Since he was old enough to know, big boy
Doing a man's work, though a child at heart—
He saw all spoiled. 'Don't let him cut my
    hand off—
The doctor, when he comes. Don't let him,
    sister!'
So. But the hand was gone already.
The doctor put him in the dark of ether.
He lay and puffed his lips out with his
    breath.
And then—the watcher at his pulse took
    fright.   30
No one believed. They listened at his heart.
Little—less—nothing!—and that ended it.
No more to build on there. And they, since
    they
Were not the one dead, turned to their affairs.

To Earthward

Love at the lips was touch
As sweet as I could bear;
And once that seemed too much;
I lived on air

That crossed me from sweet things,
The flow of—was it musk
From hidden grapevine springs
Down hill at dusk?

I had the swirl and ache
From sprays of honeysuckle   10
That when they're gathered shake
Dew on the knuckle.

I craved strong sweets, but those
Seemed strong when I was young;
The petal of the rose
It was that stung.

Now no joy but lacks salt
That is not dashed with pain
And weariness and fault;
I crave the stain   20

Of tears, the aftermark
Of almost too much love,
The sweet of bitter bark
And burning clove.

When stiff and sore scarred
I take away my hand
From leaning on it hard
In grass and sand,

The hurt is not enough:
I long for weight and strength   30
To feel the earth as rough
To all my length.

Acquainted with the Night

I have been one acquainted with the night.
I have walked out in rain—and back in rain.
I have outwalked the furthest city light.

I have looked down the saddest city lane.
I have passed by the watchman on his beat
And dropped my eyes, unwilling to explain.

I have stood still and stopped the sound of
    feet
When far away an interrupted cry
Came over houses from another street,

But not to call me back or say good-bye;   10
And further still at an unearthly height,
One luminary clock against the sky

Proclaimed the time was neither wrong nor
    right.
I have been one acquainted with the night.

The Draft Horse

With a lantern that wouldn't burn
In too frail a buggy we drove
Behind too heavy a horse
Through a pitch-dark limitless grove.

And a man came out of the trees
And took our horse by the head
And reaching back to his ribs
Deliberately stabbed him dead.

The ponderous beast went down
With a crack of a broken shaft.   10
And the night drew through the trees
In one long invidious draft.

The most unquestioning pair
That ever accepted fate

And the least disposed to ascribe
Any more than we had to to hate,

We assumed that the man himself
Or someone he had to obey
Wanted us to get down
And walk the rest of the way.   20

CARL SANDBURG

Four Preludes on Playthings of the Wind

"The Past Is a Bucket of Ashes."

1

The woman named Tomorrow
sits with a hairpin in her teeth
and takes her time
and does her hair the way she wants it
and fastens at last the last braid and coil
and puts the hairpin where it belongs
and turns and drawls: Well, what of it?
My grandmother, Yesterday, is gone
What of it? Let the dead be dead.

2

The doors were cedar   10
and the panel strips of gold
and the girls were golden girls
and the panels read and the girls chanted:
    We are the greatest city,
    and the greatest nation:
    nothing like us ever was.

The doors are twisted on broken hinges,
Sheets of rain swish through on the wind

where the golden girls ran and the
  panels read:
We are the greatest city,   20
the greatest nation,
nothing like us ever was.

3

It has happened before.
Strong men put up a city and got
  a nation together,
And paid singers to sing and women
  to warble: We are the greatest city,
    the greatest nation,
    nothing like us ever was.

And while the singers sang   30
and the strong men listened
and paid the singers well,
  there were rats and lizards who listened
  . . . and the only listeners left now
  . . . are. . . the rats. . . and the lizards.
  And there are black crows
  crying, "Caw, caw,"
  bringing mud and sticks
  building a nest
  over the words carved   40
on the doors where the panels were cedar
and the strips on the panels were gold
and the golden girls came singing:
    We are the greatest city,
    the greatest nation:
    nothing like us ever was.

The only singers now are crows crying, "Caw,
    caw,"
And the sheets of rain whine in the wind and
    doorways.
And the only listeners now are . . . the rats . . .
    and the lizards.

4

The feet of the rats   50
scribble on the doorsills;
the hieroglyphs of the rat footprints
chatter the pedigrees of the rats

and babble of the blood
and gabble of the breed
of the grandfathers and the great-
    grandfathers
of the rats.

And the wind shifts
and the dust on a doorsill shifts
and even the writing of the rat footprints   60
tells us nothing, nothing at all
about the greatest city, the greatest nation
where the strong men listened
and the woman warbled: Nothing like us
    ever was.

Broken-Face Gargoyles

All I can give you is broken-face gargoyles.
It is too early to sing and dance at funerals,
Though I can whisper to you I am looking
    for an undertaker humming a lullaby and
    throwing his feet in a swift and mystic
    buck-and-wing, now you see it and now
    you don't.

Fish to swim a pool in your garden flashing a
    speckled silver,
A basket of wine-saps filling your room with
    flame-dark for your eyes and the tang of
    valley orchards for your nose,
Such a beautiful pail of fish, such a beautiful
    peck of apples, I cannot bring you now.
It is too early and I am not footloose yet.

I shall come in the night when I come with a
    hammer and saw.
I shall come near your window, where you
    look out when your eyes open in the
    morning,
And there I shall slam together bird-houses
    and bird-baths for wing-loose wrens and
    hummers to live in, birds with yellow wing
    tips to blur and buzz soft all summer.   10

So I shall make little fool homes with doors,
   always open doors for all and each to run
   away when they want to.
I shall come just like that even though now
   it is early and I am not yet footloose,
Even though I am still looking for an
   undertaker with a raw, wind-bitten face
   and a dance in his feet.
I make a date with you (put it down) for
   six o'clock in the evening a thousand years
   from now.

All I can give you now is broken-face
   gargoyles.
All I can give you now is a double gorilla
   head with two fish mouths and four eagle
   eyes hooked on a street wall, spouting
   water and looking two ways to the ends
   of the street for the new people, the young
   strangers, coming, coming, always coming.

      It is early.
      I shall yet be footloose.

WALLACE STEVENS

Le Monocle de Mon Oncle

"Mother of heaven, regina of the clouds,
O sceptre of the sun, crown of the moon,
There is not nothing, no, no, never nothing,
Like the clashed edges of two words that
   kill."
And so I mocked her in magnificent measure.
Or was it that I mocked myself alone?
I wish that I might be a thinking stone.
The sea of spuming thought foists up again
The radiant bubble that she was. And then
A deep up-pouring from some saltier well   10
Within me, bursts its watery syllable.

II

A red bird flies across the golden floor.
It is a red bird that seeks out his choir
Among the choirs of wind and wet and wing.
A torrent will fall from him when he finds.
Shall I uncrumple this much-crumpled
   thing?
I am a man of fortune greeting heirs;
For it has come that thus I greet the spring.
These choirs of welcome choir for me
   farewell.
No spring can follow past meridian.   20
Yet you persist with anecdotal bliss
To make believe a starry *connaissance*.

III

Is it for nothing, then, that old Chinese
Sat tittivating by their mountain pools
Or in the Yangtse studied out their beards?
I shall not play the flat historic scale.
You know how Utamaro's beauties sought
The end of love in their all-speaking braids.
You know the mountainous coiffures of Bath.
Alas! Have all the barbers lived in vain   30
That not one curl in nature has survived?
Why, without pity on these studious ghosts,
Do you come dripping in your hair from
   sleep?

IV

This luscious and impeccable fruit of life
Falls, it appears, of its own weight to earth.
When you were Eve, its acrid juice was sweet,
Untasted, in its heavenly, orchard air.
An apple serves as well as any skull
To be the book in which to read a round,
And is as excellent, in that it is composed   40
Of what, like skulls, comes rotting back to
   ground.

---

l. 22. *connaissance:* acquaintance, knowledge.
l. 27. *Utamaro:* Japanese designer of color prints (1754–1806), whose drawings of women are renowned for grace of line and color.

But it excelts in this, that as the fruit
Of love, it is a book too mad to read
Before one merely reads to pass the time.

V

In the high west there burns a furious star.
It is for fiery boys that star was set
And for sweet-smelling virgins close to them.
The measure of the intensity of love
Is measure, also, of the verve of earth.
For me, the firefly's quick, electric stroke   50
Ticks tediously the time of one more year.
And you? Remember how the crickets came
Out of their mother grass, like little kin,
In the pale nights, when your first imagery
Found inklings of your bond to all that dust.

VI

If men at forty will be painting lakes
The ephemeral blues must merge for them
  in one,
The basic slate, the universal hue.
There is a substance in us that prevails.
But in our amours amorists discern   60
Such fluctuations that their scrivening
Is breathless to attend each quirky turn.
When amorists grow bald, then amours shrink
Into the compass and curriculum
Of introspective exiles, lecturing.
It is a theme for Hyacinth alone.

VII

The mules that angels ride come slowly down
The blazing passes, from beyond the sun.
Descensions of their tinkling bells arrive.
These muleteers are dainty of their way.   70
Meantime, centurions guffaw and beat
Their shrilling tankards on the table-boards.
This parable, in sense, amounts to this:
The honey of heaven may or may not come,

---

l. 66. *Hyacinth:* boy beloved by Apollo and Zephyr, who
preferred Apollo. Zephyr drove Apollo's quoit to Hyacinth's head and killed him. His blood became the
flower bearing his name.

But that of earth both comes and goes
  at once.
Suppose these couriers brought amid their
  train
A damsel heightened by eternal bloom.

VIII

Like a dull scholar, I behold, in love,
An ancient aspect touching a new mind.
It comes, it blooms, it bears its fruit and
  dies.   80
This trivial trope reveals a way of truth.
Our bloom is gone. We are the fruit thereof.
Two golden gourds distended on our vines,
Into the autumn weather, splashed with frost,
Distorted by hale fatness, turned grotesque.
We hang like warty squashes, streaked and
  rayed,
The laughing sky will see the two of us
Washed into rinds by rotting winter rains.

IX

In verses wild with motion, full of din,
Loudened by cries, by clashes, quick and
  sure   90
As the deadly thought of men accomplishing
Their curious fates in war, come, celebrate
The faith of forty, ward of Cupido.
Most venerable heart, the lustiest conceit
Is not too lusty for your broadening.
I quiz all sounds, all thought, all everything
For the music and manner of the paladins
To make oblation fit. Where shall I find
Bravura adequate to this great hymn?

X

The fops of fancy in their poems leave   100
Memorabilia of the mystic spouts,
Spontaneously watering their gritty soils.
I am a yeoman, as such fellows go.
I know no magic trees, no balmy boughs,
No silver-ruddy, gold-vermilion fruits.
But, after all, I know a tree that bears
A semblance to the thing I have in mind.

It stands gigantic, with a certain tip
To which all birds come sometime in their
    time.
But when they go that tip still tips the
    tree.   110

XI

If sex were all, then every trembling hand
Could make us squeak, like dolls, the wished-
    for words.
But note the unconscionable treachery of fate,
That makes us weep, laugh, grunt and groan,
    and shout
Doleful heroics, pinching gestures forth
From madness or delight, without regard
To that first, foremost law. Anguishing hour!
Last night, we sat beside a pool of pink,
Clippered with lilies scudding the bright
    chromes,
Keen to the point of starlight, while a frog 120
Boomed from his very belly odious chords.

XII

A blue pigeon it is, that circles the blue sky,
On sidelong wing, around and round and
    round.
A white pigeon it is, that flutters to the
    ground,
Grown tired of flight. Like a dark rabbi, I
Observed, when young, the nature of
    mankind,
In lordly study. Every day, I found
Man proved a gobbet in my mincing world.
Like a rose rabbi, later, I pursued,
And still pursue, the origin and course   130
Of love, but until now I never knew
That fluttering things have so distinct a
    shade.

The Idea of Order at Key West

She sang beyond the genius of the sea.
The water never formed to mind or voice,
Like a body wholly body, fluttering
Its empty sleeves; and yet its mimic motion
Made constant cry, caused constantly a cry,
That was not ours although we understood,
Inhuman, of the veritable ocean.

The sea was not a mask. No more was she.
The song and water were not medleyed sound
Even if what she sang was what she heard, 10
Since what she sang was uttered word by
    word.
It may be that in all her phrases stirred
The grinding water and the gasping wind;
But it was she and not the sea we heard.

For she was the maker of the song she sang.
The ever-hooded, tragic-gestured sea
Was merely a place by which she walked to
    sing.
Whose spirit is this? we said, because we
    knew
It was the spirit that we sought and knew
That we should ask this often as she sang. 20

If it was only the dark voice of the sea
That rose, or even colored by many waves;
If it was only the outer voice of sky
And cloud, of the sunken coral water-walled,
However clear, it would have been deep air,
The heaving speech of air, a summer sound
Repeated in a summer without end
And sound alone. But it was more than that,
More even than her voice, and ours, among
The meaningless plungings of water and the
    wind,   30
Theatrical distances, bronze shadows heaped
An high horizons, mountainous atmospheres
On sky and sea.
                It was her voice that made
The sky acutest at its vanishing.
She measured to the hour its solitude.

She was the single artificer of the world
In which she sang. And when she sang, the
   sea,
Whatever self it had, became the self
That was her song, for she was the maker.
   Then we,   40
As we beheld her striding there alone,
Knew that there never was a world for her
Except the one she sang and, singing, made.

Ramon Fernandez, tell me, if you know,
Why, when the singing ended and we turned
Toward the town, tell why the glassy lights,
The lights in the fishing boats at anchor there,
As the night descended, tilting in the air,
Mastered the night and portioned out the sea,
Fixing emblazoned zones and fiery poles,   50
Arranging, deepening, enchanting night.

Oh! Blessed rage for order, pale Ramon,
The maker's rage to order words of the sea,
Words of the fragrant portals, dimly-starred,
And of ourselves and of our origins,
In ghostlier demarcations, keener sounds.

The Candle a Saint

Green is the night, green kindled and
   apparelled.
It is she that walks among astronomers.

She strides above the rabbit and the cat,
Like a noble figure, out of the sky,

Moving among the sleepers, the men,
Those that lie chanting *green is the night*.

Green is the night and out of madness woven,
The self-same madness of the astronomers

And of him that sees, beyond the astronomers,
The topaz rabbit and the emerald cat,   10

That sees above them, that sees rise up above
   them,
The noble figure, the essential shadow,

Moving and being, the image at its source,
The abstract, the archaic queen. Green is the
   night.

william carlos williams

The Yachts

contend in a sea which the land partly
   encloses
shielding them from the too heavy blows
of an ungoverned ocean which when it
   chooses

tortures the biggest hulls, the best man knows
to pit against its beatings, and sinks them
   pitilessly.
Mothlike in mists, scintillant in the minute

brilliance of cloudless days, with broad
   bellying sails
they glide to the wind tossing green water
from their sharp prows while over them the
   crew crawls

ant like, solicitously grooming them,
   releasing,   10
making fast as they turn, lean far over and
   having
caught the wind again, side by side, head for
   the mark.

In a well guarded arena of open water
   surrounded by

lesser and greater craft which, sycophant,
  lumbering
and flittering follow them, they appear
  youthful, rare

as the light of a happy eye, live with the grace
of all that in the mind is feckless, free and
naturally to be desired. Now the sea which
  holds them

is moody, lapping their glossy sides, as if
  feeling
for some slightest flaw but fails completely. 20
Today no race. Then the wind comes again.
  The yachts

move, jockeying for a start, the signal is set
  and they
are off. Now the waves strike at them but
  they are too
well made, they slip through, though they
  take in canvas.

Arms with hands grasping seek to clutch at
  the prows.
Bodies thrown recklessly in the way are cut
  aside.
It is a sea of faces about them in agony, in
  despair

until the horror of the race dawns staggering
  the mind,
the whole sea become an entanglement of
  watery bodies
lost to the world bearing what they cannot
  hold. Broken,   30

beaten, desolate, reaching from the dead to be
  taken up
they cry out, failing, failing! their cries rising
in waves still as the skillful yachts pass over.

To Daphne and Virginia

THE SMELL OF the heat is boxwood
      when rousing us
            a movement of the air
stirs our thoughts
      that had no life in them
            to a life, a life in which
two women agonize:
      to live and to breathe is no less.
            Two young women.
The box odor   10
      is the odor of that of which
            partaking separately,
each to herself
      I partake also
                  separately.

BE PATIENT THAT I address you in a poem,
      there is no other
            fit medium.
The mind
      lives there. It is uncertain,   20
            can trick us and leave us
agonized. But for resources
      what can equal it?
            There is nothing. We
should be lost
      without its wings to
            fly off upon.
THE MIND IS the cause of our distresses
      but of it we can build anew.
            Oh something more than   30
it flies off to:
      a woman's world,
            of crossed sticks, stopping
thought. A new world
      is only a new mind.
            And the mind and the poem
are all apiece.
      Two young women
            to be snared,

odor of box,   40
        to bind and hold them
                for the mind's labors.

ALL WOMEN ARE fated similarly
        facing men
                and there is always
another, such as I,
        who loves them,
                loves all women, but
finds himself, touching them,
        like other men,   50
                often confused.

I HAVE TWO sons,
        the husbands of these women,
                who live also

in a world of love,
        apart.
                Shall this odor of box in
                the heat
not also touch them
        fronting a world of women   60
                from which they are
debarred
        by the very scents which draw them on
                against easy access?

IN OUR FAMILY we stammer unless,
        half mad,
                we come to speech at last

AND I AM not
        a young man.
                My love encumbers me.   70
It is a love
        less than
                a young man's love but,
like this box odor
        more penetrant, infinitely
                more penetrant,
in that sense not to be resisted.

THERE IS, IN the hard
        give and take

of a man's life with   80
        a woman
a thing which is not the stress itself
        but beyond
                and above
that,
        something that wants to rise
                and shake itself
free. We are not chickadees
        on a bare limb
                with a worm in the mouth.   90
The worm is in our brains
        and concerns them
                and not food for our
offspring, wants to disrupt
        our thought
                and throw it
to the newspapers
        or anywhere.
                There is, in short,
a counter stress,   100
        born of the sexual shock,
                which survives it
consonant with the moon,
        to keep its own mind.
                There is, of course,
more.
        Women
                are not alone
in that. At least
        while this healing odor is abroad   110
                one can write a poem.

STAYING HERE in the country
        on an old farm
                we eat our breakfasts
on a balcony under an elm.
        The shrubs below us
                are neglected. And
there, penned in,
        or he would eat the garden,
                lives a pet goose who   120
tilts his head
        sidewise
                and looks up at us,

649   William Carlos Williams

a very quiet old fellow
     who writes no poems.
          Fine mornings we sit there
while birds
     come and go.
         A pair of robins
is building a nest   .   130
     for the second time
         this season. Men
against their reason
     speak of love, sometimes,
         when they are old. It is
all they can do   .
     or watch a heavy goose
         who waddles, slopping
         noisily in the mud of
         his pool.   140

d. h. LAWRENCE

Cherry Robbers

Under the long dark boughs, like jewels red
   In the hair of an Eastern girl
Hangs strings of crimson cherries, as if had
    bled
   Blood-drops beneath each curl.

Under the glistening cherries, with folded
    wings
   Three dead birds lie:
Pale-breasted throstles and a blackbird,
    robberlings
   Stained with red dye.

Against the haystack a girl stands laughing
    at me,
   Cherries hung round her ears.   10
Offers me her scarlet fruit: I will see
   If she has any tears.

Piano

Softly, in the dusk, a woman is singing to me;
Taking me back down the vista of years, till
   I see
A child sitting under the piano, in the boom
   of the tingling strings
And pressing the small, poised feet of a
   mother who smiles as she sings.

In spite of myself, the insidious mastery of
   song
Betrays me back, till the heart of me weeps
   to belong
To the old Sunday evenings at home, with
   winter outside
And hymns in the cozy parlor, the tinkling
   piano our guide.

So now it is vain for the singer to burst into
   clamor
With the great black piano appassionato. The
   glamour   10
Of childish days is upon me, my manhood is
   cast
Down in the flood of remembrance, I weep
   like a child for the past.

---

l. 10. *appassionato:* impassioned.

Bavarian Gentians

Not every man has gentians in his house
in Soft September, at slow, Sad Michaelmas.

Bavarian gentians, big and dark, only dark
darkening the day-time torch-like with the
   smoking blueness of Pluto's gloom,
ribbed and torch-like, with their blaze of
   darkness spread blue

---

l. 4. *Pluto:* in Greek mythology, King of Hades, or Dis.

down flattening into points, flattened under
   the sweep of white day
torch-flower of the blue-smoking darkness,
   Pluto's dark-blue daze,
black lamps from the halls of Dis, burning
   dark blue,
giving off darkness, blue darkness, as
   Demeter's pale lamps give off light,
lead me then, lead me the way.   10

Reach me a gentian, give me a torch
let me guide myself with the blue, forked
   torch of this flower
down the darker and darker stairs, where
   blue is darkened on blueness
even where Persephone goes, just now, from
   the frosted September
to the sightless realm where darkness is
   awake upon the dark
and Persephone herself is but a voice
or a darkness invisible enfolded in the
   deeper dark
of the arms Plutonic, and pierced with the
   passion of dense gloom,
among the splendour of torches of darkness,
   shedding darkness on the lost bride and
   her groom.

---

l. 9. *Demeter:* in Greek mythology, goddess of agriculture, protectress of marriage, whose daughter Persephone was abducted by Pluto.

EZRA POUND

The Return

See, they return; ah, see the tentative
    Movements, and the slow feet,
      The trouble in the pace and the uncertain
    Wavering!

See, they return, one, and by one,
With fear, as half-awakened;
As if the snow should hesitate
And murmur in the wind,
          and half turn back;
These were the 'Wing'd-with-Awe',   10
        Inviolable.

Gods of the wingèd shoe!
With them the silver hounds,
        sniffling the trace of air!

Haie! Haie!
    These were the swift to harry;
These the keen-scented;
These were the souls of blood.

Slow on the leash,
        pallid the leash-men!   20

The River-Merchant's Wife: A Letter

While my hair was still cut straight across
        my forehead
I played about the front gate, pulling flowers.
You came by on bamboo stilts, playing horse,
You walked about my seat, playing with blue
        plums.
And we went on living in the village of
        Chokan:
Two small people, without dislike or
        suspicion.

At fourteen I married My Lord you.
I never laughed, being bashful.
Lowering my head, I looked at the wall.
Called to, a thousand times, I never looked
        back.   10

At fifteen I stopped scowling,
I desired my dust to be mingled with yours
Forever and forever and forever.
Why should I climb the look out?

At sixteen you departed,
You went into far Ku-to-yen, by the river of
        swirling eddies,
And you have been gone five months.
The monkeys make sorrowful noise overhead.
You dragged your feet when you went out.
By the gate now, the moss is grown, the
        different mosses,   20
Too deep to clear them away!
The leaves fall early this autumn, in wind.
The paired butterflies are already yellow
        with August
Over the grass in the West garden;
They hurt me. I grow older.
If you are coming down through the narrows
        of the river Kiang,
Please let me know beforehand,
And I will come out to meet you
        As far as Cho-fu-Sa.

by Rihaku

Rihaku: Chinese poet (eighth century A.D.).

In a Station of the Metro

The apparition of these faces in the crowd;
Petals on a wet, black bough.

Metro: the subway in Paris.

from **Hugh Selwyn Mauberley**

I

E. P. Ode Pour L'Election de Son Sepulchre

For three years, out of key with his time,
He strove to resuscitate the dead art

E. P. Ode . . . Sepulchre: E[zra]. P[ound]. "Ode on the
Choice of His Tomb."

Of poetry; to maintain 'the sublime'
In the old sense. Wrong from the start—

No, hardly, but seeing he had been born
In a half savage country, out of date;
Bent resolutely on wringing lilies from the
    acorn;
Capaneus; trout for factitious bait;

"Ἴδμεν γάρ τοι πάνθ' ὅσ' ἐνὶ Τροίη
Caught in the unstopped ear;   10
Giving the rocks small lee-way
The chopped seas held him, therefore,
    that year.

His true Penelope was Flaubert,
He fished by obstinate isles;
Observed the elegance of Circe's hair
Rather than the mottoes on sun-dials.

Unaffected by 'the march of events',
He passed from men's memory in *l'an
    trentiesme*
De son eage; the case presents
No adjunct to the Muses' diadem.   20

II

The age demanded an image
Of its accelerated grimace,

---

l. 8. *Capaneus:* one of the eight against Thebes who
swore he would enter the city in spite of Zeus; on
reaching the top of the wall, he was struck down by a
thunderbolt.
l. 9. "Ἴδμεν . . . Τροίη: a variation on the Sirens' song in
Homer's *Odyssey,* meaning "For we know all things
that are in Troy."
l. 10. *unstopped ear:* Odysseus, to escape the lure of
the Sirens and ultimate shipwreck, stopped the ears
of his crew and tied himself to the ship's mast.
l. 13. *Penelope:* the faithful wife of Odysseus.
l. 13. *Flaubert:* (1821–1880), author of *Madame Bovary;*
an artist who searched for precise expression.
l. 15. *Circe:* the sorceress who held Odysseus captive
and turned his crew into swine.
ll. 18–19. *l'an . . . eage:* "in the thirtieth year of his life,"
a line from *Grand Testament* by François Villon
(1431–1463?).

Something for the modern stage,
Not, at any rate, an Attic grace;

Not, not certainly, the obscure reveries
Of the inward gaze;
Better mendacities
Than the classics in paraphrase!

The 'age demanded' chiefly a mould in
    plaster,
Made with no loss of time,   30
A prose kinema, not, not assuredly, alabaster
Or the 'sculpture' of rhyme.

III

The tea-rose tea-gown, etc.
Supplants the mousseline of Cos,
The pianola 'replaces'
Sappho's barbitos.

Christ follows Dionysus,
Phallic and ambrosial
Made way for macerations;
Caliban casts out Ariel.   40

All things are a flowing,
Sage Heracleitus says;
But a tawdry cheapness
Shall outlast our days.

Even the Christian beauty
Defects—after Samothrace;

We see τὸ καλὸν
Decreed in the market place.

Faun's flesh is not to us,
Nor the saint's vision.   50
We have the press for wafer;
Franchise for circumcision.

All men, in law, are equals.
Free of Pisistratus,
We choose a knave or an eunuch
To rule over us.

O bright Apollo,
τίν ἄνδρα, τίν ἥρωα, τινα θεὸν,
What god, man, or hero
Shall I place a tin wreath upon!   60

IV

These fought in any case,
and some believing,
                    pro domo, in any case . . .

Some quick to arm,
some for adventure,
some from fear of weakness,
some from fear of censure,
some for love of slaughter, in imagination,
learning later . . .
some in fear, learning love of slaughter;   70
Died some, pro patria,
                    non 'dulce' non 'et decor' . . .
walked eye-deep in hell
believing in old men's lies, then unbelieving
came home, home to a lie,
home to many deceits,
home to old lies and new infamy;

---

l. 24. *Attic:* of Attica, part of Greece surrounding Athens.
l. 31. *kinema:* motion; cinema.
l. 34. *mousseline of Cos:* muslin of silk from Cos in Greece.
l. 35. *pianola:* player piano.
l. 36. *Sappho's barbitos:* lyre of the Greek poetess.
l. 37. *Dionysus:* god of wine and fertility.
l. 40. *Caliban . . . Ariel:* characters from Shakespeare's *The Tempest;* Caliban is a monster, Ariel a helpful spirit.
l. 42. *Heracleitus:* Greek philosopher (sixth century B.C.).
l. 46. *Samothrace:* Greek isle noted for its statue "Winged Victory" and for being the first place Saint Paul stopped on his Macedonian trip.

l. 47. τὸ Καλὸν: "the beautiful."
l. 54. *Pisistratus:* Athenian dictator (sixth century B.C.).
l. 58. τίν . . . θεὸν: a variation on a line from Pindar's "Second Ode": "What God, what hero, what man shall we praise." The first Greek word sounds like "tin."
l. 63. *pro domo:* "for home."
ll. 71–72. *pro patria . . . decor:* from Horace's *Odes* (III, ii, 13): "It is sweet and fitting to die for one's country."

usury age-old and age-thick
and liars in public places.

Daring as never before, wastage as never
    before.   80
Young blood and high blood,
fair cheeks, and fine bodies;

fortitude as never before

frankness as never before,
disillusions as never told in the old days,
hysterias, trench confessions,
laughter out of dead bellies.

V

There died a myriad,
And of the best, among them,
For an old bitch gone in the teeth,   90
For a botched civilization,

Charm, smiling at the good mouth,
Quick eyes gone under earth's lid,

For two gross of broken statues,
For a few thousand battered books.

h. d. (hilda doolittle)

Fragment Thirty-Six

I know not what to do: my mind is divided.
—SAPPHO.

I know not what to do,
my mind is reft:
is song's gift best?

Sappho: Greek poetess (fl. c. 600 B.C.).

is love's gift loveliest?
I know not what to do,
now sleep has pressed
weight on your eyelids.

Shall I break your rest,
devouring, eager?
is love's gift best?   10
nay, song's the loveliest:
yet were you lost,
what rapture
could I take from song?
what song were left?

I know not what to do:
to turn and slake
the rage that burns,
with my breath burn
and trouble your cool breath?   20
so shall I turn and take
snow in my arms?
(is love's gift best?)
yet flake on flake
of snow were comfortless,
did you lie wondering,
wakened yet unawake.

Shall I turn and take
comfortless snow within my arms?
press lips to lips   30
that answer not,
press lips to flesh
that shudders not nor breaks?

Is love's gift best?
shall I turn and slake
all the wild longing?
O I am eager for you!
as the Pleiads shake
white light in whiter water
so shall I take you?   40

My mind is quite divided,
my minds hesitate,

---

l. 38. *Pleiads:* in Greek mythology, the seven daughters
of Atlas, who were placed by Zeus among the stars.

so perfect matched,
I know not what to do:
each strives with each
as two white wrestlers
standing for a match,
ready to turn and clutch
yet never shake muscle nor nerve nor tendon;
so my mind waits   50
to grapple with my mind,
yet I lie quiet,
I would seem at rest.

I know not what to do:
strain upon strain,
sound surging upon sound
makes my brain blind;
as a wave-line may wait to fall
yet (waiting for its falling)
still the wind may take   60
from off its crest,
white flake on flake of foam,
that rises,
seeming to dart and pulse
and rend the light,
so my mind hesitates
above the passion
quivering yet to break,
so my mind hesitates
above my mind,   70
listening to song's delight.

I know not what to do:
will the sound break,
rending the night
with rift on rift of rose
and scattered light?
will the sound break at last
as the wave hesitant,
or will the whole night pass
and I lie listening awake?   80

ROBINSON JEFFERS

Apology for Bad Dreams

I

In the purple light, heavy with redwood, the
    slopes drop seaward,
Headlong convexities of forest, drawn in
    together to the steep ravine. Below, on the
    sea-cliff,
A lonely clearing; a little field of corn by the
    streamside; a roof under spared trees.
    Then the ocean
Like a great stone someone has cut to a
    sharp edge and polished to shining.
    Beyond it, the fountain
And furnace of incredible light flowing up
    from the sunk sun. In the little clearing a
    woman
Is punishing a horse; she had tied the halter
    to a sapling at the edge of the wood, but
    when the great whip
Clung to the flanks the creature kicked so
    hard she feared he would snap the halter;
    she called from the house
The young man her son; who fetched a chain
    tie-rope, they working together
Noosed the small rusty links round the
    horse's tongue
And tied him by the swollen tongue to the
    tree.   10
Seen from this height they are shrunk to
    insect size,
Out of all human relation. You cannot
    distinguish
The blood dripping from where the chain is
    fastened,
The beast shuddering; but the thrust neck
    and the legs
Far apart. You can see the whip fall on the
    flanks ...

The gesture of the arm. You cannot see the
face of the woman.
The enormous light beats up out of the west
across the cloud-bars of the trade-wind.
The ocean
Darkens, the high clouds brighten, the hills
darken together. Unbridled and
unbelievable beauty
Covers the evening world . . . not covers,
grows apparent out of it, as Venus down
there grows out
From the lit sky. What said the prophet? 'I
create good: and I create evil: I am the
Lord.'   20

II

This coast crying out for tragedy like all
beautiful places,
(The quiet ones ask for quieter suffering:
but here the granite cliff the gaunt
cypresses crown
Demands what victim? The dykes of red lava
and black what Titan? The hills like
pointed flames
Beyond Soberanes, the terrible peaks of the
bare hills under the sun, what immolation?)
This coast crying out for tragedy like all
beautiful places: and like the passionate
spirit of humanity
Pain for its bread: God's, many victims',
the painful deaths, the horrible
transfigurations: I said in my heart,
'Better invent than suffer: imagine victims
Lest your own flesh be chosen the agonist,
or you
Martyr some creature to the beauty of the
place.' And I said,
'Burn sacrifices once a year to magic   30
Horror away from the house, this little
house here
You have built over the ocean with your
own hands

Beside the standing boulders: for what
are we,
The beast that walks upright, with speaking
lips
And little hair, to think we should always
be fed,
Sheltered, intact, and self-controlled? We
sooner more liable
Than the other animals. Pain and terror, the
insanities of desire; not accidents but
essential,
And crowd up from the core:' I imagined
victims for those wolves, I made them
phantoms to follow,
They have hunted the phantoms and missed
the house. It is not good to forget over
what gulfs the spirit
Of the beauty of humanity, the petal of a
lost flower blown seaward by the
night-wind, floats to its quietness.   40

III

Boulders blunted like an old bear's teeth
break up from the headland; below them
All the soil is thick with shells, the tide-rock
feasts of a dead people.
Here the granite flanks are scarred with
ancient fire, the ghosts of the tribe
Crouch in the nights beside the ghost of a
fire, they try to remember the sunlight,
Light has died out of their skies. These have
paid something for the future
Luck of the country, while we living keep
old griefs in memory: though God's
Envy is not a likely fountain of ruin, to
forget evils calls down
Sudden reminders from the cloud:
remembered deaths be our redeemers;
Imagined victims our salvation: white as the
half moon at midnight
Someone flamelike passed me, saying,
    'I am Tamar Cauldwell, I have my desire,' 50

I. 20. 'I create . . . Lord': cf. Isaiah 45:7.
I. 23. Titan: one of a race of earth giants in Greek
mythology whose immense power was destroyed by
the Olympian gods.

I. 50. Tamar Cauldwell: character from Jeffers' poem
Tamar, a story of incest and violence, based on II Samuel 13.

Then the voice of the sea returned, when she
   had gone by, the stars to their towers.
. . . Beautiful country burn again, Point Pinos
   down to the Sur Rivers
Burn as before with bitter wonders, land and
   ocean and the Carmel water.

IV

He brays humanity in a mortar to bring the
   savor
From the bruised root: a man having bad
   dreams, who invents victims, is only the
   ape of that God.
He washes it out with tears and many
   waters, calcines it with fire in the red
   crucible,
Deforms it, makes it horrible to itself: the
   spirit flies out and stands naked, he sees
   the spirit,
He takes it in the naked ecstasy; it breaks
   in his hand, the atom is broken, the power
   that massed it
Cries to the power that moves the stars,
   'I have come home to myself, behold me.
I bruised myself in the flint mortar and
   burnt me   60
In the red shell, I tortured myself, I flew
   forth,
Stood naked of myself and broke me in
   fragments,
And here am I moving the stars that are me.'
I have seen these ways of God: I know of no
   reason
For fire and change and torture and the old
   returnings.
He being sufficient might be still. I think they
   admit no reason; they are the ways of my
   love.
Unmeasured power, incredible passion,
   enormous craft: no thought apparent but
   burns darkly
Smothered with its own smoke in the human
   brain-vault: no thought outside: a certain
   measure in phenomena:
The fountains of the boiling stars, the flowers
   on the foreland, the ever-returning roses of
   dawn.

MARIANNE MOORE

The Pangolin

Another armoured animal—scale
   lapping scale with spruce-cone regularity
      until they
form the uninterrupted central
   tail-row! This near artichoke with head and
      legs and grit-equipped gizzard,
the night miniature artist engineer is
   Leonardo's—da Vinci's replica—
      impressive animal and toiler of whom
         we seldom hear.
   Armour seems extra. But for him,
      the closing ear-ridge—
      or bare ear lacking even this
         small.10
      eminence and similarly safe

contracting nose and eye apertures
   impenetrably closable, are not;—a true
      ant-eater,
not cockroach-eater, who endures
   exhausting solitary trips through
      unfamiliar ground at night,
returning before sunrise; stepping in the
      moonlight,
   on the moonlight peculiarly, that the
      outside
   edges of his hands may bear the
      weight and save the claws
for digging. Serpentined about
   the tree, he draws   20
      away from danger unpugnaciously,
      with no sound but a harmless hiss;
         keeping

the fragile grace of the Thomas-
   of-Leighton Buzzard Westminster Abbey
      wrought-iron vine, or

---

ll. 27–28. *Thomas-of-Leighton . . . vine:* a fragment of
iron-work in Westminster Abbey [Moore's note].

rolls himself into a ball that has
    power to defy all effort to unroll it; strongly
               intailed, neat
head for core, on neck not breaking off,
           with curled-in feet.
    Nevertheless he has sting-proof scales;
           and nest
of rocks closed with earth from
        inside, which he can thus darken
Sun and moon and day and night and
           man and beast [30]
    each with a splendour
        which man in all his vileness cannot
        set aside; each with an excellence!

'Fearful yet to be feared,' the armoured
    ant-eater met by the driver-ant does not
           turn back, but
engulfs what he can, the flattened sword-
    edged leafpoints on the tail and artichoke
          set leg- and body-plates
quivering violently when it retaliates
    and swarms on him. Compact like the
        furled fringed frill
on the hat-brim of Gargallo's hollow
        iron head of a [40]
    matador, he will drop and will
    then walk away
        unhurt, although if unintruded on,
        he cautiously works down the tree,
          helped

by his tail. The giant-pangolin-
    tail, graceful tool, as prop or hand or
        broom or axe, tipped like
the elephant's trunk with special skin,
    is not lost on this ant- and stone-swallowing
          uninjurable
artichoke which simpletons thought a
        living fable
whom the stones had nourished,
        whereas ants had done [50]
so. Pangolins are not aggressive
        animals; between
dusk and day they have the not
        unchain-like machine-like

form and frictionless creep of a
           thing
    made graceful by adversities, con-

versities. To explain grace requires
    a curious hand. If that which is at all
        were not forever,
why would those who graced the spires
    with animals and gathered there to rest, on
        cold luxurious
low stone seats—a monk and monk and
        monk—between the thus
ingenious roof-supports, have slaved to
        confuse [60]
    grace with a kindly manner, time in
        which to pay a debt,
    the cure for sins, a graceful use
    of what are yet
        approved stone mullions branching
        out across
    the perpendiculars? A sailboat

was the first machine. Pangolins, made
    for moving quietly also, are models of
        exactness,
on four legs; or hind feet plantigrade,
    with certain postures of a man. Beneath
        sun and moon, man slaving
to make his life more sweet, leaves half the
        flowers worth having, [70]
needing to choose wisely how to use the
        strength;
    a paper-maker like the wasp; a tractor
        of foodstuffs,
    like the ant; spidering a length
    of web from bluffs
        above a stream; in fighting,
        mechanicked
    like the pangolin; capsizing in

disheartenment. Bedizened or stark
    naked, man, the self, the being we call
        human, writing-
master to this world, griffons a dark
    'Like does not like like that is obnoxious';
        and writes error with four [80]

r's. Among animals, one has a sense of
            humour.
Humour saves a few steps, it saves
            years. Unignorant,
   modest and unemotional, and all
            emotion,
    he has everlasting vigour,
       power to grow,
        though there are few creatures who
            can make one
      breathe faster and make one
            erecter.

Not afraid of anything is he,
   and then goes cowering forth, tread paced
            to meet an obstacle
at every step. Consistent with the   **90**
   formula—warm blood, no gills, two pairs
          of hands and a few hairs—that
is a mammal; there he sits in his own
            habitat,
    serge-clad, strong-shod. The prey of
          fear, he, always
     curtailed, extinguished, thwarted by
          the dusk, work partly done,
says to the alternating blaze,
    'Again the sun!
      anew each day; and new and new
            and new,
     that comes into and steadies my
            soul.'

joHN CROWE RANSOM

Winter Remembered

Two evils, monstrous either one apart,
Possessed me, and were long and loath at
  going:

A cry of Absence, Absence, in the heart,
And in the wood the furious winter blowing.

Think not, when fire was bright upon my
  bricks,
And past the tight boards hardly a wind
  could enter,
I glowed like them, the simple burning sticks,
Far from my cause, my proper heat and
  center.

Better to walk forth in the frozen air
And wash my wound in the snows; that would
  be healing;   **10**
Because my heart would throb less painful
  there,
Being caked with cold, and past the smart of
  feeling.

And where I walked, the murderous winter
  blast
Would have this body bowed, these eyeballs
  streaming,
And though I think this heart's blood froze
  not fast
It ran too small to spare one drop for
  dreaming.

Dear love, these fingers that had known your
  touch,
And tied our separate forces first together,
Were ten poor idiot fingers not worth much,
Ten frozen parsnips hanging in the
  weather.   **20**

Good Ships

Fleet ships encountering on the high seas
Who speak, and then unto the vast diverge,
These hailed each other, poised on the loud
  surge
Of one of Mrs. Grundy's Tuesday teas,

---

l. 4. *Mrs. Grundy:* a character from the play *Speed the Plough* by Tom Morton, used as a personification of narrow-minded conventionality.

Nor trimmed one sail to baffle the driving
    breeze.
A macaroon absorbed all her emotion;
His hue was ashy but an effect of ocean;
They exchanged the nautical technicalities.

It was only a nothing or so, and thus they
    parted.
Away they sailed, most certainly bound for
    port,   10
So seaworthy one felt they could not sink;
Still there was a tremor shook them, I should
    think,
Beautiful timbers fit for storm and sport
And unto miserly merchant hulks converted.

Judith of Bethulia

Beautiful as the flying legend of some leopard
She had not yet chosen her great captain or
    prince
Depositary to her flesh, and our defense;
And a wandering beauty is a blade out of its
    scabbard.
You know how dangerous, gentlemen of
    threescore?
May you know it yet ten more.

Nor by process of veiling she grew the less
    fabulous.
Grey or blue veils, we were desperate to study
The invincible emanations of her white body,
And the winds at her ordered raiment were
    ominous.   10
Might she walk in the market, sit in the
    council of soldiers?
Only of the extreme elders.

But a rare chance was the girl's then, when
    the Invader

Judith of Bethulia: title heroine of a book in the Apoc-
rypha, who saved her people by killing the Assyrian
general Holofernes.

Trumpeted from the south, and rumbled
    from the north,
Beleaguered the city from four quarters of
    the earth,
Our soldiery too craven and sick to aid her—
Where were the arms could countervail this
    horde?
Her beauty was the sword.

She sat with the elders, and proved on their
    blear visage
How bright was the weapon unrusted in her
    keeping,   20
While he lay surfeiting on their harvest
    heaping,
Wasting the husbandry of their rarest
    vintage—
And dreaming of the broad-breasted dames
    for concubine?
These floated on his wine.

He was lapped with bay-leaves, and grass
    and fumiter weed,
And from under the wine-film encountered
    his mortal vision,
For even within his tent she accomplished
    his derision;
She loosed one veil and another, standing
    unafraid;
And he perished. Nor brushed her with even
    so much as a daisy?
She found his destruction easy.   30

The heathen are all perished. The victory
    was furnished,
We smote them hiding in our vineyards,
    barns, annexes,
And now their white bones clutter the holes
    of foxes,
And the chieftain's head, with grinning
    sockets, and varnished—
Is it hung on the sky with a hideous
    epitaphy?
No, the woman keeps the trophy.

May God send unto our virtuous lady her
    prince.

It is stated she went reluctant to that orgy,
Yet a madness fevers our young men, and
    not the clergy
Nor the elders have turned them unto
    modesty since.   40
Inflamed by the thought of her naked beauty
    with desire?
Yes, and chilled with fear and despair.

Prelude to an Evening

Do not enforce the tired wolf
Dragging his infected wound homeward
To sit tonight with the warm children
Naming the pretty kings of France.

The images of the invaded mind
Being as monsters in the dreams
Of your most brief enchanted headful,
Suppose a miracle of confusion:

That dreamed and undreamt become each
    other
And mix the night and day of your mind;   10
And it does not matter your twice crying
From mouth unbeautied against the pillow

To avert the gun of the swarthy soldier,
For cry, cock-crow, or the iron bell
Can crack the sleep-sense of outrage,
Annihilate phantoms who were nothing.

But now, by our perverse supposal,
There is a drift of fog on your mornings;
You in your peignoir, dainty at your
    orange-cup,
Feel poising round the sunny room   20

Invisible evil, deprived, and bold.
All day the clock will metronome
Your gallant fear; the needles clicking,
The heels detonating the stair's cavern.

Freshening the water in the blue bowls
For the buckberries with not all your love,
You shall be listening for the low wind,
The warning sibilance of pines.

You like a waning moon, and I accusing
Our too banded Eumenides,   30
You shall make Noes but wanderingly,
Smoothing the heads of the hungry
    children.

l. 30. *Eumenides:* in Greek mythology, the Furies; literally, "the gracious ones."

T. S. ELIOT

The Love Song of J. Alfred Prufrock

S'io credesse che mia risposta fosse
A persona che mai tornasse al mondo,
Questa fiamma staria senza piu scosse.
Ma perciocche giammai di questo fondo
Non torno vivo alcun, s'i'odo il vero,
Senza tema d'infamia ti rispondo.

Let us go then, you and I,
When the evening is spread out against the
    sky
Like a patient etherised upon a table;
Let us go, through certain half-deserted
    streets,
The muttering retreats
Of restless nights in one-night cheap hotels
And sawdust restaurants with oyster-shells:

S'io ... rispondo: Dante, *Inferno,* xxvii: "If I thought
that my reply would be to one who would ever return
to the world, this flame would stay without further
movement; but since none has ever returned alive
from this depth, if what I hear is true, I answer you
without fear of infamy."

Streets that follow like a tedious argument
Of insidious intent
To lead you to an overwhelming
    question ...   10
Oh, do not ask, "What is it?"
Let us go and make our visit.

    In the room the women come and go
Talking of Michelangelo.

    The yellow fog that rubs its back upon the
        window-panes,
The yellow smoke that rubs its muzzle on
        the window-panes
Licked its tongue into the corners of the
        evening,
Lingered upon the pools that stand in drains,
Let fall upon its back the soot that falls
        from chimneys,
Slipped by the terrace, made a sudden leap, 20
And seeing that it was a soft October night,
Curled once about the house, and fell asleep.

    And indeed there will be time
For the yellow smoke that slides along the
        street,
Rubbing its back upon the window-panes;
There will be time, there will be time
To prepare a face to meet the faces that you
        meet;
There will be time to murder and create,
And time for all the works and days of hands
That lift and drop a question on your plate; 30
Time for you and time for me,
And time yet for a hundred indecisions,
And for a hundred visions and revisions,
Before the taking of a toast and tea.

    In the room the women come and go
Talking of Michelangelo.

    And indeed there will be time
To wonder, "Do I dare?" and, "Do I dare?"
Time to turn back and descend the stair,

With a bald spot in the middle of my hair— 40
[They will say: "How his hair is growing
        thin!"]
My morning coat, my collar mounting firmly
        to the chin,
My necktie rich and modest, but asserted by
        a simple pin—
[They will say: "But how his arms and legs
        are thin!"]
Do I dare
Disturb the universe?
In a minute there is time
For decisions and revisions which a minute
        will reverse.

    For I have known them all already, known
        them all:—
Have known the evenings, mornings,
        afternoons,   50
I have measured out my life with coffee
        spoons;
I know the voices dying with a dying fall
Beneath the music from a farther room.
    So how should I presume?

    And I have known the eyes already, known
        them all—
The eyes that fix you in a formulated phrase,
And when I am formulated, sprawling on a
        pin,
When I am pinned and wriggling on the wall,
Then how should I begin
To spit out all the butt-ends of my days and
        ways?   60
    And how should I presume?

    And I have known the arms already, known
        them all—
Arms that are braceleted and white and bare
[But in the lamplight, downed with light
        brown hair!]
Is it perfume from a dress
That makes me so digress?

1.29. *works and days:* title of a poem about the farming
year by Hesiod (eighth century B.C.).

1. 52. *dying fall:* referring to Orsino's speech in Shakespeare's *Twelfth Night* (I, i).

Arms that lie along a table, or wrap about
    a shawl.
    And should I then presume?
    And how should I begin?

         .   .   .   .   .

Shall I say, I have gone at dusk through
    narrow streets   70
And watched the smoke that rises from the
    pipes
Of lonely men in shirt-sleeves, leaning out of
    windows? . . .

    I should have been a pair of ragged claws
Scuttling across the floors of silent seas.

         .   .   .   .   .

And the afternoon, the evening, sleeps so
    peacefully!
Smoothed by long fingers,
Asleep . . . tired . . . or it malingers,
Stretched on the floor, here beside you
    and me.
Should I, after tea and cakes and ices,
Have the strength to force the moment to its
    crisis?   80
But though I have wept and fasted, wept and
    prayed,
Though I have seen my head [grown slightly
    bald] brought in upon a platter,
I am no prophet—and here's no great matter;
I have seen the moment of my greatness
    flicker,
And I have seen the eternal Footman hold my
    coat, and snicker,
And in short, I was afraid.

    And would it have been worth it, after all,
After the cups, the marmalade, the tea,
Among the porcelain, among some talk of
    you and me,
Would it have been worth while,   90
To have bitten off the matter with a smile,
To have squeezed the universe into a ball
To roll it toward some overwhelming
    question,

---

l. 92. *squeezed . . . ball:* cf. Marvell's "To His Coy Mistress," lines 41–42.

To say: "I am Lazarus, come from the dead,
Come back to tell you all, I shall tell you
    all"—
If one, settling a pillow by her head,
    Should say: "That is not what I meant at
    all.
    That is not it, at all."

    And would it have been worth it, after all,
Would it have been worth while,   100
After the sunsets and the dooryards and the
    sprinkled streets,
After the novels, after the teacups, after the
    skirts that trail along the floor—
And this, and so much more?—
It is impossible to say just what I mean!
But as if a magic lantern threw the nerves
    in patterns on a screen:
Would it have been worth while
If one, settling a pillow or throwing off a
    shawl,
And turning toward the window, should say:
    "That is not it at all,
    That is not what I meant, at all."   110

         .   .   .   .   .

No! I am not Prince Hamlet, nor was meant
    to be;
Am an attendant lord, one that will do
To swell a progress, start a scene or two,
Advise the prince; no doubt, an easy tool,
Deferential, glad to be of use,
Politic, cautious, and meticulous;
Full of high sentence, but a bit obtuse;
At times, indeed, almost ridiculous—
Almost, at times, the Fool.

    I grow old . . . I grow old . . .   120
I shall wear the bottoms of my trousers
    rolled.

    Shall I part my hair behind? Do I dare to
    eat a peach?

---

l. 94. *Lazarus:* the man Christ raised from the dead,
John 12:1–18; also the beggar carried to Abraham's
bosom, Luke 16:19–31.
l. 113. *swell a progress:* join a royal procession.
l. 117. *sentence:* judgment; opinion.

I shall wear white flannel trousers, and walk
    upon the beach.
I have heard the mermaids singing, each to
    each.

    I do not think that they will sing to me.

    I have seen them riding seaward on the
        waves
Combing the white hair of the waves blown
    back
When the wind blows the water white and
    black.

    We have lingered in the chambers of the sea
By sea-girls wreathed with seaweed red and
    brown   130
Till human voices wake us, and we drown.

Journey of the Magi

'A cold coming we had of it,
Just the worst time of the year
For a journey, and such a long journey:
The ways deep and the weather sharp,
The very dead of winter.'
And the camels galled, sore-footed, refractory,
Lying down in the melting snow.
There were times we regretted
The summer palaces on slopes, the terraces,
And the silken girls bringing sherbet.   10
Then the camel men cursing and grumbling
And running away, and wanting their liquor
    and women,
And the night-fires going out, and the lack of
    shelters,
And the cities hostile and the towns
    unfriendly
And the villages dirty and charging high
    prices:
A hard time we had of it.

At the end we preferred to travel all night,
Sleeping in snatches,
With the voices singing in our ears, saying
That this was all folly.   20

    Then at dawn we came down to a temperate
        valley,
Wet, below the snow line, smelling of
    vegetation;
With a running stream and a water-mill
    beating the darkness,
And three trees on the low sky,
And an old white horse galloped away in the
    meadow.
Then we came to a tavern with vine-leaves
    over the lintel,
Six hands at an open door dicing for pieces
    of silver,
And feet kicking the empty wine-skins.
But there was no information, and so we
    continued
And arrived at evening, not a moment too
    soon   30
Finding the place; it was (you may say)
    satisfactory.

    All this was a long time ago, I remember,
And I would do it again, but set down
This set down
This: were we led all the way for
Birth or Death? There was a Birth, certainly,
We had evidence and no doubt. I had seen
    birth and death,
But had thought they were different; this
    Birth was
Hard and bitter agony for us, like Death, our
    death.
We returned to our places, these Kingdoms, 40
But no longer at ease here, in the old
    dispensation,
With an alien people clutching their gods.
I should be glad of another death.

---

ll. 1–5.'*A cold ... winter':* lines adapted from a passage in a Nativity Sermon by Lancelot Andrewes.

from Landscapes

I. New Hampshire

Children's voices in the orchard
Between the blossom- and the fruit-time:
Golden head, crimson head,
Between the green tip and the root.
Black wing, brown wing, hover over;
Twenty years and the spring is over;
To-day grieves, to-morrow grieves,
Cover me over, light-in-leaves;
Golden head, black wing,
Cling, swing,   10
Spring, sing,
Swing up into the apple-tree.

II. Virginia

Red river, red river,
Slow flow heat is silence
No will is still as a river
Still. Will heat move
Only through the mocking-bird
Heard once? Still hills
Wait. Gates wait. Purple trees,
White trees, wait, wait,   20
Delay, decay. Living, living,
Never moving. Ever moving
Iron thoughts came with me
And go with me:
Red river, river, river.

The Dry Salvages

(The Dry Salvages—presumably les trois
sauvages—*is a small group of rocks, with a
beacon, off the N.E. coast of Cape Ann,
Massachusetts.* Salvages *is pronounced to
rhyme with* assuages. Groaner: *a whistling
buoy.)*

I

I do not know much about gods; but I think
    that the river
Is a strong brown god—sullen, untamed and
    intractable,
Patient to some degree, at first recognised
    as a frontier;
Useful, untrustworthy, as a conveyor of
    commerce;
Then only a problem confronting the builder
    of bridges.
The problem once solved, the brown god is
    almost forgotten
By the dwellers in cities—ever, however,
    implacable,
Keeping his seasons and rages, destroyer,
    reminder
Of what men choose to forget. Unhonoured,
    unpropitiated
By worshippers of the machine, but waiting,
    watching and waiting.   10
His rhythm was present in the nursery
    bedroom,
In the rank ailanthus of the April dooryard,
In the smell of grapes on the autumn table,
And the evening circle in the winter gaslight.

    The river is within us, the sea is all about
        us;
The sea is the land's edge also, the granite
Into which it reaches, the beaches where it
        tosses
Its hints of earlier and other creation:
The starfish, the hermit crab, the whale's
        backbone;
The pools where it offers to our curiosity   20
The more delicate algae and the sea anemone.
It tosses up our losses, the torn seine,
The shattered lobsterpot, the broken oar
And the gear of foreign dead men. The sea has
        many voices,
Many gods and many voices.
                            The salt is on the
                                briar rose,
The fog is in the fir trees.
                            The sea howl
And the sea yelp, are different voices

---

l. 12. *ailanthus:* "tree of heaven," a common plant difficult to root out once it has established itself.

Often together heard; the whine in the
    rigging,   30
The menace and caress of wave that breaks
    on water,
The distant rote in the granite teeth,
And the wailing warning from the
    approaching headland
Are all sea voices, and the heaving groaner
Rounded homewards, and the seagull:
And under the oppression of the silent fog
The tolling bell
Measures time not our time, rung by the
    unhurried
Ground swell, a time
Older than the time of chronometers,
    older   40
Than time counted by anxious worried
    women
Lying awake, calculating the future,
Trying to unweave, unwind, unravel
And piece together the past and the future,
Between midnight and dawn, when the past
    is all deception,
The future futureless, before the morning
    watch
When time stops and time is never ending;
And the ground swell, that is and was from
    the beginning,
Clangs
The bell.   50

II

Where is there an end of it, the soundless
    wailing,
The silent withering of autumn flowers
Dropping their petals and remaining
    motionless;
Where is there an end to the drifting
    wreckage,
The prayer of the bone on the beach, the
    unprayable
Prayer at the calamitous annunciation?

There is no end, but addition: the trailing
Consequence of further days and hours,
While emotion takes to itself the emotionless

Years of living among the breakage   60
Of what was believed in as the most reliable—
And therefore the fittest for renunciation.

There is the final addition, the failing
Pride or resentment at failing powers,
The unattached devotion which might pass
    for devotionless,
In a drifting boat with a slow leakage,
The silent listening to the undeniable
Clamour of the bell of the last annunciation.

Where is the end of them, the fishermen
    sailing
Into the wind's tail, where the fog cowers? 70
We cannot think of a time that is oceanless
Or of an ocean not littered with wastage
Or of a future that is not liable
Like the past, to have no destination.

We have to think of them as forever bailing,
Setting and hauling, while the North East
    lowers
Over shallow banks unchanging and
    erosionless
Or drawing their money, drying sails at
    dockage;
Not as making a trip that will be unpayable
For a haul that will not bear examination. 80

There is no end of it, the voiceless wailing,
No end to the withering of withered flowers,
To the movement of pain that is painless and
    motionless,
To the drift of the sea and the drifting
    wreckage,
The bone's prayer to Death its God. Only the
    hardly, barely prayable
Prayer of the one Annunciation.

It seems, as one becomes older,
That the past has another pattern, and ceases
    to be a mere sequence—
Or even development: the latter a partial
    fallacy,
Encouraged by superficial notions of
    evolution,   90

Which becomes, in the popular mind, a means
    of disowning the past.
The moments of happiness—not the sense of
    well-being,
Fruition, fulfilment, security or affection,
Or even a very good dinner, but the sudden
    illumination—
We had the experience but missed the
    meaning,
And approach to the meaning restores the
    experience
In a different form, beyond any meaning
We can assign to happiness. I have said
    before
That the past experience revived in the
    meaning
Is not the experience of one life only   100
But of many generations—not forgetting
Something that is probably quite ineffable:
The backward look behind the assurance
Of recorded history, the backward half-look
Over the shoulder, towards the primitive
    terror.
Now, we come to discover that the moments
    of agony
(Whether, or not, due to misunderstanding,
Having hoped for the wrong things or
    dreaded the wrong things,
Is not in question) are likewise permanent
With such permanence as time has. We
    appreciate this better   110
In the agony of others, nearly experienced,
Involving ourselves, than in our own.
For our own past is covered by the currents
    of action,
But the torment of others remains an
    experience
Unqualified, unworn by subsequent attrition.
People change, and smile: but the agony
    abides.
Time the destroyer is time the preserver,
Like the river with its cargo of dead Negroes,
    cows and chicken coops,
The bitter apple and the bite in the apple.
And the ragged rock in the restless waters, 120
Waves wash over it, fogs conceal it;
On a halcyon day it is merely a monument,

In navigable weather it is always a seamark
To lay a course by: but in the sombre season
Or the sudden fury, is what it always was.

III

I sometimes wonder if that is what Krishna
    meant—
Among other things—or one way of putting
    the same thing:
That the future is a faded song, a Royal Rose
    or a lavender spray
Of wistful regret for those who are not yet
    here to regret,
Pressed between yellow leaves of a book that
    has never been opened.   130
And the way up is the way down, the way
    forward is the way back.
You cannot face it steadily, but this thing is
    sure,
That time is no healer: the patient is no
    longer here.
When the train starts, and the passengers are
    settled
To fruit, periodicals and business letters
(And those who saw them off have left the
    platform)
Their faces relax from grief into relief,
To the sleepy rhythm of a hundred hours.
Fare forward, travellers! not escaping from
    the past
Into different lives, or into any future;   140
You are not the same people who left that
    station
Or who will arrive at any terminus,
While the narrowing rails slide together
    behind you;
And on the deck of the drumming liner
Watching the furrow that widens behind you,
You shall not think "the past is finished"
Or "the future is before us."
At nightfall, in the rigging and the aerial,
Is a voice descanting (though not to the ear,

---

l. 126. *Krishna:* Hindu deity, hero of the *Bhagavadgita,*
whose sayings are translated in lines 131–133 and 151–
168.

The murmuring shell of time, and not in any
    language)   150
"Fare forward, you who think that you are
    voyaging;
You are not those who saw the harbour
Receding, or those who will disembark.
Here between the hither and the farther
    shore
While time is withdrawn, consider the future
And the past with an equal mind.
At the moment which is not of action or
    inaction
You can receive this: 'on whatever sphere of
    being
The mind of a man may be intent
At the time of death'—that is the one
    action   160
(And the time of death is every moment)
Which shall fructify in the lives of others:
And do not think of the fruit of action.
Fare forward.
                    O voyagers, O seamen,
You who come to port, and you whose bodies
Will suffer the trial and judgement of the sea,
Or whatever event, this is your real
    destination."
So Krishna, as when he admonished Arjuna
On the field of battle.   170
                    Not fare well,
But fare forward, voyagers.

IV

Lady, whose shrine stands on the promontory,
Pray for all those who are in ships, those
Whose business has to do with fish, and
Those concerned with every lawful traffic
And those who conduct them.

    Repeat a prayer also on behalf of
Women who have seen their sons or husbands
Setting forth, and not returning: 180
Figlia del tuo figlio,
Queen of Heaven.

Also pray for those who were in ships, and
Ended their voyage on the sand, in the sea's
    lips
Or in the dark throat which will not reject
    them
Or wherever cannot reach them the sound
    of the sea bell's
Perpetual angelus.

V

To communicate with Mars, converse with
    spirits,
To report the behaviour of the sea monster,
Describe the horoscope, haruspicate or
    scry,   190
Observe disease in signatures, evoke
Biography from the wrinkles of the palm
And tragedy from fingers; release omens
By sortilege, or tea leaves, riddle the
    inevitable
With playing cards, fiddle with pentagrams
Or barbituric acids, or dissect
The recurrent image into pre-conscious
    terrors—
To explore the womb, or tomb, or dreams;
    all these are usual
Pastimes and drugs, and features of the
    press:
And always will be, some of them
    especially   200
When there is distress of nations and
    perplexity
Whether on the shores of Asia, or in the
    Edgware Road.
Men's curiosity searches past and future
And clings to that dimension. But to
    apprehend
The point of intersection of the timeless
With time, is an occupation for the saint—
No occupation either, but something given
And taken, in a lifetime's death in love,
Ardour and selflessness and self-surrender.

---

l. 190. *haruspicate or scry:* to foresee the future by examining entrails of sacrificed animals or crystal gazing.

---

l. 181. *Figlia . . . figlio:* "the daughter of Thy Son."

For most of us, there is only the
    unattended   210
Moment, the moment in and out of time,
The distraction fit, lost in a shaft of sunlight,
The wild thyme unseen, or the winter
    lightning
Or the waterfall, or music heard so deeply
That it is not heard at all, but you are the
    music
While the music lasts. These are only hints
    and guesses,
Hints followed by guesses; and the rest
Is prayer, observance, discipline, thought
    and action.
The hint half guessed, the gift half
    understood, is Incarnation.
Here the impossible union   220
Of spheres of existence is actual,
Here the past and future
Are conquered, and reconciled,
Where action were otherwise movement
Of that which is only moved
And has in it no source of movement—
Driven by daemonic, chthonic
Powers. And right action is freedom
From past and future also.
For most of us, this is the aim   230
Never here to be realised;
Who are only undefeated
Because we have gone on trying;
We, content at the last
If our temporal reversion nourish
(Not too far from the yew-tree)
The life of significant soil.

                    [from *Four Quartets*]

---

l. 227. *chthonic:* underworld.

ARChibALd MACLEiSh

You, Andrew Marvell

And here face down beneath the sun
And here upon earth's noonward height
To feel the always coming on
The always rising of the night

To feel creep up the curving east
The earthy chill of dusk and slow
Upon those under lands the vast
And ever climbing shadow grow

And strange at Ecbatan the trees
Take leaf by leaf the evening strange   10
The flooding dark about their knees
The mountains over Persia change

And now at Kermanshah the gate
Dark empty and the withered grass
And through the twilight now the late
Few travelers in the westward pass

And Baghdad darken and the bridge
Across the silent river gone
And through Arabia the edge
Of evening widen and steal on   20

And deepen on Palmyra's street
The wheel rut in the ruined stone
And Lebanon fade out and Crete
High through the clouds and overblown

And over Sicily the air
Still flashing with the landward gulls
And loom and slowly disappear
The sails above the shadowy hulls

And Spain go under and the shore
Of Africa the gilded sand   30
And evening vanish and no more
The low pale light across that land

Nor now the long light on the sea

And here face downward in the sun
To feel how swift how secretly
The shadow of the night comes on . . .

The End of the World

Quite unexpectedly as Vasserot
The armless ambidextrian was lighting
A match between his great and second toe
And Ralph the lion was engaged in biting
The neck of Madame Sossman while the drum
Pointed, and Teeny was about to cough
In waltz-time swinging Jocko by the thumb—
Quite unexpectedly the top blew off:

And there, there overhead, there, there, hung
    over
Those thousands of white faces, those dazed
    eyes,   10
There in the starless dark the poise, the hover,
There with vast wings across the canceled
    skies,
There in the sudden blackness the black pall
Of nothing, nothing, nothing—nothing at all.

E. E. CUMMINGS

from Chansons Innocentes

I

in Just-
spring   when the world is mud-
luscious the little
lame balloonman

whistles   far   and wee

and eddieandbill come
running from marbles and
piracies and it's
spring

when the world is puddle-wonderful   10

the queer
old balloonman whistles
far   and   wee
and bettyandisbel come dancing

from hop-scotch and jump-rope and

it's
spring
and
    the

        goat-footed   20

balloonMan   whistles
far
and
wee

from Portraits

VIII

Buffalo Bill's
defunct
    who used to
    ride a watersmooth-silver
                  stallion
and break onetwothreefourfive
             pigeonsjustlikethat
                    Jesus

he was a handsome man
             and what i want to know is
how do you like your blueeyed boy   10
Mister Death

i sing of Olaf glad and big

i sing of Olaf glad and big
whose warmest heart recoiled at war:
a conscientious object-or

his wellbelovéd colonel(trig
westpointer most succinctly bred)
took erring Olaf soon in hand;
but—though an host of overjoyed
noncoms(first knocking on the head
him)do through icy waters roll
that helplessness which others stroke   10
with brushes recently employed
anent this muddy toiletbowl,
while kindred intellects evoke
allegiance per blunt instruments—
Olaf(being to all intents
a corpse and wanting any rag
upon what God unto him gave)
responds,without getting annoyed
"I will not kiss your f.ing flag"

straightway the silver bird looked grave   20
(departing hurriedly to shave)

but—though all kinds of officers
(a yearning nation's blueeyed pride)
their passive prey did kick and curse
until for wear their clarion
voices and boots were much the worse,
and egged the firstclassprivates on
his rectum wickedly to tease
by means of skilfully applied
bayonets roasted hot with heat—   30
Olaf(upon what were once knees)
does almost ceaselessly repeat
"there is some s. I will not eat"

our president,being of which
assertions duly notified
threw the yellowsonofabitch
into a dungeon,where he died

Christ(of His mercy infinite)
i pray to see;and Olaf,too

preponderatingly because   40
unless statistics lie he was
more brave than me:more blond than you.

anyone lived in a pretty how town

anyone lived in a pretty how town
(with up so floating many bells down)
spring summer autumn winter
he sang his didn't he danced his did.

Women and men(both little and small)
cared for anyone not at all
they sowed their isn't they reaped their same
sun moon stars rain

children guessed(but only a few
and down they forgot as up they grew   10
autumn winter spring summer)
that noone loved him more by more

when by now and tree by leaf
she laughed his joy she cried his grief
bird by snow and stir by still
anyone's any was all to her

someones married their everyones
laughed their cryings and did their dance
(sleep wake hope and then)they
said their nevers they slept their dream   20

stars rain sun moon
(and only the snow can begin to explain
how children are apt to forget to remember
with up so floating many bells down)

one day anyone died i guess
(and noone stooped to kiss his face)
busy folk buried them side by side
little by little and was by was

all by all and deep by deep
and more by more they dream their sleep   30

noone and anyone earth by april
wish by spirit and if by yes.

Women and men(both dong and ding)
summer autumn winter spring
reaped their sowing and went their came
sun moon stars rain

and lay still
while he passed(as

close as i'm to you
yes closer   10
made of nothing
except loneliness

what freedom's not some under's mere above

what freedom's not some under's mere above
but breathing yes which fear will never no?
measureless our pure living complete love
whose doom is beauty and its fate to grow

shall hate confound the wise?doubt blind
    the brave?
does mask wear face? have singings gone
    to say?
here youngest selves yet younger selves
    conceive
here's music's music and the day of day

are worlds collapsing?any was a glove
but i'm and you are actual either hand   10
is when for sale?forever is to give
and on forever's very now we stand

nor a first rose explodes but shall increase
whole truthful infinite immediate us

no time ago

no time ago
or else a life
walking in the dark
i met christ

jesus)my heart
flopped over

Robert Graves

Ulysses

To the much-tossed Ulysses, never done
    With woman whether gowned as wife
        or whore,
Penelope and Circe seemed as one:
She like a whore made his lewd fancies run,
    And wifely she a hero to him bore.

Their counter-changings terrified his way:
    They were the clashing rocks, Symplegades,
Scylla and Charybdis too were they;
Now they were storms frosting the sea with
        spray
    And now the lotus island's drunken ease. 10

They multiplied into the Sirens' throng,

---

l. 1. *Ulysses:* hero of Homer's *Odyssey;* King of Ithaca.
l. 3. *Penelope:* Ulysses' wife.
l. 3. *Circe:* an enchantress who changed Ulysses' crew into swine.
l. 7. *Symplegades:* two movable rocks where the Bosporus and Black Sea meet, said to have closed together when a ship attempted to sail between them.
l. 8. *Scylla:* a rock on which a sea monster dwelt, opposite Charybdis.
l. 8. *Charybdis:* a whirlpool.
l. 11. *Sirens:* mythological monsters who enticed seamen onto dangerous rocks by the sweetness of their singing.

Forewarned by fear of whom he stood
   bound fast
Hand and foot helpless to the vessel's mast,
Yet would not stop his ears: daring their song
   He groaned and sweated till that shore was
      past.

One, two and many: flesh had made him
   blind,
   Flesh had one pleasure only in the act,
Flesh set one purpose only in the mind—
Triumph of flesh and afterwards to find
   Still those same terrors wherewith flesh
      was racked.   20

His wiles were witty and his fame far known,
Every king's daughter sought him for her
   own,
   Yet he was nothing to be won or lost.
All lands to him were Ithaca: love-tossed
He loathed the fraud, yet would not bed alone.

Leda

Heart, with what lonely fears you ached,
   How lecherously mused upon
That horror with which Leda quaked
   Under the spread wings of the swan.

Then soon your mad religious smile
   Made taut the belly, arched the breast,
And there beneath your god awhile
   You strained and gulped your beastliest.

Pregnant you are, as Leda was,
   Of bawdry, murder and deceit;   10
Perpetuating night because
   The after-languors hang so sweet.

Leda: mortal seduced by Zeus in the disguise of a
swan.

To Juan at the Winter Solstice

There is one story and one story only
That will prove worth your telling,
Whether as learned bard or gifted child;
To it all lines or lesser gauds belong
That startle with their shining
Such common stories as they stray into.

Is it of trees you tell, their months and
   virtues,
Or strange beasts that beset you,
Of birds that croak at you the Triple will?
Or of the Zodiac and how slow it turns   10
Below the Boreal Crown,
Prison of all true kings that ever reigned?

Water to water, ark again to ark,
From woman back to woman:
So each new victim treads unfalteringly
The never altered circuit of his fate,
Bringing twelve peers as witness
Both to his starry rise and starry fall.

Or is it of the Virgin's silver beauty,
All fish below the thighs?   20
She in her left hand bears a leafy quince;
When with her right she crooks a finger,
   smiling,
How may the King hold back?
Royally then he barters life for love.

Or of the undying snake from chaos hatched,
Whose coils contain the ocean,

Juan: Graves' seventh child, born December 21, 1945,
the same day of the winter solstice when, according to
tradition, the "solar heroes" of antiquity were born.
l. 9. birds . . . will: The Raven, associated with fate and
death, will "croak" the will of the legendary three Fates
who spin the thread of destiny and cut off human life
as they please.
l. 10. Zodiac: an imaginary belt in the heavens including the paths of the moon and all the principal planets.
l. 17. twelve peers: The zodiac was divided into twelve
parts or signs.
l. 19. Virgin: Virgo, the mermaid, one of the zodiac's
twelve signs.

673   Robert Graves

Into whose chops with naked sword he
    springs,
Then in black water, tangled by the reeds,
Battles three days and nights,
To be spewed up beside her scalloped
    shore?   30

Much snow is falling, winds roar hollowly,
The owl hoots from the elder,
Fear in your heart cries to the loving-cup:
Sorrow to sorrow as the sparks fly upward.
The log groans and confesses:
There is one story and one story only.

Dwell on her graciousness, dwell on her
    smiling,
Do not forget what flowers
The great boar trampled down in ivy time.
Her brow was creamy as the crested wave, 40
Her sea-blue eyes were wild
But nothing promised that is not performed.

l. 34. *Sorrow . . . upward:* cf. Job 5:7, "Man is born unto
trouble, as the sparks fly upward."

HART CRANE

from Voyages

VI

Where icy and bright dungeons lift
Of swimmers their lost morning eyes,
And ocean rivers, churning, shift
Green borders under stranger skies,

Steadily as a shell secretes
Its beating leagues of monotone,

Or as many waters trough the sun's
Red kelson past the cape's wet stone;

O rivers mingling toward the sky
And harbor of the phœnix' breast—   10
My eyes pressed black against the prow,
—Thy derelict and blinded guest

Waiting, afire, what name, unspoke,
I cannot claim: let thy waves rear
More savage than the death of kings,
Some splintered garland for the seer.

Beyond siroccos harvesting
The solstice thunders, crept away,
Like a cliff swinging or a sail
Flung into April's inmost day—   20

Creation's blithe and petalled word
To the lounged goddess when she rose
Conceding dialogue with eyes
That smile unsearchable repose—

Still fervid covenant, Belle Isle,
—Unfolded floating dais before
Which rainbows twine continual hair—
Belle Isle, white echo of the oar!

The imaged Word, it is, that holds
Hushed willows anchored in its glow.   30
It is the unbetrayable reply
Whose accent no farewell can know.

For the Marriage of Faustus and Helen

"And so we may arrive by Talmud skill
And profane Greek to raise the building up
Of Helen's house against the Ismaelite,
King of Thogarma, and his habergeons
Brimstony, blue and fiery; and the force
Of King Abaddon, and the beast of Cittim;
Which Rabbi David Kimchi, Onkelos,
And Aben Ezra do interpret Rome."
                              —THE ALCHEMIST

I

The mind has shown itself at times
Too much the baked and labeled dough
Divided by accepted multitudes.
Across the stacked partitions of the day—
Across the memoranda, baseball scores,
The stenographic smiles and stock quotations
Smutty wings flash out equivocations.

The mind is brushed by sparrow wings;
Numbers, rebuffed by asphalt, crowd
The margins of the day, accent the curbs,   10
Convoying divers dawns on every corner
To druggist, barber and tobacconist,
Until the graduate opacities of evening
Take them away as suddenly to somewhere
Virginal perhaps, less fragmentary, cool.

> *There is the world dimensional for*
> *those untwisted by the love of things*
> *irreconcilable ...*

And yet, suppose some evening I forgot
The fare and transfer, yet got by that way   20
Without recall—lost yet poised in traffic.
Then I might find your eyes across an aisle,
Still flickering with those prefigurations—

Faustus and Helen: Faustus, a hero of several medieval
legends and a play by Christopher Marlowe, was an
old philosopher who sold his soul to the devil in
exchange for knowledge and power. Helen of Troy and
Faustus meet through the devil's conjuring.
The Alchemist: a play by Ben Jonson.

Prodigal, yet uncontested now,
Half-riant before the jerky window frame.

There is some way, I think, to touch
Those hands of yours that count the nights
Stippled with pink and green advertisements.
And now, before its arteries turn dark,
I would have you meet this bartered blood. 30
Imminent in his dream, none better knows
The white wafer cheek of love, or offers words
Lightly as moonlight on the eaves meets snow.

Reflective conversion of all things
At your deep blush, when ecstasies thread
The limbs and belly, when rainbows spread
Impinging on the throat and sides ...
Inevitable, the body of the world
Weeps in inventive dust for the hiatus
That winks above it, bluet in your breasts.   40

The earth may glide diaphanous to death;
But if I lift my arms it is to bend
To you who turned away once, Helen,
      knowing
The press of troubled hands, too alternate
With steel and soil to hold you endlessly.
I meet you, therefore, in that eventual flame
You found in final chains, no captive then—
Beyond their million brittle, bloodshot eyes;
White, through white cities passed on to
      assume
That world which comes to each of us alone.50

Accept a lone eye riveted to your plane,
Bent axle of devotion along companion ways
That beat, continuous, to hourless days—
One inconspicuous, glowing orb of praise.

II

Brazen hypnotics glitter here;
Glee shifts from foot to foot,
Magnetic to their tremolo.
This crashing opéra bouffe,

---

l. 58. *opéra bouffe:* comic opera.

Blest excursion! this ricochet
From roof to roof—   60
Know, Olympians, we are breathless
While nigger cupids scour the stars!

A thousand light shrugs balance us
Through snarling hails of melody.
White shadows slip across the floor
Splayed like cards from a loose hand;
Rhythmic ellipses lead into canters
Until somewhere a rooster banters.

Greet naïvely—yet intrepidly
New soothings, new amazements   70
That cornets introduce at every turn—
And you may fall downstairs with me
With perfect grace and equanimity.
Or, plaintively scud past shores
Where, by strange harmonic laws
All relatives, serene and cool,
Sit rocked in patent armchairs.

O, I have known metallic paradises
Where cuckoos clucked to finches
Above the deft catastrophes of drums.   80
While titters hailed the groans of death
Beneath gyrating awnings I have seen
The incunabula of the divine grotesque.
This music has a reassuring way.

The siren of the springs of guilty song—
Let us take her on the incandescent wax
Striated with nuances, nervosities
That we are heir to: she is still so young,
We cannot frown upon her as she smiles,
Dipping here in this cultivated storm   90
Among slim skaters of the gardened skies.

III

Capped arbiter of beauty in this street
That narrows darkly into motor dawn,—
You, here beside me, delicate ambassador
Of intricate slain numbers that arise
In whispers, naked of steel;
                              religious gunman!
Who faithfully, yourself, will fall too soon,

And in other ways than as the wind settles
On the sixteen thrifty bridges of the city:
Let us unbind our throats of fear and pity. 100

                              We even,
Who drove speediest destruction
In corymbulous formations of mechanics,—
Who hurried the hill breezes, spouting malice
Plangent over meadows, and looked down
On rifts of torn and empty houses
Like old women with teeth unjubilant
That waited faintly, briefly and in vain:

We know, eternal gunman, our flesh
    remembers
The tensile boughs, the nimble blue plateaus, 110
The mounted, yielding cities of the air!
That saddled sky that shook down vertical
Repeated play of fire—no hypogeum
Of wave or rock was good against one hour.

We did not ask for that, but have survived,
And will persist to speak again before
All stubble streets that have not curved
To memory, or known the ominous lifted arm
That lowers down the arc of Helen's brow
To saturate with blessing and dismay.   120

A goose, tobacco and cologne—
Three-winged and gold-shot prophecies of
    heaven,
The lavish heart shall always have to leaven
And spread with bells and voices, and atone
The abating shadows of our conscript dust.

Anchises' navel, dripping of the sea,—
The hands Erasmus dipped in gleaming tides,
Gathered the voltage of blown blood and
    vine;
Delve upward for the new and scattered wine,
O brother-thief of time, that we recall.   130
Laugh out the meager penance of their
    days

---

l. 126. *Anchises:* in Roman legend, father of Aeneas,
founder of Rome.
l. 127. *Erasmus:* Dutch humanist (1466?–1536), author
of *The Praise of Folly.*

Who dare not share with us the breath
   released,
The substance drilled and spent beyond repair
For golden, or the shadow of gold hair.

Distinctly praise the years, whose volatile
Blamed bleeding hands extend and thresh
   the height
The imagination spans beyond despair,
Outpacing bargain, vocable and prayer.

National Winter Garden

Outspoken buttocks in pink beads
Invite the necessary cloudy clinch
Of bandy eyes.... No extra mufflings here:
The world's one flagrant, sweating cinch.

And while legs waken salads in the brain
You pick your blonde out neatly through
   the smoke.
Always you wait for someone else though,
   always—
(Then rush the nearest exit through the
smoke).

Always and last, before the final ring
When all the fireworks blare, begins   10
A tom-tom scrimmage with a somewhere
   violin,
Some cheapest echo of them all—begins.

And shall we call her whiter than the snow?
Sprayed first with ruby, then with emerald
   sheen—
Least tearful and least glad (who knows her
   smile?)
A caught slide shows her sandstone grey
   between.

Her eyes exist in swivellings of her teats,
Pearls whip her hips, a drench of whirling
   strands.

Her silly snake rings begin to mount,
   surmount
Each other—turquoise fakes on tinselled
   hands.   20

We wait that writhing pool, her pearls
   collapsed,
—All but her belly buried in the floor;
And the lewd trounce of a final muted beat!
We flee her spasm through a fleshless door....

Yet, to the empty trapeze of your flesh,
O Magdalene, each comes back to die alone.
Then you, the burlesque of our lust—and
   faith,
Lug us back lifeward—bone by infant bone.

[from *The Bridge*]

Langston Hughes

Strange Hurt

In times of stormy weather
She felt queer pain
That said,
"You'll find rain better
Than shelter from the rain."

Days filled with fiery sunshine
Strange hurt she knew
That made
Her seek the burning sunlight
Rather than the shade.   10

In months of snowy winter
When cozy houses hold,
She'd break down doors
To wander naked
In the cold.

Trumpet Player

The Negro
With the trumpet at his lips
Has dark moons of weariness
Beneath his eyes
Where the smoldering memory
Of slave ships
Blazed to the crack of whips
About his thighs.

The Negro
With the trumpet at his lips   10
Has a head of vibrant hair
Tamed down,
Patent-leathered now
Until it gleams
Like jet—
Were jet a crown.

The music
From the trumpet at his lips
Is honey
Mixed with liquid fire.   20
The rhythm
From the trumpet at his lips
Is ecstasy
Distilled from old desire—

Desire
That is longing for the moon
Where the moonlight's but a spotlight
In his eyes,
Desire
That is longing for the sea   30
Where the sea's a bar-glass
Sucker size.

The Negro
With the trumpet at his lips
Whose jacket
Has a *fine* one-button roll,
Does not know
Upon what riff the music slips
Its hypodermic needle
To his soul—   40

But softly
As the tune comes from his throat
Trouble
Mellows to a golden note.

Daybreak in Alabama

When I get to be a composer
I'm gonna write me some music about
Daybreak in Alabama
And I'm gonna put the purtiest songs in it
Rising out of the ground like a swamp mist
And falling out of heaven like soft dew.
I'm gonna put some tall tall trees in it
And the scent of pine needles
And the smell of red clay after rain
And long red necks   10
And poppy colored faces
And big brown arms
And the field daisy eyes
Of black and white black white black people
And I'm gonna put white hands
And black hands and brown and yellow hands
And red clay earth hands in it
Touching everybody with kind fingers
And touching each other natural as dew
In that dawn of music when I   20
Get to be a composer
And write about daybreak
In Alabama.

RobERT pEnn WARREN

Pursuit

The hunchback on the corner, with gum and
    shoelaces,
Has his own wisdom and pleasures, and may
    not be lured
To divulge them to you, for he has merely
    endured
Your appeal for his sympathy and your kind
    purchases;
And wears infirmity but as the general who
    turns
Apart, in his famous old greatcoat there on
    the hill
At dusk when the rapture and cannonade
    are still,
To muse withdrawn from the dead, from his
    gorgeous subalterns;
Or stares from the thicket of his familiar
    pain, like a fawn
That meets you a moment, wheels, in
    imperious innocence is gone.   10

Go to the clinic. Wait in the outer room
Where like an old possum the snag-nailed
    hand will hump
On its knee in murderous patience, and the
    pomp
Of pain swells like the Indies, or a plum.
And there you will stand, as on the Roman
    hill,
Stunned by each withdrawn gaze and severe
    shape,
The first barbarian victor stood to gape
At the sacrificial fathers, white-robed, still;
And even the feverish old Jew stares stern
    with authority

Till you feel like one who has come too late,
    or improperly clothed, to a party.   20

The doctor will take you now. He is burly
    and clean;
Listening, like lover or worshiper, bends at
    your heart;
But cannot make out just what it tries to
    impart;
So smiles; says you simply need a change of
    scene.
Of scene, of solace: therefore Florida,
Where Ponce de Leon clanked among the
    lilies,
Where white sails skit on blue and cavort like
    fillies,
And the shoulder gleams in the moonlit
    corridor.
A change of love: if love is a groping
    Godward, though blind,
No matter what crevice, creek, chink, bright
    in dark, the pale tentacle find.   30

In Florida consider the flamingo
Its color passion but its neck a question;
Consider even that girl the other guests shun
On beach, at bar, in bed, for she may know
The secret you are seeking, after all;
Or the child you humbly sit by, excited and
    curly,
That screams on the shore at the sea's sunlit
    hurlyburly,
Till the mother calls its name, toward
    nightfall.
Till you sit alone: in the dire meridians, off
    Ireland, in fury
Of spume-tooth and dawnless sea-heave, salt
    rimes the lookout's devout eye.   40

Till you sit alone—which is the beginning of
    error—
Behind you the music and lights of the great
    hotel:

---

l. 18. *sacrificial fathers:* referring to the invasion of Rome by the Gauls in 390 B.C. The Roman Senate Fathers sat silent and indifferent and were slain.

l. 26. *Ponce de Leon:* Spanish explorer (1460?–1521), who discovered Florida while seeking the Fountain of Youth.

Solution, perhaps, is public, despair personal,
But history held to your breath clouds like
    a mirror.
There are many states, and towns in them,
    and faces,
But meanwhile, the little old lady in black, by
    the wall,
Who admires all the dancers, and tells you
    how just last fall
Her husband died in Ohio, and damp mists
    her glasses;
She blinks & croaks, like a toad or a Norn,
    in the horrible light,
And rattles her crutch, which may put forth a
    small bloom, perhaps white.   50

_____

l. 49. *Norn:* in Norse mythology, any of the three god-
desses (Past, Present, and Future) who determined the
destiny of gods and men.

Original Sin: A Short Story

Nodding, its great head rattling like a gourd,
And locks like seaweed strung on the
    stinking stone,
The nightmare stumbles past, and you have
    heard
It fumble your door before it whimpers and
    is gone:
It acts like the old hound that used to
    snuffle your door and moan.

You thought you had lost it when you left
    Omaha,
For it seemed connected then with your
    grandpa, who
Had a wen on his forehead and sat on the
    veranda
To finger the precious protuberance, as was
    his habit to do,
Which glinted in sun like rough garnet or
    the rich old brain bulging through.   10

But you met it in Harvard yard as the
    historic steeple

Was confirming the midnight with its hideous
    racket,
And you wondered how it had come, for it
    stood so imbecile,
With empty hands, humble, and surely
    nothing in pocket:
Riding the rods, perhaps—or grandpa's will
    paid the ticket.

You were almost kindly then, in your first
    homesickness,
As it tortured its stiff face to speak, but
    scarcely mewed;
Since then you have outlived all your
    homesickness,
But have met it in many another
    distempered latitude:
Oh, nothing is lost, ever lost! at last you
    understood.   20

But it never came in the quantum glare of
    sun
To shame you before your friends, and had
    nothing to do
With your public experience or private
    reformation:
But it thought no bed too narrow—it stood
    with lips askew
And shook its great head sadly like the
    abstract Jew.

Never met you in the lyric arsenical meadow
When children call and your heart goes stone
    in the bosom;
At the orchard anguish never, nor ovoid
    horror,
Which is furred like a peach or avid like the
    delicious plum.
It takes no part in your classic prudence or
    fondled axiom.   30

Not there when you exclaimed: "Hope is
    betrayed by
Disastrous glory of sea-capes, sun-torment of
    whitecaps
—There must be a new innocence for us to be
    stayed by."

But there it stood, after all the timetables,
  all the lamps,
In the crepuscular clutter of *always, always,*
  or *perhaps.*

You have moved often and rarely left an
  address,
And hear of the deaths of friends with a sly
  pleasure,
A sense of cleansing and hope, which blooms
  from distress;
But it has not died, it comes, its hand
  childish, unsure,
Clutching the bribe of chocolate or a toy you
  used to treasure.   **40**

It tries the lock; you hear, but simply drowse:
There is nothing remarkable in that sound at
  the door.
Later you hear it wander the dark house
Like a mother who rises at night to seek a
  childhood picture;
Or it goes to the backyard and stands like an
  old horse cold in the pasture.

W. H. AUdEN

Musée des Beaux Arts

About suffering they were never wrong,
The Old Masters: how well they understood
Its human position; how it takes place
While someone else is eating or opening a
  window or just walking dully along;
How, when the aged are reverently,
  passionately waiting

Musée . . . Arts: Museum of Fine Arts.

For the miraculous birth, there always
  must be
Children who did not specially want it to
  happen, skating
On a pond at the edge of the wood:
They never forgot
That even the dreadful martyrdom must
  run its course   **10**
Anyhow in a corner, some untidy spot
Where the dogs go on with their doggy life
  and the torturer's horse
Scratches its innocent behind on a tree.

In Brueghel's *Icarus,* for instance: how
  everything turns away
Quite leisurely from the disaster; the
  ploughman may
Have heard the splash, the forsaken cry,
But for him it was not an important failure;
  the sun shone
As it had to on the white legs disappearing
  into the green
Water: and the expensive delicate ship that
  must have seen
Something amazing, a boy falling out of the
  sky,   **20**
Had somewhere to get to and sailed calmly
  on.

---

l. 14. *Brueghel's Icarus:* referring to *Landscape with the Fall of Icarus* by Pieter Brueghel the Elder (1520?–1569), based on the legend of Daedalus and Icarus, father and son who escaped from the Labyrinth by fashioning wings for flying. When Icarus flew too close to the sun, the wax holding his wings together melted, and he fell to his death in the sea.

In Memory of W. B. Yeats

(*d. Jan. 1939*)

I

He disappeared in the dead of winter:
The brooks were frozen, the air-ports almost
  deserted,
And snow disfigured the public statues;

The mercury sank in the mouth of the dying
    day.
O all the instruments agree
The day of his death was a dark cold day.

Far from his illness
The wolves ran on through the evergreen
    forests,
The peasant river was untempted by the
    fashionable quays;
By mourning tongues   10
The death of the poet was kept from his
    poems.

But for him it was his last afternoon as
    himself,
An afternoon of nurses and rumours;
The provinces of his body revolted,
The squares of his mind were empty,
Silence invaded the suburbs,
The current of his feeling failed; he became
    his admirers.

Now he is scattered among a hundred cities
And wholly given over to unfamiliar
    affections;
To find his happiness in another kind of
    wood   20
And be punished under a foreign code of
    conscience.
The words of a dead man
Are modified in the guts of the living.

But in the importance and noise of to-morrow
When the brokers are roaring like beasts on
    the floor of the Bourse,
And the poor have the sufferings to which
    they are fairly accustomed,
And each in the cell of himself is almost
    convinced of his freedom;
A few thousand will think of this day
As one thinks of a day when one did
    something slightly unusual.

O all the instruments agree   30
The day of his death was a dark cold day.

II

You were silly like us: your gift survived
    it all;
The parish of rich women, physical decay,
Yourself; mad Ireland hurt you into poetry.
Now Ireland has her madness and her
    weather still,
For poetry makes nothing happen: it survives
In the valley of its saying where executives
Would never want to tamper; it flows south
From ranches of isolation and the busy griefs,
Raw towns that we believe and die in; it
    survives,   40
A way of happening, a mouth.

III

Earth, receive an honoured guest;
William Yeats is laid to rest:
Let the Irish vessel lie
Emptied of its poetry.

Time that is intolerant
Of the brave and innocent,
And indifferent in a week
To a beautiful physique,

Worships language and forgives   50
Everyone by whom it lives;
Pardons cowardice, conceit,
Lays its honours at their feet.

Time that with this strange excuse
Pardoned Kipling and his views,
And will pardon Paul Claudel,
Pardons him for writing well.

In the nightmare of the dark
All the dogs of Europe bark,

---

l. 25. *Bourse:* Paris Bourse, or stock exchange.

l. 55. *Kipling:* Rudyard Kipling (1865–1936), English author, celebrator of the British Empire.
l. 56. *Paul Claudel:* French poet, dramatist, and diplomat (1868–1955).

And the living nations wait,
Each sequestered in its hate;

Intellectual disgrace
Stares from every human face,
And the seas of pity lie
Locked and frozen in each eye.

Follow, poet, follow right
To the bottom of the night,
With your unconstraining voice
Still persuade us to rejoice;

With the farming of a verse   70
Make a vineyard of the curse,
Sing of human unsuccess
In a rapture of distress;

In the deserts of the heart
Let the healing fountain start,
In the prison of his days
Teach the free man how to praise.

Pur

This lunar beauty
Has no history
Is complete and early;
If beauty later
Bear any feature
It had a lover
And is another.

This like a dream
Keeps other time
And daytime is   10
The loss of this;
For time is inches
And the heart's changes
Where ghost has haunted
Lost and wanted.

But this was never
A ghost's endeavor

Nor finished this,
Was ghost at ease;
And till it pass   20
Love shall not near
The sweetness here
Nor sorrow take
His endless look.

THEODORE ROETHKE

I Knew a Woman

I knew a woman, lovely in her bones,
When small birds sighed, she would sigh
    back at them:
Ah, when she moved, she moved more ways
    than one:
The shapes a bright container can contain!
Of her choice virtues only gods should
    speak,
Or English poets who grew up on Greek
(I'd have them sing in chorus, cheek to
    cheek).

How well her wishes went! She stroked my
    chin,
She taught me Turn, and Counter-turn, and
    Stand;
She taught me Touch, that undulant white
    skin;   10
I nibbled meekly from her proffered hand;
She was the sickle; I, poor I, the rake,
Coming behind her for her pretty sake
(But what prodigious mowing we did make).

Love likes a gander, and adores a goose:
Her full lips pursed, the errant note to seize;
She played it quick, she played it light and
    loose;

My eyes, they dazzled at her flowing knees;
Her several parts could keep a pure repose,
Or one hip quiver with a mobile nose   20
(She moved in circles, and those circles
      moved).

Let seed be grass, and grass turn into hay:
I'm martyr to a motion not my own;
What's freedom for? To know eternity.
I swear she cast a shadow white as stone.
But who would count eternity in days?
These old bones live to learn her wanton
      ways:
(I measure time by how a body sways).

The Waking

I wake to sleep, and take my waking slow.
I feel my fate in what I cannot fear.
I learn by going where I have to go.

We think by feeling. What is there to know?
I hear my being dance from ear to ear.
I wake to sleep, and take my waking slow.

Of those so close beside me, which are you?
God bless the Ground! I shall walk softly
      there,
And learn by going where I have to go.

Light takes the Tree; but who can tell us
      how?   10
The lowly worm climbs up a winding stair;
I wake to sleep, and take my waking slow.

Great Nature has another thing to do
To you and me; so take the lively air,
And, lovely, learn by going where to go.

This shaking keeps me steady. I should know.
What falls away is always. And is near.
I wake to sleep, and take my waking slow.
I learn by going where I have to go.

In a Dark Time

In a dark time, the eye begins to see.
I meet my shadow in the deepening shade;
I hear my echo in the echoing wood—
A lord of nature weeping to a tree.
I live between the heron and the wren,
Beasts of the hill and serpents of the den.

What's madness but nobility of soul
At odds with circumstance? The day's on fire!
I know the purity of pure despair,
My shadow pinned against a sweating wall. 10
That place among the rocks—is it a cave,
Or winding path? The edge is what I have.

A steady storm of correspondences!
A night flowing with birds, a ragged moon,
And in broad day the midnight comes again!
A man goes far to find out what he is—
Death of the self in a long, tearless night,
All natural shapes blazing unnatural light.

Dark, dark my light, and darker my desire.
My soul, like some heat-maddened summer
      fly,   20
Keeps buzzing at the sill. Which I is *I?*
A fallen man, I climb out of my fear.
The mind enters itself, and God the mind,
And one is One, free in the tearing wind.

stephen spender

An Elementary School Classroom in a Slum

Far far from gusty waves these children's
   faces.
Like rootless weeds, the hair torn round
   their pallor.
The tall girl with her weighed-down head.
   The paper-
seeming boy, with rat's eyes. The stunted,
   unlucky heir
Of twisted bones, reciting a father's gnarled
   disease,
His lesson from his desk. At back of the dim
   class
One unnoted, sweet and young. His eyes live
   in a dream
Of squirrel's game, in tree room, other than
   this.

On sour cream walls, donations.
   Shakespeare's head,
Cloudless at dawn, civilized dome riding
   all cities.   10
Belled, flowery, Tyrolese valley. Open-handed
   map
Awarding the world its world. And yet,
   for these
Children, these windows, not this world,
   are world,
Where all their future's painted with a fog,
A narrow street sealed in with a lead sky,
Far far from rivers, capes, and stars of words.

Surely, Shakespeare is wicked, the map a bad
   example
With ships and sun and love tempting them
   to steal—
For lives that slyly turn in their cramped
   holes

From fog to endless night? On their slag
   heap, these children   20
Wear skins peeped through by bones and
   spectacles of steel
With mended glass, like bottle bits on stones.
All of their time and space are foggy slum.
So blot their maps with slums as big as doom.

Unless, governor, teacher, inspector, visitor,
This map becomes their window and these
   windows
That shut upon their lives like catacombs,
Break O break open till they break the town
And show the children to green fields, and
   make their world
Run azure on gold sands, and let their
   tongues   30
Run naked into books, the white and green
   leaves open
History theirs whose language is the sun.

Thoughts During an Air Raid

Of course, the entire effort is to put oneself
Outside the ordinary range
Of what are called statistics. A hundred are
   killed
In the outer suburbs. Well, well, one carries
   on.
So long as this thing 'I' propped up on
The girdered bed which seems so like a
   hearse,
In the hotel bedroom with the wall-paper
Blowing smoke-wreaths of roses, one can
   ignore
The pressure of those names under the
   fingers
Indented by lead type on newsprint,   10
In the bar, the marginal wailing wireless.
Yet supposing that a bomb should dive
Its nose right through this bed, with one
   upon it?
The thought's obscene. Still, there are many

For whom one's loss would illustrate
The 'impersonal' use indeed. The essential is
That every 'one' should remain separate
Propped up unde   roses, and no one suffer
For his neighbour. Then horror is postponed
Piecemeal for each, until it settles on him   20
That wreath of incommunicable grief
Which is all mystery or nothing.

Seascape

(In Memoriam, M.A.S.)

There are some days the happy ocean lies
Like an unfingered harp, below the land.
Afternoon gilds all the silent wires
Into a burning music for the eyes.
On mirrors flashing between fine-strung fires
The shore, heaped up with roses, horses,
   spires,
Wanders on water, walking above ribbed
   sand.

The motionlessness of the hot sky tires
And a sigh, like a woman's, from inland
Brushes the instrument with shadowing
   hand   10
Drawing across its wires some gull's sharp
   cries
Or bell, or shout, from distant, hedged-in
   shires;
These, deep as anchors, the hushing wave
   buries.

Then from the shore, two zig-zag butterflies,
Like errant dog-roses, cross the bright strand
Spiralling over sea in foolish gyres
Until they fall into reflected skies.
They drown. Fishermen understand
Such wings sunk in such ritual sacrifice,

Recalling legends of undersea, drowned
   cities.   20

What voyagers, oh what heroes, flamed like
   pyres
With helmets plumed, have set forth from
   some island
And them the sea engulfed. Their eyes,
Contorted by the cruel waves' desires
Glitter with coins through the tide scarcely
   scanned,
While, above them, that harp assumes their
   sighs.

ELIZABETH bishop

A Miracle for Breakfast

At six o'clock we were waiting for coffee,
waiting for coffee and the charitable crumb
that was going to be served from a certain
   balcony,
—like kings of old, or like a miracle.
It was still dark. One foot of the sun
steadied itself on a ripple in the river.

The first ferry of the day had just crossed the
   river.
It was so cold we hoped that the coffee
would be very hot, seeing that the sun
was not going to warm us; and that the
   crumb   10
would be a loaf each, buttered, by a miracle.
At seven a man stepped out on the balcony.

He stood for a minute alone on the balcony
looking over our heads toward the river.
A servant handed him the makings of a
   miracle,
consisting of one lone cup of coffee
and one roll, which he proceeded to crumb,
his head, so to speak, in the clouds—along
   with the sun.

Was the man crazy? What under the sun
was he trying to do, up there on his
    balcony!   20
Each man received one rather hard crumb,
which some flicked scornfully into the river,
and, in a cup, one drop of the coffee.
Some of us stood around, waiting for the
    miracle.

I can tell what I saw next; it was not a
    miracle.
A beautiful villa stood in the sun
and from its doors came the smell of hot
    coffee.
In front, a baroque white plaster balcony
added by birds, who nest along the river,
—I saw it with one eye close to the
    crumb—   30

and galleries and marble chambers. My
    crumb
my mansion, made for me a miracle,
through ages, by insects, birds, and the river
working the stone. Every day, in the sun,
at breakfast time I sit on my balcony
with my feet up, and drink gallons of coffee.

We licked up the crumb and swallowed the
    coffee.
A window across the river caught the sun
as if the miracle were working, on the wrong
    balcony.

Roosters

At four o'clock
in the gun-metal blue dark
we hear the first crow of the first cock

just below
the gun-metal blue window
and immediately there is an echo

off in the distance,
then one from the back-yard fence,
then one, with horrible insistence,

grates like a wet match   10
from the broccoli patch,
flares, and all over town begins to catch.

Cries galore
come from the water-closet door,
from the dropping-plastered henhouse floor,

where in the blue blur
their rustling wives admire,
the roosters brace their cruel feet and glare

with stupid eyes
while from their beaks there rise   20
the uncontrolled, traditional cries.

Deep from protruding chests
in green-gold medals dressed,
planned to command and terrorize the rest,

the many wives
who lead hens' lives
of being courted and despised;

deep from raw throats
a senseless order floats
all over town. A rooster gloats   30

over our beds
from rusty iron sheds
and fences made from old bedsteads,

over our churches
where the tin rooster perches,
over our little wooden northern houses,

making sallies
from all the muddy alleys,
marking out maps like Rand McNally's:

glass-headed pins,   40
oil-golds and copper-greens,
anthracite blues, alizarins,

each one an active
displacement in perspective;
each screaming, "This is where I live!"

Each screaming,
"Get up! Stop dreaming!"
Roosters, what are you projecting?

You, whom the Greeks elected
to shoot at on a post, who struggled   50
when sacrificed, you whom they labelled

"Very combative . . ."
what right have you to give
commands, and tell us how to live,

cry, "Here!" and "Here!"
and wake us here where are
unwanted love, conceit, and war?

The crown of red
set on your little head
is charged with all your fighting-blood.   60

Yes, that excrescence
makes a most virile presence,
plus all that vulgar beauty of iridescence.

Now in mid-air
by twos they fight each other.
Down comes a first flame-feather,

and one is flying,
with raging heroism defying
even the sensation of dying.

And one has fallen,   70
but still above the town
his torn-out, bloodied feathers drift down;

and what he sung
no matter. He is flung
on the gray ash-heap, lies in dung

with his dead wives
with open, bloody eyes,
while those metallic feathers oxidize.

*   *   *

St. Peter's sin
was worse than that of Magdalen   80
whose sin was of the flesh alone;

of spirit, Peter's,
falling, beneath the flares,
among the "servants and officers."

Old holy sculpture
could set it all together
in one small scene, past and future:

Christ stands amazed,
Peter, two fingers raised
to surprised lips, both as if dazed.   90

But in between
a little cock is seen
carved on a dim column in the travertine,

explained by *gallus canit;*
flet Petrus underneath it.
There is inescapable hope, the pivot;

yes, and there Peter's tears
run down our chanticleer's
sides and gem his spurs.

Tear-encrusted thick   100
as a medieval relic
he waits. Poor Peter, heart-sick,

still cannot guess
those cock-a-doodles yet might bless,
his dreadful rooster come to mean
     forgiveness,

a new weathervane
on basilica and barn,
and that outside the Lateran

---

ll. 94–95. *gallus . . . Petrus:* literally, "[the] cock crows;
Peter weeps."

there would always be
a bronze cock on a porphyry   110
pillar so the people and the Pope might see

that even the Prince
of the Apostles long since
had been forgiven, and to convince

all the assembly
that "Deny deny deny,"
is not all the roosters cry.

In the morning
a low light is floating
in the backyard, and gilding   120

from underneath
the broccoli, leaf by leaf;
how could the night have come to grief?

gilding the tiny
floating swallow's belly
and lines of pink cloud in the sky,

the day's preamble
like wandering lines in marble.
The cocks are now almost inaudible.

The sun climbs in,   130
following "to see the end,"
faithful as enemy, or friend.

brother antoninus (william everson)

The Stranger

Pity this girl.
At callow sixteen,
Glib in the press of rapt companions,
She bruits her smatter,
Her bed-lore brag.
She prattles the lip-learned, light-love list.
In the new itch and squirm of sex,
How can she foresee?

How can she foresee the thick stranger,
Over the hills from Omaha,   10
Who will break her across a hired bed,
Open the loins,
Rive the breach,
And set the foetus wailing within the womb,
To hunch toward the knowledge of its
    disease,
And shamble down time to doomsday?

I Am Long Weaned

When I looked for good then evil came, and
when I waited for light then came darkness.
My bowels boil, and rest not.
                                    —THE BOOK OF JOB

I am long weaned.

My mouth, puckered on gall,
Sucks dry curd.

My thoughts, those sterile watercourses
Scarring a desert.

My throat is lean meat.
In my belly no substance is,
Nor water moves.

My gut goes down
A straight drop to my groin.   10

My cod is withered string,
My seed, two flints in a sack.

Some day, in some other place,
Will come a rain;
Will come water out of deep wells,
Will come melons sweet from the vine.

I will know God.

Sophia, deep wisdom,
The splendid unquenchable fount:

Unbind those breasts.   20

MURiEL RukEysER

Effort at Speech Between Two People

Speak to me.   Take my hand.   What
    are you now?
I will tell you all.   I will conceal nothing.
When I was three, a little child read a story
    about a rabbit
who died, in the story, and I crawled under a
    chair:
a pink rabbit: it was my birthday, and a
    candle
burnt a sore spot on my finger, and I was
    told to be happy.

Oh, grow to know me.   I am not happy.   I
    will be open:
Now I am thinking of white sails against a
    sky like music,
like glad horns blowing, and birds tilting,
    and an arm about me.
There was one I loved, who wanted to live,
    sailing.   10

Speak to me.   Take my hand.   What
    are you now?
When I was nine, I was fruitily sentimental,
fluid: and my widowed aunt played Chopin,
and I bent my head on the painted
    woodwork, and wept.
I want now to be close to you.   I would
link the minutes of my days close, somehow,
    to your days.

I am not happy.   I will be open.
I have liked lamps in evening corners, and
    quiet poems.
There has been fear in my life.   Sometimes
    I speculate
On what a tragedy his life was, really.   20

Take my hand.   Fist my mind in your hand.
    What are you now?
When I was fourteen, I had dreams of suicide,
and I stood at a steep window, at sunset,
    hoping toward death:
if the light had not melted clouds and plains
    to beauty,
if light had not transformed that day, I
    would have leapt,
I am unhappy.   I am lonely.   Speak to
me.

I will be open.   I think he never loved me:
he loved the bright beaches, the little lips of
    foam
that ride small waves, he loved the veer of
    gulls:
he said with a gay mouth: I love you.   Grow
    to know me.   30

---

l. 13. *Chopin:* Polish pianist and composer (1810–1849).

What are you now?   If we could touch one
    another,
if these our separate entities could come to
    grips,
clenched like a Chinese puzzle . . . yesterday
I stood in a crowded street that was live with
    people,
and no one spoke a word, and the morning
    shone.
Everyone silent, moving. . . . Take my hand.
    Speak to me.

Reading Time: 1 Minute 26 Seconds

The fear of poetry is the
fear: mystery and fury of a midnight street
of windows whose low voluptuous voice
issues, and after that there is no peace.

That round waiting moment in the
theatre: curtain rises, dies into the ceiling
and here is played the scene with the mother
bandaging a revealed son's head. The bandage
    is torn off.
Curtain goes down. And here is the moment
    of proof.

That climax when the brain acknowledges
    the world,   10
all values extended into the blood awake.
Moment of proof. And as they say Brancusi
    did,
building his bird to extend through soaring
    air,
as Kafka planned stories that draw to
    eternity
through time extended. And the climax
    strikes.

---

l. 12. *Brancusi:* Constantin Brancusi, Rumanian-born
French abstract sculptor (1876–1957).

Love touches so, that mouths after the look
    of
blue stare of love, the footbeat on the heart
is translated into the pure cry of birds
following air-cries, or poems, the new scene.
Moment of proof. That strikes long after
    act.   20

They fear it. They turn away, hand up palm
    out
fending off moment of proof, the straight
    look, poem.
The prolonged wound-consciousness after the
    bullet's shot.
The prolonged love after the look is dead,
the yellow joy after the song of the sun.

dyLan Thomas

If I Were Tickled by the Rub of Love

If I were tickled by the rub of love,
A rooking girl who stole me for her side,
Broke through her straws, breaking my
    bandaged string,
If the red tickle as the cattle calve
Still set to scratch a laughter from my lung,
I would not fear the apple nor the flood
Nor the bad blood of spring.

Shall it be male or female? say the cells,
And drop the plum like fire from the flesh.
If I were tickled by the hatching hair,   10
The winging bone that sprouted in the heels,
The itch of man upon the baby's thigh,
I would not fear the gallows nor the axe
Nor the crossed sticks of war.

Shall it be male or female? say the fingers
That chalk the walls with green girls and
    their men.
I would not fear the muscling-in of love
If I were tickled by the urchin hungers
Rehearsing heat upon a raw-edged nerve.
I would not fear the devil in the loin   20
Nor the outspoken grave.

If I were tickled by the lovers' rub
That wipes away not crow's-foot nor the lock
Of sick old manhood on the fallen jaws,
Time and the crabs and the sweethearting
    crib
Would leave me cold as butter for the flies,
The sea of scums could drown me as it broke
Dead on the sweethearts' toes.

This world is half the devil's and my own,
Daft with the drug that's smoking in a girl 30
And curling round the bud that forks her eye.
An old man's shank one-marrowed with my
    bone,
And all the herrings smelling in the sea,
I sit and watch the worm beneath my nail
Wearing the quick away.

And that's the rub, the only rub that tickles.
The knobbly ape that swings along his sex
From damp love-darkness and the nurse's
    twist
Can never raise the midnight of a chuckle,
Nor when he finds a beauty in the breast   40
Of lover, mother, lovers, or his six
Feet in the rubbing dust.

And what's the rub? Death's feather on the
    nerve?
Your mouth, my love, the thistle in the kiss?
My Jack of Christ born thorny on the tree?
The words of death are dryer than his stiff,
My wordy wounds are printed with your hair.
I would be tickled by the rub that is:
Man be my metaphor.

A Refusal to Mourn the Death, by Fire, of a Child in London

Never until the mankind making
Bird beast and flower
Fathering and all humbling darkness
Tells with silence the last light breaking
And the still hour
Is come of the sea tumbling in harness

And I must enter again the round
Zion of the water bead
And the synagogue of the ear of corn
Shall I let pray the shadow of a sound   10
Or sow my salt seed
In the least valley of sackcloth to mourn

The majesty and burning of the child's death.
I shall not murder
The mankind of her going with a grave truth
Nor blaspheme down the stations of the
    breath
With any further
Elegy of innocence and youth.

Deep with the first dead lies London's
    daughter,
Robed in the long friends,   20
The grains beyond age, the dark veins of her
    mother,
Secret by the unmourning water
Of the riding Thames.
After the first death, there is no other.

Do Not Go Gentle into that Good Night

Do not go gentle into that good night,
Old age should burn and rave at close of day;
Rage, rage against the dying of the light.

Though wise men at their end know dark
    is right,

Because their words had forked no lightning
   they
Do not go gentle into that good night.

Good men, the last wave by, crying how
   bright
Their frail deeds might have danced in a
   green bay,
Rage, rage against the dying of the light.

Wild men who caught and sang the sun in
   flight,   10
And learn, too late, they grieved it on its way,
Do not go gentle into that good night.

Grave men, near death, who see with blinding
   sight
Blind eyes could blaze like meteors and be
   gay,
Rage, rage against the dying of the light.

And you, my father, there on the sad height,
Curse, bless, me now with your fierce tears, I
   pray.
Do not go gentle into that good night.
Rage, rage against the dying of the light.

Fern Hill

Now as I was young and easy under the apple
   boughs
About the lilting house and happy as the
   grass was green,
   The night above the dingle starry,
      Time let me hail and climb
   Golden in the heydays of his eyes,
And honoured among wagons I was prince of
   the apple towns
And once below a time I lordly had the trees
   and leaves
      Trail with daisies and barley
   Down the rivers of the windfall light.

And as I was green and carefree, famous
      among the barns   10

About the happy yard and singing as the farm
      was home,
   In the sun that is young once only,
      Time let me play and be
   Golden in the mercy of his means,
And green and golden I was huntsman and
      herdsman, the calves
Sang to my horn, the foxes on the hills barked
      clear and cold,
      And the sabbath rang slowly
   In the pebbles of the holy streams.

All the sun long it was running, it was lovely,
   the hay
Fields high as the house, the tunes from the
      chimneys, it was air   20
   And playing, lovely and watery
      And fire green as grass.
   And nightly under the simple stars
As I rode to sleep the owls were bearing the
      farm away,
All the moon long I heard, blessed among
      stables, the nightjars
   Flying with the ricks, and the horses
      Flashing into the dark.

And then to awake, and the farm, like a
      wanderer white
With the dew, come back, the cock on his
      shoulder: it was all
   Shining, it was Adam and maiden,   30
      The sky gathered again
   And the sun grew round that very day.
So it must have been after the birth of the
      simple light
In the first, spinning place, the spellbound
      horses walking warm
   Out of the whinnying green stable
      On to the fields of praise.

And honoured among foxes and pheasants by
      the gay house
Under the new made clouds and happy as the
      heart was long
   In the sun born over and over,
      I ran my heedless ways,   40

My wishes raced through the house
    high hay
And nothing I cared, at my sky blue trades,
    that time allows
In all his tuneful turning so few and such
    morning songs
  Before the children green and golden
    Follow him out of grace,

Nothing I cared, in the lamb white days,
    that time would take me
Up to the swallow thronged loft by the
    shadow of my hand,
  In the moon that is always rising,
    Nor that riding to sleep
  I should hear him fly with the high
    fields   50
And wake to the farm forever fled from the
    childless land.
Oh as I was young and easy in the mercy of
    his means,
  Time held me green and dying
  Though I sang in my chains like the sea.

MARGARET WALKER

For My People

For my people everywhere singing their
  slave songs repeatedly: their dirges
  and their ditties and their blues and
  jubilees, praying their prayers nightly
  to an unknown god, bending their
  knees humbly to an unseen power;

For my people lending their strength to
  the years, to the gone years and the
  now years and the maybe years, washing ironing cooking scrubbing sewing 10

mending hoeing plowing digging
  planting pruning patching dragging
  along never gaining never reaping
  never knowing and never understanding;

For my playmates in the clay and dust
  and sand of Alabama backyards playing baptizing and preaching and doctor and jail and soldier and school
  and mama and cooking and playhouse 20
  and concert and store and hair and
  Miss Choomby and company;

For the cramped bewildered years we
  went to school to learn to know the
  reasons why and the answers to and
  the people who and the places where
  and the days when, in memory of the
  bitter hours when we discovered we
  were black and poor and small and
  different and nobody cared and no- 30
  body wondered and nobody understood;

For the boys and girls who grew in spite
  of these things to be man and woman,
  to laugh and dance and sing and play
  and drink their wine and religion and
  success, to marry their playmates and
  bear children and then die of consumption and anemia and lynching;

For my people thronging 47th Street in 40
  Chicago and Lenox Avenue in New
  York and Rampart Street in New
  Orleans, lost disinherited dispossessed
  and happy people filling the cabarets
  and taverns and other people's pockets
  needing bread and shoes and milk and
  land and money and something—
  something all our own;

For my people walking blindly spreading
  joy, losing time being lazy, sleeping 50
  when hungry, shouting when burdened, drinking when hopeless, tied

and shackled and tangled among ourselves by the unseen creatures who
tower over us omnisciently and laugh;

For my people blundering and groping and floundering in the dark of
churches and schools and clubs and
societies, associations and councils
and committees and conventions, dis- 60
tressed and disturbed and deceived
and devoured by money-hungry glory-
craving leeches, preyed on by facile
force of state and fad and novelty,
by false prophet and holy believer;

For my people standing staring trying to
fashion a better way from confusion,
from hypocrisy and misunderstanding, trying to fashion a world that will
hold all the people, all the faces, all 70
the adams and eves and their countless generations;

Let a new earth rise. Let another world be
born. Let a bloody peace be written
in the sky. Let a second generation full
of courage issue forth; let a people
loving freedom come to growth. Let a
beauty full of healing and a strength
of final clenching be the pulsing in our
spirits and our blood. Let the martial 80
songs be written, let the dirges disappear. Let a race of men now rise
and take control.

Whores

When I grew up I went away to work
where painted whores were fascinating
   sights.
They came on like whole armies through the
   nights—
their sullen eyes on mine, their mouths a
   smirk,

and from their hands keys hung suggestively.
Old women working by an age-old plan
to make their bread in ways as best they can
would hobble past and beckon tirelessly.

Perhaps one day they'll all die in the streets
or be surprised by bombs in each wide bed; 10
learning too late in unaccustomed dread
that easy ways, like whores on special beats,
no longer have the gift to harbor pride
or bring men peace, or leave them satisfied.

Gwendolyn brooks

The Children of the Poor

1

People who have no children can be hard:
Attain a mail of ice and insolence:
Need not pause in the fire, and in no sense
Hesitate in the hurricane to guard.
And when wide world is bitten and bewarred
They perish purely, waving their spirits hence
Without a trace of grace or of offense
To laugh or fail, diffident, wonder-starred.
While through a throttling dark we others
   hear
The little lifting helplessness, the queer 10
Whimper-whine; whose unridiculous
Lost softness softly makes a trap for us.
And makes a curse. And makes a sugar of
The malocclusions, the inconditions of love.

2

What shall I give my children? who are poor,
Who are adjudged the leastwise of the land,

Who are my sweetest lepers, who demand
No velvet and no velvety velour;
But who have begged me for a brisk contour,
Crying that they are quasi, contraband   20
Because unfinished, graven by a hand
Less than angelic, admirable or sure.
My hand is stuffed with mode, design, device.
But I lack access to my proper stone.
And plenitude or plan shall not suffice
Nor grief nor love shall be enough alone
To ratify my little halves who bear
Across an autumn freezing everywhere.

3

And shall I prime my children, pray, to pray?
Mites, come invade most frugal vestibules   30
Spectered with crusts of penitents' renewals
And all hysterics arrogant for a day.
Instruct yourselves here is no devil to pay.
Children, confine your lights in jellied rules;
Resemble graves; be metaphysical mules;
Learn Lord will not distort nor leave the fray.
Behind the scurryings of your neat motif
I shall wait, if you wish: revise the psalm
If that should frighten you: sew up belief
If that should tear: turn, singularly calm   40
At forehead and at fingers rather wise,
Holding the bandage ready for your eyes.

4

First fight. Then fiddle. Ply the slipping string
With feathery sorcery; muzzle the note
With hurting love; the music that they wrote
Bewitch, bewilder. Qualify to sing
Threadwise. Devise no salt, no hempen thing
For the dear instrument to bear. Devote
The bow to silks and honey. Be remote
A while from malice and from murdering.   50
But first to arms, to armor. Carry hate
In front of you and harmony behind.
Be deaf to music and to beauty blind.
Win war. Rise bloody, maybe not too late
For having first to civilize a space
Wherein to play your violin with grace.

5

When my dears die, the festival-colored
    brightness
That is their motion and mild repartee
Enchanted, a macabre mockery
Charming the rainbow radiance into
    tightness   60
And into a remarkable politeness
That is not kind and does not want to be,
May not they in the crisp encounter see
Something to recognize and read as
    rightness?
I say they may, so granitely discreet,
The little crooked questionings inbound,
Concede themselves on most familiar ground,
Cold an old predicament of the breath:
Adroit, the shapely prefaces complete,
Accept the university of death.   70

ROBERT LOWELL

Children of Light

Our fathers wrung their bread from stocks
    and stones
And fenced their gardens with the Redman's
    bones;
Embarking from the Nether Land of
    Holland,
Pilgrims unhoused by Geneva's night,
They planted here the Serpent's seeds of
    light;

Children of Light: derived from Luke 16.
l. 4. *unhouseled:* not having received Communion.
l. 4. *Geneva:* the center of Calvinistic doctrine, a strong
influence on Puritanism.

And here the pivoting searchlights probe to
  shock
The riotous glass houses built on rock,
And candles gutter by an empty altar,
And light is where the landless blood of Cain
Is burning, burning the unburied grain.   10

The Dead in Europe

After the planes unloaded, we fell down
Buried together, unmarried men and women;
Not crown of thorns, not iron, not Lombard
  crown,
Not grilled and spindle spires pointing to
  heaven
Could save us. Raise us, Mother, we fell down
Here hugger-mugger in the jellied fire:
Our sacred earth in our day was our curse.

Our Mother, shall we rise on Mary's day
In Maryland, wherever corpses married
Under the rubble, bundled together? Pray   10
For us whom the blockbusters marred and
  buried;
When Satan scatters us on Rising-day,
O Mother, snatch our bodies from the fire:
Our sacred earth in our day was our curse.

Mother, my bones are trembling and I hear
The earth's reverberations and the trumpet
Bleating into my shambles. Shall I bear,
(O Mary!) unmarried man and powder-
  puppet,
Witness to the Devil? Mary, hear,
O Mary, marry earth, sea, air and fire;   20
Our sacred earth in our day is our curse.

Skunk Hour

(*For Elizabeth Bishop*)

Nautilus Island's hermit
heiress still lives through winter in her
    Spartan cottage;
her sheep still graze above the sea.
Her son's a bishop. Her farmer
is first selectman in our village;
she's in her dotage.

Thirsting for
the hierarchic privacy
of Queen Victoria's century,
she buys up all   10
the eyesores facing her shore,
and lets them fall.

The season's ill—
we've lost our summer millionaire,
who seemed to leap from an L. L. Bean
catalogue. His nine-knot yawl
was auctioned off to lobstermen.
A red fox stain covers Blue Hill.

And now our fairy
decorator brightens his shop for fall;   20
his fishnet's filled with orange cork,
orange, his cobbler's bench and awl;
there is no money in his work,
he'd rather marry.

One dark night,
my Tudor Ford climbed the hill's skull;
I watched for love-cars. Lights turned down,
they lay together, hull to hull,
where the graveyard shelves on the town....
My mind's not right.   30

A car radio bleats,
"Love, O careless love...." I hear
my ill-spirit sob in each blood cell,
as if my hand were at its throat....

I myself am hell;
nobody's here—

only skunks, that search
in the moonlight for a bite to eat.
They march on their soles up Main Street:
white stripes, moonstruck eyes' red fire   40
under the chalk-dry and spar spire
of the Trinitarian Church.

I stand on top
of our back steps and breathe the rich air—
a mother skunk with her column of kittens
    swills the garbage pail.
She jabs her wedge-head in a cup
of sour cream, drops her ostrich tail,
and will not scare.

---

l. 35. *I . . . hell:* See Satan's speeches in Milton's *Paradise Lost*, Book IV, lines 73–78, 506–511.

RichARd wilbuR

Juggler

A ball will bounce, but less and less. It's not
A light-hearted thing, resents its own
    resilience.
Falling is what it loves, and the earth falls
So in our hearts from brilliance,
Settles and is forgot.
It takes a skyblue juggler with five red balls

To shake our gravity up. Whee, in the air
The balls roll round, wheel on his wheeling
    hands,
Learning the ways of lightness, alter to
    spheres
Grazing his finger ends,   10

Cling to their courses there,
Swinging a small heaven about his ears.

But a heaven is easier made of nothing at all
Than the earth regained, and still and sole
    within
The spin of worlds, with a gesture sure and
    noble
He reels that heaven in,
Landing it ball by ball,
And trades it all for a broom, a plate, a table.

Oh, on his toe the table is turning, the
    broom's
Balancing up on his nose, and the plate
    whirls   20
On the tip of the broom! Damn, what a show,
    we cry:
The boys stamp, and the girls
Shriek, and the drum booms
And all comes down, and he bows and says
    goodbye.

If the juggler is tired now, if the broom stands
In the dust again, if the table starts to drop
Through the daily dark again, and though
    the plate
Lies flat on the table top,
For him we batter our hands
Who has won for once over the world's
    weight.   30

A Voice from under the Table

To Robert and Jane Brooks

How shall the wine be drunk, or the
    woman known?
I take this world for better or for worse,
But seeing rose carafes conceive the sun
My thirst conceives a fierier universe:
And then I toast the birds in the burning trees

That chant their holy lucid drunkenness;
I swallowed all the phosphorus of the seas
Before I fell into this low distress.

You upright people all remember how
Love drove you first to the woods, and there
    you heard   10
The loose-mouthed wind complaining *Thou*
    and *Thou;*
My gawky limbs were shuddered by the word.
Most of it since was nothing but charades
To spell that hankering out and make an end,
But the softest hands against my shoulder-
    blades
Only increased the crying of the wind.

For this the goddess rose from the midland
    sea
And stood above the famous wine-dark wave,
To ease our drouth with clearer mystery
And be a South to all our flights of love.   20
And down by the selfsame water I have seen
A blazing girl with skin like polished stone
Splashing until a far-out breast of green
Arose and with a rose contagion shone.

"A myrtle-shoot in hand, she danced; her hair
Cast on her back and shoulders a moving
    shade."
Was it some hovering light that showed her
    fair?
Was it of chafing dark that light was made?
Perhaps it was Archilochus' fantasy,
Or that his saying sublimed the thing he
    said.   30
All true enough; and true as well that she
Was beautiful, and danced, and is now dead.

Helen was no such high discarnate thought
As men in dry symposia pursue,
But was as bitterly fugitive, not to be caught
By what men's arms in love or fight could do.

---

l. 29. *Archilochus:* Greek lyric poet and satirist (fl. 650
B.C.).
l. 33. *Helen:* Queen of Sparta, seized by Paris of Troy,
precipitating the Trojan War.

Groan in your cell; rape Troy with sword
    and flame;
The end of thirst exceeds experience.
A devil told me it was all the same
Whether to fail by spirit or by sense.   40

God keep me a damned fool, nor charitably
Receive me into his shapely resignations.
I am a sort of martyr, as you see,
A horizontal monument to patience.
The calves of waitresses parade about
My helpless head upon this sodden floor.
Well, I am down again, but not yet out.
O sweet frustrations, I shall be back for more.

In the Smoking-Car

The eyelids meet. He'll catch a little nap.
The gizzled, crew-cut head drops to his chest.
It shakes above the briefcase on his lap.
Close voices breathe, "Poor sweet, he did his
    best."

"Poor sweet, poor sweet," the bird-hushed
    glades repeat,
Through which in quiet pomp his litter goes,
Carried by native girls with naked feet.
A sighing stream concurs in his repose.

Could he but think, he might recall to mind
The righteous mutiny or sudden gale   10
That beached him here; the dear ones left
    behind . . .
So near the ending, he forgets the tale.

Were he to lift his eyelids now, he might
Behold his maiden porters, brown and bare.
But even here he has no appetite.
It is enough to know that they are there.

Enough that now a honeyed music swells,
The gentle, mossed declivities begin,
And the whole air is full of flower-smells.
Failure, the longed-for valley, takes him in.   20

jAMES dickEy

The Firebombing

Denke daran, dass nach den grossen
    Zerstörungen
Jedermann beweisen wird, dass er
    unschuldig war.
                —GÜNTER EICH
Or hast thou an arm like God?
                —THE BOOK OF JOB

Homeowners unite.

All families lie together, though some are
          burned alive.
The others try to feel
For them. Some can, it is often said.

Starve and take off

Twenty years in the suburbs, and the palm
          trees willingly leap
Into the flashlights,
And there is beneath them also
A booted crackling of snailshells and coral
          sticks.
There are cowl flaps and the tilt cross of
          propellers,   10
The shovel-marked clouds' far sides against
          the moon,
The enemy filling up the hills
With ceremonial graves. At my somewhere
          among these,

Snap, a bulb is tricked on in the cockpit

And some technical-minded stranger with my
          hands

Günter Eich: German playwright and poet (b. 1907); the verses can be translated as "Think of it: after the great destruction,/Everyone will prove that he wasn't guilty."

Is sitting in a glass treasure-hole of blue
          light,
Having potential fire under the undeodorized
          arms
Of his wings, on thin bomb-shackles,
The "tear-drop-shaped" 300-gallon drop-tanks
Filled with napalm and gasoline.   20

Thinking forward ten minutes
From that, there is also the burst straight out
Of the overcast into the moon; there is now
The moon-metal-shine of propellers, the
          quarter-
moonstone, aimed at the waves,
Stopped on the cumulus.

There is then this re-entry
Into cloud, for the engines to ponder their
          sound.
In white dark the aircraft shrinks; Japan

Dilates around it like a thought.   30
Coming out, the one who is here is over
Land, passing over the all-night grainfields,
In dark paint over
The woods with one silver side,
Rice-water calm at all levels
Of the terraced hill.
                Enemy rivers and trees
Sliding off me like snakeskin,
Strips of vapor spooled from the wingtips
Going invisible passing over on   40
Over bridges roads for nightwalkers
Sunday night in the enemy's country
          absolute
Calm the moon's face coming slowly
About
          the inland sea
Slants is woven with wire thread
Levels out holds together like a quilt
Off the starboard wing cloud flickers
At my glassed-off forehead the moon's now
          and again
Uninterrupted face going forward   50
Over the waves in a glide-path
Lost into land.

Going; going with it

Combat booze by my side in a cratered
        canteen,
Bourbon frighteningly mixed
With GI pineapple juice,
Dogs trembling under me for hundreds of
        miles, on many
Islands, sleep-smelling that ungodly mixture
Of napalm and high-octane fuel,
Good bourbon and GI juice.   60

Rivers circling behind me around
Come to the fore, and bring
A town with everyone darkened.
Five thousand people are sleeping off
An all-day American drone.
Twenty years in the suburbs have not shown
        me
Which ones were hit and which not.

Haul on the wheel   racking slowly
The aircraft blackly around
In a dark dream   that   that is   70
That is like flying inside someone's head

Think of this   think of this

I did not think of my house
But think of my house now

Where the lawn mower rests on its laurels
Where the diet exists
For my own good   where I try to drop
Twenty years, eating figs in the pantry
Blinded by each and all
Of the eye-catching cans that gladly have
        caught my wife's eye   80
Until I cannot say
Where the screwdriver is   where the children
Get off the bus   where the new
Scoutmaster lives   where the fly
Hones his front legs   where the hammock
        folds
Its erotic daydreams   where the Sunday
School text for the day has been put   where
        the fire

Wood is   where the payments
For everything under the sun
Pile peacefully up,   90

But in this half-paid-for pantry
Among the red lids that screw off
With an easy half-twist to the left
And the long drawers crammed with dim
        spoons,
I still have charge—secret charge—
Of the fire developed to cling
To everything: to golf carts and fingernail
Scissors as yet unborn   tennis shoes
Grocery baskets   toy fire engines
New Buicks stalled by the half-moon   100
Shining at midnight on crossroads   green
        paint
Of jolly garden tools   red Christmas ribbons:

Not atoms, these, but glue inspired
By love of country to burn,
The apotheosis of gelatin.

Behind me having risen the Southern Cross
Set up by chaplains in the Ryukyus—
Orion, Scorpio, the immortal silver
Like the myths of king-
insects at swarming time—   110
One mosquito, dead drunk
On altitude, drones on, far under the engines,
And bites between
The oxygen mask and the eye.
The enemy-colored skin of families
Determines to hold its color
In sleep, as my hand turns whiter
Than ever, clutching the toggle—
The ship shakes   bucks
Fire hangs   not yet fire   120
In the air above Beppu
For I am fulfilling

An "anti-morale" raid upon it.
All leashes of dogs
Break under the first bomb, around those
In bed, or late in the public baths: around
        those

Who inch forward on their hands
Into medicinal waters.
Their heads come up with a roar
Of Chicago fire: 130
Come up with the carp pond showing
The bathhouse upside down,
Standing stiller to show it more
As I sail artistically over
The resort town followed by farms,
Singing and twisting
All the handles in heaven   kicking
The small cattle off their feet
In a red costly blast
Flinging jelly over the walls   140
As in a chemical war-
fare field demonstration.
With fire of mine like a cat

Holding onto another man's walls,
My hat should crawl on my head
In streetcars, thinking of it,
The fat on my body should pale.

Gun down
The engines, the eight blades sighing
For the moment when the roofs will
                    connect   150
Their flames, and make a town burning with
                    all
American fire.
                              Reflections of houses catch;
Fire shuttles from pond to pond
In every direction, till hundreds flash with
                    one death.
With this in the dark of the mind,
Death will not be what it should;
Will not, even now, even when
My exhaled face in the mirror
Of bars, dilates in a cloud like Japan.   160
The death of children is ponds
Shutter-flashing; responding mirrors; it
                    climbs
The terraces of hills
Smaller and smaller, a mote of red dust
At a hundred feet; at a hundred and one it
                    goes out.
That is what should have got in
To my eye

And shown the insides of houses, the low
                    tables
Catch fire from the floor mats,
Blaze up in gas around their heads   170
Like a dream of suddenly growing
Too intense for war. Ah, under one's dark
                    arms
Something strange-scented falls—when those
                    on earth
Die, there is not even sound;
One is cool and enthralled in the cockpit,
Turned blue by the power of beauty,
In a pale treasure-hole of soft light
Deep in aesthetic contemplation,
Seeing the ponds catch fire
And cast it through ring after ring   180
Of land: O death in the middle
Of acres of inch-deep water!   Useless

Firing   small arms
Speckles   from the river
Bank   one ninety-millimeter
Misses   far down   wrong petals   gone

It is this detachment,
The honored aesthetic evil,
The greatest sense of power in one's life,
That must be shed in bars, or by whatever 190
Means, by starvation
Visions in well-stocked pantries:
The moment when the moon sails in between
The tail-booms   the rudders nod   I swing
Over   directly over the heart
The *heart* of the fire. A mosquito burns out
                    on my cheek
With the cold of my face   there are the eyes
In blue light   bar light
All masked but them   the moon
Crossing from left to right   in the streams
                    below   200
Oriental fish form quickly
In the chemical shine,
In their eyes one tiny seed
Of deranged, Old Testament light.

Letting go   letting go
The plane rises gently   dark forms

Glide off me   long water   pales
In safe zones   a new cry enters
The voice box of chained family dogs

We buck   leap over something   210
Not there   settle back
Leave it   leave it clinging and crying
It consumes them in a hot
Body-flash, old age or menopause
Of children, clings and burns
                                        eating through
And when a reed mat catches fire
From me, it explodes through field after field
Bearing its sleeper   another

Bomb finds a home   220
And clings to it like a child. And so

Goodbye to the grassy mountains
To cloud streaming from the night engines
Flags   pennons   curved silks
Of air   myself streaming also
My body covered
With flags, the air of flags
Between the engines.
Forever I do sleep in that position,
Forever in a turn   230
For home that breaks out streaming banners
From my wingtips,
Wholly in position to admire.

O then I knock it off
And turn for home over the black complex
                        thread worked through
The silver night-sea,
Following the huge, moon-washed
                        steppingstones
Of the Ryukyus south,
The nightgrass of mountains billowing softly
In my rising heat.   240
                        Turn and tread down
The yellow stones of the islands
To where Okinawa burns,
Pure gold, on the radar screen,
Beholding, beneath, the actual island form
In the vast water-silver poured just above
                        solid ground,

An inch of water extending for thousands of
                        miles
Above flat ploughland. Say "down," and it is
                        done.

All this, and I am still hungry,
Still twenty years overweight, still unable   250
To get down there or see
What really happened.
                        But it may be that I could not,
If I tried, say to any
Who lived there, deep in my flames: say, in
                        cold
Grinning sweat, as to another
As these homeowners who are always
                        curving
Near me down the different-grassed street:
                        say
As though to the neighbor
I borrowed the hedge-clippers from   260
On the darker-grassed side of the two,
Come in, my house is yours, come in
If you can, if you
Can pass this unfired door. It is that I can
                        imagine
At the threshold nothing
With its ears crackling off
Like powdery leaves,
Nothing with children of ashes, nothing not
Amiable, gentle, well-meaning,
A little nervous for no   270
Reason   a little worried   a little too loud
Or too easygoing   nothing I haven't lived
                        with
For twenty years, still nothing not as
American as I am, and proud of it.

Absolution? Sentence? No matter;
The thing itself is in that.

703   James Dickey

jAmES WRiqHT

At the Executed Murderer's Grave

(FOR J. L. D.)

Why should we do this? What good is it to us?
Above all, how can we do such a thing?
How can it possibly be done?
                                        —FREUD

1

My name is James A. Wright, and I was born
Twenty-five miles from this infected grave,
In Martins Ferry, Ohio, where one slave
To Hazel-Atlas Glass became my father.
He tried to teach me kindness. I return
Only in memory now, aloof, unhurried,
To dead Ohio, where I might lie buried,
Had I not run away before my time.
Ohio caught George Doty. Clean as lime,
His skull rots empty here. Dying's the best 10
Of all the arts men learn in a dead place.
I walked here once. I made my loud display,
Leaning for language on a dead man's voice.
Now sick of lies, I turn to face the past.
I add my easy grievance to the rest:

2

Doty, if I confess I do not love you,
Will you let me alone? I burn for my own lies.
The nights electrocute my fugitive,
My mind. I run like the bewildered mad
At St. Clair Sanitarium, who lurk,   20
Arch and cunning, under the maple trees,
Pleased to be playing guilty after dark.
Staring to bed, they croon self-lullabies.
Doty, you make me sick. I am not dead.
I croon my tears at fifty cents per line.

3

Idiot, he demanded love from girls,
And murdered one. Also, he was a thief.

He left two women, and a ghost with child.
The hair, foul as a dog's upon his head,
Made such revolting Ohio animals   30
Fitter for vomit than a kind man's grief.
I waste no pity on the dead that stink,
And no love's lost between me and the
    crying
Drunks of Belaire, Ohio, where police
Kick at their kidneys till they die of drink.
Christ may restore them whole, for all of me.
Alive and dead, those giggling muckers who
Saddled my nightmares thirty years ago
Can do without my widely printed sighing
Over their pains with paid sincerity.   40
I do not pity the dead, I pity the dying.

4

I pity myself, because a man is dead.
If Belmont County killed him, what of me?
His victims never loved him. Why should we?
And yet, nobody had to kill him either.
It does no good to woo the grass, to veil
The quicklime hole of a man's defeat and
    shame.
Nature-lovers are gone. To hell with them.
I kick the clods away, and speak my name.

5

This grave's gash festers. Maybe it will
    heal,   50
When all are caught with what they had to do
In fear of love, when every man stands still
By the last sea,
And the princes of the sea come down
To lay away their robes, to judge the earth
And its dead, and we dead stand undefended
    everywhere,
And my bodies—father and child and
    unskilled criminal—
Ridiculously kneel to bare my scars,
My sneaking crimes, to God's unpitying stars.

6

Staring politely, they will not mark my face 60

From any murderer's, buried in this place.
Why should they? We are nothing but a man.

7

Doty, the rapist and the murderer,
Sleeps in a ditch of fire, and cannot hear;
And where, in earth or hell's unholy peace,
Men's suicides will stop, God knows, not I.
Angels and pebbles mock me under trees.
Earth is a door I cannot even face.
Order be damned, I do not want to die,
Even to keep Belaire, Ohio, safe.   70
The hackles on my neck are fear, not grief.
(Open, dungeon! Open, roof of the ground!)
I hear the last sea in the Ohio grass,
Heaving a tide of gray disastrousness.
Wrinkles of winter ditch the rotted face
Of Doty, killer, imbecile, and thief:
Dirt of my flesh, defeated, underground.

ANNE SEXTON

Some Foreign Letters

I knew you forever and you were always old,
soft white lady of my heart. Surely you
    would scold
me for sitting up late, reading your letters,
as if these foreign postmarks were meant for
    me.
You posted them first in London, wearing
    furs
and a new dress in the winter of eighteen-
    ninety.
I read how London is dull on Lord Mayor's
    Day,
where you guided past groups of robbers, the
    sad holes

of Whitechapel, clutching your pocketbook,
    on the way
to Jack the Ripper dissecting his famous
    bones.   10
This Wednesday in Berlin, you say, you will
go to a bazaar at Bismarck's house. And I
see you as a young girl in a good world still,
writing three generations before mine. I try
to reach into your page and breathe it back . . .
but life is a trick, life is a kitten in a sack.

This is the sack of time your death vacates.
How distant you are on your nickel-plated
    skates
in the skating park in Berlin, gliding past
me with your Count, while a military band 20
plays a Strauss waltz. I loved you last,
a pleated old lady with a crooked hand.
Once you read *Lohengrin* and every goose
hung high while you practiced castle life
in Hanover. Tonight your letters reduce
history to a guess. The Count had a wife.
You were the old maid aunt who lived with us.
Tonight I read how the winter howled
    around
the towers of Schloss Schwöbber, how the
    tedious
language grew in your jaw, how you loved the
    sound.   30
of the music of the rats tapping on the stone
floors. When you were mine you wore an
    earphone.

This is Wednesday, May 9th, near Lucerne,
Switzerland, sixty-nine years ago. I learn
your first climb up Mount San Salvatore;
this is the rocky path, the hole in your shoes,
the yankee girl, the iron interior
of her sweet body. You let the Count choose
your next climb. You went together, armed
with alpine stocks, with ham sandwiches 40

---

l. 12. *Bismarck:* Otto E. L. von Bismarck (1815–1898),
Prussian prince and chancellor who unified Germany.
l. 23. *Lohengrin:* in German legend, a knight of the Holy
Grail, son of Parsifal; also, title character of an opera
(1850) by Richard Wagner.

and *seltzer wasser*. You were not alarmed
by the thick woods of briars and bushes,
nor the rugged cliff, nor the first vertigo
up over Lake Lucerne. The Count sweated
with his coat off as you waded through top
    snow.
He held your hand and kissed you. You
    rattled
down on the train to catch a steamboat for
    home;
or other postmarks: Paris, Verona, Rome.

This is Italy. You learn its mother tongue.
I read how you walked on the Palatine
    among   50
the ruins of the palaces of the Caesars;
alone in the Roman autumn, alone since July.
When you were mine they wrapped you out
    of here
with your best hat over your face. I cried
because I was seventeen. I am older now.
I read how your student ticket admitted you
into the private chapel of the Vatican and how
you cheered with the others, as we used to do
on the Fourth of July. One Wednesday in
    November
you watched a balloon, painted like a silver
    ball,   60
float up over the Forum, up over the lost
    emperors,
to shiver its little modern cage in an
    occasional
breeze. You worked your New England
    conscience out
beside artisans, chestnut vendors and the
    devout.

Tonight I will learn to love you twice;
learn your first days, your mid-Victorian face.
Tonight I will speak up and interrupt
your letters, warning you that wars are
    coming,
that the Count will die, that you will accept
your America back to live like a prim thing 70

---

on the farm in Maine. I tell you, you will
    come
here, to the suburbs of Boston, to see the
    blue-nose
world go drunk each night, to see the
    handsome
children jitterbug, to feel your left ear close
one Friday at Symphony. And I tell you,
you will tip your boot feet out of that hall,
rocking from its sour sound, out onto
the crowded street, letting your spectacles
    fall
and your hair net tangle as you stop
    passers-by
to mumble your guilty love while your ears
    die.   80

For Johnny Pole on the Forgotten Beach

In his tenth July some instinct
taught him to arm the waiting wave,
a giant where its mouth hung open.
He rode on the lip that buoyed him there
and buckled him under. The beach was strung
with children paddling their ages in,
under the glare of noon chipping
its light out. He stood up, anonymous
and straight among them, between
their sand pails and nursery crafts.   10
The breakers cartwheeled in and over
to puddle their toes and test their perfect
skin. He was my brother, my small
Johnny brother, almost ten. We flopped
down upon a towel to grind the sand
under us and watched the Atlantic sea
move fire, like night sparklers;
and lost our weight in the festival
season. He dreamed, he said, to be
a man designed like a balanced wave ...   20
how someday he would wait, giant
and straight.

Johnny, your dream moves summers
inside my mind.

He was tall and twenty that July,
but there was no balance to help;
only the shells came straight and even.
This was the first beach of assault;
the odor of death hung in the air
like rotting potatoes; the junkyard   30
of landing craft waited open and rusting.
The bodies were strung out as if they were
still reaching for each other, where they lay
to blacken, to burst through their perfect
skin. And Johnny Pole was one of them.
He gave in like a small wave, a sudden
hole in his belly and the years all gone
where the Pacific ocean chipped its light out.
Like a bean bag, outflung, head loose
and anonymous, he lay. Did the sea move
     fire   40
for its battle season? Does he lie there
forever, where his rifle waits, giant
and straight? . . . I think you die again
and live again,

Johnny, each summer that moves inside
my mind.

For God While Sleeping

Sleeping in fever, I am unfit
to know just who you are:
hung up like a pig on exhibit,
the delicate wrists,
the beard drooling blood and vinegar;
hooked to your own weight,
jolting toward death under your nameplate.

Everyone in this crowd needs a bath.
I am dressed in rags.
The mother wears blue. You grind your
     teeth   10

and with each new breath
your jaws gape and your diaper sags.
I am not to blame
for all this. I do not know your name.

Skinny man, you are somebody's fault.
You ride on dark poles—
a wooden bird that a trader built
for some fool who felt
that he could make the flight. Now you roll
in your sleep, seasick   20
on your own breathing, poor old convict.

x. j. kennedy

Inscriptions After Fact

for Frank Brownlow

I Declare War Against Heaven

Not in silk robes but the hard hides of bulls,
Tusk of the boar and the stiff quill of the
     swan
Gods garb them, tread our world. Run,
     woman, run
Lest trolled in bed you bear strange
     bellyfulls.

Truant from home stars and from right
     spouse,
A god by self conceived and of self born
Sets out of manhood, halts in the halfway
     house
Of beast. But it is man he caps with horn.

---

l. 3. *Gods garb them:* referring to the disguises the
Greek god Zeus took on in illicit pursuit of women—as
a bull in pursuit of Europa, as a swan with Leda, and so
forth.
l. 8. *horn:* According to superstition, a cuckolded man
grew horns at his temples.

Between what stubs one's knuckle and what
  but seems,
Between goat-paddock and god-rampant
  heaven,   10
Must man contend two ravening extremes
For his own women?

Shall he not rage who, having tied a bib
Round a fair boy that he thinks of his own
  make,
Fed him his porridge, taught him patty-cake,
Finds a constrictor throttled in his crib?

What child under a rooftree can sleep safe
While skies uncoil and phalloi slither down?
Will woman, the onslaught of a swan once
  known,
Think man a goose and give him up for life? 20

Drive! drive them back! Breast them with
  bow-
Sprits taut, stand fast, O rout them back to
  Heaven!
Let not a man-jack among them batter
  through!
Then kneel once more, slay beasts to be
  forgiven.

II   Lilith

Adam's first wife had soft lips but no soul:
He looked her in the eye, back looked a hole.
Her small ear lay, a dry well so profound
No word he pebbled in it drew a sound.

Could he complete what God had left half-
  wrought?
He practiced in a looking lake, he taught   30
Stray rudiments of wriggle, where to stand
Her liltless feet. She handed him her hand.

Her breasts stood up but in them seemed
  to rise
No need for man. He roamed lone in her
  thighs
And inmost touching, most knew solitude:
In vacant rooms, on whom can one intrude?

O let down mercy on a poor man who clings
To echoes, beds him with imaginings!
Sweet Lord, he prayed, *with what shade do I*
  lie?
Second came she whom he begot us by.   40

III   The Sirens

Stayed in one place and did no work
But warble ditties a bit loose,
Strike poses, primp, bedeck their rock
With primrose boxes. Odysseus

Salt-lipped, long bandied before winds,
Heard in his loins a bass chord stir,
Said to his men, 'Men, stop your ears—
I need not, being an officer.'

Under the deaf indifferent tread
Of wood on water, round each oar   50
Broke like the grapes of Ilium
Ripening clusters of blue air

And when those soft sounds stole, there grew
The notion as he champed his bit
That love was all there was, and death
Had something to be said for it.

Roared as the music sweetened, railed
Against his oarsmen's bent wet slopes,
Imprisoned in propriety
And pagan ethic. Also ropes.   60

Sails strummed. The keel drove tapestries
Of distance on the sea's silk-loom
Leaving those simple girls beyond
Woven undone rewoven foam

To wonder: had they lost their touch?
Unbroken yet, a woof of sea
Impelled him to his dying dog,
Pantoufles, and Penelope.

Sirens: based on the episode in the *Odyssey* in which
Ulysses, returning to Ithaca and his wife, Penelope,
passed the singers who lured mariners to their death
on dangerous rocks.

IV Narcissus Suitor

He touched her face and gooseflesh crept—
He loved her as it were   70
Not for her look though it was deep
But what he saw in her.

Drew her up wobbling in his arms,
Laid lips by her smooth cheek
And would have joined the two of him
In one cohesive Greek

When soft by his obdurate ear
Like lips, two ripples pursed—
These syllables distinct and pure
Bubbled to air, and burst: 80

'Oh keep your big feet to yourself
Good sir, goddammit stop!
I'm not that sort of pool at all!
I'll scream! I'll call a cop!

'Settle me back in my right bed
Or you shall edge your skiff
Through ice as limber as your eyes,
As blue, as frozen stiff.'

V Theater of Dionysus

Athens, U. S. Sixth Fleet, March 1953

By the aisle on a stone bench
In the Theater of Dionysus   90
I make a flock of Greek kids smile
Sketching them Mickey Mouses

Where beery Aristophanes
By sanction till night's fall
Ribbed Eleusinian mysteries
With queer-joke and pratt-fall.

On high from the sacked Parthenon
A blackbird faintly warbles.
Sellers of paperweights resell
The Elgin marbles.   100

Here where queen-betrayed
Agamemnon had to don
Wine-purple robes, boys in torn drabs
Try my whitehat on,

Over stones where Orestes fled
The sonorous Furies
Girls hawking flyspecked postcards
Pursue the tourist.

Here in her anguish-mask
Andromache   110
Mourned her slain son—'Young man,
Aren't you from Schenectady?'

As I trudge down, a pebble breaks
Rattling across stone tiers,
Scattering echoes: do I kick
A watcher's skull downstairs?

Silence imponders back
As I take the stage, the pebble
Stilled on a lower tier.
Trailing home now, the child rabble.   120

I stand in the center of the stage,
Could speak, but the sun's setting
In back of neon signs. Night unsheathes
Her chill blade. Better be getting

Back to the destroyer, radared bark,
No thresh of oars, sails with gods' crests—
Does the wind stir through the dark
Or does a throng of ghosts?

Narcissus Suitor: based on the myth of the young man
who fell in love with his own reflection in a pool.
l. 93. *Aristophanes:* Greek comic poet (450?–385? B.C.).
l. 95. *Eleusinian mysteries:* secret religious rites of ancient Greece, celebrated every spring at Eleusis and
symbolizing the annual death and resurrection of vegetation.

l. 102. *Agamemnon:* title hero of a play by Aeschylus,
Greek tragedian (525–456 B.C.). Agamemnon was murdered by his wife, Clytemnestra, and her lover, Aegisthus.
l. 105. *Orestes:* son of Agamemnon, who avenged his
father's death and was pursued by the Furies for
doing so.
l. 110. *Andromache:* wife of Hector in Homer's *Iliad*.

I run. Inaudible laughter drives
Offstage my spirit   130
As in the parched grass, wind routs
A white shiver before it.

GREGORY CORSO

Ode to Coit Tower

O anti-verdurous phallic were't not for
    your pouring height looming in tears
    like a sick tree or your ever-gaudy-
    comfort jabbing your city's much
    wrinkled sky you'd seem an absurd
    Babel squatting before mortal millions
Because I filled your dull sockets with my
    New York City eyes vibrations that
    hadn't doomed dumb Empire State
    did not doom thee   10
Enough my eyes made you see phantasmal
    at night mad children of soda caps
    laying down their abundant blond
    verse on the gridiron of each other's
    eucharistic feet like distant kings
    laying down treasures from camels
Illuminations hinged to masculine limbs
    fresh with the labor sweat of cablecar
    & Genoa papa pushcart
Bounty of electricity & visions carpented 20
    on pig-bastard night in its spore like
    the dim lights of some hallucinating
    facade
Ah tower from thy berryless head I'd a
    vision in common with myself the
    proximity of Alcatraz and not the hip
    volley of white jazz & verse or verse &

Coit Tower: located in San Francisco

jazz embraced but a real heart-rending
    constant vision of Alcatraz marshalled
    before my eyes   30
Stocky Alcatraz weeping on Neptune's
    table whose petrific bondage crushes
    the dreamless seaharp gasping for song
    O that that piece of sea fails to dream
Tower I'd a verdure vagueness fixed by a
    green wind the shade of Mercy lashed
    with cold nails against the wheat-
    weather Western sky weeping I'm sure
    for humanity's vast door to open that
    all men be free that both hinge and   40
    lock die that all doors if they close
    close like Chinese bells
Was it man's love to screw the sky with
    monuments span the bay with orange
    & silver bridges shuttling structure
    into structure incorruptible in this
    endless tie each age impassions be it
    in stone or steel either in echo or half-
    heard ruin
Was it man's love that put that rock there 50
    never to avalanche but in vision or
    this imaginary now or myself stand-
    ing on Telegraph Hill Nob Hill
    Russian Hill the same view always
    Alcatraz like a deserted holiday
And I cried for Alcatraz there in your
    dumb hollows O tower clenching my
    Pan's foot with vivid hoard of Danne-
    mora
Cried for that which was no longer sov-   60
    ereign in me stinking of dead dreams
    dreams I yet feign to bury thus to
    shun reality's worm
Dreams that once jumped joyous bright
    from my heart like sparks issued from
    a wild sharper's wheel now issued no
    longer
Were't not for cities or prisons O tower
    I might yet be that verdure monk
    lulling over green country albums   70
    with no greater dream than my youth's
    dream
Eyes of my hands! Queen Penthesileia
    and her tribe! Messenger stars Doctor

Deformous back from his leprosy and
woe! Thracian ships! Joyprints of
pure air!
Impossible for me to betray even the
simplest tree
Idiotic colossus I came to your city dur- 80
ing summer after Cambridge there
also no leaf throbbed between my fingers no cool insect thrilled my palm
though I'd a vision there Death seated
like a huge black stove
Inspired by such I came to your city
walked Market Street singing hark
hark the dogs do bark the beggars are
coming to town and ran mad across
Golden Gate into Sausalito and fell 90
exhausted in a field where an endless
scarecrow lay its head on my lap
How happily mad I was O tower lying
there amid gossipy green dreaming of
Quetzalcoatl as I arched my back like
a rainbow over some imaginary gulph
O for that madness again that infinitive
solitude where illusion spoke Truth's
divine dialect
I should have stayed yet I left to Mexico 100
to Quetzalcoatl and heard there atop
Teotihuacan in T-prophetic-Cuauhxi-
calli-voice a dark anthem for the coming year
Ah tower tower that I felt sad for Alcatraz
and not for your heroes lessened not
the tourist love of my eyes
I saw your blackjacketed saints your Zens
potsmokers Athenians and cocksmen
Though the West Wind seemed to harbor 110
there not one pure Shelleyean dream
of let's say hay-
    like universe
       golden heap on a wall of fire
sprinting toward the gauzy eradica-
tion of Swindleresque Ink

Don't Shoot the Warthog

A child came to me
swinging an ocean on a stick.
He told me his sister was dead,
I pulled down his pants
and gave him a kick.
I drove him down the streets
down the night of my generation
I screamed his name, his cursed name,
down the streets of my generation,
and children lept in joy to the name   10
and running came.
Mothers and fathers bent their heads to hear;
I screamed the name.

The child trembled, fell,
and staggered up again,
I screamed his name!
And a fury of mothers and fathers
sank their teeth into his brain.
I called to the angels of my generation
on the rooftops, in the alleyways,   20
beneath the garbage and the stones,
I screamed the name! and they came
and gnawed the child's bones.
I screamed the name: Beauty
Beauty Beauty Beauty

LeRoi Jones

Notes For A Speech

African blues
does not know me. Their steps, in sands
of their own
land. A country
in black and white, newspapers
blown down pavements

of the world. Does
not feel
what I am.
                    Strength   10
in the dream, an oblique
suckling of nerve, the wind
throws up sand, eyes
are something locked in
hate, of hate, of hate, to
walk abroad, they conduct
their deaths apart
from my own. Those
heads, I call
my "people."   20
                    (And who are they. People. To
                                    concern
myself, ugly man. Who
you, to concern
the white flat stomachs
of maidens, inside houses
dying. Black. Peeled moon
light on my fingers
move under
her clothes. Where
is her husband. Black   30
words throw up sand
to eyes, fingers of
their private dead. Whose
soul, eyes, in sand. My color
is not theirs. Lighter, white man
talk. They shy away. My own
dead souls, my, so called
people. Africa
is a foreign place. You are
as any other sad man here
american.   40

of muscle.   A position
for myself: to move.

Duncan
told of dance. His poems
full of what we called
so long for you to be. A   10
dance. And all his words
ran out of it. That there
was some bright elegance
the sad meat of the body
made. Some gesture, that
if we became, for one blank moment,
would turn us
into creatures of rhythm.

I want to be sung. I want
all my bones and meat hummed   20
against the thick floating
winter sky. I want myself
as dance. As what I am
given love, or time, or space
to feel myself.

The time of thought. The space
of actual movement. (Where they
have taken up the sea, and
keep me against my will.) I said, also,
love, being older or younger   30
than your world. I am given
to lying, love, call you out
now, given to feeling things
I alone create.
And let me once, create
myself. And let you, whoever
sits now breathing on my words
create a self of your own. One
that will love me.

The Dance

The dance.
                    (held up for me by
an older man.   He told me how.   Showed
me. Not steps, but the fix

---

l. 7. *Duncan:* Robert Duncan (b. 1919), poet; perhaps a
specific reference to his poem, "A Dancing Concerning a Form of Women."

ishmael reed

The Gangster's Death

how did he die/ O if i told you,
you would slap your hand
                       against your forehead
and say good grief/ if i gripped you
by the lapel and told how they dumped
    thalidomide hand grenades
into his blood stream and/
                 how they injected
a cyst into his spirit the size of an egg
which grew and grew until floating   10
    gangrene encircled the globe
and/ how guerillas dropped from trees like
mean pythons
               and squeezed out his life/
so that jungle birds fled their perches/
so that hand clapping monkeys   tumbled
    from branches and/
how twelve year olds snatched B 52's
    from the skies with their bare hands and/
how betty grable couldn't open a hershey bar   20
    without the wrapper exploding and/
how thin bent women wrapped bicycle chains
    around their knuckles saying
    we will fight until the last bra or/
    give us bread or shoot us/ and/
how killing him became child's play
in Danang in Mekong in Santo Domingo

       and how rigor mortis was sprinkled
in boston soups
                giving rum running families   30
stiff back aches
so that they were no longer able to sit
at the elbows of the president
with turkey muskets   or/ sit
on their behinds watching the boat races
off Massachusetts through field glasses but/
how they found their duck pants
    pulled off in the get-back-in-the-alleys
    of the world and/

how they were routed by the people
    spitting into their palms
    just waiting to use those lobster pinchers
    or smash that martini glass and/
how they warned him
             and gave him a chance
    with no behind the back dillinger
    killing by flat headed dicks but/
how they held megaphones
          in their fists
    saying   come out with your hands up and/
how refusing to believe the jig was up
    he accused them
             of apocalyptic barking
    saying out of the corner of his mouth
    come in and get me and/
how they snagged at his khaki legs
    until their mouths were full
    of ankles and calves and/
how they sank their teeth into his swanky jugular
    getting the sweet taste of max factor
    on their tongues and/
how his screams were so loud
    that the skins of eardrums blew off
    and blood trickled
           down the edges of mouths

and people got hip to his aliases/
             i mean/
democracy and freedom began bouncing
all over the world
        like bad checks
as people began scratching their heads
and stroking their chins
as his rhetoric stuck in his fat throat
      while he quoted
men with frills on their wrists
and fake moles on their cheeks
and swans on their snuff boxes
    who sit in Gilbert Stuart's portraits
    talking like baroque clocks/
    who sit talking turkey talk
  to people who say   we don't want
          to hear it
as they lean over their plows reading Mao
wringing the necks of turkeys
    and making turkey talk gobble

40

50

60

70

80

in upon itself
in Mekong and Danang and Santo Domingo
and

Che Guevara made personal appearances everywhere

Che Guevara in Macy's putting incendiary flowers
on marked down hats   and women
scratching out each other's eyes over ambulances
Che Guevara in Congress putting tnt shavings
in the ink wells   and politicians
tripped over their jowls trying to get away
Che Guevara in small towns and hamlets
where cans jump from the hands of stock clerks
   in flaming super markets/
where skyrocketing devil's food cakes
   contain the teeth of republican bankers/
where the steer of gentleman farmers
   shoot over the moon like beefy missiles
                          while undeveloped people
stand in road shoulders saying
fly Che fly bop   a few for us
      put cement on his feet
      and take him for a ride

O Walt Whitman
visionary of leaking faucets
great grand daddy of drips
   you said I hear america singing
but/ how can you sing when your throat is slit
and O/ how can you see when your head bobs
      in a sewer
in Danang and Mekong and Santo Domingo

and look at them weep for a stiff/
                          i mean
a limp dead hood
Bishops humping their backsides/
folding their hands in front of their noses
forming a human carpet for a zombie
men and women looking like sick dust mops/
   running their busted thumbs
   across whiskey headed guitars/
weeping into the evil smelling carnations
   of Baby Face McNamara
   and Killer Rusk
whose arms are loaded with hijacked rest

90

100

110

120

in peace wreaths and/
look at them hump this stiff in harlem/
sticking out their lower lips/
and because he two timed them/
    midget manicheans shaking their fists
    in bullet proof telephone booths/
    dialing legbar on long distance
    receiving extra terrestrial sorry
               wrong number
seeing big nosed black people land in space ships/
seeing swamp gas/
shoving inauthentic fireballs down their throats/
bursting their lungs on existentialist rope skipping/
    look at them mourn/
drop dead egalitarians and CIA polyglots
  crying into their bill folds
  we must love one another or die

while little boys wipe out whole regiments with bamboo
                       sticks
while wrinkled face mandarins store 17 megatons in Haiku

for people have been holding his death birds
on their wrists and his death birds
make their arms sag with their filthy nests
and his death birds ate their baby's testicles
and they got sick and fed up
with those goddamn birds
and they brought their wrists together and blew/
                 i mean/
puffed their jaws and blew and shooed
  these death birds his way
and he is mourned by
drop dead egalitarians and CIA polyglots and
midget manicheans and Brooks Brothers Black People
  throwing valentines at crackers
  for a few spoons by Kirk's old Maryland engraved/
  for a look at Lassie's purple tongue/
  for a lock of roy roger's hair/
  for a Lawrence Welk champagne bubble

as for me/ like the man said
i'm always glad when the chickens come home to roost

About the Authors

Anonymous Ballads of the Middle Ages are songs that tell stories; generally they concentrate upon a single incident: historical ("Sir Patrick Spens"), supernatural ("The Daemon Lover"), or tragic ("Edward"). Often they plunge immediately into the incident, omitting background, explanatory details, and explicit editorial comment. Transitions from episode to episode, from description to dialogue, are abrupt. Diction and imagery tend to be plain; the single rhetorical device common to most ballads is repetition, calculated to intensify the drama or ironies of the incident. For further critical or historical information, consult: Francis James Child, ed., *English and Scottish Ballads*, five volumes (Boston, 1883–1898); Gordon H. Gerould, *The Ballad of Tradition* (Oxford, Eng., 1932); Francis B. Gummere, *The Popular Ballad* (Boston, 1907); Louise Pound, *Poetic Origins and the Ballad* (New York, 1921); Evelyn K. Wells, *The Ballad Tree* (New York, 1950).

Anonymous Lyrics of the Middle Ages range over four centuries, from the mid-twelfth to the mid-sixteenth. They were composed by ecclesiasts, gentlemen, minstrels, and troubadours; and their subject matter is as varied as the backgrounds of their authors. Celebrations of the seasons ("Sumer Is Icumen In"), of love ("Western Wind"), and of mythic-religious relationships ("The Corpus Christi Carol") are perhaps most common among them. For further critical or historical information, consult: H. T. Chaytor, *Troubadours and England* (Cambridge, Eng., 1923); R. T. Davies, *Medieval English Lyrics* (London, 1963); A. K. Moore, *The Secular Lyric in Middle English* (Lexington, Ky., 1951).

Sir Thomas Wyatt (1503?–1542) was a courtier and royal ambassador under the reign of Henry VIII (1491–1547). He read and studied the works of earlier Italian poets, notably Petrarch (1304–1374), during his travels on the Continent, and he brought their rhyme schemes and subject matter back to England. "My Galley," a translation of Petrarch's Sonnet CLVI, exemplifies one of the dominant forms of the sixteenth century: the sonnet (or "little song"), a lyric of fourteen lines, divided into an octave (eight lines rhyming *abba abba* and establishing the poet's theme) and a sestet (six lines rhyming variously on some pattern of *cde cde* and resolving the theme). Generally the sonnet unfolds the story of the poet's hopeless love for a beautiful but disdainful lady who must be carefully wooed but is seldom won. In this concentration on the intensely personal, however transformed by poetic artifice, the poet reflects the Renaissance emphasis on the individual. Wyatt's best poetry is his "English" work, those poems for which no specific foreign model has been found; "They Flee from Me" (written in rime royal, a seven-line stanza rhyming *ababbcc*) and "My Lute, Awake" (doubtlessly set to music and sung, with lute accompaniment) are examples. For further biographical, critical, or historical information, consult: A. K. Foxwell, *A Study of Sir Thomas Wyatt's Poems* (New York, 1964); Kenneth Muir, *Life and Letters of Sir Thomas Wyatt* (Liverpool, 1963); and Patricia Thomson, *Sir Thomas Wyatt and His Background* (Stanford, 1964).

Sir Walter Raleigh (1552?–1618), best known for his American expeditions and his piracies against the Spanish during the reign of Queen

Elizabeth I (1533–1603), wrote poetry as well, little of which survives. It was highly acclaimed by his contemporaries. His "Nature, That Washed Her Hands in Milk" is an example of the creative use of sonnet conventions: Raleigh's six-line stanzas (rhyming *ababcc*) employ images used by many other poets (for example, Edmund Spenser and Sir Philip Sidney), and the traditional elaborate themes (a lady's incredible beauty and pride, the cruelty of time, and so on), but express unique emotions. Presumably addressed to Elizabeth, the poem seems a sincere statement of Raleigh's love for his queen, although such flattery had become a court convention. For further biographical, critical, or historical information, consult: Irvin Anthony, *Raleigh and His World* (New York and London, 1934); M. C. Bradbrook, *The School of Night: A Study in the Literary Relationships of Sir Walter Raleigh* (New York, 1965); and Walter F. Oakeshott, *The Queen and the Poet* (London, 1960).

Edmund Spenser (1552?–1599) spent most of his life in Ireland as secretary to the Lord-Deputy, writing poetry and trying to find a patron at court. Like many other Renaissance poets, he worked from classical models; his first notable work was *The Shepheardes Calendar* (1579), a collection of twelve eclogues, or studies of country life, a form popularized by the Roman poets Virgil and Horace. His major poem is the unfinished *Faerie Queene* (1590; 1596), an attempt at a modern epic woven around the mythical figure of King Arthur and dedicated to Queen Elizabeth I. The sonnet sequence *Amoretti* was published in 1595; its poems follow the familiar pattern of the poet addressing a reluctant lady. "Epithalamion," a wedding song (presented as a gift from Spenser to his bride, Elizabeth Boyle, 1594), was also published in 1595 and recounts the joyful, unconventional ending of the poet's love. To the common Renaissance poetic forms Spenser contributed a wealth of detail: his descriptions are lush, his elabora-

tions and allusions intricate. For further biographical, critical, or historical information, consult: B. E. C. Davis, *Edmund Spenser: A Critical Study* (Cambridge, Eng., 1933); J. R. Elliott, *The Prince of Poets: Essays on Edmund Spenser* (New York, 1968); and William Nelson, *The Poetry of Edmund Spenser: A Study* (New York, 1963).

Sir Philip Sidney (1554–1586), considered the epitome of an English Renaissance gentleman, was a poet, scholar, courtier, diplomat, and soldier. His major writings are equally diverse: *The Defence of Poesy*, a treatise on writing that is generally regarded as the foundation of English literary criticism; *Arcadia*, a fantastic prose-verse romance, one of the earliest in England; and *Astrophel and Stella*, a unified sequence of sonnets and songs recounting Sidney's unhappy relations with Penelope Devereux. The poems of the latter work are tied together as a narrative, and often focus on the psychology of the lover rather than on the circumstances of his love. For further biographical, critical, or historical information, consult: Frederick S. Boas, *Sir Philip Sidney: Representative Elizabethan* (London, 1955); John Buxton, *Sir Philip Sidney and the English Renaissance*, second edition (London and New York, 1966); David Kalstone, *Sidney's Poetry: Contexts and Interpretations* (Cambridge, Mass., 1965); and Robert L. Montgomery, *Symmetry and Sense: The Poetry of Sir Philip Sidney* (Austin, 1961).

William Shakespeare (1564–1616), in addition to writing some thirty-seven highly regarded plays, also won himself a reputation as a narrative and lyric poet, specifically through the publication of *Venus and Adonis* (1593), *The Rape of Lucrece* (1594), and his 154 *Sonnets* (1609). The latter, largely written in a rhyme scheme (*abab cdcd efef gg*) now identified by Shakespeare's name, have not the ordered narrative effect of Spenser's or Sidney's work; while they may entertain traditional subjects, frequently with conventional figures of speech, the poems are remarkable for the breadth and power of their expressed emotions and the variety as well as complexity of their themes. Love, whether in its more attractive (Sonnet XXIX) or corrupt (XCIV, CXVIII, CXXXVIII, CLI) aspects; the approach of old age (LXXIII); and conscience and sin (CXLVI), provide only a few examples of Shakespeare's scope of subject, tone, and treatment. For further biographical, critical, or historical information, consult: Gerald E. Bentley, *Shakespeare: A Biographical Handbook* (New Haven, 1961); Frank E. Halliday, *Shakespeare: A Pictorial Biography* (London, 1964); Edward Hubler, *Shakespeare's Songs and Sonnets* (New York, 1959); Edward Hubler, et al., *The Riddle of Shakespeare's Sonnets* (New York, 1962); G. Wilson Knight, *The Mutual Flame* (London, 1955); Allardyce Nicoll, *Shakespeare: An Introduction* (New York, 1952); and J. Dover Wilson, *An Introduction to the Sonnets of Shakespeare* (New York, 1964).

Ben Jonson (1573?–1637), like his contemporary Shakespeare, was equally esteemed for his plays and his poetry. His emphasis in both was always on the classical: on conciseness, orderliness, precision of form, and tradition. Thus his best-known plays—*Volpone* (c. 1606), *The Alchemist* (1610), and *Bartholomew Fair* (1614)—are satiric comedies rooted in classical Roman precedents. Jonson's poetry is also dominated by his love of the ancients: "On My First Sonne" is modeled on Martial's epigrams, terse, witty, often satiric poems of praise or dispraise; "Inviting a Friend to Supper" is a rendering of Horace's verses, suggestive of common speech, realistic and abundant in commonplace detail. In his return to earlier models, Jonson was a great influence on his contemporaries: he is said to have started the "Cavalier" school of poetry, distinguished by its simplicity, clarity, grace, and balance. More than one poet—notably Robert Herrick—wished to be included in the "tribe of Ben." For further biographical, critical, or historical information, consult: Mar-chette G. Chute, *Ben Jonson of Westminster* (New York, 1953); G. B. Johnston, *Ben Jonson: Poet* (New York, 1945); Elmer E. Stoll, *Poets and Playwrights: Shakespeare, Jonson, Spenser, Milton* (New York, 1965); and Wesley Trimpi, *Ben Jonson's Poems: A Study of the Plain Style* (Stanford, 1962).

John Donne (1573–1631) published only a few occasional poems during his lifetime, but between 1633, when *Songs and Sonnets* was first published, and 1669, his work grew to seven editions. To the young poets of the early seventeenth century, Donne was "a king that ruled as he thought fit/The universal monarchy of wit." His influence can be felt in modern poets as diverse as T. S. Eliot, Archibald MacLeish, John Crowe Ransom, and Dylan Thomas. Donne's appeal lies in his ability either to telescope (as in "a bracelet of bright hair about the bone" in "The Relic") or to elaborate (as in the comparison of "Air and Angels") startling images; to depict accurately the tension between ideals and reality; to mingle the solemn, sardonic, and whimsical in the same breath; to mold and match verse patterns to his individual thought and feeling. Similar qualities, though tempered by their authors' differing personalities, are to be found in the poems of Robert Herrick, George Herbert, and Andrew Marvell. For further biographical, critical, or historical information, consult: Alfred Alvarez, *The School of Donne* (New York, 1962); Joan Bennett, *Five Metaphysical Poets: Donne, Herbert, . . . Marvell*, third edition (Cambridge, Eng., 1964); Helen L. Gardner, *John Donne: A Collection of Critical Essays* (Englewood Cliffs, 1962); James B. Leishman, *The Monarch of Wit* (London, 1962); George Williamson, *The Donne Tradition* (Gloucester, Mass., 1961).

Robert Herrick (1591–1674) is generally considered the best of the followers of Ben Jonson. His poems reflect the quiet of his life as a country parson as well as his study of classical models, especially Anacreon, Catullus,

Horace, and Martial, and his interest in the course of life around him. Herrick's subject matter is perhaps more restricted than Jonson's: his favorite theme—as evidenced in "Corinna's Going a Maying"—is *carpe diem* (literally, "seize the day"), a belief that the pleasures of life in the present world are brief but unique and therefore to be made the most of and not wasted. But Herrick surpasses Jonson in his ability to project himself as a "free-born Roman," in his "delight in disorder," in his spirit of sensuous abandon. For further biographical, critical, or historical information, consult: Frederic W. Moorman, *Robert Herrick: A Biographical and Critical Study* (London, 1910); and Roger B. Rollin, *Robert Herrick* (New York, 1966).

George Herbert (1593–1633) is generally regarded as a disciple of John Donne. Like Donne, he did not publish his work during his lifetime, and he demonstrates an extraordinary facility with metrics (one editor notes that of the 169 poems in Herbert's volume *The Temple*, "116 are written in meters which are not repeated"). Herbert's dramatization of spiritual conflicts—the debate between body and soul—also calls Donne to mind; however, the two poets differ in tone and imagery. Herbert's *conceits* or comparisons center almost entirely around the church, specifically Anglican ritual, liturgy, and church building; his tone is generally that of a hymnist: simple, quiet, and direct. For further biographical, critical, or historical information, consult: Marchette G. Chute, *Two Gentle Men: The Lives of George Herbert and Robert Herrick* (New York, 1959); Mary E. Rickey, *Utmost Art: Complexity in the Verse of George Herbert* (Lexington, Ky., 1966); Joseph H. Summers, *George Herbert: His Religion and Art* (Cambridge, Mass., 1968); and Rosemond Tuve, *A Reading of George Herbert* (Chicago, 1965).

John Milton (1608–1674), called by some the last great figure of the English Renaissance, was both poet and government servant; he temporarily laid aside his dream of writing a great epic poem to become Secretary in Foreign Tongues to the Council of State (a position somewhat like that of Secretary of State) under Oliver Cromwell's Commonwealth, 1649–1660. His blindness (1651) did not prevent him from realizing his earlier ambition after the Commonwealth's fall; in 1667 he published *Paradise Lost*, certainly the summit of his poetic career. "Lycidas," which predates Milton's government activities, belongs to the tradition of the pastoral elegy, a lament written under the guise of a rustic author using shepherds as characters and an idyllic rural life as setting. (And although Milton's "Lycidas" may have exerted no direct influence on the following poems, simply for deeper comprehension, comparison, and contrast it should be read beside Whitman's "When Lilacs Last in the Dooryard Bloom'd" and W. H. Auden's "In Memory of W. B. Yeats.") "On the Late Massacre in Piedmont," which belongs to Milton's Commonwealth period, shows how he, along with Donne, revitalized the sonnet form by extending its scope to deal with religious or political subjects. For further biographical, critical, or historical information, consult: Don C. Allen, *The Harmonious Vision: Studies in Milton's Poetry* (Baltimore, 1954); Douglas Bush, *John Milton: A Sketch of His Life and Writings* (New York, 1964); James H. Hanford, *John Milton: Englishman* (New York, 1949); James H. Hanford, *John Milton: Poet and Humanist* (Cleveland, 1966); and Louis L. Martz, *Milton: A Collection of Critical Essays* (Englewood Cliffs, 1966).

Andrew Marvell (1621–1678), like Milton a poet and government servant, exerts a great charm on modern writers, if only to judge by their many citations to his graceful, witty "To His Coy Mistress": it is this poem that is quoted in one of the café scenes of Ernest Hemingway's *A Farewell to Arms*, gave Robert Penn Warren the title to his work *World Enough and Time*, and figures prominently in Archibald MacLeish's "You, Andrew Marvell" and T. S. Eliot's "The Love Song of J. Alfred Prufrock." Along with "The Definition of Love" and "The Garden," "To His Coy Mistress" offers many examples of Marvell's ability to strike comparisons, brief or extended, in the manner of Donne and his disciples. However, Marvell's poetry seems to blend Donne's jagged thought with Ben Jonson's smoothness of line. For further biographical, critical, or historical information, consult: M. C. Bradbrook, *Andrew Marvell* (Cambridge, Eng., 1961); Lawrence W. Hyman, *Andrew Marvell* (New York, 1964); J. B. Leishman, *The Art of Marvell's Poetry* (London, 1966); and Harold E. Toliver, *Marvell's Ironic Vision* (New Haven, 1965).

John Dryden (1631–1700) is perhaps the first modern man of English letters; he was a prolific author of sound, readable literary criticism, and was adept not only in drama (*Marriage à la Mode*, 1672; *All for Love*, 1677) but in translation, satiric verse (*Absalom and Achitophel*, 1681; *MacFlecknoe*, 1682), and the lyric. "Alexander's Feast," an example of the latter, written three years before Dryden's death, shows the late seventeenth-century's increasing concern for matching the sound and the sense of verse; that is, verse—as Alexander Pope was later to phrase it—in which "the sound must seem an echo to the sense." The critic Mark Van Doren has called the poem "immortal ragtime," but Handel thought it worthy of a musical setting. For further biographical, critical, or historical information, consult: Louis I. Bredvold, *The Intellectual Milieu of John Dryden* (Ann Arbor, 1934); T. S. Eliot, *John Dryden: The Poet, The Dramatist, The Critic* (New York, 1966); Arthur W. Hoffman, *John Dryden's Imagery* (Gainesville, 1962); Earl R. Miner, *Dryden's Poetry* (Bloomington, 1967); Bernard N. Schilling, *Dryden: A Collection of Critical Essays* (Englewood Cliffs, 1963); and Mark Van Doren, *John Dryden: A Study of His Poetry* (Bloomington, 1967).

Alexander Pope (1688–1744) perfected the heroic couplet, a rhyming two-line unit of twenty syllables, in a series of poems of startling variety. In the first half of his career he formulated an aesthetic of poetry for his age (*Essay on Criticism*, 1711), carried on the mock-epic tradition (in *Rape of the Lock*, 1712, 1714; *Dunciad*, 1728–1743) initiated by Dryden, and translated Homer's *Iliad* (1720) and *Odyssey* (1726). In the second half of his career—to use Pope's own words—he "stoop'd to truth and moralized his song" in poems generalizing on the universe and social conduct (*Essay on Man*, 1733–1734; *Moral Essays*, 1731–1735; *Imitations of Horace*, 1733–1738). "Epistle II. To a Lady" belongs to this second phase and is an epitome of all the characteristics of what is called Neoclassical verse: it is didactic, satiric, witty, technically precise, and calculatingly poised. For further biographical, critical, or historical information, consult: Reuben A. Brower, *Alexander Pope: The Poetry of Allusion* (Oxford, Eng., 1959); G. Wilson Knight, *Laureate of Peace* (London, 1954); Maynard Mack, *Essential Articles for the Study of Alexander Pope*, revised and enlarged edition (Hamden, Conn., 1968); George Sherburn, *The Early Career of Alexander Pope* (Oxford, Eng., 1934); G. Tillotson, *On the Poetry of Pope*, second edition (Oxford, Eng., 1950); Austin Warren, *Alexander Pope as Critic and Humanist* (Gloucester, Mass., 1963).

William Blake (1757–1827) was not only a poet but a painter and engraver as well. Each of his volumes—*Poetical Sketches* (1783), *Songs of Innocence* (1789), *The Marriage of Heaven and Hell* (1790), *Songs of Experience* (1794)— Blake personally manufactured, cutting both his verses and engravings into copper plates and illuminating the pages themselves in water colors. The revolution he effected in aesthetics matched the equally revolutionary ideas his verse celebrated: believing in man's essential dignity, Blake called for him to free himself of convention and to trust his intuition to realize self-fulfillment. His use of private symbolism, the guise of a child, and the intense incantatory voice of the prophet underscore his unique message. These techniques show their influence on successive poets as diverse as William Butler Yeats and E. E. Cummings. For further biographical, critical, or historical information, consult: Hazard Adams, *Blake and Yeats: The Contrary Vision* (Ithaca, 1955); Hazard Adams, *William Blake: A Reading of the Shorter Poems* (Seattle, 1963); Jacob Bronowski, *Blake and the Age of Revolution* (New York, 1965); Northrop Frye, *Blake: A Collection of Critical Essays* (Englewood Cliffs, 1966); Northrop Frye, *Fearful Symmetry: A Study of William Blake* (Princeton, 1947); and Jean H. Hagstrum, *William Blake, Poet and Painter* (Chicago, 1964).

Robert Burns (1759–1796), the most beloved poet of the Scots, fulfilled the late eighteenth-century Romantic hope of finding a true "noble savage" poet: that is, a common man, of the people and close to nature, largely self-taught, employing a purely everyday idiom or dialect in simple verse forms to communicate with other men. The ballad and the song—forms that owe their invention to the people rather than to one individual—are Burns's province; and he expresses his sentiments in them with the qualities they require: simplicity, sincerity, vividness, and an insistent rhythmic emphasis that urges the audience to sing rather than read. For further biographical, critical, or historical information, consult: Thomas Crawford, *Burns: A Study of the Poems and Songs* (Edinburgh, 1960); John D. Ferguson, *Pride and Passion: Robert Burns, 1759–1796* (New York, 1964); and William Montgomerie, *Robert Burns: New Judgments; Essays by Six Contemporary Writers* (Glasgow, 1947).

William Wordsworth (1770–1850) was born in the English Lake Country and matured during the French Revolution. With Samuel Taylor Coleridge he published *Lyrical Ballads* (1798), the second edition of which (1800) is considered the beginning of English Romanticism, although the work of Blake and Burns had preceded it. But the *Preface* to the second edition clearly announced the poets' revolutionary break with typical eighteenth-century literary practices: Wordsworth and Coleridge viewed themselves as men speaking to other men, the former selecting a natural subject (as in "Lines Composed a Few Miles Above Tintern Abbey") and presenting it with the freshness of a new vision, the latter presenting the incredible (as in "The Rime of the Ancient Mariner") as if it were an everyday occurrence. Poetry, for them, was "the spontaneous overflow of powerful feelings," arising from "emotion recollected in tranquillity"; its language should be a "selection of the real language of men in a state of vivid sensation." Whether or not Wordsworth was consistent in his beliefs (and Coleridge claimed he was not), and whether or not his consistency produces failures (and numerous critics say it does), Wordsworth's best work, dating from 1797 to 1812, lovingly and convincingly depicts man's closer communion with nature, as he progresses from childhood to maturity. For further biographical, critical, or historical information, consult: John F. Danby, *The Simple Wordsworth: Studies in the Poems, 1797–1807* (New York, 1961); Helen Darbishire, *The Poet Wordsworth* (Oxford, Eng., 1950); Albert S. Guerard, *English Romantic Poetry: Ethos, Structure, and Symbol in Coleridge, Wordsworth, Shelley, and Keats* (Berkeley, 1968); Bernard Groom, *The Unity of Wordsworth's Poetry* (New York, 1966); Herschel Margoliouth, *Wordsworth and Coleridge, 1795–1834* (Hamden, Conn., 1966); and David Perkins, *The Quest for Permanence: The Symbolism of Wordsworth, Shelley, and Keats* (Cambridge, Mass., 1959).

Samuel Taylor Coleridge (1772–1834) is significant both as a poet and critic. Indeed, both roles were so bound together in him that one comments on the other. In his literary auto-biography, *Biographia Literaria* (1817), Coleridge explained that he sought, especially through his poetry dealing with the supernatural, to give "a semblance of truth sufficient to procure for these shadows of imagination that willing suspension of disbelief for the moment which constitutes poetic faith." He sometimes employs a very simple poetic structure (as in the ballad form of "The Rime of the Ancient Mariner"), sometimes subconsciously fuses images from his copious reading (as in "Kubla Khan"), sometimes recollects childhood anxieties and superstitions (as in "Frost at Midnight"). Coleridge, at his best, always invokes the landscape of the subconscious and compels the reader to find himself in sudden, strange surroundings. For further biographical, critical, or historical information, consult: Walter J. Bate, *Coleridge* (New York, 1968); Kathleen Coburn, *Coleridge: A Collection of Critical Essays* (Englewood Cliffs, 1967); and John L. Lowes, *The Road to Xanadu: A Study in the Ways of the Imagination* (Boston and New York, 1927).

Percy Bysshe Shelley (1792–1822), like William Blake, was an iconoclast. An aristocrat expelled from Cambridge for his pamphlet *The Necessity of Atheism* (1811) and self-exiled from England after deserting his wife for another woman, he sought, in verse of great sensuous sound, metrical variety, and prophetic ardor, to move man to revolt against tyranny and cruelty and live by love and reason alone. "Hymn to Intellectual Beauty" (1816) and "Ode to the West Wind" (written in five *terza rima* stanzas rhyming *aba, bcd, cdc, ded, ee;* 1819) elaborate Shelley's convictions in the perfectibility of man. His convictions have been appreciated by other poets such as Robert Browning, Stephen Spender, and Gregory Corso. For further biographical, critical, or historical information, consult: Kenneth N. Cameron, *The Young Shelley: Genesis of a Radical* (New York, 1962); Edward Dowden, *The Life of Percy Bysshe Shelley* (New York, 1966); George M. Ridenour, *Shelley: A Collection of Critical Essays* (Englewood Cliffs, 1965); and Bennett Weaver, *Toward the Understanding of Shelley* (Ann Arbor, 1932).

John Keats (1795–1821) was especially influenced by Spenser and Shakespeare. "The Eve of St. Agnes" is written in the stanza form Spenser invented for his epic *The Faerie Queene,* nine lines rhyming *ababbcbcc,* the last line containing twelve syllables rather than ten; "Ode to a Nightingale" employs a stanza form that intentionally combined the virtues of both the Shakespearean and Petrarchan sonnets (ten lines divisible into a quatrain and a sestet). Keats differs from both Spenser and Shakespeare in being perhaps the most sensuous poet in the English language: his verse is almost literally to be tasted ("beaded bubbles winking at the brim,/ And purple-stainèd mouth"), to be heard ("The silver, snarling trumpets 'gan to chide"), to be felt chillingly, as he offers "This Living Hand": "see here it is—/ I hold it towards you." For further biographical, critical, or historical information, consult: Walter J. Bate, *John Keats* (New York, 1966); Walter J. Bate, *Keats: A Collection of Critical Essays* Englewood Cliffs, 1964); Walter J. Bate, *Negative Capability: The Intuitive Approach in Keats* (Cambridge, Mass., 1939); Douglas Bush, *John Keats: His Life and Writings* (New York, 1966); Richard H. Fogle, *The Imagery of Keats and Shelley: A Comparative Study* (Hamden, Conn., 1962); and I. A. R. Jack, *Keats and the Mirror of Art* (Oxford, Eng., 1967).

Alfred, Lord Tennyson (1809–1892) wrote the 181 poems (all in "envelope" quatrains, the rhymes of lines one and four "enclosing" the rhymes of lines two and three) of *In Memoriam* (1850) to commemorate the death of his dearest friend, Arthur Hallam, in 1833. Tennyson often referred to the work as "The Way of the Soul"; it is, in critic A. C. Bradley's words, "a journey from the first stupor and confusion of grief, through a growing acquiescence often disturbed by the recurrence of pain, to an almost unclouded peace and joy. . . . The soul, at first, almost sunk in the feeling of loss, finds itself at last freed from regret and yet strengthened in affection. . . . The world, which once seemed to it a mere echo of its sorrow, has become the abode of that immortal love, at once divine and human, which includes the living and the dead." For further biographical, critical, or historical information, consult: Jerome H. Buckley, *Tennyson: The Growth of a Poet* (Cambridge, Mass., 1960); John D. Jump, *Tennyson: The Critical Heritage* (New York, 1967); and John Killham, *Critical Essays on the Poetry of Tennyson* (New York, 1960).

Robert Browning (1812–1889) achieved excellence in both lyrics and narrative verse. The companion poems "Meeting at Night" and "Parting at Morning" are examples of the former; "The Bishop Orders His Tomb," "Andrea del Sarto," and " 'Childe Roland to the Dark Tower Came' " of the latter. Browning's narratives usually take the form of a soliloquy (as in " 'Childe Roland' ") or a dramatic monologue, and in the field of the dramatic monologue Browning's poems are perhaps the most widely read. In this particular form one character speaks throughout the poem, usually at some critical moment in his life. At least one other person is present, but the reader can judge the silent character's reactions to the speaker only through his own. Frequently the speaker reveals more of himself, for better or worse, than he realizes; and a realistic tension between the speaker and the observer-reader builds gradually to a climax. Elements of the dramatic monologue, variously used, can be found in the works of Matthew Arnold, Carl Sandburg, H. D., John Crowe Ransom, and T. S. Eliot. For further biographical, critical, or historical information, consult: William C. DeVane, *A Browning Handbook*, second edition (New York, 1955);

Philip Drew, *Robert Browning: A Collection of Critical Essays* (London, 1966); Park Honan, *Browning's Characters: A Study in Poetic Technique* (New York, 1961); and Roma A. King, *The Bow and the Lyre: The Art of Robert Browning* (Ann Arbor, 1964).

Walt Whitman (1819–1892), a prolific writer in verse and prose, was brought up on Long Island. He had five years of school, and worked variously as an office boy, printer's apprentice, schoolmaster, printer, editor, and journalist. *Leaves of Grass,* a volume to which Whitman continually added for over thirty years, remains his masterpiece. This work, a celebration of nineteenth-century American democracy and nationalism, was denounced and occasionally banned until the last decade of Whitman's life; but its influence on modern American poets is great; Carl Sandburg, Wallace Stevens, and Hart Crane are only a few of the descendants of the Whitman tradition. Whitman's originality lies in his evolution of "free verse." This verse form is seemingly unrestricted by externally imposed metrical patterns, built rather upon operatic repetition and catalogues of brief pictures that combine with Whitman's theme to produce a tone of grandeur, and a vision not only of America's scope but otherworldliness. For further biographical, critical, or historical information, consult: Gay W. Allen, *The Solitary Singer: A Critical Biography of Walt Whitman* (New York, 1955); Gay W. Allen, *Walt Whitman Handbook* (New York, 1962); William E. Barton, *Abraham Lincoln and Walt Whitman* (Port Washington, N.Y., 1965); Basil De Selincourt, *Walt Whitman: A Critical Study* (New York, 1965); and Roy H. Pearce, *Whitman: A Collection of Critical Essays* (Englewood Cliffs, 1962).

Matthew Arnold (1822–1888) is perhaps better regarded today as a critic than as a poet. His important poetry was written before he was forty-five but did not meet his own ideals, and he abandoned it to pursue social criticism (as in *Culture and Anarchy*, 1869; *Literature and Dogma*, 1873; *Discourses in America*, 1885). Arnold believed himself to possess "less poetical sentiment than Tennyson, and less intellectual vigor and abundance than Browning." Nevertheless, he felt that he had "perhaps more of a fusion of the two" than either poet and had "more regularly applied that fusion to the main line of modern development." Certainly his experimenting with stanzaic forms, metres, and irregular rhymes (as in "Philomela"), and his expression of "Wandering between two worlds, one dead,/ The other powerless to be born" (in "Stanzas from the Grande Chartreuse"), link him securely with his contemporaries as well as with the modern era of Ezra Pound, T. S. Eliot, Archibald MacLeish, and W. H. Auden. For further biographical, critical, or historical information, consult: Paull F. Baum, *Ten Studies in the Poetry of Matthew Arnold* (Durham, N.C., 1958); Edward K. Brown, *Matthew Arnold: A Study in Conflict* (Chicago, 1948); E. K. Chambers, *Matthew Arnold: A Study* (Oxford, Eng., 1947); Arthur D. Cullers, *Imaginative Reason: The Poetry of Matthew Arnold* (New Haven, 1966); E. D. H. Johnson, *The Alien Vision of Victorian Poetry: Sources of the Poetic Imagination in Tennyson, Browning, and Arnold* (Hamden, Conn., 1963); and Lionel Trilling, *Matthew Arnold*, second edition (New York, 1965).

George Meredith (1828–1909) achieved notable success in criticism (*On the Idea of Comedy and the Uses of the Comic Spirit*, 1877), the novel (*The Ordeal of Richard Feverel*, 1859; *The Egoist*, 1879; *Diana of the Crossways*, 1884–1885), and poetry. In the latter genre *Modern Love* (1862), a sequence of fifty sixteen-line "sonnets" frankly tracing the estrangement of Meredith and his wife, ranks as one of his best works. In his emphasis on thought (almost to the point of writing verse essays), in his ellipses, condensations, and rapid flow of new figures of speech, Meredith points ahead to practices of early twentieth-century verse. For further biographical, critical, or historical information, consult: Siegfried Sassoon, *Meredith* (London, 1948); Lionel Stevenson, *The Ordeal of George Meredith: A Biography* (New York, 1967); and George M. Trevelyan, *The Poetry and Philosophy of George Meredith* (New York, 1966).

Dante Gabriel Rossetti (1828–1882), an admirer of Shelley, Keats, and Browning, was both a painter and a poet. Discovering that Keats had thought early Italian painters superior even to Raphael, and believing Keats to be correct, Rossetti and others formed the Pre-Raphaelite Brotherhood, seeking to reestablish the spirit of individuality and freedom, as exemplified in William Blake's work, in English art. Sincerity, noble conception, and meticulous accuracy in idea and portrayal were the Brotherhood's ideals. Rossetti sought these same qualities in his sophisticated and quite graphic verse, of which "Troy Town" and "Body's Beauty" may serve as startling examples. For further biographical, critical, or historical information, consult: Sir Max Beerbohm, *Rossetti and His Circle* (London, 1922); Oswald Doughty, *Dante Gabriel Rossetti: A Victorian Romantic*, second edition (London, 1960); Gordon H. Fleming, *Rossetti and the Pre-Raphaelite Brotherhood* (London, 1967).

Emily Dickinson (1830–1886) was advised to "delay to publish" her poetry, and it was only after her death—indeed, as late as 1945—that Dickinson's full impact began to make itself felt. A recluse who scribbled her work (with many alternate versions) on backs of envelopes or old scraps of paper and stored them in bundles in her room, Dickinson effected a private revolution in letters as impressive as the public one of modern poets unfamiliar with her work. Her poetry is marked by brevity (two words like "Obviate parade" do the work of a sentence or paragraph), striking word-play ("Zero at the Bone"), solid but ambiguous figures of speech ("A Quartz contentment, like a stone"), deliberately broken rhymes, metrical irregularities, and sudden shifts of tone. For further biographical, critical, or historical information, consult: Caesar R. Blake and Carlton F. Wells, *The Recognition of Emily Dickinson: Selected Criticism Since 1890* (Ann Arbor, 1964); Albert J. Gelpi, *Emily Dickinson: The Mind of the Poet* (Cambridge, Mass., 1965); Clark Griffith, *The Long Shadow: Emily Dickinson's Tragic Poetry* (Princeton, 1964); Thomas H. Johnson, *Emily Dickinson: An Interpretive Biography* (Cambridge, Mass., 1955); Klaus Lubbers, *Emily Dickinson: The Critical Revolution* (Ann Arbor, 1968); and Richard B. Sewall, *Emily Dickinson: A Collection of Critical Essays* (Englewood Cliffs, 1963).

Thomas Hardy (1840–1928) first made his mark as a writer with his novels, *The Return of the Native* (1878), *The Mayor of Casterbridge* (1886), *Tess of the D'Urbervilles* (1891), and *Jude the Obscure* (1896). *Jude*'s tragic pessimism provoked such indignation that Hardy abandoned the novel for poetry. The poetry depicts the same world as Hardy's novels: a universe in which man and nature appear at odds with each other (as in "The Subalterns"), in which religious faith has faded (as in "The Oxen"), and in which man finds himself the ironic pawn of chance, accident, coincidence. Spare, often harsh, colloquial and archaic diction underscore Hardy's grim vision. For further biographical, critical, or historical information, consult: Ernest Brennecke, *Thomas Hardy's Universe: A Study of a Poet's Mind* (New York, 1966); Samuel C. Chew, *Thomas Hardy: Poet and Novelist* (New York, 1964); and Samuel L. Hynes, *The Pattern of Hardy's Poetry* (Chapel Hill, 1961).

Gerard Manley Hopkins (1844–1889), a Jesuit priest, published none of the small body of poetry he saved at the time he entered the Order (1868). Influenced by the poetry of Donne and Herbert (his sonnets on spiritual conflicts recall Donne's especially), Hopkins sought to project the individualizing quality (what he called the "inscape") of persons, emotions, or nature aroused in himself (the "instress"). The unique, the "original, spare, strange" required, Hopkins believed, a "sprung" rhythm based on accent only, patterned by alliteration and internal rhyme. Ellipses, interchanges of parts of speech, economical phrases, and metaphors within metaphors mark all of his poetry, and have profoundly affected poets such as T. S. Eliot, W. H. Auden, and Dylan Thomas. For further biographical, critical, or historical information, consult: Robert Boyle, *Metaphor in Hopkins* (Chapel Hill, 1961); Geoffrey H. Hartmann, *Hopkins: A Collection of Critical Essays* (Englewood Cliffs, 1966); Alan Heuser, *The Shaping Vision of Gerard Manley Hopkins* (Hamden, Conn., 1968); and John Pick, *Gerard Manley Hopkins: Priest and Poet*, second edition (New York, 1966).

William Butler Yeats (1865–1939), winner of the Nobel Prize in 1923, began his career as a poet influenced by Blake, Keats, Tennyson, and Pre-Raphaelite artists like Dante Gabriel Rossetti. His early work, heavily imbued with Irish fairy tales and Celtic folklore, was delicate, lovely, sensuous, and extremely musical (as, for example, "The Cap and Bells"). With his volumes *The Green Helmet* (1910), *Responsibilities* (1914), and *The Wild Swans at Coole* (1919), a change of tone, if not of subject matter, occurred. Yeats's phrasing became more taut, his ornamentation more sparse, the speaking voice more conversational. The changes can be variously accounted for by Yeats's own maturation, his marriage in 1917, and his association with Ezra Pound, which began in 1908. Whatever the causes, Yeats's handling of myth became more complex and profound (as in "Among School Children"), his images sharper, and his influence on younger poets far-reaching. There are echoes of Yeats's techniques in the verse of Wallace Stevens, W. H. Auden, Stephen Spender,

Adrienne Rich, and Robert Mezey. For further biographical, critical, or historical information, consult: Richard Ellmann, *The Identity of Yeats*, second edition (New York, 1964); Richard Ellmann, *Yeats: The Man and the Masks* (New York, 1948); James Hall and Martin Steinmann, *The Permanence of Yeats* (New York, 1961); Alexander N. Jeffares, *William Butler Yeats: Man and Poet* (New York, 1966); and John E. Unterecker, *Yeats: A Collection of Critical Essays* (Englewood Cliffs, 1963).

Edwin Arlington Robinson (1869–1935) began his writing career by studying the verse of Thomas Hardy, and like Hardy, saw man to be doomed as he moves according to a universal scheme he cannot comprehend, his only consolation an honest perception of his true fate. Robinson made his first great impression in American poetry with his fourth volume, *The Man Against the Sky* (1916), whose title poem reveals his essential characteristics as well as his differences from his predecessor: in theme, a search for meaning in a meaningless universe; in technique, a dramatization of this search in terms of one's psychological reactions. Simple diction, incisive phrasing, and lucid psychological portraiture are Robinson's hallmarks in this volume and in *Merlin* (1917), *Lancelot* (1920), and *Tristram* (1927). These qualities, applied with equal success to "The Clerks" and "The Sheaves," reveal Robinson's dedication to his craft, and poets like Robert Frost and Robinson Jeffers have acknowledged their debt to him. For further biographical, critical, or historical information, consult: Wallace L. Anderson, *Edwin Arlington Robinson: A Critical Introduction* (Cambridge, Mass., 1968); Robert P. T. Coffin, *New Poetry of New England: Frost and Robinson* (New York, 1964); and Yvor Winters, *Edwin Arlington Robinson* (Norfolk, Conn., 1946).

Robert Frost (1874–1963) is noted for his New England background, which imbues even those poems of his without a specific setting.

Whether working in blank verse (as in " 'Out, Out—' "), quatrains (as in "To Earthward"), or terza rima (as in "Acquainted with the Night"), Frost molds his austere lines to reflect the voices of humans whose harsh life is eked out by scratching about on barren rocky hillsides, lonely farms, or near-deserted towns. "The Draft Horse," from Frost's last volume, *In the Clearing* (1962), is perhaps the epitome of Frost's stated intentions. In an often-quoted passage, he said: "There are two types of realist—the one who offers a good deal of dirt with his potato to show that it is a real one; and the one who is satisfied with the potato brushed clean. I'm inclined to be the second kind.... To me, the thing that art does for life is to clean it up, to strip it to form." For further biographical, critical, or historical information, consult: Reuben A. Brower, *The Poetry of Robert Frost: Constellations of Intention* (New York, 1963); James M. Cox, *Robert Frost: A Collection of Critical Essays* (Englewood Cliffs, 1962); John F. Lynen, *The Pastoral Art of Robert Frost* (New Haven, 1960); Elizabeth S. Sergeant, *Robert Frost: The Trial by Existence* (New York, 1960); James R. Squires, *The Major Themes of Robert Frost* (Ann Arbor, 1963); and Lawrance R. Thompson, *Robert Frost: The Early Years, 1874–1915* (New York, 1966).

Carl Sandburg (1878–1967), one of the true descendants of Whitman, left school at thirteen and went to work on a milk wagon, then for six years worked as a porter in a barber shop, a scene-shifter in a theatre, a truck-handler in a brickyard, a turner-apprentice in a pottery, a dishwasher, and a harvest hand. His writing career received its impetus with the publication of the famous "Chicago" and other poems in a 1914 issue of *Poetry*. Volumes of his poems began to appear in rapid succession: *Chicago Poems* (1916), *Cornhuskers* (1918), *Smoke and Steel* (1920), *Slabs of the Sunburnt West* (1922), to name but a few. The titles indicate Sandburg's Whitmanesque intentions to celebrate the whole of America, agricultural and industrial. His monumental six-volume biography of Abraham Lincoln (1926; 1939) and his collections of tales and ballads are also apostrophes to the American common man. For further biographical, critical, or historical information, consult: Richard Crowder, *Carl Sandburg* (New York, 1964); Joseph Haas, *Carl Sandburg: A Pictorial Biography* (New York, 1967); and Carl Sandburg, *Always the Young Strangers* (New York, 1953).

Wallace Stevens (1879–1955) believed that an individual's "ideas of order" correspond with the innate order in nature and the universe. So passionately did he seek a correspondence that he did not issue a collection of verse until he reached his early forties (*Harmonium*, 1923), and then he further revised and enlarged this collection twice (1931 and 1937). This passion for precision carries over into Stevens' individual poems, and is indicated, as in "Le Monocle de Mon Oncle," by the mosaic-like Impressionist pictures he presents ("We hang like warty squashes, streaked and rayed" or "a pool of pink/ Clippered with lilies scudding the bright chromes"), by puns (on the word "greet"), explicit and implicit allusions (to Utamaro, Eve, Hyacinth, and, in stanza ten, possibly to Yeats), and sound closely wedded to thought ("the firefly's quick, electric stroke/ Ticks tediously the time of one more year"). For further biographical, critical, or historical information, consult: James Baird, *The Dome and the Rock: Structure in the Poetry of Wallace Stevens* (Baltimore, 1968); Marie Borroff, *Wallace Stevens: A Collection of Critical Essays* (Englewood Cliffs, 1963); Frank A. Doggett, *Stevens' Poetry of Thought* (Baltimore, 1966); Daniel Fuchs, *The Comic Spirit of Wallace Stevens* (Durham, N.C., 1963); and William V. O'Connor, *The Shaping Spirit: A Study of Wallace Stevens* (New York, 1964).

William Carlos Williams (1883–1963) would have pleased Whitman because of his "melting pot" background; his father was English by birth and his mother a Basque of Dutch-Spanish-Jewish lineage. In addition, Williams worked closely with people, both as a doctor and a poet. Considering these facts, it is not surprising to find Williams a strongly individualistic poet, rejecting, as Wallace Stevens observed, "the accepted sense of things." So intense is his almost clinical passion for the "real" that, despite Williams' idiomatic and purposely nonmelodic expression, the "real" takes on the air of the "unreal." "The Yachts" appear "youthful, rare/ as the light of a happy eye"; in "To Daphne and Virginia," loveless old men watch "a heavy goose/ who waddles, slopping/ noisily in the mud of/ his pool." For further biographical, critical, and historical information, consult: James K. Guimond, *The Art of William Carlos Williams: A Discovery and Possession of America* (Urbana, 1968); Vivienne Koch, *William Carlos Williams* (Norfolk, Conn., 1950); Joseph Hillis Miller, *William Carlos Williams: A Collection of Critical Essays* (Englewood Cliffs, 1966); Linda W. Wagner, *The Poems of William Carlos Williams: A Critical Study* (Middletown, Conn., 1964); and William Carlos Williams, *I Wanted to Write a Poem: The Autobiography of the Works of a Poet* (Boston, 1967).

D. H. Lawrence (1885–1930), in addition to his fiction, wrote verse, which was collected in two volumes (1929), then enlarged by a posthumous volume in 1933. In his poems, as in his stories, Lawrence pursues his elaboration of instinctual life in various guises: as dramatic projection in "Cherry Robbers," as autobiographer in "Piano," and as both, with the intention of merging real and unreal worlds, in "Bavarian Gentians." For further biographical, critical, or historical information, see the books listed under Lawrence's name in the section on fiction earlier in this anthology.

Ezra Pound (b. 1885) is perhaps the twentieth-century's most controversial American poet:

to some he is a man whose ability for cultivating and promoting the talents of others (such as T. S. Eliot) exceeds his ability to writing lasting poetry. To others he is a poet of the first rank, whose frenetic, telegraphic style, riddled with puns (often obscene), several languages (T. S. Eliot once quipped that Pound was the best American-English poet writing in Chinese), and dissolving of allusions into still other allusions, is magnificent. Whatever the verdict, Pound knows, assimilates, and appreciates poetry of every age and variety: the speech of Browning and the music of Yeats are evident in his early work; he could offer constructive criticism to poets as dissimilar as Robert Frost and T. S. Eliot; his influence on William Butler Yeats, William Carlos Williams, Hart Crane, and Archibald MacLeish, to name but a few, is obvious. If, as Eliot said, James Joyce made the modern world intelligible for novelists, the same may be said, without exaggeration, of Pound's service to modern poets. For further biographical, critical, or historical information, consult: Donald A. Davie, *Ezra Pound: Poet as Sculptor* (London, 1965); T. S. Eliot, *Ezra Pound: His Metric and Poetry* (New York, 1917); George S. Fraser, *Ezra Pound* (New York, 1965); K. L. Goodwin, *The Influence of Ezra Pound* (London, 1966); Thomas H. Jackson, *The Early Poems of Ezra Pound* (Cambridge, Mass., 1968); Hugh Kenner, *The Poetry of Ezra Pound* (London, 1951); and Charles Norman, *The Case of Ezra Pound* (New York, 1968).

H. D. (Hilda Doolittle, 1886–1961) belonged, with Ezra Pound, to a group of English and American poets (1909–1917) who called themselves Imagists. Their ideas, set forth in a preface to their anthology *Some Imagist Poets* (1915), were that poetry should satisfy the criteria for good written prose and that it should present objects exactly rather than diffusely. The language of their verse was to be entirely that of common speech, their choice of subject matter absolutely unre-

stricted, their rhythms and metres disciplined but arbitrary rather than padded out to meet an initially imposed pattern. H. D.'s "Fragment 36," inspired by some famous lines of the Greek poetess Sappho, fulfills the Imagists' criteria, and reveals H. D.'s sensuous focus as well as her mastery of scattered and concealed rhyme and of repetition to achieve continuity. For further biographical, critical, or historical information, consult: H. D., *Bid Me to Live* (New York, 1960); Vincent Gerard Quinn, *Hilda Doolittle (H. D.)* (New York, 1968).

Robinson Jeffers (1887–1962) became known only with the publication of his third volume, *Tamar and Other Poems* (1925), but his fame was so instantaneously achieved that the book was enlarged and reprinted (as *Roan Stallion, Tamar, and Other Poems*) in a year's time. This work—as well as those quickly to follow, such as *The Women at Point Sur* (1927), *Cawdor* (1928), *Dear Judas* (1929)—reveals Jeffers' identifying hallmarks: the rugged, fog-bound California coast as setting; passionate characters swept up in monstrous crimes; Whitmanesque free verse—except that it was stark, often savage, minus Whitman's catalogues and optimistic philosophy. Jeffers' identifying hallmarks: the rugged, republics perish, the earth dies, the sun blackens, man survives on cruelty to other men, other animals, and nature. "Apology for Bad Dreams" may be regarded as the foundation for Jeffers' vision. For further biographical, critical, or historical information, consult: Melba B. Bennett, *The Stone Mason of Tor House: The Life and Work of Robinson Jeffers* (Los Angeles, 1966); Frederic I. Carpenter, *Robinson Jeffers* (New York, 1962); Rudolph Gilbert, *Shine, Perishing Republic: Robinson Jeffers and the Tragic Sense in Modern Poetry* (New York, 1965); and James R. Squires, *The Loyalties of Robinson Jeffers* (Ann Arbor, 1956).

Marianne Moore (b. 1887) has produced a slender amount of verse that has commanded a tremendous respect from her contemporaries. T. S. Eliot expressed his admiration for her in his introduction to her *Selected Poems* (1935), and W. H. Auden jests that he rummages through her verse in search of images and themes. Like William Carlos Williams, Miss Moore has a passion for analyzing the "real" object in its every detail; but her stanzas, actually verse paragraphs patterned on accent rather than traditional metres, are more fastidious, indeed almost geometrically precise. Her images may at times recall H. D.'s, but in the end they coalesce to produce a witty, ironic statement about man and his relation to other animals and nature. "The Pangolin" is about as long a poem as Miss Moore has ever written, and clearly reveals her distinctive traits. For further biographical, critical, or historical information, consult: Bernard F. Engel, *Marianne Moore* (New York, 1964); Andrew K. Weatherland, *The Edge of the Image: Marianne Moore, William Carlos Williams, and Some Other Poets* (Seattle, 1967).

John Crowe Ransom (b. 1888), like Marianne Moore, has produced a spare number of poems; with each succeeding edition they threaten to become even sparer, as Ransom excises earlier work he no longer likes. What remains, however, reveals a man obviously capable of honest self-appraisal, whose humor is spiced with a dash of vinegar and whose creation of tension is, at the least, haunting and piercing (as, for example, in "Judith of Bethulia" and "Prelude to an Evening"). These qualities are exhibited in (though not wholly explained by) Ransom's whimsical rhymes (daisy-easy, orgy-clergy), his precise but daring description locked in equally precise and daring phrasing ("A macaroon absorbed all her emotion;/His hue was ashy but an effect of ocean"), and his never-failing tone of subtle irony. For further biographical, critical, or historical information, consult: Karl F. Knight, *The Poetry of John Crowe Ransom: A Study of Diction, Metre, and Symbol* (London, 1964); John L. Stewart, *The Burden of Time* (Princeton, 1965).

T. S. Eliot (1888–1965), a Nobel Prize winner in 1948, published his first volume of poems, *Prufrock and Other Observations*, in 1917. The title poem, both in theme and in technique, acts as a guide to the development of Eliot's career as a whole, for its speaker represents a paralyzed individual in a decaying society. Fragments of other authors' works, titles, and heroes' actions float on his stream of perception, commenting by free association or comparison on Prufrock's condition. Allusion, concentration, the fusion of intense intellectual discipline and cultural memory have been the chief characteristics of Eliot's poetry from "Prufrock" to "The Hollow Men" (1925) and "The Dry Salvages" (from *Four Quartets*, 1943). These qualities Eliot elaborated in several controversial books of literary criticism (*The Sacred Wood*, 1920; *Homage to John Dryden*, 1924; *For Lancelot Andrewes*, 1928), and are carried over into Eliot's less successful experiments in verse drama (*Murder in the Cathedral*, 1935; *The Family Reunion*, 1939; *The Cocktail Party*, 1949). So pervasive has his influence been (on poets like Archibald MacLeish, Robert Penn Warren, and Robert Lowell), and so respected are his craftsmanship, integrity, and power, that some critics refer to the first half of the twentieth century as the Age of Eliot. For further biographical, critical, or historical information, consult: Elizabeth Drew, *T. S. Eliot: The Design of His Poetry* (New York, 1960); Northrop Frye, *T. S. Eliot* (New York, 1966); Helen L. Gardner, *The Art of T. S. Eliot* (London, 1968); Hugh Kenner, *The Invisible Poet: T. S. Eliot* (New York, 1964); Hugh Kenner, *T. S. Eliot: A Collection of Critical Essays* (Englewood Cliffs, 1962); Francis O. Matthiessen, *The Achievement of T. S. Eliot*, third edition (New York, 1958); Allen Tate, *T. S. Eliot: The Man and His Work* (New York, 1966); and George Williamson, *A Reader's Guide to T. S. Eliot*, second edition (New York, 1966).

Archibald MacLeish (b. 1892) graduated from Harvard Law School, but abandoned his practice in 1923 to devote himself to writing. After a five-year sojourn in Paris, studying the early work of Pound and Eliot, MacLeish determined to return to America and write an epic employing modern anthropology and psychology to depict a great civilization's crisis. *Conquistador* (1932), the resulting poem recounting the conquest of the Mexican Aztecs by Cortez, won the Pulitzer Prize and secured MacLeish's fame. Around the same time, and even more so thereafter, MacLeish's sense of public service increased, and he contributed articles, broadcasts, lectures, and plays against fascism, the irresponsible financial world, and writers he felt to be detached from the crises of modern society. Among other offices, MacLeish has served as Librarian of Congress (1939–1944) and Assistant Secretary of State (1944–1945). MacLeish's poems, long or short, have in the main reflected his concern for the well-being of civilization; his best are built on conceits or extended comparisons (as in the evocation of the night in "You, Andrew Marvell" or the big-top circus in "The End of the World"). For further biographical, critical, or historical information, consult: Signi L. Falk, *Archibald MacLeish* (New York, 1966).

E. E. Cummings (1894–1962), like Archibald MacLeish and Robert Graves, served in World War I; afterwards he trained in painting, and in 1923 published his first volume of poems, *Tulips and Chimneys*, which revealed his painter's eye not only for arranging pictures but for rearranging typography as well. In a Cummings poem a word may be broken into its syllables and the syllables placed separately about the page, a capital letter may appear in the middle of a word, one sentence unit may run into another without initial or terminal punctuation. However, in most cases, Cummings' rearrangement will be seen to imply a method adapted in deference to his subject or intention; thus, for example,

Buffalo Bill shoots a gallery of "onetwothreefourfive pigeonsjustlikethat." Cummings' rearrangement of typography and rules of grammar are meant, among other things, to indicate the poem's movement and tone, and to secure the reader's immediate participation in both. For further biographical, critical, or historical information, consult: Norman Friedman, *E. E. Cummings: The Art of His Poetry* (Baltimore, 1960); Norman Friedman, *E. E. Cummings: The Growth of a Writer* (Carbondale, 1964); Charles Norman, *E. E. Cummings: The Magic-Maker* (New York, 1964); and Robert E. Wegner, *The Poetry and Prose of E. E. Cummings* (New York, 1965).

Robert Graves (b. 1895), a captain in the Royal Welch Fusiliers during World War I, has written criticism of many of the major English poets, has proven himself expert in the translation of world literature, and has always demonstrated a marked affinity for the explication and syncretizing of myths, national and universal (*The White Goddess*, 1948). Additionally, he has to his credit a host of witty, provocative historical novels, among which the better known are probably *I, Claudius* (1935) and *Wife to Mr. Milton* (1943). But, if Graves has many interests and many talents, he recognizes but one calling: poetry. His occupations subserve his one desire to compose poetry with delight, at the white heat of lyrical impulse, without regard for future gain or distinction. He writes his poetry from and about love; and among modern lyricists, Graves is unsurpassed for a pure poetry of intense, sensuous particulars that suggest, through myth and allusion, the undercurrents and crosscurrents of man's general experience and racial memories. For further biographical, critical, or historical information, consult: John M. Cohen, *Robert Graves* (New York, 1965); Douglas Day, *Swifter than Reason: The Poetry and Criticism of Robert Graves* (Chapel Hill, 1963); and Robert Graves, *Good-bye to All That* (New York, 1930).

Hart Crane (1899–1932) issued only two volumes of poetry during his lifetime, *White Buildings* (1926) and *The Bridge* (1930). In the first volume the influence of Wallace Stevens and T. S. Eliot is apparent, and in the second Blake, Whitman, and Dickinson make their presence felt; but, in both works, Crane always rises above being an imitator. Indeed, Crane's voice and technique are distinctly his own. Searching for (and perhaps failing to find) a theme to give unity to his work as a whole, Crane preferred the "logic of metaphor" and *synaesthesia* (the use of one sensory impression to imply another, as in "Belle Isle, white echo of the oar" in "Voyages: VI") to "so-called pure logic." And it is the strongly individualistic, cinematic flow of images, strange colors, sounds, and actions fused in clipped, crisp syntax that distinguishes Crane's work from all others', even from poetry as heavily indebted to Crane's as that of Dylan Thomas. For further biographical, critical, or historical information, consult: Herbert A. Leibowitz, *Hart Crane: An Introduction to the Poetry* (New York, 1968); Richard W. B. Lewis, *The Poetry of Hart Crane: A Critical Study* (Princeton, 1967); and Brom Weber, *Hart Crane: A Biographical and Critical Study* (New York, 1948).

Langston Hughes (1902–1967) has been called both the Poet Laureate of Harlem and the Poet Laureate of the Negro People. Both titles attest to Hughes' professed dedication to exploring the "soul-world" of his people: the consciousness, emotions, and thinking of American blacks. The largeness of Hughes' intention is matched by his prolific and varied output, for he composed not only verse but also fiction, drama, essays, histories, and anthologies. The verse shows, particularly at the outset of Hughes' career, the influence of the Whitman-Sandburg free line, but from beginning to end—in over a dozen volumes—the rhythm is distinctively that of Negro jazz and blues, fervent, syncopated, changeable, and forcefully direct. For further biographical and critical information, consult: Arthur P. Davis, "The Harlem of Langston Hughes' Poetry," *Phylon*, XIII (Winter 1952), 276–83; James A. Emanuel, *Langston Hughes* (New York, 1967); James Presley, "The American Dream of Langston Hughes," *Southwest Review*, XLVIII (Autumn 1963), 380–6; Special Langston Hughes Number, *CLA Journal*, XI (June 1968); Special Supplement on Langston Hughes, *Freedomways*, VIII (Spring 1968).

Robert Penn Warren (b. 1905), perhaps better known as a novelist (*All the King's Men*, 1946) and a critic (*Coleridge's Rime of the Ancient Mariner*, 1946) than for his poetry, has fused his gifts for narration and criticism best in several volumes of verse: *Brother to Dragons* (1953), *Promises* (1957), *You, Emperors and Others* (1960), and *Audubon: A Vision* (1969). Warren's poetry depicts the modern world as a "moment of mania"; original sin, alienation, or terror arising from one's sense of corruption and guilt, are his usual preoccupations. These subjects Warren elaborates in a series of vignettes (the title "Original Sin: A Short Story" is significant in describing Warren's technique as well as his subject), told in a seemingly casual style, alternately grim and light. For further biographical or critical information, consult: Charles H. Bohner, *Robert Penn Warren* (New York, 1964); Leonard Casper, *Robert Penn Warren: The Dark and Bloody Ground* (Seattle, 1960); John L. Langley, *Robert Penn Warren: A Collection of Critical Essays* (New York, 1965); and Victor H. Strandberg, *A Colder Fire: The Poetry of Robert Penn Warren* (Lexington, Ky., 1965).

W. H. Auden (b. 1907), according to his friend and collaborator Christopher Isherwood, is the kind of poet to whom one might say "'Please write me a double ballade on the virtues of a certain brand of toothpaste, which also contains at least ten anagrams on the names of well-known politicians, and of which the refrain is as follows...'" Within 24 hours, your ballade would be ready—and it would be good." Isherwood's comment should not be taken to mean that Auden is a facile writer but rather that he is a tireless experimentalist. There is no traditional form he has not tried, no jargon, colloquialism, or formalism in English he cannot effortlessly raise to eloquent speech; irony (as in "Musée des Beaux Arts"), tribute (as in "In Memory of W. B. Yeats"), lyric (as in "Pur"), suit him as well as "charade" (*Paid on Both Sides*, 1930), epistle (*Letters from Iceland*, 1937; *New Year Letter*, 1941), cantata (*For the Time Being*, 1944), and "eclogue" (*The Age of Anxiety*, 1947). For further biographical or critical information, consult: Joseph W. Beach, *The Making of the Auden Canon* (Minneapolis, 1957); John G. Blair, *The Poetic Art of W. H. Auden* (Princeton, 1965); Herbert Greenberg, *Quest for the Necessary: W. H. Auden and the Dilemma of Divided Consciousness* (Cambridge, Mass., 1968); Monroe K. Spears, *Auden: A Collection of Critical Essays* (Englewood Cliffs, 1964); and Monroe K. Spears, *The Poetry of W. H. Auden: The Disenchanted Island* (New York, 1963).

Theodore Roethke (1908–1963) absorbed stylistic elements from the works of Whitman, Yeats, Eliot, Pound, and Dylan Thomas into his own poetry; but W. H. Auden was among the first, in a frequently-quoted statement, to pinpoint Roethke's individuality: "Many people have the experience of feeling physically soiled and humiliated by life; some quickly put it out of their minds, others gloat narcissistically on its unimportant details; but both to remember and to transform its humiliation into something beautiful, as Mr. Roethke does, is rare." Frank, "naked to the bone" psychological exploration of the self to realize the visionary within permeates almost all of Roethke's verse; it is especially notable in "I Knew a Woman," "In a Dark Time," and "The Waking," a *villanelle*. For further biographical or critical information, consult: Karl Malkoff, *Theodore Roethke: An Introduction to the Poetry* (New York, 1966); Wil-

liam J. Martz, *The Achievement of Theodore Roethke: A Comprehensive Selection of His Poems with a Critical Introduction* (Glenview, Ill., 1966); Ralph J. Mills, *Contemporary American Poetry* (New York, 1965), pp. 48–71; Allan Seager, *The Glass House: The Life of Theodore Roethke* (New York, 1968); and Arnold Stein, *Theodore Roethke: Essays on the Poetry* (Seattle, 1965).

Stephen Spender (b. 1909), in addition to writing poetry, has been prolific in drama (*Trial of a Judge*, 1938), fiction (*The Burning Cactus*, 1936), criticism (*The Destructive Element*, 1935), and autobiography (*World Within World*, 1951). Frequently coupled with Auden, his contemporary, and compared to Shelley for iconoclasm, Spender resembles both poets only in his great knowledge of poetic traditions, and Shelley in his warm humanitarian zeal; his poetry is very much his own. To traditional forms Spender brings a consideration of the early machine age, its poverty and wars; but the objects of "An Elementary School Classroom in a Slum" or an air raid are not catalogued as interesting in themselves, but rather for the "thoughts" they inspire and the life they symbolize. For further biographical or critical information, consult: Philip L. Gerber and R. J. Gemmett, "A Conversation with Stephen Spender: The Creative Process," *English Record*, XVIII: 4 (1968), 2–10; Stephen Spender, *Life and the Poet* (London, 1942); and Stephen Spender, *The Making of a Poem* (London, 1955).

Elizabeth Bishop (b. 1911) was born in New England but has traveled extensively, especially in tropical climates. The two backgrounds seem to combine in her work to produce, as in "Roosters," austere lines packed with rich, continually unfolding images. In her patience with exactness, her building details to form a final philosophical question or statement, Miss Bishop's work may recall Marianne Moore's; but Bishop's tone is frequently sterner, more satirical, and she is not averse to working, as in "A Miracle for Breakfast," within quite ancient poetic molds. (In "Miracle" Bishop employs the *sestina*, an originally Provençal verse form consisting of six six-line stanzas and a three-line envoi, repeating the end words of the first stanza throughout. A variation on this form occurs in the second part of T. S. Eliot's "The Dry Salvages.") Bishop's first two volumes are collected in *Poems: North and South & A Cold Spring* (1955); she has also published another volume entitled *Questions of Travel* (1965), and *Complete Poems* (1969). For further biographical or critical information, consult: Ashley Brown, "An Interview with Elizabeth Bishop," *Shenandoah*, XVII:2 (1966), 3–19; Ralph J. Mills, *Contemporary American Poetry* (New York, 1965), pp. 72–83; and, in the Twayne series, Anne Stevenson, *Elizabeth Bishop* (New York, 1966).

Brother Antoninus (William Everson, b. 1912) admits to being influenced by another Californian, Robinson Jeffers, and shows in his sensitivity to elemental nature some connection to Walt Whitman and D. H. Lawrence. Converted to Catholicism in 1949, and later entering the Dominican Order, Brother Antoninus is especially convincing when he portrays the torment of spiritual and physical conflict (as in "I Am Long Weaned"); through his unflinching self-examination, he has laid the foundations for the "confessional," more autobiographical poetry of Robert Lowell and Anne Sexton to follow. Brother Antoninus' major verse is collected in *Single Source: The Early Poems of William Everson, 1934–1940; The Crooked Line of God: Poems, 1949–1954; The Hazards of Holiness: Poems, 1957–1960.* He has recently left the Dominican Order and married. For further biographical or critical information, consult: Harry J. Cargas, "An Interview with Brother Antoninus," *Renascense*, XVIII (1966), 137–45; Ralph J. Mills, *Contemporary American Poetry* (New York, 1965), pp. 84–100; and William E. Stafford, *The Achievement of Brother Antoninus: A Com-*

prehensive Selection of His Poems with a Critical Introduction (Glenview, Ill., 1967).

Muriel Rukeyser (b. 1913) has enjoyed an active public life for a prolific writer of verse and prose. In the early 1930s she was a member of committees investigating Negro and labor problems, and took a ground-course at Roosevelt Aviation School. Besides a biography (*Willard Gibbs*, 1942) and several other mixed verse-prose works, she has issued many collections of poems, the most memorable of which are *Theory of Flight* (1935), *U. S. 1* (1938), *A Turning Wind* (1939), *The Soul and Body of John Brown* (1940), *Beast in View* (1944), *The Green Wave* (1948), and *Body of Waking* (1958). Like Crane, Auden, and Spender, Rukeyser explores the objects, habits, and speech of modern society to symbolize its tensions and frustrations. Even the modern penchant for scientific exactness becomes a symbolic—and ironic—revelation as Rukeyser entitles a poem about poetry "Reading Time: 1 Minute 26 Seconds." There is no criticism of Miss Rukeyser's work at present.

Dylan Thomas (1914–1953) once remarked that his poems were written "in praise of God by a man who doesn't believe in God." This paradox illuminates the central character of Thomas' verse, from the early "If I Were Tickled by the Rub of Love" to the relatively late "Fern Hill." If Thomas elaborates religious themes similar to Donne's and Herbert's, in an image-spinning style reminiscent of Hopkins or Crane, his perception is absolutely fixed on the relentless life force that destroys as it creates. From birth to love and death only this force is real to Thomas, and despite efforts to rise above his perception and transform it into action and the faith on which action is based, he must continue to "sit and watch the worm beneath [his] nail/ Wearing the quick away"; or, as he advises his father (in "Do Not Go Gentle into that Good Night") to "rage against the dying of the light," recognizing himself (as in "Fern Hill") as "green and dying" though he sings in his "chains like the sea." For further biographical or critical information, consult: John Ackerman, *Dylan Thomas: His Life and Work* (New York, 1964); Constantine FitzGibbon, *The Life of Dylan Thomas* (Boston, 1965); Ralph Maud, *Poet in the Making: The Notebooks of Dylan Thomas* (New York, 1967); Louise Murdy, *Sound and Sense in Dylan Thomas's Poetry* (The Hague, 1966); Elder Olson, *The Poetry of Dylan Thomas* (Chicago, 1954); E. W. Tedlock, *Dylan Thomas: The Legend and the Poet; A Collection of Biographical and Critical Essays* (London, 1961): and William Y. Tindall, *A Reader's Guide to Dylan Thomas* (London, 1962).

Margaret Walker (b. 1915) first caught public attention when her volume of verse, *For My People* (1942), was published as a result of her winning the Yale University Younger Poets contest. A newspaper reporter, social worker, magazine editor, and teacher, her only other major publication is the long novel *Jubilee* (1966). Both works, however, were substantial enough to earn her the recognition of younger writers as the seminal influence on the poets of protest in the 1960s. Miss Walker's influence and talent can be partially measured by the vastly differing forms in which she can compose easily: the Whitman-Sandburg long-breathed hymn built on suspension, catalogs, and repetition (as in "For My People") or the self-contained, traditional sonnet ("Whores"). At present there is no significant criticism of her work available.

Gwendolyn Brooks (b. 1917), when asked why she wrote poetry, responded: "I like the concentration, the crush.... I like to vivify the *universal* fact, when it occurs to me. But the universal wears contemporary clothing very well." A writer of verse since the age of seven and a published poet since thirteen, she has won some award for almost every volume she has composed. Each volume is another realization of her stated purpose. "The Children of

the Poor," to use but one example, shows Brooks revitalizing the sonnet sequence both in clean, clear, unpretentious lines and contemporary subject matter. As in most cases, however, simplicity is deceptive; hers is achieved by a taut fusion (particularly in the sonnets anthologized here) of a dominant image with submerged allusions and an elliptical, alliterative language. For further biographical or critical information, consult: Frank London Brown, "Chicago's Great Lady of Poetry," *Negro Digest*, XI (December 1961), 53–7; Arthur P. Davis, "The Black and Tan Motif in the Poetry of Gwendolyn Brooks," *CLA Journal*, VI (December 1962), 90–7; Arthur P. Davis, "Gwendolyn Brooks: A Poet of the Unheroic," *CLA Journal*, VII (December 1963), 114–25; Stanley Kunitz, "Bronze by Gold," *Poetry*, LXXVI (April 1950), 52–6; and Charlemae Rollins, *Famous American Negro Poets* (New York, 1965).

Robert Lowell (b. 1917), after T. S. Eliot and W. H. Auden, has probably managed to gain the largest contemporary audience of poetry readers, and to sustain it with a line of publications indicating not only promise fulfilled but even more capacity to grow. From *Lord Weary's Castle* (1946), *The Mills of the Kavanaughs* (1951), and *Life Studies* (1959) to *Notebook 1967–68*, Lowell has moved from tightly-controlled traditional forms to freer ones, from almost wholly objective portrayals of religious and universal turmoils to what appear to be autobiographical "confessions" that become universal issues through the technique of association. "Skunk Hour," with its scattered rhymes and changing metres, its snapshots, the fragment of "Love, O careless love" bleating from a "love-car," and the climactic allusion to Milton's *Paradise Lost* in "I myself am hell," will indicate the nature and extent of Lowell's growth from the time he wrote "Children of Light" and "The Dead in Europe." For further biographical or critical information, consult: A. Alvarez, "A Talk with Robert Lowell," *Encounter*, XXIV:2

(1965), 39–43; William J. Martz, *The Achievement of Robert Lowell: A Comprehensive Selection of His Poems with A Critical Introduction* (Glenview, Ill., 1966); Jerome Mazzaro, *The Poetic Themes of Robert Lowell* (Ann Arbor, 1965); Ralph J. Mills, *Contemporary American Poetry* (New York, 1965), pp. 134–59; Thomas Parkinson, *Robert Lowell: A Collection of Critical Essays* (Englewood Cliffs, 1968); and Hugh B. Staples, *Robert Lowell: The First Twenty Years* (New York, 1962).

Richard Wilbur (b. 1921) has produced a body of verse reminiscent of Ben Jonson's and Robert Herrick's in its polish, wit, and precision. Wilbur's eye is alert to things of this world, but his imagination rarely fails to find something extraordinary in contexts usually taken for granted. Relations are suggested economically and subtly, as with the phrase "Poor sweet" or the word "concurs" in "In the Smoking-Car," both of which not only make thematic connections but also indicate sounds or movement. Wilbur's major collections include *The Beautiful Changes and Other Poems* (1947), *Ceremony and Other Poems* (1950), *Things of This World* (1956), *Advice to a Prophet and Other Poems* (1961). For further biographical or critical information, consult: Donald L. Hill, *Richard Wilbur* (New York, 1967); Frederic E. Faverty, "Well-Open Eyes; or, The Poetry of Richard Wilbur," in *Poets in Progress*, 23, 59–72; Ralph J. Mills, *Contemporary American Poetry* (New York, 1965), pp. 160–75; and Richard Wilbur, "On My Own Work," *Shenandoah*, XVII:1 (1965), 57–67.

James Dickey (b. 1923) has written five volumes of poetry: *Into the Stone* (1960), *Drowning with Others* (1962), *Helmets* (1963), *Buckdancer's Choice* (in which "The Firebombing" appeared, 1965), and *Poems, 1957–1967*. A pilot in both World War II and the Korean War, decorated three times for bravery and afterward a successful businessman, Dickey gave himself entirely to poetry in 1961. "The Firebombing," one of his most ambitious long poems, summarizes his experiences past and present and attempts a reconciliation between them; it concludes with a perception unusual to such poetry but indicative of the kind of artistic purpose and moral integrity Dickey brings to bear on almost all his work thus far. He has written one novel, *Deliverance* (1970). For further biographical or critical information, consult: Carolyn Kizer and James Boatwright, "A Conversation with James Dickey," *Shenandoah*, XVIII:1 (1966), 3–28; Lawrence Lieberman, *The Achievement of James Dickey: A Comprehensive Selection of His Poems with a Critical Introduction* (Glenview, Ill., 1968); and Ralph J. Mills, "The Poetry of James Dickey," *Tri-Quarterly*, XI (1968), 231–42.

James Wright (b. 1927) won recognition when his first volume of poetry, *The Green Wall* (1957), was chosen by W. H. Auden as an award-winning volume for the Yale Series of Younger Poets. In that volume as in those that have followed—*Saint Judas* (1959), *The Branch Will Not Break* (1963), *Shall We Gather at the River* (1968)—Wright has shown his kinship to Robinson and Frost in his care for the accurate portrayal of people and events around him (usually in the American Midwest). His independence, however, is asserted in his sympathy with the alienated of American society, in his ability to identify himself with his subject (as in "At the Executed Murderer's Grave"), and in his tone and technique of directness, which rejects smoothness of line or rhythm and obvious rhyme. For further biographical or critical information, consult: Ralph J. Mills, *Contemporary American Poetry* (New York, 1965), pp. 197–217.

Anne Sexton (b. 1928), in three works, *To Bedlam and Part Way Back* (1960), *All My Pretty Ones* (1962), and *Live or Die* (1966), has continued the "confessional" strain of contemporary poetry initiated by Brother Antoninus and Robert Lowell, under whom she studied during the 1950s. Sexton's world is one of skepticism, nightmare, and torture: during her own illness she seeks to know Christ, "hung up like a pig on exhibit" (in "For God While Sleeping"); she recalls her brother among the war dead, left "to blacken, to burst through their perfect/skin" ("For Johnny Pole on the Forgotten Beach"); a maiden aunt has a nervous breakdown triggered by sudden deafness ("Some Foreign Letters"). Each incident is partially derived from a personal experience, and in each Sexton attempts to identify herself with what is dead or lost; in the end she learns what everyone experiences, but may not express, from similar situations. In her poetry Sexton's individual experiences become, through honest analysis, public and applicable to all. For further biographical or critical information, consult: Robert Boyers, *"Live or Die:* The Achievement of Anne Sexton," *Salmagundi*, II:1 (1967), 61–71; Beverly Fields, "The Poetry of Anne Sexton," in *Poets in Progress*, edited by Edward Hungerford (Evanston, Ill., 1967), pp. 251–85; Patricia Marx, "Interview with Anne Sexton," *Hudson Review*, XVIII (1965), 560–750; and Ralph J. Mills, *Contemporary American Poetry* (New York, 1965), pp. 218–34.

X. J. Kennedy (b. 1929), who has taught at four American universities, began to write poetry while he was in the Navy. His volume of poems, *Nude Descending a Staircase* (in which "Inscriptions after Fact" appeared), was the Lamont Poetry Selection for 1961. "Inscriptions after Fact," a suite of five poems that toy variously with classical myths, shows that Kennedy is as adept as Wilbur at word play, precise metrical patterns, and high glossy finish. But, obviously, Kennedy's sense of humor is keener, indeed often more outrageous, than Wilbur's. On that score, however, it is good to remember Kennedy's own statement: he says that he has "been accused of being a wit, which charge these days is like that of Lesbianism. I am never after laughs for their own sake." For further biographical or critical information, consult: Glauco Cam-

bon, "[Review of] *Nude Descending a Staircase," Wisconsin Studies in Contemporary Literature*, III:2 (1962), 108–13; Theodore Holmes, "Wit, Nature and the Human Concern," and *Poetry*, C (August 1962), 319–22.

Gregory Corso (b. 1930) emerged in the 1950s, with novelist Jack Kerouac and poets Lawrence Ferlinghetti and Allen Ginsberg, as one of "The Holy Barbarians" or "Beatniks" whose activities centered around San Francisco (the setting of Corso's "Ode to Coit Tower"). The poetry of this group, claiming Dylan Thomas as its champion and deriving its techniques from William Carlos Williams and Ezra Pound, blended jazz, fragments of Zen philosophy, and slang in an attempt to shock middle-class American society. Specifically, the Beat poets objected to the complacency or apathy of the average man in a society of sterile universities, commercialism, world-rupturing bombs, and congressional witch-hunts. The poetry of the Beats is largely that of satire and vituperation, but beneath it all runs the desire to scream, with the speaker of Corso's "Don't Shoot the Warthog," the name of *"Beauty Beauty Beauty."* There is no criticism of Corso's poetry at present, but Donald M. Allen's *The New American Poetry 1945–1960* (New York, 1960) provides not only an anthology but helpful statements by many of its contributors. Also, consult: Corso's "Notes from the Other Side of April: With Negro Eyes, with White—Four Moments from a Poet's Life....," *Esquire*, LXII:1 (1964), 86–7, 110; and his volumes of verse: *Vestal Lady on Brattle* (1955); *Gasoline* (1958); *Happy Birthday of Death* (1960); *Long Live Man* (1962); and *There Is Yet Time to Run Back Through Life and Expiate All That's Been Sadly Done* (1965).

LeRoi Jones (b. 1934) has been active as an anthologist (*Black Music*, 1967; *Black Fire*, 1968), a dramatist (*Dutchman and The Slave*, 1964; *Baptism and The Toilet*, 1967), an essayist (*Home: Social Essays*, 1966), a novelist (*The System of Dante's Hell*, 1965), a short-story writer (*Tales*, 1967), and a poet (*Preface to a Twenty Volume Suicide Note*, 1961; *The Dead Lecturer*, 1964; *Black Arts*, 1967). Considered one of the avant-garde writers in his youth, Jones later became a "missionary of Blackness," rejecting the aesthetics and culture of white America, urging the study of African and Arabic languages to bring blacks together as a separate group and force in the United States. At present, most criticism of Jones deals with his drama.

Ishmael Reed (b. 1938) gained attention, especially among college underground circles, with his first novel, *The Free-Lance Pallbear-* ers (1967). His growing reputation has been sustained by a second novel, *Yellow Back Radio Broke-Down* (1969), contributions to various anthologies of poetry, and lectures on many American campuses. Reed's work, both in verse and prose, is a satiric blending of classical myths and American folklore in a streamlike, surrealistic setting and a language that combines academic jargon and black street dialect. "The Gangster's Death" was first anthologized in *Where Is Vietnam?* (1967) and is an epitome of Reed's distinctive qualities, particularly in its militant movement from beginning to end, its alternately angry and flippant tone, and its brutal vision of horror. At present there is no significant criticism of Reed's work available.

A Selected Bibliography of Further Readings in Fiction, Drama, and Poetry*

FICTION

Aldridge, John W., ed. *Critiques and Essays on Modern Fiction, 1920–1951.* New York: Ronald Press, 1952.

Allen, Walter. *The English Novel: A Short Critical History.* New York and London: Dutton, 1954.

Anderson, Sherwood. *Memoirs.* New York: Harcourt Brace Jovanovich, 1942.

————. *Notebook.* New York: Boni & Liveright, 1926.

————. *A Story Teller's Story.* Garden City: B. W. Huebsch, Inc., 1924.

Arvin, Newton, ed. *The Heart of Hawthorne's Journals.* New York: Barnes & Noble, 1967.

Auerbach, Erich. *Mimesis: The Representation of Reality in Western Literature.* Translated by Willard R. Trask. Garden City: Doubleday Anchor Books, 1957.

Blackmur, Richard P., ed. *Henry James: The Art of the Novel.* New York: Scribners, 1962.

Booth, Wayne C. *The Rhetoric of Fiction.* Chicago: University of Chicago Press, 1961.

Brod, Max, ed. *The Diaries of Franz Kafka.* Translated by Joseph Kresh. Two Volumes. New York: Schocken Books, 1948–49.

Forster, E. M. *Aspects of the Novel.* London: Harcourt Brace Jovanovich, 1949.

Kipling, Rudyard. *Something of Myself.* Garden City: Doubleday, Doran, 1937.

Koteliansky, Samuel S., ed. *Anton Tchekhov: Literary and Theatrical Reminiscences.* New York: B. Blom, 1965.

Lawrence, D. H. *Apocalypse.* New York: Viking Press, 1960.

Leavis, F. R. *The Great Tradition.* New York: New York University Press, 1963.

Lubbock, Percy. *The Craft of Fiction.* New Edition. London: Jonathan Cape, 1954.

Murry, J. Middleton. *Katherine Mansfield: Journal.* Definitive Edition. London: Constable, 1954.

O'Connor, William Van, ed. *Forms of Modern Fiction.* Minneapolis: Indiana University Press, 1948.

Roberts, Morris, ed. *Henry James: The Art of Fiction, and Other Essays.* New York: Oxford University Press, 1948.

Van Ghent, Dorothy. *The English Novel: Form and Function.* New York: Harper & Row, 1964.

West, Ray B., Jr., and Stallman, R. W., eds. *The Art of Modern Fiction.* New York: Holt, Rinehart & Winston, 1949.

Wright, Walter F., ed. *Joseph Conrad on Fiction.* Lincoln, Nebraska: University of Nebraska Press, 1964.

---

* Publication dates listed here, and those listed in the individual authors' bibliographies, are generally for recent editions; works cited in the individual bibliographies are not repeated in this list.

DRAMA

Bentley, Eric. *The Playwright as Thinker.* New York: Harcourt Brace Jovanovich, 1960.

Butcher, S. H. *Aristotle's Theory of Poetry and Fine Art.* New York: Dover Publications, 1951.

Clark, Barrett H., ed. *European Theories of the Drama.* Rev. ed. New York: Crown Publishers, 1965.

Cole, Toby, ed. *Actors on Acting.* New York: Crown Publishers, 1949.

————. *Directors on Directing.* Indianapolis: Bobbs-Merrill, 1963.

————. *Playwrights on Playwriting.* New York: Hill & Wang, 1960.

Cook, Albert S. *The Dark Voyage and the Golden Mean.* New York: W. W. Norton, 1966.

Cooper, Lane. *An Aristotelian Theory of Comedy.* New York: Harcourt Brace Jovanovich, 1922.

Eastman, Max. *Enjoyment of Laughter.* New York: Simon & Schuster, 1936.

Feibleman, James. *In Praise of Comedy.* New York: Russell, 1962.

Fergusson, Francis. *The Human Image in Dramatic Literature.* Garden City: Peter Smith, 1957.

————. *The Idea of a Theatre.* Garden City: Doubleday Anchor Books, 1953.

Gassner, John, ed. *Ideas in the Drama.* New York: AMS Press, 1964.

————. *Masters of the Drama.* 3rd ed. New York: Dover Publications, 1954.

Grotjahn, Martin. *Beyond Laughter.* New York: McGraw-Hill Book Co., 1957.

Huizinga, Johan. *Homo Ludens.* Boston: Beacon Press, 1955.

Kitto, H. D. F. *Greek Tragedy.* 3rd ed. London: Doubleday Anchor Books, 1966.

Koestler, Arthur. *Insight and Outlook.* New York: Peter Smith, 1949.

Krutch, Joseph Wood. *"Modernism" in Modern Drama.* Ithaca, N.Y.: Cornell University Press, 1966.

Lucas, F. L. *Tragedy.* Rev. ed. New York: Macmillan, 1965.

McCollum, William. *Tragedy.* New York: Macmillan, 1957.

Meyers, Henry Alonzo. *Tragedy: A View of Life.* Ithaca, N. Y.: Cornell University Press, 1956.

Michel, Laurence, and Sewall, Richard Benson, eds. *Tragedy: Modern Essays in Criticism.* Englewood Cliffs, N. J.: Prentice-Hall, 1963.

Nagler, A. M., ed. *A Source Book in Theatrical History.* New York: Peter Smith, 1959.

Nicoll, Allardyce. *An Introduction to Dramatic Theory.* 4th rev. ed. London: G. G. Harrap, 1958.

Nietzsche, Friedrich. *The Birth of Tragedy.* Translated by Francis Golffing. Garden City: Doubleday, 1956.

Olson, Elder. *Tragedy and the Theory of Drama.* Detroit: Wayne State University Press, 1961.

Potts, L. J. *Comedy.* London: Hutchinson, 1966.

Rowe, Kenneth Thorpe. *A Theatre in Your Head.* New York: Funk & Wagnalls, 1960.

Sewall, Richard Benson. *The Vision of Tragedy.* New Haven, Conn.: Yale University Press, 1959.

Smith, Willard. *The Nature of Comedy.* Boston: R. G. Badger, 1930.

Steiner, George. *The Death of Tragedy.* London: Hill and Wang, 1963.

Swabey, Marie Collins. *Comic Laughter.* New Haven, Conn.: Yale University Press, 1961.

Sypher, Wylie, ed. *Comedy: An Essay on Comedy, by George Meredith. Laughter, by Henri Bergson. The Meaning of Comedy, by Wylie Sypher.* Garden City: Doubleday, 1956.

Thompson, Alan Reynolds. *The Anatomy of Drama.* 2nd ed. Freeport, N.Y.: Books for Libraries, Inc., 1968.

————. *The Dry Mock: A Study of Irony in Drama.* Berkeley: University of California Press, 1948.

POETRY

Abrams, Meyer H. *The Mirror and the Lamp: Romantic Theory and the Critical Tradition.* New York: W. W. Norton, 1953.

Bodkin, Maud. *Archetypal Patterns in Poetry.* London: Oxford University Press, 1965.

Brooks, Cleanth. *The Well Wrought Urn: Studies in the Structure of Poetry.* New York: Harcourt Brace Jovanovich, 1964.

Bush, Douglas. *Mythology and the Renaissance Tradition in English Poetry.* New rev. ed. New York: W. W. Norton, 1963.

————. *Mythology and the Romantic Tradition in English Poetry.* Cambridge, Mass.: W. W. Norton, 1937.

————. *Pagan Myth and Christian Tradition in English Poetry.* Philadelphia: American Philosophical Society, 1968.

Crane, Ronald. *The Language of Criticism and the Structure of Poetry.* Toronto: University of Toronto Press, 1953.

Drew, Elizabeth. *Discovering Poetry.* New York: W. W. Norton, 1933.

Eastman, Max. *Enjoyment of Poetry, with Other Essays in Aesthetics.* New York and London: Charles Scribner's Sons, 1939.

Eliot, T. S. *On Poetry and Poets.* New York and London: Farrar, Straus & Giroux, 1957.

————. *Selected Essays.* New York and London: Harcourt Brace Jovanovich, 1951.

Empson, William. *Seven Types of Ambiguity.* 3rd ed. London: New Directions, 1953.

Fraser, G. S. *The Modern Writer and His World: Continuity and Innovation in Twentieth-Century Literature.* New York: F. A. Praeger, 1964.

Frye, Northrop. *Anatomy of Criticism: Four Essays.* New York: Atheneum, 1957.

Hough, Graham. *The Last Romantics.* New York and London: Barnes & Noble, 1961.

Jarrell, Randall. *Poetry and the Age.* New York: Random House, 1955.

Kreuzer, James R. *Elements of Poetry.* New York: Macmillan, 1958.

Krieger, Murray. *The New Apologists for Poetry.* Minneapolis: University of Minnesota Press, 1956.

Leavis, F. R. *New Bearings in English Poetry: A Study of the Contemporary Situation.* Ann Arbor: University of Michigan Press, 1960.

————. *Revaluation: Tradition and Development in English Poetry.* New York: W. W. Norton, 1947.

Lucas, F. L. *Ten Victorian Poets.* Cambridge, England: Shoe String Press, Archon Books, 1940.

Praz, Mario. *The Romantic Agony.* Translated by Angus Davidson. 2nd ed. Cleveland: Peter Smith, 1967.

Ransom, John Crowe. *The World's Body.* New York and London: Louisiana State University Press, 1938.

Richards, I. A. *Practical Criticism: A Study of Literary Judgment.* New York: Harcourt Brace Jovanovich, 1962.

————. *Principles of Literary Criticism.* 2nd ed., with two new Appendices. London: Harcourt Brace Jovanovich, 1955.

Smith, Hallett. *Elizabethan Poetry: A Study in Conventions, Meaning, and Expression.* Cambridge, Mass.: Harvard University Press, 1952.

Stauffer, Donald A. *The Nature of Poetry.* New York: W. W. Norton, 1946.

Sutherland, James R. *A Preface to Eighteenth-Century Poetry.* Oxford: Oxford University Press, 1962.

Trilling, Lionel. *The Liberal Imagination: Essays on Literature and Society.* New York: Doubleday Anchor Books, 1953.

Tuve, Rosemond. *Elizabethan and Metaphysical Imagery: Renaissance Poetic and Twentieth-Century Critics.* Chicago: University of Chicago Press, 1965.

Wellek, René and Warren, Austin. *Theory of Literature.* 3rd ed. New York: Harcourt Brace Jovanovich, 1963.

Glossary

Act: the major division of the action of a play, which may contain one or more *scenes* (which see).

Alexandrine: a line of iambic hexameter (six iambic feet), as in the closing line to each stanza of Keats' "The Eve of St. Agnes"; for example, "To think how they may ache in icy hoods and mails."

Allegory: a form, based on *metaphor* (which see), in which one thing is described in terms of another; or a narrative in which each character represents a specific quality such as chastity, faith, or fortitude. There are allegorical elements in Kipling's "*They*," Kafka's "The Judgment," George Herbert's "Redemption" or "Love (III)," and John Milton's "Lycidas."

Alliteration: the repetition of the initial consonants of words or syllables, as in Spenser's "Epithalamion"; "Your string coulde soone to sadder tenor turne."

Allusion: a conscious, brief reference to something literary or historical outside the work proper, for purposes of ornamentation and/or enrichment of meaning by comparison or contrast; as, for example, the poem referred to in Elizabeth Bowen's title, "Mysterious Kôr"; historical events in Molière's *Tartuffe*; the contemporary figures in Pope's "Epistle II."

Ambiguity: the intentional or accidental suggestion of more than one meaning; as, for example, in the use of the smile in Hawthorne's "Wakefield"; the title character's "madness" in Pirandello's *Henry IV*; the final line in Anne Sexton's "For God While Sleeping."

Amphitheatre: a seating area for an audience consisting of steeply raked seats arranged roughly in a semicircle, often outdoors.

Anapest: a metrical *foot* (which see) of three syllables, the first two unstressed, the third stressed, as in COM-PRE-HEND.

Antagonist: in fiction and drama, the (frequently unsympathetic) character or force usually in conflict with the *protagonist* (which see).

Antithesis: the expression of strongly contrasting ideas within the same grammatical unit; the opposition of positive and negative; as, for example, in Pope's "Epistle II": "A teeming Mistress, but a barren Bride."

Apostrophe: a direct address to an absent person or abstract quality, as in the last section of Whitman's "Crossing Brooklyn Ferry," or the opening lines of Wallace Stevens' "Le Monocle de Mon Oncle."

Aside: a character's speech that is understood by, and frequently addressed to, the audience, but is not to be heard by the other characters on stage with him.

Assonance: the correspondence or repetition of a vowel sound in two stressed syllables, similar to, and often used as, *rhyme* (which see); for example, in an alternate version of Emily Dickinson's "I taste a liquor never brewed": "And Saints—to windows run—/ . . . From Manzanilla come!"

Ballad: a verse form of two types, *folk* and *literary*, the first anonymous, the second a conscious imitation of the first. In general, both types are narrative song-poems, usually relating a single, dramatic incident, using repetition and *refrains* (which see), conventional figures of speech, dialogue without transitions. Examples of the folk ballad can be found under Anonymous Ballads of the Middle Ages. Coleridge's "Rime of the Ancient Mariner," Keats' "La Belle Dame sans Merci," and Rossetti's "Troy Town" are examples of the literary ballad.

Ballad Stanza: a four-line stanza, common to the folk ballad, in which lines 1 and 3 are written in iambic tetrameter (four iambic feet) and lines 2 and 4 are written in iambic trimeter (three iambic feet). The second and fourth lines generally rhyme, but the first and third may not.

Blank Verse: unrhymed iambic pentameter (five iambic feet), used, for example, in Wordsworth's "Lines Composed a Few Miles Above Tintern Abbey," Browning's "The Bishop Orders His Tomb," Edwin Arlington Robinson's "The Man Against the Sky," and Frost's "Out, Out—.' "

Blocking: the process (usually during rehearsal of the play) of setting the movements and gestures of the actors; the movements and gestures themselves.

Box Set: an interior setting on a *proscenium-arch* stage (which see) intended as a realistic reproduction of a room.

Cacophony: the purposeful arrangement of sounds to produce a sense of harshness, as, for example, in T. S. Eliot's "Journey of the Magi": "And the camels galled, sore-footed, refractory." The opposite of cacophony is *euphony* (which see).

Caesura: a pause within a line of poetry that may occur at any place, although it usually falls near the middle.

Carol: originally, a song for a circle dance, as around the Christmas crib in the Middle Ages; later, a traditional Christmas or drinking song.

Catalog: a list of objects (flowers, sensory perceptions, etc.) used in poetry to achieve grandeur (as in Milton's "Lycidas," Whitman's "Crossing Brooklyn Ferry") or to create tension (as in Eliot's "The Love Song of J. Alfred Prufrock").

Catastrophe: generally, the resolution of a *tragedy* (which see), usually toward its end,

involving the death or defeat of the *protagonist* (which see).

Chorus: in Greek drama, a group of actors who, as a unit, comment on the action of the play through chanting and dancing; or, in poetry, a group of verses, repeated like a *refrain* (which see) at the close of a *stanza* (which see), as, for example, in Dryden's "Alexander's Feast."

Comedy: a term used generally for drama that seeks to amuse or that ends happily or in a successful resolution for the protagonist.

Conceit: usually, an extended, striking analogy or *metaphor* (which see), comparing unlike objects, sometimes encompassing an entire poem, as in Wyatt's "My Galley" or Ransom's "Good Ships."

Conflict: in fiction and drama, the basic opposition of two forces in the *plot* (which see); the working out of the conflict is the basis of plot.

Consonance: the correspondence or repetition of a consonantal sound in two stressed syllables, similar to, and often used as, *rhyme* (which see); as, for example, in Yeats' "Among School Children": "In momentary wonder stare upo<u>n</u>/ A sixty-year-old smiling public ma<u>n</u>." When employed in this manner, the rhyme may be variously called *approximate, dissonant, half, imperfect, near, oblique, off, partial,* or *slant.*

Couplet: two lines, usually of the same length, that rhyme; as, for example, the closing lines of Shakespeare's sonnets; Herrick's "Love What It Is;" Pope's "Epistle II." Pope's couplets are called heroic in that he often used them, along with Dryden, to relate tales in the tradition of the *epic* (which see).

Crisis: a term generally used to designate the point in a play in which the conflict arrives at an irreversible situation, making the final outcome no longer in doubt.

Dactyl: a metrical foot of three syllables, the first stressed, the second and third unstressed; as, for example, in HÁP-PĬ-LȲ.

Dénouement: the final unraveling or outcome of the plot of a play.

Dialogue: the words spoken by the characters of a play.

Dilemma: a situation, usually in drama, in which a character finds he must choose between equally unattractive alternatives.

Dimeter: a line of verse having only two metrical feet.

Director: the person charged with the overall artistic production of a play.

Downstage: toward the audience.

Dramatic Monologue: a poem in which a single speaker, usually a projected character rather than the poet, reveals himself to one or more silent person(s) at some crucial moment in his life; as, for example, in Browning's "The Bishop Orders His Tomb" or "Andrea del Sarto."

Elegy: a classical verse form usually devoted to meditations on death (as in Whitman's "When Lilacs Last in the Dooryard Bloom'd" or as in Auden's "In Memory of W. B. Yeats"), love (as in Donne's "To His Mistress Going to Bed"), war (as in Dickey's "The Firebombing"), etc. When the characters are portrayed as rustics and the setting is rural (as in Milton's "Lycidas"), the form is called a *pastoral elegy.*

Elision: in poetry, the running together of two words, usually by omitting the final vowel sound of a word preceding a word with an initial vowel sound, for a specific effect or in order to achieve conformity of meter; as, for example, in Herrick's "Corrina's Going A-Maying": ". . . yet w'<u>are</u> not a Maying."

Epic: a long narrative poem, written in a formal style, which generally depicts a national hero or elaborates the traits and hopes of a nation. It includes an invocation to the Muse for inspiration, a statement of theme, a tradition for beginning in the "middle of things" or action (*in medias res*), gods and supernatural beings, great deeds, and great *similes* and *catalogs* (both of which see). Homer's *Iliad* and *Odyssey* and Virgil's *Aeneid* are examples of the classical epic; Whitman's *Leaves of Grass* and Crane's *The Bridge* are examples of the modern. Some poets have applied the epic form to a trivial event for satirical effect, a form called *mock epic.*

Epigram: a brief witty or sarcastic statement; as, for example, in Herrick's "Love What It Is."

Epigraph: a quotation preceding a play, poem, or story, usually taken from another author, to summarize the theme of the present work or to make a comparison or contrast of themes and attitudes; as, for example, in Wordsworth's "Ode: Intimations of Immortality" or T. S. Eliot's "The Love Song of J. Alfred Prufrock."

Episode: in Greek drama, the scenes of action between the singing and dancing of the chorus.

Epitaph: like an epigram, a short statement, but usually on death; as, for example, in Ben Jonson's "On My First Sonne."

Epithet: a word or phrase, usually an adjective, frequently repeated and describing a person or object by a prominent characteristic, most often used in *ballads* and *epics* (both of which see); for example, the "bright-eyed" mariner of Coleridge's "Rime of the Ancient Mariner."

Euphony: the purposeful arrangement of sounds to produce a sense of pleasure; as, for example, in John Keats' "The Eve of St. Agnes": "In blanchèd linen, smooth, and lavendered."

Farce: a form of comedy, intended to amuse, usually depending on coarse humor, fast action, and improbable situations.

Feminine Ending: an extra, unstressed syllable often ending a line of poetry.

Feminine Rhyme: a rhyme of two or more syllables; as, for example, in <u>sever</u> and <u>forever</u>.

Flat Character: in fiction and drama, a character with next to no different sides to his personality, purposely developed only enough to be credible.

Foil: a character in a story or play used to contrast with another character.

Foot: the basic rhythmic unit in a line of metrical poetry, consisting of one stressed syllable and usually one or more unstressed syllables; the commonest feet in English poetry are the *anapest, dactyl, iamb,* and *trochee* (all of which see).

Foreshadowing: an indication early in a story or a play, by statement, action, or *symbol* (which see), of a subsequent and often unhappy event.

Free Verse: poetry, often called *cadenced verse,* which follows patterns of natural speech rhythms rather than fixed metrical patterns; as, for example, in any of Whitman's poems, H. D.'s "Fragment 36," or T. S. Eliot's "The Dry Salvages."

Haiku: a Japanese verse form consisting of three lines of verse totaling seventeen syllables; for an example based on this form, see Ezra Pound's "In a Station of the Metro."

Heptameter: a line of verse having seven metrical feet.

Hexameter: a line of verse having six metrical feet.

Hovering Accent: two consecutive syllables both stressed, as in "Oh, no!"; also called *distributed stress.*

Hubris (Hybris): overweening pride, which in Greek tragedy leads to insolence toward the gods and self-destruction.

Hyperbole: a figure of speech using intentional overstatement or exaggeration to emphasize meaning; as exemplified by Marvell throughout "To His Coy Mistress."

Iamb: a metrical *foot* (which see) of two syllables, the first unstressed, the second stressed; as, for example, in CŎN-CEÍVE.

Image: a picture conceived in the imagination; a mental reproduction or literary imitation of a sensory experience meant to evoke the same experience in a reader or the audience.

Imagism: a movement by American and English poets (1909–1917), reacting against practices of late nineteenth-century poets, seeking to make precise images the basis of their poetry, demanding absolute freedom in choice of subject, rhythm, and development. See Ezra Pound's "In a Station of the Metro," H. D.'s "Fragment 36," and the section on the fog in T. S. Eliot's "The Love Song of J. Alfred Prufrock."

Irony: generally, in poetry, the figure of speech or mode of expression in which the actual or literary meaning of the words is the opposite of, or in strong contrast with, the intended meaning; in drama and fiction, frequently the combination of incongruous events, or of a character of a strong disposition in a setting alien to him. The device is common, so there are many examples of it in the present anthology; one example in each genre, however: Chekhov's "The Darling," Euripides' *The Bacchae* Shakespeare's Sonnet XCIV.

Leonine Rhyme: an internal rhyming of the last syllable before the *caesura* (which see) with the last syllable in the line, as frequently exemplified by Coleridge's "Rime of the Ancient Mariner": "The guests are met, the feast is set."

Lyric: from Greek, a poem sung to the accompaniment of a lyre; generally any poem with a single speaker expressing a deeply felt thought or emotion, such as an *elegy, ode,* or *sonnet* (all of which see).

Masculine Rhyme: a rhyme of only one syllable; such as bat and cat; believe, conceive.

Melodrama: a term with various meanings but principally used to denote a serious play that fails to be a *tragedy* (which see).

Metaphor: a figure of speech in which a comparison between two generally dissimilar things is implied or suggested. The device is common, so there are many examples of it in the present anthology; one example, in each genre, however: Henry James' "The Altar of the Dead," Euripides' *The Bacchae*, Wordsworth's "Ode: Intimations of Immortality."

Metaphysical Poetry: verse of the early seventeenth century characterized by the treatment of philosophical subjects in varying but complex stanza forms, with extended and striking *conceits* (which see). The verse of Donne, Herbert, and Marvell to a lesser extent is usually called Metaphysical.

Meter: the rhythm of a line of poetry resulting from the recurrence of specific rhythmic units called *feet* (see *foot*).

Metonymy: a figure of speech in which the name of one thing is substituted for another closely related thing; as, for example, in Shakespeare's Sonnet CXLVI, "Poor soul, the center of my sinful *earth*," in which *earth* replaces *body* (=dust).

Monologue: a speech in which the only character on stage addresses the audience directly.

Myth: a story of unknown origin describing supernatural events or heroic events that explain such things as how creation, life and death, and various other phenomena came to be. Many dramatists, poets, and short-story writers base their works on myths and mythological characters, or allude to them; for example, Euripides' *The Bacchae*, Milton's "Lycidas," Arnold's "Philomela," Yeats' "Among School Children," D. H. Lawrence's "Bavarian Gentians," Ezra Pound's "The Return," Robert Graves' "Ulysses," "Leda," and "To Juan at the Winter Solstice."

Octave: the first eight lines of a Petrarchan *sonnet* (which see), rhyming *abbaabba*, in which a question is raised or a problem set forth; as, for example, in Wyatt's "My Galley Chargèd with Forgetfulness." The answer or resolution is developed in the final six lines

of the poem, called the *sestet* (which see).

Ode: a formal lyric, originally of scope and subject matter suitable for chanting by a Greek chorus; its structure is free: authors may create a stanza form and repeat it throughout, as, for example, in Shelley's "Ode to the West Wind" or Keats' "Ode to a Nightingale"; or they may prefer free development of stanzas different in length in the same poem, as, for example, in Wordsworth's "Ode: Intimations of Immortality" or Corso's "Ode to Coit Tower." Dryden's "Alexander's Feast" is called a Pindaric Ode, after Pindar the Greek poet.

Onomatopoeia: the use of words that create in their sounds the meaning or sense intended; as, for example, with *bang, buzz, hiss, scratch, thwack.*

Orchestra: in the Greek theatre, a level round area between the *skene* and the *amphitheatre* (both of which see), on which the chorus performed.

Ottava Rima: an eight-line stanza of iambic pentameter (five iambic feet), rhyming *abababcc*; as, for example, in Yeats' "Among School Children."

Pantomime: a play or part of a play given without words.

Paradox: a statement in which one element seems incongruous with another, though both are true; as, for example, in T. S. Eliot's "The Dry Salvages": "And the way up is the way down, the way forward is the way back."

Parody: a conscious imitation of a writer's style or a type of writing for comic or satiric effect. John Crowe Ransom parodies the Petrarchan conceit (lover=ship, as in Wyatt's "My Galley") in "Good Ships," and Wallace Stevens parodies himself in "Le Monocle de Mon Oncle."

Pathetic Fallacy: the attribution of human characteristics to inanimate objects; as, for example, with the effects of Edward King's death on nature, as described by Milton in "Lycidas."

Pentameter: a line of verse having five metrical feet.

Persona: an author's voice or mask as opposed to his private personality; the narrator imagined by the poet or fiction writer to speak the words of his poem or story.

Personification: a figure of speech that gives human characteristics to nonhuman things or abstract qualities; as, for example, in Marvell's treatment of love in the first stanza of "The Definition of Love."

Plot: in fiction, drama, or narrative poetry, a planned series of interrelated actions or events by which a conflict of forces is instigated, developed, and resolved.

Problem Play: a drama centered on a political, psychological, or social issue.

Properties (Props): objects of any kind used in a play.

Proscenium-Arch Theatre: the most frequent type of realistic theatre in the twentieth century; an indoor theatre in which the audience is seated in rows before a raised stage with a frame through which the audience views the action.

Protagonist: in fiction and drama, the leading character or hero in the conflict, to whom the audience or reader gives most sympathy.

Pun: the use of a word that has two different meanings to achieve a comic effect, irony, or emphasis; as, for example, in Shakespeare's use of the word *lie* in Sonnet CXXXVIII.

Quatrain: a stanza of four lines, rhymed or unrhymed.

Realism: a type of play or story that attempts to preserve the surface of actuality and to maintain cause-effect relationships in its plot structure.

Refrain: a word, phrase, or clause repeated at various places in a poem, most usually at the end of a stanza; as, for example, in Rossetti's "Troy Town."

Repartee: exchange of dialogue in rapid succession, usually for comic or witty effects.

Rhyme: the repetition or correspondence of sounds in stressed syllables in lines of poetry. Rhyme may occur within a line (internal), at the ends of lines (end), or at the beginnings of lines (initial). It may be assonantal (run-come), consonantal (upon-man), perfect, or slant, and occur on one syllable (masculine) or more (feminine). The pattern of end rhymes is called a *rhyme scheme*, and is identified by letters of the alphabet.

Rhythm: the repetition of stressed and unstressed syllables in lines of poetry at regular or expected intervals. Metrical rhythm is based on about five different units: the *iamb, anapest, trochee, dactyl,* and *spondee* (all of which see). In *sprung rhythm,* rhythm is regular only in the accented syllables. Free verse rhythm is more varied, emphasizing the cadences of natural speech.

Rime Royal: a stanza with seven lines of iambic pentameter (five iambic feet), rhyming *ababbcc;* as, for example, in Wyatt's "They Flee from Me" or Yeats' "A Bronze Head."

Round Character: in a story or play, a character so fully developed by the author as to seem almost human.

Satire: a work, in prose or verse, which holds a person, institution, nation, or idea up to ridicule. There are satirical elements in Roth's "Novotny's Pain," Moliere's *Tartuffe,* and Burns' "Holy Willies Prayer."

Scansion: the analysis of the rhythm of a poem, consisting of marking stressed and unstressed syllables and dividing them into metrical feet: *monometer* (one foot), *dimeter* (two feet), *trimeter* (three), *tetrameter* (four), *pentameter* (five), *hexameter* (six), *heptameter* (seven), etc.

Scene: a term with several meanings—the physical setting of a story, play, or narrative poem; in drama, an episode or division of an act, or the actual unit on stage surrounding the actors.

Sestet: the final six lines of a Petrarchan sonnet, usually rhyming *cdecde* or in some other combination of three rhymes.

Sestina: a verse form of six unrhymed six-line stanzas with the same terminal words, in different orders, followed by a tercet (three lines), using three to six of the terminal words; as, for example, in T. S. Eliot's "The Dry Salvages" or Elizabeth Bishop's "A Miracle for Breakfast."

Set: the scenery used in a play.

Simile: a direct comparison of two generally dissimilar objects, usually preceded by the words *like* or *as*. The device is common, so there are many examples of it in the present anthology; one example in each genre, however: Jean Toomer's "Theater," Euripides' *The Bacchae*, Ishmael Reed's The Gangster's Death."

Skene: in the Greek theatre, a building facing the audience, often representing a palace or temple and containing doors through which actors made entrances and exits.

Soliloquy: a speech by a character alone on the stage, usually representing his thinking at the time.

Sonnet: a lyric poem of fourteen lines, usually in iambic pentameter (five iambic feet), organized either according to the Petrarchan or Italian rhyme pattern (octave—*abbaabba;* sestet—*cdecde* or some combination of three rhymes) or according to the Shakespearean or English rhyme pattern (three quatrains—*abab cdcd efef;* one couplet—*gg*).

Spenserian Stanza: nine lines, rhyming *ababbcbcc,* the first eight lines in iambic pentameter (five iambic feet), the last an alexandrine (six iambic feet). Invented by Edmund Spenser for his poem *The Faerie Queene,* the stanza is used by Keats in "The Eve of St. Agnes."

Spondee: a foot consisting of two consecutive stressed syllables; as, for example, ICE-STORM.

Sprung Rhythm: a term invented by Gerard Manley Hopkins to describe the meter of poetry that has a fixed number of stressed syllables to a line but a varying number of unstressed syllables; the stressed syllable always comes first in the foot.

Stanza: a grouping of lines in a poem according to the number of lines, rhyme scheme, or thought expressed, usually repeated throughout the poem. Common stanzas are the *couplet, tercet, quatrain* (all of which see).

Stichomythia: in Greek and later verse drama, a series of speeches in which two characters utter one line of verse apiece.

Stock Character: in a story or play, a character who has appeared so frequently in many authors' works that his nature and appearance are well known; e.g., the cruel stepmother, the quack doctor, etc.

Symbol: an image or object used to represent or suggest something more complex or abstract; characters, settings, and situations may be used symbolically, as with Coleridge's mariner in "The Rime of the Ancient Mariner," the estate in Kipling's *"They,"* or the building and climbing in Ibsen's *The Master Builder.*

Synaesthesia: the description of one kind of sense perception in words that usually describe another; as, for example, in the second stanza of Keats' "Ode to a Nightingale," when the wine is described as "tasting" of "Dance, and Provençal song...."

Syncope: the omission of a letter or syllable within a word; as, for example, *e'er* for *ever.*

Synecdoche: a figure of speech which uses a part to represent the whole or vice versa; as, for example, in the third stanza of Marvell's "The Garden" when "white" and "red" (complexions) are used in place of *women.*

Tercet: a stanza containing three lines which may, but do not always, rhyme consecutively; as, for example, in Herrick's "Upon Julia's Clothes."

Terza Rima: a stanza form employing tercets (three lines), rhyming in an interlocking manner, *aba, bcb, cdc,* and so on; as, for example, in Shelley's "Ode to the West Wind" and Frost's "Acquainted with the Night."

Tetrameter: a line of verse having four metrical feet.

Theme: the central or controlling idea underlying a short story, play, or poem; a work's thesis.

Tone: an author's attitude toward his subject —e.g., serious, whimsical, ironic.

Tragedy: a serious play, usually formal in style, in which the protagonist moves from relatively good to bad fortune and in which the events have broad significance beyond the protagonist's immediate fate.

Tragicomedy: a play that begins with a potentially tragic conflict but ends relatively happily.

Trimeter: a line of verse having three metrical feet.

Understatement: the deliberate expression of a subject with less emotion or description than the subject calls for, often used for ironic effect, and also called *meiosis.*

Upstage: away from the audience.

Villanelle: a verse form consisting of five tercets (three-line stanzas) and one quatrain (a four-line stanza), having two rhymes only. The opening line is repeated at the ends of the second and fourth stanzas, and the third line at the ends of the third and fifth. The two refrain lines conclude the poem. For examples, see Roethke's "The Waking" and Thomas' "Do Not Go Gentle into That Good Night."

Well-Made Play (also called **pièce bien faite**): a play with a tight plot structure in which every detail contributes directly to the development and resolution of the conflict.

Zeugma: the grammatical linking of two words by another word by using the later word in two different senses, usually for an ironic effect; as, for example, in Pope's "Epistle II": "Or her, whose life the *Church* and *Scandal share.*"

Index of Authors' Names, Titles, and First Lines of Poems

A NOTE ON THE TYPE

The text of this book was set on the Linotype in Aster,
a typeface designed by Francesco Simoncini for
Ludwig and Mayer, the German type foundry. Starting
out with the basic old-face letterforms that can be
traced back to Francesco Griffo in 1495, Simoncini
emphasized the diagonal stress by the simple device of
extending diagonals to the full height of the letterforms
and squaring off. By modifying the weights of the
individual letters to combat this stress, he has
produced a type of rare balance and vigor.

Composed by Cherry Hill Composition, Inc.,
Pennsauken, N.J.
Printed and bound by The Colonial Press, Clinton, Mass.